The Letters of William Lloyd Garrison

EDITED BY

WALTER M. MERRILL AND LOUIS RUCHAMES

PUBLISHER'S NOTE

A word of explanation about the cooperation of the editors of this edition. Some time before 1960, each of the editors, unknown to the other, had embarked on the task of editing Garrison's letters. Each had secured a publisher: Professor Merrill, Harvard University Press; Professor Ruchames, University of Massachusetts Press. On learning accidentally of one another's efforts, the editors decided to cooperate in issuing one edition. The University of Massachusetts Press and Harvard University Press, after mutual discussions, concluded that the latter should assume the responsibility for publishing the work.

In arriving at their decision to cooperate, the editors agreed to combine the letters which each had gathered separately as well as to unite in a systematic search for letters that had thus far been overlooked. Repositories of manuscript letters, including libraries, state and local historical societies, and manuscript dealers, in the United States and abroad, were checked. In a number of instances, collections of uncatalogued letters were also searched and additional letters found. During the past two years, several hundred new letters have been discovered and incorporated in the collections. Thus, whereas the original plan called for an edition of four volumes, it appears that ultimately the number of volumes will reach six and perhaps eight.

In the allocation of responsibilities, the editors have divided the material by periods as follows:

1822–1835 — Walter M. Merrill	1850–1860 — Louis Ruchames
1836–1840 — Louis Ruchames	1861–1869 — Walter M. Merrill
1841–1849 — Walter M. Merrill	1870–1879 — Louis Ruchames

Each editor assumes complete responsibility for his volumes.

Garrison at about thirty-five

The Letters of
William Lloyd Garrison

Volume II

A HOUSE
DIVIDING
AGAINST
ITSELF

1836-1840

EDITED BY LOUIS RUCHAMES

The Belknap Press of Harvard University Press

Cambridge, Massachusetts   1971

© Copyright 1971 by the President and Fellows of Harvard College
All rights reserved
Distributed in Great Britain by Oxford University Press, London
Printed in the United States of America
Library of Congress Catalog Card Number 75–133210
SBN 674–52661–9
Book design by David Ford

To

Sidney Kaplan

PREFACE

ILLIAM LLOYD GARRISON may be said to be the Founding Father of the American civil rights movement. Notwithstanding earlier sporadic efforts on behalf of freedom and equality for Negroes, it was Garrison, more than anyone else, who in 1831 initiated the movement which sought the abolition of slavery in the South and the achievement of equality of rights and opportunities for the free Negro everywhere.

Participants in the civil rights movement today are the lineal descendants of the antislavery men and women who wrought against overwhelming odds during the decades before the Civil War and immediately thereafter. The issues of today are in many respects similar, if not identical, to those which confronted the abolitionists during the previous century. A study of their lives, writings, and actions has much to teach us as we confront the problems of our own day.

Garrison's letters, in particular, provide a wealth of instruction. They begin in 1822, when Garrison was seventeen, and they end in 1879, the year of his death. From about 1830, when he first gave public utterance to the slogan of immediate and unconditional emancipation, to the last year of his life, issues involving the rights of the Negro, the nature of slavery, the tactics and strategy of the antislavery movement, the meaning of racial differences, and a host of other related themes are referred to and commented upon in his letters.

The letters also offer an insight into the mind and life of an outstanding figure in American history, a reformer-revolutionary who sought radical changes in the institutions of his day — in the relationship of the races, the rights of women, the nature and role of religion and religious institutions, and the relations between the state and its citizens; and who, perhaps as much as any other single individual, as Abraham Lincoln pointed out shortly before his own death, was ultimately responsible for the emancipation of the slaves.

The letters are also important *sui generis*, as the expression of a vigorous letter writer, whose letters reflect his strength of character and warm humanity, and who appears here not only as the journalist, the reformer, and the leader of men, but also as the loving husband and father, the devoted son and son-in-law, the staunch friend, and the formidable opponent.

ACKNOWLEDGMENTS

I wish to express my deepest appreciation to the many persons — librarians, curators, scholarly predecessors, colleagues, autograph dealers, research assistants, typists, historical societies, universities, and friends — who have contributed to the preparation of this volume.

I am deeply indebted to the following institutions for furnishing photocopies of Garrison letters included in this volume and for permission to publish them: American Missionary Association Archives in the Amistad Research Center, Fisk University, Nashville, Tennessee; Berea College Library, Berea, Kentucky; Boston Athenaeum; Boston Public Library; Chicago Historical Society; Essex Institute, Salem, Massachusetts; Friends' Historical Library, Swarthmore College, Swarthmore, Pennsylvania; Haverford College Library, Haverford, Pennsylvania; Houghton Library, Harvard University; Library of Congress; Lilly Library, Indiana University; Massachusetts Historical Society; National Archives and Record Service, Naval Records Collection, Washington, D.C.; New York Public Library; Pennsylvania Historical Society; Smith College Library, Northampton, Massachusetts; University Library, Cambridge, England; Waterloo Library and Historical Society, Waterloo, New York; Wichita State University, Wichita, Kansas. I am indebted, similarly, to Mr. Robert L. Huttner, of Chicago, for the use of two Garrison letters in his possession.

The following persons were most helpful in providing information and research assistance: James T. Abajian, California Historical Society; John Alden, Boston Public Library; Mrs. Marion Bates, Ohio Historical Society; John B. Blake, National Library of Medicine, Bethesda, Maryland; Mrs. Hendon Chubb, West Orange, New Jersey; Clarkson A. Collins, 3rd, Rhode Island Historical Society; Caroline Dunn, Indiana Historical Society; Thomas R. Cripps, Morgan State College, Baltimore, Maryland; Mark G. Eckhoff, National Archives and Records Service; Paul Faler, University of Massachusetts at Boston; John Hope Franklin, University of Chicago; Eleanor Garrison,

Acknowledgments

Santa Barbara, California; Lloyd K. Garrison, New York, N.Y.; Zoltan Haraszti, emeritus Keeper of Rare Books, Boston Public Library; Edith Hazelton, Mildred Leavitt and Diana Small, New England Historical Genealogical Society; Thompson R. Harlow, Connecticut Historical Society; Mrs. Emma Kaplan, Reference Librarian, Elizabeth S. Duval and Mary-Elizabeth Murdock, Curators, Sophia Smith Collection, Smith College Library; Albert T. Klyberg, Rhode Island Historical Society; Alan D. MacKinnon, Vermont Historical Society; Pamela McNulty, Marine Historical Society, Mystic, Connecticut; James M. McPherson, Princeton University; Mrs. Robert M. May, Groton, Massachusetts; Mrs. Harold Merriam, North Brookfield, Massachusetts; Ellen M. Oldham, Boston Public Library; Loretta E. Phaneuf, Free Public Library, New Bedford, Massachusetts; Mrs. Charles A. Potter, Essex Institute, Salem, Massachusetts; Benjamin Quarles, Morgan State College; Duncan Rice, University of Aberdeen; Juliette Tomlinson, Connecticut Valley Historical Museum; Mrs. Robert C. White, Vermont Historical Society; Walter M. Whitehill, Boston Athenaeum.

The American Council of Learned Societies and the American Philosophical Society have each provided two generous grants-in-aid for research. I am indebted most of all to the University of Massachusetts for the major portion of the financial support which I have received as well as for assistance and encouragement in numerous other forms.

I wish to thank Mrs. Leone Stein, the editor of the University of Massachusetts Press, for her early assistance and encouragement as well as for her continued interest. I am grateful, too, to my colleague and friend, Professor Sidney Kaplan, of the Department of English at the University of Massachusetts in Amherst, who has been an unfailing source of understanding and encouragement.

Professor Walter M. Merrill, who is editing alternate volumes of the Garrison letters, has been of great help in the process of gathering letters, exchanging information, including transcriptions, photocopies, and lists, and in many editorial matters.

The late Thomas J. Wilson, director of the Harvard University Press at the time this project was initiated, was most helpful in many respects, as has also been Mark Carroll, its present director.

Mrs. L. J. Kewer, Chief Editor for Special Projects of the Harvard University Press, has been a vital source of information and wisdom. I am also grateful to Mrs. Carl A. Pitha of the Harvard University Press for her invaluable help.

My colleagues at the University of Massachusetts–Boston, Professors Paul Boller, Thomas N. Brown, Paul Gagnon, and Richard Powers, have been a source of continuing encouragement and support.

Acknowledgments

My wife, Miriam, has borne the trials and tribulations of my work, with fortitude, devotion and love.

Mrs. Dorothy Koval, my research assistant these many years, has provided indispensable assistance in the completion of this first volume and in numerous other areas related to the entire project, including the compilation of the Index. Her devotion and concern far exceed any expression of gratitude that I can offer.

Louis Ruchames

Boston
April 1971

CONTENTS

List of Illustrations   xvii

Editorial Statement   xix

Abbreviations and Short Titles   xxi

Short Biographies of Antislavery Men and Women   xxii

I AFTERMATH OF THE BOSTON MOB: 1836   1

1. To Henry E. Benson, January 9, 1836
2. To George W. Benson, January 11, 1836
3. To Henry E. Benson, January 16, 1836
4. To Samuel J. May, January 17, 1836
5. To Samuel J. May, January 17, 1836
6. To Henry E. Benson, January 26, 1836
7. *To the President of the Anti-Slavery Convention to be
    held at Providence, Feb. 2*, January 30, 1836
8. To Isaac Knapp, February 3, 1836
9. To Oliver Johnson, February 10, 1836
10. To Lewis Tappan, February 12, 1836
11. To William Goodell, February 26, 1836
12. To Dutee J. Pearce, February 26, 1836
13. To Lewis Tappan, February 29, 1836
14. To Helen E. Garrison, March 5, 1836
15. To Helen E. Garrison, March 7, 1836
16. To George W. Benson, March 15, 1836
17. To James G. Birney, April 6, 1836
18. To George W. Benson, April 10, 1836
19. To Henry C. Wright, April 11, 1836
20. To Helen E. Garrison, April 16, 1836
21. To Helen E. Garrison, April 18, 1836
22. To Friends of the Anti-Slavery Movement, April 18, 1836
23. To William H. Scott, April 20, 1836
24. To Helen E. Garrison, May 5, 1836
25. To Helen E. Garrison, May 6, 1836
26. To Helen E. Garrison, May 10, 1836

Contents

27. To Isaac Knapp, May 11, 1836
28. To Helen E. Garrison, May 21, 1836
29. To George Thompson, May 24, 1836
30. To Helen E. Garrison, May 25, 1836
31. To Helen E. Garrison, May 30, 1836
32. To Helen E. Garrison, June 1, 1836
33. To Henry E. Benson, June 8, 1836
34. To William Chace, June 11, 1836
35. To Henry E. Benson, June 14, 1836
36. To Samuel J. May, June 19, 1836
37. To Isaac Knapp, June 22, 1836
38. To George W. Benson, June 28, 1836
39. To Helen E. Garrison, July 2, 1836
40. To Isaac Knapp, July 5, 1836
41. To Henry E. Benson, July 14, 1836
42. To Isaac Knapp, July 16, 1836
43. To Isaac Knapp, July 19, 1836
44. To Henry E. Benson, July 28, 1836
45. To the *New England Spectator*, July 30, 1836
46. To Henry E. Benson, August 4, 1836
47. To David L. Child, August 6, 1836
48. To Henry E. Benson, August 11, 1836
49. To George W. Benson, August 18, 1836
50. To Henry E. Benson, August 18, 1836
51. To Isaac Knapp, August 19, 1836
52. To Henry E. Benson, August 21, 1836
53. To Isaac Knapp, August 23, 1836
54. To Effingham L. Capron, August 24, 1836
55. To Henry E. Benson, August 27, 1836
56. To George W. Benson, September 19, 1836
57. To Samuel J. May, September 23, 1836
58. To George Benson, September 28, 1836
59. To Henry E. Benson, November 4, 1836
60. To Helen E. Garrison, November 22, 1836
61. To Henry E. Benson, December 3, 1836
62. To Henry E. Benson, December 17, 1836
63. To Mrs. Sarah T. Benson, December 24, 1836
64. To Sarah Benson, December 31, 1836

II CLERICAL DISAFFECTION: 1837

199

65. To George W. Benson, January 4, 1837
66. To George W. Benson, January 8, 1837
67. To Caleb Cushing, January 12, 1837
68. To Mary Benson, January 14, 1837
69. To Anna Benson, February 4, 1837

Contents

70. To George W. Benson, February 17, 1837
71. To Amos A. Phelps, February 21, 1837
72. To Helen E. Garrison, March 2, 1837
73. To the Editor of the Courier, March 4, 1837
74. To the Editor of the Courier, March 11, 1837
75. To Samuel J. May, March 14, 1837
76. To the Editor of the Courier, March 18, 1837
77. To the Editor of the Courier, March 24, 1837
78. To George W. Benson, April 3, 1837
79. To Mrs. Sarah T. Benson, April 8, 1837
80. To Caleb Cushing, April 11, 1837
81. To Henry C. Wright, April 16, 1837
82. To Helen E. Garrison, May 6, 1837
83. To Amos A. Phelps, May 23, 1837
84. To John Farmer, June 6, 1837
85. To George W. Benson, June 14, 1837
86. To Helen E. Garrison, July 1, 1837
87. To Isaac Knapp, August 9, 1837
88. To Orson S. Murray, August 11, 1837
89. To Oliver Johnson, August 14, 1837
90. To J. H. Kimball, August 16, 1837
91. To George W. Benson, August 26, 1837
92. To James T. Woodbury, August 28, 1837
93. To Lewis Tappan, September 13, 1837
94. To George W. Benson, September 16, 1837
95. To George W. Benson, September 23, 1837
96. To Isaac C. Taber, October 9, 1837
97. To James P. Boyce, October 10, 1837
98. To George W. Benson, October 20, 1837
99. To the Editor of the Spectator, October 20, 1837
100. To Elizur Wright, Jr., October 23, 1837
101. To Phoebe Jackson, November 6, 1837
102. To Elizabeth Pease, November 6, 1837
103. To Mrs. Hannah Fifield, November 21, 1837
104. To George W. Benson, December 9, 1837
105. To Samuel J. May, December 30, 1837

III BROADENING INTERESTS — PEACE AND
NONRESISTANCE: 1838   333

106. To Edward M. Davis, January 8, 1838
107. To George W. Benson, January 15, 1838
108. To Mrs. Sarah T. Benson, January 20, 1838
109. To Mrs. Sarah T. Benson, March 5, 1838
110. To George W. Benson, March 10, 1838
111. To George W. Benson, April 7, 1838

Contents

112. To Samuel J. May, April 24, 1838
113. To Helen E. Garrison, May 4, 1838
114. To Helen E. Garrison, May 7, 1838
115. To George Thompson, May 7, 1838
116. To Isaac Knapp, May 8, 1838
117. To Helen E. Garrison, May 12, 1838
118. To Mrs. Sarah T. Benson, May 19, 1838
119. To George W. Benson, May 25, 1838
120. To Francis Jackson, June 18, 1838
121. To Edmund Quincy, June 19, 1838
122. To Francis Jackson, June 28, 1838
123. To Samuel J. May, July 13, 1838
124. To Oliver Johnson, August 14, 1838
125. To Erasmus D. Hudson, September 8, 1838
126. To Samuel J. May, September 8, 1838
127. To Helen E. Garrison, September 21, 1838
128. To Mary Benson, September 22, 1838
129. To Helen E. Garrison, September 23, 1838
130. To Sarah Benson, September 24, 1838
131. To Samuel J. May, September 24, 1838
132. To George W. Benson, September 29, 1838
133. To Samuel J. May, October 30, 1838
134. To Mary Benson, December 23, 1838

IV POLITICS AND WOMEN — DIVISIONS WITHIN
THE RANKS: 1839   412

135. To Samuel J. May, January 4, 1839
136. To George W. Benson, January 5, 1839
137. To Mary S. Parker, January 8, 1839
138. To George W. Benson, January 14, 1839
139. To Harriet Foster, January 14, 1839
140. To John Quincy Adams, February 8, 1839
141. To Mary Benson, February 10, 1839
142. To Friends of Non-Resistance, March 1, 1839
143. To James Mott, March 4, 1839
144. To George W. Benson, March 19, 1839
145. To the Abolitionists of Massachusetts, March 30, 1839
146. To Harriet Foster, April 8, 1839
147. To Arthur and Lewis Tappan, April 8, 1839
148. To Helen E. Garrison, April 22, 1839
149. To Helen E. Garrison, May 5, 1839
150. To the Executive of the American Anti-
      Slavery Society, May 13, 1839
151. To Henry C. Wright, May 20, 1839
152. To Nathaniel P. Rogers, May 21, 1839

Contents

153. To the Editor of the Emancipator, May 31, 1839
154. To Wendell Phillips, June 4, 1839
155. To George W. Benson, June 15, 1839
156. To Samuel J. May, June 22, 1839
157. To Amos A. Phelps, July 9, 1839
158. To the Abolitionists of Massachusetts, July 17, 1839
159. To Samuel Osgood, August 2, 1839
160. To Oliver Johnson, August 5, 1839
161. To George Thompson, August 23, 1839
162. To Edmund Quincy and Henry C. Wright, September 14, 1839
163. To George W. Benson, September 30, 1839
164. To Lewis Tappan, *et al.*, November 1, 1839
165. To an Unidentified Friend, December 2, 1839
166. To the Executive Committee of the American Anti-Slavery Society, December 6, 1839
167. To James K. Paulding, December 14, 1839
168. To the Hon. Caleb Cushing, December 16, 1839

V THE GREAT SCHISM AND THE EUROPEAN PILGRIMAGE: 1840

553

169. To George W. Benson, January 4, 1840
170. To Caleb Cushing, February 10, 1840
171. To Charles Stearns, February 10, 1840
172. To the Abolitionists of the United States, February 28, 1840
173. To Caleb Cushing, March 6, 1840
174. To Gerrit Smith, March 27, 1840
175. To Delegates of the Massachusetts Anti-Slavery Society, April 9, 1840
176. To Joshua T. Everett, April 14, 1840
177. To the Abolitionists of the United States, April 24, 1840
178. To George Bradburn, April 24, 1840
179. To Nathaniel P. Rogers, April 24, 1840
180. To Lucretia Mott, April 28, 1840
181. To Richard P. Hunt, May 1, 1840
182. To Gerrit Smith, May 8, 1840
183. To Oliver Johnson, May 12, 1840
184. To Helen E. Garrison, May 15, 1840
185. To Helen E. Garrison, May 16, 1840
186. To Helen E. Garrison, May 19, 1840
187. To Helen E. Garrison, May 20, 1840
188. To Helen E. Garrison, May 21, 1840
189. To George W. Benson, May 21, 1840
190. To Oliver Johnson, May 22, 1840

Contents

191. To an Unidentified Correspondent, May 22, 1840
192. To Helen E. Garrison, May 28, 1840
193. To Maria W. Chapman, June 3, 1840
194. To James Garrison, June 4, 1840
195. To an Unidentified Correspondent, June 12, 1840
196. To Edmund Quincy, June 13, 1840
197. To Helen E. Garrison, June 14, 1840
198. To an Unidentified Correspondent, June 14, 1840
199. To Helen E. Garrison, June 15, 1840
200. To Helen E. Garrison, June 15, 1840
201. To Helen E. Garrison, June 29, 1840
202. To Helen E. Garrison, July 3, 1840
203. To Oliver Johnson, July 3, 1840
204. To Oliver Johnson, July 0, 1840
205. To Elizabeth Pease, July 13, 1840
206. To Helen E. Garrison, July 23, 1840
207. To Marcus Gunn, July 27, 1840
208. To Joseph Pease, August 3, 1840.
209. To George W. Benson, August 18, 1840
210. To Anti-Slavery Friends and Coadjutors, August 19, 1840
211. To James G. Barbadoes, Thomas Cole, J. T. Hilton, August 19, 1840
212. To Henry C. Wright, August 23, 1840
213. To Elizabeth Pease, August 31, 1840
214. To Elizabeth Pease, September 1, 1840
215. To Joseph Pease, September 1, 1840
216. To Nathaniel P. Rogers, September 4, 1840
217. To Amos Farnsworth, September 6, 1840
218. To Samuel J. May, September 6, 1840
219. To Mrs. Henry Walker, September 8, 1840
220. To George W. Benson, September 17, 1840
221. To James Garrison, September 17, 1840
222. To Phebe Jackson, September 19, 1840
223. To Elizabeth Pease, September 30, 1840
224. To Joseph Pease, September 30, 1840
225. To Maria W. Chapman, October 5, 1840
226. To His Editorial Chair, October 6, 1840
227. To Maria W. Chapman, October 13, 1840
228. To John A. Collins, October 16, 1840
229. To George W. Benson, November 1, 1840
230. To John A. Collins, December 1, 1840
231. To Elizabeth Pease, December 1, 1840

Index of Recipients   733
Index   735

LIST OF ILLUSTRATIONS

Frontispiece

William Lloyd Garrison at about the age of thirty-five. From a daguerreotype by T. B. Shew; on stone by Albert Newsam; P. S. Duval, lithographer, Philadelphia, *circa* 1840

Courtesy of the Sophia Smith Collection, Smith College Library, Northampton, Massachusetts.

Following page 328

The Liberator, January 9, 1836, first page.

Courtesy of the Harvard College Library.

The pro-slavery riot of November 7, 1838, Alton, Illinois, during which the Reverend Elijah P. Lovejoy was killed. From a woodcut made in 1838.

Courtesy of the Library of Congress.

Following page 534

The Liberator, July 20, 1838, first page. The burning of Pennsylvania Hall is discussed in the lead column.

Courtesy of the Harvard College Library.

William Lloyd Garrison to Lewis Tappan, Arthur Tappan, Joshua Leavitt, or James G. Birney, New York City, November 1, 1839 (letter number 164). The seal on this letter is taken from the seal of the Committee for the Abolition of the Slave Trade, formed in Britain in May 1787, from which Josiah Wedgwood struck a medallion in 1787 (see letter number 115, note 1).

Courtesy of the American Missionary Association Archives in the Amistad Research Center, Fisk University, Nashville, Tennessee.

Following page 666

Nathaniel Colver, Samuel Gurney, and Thomas Clarkson, portrait studies by Benjamin Robert Haydon, the English artist, on the occasion of the World's Anti-Slavery Convention in London, June 1840. Colver and Gurney were delegates to the convention; Clarkson was president of the convention.

Courtesy of Willard B. Pope, Burlington, Vermont.

xvii

List of Illustrations

The World's Anti-Slavery Convention, June 1840. The painting, now in the National Portrait Gallery, London, is by Benjamin Robert Haydon and shows Thomas Clarkson as he "drew tears from every eye at the close of his presidential address" (Anna M. Stoddart, *Elizabeth Pease Nichol*, London and New York, 1899, page 124). Elizabeth Pease is sitting on Clarkson's right.

Reproduced from Stoddart, by courtesy of the Library of Congress.

EDITORIAL STATEMENT

THIS VOLUME contains all the available letters written by Garrison from the beginning of 1836 to the end of 1840. The originals were either in Garrison's own handwriting, or appeared in newspapers under Garrison's name, or have been found in typescripts or handwritten copies prepared by others from the originals. The exact source is indicated in the notes.

The letters are arranged in five yearly periods, with each year prefaced by a short essay which provides a context for understanding the letters of that year. Where there are two or more letters per day, they are arranged in alphabetical order according to the surname of the recipient.

1. Each letter is numbered according to its position in the sequence of letters.

2. The name of the recipient, in its usual spelling, is printed at the head of each letter. Titles are excluded from the caption unless their presence helps to differentiate two persons of the same name.

3. Each letter is given a date line using Garrison's original words, the editor having supplied additional information, as in conjectural dates and place names, in square brackets. Where Garrison noted the place and date at the close of a letter, these are also included, in brackets, at the beginning.

4. The salutation is uniformly placed and follows Garrison's original wording.

5. The editor has sought to provide an accurate text of each letter as presented in its source. Obvious slips, such as the misspelling of a word or the inadvertent repetition of a word or phrase, have been silently corrected.

6. The complimentary close and signature are presented as in the source, but uniformly placed.

7. Postscripts are uniformly placed after Garrison's signature. Marginal notations intended as postscripts are similarly placed, with a note indicating their original position in the manuscript.

8. Certain editorial situations are indicated by the following symbols:

⟨Cancellation⟩

[. . .] Unrecoverable matter. If the material is more than four or five words long, its nature and extent are explained in the notes.

[   ] Editorial insertion.

[   ] Garrison's brackets.

☞ ☜ Garrison's method of emphasis.

Descriptive Notes

1. The source of the letter is provided immediately following the text; abbreviations used are ALS for "autograph letter signed," and AL for "autograph letter" unsigned. A source other than an autograph is always described.

2. Known previous publications of a letter, whether in whole or in part, have been indicated.

3. Efforts have been made to identify all recipients either in notes or in introductory essays.

Notes

1. Notes, numbered consecutively, are placed immediately after the descriptive notes.

2. The editor has attempted to identify persons referred to in the texts of the letters and to explain references and allusions not immediately clear in their contexts. Whenever possible, Garrison's quotations have been identified. The Contents and the Index of Recipients should serve as convenient guides.

ABBREVIATIONS AND SHORT TITLES

ACAB. James Grant Wilson and John Fiske, eds. *Appletons' Cyclopedia of American Biography* (New York: D. Appleton and Company, 1888–89), 6 volumes.

BDAC. James L. Harrington, *Biographical Directory of the American Congress, 1774–1961* (Washington, D.C.: Government Printing Office, 1961).

CVDE. William Bridgwater, Editor-in-Chief, *The Columbia-Viking Desk Encyclopedia* (New York: Dell Publishing Co., 1966).

DAB. Allen John and Dumas Malone, eds., *Dictionary of American Biography* (New York: Charles Scribner's Sons, 1928–1936), 20 volumes.

DNB. Leslie Stephen and Sidney Lee, eds., *Dictionary of National Biography* (New York and London: Macmillan and Company and Smith, Elder and Company, 1885–1912), 63 volumes, and supplements.

DUSH. J. Franklin Jameson, ed., *Dictionary of United States History, 1492–1894* (Boston: Puritan Publishing Co., 1894).

EB. Warren E. Preece, ed., *Encyclopaedia Britannica* (Chicago *et al.*: William Benton, publisher, 1968), 23 volumes.

EE. Andrew Boyle, ed., *The Everyman Encyclopaedia* (New York: E. P. Dutton & Company, 1913), 12 volumes.

Letters, I. The Letters of William Lloyd Garrison, vol. I, Walter M. Merrill, ed. (Cambridge, Mass.: The Belknap Press of Harvard University Press, 1971).

Life. W. P. and F. J. Garrison, *William Lloyd Garrison, 1805–1879: The Story of His Life, Told by His Children* (New York: 1885–1889).

NCAB. National Cyclopaedia of American Biography (New York: James T. White and Co., 1898–1968).

Ruchames, *The Abolitionists.* Louis Ruchames, *The Abolitionists: A Collection of Their Writings* (New York: Capricorn Edition, 1964).

Union List of Newspapers. Winifred Gregory, ed., *American Newspapers, 1821–1936: A Union List of Files Available in the United States and Canada* (New York: H. W. Wilson & Co., 1937).

Union List of Serials. Edna Brown Titus, ed., *Union List of Serials in Libraries of the United States and Canada,* 3d edition (New York: H. W. Wilson & Co., 1965).

Weld-Grimké Letters. Gilbert H. Barnes and Dwight L. Dumond, eds., *Letters of Theodore Dwight Weld, Angelina Grimké Weld and Sarah Grimké, 1822–1844* (Gloucester, Mass.: 1965).

SHORT BIOGRAPHIES OF
ANTISLAVERY MEN AND WOMEN

The Benson Family

Helen Eliza Benson, whom Garrison married in September 1834, was one of a family of ten — six daughters and two sons — then living in Brooklyn, Connecticut.

The father, George Benson (1752–1836), had been a prominent merchant and civic leader in Providence, Rhode Island, where he was a member of the distinguished firm of Brown, Benson, & Ives. Although raised as a Baptist, he was closely attached to the views and customs of the Society of Friends and while never a member of the society, did attend their meetings in Providence. His antislavery interests extended as far back as the immediate post-Revolutionary period. In 1789–1790, he helped found and incorporate the Providence Society for the Abolition of the Slave Trade, of which he later became secretary. In 1792, he was made an honorary member of the Pennsylvania Society for Promoting the Abolition of Slavery, the first American antislavery society, which had first been founded in 1775. On retiring from business activity, he moved with his family to a farm in Brooklyn, Connecticut, in 1824. He attended Samuel J. May's Unitarian church in Brooklyn regularly for many years and formed with May the Windham County Peace Society, of which May was corresponding secretary and Benson the president. Benjamin Lundy stayed at Benson's home after speaking at a meeting in Brooklyn in 1828. In 1833, after the death of John Kenrick, Benson was chosen president of the New England Anti-Slavery Society, and re-elected unanimously in 1834.

The mother, Sarah Thurber Benson (1770–1844), described by Samuel J. May as "one of the most motherly of women," was a shy, quiet woman who was deeply devoted to her family and her home. Of their eight children the first five were girls.

Frances, the eldest (1794–1832), had died before Garrison knew the family. In his *Memoir*, Samuel J. May characterizes her as "very Orthodox."

Mary (1797–1842) was deeply interested in various reform movements of the day, especially antislavery. In 1838, she attended the Annual Convention of American Anti-Slavery Women in Philadelphia. Her religious convictions were close to the Quakers, whose Society she joined in 1829. Garrison often wrote to her about developments in the antislavery movement.

She died while staying with the Garrisons in Boston. *The Liberator*, noting her death, remarked that "in all the righteous reforms of the age, she took a deep interest; and the last efforts of her industry were in behalf of the suffering slave."

Sarah Thurber (1799–1850) was characterized by Samuel J. May as "a very saint." In writing her obituary in *The Liberator*, on October 11, 1850, Garrison noted that "though constitutionally feeble, and for several years suffering the pains of martyrdom from an incurable disease, she was a model of patience, fortitude, and holy resignation. There was no movement for the renovation of society, or the overthrow of injustice and oppression, in which she did not take a deep interest. Especially, from childhood, were her feelings strongly enlisted in behalf of the millions who are held in bondage in our guilty land."

Ann Elizabeth, called Anna (1801–1843) was described by Garrison, in a letter in *The Liberator*, dated Northampton, September 17, 1843, as "among the gentlest, purest spirits that ever dwelt on earth. . . . Her heart was in all the various reforms of the age; and though, in consequence of her long protracted bodily infirmities, and of her great natural diffidence, she was unable to make herself conspicuous or active in carrying them forward, she nevertheless took a lively and an abiding interest in every effort to promote the happiness of the human race, especially in the beneficent cause of anti-slavery."

Charlotte (1803–1886) married in 1826 Henry Anthony (1802–1879) of Providence, and lived in Providence thereafter. She and Helen, Garrison's wife, were the only two of the sisters who married. Charlotte and Henry's surviving children (two had died in the year of birth) were Mary Gould (b. 1829), Sarah B. (b. 1832), George H. (b. 1835), Joseph B. (b. 1837), and Frederick Eugene (b. October 18, 1840).

George William Benson (1808–1879), one of the earliest supporters in New England of Garrison and *The Liberator*, managed the Benson family farm in Brooklyn, Connecticut, from the time it was bought, in 1824, until it was sold in 1841. During several of those years, beginning in 1831, he conducted a business, as wool and leather merchant, in Providence, Rhode Island, in partnership with William M. Chace, another *Liberator* supporter. The business became known as George W. Benson & Co. In 1833. In 1836, when his father died, he abandoned the business in order to become head of the household in Brooklyn, Connecticut. He remained there until 1841, when he sold the farm, because it was unprofitable, and moved to Bensonville (now Florence), Massachusetts. There, in 1842, he helped found the Northampton Association of Education and Industry, one of the communal experiments of the day. Although the association was dissolved in 1846, he continued to live there until 1850, when he moved to Williamsburgh, Long Island, where he started a laundry business. In 1855, he moved to New York City and became a commission broker. In 1860, he moved to Lawrence, Kansas, where he spent his last years, participated in politics, and was elected state representative. Throughout the years he was Garrison's devoted friend and collaborator, in the anti-slavery movement as well as in other areas such as peace, nonresistance and the anti-Sabbath movement.

He married Catherine (often spelled Catharine) Knapp Stetson in Waltham, Massachusetts, on December 10, 1833. Their children were Anna Elizabeth (b. Providence, September 23, 1834), Henry Egbert (b. Brooklyn, Connecticut, October 7, 1837), George (b. Brooklyn, January 7, 1839), Eliza Davis (b. Brooklyn, February 24, 1841; d. May 3, 1842), Thomas Davis (b. Northampton, September 1, 1842), Mary (b. Northampton, October 18, 1843), and Sarah (b. October 17, 1846).

Helen Eliza (1811–1876), Garrison's wife, first met him in 1833, when he spoke at the African Church in Providence. "She was," her children note in the biography of their father, "a plump and rosy creature, with blue eyes and fair brown hair, just entering, when first seen by him, her twenty-third year." She proved to be a loving and devoted wife and mother, gentle, sweet, and kindly in disposition. On the first anniversary of their marriage, Garrison wrote to her brother George: "I did not marry her expecting that she would assume a prominent station in the anti-slavery cause, but for domestic quietude and happiness. . . . By her unwearied attentions to my wants, her sympathetic regards, her perfect equanimity of mind, and her sweet and endearing manners, she is no trifling support to Abolitionism, inasmuch as she lightens my labors, and enables me to find exquisite delight in the family circle, as an offset to public adversity."

Henry Egbert (1814–1837), the youngest of the Benson children, was, like his older brother, an early reader and supporter of *The Liberator*. Several months after its appearance, Henry accepted an offer from Garrison, made at the suggestion of Samuel J. May, that he act as agent for *The Liberator*. They did not meet personally until June, 1832, at the home of Moses Brown, in Providence, Rhode Island, but, thereafter, their friendship for one another grew close and strong. Henry's efforts in securing subscribers and financial support for *The Liberator* in its early years contributed importantly to its continuance. With his brother, he helped to organize the Providence Anti-Slavery Society. During George Thompson's visit to the United States he acted as his traveling associate and secretary. He became secretary and general agent of the Massachusetts Anti-Slavery Society in July 1835. After his attendance at the convention of the Rhode Island Anti-Slavery Society in February 1836, held in subzero weather, he took ill, recovered, but then suffered a relapse and died on January 6, 1837.

Maria Weston Chapman

Maria Weston Chapman (b. July 25, 1806, in Weymouth, Massachusetts; d. July 12, 1885) married Henry Grafton Chapman, a Boston merchant, in 1830. With her husband, who died in 1842, she joined the antislavery movement in 1834 and became one of Garrison's staunchest supporters and collaborators. Garrison's sons, in the biography of their father, write that "on her, more than on any other woman, the conduct of the cause rested." She was the living spirit of the Boston Female Anti-Slavery Society and edited the annual reports of the society, published between 1836 and 1840 under the title *Right and Wrong in Boston*. She contributed frequently to *The Liberator*, the *National Anti-Slavery Standard*, the *Liberty Bell*, which she edited from 1839 to 1846, and other antislavery publications. On various occasions through the years, during Garrison's illness or absence from Boston, she and Edmund Quincy edited *The Liberator*. In 1840, she was elected to the Executive Committee of the American Anti-Slavery Society, as were Lucretia Mott and Lydia Maria Child. James Russell Lowell, in a poem describing an Anti-Slavery Bazaar held in Boston on December 22, 1846, characterized her as

> "The coiled-up mainspring of the Fair,
> Originating everywhere
> The expansive force without a sound
> That whirled a hundred wheels around. . . ."

Francis Jackson

Francis Jackson (b. March 7, 1789, in Newton, Massachusetts; d. November 14, 1861) was Garrison's close friend and collaborator from the mid-1830's to the end of his life. He was a soldier in the War of 1812 at Fort Warren in Boston harbor, and in subsequent years participated actively in Boston municipal affairs. A man of means, for twenty-five years he gave strong financial support to Garrison in meeting *The Liberator's* debts and participated with other antislavery businessmen in supervising *The Liberator's* finances. In October, 1835, when the Boston mob forced adjournment of the annual meeting of the Boston Female Anti-Slavery Society, amid cries of "lynch Garrison," Jackson courageously invited the ladies to meet in his home. They did meet there on November 19. Jackson's reply to a letter of thanks from the Massachusetts Anti-Slavery Society for having the meeting in his home is a remarkable defense of the right of free speech. For many years, he was president of the Massachusetts Anti-Slavery Society, as well as of the New England Anti-Slavery Conventions, and a vice-president of the American Anti-Slavery Society. He accepted Garrison's policy of "no union with slaveholders" and joined in denouncing the Constitution as "a covenant with death and an agreement with hell." In 1844, he resigned his commission as justice of the peace, expressing regret at his having taken the oath of office to support the United States Constitution and affirming publicly that he could not obey the Constitutional provision for the return of fugitive slaves. At his death, he left $10,000 for aid to Negro freedmen, a liberal bequest to Garrison, and $5,000 to the Woman's Rights Movement.

Oliver Johnson

Oliver Johnson (b. December 27, 1809; d. December 10, 1889) was one of Garrison's earliest collaborators. In 1828 and 1829, as a printer's apprentice in the Montpelier, Vermont, office of the Vermont *Watchman*, he first came under Garrison's influence by reading the *Journal of the Times*, which Garrison was then editing at Bennington, Vermont.

It was in the same building in which Garrison edited *The Liberator* that Johnson, using *The Liberator* press, also edited the *Christian Soldier*, an anti-Universalist religious paper. He began issuing his paper in 1831, within a week of the first issue of *The Liberator*. A warm friendship and close collaboration in anti-slavery matters developed between the two which continued throughout their lives. Johnson was one of the founders of the New England Anti-Slavery Society in 1832, and became its traveling agent in 1836. On various occasions, during periods of Garrison's illness, as in the summers of 1837 and 1838, or during Garrison's trips to Europe, as in 1833 and 1840, Johnson edited *The Liberator*. After assisting Horace Greeley on the New York *Tribune* from 1844 to 1848, he edited the *Anti-Slavery Bugle* of Salem, Ohio (not Massachusetts, as given in the *DAB*), and later the *Pennsylvania Freeman*, another antislavery newspaper. In 1853, he became associate editor of the *National Anti-Slavery Standard*, published in New York as the official organ of the American Anti-Slavery Society. He held the post until the end of the Civil War. Among the publications which he helped to edit after the war, were the *Independent*, the *New York Weekly Tribune*, and the *New York Evening Post*.

As was also true of Garrison, Johnson was active in many of the reform movements of his day, including woman's rights and peace. He wrote several books, the most important of which was *William Lloyd Garrison and His Times* (1880). His wife, Mary Ann (1808–1872), also active in reform, was for a time assistant matron in the female state prison, Sing Sing, New York.

Isaac Knapp

Isaac Knapp (b. January 11, 1804; d. September 14, 1843), born in Newburyport, Massachusetts, was Garrison's boyhood friend and one of his earliest collaborators. A printer by trade, Knapp bought the *Northern Chronicler* of Newburyport in June 1825, changed its name to the *Essex Courant*, and published it until March 1826, when he retired because of ill health. Garrison bought the paper from him, changed its name to the *Free Press* and published it for six months. *The Liberator*, when it first appeared, in January 1831, was issued by Garrison and Knapp as partners, the names of both appearing on its front as publishers, with Garrison listed also as editor and Stephen Foster as printer. It was Knapp's responsibility to manage *The Liberator*'s finances. Knapp also helped found the New England Anti-Slavery Society in 1832. The partnership of Garrison and Knapp ended at the close of 1835 with Knapp becoming *The Liberator*'s sole publisher and assuming all its financial responsibilities. In the ensuing years, Knapp served as *The Liberator*'s printer, but he seems to have been overwhelmed by his responsibilities, and his management of its finances proved less than satisfactory. In 1838, as a result of an agreement with Garrison and a group of other Abolitionists, Knapp relinquished control of *The Liberator*'s business management but continued as its printer. During his latter years, Knapp seems to have deteriorated physically and morally. He married a young girl whose demands sent him deeply into debt. He drank and gambled recklessly. In 1841, Garrison and his friends bought out Knapp's remaining interest in *The Liberator*. Knapp later repented the settlement, claiming that he had been defrauded. In retaliation, he published, on January 8, 1842, the first and only issue of a rival newspaper, *Knapp's Liberator*. He died less than two years later.

Samuel Joseph May

Samuel Joseph May (b. September 12, 1797; d. July 1, 1871), Boston-born and descended on his mother's side from Judge Samuel Sewall, was a Unitarian clergyman and early supporter of Garrison's antislavery efforts. Ordained in 1822, May had assisted the great Unitarian clergyman William Ellery Channing, and then served churches at Brooklyn, Connecticut (1822–1835), South Scituate, Massachusetts (1836–1842), and Syracuse, New York (1845–1867). From 1842 to 1844, in response to a request from Horace Mann, he was principal of the Normal School at Lexington, Massachusetts. May met Garrison in 1830, on the night of an antislavery lecture by the latter in Boston, and became his devoted follower. He participated in the founding of the New England Anti-Slavery Society in 1832, and of the American Anti-Slavery Society in December, 1833. He gave aid to Prudence Crandall and defended her right to keep a school for Negro girls in Canterbury, Connecticut. In 1835 and 1836, he served as general agent and secretary of the Massachusetts Anti-Slavery Society. In Syracuse, his home was a station for Negroes attempting to reach Canada on the Underground Railroad and in 1851 he took part in a successful public rescue of a Negro slave being detained by the authorities in Syracuse for shipment back to slavery. Among his other reform interests were the rights of woman, peace, and temperance. He and Garrison were close friends until his death.

James and Lucretia Mott

James and Lucretia Coffin Mott were pioneer abolitionists who made signal contributions to the antislavery cause. Both were descendants of Quakers. James Mott (b. June 20, 1788; d. January 26, 1868) was born in North Hempstead, Long Island, New York; Lucretia (b. January 3, 1793; d. November 11, 1880) was born on the island of Nantucket. They met in the Friends' boarding school at Nine Partners, near Poughkeepsie, New York, where both James and Lucretia were students and teachers. They were married on April 11, 1811, and had six children, of whom five lived to maturity.

James tried his hand at various business ventures and finally succeeded in the cotton commission business in Philadelphia during the 1820's. He abandoned it in 1830 because of its connection with slavery, and entered the wool commission business where he prospered until his retirement in 1852. Lucretia, at the age of twenty five, displayed marked talents as a preacher at Quaker meetings and was made a minister of the society, aligning herself, as did her husband, with the Hicksite group. She became widely known for her preaching, traveling to Quaker meetings all over the country.

James and Lucretia Mott were early opponents of slavery. They were present at the founding convention of the American Anti-Slavery Society in Philadelphia in 1833, with James participating as a member. Soon afterward, Lucretia helped form the Philadelphia Female Anti-Slavery Society, of which she became and remained president for many years. They both attended the world anti-slavery convention in London in 1840, with James publishing his reminiscences in 1841 in a small book entitled *Three Months in Great Britain*. With the passage of the Fugitive Slave Law of 1850, their home became a refuge for runaway slaves. Their interest in the antislavery movement continued until emancipation.

Both Lucretia and James Mott were active at the first woman's rights convention at Seneca Falls, New York, in 1848, with Lucretia one of its prominent promoters and James presiding over some of its sessions.

Amos Augustus Phelps

Amos Augustus Phelps (b. Farmington, Connecticut, November 11, 1804; d. Roxbury, Massachusetts, July 30, 1847), a graduate of Yale Divinity School, had been pastor of the Pine-Street (Trinitarian) Church in Boston, which he served from 1832 to 1834. His book, *Lectures on Slavery and Its Remedy* was published in Boston in 1834 by the New England Anti-Slavery Society. The book was an important contribution to the antislavery cause and was characterized by Oliver Johnson, Garrison's co-worker and biographer, as "of equal power and value with Mrs Child's Appeal." Phelps was also an early member of the New England Anti-Slavery Society and one of the founders of the American Anti-Slavery Society. He was general agent of the Massachusetts Anti-Slavery Society from June 1837 to December 1838. From 1839 to 1841, he was minister at the Free Church, Marlboro' Chapel. Although a close friend of Garrison for several years, the two quarreled bitterly in 1838 and 1839 over the admission of women to the Massachusetts and American Anti-Slavery Societies. He served the East Boston Maverick Chuch from March 2, 1842, to June 2, 1845.

Edmund Quincy

Edmund Quincy (b. February 1, 1808; d. May 17, 1877), Boston born, was the second son of Josiah Quincy, president of Harvard University, mayor of Boston, and congressman. A graduate of Harvard College, Edmund studied law and was admitted to the bar but never practiced. He married Lucilla P. Parker in 1833.

In 1837, outraged by the murder of Elijah Lovejoy, the antislavery editor, at Alton, Illinois, he joined the Massachusetts Anti-Slavery Society and, in the following year, the American Anti-Slavery Society. In the former organization, he was corresponding secretary from 1844 to 1853; in the latter, he held the office of vice-president in 1853 and from 1856 to 1859.

An able writer and editor, he became an editor of the *Abolitionist*, the official organ of the Massachusetts Anti-Slavery Society in 1839, and of the *National Anti-Slavery Standard*, the weekly newspaper of the American Anti-Slavery Society, in 1844. He contributed to the *Liberty Bell*, an annual antislavery volume edited by Maria Weston Chapman, as well as to the *New York Tribune*, the *Independent*, and *The Liberator*, which he also edited, from time to time, in Garrison's absence.

Influenced by Garrison's views on the nature of the Constitution and on nonresistance, he became an editor of *The Non-Resistant* in 1839. He later returned his commission as justice of the peace because of his inability to carry out the constitutional provision for the return of fugitive slaves. He was also a vigorous proponent of freedom and equality for women.

His contributions as a writer deserve to be better known. James Russell

Lowell called his writings on slavery "gems of Flemish art." In 1854 he wrote *Wensley, a Story Without a Moral.* Some of his best short stories were collected and published in 1885 in *The Haunted Adjutant and Other Stories,* and in 1867 he wrote a biography of his father, *Life of Josiah Quincy.*

In his later years, especially after the Civil War, he concentrated upon literary and civic pursuits, serving as recording secretary of the Massachusetts Historical Society, on the Board of Overseers of Harvard College, as a fellow of the American Academy of Arts and Sciences, and as a member of the American Philosophical Society.

Arthur and Lewis Tappan

Arthur and Lewis Tappan, brothers, of Northampton, Massachusetts, were businessmen-philanthropists who distinguished themselves in the antislavery and other reform movements. Owners of a silk jobbing firm in New York founded in 1826 by Arthur Tappan (b. May 22, 1786; d. July 23, 1865), who was joined in 1828 by Lewis Tappan (b. May 23, 1788; d. June 21, 1873), their original efforts were directed toward furtherance of Protestant church and missionary efforts, such as the American Tract Society and the American Sunday School Union. Their concerns included stricter Sabbath observance, temperance, and the evils of tobacco smoking and prostitution.

Their friendship with Garrison began in 1830 when Arthur Tappan freed Garrison from a Baltimore jail by paying his fine. Both brothers subsequently became warm admirers of Garrison, providing financial support for *The Liberator* for several years, and praising him publicly for his antislavery efforts. In 1833, in New York, they helped to establish the *Emancipator,* an antislavery newspaper which became the official organ of the American Anti-Slavery Society, and participated in the formation of the New York Anti-Slavery Society, and the American Anti-Slavery Society. Arthur was elected its president and held this office for many years.

The Tappans broke with Garrison in 1840 over the participation of women in antislavery activities and the issue of political action. With others of Garrison's opponents they seceded from the American Anti-Slavery Society and formed the American and Foreign Anti-Slavery Society, of which Arthur was elected president and Lewis treasurer. They supported the Liberty party candidate in 1840, and helped to establish an antislavery weekly, the *National Era,* in Washington. Although both men severed all ties with Garrison in 1840, they were reconciled in November 1863, when Garrison invited Arthur Tappan to participate in a commemorative meeting of those who had originally formed the American Anti-Slavery Society. When Lewis Tappan published the biography of his brother, *The Life of Arthur Tappan,* in 1870, he made every effort to mitigate the asperities of the conflict with Garrison and his treatment of the latter was warm and sympathetic. A letter that he received from Garrison shortly before the publication of the work reciprocated his sentiment.

George Thompson

George Thompson (b. Liverpool, England, June 18, 1804; d. Leeds,

England, October 7, 1878), an English antislavery leader, did yeoman service for the antislavery cause in the United States. His official connection with the antislavery movement began in 1831 in England, with his appointment as lecturing agent of the London Anti-Slavery Society, in the midst of the campaign for the elimination of slavery in the British West Indies. Taking as his motto "immediate and unconditional emancipation," he played an important role in influencing public opinion and in bringing about the passage of the emancipation bill in Parliament in 1833, which ended slavery in the British colonies. In 1864, John Bright, the English statesman, referred to him as "the real liberator of the slaves in the English colonies." It was during Garrison's first visit to England in 1833 that he first met Thompson and persuaded him to come to the United States to help in the antislavery effort. He arrived in this country in September 1834 and remained until December, 1835. During that time, he addressed numerous antislavery meetings and was in frequent danger of being mobbed and physically attacked. In October 1835, during the mob attack on Garrison in Boston, it was he who was as much sought after as Garrison. Thompson again came to the United States in October 1850 and remained for eight months, lecturing and seeing old friends. Although a meeting at Faneuil Hall in Boston in his honor was broken up by a band of rioters, the reception was subsequently held in Worcester and most of his other appearances met with cordial receptions. His last visit to the United States began in February 1864, when the abolitionists were perhaps at the height of their popularity. He was given an enthusiastic reception in Boston at a meeting presided over by Governor John A. Andrew, with a tremendous audience crowding the doors of the Music Hall. Even more noteworthy, perhaps, was the public reception given him at Washington, D.C., in the House of Representatives, with President Lincoln and most other members of the Cabinet present.

Thompson earlier in the war played a vital part in helping to form English opinion in favor of the northern cause and in preventing the British Cabinet from recognizing the independence of the southern Confederacy.

He also participated in the struggle to abolish the English corn laws, helped form the British India Association, defended the cause of the natives of India against the East India Company, and was a member of Parliament for several years.

Henry Clarke Wright

Henry Clarke Wright (b. Sharon, Connecticut, August 29, 1797; d. Pawtucket, Rhode Island, August 16, 1870) was a hatmaker turned minister. He studied at Andover from 1819 to 1823, when he was ordained. He ministered to the Congregational Church in West Newbury, Massachusetts, until 1833, joined the New England Anti-Slavery Society in May 1835 and met Garrison for the first time on November 6, 1835. At the end of 1836, Wright was included among the "seventy" agents of the American Anti-Slavery Society whose task was to popularize the antislavery cause. He was then appointed a Children's Anti-Slavery Agent by the American Anti-Slavery Society. As he announced in *The Liberator*, "my object is to embody our children in Anti-Slavery Societies in every church, and town, and city, in the land." (*The Liberator*, December 24, 1836.) He remained an agent until October 1837, when the executive committee of the American Anti-Slavery Society refused to renew his commission, probably "because of his peculiar peace views, and because he declined giving a pledge to confine himself to the discussion of abolitionism." (*Life*, II, 159n.) He was one of the organizers of the Peace Convention, in September 1838, which led to the formation of the New England Non-Resistance Society. He was the society's only lecturing agent and he also assisted in the editing of the *Non-Resistant*, its official organ. He took part in calling the famous Chardon-Street Convention in November 1840 and participated in its deliberations.

Wright has been called the "chief propagandist for the nonresistance cause" during the late thirties and through the 1840's. (Peter Brock, *Pacifism in the United States, from the Colonial Era to the First World War*, Princeton, 1968, p. 586.) His writings consisted of letters, essays, pamphlets, and books. Among them were the following:

> *Man-Killing, by Individuals and Nations, Wrong — Dangerous in All Cases*, Boston, 1841.
> *Ballot Box and Battle Field. To voters under the United States Government.* Boston, 1842.
> *A Kiss for a Blow*, Dublin, 1843.
> *Defensive War Proved to be a Denial of Christianity and of the Government of God; with Illustrative Facts and Anecdotes*, London, 1846.

During the 1850's, most of his efforts were concentrated within the antislavery movement, but his interest in both peace and Negro emancipation and equality continued to the end of his life.

I THE AFTERMATH OF THE BOSTON MOB: 1836

ON OCTOBER 26, 1835, George W. Benson, in a letter
to his brother, Henry, wrote:

I think brother Garrison had better dispose of his house
in Boston, store a part of his furniture in some place of
safety, and make an arrangement to board in Brooklyn
this winter, for which opinion there are several reasons: one is, he can edit
the paper much better, not being liable to constant interruption. Again . . .
it would be much pleasanter for Sister Helen, and much cheaper for all excepting yourself and Brother Knapp. . . .

There appears to my mind but one serious objection, and that is, that our
opponents may say that he does not return to Boston. That can be obviated,
however, by his going there and spending several weeks, and after that
going there occasionally as his business or inclination may require. I do not
believe that he would be in any danger of personal violence now or a few
days hence.

Garrison ultimately followed this plan. On October 23, two days
after he was mobbed, he and Helen, who was pregnant with their first
child, arrived in Brooklyn, Connecticut; on November 4, Garrison returned to Boston, and by the end of the month he was back again in
Brooklyn. He remained there except for occasional trips to Boston,
until the latter part of September 1836, when he returned to Boston
with Helen and their infant son. In *The Liberator* of October 1, 1836,
it was announced:

After a protracted sojourn in Connecticut, the editor is once more located
in Boston; consequently, letters may no longer be addressed to him at
Brooklyn, Connecticut. He is indebted to his able friend Mr. C. C. Burleigh,
for many articles of interest communicated and published during his absence. For several months past, his health has failed him, but he is now
better. . . . His thanks are due both to the publisher and the patrons of
the Liberator, for allowing him to be absent so long, with so little of complaint, although they have desired his presence continually in the city.

During Garrison's absence, the affairs of *The Liberator* [1] were conducted by Isaac Knapp, who, at the beginning of 1836, had become

1. Garrison had been issuing *The Liberator*, his weekly antislavery newspaper,
since January 1831.

1

sole publisher of the paper — previously he and Garrison had been co-partners — and had assumed all responsibility for its financial affairs. Charles Calistus Burleigh assumed most of the editorial duties. Both were helped by Henry Benson, who was then secretary and general agent of the Massachusetts Anti-Slavery Society and in charge of the society's office at 46 Washington Street, and by Samuel J. May, who was corresponding secretary and general agent of the society from the spring of 1835 to October 1836.

The end of 1835 and the beginning of 1836 witnessed strong efforts to repress the antislavery movement. Governors, legislatures, and other leaders of southern states called upon northern legislatures and men of influence to outlaw the abolitionists and prevent them from expressing their "incendiary" antislavery views, either in speech or writing. The result was that antislavery men were in constant danger of being mobbed and their meetings broken into by those who regarded them as enemies of society. Garrison's narrow escape from serious injury in October 1835 was perhaps narrower than that of others, but not all antislavery men were so fortunate and sometimes physical injury occurred.

Yet, despite constant dangers and difficulties, the antislavery movement surged forward; in its membership, in the numbers of its local branches, which were being formed at the rate of approximately one a day, and in its broadening influence. No wonder Garrison exulted in an editorial in *The Liberator* on January 2, 1836:

> Where now is . . . the American Colonization Society? Struggling in the agonies of dissolution! Look, now, at that powerful association, the American Anti-Slavery Society! Look at seven flourishing State Societies! Look at five hundred auxiliary societies, and see them multiplying daily! Look at the flood of our publications sweeping through the land. . . . See how many agents are in the field. . . . And the stream of sympathy still rolls on — its impetus is increasing — and it must ere long sweep away the pollutions of slavery.

For Garrison, the year 1836 was marked by a number of significant events. In February, his first child, George Thompson, named after the British abolitionist, was born. During the same month, Garrison delivered a scathing review of William Ellery Channing's *Slavery*. In March, together with other antislavery men and women and proponents of free speech, he appeared before the joint committee of the Massachusetts legislature, whose chairman was George Lunt, in which he affirmed the aims of the abolitionists and defended their right to speak and organize. In July he entered the lists against Lyman Beecher's views of the Sabbath, and sought to expose the inconsistency in orthodox Sabbath observance when combined with the failure to condemn slavery. In September, Garrison returned to Boston with his family, and in November, he was present in New York to participate in the training of the newly appointed seventy agents of the American Anti-Slavery Society. During the same month, in the national elections, Garrison and most of the other abolitionists found nothing to choose between the leading presidential candidates and condemned both Martin Van Buren and William Henry Harrison. The year closed with the death of George Benson, Helen's father, in his eighty-fifth year, beloved and mourned by all who knew him, for his kindness, philanthropy, and love of mankind.

1

TO HENRY E. BENSON

Brooklyn, Jan. 9, 1836.

My dear Henry:

Last evening, I was somewhat disappointed in not receiving my bundle of newspapers, but am patiently looking for it by this afternoon's stage.

Robert D. Sharpe, of Abington,[1] has paid me $2.00 for the Liberator, in advance for the present year, which I enclose. He says he has not received No. 52 of the last volume, and wishes you to send it to complete his file.

I wish you to transmit Helen's letter to me in the bundle.

The accompanying letters please convey to Miss Chapman,[2] Miss Ammidon,[3] and Miss Clark.[4]

Mr. Parrish expired while I was in Boston, and was buried on the day before my return. He retained his senses to the last, but did not converse much, through physical inability.[5]

I want to receive a copy of the second edition of Dr. Channing's book,[6] as soon as practicable.

John Edward[7] has been somewhat unwell with the mumps, but is now much better.

The slippery walking has caused several people to trip in the village. Mr. Joseph Williams[8] broke his shoulder-bone a few days since.

I suppose brother George has written to you, informing you that little Anna[9] has been sick with the scarlet fever, but is now convalescent.

All are well.

Yours,
W. L. G.

P. S. Sunday evening — The bundle has just come. I meant to have forwarded this package by the stage yesterday, but missed it by about one minute.

I hope friend Knapp [10] will keep an eye upon the doings and sayings in Congress upon our question, and publish all he can find.

Father is very much obliged to you for your present of Granville Sharpe's Life,[11] and to brother May [12] for the numbers of the Herald of Peace.[13]

I shall write a letter and send it in season to bro. May, to be read at the Annual Meeting.[14] Have you yet obtained a hall? I entreat, that the *new* Board of Managers may be elected from among *old* and *sound* materials. Let there be no electioneering after *respectable* and *influential* persons.

A piece of poetry, respecting Washington's slaves, appeared some time since in the N. Y. Evangelist, which I sent on for insertion.[15] I hope it has not been lost.

☞ Rev. Mr. Wilson [16] wishes bro. May to send him a number of Channing's works as soon as convenient. Put them into my bundle.

Will bro. May write a paragraph for the next paper about the annual meeting — in advance?

ALS: Garrison Papers, Boston Public Library.
    Henry E. Benson was Garrison's brother-in-law. See introductory biographical sketch.

    1. Robert Davis Sharpe (b. August 21, 1790; d. September 16, 1878), of Abington, Connecticut, married Syrena Robinson in 1820. He was an officer of the Windham County Anti-Slavery Society (*The Liberator*, May 7, 1836; W. C. Sharpe, *Sharpe Genealogy and Miscellany*, Seymour, Conn., 1880, p. 118).

    2. Ann Greene Chapman (d. Boston, March 24, 1837, aged thirty-five) was the daughter of Henry Chapman, the antislavery merchant, and the sister of Henry Grafton Chapman, Maria W. Chapman's husband. She was an enthusiastic supporter of the antislavery cause and active in the Boston Female Anti-Slavery Society (*Life*, II, 12, 207–208, 360).

    3. Probably Miss Melania Ammidon, who was corresponding secretary of the Boston Female Anti-Slavery Society in 1836. Born in 1809, she was the daughter of Philip Ammidon of Boston (b. 1774) and the sister of Sylvia (b. 1814). She later married the Reverend Joseph Parker of Boston; Sylvia married the Reverend Henry Parker. Both ladies were active in the Boston Female Anti-Slavery Society. (See *Right and Wrong in Boston in 1836, Annual Report of the Boston Female Anti-Slavery Society* . . . , Boston, 1836, p. 32.)

    4. Miss Mary Clark (1792–1841) of Concord, New Hampshire. There are numerous letters from her to Francis Jackson, the abolitionist, in the Boston Public Library. She was an active abolitionist in New Hampshire and helped in the issuance of the *Herald of Freedom*. She was devoted to both antislavery and peace; she wrote poetry and was a close friend of John Farmer, the Concord historian and antiquarian. Although a religious woman, she was a member of no one sect. Before her death, not believing in "priestcraft," she directed that her funeral be without ceremony or officiating clergyman; two friends, Amos Wood and John B. Chandler, officiated. (Obituary, *The Liberator*, May 21, 1841, reprinted from the *Herald of Freedom*.)

    5. John Parish (also Parrish) was born in Canterbury, Connecticut, on June

11, 1761, and died in Brooklyn, Connecticut, on December 29, 1835. A prominent lawyer in Brooklyn, he was active in the cause of temperance and was a Unitarian Congregationalist. He was one of a committee of two who invited Samuel J. May to become the Unitarian minister in Brooklyn. In 1828, May and his wife boarded with him. (Ellen D. Larned, *History of Windham County, Connecticut*, Worcester, Mass., 1880, II, 263–264, 470–473; *Memoir of Samuel Joseph May*, Boston, 1873, pp. 76, 87; Roswell Parish, *New England Parish Families, Descendants of John Parish of Groton, Massachusetts and Preston, Connecticut*, Rutland, Vt., n.d., p. 88.)

6. *Slavery.* The second edition, which appeared in late February 1836, was a revised and enlarged edition of 183 pages, as compared with the first edition's 167 pages, published in 1835. A third edition of 183 pages and a fourth, of 187 pages, appeared during the same year.

William Ellery Channing (1780–1842) was the outstanding Unitarian clergyman of his day and perhaps the greatest in American history. He was installed as minister of the Federal Street Church in Boston on June 1, 1803, and remained there until his death. Although he was antislavery in his views, he was a gradualist and opposed to immediate emancipation. He disapproved of the condemnation of slaveholders as evil men and even frowned upon antislavery organization. Samuel J. May, after graduating from Harvard in 1817, assisted Channing for several months at his Boston church and remained Channing's close personal friend and admirer despite their differences over abolitionist theory and tactics. (*DAB*; Samuel J. May, *Some Recollections of Our Antislavery Conflict*, Boston, 1869, pp. 170–185.)

7. The son of Samuel J. May. He was born in Brooklyn, Connecticut, on October 7, 1829. He was educated in schools in Lexington, Massachusetts, and Syracuse, New York, and at the Rensselaer Polytechnic Institute, at Troy, New York. He was in business in Syracuse, New York, from 1852 to 1858 and thereafter in Boston, Massachusetts. ([Samuel May], *A Genealogy of the Descendants of John May*, Boston, 1878, p. 45.)

8. Joseph Williams (b. August 14, 1793; d. September 15, 1882), a farmer of Brooklyn, Connecticut, was the descendant of an old Windham county family, the son of Samuel Williams. (*Commemorative Biographical Record of Tolland and Windham Counties, Connecticut*, Chicago, 1903, II, 992.)

9. Anna Elizabeth, the daughter of George W. Benson, born on September 23, 1834.

10. Isaac Knapp (1804–1843), Garrison's boyhood friend and his partner in the establishment of *The Liberator*. At the beginning of 1836, Knapp became *The Liberator*'s publisher with complete responsibility for its finances. See introductory biographical sketch.

11. Granville Sharp (1735–1813) was an English philanthropist who gained fame as the father of the antislavery movement in England. As a culmination of Sharp's efforts, which extended over several years, on June 22, 1772, Lord Chief Justice Mansfield issued his famous decision in the case of James Sommersett, that a slave "becomes free" on setting foot on English soil. Sharp wrote several tracts against slavery, initiated the founding of the English society for the abolition of slavery in 1787, and was a prime mover in forming a settlement for emancipated slaves in Sierra Leone. (*DNB*.) A new life of Sharp, by Charles Stuart was published by the American Anti-Slavery Society at the beginning of 1836. It was undoubtedly for this newly published book that Garrison thanked Henry on behalf of the elder Benson.

12. The Reverend Samuel Joseph May. See introductory biographical sketch.

13. The *Herald of Peace* was first issued in January 1819 by the Society for the Promotion of Permanent and Universal Peace, often called the London Peace Society. The society had been organized in June 1816. During the first two years the *Herald* appeared as a monthly, then as a quarterly. (Merle Eugene Curti, *The American Peace Crusade, 1815–1860*, Durham, N.C., 1929, pp. 14–15, 232.)

14. The Fourth Annual Meeting of the Massachusetts Anti-Slavery Society,

which convened in Boston on January 20. The Massachusetts Anti-Slavery Society was the successor to the New England Anti-Slavery Society after 1835.

15. The poem, entitled "Washington's Freed-Men," by W. B. T. (otherwise unknown), was reprinted in *The Liberator* on January 23, 1836. It was evoked by a chance meeting of W. B. T. with a group of Negro workers at George Washington's tomb at Mt. Vernon, Virginia. The Negroes were cleaning the grounds and repairing the tomb, which had fallen into disrepair through neglect by the state. He asked them if they were Washington's slaves and they replied that they were not his slaves but his servants, for he had freed them at his death. The poem extolls Washington's virtues.

The New York *Evangelist* had been founded in 1830 by Arthur and Lewis Tappan and their Association of Gentlemen to promote religious revivals, temperance and other reforms. The founding occurred during a visit to New York by Charles Grandison Finney, the Protestant evangelist, whose preaching profoundly influenced the Tappans. Joshua Leavitt, the abolitionist, became its editor in 1831. (*Weld-Grimké Letters*, I, 37n, 50n, 118–119n; Frederic Hudson, *Journalism in the United States, from 1690 to 1872*, New York and Evanston, p. 298; "Joshua Leavitt," *ACAB*.)

16. The Reverend Luther Wilson (also Willson), formerly of New Braintree, Massachusetts, was ordained a colleague pastor of the Congregational Church in Brooklyn, Connecticut, in 1813 and remained there until 1817, when he was found guilty of heresy and dismissed. He was the predecessor of Samuel J. May. He was later pastor of a church in Petersham, Massachusetts. (*Memoir of Samuel Joseph May*, pp. 82, 88–89; Larned, *History of Windham County*, II, 461–464.)

2

TO GEORGE W. BENSON

Brooklyn, Jan. 11, 1836.

My dear George:

I hastily seize my pen to say, that you deserve many a well-filled sheet from me, but are in no prospect of getting one at present — not owing to any abatement of brotherly affection, but to an increase of business. Accompanying this is a package for bro. Phelps,[1] which Mr. May [2] desired me to send to Hartford; but as I hear that he is now in your vicinity, I send it to your care.

Before I went to Boston, I sent you in a letter, by mail, a Preamble and Constitution,[3] according to your request, (although it may not have been in accordance with your wishes,) but you do not acknowledge its receipt in any of your subsequent letters. If it has miscarried, let me know. If not, I desire you, again, to curtail, modify, or reject it, as you may think proper. There is no probability that I shall be able to attend your Convention,[4] but I will send you a letter to be read, and some resolutions to be adopted, if agreeable.

As soon as you get your call printed, with the signatures, do not fail to send a copy of it, immediately, to Boston, for insertion in the Liberator.[5] I long to see it at full length — it will produce all kinds of emotions in the minds of the people — rage, astonishment, alarm, hope, joy and confidence.

What "a long spell of weather" we have had! Nothing but cloud, and wind, and sleet, and rain, for a whole week. Is the sun, therefore, extinguished? I tell you, nay. We must certainly soon see "the powerful King of day rejoicing in the east." [6] Why, then, should dull or tempestuous weather make us dolorous or disconsolate? See you not my drift? Our moral sky has long been overcast, and there have been thunderings and lightnings, and a storm of something more potent than hail-stones — to wit, brickbats. But is the sun of Truth therefore quenched? No indeed! See — the clouds are retreating, and light already begins to break forth!

Poor little Anna! Your account of her sickness, and her patience and intelligent obedience, was highly interesting. May she live to be the best specimen of human excellence since the days of Him who was immaculate!

Send your petitions to Congress, if you have any,[7] "Keep the mill a-going," as the saying is. The blustering of the southern members in Congress is ludicrous enough. The knaves and cowards! They will soon find that humanity and conscience are not so easily or willingly surrendered by us, as they would fain imagine.

We all desire to be affectionately remembered to your dear wife, to sisters Mary and Charlotte,[8] Mr. Anthony,[9] Wm. Chace,[10] &c. &c.

In good health, good spirits, great haste, and brotherly affection, I remain,

Yours truly,   Wm. Lloyd Garrison.

ALS: Garrison Papers, Boston Public Library.

George W. Benson was Garrison's brother-in-law. See introductory biographical sketch.

1. Amos Augustus Phelps (1804–1847) was then general agent of the American Anti-Slavery Society. See introductory biographical sketch

2. Samuel J May.

3. These were to be used in the formation of a Rhode Island Anti-Slavery Society. The preamble and constitution, as later adopted, were printed in *The Liberator*, February 6, 1836.

4. The convention for the formation of the Rhode Island Anti-Slavery Society was held on February 2, 1836, in Providence. It consisted of delegates from existing local antislavery societies in Rhode Island and friends of abolition from towns which had no societies.

5. The call appeared in *The Liberator* on January 16, 1836. It carried 850 signatures, from all the towns in Rhode Island except two.

6. The quotation is from *The Seasons*, "Summer," by James Thomson (1700–1748), Scottish poet.

7. Petitions for the emancipation of the slaves in Washington, D.C.

8. Helen's sisters, Mary Benson and Charlotte Anthony.

9. Henry Anthony (b. April 6, 1802; d. September 17, 1879), Charlotte's husband. They were married on October 22, 1826. It is noted in Lillie Buffum Chace

Wyman and Arthur Crawford Wyman, *Elizabeth Buffum Chace, 1806–1899, Her Life and Environment* (Boston, 1914), I, 137, that Garrison "seldom attended an anti-slavery meeting in Providence. It was suggested that he avoided public appearances in that city because the Anthonys lived there, and as they were not much in sympathy with his opinions, he did not want to irritate them by the promulgation of his ideas in their vicinity, lest it should make a breach between them and his wife; but I do not know that he was influenced by any such motive." See also Charles L. Anthony, *Genealogy of the Anthony Family from 1495 to 1904* (Sterling, Ill., 1904), pp. 236, 239.

10. William M. Chace (1814–1862) of Providence, an early abolitionist, founder and corresponding secretary of the Rhode Island Anti-Slavery Society, wool merchant and business partner of George W. Benson (*Life, passim*). He was one of Garrison's earliest "coadjutors" in the antislavery cause, becoming a devoted agent in Providence of *The Liberator* with its establishment in 1831. He later moved to New York and entered the profession of law. He became an active Republican with the organization of the Republican party and served in various civilian capacities on behalf of the northern war effort during the Civil War. He apparently never marrried. (*The Liberator*, September 5, 1862.)

3

TO HENRY E. BENSON

Brooklyn, Jan. 16, 1836.

My dear Henry:

This week the bundle came punctually, at 4 o'clock, yesterday afternoon. There was nothing of special interest in it, except your letter. Was that the cause of its prompt transmission? I suppose there would have been a copy of the Liberator, if any had been printed.

What! another "fine meeting" of the anti-slavery ladies,[1] and "no mob"! Where are the "gentlemen of wealth and standing"?[2] Why did they not throw the city into an uproar? Is this their regard for the south — their attachment to the Union? Tell it not in Charleston! publish it not in the streets of New-Orleans! lest mad McDuffie[3] should hang himself, and the Lynch Committee[4] be induced to leave the country. So doth moral courage triumph over brute force!

The presents which the ladies have voted to give to me and the Liberator are truly generous:[5] they shall be accepted, not for my emolument or to promote my ease, but to advance the cause which is so dear to all our hearts. — Such gifts possess a sacred character. By the way, I am *very* anxious to obtain a copy of the Annual Report of the Ladies' Society as soon as it is published,[6] that I may read and notice it without delay. I have no doubt it is a capital performance.

I can bear all the threats and taunts of the South, better than those refusals which have been given to your application for a meeting-house or hall, in which to hold our annual meeting. My spirit is stirred

within me, not passionately, but with lawful indignation. Never mind —
No. 46 is still ours.[7] "Don't give up the ship!"

I have almost grown tired in waiting for a copy of Channing's
second edition. If it should not come next week, I must "fire off" my
gun.

The subscription of Mr. Chapman's father,[8] towards liquidating
our debt,[9] is as generous as it is unexpected, and manifests a thorough-
going anti-slavery spirit. I am thankful to hear that the Committee
are actively endeavoring to get the whole sum made up as fast as
possible, because every thing in such a case depends upon despatch.
Whoever else may be called upon to aid, I hope friend Dole,[10] of
Hallowell, will not be appealed to again, as he has already on various
occasions contributed more liberally to the support of the paper than
any other person in like circumstances. I think each one who is requested to give any thing should be impressed with the fact, that
he is not paying for "a dead horse" — for it is not only participating
in the credit that may attach to the Liberator for what it has done in
waking up a lethargic public sentiment, but it is continuing the life
and usefulness of the paper. As soon as the sum is completed, I write
a letter of thanks to each of the subscribers, in behalf of friend Knapp
and myself.

I am very sorry to hear that "friend Yates has backed out from the
cause." [11] He was one of its earliest and most zealous supporters. He
has some reason to complain that he was ousted from the Board of
Managers: still, he ought not on that account to stand aloof from us.

If we can get along without E. M. P. Wells's subscription,[12] I shall
be glad; because I wish no man to pay money for the support of the
Liberator, if such an act goes against his conscience. It is true, he
justly owes the money — but he says he now dislikes the paper.

The accompanying packet for the editor of the Lynn Record,[13] I
wish you would drop immediately into the Boston Post Office, paying
the postage upon it, and charging the same to my account.

Let me know whether friend K.[14] has got into his new office. Tell
him to make *every thing else give way* (communications, editorials,
and all,) to the debates in Congress upon the petitions for the abolition of slavery in the D. of C.[15] The sooner we publish the debates,
the greater will be the interest in their perusal. Let him select the best
reports he can find. It is important, too, that we should publish all
official documents in opposition to our cause, instanter, that we may
not be anticipated by other papers. In the next Liberator, (i.e. Jan.
23,) if possible, insert the accompanying extract from Gov. Marcy's
message,[16] and also the correspondence between him and Gov. Gayle [17]
of Alabama, respecting Williams [18] — especially the latter.

Give as good an account of the annual meeting to the readers as the time will permit.[19]

Probably E. M. P. Wells would prefer *not* to be one of the officers of our society.[20]

Let the Vice Presidents be as influential as possible, without relying too much upon *names*. We can select them from all parts of the Commonwealth. The Managers should be the truest of the true. I should be glad to see our brother Wright one of the number.[21]

I hope the Rhode-Island call will appear in this week's Liberator.[22] It is a mighty voice. We shall expect to see you after the Convention.

We are all as well and quiet as usual in Friendship's Valley. No bird in summer is happier than

Your "fanatical" brother-in-law,

W. L. Garrison.

P.S. The N.Y. Evening Post,[23] containing the correspondence between Gov. Gayle and Gov. Marcy I have accidentally burnt up. I hope friend Knapp will not fail to get another copy of it, and append it to the extract from Marcy's message. They had better all be published together, long as they are: therefore they must be deferred to the Liberator of 30th inst.[24]

ALS: Garrison Papers, Boston Public Library. The greater part is printed in *Life*, II, 84–85.

1. The quarterly meeting of the Boston Female Anti-Slavery Society was held on January 13, 1836, at 46 Washington Street, Boston.

2. This phrase refers to the newspaper characterizations of the mob that attacked Garrison on October 21, 1835.

3. Governor George McDuffie (1790–1851) of South Carolina. In his annual message to the South Carolina legislature, published in *The Liberator*, December 12, 1835, Governor McDuffie declared that interference by abolitionists with slavery should be punishable "by death without benefit of clergy" and that abolitionists should be regarded as "enemies of the human race." He called slavery "the cornerstone of our republican edifice."

George McDuffie was representative from South Carolina in the United States House of Representatives from 1821 to 1834, when he resigned to become governor of South Carolina. After two terms as governor, he returned to his law practice, but then went back to public life as a senator from 1842 to 1846. He favored nullification, participated in the nullification convention of South Carolina in 1832, and was, of course, an enthusiastic defender of slavery as well as a violent opponent of abolition and abolitionists. (*DAB*.)

4. A reference to the mob violence then being directed against the abolitionists throughout the country. The term derived from Charles Lynch, a Virginia planter, who, at the time of the American Revolution, with the help of associates, hanged Tories by their thumbs until they shouted, "Liberty forever." It was later applied to executions, especially hangings, without trial. (*DUSH*.)

5. The Boston Female Anti-Slavery Society at their quarterly meeting on January 13 voted a gift of $50 to Garrison, "as a testimony of our esteem and also as an expression of our sympathy for the loss he sustained at our Annual Meeting in October last," and of $20 for *The Liberator*. (See letters from Lucy M. Ball

to Garrison, Jan. 30, 1836, and to Garrison and Knapp, January 19, 1836, ALS, Anti-Slavery Letters to Garrison and Others, Boston Public Library.)

6. The report was to have appeared in December 1835. On the last page of the report, the following apology was printed: "To our friends, who have been expecting the appearance of our Report since the middle of Dec., we can only lament, without being able to account for the delay of the printer." See *Annual Report of the Boston Female Anti-Slavery Society, with a Concise Statement of Events, Previous and Subsequent to the Annual Meeting of 1835* (Boston, 1836), p. 108. The title of the report is preceded by another title, *Right and Wrong in Boston*, which is the general title under which the annual reports of the society were published.

7. 46 Washington Street, Boston, was the address of the antislavery office and meeting-hall, where the October 21, 1835, riot began. The following comment is to be found in *The Fourth Annual Report of the Board of Managers of the Massachusetts Anti-Slavery Society, with Some Account of the Annual Meeting, January 20, 1836* (Boston, 1836, p. 44):

"The Fourth Annual Meeting of the Massachusetts Anti-Slavery Society was held in Boston on Wednesday, January 20. When we saw the large number of gentlemen from the country, who had come to the meeting as delegates, and friends of this righteous cause, we were filled with shame, that our liberal, liberty-loving, boastful city would not afford them an ample room. All the Churches in Boston, that have ever been let to benevolent associations, had been applied for by the Committee of arrangements and refused: also the several Halls in the city, that were thought to be large enough, and were withheld. We were therefore obliged to receive our friends in our little Hall, 46 Washington St., which must now be considered the only cradle of liberty in this metropolis."

8. Henry Chapman (b. Salem, Massachusetts, 1771; d. Boston, November 23, 1846), the father of Henry Grafton Chapman and the father-in-law of Maria Weston Chapman. The biography of Garrison by his sons notes: "the elder Chapman was the only one of those then reckoned the Boston merchants *par excellence* to make the anti-slavery cause his own: his wife paid, through the Boston Female A. S. Society, the counsel fee in the Med case . . ." (II, 49n, 447). Henry Chapman, orphaned while still a boy, was a self-made businessman who engaged in business in Boston for more than fifty years. "Great energy, a spirit of enterprise, which tempted fortune in many channels, a fertility of resource, which no difficulties exhausted, made him a successful merchant." He was one of the earliest supporters of Garrison and the antislavery enterprise. "He and his late son [Henry G. Chapman] were almost the only, if not the only, mercantile houses in the country, which sacrificed a profitable Southern business to their deep conviction of the sin of slavery" (*The Liberator*, December 4, 1846, from an obituary reprinted from the Boston *Courier*).

9. *The Liberator's* debt, at the end of December, amounted to $2500.

10. Ebenezer Dole (b. Newburyport, Massachusetts, 1776; d. Hallowell, Maine, 1847), a merchant and Garrison's distant cousin, was an early supporter of Garrison's *The Liberator* and a founder of the New England and American Anti-Slavery Societies. Garrison's earliest letter to Dole is dated Baltimore, July 14, 1830 (*Letters*, I). Dole provided financial help for Garrison on the latter's release from the Baltimore jail in 1830. (*Life*, I, 192–193, 204, 273; II, 84, 228.)

11. The Reverend James D. Yates was elected to the Board of Managers of the New England Anti-Slavery Society at its annual meeting on January 9, 1833. He was re-elected at the next annual meeting on January 15, 1834, but not renominated or elected at the society's third annual meeting on January 21, 1835, or thereafter. His name is not listed thereafter among the society's financial contributors.

12. The Reverend E. M. P. Wells (1793–1878), of Boston, was a vice-president of the New England Anti-Slavery Society as early as January 1833. He was an Episcopal minister and principal of the Boston Asylum and Farm School, of which

Mayor Theodore Lyman, Jr., was president and a principal financial supporter. Wells ended his subscription to *The Liberator* as a result of Garrison's criticism of the mayor's handling of the Boston mob of October 21, 1835. (*Life*, II, 54n; letter to Charles Follen, March 18, 1834, *Letters*, I.)

13. The Lynn *Record* was founded in January 1830 by Alonzo Lewis, whose connection with the paper ceased with the sixth number. It then became the organ of the antimasonic party. In 1833, and probably thereafter, the editor was Daniel Henshaw. The proprietor was John B. Tolman. It ceased publication in 1841. (Alonzo Lewis and James Newhall, *History of Lynn, 1620–1864*, Lynn, 1890, pp. 395, 582.)

14. Isaac Knapp.

15. District of Columbia.

16. Governor William Learned Marcy (1786–1857), of New York, lawyer and politician, was comptroller of New York in 1823–1829, associate justice of the state supreme court from 1829 to 1831, and a United States senator from December 1831 to January 1833, when he resigned to serve as governor of New York for three terms, from 1833 to 1838. (*DAB*.) The extract from his message was printed in *The Liberator*, January 30, 1836.

17. Governor John Gayle (1792–1859), of Alabama, was a prominent lawyer and politician who had served in the state legislature and on the bench as circuit judge and justice of the state supreme court. He was first elected governor of Alabama in 1831 and served two terms. He was a Harrisonian elector in 1840, was elected to Congress on the Whig ticket in 1847, and was appointed a federal judge by President Taylor two years later. (*DAB*.)

18. Ransom G. Williams, publishing agent of the American Anti-Slavery Society at New York.

On November 14, 1835, Governor Gayle of Alabama had written to Governor Marcy of New York, informing him that Ransom G. Williams had been indicted and convicted by a jury in Tuscaloosa, Alabama, of circulating the *Emancipator*, an antislavery newspaper, and spreading inflammatory remarks about slavery in the South. Governor Gayle asked that Williams, who had been tried *in absentia*, be extradited from New York to Alabama.

Governor Marcy, while expressing a strong dislike and condemnation of the abolitionists, nevertheless refused permission for Williams' extradition. (*Life*, II, 75; *The Liberator*, January 23, 1836.) The correspondence between Governor Marcy and Governor Gayle appeared in *The Liberator* on January 23, 1836. There Williams is referred to as Robert instead of Ransom.

19. The report of the annual meeting appeared in the January 23, 1836, issue of *The Liberator*.

20. Despite Garrison's seeming opposition, Wells was re-elected as a vice-president of the Massachusetts Anti-Slavery Society.

21. The Reverend Henry Clarke Wright was born in Sharon, Connecticut, on August 29, 1797, and died at Pawtucket, Rhode Island, on August 16, 1870. He was a hatmaker turned minister, who prepared for the ministry at Andover, was ordained in 1823, and lived in West Newbury, Massachusetts, until 1833. He joined the New England Anti-Slavery Society in May 1835 and met Garrison for the first time in November of the same year. He was elected a vice-president at the January 20, 1836, meeting. Louis Filler, a historian of the antislavery movement, has called him "the radical of radicals: a creator of radicalisms and the originator of many of Garrison's formulas." Wright's autobiography, entitled *Human Life: Illustrated in My Individual Experience as A Child, A Youth, and A Man*, was printed in Boston in 1849. See introductory biographical sketch.

The following were the elected officers for the ensuing year:

President: Joseph Southwick, Boston   The Reverend Moses Thacher,
Vice Presidents: North Wrentham
The Reverend E. M. P. Wells, Boston   Dr. Charles Follen, Milton

22. The call did appear in *The Liberator* of January 16.

23. The New York *Evening Post* had been established in 1801 under the editorship of William Coleman. In 1836 its editor was William Cullen Bryant, who had assumed the editorship in 1829 at Coleman's death. Although originally a Federalist paper, the *Post*, under Bryant, supported Jackson and the Democratic party. (Frank Luther Mott, *American Journalism, A History: 1690–1960*, third edition, New York, 1962, pp. 184–186.)

24. Actually, the correspondence between Governor Gayle and Governor Marcy was published in *The Liberator* on January 23, 1836. Governor Marcy's message to the New York state legislature was published in *The Liberator* on January 30, under the title, "Proposition for the Passage of Another Alien and Sedition Law."

4

TO SAMUEL J. MAY

Brooklyn, Jan. 17, 1836.

My beloved Coadjutor:

Accompanying this, I send a letter, which, if you think proper, you may read to the meeting on Wednesday next,[1] and then hand it over to friend Knapp for publication in the Liberator.[2]

Boston is yet a strong hold of slavery. By Henry's [3] letter received yesterday, it seems you have applied in vain for the use of a meeting-house or hall, in which to hold the annual meeting. Sixteen refusals successively! And yet the people of Boston are strongly opposed to slavery! Pardon my hard language — "they are liars, and the truth is not in them." [4] They stand ready, at any moment, to crush the slaves, and to co-operate with the masters. While such a city behaves so wickedly, I do think we ought to be more tender of the south — or, rather, we ought to be more impartial in our denunciations. Spare not your hypocritical and callous-hearted city, but at your meeting hold it up in all the infamy which attaches to its professions and conduct. Woe unto thee, Boston! for if the mighty works which have been done in thee, had been done in Charleston or Savannah, peradventure they had repented long ago.

I hope bold and emphatic resolutions will be adopted respecting the murderous proposition of the Nero McDuffie [5] in his message, and the equally despotic suggestions of the Dometian Marcy; [6] for every proper occasion should be seized upon to bear testimony against such dangerous documents.

Strong resolutions should also be passed against the continuance of slavery and the slave trade in the District of Columbia, and especially in reprehension of the inhuman policy and base servility of our northern representatives in Congress, upon this subject.

Our brother Thompson [7] will be greatly strengthened and gratified, if a resolution should be passed in kind remembrance of him and those who sustained his mission. — I think our bro. Stuart [8] ought also to be remembered, inasmuch as he is laboring "with all his might," [9] most nobly, successfully and disinterestedly, in our sacred cause.

Let the south be made to understand, that this is with us a high moral and religious question; that we shall as soon deny our God, and worship idols, as abandon the advocacy of the rights of man; that we are ready to go to the gibbet or the stake, sooner than forsake the cause of our enslaved countrymen; and that, above all things, we are not to be frightened or driven back by deeds of violence and blood.[10] ☞ Undeceive them, also, as to the character and numbers of the abolitionists; for they ought not to believe what is said by their northern abettors, respecting our feebleness. We ought, at all times, to speak in brave and confident language of our success and prospects; for we are authorised to do so by facts, and especially by the inherent excellence of our cause. Deliver us from a boastful, vain-glorious, self-confident spirit: but, oh! what dignity there is in christian independence! what majesty in christian resolution! what strength in christian faith! what triumph in christian endurance! Let us use, then, the dialect of christian conquerors.

In the last resort, I suppose you will hold your meeting in the Anti-Slavery Hall,[11] which is sufficiently large to hold more delegates than will attend, although but few of the people can be accommodated in it.

The Annual Report I am confident will confer credit upon your head and heart.[12] You know something of my anxiety respecting its remarks upon Dr. Channing's work: [13] let there be an impartial mixture of praise and reproof. I think our anti-slavery brethren, generally, ought to be warned to give no heed to the Dr's advice to us, to abandon our societies, to give up our watch-word immediate emancipation, to the charge of fanaticism, &c. &c. The imputation upon us ought to be repelled, that, in spite of all our toils, perils, sacrifices, ay, and *successes*, "nothing seems to have been gained"! but "perhaps something has been *lost* to the cause of freedom and humanity"! [14] *Et tu Brute?* Our enemies have never stabbed more deeply than this.

I must rely upon your kindness, (if you will allow me to do so,) to prepare an account of the meeting for the Liberator.

Would it not be well to remember Miss Martineau honorably in a resolution — applaud her moral courage, and rebuke her foul calumniators? [15]

Cheers for Rhode Island! Eight hundred and fifty names, the bone and muscle of the State, appended to the call of an anti-slavery meeting! [16] Here is fanaticism! Now for a dissolution of the Union — after so long a time! Do not fail to send delegates to Providence. Truly, "the call is strong — the response ought to be loud." A small meeting would make us appear somewhat ridiculous.

My venerated father-in-law [17] is exceedingly obliged to you for your kindness in sending the numbers of the Herald of Peace to him.

I trust you have recovered your health since Henry wrote. Helen joins with the rest of the family in sending special regards to you and Mrs. May. We are all *very* well.

Yours, affectionately,
Wm. Lloyd Garrison.

P.S. Would not Prof. Follen consent to occupy the place of E. M. P. Wells as Vice President? [18]

In case you should return to Brooklyn in the spring, it will be necessary to choose another Corresponding Secretary.

At the annual meeting, let an effort be made to obtain new members to the Society. If bro. Wright [19] could be elected one of our managers, it would meet my wishes.

I will thank you to tender our kindest remembrances to the Misses Parker and their excellent boarders.[20] — John Edward is well.

ALS: Garrison Papers, Boston Public Library; printed in part in *Life*, II, 85–87.

1. The annual meeting of the Massachusetts Anti-Slavery Society, held on January 20, 1836.

2. The letter (5), dated January 17, 1836, appeared in *The Liberator* on January 23, 1836.

3. Henry E. Benson.

4. I John 2:4. The verse reads: "He that saith, I know him, and keepeth not his commandments, is a liar, and the truth is not in him."

5. See letter 3, to Henry E. Benson, January 16, 1836.

6. Although Governor Marcy had refused the extradition of Ransom G. Williams to South Carolina, he did express his abhorrence of the abolitionists and the

need for punitive legislative enactments against them. In response to demands from various southern governors and legislatures for penal enactments against the abolitionists, he expressed the opinion that these could be legitimately carried out to prevent "the citizens of this State and residents within it from availing themselves with impunity of the protection of its sovereignty and laws, while they are actually employed in exciting insurrection and sedition in a sister State, or engaged in treasonable enterprises, intended to be executed therein" (quoted in *Life*, II, 75–76).

7. George Thompson (1804–1878), the English antislavery leader, arrived in the United States in September 1834 and remained until December 1835, when he was forced to flee the country as a result of the violence that was being directed against him. A resolution was passed which thanked the abolitionists of Great Britain for sending Thompson to the United States and thanked Thompson for his contribution to the antislavery effort. The sources for this and other information concerning the meeting are *The Fourth Annual Report of the Board of Managers of the Massachusetts Anti-Slavery Society, with Some Account of the Annual Meeting, January 20, 1836* (Boston, 1836); and *The Liberator*, January 23, 1836. See introductory biographical sketch of George Thompson.

8. Charles Stuart (1783–1865), the son of a British officer, was himself "a retired officer, on half-pay, formerly in the East India service." He settled in Utica, New York, in 1822, where he was principal of the Utica Academy. Garrison printed Stuart's exposure of the American Colonization Society in *The Liberator* in 1831. (*Life*, I, 262; *Weld-Grimke Letters*, I, 6n.)

9. *Life*, II, 86n: "and being mobbed for it — e.g., at Winfield, N.Y. . . ."

10. Resolutions to this effect were introduced and passed at the meeting.

11. At 46 Washington Street, Boston.

12. Samuel J. May prepared the annual report of the Board of Managers, which was accepted and ordered to be published.

13. William Ellery Channing's *Slavery* (Boston, 1835). The book had appeared in December. May discussed Channing's work and while he praised him for his generous remarks concerning the characters and motives of some abolitionists, criticized him for his misunderstanding of their goals and tactics.

14. Channing's remarks in *Slavery*. In the second edition, revised, and published in Boston in 1836 by James Munroe and Company, they appear on page 162. The second quotation is not quite accurate. It should read: "Perhaps (though I am anxious to repel the thought) something has been lost. . . ."

15. No such resolution was passed. Harriet Martineau (1802–1876), the prominent British author, arrived in the United States in September 1834 and stayed until August 1, 1836, when she left New York for England. Her sympathetic account of the abolitionists, especially Garrison and his friends, appeared in *The Martyr Age in America* (London, 1838). (*Life*, I, 446; II, 36–37, 55, 69–71, 97, *et passim*.)

16. See letter 3, to Henry Benson, January 16, 1836.

17. George Benson.

18. Charles Follen was elected a vice-president of the Massachusetts Anti-Slavery Society, but not in place of E. M. P. Wells.

Dr. Charles Follen was born in Germany in 1796. After teaching at the University of Jena and at the University of Basle, where he was professor of civil law, he was forced to flee Europe because of his liberal views and came to the United States in 1824. He became a teacher of German at Harvard College in 1825, and was appointed professor of German literature in 1830. In the same year he became a naturalized citizen. The publication of *The Liberator* struck a responsive chord in Follen, and soon after the formation of the New England Anti-Slavery Society he joined that organization and was elected one of its vice-presidents. As a result, he lost his position at Harvard. He next served as pastor of a Unitarian church in New York, but lost that position too, after two years, because of his antislavery preaching. Soon after being appointed pastor of a congregation

of liberal Christians in East Lexington, he lost his life in the fire of the ill-fated
steamer *Lexington*, on January 13, 1840. (Ruchames, *The Abolitionists*, p. 131.)

19. The Reverend Henry Clarke Wright.

20. The Misses Parker were four sisters, Mary S. (1801–1841), Lucy (1798–
1889), Eliza (1803–1890), and Abigail (1797–1859). They all died in Jaffrey,
New Hampshire. The most important in antislavery circles was Mary S., who was
president of the Boston Female Anti-Slavery Society for several years. Mary,
Lucy, and Eliza kept a boarding-house at 5 Hayward Place, in Boston, which was
frequented by antislavery people. The Samuel J. Mays boarded there for a while,
as did the Garrisons on some occasions. (*Life*, II, 12–15, *et passim*; obituary in
The Liberator, July 23, 1841; Albert Annett and Alice E. E. Lehtinen, *History of
Jaffrey, N. H.*, Peterboro, N.H., 1937, II, 570–571.)

5

TO SAMUEL J. MAY

Brooklyn, Jan. 17, 1836.

Rev. Samuel J. May:

My Dear Friend — My regret in not being able to attend the fourth
annual meeting of the Massachusetts Anti-Slavery Society, is equal to
the intense interest which I feel in its deliberations.

Let me say to the brethren who shall assemble together — BE BOLD
FOR GOD. These are times in which we are specially called upon not
to count our lives dear unto us — if, living, we are to be slaves ourselves, or to work at the enslavement of others. Nay, we shall be unworthy of an existence, if we suffer ourselves to be awed into silence
by the threats of oppressors. The cause which we advocate is not ours,
but GOD's; and therefore I renew the charge — BE BOLD FOR GOD. Nevertheless, it *is* ours to carry forward, instrumentally — but not ours to
choose or reject, as we may think expedient. Those who call upon us
to suspend our operations, or to keep silence, or to wait till a more
convenient season, or to stop our ears and steel our hearts to the cries
of our bleeding countrymen, make application to the wrong source.
They ought to beseech the Creator of heaven and earth to release us
from our obligations to himself and to mankind; to reverse or repeal
all the laws of his moral government; to transform us into stocks and
stones; to make the slaves in reality, what they are deemed by human
enactments, goods and chattels, implements of husbandry, and four-
footed beasts; to ordain that henceforth rebellion shall be loyalty — sin,
righteousness — and the cruel despotism of American slaveholders, the
glorious liberty of the sons of God! In all rationality, too, they ought
to petition the great Lawgiver to repeal every injunction of holy writ
like the following: — "Thou shalt not steal" [1] — "Thou shall not covet

any thing that is thy neighbor's" [2] — "Love thy neighbor as thyself" [3] — "Whatsoever ye would that men should do to you, do ye even so to them"[4] — "Envy thou not the oppressor, and choose none of his ways" [5] — "Remember them that are in bonds as bound with them" [6] — "Undo the heavy burdens, let the oppressed go free, and break every yoke" [7] — "Deliver him that is spoiled out of the hand of the oppressor" [8] — "Open thy mouth for the dumb in the cause of all such as are appointed to destruction." [9] O foolish and insane men! thus to consider obedience to God as something that policy may properly defer, or expediency lawfully annul! By ceasing to be men, shall we be independent of the Almighty? By setting up our authority in opposition to his own, shall we not be destroyed?

So, too, those who think they shall destroy our cause, if they can destroy a few of its prominent advocates — how wild and impious is their delusion! "The battle is the LORD's" [10] not ours. Why, then, do they not attempt to scale the battlements of heaven, that they may dethrone Him who is higher than the highest, and thus end the great controversy, not only in this nation, but in all nations — not only at the present period, but through all time? It is true, those battlements are high; but our enemies have "sought out many inventions" [11] — they are skilful, ingenious, adventurous — and, seemingly, confident of victory. It is true, he whom they must encounter and vanquish is, "Jehovah of hosts" [12] — "King of kings, and Lord of lords" [13] — "God over all" [14] — "The high and lofty One that inhabiteth eternity, whose name is Holy" [15] — "The Lord Almighty," [16] "who hath measured the waters in the hollow of his hand, and meted out heaven with the span, and comprehended the dust of the earth in a measure, and weighed the mountains in scales, and the hills in a balance" [17] — "all nations before him are as nothing; and they are counted to him less than nothing, and vanity." [18] But our enemies are valiant men — ambitious of great achievements — omnipotent in their own strength — having much property in "slaves and the souls of men" [19] — lifted up above all that is called God! — Ah! proud boasters, do ye grow pale, and shudder, and turn away, in view of such a fearful contest? Do ye remember the fate of Pharaoh and his hosts? of Babylon, and Tyre, and Sidon? of Sodom and Gomorrah? of an antediluvian world? — Truly, ye do well to retreat from the Majesty of Him, at whose presence it is declared, — "The earth shook and trembled; the foundations also of the hills moved and were shaken, *because he was wroth.* There went up a smoke out of his nostrils, and fire out of his mouth devoured: coals were kindled by it. He bowed the heavens also, and came down: and darkness was under his feet. And he rode upon a cherub, and did fly: yea, he did fly upon the wings of the wind. He made darkness his secret place:

18

his pavilion round about him were dark waters and thick clouds of
the skies. He sent out his arrows, and scattered them; and he shot out
lightnings, and discomfited them." [20] O ye flagitious oppressors, ye
do well to remember that "it is a fearful thing to fall into the hands of
the living God." [21] But will ye aim at no higher victims than Arthur
Tappan,[22] George Thompson, and William Lloyd Garrison? And who
and what are they? Three drops from a boundless ocean — three rays
from a noonday sun — three particles of dust floating in a limitless
atmosphere — nothing, subtracted from infinite fulness. Should ye succeed in destroying them, the mighty difficulty still remains. Still He
liveth who saith, "Vengeance is mine, I will repay." [23] Still He reigneth,
who "executeth righteousness and judgment for all that are oppressed." [24] Still He is faithful and true who declares, "For the oppression of the poor, for the sighing of the needy, now will I arise; I will
set him in safety from him that puffeth at him." [25] Still He is omnipotent
who proclaims, "Therefore thus saith the Lord; ye have not hearkened
unto me, in proclaiming liberty, every one to his brother, and every
man to his neighbor; behold I proclaim a liberty for you, saith the
Lord, to the sword, to the pestilence, and to the famine." [26] O, then,
destroy not yourselves nor your country; but take from the midst of
you the yoke, the putting forth of the finger, and speaking vanity;
and draw out your souls to the hungry, and satisfy the afflicted soul;
bring the poor that are cast out to your house, and cover their nakedness, and hide not yourselves from your own flesh; — then shall your
light rise in obscurity, and your darkness be as the noon-day. And
they that shall be of you shall build the old waste places; ye shall raise
up the foundation of many generations; and ye shall be called, The
repairers of the breach, The restorers of paths to dwell in. "For the
mouth of the Lord hath spoken it." [27]

It is indeed a mighty conflict, my dear brother, through which we
are called to pass, and we shall assuredly be overcome, unless we are
sustained by the energy of a divine love, and impressed with a fear
of God that shall make all other fears contemptible. Remember that,
but a little while since, we had to commence the work of converting
the entire nation, (so thoroughly had slavery corrupted it,) beginning
at Boston, as did the apostles at Jerusalem. Surprisingly has the truth
made progress, and multitudinous are the converts to it. Still, though
much has been done, more remains to be accomplished. The church
is yet stained with "the blood of the souls of the poor innocents" [28] —
it is yet the hiding-place and sanctuary of the ruthless monster that
feeds upon human flesh, and battens upon human agony and degradation. The decidedly pro-slavery tone of a large majority of our newspapers; the numerous public meetings that have been held in all parts

of the free States, unanimously coinciding with the corrupt sentiments of the south; the slavish language uttered in every hall of legislation; the despotic recommendations of certain Governors in their recent messages, particularly of Gov. Marcy of New-York; the indifference, nay, the positive approbation with which propositions are received by the people, to destroy the liberty of speech and of the press, and annul the right of petitioning government, that protection and perpetuity may be given to slavery; the attitude assumed in Congress, by northern and southern representatives, respecting the abolition of slavery and the slave trade in the District of Columbia; the sanction given to the robbery and censorship of the mail; the impunity with which some of our northern citizens, convicted of no crime, have been seized at the south, and without a legal trial, publicly lacerated, or cast into prison, or ignominiously put to death; the rewards offered by the south for the abduction of certain freemen of the north; the demand of southern executives upon our own, to deliver over the same individuals to a murderous fate; the proposition of the south to the north, to imprison, or put to death "without benefit of clergy," all of us who shall dare to hint that slavery is inconsistent with humanity, justice and religion, or who shall refuse to subscribe to the monstrous dogma, that "domestic slavery is the corner-stone of our republican edifice"; [29] the countenance which is given to mobs against the friends of emancipation, by men of high standing, both in Church and State; the impious justification of slavery by the southern clergy and churches; the general insensibility or perverseness of religious newspapers and periodicals; the unanimous declaration of southern oppressors, that they will never consent to the emancipation of their slaves, either immediately or ultimately, either for union or money, either for God or man; the dangers and difficulties which attend all our public attempts to plead the cause of our fettered, bleeding, guiltless countrymen; the brand of fanaticism, or treason, or robbery, which is put upon all the commandments and precepts of the bible, and upon the plainest maxims of republicanism: — these and other indications of the ferocious attachment of the people to the system of slavery, and to the company of slaveholders, portend that we are engaged in one of the mightiest moral struggles which the world has ever witnessed, and show how necessary it is that we all should have the endurance of the man of Uz,[30] the faith of Gideon, the meekness of Moses, and the intrepidity of the youthful David.

But I must pause. Brethren, "cease from man"; [31] beware of a worldly policy; do not compromise principle; fasten yourselves to the throne of God; and lean upon the arm of Omnipotence. Let your doings be characterised by the loftiness of christian independence,

and by the compassion of the Son of God. In your prayers, your resolutions, your speeches, make mention of our brethren GEORGE THOMP-
SON and CHARLES STUART, and of all our brethren in England — and,
above all things, fail not now and at all times to BE BOLD FOR GOD.

Yours, with brotherly affection,

Wm. Lloyd Garrison.

ALS: Garrison Papers, Boston Public Library. Because of lack of room, Garrison's
signature was placed along the left edge of the last page. The letter was printed
in *The Liberator* on January 23, 1836.

1. Exodus 20:15; Deuteronomy 5.19, and elsewhere in the Bible.
2. Exodus 20:17 and Deuteronomy 5:21. Garrison quotes the beginning and
end of the verse.
3. Leviticus 19:18 and in the New Testament.

4. Matthew 7:12.
5. Proverbs 3:31.
6. Hebrews 13:3.
7. Isaiah 58:6.
8. Jeremiah 21:12.
9. Proverbs 31:8.
10. I Samuel 17:47.
11. Ecclesiastes 7:29.
12. Old Testament, *passim.*

13. Revelation 19:16.
14. Romans 10:12, slightly adapted.
15. Isaiah 57:15.
16. The Bible, *passim.*
17. Isaiah 40:12.
18. Isaiah 40:17
19. Revelation 18:13.
20. II Samuel 22:8–12, 15, slightly adapted.
21. Hebrews 10:31.

22. See introductory biographical sketch of Arthur and Lewis Tappan.

23. Romans 12:19.
24. Psalms 103:6.
25. Psalms 12:5.

26. Jeremiah 34:17.
27. Isaiah 1:20; 40:5 *et passim.*
28. Jeremiah 2:34.

29. The proposition was that of Governor George McDuffie of South Carolina,
in his annual message to the South Carolina legislature at the end of 1835. The
message was published in *The Liberator*, December 12, 1835.
30. The reference is to Job.
31. Isaiah 2:22.

6

TO HENRY F. BENSON

Brooklyn, Jan. 26, 1836.

Dear Henry:

The number of delegates that attended the annual meeting pleases
and surprises me.[1] It is, by far, the largest that has yet assembled
together in Boston — excepting, of course, at our N. E. Conventions.[2]
The conduct of those who kept us out of the meeting-houses is even
more disgraceful, more intolerable, than that of the rioters last October
— I say *us*, for abolitionists are *one*. "E Pluribus Unim." [3] As so many
good speakers were present, why was not the meeting held a day
longer? I was gratified to see so full an account of its proceedings in
the last *Liberator*. I cannot understand why bro. Wright's resolution

was laid upon the table.[4] I do not see any thing that is objectionable in it.

There is scarcely a man in the nation, whose good opinion I value more than that of Wm. Goodell. Hence, I feel greatly indebted to him for his resolution and speech, in approval of the course I have pursued, and also to the meeting which adopted it so unanimously.[5] What will Joseph Tracy say now about "the Garrison party"?[6] In vain will he labor to separate those whose principles, feelings, hopes and purposes are one. You wish that I could have listened to bro. Goodell's eloquent remarks. As they were panegyrical, it would not have been proper for me to listen to them, if I could have done so.

Prof. Follen always speaks so delightfully, that I hope he will not fail to report his speech.[7] The proceedings of the meeting ought to appear in pamphlet form without delay. Were any delegates chosen to attend the R. I. Convention? If not, it is not too late for the Board to appoint a number — as our Society ought to be represented.

The subscriptions to our Society, and to the Liberator, show abundantly that abolitionists love to practice as well as to preach. The sum is unexpectedly large.[8]

The officers and managers are "true blue" — as far as I know them, thorough-working and uncompromising, except E. M. P. W. I am sorry that he was re-elected — because he who is ready to sacrifice the Liberator is commonly conceived to be lacking in soundness of faith. H. C. Wright, H. G. Chapman, and J. S. Kimball are valuable acquisitions.[9]

I shall endeavor to write a letter [10] to Vermont, according to friend Johnson's request. The trumpet of Liberty will echo finely among the Green Mountains.

What an enviable couple they must be who are able to produce a beautiful *bud of May* in freezing January! [11] Give my congratulations to bro. M. and his wife, and tell them there is a pair in Brooklyn who are resolved to present a greater phenomenon in the course of a week or two — we expect that *a whole Garrison* will then be born at a single birth! [12] Another pair, our nearest neighbors, determined to keep up the oddity of the competition, are demonstrating daily that they will shortly present to the view of a curious world, an infant that is perfectly *Gray!* [13] When will the age of wonders cease?

I have waited so long for the 2d edition of Channing, that I shall still wait patiently until a copy of it come. Rev. Mr. Wilson is very anxious to get his half dozen copies. Send them in the next bundle, if practicable.

It is truly good news to hear that the house in Brighton-street [14] is let. The iron and tin ware you may sell to the occupant — but reserve the glass lamps, as we shall want them, unless you can sell them for nearly their worth. I believe the large pair (one of the smaller pair is broken) cost $2,25 or $2,50.

Enclosed are $2, to pay for Wm. Geer's subscription for the present year.[15]

Friend Rowland Greene wishes you to stop sending Dorcas Green's paper to Bristol, R. I. and send it to Plainfield, Ct. directed to him.[16]

Miss Ball [17] has written to me, desiring to know how she shall send the fifty dollars which the Ladies' Society have generously given to me. I have written to her to pay it over to you; and if you should come to Brooklyn, please bring it with you; if not, get a fifty dollar bank-note (Boston or U. S. money) and send it to me by mail in a letter. See that it is carefully put into the Post Office.

Week before last, a piece of original poetry, highly complimentary to myself, appeared in the Liberator.[18] It ought to have been sent to the Emancipator [19] or Spectator.[20] It looks very egotistical to see such pieces in the Liberator, and I hope friend K. will be careful not to publish any more that may be communicated for the paper.[21] A defensive speech, like that of bro. Goodell, is another thing.

As friend K. has some editorial on hand, I have not sent much in this bundle. I hope he will be able to insert, *this* week the proceedings of the Convention at Northampton,[22] (a grand one it was,) and also those of the young men at Lowell.[23] [Such] meetings ought not to be slighted, being much more important in their effect than common articles. He will find the procee[dings] in this bundle — also many other articles, both literary and miscellaneous, which I wish him carefully to examine. It may puzzle him to choose among so much, but all that I send is worth something. I want every article in the Liberator to be interesting. We must make the paper the very best, if possible. Very much, therefore, depends upon choice selections. I have furnished several pieces of poetry. We have had so many long documents, of late, in the paper, that the readers probably desire to see shorter articles. Nevertheless, I want to see the extracts from Marcy's speech, and also *all* the debates in both houses of Congress upon the slavery question, published without delay. These are official acts, and belong to history.

☞ Should the Lynn Record publish a piece of poetry, headed, "There were some little souls," &c. let it be copied into the Liberator.☜ [24]

I have marked several excellent passages in the sermons of Rev. Mr. Root [25] and Rev. Mr. Cutler,[26] for early publication — one from each at a time, as may be convenient. They may be put upon the last page. Both of you must excuse me for making one letter answer for you both.

Next to the proceedings of public meetings, I wish those articles to have a preference which relate to our petitions to Congress.

It is *too bad* for you to confine yourself so long and so laboriously at the office. You ought not to do so for love or money. As for your not going to the Convention at Providence, and then coming here, I will not listen to it for a moment — not I. You ought to go to that Convention, if you have to elope by midnight. Fail not, I beseech you.

No news from George Thompson yet? Has Mrs. Thompson [26a] yet sailed? If not, where is she? I wish to know, because I ought to write to her without delay. I hope friend K. has transmitted the Liberators regularly by packet to bro. T. Think how anxious he must be to see them!

Father and mother will groan in spirit if you should not make us a visit in Brooklyn. But whether you come here or not, you must certainly go to Providence. It is a rare opportunity, and many are the attractions which call you thither. GO! If you don't I shall blame you *very much*, and still remain

Yours, lovingly,

W. L. G.

☞ Can you send me the Herald of Freedom of 9th inst.? [27]

☞ I will try to send the remainder of my sketch of Geo. Thompson for friend K. by the next mail.[28]

Will bro. May write an editorial paragraph about the R. I. Convention for Saturday's paper? [29] It ought to be mentioned — but I have no more time to write.

ALS: Garrison Papers, Boston Public Library.

1. The list of official delegates published in *The Liberator*, January 23, 1836, totaled about 150, and included an additional thirty "friends." The proceedings of the meeting were also published in this issue.

2. The reason for Garrison's surprise was that it was the first time that the organization met as the Massachusetts Anti-Slavery Society instead of, as in former years, as the New England Anti-Slavery Society.

3. Garrison's spelling.

4. The resolution held the North as responsible as the South for slavery, and condemned the North's failure to put its antislavery principles into practice.

5. The resolution introduced by William Goodell and adopted unanimously read: "*Resolved*, That while some men may with impunity *commit* crimes, which others may not boldly *reprove*, without violating the fastidious decorum of the age, we commend our brother, William Lloyd Garrison, and the Liberator, to the hearts of all who love the Gospel of peace and good will to men." Goodell (1792–1878), a founder of the American and New York Anti-Slavery Societies, was editor of the antislavery *Emancipator* in New York from 1834 to 1836, when he founded and edited the *Friend of Man*, organ of the New York Anti-Slavery Society until 1842. (*Life, passim; Weld-Grimké Letters*, I, 104n. The latter source erroneously gives Goodell's year of birth as 1782.) For Goodell's speech on behalf of his resolution, see *Fourth Annual Report of the Massachusetts Anti-Slavery Society* (Boston, 1836), pp. 54–61.

6. The Reverend Joseph Tracy (1793–1874) was a Congregational minister, editor, author, and supporter of Negro colonization who was ordained in 1821,

and served his first pastorate in Vermont. He became editor successively of the *Vermont Chronicle* in 1829, of the Boston *Recorder* in 1834, and of the New York *Observer* in 1835. He was appointed secretary of the Massachusetts Colonization Society in 1842 and continued in that office during the remainder of his life. He also became a director of the American Colonization Society in 1858. Among his published works were two books on missionary activity in Africa, published in 1840 and 1844. As a means of siphoning off support from Garrison and the Garrisonian abolitionists, Tracy and seven others had signed a call, in December 1834, for a convention to form an American Union for the Relief and Improvement of the Colored Race, to be held in Boston on January 14, 1835. The organization was to provide a refuge for those who were dissatisfied with Garrison's "harsh" and "unchristian" language and/or were not willing to condemn the Colonization Society. Its purpose, obviously, was to weaken, if not destroy, the Garrisonian movement. For additional material on the relationship between Tracy and the Garrisonians, see the letter by Henry C. Wright in *The Liberator*, August 1, 1835. (*DAB; Life*, I, 469; II, *passim*; the latter source lists 1794 as Tracy's date of birth.)

7. Follen's speech was on behalf of a resolution which he had introduced, emphasizing the equality of duties and rights of all participants in the antislavery movement: "White men and colored men, citizens and foreigners, men and women." (Follen's remarks are reported in the *Fourth Annual Report of the Massachusetts Anti-Slavery Society*, Boston, 1836, pp. 49–54.)

8. C. P. Grosvenor, of Salem, Massachusetts, a vice-president, and in the previous year assistant general agent and corresponding secretary, resolved that a collection be taken among the delegates and auxiliary organizations to pay off the society's debts. Thereupon, a sum of $105 in cash and subscriptions amounting to $1,045 were collected for the society, as well as $75 for *The Liberator*. (*Fourth Annual Report*, p. 61.)

9. E. M. P. W. was E. M. P. Wells. Henry C. Wright was elected vice-president, H. G. Chapman, treasurer, and John S. Kimball, of Boston, counsellor.

Henry Grafton Chapman (b. Boston, May 3, 1804; d. October 3, 1842) was a Boston merchant who married Maria Weston Chapman in 1830. He was the son of Henry and Sarah Greene Chapman. Henry Grafton and Maria W. Chapman were members of William Ellery Channing's congregation. They joined the abolitionists in 1834, despite the objections of Channing and the condemnation of their closest friends. (*Life*, II, 49n.)

John S. Kimball (b. Pembroke, New Hampshire, April 15, 1812; d. Boston, April 19, 1888) was variously employed in a bakery, printing shop, and post office before he studied law at Harvard. After his admission to the bar, he was a partner in the law office of Robert Rantoul in Boston for six years. His failing health forced him to abandon the practice of law and to enter business. He entered the wholesale drygoods firm of Kimball and Chace in 1838, changing its name to J. S. Kimball & Co. upon the death of his partner in 1840. He retired from active business in 1865. (Leonard A. Morrison, *History of the Kimball Family in America*, Boston, 1897, pp. 639–640.)

10. The letter (9) was dated "Brooklyn, Ct. Feb. 10, 1836," and was read at the annual meeting of the Vermont Anti-Slavery Society, which met at Middlebury on February 16 and 17.

11. The son born at this time, January 21, 1836, to the Reverend and Mrs. Samuel J. May was Joseph. He graduated from Harvard University in 1857 and from Cambridge Divinity School in 1865. He served as minister in Yonkers, New York, Newburyport, Massachusetts and, from 1876, at the Locust Street Church in Philadelphia. (Samuel May, *A Genealogy of the Descendants of John May*, Boston, 1878, pp. 23, 46.)

12. George Thompson Garrison, born February 13, 1836.

13. Mr. and Mrs. John Gray were residents of Brooklyn, Connecticut, and friends of the Bensons. Mr. Gray (1798–1859) was a temperance man who strayed occasionally. See letter from Samuel May, Jr., to Samuel J. May, dated

February 16, 1836 (May Papers, Boston Public Library). The Grays sold their home in August, with the intention of moving to Scituate to be near Samuel J. May (see letter 55, to Henry E. Benson, August 27, 1836). John Gray was publisher of the *Windham County Advertiser* in Brooklyn in 1826. (Ellen D. Larned, *History of Windham County, Connecticut*, Worcester, Mass., 1880, II, 479; M. D. Raymond, *Gray Genealogy* . . . , Tarrytown, N.Y., pp. 195–196.)

14. Garrison and his wife had lived in a rented house in Roxbury until May 1835. They then removed "to a boarding house on Guild Row (now Washington Street), near Dudley Street." Several weeks later they moved to 23 Brighton Street, near the Leverett Street Jail. (See *Life*, I, 502n.) The latter was a temporary arrangement that involved the taking over of George Thompson's lease on the house. In August, the growing threat of mob violence induced them to leave Brighton Street for Brooklyn, Connecticut, and by January 1836, they succeeded in subletting the house and storing their furniture with friends.

15. W. D. Geers (the s is in the name) was apparently a farmer living in or near Brooklyn. Garrison, in a letter to George W. Benson, November 27, 1835, (*Letters*, I), notes: "Mr. Geers talks of taking a load of pork to your market on Monday or Tuesday, should the weather prove favorable." Geers is also mentioned as a correspondent of *The Liberator* in its issue of September 29, 1832.

16. Rowland Greene (b. Old Warwick, Rhode Island, November 24, 1770; d. August 18, 1859) was the son of Thomas Greene, of Warwick, landowner and shipmaster. He married Susanna Harris on March 31, 1791. After studying medicine for some years, he moved to Plainfield, Connecticut, in 1814, where he conducted a Friends' boarding school at Black Hill, with his son Benjamin. Susan B. Anthony, the feminist leader, and Phebe Jackson of Providence, who participated in antislavery activities, were trained in the school. (Louise Brownell Clarke, comp., *The Greenes of Rhode Island*, New York, 1903, pp. 386–388.) On October 8, 1836, *The Liberator* printed "An Address" from Rowland Greene to the free people of color in New England, urging them to place their children in situations enabling them to secure an education or to learn a useful trade.

Dorcas was Rowland Greene's daughter, and the sister of Benjamin and Freelove Greene. She was born in 1809 and died in 1896. She married her cousin, Albert Daniel Greene, in 1841. (*Ibid.*, p. 547.)

17. Lucy M. Ball, treasurer of the Boston Female Anti-Slavery Society.

18. *The Liberator* of January 16, 1836. The poem, by W. C., was entitled "To William Lloyd Garrison."

19. The *Emancipator*, a weekly antislavery newspaper, was founded in 1833 by abolitionists associated with the formation of the New York City Anti-Slavery Society. Its first editor was Charles W. Denison. He was succeeded by William Goodell, who was associated with the newspaper from the beginning and continued to edit it until he was succeeded by Joshua Leavitt in 1837. The *Emancipator* became the official organ of the American Anti-Slavery Society after the formation of that organization at the end of 1833. In 1840, the secessionists from the American Anti-Slavery Society took the *Emancipator* with them and it became the official organ of the New York Anti-Slavery Society. (Dwight L. Dumond, *Antislavery: The Crusade for Freedom in America*, Ann Arbor, Mich., 1961, pp. 177, 179; Louis Filler, *The Crusade Against Slavery, 1830–1860*, New York, Evanston, and London, 1960, pp. 25, 63, 97, 136, 191.)

20. The *New England Spectator*, a religious antislavery paper, was first issued on November 5, 1834. Its editor and proprietor was William Smith Porter. Its masthead read, "A Family Paper, Designed to Promote the Study of the Bible and Family Religion, the Cause of Active Piety, the Abolition of War, Slavery, Licentiousness, &c., and the Circulation of Useful Intelligence." In 1837 it became the property of John Gulliver, a deacon in the Free Church of the Reverend Charles Fitch of Boston, and it ceased publication in 1838. (*Life*, II, 158, 175, 252 *et passim*; *Weld-Grimké Letters*, I, 427; *The Liberator*, May 4, 1838.)

21. Despite these instructions, Knapp included a second adulatory poem "To

William Lloyd Garrison," by R., dated Kingston, January 1836, in *The Liberator* of January 30.

22. The description of the proceedings was included in *The Liberator*, February 13, 1836. The convention met on January 20 for the purpose of forming an Old Hampshire Anti-Slavery Society.

23. This meeting took place on January 6, for the purpose of forming a Lowell Young Men's Anti-Slavery Society. The report of the proceedings was reprinted in *The Liberator*, February 6, 1836, from the Lowell *Times*.

24. The poem was reprinted in *The Liberator*, February 13, from the Lynn *Record*. It satirized the Boston mob of October 21, 1835, and was to be sung to the tune of "There was a Little Man and he Wooed a Little Maid." The first stanza read:

> "There were some little souls with the optics of moles;
> And they said to one another, let us try, try, try,
> If we cannot get Judge *Lynch* to serve at a pinch
> The ends of little you and little I, I, I."

The author is unknown.

25. A paragraph from the sermon of the Reverend David Root, of the Congregational Church and Society of Dover, New Hampshire, which had been delivered as a Thanksgiving sermon on November 26, 1835, appeared in *The Liberator*, January 9, 1836. Root was born in Piermont, New Hampshire, June 17, 1791, and died in Chicago on August 30, 1873. After graduating from Middlebury College in 1816, he pursued theological studies in Troy, New York, served as a missionary in Georgia, and was ordained pastor of the Second Presbyterian Church in Cincinnati, Ohio, in 1819. Resigning his charge in 1832, he became minister of the First Congregational Church in Dover, New Hampshire, in 1833, remaining until September 4, 1839. For several months thereafter, he was an agent of the anti-Garrisonian Massachusetts Abolition Society. He served in the First Church in Waterbury, Connecticut, from 1841 to 1844, and the Third Congregational Church in Guilford, Connecticut, from 1845 to 1851. He apparently retired from the ministry in 1851 and lived in New Haven for some time. (*The First Parish in Dover, New Hampshire*, Dover, 1884, pp. 100–101.)

26. The Reverend Calvin Cutler (b. Guildhall, Vermont, October 10, 1791; d. February 17, 1844), graduated from Dartmouth College and Andover Theological Seminary. He was ordained in November 1823, at the Congregational Church in Lebanon, New Hampshire, and remained there until May 1827. In October of the same year, he began preaching at Windham, New Hampshire, and was installed at the Presbyterian Church on April 9, 1828. He stayed there until the end of his life. He joined the New England Anti-Slavery Society in 1834, but regarded Garrison and Nathaniel P. Rogers as extremists. He preached his sermon on Thanksgiving Day, November 26, 1835. A paragraph of the sermon appeared in *The Liberator* on January 30, 1836. The entire sermon was later printed as a pamphlet. (Leonard A. Morrison, *The History of Windham in New Hampshire, 1719–1883*, Boston, 1883, pp. 127–128, 417–419.)

26a. Anne Erskine Spry married George Thompson in 1831. They had six children. (*DAB*.)

27. The *Herald of Freedom* was an antislavery newspaper edited by Nathaniel P. Rogers (1794–1846) of Concord, New Hampshire. The newspaper was established by the New Hampshire Anti-Slavery Society in 1835.

28. *The Liberator*, January 9, announced a forthcoming volume devoted to George Thompson, containing his letters, activities in the United States, and essays vindicating him from the attacks of his American detractors. It was to include, too, the story of the mobbing of Garrison on October 21, 1835.

29. Samuel J. May's editorial paragraph about the Rhode Island convention appeared in *The Liberator*, January 30, 1836. It urged a large attendance at the convention.

7

TO THE PRESIDENT OF THE ANTI-SLAVERY CONVENTION TO BE HELD AT PROVIDENCE, FEB. 2.

BROOKLYN, CT. JAN. 30, 1836.

My Dear Sir:

Circumstances prevent my attending your State Convention,[1] but they allow me to send a letter as a substitute for my bodily presence.

As I think of your meeting, my heart heaves within me tumultuously: every emotion is a wave, and every thought a breeze. My paper must be the bark to waft a freight of good-will to your body. May it add something to the almost empty treasury of humanity — for great expenditures are yet to be made in her sacred cause!

What shall I say respecting the call of your Convention? It burst forth in a mingled peal of a thousand voices,[2] — suddenly, — unexpectedly, — like a clarion in the clear, still noon of night. It has gone over the Alleghany mountains, and is swiftly travelling along the Mississippi, nor will its echoes cease till they have 'rung from side to side' of our extended republic. There has been no single burst like it in any other cause. Let Rhode Island have the palm — for, of all her competitors, she is now foremost in the race of freedom. When the empire State, New York, sent forth her call for an Anti-Slavery Convention,[3] it was signed by about four hundred 'good men and true' — a number that made Liberty wave her cap, and Mercy smile in gladness. But little Rhode Island has, in this instance, shown herself larger than the largest. Let her be crowned on Tuesday next. Not that *we* rely for success upon any other arm than that of Omnipotence: not that we depend upon numbers to inspire our hopes, influence our actions, or direct our course. No — but our enemies do; so that, if we cannot silence them by our arguments, we shall finally do so by our multitudinous array. Hence it is worthy of remark, that since your conventional notice appeared, with its host of signatures gathered from almost every town and village in the State, your pro-slavery newspapers, which were wont to be violent and voluble in their denunciations of the abolitionists, have all been mute.

> 'The oracles are dumb;
> No voice, or hideous hum,'[4]

is heard from any quarter. Where is their patriotism? Have they grown ashamed of their allies, — the rabble? Is the case altered now — and wherefore? Do they hope to satisfy the South, by protesting that they do not like her compliments less, but that they like the dollars of the yeomanry of Rhode Island more? O, no doubt they have good reasons for their silence, but they do not like to give them 'upon compulsion' — their *principal* reason (though it would seem to argue the sacrifice of all *principle*,) would probably be found to appertain to both PRINCIPAL and INTEREST.

What shall I say of the object of your Convention? It is to form another State Anti-Slavery Society — not for the purpose of leaving Connecticut to stand alone, (as she will from all her New England sisters, but I trust not long,) [5] but to embody the opinions of the people of Rhode Island, in opposition to American slavery. It is to roll the tide of moral influence onward to the south. It is to create a Union, by which THE UNION shall be purified from every stain of blood, and supported to the end of time by the pillars of JUSTICE, LIBERTY, HUMANITY, RIGHTEOUSNESS. For it is by the irresistible pressure of PUBLIC OPINION, that the grim monster OPPRESSION is to be hurled from his throne of skulls, and the fetters of his victims are to be broken asunder. Maine has her State Society, with numerous auxiliaries. So has New Hampshire; so has Vermont; [6] so has Massachusetts, [7] so has New York; so has Ohio; [8] so has Kentucky; [9] and so, it shall be announced in a few days, has Rhode Island! All these STATE Societies, excepting one, have been organized within two years, besides a National Society. These are the tokens of the downfall of our cause, the fewness of our numbers, and the impotence of our efforts! And what have our enemies to present as the evidence of *their* success? Why, for every score of societies that we have formed, they can produce a riot in their favor. For every speech that we have made in favor of liberty, they can show a brickbat, or a rotten egg, or a bludgeon, or a dagger, used in support of oppression. For every petition that we have put up to the Throne of Mercy, they can adduce a sneer, a threat, or a malediction! And we are discomfited, forsooth! This is the general proclamation. Then is victory discomfiture; then is continual success continual defeat; then is the rise of the tide its ebb; then is the sun near its meridian waning below the horizon! Of what, then, are we confident? Why, that Truth is more than a match for Falsehood, and that Liberty is mightier than Oppression. Of what do we boast? of our own strength and prowess? No. But of *the certain progress of humanity* — the wide regeneration of public sentiment by that 'foolishness of preaching,' [10] which is yet to bring down principalities and powers, — to emancipate a groaning world from the bondage of sin, — and to bring people of every kindred, tribe and nation into the glorious liberty of the sons of God. Who are witnesses of the mighty conflict in which we are engaged? All heaven and earth! What is our Statute Book? The Bible! Who is our leader? Not one on earth — *but* one in heaven — Jehovah of Hosts! — Therefore we will 'give unto the LORD the glory due unto his name!' [11]

But — to the *object* of your Convention. It is not a foreign, nor a local, nor a partial object. It is fraught with more than Grecian or Polish interest. It is emphatically a NATIONAL object, around which are clustering momentous consequences, — universal results. It has a great variety of aspects. It is to emancipate *two millions and a half of our own countrymen* from a domestic tyranny, incomparably more dreadful than that which caused all Egypt to be filled with plagues, and Pharaoh and his host to be destroyed in the Red Sea. It is to save a million of the gentler sex from pollution, field labor, and the lash. *It is to put an end to an impure and disgraceful amalgamation.* It is to restore the stolen babe to the arms of its frantic mother, and to reunite all the sundered ties of life. It is to suppress cruelty, stop the effusion of blood, undo the heavy burden, enlighten ignorance, destroy the cause of insurrection, abolish heathenism, place our entire population under equal laws, and suffer none to stand beyond the pale of the Constitution. It is to save, enrich and bless the south, by substituting two millions of free laborers, animated by the hope of reward and the prospect of happiness, in the place of two millions of cattle, goaded to madness by torture. It is to avert the overshadowing judgments of Almighty God from our nation, by a timely repentance. It is to rescue as many new victims of slavery in this country, annually, as are stolen from Africa by all the kidnappers in the world. It is to make the theory and the practice of the American people harmonious, and perfect in righteousness, so that we may no longer be a proverb, a hissing, and an astonishment in the earth, nor be accessary to the despotisms of the old world, nor be guilty of the awful crime of self-murder. In fine, there is no interest of man which appertains to his intellect, his soul, his well-being — to time or eternity — which it does not seek to advance; no reverence for God and his commandments which it does not studiously consult. Was ever a struggle like this?

Yet more. In one half of our country, we who abhor slavery, and are known to desire emancipation, cannot travel without perilling our *property* — SAFETY — LIVES! Yes — from one half of our boasted Union, we are excluded by the establishment of lynch law — by the prevalence of as murderous a spirit as reigned during the bloody supremacy of French jacobinism! As safely may the liberty-loving Greeks go to Constantinople, as any of us to Charleston or New Orleans! It is, then, the object of your Convention to recover the lost, invaluable *right of locomotion*, without hindrance or danger, in all parts of our country, for ourselves and our posterity — to knock off those shackles from our feet which now cripple and confine us — and to make every nook and corner of our native territory accessible to all.

Again. It is to rescue THE LIBERTY OF SPEECH from the grasp of that oppression, which now holds millions of our colored countrymen by their throats — a liberty which is becoming more and more abridged, for which GAGS and PADLOCKS are now recommended, without which men are abject as brutes, and in defence of which our fathers poured out their blood like water. Until our tongues are cut out, we will not cease to speak freely — our voices shall be heard loud as a thousand thunders, against the enslavement of our species — against their enslavers.

Again. It is to prevent the establishment of a despotic CENSORSHIP OF THE PRESS, which is now strenuously advocated even by those high in authority among us. What is a free press but the palladium of our rights? For whom is it desirable? For ourselves — our country — the whole world. When is it desirable? To-day — to-morrow — now — in this age — in all ages. How much is it worth? More than argosies of gold — as much as life itself. What shall wrest it from us? No mobs — no penal enactments — no bodily sufferings — no confiscations — *nothing but that which puts an end to our earthly existence.* We will submit to taunts, calumnies, insults, outrages, tortures — but to a censorship of the press, *especially on the subject of slavery,* WE WILL NOT SUBMIT — not if a gibbet is erected for us at the corner of every street, and the fires of martyrdom blaze in every square.

Finally. It is to save the friends of universal liberty — ourselves — from *a bloody extermination.* Let the eight hundred and fifty persons who signed the call of your Convention — and all who shall attend the Convention — and all who hold that every yoke ought instantly to be broken — remember that the south demands, in case of the failure of all other means, that they shall be 'PUT TO DEATH WITHOUT BENEFIT OF CLERGY.' [12] The spirit of southern slavery is a spirit of EXTERMINATION against all those who dare to represent it as a dishonor to our country, rebellion against God, and treason against the liberties of mankind. Now, therefore, that it has come to this — now that the alternative which slavery presents to us is, either to consent to be gagged or to be suspended upon a gallows — we shall carry on the warfare against it as men who realize that upon the energy, union and success of our efforts depend the security of our firesides, the enjoyment of civil and religious liberty, the preservation of our lives, the salvation of our country. As christian warriors, whose weapons are not carnal but spiritual, from man to man, and from rank to rank, the interrogation shall pass —

> 'Who would be a traitor-knave?
> Who would fill a coward's grave?
> Who so base would be a slave?
>   Let him turn and flee!' [13]

31

Excuse the length of this epistle — for a slaveholder (Gov. Hayne) tells us, in the language of Burke, 'you must pardon something to the spirit of Liberty' [14] — and when so grand and awful a theme as Liberty excites my mind, I know not when or where to pause. We have already been called to suffer something in this cause — we shall, unquestionably, be tried yet more severely. O, may the spirit of retaliation, and all passion and violence, be removed from our hearts; and may we have Christ so formed within us as to be enabled to return good for evil, and blessing for cursing, in all cases, under the most grievous provocation. I believe ours is the cause of God, else I would abandon it instantly. I believe we are willing that our blood should be shed, rather than that of the slaveholders. I am sure that we all deprecate insurrection among the slaves, and desire that they may be obedient to their masters *as unto God,* and patiently wait for a peaceful deliverance through the omnipotence of truth. We are stigmatized as fanatics, but our fanaticism is all embodied in the following lines of Cowper. Each one of us exclaims with him —

'I would not have a slave to till my ground,
To carry me — to fan me while I sleep,
And tremble when I wake, for all the wealth
That sinews, bought and sold, have ever earn'd.
No — dear as freedom is, and in my heart's
Just estimation prized above all price,
*I had much rather be myself the slave,
And wear the bonds, than fasten them on him.'* [15]

This is the spirit of Cowper. It is the spirit of Jesus Christ. It is, I trust, the spirit which animates us all, and which we desire to see reign in every breast, at the north and the south, in this and in all other lands, now and evermore. *It is immediate emancipation.*

Your devoted fellow-laborer,

WM. LLOYD GARRISON.

Printed in *The Liberator*, February 6, 1836; the heading is given as it appears there.

The president of the Rhode Island Anti-Slavery Society was John S. Clarke, of South Kingston, Rhode Island.

1. Garrison did attend the convention. See letter 8, to Isaac Knapp, dated "PROVIDENCE, FEB. 3d, 1836."

2. A footnote in *The Liberator* notes that "Eight hundred and fifty names were affixed to the call; but these were only the Representatives of the body, not the whole body itself."

3. The convention met at Utica, New York, on October 21, 1835, the day Garrison was mobbed in Boston. The convention at Utica was attacked by a mob and was forced to adjourn, but reconvened at the home of Gerrit Smith in Peterborough, New York. (See *Life*, I, 40n, 42; Samuel J. May presents an extended account of the convention in *Some Recollections of the Antislavery Conflict*, Boston, 1869, pp. 162–170.)

4. John Milton, "On the Morning of Christ's Nativity," in "The Hymn," stanza 19.

5. Maine, New Hampshire, Massachusetts, and Vermont had already formed state antislavery societies. Connecticut was still without one.

6. These three state societies were formed in 1834; the New Hampshire State Anti-Slavery Society had been formed at Concord on November 11–12; the Vermont Anti-Slavery Society had been formed at Middlebury on May 1. (See Dwight L. Dumond, *Antislavery: The Crusade for Freedom in America*, Ann Arbor, Mich., 1961, p. 188.)

7. *The Third Annual Report of the Board of Managers of the New England Anti-Slavery Society* (Boston, 1835), presented on January 21, 1835, notes: "In consequence of the formation of the American Anti-Slavery Society, and of the design contemplated to form State Societies in the New-England States, a design which has already been accomplished in Maine, New-Hampshire, and Vermont, the operations of the New-England Anti-Slavery Society during the past year, have been very much confined to Massachusetts. And hereafter, it will be only a State Society°" (p. 5.). The footnote reads: "Since the Report was read, the name of the association has been changed to that of the *Massachusetts Anti-Slavery Society*."

8. The Ohio State Anti-Slavery Society was organized at Putnam, April 22–24, 1835 (Dumond, *Antislavery*, p. 189).

9. The Kentucky Society for the Gradual Relief of the State from Slavery had been formed at Lexington, December 6, 1833 (Dumond, *Antislavery*, p. 199). This gave way to the Kentucky Anti-Slavery Society, formed on March 19, 1835, at Danville, Kentucky, which adopted the principle of immediate emancipation. James Birney played a leading part in the formation of both societies. (*The Liberator*, May 16, 1835.) *Life*, I, 479n, refers to the latter as "Birney's short-lived Kentucky A. S. Society."

10. I Corinthians 1:21.

11. Psalms 29:2.

12. Governor George McDuffie of South Carolina. See letter 3, to Henry E. Benson, January 16, 1836.

13. Robert Burns, "Scots, Wha Hae," stanza 3. First published in the *Morning Chronicle*, in May 1794.

14. Governor Robert Young Hayne (1797–1839) of South Carolina. Hayne was United States senator from South Carolina from 1823 to 1832 and governor of South Carolina from 1832 to 1834 (*ACAB*). In the course of his famous debate with Webster in January 1830, at the very end of the speech that he delivered in the Senate on January 26, 1830, Hayne quoted these famous words from Edmund Burke (1729–1797), the British statesman and political writer.

15. William Cowper (1731–1800), English poet, *The Task* (1785), Book II, "The Timepiece," lines 29–36.

8

TO ISAAC KNAPP

PROVIDENCE, FEB. 3d, 1836. }
Wednesday Evening 7 o'clk. }

MY DEAR KNAPP:

You will be very much surprised to learn by this hasty note, that I am now attending the Rhode Island State Anti-Slavery Society — for I did not suppose that circumstances would allow me to be present, and, accordingly, I transmitted a letter to the Convention, excusing my absence, which was read before my arrival, and which I herewith transmit to be published in the Liberator, together with several other letters, all of which have been well received by the Convention, and ordered by them to be published with their proceedings.[1] Mr. Birney's letter is peculiarly interesting, and shows how great are the perils which surround that dear friend of God, and how strongly he stands in his integrity.[2] Mr. Bourne's letter is characteristic of that early pioneer in the cause of immediate emancipation, and worthy of lasting record.[3]

This is one of the grandest Conventions ever held in this country, in any cause of benevolence. Nearly FOUR HUNDRED individuals have enrolled their names as members of the Convention, and nearly THREE HUNDRED have signed their names to the Constitution of the State Society.[4] About $2,000 were subscribed this afternoon, in the course of half an hour, to carry on the operations of the Society. Although the thermometer, yesterday and to-day, stood below zero, yet there is no lack of comfortable warmth in the Convention. Two of our number travelled afoot more than forty miles! This is a specimen of abolition zeal, perseverance and endurance. Freezing weather cannot check them — mobs cannot put them down — rewards cannot frighten them.

The Convention is holding its meetings in High-street meeting-house, a new, beautiful and spacious building. A most delightful spirit prevails among the members, and it is refreshing to look at their countenances. No State in the Union can produce a more upright and substantial body of men: they are the bone and muscle of society, in the most emphatic sense of the words. Every thing is perfectly quiet in the city, for the simple reason, probably, that the two political parties are so equally balanced in this State, that both are afraid to insult or annoy us, lest they should lose the votes of the abolitionists.

All the meetings have been very fully attended. This evening, the house is crowded with a noble audience, such as is rarely seen even in the most popular causes. Rev. Mr. Storrs,[5] of N. H. is now making a very powerful speech, to the admiration of his listeners.

I have full confidence that this letter will arrive safely, as there are no mail-robbers on the route between Providence and Boston, these felons chiefly residing in Charleston, South Carolina. In that violent and bloody city, they have a high reputation for patriotism and honesty, which they do not wish to lose by strolling abroad. Their offence, indeed, is quite insignificant, in the long catalogue of their crimes: for what is their occasional robbery of the northern mail, their unlawful seizure of our letters and newspapers, contrasted with their daily robbery of the poor and needy — their transformation of millions of human beings into live stock and creeping things? Robbery is their trade, and they know how to rob systematically. They have made it an honorable business among themselves: they subsist altogether by plunder. To rob the mail, therefore, is only to labor 'in their vocation,' on a very small scale. They make a prey of men, women and children — ay, not unfrequently of *their own children.* Is it a matter of surprise, then, that they should rifle a mail-bag? [6]

But I must close. I have no more time to write, and you will not find room for any more if I should extend my sketch.

WILLIAM LLOYD GARRISON

Printed in *The Liberator*, February 6, 1836.

1. The convention met in Providence on Tuesday, February 2, at 2 p.m. in the High Street Congregational Meeting House. On February 6, *The Liberator* published letters to the Rhode Island Convention from various antislavery leaders, including James G. Birney, George Bourne, Lewis Tappan, John Rankin, Beriah Green, and others.

2. The letter from James G. Birney was dated Cincinnati, January 22, 1836, and was addressed to Mr. William M. Chase, corresponding secretary, Providence Anti-Slavery Society. In it he wrote that "The war is raging. . . . Our dearest rights are not only menaced, but almost held at the mercy of the slave-holding part of the country.

"I cannot print my paper *here.* . . . It was but yesterday, that a wealthy slaveholder of Kentucky, called to let me know, that my Press in *Ohio* would be destroyed by a band of *his* fellow-citizens who had determined on it . . . and that my life is in continual danger. . . . If I fall in this cause, I trust it will bring hundreds to supply my place."

Birney (1792–1857), a Kentucky lawyer and Presbyterian leader, was at first a colonizationist, but was influenced by Theodore Weld to become an abolitionist in 1834, when he also accepted a secret agency from the American Anti-Slavery Society. After meeting with much hostility in Kentucky, he moved to Cincinnati, Ohio, where he established the *Philanthropist* early in 1836. He became corresponding secretary of the American Anti-Slavery Society in 1837 and remained in that post until 1840, when he seceded with other anti-Garrisonians. He was candidate of the Liberty party for President in 1840 and 1844. (*Weld-Grimké Letters*, I, 150n; *Life, passim*; Betty Fladeland, *James Gillespie Birney, Slaveholder to Abolitionist*, Ithaca, N.Y. 1955.)

3. The letter from George Bourne, dated New York, February 1, 1836, was addressed "to the Rhode Island Anti-Slavery Convention," and read, in part:

"Political discussions, and even calculations based upon self-interest will avail nothing to overthrow the monster which has so long desolated the morals and withered the energies of the Southern citizens. . . . The connection of slavery with the profession of religion, and its incorporation with the christian churches are the most gross outrage upon common sense and the gospel." He closed by urging the convention to demand of the churches in the state that they refuse to acknowledge slaveholders as "disciples of Jesus," and have no fellowship with them.

The Reverend George Bourne (1780–1845) was a pre-Garrisonian abolitionist, author of several antislavery books and pamphlets, one of which in particular, *The Book and Slavery Irreconcilable* (Philadelphia, 1816), had an important influence upon Garrison. In his early opposition to colonization and in his espousal of immediate emancipation, Bourne preceded Garrison. He was one of the founders of the American Anti-Slavery Society. (*Life*, I, postscript immediately following the preface, 306, II, 445.)

4. The constitution of the Rhode Island State Anti-Slavery Society was printed in *The Liberator*, February 6, 1836.

5. The Reverend George Storrs (b. Lebanon, New Hampshire, December 13, 1796; d. Brooklyn, New York, December 28, 1879); a Methodist minister, he was arrested on December 14 by the legal authorities of Northfield, New Hampshire, in the midst of his devotional exercises, to prevent him from preaching a sermon against slavery, in a church whose members had invited him to address them. He was charged with being "an idle and disorderly person, and wanton and lascivious in speech and behavior, a common railer and brawler, who neglects any lawful employment, and misspends his time in going about said town and county, disturbing the public peace." However, the charge did not hold and "he was dismissed." He was censured by the Methodist church in 1836 for his antislavery actions. An agent of the American Anti-Slavery Society in 1835 and 1836, he was transferred to New York by the executive committee of the society in 1837. He withdrew from the Methodist church in 1840 and joined the Adventists. During the early 1840's, he preached an extreme form of Adventism. (*The Liberator*, January 9, 1836; *Life*, II, 67–68; Dwight L. Dumond, *Letters of J. G. Birney*, New York and London, 1938, I, 256; Isaac C. Wellcome, *History of the Second Advent Message*, Yarmouth, Me., 1874, pp. 281–282.)

6. On the night of July 29, 1835, some of the leading citizens of Charleston, South Carolina, broke into the post office in that city and confiscated antislavery publications mailed from New York and brought to Charleston by the U. S. mail packet *Columbia*. On the following night, the publications were publicly burned by a mob of three thousand persons. (*Life*, I, 485.)

9

TO OLIVER JOHNSON

BROOKLYN, Ct. Feb. 10, 1836.

My Dear Friend:

I shall mingle my spirit with the brave spirits who purpose to attend the annual meeting of the Vermont Anti-Slavery Society, at Middlebury, on the 16th and 17th instant. There are many reasons why I should desire to be present with you 'in the flesh,' on that occasion. *Abolitionism is indigenous to the soil of Vermont.* Yours was the first *State* Society that was regularly organized in this country,[1] for the immediate extirpation of American slavery — a system which LORD BROUGHAM [2] brands as 'that most infernal scourge to humanity,' and which JOHN WESLEY [3] described as 'that execrable villany, which is the scandal of religion and of human nature.' Almost my first efforts in the sacred cause of UNIVERSAL EMANCIPATION, (for we are struggling to preserve our own rights, as well as to recover the liberties of southern bondmen, hence it is a common cause,) were made in Vermont, more than seven years ago. It was a suitable place, — of all others the best chosen, — to plant the standard of Liberty upon the summit of her

Green Mountains, and to blow the trump of Liberty through all her valleys. One of our opponents tells us, that the world is one great whispering gallery, whose faintest echoes reach alike the ears of the oppressed and the oppressor. No wonder, therefore, that the latter trembles when he hears the voice of humanity, and that he commands us to be silent upon peril of our lives. I remember, with lively satisfaction, how readily I procured the names of TWENTY-THREE HUNDRED of your free inhabitants, in the course of three or four weeks, to a petition praying for the abolition of slavery in the District of Columbia — the largest petition on this subject, if I mistake not, that has ever been presented to Congress, and procured at a time, moreover, when the people of other States were slumbering in the arms of indifference. 'Honor to whom honor is due.' [4] Of all the northern representatives in Congress, during its present session, who has most ably advocated the cause of insulted, down-trodden humanity, and most firmly sustained the dignity of the North? A representative from Vermont — WILLIAM SLADE.[5] I read an anecdote, some years ago, which is probably familiar to many, but which I quote as characteristic of the spirit which animates the people of your patriotic State. A slaveholder, in pursuit of a runaway slave, finding him in one of your villages, immediately pounced upon him, and brought him before the court, presenting at the same time, what he considered indubitable evidence, that the victim was his lawful *property*. Still, the judge demurred — he wanted other proof. At last, the prowling oppressor passionately desired to know of the judge, what evidence would satisfy him that the slave belonged to the claimant? '*A bill of sale from the Almighty!*' was the memorable reply.[6] These things make me love and honor Vermont. The anecdote I have related reminds me of the beautiful simile used by the great Bard of Nature:

> 'How far that little candle throws its beams!
> *So shines a good deed in a naughty world!*' [7]

Henceforth, when the American oppressor attempts to convince us that the slaves are his property, by pointing us to the color of their skin and the texture of their hair, by showing us how large a sum he has paid for their bodies and souls, by proving that they were bequeathed to him by some defunct predecessor, we will kindle at the insult, and tell him that nothing will satisfy us but A BILL OF SALE FROM THE ALMIGHTY!

For what are we battling? It is for the dignity, the equality, the enfranchisement of our common nature. Every sixth man, woman, child and babe, in the United States, — constituting a number as large as the whole population of New England, — is in bondage, and their cries are hourly borne to our ears by the free winds of heaven! If any of us were in their condition, what would be the doctrine we should desire our advocates to preach for our deliverance? What! *expatriation* to a barbarous land as the condition of our freedom! What! a *gradual* sundering of our chains! No — no. It would be the doctrine of *immediate*, TOTAL, EVERLASTING emancipation. In the mighty conflict of 1776, between the mother country and her colonies, no other doctrine was listened to, for a moment, by our patriotic sires — least of all by the independent yeomanry of Vermont, for the mountains of the earth have always been the chosen abode of LIBERTY, and no wonder that she makes them *Green* Mountains, as her footsteps press their genial soil! Was STARKE [8] a gradualist or an immediatist? Let the battle of Bennington answer! What voice is heard on the plains of Lexington and Concord — from the heights of Bunker Hill? 'INDEPENDENCE NOW — INDEPENDENCE FOREVER!' [9] Tell me, ye whose blood was freely shed to make your children free — would he not have been deemed a traitor, or a madman, who should have maintained, in view of your sufferings, perils and oppression, that the mother country ought to be *compensated*, if she should cease to tread upon your necks, and to spill your blood? Your reply would be, in the conclusive language of an eminent patriot, — 'Slavery is a *crime*, and crime is not a marketable commodity, to be bought and sold.' [10] Never was the duty of compensating oppressors urged, but in the case of the oppressors of the colored race — the most flagitious despots who have ever sought to brutalize mankind. If one of these monsters tells me, he has given one thousand dollars for his slave, that he may hold him in bondage; my reply is this — *Jesus Christ has given his life for that slave, that he may bring him into the glorious liberty of the sons of God!* I will give you an anecdote, which puts this matter of compensation in a clear light. At one of the great anti-slavery meetings in Manchester, England, just as the audience were about to disperse, an eccentric but excellent Baptist clergyman, who was standing in one of the aisles, rushed forward to the platform, and cried out vehemently — 'STOP, my friends! I've something to say to you. It's about *compensation*! Now, suppose a thief had been stealing the goods of his neighbors for days, and weeks, and months — and suppose he had filled his house with them — and suppose at last the sheriff should find him out — and suppose he should go to the house, and begin to pull the stolen goods out into the street — and suppose the neighbors who had been plundered should cluster around, and one woman should exclaim, — 'That's my cradle!' and another should say, 'That's my frying-pan!' and so all the articles should be designated by the lawful owners. Suppose the thief should reply — 'I know that's your cradle, and that's your frying-pan; and I know that I have used and abused them, without your leave; but if you take them from me, you must give me *compensation!*' What my friends, would the sheriff say to the thief? Why, this — 'Yes, you villain, you shall have *compensation* — you need not be uneasy on that score — that's just what we intend to give you — and you shall get it at *Botany Bay!*' [11] This simple illustration of a plain case electrified the vast assembly, and elicited thunders of applause. And yet how much greater is the crime of using, and abusing, and defrauding the bodies and minds of the slaves, without their leave, than of stealing and maltreating household furniture!

You remember how clamorous were the West India slaveholders for compensation, when they found that England would no longer tolerate the bloody system of slavery in any part of her dominions. This claim upon the mother country was made, in full view of the fact, that, during a period of thirty years, she had added 150 millions (sterling) to her debt, in support of the colonies; that 50,000 British subjects had, during the same space of time, been sacrificed to the climate, to guard the slave system; and that the slave population was diminishing by thousands, annually, in consequence of the cruelty of their masters!

In July, 1833, I attended an anti-slavery meeting held in Exeter Hall, London, at which were present some of the most distinguished advocates of emancipation. In the course of its proceedings, the meeting was interrupted by a Mr. LIGGINS,[12] a person connected with the West Indies, who contended that emancipation would certainly ruin the planters, because it would be impossible to pay the slaves £160,000 a week for their labor, (as all that sum would be required for that purpose,) whereas there were not more than £20,000 in the whole of the colonies. Mr. O'CONNELL instantly rose and said [13] — 'He (Mr. LIGGINS) had announced an awful fact, that the colonists could not pay wages to the slaves — that it cost them £160,000 a week. *What was this but robbing the slaves of* £160,000 *a week?* robbing them of labor worth that sum? But he told them another fact, which he (Mr. O'Connell) was rejoiced to hear, as it showed that it was inconsistent with the providence of an all great and just God, that villany should prosper; he told them that this villany was of the most beggaring description — for though the villains got £160,000 a week for nothing, yet they had not £20,000 in money! He turned to the West Indian, and asked him how he dared to rob the negro of £160,000, when instead of benefit, it was only productive of beggary? How frightful this appeared on the face of it! This £160,000 a week made £8,320,000 a year!'

You can imagine the effect of a retort like this. Remember that we have three times as many slaves as there were in the British colonies: of course, according to this calculation, the southern planters are plundering their slaves of $2,133,333 a week, or $110,933,333 a year! — and yet they want compensation, should they be compelled to be honest men!

One other fact, and I have done. The New-York Journal of Commerce [14] contains a letter from a correspondent at Antigua, who says — 'A clergyman remarked to me, that it was pretty generally conceded, that the $100,000,000 granted as a compensation to the slaveholders here, *was equivalent to a free gift;* THE VALUE OF THE PROPERTY NOT BEING DIMINISHED, BUT EVEN RISING.' This is one of the 'awful' consequences of emancipation. It seems, therefore, that the West India planters are retaining in their hands an immense sum of money, which does not belong to them, even granting that slaves are property, because they are gainers by the liberation of their victims. What, then, as honest men, ought they to do with it? Why, either to restore it to the treasury of England, or distribute it among those to whom it justly belongs — their plundered laborers.

We mean to give a rich compensation to southern slaveholders, by emancipating the slaves, viz. to substitute men for beasts, honesty for knavery, purity for lewdness, liberty for despotism, light for darkness, holiness for heathenism.

With strong affection and high regard for you, my dear friend, as one of my early and faithful coadjutors, I remain,   Yours, truly,

WM. LLOYD GARRISON.

Mr. OLIVER JOHNSON.

Printed in *The Liberator*, March 5, 1836.

1. The Vermont State Anti-Slavery Society was organized at Middlebury, May 1, 1834.

2. Henry Peter Brougham (1778–1868), of Edinburgh, Scotland, Lord Chancellor of England, was an early contributor to the *Edinburgh Review*, an ardent supporter of the British movement for the abolition of slavery, and an outstanding British statesman and writer. (*EE*.)

3. John Wesley (1703–1791), the founder of Methodism, accompanied James Oglethorpe to Georgia in 1735 as a missionary and stayed until 1738 (*ACAB*). His antislavery volume, *Thoughts on Slavery*, appeared in London in 1774, and was reprinted in New York in 1834. (Dwight L. Dumond, *Antislavery, The Crusade for Freedom in America*, Ann Arbor, Mich., 1961, p. 375.) The quotation is from Wesley's last letter, written to William Wilberforce, British antislavery leader, dated Thursday, February 24, 1791. The letter reads in part: "Unless the Divine Power has raised you up to be as Asthanasius, *contra mundum*, I see not how you can go through with your glorious enterprise, in opposing that execrable villany, which is the scandal of religion, of England, and of human nature. Unless God has raised you up for this very thing, you will be worn out by the opposition of men and devils, but, *if God be for you, who can be against you?*" (Quoted in *The Life and Times of John Wesley*, by the Reverend L. Tyerman, New York, 1872, III, 650.)

4. Romans 13:7.

5. William Slade (1786–1859) was a representative from Vermont in 1831–

1843. He was elected governor of the state in 1844. (See Garrison's letter to Helen Garrison, December 28, 1835, *Letters*, I, and *Life*, II, 68 and 68n; *BDAC*.)

6. At this point, *The Liberator* carried the following footnote: "When the reading of this letter was concluded, the Hon. Dorastus Wooster of Middlebury, rose and stated, that the transaction here referred to, took place in THE VERY ROOM where the Society was then assembled! The memorable decision was pronounced by the late judge HARRINGTON of Clarendon, a man remarkable for his unyielding firmness and practical good sense. The annunciation of this fact, as may well be conceived, produced a thrilling effect!"

Judge Theophilus Herrington (commonly known as Harrington) was born in Rhode Island (date unknown), married Betsey Buck, and in 1785 moved to Clarendon, Vermont, where he became a farmer and the father of twelve children. He represented Clarendon in the Vermont legislature in 1795 and in 1798–1803. He was chief judge of Rutland County from 1800 to 1803, when he was elected judge of the state Supreme Court, where he served until 1813. He was notoriously nonconventional, sometimes holding court barefooted. It was not until after his election to the state Supreme Court that he was admitted to the bar. He died on November 27, 1813. (Jacob G. Ullery, *Men of Vermont: An Illustrated Biographical History of Vermonters and Sons of Vermont*, Brattleboro, Vt., 1894, Part I, p. 178.)

7. Shakespeare, *The Merchant of Venice*, V, i, 90.

8. John Stark (1728–1822), a Revolutionary general and native of New Hampshire. He fought at Bunker Hill, Trenton, and Princeton. On August 16, 1777, at Bennington, he commanded the New Hampshire militia against a Hessian detachment and defeated them, contributing to the English defeat at Saratoga. (*DUSH*.)

9. These words were originally attributed to John Adams by Daniel Webster, in a speech on "Adams and Jefferson," which he delivered on August 2, 1826, in Faneuil Hall, Boston. Adams presumably made the remark in July 1776 during the debate on the adoption of the Declaration of Independence. His remarks, as presented by Webster, were: "'It is my living sentiment, and by the blessing of God it shall be my dying sentiment, Independence *now*, and INDEPENDENCE FOR EVER.'" (Edwin P. Whipple, *The Great Speeches and Orations of Daniel Webster, With an Essay on Daniel Webster as a Master of English Style*, Boston, 1894, p. 170.)

10. Although we have been unable to identify the source of this quotation, a paraphrase of it appears in the Declaration of Sentiments of the American Anti-Slavery Society: ". . . slavery is a crime, and therefore is not an article to be sold." (See Ruchames, *The Abolitionists*, p. 81.)

11. Botany Bay, an inlet five miles south of Sydney, Australia, discovered by Captain James Cook on April 29, 1770. It was originally named Sting Ray Harbor by Captain Cook and then changed by him to Botany Bay in recognition of the new plants discovered there by the naturalist Joseph Banks. In 1788, plans were projected for the establishment there of a convict colony, but were abandoned because of the poor soil and lack of water. However, the name, Botany Bay, continued to be associated with the idea of a place of penal exile in English folklore. (*EB*.)

12. Otherwise unidentified.

13. Daniel O'Connell (1775–1847), Irish statesman and lawyer, known as the "Liberator." He was elected to Parliament in 1828 and then joined the Whigs. A brilliant spokesman for Irish Catholic rights and for free trade, he was also a leading reformer and antislavery leader. In 1841, with the accession of Sir Robert Peel to power, he started agitating for Irish Independence. In 1844, he was convicted of "sedition" and spent several months in prison. (*DNB*.)

14. The New York *Journal of Commerce* was founded in 1827 by Arthur Tappan, as a commercial paper with strong religious leanings and opposed to slavery, Sabbath-breaking and intemperance. It did not accept theater or lottery adver-

tising, but did accept sometimes questionable patent medicine ads. Tappan lost heavily during his ownership, and soon sold the paper to Gerard Hallock and David Hale, who issued it at a profit. Under the new management, it was noticeably proslavery. (Frank Luther Mott, *American Journalism*, New York, revised edition, 1950, pp. 181–182, 195, 351–352.)

10

TO LEWIS TAPPAN

Brooklyn, Ct. Feb. 12, 1836.

My dear friend:

I have just received your letter of the 8th inst. and hasten to reply to it. The one which you forwarded to Boston I have not seen. I rejoice to learn, that your Committee are resolved to publish the Emancipator again weekly [1] — once a month must necessarily diminish its influence, importance and interest. You kindly request of me an opinion, respecting the fitness of B. Kingsbury, Jr. and Wm. C. Brown, both of Zion's Herald, Boston,[2] I suppose — to conduct the Emancipator. I should not recommend either. I have never regarded them as anti-slavery men, in the best and most thoroughgoing sense of the term. Brown, I have always understood, is, or was till very recently, a colonizationist. Both of these individuals possess talent, but I do not think they are adequate to sustain so responsible a station. The choice would not be a judicious one.

As to the Rev. George Allen,[3] of Shrewsbury, I do not know him, either by repute or personally. There is scarcely one man in ten thousand, even among men of ability, who has the right tact to edit a newspaper. Why not take Mr. Goodell? Or are there reasons why he is withdrawn? I should be sorry, very sorry, to see Amos A. Phelps taken from the field as a lecturer; but I can think of no person who is in all things so happily qualified to take charge of the Emancipator as himself. His style of writing is not so flowing and elegant as that of many of others; but in tact, industry, expertness, and argumentation, he is peculiarly excellent, and just the man for a first-rate editor. He is *my* choice, decidedly — and I can truly say, that I feel as deep an interest in the character and value of the Emancipator, as I do in that of the Liberator. Some other lecturer may be found to supply his place. It is a most responsible station to be editor of *such* a paper, and I trust you will not fill it hastily. Get a first-rate man, or none — but do not select either K——— or B———.

I have expressed my mind frankly to you and the Committee — of course, the letter is confidential. Destroy it as soon as you have done with it.[4] In great haste,

Yours, affectionately,

Wm. Lloyd Garrison.

ALS: Tappan Collection, Library of Congress.

1. It had been published as a monthly since August 1835 and was published as a weekly beginning in April 1836.

2. *Zion's Herald* was a Methodist newspaper established as the organ of the New England Methodists. Garrison believed that it had been established because of dissatisfaction with *The Christian Advocate and Journal*, of New York, edited by David M. Reese, a strong anti-abolitionist whom Garrison described as "a vindictive, selfish and loathsome creature" (*The Liberator*, January 16, 1836). In *The Liberator*, January 30, 1836, Garrison printed comments from Benjamin Kingsbury, Jr., editor of *Zion's Herald*, who insisted that the founding of *Zion's Herald* was not due to disagreements with the *Christian Advocate*. William C. Brown was an editor of *Zion's Herald* before Kingsbury, Jr. About 1842, Kingsbury went to Portland, Maine, to edit *The American*, a political newspaper with Democratic leanings. He filled the office of mayor in 1871–1873. (Edward H. Elwell, *Portland and Vicinity*, Portland, 1876, p. 33.)

3. The Reverend George Allen (1792–1883) was the son of the Honorable Joseph Allen of Worcester. He had been ordained in Shrewsbury on November 19, 1823, and was minister at the First Church of Christ in Shrewsbury from 1823 to 1839. He became chaplain of the State Lunatic Hospital in Worcester in 1840, a post which he still held in 1851 (E. Smalley, *The Worcester Pulpit*, Boston, 1851, pp. 527 528). In 1838, under his leadership, a convention of eighty ministers of the county was held in Worcester and issued a strong statement against slavery. Two county antislavery societies were formed, a north and a south division. George Allen was elected corresponding secretary of the South Division Society. In June 1848, he proposed the famous resolution and watchword of the Free-soil party: "Resolved that Massachusetts goes now and will ever go for free soil and free men, for free lips and free press, for a free land and a free world." (Charles Nutt, *History of Worcester and its People*, New York, 1919, pp. 492, 497.)

4. Obviously, Tappan did not follow instructions.

11

TO WILLIAM GOODELL

Brooklyn, Feb. 26, 1836.

My dearly beloved Coadjutor:

Your very kind, instructive and acceptable letter of yesterday [1] has just been received, for which I return you many thanks.

I perceive that bro. George [2] has misapprehended me, respecting my contemplated review of Dr. Channing's book. Whether I shall give my criticisms to the public through the medium of the Liberator exclusively, or whether they will appear in another form, I have not yet determined, for they remain to be written. At the longest, I shall make only a small pamphlet — not "a book." Nor is it my design to taunt the Dr. on the ground of "plagiarism," because many of his thoughts are like our thoughts, and much of his language is like our language. It would partake too much of the ridiculous, and savor too strongly of vanity or churlishness, for any abolition writer to plume himself upon having anticipated other writers in vindicating certain fundamental doctrines, appertaining to governments and the rights of man. Be assured, such a course is foreign both to my disposition and purpose. It is true, I mean to draw some parallel resemblances between Dr. Channing and certain "ultra" abolition writers, i. e. from their disquisitions and for several reasons. First — To show that the Dr. has not made any new moral discoveries, which his admirers would fain make a great doctor-of-divinity-worshipping public believe is the fact. Secondly — To show that the Dr. endorses those very principles which peculiarly characterise the abolitionists as a party, and for the dissemination of which they have been scorned, traduced, injured, and mobbed, as fanatics, madmen and traitors. Thirdly — To show that the Dr. has acted disingenuously, and evinced a want of magnanimity, in not even slightly intimating that the abolitionists, with all their zeal and fanaticism, have uniformly and consistently maintained the great essential doctrines upon which human rights find an immoveable basis. My object, in this last particular, is not so much to bring honor to any particular individuals, (though the rule is a good one — "Honor to whom honor is due,") as it is to vindicate *the anti-slavery cause*, as such, from the misrepresentations which have been cast upon it, even by some of the very men who are now lauding Dr. C's book to the skies. They who have been maligned ought to possess their souls in patience; but they certainly have a right modestly to acquit themselves, if they can.

I think you and I will agree as to the propriety and utility of such a presentation of the case.

Some other parallelisms will be drawn, which will be quite as afflicting to the Dr. & his admirers. These will show that his book abounds with inconsistencies, and neutralizes every useful truth contained in it. Abolitionists, in my opinion, have been hasty and unwise in praising the book, and taking special pains to circulate it. You will probably see in the Liberator of to-morrow, twenty-four reasons why I think they ought not to laud or commend the work.[3] The graphic picture which you have painted in your noble and disinterested speech in Boston, (a speech which ought to have been spoken in your behalf, not mine, for you are a much older and a better soldier, and without your early co-operation, the anti-slavery cause would have dragged heavily,) — I say, that picture of the effect produced upon an individual, "remotely connected with slaveholding," in reading Dr. C's

book *through*, shows plainly the inefficacy, nay, the deleterious tendency of such a give-and-take-again production. Your other objection
is a vital one — "Dr. C's separates the sinner from his sin." This is a
radical defect; and a book which is radically defective, will never
aid in reforming a radically corrupt nation.

There is one individual whom Dr. C. deigns to quote approvingly
— but he is not an abolitionist — viz. Pres. Wayland.[4]

I cannot think that Dr. C. is ignorant of the writings of abolitionists. He has long been a subscriber to the Liberator, and has been
presented with many other anti-slavery publications. The Emancipator, as the official organ of the national society, I presume he has
carefully perused; and there is the strongest probable evidence, that
your essays upon "Human Rights"[5] were before him when he wrote
his chapter upon the same subject. I shall have occasion to allude to
your essays in my review. I have read them all, carefully, with delight
and profit.

Is it said by some of our number, "It is true, Dr. C. uses us rather
ungenerously — but then, his opposing us will only cause his book
to obtain a greater circulation, and to be read more candidly"? I
answer — the cause and the advocates of the cause are closely identified. Separate them, and the cause at once encounters defeat. We
deceive ourselves, if we imagine that hostility to the abolitionists is
no evidence of hostility to emancipation. George Thompson would
never have been driven from this country, — foreigner as he was, — if
he had not branded slavery as sin, and held up the duty of immediate
repentance. Why is J. G. Birney in such peril, even in Ohio? Or why
were you tracked to Brooklyn by the blood-hounds in New-York city?
The mobocrats scarcely know a man of us personally; and, aside from
the *cause* that we espouse, they find no fault with us. Now, Dr. C.
brings two grievous (because slanderous) accusations against the
whole body of abolitionists — to wit, that they are *fanatics*, and that
something has probably been *lost* to the cause of human liberty by
their efforts!! *We* may complacently smile at such accusations: but
the reputation of Dr. C. gives them an influence disastrous to our
cause — yea, they are a two-edged sword, wounding us and our cause
by the same blow. It was the preaching of the gospel alone, that
made Peter and Paul, and Silas and Stephen, "pestilent fellows,"
"stirrers up of sedition," &c. It appears to me that Dr. C's book has
no just claim upon us to a peculiarly tender treatment: nay, it ought
to be reviewed sharply, not acrimoniously, and with all fidelity. I
wish I could persuade *you* to undertake this review, because I think
it would be more skilfully done; and if you will promise to write it,
I will desist.

What say you, my dear friend? Were my late strictures upon Gerrit

Smith merited or not? [6] His letter to Gurley [7] was not, I think, magnanimous. He seems to be wholly unwilling to allow, that he himself has erred in his views or principles at any time, but is liberal in rebuking both the Anti-Slavery and the Colonization Societies.

My copy of Wayland's Elements, (first edition,) I have left in Boston. I meant to have noticed the work ere this. The part to which you allude I had marked for review. Another edition of the work has been published, "abridged, and adapted to the use of schools and academies," a copy of which is before me. [8] The work is almost entirely re-written, and, as a *whole*, is of some value. On the subject of slavery, he is corrupt and oppressive, "If," he says, "the slave be able to take care of himself, [the master is to be judge and jury, you will observe,] the master will either immediately manumit him, — *or*, — ☞ by allowing him such wages as are just, enable him, *in process of time*, to liberate himself"!! [9] that is, will make him pay roundly for an inalienable right!

In his chapter on Benevolence, he is equally inconsistent. Speaking of injuries received, he says — "Our blessed Saviour spent his life in doing good to his bitterest enemies, unmoved by the most atrocious and most malignant injustice. So we are commanded to bless them that curse us, &c. God has made it the condition of the pardon of our offences." [10] "On our obedience to this command is suspended our only hope of salvation." [11] Yet he immediately adds — "If a man break into my house, it does not follow, that I should not take proper means to have him *put in prison*"!! [12]

☞ Go to Utica, by all means. True, you are wanted very much in Connecticut, at this crisis, and perhaps you can so arrange matters as to labor here till the May meeting. At all events, go to Utica. I would rather see you in charge of an abolition paper, or any other moral reform paper, than any other man in the range of my acquaintance. You may do much, I know, as a correspondent of the Emancipator, but you ought never to vacate the editorial chair as long as you have strength to fill it. Write me again soon.

Yours, affectionately,

Wm. Lloyd Garrison.

ALS: Berea College, Berea, Kentucky; printed in *Life*, II, 91–94.

William Goodell (1792–1878), a native of New York, engaged in business in Providence, Rhode Island, Alexandria, Virginia, and New York until 1826 when he established and edited *The Investigator and General Intelligencer*, "a general reform journal." This journal then merged with the *National Philanthropist* of Boston, which Garrison had edited, and was issued in New York from 1830 on, under the title, *Genius of Temperance*. In 1833 Goodell helped found the American Anti-Slavery Society and the *Emancipator*, of which he became the editor during the following year. In 1836 he went to Utica, the seat of the New York State Anti-Slavery Society, to edit *The Friend of Man*, an antislavery newspaper, and was its editor until 1842. He left the American Anti-Slavery Society in 1840, with the other anti-Garrisonians. He helped in the formation of the Liberty party in 1840, but left it in 1847 to form a broader reform organization, the Liberty League. His most important works on slavery and the antislavery movement were *Views on American Constitutional Law in Its Bearing on American Slavery* (1844), *Slavery and Anti-Slavery* (1852), and *The American Slave Code* (1853). Although he and Garrison severed their previous friendship as a result of disagreement over the issue of political activity, they were reconciled after the beginning of the Civil War. (Dwight L. Dumond, *Antislavery: The Crusade for Freedom in America*, Ann Arbor, Mich., 1961, pp. 264–265; *Weld-Grimké Letters*, I, 104n; *Life*, IV, 37, 382–383 *et passim.*)

1. The letter from Goodell, dated Providence, February 25, 1836, is reprinted in part in *Life*, II, 87n. Much of it was devoted to the charge that Channing had appropriated material from the abolitionists without acknowledgment. Thus "some passages in so humble a writer as myself, *appear* to have been appropriated by the great Dr. Channing, without so much as saying 'by your leave, Sir' " (ALS, Anti-Slavery Letters to William Lloyd Garrison and Others, Boston Public Library).

2. George W. Benson.

3. In its issue of February 27, 1836, *The Liberator* printed Garrison's editorial review entitled "Channing on Slavery," which presented twenty-five objections to Channing's volume. The review began: "The second edition of this work, 'revised,' has just made its appearance. A few more pages have been added, but there is no improvement in the volume, on the score of consistency or fairness." The final paragraph reads: "Here we have pointed out twenty-five objections to Dr. Channing's work, which show that it is utterly destitute of any redeeming, reforming power — that it is calumnious, contradictory and unsound — and that it ought not to be approbated by any genuine abolitionist. 'He that is not with us is against us.' "

4. Francis Wayland (1796–1865) was president of Brown University from 1827 to 1855 and had been pastor of the First Baptist Church in Boston from 1821 to 1826. Wayland was the author of *Elements of Moral Science* (Boston and New York, 1835), *Elements of Political Economy* (New York, 1837), *Moral Law of Accumulation* (Boston, 1837), and *The Limitations of Human Responsibility* (Boston, 1838). (*ACAB.*) Wayland was opposed both to slavery and to immediate emancipation. See his letter to Garrison, dated Providence, November 1, 1831, in *Life*, I, 242n–244. The quotation by Channing occurs on pages 125–127 of his *Slavery*, second edition, revised, Boston, 1836, and is from Wayland's *Elements of Moral Science*, pp. 225–226.

5. These had been published in the *Emancipator* from July to November 1835. *Life* (II, 89–90) notes: "William Goodell thought himself personally aggrieved, and that Dr. Channing had helped himself freely to the ideas contained in his monthly articles on 'Human Rights' published in the *Emancipator*, and suggested that this be shown by parallel passages in the *Liberator*."

6. Gerrit Smith (1797–1874) of Peterboro, New York, philanthropist and reformer. He first joined the American Anti-Slavery Society on November 12, 1835, as a result of the mobbing of a convention which had met in Utica, New York, in October to form a New York State Anti-Slavery Society. Until then a member of the American Colonization Society, he remained in both organizations until November 24, 1835, when he wrote to Reverend Ralph Randolph Gurley, secretary of the American Colonization Society, announcing his withdrawal from the Colonization Society, giving the reasons for his withdrawal, and explaining his recent adherence to the American Anti-Slavery Society. However, despite his withdrawal, he enclosed a check for $3,000 in fulfillment of pledges previously made to the Colonization Society (*The Liberator*, February 6, 1836). Garrison's strictures on Gerrit Smith, emphasizing the latter's inconsistency, appeared in *The Liberator*, February 13, 1836. Smith was later a supporter of John Brown and his attack on Harpers Ferry. (Ruchames, *The Abolitionists*, pp. 113–117.)

7. Ralph Randolph Gurley (1797–1872), a Yale graduate, became an agent of the American Colonization Society in 1822 in Washington, D.C., and devoted the remainder of his life to that organization as agent, secretary, vice-president, life director, preparer of the society's annual reports and for twenty-five years editor of the society's official organ, the *African Repository*. (*DAB*.)

8. The first edition was published in Boston, 1835. The other edition is Francis Wayland, *Elements of Moral Science*, abridged and adapted to the use of schools and academies by the author (Boston: Gould, Kendall & Lincoln, 1835).

9. Wayland, *Élements* (abridged edition), p. 111.

10. *Ibid.*, p. 220.

11. *Ibid.*, p. 235.

12. *Ibid.*, p. 236.

12

TO DUTEE J. PEARCE

Brooklyn, Ct. Feb. 26, 1836.

Hon. Dutee J. Pierce:

Sir — I have been requested, by the signers thereof, to transmit the accompanying petition to Congress. I commit it to your hands, feeling assured that you will present it to the H. of R. without delay. According to the decision of the House upon Mr. Pinckney's resolution,[1] it ought to be referred to the Select Committee appointed to report upon the subject of slavery and the slave trade in the District of Columbia. But I perceive that the delegates from the South are still resolved to trifle with the time and intelligence of the House, by renewing their objections to the reception of new petitions. The names which I send are not numerous, but they belong to persons, who, on the score of patriotism, sound intelligence, virtue and piety, are blessings to society and worthy of the name of Americans. The south is ignorant of the character of those, who are petitioning that the seat of government may be immediately purged from its stains of blood, or it wilfully defames that character. She ought to be admonished, that the people of the north consider this question as eminently a moral and religious one — its support, as a part of their obedience to God. It was upon the shoulders of Christianity, that the abolition of colonial slavery was carried in Great Britain. In the same manner will our system of slavery be overthrown in the D. of C., through the medium of Congress.

Allow me to suggest, that a motion ought to be made to this effect: That the Select Committee to whom, &c. &c. be instructed to report to the House, the number of petitions that may have been presented, the places and States from which they may have emanated, the number of signatures appended to each petition, and the relative proportion of male and female supplicants. This information ought to be given, that Congress and the whole country may be correctly advised upon a subject so momentous.

Unquestionably, the people at the next session of Congress will call for the abolition of slavery and the slave trade in the D. C. in a tone that will be felt and obeyed.

Hoping that the representatives from New-England will listen to the cries of the down-trodden slave, and the voice of mercy, I remain,

Respectfully yours,

Wm. Lloyd Garrison.

ALS: Pennsylvania Historical Society.

Dutee Jerauld Pearce (Garrison misspelled the name), 1789–1849, of Rhode Island, was attorney-general of Rhode Island from 1819 to 1825 and United States District Attorney in 1824–1825. He was elected as a Democrat to the United States House of Representatives from 1825 to 1837. (*BDAC.*)

1. The resolution declared, in part, that "Congress ought not to interfere in any way with the subject of slavery in the District of Columbia, because it would be a violation of the public faith: unwise, impolitic and dangerous to the Union." The vote in the House approved this part of the resolution by 129 to 74 (*The Liberator*, April 16, 1836). Henry Laurens Pinckney (1794–1863) was at this time representative from South Carolina.

13

TO LEWIS TAPPAN

Brooklyn, Feb. 29, 1836.

Esteemed Friend:

Your letter of the 25th inst. ought to have arrived here before to-day, but did not. I hasten to reply to it.[1]

It grieves me to learn, that Israel Lewis[2] is acting so base a part, especially toward those whom every colored person in the world is under the highest obligations to honor and bless — your brother and yourself. I shall also lament, if any of your difficulties have arisen in consequence of any oversight or negligence on my part — which I hope is not the case.

I will give you as intelligible and direct replies to your questions as I can, at this late period; for I had supposed, prior to the return of Mr. Paul,[3] that the understanding between us, relative to his case, was clear and definite.[4] You ask —

"1. When Mr. Paul advanced money to you in England, did you promise to repay it to A. T. or to myself?"

Answer — To Arthur Tappan, or Arthur Tappan & Co. I do not distinctly remember which. Mr. Paul loaned me £40 in England, and desired me to repay the same to your brother, I think, (perhaps to A. T. & Co. but probably this is of no consequence,) stating that A. T. was authorised to receive in trust whatever monies, collected in England for the Colonies, he (Mr. P.) might transmit to him.

"2. Did you mention the matter to A. T. or L. T. previous to the contract I made for books, &c. purchased of G. & K.?" [5]

I believe I did not. The third question is involved in the second:

"3. *When* did you first mention to A. T. or L. T. that you wished $200 to be paid to Mr. Paul? And *what* did you say or write?"

"4. When did you return from England?"

I landed in New-York, Oct. 2d, 1833. In consequence of the uproar in the city, and my anxiety to reach home, I left for Boston immediately, without being able to say much about my mission to any of the friends in N. Y. My next visit to your city was in December. A meeting of the Exec. Comm. was called, after the conventional proceedings in Philadelphia, for the purpose of hearing my statements respecting the embarrassments of the Liberator. I stated that Mr. Knapp and myself had on hand about $1000 worth of anti-slavery publications, (all of first-rate utility and value, as they really were,) which, inasmuch as we could not readily dispose of them, were a dead-weight, sinking us to the earth; and that, if the Parent Society [6] would purchase a portion of them, relief would at once be given to the Liberator; otherwise the paper must inevitably go down. I remember that all who were present expressed deep sympathy, and deplored the possibility of the paper being discontinued; but several of the committee raised some *constitutional*, or rather financial objections to the purchasing of the publications alluded to, inasmuch as the Parent Society was then *destitute of funds*. Were there any present who would make a purchase, advance the money, and take the risk of being paid by the Society whenever the state of its funds should allow? was the question propounded to the meeting. Several expressed a willingness to do so, if it were in the[ir] power. But you probably remember how distressing was the state of things at that period throughout the country. Failures were taking place continually — the banks would not discount — a frightful panic prevailed — and the oldest and most prosperous establishments trembled to their foundations. It was easier to obtain human blood than money. At last, on motion, it was voted that the Society purchase of Garrison & Knapp, publications to the amount of $440 — to be paid for as soon as possible. It was at this meeting I first stated to your brother and yourself, (I believe to the whole meeting,) that it would not be necessary to raise the whole sum of $440, inasmuch as I owed Rev. Mr. Paul, then in England, $200, (or £40, which was the exact sum I borrowed,) and which I desired, and was requested by Mr. Paul, to pay immediately into the hands of Arthur Tappan; consequently, if $240 could be raised, it would give the desired relief. In other words, if Mr. Tappan would advance $240, I would forward the whole amount of publications ordered by the Parent Society, leaving $200 in Mr. T.'s hands, nominally so indeed, but giving him the understanding that the sum of $440 was to be paid to him by the Society, ultimately, in consideration of his giving credit at my hands to N. Paul for the sum of $200, and advancing $240 to Garrison & Knapp — together making the total of $440, the amount of publications that was engaged in behalf of the Society.

I recollect that your brother expressed his willingness to make such an arrangement, so far as giving the desired credit to Mr. Paul of $200, was concerned, — taking the Society as security (on the score of G. & K.'s publications) for the payment of that sum to himself. — After a pause, you kindly and generously remarked, that you would give me a check for $240 upon Wm. J. Hubbard of Boston,[7] (am I right in the name?) who probably had that sum in his hands, you thought, belonging to you, for rents. You regarded this reserved and uncalled for sum in Boston as a providential circumstance, as you thought of it accidentally, and as you did not know where else to raise the money. This check for $240 you gave me; and the understanding between us and your brother then was, that, as soon as the books were received by the Society in N. Y. he would pass $200 to the credit of Mr. Paul, and thus settle the account between Mr. P. and myself. Your check for $240 was promptly paid by Mr. Hubbard on its presentation; and that was all Garrison & Knapp ever received for the $440 worth of publications which they immediately forwarded to New-York on my return. This arrangement saved the life of the Liberator.

Supposing that you and your brother were promptly paid $440 by the Society as soon as it had the money, and that every thing was clearly understood and satisfactorily arranged between us, and between yourselves and the Society, I thought no more of the matter, except as I think of your manifold acts of kindness shown to me in the hour of need, (both you and your brother,) that is, to feel my heart continually filled with gratitude and tender love toward you. I hope this long explanation is a satisfactory answer to your 2d, 3d, and 4th questions. Will you be good enough to inform me, whether the Society has ever paid over to you and A. T. the sum of $440, as it ought to have done, according to agreement, long ago?

"5. When did you receive $240 from me for books, &c.?"

I have already answered above. It was about the middle of December, 1833.

I am not positive, whether Mr. Paul told me that your brother was his banker in the U. S. to whom he was authorised by the colony [8] to transmit money, or whether he said I could pay A. T. to settle an old debt.

If, through any omission of mine, or any misconception between us, any loss has been sustained either by you or your brother on the ground of principal or interest, let me know, and I will make it good. It is my earnest hope that Israel Lewis will withdraw the suit, and settle the matter amicably and privately with you; for it will greatly scandalize the whole colored population to see him arrayed in court against two such benefactors as yourselves. Shame! shame!

I rejoice to hear of Weld's success, and long to see and hear him.[9] Stanton [10] is a wonderful man, worth his weight in solid gold a million times over. What! J. C. Young no longer against us — the hair-splitter, the traducer, the jesuit, the gradualist, the colonizationist! [11]

My strictures upon G. Smith [12] were certainly merited; they were written, too, after the receipt of $20 from him to help the Liberator, and also a high compliment to myself! I hope always to be favor-proof as well as storm-proof. It was to vindicate our *cause*, that I rebuked G. S. The rebuke will do him good.

Yours, truly, Wm. Lloyd Garrison.

P. S. Did you receive a small bundle from me, a few days since, for George Thompson?— Rely upon it, bro. Phelps would not make a *dry* editor. He has a fine vein of wit and humor. Perhaps, however, he had better be kept in the field as a lecturer. — I have named my son George Thompson Garrison. He is in[deed a] fine little fellow. — Did your brother ever get his $500 of Turpin[?] [13] I have never heard.

ALS: Tappan Collection, Library of Congress. See introductory sketch of Arthur and Lewis Tappan.

1. On February 25, 1836, Lewis Tappan had written to Garrison:

"Israel Lewis has sued my brother, 1. for slander, & 2. for money in his hands when suit was commenced on note of Israel Lewis and Nathaniel Paul. It is vexatious to be troubled in this way, but we must defend the suits in the usual manner. To this end, I want some facts from you. . . .[The questions which Garrison quotes in reply are asked here].

"I advanced Lewis $100.00 December 12, 1831, to enable him to pay Mr. Paul's passage, on his assuring him [that] Arthur Tappan had agreed to advance the money, but A.T. denied he had so agreed. I therefore sued Lewis (suit was brought by A. T. & Co.) and Paul. Judgment was obtained, but nothing was ever collected. Meantime I agreed to purchase $440 worth of books &c. of Garrison & Knapp, and sent them order to receive the money in Boston. They received only $240, and for a long time I did not know the reason. When you were here, some time afterwards, you stated to me, if I recall rightly, that $200 was to be paid to Mr. Paul to reimburse him for money advanced you in England. I want to know when this communication took place, and the instructions you gave me respecting the $200. Having lost all my private books and papers by the late fire I am unable to recall the facts" (ALS, Anti-Slavery Letters to Garrison and Others, Boston Public Library).

2. Israel Lewis was one of the organizers of the Negro colony of Wilberforce, near Lucan, in Canada West, where Negro refugees from Cincinnati had settled in 1829. Israel Lewis and the Reverend Nathaniel Paul raised funds in the United States and England for this colony and others, which apparently never received the funds. The colony seems to have declined after 1836. In its issue of July 16, 1836, *The Liberator* reprinted public statements by prominent Negroes, including the Board of Managers of the Wilberforce Settlement, accusing Lewis of misappropriation of funds. Lewis seems to have disappeared into ignominy after 1839, and died a pauper's death years later in Montreal. (William H. Pease and Jane H. Pease, *Black Utopia, Negro Communal Experiments in America*, Madison, Wis., 1963, pp. 57–62; Robin W. Winks, " 'A Sacred Animosity': Abolitionism in Caanda," Martin Duberman, ed., *The Antislavery Vanguard: New Essays on the Abolitionists*, Princeton, N.J., 1965, p. 308.)

3. The Reverend Nathaniel Paul, a Negro, was born in New Hampshire, and served as a Baptist minister in Albany, New York, from 1820 to 1830. He went to Wilberforce Colony with his brother Benjamin when the colony was founded. There they served as leaders, agents, and ministers. In December 1831 Paul set sail for England to gather funds for Wilberforce and to repay those who had apparently been defrauded by Lewis. He carried a letter of recommendation from John Colburne, lieutenant-governor of Upper Canada, saying that Paul had spent the last nine months in Canada establishing schools for people of color. Paul spent four years in England, Ireland, and Scotland, collecting money and lecturing. Since Paul's original plan was to remain in England no more than two years, Henry Nell, a Canadian, was sent to England by the president of Wilberforce, Austin Steward, to bring Paul back to Canada. Nell, however, after seeing Paul and urging him to return, remained in England himself instead of returning to Canada as was expected of him. Paul returned to Wilberforce and reported that he had raised over $8,000 in England, but that his expenses had equaled that amount; which meant that he had returned empty-handed. He then left Wilberforce and preached for several more years in Albany, where he died in 1839. His obituary was published in *The Liberator* of July 26, 1839. (William H. and Jane H. Pease, *Black Utopia*, pp. 50–53, 57–61.)

4. For further information on Garrison's relationship to the Reverend Nathaniel Paul and the details of the loan by Paul to Garrison, see the letter, dated Brooklyn, Connecticut, December 17, 1835, from Garrison and Knapp to Lewis Tappan (*Letters*, I).

5. Garrison & Knapp.

6. The American Anti-Slavery Society.

7. William Joseph Hubbard (b. New York, July 3, 1802; d. October 14, 1864), a lawyer, graduated from Yale in 1820 and was admitted to the Suffolk county (Massachusetts) bar in 1823. In 1828 he married Eliza Oliver Chaplin. He practiced law in Boston with Francis O. Watts, at 20 Court Street. In 1836, his home was at 72 Chestnut Street. (Edward Warren Day, compiler, *One Thousand Years of Hubbard History, 866–1895*, New York, 1895, p. 191; William T. Davis, *Professional and Industrial History of Suffolk County, Massachusetts*, Boston, 1894, p. 203.)

8. Probably Wilberforce.

9. Theodore Dwight Weld (b. Hampton, Connecticut, November 23, 1803; d. Hyde Park, Massachusetts, February 3, 1895), prominent abolitionist, entered Lane Theological Seminary, at Cincinnati, Ohio, in 1833, but left with the other students and faculty when the trustees suppressed the antislavery society at that institution. He became an antislavery lecturer, helped to train the "Seventy" agents of the American Anti-Slavery Society and took over much of the society's publicity, editing the society's book and pamphlets. His public speaking ended soon after this period with the loss of his voice. In 1838, he married Angelina Grimké, with whom he had three children. In 1841–1843, he did research in Washington, D.C., for certain antislavery members of Congress. In 1854, he estab-

lished a school at Eagleswood, New Jersey, and admitted pupils regardless of sex and color. He moved to Hyde Park, Massachusetts, in 1864, and lived there until his death. His *American Slavery As It Is: Testimony of a Thousand Witnesses* (1839) was one of the most important books in antislavery literature. (*DAB*; *ACAB*; Ruchames, *The Abolitionists*, p. 164.)

10. Henry Brewster Stanton (b. Griswold, Connecticut, June 29, 1805; d. New York City, January 14, 1887), journalist and antislavery leader, was at this time an agent of the American Anti-Slavery Society. During 1835 and 1836, he toured Rhode Island, Connecticut, and southern Massachusetts, on behalf of the antislavery movement. (*Weld-Grimké Letters*, I, 51–52n; *ACAB*.)

11. John Clarke Young (1803–1857) was president of Centre Colege, Danville, Kentucky, from 1830 until his death. Gilbert H. Barnes and Dwight L. Dumond point out: "He was the leading figure in the gradualist movement in Kentucky, and his *Address to the Presbyterians of Kentucky*, condemning slavery and offering a plan for its gradual abolition, was adopted by the Kentucky Synod and formed the basis for the gradual emancipation bill which failed of passage by only a few votes in the Kentucky legislature" (*Weld-Grimké Letters*, I, 157n). Lewis Tappan had written to Garrison on February 25, 1836: "Rev. John C. Young of Kentucky has written that he shall never say anything more against immediatism! He writes me in a very friendly manner, but does not want anything published respecting his private communications" (ALS, Anti-Slavery Letters to Garrison and Others, Boston Public Library).

12. Lewis Tappan, in his letter of February 25, had written: "Your remarks on Mr. Gerrit Smith have given uneasiness, I learn, to some Abolitionists, but they were well timed. We ought to deal kindly with such a man as Mr. Smith, but until he confesses his faults he ought to be rebuked publicly" (*ibid.*).

13. In its issue of May 17, 1839, *The Liberator* reprinted a "Remonstrance," which had originally appeared in the Greenville (South Carolina) *Mountaineer* of November 2, 1838, signed by 353 citizens of Abbeville and Edgefield, South Carolina. The "Remonstrance" was addressed to the Reverend Mr. Turpin, a missionary of the South Carolina Methodist Conference. It urged him to desist from preaching and giving religious instruction to the slave population of that area, explaining that "we regard the toleration of this instruction as the foundation of the corner stone of a *system on which will be built the superstructure of abolition.*" The "Remonstrance" had been dated June 14, 1838. The note in *The Liberator* states that Mr. Turpin died soon after the "Remonstrance" was sent to him. It was published in the Greenville *Mountaineer* after his death, which means that he died between June and November 1838. Of course, this may not be the Turpin mentioned by Garrison here.

14

TO HELEN E. GARRISON

Boston, March 5, 1836.

My dear Wife — and my precious little Babe:

It seems to me a great while since I saw you both, and I presume there has been some crying, at least on the part of one of you, since I left.

Brother May and I had a much more comfortable ride to Providence than we anticipated. Our hearts were warm, our bodies well covered, and the bricks kept our feet in a very comfortable state. We arrived just before 10 o'clock, of course too late to see brother George, but in much better season than could reasonably have been expected. We found Martin Robinson [1] at the Franklin House, of whom we ascertained that the friends in Providence were all well; and having conversed till nearly midnight, we retired to rest.

At 8 o'clock, next morning, we left for Boston in the stagecoach, (on runners,) the rail-cars being obstructed by the ice. Arrived safely at 3 o'clock, P. M. Mr. May was delighted to find his wife and his little one in prosperous health. A very kind reception was given to me by all the friends at Miss Parker's. Called immediately upon Mrs. Chapman,[2] who was exceedingly glad to see me again in the city, especially at this crisis. In the course of the afternoon, our Board of Managers held a meeting at Mr. Sewall's [3] office, with reference to the defence that we should make the next day before the Legislative Committee.[4] It was finally arranged, that Mr. May should open the defence by stating the prominent facts, respecting the rise and progress of the abolition cause, and the object and motives of those who were united together in the anti-slavery societies; and also by showing the *moral* obligations which rested upon us, as men, as patriots, and as christians, to plead for the suffering and the dumb. It was then proposed that I should next follow, vindicating ourselves from the charge of endeavoring to excite the slaves to revolt, by quoting from our official documents, those sentiments of forgiveness, submission and non-resistance, which we have so frequently inculcated. Ellis Gray Loring [5] was to follow me, proving that we had done nothing, and proposed to do nothing, that was repugnant either to the letter or the spirit of the U. S. Constitution, or the Constitution of this State; and, consequently, that the Legislature could have no authority to legislate upon the subject of abolition. Mr. Sewall was to succeed Mr. Loring, and show that not only had we not violated the Constitution, but that we had not infringed upon any statute or law of the State or of Congress — &c. &c. &c.

In the evening, I took tea at Mrs. Chapman's; after which, as I sat holding a brisk conversation with the Westons [6] and Chapmans, who should come into the room with bro. May, but our esteemed friend Wm. Goodell from Providence? It seems that he had heard of the contemplated examination, and was at once deputed by our abolition friends in P. to be present. It was at once arranged by us, that he should address the Committee on this point — what a law against abolition would *not* do, and what it *would* do — i. e. it would not put down the anti-slavery cause, nor suppress excitement, nor gag the abolitionists — it would only disgrace the Commonwealth.

That night I tarried at Mr. Chapman's, having first seen bro. Henry [7] and friend Knapp, whom I found to be in good health.

Yesterday afternoon, we went up to the State House to present ourselves and our cause before the *august* committee, &c. The gallery of the Senate was filled at an early hour with a choice and crowded assembly of ladies, who had got information that Paul and King Agrippa were to have an interview. The committee seemed, for some time, to be resolved that our meeting should be a failure, as they kept us waiting for an hour and a half longer than the appointed time. However, they at last concluded to allow us to go into the spacious hall of the House of Representatives, and our audience soon became large and *highly* respectable, many members of the legislature being present, and also the Westons, the Chapmans, Miss Martineau,[8] Miss Jeffrey,[9] Mrs. Follen,[10] Dr. Channing,[11] &c. I was introduced to Dr. C. on the spot, and shook hands with him,[12] but had no opportunity to converse with him.

Mr. May began the defence, and spoke pretty for [13] nearly an hour, but was frequently interrupted by the members of the committee, who, with one exception,[14] behaved in an insolent and arbitrary manner. Mr. Loring then spoke for about 15 or 20 minutes in a very admirable manner. Mr. Goodell then followed at some length, very ably, but was cramped by the committee. I succeeded him pretty warmly, but without interruption.[15] Prof. Follen began next, with great boldness and elegance, but had not proceeded far before he was stopped by the chairman of the committee, very impertinently,[16] who said it was a mere matter of *favor* that we were permitted to be heard at all. We resented the imputation, and asserted our *right* to be heard — and finally told the committee that we should petition the Legislature for leave to be heard as a matter of right, which we did to-day, and are to be heard next week.[17] The effect has been good for our cause. You shall hear again by the next mail.

Henry and Knapp desire to be kindly remembered to all, especially to the little babe in the way of kisses. Take good care of the dear one and of yourslf.

With abundant love,

Yours, till death,

Wm. Lloyd Garrison.

ALS: Garrison Papers, Boston Public Library; printed in part in *Life*, II, 95–97.

1. Martin Robinson, of Providence, Rhode Island, was one of the signers of the call for the founding convention of the Rhode Island Anti-Slavery Society in February, 1836. He was a stationer and paper dealer who lived at the Franklin House. (Providence *Directory*, 1836.)

2. Maria Weston Chapman. See introductory biographical sketch.

3. Samuel E. Sewall (1799–1888), a descendant of the famous Judge Samuel

Sewall, a Unitarian, lawyer, and founder of the New England Anti-Slavery Society, was then a member of the Board of Managers of the Massachusetts Anti-Slavery Society and its auditor. (*Life, passim.*)

4. The purpose of Garrison's trip to Boston was to testify before the legislative committee formed by the Massachusetts legislature in response to southern demands for the repression of the abolitionists as a menace to southern society. It was a joint committee of five, with Senator George Lunt of Eessex county as chairman. The Massachusetts Anti-Slavery Society had taken the initiative with a request that it be permitted to testify on its own behalf at a public hearing. The request was granted and March 4, 1836, was appointed as the day of the hearing. The Board of Managers of the society asked Garrison and Samuel J. May to come to Boston to testify. They made the trip together, stopping overnight in Providence. (*Life*, II, 95.)

5. Ellis Gray Loring (1803–1858) studied at the Boston Latin School, where he was a friend of Ralph Waldo Emerson. He entered the bar in 1827, and achieved quick success. He was an early supporter of Garrison and *The Liberator* and helped to found the New England Anti-Slavery Society, in which he became a leader. His participation in the antislavery movement cost him the friendship of many of Boston's leading families and the loss of numerous clients. (*Life, passim.*)

6. Warren and Ann(e?) Bates Weston, of Weymouth, Massachusetts, descendants of an old Pilgrim family, the parents of the Weston sisters, one of whom was Maria Weston Chapman. Captain Warren Weston died in Weymouth, on November 2, 1855, at the age of seventy-five. Ann Bates Weston, who was actually his second wife, died in Weymouth on May 18, 1878. Weston's first wife, whom he married in 1805, was Nancy Bates, the daughter of Joshua and Tirzah Bates, of Weymouth. It was Nancy Bates who was the mother of the prominent Weston sisters, of whom there were five: Maria (b. 1806), Caroline (b. 1808), Ann(e?) (b. 1812), Deborah (b. 1814), and Lucia (b. 1822). A son, Hervey Eliphaz, was born of the second marriage. (See obituary notice, *The Liberator*, November 9, 1855; *Life*, IV, 421 *et passim*; George Walter Chamberlain, *History of Weymouth, Massachusetts*, Weymouth, 1923, pp. 729–730; *Vital Records of Weymouth, Massachusetts, to the Year 1850*, Boston, 1910, p. 335.)

7. Henry E. Benson.

8. Harriet Martineau.

9. Louisa Jeffrey was Harriet Martineau's traveling-companion.

10. Eliza Lee Follen (b. Boston, August 15, 1787; d. Brookline, Massachusetts, January 26, 1860) was the wife of Dr. Charles Follen, who had already lost his Harvard professorship as a result of his abolitionist activities. Mrs. Follen, a Cabot, was, like her husband, a fervent abolitionist. She wrote a biographical memoir of Charles Follen which was published in 1842, as well as a number of other volumes, including *The Skeptic* (1835), *Poems* (1839), *To Mothers in the Free States* (1855), and *Anti-Slavery Hymns and Songs* (1855). (*Life, passim*; *ACAB*.)

11. William Ellery Channing.

12. *Life* carries the following note (II, 96–97):

"It was this handshaking that prompted Mrs. Chapman's remark: 'Righteousness and peace have kissed each other.' 'It was,' says Mrs. Chapman herself (MS. November, 1882), 'a mere *jeu d'esprit* whispered in the ear of Mrs. Follen, who told Harriet Martineau of it, and so it reached the ears of the Channings, and thereupon Dr. Channing said he did not know it was Mr. Garrison.' Miss Martineau's version, in her article on the 'Martyr Age of the United States,' in the *Westminster Review* for December, 1838, is, that Dr. Channing 'afterwards explained that he was not at the moment certain that it was Mr. Garrison, but that he was not the less happy to have shaken hands with him.' "

13. So in manuscript.

14. Ebenezer Moseley of Newburyport, a member of the house. For various

accounts of the proceedings, see *The Liberator*, March 12, 19, and 26, 1836.

15. *Life* (II, 97n) notes:

"Mr. Lunt, not content with his many outrageous interruptions on this occasion, had the dullness to invent another, of which he represented Mr. Garrison to have been the victim (see p. 108 of his preposterous 'Origin of the Late War,' Boston, 1866, and the citation from it in a letter to the Boston *Daily Advertiser* of Feb. 17, 1883). There is no mention of it in the official pamphlet 'Account of the Interviews which took place on the 4th and 8th of March,' etc., published by the Mass. A. S. Society. Mr. Garrison's opening ran as follows: 'Mr. Chairman, inasmuch as your honorable committee have said to the abolitionists, "Paul, thou art permitted to speak for thyself," I, for one, am disposed to reply with all sincerity, "I thank thee, King Agrippa." Yet I am not willing to consider it merely as a *favor* that we are permitted to appear before you!' (*Lib.* 6:50)."

16. "Dr. Follen had been showing the relation of cause and effect between the Faneuil Hall meeting and the mob of October 21, as foreshadowing the result of legislative resolutions censuring the abolitionists. 'Would not the mobocrats again undertake to execute the informal sentence of the General Court? Would they not let loose again their bloodhounds upon us?' He was interrupted by Mr. Lunt: 'Stop, Sir. You may not pursue this course of remark. It is insulting to this committee and to the Legislature which they represent.' This farce was repeated at the second hearing. 'Am I, then, to understand that speaking disrespectfully of mobs is disrespectful to this committee?' inquired Dr. Follen (*Lib.* 6:47; 'Life of Follen,' p. 396)." (*Life*, II, 97n.)

17. March 8, 1836.

15

TO HELEN E. GARRISON

Boston, March 7, 1836.

My beloved Helen:

A very hasty and unfinished scrawl was sent to you on Saturday evening,[1] with a promise that you should receive something better without delay. This morning, my heart was gladdened at the sight of a letter from you — gladdened beyond measure, because the epistle was not anticipated by me. It seemed to bring back the never-to-be-forgotten days of our pleasant courtship, with all their freshness of interest and fervency of love. — O, the dear little babe! "the darlings darling!" how I yearn to clasp him again to my heart! I am happy to hear that his appetite is so good, that he nurses well, and that he improves as a bed-fellow. But why does he not thrive faster? How provoking, to think that Mr. Gray's steelyards were just like father's![2] However, there is time enough yet for little George to increase in obesity. May he never be larger than Daniel Lambert,[3] nor taller than Fowell Buxton![4]

I have just received another letter from Mr. Thompson, dated Liverpool, January 14th, in which he gives the pleasing intelligence, that

Mrs. T. arrived at that port on the 11th, having had a voyage of 26 days. They were all in good health, except the little boy, who remained in a very delicate state. He expresses much gratitude to the numerous friends in Boston, New-York and Philadelphia, for their "unceasing and overwhelming kindness" to his wife and little ones. His letter is principally occupied with sharp criticisms upon Dr. Channing's book, which he seems to regard pretty much as I regard it — that is, a mixture of good and evil, light and darkness, energy and weakness. His letter will be published in the next Liberator.[5] He was to start the next day for Glasgow, in which place he had made an appointment to lecture on the 20th and the 22d January, and from thence he would proceed to Edinburgh. He writes that there is an intense anxiety pervading all classes to see and hear him. It seems that he had concluded not to lecture in Liverpool, because the friends of emancipation in Scotland were very urgent for his speedy apppearance among them.

Since my return to the city, my numerous anti-slavery friends have vied with each other in proffering their kindnesses to me. It strengthens me exceedingly to know, that their confidence and esteem have suffered no abatement, nay, that absence has but greatly augmented them. Saturday night I slept with Knapp and Henry [6] in the office, and had as comfortable a time as such a berth could possibly give, be it more or less. Sabbath forenoon, Mr. May, Henry and myself went to hear Dr. Channing preach,[7] and were happily not disappointed. The sermon was full of beauty and power, worthy to be written in starry letters upon the sky. The text was, "Thy will be done on earth as it is done in heaven." [8] The will of God, he observed, was expressed in two forms — first, outwardly, as it respects the creation. That will the elements cannot resist, but is executed with a resistless energy. Sometimes it has changed, as in the case of the miracles, which were wrought to illustrate the omniprescence and omnipotent power of the Almighty. The other revelation of his will is a moral one, and that will is unchangeable — it shall not change, though the earth is dashed asunder, and the suns and stars of the universe are blotted out. The laws of God he declared to be his best and highest gifts to man, full of benevolence and goodness. Weak as man considers himself, yet he has power to do what neither the winds nor waves, neither the earth nor sky, can do, that is, to resist the will of God — &c. &c.

I have had two long and very satisfactory interviews with Miss Martineau. She is plain and frank in her manners, and not less so in her conversation. I can assure you, that we abolitionists need not fear that she will ever print any thing, either in this country or in England, inimical to us, or in favor of the Colonization Society. She is now abiding under the roof of Dr. Channing, and no doubt will do him much good.[9] Last evening, there was a circle gathered by special invitation at Mr. Loring's house,[10] among the number being Miss Martineau, Miss Jeffrey, Mr. and Mrs. Chapman,[11] Mr. May,[12] Messrs. Rantoul and Hillard of the Legislature,[13] Dr. Follen,[14] Dr. Bradford,[15] myself, &c. &c. The evening was profitably spent in earnest discussion of some of the great topics of reform. The visiters left about half past 10 o'clock. I went home and tarried with the Chapman's.

Yesterday afternoon, Mr. May, Mr. Goodell, and myself, attended meeting in the African meeting-house, Belknap-street. Our colored friends beheld us gladly, and were particularly careful to let me know how happy they felt to hear that Mrs. G. had got a fine little son. Indeed, that eve[nt] tickles them beyond measure. We are doubly dear to them on that account. My Sonnets [16] seem to be universally admired. Mr. May said, that Mr. Alcott [17] wept as he read them, with excess of feeling.

I am writing this letter at friend Fuller's,[18] who is the same kind, disinterested man as ever, and who, with his excellent wife, desires me to send special remembrances to you. All the friends are extremely anxious to see you and the dear babe, and stand ready to give a welcome reception to you both.

Christiana [19] still remains at the Westons. I saw and spoke to her on Sabbath afternoon. She was well, and of course made many inquiries after you and yours.

The committee of the Legislature have not yet granted us a hearing again, but will probably do so in the course of a few days. Whether I shall address them again will depend upon my feelings and circumstances. Mr. Goodell leaves the city to-morrow morning. He has drawn up for us a very able Memorial, to be presented to the Legislature.

Mr. May's little Joseph is indeed a fine boy, and of course more advanced than little George. Mrs. May [20] looks remarkably well, and is as lively and voluble as ever. When I see her again, I will convey your message to her.

I have not yet seen any of the Grays, but shall probably call before I leave. And when shall I leave? I do not know exactly, but probably on Friday or Saturday, via Providence. I expect to be in Brooklyn, by your side, dearest, on Monday next. I am longing to get back.

Tell father that Henry is in good health; that the peace cause is steadily gaining ground in this quarter; that abolitionism is sweeping over the whole land, resistless, like a strong tide; and that the reign of terror we hope is nearly over. Love to dear mother and sisters. Kiss Anna [21] for me because she kisses the babe so often, and tell her I will settle the rest on my return.

The arrival of so many persons to see me so soon after my departure from Brooklyn is very singular. You need not write to me again, as it is so uncertain about my return.

Your devoted one,

Wm. Lloyd Garrison.

ALS: Garrison Papers, Boston Public Library; printed in part in *Life*, II, 98–99.

1. March 5.

2. This may refer to the fact that George Benson and Mr. Gray were of the same weight, probably both stout.

3. Daniel Lambert (1770–1809) was keeper of the jail at Leicester, England. Despite an active and athletic life, he weighed 739 pounds at the time of his death. His waistcoat measured 102 inches around the waist. His name has been used as a synonym for immensity. George Meredith describes London as "the Daniel Lambert of cities." (*EB.*)

4. Sir Thomas Fowell Buxton (1789–1845) was six feet four inches in height (R. H. Mottram, *Buxton the Liberator*, London, New York, Melbourne, Sydney: Hutchinson & Co., n.d.). A Quaker businessman, philanthropist, and reformer, he was a member of Parliament, representing Weymouth, from 1818 to 1837. Although interested in prison reform and in the need for improving the conditions of African Negroes, he was especially devoted to the cause of slave emancipation throughout the British empire and was the successor to Wilberforce, in 1824, as leader of the British antislavery movement. (*E.E.*)

5. George Thompson's letter appeared in *The Liberator*, March 12, 1836. It was dated Liverpool, January 14, 1836.

6. Henry E. Benson.

7. *Life* (II, 98) carries the following footnote: "This may have been the occasion of which Mrs. Chapman speaks (MS. November, 1882): 'It was about this time [the mob time] that Mr. Garrison expressed to us a wish to hear Dr. Channing preach, and we invited him to take a seat in the pew kindly placed at our disposal by one of Dr. Channing's friends, Mr. Stephen Higginson, and which we then occupied. Mr. Garrison accepted the invitation. Next day came a notice to us from Mr. Higginson that he could not allow us seats in his pew any longer.' "

8. Matthew 6:10.

9. At this point *Life* (II, 98–99n) comments: "During Miss Martineau's stay at Dr. Channing's, relates Mrs. Chapman (MS. November, 1882): 'I invited her with Dr. and Mrs. Channing to tea, "to meet Mr. Garrison." She came to me next day, with much satisfaction on her face, saying, "I think he'll come"; and afterwards she told me, "He would have come if you had not said to *meet* Mr. Garrison." ' Evidence of this avoidance might be multiplied. Mr. Garrison was clearly an exception to Dr. Channing's profession, in a letter to J. G. Birney, following the destruction of the *Philanthropist* (*ante*, p. 77): 'I feel myself attracted to the friends of humanity and freedom, however distant; and when such are exposed by their principles to peril and loss, and stand firm in the evil day, I take pleasure in expressing to them my sympathy and admiration' (*Lib*: 7:1). But neither after the Boston mob, nor at any other time, so far as is known, did Dr. Channing so much as address a line to Mr. Garrison. 'Abolition is still the exciting topic,' he wrote from Newport on Oct. 27, 1835 — the editor of the *Liberator* having gone to jail on Oct. 21. 'The mobs still interfere with the anti-slavery meetings, and the South alarms many at the North by threatening us with separation. *Happily, the great prosperity of the country and the pressure of business do not allow people to think much on the subject*'! ('Memoir' 3:170). No wonder this letter was suppressed in the 'Centenary edition of the 'Memoir.' "

10. During her tour of the South, Miss Martineau, while in Charleston, South Carolina, had stayed with a Dr. and Mrs. Gilman. Dr. Gilman was a Unitarian minister and Mrs. Gilman's brother-in-law was Ellis Gray Loring. (Vera Wheat-

ley, *The Life and Work of Harriet Martineau,* Fair Lawn, N. J., 1957, pp. 151–152.)

11. Henry Grafton and Maria Weston Chapman.

12. Samuel J. May.

13. Robert Rantoul, Jr. (1805–1852), a lawyer and a Democrat, had been elected to the state legislature from Gloucester, Massachusetts, in 1834 and served until 1838. He was a reformer who adhered to Jeffersonian principles and was a friend of John Greenleaf Whittier. He defended Thomas Sims, the fugitive slave, in 1852, and was a prominent opponent of the Fugitive Slave Act of 1850. He served in the United States Senate as a Democrat from February 1 to March 3, 1851, and in the House from 1851 to 1852. (*NCAB; BDAC.*)

George Stillman Hillard (1808–1879), a lawyer, orator, and scholar, was elected to the Massachusetts house for Suffolk county, in 1836, and to the senate in 1850. He was a delegate to the Massachusetts Constitutional Convention of 1853 and was United States District Attorney from 1866 to 1870. He was a close friend of Charles Sumner and opened a law practice with him in 1834. (*NCAB.*)

14. Charles Follen.

15. Dr. Gamaliel Bradford (b. November 17, 1795; d. October 22, 1839), a graduate of Harvard College in 1814, participated in the founding of the New England Anti-Slavery Society in January, 1832, and was superintendent of the Massachusetts General Hospital from 1833 until his death. (*Life,* I, 278n.) On March 26, 1836, *The Liberator* printed his speech delivered before the joint committee of the legislature. Apparently, Dr. Bradford had dropped his membership in the Anti-Slavery Society, despite his continuing sympathy with its efforts, for *The Liberator,* in printing the text of his remarks, carried the following introductory note: "Dr. Gamaliel Bradford (not a member of the Anti-Slavery Society, who was present as a spectator) asked the Chairman if he might say a word as a citizen? The Chairman assented, and Dr. Bradford pronounced an eloquent, thrilling, and impassioned, but entirely respectful appeal in favor of free discussion."

16. On February 20, 1836, *The Liberator* printed a group of five sonnets by Garrison, under the heading "Sonnets," with the inscription, "Addressed to an infant born on Saturday last, February 13, 1836." These, of course, were addressed to Garrison's first child. They express joy that Garrison now had someone to carry on his work should he himself fall in the antislavery cause and they contrast Garrison's child, born in freedom, to the Negro child, born into slavery.

17. Amos Bronson Alcott (1799–1888), author, teacher, transcendentalist, father of Louisa May Alcott, was the brother-in-law of Samuel J. May, and one of the earliest friends of Garrison and the antislavery cause. (*Life,* I and II, *passim.*)

18. John E. Fuller, of Boston, was a founder of the New England Anti-Slavery Society in January 1832. On the night of the Garrison "mob," Helen Garrison stayed at his home. Garrison often stayed there too. He broke with Garrison in January 1839. On August 30, 1839, *The Liberator* carried his advertisement publicizing a boarding house which he conducted at 24 Franklin Place in Boston. (*Life,* I and II, *passim.*)

19. Christiana may have been a maid.

20. Lucretia Flagge Coffin (d. 1865), daughter of Peter Coffin, a merchant of Portsmouth, New Hampshire, and, later, of Boston, married Samuel J. May in 1825. *Memoir of Samuel J. May* (Boston, 1873), pp. 276–280, portrays her life and character.

21. Anna Benson.

16

TO GEORGE W. BENSON

Brooklyn, March 15, 1836.

My dear brother George:

You have doubtless been wondering why I have not yet made my appearance in Providence, as I told bro. Goodell last week that I should return to this village via P. in a few days. My reasons for altering my purpose were these: I found that bro. Henry was in a miserable state of health, not having fully recovered from the ill attack which he experienced a few weeks since. He was troubled with indigestion, his head was occasionally giddy, his lungs were somewhat affected, and in the course of the day he would experience several shivering fits, which were succeeded by a dry feverish heat. — Still, he attempted to perform the arduous duties of the office, as usual, and did not readily seem disposed to give up. After much entreaty, however, on the part of Mr. May, Mr. Knapp, myself, and other friends, he was at last persuaded to accompany me to Brooklyn, that he might be withdrawn from the cares and bustle of the city, and have the kind, endearing attentions of his parents and sisters. We at first concluded to go via Providence on Saturday; but as it seemed desirable, for Henry's sake, that we should arrive in Brooklyn as soon as practicable, and as we found that we could get through on Saturday via Worcester, we accordingly changed our minds, took that course, and reached home about half past 6, P. M. The weather had changed suddenly, and was severely cold, from the effects of which Henry suffered considerably, but more particularly from the badness of the travelling between Worcester and Brooklyn, which was fatiguing enough even to a person in health, much more to an invalid. Soon after his arrival, Henry went to bed, and has not left it since, except for a couple of hours yesterday. Dr. Whitcomb [1] is administering to his necessities, and as he is a little better, we hope he will be so much restored in all this week as to be able to walk about the premises. He must be very careful of his health hereafter, for I think he is predisposed to a consumptive habit, although he is not in any danger at present. So much confinement as he has had in Boston, has unquestionably been injurious to him; and he ought to rusticate many weeks here, before he returns to the city.

I was glad to find that every member of the family was well, on my return. Helen, for the first time since her confinement, came down stairs and dined with us yesterday. The babe seems to be perfectly

well, is remarkably quiet, and grows finely. He has no lack of attendants, and, like his father, is already largely indebted on the score
of kindnesses to those around him. We think he is a pretty child, *of
course*: for was there ever a first-born child that was not pretty in the
eyes of affectionate parents? But we do not think that he is *quite*
so pretty as was your little Anna at the same age: so you and Catharine [2] need not be jealous. The conformation of his head is very much
like mine, but I do not think his features resemble those of either of
his parents, or any of the family. A few weeks are needed yet, to
develope and establish them. It is his moral image about which I
feel the most solicitude. May he early learn to put on Christ, that he
may be made perfect in righteousness, without spot or wrinkle, or any
such thing!

Bro. Goodell has told you, no doubt, the results of his visit to Boston — a visit which was very opportune, and highly serviceable to the
cause of human rights. Our abolition friends were all delighted to see
and hear him. In the interview we had with the legislative committee,
he spoke exceedingly well, better than any body else, and was for that
very reason more insolently treated by the chairman of the committee
than any of our number, not excepting even Prof. Follen.[3] He drew up
a very able defence of the principles and measures of the abolitionists,
which was adopted by our abolition committee, and is now probably
in the hands of the members of the Legislature, in a pamphlet form.[4]
Since he left, our Society sent in another memorial to the Legislature,
setting forth that our rights had been disregarded as freemen, that
the commitee would not suffer us to be fully heard in self-defence, and
remonstrating afresh against the passage of any law or resolutions in
derogation of anti-slavery men or measures. — In the Senate, the
memorial was laid upon the table. In the House of Representatives, as
soon as it was read, Mr. Walley [5] of Boston, (a member of Dr. Beecher's church,[6] I am told, and a hot-headed colonizationist,) rose and
moved, that it be not received by the House! falsely and furiously declaring, that it was insulting in its language, and that it was pre-
judging the committee — &c. &c. This bold attempt to kick the memorial
out of the chamber, and to trample under foot the sacred right of
petition and remonstrance, excited the strongest general indignation
among the members. It made at once many abolition converts, and
was overruled for good, great and lasting good. A very spirited debate
ensued, in the course of which, Mr. Walley received a severe casti-
gation, and stood alone in his infamous proposition. That debate was
worth more than a thousand dollars to our cause. George Blake [7] of
Boston, (though opposed to the abolitionists,) said that our fundamental principles were incontrovertible; that slavery could not long

continue in our land; that it stood on the same level with the Genthoo [8] sacrifices; and that he did not believe a man, or any body of men, could be found in that assembly, who would dare to propose any law, or any resolutions, censuring the anti-slavery society, or any other. Mr. Rantoul of Gloucester, Mr. Foster [9] of Brimfield, Mr. Hillard of Boston, Mr. Longley [10] of ——, all spoke in favor of our rights — also Mr. Ward [11] of Danvers, and Mr. Durfee of Fall River.[12] Mr. Durfee said he was proud to acknowledge himself as one of the proscribed abolitionists, and he thanked God that he stood where he could vindicate his own rights and the rights of others. A motion was now made to lay our memorial upon the table — ayes 204, noes 216. It was then referred to the committee. The next day a warm debate ensued in the Senate. I cherish strong hopes that our Legislature will pass no resolutions against us — a gag law is out of the question. Massachusetts is still the sheet anchor of our country.

I hope you will send me the proceedings of the R. I. Convention as soon as they are published.

Helen wishes you to send up, whenever convenient, a *basket*-cradle for little George. Charge the same to me.

If there are any *sweet* oranges in P., bro. Henry would like to have you send him a dollar's worth. You need not send them, if they are not sweet. The shaving soap you sent me is very greasy, and not fit to use.

Henry and all the rest of us are extremely desirous of seeing you, and we therefore cherish the hope that you will be able to make us a visit in a few days, with Catharine and little Anna.

Give my kindest regards to bro. Goodell, as well as to the other dear friends.

Yours, affectionately,
Wm. Lloyd Garrison.

ALS: Garrison Papers, Boston Public Library; printed in part in *Life*, II, 102, 103.

1. Dr. James B. Whitcomb (1804–1880) was secretary of the Windham County Medical Society in 1832–1835, 1842–1844, and 1846–1861. In 1867, he was president of the society. A graduate of the Medical School of Maine, he entered medical practice in Brooklyn, Connecticut, in 1826. (Richard M. Bayles, *History of Windham County, Connecticut*, New York, 1889, pp. 175–178; *General Catalogue of Bowdoin College and the Medical School of Maine, 1794–1894*, Brunswick, Me., 1894, p. 105.)

2. George Benson's wife.

3. "Dr. Follen's outspoken connection with the Abolitionists had already cost him his Harvard professorship, which was allowed to lapse without renewal (May's 'Recollections,' p. 254; Hudson's 'History of Lexington,' p. 360)." (*Life*, II, 102n.)

4. The pamphlet was published by Isaac Knapp, Boston, 1836, and was entitled "A full Statement of the Reasons which were in part offered to the Com-

mittee of the Legislature of Massachusetts," etc. A portion of Goodell's remarks were printed also in *The Liberator*, March 19 and 26, 1836.

5. Samuel Hurd Walley, Jr. (1805–1877), a banker and a Whig, was a member of the Massachusetts House of Representatives in 1836, 1840–1846, speaker of the house in 1845–1846, and a representative in Congress in 1853–1855. He was a member of the Park Street Church. (*Life*, II, 102n; *BDAC*.)

6. The Hanover Street Congregational Church of Dr. Lyman Beecher (1775–1863), the eminent clergyman. Dr. Beecher had been pastor of the church from 1826 to 1832. He was a leading opponent of Unitarianism and though mildly antislavery was also a colonizationist and an opponent of the abolitionists. In 1832 he accepted Arthur Tappan's offer of the presidency of Lane Theological Seminary in Cincinnati, Ohio, which in 1834 lost many of its students over his refusal to permit antislavery activities on campus. While accepting the post at Lane Seminary, he also become pastor of the Second Presbyterian Church in Cincinnati. In 1834 he was a leading spirit in the formation of the American Union for the Relief and Improvement of the Colored Race, which sought to displace the Garrisonian abolitionists, but the organization failed in 1836. He also persuaded New England ministers to close their pulpits and churches to abolition agents. Beecher resigned from his post at Lane in 1852 and spent the last years of his life at the home of his son, the Reverend Henry Ward Beecher, in Brooklyn, New York. (*Weld-Grimké Letters*, I, 12; *Life, passim.*)

7. George Blake (1769–1841), a lawyer, was the representative in the Massachusetts house for Suffolk county in 1801, 1829–1830, 1832, and 1835–1838. He was in the Massachusetts senate in 1831 and 1833–1834. (Reference Card, Massachusetts State Library, Boston.)

8. Genthoo or Gentoo, an archaic English word meaning Hindu.

9. Festus Foster was born in Canterbury, Connecticut, in 1776 and died in Brimfield, Massachusetts, in 1845 or 1846; a clergyman, he was in the Massachusetts house in 1831, 1832, 1835, and 1836. (Reference Card, Massachusetts State Library, Boston.)

10. Thomas Longley of Hawley (1774–1848) was a farmer and a member of the Massachusetts house in 1812–1817, 1824, 1836 and 1848; a member of the Massachusetts senate in 1819, 1823, 1825, 1827, and 1828. (Reference Card, Massachusetts State Library, Boston.)

11. Joshua Holyoke Ward of Danvers (1808–1848), was a lawyer and judge, president of the Salem, Massachusetts, Common Council, 1842–1844, and a member of the Massachusetts house in 1836–1837, 1840 and 1842. (Reference Card, Massachusetts State Library, Boston.)

12. Gilbert Hathaway Durfee of Fall River (1808–1842) was a merchant and custom house inspector, and a member of the Massachusetts house in 1836. (Reference Card, Massachusetts State Library, Boston.)

17

TO JAMES G. BIRNEY

Brooklyn, Ct. April 6, 1836.

Esteemed Coadjutor:

On the margin of your last paper, it is stated that you have not received a single number of the Liberator in exchange for the Philanthropist![1] Is it possible that you have been neglected so long? Be assured, that this almost inexplicable omission has been unintentional.

Mr. Knapp must have supposed, that he promptly entered the name of your valuable paper upon his mail-book. It is a grief and mortification to me, that such an oversight has occurred. What must you have thought of us?

I have read the Philanthropist with eagerness, delight, and to great edification. Whatever is admirable in moral courage, or impressive in dignity, or commendable in magnanimity, or attractive in modest worth, or excellent in christian urbanity, or serviceable in intellectual ability, is seen in the manner in which you have thus far conducted your paper. Your trials have been severe, multiform, numerous — but they will all prove burnishers to add to the brightness of your triumphs. It is scarcely necessary for me to say to you, DO NOT DESPAIR: for how can he "whose hope the Lord is," [2] whose shield and buckler, and rock and refuge, is Jehovah of hosts, whose strength lies in an omnipotent arm, who has truth and liberty, and the God of truth and liberty, and the friends of truth and liberty throughout the world, on his side — how can such an individual despair? With the earth rocking beneath his feet, and the ocean heaving upward to the clouds, and the tempest sweeping in wrath around him, his song will be — "God is my refuge and strength, a very present help in trouble. Therefore will not I fear, though the earth be removed, and though the mountains be carried into the midst of the sea; though the waters thereof roar, and be troubled, though the mountains shake with the swelling thereof." [3] Most assuredly, he is not a Christian, who does not "take pleasure in infirmities, in reproaches, in necessities, in persecutions, in distresses *for Christ's sake*" [4] — who does not know, experimentally, that "blessed are they who are persecuted for righteousness' sake, for theirs is the kingdom of heaven" [5] — and who does not *rejoice*, and is not *exceeding glad*, when men revile him, and persecute him, and say all manner of evil against him falsely, *for Christ's sake*.[6] It is a solemn, thrilling, soul-animating suggestion of an apostle — "Beloved, think it not strange, concerning the fiery trial which is to try you, as though some strange thing happened unto you; but rejoice, inasmuch as ye are partakers of Christ's sufferings; that, *when his glory shall be revealed, ye may be glad also with exceeding joy*." [7] It is the affecting language of another of the apostles: "For we who live are ALWAYS DELIVERED UNTO DEATH, *for Jesus' sake* — [why?] *that the life also of Jesus might be made manifest in our mortal flesh*" [8] — "For as the sufferings of Christ abound in us, so our consolation also aboundeth by Christ" [9] — "*If we suffer, we shall also reign with him*." [10]

It is absurd, it is presumptuous, for any of us to dwell upon our losses and crosses, our necessities and sacrifices, our trials and persecutions. It was said of Christ, "He hath a devil." [11] Has aught so bad been said against us? The Son of man had not where to lay his head.[12] Has any of us been reduced to this extremity? We read of "Christ *crucified*" [13] — nailed to the cross between two thieves. Who among us has thus ignominiously suffered? Of the Jews did Paul five times receive forty stripes save one, thrice he was beaten with rods, once was he stoned, &c. &c. Is there an abolitionist who would not be ashamed to compare sufferings with Paul? The early Christians "had trial of cruel mockings and scourgings, yea, moreover, of bonds and imprisonments: they were stoned, they were sawn asunder, were tempted, were slain with the sword: they wandered about in sheepskins, and goat-skins; being destitute, afflicted; they wandered in deserts, and in mountains, and in dens and caves of the earth" — truly, "of whom the world was not worthy." [14] Now let us talk of *our* sufferings! If Paul could exclaim, "These *light* afflictions!" [15] what shall we say?

I trust we shall see you at the annual meeting of the Parent Society at New-York in May. In the course of next month, the New-England Anti-Slavery Convention [15a] will be held in Boston, and the desire to have you present will be universal. If you cannot come, send us a letter to be read at the meeting. With us, "the work goes bravely on" — New-England will soon be "regenerated and disenthralled by the irresistible Genius of Universal Emancipation."

With great personal respect and affection,

Your friend and coadjutor,

Wm. Lloyd Garrison.

J. G. Birney, Esq.

N. B. Enclosed are $20, which my brother-in-law, Mr. Henry E. Benson, (who is too ill to write,) wishes me to transmit to you for the ten copies of the Philanthropist which are sent to the Massachusetts Society at Boston. He wishes you, on receipt of this, to send only 3 copies to the Society, and the remaining 7 as follows:

> Charles T. Torrey, Hingham, Massachusetts.[16]
> Charles Spear, Abington, Mass.[17]
> Academy A. S. Society, Leicester, Mass.[18]
> William Blake, Boston,   " [19]
> Rev. Samuel Ware, Amherst,   " [20]
> William Reed, Taunton,   " [21]
> G. H. Durfee, Fall River,   "

You may enclose a receipt for the $20, in one of the numbers of the Philanthropist, sent to the Mass. Society. My brother-in-law regrets that there has been any delay in transmitting the money. The accompanying bill, being a U. S. bank-note, will not of course be subject to any discount.

ALS: Pennsylvania Historical Society.

1. A weekly newspaper, the organ of the Ohio Anti-Slavery Society, *The Philanthropist* was established by Birney and edited by him from January 1, 1836, to September 1837. It was published at New Richmond, Ohio, from January 1 to April 8, 1836, and then at Cincinnati, Ohio. After 1843 it was continued as the Cincinnati *Weekly Herald and Philanthropist*. Gamaliel Bailey, who succeeded Birney as its editor, edited it until 1847, when he left Cincinnati for Washington to edit the *National Era*. (Dwight Lowell Dumond, *A Bibliography of Antislavery in America*, Ann Arbor, 1961, p. 93; Louis Filler, *The Crusade Against Slavery, 1830–1860*, New York, Evanston and Illinois, 1960, p. 78n.)

2. Jeremiah 17:7.

3. Psalms 40:1–3, with "I" substituted for "we."

4. II Corinthians 12:10.

5. Matthew 5:10.

6. Matthew 5:12 and 11 — combined and with the third person substituted for the second person.

7. I Peter 4:12–13.

8. II Corinthians 4:11.

9. II Corinthians 1:5.

10. II Timothy 2:12.

11. Matthew 11:18.

12. Matthew 8:20; Luke 9:58.

13. I Corinthians 1:23.

14. Hebrews 11:36–38.

15. II Corinthians 4:17.

15a. The Convention "Call" urged the attendance of delegates from all the antislavery societies of New England as well as interested individuals (*The Liberator*, May 21, 1836).

16. The Reverend Charles T. Torrey. See note 2 in letter 134, to Mary Benson, December 23, 1838.

17. Charles Spear, of Abington, Massachusetts, married Nancy Dixon in 1836. Their son, Charles Dixon Spear, was born on January 19, 1837. (*Vital Records of Abington, Massachusetts, to the Year 1850*, Boston, 1912.)

18. Probably the antislavery society associated with Leicester Academy. Leicester Academy was established in 1784.

19. The Boston city *Directory* for 1836 lists several William Blakes.

20. The Reverend Samuel Ware (1781–1866) was born and died in Massachusetts. He graduated from Williams College in 1808, married Lucy Parsons in 1810, and was ordained during the same year. He lived in Conway, Massachusetts, from 1827 to 1833, and in Amherst, Massachusetts, where he was also a justice of the peace, from 1833 to 1838. He later lived in South Deerfield and Sherborne, Massachusetts. (Emma Forbes Ware, *Ware Genealogy* . . . , Boston, 1901, p. 112; Carpenter and Morehouse, compilers and publishers, *The History of the Town of Amherst, Massachusetts*, Amherst, 1896, p. 336.)

21. William Reed (1778–1865), a merchant and manufacturer, was a representative of Taunton in the General Court of Massachusetts in 1819 and in the town court from 1825 to 1826. For many years, he was a deacon of the Winslow Trinitarian-Congregational Church in Taunton. (John Ludovicus Reed, *The Reed Genealogy*, Baltimore, Maryland, 1901, p. 200; Samuel Hopkins Emery, *History of Taunton, Mass.*, Syracuse, N.Y., 1893, pp. 266, 568, 647, 675.)

1 8

TO GEORGE W. BENSON

Brooklyn, April 10, 1836.

My dear George:

As the travelling seems to be considerably improved, I shall probably make my contemplated visit to Providence on Tuesday next — i.e. if I find that I shall be able to arrive before bed-time. Shall I go to sister Charlotte's, or tarry with you? Which is your preference? If decision be made in your favor, let me know by Monday's mail the number of your residence, name of the street, &c. But let me not be a burden to you in your new quarters. If business will require your absence, I can postpone my visit one week, without any inconvenience.

Bro. Henry still continues ill, although he is somewhat better to-day. He has scarcely any appetite, has frequently a severe pain in the breast, is troubled with a hard cough, suffers from urinary secretions, and has lost much flesh. His medicines do not seem to produce their legitimate effect. On the whole, he is in a precarious state of health, but we still hope for the best. It was a fortunate circumstance that I went to Boston, and succeeded in persuading him to return with me to Brooklyn. Here he has no lack of attention, and is surrounded by those who are dearest to him of all the world beside. Dr. Whitcomb, I believe, does not consider his situation as very dangerous.

Mother's health is somewhat improved, although she is still feeble, and *will* do what she ought not to do in household affairs. The girls are somewhat "tired out" with toil, and hope you will soon be successful in your inquiries after "help."

Charles Burleigh [1] made me a visit a few days since. He has been lecturing somewhat industriously, having had a sufficient amount of opposition and disturbance to prove the universality of the pro-slavery spirit, and the genuineness of his abolitionism. He left us to deliver a lecture in Elder Bullard's meeting-house in Hampton,[2] and has several invitations elsewhere. The soil of Connecticut is somewhat rocky, but when it is once broken up, and the seed well sown, a good harvest is generally the reward.

    ✿   ✿   ✿   ✿

The box of goods which you forwarded has just been received and opened. Helen and myself feel under great obligations to you and sister Charlotte for your prompt and kind attentions. Little George shall thank you when he is big enough. He is "doing finely." Is that the opposite of doing *coarsely*?

In your note to Henry, you express a hope that I will postpone my visit to P. until week after next, so that I may address the ladies' meeting. Pray, excuse me, and look up some other orator. I am as barren of ideas as the trees are of fruit. You know that I always speak in public with reluctance, especially if my remarks be *not* written down — and to *read* is a slavish mode of *speaking*, if speaking it can be called. It is so long since I made an address, that I have quite forgotten how. Where is the meeting to be held? I am rather desirous to make my visit on Tuesday next, as I shall probably start the last of this month for Philadelphia, and I wish to have a little interim in Brooklyn between the two visits. I hope to hear from you by Monday's mail.

Henry desires me to give his love to you and Catharine, and to say, that he keeps to his bed 16 hours out of the 24, that he is getting *no better* fast, that a large plaster which is on his breast is beginning to bite him like a mad horse, but he does not think it will end in hydrophobia, &c. &c.

Political abolitionists are now placed in an awkward predicament. What an outrageous letter Martin Van Buren has written to certain political rascals in North Carolina, respecting slavery in the District of Columbia![3] No consistent abolitionist can now vote for him. It seems that our alternative must now be between Webster or Harrison.[4] I should prefer the former. Van Buren, you will observe, covers the Society of Friends with the slime of his panegyric, and draws a broad line of distinction between them and the abolitionists.[5] Why? Simply, because the Friends in North Carolina are numerous, and their votes are wanted to turn the scales in favor of the magician.[6]

You will see by my paging, that my head is all confusion — and yet you want me to address the ladies!

Mr. Carter burnt over a small portion of the meadow, i.e. all the brush, yesterday.[7] It is not dry enough yet for a general conflagration. To-day the weather has a rainy aspect.

We have already procured between 30 and 40 names to the Call for the N. E. Convention, in this village. I hope pains will be taken in R. I. to procure a large number of signers.

Yesterday I sent a letter to A. T. Judson,[8] enclosing a petition from this town, praying for the abolition of slavery in the D. of C. It had 46 signatures.

Rev. Mr. Tillotson[9] gave a pretty good anti-slavery discourse to his people on Fast Day.

Upwards of 40 heads of families have joined the Willimantic A. S. Society. So much for mobbing bro. Phelps.

Edward Spalding's wife[10] has been delivered of a boy. Nothing but boys now-a-days!

Holbrook gives notice in the Aurora, that Mr. Garrison has a son, whom he calls George Thompson. He advises Mr. G. to call his next son *Benedict Arnold*. Burleigh remarked upon reading this suggestion, that, to reach the climax of infamy, Holbrook ought to have said — "Call his name James Holbrook." [11]

Yours, ever,

Wm. Lloyd Garrison.

Mr. G. W. Benson.

ALS: Garrison Papers, Boston Public Library; a paragraph of this letter is printed in *Life*, II, 82n.

1. Charles Calistus Burleigh (b. Plainfield, Connecticut, November 3, 1810; d. Florence, Massachusetts, June 13, 1878), was the son of Rinaldo Burleigh, president of the first antislavery society in Windham County, Connecticut, and Lydia Bradford, a lineal descendant of Governor William Bradford of the *Mayflower*. His article on Connecticut's anti-Negro legislation in William Goodell's *Genius of Temperance*, which appeared while he was studying law in 1833, persuaded Arthur Tappan to offer him the editorship of a newspaper, the *Unionist*, whose aim it was to defend Prudence Crandall and her school for colored girls. Admitted to the bar in 1835, Burleigh did not practice. Instead, he became an antislavery agent, lecturer, and writer. He later edited the *Pennsylvania Freeman*, an antislavery newspaper, and was elected corresponding secretary of the American Anti-Slavery Society in 1859. *Life* notes: "as an orator he was unsurpassed in fluency, logical strictness, and fervor, lacking only the measure of time and space. His tall figure, noble countenance, and unconventional dress, with sandy flowing beard and long ringlets, made his personal appearance as unique as his talents." (*Life*, I, 476n; *DAB*.)

2. Windham county, Connecticut.

3. Van Buren was then vice-president of the United States. The letter was dated Washington, March 6, 1836, and was in reply to one dated Jackson, February 23, 1836, signed by six North Carolinians who had asked him to reply to the following question: "Do you, or do you not believe that Congress has the constitutional power, to interfere with or abolish slavery in the District of Columbia?" In essence his reply was that Congress had no right to interfere with slavery in the states. As for the District of Columbia, even if Congress had a right to abolish slavery there, he denied the "propriety" of its doing so. He affirmed that, if he were President, he would be "the inflexible and uncompromising opponent of any attempt on the part of Congress to abolish slavery in the District of Columbia, against the wishes of the slaveholding states." The letters were reprinted from the Richmond *Enquirer* in *The Liberator*, April 23, 1836.

4. Daniel Webster and William Henry Harrison (1773–1841), who was elected President of the United States on the Whig ticket in 1840, and died after a month in office.

5. In the letter previously referred to, Van Buren praised the Quakers, as differentiated from the abolitionists, for their moderation and temperateness in the past and expressed the hope that, for the sake of the Union, they would limit if not abandon their attempts to outlaw slavery in the District of Columbia.

6. *Life*, II, 82n, places this word in quotes and capitalizes it.

7. A Mr. Edwin B. Carter of Brooklyn, Connecticut, was one of the publishers of the *Windham County Gazette* in 1835 and for several years thereafter. In 1840, he published *The Harrisonian*, a campaign newspaper. He moved to Danielsonville, Windham county, in 1844, and there published the *New England Arena*, "a spicy little sheet." (Ellen D. Larned, *History of Windham County, Connecticut*, Worcester, Mass., 1880, II, 479, 565.)

8. Andrew T. Judson (1784–1853), representative in Congress, a member of the Connecticut House of Representatives from 1822 to 1825, a member of the United States House of Representatives from March 1835 to July 1836, was appointed United States judge for the District of Connecticut by Jackson in 1836, and served in that position until his death in 1853. (*BDAC.*) Judson was a leader of those citizens of Canterbury whose harassment of Prudence Crandall in 1833 and 1834 forced her to close her school for Negro girls.

9. The Reverend George J. Tillotson (1805–1888), a former schoolteacher. He was installed as minister in the Trinitarian Congregational Church of Brooklyn, Connecticut, on May 25, 1831, and remained there until his dismissal on March 10, 1858. Thereafter, until 1870, he was pastor of a church in Putnam, Connecticut. From 1870 to 1873, he was minister in Plainfield, Connecticut. He was active in the American Missionary Association and helped endow a college for freedmen in Austin, Texas, named Tillotson Institute. (*Obituary Record of Graduates of Yale University Deceased from June 1880 to June 1890*, New Haven, 1890, p. 420; Larned, *History of Windham County, Connecticut*, II, 478–479, 487, 489, 569.)

10. The Spaldings were friends of the Bensons and Garrisons in Brooklyn. In 1835 Edward Spalding (b. Brooklyn, Connecticut, May 24, 1807; d. September 12, 1857) was married to Sarah Johnson, who died in 1839. The child referred to was Charles, born April 6, 1836, who died in 1842. Spalding went down with the steamer *Central America* on her homeward voyage from California. (Samuel J. Spalding, *Spalding Memorial*, Newburyport, Mass., 1872, p. 303.)

11. James Holbrook was editor of the Windham county *Advertiser* from 1827 to 1835 and of the Norwich *Aurora* in 1836. The *Aurora* was first issued by Holbrook on May 20, 1835. In July 1838 it passed into the hands of Gad S. Gilbert, who published it until 1842. The paper was then successively issued by William Trench and Trench & Conklin until August 8, 1844, when John W. Stedman became its editor, printer, and proprietor. It continued in existence until 1878. In 1839 Holbrook issued the *State Eagle*, which, in 1840, united with the *Patriot and Democrat* under the name of *Patriot and Eagle*, and ceased publication in 1842. (Larned, *History of Windham County, Connectiut*, II, 479; F. M. Caulkins, *History of Norwich, Connecticut*, Norwich, Conn., 1866, p. 583.)

19

TO HENRY C. WRIGHT

Brooklyn, April 11, 1836.

Esteemed Brother:

I hasten to reply to your very kind and urgent letter, which has just come to hand.

You write in behalf of our Board of Managers,[1] desiring me to locate myself in Boston or its vicinity, instead of remaining at a distance of "150 miles" — (Brooklyn, however, is but 70 miles from Boston.) Your reasons for my return are certainly weighty, and urged with affectionate persuasion. Happy am I to be thus estimated by you, and grateful do I feel to the Board for its generous proposal, respecting the enlargement of my salary. It is my desire to pursue that course which will best advance the holy cause of liberty, and make

the Liberator most formidable to tyrants. All that I have must be
made subservient to this end. For several reasons, I could wish to
be in Boston, some of which you have specified. It is an advantage to
an editor to be able to read the proof-sheet, and direct the arrangement, of each number of his paper. There are local incidents frequently occurring, which need to be chronicled, but which by his
absence are liable to neglect. — It is also a privilege to unite in counsel
with those whose province it is to manage the vast machinery, by
which slavery is to be ground to powder. For myself, I feel it is of
some consequence that the curious and the inquiring should see and
converse with me freely, owing to the ludicrous as well as hurtful
misapprehensions which so widely obtain, respecting my principles
and designs. This is one side of the question.

Had it not been for Mrs. G's delicate state of health, which would
not safely allow her to return to Boston after the riot in October, we
should not have remained in this village the past winter. The warm
season is now rapidly approaching, during which it is most undesirable
to be in a populous city. As few meetings can then be held, my presence
will be less necessary — i.e. my *constant* presence, because I shall visit
Boston perhaps as often as once a month, should I elect to remain
here. In the course of a few weeks, there will be *daily* intercourse between this place and Boston, so that newspapers and letters may be
forwarded either way with all celerity. — I am now residing here on
the score of economy to our cause. This is indeed a *home*, most desirable in itself, suited to my love of retirement, and of course peculiarly endearing to my dear Helen, surrounded as she is at this interesting crisis by father, mother, sisters and friends; yet she is ready,
at any moment, cheerfully to go when and where I please. In this
cause, her will is my will — my desires are her desires — we are indeed
one. Besides, I shall unquestionably be able to write more for the
Liberator, and to conduct a larger correspondence, here, than I could
in Boston, for many obvious reasons. Observe, dear brother — I only
propose to abide here through sultry Summer's reign, should our lives
be graciously spared; and by the first of September we shall return
to Boston, there to remain.

It is not necessary for me to enlarge, as, in consequence of your
letter and the proceedings of the Board, I purpose to be in Boston
on Thursday next, when we will discuss these matters face to face.

The review of Dr. Channing, in the Atlas,[2] I have not seen. If its
sentiments out-Herod Herod [3] — if they are worse than those of
M'Duffie — the more certain it is that we have begun our reform just
where it is most needed. "Why don't you go to the South?" is a
cuckow cry that is now seldom heard. — Nor have I seen the reviews

74

in the Christian Spectator [4] — I suppose they are from the pen of Leonard Bacon.[5] "Channing — Andrews — Winslow — all praised to the highest," you say. O'Connell [6] is right — a colonization stomach will eat iron like any thing — it will digest it like an ostrich.

Another slave State [7] is to be added to our Union — even without one note of remonstrance in Congress! Rely upon it, Texas too will soon be ours — and then it seems to me will follow a dissolution of the Union, or the entire subjugation of the free States to the will of the bloody South. Save us, O God!

Gratefully and affectionately yours,

Wm. Lloyd Garrison.

ALS: Garrison Papers, Boston Public Library.

1. The Massachusetts Anti-Slavery Society. On April 6, Wright had written: "there was a feeling among those present that you ought to be here where you might be seen — that 46 Washington Street was your proper home . . . there you ought to be found — especially now as the time of our Convention draws nigh & there are many calls at the room. It was suggested that your salary would not sustain you here. In answer it was said that the Board would raise your salary to a thousand dollars. I think that would be done if you would consent to come. . . . I feel that this your child the Liberator — your eldest child — is suffering, as all children do, by the father's absence. . . . Innumerable [times] is the question asked where is Garrison? And when it is answered, in Connecticut, there is a feeling that Abolitionism is losing ground." (ALS, Anti-Slavery Letters to Garrison and Others, Boston Public Library.)

2. The review referred to consisted of a series of sixteen articles which appeared in the Boston *Daily Atlas*, from March 17 to April 7, 1836, written anonymously and dated "Essex County, Mass., March, 1836." The review, although it began on a seemingly sympathetic note, ended with a strong condemnation of Channing and his views. It referred several times to Garrison as "an alien," and stated that "whenever the tendency of their [the abolitionists'] measures is to endanger the safety and peace of the South, or to dissolve the Union . . . I hope they will meet with such sympathy as will make them harmless, in whatsoever way that must be done" (March 28, 1836).

3. Shakespeare, *Hamlet*, III, ii.

4. There were three unsigned review articles in the *Christian Spectator*, 8 (no. 1), March 1836. The review of Channing's *Slavery* appeared under the heading "Present State of the Slavery Question." That of Professor E. A. Andrews, a lawyer and a former professor of ancient languages at the University of North Carolina, appeared under the title "Andrews on Slavery." Professor Andrews' book was entitled *Slavery and the Domestic Slave Trade in the United States. In a Series of Letters Addressed to the Executive Committee of the American Union for the Relief and Improvement of the Colored Race* (Boston, 1836). Garrison reviewed the book in *The Liberator*, March 5, 1836, under the title "A Pernicious Publication." His opening sentence read: "It is not a new thing for a mountain in labor to bring forth a mouse — but here a reptile has been produced, instead of so harmless a little animal." The article on Hubbard Winslow, pastor of the Bowdoin Street Church in Boston, was entitled "Winslow on Social and Civil Duties." It was a review of his book, *Christianity Applied to Our Civil and Social Relations* (Boston, 1835), a collection of sermons.

The book by Andrews, in part, emphasized the view that the abolitionists, by their agitation, had strengthened the determination of the slaveholders to maintain slavery, and were thus, in great part, responsible for the institution's continuance. Winslow, in his book, had condemned "extremist" reformers and reform societies, including the abolitionists.

5. Leonard Bacon (1802–1881), Congregational minister, author and editor, became pastor of the First Church in New Haven in 1825 and remained there until his death. Although known as an antislavery man, he was a colonizationist and an ardent champion of the American Colonization Society as well as an early opponent of Garrison. His writings on the Negro and slavery included *On the Black Population of the United States* (1823), written while he was a student at Andover, and *Slavery Discussed in Occasional Essays* (1846). He edited the *Christian Spectator* from 1826 to 1838, and was one of the founders of the *New Englander* in 1843 and of the New York *Independent* in 1848, which he later edited for a while. From 1866 to 1871 he was professor of didactic theology at Yale University, and from 1871 until his death taught American church history at the same institution. (*E.E.; Life*, I, 204, 301, 303, 448, 455, 470, 473; *Weld-Grimké Letters*, I, p. 103n; *DAB.*)

6. Daniel O'Connell.

7. Arkansas.

20

TO HELEN E. GARRISON

At bro. May's, in Hayward Place,
Boston, April 16, 1836.

My dear Helen:

Well — my name is not Jonah, ergo, I am not Jonah — nor have I run away like Jonah — nor have I been caught in a storm at sea, nor tossed overboard, nor swallowed by a whale, nor thrown up again, like Jonah. What then? If I am not Jonah, who am I? William Lloyd Garrison, to be sure; and what is more, the editor of the Liberator; and what is more, your husband, my dear; and what is more, the father of as fine a boy as any in Friendship's Valley. But of my luck — what of that? On Wednesday morning, you know, the weather was mild and pleasant, before I bade you all adieu — (how sweetly my dear babe looked me in the face as he lay upon the bed, when I gave him my farewell kiss!) — so I concluded to ride on the outside in the good society of Mr. Barnes, the driver of the stage, or rather of the horses. We had not proceeded far, however, before the breath of the sweet South was changed into a blustering "North-Easter," and down came quite a respectable company of snow-flakes upon us, which continued to multiply till at last it seemed as if the hugest feather-bed of heaven had been opened, and its contents freely given to all below — i.e. to as many as were underneath. It soon cleared up again, and then it much sooner *cleared down* — is that good English? No matter — I rode to *Thompson, Connecticut*, (is he related to *George Thompson*, do you know?) without flinching — for most truly could I sing —

"The snow, the snow, the fleecy snow,
With the sky above, and the earth below, —
'Tis here, 'tis there, 'tis every where,
It covers the ground, it fills the air, —
But if *it* will not, *I* will forbear." [1]

On getting into the stage at Thompson, I was glad to find a very neatly dressed colored female as a passenger to Worcester. Nobody knew me, I suppose, but not the slightest objection was made to her company, and she seemed to feel that she was, and of right ought to be, on an equality with us, or with any body else. We had also with us, or rather took up on our way, a fashionable and intelligent lady of Boston. As she sat on the middle seat close by the window, the driver in wielding his long whip happened to touch her bonnet lightly with the end of it, which led her to remark, that she had no particular desire to be struck. I said to her — "No, madam, it is not desirable to be struck by a whip, even accidentally — and yet, you know, there are thousands of your sex in our land, who are subjected to the lash, not accidentally but habitually." "I hope," she replied, "a head-ache, like mine, would be a protection against it." "Not at all, madam — it would be considere[d . . . to la]bor, and would probably bring punishment for idleness." She [did not] seem disposed to pursue the topic, and so our conversation e[nded] for a time.

We arrived at Worcester, just before 4 o'clock, having taken dinner at Oxford — but, in addition to the dinner, I ate up all the sweetened what-do-you-call 'em, which were put up by Sarah or Anna for the encouragement of my appetite, and support of my stomach — nor did they come amiss, nor were they superfluous, because why? Here, then, we have something to do with Jonah, or rather Jonah's luck, as the sequel will show.

At 4 o'clock, P. M. we started in the cars for Boston, in the midst of quite an ambitious snow-storm, expecting to be in Boston at 7 o'clock, of course. The snow retarded our progress somewhat; but when we had proceeded about two-thirds of the way, we were "brought all up standing," as a sailor would say — that is, we were met by several opposite trains of cars, in such a manner, at such a place and hour, and under such circumstances, as to render it almost impracticable for either party to back out or go ahead. After a long delay, we got extricated, and then went onward till we got into a similar predicament. The car in which I sat was crowded, but there was no angry growling, though there was some disappointment, on the part of the passengers. The storm pelted us all the while right merrily, now snowing, now hailing, now raining — but, as we were well sheltered, we did not mind it at all, at all. To shorten the story, let me tell you, dearest, that we were *six hours and a half* in making our trip, not arriving in this city till half past 10 o'clock at night. As it was too late to go [to] Miss Parker's, I ordered a coachman to drive me to the Marlboro' hotel — found it full; then told him to go [to] the Bromfield house — it was full; then to the Howard-street house, where I succeeded in getting lodgings, and slept that night pretty well, saving and excepting some twinges of the tooth-ache. After breakfast the next morning, I had my trunk carried to the anti-slavery office, where I found brothers Le Row [2] and Knapp, both in good health and spirits, and very much rejoiced to see me. I have since been staying at Miss Parker's.

[. . . Thur]sday evening, we had a large meeting of anti-[slavery frien]ds, both male and female, at Mrs. Chapman's, which [did] not break up till about 11 o'clock. Prof. Follen and wife, Ellis G. Loring and wife,[3] Mrs. Child,[4] Miss Ammidon, the Westons, *Miss* Chapman, Mr. Sewall, Mr. Southwick,[5] Mr. Knapp, Mr. Kimball, Mr. Fairbanks,[6] &c. were present. Mrs. Child looks in remarkably good health, and made some remarks at the ladies' meeting on Wednesday last, which manifested that she was as vigorous in spirit as in body. Her husband is at present out of the city, but will return in a few days. They are — I am sorry to say — going with friend Lundy to Matamoras, near Texas, in all next month. What a hazardous project! [7] But, to return to the meeting — as we are disappointed in getting a meeting-house or hall in which to hold the N. E. Convention, except our own little hall at 46, we discussed the expediency of having the Convention held either in Providence or Lowell. Mr. Kimball proposed that we should hire a vacant lot of ground in this city, and erect upon it a large shanty, capable of holding 2 or 3000 people — saying that he would give $25 towards it. It was generally thought, however, that, if erected, it would be torn down before we could occupy it, and would be likely to excite a mob without doing us any benefit, as the market is now getting to be somewhat glutted with deeds of violence. For several good reasons, we have concluded, if we cannot do better, to hold the Convention in Roxbury or Cambridgeport.[8]

Bro. Wright [9] is out of town. There is but one opinion among the friends, and that is in favor of my return to Boston after the annual meeting at New-York, to reside here. I am more and more satisfied that it will be my duty to return to Boston — but I will say no more upon this point until I see you.

I shall not return as soon as I expected, because I cannot properly, there is so much to be done here. I shall prepare the matter for next week's paper before I leave. On Wednesday next I hope to be in Providence — may perhaps conclude to address the ladies on Thursday — and on Friday, I hope to see you and my darling babe, and all the dear family.

Christiana has gone to Providence to make a visit to her friends, and on account of ill health. It is not probable that she will return here.

Bro. May has just gone to Hingham in the steam-boat, and will deliver addresses in Scituate and Cohasset.

There is a great deal of interest [. . .] of inquirers, as to Henry's state of health. They [. . .] and hope his recovery will be speedy. I trust he is doing well [and that] you all keep a strict watch over him to prevent any act of impr[ud]ence. Our Board, one and all, hope that he will give himself no anxiety about the concerns of the office. Every thing is going on very well.

Dr. Hildreth,[10] who attended Henry here, has told Mr. May that he will gladly be our family physician *gratis,* as long as we please. He is an excellent physician, and his offer is a very generous one.

Susan and Mary Ann Coffin [11] have just come into the room, and learning that I am writing to you, desire me to send their love to you. All in their family are well.

Mr. Lunt's Report will be suffered to lie upon the table until it rots. The Senate will not touch it. Good! [12]

Miss Martineau is now in New-York.

No further news from Thompson. Is it not strange?

Mr. & Mrs. May unite in love to you all. Little Joseph gets along finely. — O, my dear little George, how I yearn to see you again! Heaven protect you both!

Yours, most lovingly,

Wm. L. Garrison.

ALS: Garrison Papers, Boston Public Library (manuscript torn at upper corners); partly reprinted in *Life,* II, 105–106.

1. Unidentified; possibly by Garrison.

2. George LeRow of Boston was present at the antislavery convention of Old Hampshire, at Northampton, Massachusetts, on Wednesday, January 20, 1836. He delivered an address in defense of free public discussion on the subject of slavery. He also addressed the Boston Young Men's Anti-Slavery Society on February 22, 1836. Until 1834 he taught at Waterville College in Maine, and in 1835 he taught at Union College in Schenectady. (See manuscript letters from LeRow in Anti-Slavery Letters to Garrison and Others, Boston Public Library, dated October 27, 1834, and October 22, 1835; *The Liberator,* February 13 and 27, 1836.)

3. Louisa Gilman Loring (1797–1868) was an active abolitionist who contributed unstintingly of her time, energy, and money to the antislavery cause. (*Life,* I, 490; II, 69, 105; III, 79, 133, 134, 154, 179; IV, 393; see Garrison's letter to Louisa Loring, January 31, 1835, *Letters,* I.)

4. Lydia Maria Child (1802–1880) of Boston, the prominent author and antislavery spokesman. Her best-known antislavery work was *An Appeal in Favor of that Class of Americans Called Africans* (Boston, 1833). She and her husband, David Lee Child, were lifelong friends of Garrison.

James Russell Lowell wrote a very interesting character sketch of Mrs. Child at the end of 1848, in his *A Fable for Critics,* a sketch which Garrison termed "drawn 'to the life,'" and which he reprinted in *The Liberator* on January 5, 1849. A recent popular and short biography is Milton Meltzer's *Tongue of Flame, The Life of Lydia Maria Child* (New York, 1965).

5. Joseph Southwick (1791–1866), a Quaker, originally of Maine but now of Boston, was a founder of the American Anti-Slavery Society, president of the Massachusetts Anti-Slavery Society in 1835 and 1836, and a vice-president of the society for several years thereafter. (*Life*, I, 397; II, 46, *et passim*.)

6. Drury Fairbanks was then an officer of the Massachusetts Anti-Slavery Society, serving as one of its counsellors. He is listed for the first time among the counsellors in the *Second Annual Report of the Board of Managers of the New-England Anti-Slavery Society, Presented January 15, 1834* (Boston, 1834). Drury Fairbanks & Co. (shoes) was located at 34 Broad Street, Boston. His home was at 25 Oliver Street, Boston.

7. In January 1836 David and Lydia Maria Child had consented to join Benjamin Lundy in setting up a colony based on free labor at Matamoras, at the mouth of the Rio Grande, within the Mexican province bordering Texas on the south. Its original purpose was to provide a haven for free Negroes, with investments to come from wealthy white Americans who would be expected to employ free Negro labor in the growing of sugar, cotton, and rice. The project was abandoned before the trip could be made when the Texans defeated Mexico at the Battle of San Jacinto on April 21, 1836. Garrison had opposed this and previous projects of this nature by Lundy. Lundy was thus especially elated when the Childs, who were Garrisonian abolitionists, joined his project. Merton L. Dillon, in *Benjamin Lundy and the Struggle for Negro Freedom* (Urbana and London, 1966), p. 217, notes that "the Childs were Garrison's 'particular friends, and among the most active and influential of the New England abolitionists.' His [Lundy's] elation as he imagined Garrison's chagrin was understandable. 'How our friend Garrison, and a few others will relish it, I do not know,' he wrote."

For a detailed account of Lundy's project and the relationship of the Childs to it, see Dillon, *ibid*., pp. 217–220 *et passim*.

Benjamin Lundy (1789–1839), pioneer abolitionist and saddler by trade, began his antislavery activity in 1815, at Clairsville, Ohio, then his home, where he organized an antislavery group known as "The Union Humane Society." The following year he distributed a circular letter urging the organization of antislavery societies throughout the country. In January 1821 he founded *The Genius of Universal Emancipation*, published first at Mt. Pleasant, Ohio, then at Greeneville, Tennessee, and from 1824 on at Baltimore, Maryland. In 1828, on a lecture tour through the northern states, Lundy met Garrison and exerted considerable influence upon him in the direction of antislavery activity. In 1829 Garrison joined Lundy in Baltimore as associate editor of *The Genius*, but they soon parted, unable to agree upon policy and style. By the end of 1835, *The Genius*, which had been issued more and more irregularly, ceased to appear. In August 1836 Lundy began publishing *The National Enquirer and Constitutional Advocate of Universal Liberty*, which continued until March 1838, when it was taken over by John G. Whittier and renamed the *Pennsylvania Freeman*. Lundy died, after a brief illness, in Illinois, where he was then living. His last years were marked by increasing antagonism toward Garrison over the latter's views on the role of women in the antislavery movement, on religion, and editorial matters. (*DAB*.)

8. A footnote in *Life* (II, 105n) remarks: "This stirring Convention, the published call for which had 3,000 signatures (Supplement to *Lib*. May 14, 1836), and which was attended by 500 delegates, was held in the Rev. Mr. Blagden's Salem-Street Church, Boston, through no good-will of the pastor ('Right and Wrong,' 1836, [2] p. 9), whose retirement, a few months later, to become pastor of the Old South (*Lib*. 6:163), was thought to be in consequence of this Convention. Samuel Fessenden, of Portland, presided (*Lib*., 6:87)."

9. Henry C. Wright.

10. Dr. Charles Trueworth Hildreth (b. January 12, 1798; d. March 1843) was born in Haverhill, Massachusetts, studied medicine in Marietta, Ohio, from 1815 to 1818, returned to Haverhill where he continued his medical studies, went back to Ohio in 1819, and returned to Massachusetts in 1820. He thereafter

lived and practiced medicine in Boston at 3 Beach Street, and from 1836 at 1 Lagrange Place. He was a Baptist and built up a large medical profession among his fellow congregants. He was listed as a life member of the New England Anti-Slavery Society in the society's *Third Annual Report . . . , Presented January 21, 1835* (Boston, 1835), p. 72. (Samuel P. Hildreth, *Genealogical and Biographical Sketches of the Hildreth Family*, Marietta, Ohio, 1840, pp. 317–318.)

11. Peter Coffin was the father-in-law of Samuel J. May. See Garrison's letter to Samuel J. May, February 14, 1831 (*Letters*, I), in which he refers to Mr. Coffin and "the Misses Coffin," and to their home on Atkinson Street. A note in *Life* (I, 222), which identifies the Mr. Coffin as Peter Coffin, remarks: "Atkinson Street was that part of Congress now lying between Milk and Purchase Streets; the family lived, therefore, at no great distance from the *Liberator* office. They were remotely related to Joshua Coffin, the historian of Newbury, Mass."

12. This was a report by the joint special committee of the Massachusetts legislature on "so much of the Governor's message as relates to the Abolition of Slavery, together with certain documents upon the same subject, communicated to the Executive by the several Legislatures of Virginia, North Carolina, South Carolina, Georgia and Alabama." The report noted that "the right of the master to the slave is as undoubted as the right to any other property." Though regretting "the condition of slavery everywhere in the world," it condemned "the false benevolence," obviously abolition, "which, in order to liberate the slave, is willing to destroy the hope of liberty itself, by plunging the country in all the horrors of civil war, with bloodshed, anarchy and despotism, the sure attendants in its train." It recommended that the abolitionists abstain from all further discussions and actions "as may tend to disturb and irritate the public mind." The entire report was reprinted in *The Liberator*, April 9, 1836.

21

TO HELEN E. GARRISON

Boston, April 18, 1836.

Dearest of all women to me —

My very dear Helen — Doubtless, you will stare to perceive by this letter, that I am still in Boston. This is the way to be a prompt and faithful lover — husband — father — is it? I who talked of being in Brooklyn on Saturday last, all so expeditiously — all so certainly — behold, here I am as far off as ever! Do *you* begin to distrust *me?* Do *I* begin to slight *you?* Nay — you think all the better of me — I love you the more dearly: — you, because I am intent upon discharging the duties which I owe to God and man — I, because your acquiescence is so cheerfully and sweetly given, painful though a separation is to us both.

I have indeed been very busy with the paper and other matters since my return; so busy, that I have visited no body, except the Chapmans and Miss Sargent, and then rather in the way of business. Last evening I was at Miss S's, in company with Mrs. Child and several other friends, and had a very agreeable visit. Miss S. is a most excellent lady — so excellent that it is a pity (don't you think so?) she is not some good man's wife. She speaks of you affectionately, and will be glad to hail your return to the city.[1] And so will many others. Besides, they are curious to see little George, and to study his phrenological developments, if he has any. Whenever I think of this dear babe, my heart flutters like an imprisoned bird, longing to fly over every towering impediment till distance is annihilated, and home, sweet home, is once more regained — then to sing in sweeter strains, making all nature melodious. How does he look now? What is his weight? What new trait has he exhibited? O, the dear, little, precious, *mammoth* responsibility! How thankful to God ought we to be for such a gift! May he be trained up in the way he should go — for he has been brought into a most perilous world.

Next to hearing from you and the babe, I am anxious to learn how brother Henry *progresses*, (to use an active Americanism,) but cannot expect to know until my return. He has very many friends in this city, who esteem and admire him, and they long to hear of his complete restoration to health.

It is probable that I shall go to Providence on Wednesday or Thursday, and so endeavor to be by your side (where I am always happy to be) on Friday noon: it may be, however, that I shall be detained until Saturday morning; if so, I shall take the Pomfret stage.

The annual meeting of the Young Men's Anti-Slavery Society in Philadelphia takes place on the 27th instant. They have written to me, requesting me to forward a letter, to be read at the meeting. It is somewhat doubtful, whether I shall find time to comply with their solicitation.[2]

Tell bro. Henry that Le Row will have to leave the office for Schenectady in all next week. Who will supply his place, we do not know, but *somebody*. John Cutts Smith [3] is desirous to be his successor. He is a driving hand at business, but not very well qualified to keep accounts in "apple-pie" order.

We have just had a letter from bro. Phelps [4] at New-York, stating that Mr. Slade of Vermont had just sent on the agreeable information, that the bill for the admission of Arkansas as a slave State would not get through the House of Representatives, at Washington, short of three or four weeks, and that it will probably create another Missouri excitement. To-day we have had two hundred petitions printed on a letter-sheet, which will be scattered throughout the Commonwealth for signatures, remonstrating against the admission of that State with slavery into the Union.[5]

Bro. May has not yet returned from Scituate. His wife is very hoarse with a cold, but looks in very good health. Poor woman — she has no one to relieve her of the care of her children, from Sunday morning to Saturday night. Little Joseph resembles his father very strongly. He is not so pretty as our little boy — see how impartial I am in judgment! — But I suppose G. T.[6] has no special beauty in bro. May's eyes, and so our accounts or estimates are about squared.

Boston seems to me more populous and noisy than ever. The streets are crowded continually, and my ears are stunned with the din of enterprise. I wish its moral improvement kept pace with its prosperity.

Yesterday, I went to hear Dr. Channing preach in the forenoon. His sermon was a very excellent one, in vindication of the equality of man, and the duty of attempting to elevate the lowest classes of society to the highest intellectual, social and improvement.[7] He spoke in liberal terms of the working-man. It was, I should think, too republican a dose for his aristocratical congregation.

Mr. Gannett is in Leicester,[8] and is said to be in a very unhappy, an almost distracted state of mind, so as to be unfit to attend to the duties of his office.

Bro. George has written to me here, informing where he boards, and urging me to address the ladies in P—— [9] on Thursday evening.

All the Misses Parker, Mr. and Mrs. Drew,[10] (it is probable they will soon be parents,) Mrs. May, bro. Le Row, bro. Knapp, &c. &c. desire me to convey to you and Henry as much esteem as a rail-car can carry.

I trust father's and mother's health has improved since I left, and hope, through the goodness of God, to find you all well on my return. Love abundantly to every one in the family.

Yours, doatingly,
Wm. Lloyd Garrison.

ALS: Garrison Papers, Boston Public Library; printed in part in *Life*, II, 106.

1. A footnote to this sentence in *Life* (II, 106n) remarks, "to the close of a green old age Miss Henrietta Sargent was one of the most generous and attached friends of Mr. Garrison's family." Henrietta Sargent (b. November 18, 1785; d. Boston, January 11, 1871) was one of the officers of the Boston Female Anti-Slavery Society, serving as one of four counsellors, and was a member of the society's committee which sent a letter of thanks to Ellis Gray Loring for his part in the successful case of the slave child, Med. See *Right and Wrong in Boston in 1836, Annual Report of the Boston Female Anti-Slavery Society . . .* (Boston, 1836), pp. 68–71, for the exchange of correspondence between Loring and the committee. Gilbert H. Barnes and Dwight L. Dumond, in their edition of the Weld-Grimké correspondence, reproduce a letter from Miss Sargent to Angelina Grimké (I, 357–358).

2. He did find the time. See letter 23, to William H. Scott, April 20, 1836.

3. According to *Life*, John Cutts Smith was born John Smith Cutts. A Boston minister, he was a founder of the New England Anti-Slavery Society and broke with Garrison in 1841 (IV, 412; III, 38–39; see also Russel B. Nye, *William Lloyd Garrison and the Humanitarian Reformers*, Boston and Toronto, 1955, p. 56.)

4. Amos A. Phelps.

5. See letter 22, Boston, April 18, 1836, to *"Esteemed Coadjutor in the cause of Righteous Liberty."*

6. George Thompson Garrison, Garrison's new-born son.

7. So in manuscript.

8. The Reverend Ezra Stiles Gannett (1801–1871), colleague of William Ellery Channing, was extremely hostile to Garrison and his views. Harriet Martineau stayed at his home in December 1835. It was there that Garrison first met her, after having sent her a note asking for a meeting. It was to Gannett's credit that, despite his hostility to Garrison, he insisted that Miss Martineau invite the latter to Gannett's home for their meeting (*Life*, II, 69, 453 *et passim*).

9. Providence.

10. A Charles Drew was associated with the *New England Spectator*, a Congregational newspaper dedicated to reform. A Charles Drew of Boston was in drygoods in partnership with A. D. Babcock (Boston *Directory*, 1836). Garrison's letter to James P. Boyce, October 10, 1837, mentions that Drew was moving to Fairhaven, Massachusetts, where he was planning to engage in the shoe business. He is listed among the counsellors of the Massachusetts Anti-Slavery Society in 1835.

---

2 2

TO FRIENDS OF THE ANTI-SLAVERY MOVEMENT

Boston, April 18, 1836.

Esteemed Coadjutor in the cause of Righteous Liberty:

This is a great, an alarming crisis. Unless the most strenuous exertions are instantly made by the people of the free States, another slaveholding State will be added to the Union, thus bringing fresh blood-guiltiness upon all the land, and opening a new market for the traffic in *slaves and the souls of men.* Such barbarity, such impiety, is most appalling in *contemplation* — how much more insupportable in *reality*! Already the Senate of the United States, with only six dissenting voices, has voted to admit Arkansas as a slaveholding State! — Our only hope of effectual resistance lies in the House of Representatives. By information from Washington, we are rejoiced to learn, that there is no prospect of getting the bill through the House short of three or four weeks. They are determined to go into *a committee of the whole* on it, and discuss it thoroughly. *This is another Missouri question.* No pains, no expense should be spared to flood the House with remonstrances. Rouse up the inhabitants of your town — circulate petitions — call a public meeting, if practicable — send expostulatory letters to northern members in Congress, &c. &c. Stir — stir, for the bleeding slave, the honor and salvation of our country, and the approbation of Heaven! IMMEDIATE, is the watchword. Get as many signers to the accompanying petition as you possibly can, *in the course of a week at the furthest,* and forward it promptly to our representatives. Observe — it is not an *abolition* question; it has nothing to do with slavery in the southern States; it is simply and exclusively, whether we, the people of the United States, shall introduce and perpetuate slavery, in a new member of our confederacy. Call, therefore, for signatures, upon abolitionists, colonizationists, unionists, all — *all!* Delay not a moment.

Respectfully yours,
WM. LLOYD GARRISON.

Printed form letter· Villard Papers, Houghton Library, Harvard.

As Garrison notes in letter 21, to his wife, Boston, April 18, 1836, "To-day we have had two hundred petitions printed on a letter-sheet, which will be scattered throughout the Commonwealth for signatures, remonstrating against the admission of that State with slavery into the Union." The following handwritten statement appeared beneath Garrison's message and name:

"It is thought advisable by the friends of the cause that as many signatures of ladies be obtained as possible, & therefore a blank is left in the printed remonstrance for the insertion of the words 'male' or 'female' as the case may require. Call on *all* whether members of your society or not.

"In behalf of the Boston Female anti-slavery society

"Anne W. Weston Cor. Soc.

"Forward to William Lloyd Garrison 46 Washington St as soon as possible."

23

TO WILLIAM H. SCOTT
THE YOUNG MEN'S ANTI-SLAVERY SOCIETY
OF PHILADELPHIA

BOSTON, April 20, 1836.

Esteemed Friend: — I must appear by proxy at the first annual meeting of the Young Men's Anti-Slavery Society of your city.[1] This letter shall refute the doctrine of materialists, who affirm, that there is no such entity as a spiritual substance, but that mind is matter, and matter is mind. Of this I am sure, that, during the thirty years of my life, I have never been able to locate my *body* in two places — in Boston and Philadelphia — at the same time; but I have found no difficulty in letting my *mind* range here, there, every where, below all depths, and above all heights, among things terrestrial and things celestial, in the twinkling of an eye. Human thoughts and opinions may ultimately possess an earthly omnipresence.

The first public lecture I ever delivered against American slavery, was in the hall of the Franklin Institute, in Philadelphia, which I was kindly permitted to occupy three evenings gratuitously. It was immediately after my liberation at Baltimore, in 1830. My auditors were chiefly members of the Society of Friends. My lectures were full of burning rebuke, 'hard language,' and earnest expostulation, and assuredly were quite as fanatical and incendiary as any thing I have since written or spoken; yet they were handsomely lauded by Mr. Morris, of the Inquirer, who has since been so zealous both in reprobating my sentiments, and assailing the anti-slavery cause. Was he right then, or is he wrong now? [2]

Since that time, a change has come over our land. Other sentiments have become popular, new doctrines have been asserted, new estimates made of men and things, full of novel atrocity and absurd impiety. *Then* slavery, if it found some apologists, could find none to defend it as a righteous system; *now* it is widely vindicated in the Senate chamber, from the pulpit, by ecclesiastical bodies, by theological institutions, by the unanimous assent of legislative assemblies, as a system consistent with Christianity, and sanctioned by the Almighty. *Then* it was not disreputable, at least not dangerous, to express abhorrence of the practice of making merchandise of our fellow creatures; *now* he who remonstrates against that practice, is in peril of losing his property, safety, liberty and life.

When Jesus Christ forewarned his apostles, that they should be hated of all men for his name's sake, he sustained their spirits by the victorious promise, 'He that endureth to the end shall be saved.' [3] And truly did he say — 'It is enough for the disciple that he be as his master, and the servant as his lord: if they have called the master of the house Beelzebub, how much more shall they call them of his household?' [4] So we may pertinently make the inquiry — If our enemies assert that slavery is a divine institution, 'the corner-stone of our republican edifice' [5] — if they call cruelty humanity, lewdness virtue, fraud honesty, physical coercion voluntary labor, oppression disinterested benevolence; if they call latent animosity in the breasts of their victims palpable and sincere attachment, the prostration of millions of intellects the extreme exaltation of genius and knowledge, the ruin of the soul its sure preservation, the circulation of the Bible a criminal offence, the sanctity of marriage an idle conceit — what, as consistent errorists, ought they to call us, who scout their principles and hate their works? Why, fanatics, incendiaries, madmen, disturbers of the peace, to be sure — by those reproachful terms which they are heaping so liberally upon us. If they should call us honest men, discreet citizens, sound republicans, and genuine Christians, it would almost necessarily follow that we are as knavish, fanatical, oppressive and corrupt as themselves. In their vocabulary for 'treason' see 'loyalty,' for 'insanity' see 'reason,' for 'blood-thirstiness' see 'non-resistance,' for

'malignity' see 'forgiveness.' The history of eighteen hundred years
exactly verifies the declaration of the great Captain of our salvation —
'If ye were of the world, the world would love his own; but because
ye are not of the world, but I have chosen you out of the world, therefore the world hateth you.' [6] Let us not be alarmed about our reputation: let us rather rejoice that its inherent value is made manifest by
the combined slander and scorn of all the wicked in our land. To
reign with Christ, we must be crucified to the world; to save our lives,
we must lose them; to preserve and enlarge our reputation, we must
sacrifice it for righteousness' sake. As our beloved coadjutor George
Thompson once pleasantly remarked: 'When we shall have succeeded
in demolishing the great prison-house of oppression, each of us will
be able to dig up for himself, out of its ruins, a very good reputation.'
The time is swiftly approaching, when those hypocrites and time
servers, who are now so voluble and flippant in denouncing our principles and measures, will be ambitious to drag over us the foul slime
of their panegyric, and to cover us with the nauseous spittle of their
sycophancy. We may bear their abuse, but not their praise, with
complacency.

There is now another deadly foe besides slavery to be vanquished —
it is MOBOCRACY. We are crushed to the earth, as freemen, by ten
thousand tyrants instead of one. Fisher Ames most forcibly observes —
'The rage of one man will be tired by repetition of outrage, or it may
be eluded by art or by flight. It seldom smites the obscure, who are
many, but, like a gust, uproots chiefly the great trees that overtop
the forest. A mobocracy, however, is always usurped by the worst
men in the most corrupt times; in a period of violence by the most
violent. It is a Briareus with a thousand hands, each bearing a dagger;
a Cerberus, gaping with ten thousand throats, all parched and thirst-
ing for fresh blood. It is a genuine tyranny, but of all the least durable,
yet the most destructive while it lasts. The power of a despot, like
the ardor of a summer's sun, dries up the grass, but the roots remain
fresh in the soil; a mob government, like a West India hurricane,
strews the fruitful earth with promiscuous ruins, and turns the sky
yellow with pestilence. Men inhale a vapor like the Sirocco, and die
in the open air for want of respiration. It is a winged curse that en-
velops the obscure as well as the distinguished, and is wafted into
the lurking places of the fugitives. It is not doing justice to licentiousness, to compare it to a wind which ravages the surface of the earth;
it is an earthquake that loosens its foundations, burying in an hour
the accumulated wealth and wisdom of ages. Those who, after the
calamity, would reconstruct the edifice of public liberty, will be
scarcely able to find the model of the artificers, or even the ruins.

Mountains have split and filled the fertile valleys, covering them with rocks and gravel; rivers have changed their beds; populous towns have sunk, leaving only frightful chasms, out of which are creeping the remnant of living wretches, the monuments and the victims of despair.' [7]

At present, the master-spirits of misrule in our land are allowing us a temporary respite. But their malice is still deadly. 'Like salamanders, they can breathe only in fire. Like toads, they suck no aliment from the earth but its poisons. When they rest in their lurking places, [. . .] it is like serpents in winter, the better to concoct their venom; and when they are in action, it is to shed it.' [8] But, blessed be God, we have that which shall bruize [9] the serpent's head.

'If,' says Mr. Ames, 'in the nature of things, there could be any experience which would be extensively instructive but our own, all history lies open for our warning, *open like a churchyard*, all whose lessons are solemn, and chiseled for eternity in the hard stone, lessons that whisper (O! that they could thunder) to republics — "Your passions forbid you to be free!"' [10] Shall we then despair of our country? Never. For if religion and freedom cannot conquer and possess a speck of this earth, how shall we hope for the rescue and enfranchisement of the whole human race? Through Christ who strengthens them, his followers can do all things. Yours, truly,

WM. LLOYD GARRISON.

Wм. H. Scott.

Printed in *The Liberator*, June 4, 1836.

William H. Scott was a leader of the Pennsylvania Anti-Slavery Society as well as of the Philadelphia Young Men's Anti-Slavery Society. He was a merchant whose office was at 7 Commerce Street, and whose home was at 17 Morgan Street, Philadelphia. (Philadelphia *Directory*, 1836.)

1. The meeting took place on Wednesday, April 26, 1836, in the Bricklayers' Hall, corner of 13th and Race Streets. The best known of the speakers was the Reverend George Bourne (*The Liberator*, May 7, 1836).

2. The first of the three lectures was delivered on Tuesday evening, August 31, 1830. Garrison obtained the use of Franklin Hall only after great difficulty and only as he was about to admit failure and leave the city. The Philadelphia *Inquirer* commented on the speeches in its issue of September 2, 1830. Although questioning Garrison's "hard language," it described his first lecture as "elevated and impassioned, bespeaking the thorough acquaintance of the author with his subject, and evincing the deep and philanthropic interest which animated him in behalf of the poor Africans" (*Life*, I, 203).

Robert Morris, editor of the Philadelphia *Inquirer* for many years, was also a poet who was highly regarded by Edgar Allan Poe, an author, journalist, and bank president. Born in Philadelphia, he was the son of a Welsh sea-captain. At the age of twenty he assumed management of the Philadelphia *Album*, where he remained for several years. When the *Album* merged with the *Inquirer*, he continued as an editor. He became president of the Commonwealth Bank in Philadelphia in 1857, when it was founded. (*Biographical Encyclopedia of Pennsylvania of the Nineteenth Century*, Philadelphia, 1874, p. 276; Ellis P. Oberholtzer, *The Literary History of Philadelphia*, Philadelphia, 1906, p. 302; Frank Luther Mott, *A History of American Magazines, 1741–1850*, New York and London, 1930, pp. 354, 546n.)

3. Matthew 10:22.

4. Matthew 10:25.

5. Governor George McDuffie of South Carolina. See letter 3, to Henry E. Benson, January 16, 1836.

6. John 15:19.

7. From Fisher Ames's essay entitled "Laocoon, No. 1," first published in the Boston *Gazette*, April 1799, and reprinted in the *Works of Fisher Ames*, compiled by a number of his friends (Boston, 1809), pp. 96–97. Fisher Ames (1758–1808) was a prominent Massachusetts Federalist leader and orator. He served in the Massachusetts legislature and represented Massachusetts in Congress from 1789 to 1797 (*DUSH*).

8. *Works of Fisher Ames*, p. 98.

9. So in *The Liberator*.

10. From Fisher Ames's essay, "The Dangers of American Liberty," written in 1805, *Works of Fisher Ames*, pp. 387–388.

24

TO HELEN E. GARRISON

Providence, May 5, 1836.

My dear Wife:

I might, as a "lovyer," write with a more excited imagination — but could I be more prompt?

This certifies to you, that two absent husbands, to wit, George William Benson and Wm. Lloyd Garrison, arrived in this city fifteen minutes past 7 o'clock, which is an earlier hour, so the driver informs us, than the stage has arrived any time within six months. Have we not been fortunate? We had very few passengers among the number, however, was a mother with *three* children, one of them an infant at the breast, journeying to visit some friends — all alone too! One of the children was quite unwell, and vomited somewhat freely, but the little babe behaved much better than little babies usually do, under such circumstances. Of course, one little babe, "muling and puling in its mother's arms," [1] made me think of another little babe — my own — the sweetest, dearest, fairest, best, within a stone's throw of Friendship's Valley. This babe was not so pretty as ours, you know — or, rather, I know, or guess, or surmise.

Part of the way, I rode on the outside with brother George, and got thereby a tooth-ache which still troubles me, but camphor and cotton will probably soon effect a cure. — It was a very pleasant and refreshing ride, notwithstanding.

Tell bro. Henry I have just seen William Chace, who says he will write to Henry to-morrow.

Bro. George wishes to freight a part of this letter with love to Catharine and Anna in particular, and all the rest of the household in general.

In a few minutes, I shall walk up to sister Charlotte's with bro. G. to deliver my package of letters, and to ask for, and to give, information respecting family concerns.

Wm. Chace will go on to New-York with me to-morrow afternoon. We shall go in the Benj. Franklin.

Bro. Henry must be as merry as a bird, and he will then continue to grow fresh and blooming as the spring.

I have just called to see the Botanical Doctor,[2] and told him of my catarrhal complaint in the head and nose. He said to me, confidently, as if he was sure of effecting a cure, — "Call to-morrow, and I will give you something that will do you good." So, if all be well, I shall call to-morrow as directed — having more willingness to try a new medicine, than faith in its efficacy. Still, it may do me "good," as predicted by this vender of Nature's nostrums. It certainly will not, if I do not try it.

Many kisses upon the lips and cheeks of the peerless little George, and the beautiful little Anna, may be imprinted daily, and charged to my account.

Love, the kindest, tenderest, most abundant love to all the dear family. May Heaven bless and preserve you all!

In great haste, but with the strongest affection for you, my love, and hoping to hear from you or Henry, or both, at New-York, I remain,

Yours, ever,

Wm. Lloyd Garrison.

ALS: Garrison Papers, Boston Public Library.

1. "Mewling and puking in the nurse's arms"; Shakespeare, *As You Like It,* II, viii.

2. A Dr. M'Intyre, apparently of Providence. See letter 25, to Helen, May 6, 1836.

25

TO HELEN E. GARRISON

Providence, May 6, 1836.

My dear Helen:

I expected, yesterday, to be in New-York instead of Providence this morning, but have concluded to remain here until Monday afternoon at the urgency of the anti-slavery friends, and for two or three other reasons: — 1st. Because, on Monday, all abolitionists will, by agreement with the Captain of the steamboat President, be carried to New-York for $3 instead of $5 the usual fare: this is done to secure patronage, in opposition to the rival boat, the Massachusetts. 2d. Because by this delay, I hope to receive my bundle of newspapers from Boston, (having written to friend Knapp to send them to me this afternoon,) and shall thus be able to examine them, and select matter for the next paper. 3d. Because I shall also be able to write some editorial articles, and thus supply friend K. till my return. It is true, by stopping till Monday afternoon, we are not sure of arriving in New-York in season for the great meeting on Tuesday forenoon;[1] but, unless an accident should happen, or a storm prevail, there is little doubt of a speedy passage. — The President has just returned from N. York, having broken a shaft on the passage. Whether this will detain her on Monday, is not yet known — but we can go in the Massachusetts, if necessary. I should rejoice, on some accounts, to be in N. Y. to-morrow (Sabbath) and on Monday, because some of our abolition brethren will doubtless perform some public exercises on those days: indeed, a preliminary meeting of delegates is to be held on Monday afternoon.[2] But, on the whole, I am reconciled to tarrying here, for the sake of the paper. Ask bro. H.[3] if I have acted wisely? George decides in the affirmative.

Judge of my surprise, on going down to bro. George's shop on Friday morning, to find a letter from my friend Knapp addressed to him, inquiring after a runaway editor, i.e. myself, stating that he, the said Knapp, had not received a syllable of intelligence from me, the said runaway editor, since I left Boston — and wishing to know whether bro. G. could give him any information of my movements!! — It seems, therefore, that my two packages had miscarried, with all my editorials, selections, &c. No wonder friend Knapp felt uneasy, and surmised that we were ill. I immediately wrote to him from this place, regretting the accident, and informing him of my health and safety. N. B. I have just received the Liberator of to-day, and am much relieved to perceive, by the editorial articles, that my last package has been received, but the one sent week before last is probably lost irrecoverably. This I regret, because in the last package, was a long and somewhat important editorial article about Arkansas, with quotations from Harrison Gray Otis's speech in the U. S. Senate on the Missouri question, and also from his speech in Faneuil Hall,[4] which you will remember. I gave it to Barnes, the Worcester driver; and if bro. Henry should happen to see him, he may inquire about it.

I have not seen sister Charlotte since Thursday evening. Her husband was absent to New-York, as usual. She was hoarse with a cold. Little Sarah had had the measles, but was on the recovery. Charlotte apprehends that little Anna may have taken them from her, as she clasped her arms about Sarah's neck, and kissed her, when Sarah was ill, before it was known what ailed her. If Anna should be taken sick, you will of course endeavor to guard little George — although, as the measles this season are not of a malignant type, Charlotte thinks he might have them with comparative safety.

The Bank robber has been caught in New-York, and a hundred and sixty-eight thousand dollars in bills recovered. His accomplice made out to escape in one of the New York packets for Liverpool, with $10,000 in gold. The one who was arrested lost the packet by about 30 minutes only, and offered to give $1000 to any one who would put him on board of the vessel, but failed in succeeding. The Bank compromised with him, and for the sake of getting the money promised to let him go free. He has, however, been arrested again, and is now in prison, on a charge of stealing 25,000,000 dollars from one of the rail-cars between Providence and Boston some time ago. It is also supposed that he was the villain who stole the money at the door of the Providence bank, belonging to the bank in Thompson.[5]

Bro. George has put in his claim (and so have several others) for the $10,000 reward, or a portion of it, as he is confident that he gave the first information respecting the thief to the Bank Directors; and, by the terms of their advertisement, you will perceive that the reward was offered to any one who would give any information that should lead to the detection of the robber. Bro. G., however, does not really expect to recover a cent. There will probably be a law-suit about the matter.

Dr. M'Intyre, the Botanical doctor, has been prescribing for my nose, with some little success, but not much; and I have not faith enough to believe that he will do it any permanent good. He applies to it something in the shape of a jelly, and very fragrant. I shall let him try repeatedly till Monday.

It is raining somewhat violently this afternoon, but the shower is quite refreshing to man and beast.

There is a fair prospect of your having colored help secured in a few days.

I believe they are all well at Mr. Chace's. William went to N. York yesterday afternoon,

As I shall arrive so late at New-York, you must not hope to receive a letter from me.

Time goes far more slowly when I am absent from you, and I shall be truly glad when the time for my return shall be fully consummated.

In the mean time, — remembering me with all due affection and respect to father, mother, and every member of the household, — and sending you many kisses for my dear babe and yourself, I remain, with all fidelity and love,

Yours, ever,

Wm. Lloyd Garrison.

ALS: Garrison Papers, Boston Public Library. The date of this letter, written on Saturday, should have read "May 7." The "6" is crossed out, apparently by a later hand other than Garrison's, and "7" inserted above it.

1. Garrison is referring to the third anniversary meeting of the American Anti-Slavery Society, scheduled for Tuesday, May 10, at 10 a.m. in New York City.

2. This was to take place at 4 o'clock, in the office of the American Anti-Slavery Society, at No. 144 Nassau Street in Manhattan (*The Liberator*, May 7, 1836).

3. Henry E. Benson.

4. The speech in Faneuil Hall was delivered on Friday afternoon, August 21, 1835, at the meeting called by many of the leading citizens of Boston to condemn the Abolitionists. See Garrison's letter to Otis, September 5, 1835 (*Letters*, I).

Harry Gray Otis (1765-1848), Federalist political figure, represented Massachusetts in the Congress from 1797 to 1801, and in the Senate from 1817 to 1822. During the intervening years he was speaker of the Massachusetts legislature from 1803 to 1805 and president of the senate from 1805 to 1806 and from 1808 to 1811. He also participated in the Hartford Convention in 1814. (*DUSH.*)

5. On the weekend of April 16 and 17, 1836, the vault of the Merchants' Bank in Providence was robbed of approximately $180,000 in bills and gold sovereigns. The bank offered a reward of $10,000 for information leading to the capture of the thief. The abrupt departure from Providence of a carpenter named James Bell, alias Laidley, aroused suspicion among his neighbors. The police traced him to New York, where they located him through information provided by a porter who had helped Bell with his baggage. He was arrested but not prosecuted for robbing the bank because the money could not be recovered without his cooperation. However, when it was learned that he had also robbed the Boston Railroad of $24,000 (Garrison's figure of $25,000,000 is obviously an error), he was arrested and jailed (Boston *Daily Advertiser*, April 19, 20, and May 9, 1836).

---

2 6

TO HELEN E. GARRISON

New-York, May 10, 1836.

My very dear Wife:

This is Tuesday morning. I have just arrived from Providence, in company with about 200 persons, mostly delegates to the various anniversary meetings, and apparently a large majority abolitionists. Indeed, not one on board ventured to say one word in opposition to our blessed anti-slavery cause, although we knew that there were some on board, hostile to it. But our opponents are very cowardly, except they are sure that they have present with them an overwhelming majority on their side: then, indeed, they are as valiant as Hercules. Our huge, and good-humored, and kind-hearted, and worthy friend William Ladd [1] was with us, and in the course of the afternoon gave the passengers a lecture upon Peace. It was well received, but it was rather too rambling, perhaps too funny, to produce a serious impression. Lucius Manlius Sargent, the great temperance champion of Boston, author of "My Mother's Gold Ring," [2] was also in the boat. We did think of having a Temperance and an Anti-Slavery lecture delivered; but the noise of the machinery made it exceedingly difficult to hear even the loud voice of Mr. Ladd, and the project was abandoned. However, there was a good deal of discussion on various topics — such as peace, temperance, anti-slavery, the Sabbath, and even baptism. Rev. Mr. Wright [3] battled side by side with me, and we vanquished, or at least silenced all opponents, in despite of our extreme ultraism: of course, I allude to our good brother Wright of Boston. By the way, he wants to see our dear babe exceedingly, as well as its mother, and all of us together, in Boston. And, again, *en passant*, our friend Ladd has abandoned the American Union,[3a] and become a member of our Society. He says the peace men among abolitionists are worth all other peace men (the Friends excepted) in the land. He inquired very particularly after father's health, and that of all the household.

Rev. Thomas Williams was also with us, in company with all his eccentricities.[4] He was very zealous for the observance of the Sabbath, and I believe thought Christians ought to observe the seventh, instead of the first day of the week.

Among other fanatics, we had Ray Potter,[5] John Prentice,[6] and —— but it is needless to extend a long list. Bro. May was *not* with us, but went to New-York on Friday last, so report goes. I have had no time to make inquiries after him yet.

Theodore D. Weld will not be here. I am told that Gerrit Smith will be one of our speakers to-day. May he go straight forward, and then success to him! N. B. He has just given $3000 to the Oneida Institute [7] — a generous deed.

I am now at the hospitable mansion of my estimable friend Dr. Cox.[8] Within a few days, his lady has presented him with a fine boy, and both mother and child are doing well. The Dr. says, jocosely, that his children are multiplying too fast for him to write and dedicate Sonnets to each one of them. Beriah Green is also here, though I have not yet seen him.[9]

We had as quiet and beautiful passage from Providence, as the most fastidious could desire. I do not know that there was a single lady or gentleman who was at all sea-sick. Miss Buffum,[10] of Fall River, was among the females.

☞ I wish brother Henry to attend to the following matter instantly, provided his health will admit. I ought to have spoken to him about it on my last return from Boston. Friend Knapp wishes him to send on an order for a gold watch and musical box, to be delivered to him, now in the hands of a colored man — K. having purchased them, and being willing to secure Henry and the colored man in the sums that are due them. The colored man (I forget his name) says he will readily give them to Mr. Knapp, as soon as Henry says the word, i.e. by a written order. I will explain the whole matter satisfactorily to bro. Henry on my return. Knapp wishes to hear from him on the subject without delay.

The color of my nose is somewhat improved, but the nose itself is still sore internally, and cakes as usual. The botanical man thinks he can cure it.

I am all anxiety to hear from you or Henry, and shall look for a letter on Thursday or Friday. My heart yearns powerfully to see you and the dear babe, and to enjoy the sweets of domestic quietude, far from the busy haunts of men. How much I love you, I need not say; and how much I delight in the pure and peaceful society of Friendship's Vale, you well know.

There is no prospect of a breath of disturbance at our meeting to-day. The city is perfectly quiet, and the Courier & Enquirer is dumb.[11] May the great Jehovah guide, govern, and protect us all, and give us the victory over his enemies.

Yours, doatingly,

Wm. Lloyd Garrison.

ALS: Garrison Papers, Boston Public Library.

1. William Ladd (1778–1841), of New Hampshire and Maine, prominent peace advocate, a founder and president for many years of the American Peace Society. See Garrison's letter to Samuel J. May, February 14, 1831 (*Letters* I; *Life*, I, 113).

2. "My Mother's Gold Ring," first published about 1833 (the 110th edition appeared in 1836, published by William S. Damrell in Boston) was a temperance tale depicting the evils of drink. Lucius Manlius Sargent (1786–1867), of Boston and West Roxbury, was an author who was also active in philanthropic and temperance work. His published work, consisting of poetry and prose, included *Hubert and Helen, and other Verses* (1812), *Three Temperance Tales*, which passed through 130 editions (1848), and *The Irrepressible Conflict* (1861). He was also a frequent contributor to the Boston *Transcript*, under the pen-name "Sigma." In the 1850's Garrison became engaged in controversy with him through the pages of the *Transcript*. (*ACAB*; Garrison's letters to the Boston *Transcript* of May 17 and 31, 1850, printed in *The Liberator*, May 24 and 31, 1850, and of August 13 and September 8, 1857, printed in *The Liberator*, August 21 and September 11, 1857.)

3. Henry C. Wright.

3a. See note 6, letter 16, to George W. Benson, March 15, 1836.

4. The Reverend Thomas Williams (1779–1876) was a Congregational minister who resigned as minister of the Pacific Congregational Church of Providence, Rhode Island, in 1823. From that year until 1843, he preached variously in Attleboro and Hebronville, Massachusetts, Barrington, Rhode Island, Hartford, Connecticut, and East Greenwich, Rhode Island. (*Biographical Cyclopedia of Representative Men of Rhode Island*, Providence, 1881, p. 192.)

5. The Reverend Ray Potter (b. Cranston, Rhode Island, June 22, 1795; d. Pawtucket, Rhode Island, March 1, 1858) was a minister and elder of the Free-Will Baptists of Pawtucket, Rhode Island. He was a member of the Rhode Island delegation at the founding convention of the American Anti-Slavery Society in December 1833 and one of Garrison's staunch defenders thereafter. In the early months of 1837 he was involved in a scandal, in which he confessed to having had sexual relations with a member of his congregation who had become pregnant. He resigned as minister and was driven out of Pawtucket by a mob. On February 6, 1837, the Pawtucket Anti-Slavery Society, of which he was an active member, condemned his act and excluded him from the society (*The Liberator*, February 25, 1837). In succeeding years, he conducted various manufacturing activities: the manufacture of lamp-black, of glazing paper for box manufacturing, and, finally, of cardboard by machine. He began the latter in 1844 and, after prospering, sold his business in 1858. (The Reverend Massena Goodrich, *Historical Sketch of the Town of Pawtucket*, Pawtucket, 1876, pp. 105–106.)

6. John Prentice (c. 1790–1867), of Rhode Island, was a member of the Rhode Island delegation to the founding convention of the American Anti-Slavery Society in 1833. He was a merchant tailor and Congregational preacher. He was converted to Swedenborgianism in 1835 and joined the New Church in Bridgewater, Massachusetts, in 1836. (William R. Staples, *Annals of the Town of Providence*, Providence, 1843, Appendix, p. 636.)

7. Gilbert H. Barnes and Dwight L. Dumond, in the *Weld-Grimké Letters* (I, 17n), describe the Oneida Institute in New York:

"Oneida Institute's distinguishing characteristic was the manual labor system. Its establishment had been the outcome of the experience of one of its founders, George W. Gale. After his retirement from the active ministry in 1823, Gale had been sought out by several young men who had been converted in Finney's revivals and who wished to be prepared for the ministry. Between lessons in theology, Gale set them to work on his farm. The combination of agricultural labor and theological study produced such happy results that Gale, in 1827, founded a school on the same system. A farmer was hired to supervise the students' labors, and each student contributed three and a half hours a day to the farm. . . ."

8. Dr. Abraham Liddon Cox (1799–1864), a successful New York physician, a founder of the American Anti-Slavery Society and a member of its executive committee. His fifth child, Abraham Liddon, was born on April 30, 1836. (The Reverend Henry Miller Cox, *The Cox Family in America*, New York, 1912, pp. 92–93; *Life*, I, 398, 401–402, 407, 413, 415, 483.)

9. Beriah Green (1795–1874) was professor of sacred literature at Western Reserve College from 1830 to 1833, when he accepted the presidency of Oneida Institute. He was a delegate in 1833 to the founding convention of the American Anti-Slavery Society and was the convention's president (Ruchames, *The Abolitionists*, p. 35).

10. *Right and Wrong in Boston, Annual Report of the Boston Female Anti-Slavery Society, with a Sketch of the Obstacles Thrown in the Way of Emancipation by Certain Clerical Abolitionists and Advocates for the Subjection of Women in 1837* (Boston, 1837), p. 89, lists Miss Sarah G. Buffum as secretary of the Fall River Women's Anti-Slavery Society. She was a friend of the Grimké sisters. See note 3, letter 149, to Helen Garrison, May 5, 1839.

11. The New York *Courier and Enquirer*, aside from the *National Intelligencer* at Washington, was the leading newspaper of the Whig party. It was hostile to

antislavery agitation and probably helped incite the mobbings of antislavery men in 1834. James Watson Webb (1802–1884) was its editor from 1827 to 1861, when it merged with the New York *World*. (Frank Luther Mott, *American Journalism*, New York, 1950, pp. 260–261.)

27

TO ISAAC KNAPP

NEW YORK, May 11, 1836.

MY DEAR KNAPP:

On Monday last, at 12 o'clock, M. I left Providence in the Benjamin Franklin for this city, in company with upwards of one hundred and fifty persons, a large majority of whom were wending their way to the various anniversary meetings of the present week. — Among the number were our benevolent and pacific friend WM. LADD of Minot, Me. and LUCIUS M. SARGENT, the active, able and distinguished advocate of temperance. In the course of the afternoon, (Capt. Bunker cheerfully consenting to the arrangement,) Mr. LADD addressed the passengers at some length on the subject of peace, at their request, and apparently to their edification, although the address was somewhat rambling, and contained more of anecdote than close argumentation. At the close, the Rev. Mr. TRASK of Framingham,[1] called upon Mr. LADD for a more distinct and definite exposition of peace principles. He wished to know, whether the lecturer meant to enforce the doctrine, that all wars, whether offensive or defensive, were sinful, and whether he (Mr. L.) was ready to 'beard the lion in his den,'[2] i.e. to denounce the revolutionary war as unwarranted by the gospel of Christ? Mr. Trask, I believe, is of the non-resistance party, but made the inquiries for the purpose of having the company enlightened upon certain specific points. Before Mr. LADD could reply, a Mr. DUMONT[3] (who, I was told, preaches in Newport, that most defiled and obdurate town in New England, so far as slavery and the slave trade are concerned,) rose with some trepidation, and besought Mr. L. not to agitate the question of non-resistance, because, forsooth, he had been very agreeably entertained, every thing was now harmonious and pleasant, and to say any thing upon the point alluded to would probably serve to create bitter feelings and considerable division! How quickly such a man reveals his character! Although I know nothing more of Mr. D., yet I venture to surmise that he is an anti-abolitionist, an anti-moral reformer, and an anti-temperance man, in the true sense of these words — that is to say, that he is not for proscribing the use of wine; that he *is* for proscribing the persecuted

M'Dowall,[4] and the Boston Illuminator,[5] and the New York Advocate of Moral Reform; [6] and that he is opposed to the immediate abolition of slavery. Further, I *guess* he is not opposed to defensive war, or, in other words, to having blow for blow, and injury for injury, returned in a national capacity. Perhaps I am altogether in error: if so, as soon as I discover my error, it shall be corrected. — Another gentleman, sitting by his side, agreed with him precisely, but said, as for himself, he was willing to have a discussion, yet he could not agree to the doctrine of non-resistance, and would prefer to hear no debate upon it! Mr. LADD, in reply, said he did not wish to take away any of the laurels which adorned the brows of our revolutionary fathers; but he was free to confess, that, while he deemed them to have been most unjustly oppressed by the mother country, he could not reconcile their warlike measures with the pacific principles of the gospel of Christ. Having thus 'bearded the lion in his den,' he trusted he should be as well protected as was Daniel of old. Rev. THOS. WILLIAMS remarked, that Mr. LADD could not easily blight any of the laurels to which he had referred, inasmuch as they had withered long ago.

A temperance and anti-slavery discourse would have been given, had it not been that, owing to the number of passengers it was necessary, at an early hour in the evening, to prepare extra berths in the cabin.

We arrived at an early hour in the morning, after a very quiet and pleasant passage.

At 10 o'clock, our anti-slavery meeting convened in the spacious and beautiful meeting-house, corner of Thompson and Houston-streets. Not less than two thousand persons were present, — a most noble, most attentive, and most harmonious assembly, — no one molesting or attempting to make afraid. The speakers on this interesting occasion were Judge Jay,[7] Rev. Mr. Galusha,[8] Rev. Mr. Pomeroy,[9] and Gerrit Smith, Esq. Their speeches made a deep and solemn impression upon the listening throng, and will be read with admiration and profit throughout the land. But I am so occupied, that I have not time to make any suitable comments upon the proceedings. Brothers May, Wright and Southard [10] herewith send you a few lines each, giving some account of the meeting; and I send you also several slips from the office of the Evangelist, from which you may quote as fully as your limits will allow.

Yesterday, the Society voted to raise the sum of FIFTY THOUSAND DOLLARS for the expenditures of the current year; but this morning they have resolved to double the sum — and therefore it stands at

$100,000!

Upwards of $16,000 were subscribed this morning in the course of an hour, exclusive of what is to be given by our anti-slavery friends in this city. Gerrit Smith gave $2000; his gifts to the cause, through the medium of the N. Y. State Society, and in other ways, are already very munificent. On personal acquaintance, I am delighted with him as a man and a christian — but more next week.

Last evening, the Colonization Society held their meeting at the Chatham Street Chapel, to a crowded audience, made up of a very large number of our friends. The speeches were as incoherent, and weak, and wicked, and blasphemous, as the spirit of brutality and impiety could concoct.[11]

In great haste,

Your affectionate friend,
WM. LLOYD GARRISON.

Printed in the *Liberator*, May 14, 1836. As the result of a misprint, the letter as it appeared in *The Liberator* was erroneously dated 1835.

1. The Reverend George Trask (1798–1875), of Framingham, Massachusetts, was a prominent reform and peace advocate who opposed slavery and the use of tobacco as well as the participation of women in the antislavery movement. (*Life*, II, 220, 222, 277n; *Weld-Grimké Letters*, II, 686.)

2. From *Marmion*, by Sir Walter Scott.

3. The Reverend Dr. Henry A. Dumont, born in New York near the end of the eighteenth century, a graduate of Columbia College in the class of 1812 and of the Theological Department of Rutgers College in 1826, first served as pastor of a church in Albany, New York, and then became pastor of the United Congregational Church in Newport, Rhode Island, in 1833. He remained until December 1840, when he accepted a call from the Presbyterian Church in Morristown, New Jersey. He ministered there until 1845, when he returned to Newport, where he spent the remainder of his life. He was especially active on the school committee. He died in 1865. (The Reverend R. W. Wallace, *Congregationalism in Newport*, Newport, 1896, pp. 64–66.)

4. John Robert M'Dowall (b. Fredericksburgh, Upper Canada, September 20, 1801; d. 1836), a friend of Arthur Tappan, William Goodell, and Theodore S. Wright, was a Presbyterian minister in New York City who fought prostitution with such vigor that he was suspended by the presbytery on charges of "unministerial and unchristian conduct, slander and misrepresentation." Ordained in 1832, after studying at Amherst College, Union College, and Princeton, he became interested in helping prostitutes in 1829. He helped to establish shelters for reformed prostitutes, and in January 1833 he began to issue *M'Dowall's Journal*, to publicize the conditions he was seeking to combat and to secure help for his efforts. He later became involved in a conflict with the Female Benevolent Society of New York, with whom he had earlier cooperated. Apparently, he suffered much persecution for his efforts. (Robert M'Dowall, *Memoir and Select Remains of the Late Rev. John R. M'Dowall, The Martyr of the Seventh Commandment in the Nineteenth Century*, New York, 1838, *passim*.)

5. The Boston *Illuminator* was published from September 23, 1835, to July 12, 1837.

6. The New York *Advocate of Moral Reform*, established in 1835, was the organ of the Female Moral Reform Society of New York City. M'Dowall helped to circulate it. It superseded *M'Dowall's Journal*. Beginning with the thirteenth issue, it was published as the *Advocate and Family Guardian* by the American Female Guardian Society. It ceased publication in 1841 (*Union List of Serials*).

7. William Jay (1789–1858) was a son of John Jay, the first chief justice of the United States Supreme Court, and an early abolitionist. William Jay was a

member of the American Anti-Slavery Society and, for many years, part of its executive committee. Jay's writings played an important part in awakening the public conscience to the evils of slavery. His volume, *An Inquiry into the Character and Tendency of the American Colonization, and American Anti-Slavery Societies*, was published by the American Anti-Slavery Society in New York in 1835 and went through ten editions. With the division in abolitionist ranks in 1840, Jay left the American Anti-Slavery Society with the anti-Garrisonians, and helped form the American and Foreign Anti-Slavery Society (Ruchames, *The Abolitionists*, p. 96).

8. The Reverend Elon Galusha (d. 1855) was born in Shaftesbury, Vermont, son of a governor of that state, Jonas Galusha. He abandoned the study of law for the Baptist ministry and became a successful preacher in that denomination (Isaac Wellcome, *History of the Second Advent Message*, Yarmouth, Me., 1874, p. 288). After occupying pulpits in Whitesborough and Utica, New York, he moved to Rochester, remaining there from 1834 to 1837 as first pastor of the Second Baptist Church. His was the first church in Rochester to admit Negroes to its regular pews (Blake McKelvey, *Rochester, the Water-Power City, 1812–1854*, Cambridge, 1945, p. 279; William F. Peck, *History of Rochester and Monroe County, N. Y.*, New York, 1908, p. 311). He was minister of the Baptist Church in Perry, New York, from 1837 to 1841. Under his ministry, his congregation decided that they could have no fellowship with slaveholders and their apologists (Frank D. Roberts and Carl G. Clarke, *History of the Town of Perry, N. Y.*, Perry, 1915, p. 152). Galusha was a delegate of the National Baptist Anti-Slavery Convention, organized in New York on April 28–30, 1840, to the World's Anti-Slavery Convention. He was also a delegate of the American and Foreign Anti-Slavery Society to the World's Convention (*Life*, II, 356n).

9. Nathaniel Southard, writing as a member of the Massachusetts delegation at the convention, reported in *The Liberator* (May 14, 1836) that "Rev. Mr. Pomeroy of Bangor [Maine], in a very animated and impressive manner, offered some of the reasons why abolitionists do not 'give up' at the request of our opponents." On May 28, 1836, *The Liberator* printed an address that S. L. Pomeroy had delivered at the convention. Swan L. Pomeroy (b. Warwick, Massachusetts, 1799; d. 1869), a graduate of Brown University in 1820, was minister of the First Congregational Church in Bangor, Maine, from 1825 to 1848, when he was elected secretary of the American Board of Commissioners for Foreign Missions. (Albert A. Pomeroy, *History and Genealogy of the Pomeroy Family*, Toledo, Ohio, 1912, p. 422; *History of Penobscot County, Maine*, Cleveland, 1882, pp. 719–720.)

10. The Reverend Nathaniel Southard, a native of Lyme, New Hampshire, came to Boston in 1830 and soon thereafter immersed himself in various reform movements, including temperance, education, and abolition. He joined the New England Anti-Slavery Society not long after its founding and was a member of the Massachusetts delegation at the founding convention of the American Anti-Slavery Society in December 1833. He was editor of *The Midnight Cry*, an Adventist daily newspaper which later became a weekly, in New York from 1842 to 1845, when he returned to New Hampshire because of failing health. He occupied the pulpit of the Second Advent Church in Providence, Rhode Island, but resigned in 1850 because of a recurrence of ill health. He died on September 2, 1852. (Wellcome, *History of the Second Advent Message*, p. 272.)

11. A report on the proceedings of the Colonization Society meeting appeared in *The Liberator* (May 14, 1836) in a letter dated May 10, 1836, and signed "W."

2 8

TO HELEN E. GARRISON

[Providence, May 21, 1836.]

My loving [Wife:]

[. . . fa]natic! I trust y[ou . . .] [Friendship's] Vale, though one of [. . .] mother's nest, and [. . .]

We had a shower of rain last night, (it was more refreshing than copious,) and Nature to-day appears in her best attire. This, you know, is my favorite season of the year, and much did I admire (not the ride itself, but) the beautiful appearance of the fields, and orchards, and forests, between Brooklyn and Providence. If autumn's ripened fruit is better for the palate, spring's early blossoms are far more beautiful to the eye. There is nothing in the world more lovely than innocence; and what of earthly things is more innocent than Spring, with her buds, and blossoms, and flowers? — Alas! that I cannot fully enjoy the rich perfume of her breath, my catarrh in the head almost entirely destroying the sense of smell! But even our losses are sometimes gainful. Miss Martineau,[1] by being deaf, is not troubled with the gabble of voluble tongues; still, it is unquestionably better to hear than to be deaf. Cousin Eunice[2] is blind, and thereby is never called to contemplate many disagreeable scenes; still, it is better to see than to be blind. I cannot smell as acutely as formerly, and am therefore not troubled by the stench of a crowded city; still, it is better to smell than to have obstructed nostrils. Hence, I am still trying the prescriptions of Dr. Bolus,[3] and hope almost against hope to effect a cure. He has given me a bottle of medicine to carry to Boston — a large table spoon-full to be taken in the morning, another at noon, and a third at night. This is to benefit my blood. He has also given me a white powder to take in pinches as snuff, which causes much sneezing, and a copious discharge of the mucous from the head. I am also, every other night, to snuffle up a red liquid, to cleanse my head — (query, will it improve the brain?) My nose, externally, appears uncommonly respectable, and no longer libels my cold water habits.

[. . .]ing, just before [. . .]'s that evening, [. . .] it, I should have [. . .]as there; and so [w]as [. . .]mont, and several other abolitio[nists . . .] and [so] conversation was very free and spirited, and mostly confined to the question of slavery, Angelina[4] expressing her sentiments with all boldness and fidelity. Such men as Wm. Jenkins[5] were handled without mittens, yet without any particular reference.

After leaving my things at J. E. Brown's,[6] I went up to see sister

Charlotte and brother Henry, as in duty bound. — The latter seemed to be improving visibly, both in health and spirits. Our fears, in regard to the effect of his ride from Brooklyn, were groundless. He told me that he felt better the next day than he had done for many weeks previous.

Yesterday morning,[7] I had an hour's interview with A. E. Grimké,[8] at Wm. Jenkins's, brother Henry accompanying me. Of course, it was an hour that went pleasantly, profitably, rapidly. She appeared to be extremely glad to see me, and regretted that she could not go to Boston, to be present at our Convention.[9] She was just going to take a morning ride, but gave it up, and insisted upon my tarrying for conversation. I did not like to detain her long, as she was to embark for New-York at 12 o'clock, and therefore many things were not said which I wanted to say. She told me that she had been trying to induce Wm. Jenkins to manufacture free cotton exclusively! He said he could not get it. I presume he is not willing to make any efforts to get it. He just came into the room a moment, gave me his hand with a deliberate air and an equivocal smile, and then left us together. Soon after, his eldest son made his appearance, and strutted into the room as stiffly and loftily as a Lord Mayor with his official robes upon his precious carcass — not deigning to speak to Henry or myself, or mingling at all in the conversation. Deliver us from a Quaker coxcomb!

[. . .] and had a [. . .] went to see [. . .] mansion, and [. . . con]-versation. His health [. . .] d his m[ind . . .] clear and vigorous. He [10] is watching [. . .] of the Texian affairs with great interest. He inquired after you and the babe, and father, and all the household.

On leaving him, we rode down to his bridge, made a round circuit by the late Mr. Ives's [11] house, and from thence went to Pleasant Valley, to the mutual pleasure of the visiters and the visited. Friend Chace's immense family is well, without a single exception. Last evening, I spent some pleasant hours with them, leaving Henry to tarry all night. He has sent me a note this morning, in which he says, "I am in fine health and spirits." I believe he is to return this afternoon into the city. How thankful, how joyful ough[t] we to be at the prospect of his recovery!

Bros. Stanton and Murray [12] gave anti-s[lavery ad]dresses at Pawtucket last evening, conjointly. The former is to give a lecture this evening in the city, in the High-street meeting-house, and to-morrow evening another in Pawtucket.

I am sorry to learn that Beriah Green has gone back to Whitesboro', and cannot attend our Convention. We expect Stuart [13] in Boston on Tuesday, and Stanton [14] on Monday forenoon.

I still feel the effects of my New-York cold; and do not expect to be much more than the fifth wheel to a coach at the Convention. There is not much probability that I shall go to Concord. I find that I have lost four pounds of flesh within a fortnight, and nine pounds within a few months. Now, you will say with all anxiety, "Be extremely careful of your health!" I will, rely upon it. Dr. McIntyre says that the best remedy for my complaint would be to hoe potatoes, and cut loose from all exciting subjects for a time. He says my pursuit is such as unavoidably causes [. . .] much heat [. . .] fluids, and [. . .]rh. [. . .] whence [. . .] of next week. If you have, [. . .] from you soon; and say not that you have nothing worth communicating. It is very comforting to be assured of your health.

With great abundance of love to all the family, and sending innumerable kisses to you and the babe, I remain,

Lovingly yours, Wm. Lloyd Garrison.

ALS: Garrison Papers, Boston Public Library. The top and corner of the letter with the original date are torn off. A notation, probably by one of Garrison's sons, is penciled in the margin: "Providence, May 21, 1836."

1. Harriet Martineau, the British author.
2. See letter to Helen Benson, May 1, 1834 (*Letters*, I).
3. Dr. Bolus is otherwise unidentified.
4. Angelina Emily Grimké (1805–1879) and her sister Sarah (1792–1873) were members of a prominent South Carolina slaveholding family. Their father was a justice of the South Carolina Supreme Court. They became Quakers as the result of a visit to Philadelphia, renounced slavery, left the South for good and in 1835 joined the antislavery movement. In 1838, Angelina married Theodore Weld, the prominent antislavery leader. (Ruchames, *The Abolitionists*, p. 152.)
5. See letters to Helen dated March 8 and July 15, 1834 (*Letters*, I); William Jenkins was with the firm of Jenkins and Man, at 23 South Water Street. He lived at 199 Benefit Street in Providence (Providence *Directory*, 1836).
6. John E. Brown of Providence was a merchant, active in the antislavery movement, a member of the Richmond Street Congregational Church, and an especially good friend of the Reverend Amos Phelps (letters from John E. Brown to Amos Phelps, Phelps Papers, Boston Public Library). A John E. Brown is listed in the Providence *Directory* as the owner of a bookstore at 19 Market Street, and as a resident of 29 Broad Street.
7. Penciled note in margin: "Friday, May 20."
8. Angelina Emily Grimké.
9. The New England Anti-Slavery Convention, called for Tuesday, May 24, at 10 a.m. A preliminary meeting was to be held on Monday afternoon, May 23, at 4 o'clock, in the hall adjoining the antislavery office at 46 Washington Street.
10. Penciled note in margin: "(Moses Brown)." Moses Brown (1738–1836) was a Rhode Island manufacturer, philanthropist, reformer, and antislavery leader (Mack Thompson, *Moses Brown, Reluctant Reformer*, Chapel Hill, 1962). See Garrison's letter to *The Liberator*, September 13, 1832 (*Letters*, I).
11. Thomas Poynton Ives (1769–1835), a leading citizen of Providence, was a partner of Moses Brown in the internationally known firm, founded in 1797, which ultimately became the House of Brown, Benson and Ives. A man of strong ethical and religious principles, he was also a banker, a trustee of Brown University for forty-three years, and a force in the establishment of free public schools in Providence. In 1817 he was on a welcoming committee for President James Monroe's visit to the city. Ives was a protégé of George Benson, Garrison's father-in-law,

who, according to Garrison, raised him "from obscurity and indigence to mercantile renown and opulence." (*The Liberator*, December 17, 1836; *The Biographical Cyclopedia of Representative Men of Rhode Island*, Providence, 1881, p. 159.)

12. The Reverend Orson S. Murray (b. Orwell, Vermont, September 23, 1806; d. Fosters, Ohio, June 14, 1885) was a delegate to the founding convention of the American Anti-Slavery Society in 1833, editor of the *Vermont Telegraph*, and secretary of the Vermont Anti-Slavery Society. In 1836 he was living in Brandon, Vermont. See Garrison's letter to Oliver Johnson, December 20, 1863. (*Life*, I, 398, 450; II, 140, 370; IV, 87, 399.)

13. Charles Stuart.

14. Henry B. Stanton.

29

TO GEORGE THOMPSON

Boston, May 24, 1836.

My dear, courageous, faithful, indefatigable coadjutor:

If I have been disappointed in not hearing from you more frequently by letter, I am quite sure that you have not greatly marvelled at *my* long silence, knowing, as you well do, my habit of procrastination, and my growing and almost invincible repugnance to pen, ink and paper. However, this is no excuse, nor is it offered as an excuse, on my behalf; — and as for yourself, it is with joy and gratitude I acknowledge the receipt of your cheering letter of the 13th ultimo. Another has been received from you, of the same date, addressed to brother Henry. Copious extracts from both were read this morning to our New-England Convention, which thrilled and delighted a crowded and highly intelligent auditory. But more of this anon.

As I have not written to you since February 18th, (to my shame and confusion of face be the confession made,) with an immense amount of materials to make an epistle of some length and interest, I am nevertheless puzzled to know what to present to you. And, besides, I am at this juncture ill in body, and feeble in mind, and distracted with duties, and driven into a corner by the urgency of the occasion. Our mutual friend Spencer,[1] of Salem, will sail to-morrow or next day for England, and as I have just heard of his intention, you perceive how limited I am for time.

First of all, our hearts are gladdened beyond measure to learn how kindly, approvingly, enthusiastically, you have been received by a portion of the noblest men and women on the face of the globe. It has not been in the power of traducers here, nor of recreant delegates at home, to diminish the respect, or weaken the attachment of the friends of bleeding humanity for you, in the smallest degree. — No, —

blessed be God! though you have passed through a roaring furnace of affliction, even the *smell* of fire has not been found upon your garments, because a form like unto the Son of God was with you. See what it is to be valiant for the truth, to be steadfast in the truth, and to be victorious through the truth! See how much better it is to cling to principle in the darkest hour of adversity, than to go with human policy in the broad sunshine of worldly popularity!

Several numbers of the Glasgow Chronicle have been received, (the latest is April 22, containing your public announcement of the birth of G. T. Garrison, which makes me feel a little queerly,) and happy are all our abolition friends to read the reports of your eloquent lectures, and to observe the strict impartiality with which you mingle praise and blame in your remarks upon this country. As a nation, we scarcely deserve one ounce of praise, but rather an avalanche of wrath hurled from the throne of God to crush us into annihilation. Our corruption, our wickedness, our savage ferocity, are not yet fully made manifest. My heart is sick, and my hope of the salvation of this country flickering like a flame in the socket. But God reigns, and God is against the oppressor, and God shall have the victory, if the nation must first be emptied of its inhabitants — and this is my consolation. I do not despair of the power of truth, but I tremble lest that power shall be in judgment, and not in mercy. We can no more doubt that the truth will prevail, than that God is omnipotent; but *what* truth is to prevail is, in our case, extremely doubtful. It may be this, through repentance — "Your iniquities will I blot out, and your sins will I remember no more." [2] Or it may be this, through guilty stubbornness — "Then said the Lord unto me, Pray not for this people for their good. When they fast, I will not hear their cry; and when they offer burnt-offering and an oblation, I will not accept them: but I will consume them by the sword, and by the famine, and by the pestilence." [3] Already, the sword begins to devour; already, a terrible retribution is meted out to the inhabitants of a portion of the land. The numerous Indian tribes on our southern and western borders, having been robbed of their lands, and goaded to desperation by the cruel oppression of the whites, are up in arms, carrying death and desolation in their train, and not only defying but absolutely outgeneralling the U. S. troops. They have ravaged many plantations, killed many inhabitants, and emancipated a considerable number of slaves. Osceola,[4] their chief, is a warrior who may be considered the boldest, bravest, and most sagacious, since the days of king Philip of New-England.[5] In Georgia, Alabama and Florida, all is consternation among the whites. U. S. troops are mustering from all quarters to the field of strife. All belonging to Fort Independence, in this harbor, have been ordered to Georgia. — This war will cost much blood and treasure, petty as it may seem. It is thus slaveholders are bringing down vengeance upon their heads. — While I denounce war on all occasions, and under all circumstances, yet my sympathies are always on the side of the oppressed, and never with the oppressor. Heroic and dauntless as are the red men of the forest, they cannot long cope with the colossal power of this nation, and will probably be wholly exterminated in the course of a few years. But their blood will cry to heaven for redress. It covers our soil, and drenches the garments of the people.

Have you heard of a horrible transaction which has just taken place at St. Louis, Missouri? It seems an attempt was made to arrest two white persons for some misdemeanor, but a free colored person belonging to Pittsburg, Pa. interfering, they made their escape. He was immediately arrested, and as the officer was carrying him to prison, he asked what would be done with him? The reply was, that he would be sold as a slave into bondage. Upon this, he drew a knife, gave the officer a mortal stab, and badly wounded an assistant. As soon as he was secured in prison, the populace broke into his cell, dragged him out by moonlight to a tree to which they chained him, and then slowly and methodically roasted him alive, until he was consumed to ashes!! He bore his tortures with amazing fortitude, singing hymns, &c. No attempt was made to deliver him: he was burnt by common consent. Very little notice of this diabolical sacrifice has been taken in any of the newspapers. The victim was a colored man — "a nigger" — and why should any sympathy be excited, or horror expressed? "O for a lodge in some vast wilderness!" [6] "Shall I not visit for these things? saith the Lord. Shall not my soul be avenged on such a nation as this?" [7]

You will be glad to see our mutual and much esteemed friend Thomas Spencer in England. As he is to carry out with him a large quantity of anti-slavery documents, it will not be necessary, and, indeed, I have neither time nor room, to give you a detail of our anti-slavery proceedings for the last three months. Suffice it to say, the mob spirit seems to be almost wholly allayed, our labors are abundant, our victories over falsehood and prejudice very numerous, and societies are multiplying with unexampled rapidity. They number at this moment not less than SIX HUNDRED!! and you know something of the character of the men and women who compose them — the very salt of the earth — the chosen among mankind — the beloved of God. Notwithstanding the last year was the most appalling in the history of this country — notwithstanding scenes of riot were witnessed in every section of the land, and "lynch law" was superior to common law and the constitution — yet the average increase of new societies, *throughout the year*, was about one *daily*! We hope to do better this year.

Henry has not yet seen your letter. For the last two months, he has been at the borders of the grave in Brooklyn. He was first attacked with a dangerous fever (which settled in a cough upon his lungs,) and then seemed to be wasting in a gallopping consumption. Our fears and our grief were indescribable. I rejoice to add, that he is now apparently recovering, but will probably not be able again to occupy his station at the anti-slavery rooms. Mr. Knapp and myself feel inexpressibly thankful to you for having arranged matters so successfully with Joseph Phillips.[8] The books, as directed, shall be forwarded to him the first opportunity. Helen is quite ill at present, but our boy is in a fine condition. A multitude desires to be affectionately remembered to you. No room for names.

Yours, steadfastly,

Wm. Lloyd Garrison.

ALS: Garrison Papers, Boston Public Library.

1. Thomas Spencer was a leader of the Salem and Vicinity Anti-Slavery Society. He was a confectioner who had come from England in 1822 and settled in Salem. He was beloved there for a special candy that he introduced, called Gibraltars. He also lectured at the Lyceum on varied subjects. He returned to England many years later. (M. C. D. Silsbee, *A Half Century in Salem*, Boston and New York, 1887, pp. 113–115.)
2. A variation of Isaiah 43:25.
3. Jeremiah 14:11, 12.
4. Osceola (1804–1838), chief of the Seminole Indians, began the second Seminole War in 1836 as a result of the enslavement of his wife. He carried on the war for more than a year. He was captured in 1837 while negotiating a treaty under a flag of truce, and died in prison. (*DUSH.*)
5. King Philip (d. 1676), chief of the Wampanoag Indians, led the Indians in King Philip's War, 1675–1676, the most important Indian war in New England (*The Columbia Viking Desk Encyclopedia*, 1966, p. 1422).
6. William Cowper (1731–1800), *The Task*, Book II, "The Timepiece."
7. Jeremiah 5:9.
8. Joseph Phillips of London was a friend of Garrison who had helped him in his efforts against Elliot Cresson in England in 1833 (*Life*, I, 353, 365).

---

3 0

TO HELEN E. GARRISON

Boston, May 25, 1836.

My dear Helen:

In the midst of great confusion of mind, arising from seeing, and talking, and acting with a host of anti-slavery men and women from various parts of New-England, I seize a moment to reply to your affectionate and interesting letter, which was yesterday put into my hands, at noon, by a friend from Providence.

Of our Convention, I am prepared to speak in the most animating language. Thus far, its proceedings have been spirited and harmonious, and refreshing beyond measure. On Monday afternoon, as many of the delegates as had arrived in the city assembled in our Anti-Slavery Hall, for the transaction of business. On Tuesday morning, (yesterday,) the Convention was held in the Rev. Mr. Blagden's meeting-house in Salem-street,[1] at 10 o'clock. The spacious and beautiful house was crowded. Gen. Fessenden,[2] of Portland, was chosen President, and made a most excellent, though brief, introductory speech. From 400 to 500 delegates were in attendance, every State in New-England being represented; and such a body of men, ay, and women too, — for women had come from various quarters, — it is seldom are brought together on any occasion. They show, by their carriage and actions, that they constitute the moral *élite* of the land of the pilgrims. Mr. Hallett,[3] in his Daily Advocate, remarks, that the liberties of a nation cannot be otherwise than safe in the hands of such men and such women — a panegyric well bestowed, and of some value at this moment. We have had four great meetings, without the slightest disturbance, and many speakers, and many good, and some very thrilling speeches. Among the speakers have been Charles Stuart, George Bourne, Elizur Wright,[4] H. B. Stanton, Rev. T. S. Wright of New-York,[5] (our colored friend,) Rev. Mr. Wright of Boston,[6] Rev. Mr. Fitch of Hartford,[7] Rev. Mr. Root of Dover, Rev. Mr. Thurston of Maine,[8] Gen. Appleton,[9] S. J. May, Rev. Mr. Grosvenor,[10] C. C. Burleigh, Rev. Mr. Milligan of Vermont,[11] Rev. Messrs. Peckham [12] and Hill [13] of Haverhill, Rev. O. S. Murray of Vt. &c. &c. &c.

I have studiously shunned taking any part in the meetings, although earnestly entreated to speak, but wishing to stand in the back ground. You know my repugnance to speaking in public; and, happily, we have now so much talent enlisted on our side, that I am actually needed no more than a fifth wheel to a coach, that is, for speech-making. Besides, I am an old hack in the cause, and as a new broom sweeps clean, it is better to let some of our new converts have a chance. Stanton [14] has reflected great credit upon himself and his cause by his eloquent speeches; Burleigh [15] has attracted attention as usual, first, by his peculiar external appearance, and secondly, by an excellent speech; Mr. May has acquitted himself unusually well; and our colored brother Wright has won golden opinions [16] of all his listeners. The Convention has resolved to raise the sum of TEN THOUSAND DOLLARS during the present year, of which nearly EIGHT THOUSAND are already pledged! Our Boston Female Anti-Slavery Society has set a noble example of self-denial and liberality, having pledged itself, small and feeble and poor as it is, to raise One Thousand Dollars! O, Woman's heart, when properly affected, is large and full as the ocean — nay, the ocean has its limits, but her heart has none. Ah! how little is she appreciated in our world! But she is rising to the highest summit of human respect and excellence, and this is a struggle for her redemption. You will not suspect me of flattery, because I am your husband — and because I hope you are ready to testify, that my admiration is sincere.

The Convention will hold two more meetings to-morrow, and then adjourn. The New-Hampshire delegates are pressing me most earnestly to attend their meeting at Concord next week,[17] and perhaps I shall be compelled to go, but I really do not feel well enough to do so, though not positively sick, and mean to decline on this ground. Great will be the disappointment if I do not go very great.

I have just received a long and cheering letter from George Thompson,[18] which was yesterday read to the Convention, and produced a thrilling sensation. Mr. T. says that he is overwhelmed with kindnesses, and that his course in this country has been unequivocally approved. Dr. Cox has been compelled to hide his diminished head.[19] T. says, moreover, that our dear babe, with such a name as he has got, must really be a double dipped fanatic — GEORGE THOMPSON GARRISON!! He is soon to have another addition to his family. His little American boy is still living, but in feeble health. He has also written a letter to bro. Henry, in which he wishes to be kindly and gratefully remembered to all the household in Friendship's Valley. You will see these letters in the next Liberator.

Stanton, Bourne and Stuart are going to Newburyport to attend the annual meeting of the Essex County Society on Tuesday.[20] As that is my native place, I hope they will not be sparing of gospel thunder and lightning. From thence, they will go to Concord.

What arrangements I shall make relative to the Liberator, and my continuance here, I cannot tell now, as I have had no time to consult either friend Knapp or the Board on the subject. However, all desire me to remain here, and will hardly excuse my absence again. If you were in Boston with the dear babe, I should readily submit to their request — but I find separation to be very painful. It is the intention of the Board to raise my salary to $1200, provided we live in the city, so bro. May says. This will be a liberal support.

My nose looks outwardly very well, but is no better internally. I have not yet got rid of my New-York cold, though my hoarseness is measurably gone, and at night I cough a little. Otherwise, I am tolerably well. The weather has been very unpropitious for a few days past, especially to those who are affected, like myself, with a catarrhal complaint. I am extremely anxious to get back to Brooklyn, to be as quiet as possible for awhile, but do not expect to see you till the close of next week, and perhaps not till the week after. This will seem a long time to me and to you.

Mrs. May desires me to say, that she does not care about taking Mrs. Williams' daughter [21] on the condition you specify. She sends her love to you and the family, and hopes to see you soon. You can then compare your babes.

Say to sister Mary, that Effingham L. Capron and his lady are attending our Convention, and I have had several pleasant interviews with them.[22] They fully expect to see Mary and myself and wife and child, in the course of the summer, at their house. She is a lovely woman, and he a most excellent man.

I am stopping at Miss Parker's. This is certainly the paragon of boarding-houses. Every thing is as quiet and orderly as in the country. I am persuaded, no other place in the city would please us so well. But we may not be so lucky as to get in here in the fall.

Many are the inquiries after you and the sweet babe, but not so many as are my thoughts. These wing their way to you constantly. May we be sweetly resigned to the will of heaven, and be ready for every vicissitude and allotment of life! Press the boy to your bosom and kiss him often for his absent father's sake — and remember me in love to all the dear family — and believe me now, as hitherto,

Your faithful and loving husband,

Wm. Lloyd Garrison.

ALS: Garrison Papers, Boston Public Library.

1. The Reverend George Washington Blagden (b. Washington, D.C., October 3, 1802; d. New York City, December 17, 1884) graduated from Yale in 1823 and then studied for the ministry at the Andover Theological Seminary. He became pastor of the Brighton (Massachusetts) Congregational Church in 1827, and in 1830 was installed as minister of the Salem-Street church in Boston, where he remained until 1836. He married Miriam Phillips, the sister of Wendell Phillips, the abolitionist, in 1831. He was pastor of the Old South Church in Boston from 1836 to 1872, when he became pastor emeritus. He was orthodox in his theology and politics. He participated in the Massachusetts Constitutional Convention of 1853, and served as an Overseer of Harvard from 1854 to 1859. Regarding both slavery and the abolitionists, the Reverend Mr. Blagden's views were the opposite of those of his brother-in-law. In a sermon preached in 1847, Blagden denied that slavery was unchristian, affirmed that the institution was recognized in the Old and New Testaments, and suggested that the abolitionists had substituted passionate denunciation for patient and thoughtful study of slavery. Throughout his career he believed that the abolitionists lacked Christian charity. (The Reverend Charles A. Stoddard, *A Discourse Commemorative of the Rev. George Washington Blagden, D.D.*, delivered in the Old South Church, Boston, February 22, 1885, Boston, 1885, 32 pp.; see also letter 20 to Helen E. Garrison, April 16, 1836, note 8, and letter 93 to Lewis Tappan, September 13, 1837, note 4; Irving H. Bartlett, *Wendell Phillips, Brahmin Radical*, Boston, 1961, pp. 76, 97–98, 180.)

2. Samuel Fessenden (b. Fryeburg, Maine, July 16, 1784; d. March 13, 1869), a prominent lawyer and leader of the American Colonization Society in Maine,

first met Garrison in 1832 in Portland, Maine, where Garrison delivered an address. He was converted to immediate emancipation and in the spring of the following year presided at the formation of the Maine Anti-Slavery Society. (*Life*, I, 289, 299, III, 213.)

3. Benjamin Franklin Hallett (1797–1862), editor of the Boston *Daily Advocate*, "almost the only journal friendly to the abolitionists" (*Life*, II, 32n). A graduate of Brown University and a lawyer, he gained journalistic experience in Providence before coming to Boston, where he founded the Boston *Free Press and Advocate*, an anti-Masonic newspaper, in 1832. He was an influential Democratic politician for many years, later helping both Pierce and Buchanan obtain their nominations. He was a close friend of George Bancroft, the historian, with whom he worked on behalf of Democratic candidates during the early 1830's. On the last day of 1838, the *Advocate* merged with the Boston *Post*. Thereafter Hallett, while helping the *Post* editorially, devoted most of his efforts to his law practice (F. Lauristan Bullard, "The Press," in Albert P. Langtry, *Metropolitan Boston, A Modern History*, New York, 1929, pp. 549–551).

4. Elizur Wright, Jr. (1804–1885), a native of S. Canaan, Connecticut, but raised in Ohio, was professor of mathematics and natural philosophy at Western Reserve College in 1832, when Garrison's *Thoughts on African Colonization* appeared. He was deeply influenced by it and in 1833 resigned his position to become secretary of the New York City Anti-Slavery Society. He was one of the founders of the American Anti-Slavery Society and served as its domestic corresponding secretary until 1839. He resigned and edited the anti-Garrisonian *Massachusetts Abolitionist* in 1839. He then turned to insurance and contributed some pioneering studies in that field (*Life, passim; Weld-Grimké Letters*, I, 94–95n).

5. Theodore S. Wright (d. New York, March 25, 1847, in his fiftieth year), a prominent Presbyterian colored minister of New York City. According to Carter Woodson, he claimed Princeton Seminary as his alma mater and was the predecessor of Henry Highland Garnet, the prominent Negro preacher, at the Shiloh Presbyterian Church, also referred to as the First (Colored) Presbyterian Church. He was one of the two clergymen who offered prayers at the marriage of Angelina Grimké and Theodore Weld, on May 14, 1838, in Philadelphia. He was a member of the executive committee of the American Anti-Slavery Society for several years until 1840. In 1840, he was one of the seceders from the American Anti-Slavery Society and helped to form the anti-Garrisonian American and Foreign Anti-Slavery Society. His address was published in *The Liberator*, June 25, 1836. (*Life*, IV, 425; *Weld-Grimké Letters*, I, 211n; Carter G. Woodson, *Negro Orators and their Orations*, Washington, D.C., 1925, pp. 85–86; Benjamin Quarles, *Black Abolitionists*, New York, 1969, pp. 38, 45, 46, *et passim; The Liberator*, April 2, 1847.)

6. Henry C. Wright.

7. The Reverend Charles Fitch, a Congregational minister, was then in Hartford, Connecticut. Within the year he moved to Boston as pastor of the First Free Congregational Church. An active abolitionist, he broke with Garrison in August 1837, when he and five other clergymen issued an "Appeal of Clerical Abolitionists on Anti-Slavery Measures," published in the *New England Spectator* on August 2. The "Appeal" condemned Garrison and *The Liberator*, especially for various comments about church leaders and their attitudes towards slavery. Some years later, in a letter to Garrison dated Newark, January 9, 1840, Fitch expressed his regret at having participated in the "Appeal" and in the condemnation of Garrison. (*Life*, II, 139–140, 156, 177, 252, 335–337; III, 94.)

8. The Reverend David Thurston (b. February 6, 1779; d. May 7, 1865), a Congregational minister, graduated from Dartmouth College in 1804 and was ordained at the Congregational Church in Winthrop, Maine, on February 18, 1807. He remained there until October 15, 1851. A staunch Calvinist, he was president of the American Missionary Association and of the Maine branch of the American Education Society. His antislavery views and efforts originated in

the 1820's. He was a delegate to the founding convention of the American Anti-Slavery Society in December 1833, a member of the convention committee appointed to draft the Declaration of Sentiments, and was the first signer of the declaration as finally adopted. (Aaron Chester Adams, *In Memoriam, Rev. David Thurston*, Portland, 1865, 23 pp.; Stephen Thurston, *A Discourse on the Erection of a Marble Tablet . . . in Memory of Rev. David Thurston*, Portland, 1871, 31 pp. Both items are among the biographical pamphlets at the Massachusetts State Library, series I, volume 52, nos. 24 and 25; *Life*, I, 395, 399, 408.)

9. General James Appleton (b. Ipswich, Massachusetts, February 14, 1786; d. there August 25, 1862) was a colonel in the militia of Massachusetts and was made brigadier general at the close of the War of 1812. He was also a member of the Massachusetts legislature. He moved to Portland, Maine, in 1833 and was elected to the legislature of Maine in 1836. He came to be known as the father of Prohibition, having been the first to advocate the statutory prohibition of the manufacture and sale of liquors, first in a petition to the legislature of Massachusetts in 1831, then in a report to the Maine legislature in 1837. He was also active in the antislavery movement, and was elected a vice-president in the New England Anti-Slavery Convention. Before his death, he returned to his native village. (*NCAB.*)

10. The Reverend Cyrus Pitt Grosvenor (1793–1879), a Baptist minister, served churches in New Haven, Boston, and Salem from 1825 to 1834. He helped organize the Essex County Anti-Slavery Society, which had its first meeting at his home in Salem. He was one of the "seventy" antislavery agents appointed by the American Anti-Slavery Society; his field of operation was Connecticut and Massachusetts. He was later prominent in the Liberty party, and died in Albion, Michigan (Dwight L. Dumond, *Letters of James G. Birney, 1831–1857*, New York and London, 1938, p. 422n). See also Garrison's letter to Helen Garrison, March 12, 1834 (*Letters, I*).

11. The Reverend James Milligan (b. Dalmellington, Ayrshire, Scotland, August 7, 1785; d. Southfield, Michigan, January 2, 1862) arrived in the United States at the age of seventeen, graduated from Jefferson College in 1809, and was installed as minister of the Reformed Presbyterian Congregation in Ryegate, Vermont, in 1817, where he remained until May 17, 1839. He was one of the earliest abolitionists, and served as a vice-president of the New England Anti-Slavery Convention. He was also a fine classical scholar and taught school in Ryegate. He later served congregations in New Alexandria, Pennsylvania, and Eden, Illinois, until his old age. It was while living at the home of one of his sons that he died in 1862.

It may be noted, too, that his son Alexander McLeoud Milligan (1827–1885) was also active in the antislavery movement, was mobbed several times, and wrote to John Brown after the Harpers Ferry incident. Brown replied on the day before his execution. (Edward Miller and Frederic P. Wells, *History of Ryegate, Vermont*, St. Johnsbury, Vt., 1913, pp. 127, 128, 232, 445–447.)

12. The Reverend Samuel H. Peckham was installed as pastor of the North Parish Church (Congregational), in Haverhill, Massachusetts, on February 23, 1831. He was dismissed on September 10, 1838. "Much of Mr. Peckham's ministry was unquiet and unpleasant, yet in a very good degree successful" (George Wingate Chase, *The History of Haverhill, Massachusetts*, Haverhill, 1861, pp. 564–565).

13. The Reverend Stephen P. Hill was minister of the First Baptist Church in Haverhill, Massachusetts, from October 1832 to 1834, when he resigned because of ill health. He later moved to Baltimore, Maryland, and from there to Washington, D.C., where he was residing in 1861 (Chase, *The History of Haverhill, Massachusetts*, p. 589; the Reverend W. W. Everts, Jr., *History of the First Baptist Church and Sunday School of Haverhill, Mass.*, Haverhill, 1890, pp. 47–48).

14. Henry B. Stanton. The address was published in *The Liberator*, June 11, 1836.

15. Charles C. Burleigh. The address was published in *The Liberator*, June 18, 1836.

16. Shakespeare, *Macbeth*, I, vii, 32.

17. The convention was held on June 2.

18. The letter, dated April 13, 1836, was published in *The Liberator* on May 28, 1836.

19. The Reverend Dr. Francis A. Cox (1783–1853) and the Reverend Dr. James Hoby were English delegates to the Baptist General (Eighth Triennial) Convention, which met in the spring of 1835, at Richmond, Virginia. Although the Board of Baptist Ministers in and near London, England, had urged the American Baptists to support emancipation, the two delegates failed to offer their opinions at the convention. Dr. Cox, a member of the British and Foreign Anti-Slavery Society, was invited to attend the annual meeting of the American Anti-Slavery Society, and was urged to do so by Thompson, but apparently chose not to, in order to avoid being associated with the abolitionists. In a letter to Henry E. Benson, printed in *The Liberator*, dated April 13, 1836, Thompson indicated that he had publicly exposed Dr. Cox's failure to speak out against slavery while in the United States, without any reply from Dr. Cox. (*Life*, I, 480–481.)

"Hide his diminished head" is from Milton, *Paradise Lost*, Book IV, line 35.

20. The meeting convened on Tuesday, May 31. *The Liberator* (June 4, 1836) reported the meeting, and some of the problems involved in holding it:

"We are very sorry to perceive, that our birth-place is still governed by a pro-slavery spirit, or, rather, by a few individuals who fear not God and regard not man. The Essex County Anti-Slavery Society held its annual meeting in Newburyport on Tuesday last. The committee of the Temple-street meeting-house had given permission to the Society to occupy it; but, on Monday afternoon, a few factious individuals belonging to the congregation called a meeting of the *parish*, not of the *proprietors*, and after a warm debate, by a vote of 45 to 38, decided that the Anti-Slavery Society should not be permitted to convene in that house. An excellent and spacious place, however, was procured as a substitute. Mr. Charles Butler, an estimable and spirited citizen, at some hazard to his property, promptly invited the delegates and the people to assemble in his garden, having procured seats for the audience, and erected a stage and an awning for the speakers. Four or five hundred persons were present; the place and the occasion produced a thrilling effect. . . . The speakers were Charles Stuart, H. B. Stanton, C. C. Burleigh, Rev. T. S. Wright, of New York, Rev. H. C. Wright, Mr. Caples and Mr. Hilton of Boston, William Oakes, Esq. of Ipswich, and Rev. Mr. Peckham, of New Hampshire. . . . As Mr. Whittier was a delegate, we shall probably have some account of the meeting in the Haverhill Gazette of to-day."

21. Perhaps the daughter of Joseph Williams. See letter 1, to Henry E. Benson, January 9, 1836.

22. Effingham L. Capron (b. Pomfret, Connecticut, March 29, 1791; d. Providence, Rhode Island, September 16, 1859), was a Quaker who was originally hostile to Garrison. Persuaded by Arnold Buffum to take *The Liberator*, he changed his mind and decided that slavery was wrong. He was a delegate to the founding convention of the American Anti-Slavery Society. In 1838, he helped form the Non-Resistance Society and was elected its president. In 1836, and for many years thereafter, while living in Uxbridge, Massachusetts, he was a vice-president of the Massachusetts Anti-Slavery Society. (*Life*, I, 398; II, 229.)

3 1

TO HELEN E. GARRISON

Boston, May 30, 1836.

My dear Helen:

I am afflicted to-day by the receipt of dear sister Anna's letter, informing me of your illness. Necessary as it is that I should remain here a few days, perhaps a week longer, I am prompted to fly to you without an hour's delay; but as Anna writes that you were evidently better, and as she promises to send me another letter by the next mail, which I hope to receive without fail on Wednesday afternoon, I have concluded reluctantly to wait. Although we know that we are liable to sickness or to death every moment, yet we are ever taken by surprise, as if some strange thing had happened unto us — so little do we learn by the fleeting things around us!

I am afraid that as you received only one letter from me during the last week, and that being dated at Providence, my apparent delay may have created uneasiness in your mind, and thus induced your sickness, in some measure. My love, I am more unfortunate than blameworthy. You probably received a letter from me this forenoon, dated from this city as long ago as last Wednesday. Overwhelmed with the business of the Convention, I nevertheless contrived to write that letter — but, unfortunately, I did not get down to the Post Office in season by about fifteen minutes, owing to an interruption which I need not here specify. On Thursday, I endeavored to find some friend who was going in the cars to Providence, that I might get him to drop it into the P. O. that evening, so that it would thus reach Brooklyn on Friday forenoon. But no such opportunity presented itself.

I am truly grateful to dear Anna for her kindness in writing, and especially for stating your situation undisguisedly to me. Alas, that I am not by your side, cheering you with my presence, and administering to your wants! If the next letter be not in confirmation of your health, I shall hasten back without delay — on Friday or Saturday. It is painful enough to be separated from you when you are well — but your illness makes absence doubly poignant. I pray you, dearest, be as quiet in your mind as possible, and be as careful of *yourself* as you are solicitous about *my* welfare. Heaven watch over you kindly, and make this sickness profitable to us both — for it is a lesson of our mortality, admonishing us of that separation which at some day or other must inevitably take place. "The one shall be taken, and the

114

other left." [1] But let our aim and our hope be, to dwell together in heaven eternally, where parting shall be no more.

If your sickness is afflicting to me, I am measurably revived to hear that our dear babe is "well, hearty and good, and daily improving in his looks." Let us give thanks for his healthful preservation. By the way, I have just received the Glasgow Chronicle of April 22, in which a lecture of Mr. Thompson is reported, and in the course of which he read the following extract from one of my letters, to a crowded audience, and it is published in the Chronicle. It will make you feel queerly.

"I may as well conclude this letter with a piece of information, which I am sure will be received by you and Mrs. Thompson with pleasure. On Saturday last, at 12 o'clock noon, my dear Helen was delivered of a precious babe — a son — whom we have named George Thompson Garrison. The news of his birth gives great pleasure to my abolition friends, as far as it has gone, and his name not less. Methinks my hatred of slavery was feeble before I had a wife and child; but as the ties of life increase, I feel my abhorrence of the impious system constantly augmenting." [2]

This is the way they do things in England and Scotland, and whether we laugh or cry, it is all the same now.

Of course, I am not yet cured of my catarrh, though I think it is better. It is said that a city residence is better for this disease than the country, as it is made worse by the smell of flowers and vegetable matter. Perhaps there is truth in this notion. My nose still cakes internally, but not quite so much as formerly. Its external appearance is decidedly better. On the whole, my health is improving. But how gloomy and unpropitious has been the weather for the last eight days! The sun has been constantly shrouded, and all nature dispirited. It must appear more dull in Brooklyn than in Boston. Not a word have I heard from brother Henry, and I feel anxious to learn how this weather has affected him.

Our Convention was worthy of our cause. I took no part in its proceedings so far as speech-making is concerned, owing to my cold — but we had no lack of speeches, and good speeches. Rev. T. S. Wright passed a high panegyric upon me in his speech, thanking God that "the pioneer yet lives — Garrison lives!" &c. &c. But I feel, and heaven knows, that I deserve no praise.

To-morrow, the Essex County Anti-Slavery Society will hold their annual meeting to-morrow at Newburyport. This afternoon, a whole stage-load of abolition fanatics started for the scene of action — H. C. Wright, T. S. Wright, Stanton, Stuart, Bourne, Burleigh, Knapp, Caples,[3] &c. Mr. May thought of going, but did not.

I have given up all idea of attending the meeting at Concord [4] this week, though urged to go most importunately.

I have spent two evenings at the Chapman's, in the midst of large circles, very pleasantly. Anna Weston has gone to New-Bedford to keep a school. Love to all devotedly. My prayer is for your restoration. Kiss the babe. Yours lovingly,

W. L. Garrison.

ALS: Garrison Papers, Boston Public Library.

    1. Matthew 24:40.

    2. The manuscript of this letter has thus far not been found.

    3. Charles V. Caples of Boston was a mulatto schoolteacher. On November 29 he took part in a discussion with the Reverend H. Easton, of Hartford, Connecticut, at the Baptist meeting-house in Belknap Street, on the question, "Is the prejudice of the white population of the United States, as it is wrongfully exercised towards the colored people of this country, on account of their color?" (Benjamin Quarles, *Black Abolitionists*, New York, 1969, p. 34; *The Liberator*, November 26, 1836; he is also spoken of as a "young colored minister" in a letter from C. C. Burleigh to Samuel J. May, April 3, 1835, in Anti-Slavery Letters to Garrison and Others, Boston Public Library.)

    4. The New Hampshire Anti-Slavery Convention.

32

TO HELEN E. GARRISON

Boston, June 1, 1836.

My Love:

A heavy load of anxiety has been removed from my mind to-day, by the receipt of Anna's kind and affectionate letter, informing me that you still continue to improve in health, though debilitated from the effects of your fever. Assure her of my heartfelt gratitude for her prompt attention; for, had I not heard from Brooklyn to-day, I should have been miserable in the extreme.

Are you desirous of my return? So great is my solicitude to see you, as well as all the rest of the household. Here I remain an unwilling prisoner, yet willingly discharging the duties devolving upon me. I know not how to stay away much longer, yet know not how to leave conveniently. Mr. Tillson [1] is to fill Henry's place till he recovers, so that I cannot make the arrangement with Mr. Burleigh [2] respecting the Liberator. This will make my absence from this city more objectionable; nevertheless, I shall stay in Brooklyn until the heat of the summer is over. One thing I must certainly do — be more industrious as to editorial matter than heretofore, and then there will be less complaint.

The rooms now occupied by Mr. and Mrs. May, at Miss Parker's, are engaged by the partner[3] of Mr. Drew. Mr. May feels very sorry that I did not secure them; but it would only have been a bill of expense to me had I done so now, having my family in Connecticut. In the fall, I have no doubt Miss Parker will be able to accommodate us very comfortably.

It is possible I may be in Brooklyn on Saturday afternoon, via Worcester; yet you must not be disappointed if I should not come until next week. Mr. May, with his family, hopes to be in the village a week from to-morrow.

Yesterday I received another letter from my dear friend Thompson, dated Glasgow, April 29. He gives me the pleasing intelligence, that Mrs. Thompson had just presented him with another son, — a fine boy, — whom he has named Wm. Lloyd Garrison! This is returning a compliment as swiftly as the winds and waves could bring it, and nature and friendship could prepare it. Methinks, should his babe and ours be spared to behold and embrace each other with youthful ardor, that will be an interesting scene. I trust we shall live to witness it. Mrs. T. was rapidly recovering, and desired to be remembered to you kindly.

Mr. Knapp will probably return from Newburyport this evening. The meeting-house which was promised to the County Anti-Slavery Society was closed against them, and they were forced to hold their meeting in a large garden, in the open air![4] Benches were obtained, and very good audiences brought together. There was no disturbance. I have just seen Burleigh, who was present, and he reports the proceedings to have been very spirited, more so than they would have been, probably, had no opposition been made. The speakers were Stanton, Burleigh, Stuart, T. S. Wright, H. C. Wright, Mr. Taylor of Virginia,[5] Mr. Caples, Mr. Hilton,[6] &c. George Bourne gave a lecture on Popery. Shame on my native place! But she is not wholly corrupt. There are many of her children who sympathise with the downtrodden slave.

I have written eight or ten pretty long letters to England, this week, addressed to various friends. Will you not compliment me for my industry? Your praise is dearer than any person's. Ah! but I ought to accomplish still more.

Not a word yet respecting the health of brother Henry! — I shall endeavor to write to him this evening.

The Glasgow paper which Anna says was sent to me a few days since by father, probably came to hand — as one was given to me by Mr. Knapp.

To-day is the first day of Summer; yet at sunrise, the roofs of the houses were covered with white frost! How dreary the last fortnight must have been to you in Brooklyn — i.e. if the weather was as gloomy there as it has been here.

Anna writes quite flatteringly about our darling babe. It is comforting to know that he is in good health, while his mother is so feeble. Do you think he will know me on my return? If he should not, it will [not] take us long to renew our acquaintance.

"The Young Mother," is the title of a new work just published in this city by Dr. Alcott,[7] a copy of which I shall bring with me. It is an admirable and most instructive work, just what you and all mothers need. Six hundred copies were sold the first day it was published. Mrs. May recommends it very highly. Babes should be washed in tepid, not cold water, says the Dr.

Yesterday, a venerable member of the Society of Friends and his wife, living in New-Hampshire 150 miles from Boston, came to see me, bringing with them, as a present from their son, a box of maple sugar, made by himself. They desired to be specially remembered to you, on account of your trials during the riot.

Mr. Knapp will shortly publish a volume of Hymns composed and selected by Mrs. Chapman in the most admirable manner. I think there will be a quick demand for it.[8]

Kisses for the babe and yourself, and love to all the dear ones. Soon I hope to be with you in peace and joy.

Faithfully, lovingly yours,
Wm. Lloyd Garrison.

ALS: Garrison Papers, Boston Public Library.

1. Joseph Tillson had been doing odd jobs at the antislavery office. Following Henry Benson's illness, he was elected by the Board of Managers to take Henry's place as secretary and agent of the Massachusetts Anti-Slavery Society. (See Garrison's letter to Helen, November 4, 1835, *Letters*, I, and letter 33, to Henry, June 8, 1836.)

2. Charles C. Burleigh. "During his stay in Brooklyn, Charles Burleigh, more than anyone, acted as his *locum tenens*; and as Mr. Garrison's relaxed and ailing bodily condition kept him from contributing regularly to the paper, the place was no sinecure" (*Life*, II, 84).

3. Mr. Archibald D. Babcock. See letter 21, to Helen, April 18, 1836.

4. The meeting was that of the Essex County Anti-Slavery Society. The garden was the property of Charles Butler of Newburyport. See letter 30, to Helen, May 25, 1836.

5. Unidentified. He is not mentioned in the account of the meeting published in *The Liberator*, June 4, 1836.

6. John Telemachus Hilton, a Negro leader of Boston, died in Brighton, Massachusetts, on March 5, 1864, at the age of sixty-two (*The Liberator*, March 11, 1864). On August 23, 1839, *The Liberator* carried the following ad: "Anti-Slavery Intelligence Office, No. 36 Brattle St., The subscriber, in consequence of the almost daily application to him for colored help by citizens of Boston and vicinity, has been induced to try the experiment of securing good places to colored

persons of merit, by establishing the above office. Wanted immediately, two good wash women. For character, refer to Wm. L. Garrison, Wm. A. Burley, Oliver Johnson, Rev. Sam'l Snowden and Elder J. V. Himes.

John T. Hilton
Boston, Aug. 22, 1839."

Hilton was also active in seeking equal rights for the Negroes of Boston, notably in education (see Herbert Aptheker, *A Documentary History of the Negro People in the United States*, New York, 1967, I, 243–244). See Garrison's letter to Hilton, August 13, 1831 (*Letters*, I).

7. Dr. William Andrus Alcott (b. August 6, 1798; d. March 29, 1859), physician, author, and reformer, was the cousin of Bronson Alcott. After teaching school for several years, Alcott studied medicine at the Yale Medical School, receiving his diploma in 1825. Because of poor health, he was unable to practice medicine, but it was at this time that he began to write voluminously on educational and medical subjects, achieving a national reputation and publishing more than a hundred volumes. His writings on medicine were for the lay reader and were intended to popularize the laws of health; those on education sought to improve the public schools. "His name is identified with some of the most valuable reforms in education, morals, and physical training of the present century." His last years were spent in Newton, Massachusetts, where he died. (*DAB; ACAB.*)

The book by Alcott to which Garrison refers was entitled *The Young Mother, or Management of Children in Regard to Health*, published in Boston in 1836 by Light & Stearns, and consisted of 332 pages.

8. On June 18, 1836, and in subsequent issues *The Liberator* announced publication of "Songs of the Free, and Hymns of Christian Freedom," 228 pages, for sale at the antislavery office at 46 Washington Street. Describing the volume, *The Liberator* noted that "it contains 119 hymns, proper for devotional exercises, beside an excellent selection of poetry, from writers of our own and past times, calculated to awaken a love of liberty, and excite sympathy for the injured and oppressed."

33

TO HENRY E. BENSON

Brooklyn, June 8, 1836.

My dear Henry:

A fine, tender, solicitous, attentive brother-in-law is W. L. G.! Don't blame me over-much, because I am disposed to sit severely in judgment upon myself. It is too bad to be named in a christian age, (fortunately for me, in this instance, it is the age of enlightened heathenism,) that I should have left you so poor an invalid, and resided a fortnight in Boston, and not transmitted to you a single line either by way of inquiry or intelligence! It looks hardhearted — it is undeniably "scandalous," "abominable." Not a word did I send you about our great Convention, although I knew that your heart was in it, and that nothing but illness kept your body away, and that the smallest amount of information respecting it would have been highly acceptable. Nevertheless, I love you, and sympathise with you, and congratulate you if you are better for your botanical treatment. A part of the time I was quite unwell in Boston, and therefore took no *public* part in the doings of the N. E. Convention. *All* the time I was busy enough, and had to be careful that I did not neglect my wife, she expecting a letter from me every other day; and as Anna wrote me that she was quite sick, I felt that prompt epistolary attention was specially due to her. But, acknowledging that you ought to have received at least *one* letter from me, and did not, I shall make no more excuses.

Doubtless you have perceived by a late Liberator, that a letter for you, from George Thompson, has been received at Boston. A considerable portion of it was inserted in the paper:[1] another portion related to a settlement between Joseph Phillips of London and myself, respecting some anti-slavery books and seals belonging to the former, which I brought over with me for sale on commission, but which still remain unsold, with some exceptions. G. T. has acted very generously in this matter, as you will perceive when you come to understand all the circumstances. A settlement has been satisfactorily made, and thus a burden removed from my mind.

G. T. speaks of "your very interesting and affectionate letter of the 26th Feb. for which he most sincerely thanks you." He says, moreover — "I am much pleased with your letter. Your style is excellent. Go on — study to improve. You will scarcely need the notes you speak of, but I may yet send you a batch." When we write to him, he wishes us to address our letters as follows — "Care of William Sommerville, Jr. 8 St. David-Street, Edinburgh." He says he has not received a single copy of the Liberator since the arrival of Mrs. Thompson! — By the way, she has given him another pledge of affection somewhat quickly. The new comer is to be called after me — quite a friendly retort, and as prompt as it is friendly.[2] You have now about the sum total of his letter.

Our esteemed friend Thomas Spencer, of Salem, sailed for Liverpool last week, carrying with him many letters, newspapers, and all sorts of anti-slavery publications, for G. T. I sent eight or ten letters by him — another reason why I was so busy in Boston, to the neglect of Henry Egbert Benson.

Three or four more letters have just been received from friend Buffum, respecting his accounts. We have agreed to leave the matter out for arbitration, probably to the following persons — James Mott, Thomas Shipley, and Joseph Cassey.[3] It is very important that either Knapp, myself, or you, should immediately hasten on to P.[4] to state our case to the referees — otherwise, A. B.[5] will have clearly an advantage over us, in being able to make verbal statements which may require verbal answers. Now, it will be impracticable for Knapp, and difficult for me, to go on at present. How is it with you? Are you well enough to travel? And do you feel willing to visit P. without delay, at our expense, and have this unpleasant affair satisfactorily settled. If so, let me know, and Knapp also, as soon as possible. You can take all the letters of A. B., and also a written statement from me to lay before the arbitrators. Nothing more, I presume, will be needed. Should you go on to P., I will give you a letter to James Mott, who will be highly pleased to receive you under his hospitable roof.

My catarrh is decidedly better. I think it has been benefitted by Dr. McIntyre's prescriptions. My nose is improving in its appearance externally, and is somewhat better internally, so that I have some hopes of a complete cure — provided I can and do refrain from picking it. When brother George comes up to B., I wish he would bring with him some more of that preparation for my nose, as I have used up the little box which the Dr. gave me. The medicine for my blood is not all gone, as I am using it somewhat slowly. I am living very simply — abstaining from meat, tea, coffee, &c., &c. I think I shall suffer less in Boston than in Brooklyn from my catarrh, as vegetable matter is apt to affect those who have this complaint.

Dear Helen was very ill while I was in Boston, but is now better, though very far from being in good health. She is now quite slender in appearance. Our babe is blessed with good health, a good disposition, and the kind attention of many good friends. Unless a father's partiality blinds me, he is an uncommonly fine child. — Grandfather [6] dotes upon him.

Bro. May with his family comes to Brooklyn on Friday or Saturday, reluctantly but necessarily, to discharge his engagement to his people. All our abolition friends, both male and female, are lamenting over his return, but we cannot help it. I shall yet expect to see him once more wholly enlisted in our sacred cause.

I shall remain in Brooklyn until the warm weather is over. Then we must all return to Boston. Do you think you shall be able to take hold again at 46, Washington-street?

I am engaged to deliver an address on the 4th of July at Fall River. When does the Fall River boat leave Providence?

You may tell Dr. McIntyre that I could not take his medicine as he directed me, — a table spoonful three times a day, — as it created pain in my stomach like the colic. I take a spoonful about once a day. It operates as a purge.

Little Anna has been a little unwell for a week past, but nothing serious. All the rest of the family are well as usual.

What "a long spell of weather" we have had! Wind east for more than three weeks. Yesterday, it got round to West.

Our Board have elected friend Tillson to supply your place at 46, until your wishes or expectations are made known to them. They most earnestly desire your return — but should you not deem it prudent, Tillson will remain at the rooms permanently.

We are anxious to hear respecting bro. George's health, hope he will not attempt to be well when he is really ill.

With much love to him, and kind regards to Charlotte and her husband, the dwellers in Pleasant Valley, &c. &c. I remain,
Yours, affectionately,

Wm. Lloyd Garrison.

ALS: Garrison Papers, Boston Public Library.

1. *The Liberator*, May 28, 1836.
2. Garrison had named his son George Thompson Garrison.
3. Arnold Buffum (1782–1859), a Quaker of Smithfield, Rhode Island, a founder and first president of the New England Anti-Slavery Society as well as a founder of the American Anti-Slavery Society, was a hat manufacturer. In February 1834, having moved to Philadelphia, he was appointed agent for *The Liberator* in Philadelphia. Charged with securing subscriptions as well as payment, he was also called upon for advances to *The Liberator* in its moments of financial stringency. As a consequence, his bookkeeping became somewhat confused. The result was a disagreement between him, Garrison, Henry Benson, and Isaac Knapp over the amounts he had paid to *The Liberator* as well as the amounts he owed for subscriptions. In January, Garrison had terminated Buffum's position as agent, which apparently placed Buffum in a precarious financial position because of advances he had allegedly made to *The Liberator* against, as yet, unpaid subscriptions. Three arbiters, Thomas Shipley, James Mott, and William H. Scott, were agreed upon to decide the issue, with Scott taking the place of Cassey. Their decision, issued on June 21, 1836, favored Garrison. (See letters from Arnold Buffum to Henry E. Benson, January 16, 19, and June 4, 1836; to Isaac Knapp, February 15, 1836; and the judgment of the arbiters, June 21, 1836, all manuscripts at the Boston Public Library; see also letter 35, to Henry E. Benson, June 14, 1836; *Life, passim.*)

James Mott (1788–1868) was a Philadelphia Quaker, reformer, and pioneer abolitionist, a founder of the American Anti-Slavery Society. See introductory biographical sketch.

Thomas Shipley was one of the founders of the American Anti-Slavery Society and was a member of its Board of Managers until his death. He died on September 17, 1836, at the age of fifty-one. See *The Liberator*, September 24, October 22, 1836, and Garrison's letter to George Shepard, September 13, 1830 (*Letters*, I).

Joseph Cassey (b. West Indies, d. January 1848, aged fifty-nine), a Negro of Philadelphia, was an early supporter of Garrison and *The Liberator*. In 1832, he helped in the purchase and distribution of Garrison's *Thoughts on African Colonization* and also served as an agent for *The Liberator*. See Garrison's letter to Robert Purvis, June 22, 1832 (*Letters*, I; also, *Life*, I, 312, 325, 342; IV, 359).

4. Philadelphia.
5. Arnold Buffum.
6. George Benson.

3 4

TO WILLIAM CHACE

Brooklyn, June 11, 1836.

My dear friend:

I am truly obliged to your Committee of Arrangements for inviting me to go to Newport, and to you for communicating to me their desire. Whether I shall be able to comply with their invitation, I cannot now positively determine. If I go, this must be the condition — that I go, not to address the Committee,[1] but merely to be present as an abolitionist. I do not say that I will remain wholly dumb, because I cannot tell what may be the state of my feelings, or what may happen to render my feeble assistance desirable; but it will constitute no part of my design to say any thing to the Committee. For many good reasons, I think it were better for our cause that I should take no part in the proceedings. Nor do I feel that my presence would be of any special importance — not sufficiently so, at least, as to involve your Society in the expense of my journey. However, I will decide this matter when I see brother George. One reason why I wish to be excused is, that I am engaged to deliver an anti-slavery address at Fall River on the 4th of July,[2] which is rapidly approaching; and as my other engagements are numerous, and as none of the address is yet written, and as it will cost me some time and labor, I wish to remain quietly at Brooklyn.

I have, at your request, communicated the contents of your letter to bro. May, who arrived here yesterday with his family. He thinks it will not be practicable for him to be at Newport, but promises to write to you immediately.

It is very unfortunate that Weld [a] cannot go before the Committee, as I learn from bro. Henry's letter received by father yesterday. Weld is as brave as he is good; and while the mob are gnashing their teeth upon him, and brickbats are flying, I do not blame him that he is resolved to maintain his ground at Troy. Still, he has a sufficient excuse for leaving that city, to shield him from the charge of cowardice or desertion — and it is, in my opinion, vastly more important that he should be at Newport, than that he should put down all opposition at Troy — for what is Troy compared to the nation?, and it is a *national* effect at which we must aim before your legislative committee. Let Weld be written to again — tell him, if you please, what is my opinion — remind him that he can promise the Trojans, that he will come again to them shortly — tell him to plead the importance of fulfilling this prior engagement — and then let the elements at Troy be left to compose themselves once more. The leaven of sympathy, of humanity, of truth, will be working among the *dough*-faces during his absence. I am not sure that it would be Weld's duty to remain longer in Troy, seeing the civil authorities are too feeble to maintain the public peace, even if so important a case were not to be tried at Newport at this crisis. After manfully breasting the storm, so far as to display unequivocal intrepidity, I think he may properly "shake off the dust of his feet" [4] upon that city, and go to other places where the people will hear the word gladly. Such an act would be sound policy, and not in any degree allied to fear or apostacy. It would be merely shifting ground, without abandoning an iota of principle. It is not as if he were actually in the keeping of a mob, or confined in a prison, and then under these circumstances required to abjure his abolition sentiments, and be dumb. No: in such a case, it would be his duty to go to the gibbet or the stake, rather than to comply with such an impious requisition. But he is neither in the hands of ruffians, nor in prison, nor has any such test yet been required of his fidelity. Then, I say, when the tempest is raging, why attempt to *voice* it down at the expense of health, perhaps of life, when by going a short distance you may find nature tranquil, and may be heard without any painful effort, and where the people need to be as much instructed, quickened and converted, as they do in Troy? — especially, when it is so immensely important that the unblanching advocate should be elsewhere — at Newport? These are my views of what I think is the proper course for bro. Weld to pursue: still, he is better able to decide upon what is most dutiful than I am. I hope he will go before your Committee; for Newport is a strong citadel of the enemy, and abolitionists, the strongest and boldest of them, are even *invited within the walls*, and may peradventure carry the place by a single assault.

Why has Stanton gone to Troy? "To help Weld," so bro. Henry writes. Very well — provided he returns to Newport in season, *without fail* — and better yet, if he bring Weld along with him. But if you get neither, what is your dependance? "*I* am no orator as Brutus is," [5] and require preparation for such an emergency, for which I have no time. — Burleigh [6] will do admirably well, provided he is brief upon the numerous points which ought to be presented to the Committee. Mr. May probably cannot come. Goodell is number one, if you can get him.

Now, bro. William, what say you? If I purpose to be dumb, except in private interviews with persons, do your Committee of Arrangements still desire me to be present at Newport, as I am the head and front of the *offending* of the anti-slavery cause, and that I may be "the observed of all observers"? [7] If *so*, let me *know*, and I will *go*, if not too *slow* in preparing my 4th of July address and doing sundry other matters. There are rhyme and reason for you — to which I add that I am with great esteem,

Your truly obliged friend,
Wm. Lloyd Garrison.

Mr. Wm. Chace.

ALS: Garrison Papers, Boston Public Library.

1. This was a committee appointed by the Rhode Island legislature to consider demands of southern states for penal enactments against the abolitionists and petitions by the abolitionists protesting against the enactment of "a gag law." The committee chairman was Thomas W. Dorr (1805–1854), who later led the struggle for manhood suffrage in the state. The committee hearing was scheduled for June 22, 1836, in Newport.
2. Under the sponsorship of the Fall River Anti-Slavery Society.
3. The letter to Theodore Weld from the Rhode Island Anti-Slavery Society, dated Providence, May 29, 1836, inviting him to testify before the committee on behalf of the American Anti-Slavery Society, and signed by fifteen members of the executive committee of the Rhode Island Anti-Slavery Society, is reprinted in *Weld-Grimké Letters*, I, 306–308. Apparently, Weld replied initially that he might be able to attend. On June 11, writing from Troy, New York, he stated that circumstances in that city, where abolitionists were then being mobbed, did not permit him to leave (*Weld-Grimké Letters*, I, 309–310).
4. Mark, 6:11; Luke 9:5.
5. Shakespeare, *Julius Caesar*, III, ii.
6. C. C. Burleigh.
7. *Hamlet*, III, i.

35

TO HENRY E. BENSON

Brooklyn, June 14, 1836.

My dear Henry:

It appears by your favor of yesterday, that your forgiveness readily overtops my seeming negligence, and sits victorious above the height of my procrastination. Thanks! To be just is the severity of goodness; but to be generous, under provocation, is something beyond justice.

Happy am I to hear that your steps are tending towards the Temple of Health, — that you have indeed reached the vestibule, and are preparing to enter into the beautiful interior, and to offer up a sweet-smelling sacrifice on the altar of gratitude.

> "O, who can speak the vigorous joys of health,
>   Unclogged the body, unobscured the mind!
> The morning rises gay with pleasing stealth —
>   The temperate evening falls serene and kind." [1]

But it is better to have a sick body than a diseased soul — to have our physical functions impaired, than to have our minds cast down from their native vigor.

I deem it very fortunate that your strength will permit you to visit Philadelphia at this time, because the disagreement between friend Buffum and ourselves cannot be settled by correspondence, and because it would not be convenient either for Knapp or myself to make such a trip. Indeed, you are more familiar with the accounts of the Liberator, especially with the situation of Buffum's accounts, than I am, and probably than Knapp.

A bundle will be transmitted to you by the stage-driver this afternoon, in which you will find a letter for James Mott, which I have no doubt will give you a welcome reception at his house — and also a Statement from me, relative to the agreement between Buffum and myself,[2] entered into in the fall of 1834, to commence with the new year 1835. This you will lay before the Committee of Arbitration.

You ask for some instructions as to the mode of proceeding in the settlement of the accounts.

1. I hardly think it will be practicable for you to accomplish the object of your journey, so as to be in Newport on Tuesday next; although if you can, I shall be very glad — but I am afraid such rapid travelling, with the business to be done in so short a time, will be more fatiguing than your constitution is able to bear. Let me calculate — Should you start from Providence on Wednesday afternoon, you will reach New-York early on Thursday morning, if no obstacle prevent, in season to take the 7 o'clock steamboat for Philadelphia, in which city you will arrive about 2, P. M. The afternoon and evening you will need for rest — perhaps it will be necessary to let friend Buffum know at once of your arrival. On Friday and Saturday, you will have your interviews before the committee of arbitration, and perhaps succeed in getting their decision upon the merits of the case. Of course, you must tarry in P. over the Sabbath. Monday morning you can leave for New-York, and arrive at 2, P. M., spend three hours in seeing a few anti-slavery friends, and then leave in the Providence boat at 5, P.M. and arrive in Newport the next morning — or, you can tarry in N. Y. until Tuesday afternoon, and so reach Newport on Wednesday morning. All this is on the supposition that your strength will bear it, and that you succeed in making a speedy settlement in Philad. But it is more important that you should see the business finished, than that you should be in Newport, gratifying as I know it would be to you to hear the discussion. Indeed, I would recommend, if you find the visit agreeable to you, that you extend it some time — being very watchful in respect to your health and diet.

126

2. The arbiters named by friend Buffum and myself are James Mott, Thomas Shipley, and Joseph Cassey: if neither of these can attend to the matter, you and B. can choose any others whom you please.

3. Be careful not to impeach the character of friend Buffum in the smallest degree, unless he is obviously disposed to be dishonest, (which I cannot suppose,) of which the arbiters will judge. It will be better to assume that there is an honest misapprehension or mistake somewhere, and then endeavor to find it.

4. Neither party should make a statement to the arbiters unless both are present; and every thing that is to be said should be said before them.

5. Require friend Buffum to confirm or deny, *explicitly*, my statement of the agreement between us; for upon that, every thing depends.

6. Carefully read his letters, and observe the discrepancies therein, and see if he does not repeatedly recognise the agreement alluded to.

7. If he can satisfactorily make it appear that he advanced in the course of 1834, $200 beyond his receipts, then ascertain if he did not *afterwards* collect all of it, or a large portion. Again: If he really made the advance at that time, then see how much he owes us for the year 1835, according to agreement, and strike a balance accordingly. Again: If he made the advance unknown to us, and without our request, ought we to be responsible because the subscribers did not pay him? I think not — though we shall not refuse to do so.

8. Friend Buffum says there are between 5 and 600 dollars due in Philad., not yet collected. If it is all owing for the year 1835, then, according to agreement, it belongs to him; we are not responsible either for its loss or collection, but *he* is responsible to *us*.

9. Be careful to require of him an account of the money collected by him, at various periods, of mail subscribers, both in the city and in various parts of the State. I think the sum must be considerable.

10. If friend Buffum should make any statements which vitally affect the case, and you cannot answer them to the satisfaction of the arbiters, let their decision be deferred until you write to me for further information. I do not think of any thing more at present.

Remember me with all tenderness of affection to friend Mott and wife, Dr. Robt Moore and wife,[3] Lydia White,[4] the Fosters,[5] and *all* the dear friends. I need not particularise.

Tell bro. George little Anna has improved very much in health since I wrote last. Her appetite is good, and she appears very well.

We were glad to see Mr. Stetson [6] return yesterday — for every absent man is missed in a village like this. All the things sent by him were safely and promptly delivered. ☞ I cannot afford to pay the postage upon little George at present — must send him by private conveyance. He and his mother are well. My nose begins to inflame a little — the Dr's preparation comes seasonably — but my catarrh is certainly better. I trust Stanton and Weld will both be at Newport. Love to bro. George, Charlotte, the Chaces, &c.

Yours truly,

Wm. Lloyd Garrison.

ALS: Garrison Papers, Boston Public Library.

1. James Thomson (1700–1748), "The Castle of Indolence," Canto II.
2. See letter 33, to Henry E. Benson, June 8, 1836.
3. Dr. Robert Moore and his wife, Esther, lived in Philadelphia. He was a physician who, in a letter to Maria W. Chapman on November 25, 1842, wrote that he had been physically and mentally incapacitated and therefore was unable to practice medicine. The letter implies that he was probably in his seventies in 1842 (ALS, Boston Public Library).
Mrs. Moore was especially active in the antislavery and woman's rights movements. She died in November 1854. On December 8, 1854, *The Liberator* published a letter from Samuel Barry to Garrison, dated November 30, 1854, with information about her, including her posthumous description, through a medium named Henry C. Gordon, of what it was like to die. Her obituary was published in the *National Anti-Slavery Standard* on November 25, 1854.
4. Lydia White owned a free-labor produce store in Philadelphia and was one of the delegates present at the founding convention of the American Anti-Slavery Society (*Life*, I, 264, 398). She was also librarian of the Female Anti-Slavery Society of Philadelphia. See Garrison's letter to Robert Purvis, June 22, 1832 (*Letters, I*).
5. Unidentified.
6. James A. Stetson (1801–1893) was the brother of George W. Benson's wife, Catherine. He became an intimate friend of Garrison and May. Born in Scituate, Massachusetts, he moved to Brooklyn, Connecticut, in 1825, where he opened a shop for the making of carriages. He later gave up the business, worked for a while as a salesman for a silk factory in Northampton, and then returned to Brooklyn, where he settled on a farm for the rest of his life. He was a devoted Mason, a temperance man, a deacon of the Unitarian Church in Brooklyn, and later an active Republican. (*Commemorative Biographical Record of Tolland and Windham Counties, Connecticut*, Chicago, 1903, pp. 961–962.)

---

3 6

TO SAMUEL J. MAY

Providence, June 19, 1836.

My dear brother May:

I congratulate you that you did not come down with us yesterday, as I have some regard for your personal comfort, and presume you have also: if not, why then no matter if you are doomed to be (as we were) about eight hours in performing a journey of 29 miles, in a crowded coach, accompanied by a thunder-storm, the atmosphere dense and lifeless. The driver must be either a very indolent man, not caring much for the comfort or wishes of his passengers, — or, a very merciful man, rejoicing only when his horses walk slowly, or come to a stand-still. Luckily, he is only pro tem. One of our passengers endeavored to show his team how they ought to travel, and accordingly took the lead, which he kept a long distance, up hill and down hill and on a dead level, picking and eating strawberries by the way. We came up with him at last, owing to his condescension, frankly acknowledging that our four horses were no match for his two legs.

We were all fatigued enough, on and before our arrival. The road is one which familiarity cannot make tolerable. It is as formidable now as it was the first day I travelled upon it. If pugnacious men, who are fond of showing their skill and strength in pitched battle with each other, would only combine to hurl down some of the hills, and elevate some of the valleys, between Brooklyn and Providence, they would be much more usefully employed — don't you think so? As they fail to do as well for themselves and for others as they probably would under *our* control, suppose — after the fashion of slaveholders — that we enslave them, with all disinterestedness, charity and tenderness? But, no — if men will abuse the freedom which God allows them, it is no reason why other men should destroy that liberty: for, be it remembered, its *abuse* is at all times a less evil than its *destruction*.

Little George Thompson was quiet, curious and sleepy most of the time — crying but little, but perspiring so freely that when he arrived, he was "wringing wet." I was fearful that he would be a severe sufferer; but he seems very well to-day, and I hope has taken no serious cold.

Helen, and Catharine, and little Anna, complain of fatigue, but this will not hurt them.

I had a short interview with bro. George this morning. He informed me that the last accounts from Troy were, that the mobocratic spirit was still rampant in that city — that Weld had been stoned, and wounded in the leg, but could not be persuaded to leave for Newport — that Ray Potter had been sent to Troy to induce him to come, and would have succeeded if the mob had not been so violent — that Stanton has returned, and says it is probable that Phelps will be at Newport — that Stanton and Wm. Chace went to Boston yesterday, to persuade Sewall or Loring to attend, as it is deemed proper we should have a sound abolition lawyer present — that Goodell, Gerrit Smith, and Prof. Follen have been written to to be at Newport, but no answer has been received from them, nor is it expected that they will attend, either one or all. Bro. George wishes me to add, that the Committee are desirous you should come, and will most gladly defray all your expenses. They would have written to you again on Friday, but felt unwilling to urge you overmuch, as you had just returned to Brooklyn. I hope, now, you will come. We are not to have a hearing before the legislative committee until Wednesday evening, at 7 o'clock; so that you need not leave Brooklyn until Tuesday afternoon in the stage — on Wednesday afternoon, at 4 o'clock, we will go down in the steam-boat together. It is thought that, as Ben. Hazard [1] is a Unitarian, and very zealous in getting up a Unitarian church in Newport, you might be more acceptable to him than some others. Should you come, I wish you would bring your two bound volumes of anti-slavery tracts and pamphlets. Hazard will probably reply to us on the spot, and is now very busily engaged in examining all our anti-slavery documents to hunt up treason, and he thinks he shall put us down irremediably! Dorr,[2] the Chairman, is very much fairer, says we shall be fully heard, and is anxious we should bring forward our ablest men and *do our best*. An excellent reporter is engaged from New-York, and the daily journals in this city have solicited leave to publish our doings, speeches, &c. as fast as we proceed. This, then, is the time to strike a blow, and a heavy one, for liberty and justice. If you come, you can return on Friday forenoon, and thus be absent rather less than three days.

This afternoon, I went to hear the Rev. Mr. Farley [3] preach. His sermon was for a special bereavement that had taken place in his congregation. His text, however, "Our Father, which art in heaven," had little connection with his discourse. Some things he said I liked very well — but there was lack of discrimination as a whole.

It is very warm to-day — but, assuring you that my affection for you is more ardent than the weather, I remain, in the bonds of christian amity,

Yours, truly,

Wm. Lloyd Garrison.

N. B. My best regards to Mrs. May — kisses for the babe.

ALS: Garrison Papers, Boston Public Library.

1. Benjamin Hazard (b. September 18, 1770; d. March 10, 1841), of New-port, was chairman of the original legislative committee appointed by the Rhode Island General Assembly to report on the question of possible penal enactments against the abolitionists. At the January 1836 session of the legislature, his committee had originally presented a series of resolutions and a bill for enactment, which were all postponed to the May session. The committee of which Thomas W. Dorr of Providence was chairman was subsequently appointed to report on the entire matter. The letter of the Rhode Island Anti-Slavery Society to Theodore Weld, dated Providence, May 29, 1836 (see letter 34, to William Chace, June 11, 1836, note 1), commented: "Hazard (well knowing the good character of the abolitionists in this state) in order to be more secure in his attack, aims his blow principally at the American Anti-Slavery Society. He has *pledged* himself to produce the documentary evidence, published by that society, showing its *design*

to be *insubordination* on the part of the slave toward his master." (*The Liberator,* March 26, 1841.)

2. Thomas Wilson Dorr (1805–1854) became widely known for his leadership in the struggle for manhood suffrage in Rhode Island in 1840–1842. A graduate of Harvard College in 1823, he practiced law in Providence beginning in 1827. He represented Providence in the Rhode Island General Assembly from 1834 to 1837. In leading the movement for manhood suffrage, he was elected governor of the state by the dissident, prosuffrage forces in 1842, and was forced to flee the state twice. On returning in 1843 he was arrested, and sentenced by the Rhode Island Supreme Court in 1844 to imprisonment at hard labor and solitary confinement for life. Less than a year before his death, the General Assembly of Rhode Island repealed, reversed, and annulled the judgment of the court (*The Biographical Cyclopedia of Representative Men of Rhode Island,* Providence, 1881, II, 328–330.)

3. The Reverend Frederick Augustus Farley (b. Boston, June 25, 1800; d. March 24, 1892), of the Westminster Congregational Society (Unitarian) in Providence. He graduated from Harvard College in 1818, was admitted to the Boston Bar in 1821, and then studied theology at the Harvard Divinity School. He was ordained and installed as minister of the Westminster Congregational Society on September 10, 1828. Dr. William Ellery Channing delivered the sermon at the installation. Farley's connection with that church ended on August 1, 1841, when he was called to the Second Society of Unitarians, which met at Brooklyn Institute in Brooklyn, New York. His congregation, after uniting with another, became the First Congregational Unitarian Society of Brooklyn and in 1844 built the Church of the Savior, of which he was pastor until he retired in 1863. (J. Alexander Patten, *Lives of the Clergy of New York and Brooklyn,* New York, 1874, pp. 180–181; Index to Obituary Notices in the Boston *Transcript,* 1875–1899, Worcester, 1938, photocopy in New England Historic Genealogical Society, n.p.)

---

3 7

TO ISAAC KNAPP

NEWPORT, R. I. June 22, 1836.

MY DEAR KNAPP:

You will remember that, in February last, certain resolutions, with a bill, (intended as a gag-law,) in furious opposition to the abolitionists, alias 'the incendiaries,' were submitted to the Legislature of Rhode Island by BENJAMIN HAZARD of this place, a man destined to an immortality of infamy, and probably in this business *hired* by southern slaveholders. These resolutions were postponed to the session in May: they were then committed to Messrs. B. Hazard, Dorr,[1] Gavitt,[2] Hazard of Kent,[3] and Blake,[4] who were also instructed 'to consider and report upon the memorials of divers citizens of the State, relating to the subject of Free Discussion and the Liberty of the Press, and to hear such testimony as may be submitted to them by or in behalf of the petitioners.' It was subsequently voted by the Committee, that a meeting of the same be held at Newport, on Wednesday evening, June 22d, at 7 o'clock, in the Chamber of the House of Representatives; and they accordingly gave public notice to the memorialists, and all other persons interested in the subject of the aforesaid resolutions, to appear, if they should see fit, at the time and place appointed, and be heard in the premises. The R. I. State Anti-Slavery Society immediately appreciated the importance of having our principles and measures ably vindicated in this pro-slavery town, under these circumstances, and it accordingly spared no pains to bring forward on this occasion some of our ablest advocates. It was confidently expected that Theodore D. Weld would be on the spot, but the recent mobs in Troy, where he had been lecturing, induced him to remain in that city at great personal hazard, still fighting valiantly for truth and liberty. Our eloquent brother Stanton was also expected here, armed at all points, but he was suddenly taken ill, and is now under medical treatment in Providence. Bro. May would have been here promptly, but he supposed there would be no need of his assistance. Gerrit Smith was invited to attend, but was unable to do so. Yesterday, bro. Phelps and C. C. Burleigh, with an excellent reporter from New-York, came to Newport, ready for the conflict; and this afternoon, our esteemed friend D. L. Child [5] came with me to complete the list of speakers, accompanied by many abolition friends and curious observers. On our arrival, we were told, that Hazard [6] had just 'backed out' from the prospective encounter, notwithstanding he had boasted that he could prove from our documents, that we were endeavoring to excite the slaves to insurrection, bloodshed, &c. &c.; or, in other words, dreading the impression we should make upon the minds of those who should listen to us, as well as upon the public mind, he intimated to the legislature that he was very sorry the abolitionists had been invited to defend themselves from his charges — he did not wish to be tortured in listening to them — and, as Congress had effectually put a stop to their proceedings, (!!) he thought the resolutions might properly be indefinitely postponed, and the Committee discharged from any further consideration of the subject! On motion of Mr. Atwell,[7] this course was adopted by the legislature, though ably and strenuously opposed by several gentlemen, especially by Messrs. Dorr and Simmons,[8] who severely chastised B. Hazard for his cowardice and duplicity, and contended that it was neither magnanimous nor just, first to accuse men of heinous crimes, then to proffer them an opportunity to be heard in self-defence, and finally to evade the terms of the invitation.

Thus, we find ourselves masters of the field without a struggle. The enemy has precipitately fled, shooting a few Parthian arrows behind him. Victorious as we are, we regret that we are not able to open our battery of free discussion – but perhaps we shall yet succeed in discharging at least one forty-two pounder before we leave. This evening, we held a special meeting of friends to our cause, to consider what further proceedings we might take 'in the premises.' It was well attended by some of the most estimable men in the state, and, after an interesting discussion, it unanimously resolved to present a petition to the legislature to-morrow, asking for the use of the Representatives' Chamber during the recess between 12 and 3 o'clock, and at such other time as may be convenient, in order to disabuse the minds of the people in relation to the principles and purposes of the abolitionists – briefly stating the reasons for making this request. The petition will be presented to-morrow morning, and will no doubt excite considerable debate.[9] Several of our friends are somewhat confident that its prayer will be granted. If so, we hope to make a breach in this strong-hold of slavery – for Newport is the Charleston or New-Orleans of New-England.

A gentleman from Dover informs me, that the committee appointed by the New-Hampshire Legislature to consider and report upon the pro-slavery documents from the south, have not been able to agree, and the whole subject has been postponed to the next session, which is tantamount to an indefinite postponement.[10] The legislatures of Maine and New-York have adopted some weak resolutions, censuring the abolitionists; Massachusetts and Connecticut have refused to act upon the southern documents; Vermont is yet to act, and no doubt her legislature will imitate that of Pennsylvania,[11] viz. by vindicating the right of free discussion, and maintaining the duty of Congress to abolish slavery in the District of Columbia. The legislature of this State resolves to do nothing upon the subject. What will the south say now?

In great haste, yours, &c.

WM. LLOYD GARRISON.

Printed in *The Liberator*, July 2, 1836.

1. Thomas W. Dorr.
2. George W. Gavitt (1806–1886), businessman, of Westerly, Rhode Island, was elected to the General Assembly in 1836 as representative from Westerly (*Narragansett Weekly*, Westerly, July 29, 1886).
3. Thomas T. Hazard (1792–1874) of West Greenwich in Kent County, Rhode Island, represented West Greenwich in the state legislature, as representative or senator, for thirty-two years (*Representative Men and Old Families of Rhode Island*, Chicago, 1908, p. 2071).
4. James M. Blake (1809–1879) was chosen in 1836 to represent Bristol in the General Assembly of Rhode Island and remained in the assembly, with brief intermissions, until 1866. He was attorney-general from 1843 to 1851 (*The Biographical Cyclopedia of Representative Men of Rhode Island*, Providence, 1881, p. 352).

5. David Lee Child (1794–1874), husband of Lydia Maria Child and an early Garrisonian and antislavery leader, was a journalist, teacher, lawyer, and for a short period a member of the Massachusetts legislature. (Ruchames, *The Abolitionists*, pp. 18, 103–104.)

6. Benjamin Hazard of Newport.

7. Samuel Young Atwell (1796–1844), a leading member of the Rhode Island bar, was a member of the Rhode Island General Assembly from Gloucester. He had been elected in 1835 without opposition and was considered by many to be the first jurist of the state. He was speaker of the House of Representatives from 1836 to 1840. (*The Biographical Cyclopedia of Representative Men of Rhode Island*, p. 258.)

8. James Fowler Simmons (1795–1864) was a manufacturer of yarns who lived in the town of Johnston, Rhode Island. He represented Johnston in the General Assembly from 1828 to 1841. From 1841 to 1847 and from 1857 to 1862 he served in the United States Senate as senator from Rhode Island. (*BDAC*.)

9. Pursuant to a motion by Benjamin Hazard, the petition was tabled by a vote of 36 to 28. For an account of the conflict between the abolitionists and the Rhode Island legislature see *The Liberator*, July 2, 1836.

10. "The subservient element prevailed at the next session (*Lib.* 7:14, 25), but legislation against the abolitionists was discountenanced" (*Life*, II, 76n).

11. "It did, Nov. 16, 1836 (*Lib.* 6:193)" (*Life*, II, 76n).

---

3 8

TO GEORGE W. BENSON

Brooklyn, June 28, 1836.

Dear George:

Father and I sent letters to you this morning, by Danl. Robinson.[1] Before Mr. R. left, I promised our friend Gray that I would do an errand for him, which I forgot to perform. You may, therefore, tell Mr. Robinson, (and I hope that you will see him immediately,) that Mrs. Gray does not wish him to get the common straw carpeting, but that which has *blue stripes* — or, if the blue cannot be found, he may get either red or green. I hope he will not have made the purchase before you see him, as he supposes that Mrs. Gray wishes the common kind, i.e. all white.

I hinted to you, in my letter by Robinson, that I thought it would be highly serviceable to your cause in R. Island, (since the Newport affair has happened,) if your Society would print a large number of copies of Whittier's last, and perhaps most thrilling production, — "Now, by our fathers' ashes, where's the spirit," &c. and scatter it among the yeomanry and mechanics of the State — it will rouse them up like a trumpet-call. You need not put the heading over it in the Liberator — but let this be the caption of it, or something more expressive — Appeal to the Freemen of New-England. By J. G. Whittier.[2]

How is bro. Stanton? Did Phelps lecture on Monday evening? What
has been the effect of the meeting on Friday evening?

Yours,

Wm. Lloyd Garrison.

ALS: Garrison Papers, Boston Public Library.

1. Daniel Chapman Robinson (b. Brooklyn, Connecticut, June 11, 1803; d.
August 6, 1878), a shopkeeper in Brooklyn, Connecticut, was the son of Vine
Robinson, a merchant and judge of the county court (*Robinson Genealogy, De-
scendants of the Rev. John Robinson*, published by the Robinson Genealogical
Society, Salem, n. d., I, 146). See letter 55, to Henry E. Benson, August 27, 1836.

2. Whittier's poem appeared in *The Liberator*, June 25, 1836, reprinted from
the Haverhill *Gazette. It* was headed:

"LINES

"Written on the passage of Mr. Pinckney's Resolutions in the House of Representatives, and of Mr. Calhoun's 'Bill of Abominations,' in the Senate of the
United States: by J. G. Whittier."

The first two stanzas read:

"Now, by our fathers' ashes! where's the spirit
    Of the true-hearted and the unshackled gone?
Sons of old freemen, do we but inherit
                    Their names alone?

"Is the old Pilgrim spirit quenched within us?
    Stoops the proud manhood of our souls so low,
That mammon's lure or party's wile can win us
                    To silence now?"

39

TO HELEN E. GARRISON

Providence, July 2, 1836.

My dear Wife:

In the course of two days, I shall be required to address a public
audience in Fall River,[1] on a great and awful subject — but where is
my lecture? Is it only an echo that answers, "Where?" Stinted as I
am for time, I must write you a few lines, just to say that all is well
with me. Have you not a dutiful and an attentive husband? But I
must not praise myself. No — but may I not give my wife a hint to
praise me? "O you selfish creature!" What! selfish to desire the approbation of so good and gentle a partner as Helen Eliza Garrison!

I hope the old white horse carried you, and Anna, and the babe,
safely home. The particulars of the jaunt must be interesting. I cannot
ask, what did little George *say* after I left him — for, as he cannot
talk, I must inquire, what did he *cry*? Doubtless he thought it useless
to "cry aloud," or even to cry at all — at least I hope so, unless his

lungs needed the exercise. How many strawberries were gathered by the way, and who picked them? I need not ask who ate them, because it is presumable that you did justice to the fruit — and I like your taste.

The stage did not arrive at Pomfret Landing [2] until nearly half past 2 o'clock. I wandered about for more than two hours, trying to find *a few* strawberries, and was successful, they being very scarce indeed. Some of the time I sat upon a rock, and read portions of the trial of Dr. Crandall [3] — a trial which ought to make stones speak, and rocks cry out. Then I sat upon the bank of a little brawling stream, with just water enough to signify that it was not dry land. Do you ask, why I did not stop at the Post Office? Have you so soon forgotten that all incendiary publications must be thrown out of Uncle Sam's premises? [4] And if the publications, why not the grand incendiary himself? But I should not have strolled so far, had I not expected the stage momently. When it arrived, it was crowded inside — mostly with females. There was a mother with a little girl, and a babe in her arms, which talked exactly in George's dialect, and almost precisely with his tone of voice. He behaved remarkably well all the way, except as we entered the suburbs of Providence, when (in imitation of our own "little troublesome comfort,") he cried lustily for a few minutes — perhaps it was a *she,* I know not. — I was glad to get an outside seat with the driver all the way, which, in pleasant weather, is decidedly the best of all. The day was exceedingly warm, although the sun was partially enveloped in smoke, and the horses panted and sweat very much. Of necessity we rode very slowly, only four or five miles an hour, and did not arrive in Providence till about 9 o'clock. The route for scenery is a magnificent one — but, horror of horrors! it is as much more hilly than the Brooklyn road, as Mr. May is handsomer than cousin Joel! [5]

Bro. George, with true brotherly kindness, met me at the stage-house, and escorted me to his dwelling. He and Catharine are in very good health, (so I judge) — and as for little Anna, she is improving finely, having lost her death-like aspect, and now eating heartily. As yet, she has but one eye-tooth.

It is now one o'clock, and the steam-boat is not in from New-York, owing to the fog — some expect Henry, though he may stay a few days longer in New-York.

As a specimen of the growing wickedness of the times, take the fact that a military company is to arrive here by appointment to-morrow, (the Sabbath,) from New-York, and that another military company is to turn out here to escort them through the streets! In the afternoon, they are to march to Rev. Dr. Crocker's meeting-house, [6] where I suppose they have been specially invited. Guns, bayonets, swords, plumes, banners, epaulets, in church on the Sabbath! It seems a studied, and is a most aggravated profanation of the day.[7]

At 3 o'clock, I depart for Fall River in the steam-boat. This forenoon I have written about a dozen pages of my address, and must finish the remainder as I can. The God of the oppressed be with me to enlighten and strengthen me.

I have had no time to call at sister Charlotte's. Tell bro. May the anti-slavery friends will undoubtedly hold a meeting here on the 1st of August, though none on Monday next. They will be glad to have him on that occasion.

In gallopping haste, after desiring to be affectionately remembered to all the household, and to have many kisses given to our darling boy for my sake, I remain,

With great and growing affection,

Yours, ever,

Wm. Lloyd Garrison.

ALS: Garrison Papers, Boston Public Library. A paragraph of this letter is printed in *Life*, II, 107.

1. At the Annual Meeting of the Fall River Anti-Slavery Society, held at the Congregational Church on July 4. The election of officers was held at 1 o'clock in the afternoon, followed by the public exercises at 2. Garrison gave the address. "On the night of the 3d (Sunday) an effigy of straw was attached to a post on the Main Street, with a placard marked 'Garrison the Abolitionist: a fit subject for the gallows' (*Lib.* 6:111)." (*Life*, II, 107n.)

2. A settlement in the southeast section of the town of Pomfret, Connecticut. Pomfret Landing is described as "a rich, cool glen in the green valley of the rippling, rambling, laughing Mashomoquet," by R. M. Bayles, *History of Windham County, Connecticut* (New York, 1889), p. 549.

3. Dr. Reuben Crandall, a younger brother of Prudence Crandall, had gone to Washington, D.C., to teach botany. He was arrested on August 11, 1835, charged with circulating incendiary publications — some of his botanical specimens were found wrapped in old antislavery newspapers and imprisoned. Crandall was kept in prison for eight months before being brought to trial. Although acquitted, he died in 1838 as a result of tuberculosis contracted while in prison. The account of the trial was published under the following title: *The Trial of Reuben Crandall, M. D., Charged with Publishing Seditious Libels, by Circulating the Publications of the American Anti-Slavery Society. Before the Circuit Court for the District of Columbia, Held at Washington, in April, 1836, Occupying the Court for the Period of Ten Days* (New York: H. R. Piercy, 1836, 62 pp.). Another edition of 48 pages was published in Washington, D.C., during the same year.

4. Postmaster General Amos Kendall "encouraged an unofficial exclusion of abolition literature from the Southern mails by individual postmasters. . . . In his report of December 1, 1835, Kendall declared that the state laws against the circulation of incendiary publications should be obeyed by the officers of the general government." President Jackson approved this policy and on December 7, 1835, in his message to Congress, recommended passage of a law prohibiting circulation "through the mails in the Southern states of "incendiary publications intended to instigate the slaves to insurrection.'" In response to Jackson's recom-

mendation, Senator John C. Calhoun reported a bill "making it illegal for any deputy postmaster knowingly to receive and put in the mail any pamphlet, newspaper, handbill, or other printed paper, or pictorial representation, touching the subject of slavery, directed to any person or post office in those states where the laws prohibited their circulation." Although this bill was ultimately defeated in the Senate, in June 1836, by a vote of 25 to 19, "decisions on mail were finally placed in the hands of the local postmasters. Abolitionists gave up their attempt to keep the mails free." (Clement Eaton, *The Freedom of Thought Struggle in the Old South*, revised and enlarged edition, New York, Evanston, and London, 1964, pp. 200–205; Louis Filler, *The Crusade Against Slavery, 1830–1860*, New York, Evanston, and London, 1960, p. 98n.)

5. A Joel Garrison was born in 1760 in Cumberland County, New Jersey, was married twice, and apparently died in 1835 (*Descendants of John Garrison of Sumner County, Tenn.*, Denton, Texas, 1961, p. 43). No other Joel is listed in the family records. If the date of death is correct, this probably was not the Joel to whom Garrison refers.

6. Nathan Bourne Crocker (1781–1865) was ordained and became the rector at St. John's Episcopal Church in Providence in 1803. He continued there, except for a three years' absence because of ill health, until 1865. The church was located at the corner of North Maine and Church Streets. (*The Biographical Cyclopedia of Representative Men of Rhode Island*, Providence, 1881, pp. 153–154.)

7. This paragraph is reprinted in *Life*, II, 107.

40

TO ISAAC KNAPP

PROVIDENCE, JULY 5, 1836.

MY DEAR KNAPP: —

Yesterday, (for the sixtieth time!) the people of this vain and vaunting country perjured themselves afresh, in the presence of the world, by calling God to witness that they are a free people, that they abhor tyranny, and that they hold it to be a self-evident truth, that all men are created equal, and possess an inalienable right to liberty. O, the solemn farce, the comic tragedy! What a mingling of spurious patriotism and brazen hypocrisy, of glaring falsehood and open blasphemy! What ringing of bells, what waving of banners, what thundering of cannon, what blazing of bonfires, what long processions, what loud huzzas, what swaggering speeches, what sumptuous dinners, what alcoholic toasts, what drunken revels! All in grateful and honorable observance of the Fourth of July! Ah! and what crushing of intellect, what polluting of virtue, what marring of God's image, what bleeding of humanity, what yoking of new-born existence — what sighs, and groans, and lacerations, and robberies, and crime — all on the Fourth of July! A free country — and every sixth man on the soil a slave! Free — and our Capital the chief rendezvous of human fleshmongers, and the head quarters of despotism! Free — and the liberty of speech taken away even from northern freemen in one half of the Union! Free — and domestic slavery proclaimed to be 'the corner-stone of our republican edifice!' [1] Let Bedlam laugh, let Pandemonium howl exultingly! A *christian* country — and the bible denied to two millions and a half of its inhabitants! woman bleeding under the lash of the savage slave-driver! the marriage covenant annulled! Human families sold, and separated like swine in the market! 'The pride of thy heart hath deceived thee, thou that dwellest in the clefts of the rock, whose habitation is high; that saith in thy heart, who shall bring me down to the ground? Though thou exalt thyself as the *eagle*, and though thou set thy nest among the *stars*, thence will I bring thee down, saith the Lord.' [2]

But yesterday was not wholly given up to desecration. Many of the true disciples of Jesus were agonizing in prayer over THE GREAT ABOMINATION, that threatens destruction to all that is valuable in freedom, and precious in christianity. The pulpit, in very many instances, was faithful to its trust. Many an assembly was convened to learn what they might do towards breaking the yoke of bondage, and setting the American captive free. Many an advocate was found to lift up his voice on the side of justice, mercy, and equality, and to rebuke the nation for its exceeding wickedness. Many new volunteers enrolled themselves under the banner of immediate emancipation, thus truly remembering those in bonds as bound with them. And many a free-will offering, from the widow's two mites to the rich man's munificent gift, was cast into the treasury of bleeding humanity, to carry on the work of physical and spiritual redemption. We have reason to believe, that a mighty impulse was given to our noble cause, yesterday, throughout the free States. What though 'the wicked plotteth against the just, and gnasheth upon him with his teeth?' 'The Lord shall laugh at him: for he seeth that his day is coming.' [3]

Among the anti-slavery speakers, yesterday, were our faithful coadjutors, S. J. May, at Hampton, Ct.; C. C. Burleigh, in Pawtucket, R. I.; N. S. Southard, in Scituate, Mass.; and Rev. John Blain,[4] in this place. Mr. Blain's discourse is spoken of very highly. His theme was the guilt of the Church, incurred by its connection with slavery. I perceive that the Rev. Mr. Fitch, of Boston,[5] was to deliver an address in Pine Street meeting-house. Judging from his brave and eloquent remarks at the New England Convention, I presume it must have been peculiarly excellent. Some of our brethren must send us an account of the manner in which they observed the day in their several towns and villages.

It was my privilege, by the kind invitation of the Fall River Anti-Slavery Society, to address a large and attentive audience in that town, yesterday afternoon, in the Rev. Mr. Fowler's meeting-house.[6] At the close of my remarks, a collection of thirty-six dollars was taken up, and several new members were added to the Society, among them, the Methodist minister of F. R. In the evening, I had the happiness of attending the first annual meeting of the Female Anti-Slavery Society, in the Baptist meeting-house, (Rev. Mr. Bronson's,)[7] at which a Report was read, and remarks made by myself and others. Some new additions were made to this Society. The abolitionism of the Baptist church is evidently of a pure and decided character, from the fact, that slaveholding preachers are excluded from their pulpit, and slaveholding professors from their fellowship. Their pastor, Mr. Bronson, is a laborious, faithful, fearless watchman.

This was my first visit to Fall River. Its location was to me unexpectedly beautiful and attractive, and its appearance flourishing and impressive. What has made that populous village what it is? Human industry, animated by the hope of a just reward — Free Labor, compensated according to the voluntary contract between the employer and the employed — Liberty, throwing her protection around all its inhabitants, and placing them all on the broad level of Equal Rights. A very kind reception was given to me, the memory of which will be long and gratefully cherished in my heart. Never did I see the Fourth of July observed in so orderly and appropriate a manner in any other place. Not a single banner was unfurled to the breeze — at least, I saw none — no cannon roared — quietude prevailed in the streets — and there seemed to be a general consciousness that, while millions were enslaved in our midst, it would be something worse than mockery to celebrate the day with pomp and show. In the forenoon, a temperance address was delivered, and in the afternoon and evening, our cause was advocated, as mentioned above. During the previous night, some unknown but patriotic artist, (rejoicing in his liberty,) with considerable labor, but not much skill, made an effigy of straw, and suspended it upon a post in Main Street, to which was fastened a label containing these condemnatory words — 'Garrison, the abolitionist; a fit subject for the gallows.' This man of straw proved better than a town crier to urge all good citizens to attend our meeting in the afternoon. He brought many to hear and see, who else might have remained at home. I am much obliged to him, for he enabled me to put up the celestial goddess of Liberty in his stead, in the presence of the people.

My esteemed friend Harvey Chase,[8] gave me a free conveyance to Providence this morning in his carryall; and this afternoon, I was invited to attend a meeting of the Ladies' Anti-Slavery Society, and was happy to comply with the invitation. Truly, 'Woman is in the field!'

I wish to acknowledge, at the hand of Mr. Charles Wilbour,[9] of Little Compton, R. I., the receipt of $43.42, contributed by himself and other friends in that place, to liquidate the outstanding debt of the Liberator, — a debt incurred when we were struggling without means and without patronage, to wake up a nation from its sleep of death. We must show our gratitude to these kind donors, by our faithful adherence to the cause of righteous liberty.

Hastily, but heartily yours,

WM. LLOYD GARRISON.

Printed in *The Liberator*, July 9, 1836.

1. Governor George McDuffie, in his message to the legislature of South Carolina at the end of 1835; reprinted in part in *The Liberator*, December 12, 1835.

2. Obadiah 8–4.

3. Psalms 37:12–13.

4. The Reverend John Blain (b. Fishkill, Dutchess County, New York, February 14, 1795; d. Mansfield, Massachusetts, December 26, 1879), Baptist minister and evangelist, was a member of the executive committee of the Rhode Island Anti-Slavery Society. After studying at the Middlebury Academy in western New York, he was ordained and licensed to preach in 1819. Among the numerous congregations which he served were several in Rhode Island, including the Pine Street Church in Providence and churches in Pawtucket and Central Falls. (*The Biographical Cyclopedia of Representative Men of Rhode Island*, Providence, 1881, p. 259.)

5. The Reverend Charles Fitch, pastor of the Free Church in Boston.

6. This was the meeting-house of the First Congregational Church in Fall River, organized in 1816. A report of the meeting and Garrison's address appeared in *The Liberator*, July 9, 1836. The Reverend Orin Fowler (1791–1852) was a minister at Plainfield, Connecticut, from 1820 to 1829, and at Fall River from 1831 to 1850. He was elected to the Massachusetts senate in 1847 and to the thirty-first Congress in 1848. (Orin Fowler, *History of Fall River*, Fall River, Mass., as published in 1841 by the Reverend Fowler, republished in 1862 with a sketch of Fowler's life, pp. 1–6, from *Annals of the American Pulpit*, by William B. Sprague, New York, 1857, II, 648–652; *BDAC*.)

7. The Reverend Asa Bronson (d. November 29, 1866, at the age of sixty-eight), was pastor of the First Baptist Church in Fall River, Massachusetts, for eleven years, from April 4, 1833. During that period, he and his church took a strong and unequivocal position against slavery. After a two-year period in Albany, New York, he returned in 1846 to the Second Baptist Church in Fall River, and remained there until 1857. He was vice-president of the Fall River Anti-Slavery Society and was also active in the temperance movement (Henry M. Fenner, *History of Fall River*, New York, 1906, p. 113; D. Hamilton Hurd, *History of Bristol County, Massachusetts*, Philadelphia, 1883, pp. 357–358).

8. Harvey Chase (also spelled "Chace"), born August 31, 1797, in Somerset, Massachusetts, was educated as a Quaker, and lived in Fall River, Massachusetts, until 1843, when he moved to Valley Falls, Rhode Island. He was a leading businessman and manufacturer as well as an active participant in the antislavery movement (*The Biographical Cyclopedia of Representative Men of Rhode Island*, pp. 267–268).

9. Charles Wilbour (b. Little Compton, Rhode Island, August 15, 1805; d.

there, June 4, 1882) married Sarah Soule Wilbour, daughter of Governor Isaac Wilbour of Rhode Island, in 1827 (Benjamin Franklin Wilbour, *Little Compton Families*, Little Compton, 1967, p. 748).

41

TO HENRY E. BENSON

Brooklyn, July 14, 1836.

Deary Henry —

Remember them that are *sick*, as sick with them. I suppose, nay, I *feel*, that this is sometimes, if not habitually, a duty. Ever since my return from Fall River, I have been ailing with a kind of slow fever, induced by a superabundant quantum of bile upon the stomach. So "out of sorts" have I been, that you will see no editorial of mine in the next Liberator — not a line. Dr. Spalding [1] thinks my liver is affected. On Tuesday, he gave me four pills to take at a single dose, which produced (abolition like) much internal *agitation*, bringing up a large quantity of bilious matter. Every morning, I take two large pills, which are producing their legitimate effect. At present, I feel weak, but somewhat better. My catarrh is better, and nose quite well, comparatively, though I have done nothing for either for some time past.

So, you see, I can feelingly sympathize with you in your sickness. What, when diseased, a helpless creature is man — and yet, ordinarily, how proud! The loss of health is very humbling to him, for then he is not only powerless, but absolutely dependant upon all around him. A sick-bed is a capital instructer. We must be incorrigible pupils not to get knowledge under its tuition. Bodily affliction is often needed to prevent our going astray. We are too apt to forget that we are creatures of dust, soon to be scattered to the winds of heaven. Nothing is more certain than our own mortality — and yet, with strange infatuation,

"All men think all men mortal but themselves." [2]

It is certainly of very little consequence, in the sum total of time, and as it respects the space we fill in the world, whether we perish in early youth or at the age of three-score years and ten, except as we are busy in "doing good," in imitation of our Redeemer. "So teach us to number our days, that we may apply our hearts unto wisdom." [3]

A letter from father on Monday, and another from George yesterday, give us the pleasing information that you are getting better of your recent attack, daily, for which we desire to be thankful. We have at home felt much solicitude on your account, although we have from the first cherished the belief, that the eruptions on your body would ultimately prove beneficial — this was Dr. Spalding's opinion, decidedly. What a cordial to you must be the visit of your dear parents, especially because it was altogether unexpected! In this instance, our loss is your gain — for we miss them continually. Tell them that the whole household is safe and well, except the little ail which has affected W. L. G. Yesterday, little George was five months old, and weighed 16 lbs. and a half. His gums begin to trouble him, and Dr. S. opines that he may have teeth ere long. Eunice has just been informed that her two sons have eloped, nobody knows where — probably to some of the larger cities. Foolish boys! Great is their liability to be kidnapped — but they know it not.

Mr. May [4] visited us last evening. He is to exchange with Mr. Farley [5] on the Sabbath preceding the 1st of August. He has come to the conclusion not to stay in Brooklyn longer than the first of September — his congregation will probably go to pieces, not being able to support a minister. I hope he will be brought into the anti-slavery field once more, promptly, either by the National Society or by our own. His heart is in the work, and therefore he is the more needed. He has several good calls to be settled elsewhere, and perhaps, on account of his family, he will feel it to be his duty to accept of one of them. I am sorry that he came back to Brooklyn, because it has been a serious interruption to his labors, of considerable expense to him, and only tantalizing to his feelings. How little is the reward that he reaps on earth for all his self-sacrificing, benevolent exertions! May it be great in heaven!

The friends at Fall River have written to me, saying that my visit has done great good — that they intend to observe the 1st of August, and desire Stanton, May and myself to address them on that day. Stanton is in New York State, May is to be at Providence, and I do not dare, at present, to pledge that I will comply with their request.

Only think of it! Do you wonder that I cannot make (editorial) bricks without straw? I have not received any newspapers, letters, or a line of intelligence from Knapp, for the space of three weeks! Is not such delinquency a little too bad? Do you marvel that I have so much bile upon my stomach? Does he mean to force me to return to Boston? What, upon "compulsion"? — But I mean to return, if all is well, in all the month of August.

Wishing your perfect health of body and of soul, and desiring to be affectionately remembered to father and mother, and all the dear friends, I remain,

Exhaustedly but fondly yours,

　　　　　　　　　　　　　　　　Wm. Lloyd Garrison.

Mr. H. E. Benson.

ALS: Garrison Papers, Boston Public Library.

1. Probably Dr. John Spalding of Canterbury, Connecticut.
2. Edward Young (1683–1765), English poet, *Night Thoughts*, line 417.
3. Psalms 90:12.
4. Samuel J. May.
5. The Reverend Frederick Augustus Farley of Providence, Rhode Island.

42

TO ISAAC KNAPP

[July 16, 1836.]

[. . .] I am really in miserable health. Mine is a billious and liver complaint. For three or four weeks past, I have had a slow fever hanging upon me, and am now taking medicine in good earnest. I am losing flesh gradually, but constantly. Not many months since I weighed 158, now I weigh 146 lbs. [. . .] Brother Henry's health is such as to forbid all hope of his returning to resume the agency at Boston: — not that he is *dangerously* ill, at least I hope not, but his constitution is too much shattered to allow him to resume the labor, care and responsibility of that station. [. . .]

Extract, printed in *The Liberator*, July 16, 1836.
    This extract of a letter by Garrison appears as two quotations in an unsigned editorial by Isaac Knapp, which reads:
    "The friends of the Liberator will excuse the want of the usual complement of editorial matter in the columns of the Liberator, when they are informed that it is in consequence of the Editor's absence and protracted illness. He writes to the publisher — ." The first quotation follows. The editorial then continues: "He also writes, in relation to Mr. H. E. Benson, Secretary and Agent of the Mass. A. S. Society — ." The second quotation follows.

43

TO ISAAC KNAPP

BROOKLYN, July 19, 1836.

DEAR KNAPP — As you have publicly reported me on the sick-list, you may now say that I am somewhat better. I send you some strictures upon a speech recently made by Dr. Beecher,[1] at Pittsburgh, respecting the Sabbath. — If they are not so vigorous as they might be, ascribe the deficiency to my bodily debility.[2]

Yours, truly,
WILLIAM LLOYD GARRISON.

Printed in *The Liberator*, July 23, 1836. The letter is also quoted in *Life*, II, 107.

1. Dr. Lyman Beecher.

2. *Life*, II, 107 notes that "four columns of fine print followed this announcement, with no trace of bodily debility to be found in them." The four columns constituted the first in a series of three essays analyzing and criticizing Dr. Beecher's speech. The two others appeared in *The Liberator* on July 30 and August 6, 1836. Garrison began the first essay with an attack on Beecher's description of the Sabbath as "the great sun of the moral world," which Garrison characterized as "extravagant and preposterous language . . . it makes the outward observance of one day in the week . . . of paramount importance to every thing else in the moral or spiritual world, instead of being subordinate and co-operative." He suggested that it erroneously placed observance of the Sabbath above the nine other commandments and he decried any attempt to decree uniform observance of the Sabbath as impractical, "unauthorized interference" and as often leading "to cruel persecution and bigotted action." In the succeeding essays he emphasized the contradiction between Dr. Beecher's concern for the Sabbath and his toleration of slavery, which denied not only the Sabbath but the entire decalogue to two and a half million Americans.

44

TO HENRY E. BENSON

Brooklyn, July 28, 1836.

Dear brother Henry:

We somewhat expected sister Catharine and little Anna, yesterday, in the stage. Helen and myself took a trip to Killingley,[1] in order to do a little "shopping," and on the way met the stage, but saw not those in it whose presence we desired to meet. But, to our surprise and pleasure, on our return, who should we find at the dinner-table but dear George, and wife, and child, and our worthy friend Ray Potter! Right heartily did we greet each other, and a happy time we have had together. Poor dear little Anna looks like a wax-doll, and is, as you know, in extremely delicate health; but, as soon as her "teeth-cutting" is completed, she will probably thrive better.

How ardently do I desire to see you, my dear H., once more restored to health. George tells me that you are gradually improving, and my heart is glad. Be not discouraged — keep your mind cheerful, and your body will be benefitted accordingly. Endeavor to amuse and occupy yourself as much as possible, and thus make time move lightly. I know it is easier to give than to follow advice; and when we are in health, we find no difficulty in urging those who are sick to be filled with patience, resignation, and hope. Still, it is possible to meet every vicissitude of life with firmness and determination — and happy is he who can do it.

If you continue to improve in health, how should you like to make a trip to the British West-Indies, or to Hayti, in the month of October, and so remain absent during the winter? I should delight in having you visit Hayti particularly, because I am sure, that, on my account, you would be received with great kindness by the people. I could give you letters to President Boyer,[2] General Ingenac,[3] Secretary of State, and others, who would give you every facility to acquire information, and treat you with all desirable hospitality. The climate is one of the finest in the world, and the scenery among the mountains, for grandeur and beauty, unsurpassed. It matters not that you cannot speak the French language — interpreters are always at hand — and, besides, there are thousands of American colored residents, whom you will find scattered all over the island. We will talk this matter over when you come up with bro. May on Wednesday next. In the mean time, you can think it over in your mind. You can probably be sent out under the auspices of the American Anti-Slavery Society. It will be well to have a companion with you. Such a jaunt would undoubtedly be highly beneficial to your health, and also be productive of good to our blessed cause.

My health is now tolerably good, though not vigorous. The visit to Uxbridge,[4] made by sister Mary and myself last week, was as pleasant and interesting as heart could desire. O, how many warm and true-hearted friends are raised up to sustain us when we are in a course of well-doing! God is faithful to his promises, and he governs all things wonderfully. The nearer we get to him, the more happiness is ours, for time and eternity. May we love and serve him more and more faithfully.

Remember me with a brother's affection to bro. Anthony and Charlotte — and believe me that you occupy much of my thoughts, and that I desire to embrace you under the family roof.

Your sympathising, loving brother,

Wm. Lloyd Garrison.

ALS: Garrison Papers, Boston Public Library.

1. A town in Windham county, next to Brooklyn.
2. President Jean Pierre Boyer (1776–1850), a mulatto, educated in France, distinguished himself in Haiti during the British invasion of 1794–1798. Fleeing to France during Toussaint L'Ouverture's uprising, he returned in 1802 as a member of the French punitive expedition. He later helped to expel the French from the island, when they tried to re-establish slavery. He was acclaimed President of the Republic of Haiti for life in 1818 and emancipated the slaves. He was compelled to resign in 1843. He fled to Jamaica and then to Paris, where he died. (*EB*, eleventh edition.)
3. General Joseph Balthazar Ingenac (also spelled Inginac) was President Boyer's secretary general. In 1822 he addressed himself to John Quincy Adams, then secretary of state, and requested that the United States be the first to

recognize the second republic of the New World. He asked for a reply, but the copy of his letter was endorsed: "Not to be endorsed (By direction of the President). —" (Ludwell Lee Montague, *Hayti and the United States, 1714–1938,* Durham, N.C., 1940, p. 50n, quotes Cons. Let., Cape Haytien, V, State Department Archives.)

4. Massachusetts.

45

TO THE *NEW ENGLAND SPECTATOR*

[Brooklyn, Ct. July 30, 1836.]

ESTEEMED BROTHER PORTER: — Your remarks, in a late Spectator, upon an editorial article of mine respecting an observance of the Sabbath, it seems to me are not marked by that fairness and candor, which usually pervade your writings — at least, it is probable that they will be misapprehended without some further explanation, and perhaps to the injury of that great cause of human liberty, which is so dear to our hearts. Fair treatment I can scarcely expect to receive at the hands of the editors of the Boston Recorder,[1] Vermont Chronicle,[2] and Portland Mirror,[3] because they have too often made me an offender for a word, and almost every week they wrest my language; but you can have no desire to imitate them. You observe —

"We regret to see that Mr. Garrison has taken the ground he has in the last Liberator, *against* the Sabbath."

If you had quoted the first column of my remarks upon the Sabbath, that your readers might know precisely what "ground" I had assumed, and the evidence I adduced in support of it, I should not have troubled you with this letter; because it is far from my wish or design, at present, to enter into a discussion of this important subject, either in the columns of the Liberator or elsewhere. Now your readers are left to *imagine* any and every thing respecting my sentiments — just as the patrons of the Vermont Chronicle have most falsely and wickedly been made to believe, by its perverse editor, that, in relation to human governments, my views coincide with those which were cherished by the Jacobins of France, because I maintain that the followers of our dear Redeemer, whether individually or collectively, are obliged, on condition of eternal salvation, to *forgive* every injury and insult, without attempting by physical force or penal enactments, to punish the transgressor. "For, if ye forgive men their trespasses, your heavenly Father will also forgive you; but, if ye forgive not men their trespasses, neither will your Father forgive your trespasses."[4] Is this the spirit of Jacobinism? Is the infliction of physical punishment, forgiveness for Christ's sake? What Jacobin was ever willing, when smitten upon one cheek, to turn the other also? or to take joyfully the spoiling of his goods? or to lift up the prayer for his bitterest enemies, "Father, forgive them! they know not what they do?" [5] But I may not dwell upon this topic. I am not against government, whether civil or religious; but it must be the government of God in the hearts of men, all-directing, all-controlling, all-abiding — not one based upon physical strength, and maintained by powder and ball, and accompanied by stripes, and fines, and jails, and dungeons, and gibbets, and lawyers, and constables, and sheriffs. Nor am I "against the Sabbath," the true spiritual rest, into which it is the privilege of believers to enter, at all times and under all circumstances. The Christian Sabbath is not one of time; it is not dependent upon the recurrance of one day in seven; it sanctifies every moment, and, being wholly spiritual, comes not by observation. Is it not our daily prayer — "Thy kingdom come, thy will be done, *on earth* as it is in heaven?" [6] If that kingdom be within us, if that will be truly obeyed by us, we enjoy, as to times and seasons, a liberty in Christ Jesus, unknown to those under the first covenant. It may no longer be imposed upon us, "Ye ought to worship at Jerusalem," or "on this mountain," or "Ye ought to observe the first day of the week if ye would not be anathematized as an unbeliever here, and excommunicated from heaven hereafter." What then? Am I opposed to the religious observance and bodily rest of one day in seven? No — But provided it be voluntary. But when men attempt to make this strict outward observance a test of Christian character, and to decide for me how far I may walk or ride on that day, and to brand innocent and useful acts as damning crimes, I must resist the attempt as pernicious and unauthorized by the gospel of Christ. "Let every man be fully persuaded in his own mind." [7]

You seem, brother Porter, to have overlooked the main points in my strictures upon Dr. Beecher's speech at Pittsburgh. These were, as I expressly stated, "not to weaken either public or private attachment to a religious observance of the first day of the week, but to remonstrate against the unwarrantable assumption, that the Sabbath is the great moral sun of the world" — and, *particularly*, and almost exclusively, to show the glaring inconsistency of Dr. Beecher in deploring the violation of the fourth commandment, while he is giving his protecting influence to a system of slavery and heathenism, which, at a single blow, annihilates the whole decalogue, and which effectually excludes from the benefits of the Sabbath, two millions and a half of his fellow-countrymen! I did not travel out of my way to review his speech; it came to me, and I thought it might be made to subserve the cause of downtrodden humanity, by a resort to the *argumentum ad hominem.* My remarks upon the sacred character of the Sabbath were subordinate, and purely incidental. Yours affectionately,

WM. LLOYD GARRISON.

Brooklyn, Ct. July 30, 1836.

Printed in the *New England Spectator,* August 17, 1836.

William S. Porter (b. Farmington, Connecticut, October 28, 1799; d. New Haven, Connecticut, 1866) graduated from Yale in 1825 and was for a year acting professor of mathematics at Jefferson College. After studying theology at Jefferson College, he preached in Prospect, Connecticut. He next published and edited the *Spectator.* After 1837 he taught at Munson, Massachusetts, and was employed as a surveyor at Farmington, Connecticut. In 1850, he moved to New Hampshire and engaged in statistical work. He later served as editor of the *Connecticut Register.* (*New England Historical and Genealogical Register,* Boston, 1867, XXI, 373.)

1. The Boston *Recorder* was a Congregational weekly, founded in 1816 by Nathaniel Willis and Sidney E. Morse. In 1836 it was being published by Nathaniel Willis, at 9 Cornhill. Its editor, then, was Joseph Tracy. (Frank Luther Mott, *A History of American Magazines, 1741–1850,* New York and London, 1930, p. 138.)

2. The *Vermont Chronicle,* a Congregational weekly paper first issued in 1826. It was first printed at Bellows Falls, Vermont, and, after two years, at Windsor, Vermont. Its principal editor, E. Carter Tracy, died in 1862. It ceased publication in 1898. (John M. Comstock, *The Congregational Churches of Vermont and their Ministry, 1762–1914,* St. Johnsbury, Vt., 1815, p. 17.)

3. The Portland *Mirror* was the *Christian Mirror,* a Congregational weekly published in Portland, Maine, from 1822 to 1899. In 1860 it had a circulation of 2,500. The Reverend Asa Cummings was its editor for twenty-nine years, beginning in 1826. His editorial attitude toward slavery and the antislavery movement, which was cautious, sought to avoid controversy. (George Mooar, *The Cummings Memorial, A Genealogical History of the Descendants of Isaac Cummings,* New York, 1903, pp. 298–299.)

4. Matthew 6:14–15.

5. Luke 23:34.

6. Matthew 6:10.

7. Romans 14:5.

46

TO HENRY E. BENSON

Brooklyn, August 4, 1836.

My dear Henry:

From 1 o'clock to 6, yesterday afternoon, all of us, under the family roof, were awaiting your arrival with the utmost solicitude and the most earnest expectation. Father took his station at an early hour at the window, looking intently down the avenue, till he felt weary enough to lie down; while I took a long stroll on the turnpike, (via Job Maine's,[1]) hoping to encounter you and bro. May, by way of surprise. At last, just as we were about sitting down to tea, the chaise made its appearance, containing, to our disappointment, only bro. M. You can easily imagine how we all felt, after having our anticipations so strongly raised; for there is scarcely any thing so difficult to bear with cheerful resignation, as sudden *disappointment* in cases where affection and love and sympathy are deeply interested. — Your letter satisfactorily accounts for your non-appearance. We are disposed to acquiesce in the decision you have made. All things considered, you have doubtless acted prudently in determining to tarry awhile longer in Providence. A change of physicians would be a change of medical treatment, which, in your present feeble state of health, might prove detrimental. If you do not find that a sea air affects you injuriously, I should think the state of the atmosphere in Providence would not be far inferior to ours in Brooklyn.

But, when one is sick, who is like a mother? (except a loving wife, shall I not say?) Dear sister Charlotte has done, and will continue to do, all that sisterly affection can prompt — blessings rest upon her head for her uniform, ample, unwearied kindness, in the midst of the cares and responsibilities of a growing family! Brother George, too, is all-abounding in kindness, solicitude and attention. By coming here, you would gain in numbers, but could not in attachment, because we all, whether in Providence or Brooklyn, hold you in like esteem. You would exchange a brother and a brother-in-law, for a brother-in-law, and thus lose a brother; but you would gain four sisters for one, and a father and mother besides. — Nevertheless, it is not society, or local situation, or choice of relations or friends, that you need at present, so much as health; and it is a duty to remain wherever there is the best prospect of recovering the latter.

It is encouraging to learn by bro. May, that Dr. Brownell [2] does not think that your lungs are yet seriously affected; and from your letter, that your cough is better, and that the eruptions upon your hip have disappeared.

You write that you are very lonesome. My only fear was, that, in coming to Brooklyn, you would soon feel solitary, because, in a village like this, all is monotonous, and a new incident is a startling phenomenon; whereas, in Providence, every day something transpires to interest or diversify, and you get all the news promptly: — besides, in the course of a few weeks, bro. May and family, and myself and family, will be removed to Boston, (Deo volente,) so that you would be deprived of the little entertainment we might be able to furnish you.

We all feel indebted to Phebe Jackson,[3] on your account, for her unremitting kindness, as well as to other friends.

The West India trip looks too formidable to you, now. It was suggested merely in case the complete restoration of your health might seem to demand it. I should lament the necessity of such a voyage, and earnestly desire with you, that it may be safe for you to remain here through the winter. Should it be otherwise, I should hope that our mutual friend, Wm. M. Chace, would accompany you; for he would be both nurse and companion. There would be no difficulty in raising the wherewithal for you both. The approbation of the National Society would be rather a matter of form, than an obligation to perform labor. — But it is not necessary to dwell upon this subject.

Bro. May complains, that he was crowded into a corner on Tuesday evening,[4] by the protracted order of exercises, so that he failed to do justice either to himself or his theme. Considering how short are the evenings, this was unfortunate. I dare say, however, that bro. May's remarks were better than his fears decide, and that he did not spend his strength for nought.

I shall wait with impatience to see an authentic and correct version of the disturbance in Boston.[5] I had heard nothing of it till your letter came. What an eventful day was the first of August last year in Boston, to bro. Thompson! This year it is still signalized in the same city.

Helen will thank sister Charlotte to purchase two gowns for little George, blue and buff, French prints, (each a yard and a half,) and forward the bill in the bundle. Health abides under our roof — little Anna is improving. Divide my heart among you all. With much sympathy and love, I remain, yours, in brotherly ties,

Wm. Lloyd Garrison.

ALS: Garrison Papers, Boston Public Library.

1. Job Main or Maine (b. Stonington, Connecticut, 1781; d. 1861) moved to Brooklyn as a young man, became a farmer and owner of extensive tracts of land, and married Comfort Billings (*Commemorative Biographical Record of Tolland and Windham Counties, Connecticut*, Chicago, 1903, p. 1181).

2. Dr. Richmond Brownell (b. Little Compton, Rhode Island, 1790; d. Providence, October 29, 1864) practiced medicine in Providence and served as president of the Rhode Island Medical Society in 1840–1843. (Letter to editor, April 25, 1968, from Clarkson A. Collins, III, Director of Research, The Rhode Island Historical Society, Providence, R. I.; George Grant Brownell, *Genealogical Record of the Descendants of Thomas Brownell*, Jamestown, N. Y., 1910, p. 250; *Representative Men and Old Families of Rhode Island*, p. 1674. The latter sources cite 1866 as the date of death.)

3. Phoebe (also Phebe) Jackson (b. September 18, 1807; d. June 18, 1887) of Providence, Rhode Island, an active antislavery woman and a good friend of the Garrison and Benson families. She was the daughter of the Honorable Richard

Jackson, a proprietor of the Coventry Manufacturing Company and a representative in the United States House from 1808 to 1815. One of her brothers was Henry Jackson, D.D., another was Charles Jackson, governor of Rhode Island, and a third was George Jackson, who was for a time editor of the Providence *Journal*. (*The Biographical Cyclopedia of Representative Men of Rhode Island*, Providence, 1881, p. 171.)

4. *The Liberator* (July 30, 1836) carried a notice that Samuel J. May would speak at a First of August anniversary observance in Providence, on Monday, August 1, at a meeting sponsored by the Rhode Island Anti-Slavery Society. It is possible that the observance continued on Tuesday evening, as did a similar observance at Fall River, Massachusetts, and that May spoke on Tuesday instead of Monday. There is no notice in *The Liberator*, however, of a speech by May on Tuesday evening.

5. For a description of the "disturbance" in Boston, see the report in *The Liberator*, August 6, 1836, entitled "Rescue of Slaves," reprinted from the Boston *Daily Times*, followed by *The Liberator*'s comments. The incident involved the detention of two black women by the captain of the brig *Chickasaw* on the charge that they were escaped slaves. To gain their freedom, the abolitionists secured a writ of *habeas corpus*, which ultimately resulted in a hearing before Chief Justice Lemuel Shaw, who ruled that the captain had no right to detain them. He was about to free them, after announcing that "the prisoners must therefore be discharged from all further detention," when the agent for the slaveholders announced that he would attempt to have the women arrested again. At this remark, the report reads, "a general rush was made, prisoners and crowd together — down the stairs of the court house, at the door of which the prisoners entered a carriage and were driven off, before any one could prevent it. The Judge stated that they must be brought back to be regularly discharged in open court. The Counsel for the women expressed to the Judge his regret that any violation of the decorum of the court should have been committed. The colored people present had, however, acted on a mistake and a delay of five minutes would have seen the prisoners at liberty, unless, indeed, they had been taken on a fresh process from some other court."

47

TO DAVID L. CHILD

Brooklyn, August 6, 1836.

My very dear Friend:

I am truly indebted to you for your favor of the 2d instant, which was received yesterday, and which I hasten to answer without delay, although the mail does not leave for Worcester until Monday.

In your situation, it must be a difficult matter in patience to "brook the law's delay" [1] — yet, under all circumstances and trials, we must let patience have her perfect work. Deeply and thrillingly do I sympathize with you and dear Mrs. Child, not only in relation to this vexatious, and, I have no doubt, in strict equity *unjust* prosecution, but on account of the losses and sufferings which you have jointly encountered since you espoused the cause of helpless, perishing humanity against a proud, tyrannical and relentless nation. Yet, fail not still to trust in the promises of the God of the oppressed, and peace and comfort shall be yours. "Blessed is he that considereth the poor: the Lord will deliver him in time of trouble. The Lord will preserve him, and keep him alive; and he shall be blessed upon the earth: and thou wilt not deliver him unto the will of his enemies." [2]

Thanks and blessings upon your head for giving me an opportunity to discharge a fragment of that mountainous debt of kindness, which I owe both you and yours. I am delighted with your proposition.[3] Already I have written a long letter upon the subject, (seconded also by another from bro. May,) to Prof. Wright,[4] and requested him to lay it before the Executive Committee immediately, and also to inform either you or myself of their decision without delay. In writing it, I have loved you as myself, and used earnest, tender and persuasive language: its effect time must determine. But I think we may expect a favorable reply. Whether, however, bro. Phelps is to vacate his present station, I am not positively informed; but bro. May says it was rumored, a few days since in Providence, that the Executive Committee had determined to send Phelps on an agency to the British West Indies, to gather information respecting the result of the great experiment of human freedom in that quarter, as far as progress has been made. I hope the report is true; or, if not, that he will consent to give place to you as editor of the Emancipator, and go into the field as a lecturer. That important post I am sure you would fill with credit to yourself, and signal advantage to our great cause. Without flattery, (and you know me too well to believe me foolish or base enough to resort to its use,) I cherish a profound regard for your extensive acquirements, your solid talents, your vigor and originality of mind, and your disinterestedness, generosity and magnanimity of soul. The times are too mean, too sordid, and too corrupt, to appreciate "the mountain majesty of worth" — and what honest soul and christian patriot would wish to be appreciated by them? Commend us to the hatred and contempt of a degenerate people, but deliver us from their vile affection and vulgar respect! To receive their suffrages would only be obtaining so many verdicts against our honesty and uprightness. Their companionship would argue a base affinity between us. Let them tower in their littleness: they cannot rise above the level of obscurity.

I have told Prof. Wright, that we have enough in our cause who stand ready to attend to its moral and religious aspect; but there is scarcely an individual who regards, or is competent fully to unravel, its political relations and bearings. Hence, I have dwelt, in my letter to him, upon the importance of securing your assistance at this time because I believe you would do justice to that branch of our cause. Although we may not, in the technical sense of the term, become politicians ourselves, yet it is vastly important that we should watch and expose mere politicians — such men as Van Buren,[5] Calhoun,[6] Pinckney,[7] and the like — and that the latent movements of the State and National Governments, in opposition to inalienable human rights, should be made manifest before all the people.

Another uproar in Boston, on account of the seizure of two colored women by a prowling kidnapper.[8] It is impossible that such a being as a slave can exist, in equity, by the very *first* article of the Constitution of Massachusetts;[9] and I think none can be held in bondage in this country, either according to the letter or spirit of the U. S. Constitution.

Happy shall I be if I can be of any service to you or Mrs. Child at any time. I feel that I am greatly indebted to you both. O, for a large heap of money to throw it into your laps! — but "silver and gold have I none,"[10] and "blessed be nothing!"

Dear Helen unites with me in tendering much esteem and admiration to you both. Our boy is thriving finely.

    Ever yours to command,

           Wm. Lloyd Garrison.

ALS: Garrison Papers, Boston Public Library.

1. *Hamlet,* III, i. Garrison may be referring to an incident involving David L. Child, in which Child, about to board a ship for Europe, was arrested and jailed for an old debt. His friends obtained his release and he sailed in the fall of 1836. (Milton Meltzer, *Tongue of Flame, The Life of Lydia Maria Child*, New York, 1965, p. 63.)

2. Psalms 41:1–2.

3. As indicated further in this letter, his "proposition" seems to have been to undertake the editorship of *The Emancipator*, the official newspaper of the American Anti-Slavery Society, upon the proposed resignation of Amos Phelps.

4. Elizur Wright, Jr.

5. Martin Van Buren.

6. John C. Calhoun (1782–1850) was at this time United States senator from South Carolina.

7. Henry Laurens Pinckney.

8. *The Liberator*, August 6, 1836, carried several reports of the event.

9. "All men are born free and equal, and have certain natural, essential, and unalienable rights; among which may be reckoned the right of enjoying and defending their Lives and Liberties; that of acquiring, possessing, and protecting property; in fine, that of seeking and obtaining their safety and happiness."

10. Acts 3:6.

4 8

TO HENRY E. BENSON

Brooklyn, August 11, 1836.

My dear Henry:

Yesterday, the stage from Providence did not arrive till 12 o'clock — fourteen passengers furnishing some excuse to the poor jaded horses, but none to the unaccommodating and selfish stage-company. Father returned from the Post-Office, bringing with him only a New-York Sun, and quite disappointed, as usual, that he received no letter from Providence. Soon, however, our countenances were all made quite cheerful at the presence of Mr. Taylor,[1] who brought [us] a small parcel for sister Mary, and also a few pencilled lines from you, which were read with deep interest — for we cannot express to you how much solicitude we feel on your account, and wish we could promptly receive a daily bulletin informing us of the state of your health. Thanks to God for the improvement which seems to have taken place! May it be permanent. My soul yearns to see you fully convalescent, and engaged once more in the great duties of active life. In the mean time, remembering our mortality, and that afflictions are sent for our instruction, let us endeavor to cherish a child-like submission to the will of heaven, and to be resigned as well in sickness as in health. As for myself, I think I feel myself entirely crucified to this hollow world — to its honors, its offices, its applauses, its censures, its riches, its pleasures, its seductions — so that I have but a single desire to live yet a little longer, viz. that I may be instrumental in doing good, and in carrying on the strife of Christ against the empire of Satan. If, by the assurance of hope, "we know," and rejoice in the knowledge, "that if our earthly house of this tabernacle were dissolved, we have a building of God, a house not made with hands, eternal in the heavens," then may we "groan," not in view of our dissolution — O no! but "earnestly desiring to be clothed upon with our house which is from heaven: if so be that, being clothed, we shall not be found naked." [2]

I often take delight in repeating the following expressive and animating lines of Dr. Watts:[3]

> "Do flesh and nature dread to die?
>   And timorous thoughts our minds enslave?
> But grace can raise our hopes on high,
>   And quell the terrors of the grave.

What! shall we run to gain the crown,
    Yet grieve to think the goal so near?
Afraid to have our labors done,
    And finish this important war?

Do we not dwell in clouds below,
    And little know the God we love?
Why should we like this twilight so,
    When 'tis all noon in worlds above?

When we put off this fleshly load,
    We're from a thousand mischiefs free,
Forever present with our God,
    Where we have long'd and wish'd to be.

No more shall pride or passion rise,
    Or envy fret, or malice roar;
Or sorrow mourn with down-cast eyes,
    And sin defile our souls no more.

'Tis best, 'tis infinitely best,
    To go where tempters cannot come;
Where saints and angels, ever blest,
    Dwell and enjoy their heavenly home."

What ills flesh is heir to! Poor Frank Farley — to be cast down upon a bed of sickness just as he is about to be united with dear Eliza Chace! [4] The speediest recovery, submissively, be his.

Bro. May will make a visit to Boston on Friday of next week — probably I shall accompany him. Whether he intends going by the Worcester or Providence route, I do not know: however, in going or returning, P. will be visited, and, of course, yourself. As soon as it may be deemed best for you, all the household desire to see you in Brooklyn. Thus far, the weather this summer has not been very propitious to one in your condition. I presume you take good care to be warmly clad, especially with flannel: it is important that you should do so.

On Monday and Tuesday I was quite sick, so that I could not attend to my editorial duties, to any extent, for this week. My review of Dr. Beecher's speech seems to make some fluttering in certain quarters, especially my remarks upon the sanctity of the Sabbath.

I perceive that fresh attempts are making to renew the strength and popularity of the colonization scheme. Tillotson [5] made a speech in favor of it at Hampton on the fourth ultimo. Judge Robinson is full of it.[6]

Tell George his little girl is certainly much better. Our boy is very hearty, and weighs 17 lbs. We are all well. You shall have another letter from me soon.

Affectionately yours,

Wm. Lloyd Garrison.

ALS: Garrison Papers, Boston Public Library.

1. Daniel A. Taylor of Providence lived at 61 Broad Street. His business address was 10 Market Street. He was listed in the Providence *Directory* for 1841 as having moved to 11 Benevolent Street; with his business address, under the name of G. & D. Taylor, dry goods, as 13 Market Square. "In the 1865 State Census he is the only adult Daniel Taylor, and is listed as a merchant, aged 54, born in Providence." (Letter to editor, April 25, 1968, from Clarkson A. Rollins, III, Director of Research, The Rhode Island Historical Society, Providence, R.I.)

2. II Corinthians 5:1–3.

3. Dr. Isaac Watts (1674–1748), English dissenting clergyman and writer of hymns. The hymn quoted here, with two stanzas omitted, is from his *Divine Hymns, Composed on the Subjects of the Sermons*, "For Sermon XLIII, Death a Blessing to the Saints," *The Poetical Works of Isaac Watts* (Edinburgh, 1782), VII, 39–40.

4. Eliza Chace, William Chace's sister, later Mrs. Thomas Davis. *The Liberator* (December 11, 1840) notes that she was the eldest daughter of William Chace of Providence. She died on December 4, 1840, at the age of thirty-one. At the time of her death she was corresponding secretary of the Providence Female Anti-Slavery Society. The Frank Farley mentioned here may have been the brother of the Reverend Frederick Augustus Farley mentioned in letter 36, to S. J. May, June 19, 1836. On February 23, 1834, Henry Benson wrote to Garrison from Providence: "The bearer of this Mr. F. D. Farley is brother to the minister of that name in this city, and a young man of kindly and benevolent feelings. As regards our cause he is with us heart & hand. He resides in Vermont but is going to the west in the spring. Any abolition tracts which you can give away would be acceptable to him. We have furnished him with what we had to spare. Like the rest of us he is poor and penniless." (Anti-Slavery Letters to Garrison and Others, Boston Public Library.)

5. The Reverend George J. Tillotson.

6. Probably Judge Vine Robinson (b. Windham, Connecticut, July 25, 1767; d. Brooklyn, Connecticut, January 18, 1843) of Brooklyn, Connecticut, father of Daniel Robinson. Judge Robinson was a merchant and judge of the county court in Brooklyn. He filled many important offices and several times represented the town in the legislature. (*Robinson Genealogy, Descendants of the Rev. John Robinson*, published by the Robinson Genealogical Society, Salem, Mass., n.d., I, 145–146.)

49

TO GEORGE W. BENSON

Brooklyn, Aug. 18, 1836.

Dear bro. George:

A word in your ear. Accompanying this is a packet from bro. May, directed to Prof. Wright [1] at New-York. It is important that it should be sent safely and speedily to the "big city," as it encloses a long and able article on the Constitution from the pen of S. J. M.[2] for insertion in the next Am. Quarterly A. S. Review.[3] Now, without wishing to give you any trouble, it is our desire that you will forward it, if you can, by to-morrow's boat, so that it may be delivered in the course of Saturday — as Prof. W. was promised that he should have it by the 20th inst. (By the way, father enters upon his 85th year on that day. His health is excellent.)

I have sent $25.00 to sister Charlotte, to purchase sundry articles for Helen and the babe. Should there be enough left, will you discharge my bill at Dr. M'Intyre's? My nose is about healed up, and gives me no longer any trouble, although it is still somewhat red. Whether it will trouble me as winter approaches, I cannot of course predict — but hope it will not. The value of the salve, snuff, and other medicine I had of the Dr. did not probably cost him 50 cts. including a junk-bottle — however, if he does not charge me more than $5, I shall be content. I leave the settlement with you. He will probably desire something in the shape of a certificate from me — but if it were a more important case, I would give it.

Am happy to hear that you and cousin Chace have commenced lecturing in good earnest — hope you will rival Weld and Stanton. Dear Birney! what honors the vile are heaping upon him! These are notable times to live in — in God be our trust.

Ever affec. yours,

Wm. Lloyd Garrison.

ALS: Garrison Papers, Boston Public Library.

1. Elizur Wright, Jr.
2. Samuel J. May.
3. The *Quarterly Anti-Slavery Magazine* was published by the American Anti-Slavery Society, under the direction of Elizur Wright, Jr., for two years beginning in October 1835. Wright designed the magazine and edited it. It was supposed to appeal to educators, students, and professional men. (Dwight L. Dumond, *Antislavery: The Crusade for Freedom in America*, Ann Arbor, Mich., 1961, p. 266; Dumond, *A Bibliography of Antislavery in America*, Ann Arbor, Mich., 1961, p. 96.)

50

TO HENRY E. BENSON

Brooklyn, August 18, 1836.

Dear bro. Henry:

Your long and interesting letter was received and read by us all with delight, and demands our united acknowledgments. Do not be apprehensive lest there may be some complaint, because your letters are directed and addressed chiefly to me. To whomsoever sent, in the family, they are always regarded as common property, being read by all as most acceptable. The best news you can send us relates to the improvement of your health; and we are rendered truly happy to find, by your last epistle, that you are gradually getting better. It is more than probable that there will be alternate changes, either favorable or unfavorable, from week to week; but these are common in almost every disorder — so you must not be discouraged, if on some days you do not feel so well as on others. Even when we are free from positive sickness, you know it is common for us to experience, almost continually, fresh mutations of bodily feelings — yesterday strong and lively, to-day stupid and feeble — now, full of enterprise and activity — anon, disposed to apathy and inaction. This, for example, is one of my torpid, unproductive days, although every thing is fair and bright in creation. I am ashamed of myself, nevertheless.

The resignation to your lot, which is manifested in your letter, is truly commendable, and betokens a humble and filial spirit towards "our Father who is in heaven," and whose grace is able to sustain us under every disappointment and trial. May his loving-kindness be with you continually, mitigating every pain, and soothing every sorrow.

The news of bro. Weld's arrival in Providence [1] seemed almost "too good to be true" — but, after reading your account of an interview with him, I bid adieu to my skepticism. You see what reliance I place upon your veracity! — But, don't plume yourself too much on the fact of your having had the *first* peep at him — I shall probably have the *last*, as bro. Burleigh informs me Weld will visit Brooklyn on his return to New-York. — I am somewhat apprehensive, however, that he will be persuaded to return via Providence instead of our village, as he will doubtless have many urgent entreaties to do so — so, that if he should comply with them, you will have clearly the advantage over me. However, I rely a good deal upon his independence, and therefore mean to hold myself in readiness to give him a generous reception.

It seems, by the information he gave you, that the Am. Soc. will have no difficulty in procuring individuals both able and willing to perform a mission to the West-Indies. Thome would,[2] I think, do admirably well — but our friend Walker [3] is not exactly the man.

The formation of an anti-slavery society in Hayti is indeed a cheering event: but I shall be greatly surprised, if, as soon as the fact is published, it do not alarm our southern adversaries, and subject us to the charge of having entered into a "conspiracy" with the Haytians, to stir up negro rebellion in the United States! — "The plot thickens," they will say.

Bro. May leaves for Boston, via Worcester, in the morning. He desires me to say to you, that he regrets exceedingly he has been baffled in his original intention of going to-day via Providence, as he has a yearning desire to see you; but, he has had incessant calls upon his time, and a multitude of duties to perform. He hopes to be able to return through Providence, in the course of a fortnight, and desires me to send you his sympathy and warmest wishes for your speedy recovery. It is his intention not to engage in an agency again, but to accept of a call (on account of his family) which he has had to be settled over a Unitarian congregation in Scituate.[4] [T]his I communicate *sub rosa.* I am very sorry he has come to this determination, on many accounts. He says he will make special inquiries about your missing cloak. You ask me, if I do not need mine. No. Truly, you might as well look for strawberries in January, as for letters from Knapp at any season of the year. Not a line does he write to me, although I have besought him to answer some special inquiries.

A rare occurrence took place yesterday. Father consented to let me drive in a chaise down to our friend Hinckley's [5] at Plainfield. We saw Mr. Hinckley, the elder, Albert, his sister, and mother, who gave us a very cordial reception. Poor Albert is in a miserable state of health, is subject to epileptic fits, and is more or less bewildered by a strange and increasing confusion in his head. He is necessitated to abjure study, and keep very quiet.

After staying there two or three hours, we then visited our estimable friend Dr. Green,[6] whose beautiful residence seemed to delight father very much. It is needless to say, that our reception was very gracious by the whole family. Particular and kind inquiries were made respecting you. Our ride was a charming one, and no accident happened.

My remarks upon the sanctity of the Sabbath,[7] in late numbers of the Liberator, have subjected me already to much censure, as I anticipated — but truth need never be ashamed. You will see by the next paper, probably, that I take my leave of the subject, so far as the Lib. is concerned. With increasing affection, I remain,

Yours, faithfully,

Wm. Lloyd Garrison.

ALS: Garrison Papers, Boston Public Library.

1. Theodore Weld was at this time apparently engaged in a fund-raising and lecturing mission for the American Anti-Slavery Society in New England. See *Weld-Grimké Letters*, I, 330, 333, 334.

2. James Anthony Thome (1809–1873), Kentucky-born and raised on a plantation, was a student at Lane Seminary during the famous debate and left the seminary with the other students in 1834. He enrolled as a theology student at Oberlin College and graduated in 1836. He was chosen by the American Anti-Slavery Society for the mission to the West Indies to which Garrison refers. The

purpose of the mission, on which he was accompanied by J. Horace Kimball, was to study the results of the emancipation of the slaves which had taken place there in August 1834. The result of their study was a volume entitled *Emancipation in the West Indies. A Six Months' Tour in Antigua, Barbadoes, and Jamaica, in the year 1837*, published in New York in 1838 by the American Anti-Slavery Society. (*Weld-Grimké Letters*, I, 149n; Ruchames, *The Abolitionists*, p. 149.)

3. Probably Amasa Walker (1799–1875), businessman, reformer, teacher, author, and political figure. Born in Connecticut, he moved to North Brookfield, Massachusetts, with his parents, attended school there, and in 1825 he moved to Boston, where he engaged in business until 1840. He was an early member and financial supporter of the New England Anti-Slavery Society as well as of other causes, such as temperance and peace. He was a delegate to the Democratic National Convention at Buffalo, New York, in 1836 and to the first international peace conference at London in 1840. From 1842 to 1848 he taught political economy at Oberlin College, from 1853 to 1860 at Harvard University, and from 1859 to 1869 at Amherst College. He was elected on various occasions to the Massachusetts House of Representatives and the United States Congress, and was the author of several books on political economy. (*BDAC.*)

4. Samuel J. May had been the general agent and corresponding secretary of the Massachusetts Anti-Slavery Society since the spring of 1835. He was installed pastor of the church in South Scituate on October 26, 1836, and remained there six years.

5. Vincent Hinckley of Plainfield, Connecticut, was vice-president of the Windham County Anti-Slavery Society in 1836 (*The Liberator*, May 7, 1836). Albert Hinckley (1811–1864), his son, was a member of the Amherst class of 1838, though he did not graduate. See Garrison's letter to Henry Benson, September 19, 1835 (*Letters*, I).

6. Dr. Rowland Greene of Plainfield, Connecticut.

7. The reference is to his strictures on Dr. Lyman Beecher's views of the Sabbath.

51

TO ISAAC KNAPP

Brooklyn, Aug. 19, 1836.

Dear Knapp:

What do you think brother Henry reports of you? In his last letter he says — "I have written to Knapp, time and again; but I might as well address my letter to a State's prison convict, and look for an answer." There's a panegyric for you! and, diffident as you are, you will not acknowledge it to be unmerited. I can praise you on the same score — for not a word can I extort from you, except through the medium of our obliging bro. Burleigh.[1] Why, what a horror of goosequills, black ink and white paper you must cherish! Don't you lament that you have learnt to write your name? How much easier it is to make one's mark, you know! What a pity it is that "reading and writing comes by nature"![2] I, too, have a sort of repugnance to scribbling — pra[y] did I catch the disease of [y]ou, or you of me? So far as your delinquency toward me is co[ncerne]d, I readily excuse you: but poor bro. Henry being sick ma[y find] silence, after he has made an effort to hold a correspondence [with] you, hard to be borne. Do try to send him at least a few lines soon: they will be the more valuable for being rare. You know, or ought to know, that he esteems [you] highly; and now that he is cut off from society on account of his sickness, the smallest item of intelligence from any of his friends must be very acceptable. — You can tell him many things about Boston, and Boston folks, which nobody else can, and which would interest him very much. He writes that he is now somewhat better; but his dreadful cough still keeps the mastery over him, and I fear it will never be eradicated except by death. Still, I will not yet despair of his recovery — surprising cures are sometimes effected in cases which are hopeless. How would it answer for him to take a trip to the West Indies before winter sets in? —

I suppose he has sent you some account of his tour to Philadelphia, and settlement with friend Buffum. I think he managed the case with great judgment and fairness, and is therefore deserving of even something more than our thanks. The dear youth! how I yearn to see him again restored to health.

It seems to me, — judging at the distance of 80 miles, — that our Board of Managers in Boston did not take a wise step, by adopting and publishing such strong resolutions [3] respecting the petty disturbance (if it amounted even to that) in the case of the two colored females claimed as slaves. Such a course made the affair look formidable, and tended rather to encourage our enemies to "magnify a mole-hill into a mountain," than to abate their *patriotic* indignation. But it is too late to recal[l] the transaction, though not to get a moral from [it.]

On Sabbath evening last, I went to Pom[fret] with [S. J. M]ay, who delivered an excellent address on slavery in El[der] Branch's [4] meeting-house to an audience respectable in [nu]mber and appearance, and apparently much interested. — There I obtained a new subscriber for the Lib[r]. Send his paper as follows — "George Lyon, Pomfret, Ct." [5] Commence with last Saturday's paper. He paid $2.00 for one year, which I enclose.

Here is another — Russell Green,[6] West Thompson, Ct. — for six months, from next paper, Aug. 20 — paid $1.00, herewith enclosed.

Don't neglect sending these papers immediately. — Mr. Dan[l]. Green [7] of Killingley Centre informs me, that sometime ago he had a journeyman by the name of Arnold working with him who took the Liberator, and had it directed to Green and Arnold. Arnold has left him, and Mr. Green is inclined to suspect that he did not settle for the paper.

If he did not, he says he will do so, and I suppose will continue to take the paper, if it is yet sent to him — so, if you will make out the bill for what is due, (provided there is any thing due,) and send it to me in the bundle, I will get you the money.

The day before yesterday, Almira Crandall,⁸ (sister of Prudence,⁹) now Mrs. Rand, made us a visit with her husband from New-York. Her health is not very good. She seems to have been fortunate in marriage, as Mr. R. is quite a pleasant, genteel and handsome looking man, and is doing very well as a school teacher. Prudence is expected home in the course of a fortnight. She is very happy with Mr. Philleo, Almira says. Then she [is] made happy very easily, I think. We shall all be glad to [see] her.

Yesterday, I rode with father to Dr. Green's ¹⁰ [. . .] at Plainfield. We had a delightful time, and such an occurrence as a pleasure [-jau]nt was quite a phenomenon in his old age. You know I [was v]ery particular to request you to send a dozen extr[a copie]s of the Liberator to Dr. Green, when you inserted hi[s . . . p]iece signed Woolman, a few numbers back.¹¹ He [. . .] that he did not receive them. I hope you will not fa[il] to do so, at once — and if you cannot spare a dozen [copi]es, send as many as you can conveniently. They will be sent to individuals of some consequence in the Society of Friends, and will doubtless benefit the paper. Send them to the same Post Office to which his paper is regularly sent — Centre Village I believe, though I am not sure.

Friend Lundy has made a neat book of E. M. Chandler's writings — ¹² I shall notice it next week. As it is excellent to present as a token of esteem, I send you two dollars, for which forward me four copies in the bundle, and charge [the] remaining 50 cts. to me. I wish to give them away to certain friends.

I have been cherishing the hope that bro. May would consent to embark in our cause again as a general agent — but, on account of his family, he says he has concluded to accept of a call which he has had to be settled over a congregation in Scituate. All the friends will be sorry to learn this fact. I hope he will yet yield to our united entreaties. If bro. Weld is in Boston, get him to converse with bro. M. on the subject.

A few days since, I wounded my leg very severely, by jumping from a stone-wall, and striking against a sharp stump. It pains me continually, and will prove troublesome. More I would write if I had time and room. — The Sabbath question seems to make a stir. — Yours, affec.

W. L. Garrison.

ALS: Garrison Papers, Boston Public Library. Both pages of the letter are torn.

1. Charles C. Burleigh.
2. Shakespeare, *Much Ado About Nothing*, II, iii.
3. The resolutions of the Board of Managers of the Massachusetts Anti-Slavery Society were adopted on August 3, 1836. They condemned the use of force by Negroes to free two Negro women who had been claimed as slaves and had been in court awaiting determination of the case. The resolutions appeared in *The Liberator* August 6, 1836, together with reports of the incident.
4. Elder Nicholas Branch, a Baptist minister, was ordained a pastor in 1815 in the First Baptist Church of West Woodstock, Connecticut. From 1824 on, he held a series of positions in Baptist churches in Windham county (Ellen D. Larned, *History of Windham County, Connecticut*, Worcester, Mass., 1880, pp. 454, 541, 557).
5. Otherwise unidentified.
6. Otherwise unidentified.
7. Otherwise unidentified.
8. Garrison describes her elsewhere as "a beautiful girl" (see *Life*, 1, 341, 317, 344).
9. Prudence Crandall (1803–1889), a schoolteacher, of Quaker parentage, and originally of Hopkinton, Rhode Island, established a private academy for girls at Canterbury, Connecticut, in 1831. In 1833 when her school had become recognized as one of the best in the state, she admitted a Negro girl as a student and incurred the opposition of almost all the parents of her students, who threatened to withdraw their daughters from her school. When she decided to limit her pupils to colored girls only, there was great public indignation, and the town petitioned the state to enact a law prohibiting private schools for nonresident colored persons. The legislature passed the law in May and Miss Crandall was arrested and imprisoned under the law and was finally convicted. The case was carried to the state supreme court of errors, and her conviction was reversed on a technicality in July 1834. During the appeal she was the object of numerous attacks, and finally her house was set on fire and badly damaged. This convinced her that she could never succeed in continuing her school. She later married the Reverend Calvin Philleo, a Baptist clergyman, who died in 1876. They lived in several places in New York and Illinois. At the time of her death she was living in Elks Falls, Kansas, having moved to southern Kansas after the death of her husband. (*ACAB; DAB.*)
10. Rowland Green or Greene. See letter 6, to Henry E. Benson, January 26, 1836.
11. The piece appeared in *The Liberator*, July 30, 1836, and was entitled "To the Professors of Christianity, — Whose Sentiments on Slavery Are Merely Passive."
12. Elizabeth Margaret Chandler, *Poetical Works*, with a memoir of her life and character by Benjamin Lundy (Philadelphia: Howell, 1836), 180 pp. Miss Chandler had died on November 2, 1834. Originally, her family had considered asking Garrison to prepare a memoir and edition of her works, but finding sentiment against Garrison's antislavery views exceedingly strong in Philadelphia, they sought another editor. Lundy offered to edit the book, was unable to find a publisher, and published it by subscription. Another volume, consisting of Miss Chandler's essays, entitled *Essays, Philanthropic and Moral: Principally Relating to the Abolition of Slavery in America*, was published in Philadelphia in 1836 by Howell. Although the latter volume does not bear Lundy's name as editor, he may well have been its compiler. (Merton L. Dillon, *Benjamin Lundy and the Struggle for Negro Freedom*, Urbana and London, 1966, p. 214.)

5 2

TO HENRY E. BENSON

Sunday Evening,
Aug. 21, 1836.

Dear Henry:

I have just been informed that Daniel Taylor intends leaving for Providence in the morning; and, although I have been lying abed all day, and feel very feeble, in consequence of the injury done to my leg nearly a fortnight since, yet I must seize my pen a few moments, if only to say, for the thousandth time, that I love and admire you as "a brother, yea, above a brother." It is comforting to hear of the steady improvement of your health. May all your medicines be blessed by the Great Physician, and complete restoration be speedily obtained!

In jumping from the garden wall, I severely wounded my left leg, in front, a few inches below the knee, by striking against a sharp stump, which was concealed by the long grass. A gash was made about three inches in length — but I did not much regard it at the time. In the course of a week, finding the wound growing worse in spite of all I could do for it, I sent for Dr. Spalding, who, on examining it, thought it might be easily cured. But, up to this time, his remedies have been powerless, and it is more painful and troublesome than ever. Yesterday, while he was dressing it, I was barely enabled to keep from fainting by the aid of camphor, &c. As it prevents me from taking any exercise, I necessarily feel much bodily debility.

Helen has not felt well for several days past, and to-day she consulted the Dr. who gave her some medicine, which, in its operation, makes her feel very sick. All the rest of the family are in usual health. O what a blessing it is to be in possession of a vigorous body and sound limbs! Well does the poet Thomson rapturously exclaim —

> "O, who can speak the vigorous joys of health —
> Unclogged the body, unobscured the mind!
> The morning rises gay with pleasing stealth —
> The temperate evening falls serene and kind!" [1]

And yet sickness teaches us many a useful lesson, and ought to be received as an admonitory angel. "For what is our life? It is even as a vapor, which appeareth for a little time, and then vanisheth away." [2]

Have you read the discussion between Thompson and Breckinridge,[3] in the Emancipator? How false and dastardly is the charge of the latter against Prof. Wright and myself, — of publishing incendiary placards to stir up a mob! Thus far, I feel somewhat disappointed in reading the discussion. Bro. Thompson does not concentrate and present his evidence of the guilt of this whole nation, as I expected he would; and he treats the insolent Breckinridge altogether too tenderly. None but an American can fairly compete with an American, on the subject of American slavery. Yet the debate will do good.

My views of the Sabbath question, as incidentally presented in my review of Dr. Beecher's flaming speech at Pittsburgh, are exciting much comment, and subjecting me to much condemnation, as I anticipated. The only thing that I regret is, the insertion of a communication by Knapp, (written by friend Oakes,[4]) headed "The New and Old Puritans,"[5] because it is written in a manner calculated to exasperate, and not to convince. I know how important it is that I should keep the columns of the Liberator clear of sectarianism, nor have I ever intended to assail any denominational feelings or peculiarities. The Sabbath question is not sectarian, but general — yet the discussion of it is not exactly proper in the Lib[r]. I have received several letters, remonstrating with me on account of my sentiments, but chiefly on the erroneous supposition that I was about making my paper the arena of a sabbatical controversy. Some of these are expressed in kind and friendly language. Not so is the one sent to me by young Hyde[6] of this village. Although he has paid in advance up to September, he says that he does not wish to receive another number of the paper — and he considers me "a dangerous member of the community, deserving the reprobation of every lover of his country"!! — But the letter which grieves and surprises me most is that of Rev. Jonathan Farr of Harvard,[7] with whom I believe you are somewhat acquainted. He says — "I had supposed you a very pious person, and that a large proportion of the abolitionists were religious persons" — "I have thought of you as another Wilberforce[8] — but would Wilberforce have spoken thus of the day on which the Son of God rose from the dead?" — "I have supposed, that, in your great and incessant exertions in the anti-slavery cause, you were influenced by no worldly nor political motive — that yours was a holy zeal and a christian benevolence" — &c. &c. Here is christian charity for you! — Because, with Calvin, Belsham, Paley, Fox, Whitby, Barclay, Gill, Selden, Luther,[9] and many other distinguished commentators and pious men, I maintain that, under the gospel dispensation, there is no such thing as a "holy day," but that *all our time* ought to be sanctified by works of righteousness and in well-doing, — it follows, according to the insinuations of Mr. Farr, that I am *not* a pious person — that abolitionists are *not* religious — that I am influenced by worldly or political motives — that mine is *not* a holy zeal and a christian benevolence! — And yet this same individual complains in his letter as follows — "Though belonging to a denomination of Christians who are *denied the Christian name* by multitudes," &c. Surely, it is time for him to take the beam from his own eye — surely, if he is disposed to stigmatize me as an infidel, or shut me out from the pale of Christianity, because I differ with him as to the sanctity of an *outward observance* — he ought not to complain if he is treated in the same manner by others, because he differs with them as to the scheme of salvation, and the essential dignity of Jesus Christ. He asks — "Would Wilberforce have spoken thus," &c. What then? Is Christ or Wilberforce our exemplar? And I ask Mr. Farr in reply — "Would Wilberforce have denied the identity of Christ with the Father? or would he have been a Unitarian, to gain the applause of the world?" Such questions are not arguments, but fallacies, unworthy of a liberal mind. Bro. May is much grieved at Farr's letter — you will be; I think.

Tell Bro. George I will notice Prof. Farnsworth [10] in the Liberator — am much obliged to him for his facts.

Mr. May left for Boston on Friday morning, according to calculation.

We shall be very glad to see Frank and Eliza [11] in Brooklyn.

Hastily but affectionately yours,

Wm. Lloyd Garrison.

ALS: Garrison Papers, Boston Public Library. An excerpt of this letter was reprinted in *Life*, II, 110–111.

1. James Thomson, "The Castle of Indolence," Canto II.
2. James 4:14.
3. The Reverend Robert J. Breckinridge (1800–1871), of Baltimore, Maryland, was a prominent member of and spokesman for the American Colonization Society. For some of Breckinridge's charges against Garrison, Thompson, and others see the item entitled "Breckinridge's Essay" in *The Liberator*, August 13, 1836, which summarizes a letter by Breckinridge originally published in the New York *Journal of Commerce* from the London *Patriot*. On August 20, 1836, *The Liberator* published a letter from one of the secretaries of the Glasgow Emancipation Society, dated June 14, 1836, which presented some of the details of the debate between George Thompson and Breckinridge in Glasgow which began on June 13. At this meeting Breckinridge accused Elizur Wright, Jr., and Garrison of printing and publishing a placard "calling upon the mob to mob him." Additional details are given in *The Liberator*, September 3 and October 1, 1836; *Life*, I, 448–450.
4. William Oakes (1799–1848) of Ipswich, Massachusetts, graduated from Harvard College in 1820 and from the Law School in 1825. After two or three years he abandoned the practice of law for the study of natural history. He "became the most eminent botanist of his day in New England," but was also interested in geology and mineralogy. He collected specimens of almost every New England plant and in 1848 published *Scenery of the White Mountains* (Justin Winsor, ed., *Memorial History of Boston*, Boston, 1881, IV, 524).
5. The item appeared in *The Liberator*, July 30, 1836. The author's name was withheld. It was signed, "A Friend to the American Union," and dated Sunday, July 24, 1836. On August 20, under " 'New and Old Puritans,' " Garrison printed an apology. He noted "that that communication was published without our knowledge or approbation — that we did not see it till it appeared in print — that we

regretted its publication . . . the style of his article was calculated rather to irritate than convince."

6. A penciled note in the margin refers to Hyde as "a theological student at New Haven."

7. Jonathan Farr (b. Harvard, Massachusetts, 1790; d. there, 1845) graduated from Harvard Divinity School in 1821 and was a Unitarian minister at Gardner, Massachusetts, from 1831 to 1833. He wrote prolifically on theology, was an enthusiast of the temperance cause, and was a member of the Harvard School Committee in 1841–1843 (Henry S. Nourse, *History of the Town of Harvard, Massachusetts,* Harvard, 1894, pp. 165, 378, 430–431; William B. Henick, *History of the Town of Gardner,* Gardner, Mass., 1878, p. 502; *Life,* II, 451.)

8. William Wilberforce (1759–1833) was the British statesman and reformer, prominent in the abolition of the slave trade in Britain in 1807 and in the campaign for the abolition of slavery (*EE*).

9. John Calvin was the great Protestant theologian of the Reformation.

Thomas Belsham (1750–1829) was an English Unitarian theologian. Originally a Trinitarian, he became a Unitarian and, influenced by Priestley, succeeded him as minister at the Gravel Pit Unitarian Chapel in Hackney. In 1805 he was called to London, where he presided for many years at the Essex Street Chapel. He wrote *Discourses on the Evidence of the Christian Religion,* and *A New Translation and Exposition of the Doctrine of St. Paul.* (*DNB.*) Garrison reprints a long selection from Belsham in his essay on the Sabbath in *The Liberator,* August 27, 1836.

William Paley (1743–1805) was an English theologian, author of *Principles of Moral and Political Philosophy* and *A View of the Evidences of Christianity.* (*DNB.*)

George Fox (1624–1691) was the English founder of the Society of Friends, theologian and author (*EE*).

Daniel Whitby (1638–1726), minister and theological polemicist, was made perpetual curate of St. Thomas's Church and rector of St. Edmund's in Salisbury in 1669. He was a popular anti-Romish polemicist until 1682, when he published *The Protestant Reconciler,* which urged concessions to nonconformists. In 1683 the University of Oxford, in convention, ordered the book to be burned. His main work was *Paraphrase and Commentary on the New Testament* (2 vols.), 1703. His confession of Unitarianism was published posthumously as *Whitby's Last Thoughts.* (*DNB.*)

Robert Barclay (1648–1690) was an eminent English Quaker theologian and writer. His main work was *An Apology for the True Christian Divinity,* published in Latin in Amsterdam in 1676 and translated and published in English in 1678. He was a proprietor of eastern New Jersey. (*DNB.*)

John Gill (1697–1771) was an English nonconformist divine, a great Hebrew scholar, and a staunch Calvinist. He was pastor of the Baptist congregation at Horsleydown, Southwark. His main works were *Exposition of the Song of Solomon* (1728); *The Prophecies of the Old Testament Respecting the Messiah* (1728); *The Cause of God and Truth* (4 vols., 1735–1738); and *Expositions of the Bible,* (9 vols., 1746–1766). (*DNB.*)

John Selden (1584–1654) was an English jurist, scholar, and member of Parliament, and one of the most learned men of his time. He wrote expositions of rabbinical and British law. One of his most famous books was *A History of Tithes* (1617), which offended the clergy. He was imprisoned for two years, without trial or hearing, for having offended the king. (*DNB.*)

Martin Luther was the leader of the Protestant Reformation.

10. Dr. Amos Farnsworth (1788–1861), of Groton, Massachusetts, was an active abolitionist and a vice-president of the Massachusetts Anti-Slavery Society. He was a medical doctor, a graduate of the Harvard Medical School in 1814. He began his practice in Boston and moved to Groton in 1832. In a letter to Amos Phelps, October 27, 1837 (Phelps Papers, Boston Public Library), he presents

his views of Garrison. He furnished most of the financial support for starting the *National Anti-Slavery Standard* in 1840; he was with Garrison at the mobbing in 1835. As a physician, he did not believe in the use of medicine for fever. On his retirement from the practice of medicine, he cultivated vines and fruit trees, whose fruits he preserved by a secret formula which he refused to divulge to George Thompson and Silas Hawley (Silas Hawley, *Reminiscences of Groton During the Years 1839, 1840, and 1841*, Groton, 1886, p. 6 and Appendix).

11. Frank Farley and Eliza Chace, mentioned in letter 48, to Henry E. Benson, August 11, 1836.

53

TO ISAAC KNAPP

Brooklyn, Aug. 23, 1836.

Dear Knapp —

As you have a long article of mine on the Sabbath question for this week's paper — as there are many selected articles in your hands which ought, if possible, to obtain an insertion — as bro. Burleigh [1] is with you, and ready at any moment to pour out his valuable thoughts upon paper — and as I am not in a condition for writing editorials — I shall not trouble you with any matter for your next number — but mean to send you a mass on Thursday or Friday.

A fortnight ago, I wounded my leg badly by jumping from a wall against a sharp stump. It has been growing worse ever since, despite all the Dr's prescriptions. It gives me continual pain, both night and day, and wholly prevents me from taking any exercise. Probably some time must elapse before it will be cured — so that, if you had desired me to accompany bro. May to Boston, I could not have done so. I shall learn to be more careful of my shins hereafter. As soon as the wound heals, it will be time for me to take up my location in Boston. I wish, as do all the family, that y[ou] could first make us a visit here.

No doubt you have all been refreshed at the sight of bro. May's ever-pleasing countenance. It makes me feel badly to think of his being settled in another place, instead of engaging wholly in our cause — but the state of his family requires it. I shall be very anxious to see him on his return, to know what arrangements he may have made, and to learn a thousand little items of intelligence which may reach me through no other medium. Tel[l] him that Mrs. May, the babe, and Charlotte, are all well. A letter was received from him by Mrs. M. by yesterday's mail.

I hope you will be able to find room, this week, for the important Letter of Gen. Jackson,[2] respecting the movements of Gen. Gaines,[3] which you will find in some of the newspapers. Though it reads well, and seems to reprimand Gaines, I am afraid it is only a *blind* to the eyes of the people, and that no reliance ought to be placed upon it.

It seems, by a Providence paper, that another slave case took place in Boston on Thursday last — the result not stated.[4] In every such instance, I wish that friend Sewall or Loring would assume the ground maintained recently by Judge Hornblower [5] of New-Jersey — viz. — that the law of Congress, regulating the arrest of fugitive slaves, is unconstitutional, because no power is given by the Constitution to Congress to legislate on the subject — that every person in the State, white or black, free or slave, is entitled to a trial by jury — and that the color of a person should be no longer considered as presumptive evidence of slavery. But I would go further, and maintain, (all previous constructions to the contrary notwithstanding,) that by the Constitution of the U.S., as well as by that of our own State, no slave can lawfully exist in this country. Let such a pos[tulate] be decided by an appeal to the Supreme Court of the U.S. I am surprised that the first article of the Mass. Constitution is not more frequently appealed to, in proof that no person can be seized or claimed upon the soil of the State as a slave.

I was much interested in reading, in the last paper, the account of Thompson's 1st lecture in London, at Rev. Mr. Price's Chapel.[6] Hope you mean to insert the debate between Breckinridge and Thompson, because our English friends, as well as our own readers, and T. particularly, will expect to see it in our columns.[7] Thus far, bro. T. has not managed the case so conclusively as I expected he would — he treats Breckinridge too tenderly — but I will take care of B.

I meant to have sent a letter to bro. Burleigh by Mr. May, but had not time. I am largely his debtor.

[In] Saturday's bundle, you forgot to enclose a Liberator. I trust you will not this week.

Yours, hastily,

Wm. Lloyd Garrison.

P.S. Don't mention in the Liberator that I have hurt my leg!

ALS: Garrison Papers, Boston Public Library.

1. Charles C. Burleigh.

2. *The Liberator* of August 27, 1836, did print a small piece, "President Jackson and the Invasion of Texas," signed "B," which referred to the letter by President Andrew Jackson to Newton Cannon, governor of Tennessee, disapproving of the action of General Gaines. General Gaines had made a requisition on the governor of Tennessee for a large force of mounted men to assemble on the Texan frontier. Jackson stated that the ostensible reason for the requisition, namely, fear of hostilities from the western Indians, was unfounded, and that Mexico, the other possible source of hostilities, had not insulted the American flag or injured any American citizen. The letter to Governor Cannon, who was governor of Tennessee from 1835 to 1839, was dated "Hermitage, August 6, 1836," and is printed in John

Spencer Bassett, *Correspondence of Andrew Jackson* (Washington, D.C., 1931), V, 416–418.

3. Edmund Pendleton Gaines (1777–1849) had served in the War of 1812, was promoted to major general in 1814, and was commissioner to the Creek Indians in 1816. He served under Jackson in the Creek War and fought the Seminoles in 1836 (*HEUSH; ACAB*).

4. *The Liberator*, August 27, 1836, carried the following item, entitled "The Slave Case": "A case is now pending before the Supreme Judicial Court, which involves principles of immense importance to the cause of human rights. It is that of a young colored girl, brought to this city by her mistress, the wife of a citizen of New Orleans, where the girl was held as a slave. Liberty is claimed for her, on the ground that a slave brought by his master's voluntary act, into this state, thereby becomes legally free. The case came up before Judge Wilde last week, and was argued by Messrs. Loring and Sewall for, and Messrs. C. P. & B. R. Curtis, against, the girl's liberation. It was postponed to Friday of this week, when it was again argued, and very ably, by Messrs. Loring and Choate for the girl, and by the same counsel as before, on the other side. Our columns will hereafter contain a full report."

5. Judge Joseph Coerten Hornblower (b. Belleville, New Jersey, May 6, 1777; d. June 11, 1864), a lawyer and member of the New Jersey legislature, was elected chief justice by the New Jersey legislature in 1832 and served for fourteen years. The decision to which Garrison refers was in the case of *The State vs. The Sheriff of Burlington*, decided March 4, 1836. The case involved a fugitive slave. Justice Hornblower's opinion was that "the Fugitive Slave Law, enacted by Congress in 1793, which related to the surrender of slaves, being addressed to the states and conferring no jurisdiction upon Congress over the subject matter, was unconstitutional." Judge Hornblower retired from the bench in 1846 and resumed law practice in Newark. He was the first president of the New Jersey Historical Society (1845–1864) and taught law at Princeton from 1847 to 1855. At first a Federalist, then a Whig, he later became a Republican. His views were strongly antislavery. (*DAB*; R. S. Field, "Address on the Life and Character of Joseph C. Hornblower," in *Proceedings*, New Jersey Historical Society, vol. X, 1865.)

6. The account was reprinted in *The Liberator*, August 20, 1836, from the London *Patriot* of June 1, 1836. The meeting had taken place at the Reverend Thomas Price's Wesleyan Chapel in Devonshire Square. The theme of the address was American slavery and the progress of the American Anti-Slavery Society. The Reverend Thomas Price was one of the editors of the *Eclectic Review* and minister at the Wesleyan Chapel. He initiated an antislavery periodical in 1836, and edited a volume entitled *Slavery in America* . . . , published in London in 1837. (*Life*, I, 354, 356; *The Liberator*, September 3, 1836.)

7. For a letter by George Thompson, dated July 11, 1836, with comments on his debate with Breckinridge, see *The Liberator*, September 3, 1836; also, in the same issue, the item entitled "Thompson and Breckinridge."

54

TO EFFINGHAM L. CAPRON

Brooklyn, Aug. 24, 1836.

Esteemed Friends:

Every day the remembrance of our delightful visit to Uxbridge is as fragrant to our hearts, as is the perfume of a rose-garden to the smell. But we did not mean to requite your manifold kindnesses by committing an act of petty larceny. Nevertheless, we abducted a pocket handkerchief belonging to L.B.C.,[1] and now seize the first opportunity to return it, so that our consciences may not trouble us in time to come! Should you bring an action against us, we shall plead, in abatement of damages, — 1st. that we took the hdkf. aforesaid — 2d. That we were not guilty of theft in intention — 3d. that we returned the article by the first safe conveyance — and, lastly, that its possession was unknown to us until some days after our return home.

Our ride from Uxbridge to Brooklyn was indescribably beautiful. Where ever we turned our eyes, we saw such thickly clustering evidences of the beneficence, goodness and mercy of God toward the children of men, as to feel our hearts subdued by gratitude and love. We felt disposed to join in the rapturous injunction of the royal singer in Israel — "Let every thing that hath breath praise the name of the Lord!" [2] But, alas! of all the thronging millions of our race which populate the earth, how few there are who raise the voice of thanksgiving or prayer to Him whose mercy endureth forever!

Since I saw you, my health has not been good. At the present time, I am suffering from a wound in my left leg which I received about a fortnight ago, by jumping from a stone-wall against a sharp stump. At first, I paid no regard to it, although it was nearly three inches in length; but it has continued to enlarge, and is now very painful, and will be somewhat difficult to cure. Of course, it deprives me of that exercise which is needful for bodily vigor.

As I anticipated, my remarks upon the sanctity of the Sabbath, in the Liberator, are subjecting me to much censure, particularly among the *pious* opposers of the anti-slavery cause. Such papers as the New-Hampshire Observer,[3] Vermont Chronicle, Christian Mirror, and Boston Recorder,[4] are calling upon christian abolitionists to denounce and abandon so wicked a monster as the infidel Garrison, because he maintains that *all* time should be consecrated to the service of God and the good of mankind, instead of one day in seven; and because he believes that the real children of God "do enter into rest" here on earth, without being necessitated to wait for a respite until eternity dawn. The N.E. Spectator has also rebuked me; and, I am sorry to say, has declined inserting my defence, without suppressing all the argumentative and demonstrative part of it. I am not yet aware, that we have lost more than [one] subscriber since my remarks appeared in the Liberator — though doubtless many more will drop off when their subscription expires. This one is a theological student at New-Haven, who says in his letter, that he regards me as a dangerous member of [the] community, and that I ought to be reprobated by every lover of his country! Well, this is my joy and consolation — "It is a small thing to be judged of man's judgment," [5] for "The Lord knoweth them that are his." [6] I have been agreeably surprised to find that Luther, Calvin, Whitby, Foster,[7] Paley, Selden, Gill and Belsham, as well as Fox, Penn [8] and Barclay, all agree in opinion, that there is no such thing as a "holy day," under the gospel dispensation.

Sister Mary joins with me in sending grateful remembrances and kind regards to you both, to all the members of your interesting family, and to all those dear friends with whom it was our privilege and happiness to become acquainted during our pleasant sojourn at Uxbridge. My dear Helen sends you her thanks for the reception which you gave to her husband. Our babe is growing finely.

Bro. May is now in Boston. Poor dear Birney![9] how the wicked and malevolent are toiling to exalt him in the estimation of angels and all good people! Thompson is laboring nobly in England and Scotland.

With the highest esteem and respect,

Yours, affectionately,

Wm. Lloyd Garrison.

Transcript: Garrison Papers, Boston Public Library.

1. Lydia B. Capron (b. March 23, 1805), daughter of Walter and Lucy Allen, of Smithfield, Rhode Island. She married Effingham L. Capron on May 5, 1831 (*Vital Records of Uxbridge, Massachusetts*).

2. Psalms 150:6.

3. The New Hampshire *Observer* was a Congregationalist paper published in Concord, New Hampshire. It was established in 1819 with the name of New Hampshire *Depository*. Its name was later changed to *Observer*, then to *Panoplist*, and in 1855 it was the *Congregationalist Journal*. (Edwin A. Charlton, *New Hampshire As It Is*, Claremont, N. H., 1855, p. 559.)

4. For a more detailed attack by Garrison upon these newspapers, see the editorial essay entitled "Candor and Sagacity," in *The Liberator*, September 10, 1836.

5. I Corinthians 4:3.

6. II Timothy 2:19.

7. John Foster (1770–1843) was an English author and preacher. Beginning in 1792 he served as a Baptist preacher for twenty-five years, then left that office to devote himself entirely to literature. He "was a man of deep piety though the trend of his thought led him towards the abolition of all forms which he regarded as hindering religion" (*EE*).

8. William Penn (1644–1718), English Quaker, founder of Pennsylvania.

9. For two poignant accounts of Birney's tribulations at this time, see *The Liberator*, September 10 and 17, 1836.

5 5

TO HENRY E. BENSON

Brooklyn, Aug. 27, 1836.

Dear Henry:

We are *all* obliged to you for your letter to sister Mary; and though we are anxious to learn the state of your health daily, yet we are apprehensive that, in order to gratify us, you will be induced to write oftener than prudence would dictate. We would rather be deprived of your epistles, highly as we value them, than task your mind or strength in their composition.

Your last letter gives much affliction to the whole family, because it intimates the necessity of your making a foreign tour, in order, if possible, (and we trust it is,) to regain your health. For my own part, though I should on many accounts deprecate your absence, yet I am decidedly in favor of your seeking a bland and balmy climate, for a few months, and thus avoiding the severity of our approaching winter. I believe that such a trip would be incomparably more beneficial to you than all the medicine you can take in Providence. Still, we must not decide upon it hastily, although the sooner we come to a wise decision, the better. If the wound in my leg (which is now growing better) will admit of it, I will make you a visit in the course of all next week; and then we will look at all sides of the question, face to face. All that may seem for the best we will do — submitting with child-like resignation to the will of God. Keep your mind quiet, and your soul refreshed with good thoughts and right affections — and be it your daily prayer, "Thy will be done, Father in heaven, not mine." [1]

Helen is better than when I last wrote, but the care and nourishment of the babe are a severe tax upon her health. Little George has had an attack of the bowel complaint, and would send you his sympathies if he knew that you had been afflicted in a similar manner, and could give intelligent utterance to his thoughts. To-day he is twenty-eight weeks old. He has become a stout little fellow since you saw him, and is remarkably strong and agile. A short time since, bro. May and I took our babes to Daniel Robinson's shop, and weighed them in his scales. Joseph May weighed 16¼ lbs. — George Thompson 17 lbs.; the former being three weeks older than the latter. Yesterday I weighed little Anna — she has gained a little — weight 21½ lbs. G.T. now weighs 17¾ lbs.

You complain of feeling the cold exceedingly — it is not strange. We who are in tolerable health, in Brooklyn, have felt the need of a fire almost as much as in November. It seems to me as if we had not yet had either spring or summer — and, lo! the winter is close at our doors. It is said that thirteen spots are discoverable upon the disk of the sun, each of which is as large as our earth. No wonder, therefore, that the season *is as it is.*

Sister Mary says she has never before heard of the Album to which you allude — consequently, it was not sent at her request. A. J.[2] must have made a mistake.

John Gray has sold his house, land, and most of his furniture, to a Mr. Tarbox[3] at New-York, on satisfactory terms. He intends, if prac- ticable, to migrate to the spot which bro. May shall select for his abiding-place, which will be Scituate, near Boston — probably. Mr. Gray regards bro. M. as his Magnus Apollo.

Our venerable friend Moses Brown[4] seems to approach very often to the brink of the grave. He has not lived in vain — and what is better, he can never die: "He that believeth on me shall never taste death — I am the life,"[5] says the Redeemer.

As soon as you can make a trip to Brooklyn, you must make the effort. It is needless to say that father and mother, and the whole family, are yearning to see you. In the mean time, sister Anna has con- cluded to make you a visit, but she does not wish it to be generally known in P., as you know how painfully diffident she is, and with what reluctance she sees even her own acquaintance. She is indeed a lily of the valley.

Dr. Spalding has just called in to dress my leg. I have got his per- mission to leave on Monday noon for Providence, for I am extremely anxious to see you. I shall take a horse and chaise, and bring Anna with me: you may expect us, therefore, about 6 or 7 o'clock, Monday evening. We shall not leave till the mail arrives on Monday from Providence, so if you or George wish to have any orders obeyed, let us know by mail. Tell bro. George it would please Catharine, and be very agreeable to me, if he would so arrange his business as to return with me on Wednesday or Thursday, as may be most con- venient for him. Sister Anna desires me to say, that in case we should not come together, she will take the stage for P. on Tuesday — and she wishes bro. George to be at the stage-house on the arrival of the stage. But I trust we shall see you on Monday evening.

May inward peace and joy be with you unceasingly. You have my warmest sympathies, affections and prayers — but the favor of God is better than all.

Yours, truly,

Wm. Lloyd Garrison.

ALS: Garrison Papers, Boston Public Library.

1. A variation of Luke 22:42.
2. Probably Anna (Mrs. William) Jenkins, of Providence, Rhode Island.

3. Unidentified.

4. Moses Brown died on September 6, 1836, seventeen days before his ninety-eighth birthday.

5. Includes parts of various verses in John.

56

TO GEORGE W. BENSON

Brooklyn, Sept. 19, 1836.

Dear bro. George —

I shall not be able to go to Boston so early this week, with my family, as I anticipated, in consequence of not hearing from Mr. Knapp — as I am out of funds, and expected he would send me some money by to-day's mail — but am disappointed. As the weather is now very propitious, bro. Henry thinks he will tarry here no longer; he therefore proposes to take the Providence stage to-morrow afternoon, and go down as far as Phillips's,[1] where he wishes you to meet him, with Henry Anthony's vehicle, or any other you may please to select. Of course, he will stop during the night at Phillips's, and go into Providence the next forenoon. If, however, the weather should not be suitable for him to leave, — or if he should not feel well enough to leave, to-morrow, — you must submit to a disappointment. And in order to give you as little trouble as possible, he thinks you had better not leave Providence till quite late to-morrow afternoon, so that you may meet the stage, say, at Cornell's,[2] and learn of the driver whether he came down to Phillips's — and if he did not, then you could easily return to Providence the same evening, and might expect a letter from Henry by the mail, making other arrangements. Mr. May carried him to Killingley this forenoon; and yesterday afternoon I rode with him about five miles. He continues about the same — sometimes a little worse, sometimes much better.

The more I think of it, the more desirable it seems to me that you should (as you intend) go to Boston, and be with bro. Henry a day or two, while he is trying the new experiment. Your presence and countenance will give much efficacy to his medicines, and give him resolution and fortitude. And I should wish you to see, for yourself, the process of treating the patient. It would also solace all the family to know that Henry is placed under your supervision.

Catharine desires me to say, that she sent a small packet to you by the driver on Saturday. Did you receive it?

This afternoon, Mr. May's parishioners are to determine, whether, and at what time, they will dismiss him. To-morrow he goes with his wife to Hartford, as a delegate to the Temperance Convention.

It is possible that I shall go to Boston on Thursday, but not unless I get some money from K.

Yours, ever,

Wm. Lloyd Garrison.

ALS: Garrison Papers, Boston Public Library.

1. Probably a stagecoach stop.
2. Probably a stagecoach stop.

57

TO SAMUEL J. MAY

Brooklyn, Sept. 23, 1836.

Dear brother May:

I know not whether you will be surprised to find, on your return from Hartford, that I have gone to Boston with my family; [1] — certain it is when I parted from you on Tuesday, I did not anticipate quite so early a removal, else I should have taken a more emphatic leave of you. But we have been induced to go thus hastily, chiefly on bro. Henry's account, who will need our presence and support while he is experimenting afresh upon his shattered constitution. We learn that his journey to Providence was sustained without any injury to himself — further information has not yet been received from him.

I was agreeably surprised, this afternoon, to see our mutual and estimable friend Charles Burleigh, fresh from Boston, and vigorous as usual both in body and in mind. He is now on a visit to his parents. As he was in pursuit of William,[2] he did not tarry but a few minutes. He informed me that friend Knapp was still destitute of money, not having, as yet, been able to obtain a dollar of Mr. Chapman:[3] consequently, he had none to send to me. I sympathize with him, and really feel embarrassed to decide the question, whether it is my duty to return to Boston at an expense which must necessarily involve either himself or me, or both of us, yet more deeply in debt — at least, so I fear. As for myself, I cannot doubt that the Board will be disposed to sustain me as far as practicable; but, as I cannot serve the Society, as such, to any special advantage, I reluct being paid for services which are not directly rendered. Nevertheless, it is proper and needful for me to appear on the ground once more, and if I cannot stay, why, then I must retreat into the country once more. Now that my sabbatical, as well as some of my other religious sentiments are known, it is pretty certain that the Liberator will sustain a serious loss in its subscriptions at the close of the present volume; and all appeals for aid in its behalf will be less likely to prevail than formerly. I am conscious that a mighty sectarian conspiracy is forming to crush me, and it will probably succeed, to some extent. Well — from the heart I can say, "The Lord is my portion [4] — I will not fear what men can do unto me." O, the rottenness of Christendom! Judaism and Romanism are the leading features of Protestantism. I am forced to believe, that, as it respects the greater portion of professing Christians in this land, Christ has died in vain. In their traditions, their forms and ceremonies, their vain janglings, their self-righteousness, their will-worship, their sectarian zeal and devotion, their infallibility and exclusiveness, they are Pharisees and Sadducees, they are Papists and Jews.[5] Blessed be God, that I am not entangled with their yoke of bondage, and that I am not allied to them in spirit or form.

But I have no time to enlarge. For all your kindness to me and mine, and also that of your wife, I feel, and so does Helen, under high and lasting obligations. You cannot, and do not, expect a reward from me — because "silver and gold have I none," [6] and because money can be no equivalent. May you be remunerated in your own souls — constantly, immutably, forever.

I hope to have the pleasure of seeing you in Boston soon. Your borrowed books I have returned, excepting Bakewell's Geology,[7] which I venture to carry with me to Boston, for the purpose of extracting the remarks upon the creation by Prof. Silliman,[8] which I have been unable to transcribe, as they are somewhat protracted. — Now, joy and peace in the Holy Ghost be yours, and may we know experimentally what it is to be crucified to the world.

Yours, lovingly,

Wm. Lloyd Garrison.

ALS: Garrison Papers, Boston Public Library. An extract from this letter appears in *Life*, II, 113–114.

1. *The Liberator*, October 1, 1836, carried the announcement: "After a protracted sojourn in Connecticut, the editor is once more located in Boston; consequently, letters may no longer be addressed to him at Brooklyn, Ct. He is indebted to his able friend Mr. C. C. Burleigh, for many articles of interest communicated and published during his absence. For several months past, his health has failed him, but he is now better."

2. Charles's brother, William H. Burleigh (b. Woodstock, Connecticut, February 2, 1812; d. Brooklyn, New York, March 18, 1871), was converted to the antislavery movement as early as 1833, helped his brother edit the antislavery *Unionist*, and taught at Prudence Crandall's school. After serving as an antislavery agent in 1836, he edited the organ of the western branch of the Pennsylvania State Anti-Slavery Society, the *Christian Witness*, from 1837 to 1840.

He also edited the *Christian Freeman,* of Hartford, Connecticut, in 1843, and the Connecticut abolitionist organ, the *Charter Oak.* In his later years, he devoted himself to the temperance movement (*Weld-Grimké Letters,* I, 277n; *Life,* IV, 358).

3. Either Henry Chapman, the father-in-law, or Henry G. Chapman, the husband, of Maria W. Chapman.

4. This part of the quotation is from Lamentations 3:24.

5. In these remarks, Garrison, despite his liberal religious view of the Sabbath, expresses the extremely traditional, almost Fundamentalist, Protestant view of Catholicism and Christian view of Judaism.

6. Acts 3:6.

7. Robert Bakewell, *Introduction to Geology* (London, 1828).

8. Benjamin Silliman (1779–1864) was "the Nestor of American Science" and founder of the *American Journal of Science* in 1818, of which he was editor until 1838. He taught at Yale College from 1802 to 1853 (*DUSH*).

58

TO GEORGE BENSON

Boston, Sept. 28, 1836.

Dear and venerated Sir:

If I have nothing more to write about than the state of dear Henry's health, you will not deem this hasty epistle uninteresting. Doubtless bro. George has already informed you, by letter, from Providence, (as he is now in that city, but will return on Friday, and stay awhile longer,) that, up to the time he left Boston, Henry's symptoms were decidedly better. He still continues to improve, and is in very good spirits. – His pulse has been reduced from 112 to less than seventy, and is now quite regular. The inflammation in his mouth and throat has subsided, and his cough is no longer troublesome. For the last three nights, he has slept comfortably, without sweating. His appetite, moreover, is good, without being ravenous. – On the whole, there has been most certainly a decided improvement in his health, which, with the Doctor's confident assertion that he can effect a cure, furnishes strong ground for believing that his case is not hopeless. Still, after all, we may be disappointed, and heavenly wisdom will prompt us to be prepared for the result, whatever it may be. For my own part, I consider his removal to Boston as signally providential. Had he tarried a little longer in Brooklyn, Dr. Harrington [1] thinks nothing could have saved him. He is now under the hospitable roof of my excellent Quaker friend Joseph Southwick, much to his own satisfaction, where every attention is paid him, and all that he desires is realised. Mrs. Southwick is one of the best of women, a capital physician herself, and very much attached to Henry – she will be almost his own mother to him. — We ought all of us to feel very thankful to these kind and estimable friends, that they have voluntarily opened their doors to receive him in his present condition. There are few persons who like to receive an individual, not related, into their family, especially if he is an invalid, and more especially in a city like Boston. You will hardly need the suggestion, that it would doubtless be very pleasing to friend Southwick, if you should send him a letter, thanking him for what he has done, and is doing, for Henry; for he will accept of no compensation. Direct to Joseph Southwick, Esq. Boston, should you write to him.

This forenoon, our mutual friend Mr. Gray [2] left two letters at the office from sister Anna, — one for Helen, and the other for Henry, — which were very gratifying. I did not see Mr. Gray, but he promised to call again.

A bundle and a letter were also received to-day from my beloved friend and coadjutor Mr. May. How large a debt of gratitude do I owe to that dear man, as well as to many other friends! You will give him my thanks, and tell him I shall try to send him a letter by the next mail, in which I shall mention one of the most extraordinary cases of courage, self-consecration, benevolence, sagacity, and heroism, on the part of a colored man now in this city, but formerly a slave in Virginia.

On Monday evening I attended the monthly concert of prayer for slaves and slave-masters, and made some remarks to the audience. Bro. George followed me, and spoke with cogency, and to good effect. A collection of $9,28 cts. was taken up in aid of the colored man already alluded to.

The abolition men in this city are somewhat drowsy, but the women are, as usual, wide awake, and the life of the cause. I must put some goads into the former, and spur them up.

Yesterday there was a great procession in this city in honor of the late President Madison,[3] and a eulogy was pronounced by John Quincy Adams,[4] but I did not hear it. Alas, for the memory of Madison, that he left more than one hundred slaves in bondage, not having principle or generosity enough to emancipate one at his death! The world may call him a patriot — but at the bar of God he will be recognized as a man-stealer.

To-day I removed Helen and the babe from Mrs. Southwick to Miss Parker; but we are confined to one room at present. Of course, we are all yet in confusion, and it is with difficulty I have allotted to myself time enough to write these imperfect lines. You, and dear mother, and all at home, will be glad to hear that little George continues to thrive, and is thought to be a very fine child by all who see him.

Dear Helen joins with me in desiring to be affectionately remembered to you all, and to Mr. and Mrs. May. You shall have another letter soon.

> With high esteem, I remain,
> Yours, dutifully,
>
> Wm. Lloyd Garrison.

ALS: Garrison Papers, Boston Public Library.

1. Dr. Reuben Harrington, of Boston, resided at 42 Pond Street. He was first listed in the Boston *Directory* in 1835.
2. John Gray of Brooklyn.
3. James Madison had died on June 28, 1836.
4. The former President was a representative from Massachusetts in 1831 1848.

---

5 9

TO HENRY E. BENSON

Boston, Nov. 4, 1836.

Dear bro. Henry:

Letters from George and Anna have been received, announcing your safe arrival home, without any serious fatigue or inconvenience. Loving you as I do my own self, how can I but rejoice at the prospect of your recovery to health and usefulness? O, may the Great Physician be graciously pleased to cure all your maladies, that you may labor long, faithfully and profitably in his blessed service! Although you must expect to feel less well on some days than on others, yet I hope you will soon find yourself steadily improving.

I have seen Dr. Harrington several times since you left, and stated to him all the particulars about your journey. He was very much pleased with the information — says "the young man will do well enough in the sequel" — promises to visit you without fail ere long — but hopes you will stir about as much as you can, ride often, and not be afraid of fatigue. It is exercise — exercise — that you most need; and though to attempt it may sometimes seem a formidable affair — yet, never mind it. Demosthenes [1] said that action was every thing to an orator — so it is all important sometimes to an invalid.

Tell dear and venerated father that I do not mean to cheat him out of my board, although I am mortified that the amount due has not yet been sent to him. But friend Knapp — who is my bank and banker — is still sorely pinched to get what is due him, and I must therefore wait, and in so doing be under the necessity of making others wait, before my dues and their dues are settled. By the way, I could almost wish that father would put me into Brooklyn jail, for a time, because

I should then be so near you all! — There's love for you, stronger than iron bars or dungeon walls.

Since you left, I have not been very well. There is something wrong about my system, which needs to be radically affected. Within four or five days, I have been afflicted with a swelling about the right side of the neck and throat, and an abscess in both ears. My complaint is scrofulous — a humor as malignant to the body as sin is to the soul — often fatal in its termination, and perhaps to be so ultimately in my case. Rev. Mr. Himes [2] called to see me this afternoon, and advised me to go and take a course of Thompsonian medicine [3] at his friend M'Coun's; [4] and, to encourage me, he stated that a friend of his was in this city, about two years ago, so dreadfully afflicted by the same malignant disorder, that he was given up by all the physicians, and was fast sinking into the grave. He took a few courses of the T. medicine, immediately began to improve, used it faithfully all winter, and is now as hearty as any man in New-Bedford, where he resides. To-morrow I shall ask the advice of Dr. Harrington.

Our little George has also been seriously indisposed since you left, but begins to brighten up again. He has lost flesh, so as to look somewhat thin. But I suppose Helen has written Anna all the particulars.

Our friend Himes is to leave his people, and go elsewhere, owing to his abolition sentiments. A few aristocratical men in his society have created so much trouble that he feels inclined to leave them. For, believing, that

> "He is a freeman whom the truth makes free,
> And all are slaves beside" — [5]

he is determined to cling to the truth, and to preach it, without let or hindrance. He is a lovely man, and has a mind of his own, and a soul to feel and act. We shall feel his loss in this city. He wishes the enclosed bundle to be given to Mr. Kilton,[6] as soon as convenient after its arrival.

We have had a Board meeting, to see what s[hould] be done with our city, respecting the District of Columb[ia.] [7] Mr. Loring has agreed to take the 12th Ward, and all South Boston, under his supervision; Mr. Jackson (Francis) [8] will take Ward 11; I shall take Ward 10; Mr. Southwick Ward 9; Mr. Sewall Ward 8; Mr. Knapp Ward 7; Mr. Kimball Ward 6; Mr. Fuller Ward 4 — &c. If we get one thousand names altogether, we shall do pretty well.

I hope I shall feel able to attend the annual meeting at Providence on Wednesday,[9] but I fear I shall not.

I would send some of Miss Grimke's appeal [10] for distribution, but there are none in the office. It sells rapidly.

Your wine shall be forwarded in a day or two. May it do you good.

Longing to see father, mother, sisters, you, and all the household, with feelings of the strongest attachment I remain,

Yours and theirs till death,

Wm. Lloyd Garrison.

N. B. Cousin Andrew Garrison [11] was here a few days since from St. John. Poor fellow! he narrowly escaped with his life on board the Royal Tar, and lost every thing in his possession.

ALS: Garrison Papers, Boston Public Library.

1. Demosthenes was the great Greek orator of the fourth century B.C.

2. The Reverend Joshua Vaughan Himes (b. Wickford, Rhode Island, May 10, 1805), an active member of the Massachusetts Anti-Slavery Society and president of the Young Men's Anti-Slavery Society of Boston, was then pastor of the First Christian Society on Summer Street, a position which he had held since 1830 and which he left in January 1837. He was pastor of the Second Christian Society at Chardon Street from January 1837 to August 1842. It was there that the famous Chardon-Street Convention on the nature and validity of the Sabbath was held for three days, beginning on November 17, 1840. In 1839 Himes converted to Adventism, which emphasized the imminence of Judgment Day, and in 1840 he began publishing an Adventist periodical, *Signs of the Times*. At the age of fifty-eight, he moved to Buchanan, Michigan, where he established the *Voice of the West* and later moved to Chicago. In 1879 he converted to the Episcopal Church. His later years were spent in Elk Point, South Dakota, where he was a minister as late as 1894. (*A Brief Sketch of Joshua V. Himes*, an editorial from the *Union County Courier* of Elk Point, 1894, in the Biographical Pamphlets at the Atheneum, Boston, Massachusetts, vol. 55, no. 11, 8 pp.; Isaac C. Wellcome, *History of the Second Advent Message*, Yarmouth, Me., 1874, pp. 89–91.)

3. Thomsonian medicine was originated by Samuel Thomson (1769–1843), self-educated son of a New Hampshire farmer, who gained his knowledge of medicine through the experimental use of herbs gathered in the woods and fields of New Hampshire. His career was a checkered one, involving many lawsuits, a charge of murder, and imprisonment for six weeks. His system was based upon the theory that all ills are produced by cold, and that any treatment causing a rise in internal temperature of the body, as in the use of lobelia followed by cayenne pepper, would prove successful. He was an opponent of orthodox medicine, especially bleeding and administration of opium and calomel (*DAB*). For a more extensive description of the treatment, see letter 110, to George W. Benson, March 10, 1838.

4. Unidentified.

5. William Cowper (1731–1800), *The Task*, Book V, "The Winter Morning Walk," lines 733–734.

6. The Reverend George W. Kilton succeeded the Reverend Samuel J. May in the Unitarian Church at Brooklyn, Connecticut, for one year. He was an anti-slavery man who did not agree altogether with abolitionist tactics. (Richard M. Bayles, *History of Windham County, Connecticut*, New York, 1889, p. 592.)

7. Garrison is referring to the petition campaign for the abolition of the slave trade and slavery in the District of Columbia.

8. See introductory biographical sketch.

9. The first annual meeting of the Rhode Island State Anti-Slavery Society was to be held in Providence on Wednesday, November 9, at 2 p.m.

10. Angelina E. Grimké, *Appeal to the Christian Women of the Southern States* (New York, 1836).

11. Andrew Garrison (b. November 14, 1805; d. 1850), of St. Johns, Nova Scotia, was the son of Nathan and Rebecca Garrison (Nathan was the brother of Garrison's father, Abijah). He was a sheriff's clerk at about 1826 and a deputy sheriff and editor until he left the province in 1837, when he came to the United States and settled in Sauk Prairie, Wisconsin. He had married his cousin, Ann Ansley, in 1831. He set out for California in 1850, during the gold fever, and died of cholera on the way. (Wendell Phillips Garrison, *Memoranda of the Garrison Family for Three Generations*, New York, 1876, p. 4.)

6 0

TO HELEN E. GARRISON

New-York, Nov. 22, 1836.

My dear Wife:

You are safely in Providence, I trust, with our dear pledge of love, little "Dordie Tompit." [1] Not having heard, and not expecting to hear, any thing from you until my return, I feel anxious to know (and particularly because I cannot know) how you were enabled to bear your much dreaded trip back to Providence. The Ladies' Cabin, I suppose, was crowded full; but I hope you had better companions than those who accompanied you hither. I forgot to tell you, when I left you, that Ray Potter kindly said he hoped you would call upon him if he could be of any service to you.

It is still my purpose, the Lord willing, to be with you on Saturday morning; [2] but I shall find it extremely difficult to leave, and, on some accounts, shall be reluctant to leave; for the Convention is not to be dissolved until some time next week, [3] and there are many great themes yet to be discussed and illustrated. However, I am of no real service here, and can be spared without any detriment to our cause, although it is the earnest wish of all that I should remain until all the deliberations are finished. So occupied am I with our multiplied duties and meetings, that I can hardly find time comfortably to eat my meals; and as for preparing any thing for the Liberator here, it is entirely out of the question. I have just written to tell *him* so — that is, friend Knapp.

Last evening, we had a large and crowded meeting of our colored people, with many of our leading abolitionists. Several of the former addressed the meeting, in a very interesting manner. I was then called upon to make some remarks, and was received with grateful applause. I spoke about half an hour, and was followed by Weld, who delighted and moved all hearts. Seldom have I witnessed a more thrilling scene. Our hearts were one, and love reigned over all.

My bottle of Panacea will be exhausted to-day. — I know not

whether I shall try to find any in this city; nor can I yet say, whether the Panacea will prove such in my case. It has done me no harm, I am sure. Since you left, I have been tolerably well; but the scrofula is settling more in my throat. It is now in a large lump, and somewhat malignant.

Our Convention has unanimously invited the Grimkes, Angelina and Sarah, (who punctually attend our meetings,) to speak whenever they think proper, and to state such facts respecting slavery as they may choose. Sarah has just said, that, although brought up in the midst of slavery, and having conversed with hundreds of *well-treated* slaves, she has never found one who did not long to be free.

I long to hear from dear bro. Henry — hope he is still improving in health. Wm. Chace is here, attending upon the Convention, and taking minutes. I believe he does not think of returning until next week.

I am in great haste. Love to Henry, Charlotte, and family, and to bro. George. Kiss the dear babe frequently for me, and peace and joy and health be with you both.

Most affectionately yours,

Wm. Lloyd Garrison.

ALS: Garrison Papers, Boston Public Library. This letter was printed in part in *Life*, II, 117.

1. A pet name for little George Thompson Garrison.
2. November 26, 1836.
3. The convention which Garrison was attending was of the famous "seventy" agents who were engaged by the American Anti-Slavery Society, under the leadership of Theodore Weld, to spread abolition and organize antislavery societies. Actually, the total number of agents was less than seventy. As Dumond has indicated, "The theoretical number of seventy agents never became a reality. Five of those originally chosen did not go out to lecture because of illness, death, or changed circumstances. Twenty of the original ones were dropped in June 1837 because they were not successful and, in at least one case, not responsible. This was a year of economic distress in the country and a shortage of funds and rapidly increasing costs forced the society to discontinue all but the most efficient and successful agencies. The number of agents, therefore steadily declined, and, as state and local societies increased in number and importance, more and more reliance was placed upon local rather than travelling agents." (Dwight L. Dumond, *Antislavery: The Crusade for Freedom in America*, Ann Arbor, Mich., 1961, p. 185.) The agents were called to New York for instruction and orientation. They came together on November 8 and continued in session until the twenty-seventh. Weld was in charge of the convention, and the speakers included Weld, Garrison, Henry Stanton, Beriah Green, Charles Stuart, Amos Phelps, Elizur Wright, Jr., and others. The convention and the subsequent efforts of the agents represented a milestone in antislavery history. Helen Garrison had to return to Boston before the convention ended, but Garrison stayed until the end. For the original conception of the seventy agents, see Luke 10, which begins: "After these things the Lord appointed other seventy also, and sent them two and two before his face into every city and place, whither he himself would come."

61

TO HENRY E. BENSON

Boston, Dec. 3, 1836.

Dear brother Henry:

What is "the conclusion of the whole matter" among you all, in Friendship's Vale, respecting the thankfulness and affection of the notorious editor of the Liberator? You have sent him blackberry jelly, a liberal supply of apples, "shagbarks," dough-nuts, &c.; but what have you received in return? It is doubtless fortunate for him, that he can plead absence from the city, in extenuation of his silence; so that on his return, he is enabled to prove an *alibi*, which, in law, is tantamount to a verdict of "not guilty."

My wife, I suppose, has written Anna[1] an account of our trip to New-York — a city which she had long been wishing to see, not because "five thousand gentlemen of property and standing,"[2] as in Boston, once turned out to mob her husband, (you remember the uproar in October, 1833,)[3] — for she declares that she loves me dearly, and if you will not doubt her word, I will not, — but because it is the capital city of America, and swarming, of course, with all kinds of attractions. Little, however, did either of us dream, on leaving Boston, that she and our dear babe would accompany me farther than Providence; but our warm-hearted friend Lewis Tappan,[4] lay claim to us all in the cars, and declared that, nolens volens, to New-York we should all go — that he would pay our expenses in going and returning, entertain us comfortably at his house during our sojourn in the city, and allow us to remain as long or as short a period as we might choose. This was too generous an offer to be negatived; I therefore said, "Yea," and also easily persuaded Helen to reply in the affirmative. As for "Dordie Tompit," he seemed to be ready for any new adventure, and was full of fun and frolic all the way, both in the car and in the steam-boat. Soon after we left Providence, his mother began to feel sick and dizzy, on account of the motion of the boat. I went into the Ladies' Cabin, and found her with her head reposing upon her pillow, and was rejoiced to observe little George, as I thought, asleep in her birth;[5] but it turned out to be somebody's else babe. My attention was drawn to a lively little fellow crawling about the cabin with great glee, who seemed greatly to enjoy the rocking of the boat and the novelty of the scene around him. Many eyes were fastened upon him, but no one seemed to have charge of him. "Well," thought

I, "you are a smart little shaver, truly; but I wonder your mother don't observe your movements more narrowly." In a moment, he had crawled to a pile of bowls, and was in the act of pulling it down, when, deeming it time for me to interfere if no body else would, I took hold of him, drew him back, and, lo! it was my own darling babe! — for Helen was too sick to attend to him, and he was revelling in unrestrained liberty. The trip did him much service, but dear Helen thinks she shall not trust herself again upon the watery deep very soon.

My own dilatory habits aside, you may be disposed to query, why I did not write to you in New-York. The truth is, I was too busily employed in convention, and out of it, even to bestow the least attention upon my wife — i. e. I did not walk out with her once — hence, you received no letter from me. Now, a word as to the convention.

With the exception of the meeting which organized the New-England Anti-Slavery Society,[6] and that which was held in Philadelphia in 1833,[7] I regard this convention of Agents as of higher importance than any meeting or convocation which has been held to advance the anti-slavery cause. I am sure that its deliberations and proceedings have not been equalled in interest. About thirty of the fifty Agents, actually engaged, were present — all of them men of talents, amiable in their manners, and religious in their professions: — Weld [8] was the central luminary, around which they all revolved. Indeed, we must have been a very stupid body, if, among so many, and making common stock of all our minds, we could not make our sessions full of interest and pleasure. We held three meetings a day, scarcely allowing ourselves time to eat; and yet, when a fortnight had been thus incessantly occupied, it seemed as if we were but just entering upon the threshold of the great question of slavery — so exhaustless is the theme, so vast the relations involved in the well-being and freedom of man. Beriah Green, Weld and Stuart were the chief speakers, although every one present participated more or less in the discussions. I spoke repeatedly, but very briefly as I am wont to do.[9] The questions discussed were manifold — such as, What is slavery? What is immediate emancipation? Why don't you go to the south? The slaves, if emancipated, would overrun the north. The consequences of emancipation to the south. Hebrew servitude. Compensation. Colonization. Prejudice. Treatment and condition of our free colored population. Gradualism — &c. &c. All the prominent objections to our cause were ingeniously presented, and as conclusively shown to be futile.

It was a wise stroke of policy in bringing the Agents together, that they might see and hear each other, understand each other's feelings and sentiments, cheer each other's heart, and form a personal friendship with each other. It was a happy circumstance, too, that I was present with them, and that they had an opportunity to become *personally* acquainted with me; for, as I am a great stumbling block in the way of the people, or, rather, of some people, it would be somewhat disastrous to our cause if any of our Agents, through the influence of popular sentiment, should be led to cherish prejudices against me. I was most kindly received by all, and treated as a brother beloved, notwithstanding the wide difference of opinion between us on some religious points, especially the Sabbath question. My friend Lewis Tappan had some conversation with me, respecting my religious views — but, though we could by no means agree, we harmoniously agreed to differ. ☞ He did not show me his written creed, but I should have been gratified to see it.

As to your health, dear Henry. It seems by your last letter, addressed conjointly to friend Knapp and the Doctor, that you were slowly improving, on the whole — but could not speak above whisper. This temporary loss of voice convinces me yet more strongly, that yours is not an affection of the lungs, but of the throat — but I may be mistaken. You have done bravely in riding so frequently, and I dare say have been benefitted by it: but permanent relief will come slowly. How much resignation do you need, under such a long deprivation of health! Yet I trust you possess it. It is good for us to be afflicted; and in the sick-chamber, the soul is best instructed as to its wants, and the body as to its frailty.

Dr. Harrington left this city for Southbridge [10] the day that your letter was received; consequently, as he did not see it, we have not been able to send you any medicine. He is to return to-day, and friend Knapp desires me to say, that a bundle or basket shall be forwarded to you by Monday night's stage. I shall seize that opportunity to write to father and Anna, or to one of the other dear sisters. Tell father that all his requests, respecting the Liberator, Spectator,[11] &c. contained in his last affectionate letter, shall be attended to. He can never know how much I love, admire and venerate him. — The peace and joy of heaven be with him in his declining years. As the cold weather advances, I feel solicitous to learn how it affects his health, as last winter he was quite ill, in proportion to its severity. Say to mother that I cherish for her the affection, not merely of a son-in-law, but of a son indeed. She is one whose example is worthy of all praise and imitation. As for Mary, Sarah, and Anna, I sigh that I am not so situated as to be able to recompense them for their manifold kindnesses to me. I am almost ashamed to return nothing but thanks — for words are very cheap, and may be used as fluently by the ungrateful as the thankful. Yet they will not reckon me among those who profess much, while they feel none at all. The Lord bless and reward you all, in this life, and that which is to come! This benediction is heart-felt.

My own health has somewhat improved since my trip to New-York. The scrofula is not troublesome, except in my ears, and I suffer little or no pain, the swellings having disappeared. I am taking my third bottle of Swaim's Panacea — it has probably helped me. Am thinking of trying one or two courses of the Thompsonian medicine.

Mary Parker is quite ill of a lung fever. She was first attacked with an inflammation of the bowels, and is in a critical state. Her father has just had two shocks of the palsy, and will probably not survive long.[12] "What shadows we are!" [13]

Dear Helen enjoys excellent health — and as for Geo. Thompson, he is active, strong and fat, "in spite of his teeth," of which he has five. He is really *number one*. You shall hear from me on Tuesday.

> Yours, lovingly,
>
> Wm. Lloyd Garrison.

ALS: Garrison Papers, Boston Public Library. This letter was printed in part in *Life*, II, 114–17.

1. Anna Benson, Helen's sister.
2. On Monday, October 12, 1835, the Boston *Commercial Gazette*, in referring to the meeting of the Boston Female Anti-Slavery Society scheduled for October 14, at which George Thompson was expected to speak, called for resistance to the meeting and predicted that "This resistance will not come from a *rabble*, but from men of property and standing . . ."
3. The reference is to a mob that turned out for Garrison in New York on his return from England on October 2, 1833.
4. See introductory biographical sketch of Arthur and Lewis Tappan.
5. Garrison's spelling.
6. In Boston, in January 1832.
7. The founding convention of the American Anti-Slavery Society.
8. Theodore D. Weld.
9. *Life*, II, 116n, has the following note at this point: " 'You know that I always speak in public with reluctance, especially if my remarks be *not* written down — and to *read* is a slavish mode of *speaking*, if speaking it can be called' (MS. April 10, 1836, W. L. G. to G. W. Benson)."
10. Southbridge, Massachusetts.
11. Probably the *New England Spectator*.
12. Mary Parker's father, Asa Parker (b. August 5, 1757, Lunenburg, Massachusetts; d. April 13, 1838), a veteran of the Revolution, lived at various times in New Ipswich and Jaffrey, New Hampshire, where he spent the latter years of his life in a house on the Baptist Common owned by his four daughters (Albert Annett and Alice E. E. Lehtinen, *History of Jaffrey, N. H.*, Peterboro, 1937, II, 570–571).
13. Edmund Burke (1729–1797), English statesman, *Speech at Bristol on Declining the Poll* (1780).

6 2

TO HENRY E. BENSON

Boston, Dec. 17, 1836.

Dear Henry:

A week ago, to-day, I was standing by the bedside of him who is no longer in the flesh, — your venerated father.[1] It was a painful occasion; yet that hope which is as an anchor to the soul, "both sure and stead-fast," sustained us all. Nothing but christianity can reconcile us to the loss of near and dear friends; nothing but Christ revealed within us, can rob death of its sting, and the grave of its terrors. It was the consolation of afflicted Job — "I know that my Redeemer liveth, and that he shall stand at the latter day upon the earth: and though after my skin worms destroy this body, yet in my flesh shall I see God." [2] How are they to be pitied who have no hope in their death!

You will see, by to-day's Liberator, that I have given a brief, imperfect and feeble tribute to the memory of your father. A much more extended and elaborate notice ought to be prepared, without unnecessary delay. I hope you, and bro. George, and mother, and the dear sisters, will all see to it, that his letters, papers and pamphlets are carefully preserved for examination. No doubt much useful and important matter is embodied in them, which ought to be selected and published, not merely in respect to the dead, but to benefit the living.

You must be careful not to brood gloomily over your recent bereavement. Be grateful that your sire was not removed at an earlier period — and let your continual petition to your Maker be, "Thy will be done," not merely in some but in all things — not merely at a particular period, but always. It is criminal to repine at the dispensations of the Almighty. If we are creatures of clay, must we not expect our earthly tabernacle to crumble?

We shall never be able to exclaim, "O death, where is thy sting? O grave, where is thy victory?" [3] until we have first died unto sin — crucified the old man with his lusts — put on the new man who is after Christ — and risen in spirit with Him who is able to save all who believe in him. He in whom the Saviour dwells can never be surprised by calamity or death — he has entered into rest, even while in the flesh. With Paul he can say, "For me to live is Christ," i. e. to bear his cross, follow in his footsteps, and do his work — "but to die is gain" [4] — gain to be delivered from suffering, and poverty, and decay, and all the ills which flesh is heir to.

You may say to bro. George, (as I presume he will be in Brooklyn when this arrives,) that it was not his fault — I am sure it was not mine — that we (Helen, little G. T. and myself) did not get to Boston in good season on Wednesday afternooon; but, in consequence of waiting for the steam-boat train, we did not reach home till after 7 o'clock in the evening — two hours later than we should have been, had we taken the 3 o'clock train, as we might have done, and intended to do. How did that happen? brother G. will ask. Thus — the steam-boat train did not leave till a quarter to 4 o'clock, and then was detained on the road upwards of an hour in waiting for an opposite train. But no matter — it is a trivial affair, and I mention it merely to let bro. G. know how we missed a figure in our calculation — and to draw from it this moral: Never wait for a second train of cars in expectation of arriving sooner than the first at your place of destination, when there is but a single track. Luckily, our boy slept soundly all the way. He was really delighted on his return, for he seems already to discriminate between being at home and abroad, and to feel that there is a difference. His cold is much better than it was in Brooklyn, but he has not regained his rosy cheeks.

On Thursday and Friday, I called at Dr. Harrington's office, and ascertained that he was not in the city. I have seen him to-day, however, as he has just returned from Nantucket, having been called to visit a sick patient upon that island. In reply to your letter, he desired me to say, that he was sorry to learn you did not feel quite so well, though it was natural that the sickness and death of your father should have a depressing effect upon your spirits, and consequently upon your system. He most cheerfully assents to your going to Providence, and trying the Thompsonian course, and advises you to do so — desiring, however, that you would begin moderately, and as judiciously as possible; that bro. George should be with you, (in whom he has great confidence,) and that you would apprise him (Dr. H.) from time to time, of the effect of the application. He will still counsel and assist you to the utmost of his ability, and continues to speak quite encouragingly as to your recovery. Your snuff will be prepared, and sent either to Brooklyn or Providence, as you shall desire, without delay. He says it will not be at all necessary for him to be with you at Providence — let bro. G. be with you, and he will be satisfied. I trust, therefore, dear Henry, that you will leave Brooklyn with all convenient despatch, and try the new remedy, having faith in its utility, though not expecting a miracle.

On her return from Brooklyn, Helen took cold in one of her breasts, so that it became very troublesome, and threatened to break. Charlotte gave her a famous remedy, of some kind, to cure it, which had no effect whatever. Fortunately, when she got home, she found a piece of Dr. Harrington's plaster, applied it to her breast, and in thirty minutes it was cured!

I have received a letter from Gerrit Smith, enclosing a check of $50 upon the Utica Bank, as a donation to help sustain the Liberator, "which paper," he says, "is, and ever should be, dearer to the heart of the *thorough* American abolitionist, than any other anti-slavery periodical. It broke ground in our great and holy cause. It has been, and still is, a most able and eloquent defender of that cause; and whatever may have been its errors, they have not sprung from dishonesty or timidity. The discontinuance of the Liberator would be deeply reproachful to our abolitionists, and would furnish the enemy with an occasion for the wildest exultation. It would be also exceedingly cruel to yourself, to subject you to the painful necessity of seeing your paper die for the want of patronage." After the wide difference which has existed between us, and the many severe things I have written in reference to his colonization conduct, is not the donation generous, and the panegyric still more liberal? Noble man! not ashamed to praise that which he once repudiated. What would Joseph Tracy and Leonard Bacon say, were I to publish his letter? Perhaps I shall yet do so, as no prohibition is contained in it — though it is not probable that he intended it for publication. He evidently is willing I should do with it as I think proper.[5]

J. R. McDowall is dead.[6] What friend of virtue will not mourn at the tidings? He is a world's loss — yet how was he hated and persecuted! What a weight of glory is his!

Our esteemed friend Mary S. Parker is still confined to her room. I have not seen her since she was taken sick. Eliza [7] is also quite sick in the same room. As for myself, I have been very hoarse with a cold, since my return. — Am taking the Balsam of Liverwort, which helps me. Dear Helen is very well, but much confined with little George. — She, and the Parkers, and Mr. and Mrs. Drew, and friend Knapp, send love and good wishes to you in abundance. My next letter will probably [be] addressed to mother. Love to all, from the deep fountains of my heart.

Yours, truly,

Wm. Lloyd Garrison.

ALS: Garrison Papers, Boston Public Library. A paragraph appeared in *Life*, II, 88–89.

1. George Benson died on December 11, 1836, in his eighty-fifth year. Garrison paid tribute to him in *The Liberator* (December 17, 1836), in an editorial eulogy of more than a column, noting: "Mr. Benson was a rare example of moral excellence among mankind. In justness, he was an Aristides — in peaceableness, a Penn — in philanthropy, a Clarkson."

2. Job 19:25–26.

3. I Corinthians 15:55.

4. Philippians 1:21.

5. The letter, dated "City of New York, Dec. 13, 1836," was printed in *The Liberator* on December 24, 1836, with the following introduction: "In view of the sharp reproofs which I felt it to be my duty, some time since, to administer to this noble-hearted, though then erring philanthropist, for his advocacy of the Colonization Society, I feel that nothing can more happily illustrate his magnanimity and kindness toward myself, and his hearty espousal of the anti-slavery cause, than the following letter. It will be seen that it comes without solicitation, — that it was spontaneously elicited on reading an article in the Liberator, setting forth its present necessities. I trust he will excuse the liberty I take in publishing it, as it will undoubtedly prove of real service to the Liberator at the present time, and gratify a great multitude of anti-slavery friends both in this country and in England."

6. John R. M'Dowall's obituary, probably written by Garrison, appeared in *The Liberator*, December 24, 1836. In the same issue, there also appeared a letter from Henry C. Wright to Garrison, dated "New York, December 15, 1836," headed "Funeral of Mcdowall," which Wright had attended in New York.

7. Eliza Parker, her sister.

63

TO MRS. SARAH T. BENSON

Boston, Dec. 24, 1836.

Dear Mother:

Probably, for the first time in your life, you have known what it is to feel *solitary – alone –* since your bereavement, even though surrounded by children and friends. If, by the marriage union, *two* indeed become *one*, that is, in spirit and affection, how trying must be the hour when death comes to annul that union, and by a separation to make, as it were, the *one* become *two*! The continual care, which, for so many years, the infirmities of father required and received at your hands, must make his loss more deeply felt by you, than if it had been otherwise. However, we have scarcely time to lament at the loss of deceased relatives and friends, before the summons are sent to us to follow them through the dark valley of the shadow of death. There seems to be no space between time and eternity. Let us not mourn, but rejoice, even with joy unspeakable, that we are mortal — that we are permitted to die, to throw off this cumbrous load of clay, and (if reconciled to God) to be inhabitants of heaven. Jesus Christ has triumphed over death and hell, and so may we by putting him on, and walking in newness of life. It comforts me to believe, that your hope and consolation are in God. Though afflicted, you know how to be resigned; though bereaved, to be a gainer through the hopes of the gospel.

A week ago, to-day, I wrote a letter to bro. Henry; but no intelligence has been received from him, or from bro. George, or from any of you, since we left Brooklyn. That we are uneasy, on this account, you may suppose. We trust nothing adverse has taken place, though we know not how to account for the silence. As the mail leaves Brooklyn today, I shall expect to receive a letter to-morrow.

With us in Boston, nothing particular has occurred since I wrote bro. Henry. Helen and the babe are in good health, and I am also somewhat improved, as to my cold. I am still trying Swaim's Panacea for my scrofula — this being my fourth bottle. My complaint does not trouble me, except in my ears, which still continue to discharge matter, and are internally quite sore. I shall wait till after our annual meeting in January, before I try the Thompsonian remedy. Hope bro. Henry will not wait half as long.

The ladies of the Anti-Slavery Society held their annual fair on Thursday last,[1] and in one day realized the handsome sum of five hundred and forty-two dollars! — Now that money is so scarce, this is almost equal to a thousand dollars in ordinary times. The wife of Chief Justice Shaw [2] attended, and bought a variety of articles. True, she is no better than any other woman; but then her attendance shows that our cause is by no means so odious as it once was. Every thing was conducted "decently and in order" — and no higher eulogy need be paid. The articles were various, beautiful, and useful: many of them were left unsold. Little George was presented with a pair of shoes, a pair of stockings, a pair of mittens, and a very beautiful gown. Pretty well, for the young fanatic! There is really a great deal of interest felt in his welfare among anti-slavery folks of both sexes. Perhaps bro. Henry would like to know what ladies superintended the tables at the Fair. I can specify only the following: — Mrs. Child, Mrs. Chapman, Caroline and Anna Weston, Anna G. Chapman, Miss Sargeant, Miss Susan Paul,[3] Miss Winslow [4] from Portland, the Misses Ammidons, Mrs. Loring, &c.

At the last New-England Anti-Slavery Convention, the Boston Female Society nobly agreed to raise *one thousand dollars* for the Massachusetts Society within a year. They have already redeemed their pledge!

What spring-like weather we have had up to the present time! Our streets have been free of ice and snow till last night, when it snowed one or two inches deep. To-day, it has been bright and warm, the snow has about disappeared, and the evening is mild and beautiful.

I wish Mr. Gray to be informed, that his letter was promptly put into the hands of Frederick,[5] the morning after my arrival, by myself.

I intended to fill out this sheet, but as the mail closes immediately,

I must close rather abruptly. Will write again soon. Dear Helen joins with me in sending much love to all as one, and to yourself in particular.

Yours, dutifully,
Wm. Lloyd Garrison.

ALS: Garrison Papers, Boston Public Library.

1. The fair was held on Thursday, December 22, 1836, at the Artists' Gallery in Summer Street. It opened at 9:30 a.m. and continued through the evening (*The Liberator*, December 17, 1836). *The Liberator*, in its issue of January 2, 1837, published a full account of the fair, written by Lydia M. Child. The closing paragraph reported: "The amount of money received was $550; and the next morning the ladies paid all that remained of their pledge of one thousand dollars to the Massachusetts Society!"

2. Lemuel Shaw (1781–1861), jurist, graduate of Harvard College, had been a member of the Massachusetts state house in 1811–1816 and 1819, and of the state senate in 1821–1822 and 1828–1829. He served as chief justice of the Massachusetts Supreme Judicial Court from 1830 to 1860 (*Harper's Encyclopedia of United States History*). Only four months earlier, on August 26, Judge Shaw had ruled, in the case of the slave Med, that a slave brought into the free state of Massachusetts voluntarily by his master was free (*Right and Wrong in Boston in 1836, Annual Report of the Boston Female Anti-Slavery Society . . .* , Boston, 1836, pp. 64ff). Lydia M. Child, in her report of the fair in *The Liberator*, noted: "Work-bags were manufactured in commemoration of little Med's case, decided by Judge Shaw, in a manner so honorable to himself and his country. On one side was the representation of a Slave kneeling before the figure of Justice; underneath, these sentences were printed in golden letters: 'Slavery was abolished in Massachusetts by the adoption of the Bill of Rights as a part of the Constitution, A. D. 1780.' Slavery says of this law, 'Lo, 'tis cold and dead, and will not harm me.' Anti-Slavery replies, 'But with my breath I can revive it!' Then follows, 'The adjudication on the case of a slave brought into Massachusetts from another State, fifty-six years afterward, Aug. 26, A. D. 1836.' "

The Mrs. Lemuel Shaw referred to was the second wife of Judge Shaw. Her maiden name was Hope Savage and she was the daughter of Dr. Samuel Savage, of Barnstable. She and Shaw were married in 1827 and lived at 49 Mount Vernon Street, which they first occupied in 1831. She died in 1879. (Frederick Hathaway Chase, *Lemuel Shaw, Chief Justice of the Supreme Judicial Court of Massachusetts, 1830–1860*, Boston and New York, 1918, p. 70.)

3. Susan Paul (d. Boston, April 19, 1841, aged thirty-two) was the daughter of the Reverend Thomas Paul, who had been the pastor of the African Baptist Church in Belknap Street, Boston, and had died in 1831. Miss Paul was a teacher in a Negro primary school in Boston and an active member of the Boston Female Anti-Slavery Society. In the early 1830's she formed a Garrison Junior Choir, which sang at abolitionist meetings and for other worthy causes. In 1838, in Philadelphia, she was chosen one of the vice-presidents of the second antislavery convention of American women. Miss Paul's brother, bearing the name of their father, Thomas Paul, was an apprentice in *The Liberator* office and later a graduate of Dartmouth College. (*The Liberator*, April 23, 1841; Benjamin Quarles, *Black Abolitionists*, New York, 1969, pp. 27, 30.)

4. Either one of two sisters, the daughters of Nathan Winslow, of Portland, Maine: Lucy Ellen (1816–1856) who, in 1838, married Edward Fox of Portland, Maine, a judge of the Supreme Court of Maine in 1862 and 1863 and of the United States District Court in 1866; or Harriet (1819–?), who married Charles List of Philadelphia and later moved to Boston. After List's death, she married (1857) Samuel E. Sewall, the Boston abolitionist, who had been married to a third sister,

Louisa Maria. (David P. Holton and Mrs. Francis K. Holton, *Winslow Memorial,* New York, 1888, II, 886; Edward Eldridge Salisbury, *Family Memorials,* New Haven, 1885, p. 212.)

5. John Gray's brother, the Reverend Frederick Turell Gray (b. December 5, 1803; d. March 9, 1855) was a colleague pastor of the Pitts Street Church or Tuckerman Chapel, Boston, from 1834 to 1839, and subsequently was pastor in the Bulfinch Street Church (Congregational) from 1839 to at least 1854. (M. D. Raymond, *Gray Genealogy* . . . , Tarrytown, N.Y., 1887, pp. 195–196; "Churches, Ministers and Schools of Boston," *Boston Almanac,* 1854, p. 88.)

64

TO SARAH BENSON

Boston, Dec. 31, 1836.

Dear Sarah:

Although no tidings have been received from Brooklyn — direct — since we left, I again take up my pen to write a few hasty lines. On Saturday evening last, I put a letter into the Post-Office for mother, under circumstances that make me anxious to learn whether it was *duly* received — or whether it was received *at all*. It was my intention that it should arrive on Monday.

Yesterday forenoon, William Chace surprised me by his presence, and afflicted me most deeply (as well as dear Helen) by the tidings which he brought. He gave me a minute account of the state of bro. Henry's health — of his removal to Providence — of the visible change for the worse in his condition — of the unwillingness expressed, at the Thompsonian Infirmary, to make any trial in his case — of the decision of the Dr. that his lungs were gone, and that his time on earth was short — &c. &c. William came to get Dr. Harrington to go with him to P. Fortunately, the Dr. had just returned from New-Hampshire. He seemed surpised and affected at the intelligence, but thought it was a false alarm, and was as confident as ever that Henry's lungs were not badly affected. He took the cars yesterday afternoon with Wm., and will probably return this evening. Of course, Helen and myself wait for his arrival with the utmost solicitude, and with strong apprehension. We dare not any longer cherish the belief, that Henry will recover — we cannot hope against hope — and yet it is true, that while there is life there is hope, even in a desperate sense. In the case of father — a venerable patriarch, full of years, carried far beyond the measured three-score years and ten — while we could weep at his loss, and yet not feel it a very hard thing to commit him to the tomb, inasmuch as nature had run its course. But, oh! the thought of losing our dear Henry, in the bloom and prime of youth — one so amiable, so benevolent, so disinterested, so earnestly disposed, like his Saviour, to do good, so anxious to see this ruined world restored to its original perfectibility — a friend, a brother, yea, "a brother beloved" [1] — how it moves the deep fountains of the soul! how it lacerates the heart! And yet let us beware, that, in our deep affliction, we sorrow not after the manner of the world. "Shall not the Judge of all the earth do right?" [2] Is not the same sentence passed upon us all — "Dust to dust"? [3] Our Father in heaven will not be angry to see us weep at a bereavement like this; he knows our frame; he has given us affections; and Christ, our Redeemer, could weep at the grave of Lazarus, and groan in spirit in view of his death. But let our consolation be in God; let us not murmur at his dispensations — for we know that "God is love," [4] and that "he doth not willingly afflict the children of men." [5] As he sendeth rain upon the just and the unjust alike, so he sends his summons impartially into the palace of the king and the hut of the peasant — among the high and the low, the rich and the poor, the bond and the free. — Who shall lay any thing to his charge?

It may be, nevertheless, that our beloved brother may yet survive a long time, and even be restored to health again. But it is our duty at all times, while we may hope for the best, to be prepared for the worst. I am consoled to learn that Henry regards his dissolution with resignation, and is anxious only that the will of his heavenly Father may be perfected in him. I trust that he will be enabled to exclaim — "O Death, where is thy sting? O Grave, where is thy victory?" [6] "Thanks be to God, who giveth us the victory, through our Lord Jesus Christ!" [7]

All this week, our sweet little George has been extremely ill with an attack of the croup — the Dr. visiting him every day. We felt very much alarmed — but now have reason to rejoice and be grateful at his recovery. — To-day, he has been very lively, and his health seems to be almost wholly restored. Helen, in attending upon him nights, has got a bad cold and cough, and also lost her appetite. We hope nothing serious will occur.

Today the year gives up its parting breath. How many have gone down to the grave since its commencement! *We* are yet mercifully spared. "Bless the Lord, O our souls! and all that is within us, bless his holy name!" [8] Whether we shall survive another year, we know not — but let us be ready to depart, and be with Christ, "which is far better." [9]

As soon as Dr. Harrington returns, I shall learn whether my presence is desired in Providence or Brooklyn. I shall hold myself in readiness to go to either place.

I have had no letter yet from S. J. May.

Mary Parker is somewhat better. She and Lucy and Eliza desire to be remembered to Anna, and all the family. Dear Helen wishes a full heart of sympathy and love to be sent to all — says she is sorry I have stated that she is unwell — that she feels much better than she did, &c. I join with her in tender remembrances to you all, as one.

Affectionately yours,

Wm. Lloyd Garrison.

☞ Shall we not hear from one of you soon?

ALS: Garrison Papers, Boston Public Library.

1. Philemon 16.
2. Genesis 18:25.
3. *The Book of Common Prayer*, "Burial of the Dead."
4. I John 4:8.
5. Lamentations 3:33, somewhat altered.
6. I Corinthians 15:55.
7. I Corinthians 15:57.
8. Psalms 103:1, with some variation.
9. Philippians 1:23.

II CLERICAL DISAFFECTION: 1837

THE YEAR opened with the death of Henry Benson on January 6 at the age of twenty-three. Henry's devotion to the antislavery movement and his work for both the Massachusetts Anti-Slavery Society and *The Liberator* rendered his death not only a personal loss for Garrison and his wife but also a serious loss for the antislavery cause in Massachusetts.

Despite heavy financial difficulties, *The Liberator* expanded its page size to 16 x 23 inches, and its subscriptions reached 3,000 by midsummer. But public opinion, especially that represented in the leadership of the churches, continued to be hostile. An intensive effort by the abolitionists of Massachusetts to find a meeting-place for their annual meeting in a church in Boston met with total failure, and the meeting was finally held at the end of January in the loft of a stable. However, the abolitionists did gain an important victory when the Massachusetts legislature gave them permission to hold one of their sessions in the hall of the House of Representatives.

In the middle of June, faced with illness and exhaustion, Garrison took his family to Brooklyn, Connecticut, where all remained until August. Oliver Johnson assumed responsibility for *The Liberator* as sub-editor, although Garrison did contribute to it.

It was during his absence that he and *The Liberator* came under severe attack from the orthodox clergymen of the state, some of whom were abolitionists. The attacks were first elicited during a speaking tour of the state by Sarah and Angelina Grimké, the two abolitionist sisters from South Carolina who came to Massachusetts in June and remained for almost a year, speaking to ladies' antislavery societies and church groups. Their original purpose was to speak only to ladies. But with the spread of their fame, men soon joined their audiences, and conservative Christians were outraged at their daring to speak in public and to audiences of both sexes. The result was the issuance of a Pastoral Letter of the General Association of Massachusetts to the Orthodox Congregational churches, around the middle of July. The letter opposed the introduction of the slavery issue into the churches as a matter of debate, and deplored the public participation by women in the reform movement and their appearances as public "lecturers and teachers." The letter was followed by several clerical appeals, signed by ministers who had participated in the antislavery movement, which condemned Garrison's methods, his hard language, *The Liberator*'s attacks upon individual churchmen — these had taken place during Garrison's absence — for their proslavery or neutralist views on the issue of slavery, and Garrison's use of *The Liberator* for attacks upon the Sabbath, certain ministers, and various church organizations. Although the vast number of Massachusetts abolitionists closed ranks in defense of Garrison, many of the national leaders of the antislavery movement either refused to take sides or sided with Garrison's critics. The resultant controversies represented the earliest significant fissures in the antislavery movement and culminated, in 1840, in the division of the movement into two organizations.

---

6 5

TO GEORGE W. BENSON

Boston, Jan. 4, 1837.

Dear George:

A letter (with a small parcel) dated Dec. 23d, was received from you yesterday morning. Where it had been so long detained I could not ascertain. Of course, your advertisement for an Agent, &c. will be duly inserted in Saturday's paper.[1]

Much to the relief of dear Helen and myself, another letter from you came to hand this morning, giving the joyous information that our beloved Henry is considerably better. O, that the Great Physician in heaven may yet restore him to health — if it be possible — and are not all things possible with God? Almost miraculous recoveries sometimes take place — and may it be so in the present instance! Yet, living or dying, let us all feel inwardly to exclaim — "The will of the Lord be done!"[2] Why should any of us desire to live, merely to gratify our senses, and to be in the world? "No man liveth to himself"[3] — at least, no man should. Unless we are desirous to bear the cross of Christ, and to conflict with a world lying in wickedness, and to do what in us lies to bring glory to God in the highest, peace on earth, and good will to men, who will be benefitted by our existence? One of my cherished maxims is, that it can never be a calamity for a good man to go to heaven, either sooner or later. Let us feel no concern whatever as to the time of our exit from this miserable world. Let us only — *by dying to self* — be prepared to enter those mansions prepared for the righteous in glory, and all will be well.

Every day, for a week past, I have purposed to write to dear Henry — but have been prevented by constant interruptions. Helen and myself having now but a single room, (as Mary Parker requires the other,) [5] it is almost wholly out of the question to do any writing where little George is. Besides, he and Helen have been quite unwell — and as Helen has no help but myself, my time is necessarily frittered away by piece-meal, so that I bring very little to pass. I shall write to sister Sarah, and solicit her to spend some time with us in Boston, for dear Helen's sake -- although H. thinks she can get along very well without her — but she cannot, being no better than a prisoner in her room from one month's end to another. If Sarah cannot come, we must have our dear friend Eliza J. Chace, or some one else.

Little George is now pretty well again. — This morning, Helen had a violent eruption over her whole body, like the erysipelas — but the Dr. thinks it is only the *rash*, occasioned by a cold. She is better this evening, as the humor has disappeared.

To remedy Henry's costiveness, Dr. Harrington says he may take of *Lenitive Electary*,[6] (which you can obtain at any of the apothecaries,) a piece as large as a filbert daily — and more, if necessary. It is a pleasant medicine, and no doubt will answer in the present case. The Dr. was much pleased to hear of Henry's improvement, and trusts he will possess his soul in patience and hope. He would like to hear frequently how he gets along.

Tell dear Henry that he is in my thoughts continually, and that my heart is more and more attached to him. I desire to see him so much, that I am almost daily tempted to make a hurried trip to P.; but duties and engagements are so multiplying here, as to keep me fast. I am glad to hear by William Chace, that his mind is calm and placid. If I am spared, he shall certainly receive a letter from me in a few days.

The medicine was sent by the cars yesterday.

Bro. Stanton [7] is in town. He has lectured *thirty-six* times within three weeks! How many times, in the sum total, must the sixty [8] agents have spoken! He and Amos Dresser,[9] and perhaps Weld, will be at our annual meeting [10] in this city on the 25th inst. Hope some of our R. I. friends will also be present.

To-morrow our Gov.[11] will deliver his annual message. Many will be curious to compare it with that of last year.

New-Year's day, Mr. Henry Chapman (who sent Henry the wine) made me a present of a hundred dollars! That was a liberal gift indeed. I wish you and Henry only to be apprised of this fact, for certain reasons.

Helen wishes me to convey to Henry, all the sympathy and love that can dwell in a sister's heart towards a beloved and afflicted brother. She yearns to see his face again. She also unites with me in tendering love to Catharine, Charlotte, and all the dear friends as one.

Yours, most lovingly,

Wm. Lloyd Garrison.

☞ As the P.O. is closed, I cannot pay the postage. — Will remember it.

☞ When shall I have a settlement with you?

ALS: Garrison Papers, Boston Public Library.

1. The advertisement appeared in *The Liberator*, January 7, 1837, under the heading, "Agent Wanted," and read:

"A person well qualified to labor as an Anti-Slavery Lecturer and Agent in the State of Rhode Island.

"Any person wishing to engage, will please address George W. Benson, Providence, R. I.

"Papers friendly to the cause, will confer a favor, by giving the above an insertion."

2. Acts 21:14.

3. A variation of Romans 14:7.

4. A further variation of Romans 14:7: "no man dieth to himself"; for the general idea, see Galatians 2:19–20 and Romans 6:11.

5. Garrison and his family were then still living at Miss Mary S. Parker's boarding house, at No. 5 Hayward Place.

6. A soothing medicated paste, apparently used to relieve constipation.

7. Henry B. Stanton.

8. Although the agents were referred to as the "seventy," since that was the number originally sought, there never were as many as seventy.

9. The Reverend Amos Dresser (b. Peru, Berkshire county, Massachusetts, December 17 (?), 1812; d. Lawrence, Kansas, February 5, 1904) was one of the Lane Seminary students who, with Weld, Stanton and others, seceded from the seminary as a result of the controversy over free speech there. In August 1835 he was publicly whipped and then driven from Nashville, Tennessee, for having had antislavery newspapers in his possession. He wrote an account of his flogging in *The Narrative of Amos Dresser, with Stone's Letters from Natchez, — An Obituary Notice of the Writer, and Two Letters from Tallahassee, Relating to the Treatment of Slaves* (New York, 1836); and in *Narrative of the Arrest, Lynch Law Trial, and Scourging of Amos Dresser at Nashville, Tenn., August 1835* (Oberlin, 1849).

In the fall of 1836 he accepted a commission as one of the "seventy" agents of the American Anti-Slavery Society. He lectured during the winters and studied at Oberlin during the summers until the fall of 1839, when he married Adeline Smith, of Ulster County, New York. With his wife, he labored as a missionary among the emancipated slaves in Jamaica. A breakdown in the Dressers' health forced their return to the United States. Dresser later was pastor of a church near Cincinnati; he then taught for some time at Olivet Institute in Michigan. Leaving Olivet because of ill health, he next served in the Western Reserve of Ohio as an agent of the League of Brotherhood, a peace organization. After the death of his wife and two children, he remarried in 1851, spent some time in Europe lecturing on peace, temperance, and the antislavery movement, and on returning to the United States settled as a pastor in Farmington, Ohio. (Dwight L. Dumond, *Antislavery: the Crusade for Freedom in America*, Ann Arbor, Mich., 1961, p. 186; *Life*, IV, 367; Henry W. Cushman, *A Historical and Biographical Genealogy of the Cushmans*, Boston, 1855, pp. 627–632; letter from Mrs. Marion H. Bates of the Ohio Historical Society, September 22, 1969, which lists information from *Oberlin College Alumni Catalogue, 1833–1939.*)

10. The annual meeting of the Massachusetts Anti-Slavery Society.

11. Edward Everett (1794–1865), Unitarian clergyman, scholar, teacher, orator, and politician. He taught Greek literature at Harvard beginning in 1819 and edited the *North American Review*. He served five terms in Congress, from 1825 to 1835, where he expressed strong support for slavery in the South. He served as governor of Massachusetts from 1836 to 1839 and was minister to the Court of St. James's from 1841 to 1845. Elected to the presidency of Harvard in 1846, he remained in that office until 1849, when he resigned. He occupied the office of secretary of state during the last four months of President Fillmore's administration, and was immediately thereafter, in 1853, elected to the United States Senate by the Massachusetts legislature, but resigned after about a year of service. He was nominated for vice-president on the ticket of the Constitutional Union party in 1860, but supported the Union and Lincoln with great vigor during the Civil War. (*DAB*.)

66

TO GEORGE W. BENSON

Boston, Jan. 8, 1837.

Dear George:

I put a letter for you into the Post Office on Wednesday evening, which of course was not received at the time of writing your last letter.

My affliction was great to learn that the medicine for dear Henry had not been received. No wonder you thought strangely of the failure. I was as prompt and punctual as possible. Monday noon, I went to Dr. Harrington, and obtained the medicine, as he could not prepare it before that time. He said you requested it to be sent *by the cars*. It did not go that afternoon, as friend Knapp said it was necessary to get a small box made, so that the bottles might be sent safely. The whole was sent on Tuesday morning by the 8 o'clock train, and hence arrived in Providence as early as half past 10. How deeply do I regret that I did not send you a letter by mail, informing you of the fact; — but as the Dr. said you would expect the medicine by the cars, I concluded that you would be at the depot on its arrival. I trust you have got it ere this, as, if I mistake not, I stated in my letter how it was sent. Dear Henry must have felt very uneasily at the delay.

Not a particle of Dr. McIntyre's snuff is in my possession. Am sorry to learn that he is so unwell. Can he not tell you of what the snuff was made? You can keep the secret, I am sure, if he should desire you to do so.

Do let me hear frequently from you, respecting Henry's situation, especially if he should have any turn for the worse. Am truly happy to hear that he continues in a comfortable state. Should he be made whole again, what gratitude will be due by us all to God for his recovery!

Helen and George are now both doing well. — Hope you and yours are in health.

Nothing new in the city. Winter has come in earnest. How many poor creatures it finds in a suffering and destitute condition! Who has made us to differ? — Shall we not be thankful for the mercies that surround us?

Love abundantly to dear Henry, to Catharine, Charlotte, et al.
In haste, yours affectionately,

Wm. Lloyd Garrison.

N.B. Our Board [1] will apply for the Representatives' Hall in which to hold our annual meeting. The application for it will probably make some discussion.

ALS: Garrison Papers, Boston Public Library.

1. The Board of Managers of the Massachusetts Anti-Slavery Society. As mentioned in letter 65, the meeting was to take place on January 25, in Boston.

67

TO CALEB CUSHING

Boston, Jan. 12, 1837.

Hon. Caleb Cushing:

Dear Sir — I thank you for your letter of the 8th inst., and for putting the petitions [1] from Barnstable District into the hands of Mr. Reed.[2] Once more I venture to trespass upon your kindness, by sending you the accompanying petition from the town of Attleborough, Mass. Please either to present it yourself, or to place it in the hands of the representative to whom it more properly belongs. You will perceive that the signatures are all in the same handwriting, but they are all genuine, and were obtained chiefly by the Rev. Charles Simmons.[3] I wish the original petition had been forwarded to me, but suppose it was very much soiled. As you are doubtless very busy, do not trouble yourself to acknowledge the receipt of this.

To-day, the N. Y. Journal of Commerce has been received, giving a sketch of the debate in the House on Monday.[4] Mr. Adams exhibits a noble front, and will get to himself great and enduring fame. I am quite sure that he will be efficiently sustained by the entire delegation from Massachusetts, and by none more cordially or ably than by yourself.

Yours, in the cause of equal rights,

Wm. Lloyd Garrison.

ALS: Library of Congress.

Caleb Cushing (b. January 17, 1800; d. January 2, 1879) was at this time a Whig member of Congress, serving in the House from 1835 to 1843. He had earlier served in the Massachusetts house (1825, 1833 and 1834) and in the state senate in 1827. (*BDAC.*)

1. Petitions to Congress to end slavery and the slave trade in the District of Columbia.

2. John Reed (b. September 2, 1781; d. November 25, 1860), a lawyer who practiced in Yarmouth, Massachusetts, was elected as a Federalist to the Thirteenth and Fourteenth Congresses (March 4, 1813–March 3, 1817) and served again, as a Whig, from 1821 to 1841. He was lieutenant-governor of Massachusetts from 1845 to 1851. (*BDAC.*)

3. The Reverend Charles Simmons (d. North Wrentham, Massachusetts, 1856, at the age of fifty-eight) was a Congregational minister, the second minister of the Hebronville Church, near Attleboro, Massachusetts. He served there from 1832 to 1838. (John Daggett, *A Sketch of the History of Attleboro*, Boston, 1894, p. 289.)

4. The debate dealt with the question of whether the petitions for the abolition of slavery in the District of Columbia were to be laid on the table without receiving notice, as had been done during the previous year, or were to be given to the appropriate committee for its action. A summary of the debate which took place on Monday, January 9, appeared in *The Liberator*, January 14, 1837.

---

6 8

TO MARY BENSON

Boston, Jan. 14, 1837.

Dear sister Mary:

Walking down Washington-street this morning, I saw our friend John Gray going up toward Hayward Place, and accordingly hailed him. He told me that he should start for Brooklyn this afternoon: I therefore improve the opportunity to send you a few hasty lines — not that I have any thing special to communicate, but the mere assurance that dear Helen, the babe, and myself, are now in the enjoyment of health, will be gratifying to you all. Helen is filled with regret that she was not able to attend at Henry's obsequies, and she finds it difficult to realize that she is never again to behold his face in the flesh.[1] As for myself, though I have seen the dear departed one in the cold embrace of death, and have followed his remains to the tomb, yet the stern and dreadful reality seems only like some painful vision of the night. The morning has come — the light is beaming — but where is our beloved Henry? — But we must not mourn as do those who repine at the decrees of Heaven. All is right, for God has done it.

I trust you arrived home in safety. I left in the afternoon cars, but was six hours on the road, instead of two, the usual time. One of our cars broke down, and we had a narrrow escape of our limbs, if not of our lives. We had a most profane and vulgar company.

I send you to-day's Liberator. You will see that I have barely mentioned Henry's death, as I had not room to do justice to his memory this week.[2] In the next paper, I shall be more particular.

Let us hear from some one of the family as often as convenient. You may know by the appearance of this scrawl that I write in great haste.

Love to mother and all the sisters, &c.

Ever yours,

Wm. Lloyd Garrison.

ALS: Garrison Papers, Boston Public Library. This letter is to Garrison's sister-in-law.

1. Henry Benson died on January 6, 1837, at the age of twenty-three.
2. *The Liberator* of January 14, 1837, carried only a brief notice of Henry's death. His obituary appeared in *The Liberator*, January 21, 1837.

---

6 9

TO ANNA BENSON

Boston, Feb. 4, 1837.

Dear sister Anna:

I can scarcely persuade myself that so many days have elapsed since I last wrote to Brooklyn. None of you will think, I am sure, that because you are out of sight, you are out of mind. How much is he to be pitied, who finds Time lagging upon his flight, as if his wings were leaden ones — and who counts hours as days, and days as weeks! It is no paradox for me to say, that the more burdened I am with cares, responsibilities and duties, the more gaily does life pass with me, and the swifter do my moments roll. I think I know, by experience, that "it is a good thing always to be zealously affected in a good cause," and that none need to be weary in well-doing.[1] Blessed Saviour! like thee, I feel it is both meat and drink to do the will of my Father who is in heaven. Be thou ever my light, joy, life, righteousness and peace! Crucified with thee to the world, I feel within the power of thy resurrection. I join with ransomed millions in shouting, "Worthy is the Lamb!"[2]

The annual meeting of our State Society was held last week [3] in this city, and of course I was altogether too much engrossed with its concerns to indulge in correspondence. Bro. George, having been present at the first meeting in the stable-loft,[4] has no doubt given you all the particulars; and such as he has not been able to detail by his subsequent absence, you will find recorded at length in the last and in this week's Liberator.[5] It will hardly be necessary to occupy this sheet on that subject. Suffice it to say, that we had five public meetings, four of them crowded to excess, without any disturbance, and that, in genuine abolition spirit and brotherly kindness, they exceeded all that have hitherto been held in Boston. You can form but a faint idea of the life and glow which pervaded them all, by reading the speeches as reported in to-day's Liberator. One needed to be present to realize all that transpired. The utmost kindness and cordiality were extended to me by all present, and every speaker was more or less profuse in his *encomiums* upon myself and the Liberator. Whenever my name was alluded to, a round of applause was sure to follow [6] — which clearly demonstrated, not so much that any merit belongs to me, as that the meeting was deeply and thoroughly saturated with "Garrisonism." Indeed, there was a great deal too much said in my praise. If I did not *know* that I have nailed my natural vanity and love of human praise to the cross of Christ, such things would be likely to puff me up. But, "God forbid that I should glory, save in the cross of Christ, by whom I am crucified unto the world, and the world unto me." [7] It cannot but cheer my heart to know that I have secured the approbation and love of the best people in the land, because it has naturally followed my advocacy of a righteous though unpopular cause; but mere human applause is in itself no evidence of personal worth.

At the State House, our meeting was thronged to excess. One of our daily papers estimates, that not less than five thousand persons went away, being unable to obtain admittance! — It was expected that our enemies would rally strongly on that occasion: but, as a test of the character and feelings of the audience, I will merely state, that when Ellis Gray Loring, in the course of his speech, bestowed a strong panegyric upon my name,[8] a burst of applause followed from every part of the house. When it died away, a few hisses were heard in one of the galleries. These elicited another tremendous round of applause. Again a hiss was heard, and then followed another and still more powerful manifestation of enthusiastic approbation of my labors in the anti-slavery cause. — I mention this fact to show how vain have been the attempts of my enemies to make me odious even among my abolition brethren.

It will gratify bro. George, (for I suppose he is in Brooklyn, not having heard from him since the meeting,) to learn, that at the last meeting of our Society, on Friday forenoon of last week, about three hours were occupied in discussing the merits of the Liberator and its editor. The Sabbath question was also taken up. I dare not tell you, dear Anna, what fine things were said about me. To my surprise, notwithstanding that "delicate" subject, the Sabbath, was alluded to in connexion with my review of Dr. Beecher's speech, there was but one feeling manifested toward me, and that of the most enthusiastic kind. What was peculiarly pleasing, was, to find men of various sects joining in one common panegyric. — Among the speakers were, Rev. Mr. Norris,[9] Methodist; Isaac Winslow,[10] Friend; Rev. Mr. Hall,[11] Congregationalist; Rev. Mr. St Clair,[12] Unitarian — &c. &c. Bro. May poured out his soul as usual, and said that the same ball which laid Garrison low, would carry him down also. Stanton spoke nobly and generously. Well, does bro. G. ask, what was *done*, as well as *said*? Something that will delight him! It was unanimously voted, that the Massachusetts Anti-Slavery should henceforth assume the responsibility of printing and editing [13] the Liberator, and that the abolitionism of the Commonwealth should be pledged to sustain it.[14] The paper, however, is *not* to be the organ of our Society, nor is any body to control my pen. This arrangement will relieve friend Knapp and myself of a heavy burden, which has long crushed us to the earth. [It is] probable that we shall soon enlarge the paper.[15]

I find that I am, after all, occupying my sheets mainly with the details of the public meetings we have held. — A word, now, as to ourselves at home. *We are all well.* Dear E. J. Chace [16] still kindly tarries with us — and it is not a little singular, that our sweet babe has not had a sick day since she came! He grows more and more beautiful and precious. Helen is also remarkably well, and in good spirits. She and Eliza attended several of our meetings. They desire me to tell in this letter how much they love you all, and wish to be remembered, &c. &c. but you know all about it. — I forgot to say, that bro. S. J. May introduced a resolution at our last meeting, respecting the death of father and Henry, and attempted to make some remarks, but was so overcome with emotion, that he had to take his seat. Nearly all present were in tears.

Much love to all. In great haste,
Ever yours affectionately,
Wm. Lloyd Garrison.

☞ We are all in consternation here respecting a dreadful rumor about Ray Potter.[17]

ALS: Garrison Papers, Boston Public Library. Reprinted, in part, in *Life*, II, 122–123, 125–127. This letter is to Garrison's sister-in-law.

1. Galatians 4:18 and Galatians 6:9, both verses slightly adapted.
2. Revelation 5:12.
3. Wednesday to Friday, January 25–27, 1837.
4. Originally, the meeting was to be held in Congress Hall. Permission had been granted by the Free Church, which worshiped there. But the proprietor and lessee, Dr. Edward Hutchinson Robbins and J. M. Allen, respectively, revoked the permission and excluded the Free Church as well. No other hall could be obtained for the meeting. At the last minute the loft of a stable attached to the Marlboro Hotel, which was owned by Willard Sears, an abolitionist, was offered for the meeting, and the offer was accepted. The Wednesday morning and afternoon sessions were held there, while the evening session took place in the representatives' hall of the State House, permission for which had been granted by the Massachusetts house. (*Life*, II, 124–125; *The Liberator*, January 28, 1837.)
5. January 28 and February 4, 1837.
6. "'Tremendous applause' was given when an ex-slave, a native of Africa, after reciting some horrible tales from his experience, turned suddenly to Mr. Garrison with — 'Dat man is de Moses raised up for our deliverance' (*Lib.* 7:22)." (*Life*, II, 126n.)
7. Galatians 6:14, slightly adapted.
8. Loring's panegyric was:
"Five or six years ago, a poor and solitary individual of the working class came among us, with nothing to depend upon but his God and the native powers which God gave him. He raised the thrilling cry of immediate emancipation. His encouragement was at first small indeed. But the grand, the true, the vital idea of immediate freedom to the slave burned bright within him and supported him. He, too, at length, had his twelve associates, and the first Anti-Slavery Society was formed. From this small beginning, and owing mainly, I believe, under God, to the clear vision, the purity of character, the energy, and the intrepidity of that individual, our cause has advanced till it numbers 800 societies. An anti-slavery society has been formed in the United States every day for the last two years. There are 300 societies in the single state of Ohio, one of which numbers 4,000 members. Yet the individual who started this mighty movement, is rejected and scorned by the great and little vulgar of our day. No matter. Posterity will do justice to the name of William Lloyd Garrison." (Quoted from *The Liberator*, 7:23, in *Life*, II, 126n.)
9. The Reverend Samuel Norris (b. Dorchester, New Hampshire, March 8, 1801; d. South Newmarket, New Hampshire, June 23, 1880), a Methodist minister, occupied various pulpits in New England and was a minister in Salisbury, Massachusetts, in 1836, and then in Haverhill and Methuen. Because of deafness and general debility he retired from the ministry in 1840. He passed the latter years of his life in South Newmarket, New Hampshire. (Leonard A. Morrison, *Lineage and Biographies of the Norris Family in America*, Boston, 1892, p. 121.)
10. Isaac Winslow (b. Falmouth, Maine, January 1, 1787; d. July 25, 1867) and his brother Nathan were among the earliest supporters of *The Liberator* and both participated in the founding of the American Anti-Slavery Society. Isaac Winslow provided the funds to enable Garrison to publish his *Thoughts on African Colonization* in 1832. In 1840 he attended the World's Anti-Slavery Convention in London as a delegate of the Massachusetts Anti-Slavery Society. He was a sea-captain and merchant in his earlier years and was engaged in whaling with his brother Jeremiah. They were the first to introduce whale fishery in France, where they lived for some time. In his later years he lived in Danvers, Massachusetts, and then in Philadelphia. (David Parson Holton and Mrs. Frances K. Holton, *Winslow Memorial*, New York, 1888, II, 885–886; *Life*, I, 289, 300n, 398; II, 122, 353, 383, 385.)

11. The Reverend Robert Bernard Hall (b. Boston, January 28, 1812; d. Plymouth, Massachusetts, April 15, 1868) was a founder of the New England Anti-Slavery Society, as well as of the American Anti-Slavery Society, helping to draft the Declaration of Sentiments of the latter organization. Originally a friend of Garrison, he defected to Garrison's critics in 1839 and later joined a colonization society. (*Life*, I, 278, 280, 341, 398, 406, 415; II, 122, 293, 384.)

12. The Reverend Alanson St. Clair alternated between the Universalist and Unitarian denominations. He earlier belonged to a Universalist group known as "Restorationists." At this date, however, he was a Unitarian. Although a supporter of Garrison in 1837, he joined the latter's clerical critics in 1839. He was, variously, a minister in Worcester, an agent of the Massachusetts Anti-Slavery Society and, in 1839, of the American Anti-Slavery Society. (*Life*, I, II, and III, *passim.*)

13. "The context seems to show that this was a slip of the pen for 'publishing.' 'The editorial responsibility rests, as heretofore, with Mr. Garrison' (Official circular, March 8, 1837)." (*Life*, II, 122n.)

14. " 'Our *sole reliance* is now on the *prompt action* of auxiliary and other societies' (Official circular)" (*Life*, II, 122n.)

15. "This enlargement was made with the tenth number (March 4, 1837). The size of the printed page now became 16x23 inches. By mid-summer the subscribers numbered some 3,000." (*Life*, II, 123n.)

16. Eliza J. Chace, William Chace's sister, later Mrs. Thomas Davis.

17. See note 5 in letter 26, to Helen, May 10, 1836.

70

TO GEORGE W. BENSON

Boston, Feb. 17, 1837.

Dear bro. George:

It so happened that I did not see our esteemed friend Stetson [1] during his very brief sojourn in our city, and that is one reason why I sent no message by him. I should have been glad to have had an hour's chit-chit with him, in relation to a thousand and one domestic particularities, but he came and went like a true business courier, who had no time to waste in mere talk.

Dear Helen and I feel deeply concerned at the intelligence, that our revered mother has had another relapse, though we cannot but hope it will prove only a transient effect of her journey from Providence to Brooklyn. Filled as we shall be with continual anxiety, until we hear of her complete restoration, we hope some one of the dear family will write to us quite often. We are also afflicted to hear that Sarah is not in the enjoyment of health: of course, it would at present be very imprudent for her to come to Boston. As the spring advances, she will doubtless be relieved of her cough; but, meanwhile, she ought to be very careful how she exposes herself.

We have concluded to postpone our visit to Brooklyn till June. The season will then be more pleasant, and the country will present a more inviting appearance. It will also be a very favorable time to escape the hot air of a crowded city. Besides, little George's foot so troubles him, and continues to be so badly swollen, that he is not in a condition to travel. Poor little fellow! he is sadly afflicted — but behaves, on the whole, very well. The wound on his forehead is healing slowly; but whether it will leave a permanent scar or not, is yet problematical. I am most anxious about the result of the swelling in his foot.

We discharged our little girl on Saturday, much to our relief — for she gave us more annoyance than aid.

I dare say you are now congratulating yourself that you are not in business in Providence. The pressure of the times is said to be very dreadful throughout the country.[2] The hurricane is levelling to the earth many a tall oak; but, as I am nothing more than a mere weed by the wayside, I do not feel its power. "Blessed be nothing." Fire cannot burn it up — failures cannot ruin it — shipwreck cannot sink it. I sincerely pity the man, who, in a time and panic like the present, is not rich toward God, and has not laid up in heaven, treasures beyond the reach of dishonesty, and the corrupting influences of the moth.[3] I pity the man whose soul is tossed continually upon the billows of worldly excitement, and has not entered into a state of heavenly rest. What! can the state of the money market fill the mind of a christian with feverish anxiety, and destroy or diminish that peace which "passeth all understanding"?[4]

A great many reasons are given, pro and con, why pecuniary matters are in such a state of perplexity and confusion. The love of money, and the making haste to be rich, are at the bottom of the mischief. The wild and fraudulent speculations for the last two or three years have also produced much of it. Unfortunately, in the punishment, the innocent are involved with the guilty, and perhaps will suffer the most. But all the troubles in the world — aside from those which flesh is properly heir to — arise from disobedience to God. When love reigns supreme in the hearts of men, there will be very little misery in the world.

I am looking forward to our annual meeting[5] at New-York with much interest. What will be done, I know not; but I hope it will be *well* done, in love and unanimity. Strong language and bold measures should be the order of the day. We must put on "the whole armor of God,"[6] that we may be able to stand. May his wisdom guide, his love strengthen, and his benediction fall upon us!

I perceive by Anna's last letter, that she continues to mourn over our beloved Henry's departure. Most certainly, he ought to live in our memory, as precious beyond all human comparison: but we ought to beware lest our sadness degenerate into misanthropy or selfishness, for we have no right to be unhappy, let who will be taken away. Our happiness must centre in God — so that whether he gives or takes away, we may at all times be able to say, "Blessed be the name of the Lord." [7] It is as much our lot to die as it is to sleep, ay, and a far greater privilege.

We send dear mother, and the sisters, and Catharine, and yourself, a great abundance of pure love, and long for the time to arrive when we shall greet you all in the old family homestead.

Ever yours affectionately,

Wm. Lloyd Garrison.

ALS: Massachusetts Historical Society.

1. James A. Stetson, brother of George W. Benson's wife, Catherine.
2. The depression of 1837.
3. A paraphrase of Matthew 6:19–20.
4. Philippians 4:7.
5. The annual meeting of the American Anti-Slavery Society.
6. Ephesians 6:11.
7. Job 1:21.

71

TO AMOS A. PHELPS

Boston, Feb. 21, 1837.

Dear bro. Phelps:

In reply to yours of the 18th inst. allow me to say —

1. That your withdrawal from the anti-slavery cause, at the present time, and under present circumstances, (if at any time prior to the abolition of slavery,) is manifestly "out of the question." Your services *cannot* "be spared without any great injury to the good cause." The responsibilities upon the *tried* friends of emancipation are not diminishing, nor is the pressure upon them alleviated, by the many conversions that are taking place in favor of our views. If more hands are found to work the abolition ship than heretofore, still we cannot spare a single pilot. If our army be enlarged, the recruits are raw, and require much drilling: the leaders to the onset must remain in the forefront of the battle. Hence, *you* must continue at your post.

2. While it is desirable that you should be able to act in ecclesiastical bodies officially, it is more important that you should be mainly consecrated to the anti-slavery cause.

3. I do not wonder that you are "tired out with moving about from pillar to post." But our desire is, in Boston, not to keep you rambling,

but to allow you to remain as a fixture — at least, you can do pretty much as you please in regard to lecturing, travelling, &c. The most of your time will be wanted in the city.

4. Your *strong* reason for turning yourself into a country parson is poverty — nay, not poverty, but debt. But we hope to put that reason aside entirely — i. e. by making you as good an offer, in a pecuniary point of view, as you can obtain in any other situation. Although we have not had a Board meeting since your letter was received, I know that the Board will be perfectly willing for you to stipulate for your-self as to terms. Or if you decline doing so, and prefer that they should name your salary, they will undoubtedly put it at $1500, or even higher if you wish. In addition to this, you will be allowed your Sabbaths gratis — so that you can probably add $500 to the $1500 by preaching, making $2000 as the sum total. I have just been conversing with our mutual friend John E. Fuller.[1] He informs me that Rev. Mr. Fitch will undoubtedly leave the Free Church very soon, as he wants a higher salary than they can really afford to give him. Bro. F. says that Dea. Gulliver [2] talks of inviting you to take Mr. Fitch's place: he (bro. F.) thinks the following arrangement can be made, and to the perfect satisfaction of the church and congregation, viz. You can accept the agency of our Society, and yet supply the pulpit, or agree to see it supplied, for the Free Church, on the Sabbath, and thus re-ceive the customary compensation. This, I think, will be agreeable to you.

I deeply regret that the health of your dear wife is generally so delicate, as to require her to absent herself so large a portion of the year from the city. As a loving husband, I can appreciate how great a sacrifice to you both it is to be separated in this manner. On this point, I dare not urge your coming, with that freedom which I can on other points.

From this invitation to come to Boston, you must not suppose that we think you are *not* admirably calculated to occupy the editorship of the Emancipator. Far otherwise. We shall regret, on many accounts, your resignation of that post, (unless you come to Boston,) especially if bro. Goodell does not supply your place. I hope he will be induced to leave Utica.

All the Parkers reciprocate your kind expressions. Miss Lucy will endeavor to find you convenient accomodations in her house, whether you come sooner or later — whether you require one or two rooms — but, of course, she cannot pledge to this effect with positive certainty upon an uncertainty.

Our Society will be disposed to wait for you until after the May anniversary,[3] provided you will speedily engage to accept of its offer.[4]

I trust you will see your way clear to come, as a matter of duty and happiness. May you be guided by infinite wisdom to a right decision.

What a dreadful reproach has been brought upon the cause of Christ by the sinful conduct of Ray Potter,[5] that "brother beloved," with whom we have taken sweet counsel together, and whom we have regarded as among the best of mankind. The knowledge of it almost crushes the life out of my heart — I am overwhelmed with sorrow and consternation. How will hell rejoice, and heaven mourn!

You and our friends in New-York will rejoice to learn, that, on Thursday afternoon next,[6] we abolitionists are to have a hearing before a legislative committee in the *Hall of the House of Representatives*, to show cause why the Legislature should protest against the resolution of Congress, laying our petitions upon the table unread and unreferred — and why the Legislature should call for the abolition of slavery in the District of Columbia. The State House will undoubtedly be crowded. You see we keep *agitating* in this quarter. Our Society has engaged Geo. S. Hillard, as a lawyer, to speak on the occasion, and bro. Stanton will sustain him. Mr. Loring and Mr. Sewall, as well as myself, are too busy to make any preparation, and cannot speak without it. We shall probably be permitted to have two or three hearings before the committee — but shall not accept the liberty, unless we can get suitable persons to speak. — We had serious thoughts of sending Whittier or Stanton post haste to New-York for bro. Weld [7] — it is a glorious opportunity for him, if his health will permit, to do good on an immense scale. ☞ *Send him instanter*, we beseech you, even if you charge us a thousand dollars for his coming. Tell dear Weld he cannot even faintly imagine the state of things with us, and what a crisis this is with our cause in this Commonwealth. The Legislature will remain in session till the 1st of April. If bro. Weld will come, he can gain access, directly and indirectly, to six hundred representatives, who are now in the most favorable state of mind to hear him. The only person we can rely upon is bro. Stanton, but he is almost broken down with his unremitting labors, and says we must have bro. Weld at all hazards. ☞ All our friends speak through me to dear Weld with the voice of agonizing entreaty. Will he not come under these circumstances?

Let me hear from you again. My regards to your lady and all the friends.

Ever yours,

Wm. Lloyd Garrison.

ALS: Phelps Papers, Boston Public Library.

Amos Phelps was then in New York City as editor of the *Emancipator*, the organ of the American Anti-Slavery Society, a position which he had assumed in the spring of 1836. He had succeeded William Goodell, who had been its editor since 1834 and he, in turn, was succeeded by Joshua Leavitt, in the middle of 1837.

1. See letter 15, to Helen, March 7, 1836.
2. Deacon John Gulliver of the Free Church in Boston was also the owner of the *New England Spectator*, which ranged itself on the side of Garrison's clerical critics in 1837. See letter 98, to George W. Benson, October 20, 1837.
3. The May anniversary of the American Anti-Slavery Society.
4. Phelps did accept the offer, and he became general agent of the Massachusetts Anti-Slavery Society in June 1837. The announcement of his appointment appeared in *The Liberator*, June 9, 1837.
5. See letter 26, to Helen, May 10, 1836, for an account of Potter's difficulties at this time.
6. February 23, 1837. The abolitionists of Massachusetts had sent fifty or sixty petitions to the Massachusetts legislature during the previous two weeks, urging it to protest against the policy of the federal House of Representatives in refusing to discuss petitions from various northern states demanding the abolition of slavery and the slave trade in the District of Columbia. George S. Hillard and Henry B. Stanton appeared before the legislative committee referred to by Garrison to express the sentiments of those who had signed the petitions to the Massachusetts house. *The Liberator* of February 25 reported that the witnesses were cordially received by the committee.
7. Apparently, Garrison decided to make the trip to New York City himself, to see Weld about coming to Boston. See letter 72, to Helen, March 2, 1837.

7 2

TO HELEN E. GARRISON

New-York, March 2, 1837.

My dear Helen:

Much to your regret, I dare say, (for I know you love me,) and I will say to my own regret also, (for I know that I love you,) I shall not be able to get home as soon as I anticipated when I left Boston. To begin with the beginning. Jonah's luck with me, as usual. We were four hours on the rail-road to Providence, i.e. twice as long as usual. There was no stove in our car, and as the weather was excessively cold, we suffered to some extent on the score of our feet and hands. After we had got a mile beyond Canton,[1] we met the opposite train, and had to retrace our steps. Soon after, the cars separated, and away went the locomotive, John Gilpin[2] like, at a hurried speed, the engineer being ignorant for some time that we were left behind: so we had to wait till he discovered our loss, and came back to take us in tow. I parted from Miss Smith[3] at the Taunton branch.

We left Providence just before 2 o'clock in the afternoon, with about 90 passengers, (all of them but *one* strangers to me,) and a very heavy freight. The boat was the Benjamin Franklin, the slowest one on the route. The weather was cold and stormy. Arrived at New-port at 4 o'clock, and stopped there till 2 o'clock the next morning, on account of the wind blowing a tremendous gale. We then started for New-York, but did not arrive here till last evening a quarter past 8 o'clock. It was a tedious and disagreeable passage. Although we had so many passengers, I had none to sympathize with any of the feelings of my heart, on the ground either of humanity or religion. Nearly all of them were more or less engaged in card-playing, throwing dice, and such foolish and criminal acts.

I found a welcome reception at our friend Lewis Tappan's. They are all well, and inquired affectionately after you and little George. There was a meeting of the Executive Committee last evening, which I attended. Rev. Mr. Leavitt,[4] Arthur Tappan, Mr. Sunderland,[5] Prof. Wright,[6] and Rev. Mr. Cornish,[7] were present. — Not one of them knew where Weld was to be found, nor did they believe his health would allow him to go to Boston, except at the risk of his life. I have since [seen] R. G. Williams,[8] Mr. Phelps, H. C. Wright, and other friends, but nobody knows any thing of Weld's whereabouts! It is too bad for him to hide himself in this manner. It is probable, however, that I shall find him this afternoon. Had I seen him this forenoon, probably I could have returned to Boston this afternoon, as a steam-boat leaves for Providence at 3 o'clock. Another one leaves on Satur-day afternoon — so that I shall not see you till Monday forenoon. Tell the friends I shall do my utmost to bring Weld along with me, but cannot hold out any encouragement as to his coming, simply on account of the state of his health.

As the mail is about closing, I must drop my pen. Kiss dear George many times for my sake — remember me in love to all at No. 5, Hay-ward Place — and believe me

Ever yours most affectionately,
Wm. Lloyd Garrison.

N.B. I gave Eliza's [9] things to a colored man to hand over the box to William.[10]

ALS: Garrison Papers, Boston Public Library.

1. Canton, Massachusetts.
2. See the poem by William Cowper, "The Diverting History of John Gilpin, Showing How He Went Farther Than He Intended, and Came Safe Home Again," written in 1782. The poem tells the story of Gilpin's borrowed horse, who had a mind of his own and galloped off, with Gilpin upon him, to his own destina-tion.
3. Unidentified.
4. The Reverend Joshua Leavitt (1794–1873), a leading abolitionist, a founder of the American Anti-Slavery Society and a member of its executive committee, became editor of the *Emancipator,* the organ of the American Anti-Slavery So-ciety, in 1837. (*Life,* I and II *passim.*)

5. The Reverend La Roy Sunderland (b. April 22, 1804; d. May 15, 1885), a minister of the Methodist Episcopal Church, had joined the antislavery movement in 1833, founded and edited in 1836 *Zion's Watchman*, an antislavery paper for Methodists in New York, and during the same year was elected to the executive committee of the American Anti-Slavery Society. He edited *Zion's Watchman* until 1843. See Garrison's letter to Sunderland, September 8, 1831 (*Letters*, I). By 1854 he had developed a method of healing by nutrition, without the use of drugs. For a defense of his system in a letter to Garrison and an example of his advertisement, see *The Liberator*, March 31, 1854, p. 51. See also *Life*, I, 236; II, 207, 358, 474; *Weld-Grimké Letters*, I, 457–458n, 509.

6. Elizur Wright, Jr.

7. Samuel E. Cornish (b. Delaware, *c.* 1795), was a Negro Presbyterian minister of Philadelphia and New York City, who, with John B. Russwurm, the first Negro college graduate, published and edited the first Negro newspaper, *Freedom's Journal*, beginning on March 16, 1827. Other newspapers which Cornish published or edited, all of which were short-lived, were *Rights of All* in 1829, the *Weekly Advocate* in 1836, and the *Colored American*, with two other Negroes, founded in 1837. He helped found the American Anti-Slavery Society and was a member of its executive committee. John Hope Franklin regards him as the outstanding Negro journalist of the pre-Civil War period. (*From Slavery to Freedom*, third edition, New York, 1967, p. 252; Lerone Bennett, Jr., *Pioneers in Protest*, Baltimore, Maryland, 1968, pp. 59–66.)

8. Ransom G. Williams.

9. Eliza Chace.

10. William Chace, Eliza's brother.

73

TO THE EDITOR OF THE BOSTON *COURIER*

[March 4, 1837.]

Sir — A writer who should adopt the signature of BENEDICT ARNOLD, in advocating the cause of liberty, — or that of ROBESPIERRE,[1] in extolling humanity and religion, — would at least be charged with ignorance or bad taste; but should he assume the name of GEORGE WASHINGTON, in order to enforce the lawfulness of taxation without representation, and the superiority of a monarchial over a republican form of government, — or subscribe himself WILLIAM PENN in justifying the outrages of Georgia upon the Cherokee Indians, or applauding national wars, — he would excite not merely surprise at his folly, but indignation at the insult thus offered to the memory of the dead. In what terms, then, shall we speak of the rare audacity of a correspondent in the Courier, who, borrowing the name of the illustrious ALGERNON SIDNEY,[2] — a martyr even upon the scaffold in the cause of HUMAN RIGHTS, and an uncompromising enemy of slavery under every phase and color, — is bold and shameless enough to appear, not only as a scoffer at the tried friends of equal freedom, but as the applauder of that worst species of jacobinism, LYNCH LAW? He libels the dead, that he may defame the living, and is an anarchist in the guise of a patriot. What! the *spirit of* SIDNEY conjured up to justify the burning of property in the streets, the tumultuous dispersion of lawful convocations, the stoning of men and women, for opinion's sake! What! the *voice* of SIDNEY summoned to denounce those who plead for a brother in chains — for woman under the lash — for children and babes sold like swine in the market! What! the *patriotism* of SIDNEY invoked to abridge, by ruffian violence, the right of free discussion, when for asserting that right he lost his head upon the block! 'An ass will not leave his stupidity,' says the beheaded patriot, 'though he be covered with scarlet;' [3] and an apologist for jacobinism and slavery cannot conceal the malignity of his soul, though he assume the character of no less a personage than ALGERNON SIDNEY.

But your lynch-law correspondent, Mr. Editor, complains that Abolitionists abuse the liberty of speech, and declares that if they will still abuse it, he hopes 'they are only in the first stages of their agony,' arising from the mobocratic assaults of violent and wicked men. Waiving, in this connexion, all comments upon this ferocious declaration, and all evidence to show that Abolitionists are only guilty of calling things by their right names — I will quote a passage in point from the disquisitions of the *true* SIDNEY, who in his own day was forced to exclaim, 'We live in an age that makes *truth* pass for *treason;*' [4] and who further says —

'If Filmer [5] [his antagonist] might publish to the world his opinion, that all men [the colored race] are born under a necessity derived from the laws of God and nature, to submit to an absolute kingly [despotic] government, which could be restrained by no law or oath; and that he that has the power, whether he come to it by creation, election, inheritance, usurpation, or any other way, had the right; and none must oppose his will, but the persons and estates of his subjects must be indispensably subject unto it; I know not why I might not have published my opinion to the contrary, *without the breach of any law I have yet known.*' [6] 'If, nevertheless, the writer was mistaken, he might have been refuted by law, reason and scripture; and no man for such matters was ever otherwise punished, than by being made to see his error.' [7]

It seems, then, that this great patriot wished to be refuted by 'law, reason and scripture,' if he were in error; but the impostor in the Courier, assuming upon his own infallibility, is for refuting the errors of others with brickbats, rotten eggs, and a coat of tar-and-feathers! This is his method of propagating *charity*. By this kind of argumentation, all cavils are to be silenced, all errors exploded, all virulence mitigated, rudeness changed into politeness, and the opponents of the Colonization Society transformed into its warmest friends!

As your correspondent has chosen the English patriot as a model for disputants, courteous, rational, profound, well skilled in the use of language — *as I most cordially approve of his selection,* and desire no other advantage over him than to compare the insolent impostor with the real patriot himself, that his condemnation may be as terrible as his spirit is base — I shall resort to that exhaustless treasury of free thoughts, SIDNEY's *Discourses on Government,* in order to show, beyond all contradiction, that ALGERNON SIDNEY was *an Abolitionist of the modern school,* as 'fanatical,' 'incendiary,' 'denunciatory,' and 'blood-thirsty,' as even GEORGE THOMPSON himself. Let a fair verdict be rendered upon the following extracts from the incomparable work alluded to:

'The principles of liberty in which God created us, and which includes the chief advantages of the life we enjoy, as well as the greatest helps towards the felicity that is the end of our hopes in the other, is written in the heart of every man, and *denied by none but such as are degenerated into beasts.'* [8]

'The schoolmen could not but see that which all men saw, nor lay more approved foundations, than that *man is naturally free;* that he cannot justly be deprived of that liberty without cause; and that he doth not resign it, nor any part of it, unless it be in consideration of a greater good which he proposes to himself.' [9]

'*To depend on the will of a man is slavery.*[10] Liberty solely consists in an independence upon the will of another; and by the name of slave, we understand a man who can neither dispose of his person or goods, but enjoys all at the will of his master.' [11]

'In asserting the right to liberty ourselves, we allow it to all mankind. The temporal good of all men consists in the preservation of it.[12] He that oppugns the public liberty, overthrows his own, and is guilty of the most brutish of all follies, whilst he arrogates to himself that which he denies to all men.' [13]

'There can be no peace where there is no justice; nor any justice, if the government instituted for the good of a nation be turned to its ruin.' [14]

'I cannot believe God hath created man in a state of misery and slavery.[15] It is hard to comprehend how one man can come to be master of many, equal to himself in right, unless it be by consent or by force.[16] No man can justly impose any thing upon those who owe him nothing.[17] Whosoever, therefore, grounds his pretension of right upon usurpation and tyranny, declares himself to be an usurper and a tyrant, that is, an enemy to God and man, and to have no right at all.[18]

'All mankind must inherit the right, to which every one hath an equal title; and that which is dominion, if in one, when it is equally divided amongst all men, is that *universal liberty* which I assert.[19] No man by birth hath a right over another, or ever can have any, unless by the concession of those who are concerned.[20] *The equality amongst mankind is perfect.*[21] No man is, or can be, a lord amongst us, till we make him so: *by nature we are all brethren.*[22] No obedience can be due to him or them, who have not a right of commanding.[23] That government is unreasonable, and abhorred by the laws of God and man, which is not instituted for the good of those that live under it.[24] What name can be fit for those, who have no other title to the power they possess, than the most unjust and violent usurpation?[25] All that is or can be inherited by every one, is that exemption from the dominion of another, which we call liberty, and is *the gift of God and nature.*[26] This is a truth implanted in the hearts of men, and acknowledged so to be by all that have hearkened to the voice of nature, and disapproved by none but such as through wickedness, stupidity, or baseness of spirit, seem to have degenerated into the worst of beasts, and to have retained nothing of men but the outward shape, or the ability of doing those mischiefs which they have learnt from their master the devil.'[27]

'*The assertors of liberty want no other patron than God himself.*[28] Liberty produceth virtue, order, and stability: Slavery is accompanied with vice, weakness, and misery.[29] That which is not just, is not law; and that which is not law, *ought not to be obeyed.*'[30]

'The observation of the laws of nature is absurdly expected from tyrants, who set themselves up against all laws.'[31]

'Property is an appendage to liberty; and it is as impossible for a man to have a right to lands or goods, if he has no liberty, and enjoys his life only at the pleasure of another, as it is to enjoy either, when he is deprived of them.'[32]

'Unjust commands are not to be obeyed; and no man is obliged to suffer for not obeying such as are against law.[33] The weight of chains, number of stripes, hardness of labor, and other effects of a master's cruelty, may make one servitude more miserable than another; but *he is a slave who serves the best and gentlest man in the world,* as well as he who serves the worst: and he does serve him, if he must obey his commands, and depends upon his will.'[34]

'That which is unjust in the beginning, can never have the effect of justice; and it being manifestly unjust for one, or a few men, to assume a power over those who by nature are equal to them, *no such power can be just or beneficial to mankind*[35] Aristotle proves, that no man is to be entrusted with an absolute power, by shewing, that no one knows how to execute it, *but such a man as is not to be found.*'[36]

'Till the right of dominion be proved and justified, liberty subsists as arising from the nature and being of a man. The creature having nothing, and being nothing but what the Creator makes him, must owe all to him, and nothing to any one from whom he has received nothing. Man, therefore, must be *naturally free,* unless he be created by another power than we have yet heard of.'[37]

'We have heard of 'tyranny with a mischief, slavery and bondage with a mischief,' and they have been denounced by God against wicked and perverse nations, as mischiefs comprehending all that is most to be abhorred and dreaded in the world. But Filmer informs us that liberty, which all wise and good men have in all ages esteemed to be *the most valuable and glorious privilege of mankind,* is a 'mischief.' If he deserve credit, Moses, Joshua, Gideon, Samson, and Samuel, with others like them, were enemies to their country, in depriving the people of the advantages they enjoyed under the paternal care of Pharaoh, Adonibezek, Eglon, Jabin and other kings of the neighboring nations, and restoring them to that 'liberty with a mischief,' which he has promised to them. The Israelites were happy under the power of tyrants, whose proclamations were laws; and they ought to have been thankful to God for that condition, and not for the deliverances he wrought by the hands of his servants. Subjection to the will of a man is happiness, liberty is a 'mischief.' *But this is so abominably wicked and detestable, that it can deserve no answer.*[38]

'Nothing can be more absurd than to say, that one man has an absolute power above law, to govern according to his own will, 'for the people's good, and the preservation of their liberty;' for no liberty can subsist where there is such a power.[39]

'They who for the most part are the authors of great revolutions, not being so much led by a particular hatred to the man, as by a desire to do good to the public, seldom set themselves to conspire against the tyrant, unless he be altogether detestable and intolerable, if they do not hope to overthrow the tyranny.' [40]

'Tyrants are said, *'exuisse hominem,'* to throw off the nature of men, because they do unjustly and unreasonably assume to themselves that which agrees not with the frailty of human nature, and set up an interest in themselves contrary to that of their equals, which they ought to defend as their own. *Such as favor them are like to them*; and we know of no tyranny that was not set up by the *worst*, nor of any that have been destroyed, unless by the *best of men.'* [41]

The foregoing extracts are 'like apples of gold in pictures of silver.' [42] In what light do they place your correspondent, Mr. Editor, but as an arrant impostor — as (again to quote SIDNEY) 'so bitter an enemy to mankind, as to be displeased with nothing but that which tends to their good; and so perverse in his judgment, that we have reason to believe that to be good which he most abhors'? [43] All that has been written in favor of the rights of man, from the martyrdom of SIDNEY to the present time, is but a repetition of these great and glorious truths. I challenge the most industrious and subtle opponents of the anti-slavery cause, to find in the writings of modern Abolitionists, any opinions, principles, doctrines, or inferences, which conflict with, or are contrary to the sentiments uttered in the above selections from the essays of that ancient Abolitionist, ALGERNON SIDNEY.

Respectfully yours,

WM. LLOYD GARRISON.

5 Hayward Place.

Printed in *The Liberator*, March 4, 1837. The letter bears no date.

The editor of the Boston *Courier* was Joseph Tinker Buckingham (1779–1861), who had founded it in 1824 and continued to edit and publish it until 1848. The *Courier* reflected the views of the Whig party. In earlier years Buckingham had praised Garrison for his conduct of the Newburyport *Free Press* and had befriended him during his imprisonment in Baltimore. He served both in the house and senate of the Massachusetts legislature and became a Free-soiler when that party was formed. (*DAB*; Joseph Tinker Buckingham, *Personal Memoirs and Recollections of Editorial Life*, Boston, 1852; *Life*, I, 71, 179, 192, 246, 521; II, 7.)

1. Maximilien Robespierre (1758–1794), one of the most radical leaders of the French Revolution, a deist and champion of social revolution (*EE*).

2. Garrison refers to a letter which had been printed in the Boston *Courier*, signed pseudonymously Algernon Sidney, dated Boston, January 16, [1837], to Dr. William Ellery Channing. The letter commented on and condemned Channing's *Letter of William E. Channing to James G. Birney* (published in Cincinnati in 1836 and republished in Boston in 1837), which had defended the right of the abolitionists to free speech. *The Liberator*, on March 4, 1837, printed "Algernon Sidney" 's letter together with Garrison's reply.

Algernon Sidney or Sydney (1622–1683) was an English republican, member of Parliament, army officer, member of the English council of state, and author. Associated with the Whig plot against the king, he was arrested in 1683, tried for treason, and after an unfair trial found guilty and executed. His chief work, *Discourses Concerning Government*, was published posthumously in 1698 (*DNB*). A three-volume edition of his work, entitled *Discourses on Government*, was published in New York in 1805 by Richard Lee. It was this edition which Garrison probably used as his source. All future references will be to this edition, unless otherwise stated.

On March 11, 1837, *The Liberator* revealed the true name of "Algernon Sidney" in the following statement:

"Several inquiries having been made as to the real author of the scurrilous and brutal essays in the Courier, signed 'Algernon Sidney,' the following extract of a letter addressed by a friend to Samuel J. May, gives the necessary information — *Ed. Lib.*"

" 'You request information, *who* writes the silly ravings which appear over the abused name of ALGERNON SIDNEY, in the Boston Courier. Allow me to name him. This I can do, on evidence little, or nothing, short of demonstration. It is WALTER COLTON. . . . In 1822, he graduated at Yale College. He next went through the three years' course at Andover. He became a licentiate preacher; and Capt. Partridge received him as chaplain and professor of rhetoric in his military academy, Middletown, Conn. . . . During that period, he was constituted, and declared to be, a minister of the gospel — but was never installed in a pastoral charge. From Middletown, he went to the city of Washington, and there, for a short time, was editor of a newspaper. . . . Hence he obtained a chaplaincy on a U. S. frigate. After protracted lounging at Pensacola, and along the northern border of the Mexican Gulf, the ship, with C. of course, was sent into the Mediterranean. After much cruising from one end to the other of that celebrated sea, he returned. It is understood, that his chaplaincy now renders him stationary, in some connection with the navy yard at Charlestown. . . .' "

Soon after this exchange of letters Walter Colton (b. Rutland, Vermont, May 9, 1797; d. Philadelphia, January 22, 1851) moved to Washington, where he edited the *Colonization Herald*. He was one of the editors of the Philadelphia *North American* from 1840 to 1844 and territorial governor of California from 1846 to 1849. In California he established the first schoolhouse, empanelled the first jury, and established and edited the first newspaper, the *Alta Californian*. Besides writing numerous newspaper articles and pamphlets, Colton was also the author of a number of books, including *Ship and Shore, or Leaves from a Journal of a Cruise to the Levant*, 1835; *A Visit to Constantinople and Athens*, 1836; *Deck and Port, or Incidents of a Cruise in the U. S. Frigate Congress to California*, 1850. (*DAB*; George W. Colton, *A Genealogical Record of the Descendants of Quartermaster George Colton*, Lancaster, Pa., 1912, p. 224.)

3. Algernon Sidney, *Discourses on Government*, I, 375.

4. *Ibid.*, I, 86.

5. Sir Robert Filmer (c. 1589–1653), an English writer and Royalist, who expounded the doctrine of the divine right of kings. Sidney's *Discourses on Government* was directed, in great part, against Filmer's views. (*EE*.)

6. *Discourses on Government*, I, 87–88. In this and the following quotations, the italics are Garrison's.

7. *Ibid.*, I, 89–90.   8. *Ibid.*, I, 313.

9. *Ibid.*, I, 314.
10. *Ibid.*, I, 327.
11. *Ibid.*, I, 328.
12. *Ibid.*, I, 329, with variations.
13. *Ibid.*, I, 330.
14. *Ibid.*, I, 335.
15. *Ibid.*, I, 353, with variations.
16. *Ibid.*, I, 353.
17. *Ibid.*, I, 354.
18. *Ibid.*, I, 355, with variations.
19. *Ibid.*, I, 357.
20. *Ibid.*, I, 357.
21. *Ibid.*, I, 358, with variations.
22. *Ibid.*, I, 359, with variations.
23. *Ibid.*, I, 386.
24. *Ibid.*, I, 388, with variations.
25. *Ibid.*, I, 389.

26. *Ibid.*, I, 397.
27. *Ibid.*, I, 429.
28. *Ibid.*, I, 431.
29. *Ibid.*, II, 82.
30. *Ibid.*, III, 34.
31. *Ibid.*, III, 71.
32. *Ibid.*, III, 73.
33. *Ibid.*, III, 131.
34. *Ibid.*, III, 142.
35. *Ibid.*, III, 161.
36. *Ibid.*, III, 160.
37. *Ibid.*, III, 203.
38. *Ibid.*, III, 356.
39. *Ibid.*, III, 140.
40. *Ibid.*, II, 173.
41. *Ibid.*, II, 185.
42. Proverbs 25:11.

43. *Discourses on Government*, III, 352–353.

74

TO THE EDITOR OF THE BOSTON *COURIER*

[March 11, 1837.]

Sir, — Before proceeding any further in this discussion, you will allow me to premise —

1st. That when I authorized you to announce my intention of replying to 'Algernon Sidney,' I had seen only the first number of his essays. The entire series almost tempts me to retract my pledge, because sheer ruffianism and low scurrility do not admit of manly antagonism, and render an elaborate refutation superfluous. Yet — thanks, sir, to your editorial impartiality, — as I am permitted to occupy as much space in the columns of the Courier as your correspondent, personal disgust shall not deprive me of the opportunity to lift up my voice against those monsters who make merchandize of the image of God, and hold in chains and slavery a larger number of the inhabitants of this country, than is constituted by the entire population of New England.

2d. That I do not appear as the vindicator of Dr. Channing from the virulent assaults of 'Sidney.' Far from it. In consequence of the *false accusations* brought by the former against the Abolitionists, in his work on Slavery, the latter has clearly the advantage over him: and, surely, it must be painfully humiliating to be successfully confuted by such an assailant! If magnanimity be the attribute of a truly great mind, Dr. Channing has yet to make public confession, that, in his haste or his ignorance, he has done injustice both to anti-slavery men and measures. I leave his writings, with all their inconsistencies, misconceptions, aspersions, and fatal defects, to be exposed, ridiculed, and refuted, according to the taste and ability of your correspondent. But let not 'Sidney' foolishly imagine, that in convicting Dr. Channing of self-contradiction and perverse reasoning, he shall thereby bring either the Abolitionists or their sacred cause justly into disgrace. That they are impeccable I do not affirm; but wherein they are blameworthy, remains to be proved.

3d. That I shall not stoop to the degrading task of examining the offensive allusions, and repelling the obvious calumnies of your correspondent, in detail. He has piled them up in a large heap: let them be left to perish in their own corruption. A very few points challenge my attention.

In my former number, I demonstrated that the great English patriot, ALGERNON SIDNEY, who flourished two hundred years ago, and whose name your correspondent has insolently assumed, was the father of modern Abolitionism; that he was an immediate emancipationist, in the strictest sense; that, for his noble advocacy of the rights of man, he was beheaded as a traitor; that he regarded those who justify or palliate oppression, as seeming (again to quote his own language) 'through wickedness, stupidity, or baseness of spirit, to have degenerated into the worst of beasts, and to have retained nothing of man but the outward shape, or the ability of doing those mischiefs which they have learnt from their master, the devil' [hard language!]; that he declared, 'we know of no tyranny that was not set up by the worst, nor of any that has been destroyed, unless by the best men;'[1] and that, consequently, were he now living in this country, to apply his principles to the system of American slavery, he would be adjudged worthy of death, even by the imposter who figures in the Courier, not according to the sentence of Chief Justice Jeffreys,[2] but that of a still more sanguinary monster, Judge LYNCH.

In this number, I propose to give a short essay upon *throat-cutting*, in the names of God and Liberty!

Your correspondent furnishes me with a suitable text. Alluding to that sterling friend of America, and eloquent champion of downtrodden humanity, GEORGE THOMPSON, he says:

'Let one expression, *often on his lips*, (!!) suffice as a specimen of the rest (!!) — 'The slave has a right to cut the throat of his master'!! To this language the Abolitionists listened, and shouted their assent. (!!) And they listened to it, when they knew that he who uttered it was a refugee from justice,' &c. &c.

This is certainly a rare specimen of cool, deliberate lying, well becoming an advocate of Lynch law, and a defender of remorseless oppression. Four stout falsehoods in as many lines! No such expression was ever uttered by *Mr. Thompson*; of course no Abolitionist ever listened to such language; moreover, as it was never uttered, they never shouted their assent to it; and, finally, neither they nor Mr. Thompson's opponents then knew, nor have since known, that he was a refugee from justice. On the contrary, both parties know that he is admired, beloved, applauded and sustained by the combined philanthropy and piety of Great Britain; and that such men as PRICE [3] of London, JAMES [4] of Birmingham, CROPPER [5] of Liverpool, and WARDLAW [6] of Glasgow, are among his warmest friends. He is at the present time moving through England and Scotland with unexampled eclat, — a strange reception, indeed, for 'a *refugee from justice!*'

But, sir, it is not my design, nor is it necessary for me, to enter into a vindication of Mr. *Thompson*, from the low ribaldry of an anonymous calumniator, who, being ashamed of his own name, basely borrows that of a dead patriot, to give respectability to his character. I have another object in view. I wish to admit, argumentatively, that Mr. Thompson did assert that 'the slave has a right to cut the throat of his master'; that the Abolitionists as frequently shouted their assent to the doctrine; that the Liberator is endeavoring to excite a servile insurrection at the south; and that I am plotting to overthrow slavery by physical force, by the shedding of blood, by rapine and war. Admit all this to be true — who that is not, *in principle*, opposed to all violence, under any circumstances and pretexts whatever, will have the effrontery to look me in the face, and denounce me for such conduct, or to rebuke my associates? Will the polished ruffian in the Courier dare to confront me eye to eye? No indeed! not he who maintains that an assumed abuse of the liberty of speech may justly be punished by the Lynch code — that those who are calumniated may hurl rotten eggs and brickbats at the heads of their traducers, in order to make them more charitable! For if 'gentlemen of property and standing' — for example — may properly act the part of anarchists and jacobins, trample the constitution and laws under foot, and assault and disperse a small company of helpless females, on account of a difference of opinions, — or if you please, to show their disapprobation of 'hard language' and 'fanatical zeal,' — really, it seems to me, in my simplicity, that those who are subjected to a state of abject servitude, and ranked among goods, and chattels, and four-footed beasts, and creeping things, are authorised by such an example to revolt at any moment, and hurl their oppressors to the earth. It has been usually deemed a pertinent interrogation of the apostle Paul, — 'Thou that sayest, a man should not steal, dost thou steal?' [7] Ye who say, the slaves should not fight for liberty, have ye ever fought for liberty? Let Bunker-Hill give the response! Let the plains of Concord, and Lexington, and Yorktown, answer! Let the garments of this nation, dripping with blood, — let the hosts who perished untimely, during a seven years' war, in opposition to 'a threepenny tax upon tea,' — make the solemn reply! Let the revolutionary motto, 'Resistance to tyrants is obedience to God!' [8] — let the thrilling sentiment of Patrick Henry, 'Give me liberty, or give me death!' — let the stirring injunction of Gen. Warren,[9] 'My sons, scorn to be *slaves!*' — let these respond in thunder-tones!

It is an established doctrine among us, that British oppression, Russian oppression, Turkish oppression, and indeed all other oppression excepting that of our southern States, — the most detestable and intolerable of them all! — may be rightfully resisted unto blood. Who stimulated the enslaved Greeks 'to cut their masters' throats?' Who sent muskets and ammunition to the rebellious Poles, that they might blow out their masters' brains? Who encouraged the South-American insurrectionists to spill their masters' blood? Why, the citizens of Boston! southern slaveholders! the American people! and they glory in the deed. Who call heaven and earth to witness, that they 'hold these truths to be *self-evident* — that ALL MEN ARE CREATED EQUAL; that they are endowed BY THEIR CREATOR with certain INALIENABLE RIGHTS, among which are life, LIBERTY, and the pursuit of happiness?' The very same people! Who maintain, in their Declaration of Independence, that whenever governments become oppressive, it is the right, *it is the duty* of the oppressed to throw off such governments? The same people! Who, then, authorize and urge the slaves at the south to 'cut their masters' throats' without delay, as a religious and patriotic act? Why, the citizens of Boston! southern slaveholders! the American people! Impudent, sanguinary, brutally inconsistent men! Until they beat their swords into ploughshares, and their spears into pruning-hooks — spike every cannon, blow up every naval vessel, demolish every fortification, disband every military company; until they muffle every bell, quench every bonfire, disperse every procession, gag every orator, and hush every shout of joy, on the fourth of July; until they are able, in obedience to Christ, when smitten on one cheek to turn the other also to the assailant; until they repudiate in all cases the right of self-defence, alike in theory and in practice; until they shudder, instead of exulting, in view of the bloody scenes of the revolutionary war; until, in fine, they use only such weapons as a Christian people may lawfully wield, 'spiritual weapons,' in defence of their lives, liberty and property; let them not presume to arraign any man, or body of men, who shall shout in the ears of our slaves —

> 'Lay the proud usurpers low!
> Tyrants fall in every foe!

Liberty's in every blow!
Freemen be, or die!
By oppression's woes and pains,
By your sons in servile chains,
Freely drain your dearest veins,
But they shall be free!' [10]

Your correspondent, Mr. Editor, affects to shudder at the thought, that two millions and a half of enslaved Americans should rise up in vindication of their rights 'They may not shed a drop of their masters' blood, even to save a wife from pollution or a mother from torture; but their masters may shed *their* blood freely, lacerate their bodies to any extent, brand them with red hot irons, sell them as cattle in the shambles, and make havoc of their intellects and souls — and they are not even to whisper a remonstrance, but are in duty bound to combine the gentleness of the lamb with the stupidity of the ass! Would he require this of any other people on the face of the globe? Not he, the dastard! On this point, therefore, it may be pertinent to inquire, what are the sentiments of the patriotic *Sidney*, whom he has selected as his model, mouthpiece and oracle. Hear the noble martyr!

'No man can justly impose any thing upon those who owe him nothing. No obedience can be due to him or them, who have not a right of commanding. Unjust commands are not to be obeyed.' [11]

Again:

'By an established law among the most virtuous nations, every man might kill a tyrant; and no names are recorded in history with more honor than those who did it.' [12]

Seditious and sanguinary enough! Again:

'When pride had changed Nebuchadnezzar into a beast, what should persuade the Assyrians not to drive him out among beasts, until God had restored unto him the heart of a man? When Tarquin had turned the legal monarchy of Rome into a most abominable tyranny, why should they not abolish it? And when the Protestants of the Low Countries were so grievously oppressed by the power of Spain, why should they not make use of all the means that God had put into their hands for their deliverance?' [13]

Again:

'Nero or Domitian would have desired no more, than that those who would not execute their wicked commands, should patiently have suffered their throats to be cut by such as were less scrupulous. Those men who delivered their countries from such plagues were thought to have something of divine in them, and have been famous above all the rest of mankind to this day. Of this sort were Pelopidas, Epaminondas, Thrasibulus, Harmodius, Aristogiton, Philopemen, Lucius Brutus, Publius Valerius, Marcus Brutus, C. Cassius, M. Cato, with a multitude of others among the ancient heathens. Such as were instruments of the like deliverances amongst the Hebrews, as Moses, Othniel, Ehud, Barak, Gideon, Samson, Jepthah, Samuel, David,

Jehu, the Maccabees, and others, have from the Scriptures a certain testimony of the righteousness of their proceedings, when they would neither act what was evil, nor suffer more than was reasonable.' [14]

It is evident, sir, that your correspondent must take some other name, — GEORGE McDUFFIE's for instance, — if he would consistently espouse the side of tyranny. The English ALGERNON SIDNEY, not GEORGE THOMPSON, justifies every slave in 'cutting his master's throat.' But such sentiments are clearly anti-christian. I deny the right of any man to fight for liberty. For doing so, thousands will be ready to stone me, who would be quite as prompt to suspend me upon a gibbet, if I should grant such a right impartially to the black man as well as the white!

Who else authorize the slaves to 'cut their masters' throat'? — for it may not prove wholly uninstructive to pursue this interesting topic somewhat further. The 1st Article of our State Constitution is in the following words:

'All men are born free and equal, and have certain *natural*, ESSENTIAL, and UNALIENABLE RIGHTS; among which may be reckoned the right of enjoying and DEFENDING their lives and *liberties* — that of acquiring, possessing, and protecting property; in fine, that of seeking and obtaining their safety and happiness.'

To the slaves, then, according to the decision of the people of this Commonwealth, belongs 'the right of *defending their liberties*' — or, in plain English, they are licensed to engage in the business of cutting the throats of their oppressors, either by wholesale or retail.

Will it be credited, sir? — and yet *it is true* — the following article is contained in the Constitutions of at least two slaveholding States:

'The doctrine of *non-resistance* against arbitrary power and oppression is ABSURD, SLAVISH, and *destructive to the good and happiness of mankind*!!'

Surely, sir, the slaves can desire no better warrant for cutting their masters' throats than the above — for they derive it from the masters themselves! To reverse its phraseology: — 'The doctrine of RESISTANCE against arbitrary power and oppression is reasonable, soul-inspiring, and preservative of the good and happiness of mankind!' This sentiment is manifestly pregnant with the spirit of butchery. It virtually says to the slaves — 'Rise, and slay your oppressors, that freedom and happiness may be yours!' And yet it is not only endorsed by southern slaveholders, but deemed so rational and excellent as to be conspicuously inserted in the Constitutions, or rather Bills of Rights, of Tennessee and Maryland! Now, let fresh charges be rung about 'the incendiary Liberator,' and the sanguinary language of GEORGE THOMPSON! Suffice it to say, that no such sentiment can be found in any of the multitudinous publications of the American Anti-Slavery Society, and its eight hundred auxiliaries. The *credit* of instigating the slaves to revolt belongs to the slaveholders; and, as if they apprehended that the slaves would refuse to carry the theory of resistance into practice, they multiply the number of their stripes, increase the weight of their burdens, and resort to every exasperating infliction, in order to infuse courage and desperation into their hearts, so that ample justice may be done to the enemies of liberty! By their acts and their words they say to their victims —

> 'Hereditary bondmen! know ye not,
> Who would be free, themselves must strike the blow!' [15]

Infatuated men! thus to kindle a flame that may ere long consume you to ashes!

Who next is found bidding the slaves to "cut their masters' throats?" THE STATE OF VIRGINIA! And by a "pictorial" example too! If any person will take the trouble to get a copy of the Richmond Whig, he will find affixed to the title the Coat of Arms of the Ancient Dominion. It represents the figure of LIBERTY, standing proudly erect, her foot upon the prostrate body of TYRANNY, whose head she has severed with her sword! The motto reads — "*Sic semper tyrannis*" — *So always to tyrants*! What a design and motto for the banner of another Nat Turner!

Mr. Editor, doubtless you exchange with the Augusta (Georgia) Chronicle. Will you send a copy of that "incendiary" print to "Algernon Sidney?" Above and below the title, 'AUGUSTA CHRONICLE,' he will find, thickly interspersed, a variety of mottoes, all permanently engraved with suitable flourishes — mottoes as seditious and fanatical as can be gleaned from all the anti-slavery publications put together, and a little more so! Among them are the following: — 'Freedom of Industry! Freedom of Conscience! FREEDOM OF SPEECH! FREEDOM OF THE PRESS! ° Nullification! Every Thing for the Right! *No Monopolies*! Intelligence is Liberty! Ignorance is Slavery! LIBERTY! NO SERVILE SUBMISSION!'

How such a paper is allowed to be printed in Georgia, is a matter of astonishment to me, as I think it will be to your readers.

° To show that the Chronicle practically enforces this motto, I make the following extracts from its editorial department: — 'He [Amos Dresser] should have been hung up as high as Haman, to rot upon the gibbet, until the wind whistled through his bones.' — 'The cry of the whole South should be, DEATH, INSTANT DEATH, to the Abolitionist, *wherever he is caught*.' 'Northern Abolitionists are a class of desperate fanatics, who, to accomplish their unhallowed ends, are ready to sacrifice our lives, and those of our wives and children.' 'Keep their publications from among us, and HANG every emissary that dare step a lawless foot upon our soil — cut off all trade with every northern house connected with them,' &c. &c.

Another case in point. The message of Gov. Mason,[16] of Michigan, has just fallen under my notice, in which, after commenting upon the alleged injustice shown to that Territory by Congress, he boldly says —

'Yet there is, fellow citizens, perhaps, a remedy left us, which *tyranny* may drive a people to adopt. It is *the natural right of resistance to oppression, inherent in every community*: it is the *ultima ratio* of a desperate and oppressed people, *whose edict must be written in blood.*'

I know not, Mr. Editor, what construction your correspondent would place upon such a paragraph, but I am quite sure that every bondman who could read it would readily construe it thus — 'Slaves, cut your masters' throats! Your edict must be written in BLOOD!'

But not to multiply examples: one more shall suffice. Last year, a riotous meeting was held in Cincinnati to put down, by mob law, that amiable and exalted philanthropist, JAMES G. BIRNEY,[17] for the alleged reason that his writings were calculated to excite discontent in the bosoms of the slaves: the true reason was, they hated the colored race, and contemplated building a railroad from Cincinnati to Charleston! [18] A few weeks afterward, another meeting was held, composed substantially of the same materials, and addressed by some of the same orators, *in favor of Texas* — at which, mirabile dictu! the following 'treasonable' resolutions were adopted:

'Resolved, That we regard every war, designed for the subversion of Tyranny and establishment of Liberty, as a *holy* war, entitled to the strong sympathy and ardent support of every freeman.

Resolved, That all laws, international or ☞ domestic, ☜ having a tendency to enslave mankind, *or any portion of the human family*, are unnatural, *a libel upon Heaven* — and being instruments enacted by tyrants, for their own benefit, ought not to be recognized by freemen as an obstacle preventing them from lending their assistance to the Texans, OR ANY OTHER PEOPLE STRUGGLING FOR LIBERTY.' [19]

Sir, is not the ancient maxim likely to be fearfully verified in our midst, that whom the Gods purpose to destroy, they first make mad? Our country is at present one vast Bedlam.

Thus, sir, I have identified the real incendiaries, conspirators and revolutionists, who, by the power of example, by the sanction of right, by express authority, by murderous incitement, and by every incentive that can rouse human passion and gratify revengeful feelings, are habitually guilty of stimulating the slaves at the South to 'cut their masters' throats,' and deliver themselves, at whatever peril or sacrifice, from a horrible bondage. In my next number, I propose to show, that the Abolitionists are the only party in this country, who, while they rebuke the oppressor, deny to the oppressed the right of redressing their wrongs, by a bloody process. Allow me to conclude this communication, by quoting the impressive and startling reflections of Mr. JEFFERSON upon this very subject:

'With what *execration* should the statesman be loaded, who, permitting one half the citizens thus to trample on the rights of the other, transforms those into despots, and these into enemies, destroying the morals of the one part, and the amor patriae of the other! — And can the liberties of a nation be thought secure, when we have removed their only firm basis, a conviction in the minds of the people, that *these liberties are of the gift of God?* THAT THEY ARE NOT TO BE VIOLATED BUT WITH HIS WRATH? Indeed, I tremble for my country, when I reflect that God is just: that his justice cannot sleep forever. that, considering numbers, nature, and natural means only, a revolution of the wheel of fortune, an exchange of situation, is among possible events: that it may become probable by supernatural interference! *The Almighty has no attribute which can take side with us in such a contest.'* [20]

Respectfully yours,
WM. LLOYD GARRISON.

5 Hayward Place.

Printed in *The Liberator*, March 11, 1837.

Garrison's letter was reprinted from the Boston *Courier* beside another letter by "Algernon Sidney," dated "Boston, January 20," from the Boston *Courier*.

1. Sidney, *Discourses on Government*, II, 185.
2. George Jeffreys, first Baron Jeffreys of Wem (1648–1689), English lord chancellor. At the inquests and trials following the Duke of Monmouth's rebellion in 1685, he caused about 300 men to be hanged and hundreds of others to be transported, imprisoned or whipped. (*CVDE.*)
3. The Reverend Thomas Price.
4. The Reverend John Angell James (1785–1859) became minister of the Carr's Lane Chapel in Birmingham in 1805, and was still preaching there in 1837. He was active in public affairs in Birmingham, serving as chairman of the Board of Education from 1838 to his death. His best-known work was *The Anxious Enquirer After Salvation*, published in 1834. (*EE.*)
5. James Cropper (1773–1840), a wealthy Quaker merchant, was founder of the firm of Cropper, Benson and Company, an early opponent of slavery in the British West Indies, and a member and leader of the radical wing of the British antislavery movement, called the Agency Committee of the Anti-Slavery Society. He had been an agent of *The Genius of Universal Emancipation*, providing numerous reports of British antislavery efforts. He had been influenced by Garrison's *Thoughts on African Colonization* and during Garrison's trip to England welcomed him and opened many doors for him. They remained friends throughout Cropper's lifetime. For Garrison's appreciation of him, see *The Liberator*, March 27, 1840. (*Life, passim.*)
6. Dr. Ralph Wardlaw (1779–1853), an eminent nonconformist divine, was ordained a Congregational minister in 1803. He served in the North Albion Street Chapel in Glasgow for about twenty years, when he and his congregation moved to a chapel on West George Street. He was also a tutor in the Glasgow Theological Academy. His works include *Man's Responsibility for his Belief* and *Lectures Against Religious Establishments*. He was active also in the Glasgow Emancipation Society and presided at a series of public discussions between George Thompson and R. J. Breckinridge over the question of slavery. (*Life*, II, 399; III, 4, 363; *DNB.*)
7. Romans 2:21.

8. Jefferson. Found among his papers after his death.

9. General Joseph Warren (1741–1775) of Boston was a physician, orator, and revolutionary agitator against the British. President of the Massachusetts Provincial Congress in 1774, he was commissioned major-general by the Massachusetts Congress in 1775, and was killed at the battle of Bunker Hill. (*DUSH.*)

10. From Robert Burns, "Scots Wha Hae"; Garrison reverses the original order of the stanzas, and varies the text slightly.

11. Algernon Sidney, *Discourses on Government*, I, 354.

12. *Ibid.*, II, 234.

13. We have been unable to find this quotation in the *Discourses on Government*.

14. *Discourses on Government*, I, 325–326.

15. Lord Byron, *Childe Harold*, Canto II, stanza lxxvi.

16. Governor Stevens Thomson Mason of Michigan (b. October 27, 1811; d. January 4, 1843) was the first governor of Michigan. His father, John Mason, was appointed by President Andrew Jackson to be the secretary of the Michigan Territory. At the age of nineteen he succeeded his father as secretary, holding that position until 1836, when he was elected governor. He was a champion of public education and opposed imprisonment for debt as well as solitary confinement. He moved to New York in 1841, where he practiced law until his death. (*DAB.*)

17. This refers to a meeting held on January 22, 1836, at the courthouse in Cincinnati, which was called to prevent publication of James Birney's antislavery newspaper, the *Philanthropist*, as well as to suppress the Cincinnati Abolition Society. Among those who signed the printed call for the meeting were N. C. Read, prosecuting attorney and Democratic politician; Robert T. Lyttle, surveyor of the Land Office and ex-congressman; and Morgan Neville, receiver of the Land Office. The meeting failed of its intended purpose when Birney, who was present, rose after it had begun and defended his views and his newspaper. (William Birney, *James G. Birney and His Times*, New York, 1890, pp. 204; Betty Fladeland, *James Gillespie Birney: Slaveholder to Abolitionist*, Ithaca, N.Y., 1955, pp. 130–132.)

18. "In 1836 the Charleston railway was chartered from Cincinnati, through Kentucky, Tennessee, North Carolina, Georgia, South Carolina through Charleston. The project, as a *whole*, failed in consequence of the great burdens laid on the charter as *conditions*, by the State of Kentucky. It has, nevertheless, been in *progress* toward completion ever since, until it is now, on the southern side, more than half completed." (Charles Cist, *Sketches and Statistics of Cincinnati in 1851*, Cincinnati, 1851, pp. 132–133.)

19. The meeting at which these resolutions were adopted took place on March 23, 1836, at the Exchange in Cincinnati. The two resolutions were submitted by N. C. Read. Additional ringleaders of this meeting, who also signed the call for the January 22 meeting, were Robert T. Lyttle and Morgan Neville. (*The Liberator*, April 30, 1836.)

20. *Notes on Virginia*, Query XVIII, "Manners"; Garrison's italics and small capitals.

75

TO SAMUEL J. MAY

Boston, March 14, 1837.

Dear brother May:

My best affections are tendered to you and yours. But I have only a minute or two to occupy, as our esteemed friend, Mr. Williams [1] of

Brooklyn, is expecting the stage to call for him instantly. Bro. Stanton and Whittier are yet in the city, plotting and contriving, as usual, in order to make fanaticism the order of the day. On Sabbath evening, I lectured in the Friends' meeting-house in Lynn, to one of the most crowded audiences I have ever seen. Probably two thousand persons were present, and a multitude were excluded for want of room. My remarks were chiefly confined to the Friends. I rebuked them plainly to their faces, for their lukewarmness and exclusive spirit. They bore it pretty well from me.[2]

The Quarterly Meeting of our State Society is to be held in Lynn a fortnight from to-day.[3] You must, if possible, attend it. We shall adjourn it from Lynn to Boston, in order to have another chance at our Representatives, before they go home to their constituents. Every thing in the Legislature promises fair. An almost incredible change has taken place since last year.

What a horrible avowal is that of Van Buren in his Inaugural Address![4] We must make it a millstone about his neck.

I have just received a very long and affectionate letter from our beloved friend Thompson. He mourns that he receives no letters from me, but blames himself, and not me — generous soul! I, only, deserve censure.

Hope you will not fail to be at the annual meeting in New-York in May.[5] It will be a great and momentous occasion.

You will see what liberties I have taken with the article[6] you sent me respecting Algernon Sidney, alias Walter Colton. He *is* the author.

Mrs. Benson has been very sick in Providence, but is now convalescent. Dear Helen sends her love to you and Mrs. May. Our boy now goes alone, and thrives finely.

In a hurry, yours, lovingly,

Wm Lloyd Garrison.

ALS: Garrison Papers, Boston Public Library.

1. Joseph Williams.

2. *The Liberator*, March 11, 1837, carried a notice that "Mr. Garrison will deliver an address on slavery in the Friends' Meeting House in Lynn, to-morrow (Sabbath) evening, at 7 o'clock." On March 18, 1837, *The Liberator* printed a short item by Garrison entitled "Abolition in Lynn," in which Garrison wrote, in part:

". . . It is refreshing to escape from this crowded metropolis, — in which the extremes of wealth and poverty are constantly meeting the eye, and Aristocracy sits enthroned, — and visit a place like Lynn, the headquarters of equality. . . . Its inhabitants are proverbially industrious and productive, and having no lordly masters to rob them of their earnings, they contrive to take care of themselves in a very comfortable manner; and if they work a great deal, they also think and read a great deal. They patronize the press extensively, and use and defend the liberty of speech without fear and without partiality. Yet they are the people, whom the slaveholding despots at the south dare to rank, even upon the floor of Congress, below the benighted and grovelling slaves who cannot lay claim to their own bodies.

"It was our privilege to deliver an address on slavery in the Friends' meeting-house in Lynn, on Sabbath evening last. The building is large and commodious, and it was thronged to overflowing, notwithstanding the badness of the travelling and the cloudiness of the weather. Nearly two thousand persons were present. Mr. Stanton accompanied us, and it was generally expected that he would also address the meeting, but he declined doing so — greatly to the disappointment of the audience, and particularly to our regret, as our remarks were almost wholly addressed to the Friends, by way of rebuke and exhortation as a Society, and not adapted to a large portion of the assembly, belonging to other denominations. Mr. Stanton, however, gave a lecture in the same meeting-house on Thursday evening last. Plain and pungent as were our reproofs, the Friends received them in a kind manner; for their ancient spirit is beginning to manifest itself in holy zeal and active labors in behalf of the oppressed, and they have no desire to excuse the past apathy of their Society. We trust their meeting-house in this city will be opened to the cause of bleeding humanity without delay."

3. The quarterly meeting of the Massachusetts Anti-Slavery Society was to be held in Lynn on Tuesday, March 28, 1837. This meeting proved most notable as the scene of the maiden antislavery speech of Wendell Phillips, the great abolitionist and friend of Garrison.

4. Probably refers to President Martin Van Buren's affirmation of his opposition to any attempt to abolish slavery in the District of Columbia "against the wishes of the slaveholding states" as well as to interference with slavery in the South.

5. The annual meeting of the American Anti-Slavery Society.

6. The item appeared in *The Liberator*, March 11, 1837, p. 43. It carried the following heading: "Several inquiries having been made as to the real author of the scurrilous and brutal essays in the Courier, signed 'Algernon Sidney,' the following extract of a letter addressed by a friend to Samuel J. May, gives the necessary information. — *Ed. Lib.*" Most of the text of the article has been quoted in note 2, letter 73, to the Editor of the Boston *Courier*, March 4, 1837.

---

7 6

TO THE EDITOR OF THE BOSTON *COURIER*

[March 18, 1837.]

Sir, — If I have failed to convict the Southern slaveholders, and their Northern abettors, of instigating the slaves 'to cut their masters' throats,' it is not because I have exhausted my stock of evidence. In the present case, the argumentum ad hominem is alone sufficient to put to shame the most impudent asperser of the Abolitionists. If whipping, starving, plundering, chaining, brutalizing human beings, daily and hourly, by a systematic process; if trading in 'slaves and souls of men,'[1] by wholesale and retail, and selling them in lots to suit purchasers; if ruthlessly tearing asunder the husband from his wife, and parents from their children, to meet no more on earth (an every day occurence at the south;) if such treatment cannot furnish inducements strong enough to cause a revolt, on the part of the victims; certainly, the proclamation of the 'self-evident truths' of the Declaration of Independence, the ringing of bells, the kindling of bonfires, and the firing of cannon, on the Fourth of July, annually; our patriotic orations, toasts and songs — Bunker-Hill, Lexington, New Orleans, can more than supply the deficiency! For,

1. The American people, in *theory*, maintain that all men are created equal, and endowed by God with an inalienable right to liberty; and in *practice*, they have repeatedly declared, that all tyrants ought to be extirpated from the face of the earth. They have given to their slaves, the following sums for solution: — If the principle involved in a 'three penny tax on tea,' justified a seven years' war, how much blood may be lawfully spilt, in resisting the principle, that one human being has a right to the body and soul of another, on account of complexional differences? Again: — If the impressment of six thousand American *seamen*, by Great Britain, was a sufficient warrant for a bloody struggle with that nation,[2] and the sacrifice of hundreds of millions of capital, in self-defence, how many lives may be taken by way of recompense, or, in more popular phraseology, *how many throats may be cut*, on account of the enslavement of more than two millions of American *laborers*?

2. The rights of man, and the cuticle of his skin, have, clearly, no relation to each other. His rights belong to him, as one created but a little lower than the angels, as an intellectual, moral, and accountable being: they can be wrested from him only by destroying his immortality. Let that which is immortal put on mortality, and cease to be indestructible, and man becomes a brute; his rights must give place to merely animal instincts. Hence, if one man has a natural right to liberty, all possess that right, without abridgement or modification. Hence, too, if any man has a right to fight for liberty, this right equally extends to all men subjected to bondage. In claiming these rights for themselves, the American people necessarily allow them to all mankind. If, therefore, they tyrannize over any part of the human race, they voluntarily seal their own death-warrant, and confess that they deserve to perish.

> 'What is the lesson that ye teach to men,
>   On whom the sun has burnt a deeper hue?
> Is it the maxim of the holy pen?
>   *Do ye to them as they should do to you?*
>   Would ye behold your wives, your children sue
> In vain for heaven's sweet freedom, from a heart
>   Devoid of all to human feeling due?
> Then stretched in torture, with a demon's art,
> From all their reeking veins behold the life-blood start?

'What are the banners ye exalt? — the deeds
That raised your fathers' pyramid of fame?
Ye show the wound that still in history bleeds,
And talk exulting of the patriot's name —
Then, *when your words have waked a kindred flame,*
And slaves behold the freedom ye adore,
And deeper feel their sorrow and their shame,
Ye double all the fetters that they wore,
And press them down to earth, till hope exults no more!' [3]

3. 'Thou, therefore, which teachest another, teachest thou not thy-self?' [4] If Abolitionists do not hold to the doctrine of non-resistance, it does not belong to this nation to rebuke them. If they adopt the principles and sentiments of the people, it is not for the people to denounce them as traitors and cut-throats. Pupils are not supposed to be wiser and better than their teacher.

In the present number, I have promised to show, that 'the Abolitionists are the only party in this country, who, while they rebuke the oppressor, deny to the oppressed the right of redressing their wrongs by a bloody process' — and that they do so on the ground of *principle,* and not because they are partial, or cowardly, or inconsistent.

In the first place, Mr. Editor, allow me to lay before your readers the sentiments of GEORGE THOMPSON, whom your correspondent has so basely slandered, in relation to physical violence. In a public discussion, held in Boston on the evening of April 4th, 1835, Mr. Thompson said [5] —

'If the political principles of any nation could justify a resort to violence, in a struggle against oppression, they were the principles of this nation, which teaches that resistance to oppression is obedience to the laws of NATURE and of GOD. Yet, if he (Mr. Thompson) could make himself heard from the Bay of Boston to the frontiers of Mexico, he would call upon every slave to commit his soul to God, and abide the issue of a *peaceful* and *moral* warfare in his behalf. He believed in the existence, omniscience, omnipotence, and providence of God. He believed that every thing that was good might be much better accomplished *without blood* than with it. He would say to the enslaved, 'Hurt not a hair of your master's head. It is not consistent with the will of your God, that you should do evil that good may come. In that book in which your God and Saviour has revealed his will, it is written — LOVE your enemies, BLESS THEM that CURSE you, DO GOOD TO THEM that *hate* you, and PRAY FOR THEM which despitefully use you and persecute you, that ye may be the children of your Father which is in heaven.[6] AVENGE NOT YOURSELVES, but rather *give place unto wrath.*' [7]

He (Mr. Thompson) would, however, remind the MASTER of the awful import of the following words: 'VENGEANCE IS MINE; I WILL REPAY SAITH THE LORD.' [8]

To the SLAVE he would continue — 'Therefore, if thine enemy hunger, feed him; if he thirst, give him drink. Be not overcome of evil, but overcome evil with good.' [9]

Mr. Thompson also quoted Eph. vi. 5; [10] Col. iii. 22; [11] Titus ii. 9; [12] I. Peter ii. 18–23.[13] In proportion, however, as he enjoined upon the SLAVE patience, submission, and forgiveness of injuries, he would enjoin upon the MASTER the abandonment of his wickedness. He would tell him plainly the nature of his great transgression — the sin of robbing God's poor, withholding the hire of the laborer, trafficking in the immortal creatures of God. He did not like the fashionable, but nevertheless despicable practice of preaching OBEDIENCE TO SLAVES, *without* preaching REPENTANCE TO MASTERS. He (Mr. Thompson) would preach forgiveness, and the rendering of good for evil, to the slaves of the plantation; but before he quitted the property, he would, if it were possible, thunder forth the threatenings of God's word in the ears of the master. *This was the only consistent course of conduct.* In proportion as we taught *submission to the slave*, we should enjoin *repentance and restitution upon the master.* Nay, more — if we teach submission to the slave, we are bound to exert our own peaceful energies for his deliverance.

Shall we say to the slave, 'Avenge not yourself,' and be silent ourselves in respect to his wrongs?

Shall we say, 'Honor and obey your masters,' and ourselves neglect to warn and reprove those masters?

Shall we denounce 'carnal weapons,' [14] which are the only ones the slaves can use, and neglect to employ our moral and spiritual weapons in their behalf?

Shall we tell them to 'beat their swords into ploughshares, and their spears into pruning-hooks,' [15] and neglect to give them the 'sword of the spirit, which is the word of God?' [16]

Let us be consistent. The principles of peace and the forgiveness of injuries are quite compatible with a bold, heroic and uncompromising hostility to sin, and a war of extermination with every principle, part and practice of American slavery. *I hope no drop of blood will stain our banner of triumph and liberty.* I hope no wail of the widow or orphan will mingle with the shouts of our jubilee. I trust ours will be a battle which the PRINCE OF PEACE can direct, and ours a victory which angels can applaud.

A gentleman present (not an Abolitionist) said, in reply to Mr. Thompson, 'he believed that, by coming down to the Scriptures, it would be found that the slaves had a right to resort to arms.' [17] Mr. Thompson inquired — 'He was surprised and pained in listening to the sentiments which had just been advanced — sentiments which, *in the name of the Abolitionists of this country,* HE UTTERLY DISCLAIMED — sentiments which he trusted the gentleman himself would abandon forever.' [18]

In his public denial of the charges of the slanderer Kaufman,[19] at Andover, Mr. Thompson declared —

'I hold in utter abhorrence the shedding of blood, and would, if I had the power, inculcate upon the mind of every slave in the world, the apostolical precept, 'Resist not evil.' These doctrines I hold in common with the advocates of immediate emancipation universally.' [20]

Since his return to England, Mr. Thompson has lectured frequently upon the subject of Peace. In a speech which he delivered at New-castle-upon-Tyne,[21] he used the following 'hard' and 'incendiary' language before a people intoxicated with the love of military glory. The extract displays great moral courage, as well as illustrates his pacific principles. It does not appear that any attempts were made to lynch him for thus 'defaming' his native country.

'He (Mr. Thompson) carried his Peace principles to the fullest possible extent. He considered war unlawful, under all possible, all conceivable circumstances. He confessed, that in looking over the face of his beloved country, he could not join with those who called it a Christian country. In every direction, he saw the paraphernalia of war, offensive and defensive. Our history was a history of bloody wars. The demon of desolation had deprived us of 400,000,000*l.* sterling of treasure, and 200,000,000 of our sons. Call us a nation of civilized *savages*, of wholesale *butchers*, of sanguinary, unappeasable *murderers* — but call us not a nation of *Christians*, till we have more consistently exemplified the doctrines of the Prince of Peace!' [22]

This is a new mode of propagating insurrectionary doctrines. Such sentiments, in the time of our revolutionary war, would have subjected him who cherished them to a worse charge than that of *tory.*

The Liberator has the reputation of being an incendiary publication. In its very first number,[23] its editor attempted to instigate the slaves to revolt in the following 'spirit-stirring' lines! [24]

> Not by the sword shall your deliverance be;
>   Not by the shedding of your masters' blood;
> Not by rebellion, or foul treachery,
>   Upspringing suddenly like swelling flood:
>   Revenge and rapine ne'er did bring forth good.
> *God's time is best* — nor will it long delay:
>   Even now your barren cause begins to bud,
> And glorious shall the fruit be! — Watch and pray,
> For, lo! the kindling dawn that ushers in the day!'

In its Prospectus, the Liberator held the following language: —

'We hope to be successful in our attempts to abolish slavery — not by exciting or encouraging the slaves to rebel, for that would be perfidious and wicked; not by a physical interposition on the part of the free States, for that would be productive of war and anarchy; not by an unlawful exercise of political power, for that would be despotism; but by pricking the *consciences* of the masters — by faithfully showing them their guilt, infatuation and danger,' &c. &c.[25]

The true secret of all the uproar at the South, is, a *troubled conscience.* Hear Gen. Duff Green:

'We do not believe that the Abolitionists intend, *nor could they if they would,* excite the slaves to insurrection. We believe that we have most to fear from the organized action upon the CONSCIENCES and fears of the slaveholders themselves. Our *greatest cause of apprehension* is, from the operation of the morbid sensibility (!) which appeals to the CONSCIENCES of our own people, and would make them the *voluntary* instruments of their own ruin.'!![26]

Mr. Calhoun, in a speech in the United States Senate, last year, said —

'Does the South expect the Abolitionists will resort to arms — will commence a crusade to liberate our slaves by force? Is this what they mean when they speak of the attempt to abolish slavery? Let me tell our friends of the South who differ from us, that the war which the Abolitionists wage against us is of *a very different character,* and FAR MORE EFFECTIVE — it is urged not against our *lives,* but our *character.*'[27]

This is a sufficient refutation of the murderous charges brought against the Abolitionists. But my limits will not admit of comments.

The New-England Anti-Slavery Society, the parent of all others, set forth this declaration in the first preamble to its Constitution:

'We declare that we will not operate on the existing relations of society by other than peaceful and lawful means, and that we will give no countenance to violence or insurrection.'[28]

In its address to the people of the United States, it also declared —

'The object of our Society is neither war nor sedition. We hope ever to imbibe the spirit of Him who says, 'Resist not evil' — 'they that take the sword shall perish with the sword.' Governed by such a spirit, the weapons of our warfare can never be carnal. The only influence we can exert must be that of *moral suasion,* and not of *coercion.* In the truth, and the God of truth, alone, we trust for the success of our exertions; and with the truth, and and in the name of the God of truth, we plead for the cause of humanity.[29]

The third article of the Constitution of the American Anti-Slavery

Society, is in the following words, which have been repeated in almost all the constitutions of its auxiliaries:

'This Society will never, in any way, countenance the oppressed in vindicating their rights by resorting to physical force.' [30]

The following is the language of the Declaration of Sentiments of the National Anti-Slavery Convention held in Philadelphia, in December, 1833. Alluding to our revolutionary fathers, it says —

'*Their* principles led them to wage war against their oppressors, and to spill human blood like water, in order to be free. Ours forbid the doing of evil that good may come, and lead *us* to reject, and to entreat the *oppressed* to reject, the use of all carnal weapons for deliverance from bondage — relying solely upon those which are spiritual, and mighty through God to the pulling down of strong holds.
Their measures were physical resistance — the marshalling in arms — the hostile array — the mortal encounter. *Ours* shall be such only as the opposition of moral purity to moral corruption — the destruction of error by the potency of truth — the overthrow of prejudice by the power of love — and the abolition of slavery by the spirit of repentance.' [31]

A correspondent of the Liberator uses the following 'inflammatory' language:

'Do slaveholders deserve death at the hand of their abused slaves? To this question, Abolitionists answer, No! no! We have no fellowship with such a doctrine, nor with any one who holds or preaches it. We believe it is a doctrine of devils, fit only to stand in the creed of murdering tyrants, who glory in their power to trample in the dust all the dearest rights of man. Our glorious motto is — NON-RESISTANCE. We distinctly say to slaveholders and their abettors — in this warfare we shall never appeal to physical force, either to procure freedom for the objects of your oppression, or to protect ourselves from your vengeance. Your mobs, your robberies, your burnings, your clubs and brickbats, your scourges, your gibbets and murders, will meet with no resistance but such as Christ, our great leader, offered to his murderers — 'Father, forgive them; they know not what they do.' We can *die* in pleading the cause of our oppressed brethren — the cause of Christ; but we will not, we cannot fight with carnal weapons. And let our brethren in bonds be solemnly assured, that no Abolitionist will ever assist them to gain their freedom by shedding the blood of their oppressors. We abhor that bloody principle which leads men to resort to murder to defend or regain their liberty, as we abhor slavery itself.' [32]

In August, 1835, the Massachusetts Anti-Slavery Society put forth an Appeal to the Public, in which the following paragraph is found:

'Nothing can be further from our wishes than to excite the slave population. We should consider any action of this kind as far worse than useless — as highly dangerous, and as little less criminal than murder. Why should we seek to promote insurrection? What should we not lose by it? As merchants and mechanics, as citizens and parents, as patriots and Christians, we have as much to risk as others in community; and we know that such an event would be the greatest calamity to the slaves, and to the cause of freedom. ° ° ° The attempt is made to delude the community into the belief, that Abolitionists are willing to secure the emancipation of the slaves, at the expense of the safety of the whites. We deny this charge in the most pointed manner. We have never advocated the right of physical resistance, on the part of the oppressed. We assure our assailants, that we would not sacrifice the life of a single slaveholder, to emancipate every slave in the United States. On the contrary, we are fully persuaded that the triumph of our principles is the only means of tranquillity or safety for our country.' [33]

At a quarterly meeting of this Society, held October 5th, 1835, the editor of the Liberator offered the following resolutions, which were supported by the mover, by Mr. Thompson, and other individuals, and unanimously adopted:

'Whereas, the southern planters are slanderously reporting of northern Abolitionists, that they are in favor of a servile insurrection among the slave population, and are ready to assist them in obtaining their liberty by violence; and whereas, such reports are calculated to deceive the slaves, and may encourage them to resort to rebellion and massacre, by relying upon our co-operation: therefore

Resolved, That we solemnly warn our colored brethren, bond and free, *not to believe these charges* — FOR THEY ARE NOT TRUE.

Resolved, That by patient endurance of their wrongs, and unwavering trust in the promises of God, the slaves will hasten the day of their peaceful deliverance from the yoke of bondage — for God will continue to raise up friends and advocates to plead their cause, and by the power of TRUTH will make them free indeed; whereas, by violent and bloody measures, they will prolong their servitude, and expose themselves to destruction.

Resolved, That the conduct of southern slaveholders, in filling the ears of their ignorant victims with insurrectionary charges against the friends of immediate emancipation, is alike cruel and suicidal; and that *they alone will be responsible for all the consequences of a servile war*, should the slaves revolt against them.

Resolved, That inasmuch as we have no access to the slave population, and as a measure of *safety to themselves* and of justice to us, we earnestly entreat the holders of slaves to convey the spirit of these resolutions to all under their authority, and to assure them that these are the sentiments of all true Abolitionists universally.' [34]

Contrast the spirit of these resolutions with that which breathes in the following extract from the 'Remarks on Dr. Channing's Slavery,' [35] the author of which gravely charges Dr. Channing with using *incendiary* language, in his work on slavery!! The reviewer says —

'If, when a man is unjustly made a slave for life, and his wife and children are made slaves with him, he may not rise, in his strength or his madness, and shake off his chains, and stand guiltless before God, *with the blood of the oppressor on his hands*, it is in vain to talk about human rights . . . It is absurd to tell of wrongs without a remedy. For every human wrong, there is a remedy; by law, when the law provides one, and by resistance, when, under the color of law, instead of a remedy we find only a wrong . . . Could we doubt a moment about this, if the law of Carolina should propose to detain every white traveller passing through its territory, and turn him on the plantation as a slave? Is there a heart in New England, that would not beat high with sympathy for the abused white man? *Is there an arm that would not reach him a dagger, if it could?* Is there a tribunal on earth, or any law of heaven, that would not excuse — excuse, did I say? — that would not *command* him to watch for his opportunity, and *make himself free?* . . . The sentiment, that the individual is in no case to offer resistance to government, is fit only for a slave. It is the doctrine of passive obedience and non-resistance which was scouted from all human creeds, with the same breath that blew away the divine right of kings, and the dogmatical pretensions of the clergy . . . If any government, foreign or *domestic*, was to doom the free-born and gallant sons of our Commonwealth to slavery, and there was one of them that should tell you that government must not in such case be resisted, he would be fit for the slavery to which he was destined — ay, truly, to be the *slave of slaves.*'

Incredible as it may seem, and as a startling proof of southern infatuation, it is said that whole editions of the pamphlet containing the above truly 'inflammatory' sentiments, were eagerly purchased by the slaveholders, and distributed exultingly through the South! It is not known, however, that the dissuasive resolutions of the Massachusetts Society were ever laid before the eyes, or conveyed to the ears, of the southern slaves. If the throats of the masters should be cut by their victims, surely they can blame none but themselves.

In 1835, the United States mail was deliberately robbed of a portion of its contents by a committee of the citizens of Charleston. The stolen documents were publicly burnt in the streets, as 'most inflammatory and incendiary — and insurrectionary in the highest degree,' according to the statement of the Postmaster in that city; though it is evident, as they were taken directly out of the mailbag and burnt, that he knew nothing of their contents, except that they were anti-slavery publications. In one of these 'incendiary' papers was the extract from the Declaration of Anti-Slavery Sentiments already quoted above! In another was the following advice — 'Let our ONLY weapons be TRUTH and KINDNESS, and, *by the blessing of God*, the cause must sooner or later triumph.' In a third was this sentiment from the pen of Mr. Birney — 'The most effectual mode of PRESERVING TRANQUILLITY among the slaves of the South will be a knowledge of the fact, that efforts of a *peaceful* and *Christian* character are making in their behalf. The slaves with whom I have conversed on the subject of the PRESENT EFFORTS, have, *without exception*, looked upon their *sober* and *peaceful* demeanor as an essential contribution on their part to success.' In a fourth, the Emancipator, was the following 'insurrectionary' verse: —

'O ye slaves whom massas beat!
Ye are stained with guilt within:
As ye hope for mercy sweet,
So forgive your massas' sin.'

Once more, sir, let your readers contrast the spirit of the foregoing sentiments with that evinced in the following extract from the Address of the Anti-Tariff Nullification Convention of South Carolina in 1832, which was written by george mcduffie: —

'If it had pleased God to cover our eyes with ignorance; if he had not bestowed upon us the understanding to comprehend the *enormity of the oppression* [i.e. the Tariff!] under which we labor, we might submit to it, without absolute degradation and infamy. But the gifts of Providence cannot be neglected or abused with impunity. *A people who deliberately submit to oppression, with a full knowledge that they are oppressed, are fit only to be slaves.* No tyrant ever made a slave — no community, however small, having the spirit of freemen, ever yet had a master'!! 'It does not belong to freemen to count the costs, and calculate the hazards of vindicating their *rights*, and defending their *liberties*'! — 'It is a question of LIBERTY, on the one hand, and of SLAVERY, on the other. If we submit to this system of unconstitutional (!) OPPRESSION, we shall voluntarily sink into *slavery*, and transmit that IGNOMINIOUS INHERITANCE to our children. We will not, we dare not submit to this degradation. We stand upon *the principles of everlasting justice*, and no human power shall drive us from our position'!!

The above are the sentiments of the madman [36] who has recently proclaimed, that 'no human institution is more manifestly consistent with the will of God than domestic slavery' — 'instead of being a political evil, it is the corner-stone of our *republican edifice*' — 'no *patriot* will tolerate the *idea* of emancipation, *at any period, however remote,* or on any conditions of pecuniary advantage however favorable' — 'the laws of every community should punish this species of interference [remonstrating against oppression] by DEATH WITHOUT BENEFIT OF CLERGY'!! *Quem Deus,* &c.[37]

Once more, and I have done with this part of the subject. A great Anti-Slavery Convention, for the State of Pennsylvania, has just been held at Harrisburg. In a letter from John G. Whittier, giving an account of its proceedings, and published in the New-York Evangelist of the 11th inst., is the following statement: —

'Thus far, every thing has gone on harmoniously, *with a single exception.* A gentleman of the bar objected to the terms in the Constitution of the State Society, 'it will not countenance the use of violence on the part of the oppressed, for the redress of their wrongs.' He contended that the slaves *had* a right to throw off the yoke, even by violence — to fight *their* way to freedom, as well as the soldiers of 1776. *Finding himself unsupported by the Convention,* he left his place as one of its delegates, declaring that *the*

Convention had resolved itself into a Quaker meeting, and he had nothing more to do with it.'

Sir, who are the incendiaries and madmen in our land? O that the stirring appeal of WHITTIER might rouse this nation to a sense of its guilt and danger, and bring it to immediate repentance!

'Up, then, in Freedom's manly part,
   From grey-beard eld to fiery youth,
And *on the nation's naked heart,*
   SCATTER THE LIVING COALS OF TRUTH!
Up — while we slumber, deeper yet
   The shadow of our fame is growing:
Up — while ye pause, our sun may set
   In blood, around our altars flowing!
Oh rouse ye — ere the storm comes forth —
   The gathered wrath of God and man —
Like that which wasted Egypt's earth,
   When hail and fire above it ran.
Hear ye no warnings in the air?
   Feel ye no earthquake underneath?
Up — up — why will ye slumber where
   The sleeper only wakes in death?
Up now for Freedom! — *not in strife,*
   Like that your sterner fathers saw —
The awful waste of human life —
   The glory and the guilt of war.
But break the chain — the yoke remove —
   And smite to earth Oppression's rod,
With those mild arms of TRUTH *and* LOVE,
   Made mighty through the living God!' [38]

Respectfully yours,
WM. LLOYD GARRISON.

5, Hayward Place.

Printed in *The Liberator,* March 18, 1837. Garrison's letter was reprinted from the Boston *Courier* beside a letter by "Algernon Sidney," dated "Boston, January 27," from the Boston *Courier.*

1. Revelation 18:13.
2. The War of 1812.
3. Unidentified.
4. Romans 2:21.
5. The ensuing remarks by George Thompson were first printed in *The Liberator,* April 18, 1835, under the title, "Debate on the Peace Question."
6. Matthew 5:44–45.
7. Romans 12:19.
8. Romans 12:19.
9. Romans 12:20, 21. The end of verse 20, "for in so doing thou shalt heap coals of fire on his head," has been omitted.
10. "Servants be obedient to them that are your masters according to the flesh, with fear and trembling, in singleness of your heart, as unto Christ."

11. "Servants, obey in all things your masters according to the flesh; not with eyeservice, as men-pleasers; but in singleness of heart, fearing God."

12. "Exhort servants to be obedient unto their own masters, and to please them well in all things; not answering again."

13. "Servants, be subject to your masters with all fear; not only to the good and gentle, but also to the froward," and so on.

14. II Corinthians 10:4.

15. Isaiah 2:4; Micah 4:3.

16. Ephesians 6:17.

17. *The Liberator*, April 18, 1835.

18. *Ibid.*

19. Abram Kaufman, Jr. (d. Charleston, South Carolina, August 28, 1839), was a student at Andover Theological Seminary when George Thompson spoke at Andover, Massachusetts, in July 1835. In a communication to the New York *Commercial Advertiser*, which was widely reprinted, Kaufman accused Thompson of saying: "If we preached what we ought, or if we taught the slaves to do what they ought, we would tell every one of them to cut their masters' throats." Thompson denied the charge and was supported in his denial by others who were present, including such antislavery men as La Roy Sunderland and Amos Phelps, as well as a member of the Andover faculty, Professor Jarvis Gregg. (*Letters and Addresses by George Thompson, During his Mission in the United States, From Oct. 1st, 1834, to Nov. 27, 1835*, Boston, 1837, pp. 93–98; *The Liberator*, December 5, 1835.)

20. Letter from George Thompson to the editor of the *Daily Atlas*, Boston, September 30, 1835, printed in *The Liberator*, October 3, 1835.

21. The meeting at which Thompson spoke was held on April 7, 1836.

22. The report of Thompson's speech appeared in *The Liberator*, June 25, 1836.

23. January 1, 1831.

24. The last stanza of a poem by Garrison entitled "Universal Emancipation."

25. The prospectus issued by Garrison in August 1830 does not include this paragraph (see *Life*, I, 199–202). Either Garrison's memory failed him, or he was referring to another prospectus.

26. Duff Green (1791–1875) was an influential editor and politician. During Jackson's first term, he edited the *U. S. Telegraph,* which was regarded as an administration organ. He later broke with Jackson, supporting Clay in 1832 and Calhoun in 1836. He was regarded as a spokesman for the radical slaveholding interests. (*DUSH; DAB.*) The quotation may have come from the Washington *Reformer*, a "states-rights reform journal" Green was editing.

27. John C. Calhoun, "On the Abolition Petitions," delivered in the Senate, March 9, 1836. Garrison's quotation departs slightly from the original. See Richard K. Crallé, ed., *The Works of John C. Calhoun* (New York, 1853), II, 483–484.

28. *Constitution of the New-England Anti-Slavery Society: with an Address to the Public* (Boston, 1832), p. 3.

29. *Ibid.*, p. 7. Between the end of the first sentence of this quotation and the beginning of the second, Garrison has omitted several lines of the original.

30. Printed in *Life*, I, 414.

31. The entire Declaration of Sentiments is printed in Ruchames, *The Abolitionists*, pp. 78–83. The paragraphs quoted by Garrison appear on p. 79.

32. *The Liberator*, October 10, 1835. The letter is signed "Wickliffe." Garrison quotes the letter with some omissions.

33. Printed in *The Liberator*, August 22, 1835.

34. *The Liberator*, October 10, 1835.

35. *Remarks on Dr. Channing's Slavery*, by a Citizen of Massachusetts, Boston, 1835, 48 pp. Although published anonymously, the author was James T. Austin.

36. Refers to George McDuffie. The following quotations are from his annual

message to the legislature of South Carolina. (*The Liberator*, December 12, 1835.)

37. *Quem deus vult perdere prius dementat* (Whom God wishes to destroy he first makes mad): one form of an ancient Greek and Roman proverb variously ascribed to Sophocles, Euripides, and Æschylus. (Burton Stevenson, *The Home Book of Proverbs, Maxims and Familiar Phrases*, New York, 1948, p. 1500.)

38. The last stanzas but one of John Greenleaf Whittier's poem, "Stanzas," one of a series of poems published from 1833 to 1848, under the title *Voices of Freedom*.

---

7 7

TO THE EDITOR OF THE BOSTON *COURIER*

[March 24, 1837.]

Sir — The time I have allowed to elapse since the publication of my third rejoinder to the Letters of ALGERNON SIDNEY, has been too busily occupied by more pressing duties and engagements, to enable me to finish the controversy with desirable promptitude. I regret this delay the less, as it has enabled 'SIDNEY' to complete the whole series of his verbose, rhetorical and foul epistles; and as it was primarily your choice, that he should finish his numbers, before a replication was made to them — though, at that time, you supposed they would not exceed three or four. I must be permitted to say, that, in giving them a careful perusal, I have been amazed at the palpable disregard of principle, the horrid perversion of truth, manifested by their author; especially as his signature no longer hides his real name from public knowledge, for he is recognized as a professed minister of Jesus Christ. If I were anxious to advance the cause of human freedom by any means whatever, I should rejoice at the publication of his atrocious libels upon God and man; but my spirit saddens to witness such depravity, emanating from a heart that ought to be without guile, and defiling a man who affects to believe that his name is 'written in the Lamb's Book of Life.'[1] Dreadful delusion! With his present temper, how can he expect to enter the kingdom of heaven? For, 'if a man say, I love God, and hateth his brother, he is a liar, and the truth is not in him.'[2] May he cease to be the apologist of tyrants, the calumniator of the friends of righteous liberty, and the sanctifier of the war-system!

The subject of this communication is ABUSIVE LANGUAGE.

He who undertakes to teach lessons of mildness and forbearance to the violent and uncharitable, should himself be a pattern, in some respects at least, worthy of imitation, if not faultless and impeccable. It is the harlot who is sometimes most voluble in praise of virtue, and cowards make the loudest pretensions to courage. The biting retort of the apostle to the cavilling Jews, is not less applicable in our day to certain blind and corrupt accusers, than it was eighteen hundred years ago: — 'Behold, thou art called a Jew, and restest in the law, and makest thy boast of God, and knowest his will, and approvest the things that are more excellent, being instructed out of the law; and art confident that thou thyself art a guide of the blind, a light of them which are in darkness, an instructor of the foolish, a teacher of babes . . . thou, therefore, which teachest another, teachest thou not thyself? . . . Thou that makest thy boast of the law, through breaking the law, dishonorest thou God? For the name of God is blasphemed among the Gentiles, THROUGH YOU.' [3]

One of the heaviest charges brought by your docile correspondent, ALGERNON SIDNEY, against the Abolitionists, is, that they indulge in unchristian censures and rude epithets, as often as they write or speak on the subject of slavery. Nay, so uncharitable are they, habitually, towards those gentle, disinterested, benevolent and holy slaveholders who inhabit the southern section of our free and democratical country, and who sell the flesh of woman by the pound, and exchange a man for a horse — so incorrigibly determined are they not to confound oppressors with patriots, nor men-stealers with honest men, that 'SIDNEY' fervently hopes, in the excess of his lamb-like disposition, that 'if their sufferings [from mobs — to wit, having their persons maltreated, their property burnt in the streets, and their lives put in jeopardy,] have not taught them a little of that charity which belongs to religion and humanity, they are only in the first stages of their agony.' He is a professed *minister of the gospel*, (if I am correctly informed as to the real name of 'SIDNEY',) who thus exults over the brutal and bloody excesses of Lynch law upon the persons and property of men who cannot return blow for blow, and of women whose very helplessness, instead of contributing to their protection, exposes them to insult and outrage!! He is 'a child of God,' 'an heir of heaven,' 'a follower of the Prince of Peace,' ostensibly, who sneers at that heroic little band of intelligent, respectable and pious females the Boston Female Anti-Slavery Society, in the following manly style and veracious language: — 'A few *dismayed* women [referring to the mob in Boston in October, 1835, which has covered this city with a cloud of infamy, and which was confronted by these women, with such unblenching courage, holy fortitude, and heaven derived serenity, as to secure to them the admiration and applause of the wise and good on both sides of the Atlantic,] — a few *dismayed* (!) women, who had left their knitting-needles and *ragged* children to attend to the affairs of the nation'!! This sneer is evidently more becoming a southern slave-driver, than 'a watchman upon the walls of Zion.' He is, nevertheless, 'a preacher of righteousness,' who thinks that the Lynch Code is better than the Gospel, to teach the Abolitionist, 'a little of that charity which belongs to religion and humanity'! If in 'the first stages of their agony,' under its administration, they have not been transformed in the temper of their minds, so as to regard as a patriot and christian, him who banishes the Bible from the hand of his fettered slave, and ranks him among the brute creation, he hopes mobbing has but just commenced in our land! Of course, Mr. Editor, a man who justifies the rabble in throwing rotten eggs and brickbats at the heads of men and *women* even, because they will not make any compromise with oppression, is of all men best qualified to teach lessons of moderation, and to show by example as well as precept how to avoid the use of 'hard language' in controverting false opinions! Remembering that the Abolitionists are found among all religious sects and political parties — that, aside from their views in regard to slavery, (which are precisely consonant with those of the Declaration of Independence,) they rank among the most intelligent, peaceable and upright citizens — that their principles and measures are approbated by such men as William Jay, Arthur Tappan, Gerrit Smith, James G. Birney, Beriah Green, N. S. S. Beman,[4] Samuel J. May, and a great multitude of patriotic and pious citizens — that they are hated and proscribed by the selfish, the proud, the intemperate, the profane, the brutal, the time-serving, and the self-righteous, universally — and that they have refused to return evil for evil, or to protect themselves by a resort to the *lex talionis*,[5] when assailed by bloody-minded men — remembering all these facts, we are now prepared to listen to the charges brought against them and their cause by their very 'charitable' opponent and dove-like instructor in the use of mellifluent epithets, the pseudo ALGERNON SIDNEY!

And, first, we will look at his liberal description of Abolitionism. Now, in his view, it is a bloody monster — 'Before Abolitionism shook its gory locks,' &c. &c. Anon, by the aid of a sprightly metempsychosis, it is as formidable as the sea-serpent, if not 'very like a whale' [6] — 'Abolitionism is a huge, *enormous* snake, that hath a *prodigious* rattle in its tail.' Frightful enough! but the worst is not yet — another transmigration! — 'The *shaking* (!) footstep of the Moloch of Abolitionism now threatens this Union, and its history may yet be written in groans and blood.' This is appalling: happily, however, the magician suddenly transforms this all-devouring god into a great lake, and quenches its fires with a multitude of waters — 'The streams of Fanaticism, the brawling brooks of Radicalism, the impetuous torrents of Ultraism, have all disgorged themselves into the great lake of Abolitionism.'

This view is lively, picturesque, overwhelming — reminding one of the wildest scenery, and somewhat poetical withal: but a sketch is not an argument, nor is fancy demonstration. Tropes and figures may serve to embellish an essay, but facts and arguments are needed to convince the understanding. Again — 'Abolitionism is a species of nightmare.' True — to the conscience-stricken slaveholder. Once more — 'You might as well attempt to filter night of its darkness, as Abolitionism of its fanatical follies.' The comparison is murky. Finally — 'Tumbled and tost in the wild fanatical dreams of Abolitionism,' &c. It is the accusation which is insane. In this manner is 'charity' made to dance 'through all the mazes of metaphorical confusion' by its distinguished patron.

It is in such mild language, that 'SIDNEY' ridicules and denounces the sacred cause of bleeding humanity, involving as it is does, in this country alone, the lives, liberty, happiness, bodies, intellects and souls of a sixth-part of our immense population! — a cause which is pregnant with the life of God, sustained by his omnipotence, and pledged to be victorious by his word! — a cause cordially embraced by christian zeal, and holy love, and steadfast faith, wherever man pines in servitude, or wears upon his heel the galling fetter of slavery. The fancied resemblances of 'SIDNEY,' being absurd, allow of ironical treatment; but being also wicked and malignant, they should excite feelings of righteous displeasure in every humane breast.

Having taught the Abolitionists how to be 'charitable,' in his attack upon their enterprise, your patriotic correspondent, Mr. Editor, next ventures, somewhat timidly it may be, to sketch their portraits, using only the softest colors and drawing the most delicate lines, lest he should 'overstep the modesty of nature,' [7] and make a hideous caricature instead of an exact likeness. He takes his pencil and brush, and after eight or ten long sittings, declares that he has succeeded perfectly in painting the features of the Abolitionists. 'Look at this picture — is it like? Like what?'

1. He represents them as 'men, who, by a lawless violence of language, excite a popular tumult.'

2. 'Utterly lost to truth and candor.'

3. 'Kindling and exasperating the great mass — awakening a blind indignation towards the South — stirring up commotions — and exciting mobs.'

4. 'Evil-minded persons lurking about your houses, trying to alienate and embitter the minds of your servants, enticing them to lie away the purity of your domestic reputation, or introduce poisons into your food, that must result in the death of every member of your family.' [a comparison.]

5. He speaks of their 'cowardice' and 'infamy,' their 'Billingsgate

abuse,' 'their incendiary publications,' 'their flagrant enormities,' gives 'another proof of the dishonesty of these men,' and warns Dr. Channing against 'the bitter fruits of their ingratitude and baseness.'

6. He brands them as 'calumniators,' 'frantic men,' — says that 'they have impudence, intolerance, and mendacity enough, heaven knows' — 'degraded the right of speech into licentiousness' — 'intentionally produced impressions flagrantly false — practised deliberate, systematic imposition — in the name of religion and humanity, violated truth — forfeited their claims to moral honesty, and are wholly unworthy sympathy, respect and confidence.'

7. 'Foul, opprobrious terms pollute all their pages; no, they do not *pollute* the page — the envenomed reptile is only in the slime and filth of its own native element' — they discharge 'a torrent of opprobrious epithets, more becoming a demon than a Christian' — 'their real object is not to move on the moral convictions of the South, but to arouse the indignant passions of the North.'

8. 'To suppose these persons *honest* in these denunciatory measures, would impeach their understanding to a degree that would leave them only a claim to our commiseration.'

9. 'They import a profligate foreigner, reeking with execrations. They *know* him to be a felon, a knave, a villain, a refugee from justice, belching out his bile and blasphemies.'

10. They are 'reckless impostors, apostates from truth, moral cut-throats.'

11. They are 'reptiles — strange reptiles — spitting, hissing, trailing their slime.'

12. The editor of the Liberator is 'a spiteful porcupine' — 'every sentence falls from his tongue a scorpion, armed with its rattle and fang.'

Now, Mr. Editor, if under such an instructor as ALGERNON SIDNEY, — backed by a thousand LYNCH assistants in the school of good manners, — Abolitionists do not hereafter learn to be more 'charitable' in their estimate of southern slavery, and to speak of the robbers of their race in honeyed accents, then it must be evident to all, that they are stupid and incorrigible to a marvel. I have thus driven back to its hive, for the inspection of the curious and the safety of the innocent, this swarm of spiteful calumnies — to be smothered *en masse* without difficulty or delay. But, seriously — if the allegations brought by 'SIDNEY' against the Abolitionists be true, then a more base or ferocious body of men cannot be found on the face of the earth: if they are not true, then they evince, on the part of their author, a spirit worthy the 'Father of lies.' [8] As he has not attempted, in a single instance, to sustain them by evidence drawn from the writings of Abolitionists, and as they are applied indiscriminately and without exception, it is sufficient to brand them as wanton libels upon the character of philanthropic and christian men.

Your readers will observe, that, while 'SIDNEY' has dealt merely in general assertions, I have *demonstrated*, by plenary evidence, first, that the English patriot, whose name he has so basely prostituted, was *an Abolitionist of the modern school*; secondly, that the real instigators of servile insurrections and the justifiers of murder, in cases of oppression, are southern slaveholders and their allies; and that Abolitionists hold to the doctrine of non-resistance, and deny the right of the slaves to redress their wrongs by violence. In the present number, I have proved that your correspondent is not qualified to instruct others in the use of 'charitable' language.

Yours respectfully,
WM. LLOYD GARRISON.

5, Hayward Place.

Printed in *The Liberator*, March 24, 1837. This letter appeared in *The Liberator* by the side of a letter by "Algernon Sidney," dated "Boston, Feb. 1st," reprinted from the Boston *Courier*.

1. Revelation 21:27.
2. I John 4:20, 2:4.
3. Romans 2:17–24.
4. Nathaniel Sydney Smith Beman (1785–1871), a minister, began his career as a Congregationalist. In 1822 he accepted a call as pastor of the Presbyterian Church in Troy, New York, and remained there for forty years. For many years he was the leader of the liberal faction in the Presbyterian church. With the division of the New and Old School factions, he led the New School delegates from the General Assembly. (*Weld-Grimké Letters*, I, 33n and *passim*.)
5. The law of revenge.
6. Shakespeare, *Hamlet*, III, ii.
7. *Ibid.*
8. John 8:44; Thomas Moore (1779–1852), Irish poet, "A Case of Libel," stanza 16.

78

TO GEORGE W. BENSON

Boston, April 3, 1837.

Dear bro. George:

What do you think of me at Brooklyn? What sort of an estimate do you place upon my affection? Or how much do you suppose I care for you all? Really, I am ashamed of myself, to think that so many weeks have elapsed since I wrote to you; and I readily concede that you are warranted in using very "hard language" toward me. Call me "neglectful," "procrastinating," "forgetful," any thing but a recreant to friendship and brotherly love. — I have been very much absorbed with my own concerns, and am astonished to find how swiftly time can fly with a great pack of business upon its back. All ye dear ones in Friendship's Valley, believe me I love you none the less because I write to you so seldom. Ye are indeed dear, very dear to my heart.

We have had, and are yet having, lively times in our Legislature on the subject of slavery. You will see, by the last Liberator,[1] how the question has been carried — in one branch by a vote of 378 to 16,[2] in the other by a vote of 33 to none![3] in our favor, too! It is the most extraordinary change in political action, on a moral subject, in the annals of legislation. However, a strong effort is now making, by our enemies, to suppress all the resolutions upon the final vote for recurrence. It is not probable that they will succeed, but our majority will be reduced. No matter: the old Commonwealth of Massachusetts will do her duty in grand style, and pioneer the way for her sister States in the cause of emancipation. We shall secure this session, undoubtedly, the right of trial by jury to runaway slaves.[4]

Helen and the babe are in pretty good health. The latter has been troubled with a swelling of his right foot for some time past — the cause of it we cannot exactly determine. Dr. Hildreth is prescribing for it. A few days since, Helen began to wean George, and has succeeded without any difficulty.

For a [few] weeks past, we have had a little girl to assist us, but she is negligent and of no service, and we must therefore dismiss her. I wish you would say to sister Sarah, that we desire her, if convenient and agreeable, to make us a visit without delay, and remain with us till about the 1st of June, (after the New-England Convention,) when, the Lord willing, we will take a trip to Brooklyn, and spend June and July with you. I really hope she will be disposed to come — her presence would gladden us exceedingly.

We have just met with a very severe loss to our cause in the death of Ann G. Chapman.[5] She died somewhat suddenly. We could have better spared five hundred women in our ranks. She bequeathed 1000 dollars to the Am. Anti-Slavery Society — 100 to me — 100 to S. J. May — 100 to H. B. Stanton — 100 to the colored Samaritan Asylum,[6] &c. She was the dear girl who took so deep an interest in Henry's sickness. Bro. May came up to her funeral at her request, and performed the solemn services. Truly, in the midst of life, we are in the midst of death.

I am constrained to bring this letter abruptly to a close, as the mail closes in a few minutes. — Let me hear from you soon. I long to know what is the state of dear Mother's health — whether she is at Brooklyn — how you all do, &c. &c. Love abundantly to sisters Mary, Sarah, and Ann, Catharine, &c. &c. Mr. May and wife talk of visiting Brooklyn with us in June.

Yours most lovingly,
WM. LLOYD GARRISON.

☞ Do you think of attending the anniversary at New-York? — [7] I had an excellent, most affectionate, and animating letter from my dear friend Rowland Greene a few days since.

ALS: Garrison Papers, Boston Public Library. A paragraph of this letter was reprinted in *Life*, II, 128.

1. March 31, 1837.

2. On March 21, 1837, the Massachusetts House of Representatives, by a vote of 378 to 16, condemned the United States House of Representatives for having passed a resolution in January 1837 that "all petitions, memorials, resolutions, propositions, or papers, relating in any way or to any extent whatever to the subject of slavery, or the abolition of slavery, shall, without being either printed or referred, be laid on the table, and no further action whatever shall be had thereon." The Massachusetts house, in its resolution, characterized slavery as "a great social, moral and political evil," indicted the resolve of the federal House as "a virtual denial of the right of petition," "an assumption of power and authority, at variance with the spirit and intent of the Constitution of the United States, and injurious to the cause of freedom and free institutions"; and a repudiation of "the inherent, absolute, and inalienable rights of man," and affirmed that Congress, "having exclusive legislation in the District of Columbia, POSSESS THE RIGHT TO ABOLISH SLAVERY IN SAID DISTRICT . . ." The resolution was reprinted in *The Liberator*, March 24, 1837.

3. On March 29, 1837, the Massachusetts senate voted 35 (not 33) to 0 in favor of a resolution that "Congress having exclusive legislation in the District of Columbia, possesses the right to abolish slavery and the slave trade therein; and that the early exercise of such right is demanded by the enlightened sentiment of the civilized world, by the principles of the Revolution, and by humanity." (*The Liberator*, March 31, 1837).

4. "This significant measure passed both houses almost without dissent (*Lib.* 7:65-67)" (*Life*, II, 128n).

5. She died on Friday, March 24, 1837. Her will, dated February 1, 1837, read in part:

"Whilst I live, I have solemnly devoted myself to the cause of Truth, Justice, Freedom; and dying, I would yet bless it, in its onward course.

"Believing that the American Anti-Slavery Society is most beneficial to the slave, and is advancing rapidly the coming of Christ's kingdom, I leave to its Treasurer, Mr. John Rankin, or his successor in that Office, the sum of one thousand dollars for the use of the Society.

"To the Samaritan Asylum, one hundred dollars.

"To the Boston Female Anti-Slavery Society, one hundred dollars.

"I trust that when the hour of death comes, my mind will be, as it is now, convinced that the way to serve God, and secure his favor, is by making the cause of his oppressed children my cause. And then I shall not have lived in vain." This extract from her will, as well as various eulogies to Miss Chapman, was printed in *The Liberator*, April 7, 1837.

6. The following notice, which appeared in *The Liberator* on March 4, 1837, under the heading, "The Boston Samaritan Asylum for Indigent Colored Chil-

dren," reported: "It may not be known to the friends of the colored people, that there is in the city an Asylum for colored children. It is situated in Poplar street Court, and has twelve children connected with it. Visitors are admitted on Wednesday and Saturday afternoons.

"The funds of the society are exceedingly limited. Many children are waiting to be received, who cannot be admitted for *want* of the *means necessary* to their support.

"The annual subscription is one dollar. Life membership *ten dollars.* Could not those who are favorable to the cause become annual subscribers or life members? Any articles of furniture, bedding, or provisions will be gratefully received. Friends in the country who have anything to give can send them directed to the Samaritan Asylum, to the Anti-Slavery Office No. 25, Cornhill."

7 Probably the anniversary meeting of the American Anti-Slavery Society held in New York on May 9, 1837.

79

TO MRS. SARAH T. BENSON

Boston, April 8, 1837.

Dearly beloved mother:

I am apprehensive that you have been disposed to consider me somewhat undutiful as a son, on account of my protracted silence: yet I hope you do not graduate my affection by the number of epistles which you receive from me. Had I fully understood how ill you were, I should not only have written ere this, but probably have made a visit to Providence on purpose to see you; but I had supposed that you had fully recovered, and returned to Brooklyn some time since. It is seldom, now, that we receive information from any of the dear family in Friendship's Valley. Bro. George is doubtless very busy — and my own silence has, I presume, been considered a sufficient apology for an interruption of our correspondence.

Most deeply do I sympathize with you in your sickness, and not less do I rejoice to learn that you are now convalescent. How many admonitions have been given to us all, within a short time, to be prepared for our final change! The death of father — the early removal of our beloved Henry — your recent illness — these are special lessons, teaching us "what dying worms are we." But they ought not to excite gloomy sensations within us. It is perfectly absurd, irrational and unwise for us to complain that we are mortal; for who would live always in a vale of tears, a world of wo, a tabernacle of clay? Who would be always on a weary pilgrimage, and never arriving at the desired haven of rest? "The sting of death is sin." [1] Let us be crucified to sin, then, and rise with Christ from the dead, and death will have no power to alarm or distress us. It will then come as a welcome messenger in

God's good time, and we shall feel that though "to live is Christ, to die is gain." [2]

Of domestic intelligence, I have nothing special to communicate. Dear Helen and myself continue in good health — the chains that bind us we still find to be silken — our hearts are knit together in love — and our quantum of matrimonial happiness is even more than we anticipated. Our darling boy is our delight, and the admiration of all who see him. His general health is robust; but, for a few weeks past, his right foot has been badly swollen, though not very painfully so — from what cause, we are at a loss to determine. A few days since, the poor little fellow met with a bad accident. While we were at dinner, he fell out of Rebecca's arms, (a little girl we have in our employ,) and struck upon the sharp edge of a chair, making a gash in his forehead an inch long, which penetrated to the bone. The Dr. sewed it up, covered it with sticking plaster, and bandaged the head tightly. Last evening, as we went down to tea, Rebecca put him into his carriage to haul him about the room, but unfortunately upset the carriage, and threw him out headlong, the precious sufferer falling upon his former wound, bruising his nose and face, and causing such a general swelling of the features as to alter his appearance essentially. He passed, however, a tolerably good night, and we hope nothing serious will arise from the injury. Helen did not wish me to inform you of the accident, lest you might think she was to blame on the score of carelessness; but, as it was not her fault any more than it was mine, and not the fault of either, I have deemed it proper to give you the above information. We shall immediately dismiss Rebecca, as she does not answer our purpose; and we shall be very happy, and esteem it quite a favor, if dear sister Sarah can make it convenient to visit us, and remain with us till the 1st of June, (only six weeks,) when, if all be well with us, we purpose to visit Brooklyn, and remain there during the months of June and July. I have written to bro. George, asking him to make Sarah acquainted with our wishes.

Much gloom has been thrown over the anti-slavery circle in this vicinity by the sudden death of one of the loveliest females with whom it has been my privilege to become acquainted — Ann Greene Chapman. She it was who took so lively an interest in bro. Henry's sickness, and who used so frequently to send him fruit, &c. &c. When I think of them both, (and they are continually in my memory,) their decease seems an illusion. I can only fancy that they have gone on a short journey, and will return speedily. But I would not reverse the decree of Heaven, by bringing them back, if I could. I trust they are in the realms of glory, enjoying a full measure of unalloyed bliss. Miss Chapman was of more value to our cause in this city, than any other female.

She left $1000 to the American Anti-Slavery Society; $100 to the Colored Samaritan Asylum; and to Henry B. Stanton, Saml. J. May, and myself, $100 each.

I hear that sister Charlotte's family has had much sickness since I was in P.[3] last. Happily, none have fallen a prey to the universal Destroyer. Give my tender sympathies and affectionate remembrances to her and her husband. I also send a large share of my esteem to my friends the Chaces. I am rejoiced to hear that Phebe Jackson is espousing the anti-slavery cause with christian ardor and boldness Her happiness will be augmented in proportion to her efforts.

Tell dear Anna that we hope to receive a line from her before your return to Brooklyn.

Our spring is gradually advancing — but the seasons can neither increase nor diminish the respect and affection of

Yours, dutifully,

WM. LLOYD GARRISON.

ALS: Massachusetts Historical Society.

1. I Corinthians 15:56.
2. Philippians 1:21.
3. Providence, Rhode Island.

---

8 0

TO CALEB CUSHING

Boston, April 11, 1837.

Hon. Caleb Cushing:

Sir, — A Quarterly Meeting of the Massachusetts Anti-Slavery Society was held in Lynn on the 28th ultimo, at which the following resolution was offered by Wendell Phillips, Esq. of Boston, and sustained by him in a brief but eloquent speech: [1]

"Resolved, that the exertions of John Quincy Adams, and the rest of the Massachusetts delegation who sustained him in his defence of the citizens' right of petition, deserve the deepest gratitude and the warmest admiration of every American."

The vote upon the above resolution was taken by rising. The immense audience, male and female, rose spontaneously upon their feet in its favor — but no one more cordially than did

Your co-worker against oppression,

Wm. Lloyd Garrison,

Cor. Sec. of the Mass. A. S. Soc.

N. B. I was instructed by the meeting to communicate the above resolution to Mr. Adams, Mr. Lincoln,[2] and yourself.

ALS: In possession of Robert L. Huttner, Chicago, Illinois.

1. It was on March 28, 1837, at this quarterly meeting of the Massachusetts Anti-Slavery Society, that Wendell Phillips (1811–1884), who was to devote his life to the antislavery movement as a co-worker and close friend of Garrison, delivered his maiden address in the antislavery cause. The son of the first mayor of Boston, John Phillips, and a graduate of Harvard College in 1831, he abandoned the profession of law, where he had a brilliant future, to devote all his efforts to antislavery. (Ruchames, *The Abolitionists*, pp. 141–142.)

2. Levi Lincoln (b. October 25, 1782; d. May 29, 1868) was a Whig member of Congress from Worcester, Massachusetts, serving in the House of Representatives from February 17, 1834, to March 16, 1841. He had been governor of the State from 1825 to 1834, an associate justice of the state supreme court in 1824 and lieutenant-governor of Massachusetts in 1823. (*BDAC*.)

81

TO HENRY C. WRIGHT

Boston, April 16, 1837.

My dear Brother:

I am most heartily obliged to you for your frequent letters and communications. Not only are they satisfactory to me, but widely beneficial to the anti-slavery cause. Your affecting account of the arrest and trial of poor Dixon has come safely to hand, and shall be published in Saturday's Liberator.[1] It is an atrocious case. There really does not seem to be any more protection for the liberty of our free colored brethren and sisters in New-York than in New-Orleans: — nay, I doubt whether half as many attempts at kidnapping are made in the latter as in the former city. The brutal monsters at the South cannot desire a more stony-hearted, corrupt and violent magistracy than exists in the Commercial Emporium. The "Plaindealer"[2] says that Justice Bloodgood, while fulminating the anathemas of justice from the bench, had on the table before him a pair of enormous pistols, which he frequently flourished in illustration of his discourse!! — and that, "among many other similar ferocities of speech, he frequently expressed his regret that he had neglected to take his percussion caps with him into the Park, as he should have liked no better sport than to shoot a half a dozen of the damned niggers, and send them to hell!" What a judicial monster!

It is a great disappointment to me to hear that dear bro. Weld will be absent from New-York during the anniversary week. We need the aid of his sagacious, far-reaching, active mind on that occasion: yet I grant that the preservation of his health and life is of more consequence. May he obtain a speedy restoration, and be more provident of his bodily energies in time to come! I long to know that he has embraced our ultra pacific views, and is ready to stand boldly forth in their defence. You cheer my heart by the information that our be-loved sisters, Sarah and Angelina E. Grimké, are now satisfied that the followers of Him, who, when he was reviled, reviled not again, and when nailed to the cross exclaimed respecting his murderous enemies, "Father, forgive them, they know not what they do!" [3] — are not authorised to combine together in order to lacerate, sue, imprison, or hang their enemies, nor even as individuals to resort to physical force to break down the heart of an adversary. And, surely, if they cannot do these things as a body, or in their private capacity, they have no right to join with the ungodly in doing them. The remedy, however, will not be found in any thing short of faith in our Lord Jesus Christ. Human governments will remain in violent existence, as long as men are resolved not to bear the cross of Christ, and to be crucified unto the world. But in the kingdom of God's dear Son, holi-ness and love are the only magistracy. It has no swords, for they are beaten into ploughshares — no spears, for they are changed into prun-ing-hooks — no military academy, for the saints cannot learn war any more — no gibbet, for life is regarded as inviolate — no chains, for all are free. And that kingdom is to be established upon the earth — for the time is predicted when the kingdoms of this world will have become the kingdoms of our Lord and of his Christ.[4]

When they visit us in this quarter, we shall give those excellent women a welcome reception. You may tell them that the "Friends" in New-England are fast ceasing to be abolitionists *ex officio*, and are becoming such in spirit and in truth.

I shall endeavor — Deo volente — to be in New-York the week preceding the anniversary meeting. If we can find time, we will then freely interchange our religious views. My own are simple, but they make havoc of all sects, and rites, and ordinances of the priesthood of every name and order. Let me utter a startling assertion in your ear — There is nothing more offensive to the religionists of the day, than *practical holiness* — and the doctrine, that total abstinence from sin, in this life, is not only commanded but necessarily attainable, they hate with a perfect hatred, and stigmatize entire freedom from sin as a delusion of the devil! — Nevertheless, "he that is born of God cannot commit sin" [5] — "he that committeth sin is of the devil." [6] "How shall we who are dead to sin live any longer therein?" [7] "There is therefore now no condemnation to them who are in Christ Jesus, who walk not after the flesh, but after the Spirit. For the law of the Spirit of life in Christ Jesus hath made us free from the law of sin and death." [8] "Now, if any man have not the Spirit of Christ, he is none of his." [9] "For by one offering he hath *forever perfected* them who are sanctified." [10] "If any man be in Christ Jesus, he is a new creature." [11]

I have many things to say to you, but no time now. — What anxiety, and distress, and confusion, among bankers, and brokers, and merchants, and speculators, at the present time! — [12] I pity all those who have not treasures laid up in heaven. — O the emptiness of this sin-stricken world!

This is the spring of the year — but my affection for you is ripe with the fruits of autumn.

The peace of God, which passeth all understanding, abide with you forever.

Yours, in holy bonds,
Wm. Lloyd Garrison[.]

N.B. The Vermont Chronicle, New-York Observer, and Leonard Bacon in the New-Haven Religious Intelligencer,[13] are out upon certain articles of yours in the Liberator. They are "out" in a double sense — out in their columns, and out of their minds.

ALS: Garrison Papers, Boston Public Library. Most of this letter is reprinted in *Life*, II, 148–150.

1. Henry C. Wright's account, in the form of two letters, dated April 12 and 13, respectively, appeared in *The Liberator*, April 21, 1837. They told of the arrest and trial in New York City of one William Dixon, a Negro about thirty years old, who was charged with being a fugitive slave, having escaped from his owner, a Dr. Walter T. Allender of Baltimore, Maryland, in 1832. Though Dixon had witnesses who testified that he had worked for them in New York in 1830, two years before he was supposed to have escaped, he was not released. Dixon's lawyer, in turn, served a writ of false imprisonment on Allender, which made it necessary that the case be decided by a jury trial. Other accounts published in the same issue of *The Liberator* indicated that an attempt was made by a large number of Negroes to release Dixon by force as he was being taken from the courtroom to jail, but the effort failed. Justice Bloodgood, who presided at the trial, was beaten during the attempt, which may have accounted for his keeping two pistols before him during the trial.
2. The New York *Plaindealer*, a political newspaper published from December 3, 1836, to September 30, 1837. Its editor was William Leggett, formerly of the New York *Evening Post*, a radical and a Jacksonian. (*ACAB.*)
3. Luke 23:34.
4. Revelation 11:15, slightly altered.
5. I John 3:9, slightly altered.
6. I John 3:8.
7. Romans 6:2.
8. Romans 8:1, 2.
9. Romans 8:9.
10. Hebrews 10:14.
11. II Corinthians 5:17.
12. This refers to the economic depression of 1837, which began soon after the inauguration of President Martin Van Buren.
13. The New Haven *Religious Intelligencer* superseded the *Connecticut Evangelical Magazine and Religious Intelligencer* in 1816. It continued publication, perhaps intermittently, until October 7, 1837. (*Union List of Serials.*)

8 2

TO HELEN E. GARRISON

New-York, May 6, 1837.

My dear Wife:

Not the less dear because I am in the great American Babylon,[1] and you are in the Literary Emporium.[2] But I cannot love you in one place better than in any other — nor dislike you any where, unless, indeed, you become a very different woman from what you now are.

Well — we left No. 5, Hayward Place, in a great hurry, you know — not sure that we should arrive in season at the Depot, but we did. Waited 10 minutes before starting, and had time to eat two oranges which I bought for you, and two cakes which I intended for Dordie Toppy[3] — that was my dinner, and, so far as the oranges appertained to it, you will admit was a very good one. Felt perfectly satisfied myself. Found several abolition friends in the car — among them, Amasa Walker, and two female delegates from Salem, and one from Roxbury. Took Julia Williams[4] in with us as a matter of course, but expected she would be ordered out, as some of the passengers and by-standers cast certain significant glances at each other. On the whole, they probably supposed, or at least were willing to think, that she was our servant. Arrived in Providence at half past 3. Ushered the ladies, Miss Julia included, into the Ladies' Cabin, and secured them berths. We afterward managed it very well. Had Miss Williams gone down to tea last evening, or to breakfast this morning, no doubt a great commotion would have been stirred up — to prevent which, and to keep the secret to ourselves, we had tea and breakfast brought up to her, and Mary[5] took hers in the same manner. We had rather a rough passage, and the ladies were all more or less sick — Mary very slightly, however. In the night, the weather was very thick — we had much thunder and lightning, and some rain. The boat was struck by a squall, and laid over on her side, (and I believe slightly struck the shore,) so as to alarm some who were awake; but I was asleep, and knew nothing of the affair. We arrived safely, however, this morning, at 8 o'clock — baggage all safe. Took a carriage, and drove to the Anti-Slavery Rooms, to know what to do with my female friends. Saw bro. Stanton, Gould,[6] Goodell, &c. &c.; but no provision had been made for any body. Knew not what to do, nor where to drive to. Finally, drove to the Graham boarding-house, — full, — could not accommodate even one of us. Drove to another house in John-street, where I succeeded in leaving Miss Pope.[7] Then drove to Read-st. to bro. Phelps,[8] and left Mary, to be accommodated somehow and any how. Then drove to a colored boarding-house in Leonard-st. and left Miss Williams. Then had myself driven (not in a slaveholding sense, but "with my own consent,") to Dr. Cox's,[9] in Prince-st. Saw the Dr., but not Mrs. C. He inquired particularly about little George's case — does not believe it is the scrofula — and thinks it ought not to have been lanced. Hopes I will get some skilful surgeon to look at it — &c.

I am now at the Anti-Slavery Office, and delegates are coming in fast. Cannot learn that any thing has been done respecting the Ladies' Convention. The Grimke's have not returned from Philadelphia, and much dependence on the score of arrangements has been placed upon them. They will probably be here on Monday; and I suppose the female delegates will hold a preliminary meeting on Monday afternoon, in the Sessions' room of the Tabernacle Church. Weld left the city for Hartford a few days since, and will not be here during the meetings. — This step was required by the state of his health.

I forgot to say that the hackman (colored) charged me three dollars and a half hack hire for our ride from the boat — paid him $3 — at least one more than he ought to have received.

If you should receive this letter to-morrow (Sunday) afternoon or evening, and friend Knapp should be the bearer of it, tell him to be sure and send as many copies of my Annual Report [10] as friend Southard or May can bring conveniently. Hope he will attend to this. Tell him bro. Stanton was much pleased to get his box of Reports.

Poor, dear little George! How I have mourned to think that his foot was probed and lanced afresh yesterday. Hope the symptoms are no worse. Kiss the little sufferer again and again for the sake of his loving father, and of

Your affectionate husband,

Wm. Lloyd Garrison.

☞ Love to all at home.

ALS: Garrison Papers, Boston Public Library.

1. Garrison was in New York for the annual meeting of the American Anti-Slavery Society, which was held on May 9.

2. Boston.

3. Nursery lingo for their infant son George Thompson, previously referred to as Dordie Tompit.

4. Apparently a Negro woman, who may have been a delegate to the Ladies' Anti-Slavery Convention, which was held in New York at the same time as that of the American Anti-Slavery Society. The meeting was presided over by Mary Parker, and comprised seventy-one delegates (*Life*, II, 131).

5. Mary Parker.

6. Probably Joseph D. Gould, one of the Lane rebels, who became one of the "seventy" antislavery agents, and was especially successful at fund-raising (*Weld-Grimké Letters*, I, 334n).

7. Eliza Pope (b. December 1, 1802; d. May 31, 1885) daughter of Frederick and Mary Pope, lived in Dorchester all her life, an invalid for many years. She never married, was one of the earliest members of the Baptist Church in Dorchester, and was active in the antislavery movement. (Charles Henry Pope, *A History of the Dorchester Pope Family*, Boston, 1888, p. 163; see also her letter to Maria W. Chapman, September 28, 1840, Weston Papers, Boston Public Library.)

8. Amos Phelps.

9. Dr. Abraham L. Cox.

10. The annual report of the Board of Managers of the Massachusetts Anti-Slavery Society, written by Garrison as corresponding secretary of the society, and presented to the annual meeting on January 25, 1837.

83

TO AMOS A. PHELPS

Boston, May 23, 1837.

Dear bro. Phelps:

Your letter of the 16th, signifying your willingness to act as the General Agent of the Massachusetts Anti-Slavery Society, on certain specified terms, has given us all much pleasure. I meant to have sent you a reply on Saturday; but friend Southard [1] did not succeed in getting a board meeting together, and I thought it would be useless to send you back an indefinite answer. Yesterday afternoon, however, we had a meeting of the Board, and your letter was read to them. It was then voted, unanimously, that the terms stipulated in your letter, for one, two and three years, be complied with. As to the $400 in advance, and *instanter*, we hardly knew what to do, our treasury being empty, and money being as scarce as pity for the colored race. A committee was raised, however, to obtain as much as possible by to-day at 12 o'clock, at which time the steam-boat mail closes. The result is, the enclosed Draft for two hundred dollars. The remainder of the $400 will be made up promptly in the course of a fortnight. We earnestly hope that the enclosed will enable you to come on, *especially to our Convention*,[2] even if you should be necessitated to return to New-York for a short time. You can leave N. Y. as late as Monday afternoon at 5 o'clock, and arrive here at the time the Convention will open — but we should prefer to see you, if convenient, on Saturday. Do make one of our number on this momentous occasion. Our Convention will be held in the Methodist church, Piedmont-st.[3] formerly Mr. Sabine's — all others have been refused to us. Shame upon the Salem-street society! How our enemies will taunt us! Mr. Towne,[4] I understand, is opposed to our having the house, for *prudential* reasons! He recently declined making a prayer at a meeting in behalf of the

Colored Samaritan Asylum. God will confound such a time-serving policy. You will see, by the next Liberator, what kind of refusals we have received from all quarters.

☞ You will receive this to-morrow forenoon. You will greatly oblige me by sending me, if you can, by the mail of *to-morrow* afternoon, a proof-sheet of the resolutions and doings of the annual meeting,[5] which I presume will appear in the next Emancipator — so that I shall receive them by Thursday, 1 o'clock, and thus be enabled to insert them in the Liberator this week.[6] I shall look for them anxiously, and keep my columns open, waiting.☜

If bro. Stanton is in New-York, tell him I am very desirous that he should see Dr. Cox, and get an accurate copy of R. J. Breckinridge's will in his possession, (a queer document,) emancipating his slaves prospectively. If he has left, will you do me this favor?

I am almost feverish to learn the proceedings of the General Assembly.[7] It seems that Witherspoon[8] has not been re-elected moderator, but Elliot of Ohio.[9] This is another sign of the times. I pray that our abolition friends in that body may be faithful and fearless. They have two formidable opponents in R. J. Breckinridge, and Plumer of Virginia:[10] yet why should they fear, or hold back?

Of course, should you come to the Convention, we shall expect you and yours at no. 5, Hayward Place.

Yours, Lovingly,

A. A. Phelps. Wm. Lloyd Garrison.

ALS: Phelps Papers, Boston Public Library.

1. Nathaniel Southard, the recording secretary of the Massachusetts Anti-Slavery Society.
2. The New England Anti-Slavery Convention was to begin on Tuesday, May 30, in Boston.
3. Also called the Church Street Church. *The Liberator*, May 26, 1837, printed replies from the various churches to which application had been made for their use by the convention. All but the Church Street Church refused. The Board of Stewards of that church granted permission, unanimously.
4. The Reverend Joseph Hardy Towne (b. Salem, Massachusetts, May 22, 1805; d. July 30, 1897) was a graduate of Yale University in 1827, and served as minister of the Salem Street Church from 1837 to 1843. He was later co-author of the anti-Garrisonian "Clerical Appeal." (Justin Winsor, ed., *Memorial History of Boston*, Boston, 1881, III, 416–418; Edwin Eugene Towne, *The Descendants of William Towne*, Newtonville, Mass., 1901, p. 150.)
5. Of the American Anti-Slavery Society.
6. They appeared in *The Liberator*, June 2, 1837.
7. Refers to the convention of the General Assembly of the Presbyterian church, held during the last week in May in Philadelphia. The Presbyterian church was then divided into two primary factions, called Old School and New School, each vying for control of the General Assembly. The differences were doctrinal as well as political, with the Old School representing a conservative point of view. Politically, Old School Presbyterians, although differing somewhat in their views of slavery, were agreed that slavery was not an issue on which the church

should take a stand. Most southern Presbyterians were in this group. The New School Presbyterians included a larger proportion of antislavery men and were more inclined to permit individual churches to take a stand against slavery, though many among them were reluctant to have the church as a whole condemn slavery. (Zebulon Crocker, *The Catastrophe of the Presbyterian Church in 1837, including a full view of the Recent Theological Controversies in New England*, New Haven, 1838, *passim*; Ernest Trice Thompson, *Presbyterians in the South*, Richmond, Virginia, 1963, I, 392–394.)

8. Dr. John Witherspoon, pastor of the Presbyterian Church of Camden, South Carolina, was a slaveholder and conservative in politics as well as in religion. He was chosen moderator by the Presbyterian General Assembly of 1836. At that time he wrote to Dr. Thomas Smith of Charleston, South Carolina: "It is said that there are 150 abolitionists on the floor of the Assembly. I can scarcely believe this and yet I am convinced *they be very many. . . .* I say, Sir, let the *South look well to her interests.*" (Quoted in Ernest Trice Thompson, *Presbyterians in the South*, I, 386; Robert Ellis Thompson, *A History of the Presbyterian Churches in the United States*, New York, 1907, p. 112; Zebulon Crocker, *The Catastrophe of the Presbyterian Church in 1837*, p. 64.)

9. Dr. David Elliot or Elliott (b. Pennsylvania, Feb. 6, 1787) was then professor of theology at Western Theological Seminary in Allegheny, Pennsylvania. He was elected moderator at the General Assembly in 1837. (*Presbyterian Reunion: A Memorial Volume, 1837–1871*, New York, 1871, pp. 528–530.)

10. William Swan Plumer (b. July 26, 1802; d. October 22, 1880), a Presbyterian clergyman, graduated from Princeton Theological Seminary in 1826, and was pastor of a Presbyterian church in Petersburg, Virginia, from 1831 to 1834 and of the First Presbyterian Church in Richmond, Virginia, from 1834 to 1847. He served the Franklin Street Presbyterian Church in Baltimore, Maryland, from 1847 to 1854, and for eight years thereafter was professor of theology at the Western Theological Seminary in Allegheny, Pennsylvania. In the 1837 controversy within the Presbyterian church between the Old School and New School he was the outstanding debater and leader on the Old School side. (*DAB.*)

84

TO JOHN FARMER

Boston, June 6, 1837.

Dear Sir:

If I could believe that my presence at the annual meeting of your State Anti-Slavery Society [1] would be of essential importance, I would hasten to Concord, — busily occupied as I am, at the present time, with pressing duties in the city: but, as you are to have with you our distinguished coadjutor James G. Birney, and our invaluable friend William Goodell, as well as other able advocates of our much persecuted, yet very thriving cause, this brief and hasty letter must answer as a substitute for my personal attendance.

Let me admonish you all, not to waste your time in discussing points which are not of IMMEDIATE AND VITAL IMPORTANCE. I would humbly suggest, that, to dwell upon the "self-evident truth," that *all men are created free and equal* — to attempt to prove, by an elaborate train of metaphysical reasoning, that to transform a human being into a beast or an article of merchandize, is a sinful act — to linger about the simple and obvious proposition, that to withhold the Bible, and all moral and intellectual culture, from "our fellow-countrymen in chains," who are "slaves in a land of light and law," [2] is a dreadful outrage upon the MIND and SOUL — or even to spend time in discussing the safety and practicability of immediate emancipation, or the absurdity and cruelty of the colonization scheme — would be, AT THE PRESENT CRISIS, in your meeting, not clearly to discern the "signs of the times," [3] but to overlook matters of far more IMMEDIATE importance. I do not know but I shall excite much surprise among you in declaring, that never have I regarded the anti-slavery cause to be in such peril — never have I had so little hope of the peaceful overthrow of slavery in our midst — never have I regarded the existence of this nation in so much jeopardy, as at the present time. There is every probability that we are speedily to be involved in a war with Mexico, ostensibly to redress injuries, but really to extend slavery and the slave trade. As a nation, we have evinced the basest perfidy toward Mexico; we have openly violated the faith of treaties; we have encouraged our citizens to invade and revolutionize a part of her territory; we have rashly and impudently recognized the independence of that territory; and we have been fertile in devising plots and expedients to provoke her to declare war against us. I need not portray to you what will be the horrors of such a war; nor in what manner, or to what extent, it will cripple all the benevolent and religious enterprises of the day — for when a nation is at war, the brotherhood of mankind is forgotten or denied, good will toward men is turned into malevolence, and false honor and the demon of revenge make havoc of all that is lovely and of good report.

But the crowning calamity which threatens us, is the annexation of Texas to our Union, at the session of Congress in September next.[4] Should this awful event happen, I do not see any hope for the slaves at the south — for the freemen of the North — or for our guilty, though still beloved country. I fear the time for repentance and reformation will have passed forever. And yet there cannot be the slightest doubt, that the plot is already perfected — and that the extra session alluded to, is to carry it into execution. You will perceive, by the resolutions passed at the annual meeting of the Parent Society at New-York,[5] and by the New-England Convention in this city, the deep and solemn interest which was felt in this tremendous question by the delegates assembled on those occasions. I hope those resolutions, in reference to Texas, will be read at your meeting — that they will occupy your thoughts, and incite you to action — that you will adopt similar ones, and lay your plans to rouse up the people of New-Hampshire, without distinction of sect or party, to protest against the admission of Texas into the Union.[6] In comparison with this topic, all others are of trifling importance at this crisis. Bend all your energies and means to prevent so direful a catastrophe.

My heart is overflowing on this subject — but I must stop, for I have neither time nor room to give it utterance.

With high esteem and fraternal regard, I remain,

Your friend and coadjutor,

Wm. Lloyd Garrison.

John Farmer.

ALS: Massachusetts Historical Society; printed in *The Liberator*, June 16, 1837.

John Farmer (b. Chelmsford, Massachusetts, June 12, 1789; d. Concord, New Hampshire, August 13, 1838) was a neighbor of Nathaniel P. Rogers in New Hampshire; an early abolitionist who was a founder and corresponding secretary of the New Hampshire Anti-Slavery Society; an historian and genealogist who was the author of many studies in history and genealogy, including *Belknap's History of New Hampshire, Genealogical Register of the First Settlers of New England, Histories of Billerica and Amherst*, etc. Although at first a schoolmaster, he later became a druggist. (*Life*, I, 454; II, 60, 451; *HEUSH*; *Weld-Grimké Letters*, I, 472.)

1. The New Hampshire Anti-Slavery Society. A report of the meeting appeared in *The Liberator*, June 16, 1837.

2. Both this and the preceding quotation are from John Greenleaf Whittier's "Stanzas," in *Voices of Freedom*.

3. Matthew 16:3.

4. In a short item entitled "Annexation of Texas to the U. S.," *The Liberator*, on June 9, 1837, noted: "There cannot be a shadow of doubt, that this question will be presented to Congress, at the extra session which the President has called. Will its opponents now *bestir themselves* in forwarding memorials to that body, protesting against the measure? . . . . Let meetings be held, and resolutions, addresses, remonstrances, &c., be published immediately, in every city, town, and settlement, where a half-dozen individuals can be found to raise their voice against the unhallowed scheme."

5. These resolutions were introduced by Garrison and were adopted by the convention. They called for public opposition to the admission of Texas into the Union, and for a country-wide campaign by the American Anti-Slavery Society to build such opposition and to defeat all efforts in Congress to admit Texas. (*The Liberator*, June 2, 1837.)

6. Resolutions to that effect were introduced and passed at the meeting. See *The Liberator*, June 16, 1837.

85

TO GEORGE W. BENSON

Boston, June 14, 1837.

My dear George:

It does my heart good to see your plain, unambitious handwriting once more, in the letter from you which is now before me. It is very brief indeed, and business-like, showing that you feel the importance of making hay while the sun shines, like a good and thrifty farmer. It is enough that you say — "I anticipate your visit with much pleasure." What more could you have said, had you filled your entire sheet with professions of friendship? I will add, that for some weeks I have been longing, like a child absent from home, to see you all under the dear family roof. *All*, did I say? It yet seems difficult for me to realize, that two of the number have taken their flight to a fairer clime — that the ripened shock of corn and the blooming flower have fallen to the earth. Thanks be to God, it is only mortality swallowed up of life. But those that remain in this earthly tabernacle, I hope to see on Saturday afternoon, bringing with me my dear affectionate Helen, and my darling boy, both of whom need the beneficial influences of a country residence. We hope to be able to tarry with you a few weeks, without meaning to be burdensome to you. During my absence, my friend Oliver Johnson will act as sub-editor of the Liberator,[1] and thus keep its concerns in good order. Of course, I divide my salary with him. I shall try to write for the paper every week, so that no complaint may arise on account of my absence.

I have just settled dear Henry's account with Mr. Chapman.[2] A mistake of four dollars was discovered in his favor — making the whole amount $17,82 — not so large as I supposed it would be. Of this sum, agreeably to your request, I have paid Mr. Southard $16, leaving a balance of $1,82 in my hands, which I will put into your hands when we meet. I shall bring with me all the numbers of the Youth's Cabinet, up to the present week. It is a very interesting publication — and friend Southard is just the man to be its editor.[3]

The anti-slavery cause, in the Commonwealth, continues to be in a thriving condition. Our late New-England Convention was a prime one — the proceedings of which will soon be laid before the public.[4] It was a regular "protracted meeting" — i.e. just "four days," in duration, viz. Tuesday, Wednesday, Thursday and Friday.[5] We are now preparing to make a mighty agitation on the subject of Texas — and unless every effort be put forth, and every man be found at his post, to prevent the annexation of that republic of thieves, cut-throats and men-stealers to our Union, I fear we, and those who now live, will never see slavery peacefully abolished. May Heaven confound every attempt to make that blood-stained territory a part of our own!

The Liberator has now a pretty fair circulation — at least three thousand subscribers — despite all the machinations of sectarian cavillers and pro-slavery opposers. Its expenses, however, are very great, in consequence of the enlargement of its sheet, and the low price at which it is afforded.

We have been very fortunate in securing the services of bro. Phelps as our General Agent. He is expected in Boston on Saturday, to commence his labors in good earnest. Whittier has just gone to New-York, to relieve Stanton from the drudgery of epistolary correspondence, and enable him to come to Massachusetts for a few weeks, in order to complete the victory commenced last year — revolutionize John Quincy Adams's District — drive the Texas question, &c. Stanton is the Napoleon of our cause.

Mr. Adams is now at Quincy. He has lately had quite a "visitation" from several abolition fanatics, and received them all with respect and cordiality. First, James G. Birney and Francis Jackson had a long interview with him — then John G. Whittier and W. L. Garrison — then Angelina E. and Sarah M. Grimké — and then Wm. Goodell. I will tell you something about these visits hereafter.

I have been invited to go to Coventry next week, to address the women of that village, who have sent me six dollars to defray my expenses — and Wm. M. Chace writes me that my presence is much needed, at about the same time, at some public meetings which are to be held in various places in that State.[6] I do not know that I shall accept of either of the invitations — perhaps I shall of *all*.

There was a tremendous riot in this city on Sunday afternoon last — exceeding in violence any that has ever gone before it. It took place between the Irish and some engine companies — the latter being chiefly to blame. Many of the former got most dreadfully bruised — their houses were sacked, and the most dastardly outrages perpetrated upon their property — yet they were the only individuals arrested as offenders, and dragged off to jail. The spirit felt toward the poor Irish is almost as ferocious as toward the colored race.

I believe Helen has done what little shopping was requested of her in Anna's letter. It has been a real pleasure to her to make the purchases.

Mary Ann Coffin [7] is to accompany us to Brooklyn on Saturday. She is to stay with Lucy Scarborough [8] awhile.

It may be that something will transpire, so as to prevent our coming on Saturday. If so, we shall seize the next opportunity. Give yourselves no uneasiness, should there be a failure.

My next letter will probably be a living epistle. A great deal of love to Catharine, dear mother, Mary, Sarah, Anne, &c.

Yours, lovingly,
Wm. Lloyd Garrison.

ALS: Garrison Papers, Boston Public Library.

1. On June 16, 1837, *The Liberator* announced: "The Editor will leave the city to-morrow, for a temporary residence in the country. During his absence, he

will continue to devote his time mainly to the editorial department of the Liberator. Letters intended for his private perusal may be addressed to him at Brooklyn,
Connecticut; but all communications, prepared for insertion in the Liberator,
must be directed to Boston as heretofore. He has engaged a friend, well qualified
for the task, to act as sub-editor until his return."

2. Probably Maria W. Chapman's father-in-law, Henry Chapman, who was often
involved in making contributions to *The Liberator* and in helping to pay its debts.

3. *The Liberator*, on May 12, 1837, carried an announcement of the planned
publication of *Youth's Cabinet*, as well as a lengthy prospectus describing its aims
and purposes. The announcement read: "*Youth's Cabinet* will be published every
Friday, at no. 25, Cornhill, Boston, Mass. N. Southard, editor. Terms, $1 per
annum in advance. — $1.25 if not paid before the publication of the 14th number

"Agents, who obtain subscribers and forward the money, free of expense, in
advance, will be allowed a discount of 20 per cent."

The prospectus explained that the newspaper's purpose was to promote "the
physical, intellectual, moral, and religious education of children." The prospectus
was dated Boston, April 28, 1837.

4. A summary of the proceedings appeared in *The Liberator* on June 2, 1837.
Additional material related to the convention appeared in *The Liberator* on
June 23, June 30, and July 7, 1837.

5. May 30–June 2.

6. Rhode Island.

7. See letter 20, to Helen, April 16, 1836.

8. Lucy Scarborough (b. April 16, 1816, in Brooklyn, Connecticut) was the
daughter of Philip (b. February 24, 1788) and Deidama Scarborough of Brooklyn, Connecticut. Philip Scarborough was a farmer. In 1850 Lucy married Daniel
Thaxter, an optician, of Hingham, Massachusetts. Theodore Parker performed the
marriage ceremony. (Typescript of Brooklyn Vital Records, in Massachusetts Historic Genealogical Society, Boston, pp. 58, 59.)

---

8 6

TO HELEN E. GARRISON

Brooklyn, July 1, 1837.

My dear Helen:

I have often thought that a man must feel queerly, who has had a
leg amputated; but what is the subtraction of a leg, compared to the
loss of his "better half"? If we twain are *one*, (as I have been imagining
ever since S. J. May bound us together,) [1] how is it that you are in
Providence, and I am in Brooklyn, at the same instant? Why, the
Siamese twins never deem a separation between themselves possible;
and is the ligament that makes them indissoluble, of a firmer texture
than that which holds husband and wife together? Ah! the solution of
the enigma is easy — our *hearts* are one, not our *bodies*, so that we
can be in full communion with each other at a distance of thirty miles.

Then I have another bodily bereavement. Where is my sweet babe?
I may listen in vain to hear his tiny footsteps — to catch the sound of
his merry voice. Mother and child both gone! Well, I can spare you,

for a short time at least, without being *very* unhappy. I have not shed a tear on your account, since your departure; and yet I am not naturally hard-hearted. I have not wrung my hands in mournful mood; and yet I love you, without a peradventure. Nevertheless, I have missed you so much as to feel somewhat lonely — and shall rejoice when we become united again.

If convenient, you must send me a few lines by the mail on Monday. We (i.e. myself and the rest of the household) have no uneasiness on account of your safety, and presume that your ride was completed at a seasonable hour. After all, the weather was not so good (or, rather, was not so pleasant, for it is always good, i.e. such as the most benevolent Being in the Universe is disposed to give,) as we supposed it would be when you left. It rained here slightly toward night, and probably gave you a sprinkling on the way.

I have risen this morning at 4 o'clock, to devote an hour to you. Yesterday was the warmest, and, on the whole, the most agreeable day I have experienced this season. The sun is rising splendidly this morning — a glorious incendiary; the birds are carolling forth their sweetest notes, though some of them are busy stealing the cherries in front of my window, and I do not believe that even the thieves in London are more expert in their business. Every thing is vocal with joy, and the universal exclamation seems to be — "How manifold are thy works, O Lord of hosts! In wisdom hast thou made them all.[2] Let every thing that hath breath praise the name of the Lord!" [3]

Last evening, Mr. and Mrs. Kilton,[4] with their children, spent an hour with us. She reminded me of Sarah Gray,[5] in her form and features, though she is somewhat taller. Her little boy George gave me a bag, containing forty-three cents, (a present both heavy and valuable,) to be used in emancipating little slave children. Her youngest babe is very sprightly, and has an uncommonly large head. If cousin William [6] had been present, he would have decided upon its phrenological proportions, and made me wiser than I am now. *En passant* — Ask him to examine your cranium, my dear, and decide upon your character as a wife and mother.

Yesterday the mail arrived from Boston, bringing me neither letter nor newspaper. It is strange that among so many at head-quarters, not one is so thoughtful as to send me any intelligence, written or printed. My vanity begins to be alarmed: nobody seems to miss me, whereas I thought I was of some little consequence in Boston, if not in the world. But so it is, Helen: men, and without slander it may be affirmed that women too, are generally disposed to over-estimate their own importance — and it is proper, therefore, that they should be made to see and feel what pigmies they are in this tall universe.

Not only do I receive nothing from Boston by the mail, but friend Knapp still *remembers to forget* to send me a bundle. This afternoon, however, I confidently expect one by the Worcester stage. Should I be again disappointed, — *I shall be very patient.*

Yesterday I received another letter from Miss Peck [7] at Coventry, in the name of the Kent County Ladies' Anti-Slavery Society, saying that they were somewhat disappointed in my not coming last Sabbath, and expressing the hope that I would visit them a week from to-morrow, (9th July,) if convenient — if not, at whatever time I may select. I shall propose the 30th inst.

There has nothing unusual transpired since you left; for Brooklyn is not able to compare with London in bustle and variety of incident, although it has higher hills, more grass, and finer trees. — The cows have been regularly milked, and turned into the pasture, — (they live, you know, on the Graham system.) [8] The motherly hens have exercised a proper watchfulness over their tender brood, while the patriarch himself has stalked about majestically, sounding his shrill horn at earliest dawn of day. The pigs have slept in inglorious ease, or given an occasional squeal of discontent whenever their mother has refused to pamper them. The colt is full of his antics, and seems determined to confer so much credit on his dam as to make the old adage true beyond all cavil, that "the *grey* mare is the better horse" [9] — though, in this instance, she happens to be of a *dun* color — but abolition colts care nothing about *color.*

Apropos — a word as to this hot weather. Mother and the girls think you had better relieve little George of some of his flannel, for now is the season to obtain emancipation. If the weather should alter materially, you can govern yourself accordingly.

"How do you come on with your Address?" [10] Answer: I have begun it — and have left the exordium to write to you. — It will be a laborious job for me to finish the *mechanical* part of it.

I can hardly tell you, whether I shall take the Pomfret stage on Monday, or leave here on Tuesday morning in a carryall. I shall choose the latter mode of travelling, provided I can hire a horse, which is somewhat doubtful, as there is to be a special turn out for a ride in this village on the 4th. — Still, I shall hope to succeed. It is not probable that bro. George will be able to go down with me, and Sarah is somewhat apprehensive that it will be too fatiguing for her to go and come in so short a time, though she would like to visit P. [11] We must calculate to return on Wednesday. Our beloved friend E. J. Chace [12] we hope will come with us.

You can tell the dear friends in Pleasant Valley, that my friendship for them is as green and ardent as the season; that I feel deeply indebted to them for their many kindnesses to me and mine; and that I anticipate my journey to P. with a great deal of pleasure, as it will enable me to see and talk with them face to face.

Cover the face of my darling boy with kisses, and tell him that father is coming.

All the household desire to freight this letter with affectionate remembrances to you and all the members of our friend C's [13] family.

Most affectionately, yours, ever,

Wm. Lloyd Garrison.

ALS: Garrison Papers, Boston Public Library.

1. On September 4, 1834.
2. Psalms 104:24.
3. Psalms 150:6.
4. See letter 59, to Henry E. Benson, November 4, 1836.
5. Mrs. John Gray, Jr., the former Sarah S. Paine, who married John Gray, Jr., of Brooklyn, Connecticut, on March 4, 1833, the ceremony being performed by Samuel J. May. (Typescript of Brooklyn Vital Records, New England Historic Genealogical Society; see letter 6, to Henry E. Benson, January 26, 1836.)
6. In a letter to Helen dated September 21, 1870 (Garrison Papers, Boston Public Library), Garrison writes: "I presume the Mrs. Garrison who called upon you is the wife of William Garrison, who claimed to be my cousin, who called upon us many years ago, and who gave me the picture of West India scenes hanging up in our sleeping room." This may be the cousin referred to here, but we cannot identify him further.

Garrison also had a cousin William who had died in Nova Scotia in February 1837, and a cousin Edwin William (1804–c. 1844), the son of his father's brother Nathan. Helen had a cousin named William Collins Benson (1791–1858), the son of her father's brother John, who was a farmer in northern New York. A William P. R. Benson is listed as a house-carpenter at Peck's Wharf in the Providence *Directory* for 1836–1837. Whether or not he was related to Helen is unknown. (Wendell Phillips Garrison, *Memoranda of the Garrison Family for Three Generations*, New York, 1876, pp. 3, 4; *The Benson Family of Newport, Rhode Island*, privately printed, New York, 1872, p. 30.)
7. Probably one of the daughters of Perez Peck of Coventry, Rhode Island, an active antislavery man. The eldest was Harriet (b. April 19, 1815; d. May 23, 1840), next came Mary Ann (b. July 15, 1816), then Lydia H. (b. Dec. 31, 1817) and finally Joanna (b. Sept. 13, 1821), who may have been too young to be an antislavery leader. (Ira B. Peck, *Genealogical History of the Descendants of Joseph Peck*, Boston, 1868, p. 80.)
8. The Graham movement was founded by Sylvester Graham (1794–1851), an American reformer, temperance lecturer, and advocate of vegetarianism. A Presbyterian minister, he became interested in the relationship between alcoholism and diet and concluded that alcoholism could be cured by a vegetarian diet. In 1839 he published the *Graham Lectures on the Science of Human Life*, and *Bread and Bread-Making*. (*ACAB*.) *The Liberator*, June 16, 1837, carried an essay on the program of activities of a Graham House.
9. "The saying, 'the grey mare is the better horse,' is found in Camden's *Remains, Proverb Concerning Britain*. (1605, reprint of 7th ed. 1870.) Also in *A Treatyse shewing and declaring the Pryde and Abuse of Women Now a Dayse* (1550)." *Hoyt's New Cyclopedia of Practical Quotations*, completely revised and greatly enlarged by Kate Louise Roberts (New York and London, 1923), p. 870, no. 6.
10. Garrison was scheduled to deliver an address at a July 4 antislavery meet-

ing in Providence at the High-Street meeting-house, under the sponsorship of the Providence Anti-Slavery Society. A description of the meeting and a summary of Garrison's address appeared in *The Liberator*, July 28, 1837, under the heading, "Fourth of July in Providence."

11. Providence.
12. Eliza J. Chace.
13. William Chace.

8 7

TO ISAAC KNAPP

Brooklyn, Aug. 9, 1837.

My dear Knapp:

What is in the wind now? Only think of a public "clerical" admonition! Do not ecclesiastical terrors take hold of you, as publisher of the Liberator? Have you done penance, and obtained absolution? For my own part, I am growing more and more irreverent, and must be given over as incorrigible. Surely, you must be a pugnacious man to employ such an Ishmaelitish editor. "Wo is me, my mother! for I was born a man of strife." [1] What latent feelings, think you, have stirred up Messrs. Fitch and Towne to make such a strange "Appeal"? [2] Tell me whether there is not some sectarian ill-will, some "clerical" apprehension, at the bottom of this movement. You are very good, as a Yankee, in guessing — but perhaps the facts in the case are too palpable to need a single surmise. My review [3] of the "Appeal" will probably ensure you the loss of a few subscribers, and perhaps add a few more to your list. It was written in more haste than I could have wished, but as I expected to be in Boston before commencing it, it was delayed till but a little time was left to me. I forwarded it to Boston, in parcels, by three different conveyances: — the first, in two letters by mail on Tuesday — the second, yesterday noon, via Worcester, by Rev. Mr. Martin [4] of New-York, who promised to deliver it promptly on his arrival — the third this morning, via Providence, by a friend, to be dropped into the P. O. in that city; so that I suppose you will have received the whole to-night. I shall be sorry if any of it should happen to be lost or mislaid. Whether you will think it best to delay the paper for it this week, I cannot tell, but shall be satisfied with your decision, either way — though I think the sooner the rejoinder appears, the better. See to it that the proof of it is read correctly. The "Appeal," I fear, will do some injury to our cause, as it will doubtless be used to some purpose by our enemies.

I do not remember whether I have told you how very much like a hospital our house has been within the last fortnight. Helen was first taken sick, and had a severe time of it — then I followed, so as to be unable to do any thing — next, sister Mary was violently attacked — and finally sister Anna was seized with a more alarming illness than either of us all. Happily, we are all better, and have discharged the physician. Some persons would say, that we ought to be very thankful to God for his special mercy in restoring us to health; but there is nothing special or miraculous in a restoration like this. Medicine had its legitimate effect, and that is the sum total of the whole matter. What then? Are we not grateful to God? Certainly. But for what? Why, for providing remedies, in his bountiful providence, that have been successful in the removal of our complaints. Now, that gratitude is purely spasmodic which is elicited only by some rare occurrence. As for myself, I am thankful in sickness and in health — in pain and in ease — in adversity and in prosperity. Nothing comes amiss. I have perpetual tranquillity, but no spasms — never ceasing light, but no darkness. I have but one wish — "Thy will be done on earth as it is done in heaven." [5] My rejoicing is in the Lord always. My peace is like a deep river — my rest perfect.

Doubtless, you are busy, very busy, but send me a few lines, if you can, in Saturday's bundle. Tell me something about your visit to New-buryport — how the friends were in Temple-street — how abolitionism flourishes in that place, and what new converts have been made — how Mrs. Knapp was pleased — whether you visited Plum Island [6] and the Essex Merrimac Bridge, at which latter place you once got surfeited upon hot mince pie, though I consumed double the quantity with impunity — how the Grimke's succeeded — how Mr. Adams's [7] oration was relished — &c. &c.

I have not yet been to Coventry! Three times have I disappointed the friends in that place, but have made another appointment, (20th inst.) which I hope to fulfil without fail. On the 21st, I am to address the Windham Co. Society in Hampton, [8] six miles from this village — and hope to be in Boston on the evening of the 23d. Whether Helen and the babe will return with me, will depend upon circumstances. Bro. George is anxious that I should go into a Thompsonian Infirmary, and I think I must. My health is not good — my liver is badly affected — and my scrofula in the neck, throat and head is troublesome.

Will you request bro. Phelps to tell Lucy Parker, that, contrary to what I wrote her last week, I have concluded to remain here a fort-night longer? How does he fancy the "Appeal"? and what does bro. Fuller [9] say of his pastor?

Bro. Southard, I hope, will not remove to New-York. My best regards to him. How does the Almanac sell? [10] What number of sub-scribers to the Youth's Cabinet?

Bro. Johnson must hold on, if he can, until my return; but if he cannot, bros. Phelps and Southard must assist you a little. As I have got to write two anti-slavery addresses before the 20th, (a severe task, mechanically, at least) you must not expect much editorial from my pen until after that time. I shall, however, forward you some of my *cuttings*.

Do you send a Liberator to Sarah A. Searl,[11] Natick, R. I.? If not, send it regularly, with some back numbers, and I will tell you the rest when I see you.

☞ Don't forget the bundle on Saturday — and, if you can, (but I do not expect it,) send in it a copy of this week's paper.

Love to all the friends.

Yours, faithfully,

Wm. L. Garrison.

ALS: Garrison Papers, Boston Public Library. The opening lines of this letter were printed in *Life*, II, 138–139.

1. Jeremiah 15:10, slightly modified.
2. "Appeal of Clerical Abolitionists on Anti-Slavery Measures" was published in the *New England Spectator*, August 2, 1837, and reprinted in *The Liberator*, August 11, 1837. It carried the signatures of five clergymen: Charles Fitch, Boston; David Sanford, Dorchester; William M. Cornell, Quincy; Jonas Perkins, Weymouth; and Joseph H. Towne, Boston. Only Towne and Fitch had been associated with the antislavery movement and they, apparently, were the document's authors. (See *Life*, II, 136–137.) At the time Fitch was the pastor of the First Free Congregational Church and Towne was the pastor of the Salem Street Congregational Church. The "Clerical Appeal" expressed several grievances: (1) attacks in *The Liberator* upon a southern minister, the Reverend Mr. White, who had preached in Boston and had been accused in *The Liberator* of being a slaveholder; (2) "Insinuations," in *The Liberator*, that the Reverend George W. Blagden, who had been pastor of the Salem Street Congregational Church, was a slaveholder; (3) "Demands" by *The Liberator* that ministers read antislavery notices in their pulpits; (4) the tendency among abolitionists to divert support from "Foreign and Home Missions" and "Tract and Bible and Education Societies" to the antislavery cause; (5) the "abuse which is heaped upon ministers of the gospel, and other excellent Christians, who do not feel prepared to enter fully into the efforts of anti-slavery societies."
    In the issue of *The Liberator* which printed the "Clerical Appeal," there also appeared a reply by Oliver Johnson, as editor *pro tem* of *The Liberator*. The next number of *The Liberator* (August 18) carried further replies by Amos A. Phelps, then general agent of the Massachusetts Anti-Slavery Society, and by Garrison.
3. Garrison's review appeared in *The Liberator*, August 18, 1837, under the title, "A Layman's Reply to a Clerical Appeal." It occupied the entire first page and two columns of the second page.
4. Unidentified.
5. Matthew 6:10.
6. A small island near Newburyport, Massachusetts, most of which is now a wildlife sanctuary.
7. John Quincy Adams delivered an antislavery address at Newburyport on July 4. A summary of the address was reprinted from the Salem *Register* in *The Liberator* on July 14, 1837.

8. A notice in *The Liberator* on August 4, 1837, stated that "a special meeting of the Windham County (Connecticut) Anti-Slavery Society, will be held at the Town Hall in Hampton, on Monday, the 21st of August, at 1 o'clock, P. M., relative to the annexation of Texas to the American Union. It is expected that George Bourne of New York, Wm. Lloyd Garrison of Boston, and several gentlemen of the County, will address the meeting." The notice was entitled, "Connecticut, to the rescue!"

9. John E. Fuller was a member of the Reverend Charles Fitch's congregation.

10. On June 30, 1837, and in several subsequent issues, *The Liberator* printed a notice with the heading "American Anti-Slavery Almanac for 1838, N. Southard, Editor." The notice read: "The American Anti-Slavery Almanac, for 1838, will be published on the 1st of July next. No pains or expense have been spared in producing a valuable Abolition Tract. The calculations and engravings cost $150. It will contain articles from the most prominent friends of Abolition in the country. It also comprises facts and information concerning slavery which cannot fail to render it interesting to the friends of Abolition, and a terror to slaveholders.

"The calculations are got up with great care, by an experienced gentleman, who has been for many years devoted to the subject of astronomy. On each calendar page, there is to be an appropriate engraving, representing slavery in its different stages. There is also an elegant frontispiece on the title page. . . .

"D. K. Hitchcock, Publisher,
Boston, May 26,   No. 9, School-st."

11. Unidentified.

88

TO ORSON S. MURRAY

Brooklyn, Ct. August 11, 1837.

Beloved Brother:

I thank you for communicating to me the pleasing intelligence, that a State Convention, to deliberate upon the subject of PEACE, is to be held at Middlebury [1] during the present month. If my engagements would permit, I should be most happy to attend the Convention as a silent member at least, if not to take a part in its discussions; for though abolitionists are accused (falsely accused, I think) of being too much, nay, *wholly* absorbed in the anti-slavery cause, — I, for one, (to whom this charge may *seem* to apply with special propriety,) deny that my thoughts are concentrated upon a single point, or that I deem an interest in the emancipation of my enslaved countrymen to be paramount to all other obligations. In giving my attention to the degradation and misery of two millions of American bondmen, I do not forget mankind. My mind is busy in the investigation of many subjects, which, in their full elucidation and practical bearings, are destined to shake the nations. The subject of PEACE is among them, and peculiarly dear to me.

The sweetest strain of melody that mortals have ever heard, burst forth in the angelic song — 'Glory to God in the highest, and on earth *peace*, good will towards men.' [2] The prophet takes his harp and sings — 'How beautiful upon the mountains are the feet of him that bringeth good tidings, that publisheth *peace!*' [3] Christ appears as the Prince of *Peace*, of the increase of whose government and *peace*, (the prophecy runs,) there shall be no end. The legacy that he bequeathed to his disciples was *peace* — 'Peace I leave with you, my peace I give unto you.' [4] The kingdom of God is righteousness and *peace*. The fruit of the spirit is love, joy, *peace*, long-suffering, gentleness. God hath called us to *peace*, and to have *peace* one with another, and to follow *peace* with all men. He styles himself the God of *peace*. 'Blessed are the *peace-makers*, for they shall be called the children of God.' [5]

Who is a *peace* man? Surely, not he who will fight to redress injury, or avert calamity. Not he who holds a military station, or commands a naval ship. Not he who appears on muster day, 'armed and equipped as the law directs,' for the performance of military duty. Not he who, as a Senator or Representative, votes for the building of fortifications or naval vessels. Not he who fills the station of 'commander-in-chief of all the military forces.' * Not he who gives his sanction to that thoroughly anti-christian institution, the Academy at West Point, and approvingly fires a cannon. He may, indeed, be a *Doctor of Divinity*, but not a man of *peace*.† Not he who usurps authority over

---

* The following are the words of a Section in the Constitution of Massachusetts: — 'The Governor of this Commonwealth, for the time being, shall be the commander-in-chief of the army and navy, and of all the military forces of the State, by sea and land; and shall have full power, by himself, or by any commander, or other officer or officers, from time to time, to train, instruct, exercise and govern the militia and navy; and for the special defence and safety of the Commonwealth, to assemble in martial array, and put in warlike posture the inhabitants thereof; and to lead and conduct them, and with them to encounter, repel, resist, expel, and pursue, by force of arms, as well by sea as by land, within or without the limits of this Commonwealth, and also to KILL, SLAY, and DESTROY, if necessary, and conquer, by all fitting ways, enterprises and means whatsoever, all and every such person and persons, as shall, at any time hereafter, in a hostile manner, attempt or enterprize the destruction, invasion, detriment, or *annoyance* of this Commonwealth; and to use and exercise, over the army and navy, and over the militia in actual service, the *law martial*, in time of war or invasion, and also in time of rebellion declared by the Legislature to exist, as occasion shall necessarily require; and to take and surprise, *by all ways and means whatsoever*, (!) all and every such person or persons with their ships, arms, ammunition, and other goods, as shall, in a hostile manner, invade, or attempt the invading, conquering, or *annoying* this Commonwealth;' &c. &c. It is evident, from this Section, that no man can be Governor of Massachusetts, and execute or swear to execute the provisions of the Constitution, and at the same time be a Christian. 'If any man have not the spirit of Christ, he is none of his.' 'Let God be true, though every man a liar.' I repeat it, *no man can be a Christian who consents to be Governor of Massachusetts, and to support its present Constitution.*

† See an account of a recent visit of President Wayland to West Point, in the New-York Spectator and in the Vermont Telegraph.

his fellow-man, and denies the equality of our race. Not he who delights to celebrate the deeds of Bunker Hill, of Saratoga,[6] and of Monmouth! ‡ Not he who cannot forgive the worst of injuries, the most flagrant of insults, but demands an eye for an eye, and a tooth for a tooth, at the hands of government. Not he who regards his country, or his own countrymen, to the disparagement or injury of a foreign nation or people. Not he who is one only in the *abstract*.

Who, then, is a *peace* man? He who is made perfect in love; who loves his neighbor as himself, whether that neighbor resides upon 'Greenland's icy mountains,'[7] or wanders upon 'India's coral strand;'[8] who is willing to be always delivered unto death for Jesus' sake; who can take joyfully the spoiling of his goods, and glory in tribulation; who when smitten on the one cheek, can turn the other also — when reviled, revileth not again; who loves his enemies, blesses those who curse him, does good to those who hate him, and prays for those who despitefully use him and persecute him;[9] who is harmless as a dove, and like a lamb in the midst of wolves; who rejoices to be a partaker of Christ's sufferings; who, when he suffers, threatens not, but committeth himself to him who judgeth righteously; who will not fight under any circumstances, or for any pretences whatsoever; the weapons of whose warfare are not carnal, but spiritual; whose loins are girt about with truth, who puts on the breast-plate of righteousness, whose feet are shod with the preparation of the gospel of peace, and who takes the shield of faith, the helmet of salvation, and the sword of the Spirit.[10] He, and he only, is a *peace* man.

I presume the object of the Convention at Middlebury is not merely to discuss the subject of peace, but also to decide upon the expediency of organizing a State Peace Society. Allow me, then, to make a few suggestions. See to it, with ceaseless vigilance and holy jealousy, that you build upon a sure foundation. Do not make the American Peace Society ¶ and its auxiliaries, your pattern. They are radically defective in principle, and based upon the sand; and, in my opinion,

‡ Our fathers deserve to be eulogized for their hatred of oppression, but they had no right, *as Christians*, to slaughter their oppressors. If they had, then our southern slaves have a better right to cut throats and destroy life than any other people on the face of the earth, because their yoke is heavier, their chains more galling, and their sufferings more intolerable.

¶ I think I have understood that the American Peace Society incorporated the doctrine of non-resistance into its Constitution in May last. If this be so, let it have the credit; yet that must fall almost exclusively upon WILLIAM LADD; for at the last annual meeting of that Society, the chairman, in pronouncing a well-merited eulogium upon Mr. Ladd, said that *he* constituted, in fact, the American Peace Society! I hope to be more deeply engaged in the cause of Peace by and by, than I can at present; and, unless they alter their present course, the first thing I shall do will be to serve our Peace Societies, as I have done the Colonization Societies.

will do just as much towards suppressing the spirit of violence among men, as the Colonization Society will do in abolishing prejudice and slavery — that is to say, they are mischievous, instead of being beneficial, because they occupy the ground without being able to effect the object. What a farce it is to see a Peace Society enrolling upon its list of members, not converted, but belligerous commanders-in-chief, generals, colonels, majors, corporals, and all! What a wonderful reform may be expected where there are none to be reformed! Five or six years ago, I heard my esteemed and truly philanthropic friend, WILLIAM LADD, of Minot, (Me.) deliver a Peace address in Boston. After exhibiting the astonishing costliness of war, and vividly portraying its manifold horrors, and showing how many wars had been waged for purposes alike paltry and criminal, he concluded by making an appeal in behalf of the American Peace Society, telling the audience in a very emphatic manner not to misunderstand him — that that Society was not 'a Quaker Society' — that it did not meddle with the question of defensive war — &c. &c. I told him the next day, that I was truly grieved to see him wasting his time, his talents, and his means, in the advocacy of such a Society, and that no reform could possibly be accomplished by it. 'For,' said I, 'if your audience, last evening, had been composed entirely of military men, they would have found no fault with your discourse, but rather have given their assent to all its statements. You said that war is ruinous to morals. Granted, would be their reply. That it sheds much blood, destroys many victims, makes many widows and orphans. Granted. That it is a terrible calamity, in all its aspects. Granted. That it is often frightfully expensive — often waged under the most frivolous pretences — and that we should all aim to promote peace between the nations of the earth. Granted. So far, you and they would agree. Did you go any further? No. What did you tell them they might do, in case the American flag should be insulted, or the country invaded? Did you proclaim the utter unlawfulness of resorting to arms in such cases? No. Did you reprobate defensive war? No. You wished them to remember that yours was not *a Quaker Society* — in other words, that it was dumb on those radical points, and *charitably* left every man to decide for himself — nay, not wholly dumb, for in its publications the doctrine of non-resistance is repudiated. You have no body to reform, friend Ladd. Be assured that, until you occupy other ground — until your cause is honored with lynch law, a coat of tar and feathers, brickbats and rotten eggs — no radical *reform* can take place, to the ushering in of that period when 'swords shall be beaten into ploughshares, and spears into pruning-hooks, and men shall not *learn war* any more.' [11] This was, substantially, what I told him. He is now, I rejoice to know, an 'ultra,' 'reckless,' 'fanatical' advocate of Peace, and will not, as a true *peace* man, *fight shy* any more.

Again. Do not hope, should you organize a Society on right principles, to see it popular in its infancy. In the nature of things, and according to the present state of public sentiment, it must be the slowest and most difficult of all reforms, and yet the cause has infinite vitality in itself. It is easy, comparatively, to be an abolitionist, and to convert men to abolitionism, — because it is to sympathize with an oppressed and deeply injured people, and common humanity requires it. It is easier still to be a cold water man, — because it is very injurious to personal health, and also to morals, to drink alcoholic liquors. It is easiest of all to be in favor of foreign missions, — because but a small sacrifice of money is required. But to be a Peace man, in the true acceptation of that term, is to be forever powerless (physically) against injury, insult, and assault — to trust solely to the living God for protection — to be incapable of returning blow for blow, either personally or by proxy. Moreover, it is to oppose all military preparations, and call for the demolition of all our fortifications, naval ships, &c. Do you suppose many mighty, many noble, many wise, will *first* be willing to bear this cross, and to conduct this enterprise? I tell you, nay. — It must be done by the 'foolish,' the 'weak,' and the 'base.' [12] Yet the American Peace Society sprung into existence under the auspices of Governors, Generals, and the Rabbies of the land, as its patrons and supporters! — a proof, in itself, that it had no reforming principle in its constitution — for such men *never* take the lead in the unpopular and disgraceful task of reforming mankind.

May the God of peace be felt, acknowledged and obeyed in your Convention, that his blessing may rest upon you all, is the prayer of

Yours, in the gospel of peace,

WM. LLOYD GARRISON.

Orson S. Murray.

Printed in *The Liberator*, September 8, 1837 (from the *Vermont Telegraph*.)

For information about Orson S. Murray see letter 28, to Helen E. Garrison, May 21, 1836.

1. Vermont.
2. Luke 2:14.
3. Isaiah 52:7.
4. John 14:27.
5. Matthew 5:9.
6. After a series of defeats by American troops under Horatio Gates and Benedict Arnold, General John Burgoyne, the English commander, surrendered to the American forces at Saratoga, New York, on October 17, 1777.

At the battle of Monmouth Courthouse on June 28, 1778, Washington turned a flight by American troops under General Charles Lee into a drawn battle.

7. From the hymn "From Greenland's Icy Mountains," by Bishop Reginald Heber (1783–1826), of England.

8. *Ibid.*
9. A paraphrase of Luke 6:27–28.
10. Ephesians 6:14–17.
11. Isaiah 2:4.
12. Garrison refers to I Corinthians 1:26–28.

89

TO OLIVER JOHNSON

BROOKLYN, August 14, 1837

MY DEAR FRIEND:

What an oath-taking, war-making, man-enslaving religion is that which is preached, professed, and practised in this country! It is like 'clouds without water, carried about of winds; trees whose fruit withereth, without fruit, twice dead, plucked up by the roots; raging waves of the sea, foaming out their own shame.' [1] Its main pillars are Judaism and Popery,[2] and no wonder the crazy superstructure is tottering to its fall. But God is preparing something better, to redeem, regenerate, and give rest to this troubled world. Out of the ruins of the various religious sects, (for they are all to be destroyed by the brightness of the coming of Christ,) materials of holiness shall be gathered to build up a spiritual house, and to constitute a royal priesthood. Below is a poetical effusion, on the subject of CHRISTIAN REST, to which my mind and head have just given birth.[3]

Yours, in the bonds of love,

W. L. G.

Printed in *The Liberator*, August 25, 1837.

1. Jude 12–13.
2. Garrison's interpretation of Judaism and Catholicism is an extreme fundamentalist Protestantism which cannot find anything of value in either of its predecessors.
3. The poem by Garrison, which appeared below the letter, was entitled "True Rest" and occupied the better part of the column. It was included, with slight alterations, under the title of "Christian Rest," in the collection of "Sonnets and Other Poems by William Lloyd Garrison" published in Boston by Oliver Johnson in 1843.

90

TO JOSEPH H. KIMBALL

BROOKLYN, Ct. Aug. 16, 1837.

J. H. KIMBALL,

My dear Coadjutor, — Although your friendly and spirit-stirring letter, inviting me to attend the Young Men's State Anti-Slavery Convention, to be held in Concord on the 22d inst.[1] was received at an early date, I had previously made an engagement to address the people of this county on the 21st, in relation to the admission of Texas into the Union, and am therefore obliged to forego the thrilling pleasure of taking a part in your deliberations. Not having yet completed half of three-score years and ten, I may be allowed, on the score of age, to rank myself as A YOUNG MAN with the members of your convention; and by affinity of sentiment, and kindred zeal in defence of the weak against the powerful, in love of country and of universal liberty, I claim to have my name enrolled upon your list. *E. Pluribus Unum.*

The rallying together of a portion (a large portion, I hope, but whether large or small, the *best* portion) of the young men of New Hampshire, at this tremendous crisis, for the purpose of deliberating upon the best plan to be adopted for the preservation of our own liberties, and for the emancipation of the millions who are in our midst as slaves, is equally a test and an exhibition of character, at once patriotic and magnanimous. In venturing to style them the *best* portion of the young men of New Hampshire, (including, of course, those who shall unavoidably be absent) my object is neither to flatter *them* nor to disparage *others*, but simply to anticipate the sure and honorable verdict of an enlightened, impartial and enfranchised posterity. Personally, with very few exceptions, I know them not; and yet, so exactly do I know what qualities are indispensable, in troubled and perilous times, to make men, whether young or old, willing to stand forth and unflinchingly "bide the peltings of the pitiless storm'[2] — willing, for the sake of truth and in the cause of right, to make themselves of no reputation, and to be the martyrs of the age in which they live — I am almost certain that an extraordinary share of physical endurance, intellectual endowment, moral courage, and christian philanthropy, will be found in the convention, 'our enemies themselves being judges.'[3] I may therefore most appropriately adopt the language of the venerable apostle who was banished to Patmos — 'I write unto you, YOUNG MEN, because ye are STRONG.'[4] I trust it may be added with as much propriety — 'FOR THE WORD OF GOD ABIDETH IN YOU, and ye have overcome the wicked one.'[5]

There have been dark and gloomy periods in the history of this nation, but none so dark, none so gloomy, none so full of solemnity as the present. The suspense was indeed awful throughout the revolutionary struggle — for the conflict between liberty and despotism was most unequal, and at times seemed to be approaching a fatal termination. Washington, and Adams, and Hancock, were outlaws. The men who gave their signatures to the declaration of independence knew not but an ignominious death upon the gallows would be their fate. Those who battled for their rights were regarded and threatened as traitors. But the people of the colonies, as a body, were united — a thousand natural advantages, arising from their remoteness from the mother country, were on their side — the colossal power of France came seasonably to their assistance — and, terminate as that contest might, their ultimate independence in the course of time was certain. The embargo and the war of 1812–15, constituted another trying period, but less appalling in its aspect, and far less doubtful in its issue, than that of the revolution. At each of those periods, however, some of the wisest and most patriotic found their hearts occasionally failing them for fear, and for looking after those things which seemed to threaten the destruction of the land. What, then, ought to be the feelings of every lover of his country, every friend of his race, at the present time?

Will it be asked, what reason is there for sadness or dismay? why should we not eat, drink, and be merry? are we not a mighty and prosperous people? who can do us any harm? Such questions *are* asked, daily, not by men of reflection and foresight — not by those who realize, in the total overthrow of ancient nations, how fearful a thing it is for a guilty people to fall into the hands of the living God,[6] and especially to contend with Jehovah of hosts, as if he were such an one as themselves — but they are asked by the affectedly wise, who wear the cap and bells of folly as a crown of wisdom; by the basely selfish, who think of nothing, care for nothing, aim at nothing, but the promotion of their own private ends; by the shamelessly corrupt, whose hearts are more indurated than granite; by the culpably ignorant, who are willing to be led by the nose like beasts, whenever and wherever aspiring demagogues may elect; by the stupidly indifferent, who deprecate nothing so much as excitement, and whose cry is, 'Yet a little more sleep, a little more slumber, a little more folding of the hands to sleep;'[7] by the hypocritically patriotic, who theorize like angels, but act like devils. To all these questions, the prophet Nahum [8] furnishes an apposite and most emphatic reply: — 'Wo to the bloody land! it is all full of lies and robberies; *the prey departeth not*; the noise of the WHIP, and the noise of the rattling of the wheels, and of the prancing horses, and of the jumping chariots. . . . Art thou, [Columbia!] better than populous No, that was situate among the rivers, that had the waters round about it, whose rampart was the sea, and her wall was from the sea? Ethiopia and Egypt were her strength, *and it was infinite*; Put and Lubim were her helpers. Yet she was carried away, she went into captivity: her young children also were dashed to pieces at the top of all the streets: and they cast lots

for her honorable men, and all her great men were bound in chains.
. . . There is no healing of thy bruise; thy wound is grievous: all that
hear the bruit of thee shall clap the hands over thee: for upon whom
hath not thy wickedness passed continually?'

What shall we say of the discernment or understanding of those,
who, because the globe turns quite regularly on its axis, and the sun
rises and sets precisely as it has been wont to do since the creation,
and the moon gives her borrowed light without any diminution, and
the seasons alternate with no perceptible variation, and the trees bud
and blossom and bear fruit abundantly, and seed time and harvest
fail not, and the earth looks as green and beautiful as ever, and the
face of the heavens is perfectly serene — are so infatuated as to dream
that all is safe in the moral world, and that the pillars of our republic,
like those of the universe, will stand securely until come 'the wreck
of matter and the crush of worlds?' [9] Alas! that they constitute so large
a number of our population! 'Our fate,' says an eminent statesman, 'is
not foretold by signs and wonders: the meteors do not indeed glare
in the form of types, and print it legibly in the sky: but our warning
is as distinct, and almost as awful, as if it were announced in thunder
by the concussion of all the elements.' [10] Was the globe arrested in its
revolution when Edom was cast down, and the light of his glory extinguished as in a moment? — Edom, who dwelt in the clefts of the
rock, whose habitation was high, who exalted himself as an eagle, and
set his nest among the stars; and who said in the pride of his heart,
Who shall bring me down to the ground? [11] Did not the sun shine
brightly, and the moon reflect his beams, when Tyre was made a desolation and a terror? — Tyre, who filled many people, and enriched the
kings of the earth with the multitude of her riches and of her merchandise, and was the renowned city strong in the sea, the anointed
cherub upon the holy mountain of God.[12] Were the seasons utterly
changed, when Babylon was spoiled, and became heaps, and a dwell-
ing-place for dragons, an astonishment and a hissing, without an
inhabitant? — Babylon, who had her princes and her wise men, her
captains, and her rulers, and her mighty men, and her broad walls,
and her high gates.[13] Was the earth smitten with barrenness when
Jerusalem was made to swim in the blood of her inhabitants, and her
temples and palaces were burned with fire, and she was utterly wasted?
— Jerusalem, the chosen of the Lord, and the glory of the nations! [14]
No. In none of these instances of judicial visitation on account of
national transgressions, did Nature, by changing her laws or altering
her aspect, give premonitory warnings that destruction was at hand.

So in regard to this country. The stars shine brightly over our heads,
the ground upon which we tread is firm, and our rivers are sending

their waters peacefully to the sea. Are we therefore safe? *We are upon the brink of a fatal precipice*! Another step, and, as far as human foresight can reach, ALL IS LOST. What constitutes our guilt, and wherein is our condemnation as a people? 'Our hands are defiled with blood, and our fingers with iniquity; our lips have spoken lies, our tongue hath muttered perverseness. None calleth for justice, nor any pleadeth for truth.[15] The act of violence is in our hands,[16] and we make haste to shed innocent blood.[17] As for our iniquities, we know them; in transgressing and lying against the Lord, and departing away from our God, speaking oppression and revolt, conceiving and uttering from the heart words of falsehood. And judgment is turned away backward, and justice standeth afar off: for truth is fallen in the street, and equity cannot enter. Yea, truth faileth; and *he that departeth from evil maketh himself a prey.*' [18]

This is our condition, this our criminality, and this our liability to punishment. Blessed be God, however, the above description is not literally correct in every particular. There are some who call for justice, and not a few who plead for truth, and the number is increasing continually. There are trumpet-tones issuing from the hills and fastnesses of the GRANITE STATE,[19] and the ROCKY MOUNTAINS are sending back their echoes!

Young men of New-Hampshire! Remember the guilt of your country! For two hundred years her soil has been stained with human blood — blood warm and fresh, — the blood of innocence! She is now engaged in completing the extinction of the red men of the forest, once the occupants and owners of her soil, once multitudinous and powerful! For a period of almost two centuries, she illuminated all Africa with the flames of midnight conflagrations, kidnapped hundreds of thousands of her sable children, and made the Atlantic ocean populous with dead victims! She has buried like dogs, at least two millions of slaves, who were doomed to drag out a miserable existence in chains and slavery, on her own soil, until emancipated by death! She is yet holding in an iron bondage more than two millions of the descendants of Africa, waxing worse and worse in cruelty, growing more and more desperate in spirit, and hardening her heart continually against God! From this vast multitude, she withholds the Bible, all personal and civil rights, the sanctity of marriage, even the knowledge of the alphabet, all protection by law, and ranks and treats them as cattle and creeping things — selling woman by the pound, the infant from its nursing mother, and parents from their children, in lots to suit purchasers! She has purchased of foreign nations territories of immense extent, for the express purpose of extending slavery and the slave trade! Not satisfied with these, she has recently invaded a foreign

territory in violation of her national faith, revolutionized and con-
quered it, acknowledged its independence, and now intends annexing
it to her soil, for the same diabolical purpose — namely, to speed the
'trade in slaves and the souls of men!' [20]

Remember the situation of your country! — Recreant to her own
heaven-attested principles! Perjured before a horror-stricken world!
A byword and a hissing among the monarchists and despots of Europe!
Now fearfully exposed to the exterminating judgments of heaven!

Remember that LIBERTY is crucified in your country, and all her
true worshippers are branded as madmen, fanatics, and incendiaries!
That the constitution is trampled under foot, 'a blurred and tattered
parchment,' by a slaveholding faction and their northern adherents!
That the 'self-evident truths' embodied in the declaration of independence are now ridiculed by the rulers in church and state, as
'rhetorical flourishes' and 'splendid absurdities!' That the inalienable
rights of man are legally made to depend upon the color of his skin!
That freedom of speech and the press, without which men had better
be in their graves, is not tolerated in one half of the Union, and
scarcely permitted even upon the GRANITE HILLS of *republican* New
Hampshire! That the Union itself gives no protection to those who
dare to believe, ay, and to *say*, that slaveholding is in all cases a sin
against God, and war upon mankind! — That a price is set by southern
legislatures upon the heads of northern freemen, guilty of no crime!
That it is death by lynch law, and a penitentiary offence by express
statute, to obey the scriptural injunction — 'Open thy mouth for the
dumb, in the cause of all such as are appointed to destruction. Open
thy mouth, judge righteously, and *plead the cause of the poor and
needy.*' [21] That the sacred right of petition is struck down to the earth
by the despotic arm of Congress! That Texas is knocking for admission
into the Union, to aid in subjugating the freemen of the North, and
compel them to wear a southern yoke! That anarchy prevails in all
parts of the land, mob-law against the advocates of liberty being
sanctioned and administered by judges, lawyers, and the officers of
government, both in church and state, as well as by the ignorant
multitude! That even in New Hampshire, — so excessively boastful of
her regard for democracy — a talented, respectable and beloved minister of the gospel, while in the solemn act of prayer, has been dragged
from the pulpit by men clothed in the panoply of law, tried and condemned as a vagabond and brawler, and sentenced to imprisonment,
merely because he intended to express his views upon the subject
of southern slavery, and to examine that horrid system in the light of
revelation, and to measure it by our republican standard! [22] And
remember, too, that by assembling together as an anti-slavery con-

vention, each and all of you, on being apprehended in any State south of the Potomac, would be deemed worthy of stripes, and covered with a coat of tar and feathers, thrown into a loathsome prison, and perhaps suspended upon gibbets, even without the form of a trial by law! You would be safer in the hands of Turks and Arabs, of the pirates of the deep, than in those of American slaveholders!

Remember, then, the high, solemn and affecting responsibilities which now rest upon you — responsibilities which you cannot evade but at the peril of your souls, and to the certain destruction of your country. You are young men, and are therefore more deeply interested in the future, than if your locks were whitened with age. You are young men, into whose hands the reins of government are soon to fall, unless indeed tyranny shall succeed in overshadowing all the land; and whatever of reform is necessary to be done must be accomplished by you; for labor is not for the aged who are weak, but for young men who are strong. Should you be reproached for being engaged in the work of reformation, reply in the words of THOMAS JEFFERSON, who is venerated as an oracle by the democrats of New Hampshire — 'This enterprise is for the *young* — for those who can follow it up, and bear it through to its consummation.' Your State needs to be thoroughly regenerated. Not Georgia itself is more obsequious to southern despotism in Congress, than New Hampshire. Look at the conduct of your representatives, going all lengths with the south in opposition to the abolition of slavery and the slave trade in the District of Columbia, and in casting the petitions of the people back into their faces! [23] Look at their vote in favor of admitting Arkansas into the Union as a slaveholding State! [24] — Look at the extraordinary conduct of your *republican* legislature! [25] Look at the still more extraordinary message of your *republican* governor! [26] Tell your people that they must act as consistent democrats, or be branded as hypocrites and liars — and let them see to it that their representatives do not trample upon liberty, equality, and the rights of man. Whoever apologizes for oppression, and takes the side of the strong against the weak, and denies that all men are born free and equal, is not a democrat, but (if he pretends to be one) is a political wolf in sheep's clothing. Beware of such a man, and trust him not!

The question, whether it is best to organize yourselves into a State Society, is an important one, and will doubtless be fully discussed by you. My own convictions are, that *you ought to organize*, either as a society or as a convention to meet annually — but at all events TO ORGANIZE. My reasons are, briefly, because 'in union there is strength' [27] — because nothing effectual has been done in this cause except by organization — and because there is nothing which the slaveholders and their allies deprecate and fear more than our *combined* forces; and the fact that they are striving by every political and sectarian artifice *to divide us*, shows us clearly what is our duty — for it is a safe rule to disregard their advice in every thing except stirring up their slaves to revolt, and justifying them in fighting for liberty!

This letter is very prolix — but you will readily 'pardon something to the spirit of freedom.' [28]

Your faithful coadjutor,
WM. LLOYD GARRISON

Printed in *The Liberator*, September 1, 1837.

Joseph Horace Kimball (1813–1838) was in 1836 editor of the *Herald of Freedom*, recently founded at Concord, New Hampshire (Nathaniel P. Rogers did not become its sole editor until 1838). At the end of 1836 and the beginning of 1837, Kimball accompanied James A. Thome to the West Indies, from which there emerged their report, *Emancipation in the West Indies: A Six Months Tour in Antigua, Barbadoes and Jamaica in 1837*, published in New York in 1838 by the American Anti-Slavery Society. (His obituary, entitled "Another Severe Bereavement," appeared in *The Liberator*, April 20, 1838; see also *Weld-Grimké Letters*, I, 484n.)

1. A detailed summary of the proceedings of the convention appeared in *The Liberator* on September 1, 1837, reprinted from the New Hampshire *Herald of Freedom*.

2. Shakespeare, *King Lear*, III, iv. 28.

3. Deuteronomy 32:31.

4. I John 2:14.

5. *Ibid.*

6. Hebrews 10:31, paraphrased.

7. Proverbs 6:10, slightly changed by the addition of "more" in each of the three clauses.

8. Nahum, Chapter 3, *passim.*

9. Joseph Addison (1672–1719), English essayist, poet, and playwright, *Cato*, I, v, 28.

10. Unidentified.

11. The description of Edom is adapted from Jeremiah 49:16–22 and Obadiah 3–4.

12. On Tyre, see Isaiah 23.

13. On Babylon, see Jeremiah 51:37.

14. On Jerusalem, see Jeremiah 39, 52.

15. Isaiah 59:3–4. The original speaks of "your" instead of "our."

16. Isaiah 59:6. The original speaks of "their" instead of "our."

17. Isaiah 59:7. Garrison substitutes "we" for the original "they."

18. Isaiah 59:12–15.

19. New Hampshire.

20. Revelation 18:13. In the previous lines, Garrison is referring to Texas.

21. Proverbs 31:8–9.

22. John N. McClintock, in *History of New Hampshire*, Boston, 1888, p. 572, reports: "A Methodist minister, engaged to give an anti-slavery lecture in Northfield, was arrested as a common *brawler*, and dragged from his knees and the pulpit as he was opening his meeting with prayer." The minister was George Storrs. See note 5 in letter 8, to Isaac Knapp, February 3, 1836.

At the time, certain communities in New Hampshire had enacted ordinances prohibiting the use of the pulpit for the preaching of antislavery sermons. One such community is referred to in the following resolution adopted by the Young Men's Anti-Slavery Convention in 1837.

"Resolved, that the resolution passed at the recent county association in Littleton in this state, shutting up the pulpit against the advocate of the perishing slave, is alike hard hearted and regardless of the sufferings of our countrymen in bondage, and in violation of the rights and property of pew-holders, and of the right of 'free discussion' " (*The Liberator*, September 1, 1837).

23. Franklin Pierce, who was later to serve as President of the United States, was a representative of New Hampshire from 1833 to 1837 and was a member of the committee of the United States House of Representatives which, on February 8, 1836, reported on the petitions to Congress to abolish slavery in the District of Columbia. The committee, whose chairman was Henry Laurens Pinckney of South Carolina, proved hostile to any attempt to abolish slavery in the District of Columbia and to the petitions themselves. In the three resolutions which it recommended to the House, it denied Congress's constitutional authority to interfere with slavery in any southern state, it recommended that "Congress ought not to interfere in any way with the slavery in the District of Columbia," and it urged "that all petitions, memorials . . . relating in any way or to any extent whatever, to the subject of slavery, or the abolition of slavery, shall, without either being printed or referred, be laid upon the table, and that no further action whatever shall be had thereon." The resolutions were adopted by the House on May 26, 1836. For a copy of the committee's report, see *The Liberator*, June 4, 1836.

24. Arkansas became a state on June 15, 1836. The vote in Congress to admit Arkansas took place on June 13. The New Hampshire delegation in the House consisted of Benning M. Bean, of Moultonboro; Robert Burns, of Plymouth; Franklin Pierce, of Hillsboro; Joseph Weeks, of Richmond; and Samuel Cushman, of Portsmouth. All except Cushman voted for the admission of Arkansas as a slave state. Cushman, apparently, did not vote.

25. On January 11, 1837, a select committee of the New Hampshire House of Representatives presented a report on the abolitionists to the house and recommended the passage of five resolutions, of which the first three read:

"*Be it resolved by the Senate and House of Representatives in General Court convened,* That we recognize the constitutional right of the several States of the Union to exercise exclusive jurisdiction within their own limits, on the subject of domestic slavery.

"*Be it further resolved,* That Congress cannot, without a violation of the public faith, abolish slavery in the District of Columbia, unless upon the request of the citizens of that District, and of the States by whom that territory was ceded to the General Government.

"*Be it further resolved,* That as the Union of the States can only be maintained by abstaining from all interference with the laws, domestic policy, and peculiar interests of every other State, the conduct of those who would coerce our fellow citizens in other States into the abolition of slavery, by inflammatory appeals addressed to the fears of the masters and the passions of the slaves, is in the highest degree censurable as tending to alienate one portion of our countrymen from another, and to introduce discord into our sister States, and as a violation of that spirit of compromise in which the constitution was framed, and a due observance of which is necessary to the safety of the Union. . . ."

The resolutions were adopted by overwhelming majorities.

The entire report, including the resolutions, appeared in *The Liberator*, February 11, 1837.

26. Governor Isaac Hill (1788–1851) had been a United States senator from New Hampshire from 1831 to 1836 and was governor of the state from 1836 to 1839. In his message to the state legislature in June 1836 he attributed the origin of slavery to the fact that "the whites found the colored race unaccustomed to

take charge of their own conduct, and fit only for servitude." Moreover, "it is considered disreputable for the master to maltreat his slave — as much or more so as it is in New England for the master to abuse his apprentice, or for an employer to impose hardships on those whom he has in charge." He affirmed that "the obligation of the whole country is to protect the RIGHTS which the slaveholder has in the slave. . . . It is not to be wondered that the master should feel obliged to deny the slave the means of instruction, when he knows that teaching him to read and write will increase his ability and his inclination to do his master injury." (Extracts from the message were printed in *The Liberator,* June 25, 1836; see also *BDAC.*)

27. Æsop, "The Bunch of Sticks."
28. Edmund Burke, *Speech on Conciliation with America, 22 March 1775.* Garrison substitutes "freedom" for "liberty."

---

9 1

TO GEORGE W. BENSON

Boston, Aug. 26, 1837.

Dear bro. George:

We arrived in Boston at quarter before 7 o'clock on Wednesday evening,[1] and found an almost empty house. Eliza and Mary S. Parker have gone to visit their parents. The only boarders besides ourselves, are bro. Phelps, Mr. Babcock,[2] and a young man. Bro. P. started yesterday morning for Farmington,[3] but could not go conveniently by the way of Brooklyn. I have seen a good many of our best abolition friends since my return, and have received a very cordial greeting from them all. The Fitch [4] party would be "less than nothing," were it not for the co-operation of our enemies with it. Bro. Fuller [5] assures me that there are not more than *three* members in the Free Church who can swallow the Appeal. Mr. Fitch will not probably remain here long. Bro. Whittier arrived here yesterday from New-York. I learn from him that our friends in New-York will not be disposed to make themselves a party in this controversy — though I do not see how they can fairly stand aloof from it. It behooves them to remember, that "silence gives consent" — and if they refuse to answer the Appeal, the enemy will construe their silence into a virtual approval of it. Bro. Stanton is also here, but expects to leave for N. Y. on Monday or Tuesday. He is somewhat cautious about committing himself, though he is disposed to stand by us. Father Bourne [6] left to-day noon for N. Y. I have just read a letter from our friend Lewis Tappan, addressed to bro. Phelps, in reference to the "clerical" disaffection. He says H. C. Wright will be recalled by the Executive Committee, unless he ceases interweaving his "no government" views with abolitionism.[7] He thinks it is unfortunate that the Massachusetts Anti-Slavery Society is connected at all with the Liberator, as it gives the enemy some advantage in saying, that the Society is responsible for all that I write and publish. We are to have a Board meeting on Monday,[8] expressly on this point; and what will be the result, I can hardly predict. Probably friend Knapp and myself will have to resume the pecuniary responsibilities of the paper, but these will probably be met by some of our brethren. If not, the paper cannot be sustained after the first of Jan. next.

I feel somewhat at a loss to know what to do — whether to go into all the principles of holy reform, and make the abolition cause subordinate, or whether still to persevere in the *one* beaten track as hitherto.[9] Circumstances hereafter must determine this matter.

Dear little George seems to miss his Brooklyn friends, and the old horse, the colt, the cows, and the hens, very much. He has already grown thin and pale, and is very restless. Helen will feel her confinement to two rooms as quite irksome — I wish she had somebody with her. We desire all possible love to be given to all the precious family circle.

Yours, lovingly,

Wm. Lloyd Garrison.

ALS: Garrison Papers, Boston Public Library. A portion of this letter was printed in *Life*, II, 159–160.

1. August 23, 1837. Garrison and his family had been staying in Brooklyn, Connecticut, at the Benson home, since June 17, 1837. It may well be that the furor created by the "Clerical Appeal" brought Garrison and his family back at this time.

2. Archibald D. Babcock (b. Mansfield, Connecticut, December 13, 1808), of Boston, was a partner of Charles Drew in the dry-goods business (Stephen Babcock, *Babcock Genealogy*, New York, 1903, p. 357).

3. Farmington, Connecticut, several miles west of Hartford.

4. The Reverend Charles Fitch.

5. John E. Fuller.

6. The Reverend George Bourne.

7. "Two months later, Mr. Wright's commission having expired, the Executive Committee would not renew it because of his peculiar peace views, and because he declined giving a pledge to confine himself to the discussion of abolitionism (MSS. Oct. 20, 1837, Abby Kelley to W. L. G.; Nov. 13, 1837, C. C. Burleigh to J. M. McKim)." (*Life*, II, 159n.)

8. August 28, 1837.

9. In a letter dated August 27, 1837, from Sarah Grimké to Henry C. Wright, Angelina Grimké added the following postscript: "What would'st thou think of the *Liberator* abandoning abolitionism as a *primary* object, and becoming the vehicle of *all* these grand principles? Is not the time rapidly coming for such a change; say after the contract with the Massachusetts Society is closed with the editor, the first of next year? I trust brother Garrison may be divinely directed." (*Life*, II, 161.)

9 2

TO JAMES T. WOODBURY

[August 28, 1837.]

Sir: — Your letter is a 'clerical' curiosity. To those who are acquainted with you, the most expressive term that can be applied to it — perhaps the *severest* — is to say that it is perfectly *characteristic*. In elegance of diction, refinement of taste, and serenity of temper — in brotherly kindness, christian suavity, and 'clerical' disinterestedness — in manner and matter, argument and illustration, candor and logic — it is a very rare composition. 'I never swallowed William Lloyd Garrison, and I never tried to swallow him,' is a piece of information, at once highly important and most forcibly expressed. It is a modest puff of Mr. Woodbury's bravery, independence, foresight, and sagaciousness, given by himself to himself. It is not less charitable than modest, in its 'insinuation,' ('the meanest and vilest form of lying,' *) that other persons — that abolitionists generally — have not merely *tried* to 'swallow' me, but have actually *succeeded* in swallowing me, and even made me 'the god of their idolatry.' Your distaste is not an isolated case. The robbers of God's poor, the supporters of lynch law, the chief priests, scribes and pharisees, have all been unable to 'swallow Wm. Lloyd Garrison,' and, like yourself, have never 'tried to swallow him.' In this particular, then, you are all agreed. For myself, I feel within me the instinct of self-preservation too strongly to be willing to allow either man or beast to swallow me, either in a figurative or literal sense. I desire to remain uneaten: my earnest entreaty is, that no man will think of making a meal of me, either in the gross, or in choice proportions. The conscience, humanity and good taste, displayed by you, are worthy of all praise — you have 'never tried to swallow' me — there is nothing of the cannibal in your disposition — in other words, you are not 'a wolf in sheep's clothing.' [1]

But this is too serious a matter for pleasantry. What is your disclaimer, sir, but a wanton impeachment of the self-respect, intelligence and piety of the thousands and tens of thousands of abolitionists, whose voices are cheering me on as I advance toward the citadel of slavery? You make a parade of your independence of thought and action, as if you were a prodigy — the *eighth* wonder of the world! You blow a blast through a penny trumpet, to arouse the nation to a sense of the fact, that you refuse to swallow a certain man, and are not guilty of idolatry! Your language, virtually, is as follows: — 'All

* 'Clerical Appeal.'

you who patronize the Liberator, and approve of the general course pursued by its editor, are nothing better than base and servile tools, or blind and infatuated supporters, or weak and ignorant dupes. Mr. Garrison is the god of your idolatry. You live, and move, and have your being, in him alone. His thoughts are yours — his understanding and conscience yours — his *ipse dixit* yours. You have 'swallowed' him — put him on — and he is as Christ unto you! But as for myself, *I*, James T. Woodbury, a 'clerical' teacher in Acton, make known unto you and to all the world, that *I* have never tried to swallow Wm. Lloyd Garrison. *I* have too much wisdom and strength, too much intelligence and virtue, too high a regard for the laws of God, to be tamely led by the nose, or be guilty of the sin of idolatry.' This, then, is a personal attack, not merely upon myself as one desiring to be worshipped as a god, but upon the great body of American abolitionists, who have uniformly given me the right hand of fellowship — upon such men as William Goodell, Elizur Wright, Jr., Arthur and Lewis Tappan, Beriah Green, Amos A. Phelps, James G. Birney, Gerrit Smith, and a host of others now ardently engaged in the anti-slavery cause. I leave it with these tried coadjutors and best friends of bleeding humanity to treat the aspersion as it deserves.

It is your boast that you have not swallowed the editor of this paper. Let us see. What do the slave-drivers of the South, and their northern apologists, consider as tantamount to 'swallowing Garrison'? This — the abandonment of the Colonization Society, and the adoption of the national Anti-Slavery Declaration. From the commencement of the campaign up to the present time, every man, who has joined the anti-slavery ranks, has had to endure the opprobrium of being stigmatized as 'a Garrison man,' or 'a Garrisonite,' or, in your choice phraseology, as 'swallowing Garrison.' This is personal experience and historical fact. When my friend Arthur Tappan espoused my abolition sentiments, he became, in popular language, 'a Garrisonite' — and so did James G. Birney. The rod which was held *in terrorem* over the heads of the people, by the rulers in church and state, to prevent their joining the abolition ranks, was, that by such a procedure they must be branded as 'Garrison men.' That rod is still held up, and it has frightened many a man from the performance of a high and solemn duty, because he has loved the praise of men more than the favor of God. Now, what does J. T. Woodbury say? — Hear him! — 'I am an abolitionist, *and I am so in the strictest sense of that term.*' Of course, then, you believe that the Colonization Society is the work of the devil, the prince of slaveholders; that every slaveholder is a man-stealer, whether he is a layman, priest, or doctor of divinity; that to enslave a man is to dethrone the Almighty; that immediate emanci-

pation, without compensation or expatriation, is the duty of the master
and the right of the slave; that prejudice against men on account of
their complexion is sinful; and that the cord of caste between the
white and black man ought to be burned with fire. Ask the editors of
the New York Observer, Boston Recorder, Vermont Chronicle, and
Christian Mirror, whether this is not 'swallowing Garrison.'

O! but I, James T. Woodbury, do not endorse Mr. Garrison's views
and sentiments on *other* subjects! Pray, sir, where is the abolitionist,
as an abolitionist, who does? Your disclaimer is a piece of superfluous
folly. Who in all the world ever supposed that abolitionists must be
responsible for each other's political or religious predilections? Who
ever supposed that Samuel J. May abandoned his Unitarian, or Amos
A. Phelps his Trinitarian, or John G. Whittier his Quaker principles,
by agreeing to join hands with others of a different sect for the rescue
of perishing millions? Who ever supposed that these individuals, by
becoming abolitionists, obligated themselves not to exercise their rights
of conscience and their liberty of speech in regard to other matters?
The truth is, sir, — in despite of your idle disclaimer, — you have
swallowed me to the same extent, and with as much gusto, as either
of those coadjutors; i.e. you have given your sanction to all the anti-
slavery principles and measures which I have ever advocated — and
they have done no more. It is something worse than effrontery, it is
black ingratitude for you to say — 'Desert Mr. Garrison I would, if
I ever followed him. *But I never did!*' How dare you to sacrifice truth
in this manner? You *have* followed me (if your professions have not
been hypocritical) from the colonization to the abolition ranks; from
gradual to immediate emancipation; from associating with slaveholders
as Christians to repudiating them as thieves and robbers, and 'sinners
of the first rank.' To whom, under God, are you indebted but to myself,
(and I put the interrogation in self-defence, not boastingly,) for your
present views and feelings in opposition to slavery? I remember, indeed, that you have dated your conversion to abolitionism back to the
time that you stood by Washington's tomb, (if I mistake not, a period
since my labors commenced in this sacred cause) — but I presume,
anxious as you seem to be to have the reputation of being a *thinking*
and an *independent* man, you will not pretend to say that you would
have endorsed in 1831, the sentiments which you cherish in 1837, respecting the guilt of every slaveholder, and the exact nature of slavery. But this is not material. No man may hope to be an abolitionist
'in the strictest sense of the term,' and yet escape the charge of being
'a follower of Garrison.' I admit that the charge is a false one, whenever
and wherever applied to any individual — and that to be an abolitionist
is, in that particular, to follow the Spirit of Truth; I admit that no man

can follow me, (i.e. make me his oracle, or light, or guide, instead of the Incarnate Word,) without being an idolator; but how can you say that you have not come after me in the contest with American slavery? I heard nothing of you in this cause till it had found a multitude of supporters.

Your gratuitous and hot denial that you have *swallowed* me, (what a ridiculous idea!) and that you have *followed* me, and your grievous assertion, that with some abolitionists I am 'the god of their idolatry,' evince a jealous, petulant temper, an acerbity of spirit, wholly unbecoming — I was about to say 'a clerical abolitionist,' but as I know of no such person, I will add — utterly unworthy of a professed disciple of Jesus. You seem to be almost as angry as my worst enemies, in finding that all attempts to make me odious are worse than useless. Hitherto you have cordially taken me by the hand, and inquired, 'Art thou in health, my brother?' [2] and now you are striving to stab me under the fifth rib with a sectarian dagger, a viler weapon than a Bowie knife. In the next Liberator — for I have not room to-day — I shall endeavor to show that you have worn two faces — one, friendly and smiling in my presence — the other, hostile and frowning when your back was turned. Remember that you are the assailant, and that I merely stand on the defensive.

Your complaint in the postscript to your letter, is, that I 'embody abolition,' and am 'abolition personified and incarnate,' — that is, 'with some.' What do you mean by such language? If nothing more than that my abolition principles are regarded by the friends of immediate emancipation as irrefragably true, then you are in the same predicament with them — for you profess to agree with me in those principles. If you mean, (and this is doubtless the 'insinuation' you intend to convey,) that those who co-operate with me would 'swallow' me even if I should abandon the anti-slavery ground — that if I should espouse the Colonization Society, they would still obsequiously regard me as 'abolition personified and incarnate' — then I have only to repeat, that your poisoned arrows are aimed at other bosoms besides my own, and that you are guilty of wholesale calumny. I 'embody abolition' just as a thorough-going, consistent temperance-man embodies temperance — and in no other light. Is it an abolitionist who reproaches me, and calumniates others, because my advocacy of human rights has been consistent and just, and has won the respect and confidence of a great multitude of good men? How has it happened that I have brought around me, in delightful association, men of all political parties and of all religious sects, notwithstanding the mightiest efforts have been made all over the nation to crush me to the earth, and to make me appear vile in the eyes of the people? It is a problem which has puzzled all the popularity hunters both in Church and State. But you know something of the rise and progress of the anti-slavery cause, through my humble instrumentality. I was a poor, self-educated mechanic — without important family connexions, without influence, without wealth, without station — patronized by nobody, laughed at by all, reprimanded by the prudent, contemned by the wise, and avoided for a time even by the benevolent. I stood alone, an object of wonder, pity, scorn and malevolence. You can realize nothing of the trials, discouragements and perils, through which I have had to pass. The pressure upon me was like an avalanche, and nothing but the power of God sustained me. The clergy were against me — the rulers of the people were against me — the nation was against me. But God and his truth, and the rights of man, and the promises of the Holy Scriptures, were with me; and having found a partner whose vision was as clear, whose faith was as strong, and whose self-denial was as great, as my own, I commenced that warfare which is now going on with such glorious success. From the very first moment that I buckled on my armor, I was assured that I could not maintain my ground; that I should retard, instead of aiding the cause of emancipation; that my language was not to be tolerated; that my principles and measures were wild and untenable; and that no person of sane mind would rally under my standard. The entreaties, and warnings, and prophecies, and rebukes, which my determination elicited, were numberless; and had I been influenced by them, had not God made my forehead strong against the foreheads of the people,[3] the bark of abolition would have been wrecked upon the rocks and quicksands of human expediency. I will not stop to trace the progress of this great enterprise. Suffice it to say, that its growth has been such as to astonish nations. Now, sir, if I possess any influence, it has been obtained by being utterly regardless of the opinions of mankind; if I have acquired any popularity, it has been owing to my sturdy unwillingness to seek that honor which comes from men; if I have been 'swallowed' by any body, it is because I have always refused to 'confer with flesh and blood.'[4] I have flattered no man, feared no man, bribed no man. Yet having made myself of no reputation, I have found a reputation; having refused to be guided by human opinions, I have won 'golden opinions'[5] from the best of men; having sought that honor which comes from God, I am not left without honor among my countrymen. Now, sir, are you jealous of my 'good name and fame?' Because Mordecai has been promoted, are you troubled in spirit? Do you remember who it was that was suspended upon Haman's gallows?[6]

These things are extorted from me by necessity. Like an apostle, 'I am become a fool in glorying: you have compelled me: for I ought to have been commended of you.[7] Seeing that many glory after the flesh, I will glory also. For ye suffer fools gladly, seeing ye yourselves are wise.' [8]

Your assertions that I am laboring, as editor of the Liberator, 'to overthrow the Christian Sabbath, and the Christian ministry, and the Christian ordinances, and the visible church, and all human and family governments,' and that with the cause of abolition I am 'determined to carry forward and propagate and enforce my peculiar theology,' are utterly destitute of truth. Upon all these topics, I have my own views, but I have never enforced them as an abolitionist. As to the Sabbath, I am as orthodox as was John Calvin; as to the christian ministry, I hold to a 'royal priesthood'; [9] as to the Christian ordinances, I believe in eating the flesh and drinking the blood of the Incarnate Word, and being baptized into the death of the Son of God; as to the visible church, I believe that there is such a church, but visible only to those who are gifted with spiritual vision; as to human and family governments, I agree with an apostle, that 'the powers that be are ordained of God,' [10] and that it is the religious duty of parents to bring up their children 'in the nurture and admonition of the Lord.' [11] This is my jacobinism, and these are my heresies; but they do not necessarily constitute any part of abolitionism.

You are disposed to quarrel with me as an editorial purveyor. You remember the old adage, '*De gustibus*,' &c.[12] It seems that *you* like nothing but *veal*: onions, and garlics, and spice, and pepper, are an abomination to you. I rather marvel that one who deals so freely in pepper as yourself, should not be fond of it; for no one can partake of a single dish served up by you, without finding it to taste strongly of that ingredient. Like a friend of mine, you sometimes put *cayenne* all over plum pudding. Now, my dear sir, there are two things you will please to remember: first, that the Liberator was not established to give you nothing but veal; and secondly, that though *you* do not like onions, &c. there are a great many persons who do. If you do not fancy my dishes, you need not eat them; but, in the name of vigorous appetites and good digestions, I protest against your making your taste a standard by which my customers shall regulate theirs.

WM. LLOYD GARRISON.

Boston, Aug. 28, 1837.

Printed in *The Liberator*, September 1, 1837. Much of this letter is also reprinted in *Life*, II, 155–156.

The Reverend James Trask Woodbury (b. Francestown, New Hampshire, May 9, 1803; d. Milford, Massachusetts, January 16, 1861) of Acton, Massachusetts, brother of Levi Woodbury, then secretary of the treasury, and one of the seventy agents of the American Anti-Slavery Society, had written a letter to the *New England Spectator* (it appeared there on August 23), dated August 17, 1837, in which he praised the "Clerical Appeal." Addressing himself to "Dear Brothers Fitch and Towne," he wrote: "I am an abolitionist, and I am so in the strictest sense of the term; but I never swallowed Wm. Lloyd Garrison, and I never tried

to swallow him. If that be the 'Shiboleth,' — if that be the test, I am no abolitionist and never was, though I have said and done for the cause what I have.
I have seen, as I think, in Mr. Garrison, a decided wish, nay, a firm resolve, in
laboring to overthrow slavery, to overthrow the Christian Sabbath, and the Christian ministry. His doctrine is, that every day is a Sabbath, and every man his own
minister. There are no Christian ordinances, — there is no visible church. . . .
But I am now well satisfied that with the cause of *abolition he is determined to
carry forward and propagate and enforce his peculiar theology.* He is not satisfied
to teach his readers and hearers the truth as he holds it in reference to slavery
and its abolition, but he must indoctrinate them, too, on human governments and
family government and the Christian ministry and the Christian Sabbath, and the
Christian ordinances. Slavery is not merely to be abolished, but nearly everything
else." Woodbury's letter was reprinted in *The Liberator,* September 1, 1837,
the issue which also printed Garrison's reply. (*Life,* II, *passim;* IV, 423–424.)

1. Æsop.
2. II Samuel 20:9.
3. Ezekiel 3:8, paraphrased.
4. Galatians 1:16 — "Immediately I conferred not with flesh and blood."
5. Shakespeare, *Macbeth,* I, vii, 33.
6. See the Book of Esther.
7. II Corinthians 12:11.
8. II Corinthians 11:18–19.
9. I Peter 2:9.
10. Romans 13:1.
11. Ephesians 6:4.
12. "*De gustibus non est disputandum,*" "there is no disputing concerning tastes."

---

9 3

TO LEWIS TAPPAN

Boston, Sept. 13, 1837.

My dear friend:

I have just learnt that Mr. Chapman [1] will leave in the morning for
New-York; and although it is the proper time for me to retire to rest,
I feel constrained to send you a very few lines.

The studied silence of the Emancipator, respecting the "Clerical
Appeal," fills me with surprise and regret, and, in my opinion, if it
be continued longer, will not only create much dissatisfaction on the
part of New-England abolitionists, but call for a plain rebuke through
the columns of the Liberator. What is the meaning of it? The organ
of the Parent Society ought to be the first to discern any defection
from our cause, and to sound the alarm when efforts are made to divide
our ranks. If it be a sound maxim, that "silence gives consent," then it
would seem that you in New-York approve of the "Appeal." But I am
told, by letters, that you are disposed to view the affair as strictly
local in its bearing, and personal in its discussion, and therefore you

mean to have nothing to do with it — nay, that you are wondering and lamenting that I regard it as of so much importance as to give it even a passing notice. Is this indeed so? Then I can only marvel at the short-sightedness of you all. My dear friend, is it a small matter that, in the very crisis of our campaign, sedition shows itself in our camp — bold and rampant sedition? Does it indeed not concern the Parent Society, that five clergymen, professed abolitionists, have publicly impeached the benevolence, disinterestedness and real design of the abolition cause and its "leading" advocates? Is it nothing that they have taken sides with those time-serving clergymen, who refuse to espouse the side of the down-trodden slave, because they would otherwise risk their salary or their popularity? Is it magnaminous to leave me to manage this trying case, single-handed, as if it were my own special concern, when it is as much yours as it is mine? What belongs to me I am willing to take, and able to bear; but what affects the whole cause should be a matter of common concern. How is it possible that you in New-York can persuade yourselves that either policy or duty requires you to say nothing about the "Appeal"? (I say nothing of the subsequent Protests,[2] for they are mere after thoughts, and chiefly personal and sectarian in their character.) In the "Appeal," the only complaints urged against the Liberator relate to the charge brought against Mr. White,[3] and the question propounded to Mr. Blagden.[4] So far, then, the Liberator was strictly implicated, and the matter was exclusively local and personal. But when the "Appeal" goes on to justify those clergymen who stand aloof from our cause, and who refuse to read on any occasion an anti-slavery notice; when it arraigns in general terms, (and the more cruel for being general, and not specific,) "the movements of some leading abolitionists," an opprobrious phraseology which may be applied to the active advocates of liberty in all parts of our country, when it accuses abolitionists of resorting to "the press-gang system of doing things"; when it proceeds to argue that an abolition clergyman has no right to open his mouth for the dumb in a brother's pulpit; when it insinuates that abolitionists, as a body, are inimical, or to say the least indifferent to the prosperity of the Foreign and Home Missions, and Tract and Bible and Education Societies — &c. &c. &c.; and when, in addition to the appalling fact that these sweeping charges are made not by our enemies, but by our professed friends, in a clerical capacity too, in order to give them greater weight and importance — the "Appeal" is seen eagerly and exultingly copied into the columns of the religious and political pro-slavery presses throughout the country, and a plot is going on for a distinct anti-slavery organization on sectarian grounds — I say, when all these things are considered, is it pardonable in the Emancipator and the Executive

Committee to treat the "Appeal" as if it were nothing to you or to the abolition cause? I maintain, with all seriousness and due earnestness, that you are both bound to meet these injurious aspersions promptly, and in an official capacity; and should you refuse to do so, I for one shall feel that you will have greatly misapprehended your duty, and need to be admonished by abolitionists universally.

Be assured that I do not require to be told, that it is a sad thing to see abolitionists fall out by the way. *True-hearted abolitionists never will quarrel with each other*; but remember, all are not such who profess to be. I lament, as much as any one, that there is this collision — but it is not one of *my* seeking — let the blame rest on the heads of those who have virtually abandoned our cause, if they ever belonged to it. The task of chastising Messrs. Fitch, Towne and Woodbury is not a pleasant one to me; but I am certain that by shunning it, I should have turned recreant to the cause of the perishing slave. Thanks be to God, its faithful performance has knocked sedition in the head, and abolitionists are still a united body. The Liberator, Friend of Man,[5] Herald of Freedom,[6] and Christian Witness,[7] have spoken out manfully — but the Emancipator, the organ of the Parent Society, is dumb! Strange, inexplicable, pernicious silence! — I do not ask you to vindicate the cause of the Liberator, (for I am of age, and can speak for myself,) but to *stand by the cause* whenever and wherever it is assailed, without respect to persons or stations.

Yours, affectionately,

Wm. Lloyd Garrison.

P. S. The silence of the Emancipator respecting the Andover Appeal [8] is, if possible, still more extraordinary. The allegations in that Appeal are made in a vague, general, and therefore unjustifiable manner, and will doubtless be used all over the country against our cause.

ALS: Tappan Collection, Library of Congress.

1. Probably Henry Grafton Chapman.

2. Garrison may be referring to the letter by James T. Woodbury of August 17, 1837, to which Garrison replied on August 28, and the three clerical appeals which followed the first, all in support of the first appeal. These were the "Appeal of Abolitionists of the Theological Seminary," dated Andover, Massachusetts, August 3, 1837, bearing thirty-nine signatures and reprinted in *The Liberator*, August 25, 1837; "Protest of Clerical Abolitionists, No. 2," addressed "To the Editor of the New England Spectator," signed by Charles Fitch and Joseph H. Towne, and reprinted in *The Liberator*, September 8, 1837 (Garrison replied to "Clerical Protest No. 2" in *The Liberator*, September 8, 1837); and "Protest of Clerical Abolitionists No. III," addressed "To the Editor of the N. E. Spectator," signed by Charles Fitch and J. H. Towne, and undated, reprinted in *The Liberator* on September 29, 1837.

3. The Reverend Elipha White, a southern Presbyterian minister, originally of Massachusetts (*Life*, II, 138n). The "Appeal" had stated the following concerning *The Liberator's* treatment of Mr. White:

"We cannot approve the hasty, unsparing and almost ferocious denunciation of a man who happens to come from the South, which we have recently seen in the case of Rev. Mr. White. To drag a man's name into the public prints, and hold him up to universal abhorrence, while neither time nor pains have been taken to ascertain the truth in relation to him, we think altogether unjustifiable. — We believe that Rev. Mr. White is not, and never has been, a slaveholder, in any sense of the word, neither is his wife. All that can be said is, that the father of Mrs. White does hold slaves, but we think it visiting the iniquities of the fathers upon the children too soon altogether, to call Mr. White to account at present for the sins of his father-in-law. . . ." (*The Liberator*, August 11, 1837.)

It was Oliver Johnson, editing *The Liberator* in Garrison's absence, who had accused Mr. White of being a slaveholder. In his reply to the "Appeal" in the same issue of *The Liberator*, Johnson noted:

"We were first informed by an *opponent* of the Anti-Slavery cause that Mr. White was an extensive slaveholder, and that he had preached in Park-street and Bowdoin-street churches. . . . We then took both 'time and pains' to inquire of at least eight or ten individuals, and from every one we received the assurance that he was a slaveholder. . . . We believe he has been and still is a slaveholder, to all intents and purposes. We have been informed on authority which will be satisfactory to us until Mr. White himself publicly denies the truth of the statement, that ever since his marriage, he has had in his possession one or more slaves. That his father-in-law ever executed deeds of conveyance to him of a slave or slaves, we do not say, but that he has had one or more in his possession, and entirely in his control, and that they have been regarded by himself and his relations as virtually his, we have no doubt. We have conversed within a few days with a worthy clergyman of this State, who is intimately acquainted with Mr. White, and who says that he has always understood him to be a slaveholder. . . . We understand, also, on what we shall consider satisfactory evidence till Mr. White himself denies it, that the people of his parish have given him a quantity of land which is cultivated by SLAVES, and that he is supported in part by the proceeds of their unrequited toil. The statement that he is a slaveholder, moreover, is not by any means new. We are informed that he has been spoken of as such repeatedly in the newspapers within a few years, and we are not aware that the statement has been contradicted by himself or his friends. Whether his conduct in the General Assembly of the Presbyterian Church affords evidence that he is a slaveholder, let the following extract from one of his speeches made at the last meeting of that body show:

" 'If the General Assembly have a right to assume the powers asserted in the resolution now on the table, they may say that my Presbytery shall not hold slaves. Let them do that, sir, and their authority will be disregarded. . . . No, sir — my Presbytery will NEVER — no, NEVER GIVE UP THEIR RIGHT TO HOLD SLAVES to this Assembly nor to any other Assembly than the "General Assembly of the First Born in Heaven." ' "

"The person who uttered this blasphemous speech is admitted to the orthodox pulpits in Boston, and the Rev. Mr. Fitch and his associates (professed abolitionists!) would have us consider him an abused man, because he has been represented to be a slaveholder."

4. In *The Liberator*, July 21, 1837, Oliver Johnson had inserted the following notice: "Is the REV. GEORGE W. BLAGDEN, pastor of the Old South Church, A SLAVEHOLDER? Rumor says YES. Will Mr. Blagden contradict the rumor by saying *No*, or by his silence virtually confirm it? We wait for his reply." On July 14, 1837, Johnson had inserted the following notice, beneath a letter from an anonymous antislavery person attacking Mr. Blagden: "We have heard it said that Mr. Blagden is a slave-holder! We know not whether such is the fact, and would like to be informed." The "Clerical Appeal" attacked these "insinuations" "that Rev. Mr. Blagden is a slaveholder. . . . If the conductors of the Liberator know that this gentleman is a slaveholder, and have the proofs in their possession, let them boldly assert it. But to *insinuate* such a thing before the public, while they have no proof of it!! It is a wicked, it is a base thrust at a man's reputation." Johnson replied to this condemnation by asking, "How did the signers of the

'Appeal' *know* that we had no better ground for asking whether he was a slaveholder than a mere *'guess'*? And if they did *not* know, what right had they to make such an 'insinuation'?" In his defense, he noted that "we asked it because many individuals, from various circumstances, fully believed that Mr. B. was a slaveholder. The rumor had been current in various quarters for a period of more than six months. Was it not proper in such circumstances to put the question, and call upon Mr. B. to contradict the rumor, if unfounded? But it was 'an attempt to destroy his reputation by *falsehood!*' . . . How Mr. Blagden can have any reason to complain of the question as an attack upon his reputation, we are at a loss to discover, since he maintains that slaveholding is reputable and perfectly consistent, in some cases, with Christian character. We believe that the circumstances were such as fully to justify our course; and we are not yet satisfied that Mr. B. is not what rumor says he is, a slaveholder. That we have been disposed to do him full justice, the article in the last Liberator under the head "Rumor Contradicted," which was written and published before we saw or heard of the 'Appeal' will conclusively show." (August 11, 1837.)

The article by himself to which Johnson referred had appeared in *The Liberator* on August 4 and had stated:

"We have been informed by a member of the Salem St. church (formerly Mr. Blagden's,) that Mr. B. is not a slaveholder — that a member of that church sometime since asked him the question, and that Mr. B. said in reply, that he was not and never had been a slaveholder. Some other individuals, who could scarcely fail to know it, if such were the fact, have assured us that they are satisfied of the correctness of the above statement. They think it must be true. We are glad of the opportunity of so far correcting the report in question, but as that report came from sources on which we supposed reliance could be placed, and seemed withal well authenticated, and as Mr. Blagden does not see fit himself to contradict it, we cannot speak by authority in the case, but can only give the above statement for what it is worth, and will add that, on the whole, we *suppose* it to be correct."

5. Published in Utica, New York; the organ of the New York Anti-Slavery Society. On September 8, *The Liberator* reprinted an editorial from the *Friend of Man*, in defense of Garrison. It was entitled, "The Measures! The Measures!! The Measures!!!" and carried a subheading, " 'We are all opposed to slavery — but — your measures are all wrong,' Old Tune." A second editorial, "The Clerical Appeal," was reprinted in *The Liberator* on September 15.

6. The organ of the New Hampshire Anti-Slavery Society, edited by Nathaniel P. Rogers at Concord. The *Herald*'s editorial defending Garrison was entitled "Exultation of Our Enemies" and was reprinted in *The Liberator* on September 15, 1837.

7. See letter 57, to Samuel J. May, September 23, 1836, note 2. An editorial defense of Garrison from the criticisms of the "Clerical Appeal" was reprinted from the *Christian Witness* in *The Liberator*, September 1, 1837.

8. The "Appeal" issued by abolitionists of the Andover Theological Seminary on August 3, 1837, endorsing the first "Appeal" of Fitch, Towne, *et al.* It bore thirty-nine signatures.

94

TO GEORGE W. BENSON

Boston, Sept. 16, 1837.

My dear George:

In a very few minutes, Helen, and the babe, and your loving W. L. G. are to start in the steam-boat for Hingham and Scituate, to spend the Sabbath with bro. May. Of course, I have not time to give you any news. As to the kind of reception which the Clerical Appeal is receiving at the hands of our abolition brethren, you will learn very explicitly, and in a manner that will be cheering to your heart, by this week's Liberator.[1] If this sedition in our ranks should be speed-ily and effectually quelled, I think our enemies may as well surrender at discretion — or at least abandon all expectation of dividing and conquering our forces. The only thing that surprises and grieves me is, the studied silence of the Emancipator respecting this controversy. It has not said a word about it, and, I understand, does not mean to say any thing — notwithstanding the charges in the Boston and Andover Appeals are broadly made against our cause and "leading abolitionists" — and notwithstanding the religious and political pro-slavery presses are publishing the Appeal, with strong encomiums, all over the land! Silence, like this, is shameful, is criminal, and any thing but magnani-mous. I have received a singular letter from Elizur Wright, Jr.[2] in which he denounces my course in the severest manner. Could you see it, you would hardly believe that he could have penned such a letter. But it only convinces me that all is not as it should be at head-quarters, and that our friends in New-York would be glad, on the whole, to see me cashiered, or voluntarily leave the ranks. Next week, I mean publicly to rebuke the Emancipator.[3] You will perceive by the Liberator, that our State Society is to hold a quarterly meeting at Worcester on the 27th inst. I sincerely hope you will be able to attend it; for, doubtless, Woodbury, Fitch, Towne, and their party, will en-deavor to rally all their forces, and try to force through the meeting some condemnatory resolutions. I think I shall not attend, but let things take their course, uninfluenced by my presence.[4] Little George's foot does not improve any, as yet, under Dr. Hewitt's treatment.[5] We are all in very good health, and expect to have a pleasant time at Scituate. What a narrow and merciful escape dear mother and Mary had! I rejoice and sympathize with them. The cake for George, sent by John Gray, was very acceptable. I expect we shall return on Mon-day, when I shall try to write you again.

Yours affectionately,
Wm. Lloyd Garrison.

ALS: Garrison Papers, Boston Public Library.

1. *The Liberator* of September 15, 1837, carried items supporting Garrison against the "Clerical Appeals," from the *Union Herald*, a religious abolition news-paper printed at Cazenovia, New York, the *Friend of Man*, the *Herald of Free-dom*, and *Human Rights*; from several antislavery societies of Massachusetts; from W. H. Burleigh and William Adams, of Pawtucket, an early antislavery sup-porter; and from others of Massachusetts and elsewhere.

2. Garrison quotes an appreciable portion of Wright's letter in his own letter (95) of September 23, 1837, to George W. Benson.

3. No rebuke of the *Emancipator* seems to have been printed in *The Liberator* until the following, rather mild, item appeared on October 6: "The Emancipator has maintained a profound, and we are constrained to think, a most injurious silence respecting the Clerical Protests, and the movements of the anti-slavery societies in reference to them. All the abolition newspapers have spoken out, except one — the Emancipator alone is dumb! What does it mean?"

4. Garrison did attend the meeting and wrote about it in a column and a half report in *The Liberator*, October 6, 1837. He began his report by explaining: "It was not our intention to attend the meeting of the State Society at Worcester, on the 27th ultimo — as the entire absence of editorial matter in our last number plainly manifested; but at a late hour, we were induced by the entreaty of many friends to alter our determination, and accordingly took 'French leave' of our editorial chair. . . ."

5. Unidentified.

---

9 5

TO GEORGE W. BENSON

Boston, Sept. 23, 1837.

Dear bro. George:

Next to a glance at the face of an absent friend, is the sight of his handwriting — and therefore I was made happy by your letter of the 20th inst. Doubly happy indeed, because dear Anna very kindly occupied a portion of it with her neat chirography.

With regard to our meeting at Worcester on Wednesday next,[1] I cannot urge upon you to attend it, if it will interfere materially with your business. But the crisis is a momentous one, and perhaps we have never needed a stronger expression of feeling and sentiment from the thorough-going friends of our cause, than at the present time. I hope, therefore, that you will contrive, by hook or by crook, to be at Worcester; for the meeting cannot now avoid a discussion upon the "Appeal," and its decision will be looked for with great anxiety all over the land. The condemnation ought to be explicit — it ought to be strong — it ought to be decisive. Especially in view of the criminal and extraordinary course pursued by the Executive Committee and Emancipator at New-York. Be assured, we have too much sectarianism at headquarters. There appears to be "something rotten in the State of Denmark."[2] I am troubled exceedingly in spirit at what I am constrained to consider the blind, temporizing policy which the Board at New-York seem determined to pursue. Only look at it! — Five clergymen, professing to be conspicuous abolitionists, make a public appeal, in which they bring severe and vital charges, not merely against the Liberator, but abolitionists and their cause. Another appeal, backing this up, but still more grave and general in its charges, is issued at Andover, signed by thirty-nine professed friends. Then follows a letter from J. T. Woodbury, one of the "seventy agents." All these are copied exultingly into various religious and political pro-slavery newspapers, and our enemies are rejoicing in the assertion of Fitch and Towne, that nine-tenths of the abolitionists in New-England agree with them in opinion. The Friend of Man, the Herald of Freedom, the Vermont Telegraph,[3] and various anti-slavery societies, have deemed the whole affair as worthy of special notice — yet, in view of all these things, our friends in New-York have preserved unbroken silence! Will not our enemies quote the old adage — "Silence gives consent," and claim the Emancipator as *privately* favoring the Appeal? Our friends at New-York may rely upon it, that the course which they have resolved to pursue, respecting this matter, will very much displease the great body of abolitionists, and alienate them and their money from the Parent Society.

In order that you may know something of the feelings at head-quarters, I make a few extracts from a letter which I have received from Elizur Wright, Jr. — a letter, the tone and temper of which are so unlike himself, that you will find it difficult to believe that he wrote it. He says —

"I could have wished, yes, I have wished, from the bottom of my soul, that you could conduct that dear paper, the Liberator, in the singleness of purpose of its first years, without travelling off from the ground of our true, noble, heart-stirring Declaration of Sentiments — without broaching sentiments which are novel and shocking to the community, and which seem to me to have no logical sequence from the principles on which we are associated as abolitionists. I cannot but regard the taking hold of one great moral enterprise, while another is in hand and but half achieved, as an outrage upon common sense, somewhat like that of the dog crossing the river with his meat.[4] But you have seen fit to introduce to the public some novel views — I refer especially to your sentiments on government and religious perfection, and they have produced the effect which was to have been expected. And now, considering what stuff human nature is made of, is it to be wondered at, that some honest-hearted, thorough-going abolitionists should have lost their equanimity? As you well know, I am comparatively no bigot to any creed, political or theological; yet, to tell the plain truth, I look upon your notions of government and religious perfection as downright fanaticism — as harmless as they are absurd. I would not care a pin's head, if they were preached to all christendom; for it is not in the human mind, (except in a peculiar, and, as I think, diseased state,) to believe them. * * My heart sickens over your letter to Woodbury. I feel that it does injustice to him. Grant

305

that his publication was ill-natured, coarse, and acrimonious: there was still some reason — to his mind, very strong reason for it. You meet him in a way which my whole soul tells me is *sinful*. You exalt yourself too much. I pray to God that you may be brought to repent of it, as repent you must, unless my moral vision is wofully bleared. I am as confident as of my existence, that a few more such letters would open a bottomless gulf of distrust between you and the abolitionists. * * Let the Sabbath, and the theoretic theology of the priesthood, alone for the present, and with my good will, you may grind every one of them to powder, who brings his popery to sustain the slave holder. Let the government alone, till, such as it is, all are equally protected by it, and after that you may work your will upon it, for all me. But if all this cannot be done, why, come out plainly, and say you have left the old track, and are started on a new one — or, rather, two or three new ones, at once, and save us from the miserable business of making *disclaimers*.⁵ I cannot but regard the Boston controversy as wrong, wrong, wrong, *on both sides*. If strict military justice were done, I am thinking both parties would be cashiered!"

If our dear bro. E. Wright can scribble in the foregoing strain, what have we to expect from other members of the Executive Committee? — I have a letter from Lewis Tappan,⁶ in which he says —

"I deeply regretted seeing the Clerical Appeal; but after its publication, my own judgment would have been in favor of a short, well-tempered, dignified, Christ-like reply" — [thus insinuating that neither brother Phelps nor myself have exhibited any of these qualities!] — "Your reply to Woodbury pained me exceedingly. It was beneath you in very many respects. Without enlarging, I consider the whole proceedings most unwise and hurtful. The Executive Committee determined on maintaining silence, at least for the present, and they approve the course pursued by the editor of the Emancipator. They will not be deterred from what they deem their duty. They neither approve of the Appeal, *nor of the replies*, but lament the whole. * * Candor induces me to say, that, in my judgment, objectionable things have appeared in the Liberator, and they have been discussed, at times, with an appearance of acrimony. Questions have been mooted that had better not have been discussed, and language has sometimes been used not in accordance with the lowly spirit of the gospel. * * May the Lord preserve you and bless you, and give you the sweet temper of John united to the intrepidity and ardor of Paul."

I might make other extracts, but these must suffice. Have we not reason to feel disquieted at the New-York policy? If persisted in, will it not inevitably divide the anti-slavery ranks? In the next Liberator, I shall feel it to be an imperative duty to rebuke the Ex. Committee and the Emancipator before the public.

How much, then, is depending upon the meeting of our State Society at Worcester! Whatever it does, will tell mightily for good or evil. Whether Fitch and Woodbury will try to rally their forces on that occasion, I do not know, but think it highly probable. Should you attend, let your soul speak out as God shall give it utterance — and think not of me as your brother-in-law, but only of our glorious cause. You are, happily, too well known to be charged with being swerved or biased by our connexion. Bro. May and Phelps will be there — the Grimkes — Alvan Stewart [7] and perhaps Gerrit Smith, and many others. The meeting will probably hold two days, but perhaps only one. From Worcester, bro. May will go with his family to Brooklyn. The course of reasoning, marked out in your letter, to be given at Worcester, is very good and conclusive. I have not time or room to suggest any points. As I shall not go to Worcester myself,[8] perhaps I may find time to send you a few suggestions by bro. Phelps.

Helen and myself had a very delightful visit at bro. May's, in South Scituate, and attended two anti-slavery meetings. Mr. Davis [9] and E. J. Chace have just paid us a visit, and returned yesterday to Providence. We are all well. Blessing and joy and peace be with you all in Brooklyn.

Ever yours,
Wm. Lloyd Garrison.

P.S. Our abolition friends in Vermont are out strongly, in the Brandon Telegraph,[10] against the Clerical Appeal. Good!

P.S. I have paid Dr. Harrington $2.00 for his Antiseptic, but he carried it with him to Southbridge — he promises to send it to you by the way of Thompson in the course of a week. Says he shall sell his farm in a few weeks — is very anxious that you should buy it. He had no plaster on hand when I called to see, but was going to spread some in a day or two. You shall have a strip soon.

ALS: Garrison Papers, Boston Public Library. The greater portion of this letter is reprinted in *Life*, II, 167–170.

1. September 27, 1837.

2. *Hamlet*, I, iv.

3. See *The Liberator*, September 29, 1837, for an item from the *Vermont Telegraph*.

4. At this point, *Life*, II, 168, has the following note: "It was about this time that Mr. Wright first made acquaintance with La Fontaine's Fables, and began the metrical version of them which is today the best in the language (see the advertisement to the first edition, 1841)."

5. At this point, *Life*, *ibid.*, notes: "Mr. Wright was not quite so frank to Mr. Garrison as to Mr. Phelps, to whom, on Oct. 26, 1837, he wrote: 'I have just received a letter from Garrison which confirms my fears that he has finished his course *for the slave*. At any rate, *his* plan of rescuing the slave by the destruction of human laws is fatally conflictive with ours. Only one of them can lead to any good result. Still, if he would run up his *perfection flag*, so that Abolitionists might see what they are driving at, shouting for him, he would not

do us much hurt. *I have conjured him to do so. Honesty requires it of him'* (2d Annual Report Mass. Abolition Society, in *Free American*, 3:57)."

6. Lewis Tappan had written to Garrison on September 4, 1837, and had discussed the latter's feeling of anger at the executive committee of the American Anti-Slavery Society and the *Emancipator* for their silence on the clerical controversy. The entire letter is reproduced in *Life*, II, 163–166. However, the ensuing quotation is, as *Life* suggests at this point (II, 169), from a letter which apparently followed that of September 21.

7. Alvan Stewart (1790–1849) was a prominent lawyer of Utica, New York, who helped found the New York State Anti-Slavery Society in 1835. In 1838 he sought to commit the American Anti-Slavery Society to the doctrine that the federal government had jurisdiction over slavery in the states, but failed narrowly. He later helped to organize the Liberty party. Neither he nor Gerrit Smith attended the Worcester meeting. The Reverend Joshua Leavitt, editor of the *Emancipator*, was the sole representative there of the American Anti-Slavery Society. (*Life*, II, 170n.)

8. Garrison finally did attend the convention at the insistence of his friends. *Life*, II, 170, notes: "He was, however, much engaged on the business committee, and did not hear the debates, and spoke only to the question of Texas. His appearance there was the signal for 'some spontaneous rounds of approbation.'"

9. Thomas Davis (b. Dublin, Ireland, Dec. 18, 1806; d. Providence, Rhode Island, July 26, 1895) emigrated to the United States from Ireland in 1817 and made his home in Providence, where he engaged in manufacturing jewelry. He later married Eliza J. Chace, William Chace's sister. An antislavery Democrat, he was a member of the state senate from 1845 to 1853, and a representative in Congress from 1853 to 1855. Eliza Chace was a very close friend of Helen Garrison. (*BDAC*.) After Eliza Chace's death, Davis married Pauline Wright, a widow, friend of Elizabeth Cady Stanton and of Stephen and Abby Kelley Foster (Lillie Buffum Chace Wyman and Arthur Crawford Wyman, *Elizabeth Buffum Chace, 1806–1899, Her Life and Its Environment*, Boston, 1914, I, 119).

10. Edited by Orson S. Murray.

96

TO ISAAC C. TABER

Boston, Oct. 9, 1837.

Respected Friend:

This morning, I gave my much esteemed friend Alanson St. Clair a very brief note, by way of introduction to you; but I had no time to tell you why it is I must forego the pleasure of being at your county meeting the present week. The truth is, there is no person in Boston to whom I can entrust the editorial charge of the Liberator during my absence; and no one who is not intimately familiar with the details of a printing-office, can realize how indispensable is the presence of the editor. Especially is it difficult for me to be absent, even for a day, at the present time. When I say that I long to see my brethren in New-Bedford, both white and colored, and deeply regret that circumstances are such as to hinder me from visiting them, it is not a commonplace expression, but the sincerity of earnest desire. How soon I may be permitted to see them, face to face, I know not — perhaps never on earth; but, O! the joy of hoping to spend a blissful eternity with all who are, in deed and in truth, the followers of the Lamb of God — heirs of God, and joint-heirs with Christ Jesus!

I find that I have erroneously called your *quarterly* meeting the *annual*, in the Liberator.[1] The notice in the Fall River paper says it is to be held on the 11th inst. As your letter stated the 12th, I presume you were correct.

I had thought of preparing a letter to be read at your meeting, but am too much pressed for time to be able to send you any thing worth reading. Should the people attend in any considerable number, you will doubtless have an interesting occasion. Bro. St. Clair, and Russell,[2] and Alexander,[3] constitute a formidable abolition trio, and are very bold and zealous men for God and his cause. You must "make the most" of their visit. They are all good speakers, and will not fail, I think, to declare the whole counsel of God on the subject of slavery — northern criminality — &c. &c. Happily, too, they are very much emancipated from the thraldom of sectarianism, and have no peculiar "clerical" sensitiveness. As bro. St. Clair is very poor, and is laboring *abundantly* in the cause without any desire or expectation of remuneration — and as he has expended some fifty or seventy-five dollars out of his own pocket to defray his travelling expenses, and is now utterly unable to do any thing more in this way — I encouraged him to expect that you would see to it that our New-Bedford friends make good his expenses in attending the Convention. It is very important that good speakers should be present at *county* meetings in particular, and hence it is *good economy for the cause* to pay the expenses of such as shall attend from abroad.

Should any action be taken upon the "Clerical Appeal," I trust it will be decisive. Bro. St. Clair will tell you what an interesting meeting was held last week by the Essex County Anti-Slavery Society, in New-Rowley.[1]

With much esteem I remain,

Your friend,

Wm. Lloyd Garrison.

I. C. Taber.

N. B. I have not seen bro. Phelps, and do not know, therefore, whether he will be with you.

ALS: Merrill Collection of Garrison Papers, Wichita State University Library.

Isaac C. Taber (b. New Bedford, Massachusetts, February 18, 1815; d. there, September 29, 1862) is listed as a bank clerk in the New Bedford *Directory* for 1836. He was also, at the time, and for several years afterward, a counsellor of the New Bedford Young Men's Anti-Slavery Society. He was active in civic affairs, serving as a trustee of the New Bedford Atheneum and as a director of the New Bedford Port Society for the Moral Improvement of Seamen. He later became mayor of New Bedford. (George L. Randall, *Taber Genealogy*, New Bedford, 1924, p. 126; *The New Bedford Directory . . . and The Register*, New Bedford, 1839, pp. 31, 33.)

1. *The Liberator*, October 27, 1837, in an account of the meeting in New Bedford of the Bristol County Anti-Slavery Society, named the officers elected at the meeting and the resolutions that were adopted. The notice which Garrison mentions appeared in *The Liberator*, October 6, 1837.

2. The Reverend Philemon R. Russell was the first minister of the Christian Church of Lynn, on Silsbee Street, from 1835 to 1840. He was the author of *Series of Lectures to a Universalist; Universalism Examined and Refuted* (2nd edition, Exeter, 1842). He lectured for the American Anti-Slavery Society in Massachusetts in 1838 and 1839. (Alonzo Lewis and James R. Newhall, *History of Lynn*, Boston, 1865, pp. 402, 584.) In 1837, he lectured for the Massachusetts Anti-Slavery Society and was a local agent of the American Anti-Slavery Society. (Dwight L. Dumond, ed., *Letters of James Gillespie Birney, 1831–1857*, Gloucester, Mass., 1966, I, 450–451n.)

3. Benjamin Quarles, *Black Abolitionists* (New York, 1969), p. 124, mentions a Negro abolitionist, S. R. Alexander, as a speaker at a Negro meeting in Boston in 1843. This may or may not be the "Alexander" to whom Garrison refers.

4. Garrison mentioned the meeting in *The Liberator*, October 6, 1837.

---

9 7

TO JAMES P. BOYCE

Boston, Oct. 10, 1837.

My dear Boyce:

The remembrance of my visit to your house is as pleasant as the perfume of a bed of roses. Since I was there, I learn that your dear wife has been brought very low, almost to the grave itself, by sickness; and hence I have deeply sympathized with you in your affliction, and can also rejoice with you at the prospect of her recovery. However, may we all be enabled to say with an apostle, "For me to live is Christ, but to die is gain" [1] — for there is no escape, finally, from "the inevitable hour" [2] of a mortal dissolution, and it behooves us to be at all times prepared for it. Remember me with tenderness and gratitude to your afflicted wife.

My excellent friend, Mr. Charles Drew,[3] formerly a merchant in this city, is about to establish himself in the shoe line at Fairhaven.[4] He is a highly trust-worthy and truly pious man, and has long been a genuine friend of the abolition cause. He inquired of me to-day, whether I knew any of the shoe-dealers in Lynn, and who among them were most conspicuous as conscientious and upright men. I told him that, as far as I knew, they were all reputedly men of integrity; but I could give him a letter of introduction to one of them, upon whom the utmost reliance might be placed, and who would give him all requisite information. That one is yourself. You will not need a more formal introduction to each other.

Yours, with lively esteem,

Wm. Lloyd Garrison.

Transcript: Garrison Papers, Boston Public Library.

James P. Boyce (1805–1885), of Lynn, Massachusetts, was an abolitionist and a nonresistant (*Life*, II, 228; IV, 356). He was a shoe manufacturer (as was his father, Jonathan Boyce), a Quaker, and a prominent founder and participant in the Old Silsbee Street Debating Club. The club was devoted to debating all moral, social, and political issues of the time. With James N. Buffum and William Bassett, Boyce was one of the leaders of the antislavery group within the club. He married Julia Ann Purrinton, June 16, 1830. He was reputed to have had an excellent sense of humor and "a keen sense of the ludicrous." It may be noted that, at the time, every shoe shop in Lynn was "an incipient debating club." (David N. Johnson, *Sketches of Lynn*, Lynn, 1880, pp. 105, 194–195, 200, 219–220; *Vital Records of Lynn*, Salem, 1905, I, 58; II, 52.)

1. Philippians 1:21.
2. Thomas Gray (1716–1771), English poet, "Elegy in a Country Churchyard."
3. See letter 21, to Helen, April 18, 1836, where Garrison mentions Mr. and Mrs. Drew.
4. Massachusetts.

---

9 8

TO GEORGE W. BENSON

Boston, Oct. 20, 1837.

My dear George:

I proffer you a thousand congratulations upon the birth of your dear babe, and especially as the child proves to be a son. Not that I am in the slightest degree prejudiced against the female sex; not that I am a heretic, or an infidel, as to the equality of our race, as you very well know; but as your first was a girl, why should I not be glad that your second is a boy? May he be a better man than his father! Don't sue me for constructive defamation, now! Don't remind me of the "clerical" assertion, that "insinuation is the meanest and vilest form of lying"! I repeat the wish — May he be a better man than his father!

With regard to his name. I know it is difficult to decide between the predilections of filial love and brotherly attachment; but I think there is a *bona fide* promise, which was made to your venerated father, that remains to be performed — viz. to call your next babe, if a boy, George Benson. You recollect, of course, how we compromised matters with regard to George Thompson Garrison: it was evident that nothing reconciled father to the change of name but the promise you gave him that you would, if it should ever be in your power, perpetuate the worthy name by which he was called. Besides — I am so anti-Malthusian as to hope that this is not the only son you are to have. Let your next, then, bear dear Henry's name *in full* — thus father and brother will be exactly perpetuated in the memory of other generations. Of course, you will give no heed to this suggestion, unless it is agreeable to all. [Helen jogs my elbow, at this point, and intimates, should heaven be so kind as to give us another son, he shall be called after the name of our precious, departed Henry. Sufficient unto the day, &c.]

In congratulating you, I of course mean to congratulate Catharine also. Happy couple! If you love such "little responsibilities" half as well as I do, your hearts must have thrilled with pleasure and gratitude at the baby-advent. May the son be a better man than his father! And I might add, perhaps, if I were in the Emerald Isle, a better *man* than his *mother!*

At this sedate and instructive season of the year, now that the forest is in the sere and yellow leaf,[1] and a suspension of rivalry has taken place between Summer and Winter, I very much desire to be with you in Brooklyn, not with my editorial pack upon my back, but emancipated like Bunyan's pilgrim, with a light, elastic step, a smiling countenance, a bright eye, ready for some adventure, but divested of all quixotism and romance. How does the big oak tree look now? Has not the glory departed from the majestic elm in front of Judge R's?[2] But I know that the costume of Nature, though changed entirely, is still beautiful. Look at the trees! What painter is like unto Jack Frost? How delicate is his coloring! How he excels in perspective! —— But he will pinch my nose, by and by — why then should I praise him? To show my magnanimity, certainly.

Truly, there is but one step from the sublime to the ridiculous — from pathos to bathos — from what is true to what is false. Hence I descend to the Clerical Appeal. Was ever treachery so signally punished as in the case of the signers of that unfortunate document? What an avalanche of condemnation has fallen upon their heads, grinding them to powder? What expressions of regard for the Liberator and its editor have been extorted by their conduct? But the conspiracy is not wholly quelled, as you will perceive by the attempt of Dea. Gulliver[3] to get up a separate organization. The clergy (meaning the colonization and union[4] portion of them, together with such deserters as Fitch, Towne and Woodbury,) are very busily engaged in holding caucusses, corresponding with each other, and laying plots to carry their point against us. There is a tremendous accumulation of power in their hands, and they are able to wield it with great effect; but, happily, the charm of their infallibility is dispelled, and the people are beginning to see that they may refuse to kiss their feet, and yet obtain salvation. I do not mean, needlessly, to protract the controversy that is now going on; but it is really of great service to our cause to publish the proceedings of anti-slavery societies, condemnatory of the Appeal, and in favor of the Liberator.[5] There are a great many encomiums heaped upon me, which are altogether unmerited, but they are useful in refuting the charge that I am growing unpopular with the abolitionists. If my enemies don't wish to see me praised, let them cease attacking me.

It is not my intention, at present, to alter either the general character or course of the Liberator. My work in the anti-slavery cause is not wholly done: as soon as it is, I shall know it, and shall be prepared, I trust, to enter upon a mightier work of reform. *The cause must be kept in the hands of laymen,* or it will not be maintained.

Bro. May's visit to Brooklyn must have been as refreshing to you all as Spring itself. Lovely man! where shall we find his superior in all that is amiable, disinterested, pure and good? We expect him in this city next week.

George Thompson is in vigorous health — a stout, noisy, rampant boy — but his foot, alas! remains in a bad condition. Dear Helen is in fine spirits, and accompanies me in expressions of the purest love and strongest attachment to all the household.

Your loving brother,

Wm. Lloyd Garrison.

N. B. Hope you will not fail to attend the State meeting in Providence.[6]

ALS: Garrison Papers, Boston Public Library. A portion of this letter is printed in *Life*, II, 173–174.

1. *Macbeth*, V, iii.

2. Judge Vine Robinson, of Brooklyn, Connecticut.

3. Deacon John Gulliver, one of the Reverend Charles Fitch's deacons in the Free Church of Boston, had recently bought the *Spectator* and was emphasizing its use as an anti-Garrison publication. He was also one of the leading spirits in seeking to create an anti Garrison abolitionist organization in Massachusetts. At the Worcester convention, on September 27, Deacon Gulliver delivered a strong attack on Garrison, which was, in effect, repudiated by the convention's support of Garrison. Gulliver's speech and Garrison's comments were published in *The Liberator*, October 20, 1837. Although Gulliver did not urge the formation of a rival organization in his Worcester address, the *Spectator* did print material urging the creation of a new organization. See *The Liberator*, October 20, 1837, for the piece entitled "New Anti-Slavery Organization." (*Life*, II, 158, 171–173, 177.)

4. American Union for the Relief and Improvement of the Colored Race.

5. Resolutions by antislavery societies in support of Garrison and in condemnation of the "Clerical Appeal" are to be found in *The Liberator*, October 13, 20, and 27, 1837, as well as in subsequent issues.

6. The annual meeting of the Rhode Island State Anti-Slavery Society, on

Wednesday, November 8, 1837. Garrison was also planning to be there (*The Liberator*, November 3, 1837).

---

9 9

TO THE EDITOR OF THE SPECTATOR

[October 20, 1837.]

Sir — In the days of Jesus Christ on earth, there were certain scribes and Pharisees who 'watched him whether he would heal on the Sabbath-day; *that they might find an accusation against him.*' [1] Knowing their intentions, he nevertheless performed his work; 'and they were filled with madness; and communed one with another what they might do to Jesus.' [2] They were *very pious* people, and zealous for *the law.* It is evident from the editorial article in your last paper, — '*Errors of Influential Men,*' — that, had you been living in those days, it is not impossible that you would have been found among the number of those malignant spies and taunting hypocrites. It seems that, *all at once*, you are filled with consternation, lest there should not be a due observance of the first day of the week, especially by the colored population of Boston! — and that, in imitation of your sabbatical prototypes and Jewish predecessors, you have been watching so humble a person as myself, in order to accuse me before all the people. For the last three years, you have professed a brotherly regard for me; you have seen me in private and in public; you have heard my conversation, and observed my deportment; you have written something to my credit, nothing to my disparagement; and you have admitted into the columns of the Spectator, many high encomiums upon me as a man, a philanthropist, and a Christian. For a very considerable portion of that time, you have not been ignorant of my views of the Sabbath, but have known that they correspond with the views of Calvin and other reformers, of many eminent commentators, of a multitude of pious men among the various sects, and of the Society of Friends as a body; yet you have sounded no alarm, nor manifested the least moral sensibility on the subject, until recently. Now you have arraigned me as a Sabbath-breaker! And why have you done so? I will tell you. You have betrayed the cause of humanity, and now you naturally take refuge in formal hypocrisy. Why, then, should you not begin to defame and persecute? Your motives are manifest. Your new-born zeal for the Sabbath is simply personal hostility — it has reference exclusively to my overthrow, and the suppression of the Liberator. You *know* that you were not actuated by a kind spirit, in writing the editorial article now under consideration. With gospel simplicity and plainness, I charge you with being a deceitful and bigoted man. This will sound harshly in your ear — but the Lord judge between us. Do not misapprehend me. I complain of the obvious design of your present attack, not of your affected regard for the Sabbath. I complain of your holy impertinence and pharisaical proscription being manifested upon abolition ground. I complain of you for attempting to introduce sectarian tenets and denominational strifes into the cause of bleeding humanity. — Again, see that you apprehend my meaning. I do not say that, because you are professedly engaged in the anti-slavery enterprise, you are obligated to suppress your sentiments on other subjects. No. Vindicate the Sabbath, if you will; extol the 'Christian ordinances,' and eulogize the clergy, as often as you desire. But do so in your character as an orthodox congregationalist, not as an abolitionist. You are false to the agreement which binds us together as the friends of immediate emancipation, and which makes us all ONE in the cause of liberty, notwithstanding our religious and political differences, in pointing the finger of sectarian reproach at a brother. — What greater outrage could be committed upon the feelings of a convention, assembled to promote a common object, than the following episode in Dea. Gulliver's speech at the Worcester meeting? — 'Mr. Garrison has never confessed Christ [i.e. never taken a creed upon his lips!] [3] before men, and is living in the habitual neglect of Christian ordinances. . . I go for the Christian Sabbath, and the gospel ministry; and I will *not go* with those who go against them.' Neither you nor deacon Gulliver will doubt that I am as tenacious of my religious opinions as any man. Suppose I had retorted in this instance, by declaring that I would not go with dea. G. for the emancipation of my enslaved countrymen, because he regards only one day in seven as holy, and is in favor of perpetuating carnal ordinances? If he was justified in his attack, should I not have been in such a defense? But had I betrayed so proscriptive a spirit, HUMANITY would have charged me with having abandoned her sacred cause, and the DEMON OF OPPRESSION exulted over my defection.

With the spirit of an Inquisitor, you have ventured to arraign and condemn me as a heretic. According to your charges, I am 'one who sets lightly by the Sabbath.' Just as lightly as did John Calvin: what do you think of *him*? As lightly as did the Son of God: will you take counsel with the Herodians against me, how you may destroy me? Let me tell you a gospel secret: no man who has not consecrated *all* his time to the service of God, has ever consecrated a seventh part of it. I will tell you another: no man who reverently regards all days as holy unto the Lord, will desecrate either the first or seventh day of the week. I will tell you a third: 'The law of the Spirit of Life in Christ Jesus hath made me free from the law of sin and death' [4] — 'for Christ is the end of the law for righteousness, to every one that believeth.' [5] I will also remind you of an apostolic admonition: — 'Let no man judge you in meat or in drink, *or in respect of a holy day*, or of the new moon, *or of the Sabbath days*; which are a shadow of things to come; but THE BODY IS OF CHRIST.' [6] Do these spiritual enigmas puzzle you? Most certainly, you do not understand one of them! Why? Because you are nothing but a legalist! You are endeavoring to obtain righteousness by THE LAW, and therefore are carnally minded. What is your 'eternal life'? The ten commandments! What is the standard of your obedience? The same! You seem to be ignorant that 'now we are *delivered* from the law, that being *dead* wherein we were held; that we should serve *in newness of spirit*, and not in *the oldness of the letter*.' [7]

Again: You say of me, 'One day with him is as good as another.' True — and all days, in my estimation, are sacred! I have surrendered up all my time to God, and dedicated it all to his service. Can I do better?

Again: 'He neglects the house of God on that sacred day.' This is not true. It is one of your legal impostures to represent a building made of bricks and mortar as 'the house of God.' There is no such holy locality, or holy building, on earth; and if you were not groping in Jewish darkness,[7a] you would perceive this truth. 'The hour cometh, when ye shall neither in this mountain, nor yet at Jerusalem, worship the Father.[8] The hour cometh, *and now is*, when the *true* worshippers shall worship the Father *in spirit and in truth*: for the Father seeketh such to worship him.' [9] Do you know what that means? If so, interpret it, I pray you. Does it mean that 'the true worshippers' will flock every Sunday to hear Mr. Charles Fitch preach, (for that seems to be the *Ultima Thule* [10] of your religious anxiety,) or some other 'orthodox' divine? 'If any man shall say unto you, Lo, here is Christ, or there, believe it not.[11] If they shall say unto you, Behold, he is in the desert; go not forth: behold, he is in the secret chambers; believe it not.' [12] But, according to your pagan notion, neither God nor Christ is to be found, except at Amory Hall, or some other *orthodox* 'house of God'! Or, in other words, whoever habitually absents himself from your 'religious meetings,' knows nothing of spiritual worship! Hearken: 'Every house is builded by some man; but he that built all things is God.[13] Christ [was faithful] [14] as a Son over his own house: *whose house are we*, if we hold fast,' [15] &c. Again: Our high-priest is 'a minister of the *true* sanctuary, and of the *true* tabernacle, which the *Lord* pitched, and not *man*.' [16] — 'Then verily, the first covenant had also ordinances of divine service, and *a worldly sanctuary*. . .[17] The Holy Ghost this signifying, that the way into the holiest of all was not made manifest, while as the first tabernacle was yet standing. . .[18] But Christ being come, a high priest of good things to come, *by a greater and more perfect tabernacle*, NOT MADE WITH HANDS,' [19] &c. 'The Most High dwelleth not in temples made with hands.' [20] ['What! not in *our* meeting-houses?' No!] [21] 'Heaven is my throne, and earth is my footstool: what house will ye build me? saith the Lord.' [22] An 'orthodox' house, is your response! 'Know ye not that ye are the temple of God . . . for the temple of God is holy, which temple ye are.' [23] In describing the New Jerusalem, the spiritual kingdom of Christ upon earth, John says, 'I saw no temple therein: for the Lord God Almighty and the Lamb are the temple of it.' [24] It is impossible, then, for me to neglect that which does not exist, namely, a 'house of God,' *made with hands*. If, therefore, the temple be destroyed, and not one stone left upon another, what becomes of the temple worship? 'God is a spirit; and they that worship him must worship him in spirit and in truth.' [25] Hence, to worship God acceptably, it is not necessary for the spirit to be colonized or transported by the body up to this 'mountain, or at Jerusalem,' — to Amory Hall, or Belknap-street meeting-house. You say that it is! and thus give the lie to the Holy Ghost. For if you do not mean to say this, then why this hue-and-cry about going to meeting — especially to *your* meeting? *Cui bono?* [26] Besides: by what *honorable* and *disinterested espionage* have you ascertained how often I attend, or how often I neglect public worship? Who keeps *tally?* Who is your informant respecting my manner of observing the Sabbath? To your charge, I refuse to plead either guilty or not guilty. I refer to it simply as a specimen of your pharisaical impertinence. You further state — 'He writes and reads and visits as on other days,' &c. How do you know what I write or read, or where I visit?

Again: You announce, as a fact, that I 'do my own pleasure on that sacred day.' This is a libel upon that Spirit which has translated me from darkness into marvellous light. It pours contempt upon that cross, 'by which the world is crucified unto me, and I unto the world.' [27] My meat and drink is to do the will of my heavenly Father. It is not my object, on any day, to 'do my own pleasure,' in a worldly sense. My joy is, that I am a partaker of Christ's sufferings; my happiness is, to be reproached for the name of Christ; my life is, to be always delivered unto death for Jesus' sake; my reputation is, to be ranked among madmen, fanatics, and incendiaries; my *pleasure* is, 'in infirmities, in reproaches, in necessities, in persecutions, in distresses for Christ's sake.' [28] The things of this world — its pursuits, its honors, its emulations, its fortunes, its reputations — I tread under my feet.

The overthrow of Satan's empire, and the triumphant establishment of the Redeemer's kingdom on earth, constitute the 'ruling passion' of my soul. Remember, this language is not uttered for effect, or boastingly. Few men in the world have less to do with profession than myself; nay, my *crime* is, that I have not made what is called 'a public profession of religion.' But of what value are professions where fruits are wanting? or what need of professions where fruits abound?

Malignant as is your attack upon my religious character, I should probably have suffered it to pass without a reply, had you not at the same time grievously slandered my colored brethren of this city. Do you not *know* that all you have uttered respecting their attendance upon public worship is gross misrepresentation? I know it, and they know it, if you do not. Now, I will venture the opinion, that a larger proportion of them are at this time in the practice of going to meeting on the Sabbath, than in any former year; but I have made no inquiry on the subject whatever. Very few of them know any thing of my sabbatical views; then, those who do, disagree with me in sentiment; moreover, in all my intercourse with them, I have never in a single instance spoken of the spiritual meaning of the Sabbath, nor endeavored to lessen their reverence for the first day of the week as a holy day. They do not know, and it is a matter of perfect indifference to them, where or when I attend public worship; nor are they influenced by me in the observance of 'the day of rest,' in the smallest degree. This assertion, I am sure, they will confirm to a man. Hence, your charge against them is based on nothing better than misrepresentation. I quote your words:

'We have been led to this subject, by the recent conduct of many of our colored brethren, who neglect the house of God. A short time since, many attended public worship with the Free church; but more recently, few are found there. It might, we thought, be accounted for by the wrong apprehension, that the pastor had lost his friendship for them, and consequently they resorted to other places of worship. But no, they are no where else found in the house of God. A recent visit to the church in Belknap-street, the place where the venerated Paul [29] was wont to proclaim Christ and him crucified to crowded auditories, discloses the alarming fact that its seats are almost deserted.'

I have never read a paragraph, having premises and conclusions more directly at variance with truth and honesty than the above. It bears *prima facie* evidence of sectarian *malice prepense* — all for 'the glory of God, and the good of souls,' of course! For does not the end sanctify the means?

In the first place, you underrate the sagacity and discernment of the people of color, if you suppose they cannot tell, without ascertaining my opinion, who is 'an apostate from anti-slavery principles,' or who deserves 'to be drummed out of the camp' of Liberty. Instinct with them is indeed 'a great matter.' For more than thirteen years, before they ever saw or heard of me, it was not in the power of all the clergymen in the land, or of the professed enemies of slavery, to convince them that the Colonization Society was a benevolent association, or that it was their duty to suffer themselves to be transported to the burning shores of Africa. And there are two facts upon which you may rely: the first is, that let who will among their white friends turn recreant to their cause, they will be true to themselves: the other is, that they are never deceived by mere professions of friendship, but intuitively judge of men by their fruits. Hence, they now (in common with a large portion of the members of the Free Church, and with abolitionists generally,) justly regard Mr. Fitch as being disloyal to the anti-slavery cause, and as having cruelly assailed the character of some of their earliest and most devoted advocates.

Again: Nothing can be more unfair than your reference to the 'Belknap-street church.' When the eloquent Thomas Paul acted as pastor, it was the chief, I believe the only place provided exclusively for the worship of our colored population in this city: of course, (and particularly on account of his extraordinary powers as a preacher,) it was well attended. How is it now? It appears that you have been up 'to spy out the nakedness' [30] of this meeting-house, and your report is, that 'its seats are almost deserted' — and you are noble and generous enough to ascribe this change to my 'pernicious influence'! Monstrous deception! Why do you hide the fact, (or, if you are ignorant of it, why have you rashly ventured to make me responsible for it?) that, ever since Mr. Paul's decease, the church and congregation have been torn with factions and divisions? Pew-doors have been nailed up — members have gone to law with each other — rival parties have placed each other under the ban of excommunication — and, consequently, many have been driven away, not from public worship, but from that meeting-house. It is with great reluctance that I allude to these unhappy bickerings; on which side lies the blame, I know not; nor do I know whether harmony or discord reigns at the present time in that society; but this simple statement solves the enigma, why the house is now comparatively empty.

Again: Why are you so disingenuous as to hide the fact, that, instead of *one* house, as formerly, there are now *several* houses exclusively appropriated to their religious worship — and all, more or less, numerously attended? Especially, why do you wilfully refuse to state, that the building so long, ably and successfully occupied by my beloved colored brother SAMUEL SNOWDEN [31] has been constantly thronged to such excess by our colored friends, that its dimensions have been enlarged to twice its original size? He is the Thomas Paul of our day in attractiveness, — though entirely different in his style of preaching, — and draws multitudes to hear him. Besides, a considerable number of colored persons attend the various places of worship set apart particularly for those 'whose skins are not colored like their own.'

I have thus attempted to vindicate my own character, and, what is equally dear to me, that of my colored brethren in this city, from your aspersions. I wait to hear what you can say in self-defence. It remains to be seen, whether you have sufficient candor to perceive your injustice, and sufficient magnanimity to make reparation by confessing it.

I remain, as hitherto, the friend of truth, humanity and freedom,

WM. LLOYD GARRISON.

Boston, Oct. 20, 1837.

Printed in *The Liberator*, October 27, 1837.

This letter was in reply to an editorial that had appeared in the *New England Spectator* on October 18, 1837. Garrison reprinted the editorial and followed it with his letter. However, above the editorial, which appeared in the "Refuge of Oppression" section of *The Liberator*, Garrison commented: "The following unmanly and most extraordinary attack upon the Editor of the Liberator and the colored population of Boston, appears in the New-England Spectator of the 18th inst. To suffer it to pass unnoticed would not be just to those whose cause I advocate, — and to reply to it in intelligible and emphatic language, I shall be compelled to utter sentiments which are foreign to the anti-slavery enterprise, for which that enterprise is not responsible, and with which I am conscious 'nine-tenths' of my abolition brethren will hold no fellowship. But I roll the responsibility of this digression upon those who have commenced the attack." The editorial, entitled "Errors of Influential Men," had noted that the colored population of Boston were not attending church services on Sunday and blamed their remissness upon Garrison's heretical views of the Sabbath. The editor of the *Spectator* was then, and had been for several years previously, William S. Porter. (*Life*, II, 175.)

1. Luke 6:7.
2. Luke 6:11.
3. The words in brackets are Garrison's.
4. Romans 8:2.
5. Romans 10:4.
6. Colossians 2:16, 17.
7. Romans 7:6.
7a. Another example of Garrison's Anti-Jewish Protestant Fundamentalism, with no indication that the Old Testament was a Jewish book or that the prophets, whose sensitivity to injustice Garrison shared, were themselves Jews.
8. John 4:21.
9. John 4:23.
10. Thule was the name given by the ancients to the most northerly land of Europe. The phrase, "Ultima Thule," is a metaphorical expression for the ultimate goal of human effort.
11. Matthew 24:23.
12. Matthew 24:26.
13. Hebrews 3:4.

14. The brackets are Garrison's.
15. Hebrews 3:6.
16. Hebrews 8:2.
17. Hebrews 9:1.
18. Hebrews 9:8.
19. Hebrews 9:11.
20. Acts 7:48.
21. The words in brackets are Garrison's.
22. Acts 7:49.
23. I Corinthians 3:16, 17.
24. Revelation 21:22.
25. John 4:24.
26. "To whose advantage."
27. Galatians 6:14.
28. II Corinthians 12:10.

29. The Reverend Thomas Paul, Negro pastor of the African Baptist Church in Belknap Street since 1809, when he formed it, died on April 13, 1831, of consumption, at the age of fifty-one. An obituary in *The Liberator* noted: "Few men ever deserved a higher eulogy than Mr. Paul. In his manners, he was dignified, urbane and attractive; — his colloquial powers were exuberant and vigorous; — his intellect was assiduously cultivated. . . . As a self-made man (and, in the present age, every colored man, if made at all, must be self-made,) he was indeed a prodigy. His fame, as a preacher, is exceedingly prevalent; for his eloquence charmed the ear, and his piety commended itself to his hearers." (*The Liberator,* April 16, 1831; John Hope Franklin, *From Slavery to Freedom, A History of Negro Americans,* third edition, New York, 1967, p. 163.)

30. See Genesis 42:9, 12.

31. The Reverend Samuel Snowden, a Methodist, had been pastor of the May-Street (later called Revere-Street) Church since 1826. Oliver Johnson, in *William Lloyd Garrison and His Times* (Boston, 1880), pp. 71–72, describes him as "one of the brightest, wittiest and best men, black as he was, that ever entered a pulpit. His genius was not below that of Father Taylor, who was also a preacher to seamen, and a Methodist; but of course 'nigger' sailors could not worship with white ones on terms of equality in Boston, and so Father Snowden found his sphere. His prayers were as full of salt and as nautical in their phraseology as those of his white brother. The Abolitionists were proud of him, and his prayers were as remarkable for their oddity as for their fervor."

100

TO ELIZUR WRIGHT, JR.

October 23, 1837.

My dear brother, — I am indebted to you for two long letters,[1] to which, perhaps, I shall reply at equal length, at some leisure hour. The first — though written I am sure, with the most friendly feelings — excited my surprise far more than the Clerical Appeal, and, you will pardon me for saying, was as illogical in its reasoning as it was cruel in its impeachment of my motives. Elizur Wright, Jr. never wrote that letter — some other spirit than your own free born, generous, independent spirit, prevailed with you for the time being and made you indite that strange composition, [. . .]

Transcript: Excerpt, Elizur Wright Papers, Library of Congress. This is all that remains of the original letter.

1. An extract of the first letter was given by Garrison in letter 95 of September 23, 1837, to G. W. Benson. The second letter, dated October 10, "desired the use of Mr. Garrison's name for the list of contributors to the enlarged *Quarterly Anti-Slavery Magazine,* which Mr. Wright edited with marked ability. On this head the reply (dated Oct. 23, 1837; see 2d Ann. Report Mass. Abolition Society) was favorable, and, for the rest, covered both letters" (*Life*, II, 178n). A third letter from Wright to Garrison, dated "New York, Nov. 6, 1837," is printed in *Life*, II, 178 181.

101

TO PHOEBE JACKSON.

Boston, Nov. 6, 1837.⎫
Monday evening. ⎬

Esteemed Friend:

My letter of last evening probably was received by you to-day. Our respected friends, S. M. and A. E. Grimke,[1] arrived in this city this forenoon. I immediately called to see them, but found Angelina quite unwell, and so completely prostrated by her arduous labors in Plymouth County, as to be unable to see any one. Sarah is also suffering in a similar manner, though not to the same extent. — She told me that they would not be able to visit Providence at the present time, but must retire into solitude to recover their exhausted energies. It is a case of self-preservation; and though you and our dear friends in Providence will be greatly disappointed in consequence of their absence, yet we shall all prefer their complete restoration to health to our own gratification. They duly appreciate your kindness in offering to entertain them at your house. Bro. May writes that they have been lecturing with great power and success, to crowded audiences, in his vicinity.[2] But they have been overtasked.

I thought you would wish to be apprised of this disappointment without delay, and have therefore anticipated telling you of it by word of mouth on Wednesday morning, when I hope to be in P.[3] with Miss Lucy P.[4]

With great esteem,
Yours truly,
Wm. Lloyd Garrison.

P. Jackson.

ALS: Library of Congress.

1. Sarah Moore Grimké and Angelina Emily Grimké had come to Massachusetts at the end of May 1837 at the invitation of the Massachusetts Anti-Slavery Society to present their anti-slavery message to the women of Massachusetts. As Oliver Johnson recounts the story, "they went from place to place, as the way opened before them, speaking sometimes in private parlors, sometimes in vestries or halls, and occasionally in a church. It mattered not whether the place were large or small, it was sure to be overcrowded." Soon men as well as women began to attend their meetings, thus breaking the prohibition against women publicly addressing mixed audiences of men and women. This aroused strong criticism among orthodox Congregational clergymen of the state and contributed toward evoking the "Pastoral Letter of the General Association of Massachusetts to the Congregational Churches under their care," July 28, 1837, written, for the most part, by the Reverend Nehemiah Adams. Although it did not name names, the letter attacked both Garrison and the Grimké sisters for their public activities. These attacks were continued in the "Clerical Appeal" from Andover Theological Seminary. Although the Grimké sisters counterattacked in public statements, there is little doubt that the attacks upon them and the doubts even among some abolitionists as to the morality of women speaking in public caused them much concern and aggravation, and, combined with their crowded speaking schedule, helped bring them to a state of exhaustion within a few months. For the history of their work in Massachusetts, see Oliver Johnson, *William Lloyd Garrison and His Times* (Boston, 1880), pp. 258–270; Gerda Lerner, *The Grimké Sisters from South Carolina, Rebels Against Slavery* (Boston, 1967), pp. 163–204.

2. The sisters had stayed at the home of Samuel J. May in South Scituate for eight days, until November 5. During that period, they spoke from several pulpits in Plymouth county, addressing audiences in Scituate, South Scituate, Duxbury, Hanover, and, on the evening of November 5, in Hingham. May has given an account of their labors during those days in *Some Recollections of Our Antislavery Conflict* (reprinted in New York, 1968), pp. 234–236.

3. Providence.

4. Lucy Parker.

102

TO ELIZABETH PEASE

Boston, Nov. 6, 1837

Esteemed Friend:

There are many of my countrymen, who regard me as a rash disturber of the peace of society, scarcely fit to be tolerated upon my native soil; and though they have not said of me what was charged against my Master, namely, that "he hath a devil," [1] yet they do not scruple to give me the apostolic character of being "a seditious and pestilent fellow." [2] How does it happen, then, that you, a stranger to me personally, a "foreigner" on the other side of the Atlantic, are disposed to cherish a good opinion of me, to approbate my labors, and even to aid me in my "incendiary" and "fanatical" purposes by a generous donation? Ought not my own countrymen to know me better than a resident in England? Their testimony is very strong against

me; it is unequivocal; it goes to impeach my sanity, if not to injure my
moral character. Ah! they are not disinterested witnesses. I have not
only accused them of being hostile to the rights of man, and, in rank-
ing immortal souls among cattle and creeping things, of having
exalted themselves above all that is called God, but I have sustained
the dreadful accusation by plenary evidence: hence their hatred of
me. The act of violence is in their hand, and they know it; their feet
run to evil, and they make haste to shed innocent blood; and whosoever among them that departeth from evil, maketh himself a prey; [3]
for truth has fallen in the street,[4] and equity cannot enter.

My beloved and invaluable coadjutor, Angelina E. Grimké, has
promptly conveyed to me the five guineas which you were pleased
to transmit in the letter she has recently received from you. I receive
the gift as a token of your sympathy for the suffering and the dumb
in this recreant land, whose cause it is my happiness to advocate, and
for whose deliverance from bondage all that I have and am is pledged,
without any reservation whatever. My heart is grateful in view of your
kindness, and especially to know that I possess your esteem; but you
shall not be burdened with mere words in return. Deep and genuine
emotion has no "set phrase of speech."

With regard to the present state of the anti-slavery question in this
country, you will be pleased to learn that the friends of the slave are
daily multiplying in all parts of the non-slaveholding States; that there
are now not less than twelve hundred anti-slavery societies in existence; that the spirit of lawless violence is in a great measure
subdued, not by the arm of law, but by the power of truth and the
victorious endurance of suffering innocence; that, in New-England,
all organized opposition to our cause has vanished; that our efforts
are unceasing to gain a complete mastery over the public sentiment
of the nation; and that in Massachusetts, where, only two years since,
ABOLITION was a mere foot-ball among all political parties to show
their contempt and dexterity in kicking it, these same parties are now
"bowing and scraping" to us, with cap-in-hand, at every new election,
knowing as they do that we hold the balance of power in our hands,
and can award victory or defeat according to their espousal of the
cause of liberty.

Upon the slaveholding States, we make no perceptible impression.
No opponent of slavery can tread upon their soil, as an abolitionist,
without the risk of martyrdom. I have relinquished the expectation,
that they will ever, by mere moral suasion, consent to emancipate
their victims. I believe that nothing but the exterminating judgments
of heaven can shatter the chain of the slave, and destroy the power
of his oppressor. The wildest animals may be tamed, in the course of

time; but tyrants, as all history shows, must be destroyed. I am clear, moreover, in the conviction, that, though astonishing changes have taken place in favor of emancipation among the people of the nominally free States within the last five years, the fate of this nation is, nevertheless, sealed. Repentance, if it come at all, will come too late. Our sins have gone up over our heads, and our iniquities unto the clouds, and a just God means to dash us in pieces as a potter's vessel is broken.[5] As a nation, our pride is intolerable, our infatuation amazing. "All men," says the great moral poet,[6] "think all men mortal but themselves": — and we *republicans*, we CHRISTIANS, we who have so bravely fought for LIBERTY, find no difficulty in persuading ourselves that we are immortal! All other people, of whatever language, tribe, country or clime, may perish; but WE can never waste nor decay. Time shall not be able to erase a single stripe, or obscure a single star, upon our banner. We are a vain people, and our love of adulation is excessive. We imagine, and are constantly taught to believe, that our flight, like a strong angel's, is onward and upward, without pause, without weariness; that though an earthquake should shake all Europe, and engulph empires, it could not disturb a platter on our shelves; and that the sun of our freedom shall be coeternal with the orb of day. Like ancient Edom, our habitation is high; we have exalted ourselves as an eagle, and set our nest among the stars; and we are saying in the pride of our hearts, "Who shall bring us down to the ground?"[7]

But, it is in vain that we boast of our Constitution, our glorious Union, our republican institutions. It is worse than idle for us to say, that we are "in the full tide of successful experiment."[8] The experiment has wofully[9] failed. We are madly attempting to perform impossibilities. Talk we of our national strength and prowess? As if, were it a thousand times more mighty than it is, God could not sink this nation as a mill-stone in the depths of the sea, and it shall never be missed — and thus vindicate his eternal justice, advance the cause of human liberty, promote his fear in the earth, and establish a kingdom of righteousness that shall never be destroyed! For what are the United States in the estimation of the Almighty? Do their dimensions excite his wonder? Is he impressed by their arts and sciences, their enterprise and opulence, their politics and religion, their high pretensions and solemn protestations? It is as true and as certain now, as it ever was, that "the nation and kingdom that will not serve him shall perish; yea, those nations shall be utterly wasted."[10] It has been confidently asserted, that if our experiment fail, all hope will be taken from the earth. As if down-trodden, benighted man, wherever pining in chains, or grovelling in degradation, — despite all the mutations of earthly empires, — will not ultimately rise up in majesty, emerge into light, and stand forth "redeemed, regenerated and disenthralled"! As if, come what may of this republic, it were doubtful whether the kingdoms of this world will ever become the kingdoms of our Lord, and of his Christ! [11]

While, therefore, my hope of the peaceful and voluntary overthrow of slavery in the southern states of this nation is very feeble, my faith in the promises of God, that he will maintain the cause of the afflicted and the right of the poor, and that he will deliver the oppressed out of the hand of the spoiler, is unfaltering, invincible. And while it is my earnest prayer, that the judgments of Heaven may be averted from us, by timely repentance — still, if our destruction is to come, I am ready to say, "O give thanks unto the Lord, for he is good; for his mercy endureth forever. To him that overthrew Pharaoh and his hosts; for his *mercy* endureth forever!" [12]

As in England, so in this country — the women have done and are doing more for the extirpation of slavery than the other sex. In their petitions to Congress, they outnumber us at least three, perhaps five to one. At the recent session of that body, a million of names were sent in, in the course of a month, remonstrating against the annexation of Texas to the United States. Of that immense number, a very large proportion were females. Our gifted friends, the Grimkés, are exerting an almost angelic influence wherever they go. Their public lectures are thronged by both sexes, and their triumph over prejudice and error has been most signal.

It is now more than eight years since I entered upon this mighty work. The more I labor, the less weary I grow. Rely upon it, American abolitionists will never give up the conflict through fatigue, pusillanimity, or apathy. Come what may, they can no more be divorced from the cause, than they can give up their allegiance to God. Some of them may — nay, some of them have, in a trying hour, turned recreant; but the great body fear God, and will keep his commandments.

The many dear friends in England, with whom it was my privilege to become acquainted, are none of them forgotten by me. My heart swells, and my eyes moisten as I think of their kindness. It is not probable that we shall ever meet again on earth — O may we all meet in heaven, to be parted no more!

Your grateful and admiring friend,
Wm. Lloyd Garrison.

Transcript, Garrison Papers, Boston Public Library. A portion of this letter was reprinted in *Life*, II, 183–184.

Elizabeth Pease (b. Feethams, Darlington, England, January 5, 1807; d.

1897) was the daughter of Elizabeth Beaumont and Joseph Pease, a wealthy Quaker, woolen manufacturer, railroad promotor, philanthropist, and antislavery reformer. He was the first Quaker member of the House of Commons.

An abolitionist like her father, Elizabeth's interest in the American antislavery movement began in the 1830's and continued to the end of the Civil War. She corresponded with many American antislavery leaders, including Garrison, Wendell Phillips and his wife, Angelina and Sarah Grimké, Lucretia Mott, and others. An introduction to Garrison through a gift of five guineas to the antislavery cause marked the beginning of a deep and lifelong friendship.

In 1846 Garrison named his newborn daughter Elizabeth Pease. Garrison's biography by his sons lauds Miss Pease's "sagacity, sound judgment, practical business talent, and unfailing grasp of principles. She was the Mrs. Chapman of the British agitation." In 1853 she married Professor John Nichol, of Glasgow Observatory, an astronomer, a widower, and the father of two grown children. Because Professor Nichol was not a Quaker, the marriage resulted in her exclusion from the Society of Friends.

On January 7, 1842, the following sonnet by Garrison appeared in *The Liberator*:

> "TO ELIZABETH PEASE, OF DARLINGTON, ENGLAND
> A native dignity and gentle mien;
>   An intellect expansive, clear and strong;
>   A spirit that can tolerate no wrong;
> A heart as large as ever yet was seen;
> A soul in every exigence serene,
>   In which all virtuous excellencies throng; —
>   These, best of women! all to thee belong;
> What more of royalty has England's queen?
> Thy being is absorbed in doing good,
>   As was thy Lord's, to all the human race;
> With courage, faith, hope, charity endued,
>   All forms of wretchedness thou dost embrace;
> Still by thy work of light and love pursued,
>   And thy career shall angels joy to trace."

(*Life*, II, III and IV, *passim*; Anna M. Stoddart, *Elizabeth Pease Nichol*, London and New York, 1899.)

1. John 10:20.
2. Acts 24:5, slightly emended.
3. Isaiah 59:6–7, 15.
4. Isaiah 59:14.
5. Psalms 2:9, paraphrased.
6. Edward Young (1683–1765), English poet and dramatist. The quotation is from his best-known work, *The Complaint; or Night Thoughts on Life, Death, and Immortality* (1742–1744), "Night I," line 424.
7. Obadiah 3–4.
8. Thomas Jefferson, *First Inaugural Address*, March 4, 1801.
9. Another transcript of this letter substitutes "wholly" for "wofully."
10. Isaiah 60:12.
11. Revelation 11:15.
12. Psalms 136:1, 15 and *passim* in the Old Testament.

103

TO MRS. HANNAH FIFIELD

Boston, Nov. 21, 1837.

Esteemed Friend:

I have been hesitating — too long, certainly — as to the time I should visit Weymouth, for the purpose of delivering an anti-slavery address, in compliance with the kind and reiterated request of the anti-slavery societies in Weymouth. I would name a week from next Sabbath evening for the address, if that time should be agreeable to you all.[1] Undoubtedly, more persons will be enabled to attend on such an evening, than on any other in the week; and I should hope there will be nothing in my address unworthy of the *sacredness* of that evening which is generally attached to it. "It is lawful *to do well* on the Sabbath day"[2] — and, consequently, on the *evening* of the Sabbath: for incomparably better is a man than a sheep.

The martyred Lovejoy![3] almost the last to come into our ranks, and the first to fall as a victim! He has perished in the cause of God and of bleeding humanity; but I am shocked and filled with sorrow to learn, that he first took life before he lost his own,[4] and that this reliance for victory in the darkest hour of the conflict was upon powder and ball. Alas! Alas! If the Son of God could suffer himself to be led as a lamb to the slaughter, and to be nailed unresistingly to the accursed cross, surely we are bound to imitate his example even unto death, and by so doing we shall be eternally victorious.

Yours, respectfully,

Wm. Lloyd Garrison.

ALS: In possession of Robert L. Huttner, Chicago, Illinois.

As indicated on the address, on the reverse side of the letter, Mrs. Hannah Fifield was corresponding secretary of the Female Emancipation Society of Weymouth, Massachusetts. She was born Hannah Cranch Bond in Portland, Maine, on April 13, 1787. She was living in Dorchester, Massachusetts, when she married Dr. Noah Fifield in 1820, and moved to Weymouth, Massachusetts, where he was a physician from 1806 until his death in 1867. They had three children. After her husband's death she apparently moved back to Dorchester. (George Walter Chamberlain, *History of Weymouth, Mass.*, Weymouth, 1923, II, 621; III, 225.) She attended the second annual meeting of the New England Non-Resistance Society in September 1840 (*The Non-Resistant*, October 14, 1840).

1. *The Liberator* of December 8, 1837, carried the following announcement regarding the meeting: "By the joint invitation of the anti-slavery societies in Weymouth and Braintree, it was our privilege to address a large assembly on Sabbath evening last, in the Rev. Mr. Perkins's meeting-house, on the subject of slavery. The spacious house was entirely filled — and it has never been our lot to address a more attentive audience. At the close of the lecture, the sum of

THE LIBERATOR.

VOL. VI.]   OUR COUNTRY IS THE WORLD—OUR COUNTRYMEN ARE ALL MANKIND.   [NO. 2.

BOSTON, MASSACHUSETTS.]   [SATURDAY, JANUARY 9, 1836.

THE LIBERATOR

IS PUBLISHED WEEKLY, AT
NO. 46, WASHINGTON STREET, BY
ISAAC KNAPP.

W. J. LLOYD GARRISON, EDITOR.

TERMS.

REFUGE OF OPPRESSION.

SOUTHERN VIEWS OF SLAVERY.

The resolutions of the Edgefield (S. C.) Baptist Association are given below, which received the unanimous voice of the Association.

SYNOD OF PHILADELPHIA.

COMMUNICATIONS.

PHILADELPHIA VINDICATED.

No. I.

William Lloyd Garrison, as a bold and faithful sentinel on the ramparts of Liberty, who has cried aloud and spared not, may feel assured that a deep sympathy and a lively interest is awakened in the breasts of thousands for his welfare, amid the trials and tribulations through which he is passing; and perhaps it may prove some alleviation to learn, that the clouds which have been lowering o'er our house,' and threatening to taint the moral atmosphere of our fair city, are passing away.

ABOLITION.

HOLSTON ANNUAL CONFERENCE.

SYNOD OF MISSOURI ABOLITIONISM.

The Synod of Missouri, in its late session at Marion College, passed the following preamble and resolutions in condemnation of the course pursued by the Abolitionists:

SOUTHERN CHRISTIANS AND ABOLITIONISM.

The Synod of West Tennessee, at their late session, adopted the following:

VIRGINIA BAPTISTS, ON ABOLITION.

SEVERITY OF THE ABOLITIONISTS.

THE WORKING-MEN AND THE ARISTOCRACY.

THE PRO-SLAVERY RIOT OF NOVEMBER 7, 1837, ALTON, ILL. DEATH OF REV. E. P. LOVEJOY. FROM WOODCUT MADE IN 1838.

$25.71 was generously contributed for the benefit of Mrs. Lovejoy and family."

2. Mark 3:4; Luke 6:9.

3. This phrase refers to the death of Elijah Lovejoy (1802–1837), the anti-slavery editor, at Alton, Illinois, on the night of November 7, 1837, during an attack by a mob on the warehouse housing his press. Lovejoy and several other armed antislavery men were defending the building. The news of Lovejoy's death did not reach Boston until Sunday, November 19. (*Life*, II, 186n.) It was not until approximately two years before his death that Lovejoy associated himself publicly with the principles of the American Anti-Slavery Society. (Merton Dillon, *Elijah P. Lovejoy, Abolitionist Editor*, Urbana, 1961, pp. 51–56, 62; Edward Beecher, *Narrative of Riots at Alton*, introduction by Robert Merideth, Dutton Paperback, New York, 1965, originally published at Alton in 1838; p. xiv.)

4. Edward Beecher, *ibid.*, p. 64, notes: "A few guns were then fired by individuals from within [the warehouse, where Beecher and his friends were besieged], by which Lyman Bishop, one of the mob, was killed. The story that he was a mere stranger waiting for a boat, and that Mr. Lovejoy shot him, are alike incapable of proof. He was heard during the day, by a person in whose employ he was, to express his intention to join the mob."

1 0 4

TO GEORGE W. BENSON

Boston, Dec. 9, 1837.

My dearly beloved George:

What was the date of my last letter, I do not remember; but too much time has elapsed since it was written, to render an excuse for my silence valid — that I *feel*. Why, how swiftly the seasons revolve! Tell me, do they increase in their impetus as we grow older? Strange we can never tell the exact day — week — month — ay, even the year, in which we bade adieu to boyhood, youth, and manhood! Four times eight are thirty-two — eight times four are ditto — what then? The use of arithmetic is here: To-morrow, December 10th, I complete my 32nd year. It ought to have been a better life for so long a one — and yet how short it appears! How the soul revels in its immortality! It is its clayey tenement, not itself, that wastes and perishes. *Its* age is eternity. Partaking of the nature of God, it cannot die. With it, as with Him, (grateful and glorious thought!) one day is as a thousand years, and a thousand years as one day! Though it has had a beginning, it shall not have an end. Now, if it be only assimilated in love to Him who is Love, how inconceivably happy its existence! But if alienated from Him by wicked works, how miserable!

What does mother think of her Boston son? I know she possesses a charitable and benign spirit, and will not censure me too severely for my procrastinating habits. That I esteem, admire and love her, is most certain; but then it might be clearer, or at least more tangible evidence of this, if my remembrances were forwarded to her, "in black and white," (lawful epistolary amalgamation,) a little oftener. I protest, however, against a verdict being made up on such ground. Affection is not to be measured by the ream — mine is not, I am sure. It is an exhaustless fountain, welling over the brim, and fertilizing the garden of the heart. To bottle it up, and send it by mail, is not the best way to try its quality. Dear mother! may the sweet sunshine of heaven never cease to illumine her path, quite beyond the dark and narrow vale of Time!

How is dear Mary? Happy, I presume, in the circle of her own thoughts. Beyond the family household, how few there are in Brooklyn with whom she can take sweet counsel! [1] The world is multitudinous — its population, like the waves of the sea, and as the sand upon the sea-shore innumerable — yet how few there are whose spirits "mingle into one, like kindred drops"! [2] This is all-sufficient evidence, that mankind are not in a state of happiness. We were made to love each other, with a pure heart fervently. But how can even *two* walk together, except they be agreed? [3] It is a happy circumstance, however, that in God is infinite fulness; and what the loving soul is defrauded of here by the wickedness of our race in refusing to join in Christian fellowship, is made up by his superabounding grace. Give a brother's love to her, and assure her that I realize sweet communion with her, even at this long distance — which, by the way, is no distance at all to the spirit.

As for dear Anna, so gentle and so good — good, as found in the likeness of her Redeemer — my salutations to her, with all the freshness and earnestness of a new-born love. Little heeds her spirit the turmoil of this crazy world. She does not live for time. Her companions are not those of sense, but spiritual existencies — Truth, Purity, Joy, Resignation, Love. How dear she is to my heart! Is she well?

Dear Sarah — the last, not the least of the sisters under the family roof, for they are all equally precious — she is doubtless still ceaseless in well-doing, sympathizing with the distressed, ready to engage in every good work, and peaceful as a river in the even flow of her amiable spirit. Give her a brother's right hand of fellowship for me, with a large and sincere heart in it.

As for Catherine, I love her for your own sake and her own. My best remembrances to her, and scores of kisses for little Anna and the babe.

Nothing has transpired, of consequence, in our family circle. My own health is excellent — dear Helen's not less so — and as for George Thompson, with his plump and rosy cheeks, and sturdy frame, and boyish glee, he is health and happiness personified. I do love him prodigiously, because he is, in my eyes, a prodigy — of course.

Yesterday forenoon, we had a tremendous meeting in Faneuil Hall — not less than 5,000 persons present — with reference to the Alton tragedy. There was a good deal of feeling in the audience, and some would have been glad to get up a row; but, happily, all went off pretty quietly. Dr. Channing made some excellent introductory remarks — Wendell Phillips, George Bond,[4] and Geo. S. Hillard, also made admirable speeches. The Attorney General Austin's speech [5] was as vile and inflammatory as possible, and came very [near] producing a mobocratic explosion. He was replied to by Phillips with great effect. — Several excellent resolutions,[6] drawn up by Dr. Channing, were passed with unexpected unanimity. The triumph has been a signal one for our side. [See next Liberator.] [7]

Your book on Agriculture, and some others, shall be forwarded the first opportunity.

The mail closes directly. Adieu!

Lovingly yours,
Wm. Lloyd Garrison.

ALS: Garrison Papers, Boston Public Library. A portion of this letter was printed in *Life*, II, 189n.

1. Psalms 55:14.
2. William Cowper, *The Task*, Book II, "The Time-piece," line 17.
3. Amos 3:3.
4. George Bond was a prominent Boston businessman and civic leader, an early director of the Boston and Worcester Railroad, an incorporator of the New England Mutual Life Company in 1835, and a leading member of the Brattle Street Church (*Memorial History of Boston*, IV, 129, 191; Frank Otto Gatell, *John Gorham Palfrey and the New England Conscience*, Cambridge, Mass., 1963, pp. 64, 79.)
5. James T. Austin, the attorney-general of the state and a member of Dr. William Ellery Channing's congregation, had not been scheduled to speak. He was sitting in the gallery when, following the address by George S. Hillard, he insisted upon speaking. His address opposed all that the meeting was called to uphold. He insisted that Lovejoy "died as the fool dieth," he suggested that the emancipation of the slaves was comparable to turning loose wild beasts of a menagerie, and he justified the mob's attack on Lovejoy and his press as comparable to the Boston Tea Party during the Revolution.
6. These were principally affirmations of freedom of speech and of the press.
7. *The Liberator*, December 15, 1837, carried the texts of the speeches delivered at the rally.

105

TO SAMUEL J. MAY

[Boston, December 30, 1837]
Saturday Morning.

Dear Brother May:

I think it best to defer the publication of your letter to me,[1] respecting bro. Lovejoy's conduct, until I hear from you again. Your premises are wholly unsound, and therefore your strictures are not in place. You take it for granted, that those who signed the Declaration of Sentiments at Philadelphia, and abolitionists generally, have obligated themselves not to defend their own lives and liberties — not even to support civil government. — Certainly, such is not the fact. I presume *you* are hardly prepared to say, that abolitionists ought not to sustain civil government; and yet, what was bro. Lovejoy's act? He died, not as an abolitionist, but as one of the police of Alton, regularly enrolled by the Mayor, with others, to sustain the supremacy of law against anarchists and ruffians. When he fell, and the murderers triumphed, government fell. All the facts in the case prove this. I think none but those who repudiate all human governments, sustained by physical force, can consistently reprobate Lovejoy's conduct. The Emancipator has no right to disclaim the act, and I think its course has been consistent.[2] Abolitionists hold to human governments, and to the right of self-defence, as a body; hence, their official organ cannot denounce bro. L. for giving his aid to the civil authority, at its request. I wish it were otherwise — I wish all in our ranks could be led to see, that civil government — a government upheld by military power — is not justified *among Christians*; but that question remains to be settled. Those who agree in sentiment with the Grimke's, H. C. Wright, and myself, will lament the conduct of our Alton friend[s], but all who do not agree with us ought to applaud them. Let me hear from you again. I will most cheerfully insert your letter; but I think it can be shown to be radically unsound.

W. L. G.

ALS: Garrison Papers, Boston Public Library. This letter was written by Garrison at the close of a letter by George W. Benson to Samuel J. May. It was addressed South Scituate, Massachusetts.

1. The letter was dated December 26, 1837; it does not seem to have been printed in *The Liberator*. It is to be found among the Anti-Slavery Letters at the Boston Public Library.

2. *The Emancipator*, December 28, 1837, printed a letter from Samuel J. May to Beriah Green, dated December 11, 1837, in which May expressed views similar to those of his letter of the same date to Garrison. In the same issue, *The Emancipator*, in presenting a letter from Owen Lovejoy, the brother of Elijah Lovejoy, which gave certain particulars of the latter's death, remarked: "the more light appears, the more manifest it becomes that the defenders of the press were strictly within the law and that their course was as justifiable as it would have been if the mayor himself had been at their head." The letter was reprinted in *The Liberator*, January 5, 1838.

III BROADENING INTERESTS — PEACE AND NONRESISTANCE: 1838

IN JANUARY, a second son, William Lloyd Garrison, Jr., was born into the growing Garrison family. Until June, Garrison and his family stayed at Miss Parker's, at 5 Hayward Place in Boston. Garrison attended the annual meeting of the Massachusetts Anti-Slavery Society in January, delivering his annual report piecemeal, and the meeting of the American Anti-Slavery Society in May, at which he arrived a bit late. He was present at the wedding of Angelina Grimké and Theodore Weld, on May 14, 1838, and subsequently at the Annual Convention of American Anti-Slavery Women, which was held at the newly dedicated Pennsylvania Hall, and which culminated in a riot and the burning of the hall. In June, Garrison took his family to Brooklyn, Connecticut, as he had done the previous year, and remained with them until September, when he returned to Boston to rent the home of Amos Phelps, whose wife had died. Perhaps the most noteworthy event of the latter part of the year was the holding of the Peace Convention in Boston on September 18, 19, and 20. Garrison wrote its "Declaration of Sentiments." The convention culminated in the formation of a Non-Resistance Society, which abjured the use of all force by governments, organizations, and individuals, and which led to further antagonism toward Garrison. Garrison remarked in *The Liberator* concerning the convention that "mankind shall hail the 20th of September with more exultation and gratitude than Americans now do the 4th of July." (*Life*, II, 229.)

106

TO EDWARD M. DAVIS

Boston — Jan. 8th — 1838 —

My dear friend

* * * * * In advocating the cause of emancipation, my endeavor has been to speak the truth of God in its simplicity and power; not to indulge in defamation, or to deal out flattery; not to conceal our danger, or to gild our crimes. I cannot patiently argue the question of slavery, as a matter of uncertainty as to its exact turpitude. While the chains of millions of my enslaved countrymen are clanking in my ears, and their cries are disturbing the repose of the nation, and I know that their bodies and spirits (which are God's) are daily sold under the hammer of the Auctioneer as articles of merchandize; I need no nice adjustment of abstractions, no metaphysical reasonings, to convince me, that such scenes are dreadful, and such practices impious. All that belongs to my manhood, all that is nature within me, my whole animal and spiritual organization, settles the question instantly.

* * * * * *

But I do say, that those pharisaical cavillers at the language, spirit, and measures of abolitionists; those affectedly judicious and moderate souls, who manifest that they have no flesh in them for the slaves at the South, and whose sympathies are all on the side of the slaveholders; they know that it is nothing but the sable hue of the skin, and the crisped hair of the victims, that make all the difference between the propriety of our conduct as abolitionists, and that of our revolutionary fathers, which they applaud. Now, if in seeking to break the fetters of our colored countrymen, we had resorted to violence, instead of argument, entreaty and rebuke; if we had stimulated the slaves to revolt, and assert their rights at all hazards; if we had held up before their eyes the example of Washington and Lafayette, who could justly have reproached us? — Surely not those who talk exultingly of Bunker Hill; not those who believe that it is glorious to die in the cause of liberty on the battle-field. But, thanks be to God, "the weapons of *our* warfare are not carnal, but spiritual." [1]

Yours in eternal hostility to every form of oppression,

Wm. Lloyd Garrison.

Extract, transcribed by Mrs. Davis: Garrison Papers, Boston Public Library.

Edward M. Davis (b. Philadelphia, July 21, 1811; d. Boston, November 26, 1887) married Maria, the second daughter of James and Lucretia Mott, in 1836. The young couple lived next door to the Motts. Davis was an abolitionist and a participant in the Non-Resistance movement. In 1846 he paid for the publication of Adin Ballou's nonresistance pamphlet, *Christian Non-Resistance in All its Important Bearings*, in Philadelphia. In 1850, Davis and Thomas Mott, his brother-in-law, bought a farm eight miles north of the city, where they both moved with their families. Though a Quaker and a nonresistant for many years, Davis served as an officer in the Union army during the Civil War. (*Life*, II, 124, 211; III, 221; IV, 339, 366; Anna D. Hallowell, *James and Lucretia Mott*, Boston, 1884, pp. 130, 326; Peter Brock, *Pacifism in the United States, From the Colonial Era to the First World War*, Princeton, N.J., 1968, p. 585n.)

1. II Corinthians 10:4.

107

TO GEORGE W. BENSON

Boston, Jan. 15, 1838.

Dear bro. George:

It is an old adage, that time is precious. So it is; especially when but five minutes, or so, are allowed one brother to write to another. Elder Coe,[1] of Salem, (of the Christian denomination,) an active and thorough-going abolitionist, leaves in the cars immediately for Brooklyn, via Providence. I seize the opportunity, therefore, to send you (what ought to have been sent long since) Chaptal's Chymistry,[2] Bassett's Letter,[3] Lovejoy's Portrait,[4] &c., all which you will do me the favor to accept as a New Year's token of love, though a very insignificant one. The extra copies of the Liberator, which you wanted, were all distributed, as well as the petitions to Congress. Hope you will see to it that remonstrances against Patton's resolution[5] are forwarded from your county without delay. Twenty, thirty or forty signatures to a petition will answer very well.

The annual meeting of our Society occurs next week[6] — the annual report not yet commenced![7] That fact will make you laugh. I would cry, if that would do any good. If you can, be sure to be on hand at our meeting. We expect to get Faneuil Hall for a Texas meeting, at the same time.[8] Bro. Colver must come,[9] at all events — tell him so, in the name of the Commonwealth of Massachusetts.

I have yet but one child "in the world" — am expecting another immortal gift every day. We are all well and happy. The prospects of the Liberator are bright. Providence is supplying my wants bountifully.

With the dearest remembrances to all at home, I remain,

Affectionately yours,

Wm. Lloyd Garrison.

ALS: Garrison Papers, Boston Public Library.

1. The Reverend William Coe (b. Hopkinton, Rhode Island, May 11, 1804; d. Worcester, Massachusetts, September 9, 1872) married Eliza A. Nichols of Portland, Maine, in 1835. A dedicated abolitionist, he named one of his sons (b. September 1838) after Garrison, another after Wendell Phillips, and a third after Charles Follen. He apparently lived in Salem, Massachusetts, in Brooklyn, Connecticut, and finally in Worcester, Massachusetts. (Henry F. Coe, *Descendants of Matthew Coe*, Boston, 1894, pp. 21–23.) On February 16, 1839, *The Non-Resistant* published a letter from Coe to Garrison in which Coe wrote that although he considered himself a peace man, he was not yet prepared to adopt the Declaration of Sentiments of the New England Non-Resistance Society or its views of government and the church.

2. Jean Antoine Chaptal, Comte de Chanteloup (1756–1832), French chemist and statesman, was the author of several works on chemistry. (*EE.*)

3. William Bassett (1803–1871) of Lynn (son of Isaac Bassett), city clerk of Lynn from 1850 to 1852 and cashier of the First National Bank in Lynn from 1853 to 1871, was active in the antislavery and peace movements. In 1837, he had publicly criticized the New England Quaker leaders for their conservative social and political views, especially their coolness toward antislavery societies, in a pamphlet entitled *Letter to a Member of the Society of Friends in Reply to Objections Against Joining Anti-Slavery Societies* (Boston, 1837). The pamphlet was printed by Isaac Knapp. Bassett's argument with the Quaker authorities continued for three years, in articles and pamphlets. Bassett, who had been raised as an orthodox Quaker, was finally disowned by the society in 1840. He became a devoted Unitarian. (Thomas E. Drake, *Quakers and Slavery in America*, New Haven, 1950, pp. 157, 159–160; James R. Newhall, *History of Lynn, 1864–1890*, Lynn, 1890, pp. 111–112.)

4. A portrait, unidentified, of Elijah Lovejoy.

5. A gag-rule, named after John Mercer Patton (1796–1858), a representative from Virginia, who introduced the resolution into the United States House of Representatives. It forbade even the reading of antislavery petitions, and was adopted on December 21, 1837 (*Life*, II, 197n).

6. The annual meeting of the Massachusetts Anti-Slavery Society was to be held on January 24 and 25.

7. Garrison was supposed to present it.

8. *The Liberator*, on January 19, 1838, announced: "We rejoice that the Mayor and Aldermen have granted the use of Fanueil Hall, on Thursday next, 25th inst. (in the forenoon,) on the petition of Jonathan Phillips and others, for a meeting in opposition to the annexation of Texas to the American Union . . ."

9. The Reverend Nathaniel Colver (b. Orwell, Vermont, May 10, 1794; d. Chicago, September 25, 1870) was at first a friend of Garrison, but joined his opponents over the issues of nonresistance and the participation of women in the antislavery movement. He was pastor of the First Free Church (Baptist) in Boston from 1839 to 1851, and was appointed one of the "seventy" in March 1836. (*Life*, vols. II and III, *passim*; Dwight L. Dumond, ed., *Letters of James Gillespie Birney, 1831–1857*, Gloucester, Mass., 1966, p. 344n.)

108

TO MRS. SARAH T. BENSON

Boston, Jan. 20, 1838.

Dear Mother:

The new year opens upon me in a shower of mercies. Friends (known and unknown) are liberally supplying my temporal wants, and every thing looks propitious. True, what is hid in the future, none can tell; but surely we may both confidently and gratefully speak of the present. Join with me, dear mother, and all ye dear ones, at the birth of another son — as fine and vigorous a babe, excellent in all his proportions, as the fondest parent could desire to see. Last night, at 12 o'clock, dear Helen was safely delivered, in about two hours (instead of 12 or 14, as in the case of George Thompson) — and though she thinks she suffered more, for the time being, than she did before, yet she behaved nobly, and is now doing remarkably well. She has a careful, attentive, experienced, *motherly* nurse, and will lack for nothing. You may therefore feel the utmost relief of mind, in regard to her situation. — The babe as much resembles George Thompson as two twin-cherries upon one stem — at least, in our eyes. Helen says it seems like having G. T. as of old by her side. A hearty little fellow he is, considering his brief sojourn in this hungry world; for he has been nursing with extreme avidity to-day, and is disposed to grumble if he does not get as much as he wants. There is, however, no lack of supply. He weighed 9 lbs. When bro. George wrote me an account of the birth of his son, he boasted that the little fellow weighed 8½ lbs. and challenged me to do better. Just tell him, for me, that I have not only taken up the gauntlet he threw down, but also taken the palm of victory. As for George Thompson, his brother throws him into ecstacies. He smooths his bald head very tenderly, covers his fat cheeks with kisses, throws his arms around him, and performs a variety of other brotherly pranks. George is a noble boy — and very beautiful withal! There is nothing like him in all this great city! Now, don't smile. I have tried to be very impartial in comparing him with other children — and here is the proof that I have succeeded. Well, so it *has* been, long enough to make the time-honored adage — "Every man thinks his own geese are swans" — so it *will* be, in time to come. What am I, that I should not be as weak and vain as other people? — Still, George Thompson is a paragon among the rising generation — that's certain! What will his brother be?

Come, let us have the collective opinions, preferences and decisions of the whole household in Brooklyn. What name shall be given to our baby? Ichabod, Abijah, Jonah, Aminidab, are all good scriptural names, but they are not "popular" — and as these are the days of expediency, we ought to be very "judicious," "prudent," "moderate," and "careful," you know, in bestowing a name, so as not to offend. Now, so reckless of consequences is my wife, — so anxious to show her contempt of public opinion, — so determined that he shall bear an odious name, — that she says it is her wish to call him — William Lloyd Garrison. And my friend Dr. Hildreth [1] says it must be so — the Parkers say so too, and other friends. Now, dear mother, is it right, on the principle of doing as you would be done by, to be so cruel? Make up your verdict in Brooklyn, and see if I do not abide by it.

As I am disposed to be eulogistic, I may add, that the babe is really a very fair child, with a clear skin; though I must confess that his nose, at present, is somewhat broad and flat. He has very little hair, and that is white. His eyes are pronounced to be dark blue.

Helen desires me to say, that our Irish "help," "domestic," more justly *sister*, is an excellent girl, neat, quiet, industrious, kind, and good-natured. We have been fortunate in getting her.

Tell bro. George he has now an additional inducement to come to Boston, to attend our annual meeting. I really hope he will be here. Let him come to Miss Parker's — we can accommodate him as well as not. Tell him by all means to send bro. Colver along.

Helen joins with me in freighting the mail with loving remembrances to all the family as one.

Your happy one,

Wm. Lloyd Garrison.

ALS: Massachusetts Historical Society. Mrs. Sarah Thurber Benson was Helen Garrison's mother.

1. Dr. Charles Trueworth Hildreth. See letter 20, to Helen Garrison, April 16, 1836.

109

TO MRS. SARAH T. BENSON

Boston, March 5, 1838.

My dear Mother:

I know you too well to think, for one moment, that you have up-braided me on account of the fewness of the letters which I transmit to the dear family circle in Brooklyn; but because you are disposed to be kind and forgiving, it by no means follows that I am not deserving of some strong motherly rebukes. Certainly, some one of the family ought to receive a few lines from me as often as once a week; and to write them seems but the labor of a very few moments; but, somehow, you know I am given to procrastination, (even in cases where my love is alike undoubted and unequivocal,) — and other engagements continually pressing upon me, week after week passes without your receiving what is, by every filial consideration, your due — to wit, a letter from W. L. G.

Before this arrives, you will probably have received a letter from Helen, by our friend Daniel Clapp,[1] who called to see us on Friday last, in company with Perez Peck[2] of Coventry. Of course, you are apprised of the fact, that for two or three weeks past I have been severely troubled with what is supposed to be an attack of the scrofula in my head. I have suffered a good deal of anguish, and although somewhat relieved at present, am by no means well. I feel wholly incapacitated to attend to my editorial labors, both reading and writing being painful to me, and my head being filled with confusion instead of order. Indeed, it is quite an effort for me to write this letter. Bro. George has written to me, with all a brother's earnestness and affection, urging me to try a full course of the Thompsonian treatment, and encouraging me to "go ahead" by a recital of the benefit he has recently experienced at the infirmary in Providence. Most of my friends here are afraid to have me make the experiment; but bro. G. tells me to mind nobody but himself, for he will ensure a speedy cure — to throw aside prejudice, &c. &c. Tell him that, instead of being prejudiced against, I have long been in favor of the steaming process. Tell him, further, that though *he* may have found relief in *his* case, it does not necessarily follow that *I* shall in *mine*. But tell him, finally — and that is all he will ask — that I have made up my mind to go into a Thompsonian infirmary on Thursday next, under bro. Himes's [3] auspices, and mean to make a thorough trial. Bro. H. is of opinion, that I shall need a good many courses to effect a permanent cure, but he is sanguine, like bro. George, that I shall immediately derive benefit to my system. I can but try, at all events. You shall be informed of the result without delay.

It is very amusing to listen to the many kind but conflicting suggestions of my friends. One knows of a notable cure of scrofula that was effected by the patient drinking freely of lime water. Another proposes the external and internal use of nitric acid as a remedy. A third recommends a solution of arsenic, sometimes called "Fowler's tasteless tooth-ache drops." A fourth advises the use of Swaim's Panacea. A fifth says there is nothing like sarsaparilla tea — sarsaparilla syrup — sarsaparilla pills. (By the way, I have used several bottles of the syrup, but in vain.) A sixth says, try lobelia and steaming. — A seventh says, be a Grahamite, take no medicine, and you will soon be better. (I live in a very simple manner.)

The disorder seems to be wholly confined to my ears, externally swelling them, and internally causing a high state of inflammation, the discharge of matter, &c. Hence, it affects my brain, so as to render its exercise not only difficult but hazardous.

I felt distressed to hear that bro. George had been ill, but was greatly relieved by his letter. I am afraid that he will get the notion into his head, that a dose of lobelia and a hot bath will save him at any moment, and that thus he will grow careless of his health, and labor too abundantly. Remind him that death is the portion of us all, and beseech him to take good care of himself.

My heart is with you all in Brooklyn, and the desire I feel to see you once more in the flesh is very strong. Whether we shall ever meet again on earth, is of course among the uncertainties of life; still, we may cherish the hope. One thing is sure — separate we must, eventually; and for this occurrence we should be at all times prepared. But death cannot disunite those souls in whom dwelleth the love of God, for they have "eternal life."

How your parental heart would leap for joy, if you could see our dear babe! He is really a noble boy, and excites the admiration of all who see him. I think George Thompson, beautiful as he was as an infant, was not so fair and bright looking as is his brother. Both of them are precious, beyond all estimation. Loving them with a father's love, how can I help abhorring that hideous system of slavery, which would make them, if their skin was of a different hue, mere chattels, to be torn from my arms at any moment?

I feel under additional obligations to bro. George, for his letter informing me of the proceedings of the Anti-Slavery Convention in Hartford.[4] Connecticut seems to be nobly coming up to the rescue. Leap in your chains, ye slaves!

From sister Mary, at Providence, I hear nothing. — Dear Helen is well, and unites with me in proferring loving remembrances to all at home.

Affectionately,

Wm. Lloyd Garrison.

ALS: Garrison Papers, Boston Public Library.

1. Probably Daniel Clapp of Pomfret, Connecticut, a Quaker preacher (Ebenezer Clapp, comp., *The Clapp Memorial*, Boston, 1876, p. 293).

2. Perez Peck (b. Rehoboth, Rhode Island, 1786), a successful and well-to-do mechanic who owned a celebrated machine shop established in 1810 in the village of Anthony, Town of Coventry, Kent county, Rhode Island. He was a devoted member of the Society of Friends. In 1828, he helped draft the constitution and by-laws of the Coventry Temperance Union. He lived to be almost ninety years old. (Robert Grieve, *An Illustrated History of Pawtucket, Central Falls and Vicinity*, Pawtucket, 1897, p. 441.)

3. The Reverend Joshua B. Himes. See letter 59, to Henry E. Benson, November 4, 1836.

4. On March 2, 1838, *The Liberator* carried the following notice: "On Wednesday, a State convention was to be held at Hartford, to form a Connecticut A. S. Society. The call to the convention was signed by *seventeen hundred and sixty-seven* persons, from *eighty-seven* different towns. A large portion of the signers were legal voters."

1 1 0

TO GEORGE W. BENSON

Boston, March 10, 1838.

My dear George:

Whether this will find you at home, or not, is of course uncertain; but no matter. Although it is not designed for the *public* eye, yet it may be read by all the *private* eyes that brighten the dwelling in "Friendship's Valley." "E pluribus unum!" We *many*, are *one*.

Well, the deed is done, — the experiment has been tried, — black pepper, cayenne, lobelia, hot drops, and a steam-bath, have done their worst; and still I am in the land of the living, as this letter plainly shows! What a miraculous escape from the hands of those merciless destroyers of our race, the Thompsonian quacks! How is it? Am I immortal? If they have not killed me, does it not follow that I am something more than bullet-proof — to wit, immortal? ay, even in this my fleshly tabernacle?

All this badinage is only a puff preliminary — a startling exordium, by way of giving a keener relish for the whole discourse which follows. Therefore, be very much at ease.

Influenced mainly by your advice, which was seconded by many of my friends in the city, others however protesting against the experiment, with full purpose of soul I bent my steps resolutely towards a Thompsonian infirmary, kept by Dr. Clark[1] in Pleasant-street, in company with bro. Himes, on Thursday morning last. I was suffering with the inflammation in my head, my ears being very sore, and a swelling on each side of the face adjacent. Bro. Himes very kindly offered to take a course with me, partly as an amateur performance to encourage me in making "the perilous adventure" — and partly because his health required it. We began our preliminary operations at 10 o'clock, the first dose being a cup of Thompsonian "coffee" — then other drinks — then a steaming, the thermometer ranging from 110 to 114. — Never did I know what it is to perspire until then! What a shower of rain poured from my neck to my heels! Very pleasant withal, and raising the "circulating medium" to something above par. I remained in the bath about 15 minutes, then went dripping to bed, where I remained till about 3 o'clock, P. M. ever and anon drinking hot liquids to make me vomit and sweat the more freely. During this time, bro. Himes and myself (both being in the same predicament) kept up a running fire of conversation, "from grave to gay, from lively to severe,"[2] occasionally pausing a moment to repudiate from our stomachs what the lobelia and cayenne, in their searching operation, had found hostile to our welfare and security. Although in a high state of perspiration, and constantly being dosed with hot drops and what not, I felt not only "as calm as a summer's morning," but really in a state reaching at least ten degrees beyond Point Comfortable. Had it not been for the flippancy of our tongues, I should have slept most sweetly; but having so excellent a companion as bro. H., I could not afford to "give day to night." At about 3 o'clock, we left our beds, took another bath for about 10 minutes, was then baptized with cold water, came out, dressed ourselves, went down into the sitting room, each of us "like a giant refreshed from wine," [3] or rather from *steaming* — and in a short time, behold us, with other patients, sitting at the dinner-table, with vigorous appetites, and a good beefsteak before us! The pain in my head was greatly relieved, and I felt more than 50 per cent better. In the evening, I rode home, and have felt ever since in an improving condition. I intend to take several courses, until I know whether a radical cure can be effected, or not — probably one a week. So much for experiment No. I.

Dear Helen was in great trepidation until my return, but is now thankful I went. It is surprising how soon the swelling in my face has been reduced, and the gathering in my ears dispersed. "Richard is not himself again," [4] *wholly*, but I am certainly better than I had any reason to expect under the best treatment.

You must have had a fine time at Hartford, despite the lawless conduct of a portion of the "brotherhood." What say you — was Dr. Hawes [5] "up to the mark" on the occasion? I feel anxious to know precisely how he acted.

The committee of the Odeon,[6] (of which the mayor of the city is chairman,) have to-day decided that that immense building shall be granted to the Boston Female A. S. Society, for a course of lectures on slavery from Angelina E. Grimke. So rolls the tide onward! The effort of A. E. G., before our legislative committee,[7] has been of incalculable benefit to the cause.

If you see bro. Colver, express to him my admiration of his zeal, boldness, eloquence and success, in the great and sacred enterprise so dear to us all.

Our boys are thriving finely — wish to see yours very much — cover his face with kisses for me. Love to all.

Ever yours,

Wm. Lloyd Garrison.

ALS: Garrison Papers, Boston Public Library.

1. The *Boston True Thomsonian* for July 15, 1841, carried the following advertisement:

"To the Public. Doctor William Clark having returned to this city and opened a Thomsonian Infirmary at No. 12 South Cedar street, respectfully informs his numerous friends and the public generally, that this establishment has been fitted up with express reference to the accommodation and comfort of the invalid. It is very pleasantly situated at the southerly part of the city, in a quiet spot, free from noise; and where the east winds so annoying to patients, have but little or no effect. Dr. C. has been engaged in the Botanic practice for the last seven years with great success, as thousands will testify. Medicines put up with directions for use, adapted to all complaints. Advice gratis. . . .

The above establishment will be conducted on pure temperance principles, as no alcohol will be used in tinctures, bitters, or any other remedial liquid that is taken internally. The subscriber being satisfied that one prolific source of intemperance is the use of alcohol in medicine, which, to say the least, very seldom effects any good. . . ."

In September 1841 Dr. Clark was a delegate from Massachusetts to the New England Thomsonian Convention. He contributed several articles to Thomsonian journals about the harmfulness of alcohol in medicine and the use of lobelia. In 1843 he moved his infirmary to 82 Carver Street, Boston. He assured the readers of his notice that he had "never lost any patients with the following complaints, *viz.·* typhus fever, scarlet fever, canker rash, erysipelas, measles, cholera infantum, or cholera morbus." He also offered them medicated steam baths, and Clark's Unicorn Candy, for coughs, etc. (*Boston True Thomsonian*, September 1, 1841, March 15, 1843, *et passim*; *The Thomsonian Scout*, Burlington, Vt., May 15, 1842.)

2. Alexander Pope, *Essay on Man*, Epistle, IV, line 380.

3. *Book of Common Prayer*, Psalms 78:66.

4. "Richard's himself again," Shakespeare, *Richard III*, V, iii, altered by Colley Cibber (1671–1757), English poet-laureate, dramatist, and actor.

5. The Reverend Joel Hawes (1789–1867) of Hartford, Connecticut, a graduate of Brown University and Andover Seminary (1817), was ordained minister of the First Church (Congregational) in Hartford in 1818 and married during the same year. In 1827 he published *Lectures to Young Men*, a popular volume reprinted many times. He received an honorary D.D. from Brown University in 1831. He was elected a corporate member of the American Board of Foreign Missions in 1838. (For further information see Edward A. Lawrence, D.D., *The Life of Joel Hawes, D.D.*, Hartford, 1873; *NCAB*.)

6. The history of the Odeon dates back to 1794 when the first theater in Boston was built and was variously known as the Federal Street Theater, the Boston Theater, and Old Drury. The building was destroyed by fire in 1798 but was rebuilt and opened during the same year. In 1833, it was closed as a theater and leased to the Society of Free Inquirers. The next year the Academy of Music obtained possession of it and the name was changed to the Odeon. Religious services were held there on Sundays. The building was designed by Charles Bulfinch. (Samuel Adams Drake, *Old Landmarks and Historic Personages of Boston*, Boston, 1873, p. 259.)

7. *The Liberator*, March 2, 1838, printed a letter from Maria Weston Chapman in which she described Angelina Grimké's address before the Massachusetts legislative committee on slavery during the preceding week. *The Liberator* also printed selections from the address.

111

TO GEORGE W. BENSON

Boston, April 7, 1838.

Dear bro. George:

This letter shall testify, that I am at least able to hold my pen, though it may not prove that my head is in better order than it has been for some weeks past. Yours of the 1st inst., was not received till yesterday. What a fanatical Thompsonian you are! So much for first getting crazed by abolitionism! Nevertheless, Dr. Benson, I thank you for your medical advice. You are almost tempted to believe that I have grown disheartened, or frightened, or neglectful, or indifferent, or something quite as disreputable. Fie on you! Don't you know that the organ of firmness (and, consequently, of endurance) is almost as large as a hen's egg on the top of my cranium? Am I the man, therefore, once having screwed my courage up to the sticking point, — once having encountered them victoriously, — to be afraid of lobelia, cayenne, black coffee, raspberry tea, composition powders and bitters, and a perpendicular steam-box? You write that you are daily expecting a report from me of experiment No. 2. No. 2, forsooth! Why, I have already gone through five entire courses — which, certainly, make *five* experiments. Is not that doing bravely? Is it not following-up that anti-republican enemy, the "King's evil," vigorously, actively, unyieldingly? Well, the result of the campaign, thus far — how many killed, how many wounded, and so on? Or, in other words, "how do you feel now?" Not any worse, certainly — but some better. Not so well as I could wish — not so well as I must be before I can be of much service in the editorial line — not so well as I hope to be, after a few more courses. My head is still confused, and the discharges still continue from my ears. But I am relieved of much pain — my appetite and digestion are both good — and my whole system is doubtless in better order than formerly. I shall take a course once a week regularly, till I remove to Brooklyn.

I am exceedingly anxious to attend the annual meeting at New-York,[1] because some important matters must be discussed, some new measures proposed, and perhaps a different organization made, so as more equally to distribute the power at head quarters among the different State societies. It will be a great, a momentous occasion. Yet I am apprehensive that my health will not allow me to go, safely — for excitement of the brain is what I cannot easily bear at present. Besides, I am expected to go to Philadelphia, to deliver a public address there on a special occasion; and there will be another week of excitement. Hence, just now, I cannot tell how it will be with me. The chances are about equal, that Helen and the boys will be with you about the 1st of May, or the 1st of June. If I should not be able to go to New-York, you need not expect us till the 1st of June — if otherwise, the 1st of May.

The advertisement respecting the School, in your former letter, was entirely forgotten; and had you not reminded me of it in your last, would have failed of getting an insertion in the Liberator. It shall appear next week,[2] together with a notice of your meeting at Brooklyn.[3]

Friend Knapp yesterday sent 50 copies (I told him to add the other 25) of Boyle's Letter,[4] to you at Providence. Probably you had left for Brooklyn before they arrived. I was glad to hear that Mr. Pearl[5] read it with interest, and hope it will lead him to further investigation. As yet, the Letter has been very quietly received by our subscribers; and I have been surprised that it has created no more excitement. However, the leaven must have time to work. I dare say there will be a stir about it in due time. And yet it is so powerfully written, and contains so much truth, that it cannot easily be ridiculed or refuted. Neither the Christian Mirror, N. Y. Observer, nor N. E. Spectator, has said a word about it. The last Vermont Chronicle, however, has some extracts from it, &c. As friend Knapp printed 2000 copies of it, I feel anxious he should dispose of them for his own sake, as well as for its inherent value. He puts them at cost price — $5 per hundred.

The Grimkes are doing a mighty work here, weekly, in the presence of assembled thousands.[6] Praise the Lord, all ye his servants![7]

We have kissed the babes for you, repeatedly. They are both well, as is dear Helen.

With unabated affection for you all, I remain,

Yours lovingly till death,
Wm. Lloyd Garrison.

ALS: Garrison Papers, Boston Public Library.

1. The Annual Meeting of the American Anti-Slavery Society.

2. The advertisement appeared in *The Liberator*, April 13, 1838. Carrying the heading, "Family Boarding School," it read:

"A gentleman, every way qualified, who has a delightful situation, in a pleasant town in Connecticut, where public sentiment will sustain him, proposes to open a family boarding school for boys, irrespective of color; where they shall be taught all the branches of an English or liberal education. The school to commence as soon as ten scholars are engaged, and the number to be limited to twenty.

"For further particulars, address G. W. Benson, Brooklyn, Conn. April 3, 1838."

3. The meeting was of the Windham County Anti-Slavery Society, and was to be held in Brooklyn on Thursday, April 26, at 10 a.m. The notice appeared in *The Liberator*, April 13, 1838, and was signed by "G. W. Benson, Cor. Sec."

4. This was a letter which had been printed in *The Liberator*, March 23, 1838, under the heading "Letter to Wm. Lloyd Garrison, Touching the 'Clerical Appeal,' Sectarianism, and True Holiness." The letter was written from Rome, Ashtabula County, Ohio, and was addressed to "Dearly Beloved Garrison." It was signed by James Boyle and was a fervent defense of Garrison against his clerical opponents. Garrison then published it in pamphlet form, with a preface and his poem "Christian Rest."

Life, II, 286n, presents the following information about Boyle:

"The Rev. James Boyle — a native of Lower Canada, born and bred a Catholic; afterwards, turned Protestant, a prominent revivalist preacher in Vermont, and in 1834 temporarily supplying the Free Church at Hartford, Conn. (being succeeded by Charles Fitch); finally, a New Haven Perfectionist in intimate relations with J. H. Noyes " In 1830, Boyle became lecturing and financial agent of the Ohio Anti-Slavery Society.

5. Mr. Phillip Pearl, of Hampton, Windham county, was a lawyer, abolitionist, and vice-president of the Connecticut Anti-Slavery Society. He had been a member of the Connecticut senate and was in 1840 presidential elector for Connecticut. In 1841, he was president of the executive committee of the Windham County Anti-Slavery Society. (*Weld-Grimké Letters*, I, 397; *The Liberator*, February 12, 1841.)

6. This refers to a series of antislavery lectures that Angelina and Sarah Grimké delivered at the Odeon in Boston to large audiences.

7. Possibly Revelation 19:5.

112

TO SAMUEL J. MAY

Boston, April 24, 1838.

Beloved bro. May:

I have not been prompt in replying to yours of the 16th, simply because I have been "all at sea" as to the probability of my going to New-York.[1] Even now, I am unable to decide whether it will be wise or expedient for me to be drawn into such a whirlpool of excitement as will engulph the great city of Babylon during the anniversary week. Although I have derived some benefit from the Thompsonian treatment, yet the complaint in my head almost wholly unfits me for mental effort. — The [le]ast excitement makes my brain reel as if I had drunk a full potation of liquor. I am useless as an editor, useless as a speaker; and therefore not worth much, "either in the gross or by detail." The friends here are very desirous that I should be in New-York; and, truly, "the spirit is willing, but the *head* is weak." [2] Every thing will depend upon my feelings next Monday. Greatly rejoiced am I to know that you purpose to wend your way to head-quarters, and much shall I covet your company, if I may be permitted to take the same journey. A week from to-day (Tuesday) would be the one most convenient for me to leave Boston. But the probability now is against my going. I hope you will come to the city, nevertheless, on Monday next; for there are many things I want to say to you, particularly if I am to be left behind.

Have you read Brownson's article on slavery in the 2d No. of his Quarterly?[3] If so, don't you think it wholly unworthy of a sound mind, and is it not deserving of severe treatment at the hands of abolition critics? I have lost all my confidence in B. as a reformer. Poor man! my strictures upon him make him feel badly. He has addressed a long letter to me through the columns of the Reformer,[4] a copy of which may have been sent to you. It is written with much feeling, and is spiced very freely with inconsistency and egotism. I shall publish it, with comments, in the Liberator.

Yesterday, the Grimkés bade farewell to Boston, and to the Commonwealth, having accomplished more for the cause of God's suffering ones, in the course of a year, than any of us realize, or dare to measure. Helen went with me down to the cars to see them depart, where we found Mr. and Mrs. Child, Mrs. Chapman, Mary Chapman, Caroline Weston, Mrs. Loring, the Southwicks, Mr. Fuller, Mr. Philbrick,[5] &c. &c. Sarah was to lecture in Providence last evening. They will leave P.[6] for Philadelphia on Wednesday, but do not expect to be present at the meetings in New-York. Angelina's closing lecture at the Odeon, last Thursday evening,[7] was the keystone of the arch. Its peroration was of a melting and thrilling character. The audience was truly immense, and her mastery over it was wonderful.

My annual report is at last out. Bro. Phelps wrote a protest against that part of it relating to the Clerical Appeal, and had it printed — but I am happy to say, both for his sake and the cause, has concluded to suppress it. More on this subject when I see you.

It is now so late, that I presume my volume of Lovejoy,[8] if sent to you, would arrive too late to have you read it before Monday. It is an interesting volume, but contains nothing new respecting the Alton tragedy. Perhaps I shall conclude to send it to you by the next stage.

Bro. St. Clair[9] lectured last evening at Hingham, and then came home, arriving here about 12 o'clock. He started before breakfast for Lowell, to attend the Middlesex county meeting this day. I did not see him, and therefore know not what has been his success. He is a driver indeed — not a *slave*-driver.

Mary Parker thinks of attending the Convention of Women at Philadelphia.

AL: Garrison Papers, Boston Public Library. The end of this letter is missing.

1. This refers to the fifth annual meeting of the American Anti-Slavery Society, called for Tuesday, May 8, in New York City. The business meeting was to take place during the previous week, beginning on Wednesday, May 2, 1838.

2. Garrison's variation of "The spirit indeed is willing but the flesh is weak" (Matthew 26: 41).

3. *The Boston Quarterly Review*; portions of the article were reprinted in *The Liberator*, May 11, 1838. Orestes Augustus Brownson (b. Stockbridge, Vermont, September 16, 1803; d. Detroit, Michigan, April 17, 1876), reformer, Protestant minister, author, and eventual Catholic convert, joined the Presbyterian church in 1822, became a Universalist minister in 1826, and for several years preached in various churches in Vermont, New Hampshire, and New York. After withdrawing from that denomination because of his too-liberal theological views, he became a free-lance minister and writer. For a while, he associated himself with such reformers as Robert Dale Owen and Fanny Wright, and helped organize the short-lived Workmen's party. He then joined the Unitarian denomination serving a parish at Walpole, New Hampshire, in 1832–1834, and another at Canton, Massachusetts, in 1834–1836. In 1836, he organized his own church among Boston workers, calling it The Society for Christian Union and Progress, and published his first book, a condemnation of both Catholicism and Protestantism, entitled *New Views of Christianity, Society and the Church*. In January 1838, he established the *Boston Quarterly Review*, which developed into an influential organ of the Massachusetts Democrats. He merged the *Review* with the *Democratic Review* of New York in 1842, but resumed his own journal in 1844, naming it *Brownson's Quarterly Review*. During the same year, he converted to Catholicism. The *Review* continued publication until 1864. (*ACAB; DAB.*)

4. The letter, dated Mount Bellingham, April 14, 1838, was reprinted in *The Liberator*, May 11, 1838.

Brownson became the editor of the *Boston Reformer* in July 1836. It was a weekly journal of the new humanitarianism. Its motto was "We know no party but mankind," which he interpreted as " 'We know no party but Brownson,' and he rode the *Reformer* as a hobby horse, from which he tilted at whatever was for the moment vexing him. Its columns were filled with reports of his sermons, brief articles by himself and paragraphs from other journals praising or (more generally) denouncing him. But, beneath these Brownsonian trappings of flippancy, pugnacity and arrogance, the *Reformer* had a markedly moral tone. Its editor planned to save both religion and reform by uniting them." (Arthur M. Schlesinger, Jr., *A Pilgrim's Progress: Orestes A. Brownson*, Boston, 1939, pp. 64–65.)

5. Samuel Philbrick (b. Seabrook, New Hampshire, February 4, 1789; d. Brookline, Massachusetts, September 19, 1859), of Quaker parents, engaged in business in Lynn, Massachusetts, beginning in 1816, and moved to Boston in 1830, where he entered the leather business. As early as 1829, he served as an agent of Benjamin Lundy's *Genius of Universal Emancipation*. He was treasurer of the Massachusetts Anti-Slavery Society for almost twenty years and proved a devoted friend and supporter of Garrison. (Reference Card, Rare Book Department, Boston Public Library; Thomas Philbrick, *Genealogy of the Philbrick and Philbrook Families*, Exeter, N.H., 1886, p. 58.)

6. Providence, Rhode Island.

7. March 22. *The Liberator*, on March 30, 1838, wrote of this meeting, "there were not less than three thousand persons present; and such was the pressure of the curious multitude, that it was found necessary to shut the iron gates, after the spacious building was crammed, to prevent further admittance. The attention of the audience was unbroken, and a deep and salutary impression evidently made upon many minds."

8. Probably the volume by Joseph C. and Owen Lovejoy, *Memoir of the Rev. Elijah P. Lovejoy; Who Was Murdered in Defense of the Liberty of the Press, at Alton, Illinois, Nov. 7, 1837* (New York, 1838). This volume was published with a foreword by John Quincy Adams, and had been commissioned by the executive committee of the American Anti-Slavery Society (Merton L. Dillon, *Elijah P. Lovejoy, Abolitionist Editor*, Urbana, 1961, p. 178).

9. The Reverend Alanson St. Clair. See letter 69, to Anna Benson, February 4, 1837.

113

TO HELEN E. GARRISON

New-York, May 4, 1838.

My dear Helen:

If I send you a line the very first opportunity, I am sure you will say, I could have done no better.

I arrived here this morning at 6 o'clock, having had a remarkably good passage. The distance from Boston to Providence, or rather from Boston to Stonington,[1] about 90 miles, was accomplished in about 5 hours. We left Stonington in the famous steam-boat Lexington, the moon and the stars shining brilliantly. I had a very good birth, and slept pretty soundly all night. The company was numerous, but I knew not an individual on board, and kept very quiet all the way. Bro. George left yesterday for New-Haven, to see about the Legislature, and will not return. I am quite disappointed, in consequence. He supposed I should not be here. I have seen and shaken hands with Gerrit Smith, J. G. Birney, Judge Jay,[2] Beriah Green, Lewis Tappan and family, Alvan Stewart, H. B. Stanton, Wm. M. Chace, S. J. May, Thomas Davis, and a host of others. This forenoon, there has been a very animated discussion between Alvan Stewart and Judge Jay before the delegates, respecting the constitutionality of slavery. It was very ably debated, but I think Jay had the best of the argument.[3] Last evening, there was a discussion, I am told, on a *peace* resolution offered by Whittier, but it was voted down![4] — Bro. Leavitt[5] made quite a war-like and very eloquent speech, and was replied to by bro. May. Bro. St. Clair is here, well, and busy enough, I assure you. Tell his wife that I gave him the letter and things for him, *promptly*. Mary's letter to Julia Ann Tappan[6] was also handed to her this forenoon. As yet, we have hardly got the steam up, but shall no doubt soon — and, I trust, without bursting our boiler. Messrs. Chapman, Phillips, Loring and Philbrick will return home to-morrow afternoon. Bro. Weld is not here — but I have received an invitation to the wedding, signed by himself and Angelina.[7] They wish you also to be present. I have a similar invitation for Mary. Tell her I shall be on the look-out for her on Tuesday, via Providence. There are several Philadelphia friends here, who seem to be very glad that I am going to the "city of brotherly love."

I know not, yet, where I shall stop in this city, having had no invitation — shall probably have to pay my board. These hasty lines have been written in the midst of great confusion, and are hardly legible. You shall hear from me again soon. I feel very well. Hope the dear boys are no worse for their cold — cover their soft cheeks with kisses for me. It is painful to be separated, even for an hour. My kind remembrances to all at home.

Yours, lovingly,

Wm. Lloyd Garrison.

ALS: Garrison Papers, Boston Public Library.

    1. A seaport in the southeast corner of Connecticut, near Rhode Island.

    2. William Jay.

    3. A report of the proceedings of May 2, 3, 4, 5, 7, and 8 appeared in *The Liberator*, May 18, 1838. The debate was over a motion introduced by Alvan Stewart, "That the clause of the 2d article of this Society be struck out which admits 'that each state in which slavery exists has, by the Constitution of the United States, the exclusive right to legislate in regards to its abolition in said state.'" Approval of the amendment would have meant an affirmation of the right of the national government to prohibit or abolish slavery in any of the slave states.

    4. The report of the proceedings does not mention a resolution by Whittier but it does note a resolution by Samuel J. May that was voted down by a vote of 44 to 19. The resolution read:

    "That we earnestly desire that the agents and members of this Society, while engaged in advocating the pure and pacific principles of emancipation, may continue patient under their manifold provocations, forgiving their enemies, not relying upon physical strength for their defence against the violence of others, but by their patient endurance of evil, evince that the spirit of their whole mission was one of 'peace on earth and good will to men.'"

    5. The Reverend Joshua Leavitt.

    6. Julia Tappan was the eldest daughter of Lewis Tappan.

    7. The wedding of Theodore Weld and Angelina Grimké was held on May 14, 1838, in Philadelphia.

114

TO HELEN E. GARRISON

New-York, May 7, 1838.

My dear Wife —

    I must write a few lines to you, either in the midst of the debates of the convention, or else be wholly silent, which latter alternative would not be so agreeable to you. First of all, you will feel most anxious about the state of my health. Let me say, then, that I am none the worse for my visit — perhaps a little better. The excitement of our meetings has not affected my poor brain half as much as I apprehended it would; but then, you must understand, that I have as yet taken no part in the debates, except in uttering a few sentences. In my letter of Friday, I wrote that I had no abiding place pointed out to me, during my stay here. Since then, I have been under the roof of our ever hospitable friend Thomas Truesdell,[1] where are also abiding, friends H. C. Wright and Wm. Adams of Pawtucket.[2] Mrs. Truesdell is, as usual, pleasant and smiling. To-morrow morning, I shall endeavor to be at the steam-boat landing, to welcome a portion of the American women who are soon to do the nation some service in the city of brotherly love.

This forenoon, I have been "as busy as a bee" in writing letters of introduction (seven in number) to friends in Paris and England, for James Mott's son-in-law, E. M. Davis, to send by the great steam-ship which sails at 2 o'clock for London, this day. I intend to see that transatlantic wonder start on her journey across the Atlantic.

The debates in our meetings have been quite spirited on several topics. Alvan Stewart came pretty near carrying his point, in opposition to Judge Jay, respecting an amendment of our Constitution.[3] I am glad, on the whole, he did not succeed, for a variety of reasons. The vote was a very close one — the leading abolitionists being about equally divided in opinion. With that exception, I believe all our resolutions have been adopted with great unanimity.

Sectarianism has received another hearty blow at the hands of the delegates — particularly with reference to any new organization.[4] Our New Ipswich friend, Mr. Lee,[5] has not opened his lips, nor any one on his side of the house. So far, therefore, "all's well."

Monday evening.

I have just returned from a large meeting of the colored friends in Zion's Church, very many of whom were induced to attend by knowing that I would be present. The meeting was addressed by Beriah Green, Alvan Stewart, Rev. Mr. Cross,[6] Charles W. Denison,[7] and myself. It was an interesting occasion. The manner in which these dear colored friends throng around me is very affecting to my feelings. Their expressions of attachment and gratitude are of the strongest kind. O what a reward for the very little I have done on their behalf!

Tuesday morning.[8]

I went down in good season this morning, to the Battery, to welcome Mary and her companions on their arrival. Bros. Johnson, Fuller, Chace and Adams went with me.[9] We had to wait about an hour for the arrival of the boat, but had a most delightful walk and very animated conversation during this time. Our friends arrived a few minutes past 7 — all safe and in good spirits — and were soon transmitted to their several quarters. I had seen Rebecca Spring,[10] (who, by the way, sends her best regards to you,) and made arrangements with her for accommodating Mary — but, it seems, the Tappans had already anticipated me, and so she went to their house. Mrs. Johnson [11] was in the company.

Speaking of the manifest regard which our colored friends cherish for me, it is pleasing to add, that, notwithstanding I am now known to entertain peculiar religious sentiments, hostile to all church organizations, &c. &c. yet I have been most kindly treated by all classes, ministers as well as laymen, among our white delegates. — There is no evidence of coldness on the part of a single individual, but all take me by the hand with apparent cordiality.

Tuesday, 4 o'clock.

Our great meeting was held this forenoon in the Tabernacle, and continued for more than four hours. The audience was a noble one, and the effect of the speeches most excellent. Prayer was made by Rev. Timothy Merritt [12] of Lynn; a portion of Scripture was read by Rev. E. M. P. Wells; bro. Stanton read a portion of the Annual Report, which I moved to print, making a few remarks. The first speech was made by Mr. Birney;[13] the second by Edmund Quincy; the third by Dr. McCune Smith,[14] a colored young friend; the fourth by Gerrit Smith; and the fifth by Alvan Stewart. These were *all* capital. Lewis Tappan read several interesting letters, one from John Quincy Adams, and another from Edward Beecher.[15] Every body seemed to be delighted with the meeting. I presume it was the largest that will be held in this city during the present week.

As soon as I got into the cabin of the steam-boat, Mary handed me your affectionate letter, which I read with a father's and a husband's interest and love. My dear, sweet babe! to be thus afflicted so soon after coming into this state of being — and through the instrumentality of his own brother! It almost tempts me to return home instantly, and not to go to Philadelphia; for I shall be filled with apprehension, if I stay. But, should he grow in any degree worse, let me know of it without delay; and by all means, in that case, call in Dr. Hildreth, and take his advice. I need not enjoin upon you to watch over him as for his life, for there is more danger that you will be over-anxious, than that you will be even slightly negligent. Your affections for husband and children are sincere and strong — your chief danger lies here — that you prize them all too highly — so that, if any of them should be taken from you, you will find it hard to be resigned to the will of heaven. On this point, be on your guard.

Separation from you, dear wife, even for so short a time, gives leaden wings to the hours. I would prefer not to be absent, were it not that I ought not to be selfish as to consult my own feelings alone, and that I may be in some degree made useful by coming here. Gladly shall I return to your embrace, and to the alluring company of my dear prattling babes. If William should grow no worse, it is probable that you will not see me till a week from next Saturday. It is uncertain whether I shall return by the way of Brooklyn. I expect bro. George will be here to-morrow or on Thursday, drumming up speakers for the New-Haven meeting. He left here before I arrived — consequently I did not see him, as you suppose in your letter. — He told friend Truesdell, confidentially, that he had made something like two or three thousand dollars recently, by the sale of mulberry trees.

Tell Lucy [16] I shall gratefully appreciate all her kindnesses during my absence.

As you enjoined it upon me, by promising me another letter if I obey you, I have committed your letter to the flames — so, be sure to write to me, without delay, directing your letter to Philadelphia. Love to all at home.

With love unceasing, ever yours,

Wm. Lloyd Garrison.

ALS: Garrison Papers, Boston Public Library. A portion of this letter was reprinted in *Life*, II, 209–210.

1. Thomas Truesdell was a Negro abolitionist who had a large home in Brooklyn Heights in New York. Garrison stayed there at least one other time. See *Life*, II, 356n; reference card, Rare Book Room, Boston Public Library.

2. "A most worthy Scotch Quaker, from Pawtucket, a Rhode Island delegate (see *Lib.* 10:165)." (*Life*, II, 357n.) William Adams, a Pawtucket grocer, was a native of Paisley, Scotland, who left that country at about 1820 to come to the United States. He was a Quaker "by profession, but not by birth or membership." A delegate to the World's Anti-Slavery Convention in England in 1840, he was then described as "a primitive looking Quaker, such as is rarely to be met with in Ireland in these latter times. His broad-brimmed hat, pepper-and-salt colored garb, and simple address, strongly remind us of the days of our youth. . . ." Adams, a nonresistant and upholder of "women's rights," joined Garrison in sitting in the gallery of the convention in protest against the convention's refusal to permit the participation of women. His three sons, William Tindall, Robert, and Charles P. Adams were also active abolitionists and reformers. (*The Liberator*, October 16, 1840, reprints a sketch of "William Adams of Pawtucket," from the *Dublin Weekly Herald*; Robert Greave, *An Illustrated History of Pawtucket, Central Falls and Vicinity*, Pawtucket, 1897, pp. 122, 240.)

3. Alvan Stewart's motion, which was supported by Gerrit Smith and others, was opposed by William Jay, Wendell Phillips, and Ellis G. Loring. It was defeated by a very close vote. See note 3 in preceding letter.

4. This refers to two resolutions introduced by Oliver Johnson, which were adopted unanimously:

"Resolved, That it is the glory of the anti-slavery cause, that its principles are of such fundamental importance to the whole human family, that men who differ widely from each other on political and theological subjects, can labor harmoniously together for its promotion, and that no political party, or religious denomination, which is not in itself corrupt, has any thing to fear from its progress or final triumph.

"Resolved, That while we hail with joy the efforts of our brethren of any religious denomination in which slavery exists, to purify their own church from the sin of slavery; we should deprecate the formation of any Anti-Slavery Society, which imposes a religious or political test for the purpose of rendering the anti-slavery cause subservient to the interests of a sect or party, or of opposing existing organizations." (*The Liberator*, May 18, 1838.)

5. Samuel Lee (b. Kensington, Connecticut, March 18, 1803) was graduated from Yale College in 1827 and from the Yale Theological Seminary in 1830. He was a minister in Sherborn, Massachusetts, from 1830 to 1836. In 1836, he became minister at the First Congregational Church at New Ipswich, New Hampshire. He served there until 1860, and continued living in the town until his death in 1881. (Charles H. Chandler, *The History of New Ipswich, N. H.*, Fitchburg, Mass., 1914, pp. 127, 129, 514.)

6. The Reverend John Cross (*Life*, II, 210). Sarah and Angelina Grimké, in a letter to Henry C. Wright, dated Groton, Massachusetts, August 12, 1837, refer to a "Brother Cross," of Boxboro. A footnote identifies him as the Reverend John Cross (*Weld-Grimké Letters*, I, 419–421). However, a search of the town histories of Boxboro reveals only the Reverend Joseph Warren Cross (born in 1811), who was called to the Evangelical Congregational Society of Boxboro in 1834 and served until 1839. He also served on the local school board in 1838. For a while, he was secretary of the Middlesex Anti-Slavery Society. He opposed the participation of women in antislavery societies. At the age of eighty he was living in West Boylston, Massachusetts. (D. Hamilton Hurd, *History of Middlesex County*, Philadelphia, 1890, p. 779.)

7. The Reverend Charles Wheeler Denison (b. Stonington, Connecticut, November 5, 1812; d. Washington, November 13, 1881), editor of the *World*, a newspaper published in Philadelphia. During 1833, he helped William Goodell in editing the *Emancipator*. He was a delegate from the New York City Anti-Slavery Society at the founding convention of the American Anti-Slavery Society in 1833 and seceded in 1840, with the opponents of Garrison, over the participation of women in the society (*Life*, I, 398, 406, 415; II, 198, 210, 348, 349, 450; *Weld-Grimké Letters*, I, 123n.)

8. May 8, 1838.

9. Oliver Johnson, John E. Fuller, William M. Chace, and William Adams.

10. Rebecca Spring was the daughter of the Quaker abolitionist, Arnold Buffum, and the wife of Marcus Spring, a wealthy New York merchant. Marcus Spring was the moving spirit of the group that in 1853 founded the cooperative community known as "Raritan Bay Union," at Eaglewood, New Jersey. (*Two Quaker Sisters, From the Original Diaries of Elizabeth Buffum Chace and Lucy Buffum Lovell*, with an introduction by Malcolm R. Lovell, New York, 1937, xxvi–xxviii; Gerda Lerner, *The Grimké Sisters from South Carolina*, Boston, 1967, pp. 316–318.)

11. Mrs. Oliver Johnson.

12. The Reverend Timothy Merritt (1775–1845) was born in Barkhamstead, Connecticut, the son of James and Hannah Merritt, Methodists. He began preaching as early as 1794 and in 1796 entered the Methodist traveling connection as a circuit preacher. Beginning in 1803, he preached in Maine for about ten years, then returned to Connecticut for three or four years. In 1817–1818 and in 1825–1826, he preached in Boston. He helped edit *Zion's Herald* in Malden in 1831, and from 1832 to 1835, in New York, he was assistant editor of the *Christian Advocate and Journal*. He was minister of the Methodist Church in Lynn from 1835 until his death. His biographer writes that he was an abolitionist on principle but, "while he contended earnestly and labored diligently on this subject, he avoided all offensive personalities and asperities of temper." (The Reverend G. F. Cox, D.D., "Timothy Merritt," in William B. Sprague, *Annals of the American Pulpit*, New York, 1860, VII, 273–276.)

13. James G. Birney.

14. Dr. James McCune Smith, of New York, a Negro physician, received his medical degree from the University of Glasgow in 1837 and thereafter practiced medicine in New York until his death in 1874. In 1839 he was assistant editor of the *Colored American*. His published works included *Lecture on the Haytian Revolution, with a Sketch of Toussaint L'Ouverture* (New York, 1841), and

Civilization: Its Dependence on Physical Circumstances, published in the *Anglo African* (1859). (*Weld-Grimké Letters*, II, 811n.)

15. Edward Beecher (1803–1895), the son of Lyman Beecher, the noted Orthodox Congregational clergyman, and brother of Henry Ward and Harriet, graduated from Yale in 1822, became pastor of the Park Street Church in Boston in 1826, and in 1830 accepted an invitation to assume the presidency of the newly established Illinois College in Jacksonville, Illinois. Beecher had sat on the platform when Garrison, on July 4, 1829, delivered an address at Park Street Church, by invitation of the Congregational societies of Boston. At that time, Garrison was a supporter of Negro colonization and gradual emancipation. Despite Garrison's subsequent repudiation of these opinions, Beecher was essentially in agreement with them and maintained them until 1835, when he finally accepted the abolitionist principle of immediate emancipation and came to identify himself more and more with the abolitionists. Perhaps the greatest factor in this conversion was the conflict at Lane Seminary, of which Lyman Beecher was president, between the administration and the antislavery students who finally seceded. Edward Beecher and Elijah Lovejoy met at Illinois College in 1834, and became very close friends. Immediately after Lovejoy's death, Beecher wrote an account of the events leading up to it, entitled *Narrative of Riots at Alton; in connection with the death of Rev. Elijah P. Lovejoy* (Alton, George Holton, 1838, 159 pp). In 1838, Beecher was elected a manager of the Illinois Anti-Slavery Society and became an agent of the American Anti-Slavery Society in Illinois. He was never a Garrisonian. In fact, he was critical of Garrison and in 1840 was one of those who seceded from the American Anti-Slavery Society to form the American and Foreign Anti-Slavery Society, whose executive committee he joined. For an excellent account of Beecher's life, from which the above facts are taken, see the introductory essay by Robert Merideth, ed., in *Narrative of Riots at Alton*, by Edward Beecher (New York, E. P. Dutton & Co., Inc., 1965, paperback).

16. Lucy Parker.

115

TO GEORGE THOMPSON

New-York, May 7, 1838.

My beloved coadjutor and dearest of friends —

I know not whether you are acquainted with the bearer of this — Edward M. Davis, of Philadelphia, a son-in-law of James and Lucretia Mott, with whom you have had delightful intercourse. He intends travelling a short time in France and England. Of course, he carries with him from his pleasant home the heart of a stranger; and he is therefore desirous to become acquainted with some of those transatlantic lovers of humanity, who recognize in every human being the image of God, and "a man and a brother." [1]

I am here attending the anniversary of the American Anti-Slavery Society, in company with a goodly number of delegates from all parts of the free States, made perfect in abolitionism. You can have no just idea of the mighty change that has been wrought in public sentiment since you toiled and suffered among us. But I cannot go into any particulars. I humble myself in the dust before you, on the score of delinquency as to epistolary correspondence with you. Oh, be assured, my silence is no evidence whatever that I do not love you as I do my own soul — I am certain that it would be sin in me to admire and love you to any greater degree, for then I should become an idolator. A thousand thanks to you for the newspapers transmitted to me, from time to time, containing accounts of the mighty movements going on in England for the overthrow of the hideous apprenticeship. Down with it, for it is accursed of God! As soon as that is ended, all the abolitionists here are anticipating, with joyful expectation, that you will return to this country.

Theodore D. Weld and Angelina E. Grimke are to be married next week. There is a splendid alliance of mind!

My health has not been good for many months. My little boy George Thompson is a very beautiful and noble child, full of promise, and a pet among abolition friends. I have another son, a few weeks old, named Wm. Lloyd — *of course*, a fine babe — for my geese must necessarily all be swans. My dear Helen is well — we often talk of you and yours, longing for the time that we may behold you again.

There is to be another anti-slavery convention of American women next week. It will be held in Philadelphia. Mrs. Chapman, Mrs. Child, Miss Parker, &c. &c. are to be present.

I lament that I have not time to fill this sheet — but the letter-bag closes immediately, and I must stop.

Desiring to be most kindly remembered to Mrs. Thompson, and assuring you of my ever growing attachment to you, I remain,

Your faithful coadjutor,

Wm. Lloyd Garrison.

Geo. Thompson.

ALS: Garrison Papers, Boston Public Library.

1. "Am I not a man and a brother?" was the motto on a medallion struck by Josiah Wedgwood, British master-potter and abolitionist, in 1787. The medallion pictured a Negro in chains, with one knee on the ground and both hands lifted up to heaven. Its design was taken from the seal of the Committee for the Abolition of the Slave Trade, formed in Britain in May 1787. (Ann Finer and George Savage, editors, *The Selected Letters of Josiah Wedgwood*, London, 1965, p. 311; Thomas Clarkson, *The History of the Rise, Progress, and Accomplishment of the Abolition of the African Slave Trade by the British Parliament*, London 1808, I, 450–451.)

116

TO ISAAC KNAPP

NEW YORK — *Tuesday afternoon.*
[May 8, 1838]

DEAR FRIEND KNAPP:

The great anniversary meeting of the American Anti-Slavery Society, was held this forenoon in the Broadway Tabernacle, and has undoubtedly given a fresh impulse to our holy enterprise, in connection with the very important business meetings of the delegates. The audience was worthy of the occasion, and at the end of four or five hours from the time of assembling, seemed reluctant to depart. The meeting was opened with prayer by the Rev. Timothy Merritt, of Lynn. A select and very pertinent portion of scripture was read by Rev. E. M. P. Wells, of Boston. John Rankin,[1] the Treasurer of the Society, made a report, by which it appeared that the total receipts into the treasury from May 7, 1837, to May 7, 1838, had been more than *forty-three thousand dollars*, notwithstanding the terrible depression of the times, and the expenditure more than *forty-five thousand* — leaving the Society somewhat in debt. Henry B. Stanton read a highly interesting portion of the Annual Report of the Executive Committee, in which it was stated that the increase of new societies for the past year had averaged one a day. The total number of publications, printed during the same time, amounted to 646,000! Thirty-eight travelling agents had been in the field, making in the aggregate an amount of labor equal to twenty-seven years. The whole number of persons, whose signatures had been forwarded to the House of Representatives at Washington, praying for the abolition of slavery in the District of Columbia, had been ascertained to be — of men, 213,394 — and of women 201,077; and nearly as many to the Senate! But I have not time to go into further particulars.

Speeches were made by James G. Birney, Edmund Quincy of Boston, Dr. James McCune Smith, of this city, Gerrit Smith of Peterboro', and Alvan Stewart of Utica.

In haste, yours, &c.

G.

Printed in *The Liberator*, May 11, 1838.

1. John Rankin, a wealthy New York merchant and reformer who was an associate of the Tappans and a founder of the *New York Evangelist*. He helped to found the New York City Anti-Slavery Society and the American Anti-Slavery Society. He was a member of the latter society's executive committee and treasurer for several years until 1838. (*Weld-Grimké Letters*, I, 149n; *Life*, I, 398n *et passim*.)

117

TO HELEN E. GARRISON

Philadelphia, May 12, 1838.

My dear and loving Helen:

I wrote to you a letter from New-York on Wednesday last,[1] which I entrusted to a friend, and hope it reached Boston seasonably. On the evening of that day, I attended a colonization meeting, which was very much crowded, many of our abolition friends being present. Several characteristic thrusts were made at the abolitionists, of course; but it was a spiritless affair. On Thursday morning, bro. H. C. Wright and myself left for this city, and arrived here at half past 2 o'clock — J. G. Whittier and Rev. Mr. Root[2] and wife being with us. Instead of going to James Mott,[3] (who I knew would be fully supplied with guests,) at the earnest solicitation of bro. Wright, I accompanied [him] to the house of a Quaker friend, named Edward Needles,[4] who, with his excellent wife,[5] received us with unbounded cordiality. Here I have every thing heart could wish. Bro. Wright has had his two eldest daughters-in-law boarding in this delightful family for several months past. They are "Garrison abolitionists" of the most ultra stamp, upon almost all subjects. The eldest has a noble countenance; but the youngest has the most enterprise and activity — being an accomplished scholar, versed in the languages, and full of striking traits of character. With Mrs. Needles, you would be delighted, and could not but feel yourself almost as much at home as under your mother's roof; and as for her husband, no man could exhibit more kindness and hospitality. They both (in common with many others) very much regret that I did not bring you and the babes along with me; for they are extremely anxious to see you all. On Thursday evening,[6] a considerable number of sterling male and female friends came to see us — among whom were James Mott and wife, Sarah and A. E. Grimke, David Root and wife, &c. &c. Abolition, Peace, Woman's Rights, Holiness, were the fruitful and important themes of the evening, — and, of course, our tongues were as busy as our hearts were warm. Friends are continually calling to see us. After breakfast yesterday (Friday) morning, I went to see the noble edifice which our friends have erected for free discussion, called "Pennsylvania Hall," which has just been completed, and in which all our meetings will be held next week. The hall is the largest in this city, and one of the most commodious in the republic. It will seat more than 2000 persons, and is indeed honorable to the moral enterprise of the age.[7] In the course of the forenoon, bro. Wright and I visited our beloved friends the Grimkes, and had considerable conversation about the approaching marriage. I frankly told Angelina my feelings, and expressed my fear that bro. Weld's sectarianism would bring her into bondage, unless she could succeed in emancipating *him*. She heard my remarks very pleasantly, and trusted "the experiment," as she termed it, would prove mutually serviceable. How far she will feel it her duty to comply with his sabbatical notions, observance of forms, church-going worship, &c. I do not know. When I asked her, whether she should join with him in what is called "family worship," i.e. formal offering of prayer morning and evening, she answered in the affirmative. If so, I fear she will be prepared to go further. For I did hope that she had been led to see, that, in Christ Jesus, all stated observances are so many self-imposed and unnecessary yokes; and that prayer and worship are all embodied in that pure, meek, child-like state of heart, which affectionately and reverently breathes but one petition — "Thy will be done, on earth as it is in heaven." Religion, dear Helen, is nothing but love — perfect love toward God and toward man — without formality, without hypocrisy, without partiality — depending upon no outward form to preserve its vitality, or prove its existence. May you know its abiding operation.

Last evening, I took tea with bro. Wright and the Grimkes at Robert Douglass's house,[8] (a colored friend,) — after which, we went to hear Joseph John Gurney [9] preach at the Arch-street meeting-house. He is a distinguished orthodox Friend from England, with whom I became slightly acquainted in London. The spacious house was crowded to overflowing — but I derived no edification from the sermon, the object of which seemed to be to warn the young Friends not to fall into the Hicksite heresy. He is, in his personal appearance, a fine specimen of English corporosity, having "a fair round belly, with good capon lined." [10] During his long and tedious harangue, he stood fixed like a statue, with his hands lazily flung behind him, and singing his badly enunciated words in the usual absurd and unnatural manner of Quaker preachers. Although he was a flaming abolitionist in England, he has acted in this country very much as Cox and Hoby [11] did, having scarcely opened his lips since his arrival on the subject of slavery. He is very staid and formal in his movements — and on sitting down at the conclusion of his discourse, manifested as much care as if he had a score of eggs under him. I went with bro. Wright,[12] this morning, to see him; but, anticipating a visit from me, he obviously chose to be absent, and so our call was in vain. He leaves the city to-day. When will England send us another man, like George Thompson, able to stand erect on our slave-cursed soil?

Yesterday afternoon, a number of our abolition friends arrived from New-York — among them Alvan Stewart, St. Clair,[13] Mr. Fuller [14] and wife, dear Mary,[15] &c. On board the steam-boat from Bordentown to Philadelphia, our friends obtained leave of the captain to hold a discussion in the cabin on slavery. Several slaveholders were on board. Alvan Stewart had not spoken more than a minute or two, before they began to shout, "Down with him! Hustle him out! Throw him overboard!" This induced the captain to break up the meeting — but our friends carried on the discussion in private parties until they arrived in the city. When I came on, I was introduced to a slaveholder of Alabama, who shook me by the hand with great courtesy. I took a severe cold by the way, and am very hoarse at present. It generally happens that I lose my voice by the time I land in Philadelphia from Boston. Bro. Wright has also a bad cold. Yesterday I bought a bottle of Mrs. Gardner's Balsam of Liverwort, and already begin to feel its salutary influence. My head continues about the same — it is no worse — my ears discharging as usual, but my nose not troubling me. You need not be at all anxious about me. I cannot be in better hands, and mean to take all due care of myself. Mary is well, and in good spirits.

I have received no letter from you since the one you sent by Mary, but shall expect one, to-night, on the arrival of Mrs. Chapman,[16] or by the next mail. My heart yearns to be with you and the dear babes — for, although I am happy here, I am always happier at home, by your own dear side, with my darling children in my arms.

The wedding between Theodore and Angelina will be consummated on Monday evening next.[17] Neither Whittier nor any other Quaker can be present to witness the ceremony, on pain of excommunication from the Society of Friends. What an absurd and despotic rule! Sarah must be cut off for being with Angelina when married! Only think of it! [18]

Dear wife, I feel anxious to know how you are in health, and what is the condition of dear little Willie, and also my darling George. Do let me hear from you, if you have not yet written. I shall not leave here till Friday morning next on my way home — and hope to embrace you in love on Saturday. Love to cousin Lucy and Eliza.

Yours, devotedly,
Wm. Lloyd Garrison.

ALS: Garrison Papers, Boston Public Library. With the exception of the final paragraph and two other deletions, this letter was reprinted in *Life*, II, 211–213.

1. May 9, 1838.

2. The Reverend David Root. See letter 6, to Henry E. Benson, January 26, 1836.

3. "Who had invited him (MS. April 21, 1838, E. M. Davis to W. L. G.)" (*Life*, II, 211n).

4. The house was at the corner of Twelfth and Race Streets. Edward Needles (b. Talbot county, Maryland, August 2, 1782; d. March 5, 1851) was a Philadelphia abolitionist and Quaker. In 1848, in Philadelphia, he published *An Historical Memoir of the Pennsylvania Society for Promoting the Abolition of Slavery, the Relief of Free Negroes Unlawfully Held in Bondage, and for Improving the Condition of the African Race*, 116 pp.; the following year, there appeared in Philadelphia his sixteen-page pamphlet, *Ten Years' Progress: or, A Comparison of the State and Condition of the Colored People in the City and County of Philadelphia from 1837 to 1847.* (*Life*, I, 90n; II, 211, 467.) On April 20, 1839, *The Non-Resistant* published a letter from him, dated March 12, 1839, which expressed his sympathy with the nonresistance movement.

5. Mary Hathaway Needles, who died August 26, 1873, at the age of eighty-six (*Life*, II, 211, 467).

6. May 10, 1838.

7. *Life*, II, 211n, remarks: "The Hall was erected on the southwest corner of Sixth and Haines Streets. Its estimated cost was $40,000, divided into two thousand shares of twenty dollars each. It was not intended to be used exclusively for anti-slavery purposes ('History of Pennsylvania Hall,' pp. 3–6)."

8. Robert Douglass (1809–1887) was a portrait painter by profession, the brother of Sarah H. Douglass of Philadelphia, a very close friend of Sarah and Angelina Grimké. In 1838, Robert applied for a passport to visit England in order to secure further instruction in portrait painting. He was refused a passport by the secretary of state, who contended that by the new constitution of Pennsylvania Negroes were not citizens and, therefore, not entitled to passports. (*Weld-Grimké Letters*, II, 792.) Actually, he had already sailed for England by the time the passport was refused. He was back in the United States by 1842. (Transcript of letter from Garrison to Sarah M. Douglass, March 18, 1842, Garrison Papers, Boston Public Library; reference card, Rare Book Room, Boston Public Library.)

9. Joseph John Gurney (1788–1847), an English Quaker, a nonresistant, and an antislavery man. Garrison, during his trip to England in 1840, in speaking at a public soirée in London, denounced Gurney and other supposed antislavery men who refused to condemn slavery during their visits to the United States (*Life*, II, 384n, 459). Gurney was the author of *A Winter in the West Indies, Described in Familiar Letters to Henry Clay of Kentucky*, published in London in 1840.

10. Shakespeare, *As You Like It*, II, vii.

11. See letter 30, to Helen Garrison, May 25, 1836.

12. Henry C. Wright.

13. Alanson St. Clair.

14. John E. Fuller.

15. Mary Benson.

16. Maria W. Chapman.

17. May 14, 1838.

18. "It is characteristic of the time that the bridal guests at this ceremony were reported in the public prints to have consisted of six whites and six blacks (*Lib.* 8:91)!" (*Life*, II, 213n.)

118

TO MRS. SARAH T. BENSON

Boston, May 19, 1838.

Dearly beloved Mother:

After an absence from home of nearly three weeks, I arrived here this morning, in much better condition, as to my health and spirits, than when I left. A kind Providence had taken care of my cherished wife and children. George has certainly grown taller, and little Willie looks finely. We have had great doings in Philadelphia, during the present week, which will make that city memorable. Some account will reach you, by the newspapers, before the arrival of this hasty letter; and, fearing that it may serve to create uneasiness at Brooklyn, as to my personal safety, I seize my pen — tired as I am — to say, that, although Satan has come down in great wrath in the "city of brotherly love," knowing that his time is short, yet he has not been permitted to harm a hair of our heads.

On Monday last,[1] the Pennsylvania Hall, a very large and beautiful building just erected principally by the abolitionists of Philadelphia, was dedicated to Free Discussion, Virtue, Liberty and Independence, in an eloquent address by David Paul Brown [2] of that city, an eminent lawyer, though not a sound abolitionist. The anti-slavery delegates of men and women occupied the hall several times, and had large and interesting meetings. On Wednesday evening,[3] the public were informed that Wm. Lloyd Garrison, Maria W. Chapman of Boston, and Angelina E. Grimke Weld, would address the people in that hall. There was an immense audience on the occasion — some drawn there for deeds of violence, others to gratify their curiosity by seeing the speakers, especially "the notorious Garrison," your "fanatical" son-in-law — but the greater portion evidently came to hear the cause of human rights pleaded in good old Saxon language. The floor of the hall was densely crowded with women, some of the noblest specimens of our race, a large proportion of whom were Quakers. The side aisles and spacious galleries were as thickly filled with men. Nearly three thousand persons were in the hall. There seemed to be no visible symptoms of a riot. When I rose to speak, I was greeted with applause by the immense assembly, and also several times in the course of my remarks. As soon, however, as I had concluded my address,[4] a furious mob broke into the hall, yelling and shouting as if the very fiends of the pit had suddenly broke loose. The audience rose in some confusion, and would undoubtedly have been broken up, had it not been for the admirable self-possession of some individuals, particularly the women. The mobocrats finding that they could not succeed in their purpose, retreated into the streets, and surrounding the building, began to dash in the windows with stones and brickbats. It was under these appalling circumstances, that Mrs. Chapman rose, for the first time in her life, to address a promiscuous assembly of men and women — and she acquitted herself nobly. She spoke about ten minutes, and was succeeded by A. E. G. Weld, who occupied nearly an hour. As the tumult from without increased, and the brickbats fell thick and fast, (no one, however, being injured,) her eloquence kindled, her eye flashed, and her cheeks glowed, as she devoutly thanked the Lord that the stupid repose of that city had at length been disturbed by the force of truth. When she sat down, Esther Moore [5] (a Friend) made a few remarks — then Lucretia Mott, and finally Abby Kelley,[6] a noble young woman from Lynn.[7] The meeting broke up about 10 o'clock, and we all got safely home. The next day, the street was thronged with profane ruffians and curious spectators — the women, however, holding their meetings [8] in the hall all day, till towards evening. It was given out by the mob, that the hall would be burnt to the ground that night. We were to have a meeting in the evening — but it was impossible to execute our purpose. The mayor induced the managers to give the keys of the building into his hands. He then locked the doors, and made a brief speech to the mob, assuring them that he had the keys, and that there would be no meeting, and requesting them to retire. He then went home — but the mob were bent on the destruction of the hall. They had now increased to several thousands, and soon got into the hall by dashing open the doors with their axes. They then set fire to this huge building, and in the course of an hour it was a solid mass of flame. The bells of the city were rung, and several engines rallied, but no water was permitted to be thrown upon the building. The light of the fire must have been seen a great distance. At midnight, by the advice of friends, I left the city with a friend in a carriage, and rode to Bristol a distance of 20 miles, where I took the steam-boat next morning for home.[9] Awful as is this occurrence in Philadelphia, it will do incalculable good to our cause; for the wrath of man worketh out the righteousness of God. Our friends are all in excellent spirits, shouting, Alleluia! for the Lord God omnipotent reigneth! [10] Let the earth rejoice!

Excuse the blotted appearance of this sheet. I have just stepped out of the room, and on my return find my dear mischievous boy

George using my pen on this page with great freedom. I have much more to say, but no time, as the mail closes immediately.

Yours, affectionately,

Wm. Lloyd Garrison.

N. B. Helen joins in love to the family circle. I will write again shortly.

ALS: Garrison Papers, Boston Public Library. Much of this letter is printed in *Life*, II, 213–217.

1. May 14, 1838.
2. David Paul Brown (1795–1872) is referred to in *Weld-Grimké Letters* (I, 276n) as a "prominent lawyer of Philadelphia, and occasional speaker at the antislavery assemblies. Abolitionism was but one of his numerous reforms. See his reminiscences, *The Forum, or Forty Years Full Practice at the Philadelphia Bar* (1856)." Brown's speech was printed in *History of Pennsylvania Hall* (Philadelphia, 1838), pp. 13–35.
3. May 16, 1838.
4. Printed in *History of Pennsylvania Hall*, pp. 117–123. Of the subsequent addresses, that by Angelina Grimké Weld is summarized fully while those by Maria Chapman, Abby Kelley, and Lucretia Mott are only referred to. Mrs. Moore (see n. 5) is not mentioned. (*Ibid.*, pp. 123–127.)
5. Esther Moore was the wife of Dr. Robert Moore. See letter 35, to Henry E. Benson, June 14, 1836.
6. Abby Kelley (1811–1887), a descendant of Irish Quakers, lived from infancy in Worcester. She taught at Worcester and Millbury and in a Friends' school in Lynn, Massachusetts. She was also secretary of the Lynn Female Anti-Slavery Society. *Life* notes: "Her speech so affected Theodore D. Weld that, at the close of the meeting he urged her to take the field as an anti-slavery lecturer; and, laying his hand upon her shoulder, he said, in his vehement way, 'Abby, if you don't, God will smite you!' She obeyed his voice (and her own internal prompting) in the spring of 1839." (II, 216n.) Thereafter, she became increasingly active in the Massachusetts and American Anti-Slavery Societies in various peace conventions and, in later years, in the movement for woman suffrage. She married Stephen S. Foster in 1845. They lived on a farm near Worcester until his death in 1881. (*ACAB*.)
7. In the printing of the letter in *Life*, the paragraph is divided at this point. The original continues the paragraph.
8. These were the meetings of the Anti-Slavery Convention of American Women.
9. At this point, *Life* (II, 217) has the following note:
"From the Needles's, whose mob-threatened home he quitted, on the night of the burning of the hall, with the 'parting benediction, "Peace be with you," ' Mr. Garrison took refuge, by invitation, at the friendly house of Morris L. Hallowell, No. 240 North Sixth St., where the Junior Anti-Slavery Society had gathered to meet Henry C. Wright. About two o'clock the next morning (May 18) a covered carriage was driven to the door, into which he got and was spirited away. Joseph Parrish, Jr., Israel H. Johnson, and Robert Purvis bore the chief part in this deliverance. The mob violence continued for several days and ended, as usual, by alarming the 'respectable' sympathizers with it ('History of Pennsylvania Hall,' p. 141; *Lib.* 8:87)."
10. Revelation 19:16.

119

TO GEORGE W. BENSON

Boston, May 25, 1838.

Dear George:

It is a week, this day, since I left Philadelphia, unharmed by flaming fire, uninjured by ruffian violence; for the mercy of the Lord endureth for ever! Trust not in appearances — not even where all looks sober, placable, tranquil. "The city of brotherly love," forsooth! where freedom of speech is hunted in the streets like a felon, and it is at the peril of one's life a word is spoken in behalf of the perishing slave, and riot and arson reign supreme over law and order! Howbeit, out of the wrath of man shall come the praise of God. Why, then, do the heathen rage? or mobocrats imagine a vain thing? [1]

The spirit of mobocracy, like the pestilence, is contagious; and Boston is once more ready to re-enact the riotous scenes of 1835. — The Marlboro' Chapel having just been completed,[2] and standing in relation to our cause just as did Pennsylvania Hall, is an object of pro-slavery malevolence. Ever since my return, threats have been given out that the Chapel should share the fate of the Hall. Last evening was the time for its dedication; and so threatening was the aspect of things, four companies of light infantry were ordered to be in readiness, each being provided with 100 *ball* cartridges, to rush to the scene of riot on the tolling of the bells. The lancers, a powerful body of horsemen, were also in readiness. During the day, placards were posted at the corners of the streets, denouncing the abolitionists, and calling upon the citizens to rally at the Chapel in the evening, in order to put them down. An immense concourse of people assembled, a large proportion doubtless from motives of curiosity, and not a few of them with evil designs; but, owing to the strong military preparations, the multitude refrained entirely from any overt acts of violence. They did not disperse till after 10 o'clock, and during the evening shouted and yelled like a troop of wild savages. Some ten or twelve were seized, and carried to the watch-house, and this morning fined for their disorderly conduct. To-day, the public mind is more tranquil. It is possible, however — perhaps probable — that we shall be disturbed at our meetings next week; but we can beat our opponents at least two to one at that game. Non-resistance *versus* brickbats and bowie-knives! Omnipotence against a worm of the dust! Divine law against lynch law! How unequal!

What kind of a dedication discourse do you suppose Charles Fitch [3] — the flaming abolitionist — gave last evening? Remember that the Chapel was founded mainly by abolitionists, upon the rock of universal emancipation, and to advance the cause of humanity and free discussion. It was to be expected, therefore, that the dedicatory address would set forth the reasons for the erection of such a building, and contain some stirring abolition sentiments — though, peradventure, they might partake of an "evangelical" character. But, no! Charles Fitch has proved that he cares as little for the cause he once so furiously espoused, as he is ignorant of true righteousness Ridiculous as it may seem, and incredibly out of place, it is nevertheless true that he gave a hum-drum discourse about the Sabbath, infant sprinkling, and the sacrament! Not a word about the object for which the Chapel was erected — not a syllable, either in the sermon or prayers, about the poor slave!

I have to communicate sad, heart-rending tidings about our dear and noble-spirited Mrs. Maria W. Chapman. Probably by the time this reaches you, she will be no more. How awful, how sudden this transition from active life to inanimate clay! Mrs. C. took a very active part in the Anti-Slavery Convention of Women in Philadelpia, and was consequently in a high state of mental excitement, which has resulted in a brain fever. She got as far as Stonington on her return home, where she now lies — a raving maniac. There is no hope of her recovery.[3a] Her loss to our cause will be greater than any we have experienced. As a personal friend, I shall miss her cheering countenance and ready aid, exceedingly. Just before she left for P.[4] she was making vigorous and successful efforts to secure a salary for me, and had got the arrangements partly completed. I know not now what I shall do. I earnestly hope, for many good reasons, and especially on my own account, that you will not fail to attend our Convention [5] next week. Between you and bro. May, something definite might be brought about as to my salary. Do come, if possible — otherwise, there is no prospect that Helen and myself will be able to visit Brooklyn this summer; for bro. Johnson [6] cannot take my place, unless I guarantee to him an adequate salary — and how can I pay him, unless I am paid myself? Friend Knapp is not, and will not be able to do any thing for me, even to the amount of a farthing. I am indebted to Lucy [7] for board; and had to borrow thirty dollars of her, besides, to go to New-York and Philadelphia. If you can come, there will be no difficulty about an arrangement.

I regret to say that Ann, the excellent young woman who is living with us, and who encouraged us to hope that she would accompany us to Brooklyn, has changed her mind, in consequence of her mother being in poor health, and thinking she would be homesick so far distant from her parents. Helen says she shall not be willing to go to Brooklyn, unless help can be procured for mother. Let us hear from you, soon, if you cannot visit us. Should you come, you will of course put up with us.

I want to hear something about your meetings at New-Haven. Shame on your Legislature, with regard to the right of suffrage! [8] I am surprised that so small a minority voted in favor of striking out the word "white." The representatives from Windham county acted manfully — i.e. a majority of them.

Yesterday Helen and myself called to see Abby Alcott.[9] She is desirous of going into the country, this summer, with her three children — and would much prefer going to Brooklyn, if she can be accommodated with board. Helen told her that perhaps Lucy Scarborough [10] would be willing to take her at a low rate, as Mr. Alcott is very poor at present. Will you make inquiries of Lucy, and let me know the result when you write? Abby eats no meat, drinks neither tea nor coffee, and is a practical Grahamite. She would delight to be in B. with us this season. We sympathize with her very much.

Good by, dear George! Kiss your little ones for us — ours are doing finely. My health is better, and Helen is very well. Love abundantly to Catharine, mother, sisters, all.

Yours, ever in love,

William Lloyd Garrison.

ALS: Garrison Papers, Boston Public Library. A substantial portion of this letter is reprinted in *Life*, II, 218–219.

1. Psalms 2:1, with "mobocrats" substituted for "people."

2. The Marlboro' Chapel was built as the result of a meeting in Boston on June 22, 1835, which decided on the erection of a Free Church building, "in which all the great moral questions of the day may be discussed without let or hindrance." A new congregation, including many antislavery men and women, which was to worship in the building, had already been formed (*Life*, I, 481–482).

3. See letter 30, to Helen, May 25, 1836.

3a. Mrs. Chapman did recover.

4. Philadelphia.

5. The New England Anti-Slavery Convention convened on May 30 in Boston.

6. Oliver Johnson.

7. Lucy Parker.

8. On May 22, 1838, the House of Representatives of Connecticut, by a vote of 165 to 33, turned down a resolution that the clause in the state constitution specifying those entitled to vote be amended to eliminate the word "white." The representatives from Windham county were the only ones who voted, in the majority, in favor of the resolution. Their vote in favor was 14 to 7 (*The Liberator*, June 8, 1838).

9. Abigail Alcott (1800–1877), the wife of Bronson Alcott and sister of Samuel J. May. She married Alcott on May 23, 1830, and was a tower of strength to

him throughout almost fifty years of married life. Odell Shepard, Alcott's biographer, remarks that she "never ceased, even in the occasional collapses of an imperfectly controlled tongue and temper, to think him the best and greatest man she had ever known." Her self-sacrificing devotion and constant encouragement of her husband helped make it possible for him to meet the many difficulties and failures that confronted him throughout his lifetime. (Odell Shepard, ed., *The Journals of Bronson Alcott*, Boston, 1938, xvi; see also Odell Shepard, *Pedlar's Progress, The Life of Bronson Alcott*, Boston, 1937, *passim*.)

    10. See letter 85, to George W. Benson, June 14, 1837.

120

TO FRANCIS JACKSON

Brooklyn, June 18, 1838.

My dear friend:

Since my arrival in this quiet village on Thursday afternoon, I have been "down sick" with a violent headache, sore throat, and fresh attack of the scrofula, attended with considerable fever. Probably I over-exerted myself the day before I left Boston, in removing and storing my furniture, and thus took cold. To-day I feel better, though very weak; but, feeble as I am, I sit down *instanter* to answer your kind letter of Saturday, for which I thank you most heartily. In addition to what you propose sending to our abolition friend Stedman,[1] in reply to his inquiries respecting my religious sentiments and character, I will see to it — *Deo volente* — that he receives an epistle from me on this subject, which shall testify for itself. As my views, relative to human governments, are summarily expressed in the prospectus of the present volume of the Liberator, (which he may not have seen,) you will oblige me by forwarding to him a copy of the paper containing it, which Mr. Knapp will furnish on application. That he may also have an epitome of my religious sentiments, send him a copy of my poetical effusion, entitled "True Rest," which is appended to a letter of James Boyle to myself,[2] and which friend Knapp will put into your hands. My views of the Sabbath accord with those which were entertained by Calvin, Belsham, Priestl[e]y,[3] Penn, Fox, and Barclay, and which chiefly distinguish the Society of Friends from other religious sects. As a christian, I hold to the sanctification of seven days in a week, instead of one day in seven, as under the Jewish institution. I discard all human creeds, and all ecclesiastical combinations, and all observances of times and seasons, and all rites, ceremonies, forms and ordinances, as constituting no part of christianity, and as being contrary to that liberty wherewith Christ makes his people free. I deny that there is, now, any worldly sanctuary or ordinances of divine service, or any priestly office, except that which is exclusively occupied by him "who is set on the right hand of the throne of the Majesty in the heavens." [4] I believe that the worship of God is not a thing of time or place — is neither a spasmodical nor formal observance — appertains to no particular locality or select building — but is simple, unbroken, perpetual obedience of the heart, and entire consecration of body and soul, mind and strength, reputation and property, to the service of God, "which is our *reasonable* service." [5] I believe that prayer is the breath of the soul, not to be repeated at set times, or resorted to as a papist counts over his beads, but that all prayer is comprehended in a single sentence "THY will be done *on earth*, as it is done IN HEAVEN." I am not a Trinitarian, Unitarian, Baptist, Methodist, Swedenborgian, Friend, Perfectionist, or member of any other sect, but simply, in profession, determined like Paul to know nothing but "Christ, and him crucified." I believe in passing from death unto life — in being born of God — in becoming a new creature in Christ Jesus — in being crucified to the world — in present, perfect, and perpetual deliverance from sin — in unswerving allegiance to the one great Law-giver of heaven and earth, whose glorious name is Love — &c. &c.

It seems I have been denounced, by a clerical itinerant in Vermont, (in order, I suppose, to make it appear that, *ergo*, abolition *cannot* be right, and, *ergo*, slavery *must* be "a divine institution," at least under certain circumstances,) as "a Sabbath-breaker, an enemy to the christian religion, a disturber of the peace of society, [that charge is true,] and a violator of all law, both human and divine"!!! Be assured, I smile at all this: it is a stereotyped slander, worn out many times by incessant use, and as often recast, to be used on all occasions, being excellently adapted, like the American almanac, to all parts of the country. My dear coadjutor, of one thing I have been as fully convinced, for many years, as I am of my existence — namely, that "it is a small thing to be judged of man's judgment" [6] — and my consolation and joy have been, for an equal period, that "the Lord knoweth them who are his." [7] Who this new asperser of my character is, I know not; and, certainly, I have little curiosity to know. — If he has sinned ignorantly, he is to be pitied; if malignantly, it is for him to repent, and sin no more. Before I rallied under the banner of Christ, he forewarned me that the servant could not be greater than his lord; and that, as *he* had been persecuted, *I* must also expect persecution. "If they have called the master of the house Beelzebub, how much more shall they call them of his household?" [8] I am accused of being a Sabbath-breaker — so was Jesus. Of being inimical to government — so was Jesus. Of being a disturber of the peace of society — so was Jesus. Of being hostile to the religion of the land — so was Jesus. He was accused, moreover, of being a blasphemer, a wine-bibber and gluttonous, and of having a devil! I am not aware that these additional allegations have been brought against *me.* Herein is my vindication.

For your readiness to "vindicate my character as a man and a christian," I thank you — and feel peculiar satisfaction, inasmuch as you mean to speak of my *acts*, rather than of my *professions*. I admire your catholic and discerning spirit. You "know nothing concerning my religious opinions," yet are not afraid to testify to that which you have known and seen in me. So Christ bids us judge of all men — "By their *fruits* shall ye know them." [9]

With great esteem, and unfeigned gratitude for your many kindnesses, I remain,

Your much obliged friend,
Wm. Lloyd Garrison.

ALS: Garrison Papers, Boston Public Library.

1. On June 13, Jesse Stedman, of Chester, Vermont, an antislavery man, had written to Francis Jackson to inquire about charges that had been made against Garrison from the pulpit by a Vermont minister. Garrison had been accused of being "a Sabbath breaker, an enemy to the christian religion, a disturber of the peace of society, a violator of all law, both human and divine." (*Life*, II, 250.) Jackson replied in a letter dated June 20, 1838, calmly and thoughtfully exposing the falseness of the charges. The major portion of Jackson's letter was reprinted in *Life*, II, 250–252. "There is a record of the marriage of a Jesse Stedman to Sally Ingram of Chester, Vermont, May 29, 1803." (Letter to Louis Ruchames from Mrs. Robert C. White, Vermont Historical Society, June 12, 1968.)

2. See letter 111, to George W. Benson, April 7, 1838, note 4. The poem, "True Rest," appeared in *The Liberator*, August 25, 1837. It was later reprinted under the title "Christian Rest," in *Sonnets and Other Poems by William Lloyd Garrison*, published in Boston by Oliver Johnson in 1843.

3. Joseph Priestley (1733–1804), English theologian and scientist, whose home and scientific materials were destroyed because of his sympathy with the French Revolution, and who migrated to the United States in 1794. Although originally a Presbyterian, he early in life identified himself with Unitarianism. (*CVDE.*)

4. Hebrews 8:1.

5. A variation of Romans 12:1.

6. A variation of I Corinthians 4:3.

7. II Timothy 2:19.

8. Matthew 10:25.

9. Matthew 7:20.

121

TO EDMUND QUINCY

Brooklyn, June 19, 1838.

My dear friend:

I have been so ill since my arrival in this village, as to be confined to my bed almost up to the present hour. Yesterday I began to mend, and this morning feel considerably better, having enjoyed a very delightful ride. The mail for Boston leaves Brooklyn only three times a week; and as I was too feeble to reply to your kind letter on Saturday, I can do no better than seize this next succeeding opportunity to say how much I am obliged to you for your prompt attention, your generous and disinterested kindness, and your fresh overture of personal friendship — all which are appreciated by me according to their high value. A profusion of thanks would be no evidence of my gratitude; and even if it would, I am sure you would much rather not receive it.

The donation of our New-Bedford friend Robeson [1] is to me as unexpected as it is liberal — and the more remarkable, as I have had no personal acquaintance with him, except a mere introduction in one of our anti-slavery meetings. It seems he would be gratified if I would accept of it as a present. This I will do, in the spirit of my mind; and yet you must not fail to put it down as a component part of my salary for the present year. You may retain it in your hands, with such other sums as shall be collected, until I write you specifically on the subject — paying over, however, to my friend Oliver Johnson, (who is now editor *de facto*,) whatever he may require, without any further order from me.

It is quite probable, that, since the burning of Pennsylvania Hall, Philadelphia has swarmed with calumnies against abolitionists in general, and myself in particular. Even "killing is no murder," [2] if only such madmen as ourselves fall victims to popular fury; — and why should we marvel, if those who committed the horrid deed of arson, should now attempt to charge the guilt of it upon innocent men? Well, dear friend, my shoulders are broad enough to bear all that can be piled upon them. Like another Atlas, I can sustain a whole globe of contumely and reproach, and stand more erect than himself. I am covetous of all the responsibility that belongs to me in this matter — ever carrying with me "a conscience void of offence, both toward God and toward man." [3] So fertile are my enemies in misrepresenting my language, spirit and actions, that I shall find it difficult to determine, in my own mind, as to the charges which my friend Robeson heard alleged against me in the city of negro hatred. Nevertheless, I will write to him on the subject, and also to thank him for his donation in aid of the Liberator.

Our mutual friend Jackson [4] informs me, by letter, that a clerical opponent in Vermont has recently denounced me, from the pulpit, as "a sabbath-breaker, an enemy to the christian religion, a disturber of the peace of society, and a violator of all law, both human and divine"!! These mild and charitable accusations are probably intended to contrast favorably with my "hard language" against the traffickers in "slaves and souls of men." [5] I need not say to *you*, that they are all false, excepting one. It would be useless for me to deny that I am "a disturber of the peace of society"; — but when I remember that those, "of whom the world was not worthy," [6] the simple-minded, courageous apostles of our Lord, were guilty in like manner, I feel quite hardened on that score, and am resolved neither to repent, nor to ask forgiveness of that capital transgression against the kingdoms of this world. "Wo is me, my mother! for thou hast borne me to be a man of strife!" [7]

Dr. Channing is mistaken. It is possible even for an abolitionist to take advice. Why, *I* am one of the most docile creatures in the world! True, I am resolved never to believe that slavery is a divine institution, or that slaveholders are fulfilling the royal law of love: but am I therefore to be ranked among proud, egotistical, self-willed, and most obstinate bigots? Preposterous! Because I declare that fire shall not burn this heresy out of me — to wit, that slaveholding is under all possible circumstances sinful — does it logically follow, Dr. Channing, that the advice of my friend Edmund Quincy, to "throw physic to the dogs," [8] use an air-bath every morning, and as often take an ablution in Eastern fashion, &c. &c. &c. for my especial benefit as an invalid, will be rejected by me? No — no! I thank you, my friend, and mean to "take your advice." Lobelia and cayenne I have none on hand, having been too busy in Boston, up to the hour of my departure, to go to the Thompsonian infirmary to get a supply — which, doubtless, will be very good intelligence to you and some of my other friends, whose faith, peradventure, in those unrivalled medicines is not so great as a grain of *mustard* seed. Believe me, notwithstanding so much cayenne has got into me, I am very cool and lamb-like, and mean to hurt nobody.

Little George Thompson is uncommonly buoyant and happy in his new home, and would very much like to have a companion in your dear little son. Will you send him along?

Mrs. Garrison reciprocates your expressions of friendship, and desires to be kindly remembered to Mrs. Quincy and yourself. Of course, all the best wishes of my heart cluster around your household. In storm or sunshine, I remain,

Yours with large esteem, and gratefully,
Wm. Lloyd Garrison.

ALS: Garrison Papers, Boston Public Library.

1. Andrew Robeson (b. Philadelphia, 1787; d. Boston, 1862), of New Bedford, Massachusetts, moved to New Bedford in 1817, where he carried on a business in whaling and its products. A banker as well as manufacturer, in 1824 he established the first calico printing works in the country, in Fall River, Massachusetts. He was a Quaker, an abolitionist, and a supporter of Garrison. In 1840, he made another contribution — $150 — to help pay Garrison's salary as editor of *The Liberator*. (*Life*, II, 432–433n; Kate Hamilton Osborne, *An Historical and Genealogical Account of Andrew Robeson* . . . , Philadelphia, 1916, pp. 144–145.)

2. Title of pamphlet, "Killing no Murder Briefly Discourst in Three Questions," 1657, ascribed to Edward Sexby (d. 1658), an Englishman (*The Oxford Dictionary of Quotations*, second edition, London, 1955, p. 422).

3. Acts 24:16.

4. Francis Jackson.

5. Revelation 18:13.

6. Hebrews 11:38.

7. Jeremiah 15:10, somewhat altered.

8. *Macbeth*, V, iii.

122

TO FRANCIS JACKSON

Brooklyn, June 28, 1838.

Respected friend:

You have laid me under additional obligations, by taking the trouble, in the midst of your numerous engagements, to transcribe and send me your entire letter to Jesse Stedman, in vindication of my character from the aspersions of an unknown assailant. The manner in which you have replied to those aspersions, cannot be otherwise than gratifying to me. Your good opinions are the more valuable, because they are predicated upon my practice, not upon any creed I may have taken upon my lips. "By their *professions* ye shall know them," is the modern reading of Christ's infallible rule.[1] I think it was the venerable Dr. Lathrop,[2] who, on being interrogated in a stage-coach by a pert student of divinity, "How much religion have you got?" replied, "None to *boast* of, young man." So with Paul, I make this simple answer to all inquiries respecting my religious sentiments — "By the grace of God, I am what I am."[3] If pride, ambition, and every sinful propensity, have been slain within me;

if love, joy, peace, long-suffering, gentleness, goodness, faith, meekness, temperance, "the fruit of the Spirit," dwell in me, it is solely "by the grace of God." But, if it be otherwise with me; if I do not manifest this likeness to Christ *in my life*; then a formal observance of one day in seven, or a participation in religious rites and ordinances, or a subscription to a particular creed, will serve to mark me as a hypocrite, but can avail nothing more. To my own master, I stand or fall. I know that he will uphold me forever.

It gives me not the slightest uneasiness as to what men say or think of me; though I am often amused at the glaring inconsistency of their charges, as brought against me in a single breath. A notable instance of this kind was seen in the attack of Messrs. Fitch and Towne, I believe in their second Clerical Protest.[4] In one paragraph, they accused me of being an infidel and jacobin, because of my sabbatical views; yet they acknowledged that I held to keeping, "not *one* in *seven*, but ALL days HOLY"!! A rare specimen of jacobinism, truly! In another paragraph, they denounce me because I maintain that christians are bound to live perfectly holy! What! an infidel eschewing all sin as of the devil, and contending for perfect righteousness in Christ Jesus! — So much for the blindness and bitterness of sectarianism.

You truly remark, in your letter to Mr. Stedman, that my *character* "has never been impeached," my enemies contenting themselves with bringing vague accusations against me respecting my speculative opinions. This is true — and not less remarkable than true — not that there remains any thing to be discovered injurious to my reputation, but because it is seldom that a reformer, however humble may be his sphere of action, escapes being arraigned by the tongue of malice for some special transgression. Who has had more infuriated and malignant foes than myself? For the last eight or ten years, they have endeavored to make me hideous in the eyes of my countrymen, and have even conspired to take away my life. Yet the sum total of allegations urged to prove that I am [a] very bad man is the senseless cry of "He's an infidel! he's a sabbath-breaker! he's against all law, both human and divine! he's a perfectionist, believing that men ought to live perfectly holy!" &c. &c. All this, of course, amounts to nothing, except that it is a confession, on their part, that they know not what else to say.

It seems, by a letter I have just received from bro. Johnson,[5] that I am expected to "stand the hazard of the die"[6] in the Marlboro' Chapel, next Wednesday, July 4th.[7] For this, I am totally unprepared, having taken it for granted that a substitute would be procured, on account of my continued feebleness of health. Of course, I must try to come; but I fear greatly as to the effort — it must necessarily be so hastily written and imperfectly prepared. This forenoon I have been lying upon my bed, with a slow fever upon me, and have scarcely felt adequate to the task of penning these few hasty lines. But — *nil desperandum.*

Hoping to see you next week, I remain, in the bonds of christian fellowship,

Your admiring friend,
Wm. Lloyd Garrison.

Francis Jackson.

ALS: Garrison Papers, Boston Public Library.

1. Matthew 8:20 — "by their fruits ye shall know them" — is the rule Garrison refers to.

2. Dr. John Lathrop or Lothrop (1740–1816), minister of the Second Unitarian Church in Boston from 1768 to 1816, was a scientist as well as a theologian. He was the recipient of honorary degrees from Harvard and Edinburgh and was a Fellow of the Corporation of Harvard College from 1778 to 1815. He was elected a member of the American Academy in 1790 and wrote on a variety of scientific themes. (Justin Winsor, ed., *Memorial History of Boston*, Boston, 1881, IV, 511; *ACAB*.)

3. I Corinthians 15:10.

4. The first "Clerical Protest" was reprinted in *The Liberator*, August 11, 1837. The second "Clerical Protest" appeared in *The Liberator*, September 8, 1837.

5. Oliver Johnson.

6. Shakespeare, *Richard the Third*, V, iv.

7. *The Liberator*, June 29, 1838, with Oliver Johnson acting as editor pro tem, carried the following announcement: "The Massachusetts Anti-Slavery Society will hold a public meeting at the Marlboro' Chapel on Wednesday, July 4, at 9 o'clock A.M. An address is expected from Wm. Lloyd Garrison."

123

TO SAMUEL J. MAY

Brooklyn, July 13, 1838.

Beloved Friend:

As Mrs. May intends leaving us this morning for "home, sweet home," I must send you a few lines, in spite of the boisterousness of George Toppy, and the helplessness of little Willie [1] — not in the hope of communicating a single item of intelligence, for there is none here, although there are some intelligent people, *of course* — but simply to say, that, as my love for you was never selfish, so neither time nor distance can diminish it. I lament, on my own account, that we do not live within hailing distance of each other. It would be very pleasant to me to see your countenance every morning, and to enjoy your society every day. Whether we shall one day be permanently located by the side of each other, is among things problematical; but I feel an assurance that, spiritually, we shall be united forever. These gross, material bodies of ours are not easily transported from one region to another, especially over such hills and mountainous elevations as abound in Connecticut; but mind is a swifter courier than the wind, and no discovery is yet to be made to give it additional velocity. The lightning that cometh out of the east, and shineth even unto the west,[2] is a laggard compared to it. Hence, I am with you, even now — i.e. all of me that is imperishable. Yet I want to see you in the flesh as well as in the spirit; and many there are in this vicinity, who feel the same yearning desire. For who, that has seen you once, does not desire to behold your face again? If there be such a person, I know him not — do you?

I am mistaken in saying, that I have no intelligence to communicate. The piece of land in front of our garden, (less than half an acre in extent,) has at last been mown, and the hay got into the barn, without any rain having fallen upon it! — The like event not having been known within the memory of — I don't know how many persons.

But here the stage comes — I meant to have written you a long letter, and will by and by.

All the family freight this letter heavily with affectionate remembrances.

Your loving friend,
Wm. Lloyd Garrison.

ALS: Garrison Papers, Boston Public Library.

    1. Garrison's two sons, "Toppy" being a nickname.
    2. Matthew 24:27.

124

TO OLIVER JOHNSON

Brooklyn, August 14, 1838.

My Dear Friend: Having been invited, by my colored brethren in New York, to deliver an address in the Broadway Tabernacle on the first of August, in commemoration of the wonderful deliverance of the West India slaves from their terrible thraldom by the strong arm of Jehovah, I left Brooklyn for that city, via Hartford, on the 30th ult. In Hartford, I stopped (where all travellers, who love sobriety and good order, are recommended to stop) at the Temperance Hotel, kept by Messrs. Treat [1] and Judson [2] — the only establishment of the kind in that city. Mr. Judson, I understand, is shortly to take charge of a new hotel, called the Pavilion, in New-Haven, which will be conducted on the same principle. Mr. Treat is a straight-forward, unassuming, pious man, with whom duty is paramount to interest, and the fear of God infinitely more important than the favor of man. He has made his name precious and durable by the fact, that when the State Anti-Slavery Convention were denied the use of the City Hall after it had been granted to them, and could not readily obtain any other place in which to hold their meetings, he promptly offered them the use of his large dining hall, at considerable peril to his establishment, as a riotous spirit was abroad in Hartford, breathing out hostility toward any who should evince the least sympathy for the cause of bleeding humanity, or for any of its friends. By that fearless proceedure, he has most honorably identified himself with the history of Connecticut. It is at such a crisis, and under such trying circumstances, that the spirit of a man is tested, and his religious character demonstrated — tried as by fire. If the friends of the Temperance cause are bound, by their professed attachment to that cause, to give this hotel preference over any other in Hartford — equally should those who cherish freedom of speech, and a holy abhorrence of slavery, extend their patronage to it whenever they have opportunity.

A very pleasing incident occurred on the evening of my arrival in Hartford. As I sat in the parlor, reading the morning papers, an intelligent looking individual, (rather younger than myself) handed me a slip of paper, on which was pencilled, interrogatively, 'Is this William Lloyd Garrison?' — the writer adding that he thus judged, in consequence of having seen a portrait resembling me. I nodded my head in the affirmative, at once perceiving that he was a mute. He then took his pencil, and with great rapidity wrote down to this effect — that he was very happy to see me, he being one of the teachers in the Deaf and Dumb Asylum; he hoped I should find time to visit that institution before I left the city, as it would be gratifying to the pupils, as well as to Mr. Weld,[3] the Principal, brother of our beloved Theodore. I was, unfortunately, too much engaged to accept of this invitation, or even to see any of my abolition or colored friends. Mr. Booth (for such I afterward ascertained is his name) stated to me a novel and interesting fact. There are at the Asylum, some twelve or fourteen mutes from the slaveholding States. He said, (talking, of course, with his pencil,) that they had frequently confirmed, by direct and indirect testimony, all I had charged upon the slave system. These are new and rare witnesses. I regret that my time would not allow me to see them. If we, who can both hear and speak, will not testify against the abominations of American slavery, then shall the deaf and dumb be witnesses for God and humanity; or, in case they refuse to testify, then shall the stones in the streets cry aloud.

I left Hartford in the steamboat Bunker Hill, and greatly enjoyed the beauty of the scenery to the mouth of the Connecticut, allowing nothing to escape my notice that was within the scope of vision. Every thing looked pleasant and beautiful. It was a free soil that I gazed upon, cultivated by the labor of freemen, and producing an abundant harvest. The farmers were busily engaged, to the very brink of the river, in securing their hay, not a slave or a slave-driver, not a yoke or a chain, being seen among them. Ah! if there had been, how altered would have been the scene!

In New York, I enjoyed the hospitality (not for the first or second time) of my esteemed friend THOMAS TRUESDALL,[4] formerly of Providence. The first of August was a bright and warm day — the sun rising in the morning resplendently, as if rejoicing over the glorious event that had transpired in the West India islands. The emotions of my heart were unutterable. How ought the whole land to have been filled with joyful agitation! And yet, how few of its immense population hailed the day as Freedom's noblest jubilee! Of all the New York daily papers, none but the Journal of Commerce (that murderous print!) alluded to the fact, that slavery had ended in the West Indies; and that paper had only two lines on the subject!

I did not anticipate a large audience at the Tabernacle, as the notice of the meeting was accidentally omitted in the Emancipator of the previous week, and as our colored friends deemed it best (as a matter of safety, probably — such is liberty in New York!) not to advertise it in any of the daily papers. There were, however, between three and four thousand persons present — about two-thirds colored. To the eye of the philanthropist and christian, it was a delightful spectacle. Gratitude and joy, in view of what God had wrought, seemed to pervade every bosom, and animate every countenance. Every thing was conducted in the best possible order. Prayer was offered by our colored brother, Rev. Mr. Raymond,[5] which was accompanied by a mighty power. I have seldom heard such a petition from human lips. Rev. Theodore S. Wright presided on the occasion, Arthur Tappan sitting by his side. Mr. Van Rensalaer [6] explained, in a brief and pertinent manner, why it was that the free colored people could not celebrate the fourth of July, and why they felt called upon to commemorate the first of August. My address occupied rather more than an hour and a half in its delivery.[7] It did not give perfect satisfaction to *all* who were present. I understand that Mr. Morse, of the New York

Observer,[8] did not relish some parts of it! But my colored friends responded to it *nem con*.[9] They are good judges. Though in ill health,
CHARLES C. BURLEIGH addressed the meeting for a short time, in his
usual ready and eloquent manner. The immense audience (among
whom were friends from Philadelphia, and other places,) retired
with the utmost regularity, having been notified that they would find
prepared, in the large basement of the Tabernacle, 'a table of splendid
refreshments, consisting of meats, cake, ice cream, temperance drinks,
&c. &c. all of free labor produce.' This table was kept by the wife of
our friend Van Rensalaer, assisted by a number of others. All that the
slaves can offer their friends are hominy, some tainted bacon, and a
few rotten herrings. Yet the free colored people cannot take care of
themselves! [10]

An editorial paragraph appeared in the Journal of Commerce, the
next morning, stating (to use its dignified phraseology) that 'quite
a rumpus was occasioned in the upper part of the city, last evening,
by the promenading of *a colored gemman* and a white lady, arm in arm
in Broadway.' The cry was raised, 'white woman and nigger!' and
a rabble soon joined in hot pursuit. Were any of them arrested? No
indeed! But 'both the man and the woman were taken to the watch-
house for safe-keeping!' It seems that the lady was an English woman,
'and not aware of the state of public feeling here on the subject of
color!' Pray, if prejudice against color be natural, how happens it that
no such feeling exists in England? The colored person with her was
in the employ of her brother, and she had taken him with her only
as a protector. To this account, the editors of the Journal of Commerce add, (with diabolical intent, most evidently,) that the reader
will observe that this occurrence took place on the evening of *the
first of August!* In other words, this is a consequence of West India
emancipation; you see, fellow mobocrats, to what we are coming,
if the abolitionists succeed in abolishing southern slavery; therefore,
once more resort to the torch and brickbat, to put them down! And
don't forget to aid the Colonization Society, whose noble object it is,
to ship all the 'colored gemmen' to Africa! Is my language any too
severe, when I call that paper 'a murderous print?' In New York and
Philadelphia, it is at the peril of life or limb, that white and colored
persons walk together as equals in the public streets!

On my return from New-York, I found my wife quite ill with a
fever, from which she has not yet recovered, and my youngest child
also very unwell. I got a bad cold myself, during my absence, and
have had a slow fever ever since, which has incapacitated me from
using my pen, even by way of private correspondence. Before I went
to New York, I had gained seven pounds of flesh in about five weeks,

living very abstemiously — several months having elapsed since I drank any tea or coffee, or tasted of any butter, or ate any meat. I hope to return to Boston in a short time, with renovated health. Whether sick or well, I shall ever remain,

Yours, in undying hostility to every form of oppression,

WM. LLOYD GARRISON.

OLIVER JOHNSON.

Printed in *The Liberator*, August 24, 1838.

1. Selah Treat (b. Hartland, Connecticut, 1778; d. Hartford, Connecticut, 1861) moved to Colbrook, Connecticut, in 1807, where he farmed and kept a store, and was appointed postmaster in 1812. He moved to Hartford around 1818, where he joined the First Church in 1834. He opened a temperance hotel on North Main Street and, subsequently, built the Exchange Hotel on State Street. He later sold the Temperance Hotel but continued with the latter until 1855, when he retired. (John Harvey Treat, *The Treat Family*, Salem, 1893, p. 547.)

2. Curtis Judson (b. Woodbury, Connecticut, 1812; d. Brookline, Massachusetts, June 18, 1903) is listed in the first Hartford city *Directory*, 1838, as associated with the Exchange Coffee House, 64 State Street. The New Haven *Directory* for 1840 lists him as operating the Pavilion Hotel at Eastwater and Wallace Streets, and he again appears in the Hartford *Directory*, in 1841, as associated with the City Hall, 120 Main Street. He continued to live in Hartford until 1846 when he moved to New York where, until 1881, he either operated or owned several hotels, including Judson's Hotel, the New York Hotel, Brevoort House, and Gramercy Park House. (Letter to Louis Ruchames, September 25, 1969, from Thompson R. Harlow, Director, the Connecticut Historical Society; Helen L. Judson, compiler, Judson Family Genealogy, photocopy of page on Curtis Judson.)

3. Lewis Weld (1796–1853), Theodore Weld's oldest brother, was prominent as an educator of the deaf. He was appointed principal of the Pennsylvania School for the Deaf and Dumb at Philadelphia in 1822; in 1830 he became president of the American Asylum for the Deaf and Dumb at Hartford, remaining in that position almost until his death. (*Weld-Grimké Letters*, I, 4n.)

4. See letter 114, to Helen Garrison, May 7, 1838.

5. J. T. Raymond was the pastor of Zion's Baptist Church on Spring Street, New York City, in 1838. From 1848, at least until 1854, he was minister of the Abyssinian Baptist Church on Anthony Street, in New York City. (New York City *Directories* for 1838–1839, 1840, 1848–1849, 1853–1854.) During the intervening years — from 1840 until 1848 — he apparently served as a minister in Boston. John Daniels, *In Freedom's Birthplace, A Study of the Boston Negroes* (Boston and New York, 1914, p. 452), mentions that John T. Raymond "was pastor of the old Joy Street Church, succeeding the Reverend Thomas Paul about 1840 and continuing till a few years before the war. He was a man of high character, and an active worker for anti-slavery and many of the principal reforms of the day."

6. Thomas Van Rensalaer, a Negro leader in New York City. In 1840, he provided accommodations for Garrison and other abolitionists (see letter 184, to Helen Garrison, May 15, 1840; *Life*, II, 355–356n). At the beginning of 1839, Gerrit Smith proposed that someone be sent to Liberia to investigate the state of the Negro colony there. Van Rensalaer's name was suggested, but he was turned down because of his peace, nonresistant, and Garrisonian no-government views. (See letter from Van Rensalaer to Garrison, March 24, 1839, in Anti-Slavery Letters to Garrison and Others, Boston Public Library.) He later edited the *Ram's Horn* with Frederick Douglass (Dwight L. Dumond, ed., *Letters of James Gillespie Birney, 1831–1857*, reprinted Gloucester, Mass., 1966, I, 576n). He is listed in

the New York City *Directory* as "victualler," from 1838 to 1841, as owner of a "refectory" in 1842–1843, owner of an "eating house" in 1845–1848, and as an "editor" in 1849–1850.

7. Garrison's address appeared in *The Liberator*, August 17, 1838. On August 10, *The Liberator* noted that Garrison had delivered the address in the Broadway Tabernacle, "to an audience of 3000 people," and that the address had already been published in the *Emancipator* on August 9.

8. Sidney Edwards Morse (1794–1871), son of Jedidiah Morse, the geographer, and brother of Samuel F. B. Morse, inventor of the telegraph, was an author, journalist, and inventor. A graduate of Yale in 1811, he studied law and, in 1816, founded the Boston *Recorder*, a Presbyterian newspaper, which he left after a year to enter the Andover Theological Seminary. In 1823, with his brother Richard Carey Morse, he established the New York *Observer*, another Presbyterian newspaper. According to one historian, this marked the beginning of the religious press in New York. He remained its senior editor and proprietor until 1858. He invented a process of engraving from wax, and other things, some with his brother Samuel. In 1847, he published *A Letter on American Slavery*, addressed to the editor of the Edinburgh *Witness*, July 8, 1846. It was a vigorous attack on the abolitionists as the maligners of American democracy. (*DAB*; James Grant Wilson, *The Memorial History of the City of New York*, New York, 1893, IV, 158; Frank Luther Mott, *A History of American Magazines, 1741–1850*, New York and London, 1930, p. 373.)

9. *Nemine contradicente*, "no one contradicting."

10. Sarcasm.

125

TO ERASMUS D. HUDSON

BROOKLYN, Sept. 8, 1838.

DEAR SIR: — As I am just on the eve of leaving Brooklyn for Boston, it will not be convenient for me to attend at the next monthly meeting of the Litchfield County Anti-Slavery Society at Norfolk, in compliance with your friendly importunity. Happily, at this prosperous stage of our glorious cause, my presence at every such meeting can be dispensed with, as there are now no lack of able advocates of emancipation. If once I stood alone, or was of any importance in pleading for my enslaved countrymen, that time is past. What I began in weakness, abler and better men are carrying forward with power. I am no longer an isolated drop, but swallowed up in an ocean of humane sensibility. All this is delightful to me, and in perfect accordance with my wishes. Indeed, my taste, inclination and spirit make retirement pleasant to me, rather than personal conspicuousness. For me to abandon what I have so long espoused, or to allow a diminution of ardor in its prosecution, I feel to be impossible; but, as others enlist on the same side, far better qualified than myself to manage so great an enterprise, I am anxious to retire farther and farther from public observation. It was, doubtless, a bold — and, certainly, in the estimation of many wiser men, a presumptuous act, for me to commence single-handed a work, the magnitude and difficulties of which appalled the stoutest hearts in the republic; and it would have been as insane as it was daring, if I had not had an abiding assurance that it was practicable, humane, just — worthy of universal co-operation, supported by infallible promises, and cherished by God. Though I might, and did, distrust my competency for such a task, (as my station was obscure, my influence trifling, and my ability ordinary,) yet I could not persuade myself that I should be guiltless in stopping my ears to the cries of the perishing slaves, and conniving by silence at the shocking barbarities of their task-masters. Therefore it was that my lips gave utterance to the feelings of my heart. I could not keep silence. Whether my countrymen would hear, or whether they woudl forbear, was a consideration that never once suggested itself to my mind, as a motive for action. I made use of a strong and harsh dialect, because no other would have proved effectual, even if a musical voice had been granted to me, capable of ravishing all ears by its mellifluous tones. If I blew my blasts through a ram's horn, it was because I had no skill in using a silver trumpet. My motives were pure, disinterested, benevolent, though branded as selfish and corrupt by the despisers of the colored race. I had no other interest in the overthrow of slavery, than every other citizen in the land — no other than such as grew out of my accountability to God, and my relation to mankind. It is obvious that popularity could not have been my object; and equally clear, that an unprincipled man would not concern himself, or encounter any peril, in the suppression of a huge system of wickedness, merely for the sake of notoriety. They who impeach my motives for attacking the worst of oppressors, choose to forget that the question is not one of purity of motives, but strictly of the propriety of dooming millions of our fellow-countrymen to interminable bondage, and of trading 'in slaves and the souls of men.'[1] If it could be made apparent, that the great body of abolitionists are misguided or dishonest men, their guilt would not lessen the enormity of the slave system one iota; and it is THAT SYSTEM which is now on trial before the whole world. We cannot permit, therefore, any 'travelling out of the records,' on the part of our opponents. As for myself, the great object I had in view when my voice was first lifted up on this subject, — namely, to arouse this slumbering nation to a sense of its guilt and danger, — has been fully attained. It now remains for those who have more experience, better judgments, larger intellects, and a mightier influence than myself, to go forward and perform their duty manfully. I will be content to follow them at a humble distance.

If circumstances would permit, it would be peculiarly agreeable to me to be present at your meeting on Tuesday next. It always makes me happy to be in the society of those who are endeavoring to make others happy. Especially does it mightily cheer my heart to see an assembly drawn together, regardless of what creed they may have taken upon their lips, or to what party or sect they may belong, in order to protest against the enslavement of their fellow-creatures, and to devise the best measures for letting the oppressed in our land go free. If a three-fold cord be not easily broken,[2] what must be the strength of that cord which binds men of all sects and of all parties together, for the promotion of a righteous cause? Moreover, I have a desire to see you all, face to face, because probably in no part of New England have greater pains been taken to make me appear hideous, for the criminal purpose of retarding the progress of the abolition enterprise, than in Connecticut. I have been slandered, caricatured, and denounced, in the worst manner. This would give me no uneasiness, aside from the injury it inflicts upon millions who are groaning in bondage. You may all be assured, that, personally, I have neither horns nor hoofs; and though, perhaps, not 'a marvellous proper man,' still A MAN, and no monster. Nay, it is the opinion of some of my friends, that very much is gained to our cause by a mere presentation of my person to a public assembly, as the fact is then made evident to the dullest vision, that, as far as flesh and blood, height and dimensions are concerned, I am just like other men! But the truly pharisaical enemies of abolition, stimulated by sectarian malignity, are vainly endeavoring (though with temporary success) to hinder the march of emancipation, by misrepresenting my religious views and sentiments, so as to leave the impression that I am little better than an infidel, and a jacobinical disorganizer!! Well, if such men, (the priest and the Levite, see Luke X. 30–37, inclusive,) charged my Lord and Saviour with having a devil, in the days of his sojourn on earth, why should I marvel, if indeed I am a disciple of his, at being thus aspersed? Now, I humbly conceive, the rectitude of the anti-slavery cause is not at all dependent upon the rectitude of my opinions upon any other subject, political or religious. The correctness of this proposition is self-evident. Let it be granted, that on every other question of duty I am unsound — what does the objector gain by the admission? True, it may prove that I am not what I ought to be — but how does it exonerate the slaveholder for making merchandize of those for whom Christ has died? There are enlisted in the holy cause of Temperance, men of all creeds and of no creeds, believers and unbelievers, saints and sinners; but is this a valid argument against the excellence of that cause? Would not he, who should refuse to support it on this ground, be considered a lover of the bottle, or a hypocrite? And how much better is he, who, because he does not like my sentiments on other subjects, rails against the cause of bleeding humanity? How dwelleth the love of God in any man, who despises or slights his brother on account of his complexion? We attack slaveholders, not because they belong to this or that party, or are attached to this or that sect, but because they are slaveholders — i.e. robbers of the poor, tyrants, men-stealers. We must be met and refuted upon this specific point, or the victory will be ours. It is possible for bad men to espouse a single great and glorious truth; but, surely, that truth will not be abandoned by good men on that account! No one supported our revolutionary conflict with more zeal, few with more ability, than Thomas Paine. Should Washington and his followers have surrendered at discretion to British despotism, because Paine was an infidel? What would have been thought of the sincerity or patriotism of that man, who should have urged Paine's approval of the Declaration of Independence, as the chief or only reason why he had gone over to the tory side, or was occupying neutral ground? Yet there are many persons, — some of them, too, making high pretensions to godliness, — who are so weak, shall I not rather say, so wicked, so basely hypocritical, so recreant to their duty, as to pretend that they would heartily advocate the anti-slavery cause, were it not for my advocacy of it! They shamelessly declare, that they have made up their minds, irrevocably, not to open their mouths for the suffering and the dumb, nor to plead for those who are drawn unto death and ready to be slain, so long as my voice is lifted up in behalf of these unhappy victims! As soon as *I* am silenced, they profess to be willing to cry aloud! Nay, they are anxious to obey God, to keep his commandments, to prevent their garments from being stained with 'the blood of the souls of the poor innocents;'[3] — but, alas! they cannot! — O no! I am in their way; and therefore they are necessitated to pursue a crooked and rebellious course! Are not such men convicted of impiety, out of their own mouths? Do they not show themselves to be unworthy of the confidence of the people, and disloyal to the cause of Christ? Let no one be deceived by their absurd and profligate excuses. True, they may be sincerely opposed to some of my religious sentiments; but it will be found, in every instance, that this is only a shallow pretext, and not the real difficulty in the case. They either strongly dislike the colored race, and indignantly contemn the proposition to give them equal civil and social privileges on our own soil, or they are too proud to acknowledge that they have been in the wrong, and that the persecuted abolitionists are right. In calling for the suppression of the Liberator, and for my banishment from the anti-slavery ranks, they foolishly hope, by this *ruse*, either to allay all excitement on the subject of slavery, or to extenuate their conduct for standing aloof so long from our merciful enterprise. Their motives are palpable to all who have not jaundiced visions. They cannot deceive one genuine friend of the black man: how then do they expect to impose upon the Almighty? Verily, 'by their *fruits* ye shall know them.' [4]

It will be observed, that they do not impeach my moral character, nor pretend that my walk and conversation are not exemplary. They have discovered that I do not agree with them, respecting the importance of certain creeds, and forms, and ceremonies, and what constitutes the Sabbath, or Christian rest: hence their charge of heresy against me. But what has this to do with the cause of abolition? In one breath, they accuse me of infidelity (!!) — in the next, they brand me as a Perfectionist, and declare that I believe in present and eternal deliverance from sin — that he who is born of God does not commit sin — which doctrine they reprobate, because they are conscious that *their* robes have not been made white in the blood of the Lamb. Who ever heard of an infidel contending for perfect holiness? Next, they call me a jacobin — but on what ground? Simply because I maintain, that the followers of Christ are those who have come out from 'the kingdoms of this world,' [5] which are all hostile to his kingdom — that they have no authority to punish their enemies by physical force, or to protect their persons or property by wielding carnal weapons, but are bound in all cases to return good for evil — to suffer themselves to be defrauded, deprived of their goods, injured in reputation, and even nailed to the cross, without resorting to violence in self-defence. This is 'the head and front of my offending.' [6]

But I am growing prolix. Let me say to my abolition brethren, in conclusion, that, as they do not endorse, so neither are they required to defend any of my opinions on any other subject but the extinction of slavery. Let them not allow the apologists for southern slaveholders, and the advocates of expatriation, to make *a false issue.* In banding ourselves together for the emancipation of our manacled countrymen, we ask no one to change his religious or political sentiments, but only to defend inalienable human rights, and give no countenance to oppression. We stand upon the broad platform of a common humanity; and he who is unwilling to take a similar position, for the overthrow of a vast and dreadful system of heathenism and soul-murder, plainly shows not only that divine love is inoperative in his breast, but that he has 'no flesh in his obdurate heart.'

With great esteem, I remain,

Your faithful and liberal coadjutor,

WM. LLOYD GARRISON.

E. D. HUDSON.

Printed in *The Liberator*, October 26, 1838.

Above the letter appeared the following legend: "We copy the following letter into the columns of the Liberator, because of its adaptation to other states as well as to Connecticut.

"From the Hartford Charter Oak
"LETTER FROM WM. LLOYD GARRISON

"We have obtained permission to publish the following letter, which was written in answer to an invitation of the Litchfield County Society, through their Committee, to be present at their meeting at Norfolk. It was not received in season for that meeting, but was read to the Society at its late meeting at South Cornwall."

Dr. Erasmus Darwin Hudson (b. Torringford, Connecticut, December 15, 1805; d. Riverside, Greenwich, Connecticut, December 31, 1880), abolitionist and surgeon, lived in Wolcottsville, Connecticut, and acted as an agent for *The Liberator* (*The Liberator*, October 26, 1838). In his letter of August 24, 1838, inviting Garrison to be present at the meeting, Hudson explained that local abolitionists had "most horrible and ugly ideas" about Garrison which he wished to eradicate. (Anti-Slavery Letters to William Lloyd Garrison and Others, Boston Public Library.) He graduated from the Berkshire Medical College in 1827. In 1837, he was secretary of the Torringford, Connecticut, Anti-Slavery Society. From 1837 to 1849 he was a general agent of the American Anti-Slavery Society, residing part of the time in Northampton, Massachusetts. In 1842 he also served as agent of the *National Anti-Slavery Standard*, the official organ of the American Anti-Slavery Society. He contributed to *The Liberator* and the *National Anti-Slavery Standard* and was co-editor of *The Charter Oak* (Hartford, 1838–1841). From 1850 until his death, he lived in New York City, where he devoted himself to orthopedic surgery and the invention of artificial limbs and other orthopedic appliances, some of which received awards at expositions in Europe and the United States. (*ACAB*.) Smith College has a large collection of his manuscripts, many of which are autobiographical in nature and worthy of publication.

1. Revelation 18:13.
2. Ecclesiastes 4:12.
3. Jeremiah 2:34.
4. Matthew 7:20.
5. Revelation 11:15.
6. *Othello*, I, iii.

126

TO SAMUEL J. MAY

Brooklyn, September 8, 1838.

My dear brother May:

Several weeks have elapsed since a most affectionate and truly interesting letter was received from you,[1] full of the spirit of brotherly kindness — of peace on earth, and good will to all mankind. At the time it came to hand, (July 27,) I was too busily engaged in writing my New-York address for the memorable first of August, to answer it instanter; and on my return from the commercial Babylon, I found Helen quite ill with a fever and violent cough, from the effects of which she has scarcely yet recovered. She had a narrow escape from pleurisy or lung fever. Her cough was almost incessant, day and night. I carried her through five or six courses of the Thompsonian medicines, (having a complete supply on hand,) and succeeded in removing her complaints. Our house, for some time past, has resembled a hospital. Every member of the family has been under medical treatment. During my trip to New-York, I took a violent cold, and on my return should have taken to my bed, had I not found Helen in a worse condition than myself. My necessary attendance upon her, and the care of the children during her illness, have consumed so much of my time, that I have paid no attention whatever to the subject of peace, and shall go to the Peace Convention[2] wholly unprepared to take an efficient part in its proceedings. Doubtless, there will be speakers enough without me; and yet I did hope to be able to express my views on some of the topics that might be presented for consideration. But you know that I shrink from extemporaneous discussion. Perhaps something will be elicited from me, but it will be a random fire. As to the Report you desire me to draw up,[3] I can hold out no encouragement that I shall prepare it. I trust the other friends, to whom particular topics have been assigned,[4] will not be found delinquent. What will be the result of the Convention, we cannot foresee, but have every reason to believe it will be for good.

We shall probably find no difficulty in bringing a large majority of the Convention to set their seal of condemnation upon the present militia system, and its ridiculous and pernicious accompaniments. They will also, I presume, reprobate all wars, defensive as well as offensive. They will not agree so cordially as to the inviolability of human life. But few, I think, will be ready to concede, that Christianity forbids the use of physical force in the punishment of evil-doers; yet nothing is plainer to my understanding, or more congenial to the feelings of my heart. The desire of putting my enemies into a prison, or inflicting any kind of chastisement upon them, except of a moral kind, is utterly eradicated from my breast. I can conceive of no provocations greater than those which my Lord and Master suffered unresistingly. In dying upon the cross, that his enemies might live — in asking for their forgiveness in the extremity of his agonies — he has shown me how to meet all my foes, ay, and to conquer them, or, at least, to triumph over them. Henceforth, then, I war with no man after the flesh. I feel the excellence and sublimity of that precept which bids me pray for those who despitefully use me; and of that other precept which enjoins upon me, when smitten upon one cheek, to turn the other also. Even in this, the yoke of the Saviour is easy, and his burden is light. We degrade our spirits in a brutal conflict. To talk of courts of justice, and of punishing evil and disobedient men, — of protecting the weak, and avenging the wronged, by a posse comitatus or a company of soldiers, — has a taking sound; but it is hollow in my ears. I believe that Jesus Christ is to conquer this rebellious world, as completely as the Spirit of Evil has now possession of it; and I know that he repudiates the use of all carnal weapons in carrying on his warfare. There is not a brickbat or bludgeon, not a sword or pistol, not a bowie knife or musket, not a cannon or bomb-shell, which he does not *suffer* his Universal Foe to use against him; and which he does not *forbid* his soldiers to employ in self-defence, or for aggressive purposes. If, then, the spirit of Christ dwell in me, how can I resort to those things which he could not adopt? If I belong to his kingdom, what have I to do with the kingdoms of this world? "Let the dead bury their dead." [5]

You allude, incidentally, to the Sabbath in your letter, and say you cannot accept of my opinions respecting it. How far we disagree, I know not. By your observing the first day of the week, instead of the seventh, it is evident that you do not consider the fourth commandment as binding under the gospel dispensation, at least so far as the seventh day is concerned. I find no new commandment on the subject, altering the time of worship, or the sanctification of a special day, in the New Testament. Without a "Thus saith the Lord," what men may say about it is of no weight. The soul that is sanctified, sanctifies all time. Restraints and observances are for those who cannot fully apprehend what is spiritual freedom — not for those who have obtained complete enfranchisement. It appears to me, that there is much confusion of mind, respecting the sanctity of one day in seven, in consequence of our confounding the Old and New Testaments as of equal obligation. It is the *last* will and testament of a man, and that only, that is of binding force. In giving us his, our Lord and Saviour has superseded all other preceding instruments. Now, has he enjoined upon any of his disciples the duty of observing a particular day, in a particular manner? No. Was not the Sabbath a part of the first covenant? Certainly. Are we not living under a new and better covenant? Yes. Does the new covenant provide for the observance of one day in seven? I think not. — "Let no man, therefore, judge you in meat, or in drink, or in respect of a holy day, or of the new moon, or of the sabbath." [6] But "whether ye eat or drink, or whatsoever ye do, let all be done to the glory of God." [7] Amen.

Bro. George [8] will leave Brooklyn on Tuesday, with his wife and children, and sister Sarah, on an excursion of three or four weeks to Massachusetts and New-Hampshire. He expects to arrive in your village on Thursday evening next, where he will spend a few days with his wife's relations. If perfectly convenient, sister Sarah will stay with you. She and bro. George will attend the Peace Convention. I shall leave Brooklyn on Saturday next [9] with my family, for Boston, via Providence.

Helen and all the household unite in sending their choice regards to you and Mrs. May — in which joins, of course,

Your loving friend,

Wm. Lloyd Garrison.

ALS: Garrison Papers, Boston Public Library. A portion of this letter was printed in *Life*, II, 225–226.

1. Dated July 22, 1838 (Anti-Slavery Letters to William Lloyd Garrison and Others, Boston Public Library).

2. The Peace Convention resulted from a meeting of "friends of peace," held in Boston on May 30, 1838, at which William Ladd, the prominent pacifist, presided. The meeting appointed a committee, consisting of Samuel J. May of South Scituate, Henry C. Wright of Newburyport, the Reverend George Trask of Warren, and Edmund Quincy and Amasa Walker of Boston, to call a convention in Boston "for the purpose of having a free and full discussion of the principles of Peace, and of the measures best adapted to promote this holy cause." The convention was to be held on September 18 in Marlboro' Chapel. (*Life*, II, 222–223.)

3. May had asked Garrison to draw up a report on "whether the principles of Christianity require us even to forgive public criminals, and not put them to death or keep them in prison." (*Life*, II, 223.)

4. In his letter, May had noted:

"Brother Wright will prepare one on the inviolability of human life; Quincy, on the right of others, as well as members of the Society of Friends, to have their conscientious scruples respecting military trainings, etc., duly regarded. Walker will prepare one on military parades and titles. Others have been or will be requested to write on other topics. All this should be *inter nos*." (*Life*, II, 223.)

5. Matthew 8:22.

6. Colossians 2:16.

7. I Corinthians 10:31, slightly varied.

8. George W. Benson.

9. September 15, 1838.

127

TO HELEN E. GARRISON

Boston, Friday, Sept. 21, 1838.

My dear Helen:

I have not forgotten, that I have a loving and beloved wife in Providence, and also two *very* charming little boys. But, as you may suppose, my time has been pressingly occupied with business. To begin with the beginning. We (that is, Wm. M. C.,[1] sisters, and myself) arrived in season, on Monday evening,[2] to take tea with the inmates at Hayward Place,[3] and received, of course, a very cordial welcome.

Every thing looked so natural, it scarcely seemed as if I had been absent from the city at all. Strange, that, while in less than three months, a whole empire may be ravaged, not a platter can be disturbed upon the shelf of a private dwelling. I found at home, (for it still seems like home,) Mr. and Mrs. Babcock, bro. Johnson [4] and wife, bro. St. Clair [5] and wife, and young Oliver,[6] from Baltimore — all well. Next morning, attended the Peace Convention, not knowing what to anticipate as to its complexion or numbers, and hardly attempting to imagine what would be the result of its deliberations. [I ought to have said, that we attended bro. May's lecture at the Chapel,[7] the evening of our arrival. It was delivered in the large hall, but there were very few present, and they were nearly all abolitionists. It was a good lecture.] A respectable number of delegates were in attendance. Hon. Sidney Willard,[8] of Cambridge, was elected President, and E. L. Capron and Amasa Walker Vice Pres. When the roll of members was about being made out, I rose and suggested, that, as mistakes often occur in procuring signatures, each individual should write his or *her* name on a slip of paper, &c.; thus mooting the vexed "woman question" at the very outset. There was a smile on the countenances of many abolition friends, while others in the Convention looked very grave. Several of the clergy were present, but no one rose to object. Of course, women became members, and were thus entitled to speak and vote. A business committee was then appointed, upon which Abby Kelley and a Miss Sisson [9] were placed. Mrs. Chapman was added to another committee. In the course of the forenoon, Rev. Mr. Beckwith [10] was called to order by Abby K.[11] Endurance now passed its bounds on the part of the women-contemners, and accordingly several persons (clergymen and laymen) requested their names to be erased from the roll of the Convention, because women were to be allowed to participate in the proceedings! — They were gratified in their request.[12]

In the afternoon, bro. Wright [13] opened the discussion, by offering a resolution, declaring that no man, no government, has a right to take the life of man, on any pretext, according to the gospel of Christ. He made a very able argument, and was replied to by a Rev. Mr. Powers [14] of Scituate, but in a feeble manner. In the evening, Dr. Follen [15] made a long and ingenious speech against the resolution, and contended that a man had a right to defend himself by violence. Bro. Wright spoke in reply, and was catechised, while upon the stand, pretty freely. He answered all objections very readily. Several others also addressed the meeting, very briefly, which was then adjourned. The discussion was continued with great animation the next forenoon.[16] Rev. Mr. Gannett [17] made a speech against the resolution, and moved its indefinite postponement. I replied to him in a manner that grieved him sorely. The resolution was adopted by a large majority. In the afternoon, a committee of nine was appointed to draw up a Constitution and a Declaration of Sentiments, of which I was chairman.[18] I first wrote the Constitution, radical in all things, and presented it without delay.[19] It created much discussion, which lasted during the evening, but was adopted by a decisive majority.[20] Yesterday forenoon [21] was occupied in the consideration and adoption of sundry important resolutions; but I absented myself to write the Declaration.[22] In the afternoon, it was reported to the Convention, and never was a more "fanatical" or "disorganizing" instrument penned by man. It swept the whole surface of society, and upturned almost every existing institution on earth. Of course, it produced a deep and lively sensation, and a very long and critical debate; and, to my astonishment, was adopted by those present, by a vote of more than 5 to 1.[23] It was ordered to be engrossed upon parchment, and the signatures of those who approved it are to be appended to it. It will make a tremendous stir, not only in this country, but, in time, throughout the world. All who voted for it were abolitionists. Edmund Quincy, Wendell Phillips, William Ladd, A. St. Clair, and S. J. May, declined voting either way, though almost ready to swallow it entire. Bro. May acted very inconsistently, got frightened, confused, and did some harm. After the adjournment yesterday afternoon, we formed a society, calling it the "New-England Non-Resistance Society," and electing Effingham L. Capron to be its President, myself the Corresponding, and Mrs. Chapman the Recording Secretary. Mrs. Southwick [24] and Anna Weston [25] are upon the Executive Committee. In the course of the discussions, bro. George spoke several times with much earnestness, and to great effect.

By this procedure, your husband will have subjected himself afresh to the scorn, hatred and persecution of an ungodly world; but my trust is in the God of Jacob. I know that the sentiments of the Declaration are of God, and must prevail.

Now, a word about house-keeping. It follows, that I have had no time to hunt up a house. Lucy and Mrs. Johnson [26] have examined several houses, but they are not suitable; and they are of opinion that no such house as I need can probably be obtained in the city at this time. Hearing that bro. Phelps wished to rent the house he occupies, this morning bro. George and myself went and examined it thoroughly. It is far different from what I anticipated. We liked it exceedingly. It is precisely what we want, in all respects. You know he hires all the furniture, which cost the owner not less than a thousand dollars. He pays $400 a year, and taxes, but says, if I will take it for one year, I may have it for $300; so that I can have a house neatly and completely furnished from the parlor to the attic, and go into it forthwith, at the same price I should have to pay for an ordinary house alone. There are not less than five good sleeping apartments. We need nothing, but to go in and take possession. Mrs. Bird [27] will be an excellent neighbor, on many accounts. The court is kept perfectly neat, and every thing is pleasant and agreeable to the eye and taste, except the house at the entrance of the court. Bro. Phelps says it is as quiet there as in the country. Being so retired, it will suit sister Anna. There is a good cellar, a back yard which is just the thing for George Thompson and Frederick [28] to play in — and, in fact, every convenience that we could reasonably desire.

☞ Ever since Tuesday, bro. George and myself have been enjoying the hospitality of our friends, the Southwicks. They want you to stop with them, when you come to B., until we get a house. I am not certain whether we can go into bro. Phelps's house, until the 1st of Oct. But you had better return soon.

Bro. George, and other friends, deem it a rare chance. Now, my dear, what say you? I told bro. P. I would write to you before coming to a decision, and should probably have a reply from you by Monday. If we do not take up with this offer, I see no chance of our getting a house for some time. After I hear from you, I will specify a day, or rather will you? for coming to Boston, for I long to have you and the babes with me. Bro. G. leaves in the morning for Waltham and Lowell. Love to all in P.

Your loving husband,

W. L. Garrison.

ALS: Garrison Papers, Boston Public Library. Most of this letter was printed in *Life*, II, 227–229.

1. William M. Chace.
2. Garrison had parted from his wife on Monday, September 17.
3. The lodging-house of Mary S. Parker, where Garrison and other antislavery people often stayed when in Boston.
4. Oliver Johnson.
5. The Reverend Alanson St. Clair.
6. Unidentified.
7. Marlboro' Chapel.
8. Professor Sidney Willard (1780–1856) had been a member of the anti-Garrisonian Cambridge Anti-Slavery Society, which was founded in 1834 and remained in existence for about a year, and a vice-president of the American Union. He was a follower of Dr. William Ellery Channing. (*Life*, I, 463, 470; II, 478.)
9. Susanna (or Susan) Sisson (May 21, 1800–1882), daughter of Joseph Sisson and Priscilla (Taylor) Sisson, of Pawtucket, Rhode Island, was one of seven sisters and one or two brothers. The Sissons were abolitionists, Gurneyite Quakers, and devoted followers of Garrison, except for the later period when they rallied around Nathaniel P. Rogers in his difference with Garrison. Apparently, Susan was quite homely, but she is reported to have said "that she feels as handsome as

anybody." (Letter from Albert T. Klyberg, Librarian, The Rhode Island Historical Society, June 10, 1968; Mrs. L. B. C. Wyman, *Elizabeth Buffum Chace, 1806–1899, Her Life and Its Environment*, Boston, 1914, pp. 127, 238.)

10. The Reverend George C. Beckwith (died in 1870 at the age of seventy) was a member of the executive committee of the American Peace Society. *Life* (II, 226) quotes certain "anonymous MS. minutes" concerning Beckwith's participation in a preliminary meeting of "moderate" peace men on September 17, in the evening. The minutes report that Beckwith "opened the business of the meeting. His sentiment was that the cause should be protected from the extravagance of ultra men, and that the moderate party should so manage as to secure a chairman and a majority of the business committee on their own side. A sort of vigilance committee was chosen to attend to that business. The question then arose whether the moderate party should protest, or withdraw, or both, if women should be admitted to the convention and the committees. Mr. Beckwith said he would withdraw in that case, and, the question being put, all but two voted for withdrawal." He was minister of the First Congregational Church in Lowell from 1827 to about 1829. (*Life*, II, 226–228, 443.)

11. Abby Kelley.

12. At this point, a note in *Life* reports: "Among these were Messrs. Beckwith and Stow, and three out of four of the Maine delegation, good Ebenezer Dole not excepted (Lib. 8:151)."

13. Henry C. Wright.

14. Unidentified.

15. Charles Follen.

16. September 19, 1838.

17. Ezra S. Gannett.

18. The other members of the committee were Samuel J. May, Maria W. Chapman, Edmund Quincy, William Bassett, Abby Kelley, Peleg Clark, Henry C. Wright, and James P. Boyce. (*Life*, II, 228n.)

19. For the text of the constitution, as well as the Declaration of Sentiments, and the minutes of the convention, see *The Liberator*, September 28, 1838.

20. 28 to 15. *Life* (II, 228n) notes that "the length of the session had compelled many members to return home (Lib. 8:171)."

21. September 20, 1838.

22. The text was printed in *Life*, II, 230–234.

23. The vote was 26 to 5.

24. Thankful Hussey Southwick (b. Portland, Maine, July 3, 1792; d. Grantville, Massachusetts, April 29, 1867) was the wife of Joseph Southwick (see letter 20, to Helen Garrison, April 16, 1836). She was present at the meeting of the Boston Female Anti-Slavery Society on October 21, 1835, when Garrison was mobbed. She was active in the antislavery as well as the nonresistance movement, and was a member of the committee which summoned the Chardon-Street Convention in 1840. (*Life*, II, 12, 327, 420, 422; IV, 412.)

25. See letter 14, to Helen Garrison, March 5, 1836.

26. Lucy Parker and Mrs. Oliver Johnson.

27. Unidentified.

28. Possibly Frederick Turrell Gray, Jr., the eldest son of Garrison's friend, the Reverend Frederick Turrell Gray of Boston, who was the brother of John Gray of Brooklyn, Connecticut (see letter 63, to Mrs. Sarah Thurber Benson, December 24, 1836). We do not have the son's birth date, but since the father and Garrison were about the same age, their eldest sons may have been the same age and playmates. (M. D. Raymond, *Gray Geneaology* . . . , Tarrytown, New York, 1887, pp. 195–196.) In the next letter, No. 128, to Mary Benson, September 22, 1838, Frederick is referred to again, with the implication that he was arriving with Cecilia from Brooklyn, Connecticut. This poses innumerable problems and possibilities, all insoluble, since we know nothing about Cecilia or her relationship to Frederick. There is an old Talmudic saying that certain problems are so diffi-

cult that their solution must await the second coming of Elijah the prophet, who will precede the Messiah and solve all hitherto insoluble problems.

128

TO MARY BENSON

Boston, Sept. 22, 1838.

Dear sister Mary:

Though I have been but a few days in the city, and came here with an intention to keep very quiet in spirit until we should get our household affairs settled, yet I already begin to droop with excitement, and feel as if it will not require many weeks for me to lose in bodily weight, all that I gained during my pleasant sojourn in Brooklyn. In the midst of much business, pressing upon me like an avalanche, I seize my pen a moment just to say a few words to you, in a very hurried manner.

Helen is still in Providence. I find that there are very few houses to let, of any size; Lucy Parker and Mrs. Johnson have made extensive inquiries, and think it will be very difficult for me to get just such a house as I want, for some time to come. Fortunately, I am spared all further anxiety on the subject. Bro. Phelps, having lost his wife,[1] wishes to let the house he occupies, and is very anxious that I should take it. He has it on a lease for one year longer, from the first of October. It is completely furnished, from the kitchen to the attic, in a very genteel style, by the owner of the house. The furniture cost not less than one thousand dollars. Bro. Phelps pays at the rate of $400 a year, and taxes; but says I may have it for $300. It is, in all respects, just what we want. The location is in a small court, very retired, and every thing around is almost as quiet as a country village. I have not positively engaged the house, because I first desired to know the mind of Helen respecting it. There is little doubt that we shall take it. Bro. George, and all the friends at Hayward Place, think it is a rare chance. We can go into it any moment. I have written to Helen, telling her she can come on immediately, if she wishes. As it is quite certain that she will agree with me in opinion about taking the house, I wish Cecilia [2] to be informed, that we wish her to come on to Boston without delay. — She had better leave Brooklyn on Thursday next, or, at the latest, on Saturday next, in the stage for Providence. Sister Charlotte says she can stay with her over night, and the next morning, either bro. Anthony [3] or Wm. M. Chace will go down with her to the cars. I will be at the depot in Boston, on her arrival, with a carriage, and take her at once with Frederick to our house. Tell her I will pay her expenses. Should she leave on Saturday, she will of course have to stay at C's in P.[4] until Monday morning. If any thing shall happen to detain her, it will not be very material, as there is a good colored woman living with bro. Phelps, who will stay with us till she comes. Still, I should prefer to have her leave on Thursday next, if convenient, so that she can be with us on Friday forenoon. Please write to me on the subject by Tuesday's mail.

Sister Sarah has sent word by bro. May, that she will tarry with us a short time. On her return, we shall expect to welcome mother to our home, without fail. Then you and dear Anna must follow in succession.

Am I not extremely fortunate? As there is every thing in the house that is needed, I shall not, of course, have to buy or move any furniture. This will save me an outlay, at this time, of at least two hundred dollars — besides a great deal of time and difficulty in getting every thing together. There is a snug little back yard, where Frederick and George will have rare times together. On Monday, I shall begin to get in my coal, wood, provisions, &c. &c.

Our Peace Convention has just closed,[5] and it has been full of absorbing interest. There were more than 150 persons, who enrolled their names as members — among them, quite a number of women, several of whom were immediately put upon committees. This so horrified some of the clergy, and others, that they ordered their names to be erased from the rolls. Only about ten or twelve left. A large proportion of those present were abolitionists. The discussions were very animating. Some very strong resolutions were adopted. Bro. George spoke several times with great power, and to great acceptance. Bro. May run [6] well for a time, but got strangely confused and frightened, and did not recover himself. I took a much more active part than I thought of doing. A committee of nine was appointed to draft a Declaration of Sentiments. I drew it up, and put into it all the fanaticism of my head and heart. To my amazement, it was adopted, after a warm discussion, by a vote of more than 5 to 1. It goes against every human government, all human politics, all penal enactments, and declares that no body of men have a right to imprison or destroy men for their crimes. It will make a tremendous excitement in this country and Great Britain, and undoubtedly prepare the way for fresh mobs and more persecution. But my soul is in perfect peace, for my trust is in the living God. At the close of the Convention, a New-England Non-Resistance Society was formed, of which we made Effingham L. Capron President, bro. George one of the Vice Pres., myself Cor. Sec'y, Maria W. Chapman, Rec. Sec. Mrs. Southwick and Anna Weston were placed upon the Executive Committee. The next Liberator [7] will contain some of the proceedings.

Since my arrival in Boston, I have been staying at friend South-wick's. Bro. George has also stopped at the same place. He brought little Anna in from Waltham yesterday, and left this morning for the same town, expecting to be in Lowell this evening. Anna was very homesick — Henry Egbert [8] is still in miserable health. George wishes bro. Coe [9] to be informed, that it will not be in bro. May's power to make an exchange with him this fall. I have much more to write, but no room. Give my filial love to mother, and a brother's regards to sister Anne. Accept the same for yourself.

Yours, affectionately,
Wm. Lloyd Garrison.

As the Post Office is closed, I cannot pay postage.[10]

ALS: Garrison Papers, Boston Public Library.

1. Charlotte Phelps, the first president of the Boston Female Anti-Slavery Society, died on August 31, 1838. An obituary-notice of her death appeared in *The Liberator*, September 7, 1838.
2. Apparently a servant girl.
3. Henry Anthony, Charlotte Benson's husband.
4. Charlotte's in Providence.
5. The convention ended on September 20.
6. So in manuscript.
7. September 28, 1838.
8. Henry Egbert was George Benson's child.
9. The Reverend William Coe of Salem.
10. This sentence is written along the left edge of the final paragraph.

129

TO HELEN E. GARRISON

Boston, Sabbath afternoon, Sept. 23, 1838.

My dear wife:

Bro. Johnson has just brought me your letter of yesterday. It seems that you have had as little rest as myself, on the score of sleep, since we parted. Until last night, when I slept alone for the first time, I have scarcely obtained any sleep. Ever since my arrival, I have been in a whirl of intellectual and moral excitement. I have had to perform considerable writing, and a great deal of talking. And, as a natural consequence, my brain almost overpowers my body. I feel nearly as badly as I did before I went to Brooklyn. My thirteen pounds of flesh will probably melt away at a somewhat rapid rate. The excitement in my head has called afresh the malignity of my scrofulous complaint. My nose is quite red and very badly swollen, and my ears discharge freely. In addition to all this, for the first time for several years, my eyes are inflamed and sore, so that it is very painful for me to read or write.

I sympathize with dear little Willie, inasmuch as his teeth are so troublesome. Do you rub his gums enough with the syrup? I wish you would give it a fair trial, for now is the time to test its efficacy. Paregoric ought to be used sparingly. In case he is very restless nights, and the syrup cannot soothe him, you can then give him enough to cause sleep.

The sudden illness of Mrs. Jackson [1] gives me deep concern. I trust it is not unto death. If she is attended by a "regular physician," her case is more hopeless. I wish she could be persuaded to consult the "Thompsonian quack," Dr. Brown. He might, and I have no doubt would, give her much relief, without subjecting her to a full course. — But it is not to be expected that, at her advanced period of life, she can feel confidence in giving a trial of that which is every where spoken against. Give to Phebe [2] the sympathies of my heart.

I thank you, my love, for expressing your cheerful willingness that I should engage bro. P's house. I felt sure it would be so, for you have ever manifested a desire to fall into arrangements that would be most convenient and agreeable to me. You will, I am sure, be much better pleased with the house — location and all — after we get into it, than you imagine. — Remember, you went to visit a sick woman, when every thing looked sombre and cheerless. There are several pretty yards in the Court, very nicely kept, the handsomest of which directly [3] bro. P's house. As for the rooms in the house, they are precisely, in size and number, what we desire; and all of them more neatly furnished than we should have made them. The upper rooms are very pleasant, especially those in the back part of the house. The back yard is a much better one (though small) than Lucy's, where Frederick and George can play together, without being able to get into the street. There is an immense grape vine, covering nearly the whole yard, loaded down with grapes, which will be at our disposal; so that we and our friends can have quite a treat. I regard the retirement of the situation as very desirable. Even sister Anna will not object to tarrying with us, under such circumstances.

With regard to your returning home, I have only to say, that I long to see you and the children, and also wish to be settled in our affairs without unnecessary delay; that I wish you to do just as you feel disposed — either to prolong or shorten your visit. Bro. P. says we may go into his house any day this week. I wrote a letter last night to sister Mary, and gave directions to have Cecelia leave Brooklyn on Thursday or Saturday next — telling her to leave on Thursday, if she could make it convenient. Perhaps she will not be able to come immediately; but you need not wait for her — for there is an excellent colored woman living with bro. P., who has been with him a long time, and of whom he speaks very highly, who will cook for us until she comes. Should you wish, under these circumstances, to return immediately, please write to-morrow, so that if you conclude to come on Wednesday morning, I may be at the depot to receive you. Mrs. Southwick is very urgent to have you stay a few days with her — but it will not be convenient. To-morrow I shall commence getting in wood and coal, and on Tuesday, potatoes, flour, and other articles. I shall write to sister Sarah to-morrow, and tell her we shall rejoice to see her at our house in the course of all this week, or whenever her visit at Scituate expires. She has promised to stop with us awhile, and then let mother take her place. Next week, Tuesday, I must attend the Young Men's A.S. Convention at Worcester; [4] and therefore I wish to have every thing settled this week. Tell Phebe that circumstances are such as must prevent your intended visit to her house. I do not wish you to come on Wednesday, unless it is also your desire. Should you remain till Friday, perhaps Cecelia would be able to come on with you; but it is somewhat uncertain, whether she will be able to leave Brooklyn as early as Thursday.

Wm. Chace probably saw you last evening, and told you about bro. George's leaving, with little Anna, &c.

It was a bright and warm day, yesterday, like one in June. To day it is raining dismally. I have been on the bed nearly all day, endeavoring to recover my lost sleep. This evening I am going, with bro. Johnson's,[5] to Mrs. Chapman's. We are a Publishing Committee, to prepare the doings of the Peace Convention for publication. That Convention is making a great deal of talk.

I have not had time to converse ten minutes with friend Knapp, since I came to the city; hence, nothing has been said about boarding him and his wife. It happens, very fortunately, that bro. Phelps's lease forbids any one occupying the house to take any boarders. This will settle the matter, without leaving room for any hard thoughts.

I shall depend upon hearing from you by Tuesday's mail.

Yours, lovingly,

Wm. Lloyd Garrison.

ALS: Garrison Papers, Boston Public Library.

1. Mrs. Richard Jackson of Providence, Rhode Island. Originally Nabby Wheaton, she married Richard Jackson on March 19, 1795. A successful merchant, congressman, president of the Washington Insurance Company for thirty-eight years, and a trustee of Brown University, he died on April 18, 1838. (*Biographical Cyclopedia of Representative Men of Rhode Island*, Providence, 1881, p. 171.)

2. Phebe Jackson, of Providence, Rhode Island, was the daughter of Mr. and Mrs. Richard Jackson. See letter to Henry E. Benson, August 4, 1836.

3. So in manuscript.

4. The Young Men's Anti-Slavery Convention was to take place on Tuesday and Wednesday, October 2 and 3, 1838. The call to the convention which appeared in *The Liberator* on September 14, 21, and 28, was signed by Amos Phelps, Joshua Himes, Edmund Quincy, Wendell Phillips, and Oliver Johnson, all on the Committee of Arrangements.

5. So in manuscript.

130

TO SARAH BENSON

Boston, Sept. 24, 1838.

Dear sister Sarah:

I was rejoiced to learn from bro. George, that you had expressed a willingness to stay awhile with us, before your return to Brooklyn, provided we should succeed in procuring a house immediately. It happens, most fortunately for us, that bro. Phelps wishes to let the house now occupied by him, which he has on lease one year longer from the 1st of October ensuing. It is in a small court, (the only objection to which is a huge old house at the entrance,) and in a retired situation. There are five sleeping apartments, a sitting-room, parlor, &c. The house is completely furnished, from the kitchen to the attic — carpets, beds, bedding, curtains, chairs, looking-glasses, in short, every article that we need; so that I shall not have to move any thing. or make any of those purchases which I had contemplated, in furnishing a house myself. The furniture is not owned by bro. Phelps, but by the owner of the house, who paid something like one thousand dollars for it. The court, though a very diminutive one, and therefore scarcely worthy of the name, is kept extremely neat. There is a very pretty yard directly opposite the house, attached to a humble dwelling, occupied, I believe, by an Englishman, who shows an Englishman's taste. Our back yard is small, but just the place for Geo. Thompson and Frederick to play together, as they cannot get out into the streets. There is an immense grape vine, covering a large part of the yard, on which there is now a great abundance of grapes, which bro. P. generously says we may have for our own use. He pays $400 a year for the house and furniture, but says I may have it for $300 — as he cannot do better, under present circumstances. If I were a "gentleman of property and standing," I would pay him the full amount he pays his landlord; but as I am a poor fanatic, my means will not allow me to pay more than $300.

Helen wrote to me from Providence on Saturday. Ever since I left P., little Willie's gums have proved very troublesome to him, insomuch that Helen says she has scarcely been able to obtain any rest, except by administering to him an anodyne. She writes that Phebe Jackson's mother has been taken ill very suddenly, of an inflammation of the bowels, and continues to grow worse. There does not seem to be much hope of her recovery.

Helen seems desirous to return to Boston as soon as convenient. I have therefore written to her to come in the cars on Wednesday morning — perhaps she will stay till Thursday or Friday. Bro. Phelps says we may go into his house any day this week. My object, therefore, in writing to you, is to tell you how we are situated, and that we stand ready to give you a welcome reception to our new home. I do not wish you to abridge your visit in Scituate; for it is quite certain that it will be more agreeable to you than a visit to Boston; but we shall be glad to see you on Friday or Saturday next, or as soon as you can make it convenient after that time. Please write and let me know what day you will come, and by what conveyance — whether by steam-boat or stage-coach. If by the latter, you can tell the driver to leave you at No. 2, Nassau Court, Tremont-street. If by the former, I will be at the steam-boat landing on your arrival, to take you in a carriage to our house.

Since my arrival, I have been in a whirl of social, intellectual and moral excitement. My poor brain already reels under the pressure — though my heart is as tranquil as a summer sea, and happier than any bird that ever warbled forth a song. I have had to perform considerable writing, and an immense amount of talking. As my head grows hot, my scrofulous complaint is excited to fresh malignity, and will probably give me much trouble the ensuing winter. Our Peace Convention, (of which bro. May has doubtless given you a full account,) reminded me of our early anti-slavery meetings. The discussions were free and animated, and marked by a spirit of independence. The deep solemnity of the occasion was somewhat disturbed by the broad and irresistible humor of William Ladd. He is a huge and strange compound of fat, good nature, and benevolence. He went with us nineteen-twentieths of the way, and said he expected to "go the whole" next year! Our proceedings cannot fail to cause great and prevalent excitement in this country and in Europe. I am myself astonished, and not less delighted, at the result. Great persecutions are to follow; but none shall be saved, except he endure unto the end. "The Lord is my light and salvation." [1]

I have written to Brooklyn to have Cecelia come on immediately.

In peace or war, storm or sunshine, I remain,

Yours, most lovingly,

Wm. Lloyd Garrison.

ALS: Garrison Papers, Boston Public Library.

1. Psalms 27:1.

131

TO SAMUEL J. MAY

Boston, Sept. 24, 1838.

Dear bro. May:

Peace be with you and yours — that peace which "passeth all understanding"! As there is nothing secret in the foregoing letter to Sarah,[1] I seize the opportunity to say a few words to you, upon the remainder of this sheet.

I need not say, how anxious I feel, in common with many others, that you should join the non resistance society, and affix your name to the Declaration of Sentiments; but not, of course, until every scruple has been removed from your mind — for how can even two walk together, except they be agreed? But I am certain, that there is no difference in sentiment between us. Since you left us, we have had several private meetings, (attended by our friends Quincy, Alcott, Wright, St. Clair, Johnson, Wallcut,[2] myself, &c.) in order to make the language of those two instruments (the Declaration and Constitution) as plain, unambiguous and unexceptionable as possible, consistent with the principles set forth. The verbal amendments that have been made, I think will be very satisfactory to you. Mr. Alcott says he is now prepared to sign the Declaration; so does Mr. Wallcut; so does Mr. Quincy. The two latter will also join our society. Bro. St. Clair is not yet quite clear in his mind, but will doubtless soon be heartily with us. The Declaration closes in the following strain — "Firmly relying upon the certain and universal triumph of the sentiments contained in this Declaration, however formidable may be the opposition arrayed against them, — in solemn testimony of our faith in their divine origin, — we hereby affix our signatures to it; commending it to the reason and conscience of mankind, giving ourselves no anxiety as to what may befal us, and resolving in the strength of the Lord God calmly and meekly to abide the issue."[3]

This instrument contemplates nothing, repudiates nothing, but the spirit of violence in thought, word and deed. Whatever, therefore, may be done without provoking that spirit, and in accordance with the spirit of disinterested benevolence, is not touched or alluded to in the instrument. The sum total of our affirmation is this — that, the Lord helping us, we are resolved, come what may, as christians, to have long-suffering toward those who may despitefully use and per-secute us — to pray for them — to forgive them, in all cases. This is "the head and front of our offending" [4] — nothing more, nothing less.

A word as to organizations. You know that my own mind is fetter-less — that I abjure all creeds, all political and ecclesiastical organiza-tions. How, then, can I approbate a non-resistance association? Freely enough, and with perfect consistency, because it destroys at a blow all the unnatural and artificial distinctions that obtain in society, and sunders, as by the touch of fire, all human cords by which the in-tellects and souls of men are bound. All ecclesiastical and political organizations are so constructed as to admit of rivalry, station, suprem-acy, domination, and caste; and it is made *a duty for men to join them,* and be guided by their enactments. Our association places every man upon the dead level of equality. He that would be greatest, must be the servant of all. It gives no power but that of love, and allows of nothing but suffering for Christ's sake. It has no ranks, no titles, no honors, no emoluments, to hold out to men as an inducement to sup-port it. On the contrary, it requires of every man a cheerful willing-ness to sacrifice all these, and count them as dung and dross. It denies to no man the right to think, speak and act, as his reason and conscience may dictate. It leaves every man free to act singly, or with others, as he may think best, in the promotion of universal peace. Who then can justly object to it? Its only creed is, suffering wrong meekly — its only punishment, the forgiveness of enemies, under all circumstances — its only restraint, the withholding of violence for violence.

Affectionately yours,
Wm. Lloyd Garrison.

ALS: Garrison Papers, Boston Public Library. This letter is printed, in part, in *Life*, II, 236–237.

1. Sarah Benson was then visiting the Mays in Scituate, Massachusetts.
2. Those named are Edmund Quincy, Amos Bronson Alcott, Henry C. Wright, Alanson St. Clair, Oliver Johnson, and the Reverend Robert Folger Walcutt. The Reverend Walcutt (b. Nantucket, March 16, 1797; d. Boston, March 1, 1884), a Harvard graduate, class of 1817, was a Unitarian clergyman at North Dennis, on Cape Cod, and an early antislavery man (*Life*, II, 422n, 477). Garrison mis-spells the name.
3. For the text of the declaration, see *Life*, II, 230–234.
4. *Othello*, I, iii, 80.

132

TO GEORGE W. BENSON

Boston, Sept. 29, 1838.

Dear bro. George:

I expected to see you at the Worcester Convention on Tuesday next — but learn from Cecilia, who arrived yesterday morning, that you had got back to Providence, and intended starting for Brooklyn this morning. Charlotte writes us, that dear little Henry Egbert was extremely ill — much more so than he had been. — The news is very afflicting to us; yet we cannot but hope he will recover, and live to solace his parents in their *declining* years.

We have at last got to housekeeping — though our household affairs are not all yet arranged. Bro. Phelps will not be able to remove all his furniture until Monday afternoon; and until the premises are left clear, we cannot, of course, complete our arrangements. Helen is very well pleased with the house; so that I am now relieved of anxiety on that account. The best of my furniture, that was stored, I have removed into our house; which, in addition to that which was already in it, fills us up very compactly as to room. We expect sister Sarah on Monday, though bro. May writes us that he will try to persuade her to stay in Scituate some days longer. I presume she will conclude to come on Monday. We wish dear mother to be with us as soon as convenient. So far as we are concerned, she need not wait until the return of Sarah.

You will have seen by yesterday's Liberator, that the list of officers of the new "jacobinical," "no-government" society was not published. The list is not yet completed, and the truth is, we do not know of any persons in the city, whom we [can] elect to fill up the vacancies. After you left, our friend Edmund Quincy changed his views respecting the Declaration of Sentiments, and expressed his readiness to sign it — but has once more vacillated, and thinks he is not prepared at present to endorse the entire instrument. At least, there are some doubts and difficulties that he feels, and which must be removed before he can commit himself publicly. I feel very tenderly toward him; and do not regard him any the less for his conscientious scruples. He will doubtless come out right. Bro. May says he shall write to me at length on the subject next week. I have not much hope that he will get his mind relieved in season to start with us. Indeed, we shall not have a *great* and *sudden* rush into our ranks! There are very few, in this land, in this world, who will be able to abide by the principles we have enunciated; though there may be many whose consciences must assent to their correctness. I see before us many trials through which we shall doubtless be called to pass, if we are faithful to our testimony. But let none of these things move us, or deter us from going forward. The Lord God is our sun and shield — our strength and our defence.

Since I began this letter, I have been surrounded by a troop of anti-peace men, who have so hindered me by discussions, that my time allotted to fill this sheet has been consumed three or four times over — and it is now so dark, that I must finish what I have got to say, in a very few words, for this letter must be dropped into the Post Office without delay.

I wish you to write me your opinion, respecting the probability of means being procured to sustain the Liberator, if the following arrangement should go into effect. Bro. Johnson and myself, since you left, have looked the ground all over anew. We find that it must require a book-keeper, equal to Mr. Blake, to spend all his time in taking care of the accounts. He cannot do any more. Besides this, there are about three days in the week that must be consumed in mailing the papers, &c. This bro. Johnson could attend to, and then be able to devote the remainder of the week to reading of proofs, writing the minor paragraphs for the paper, and performing many other matters that would be serviceable to the cause, and afford me very great relief. But the difficulty will be to convince those who shall contribute to support the Liberator, that a printer, book-keeper, sub-editor, and editor, are actually needed to make the concern what it ought to be. I see not how it can be done more economically, if bro. J. is to be of any assistance to me. There would be no object in merely exchanging him for Mr. Blake as book-keeper. What do you say, in view of all this? Had I better try to attend to all the editorial and mechanical concerns of the paper as I have done hitherto, and keep Mr. Blake as book-keeper? or do you think enough may be raised to support the plan I have named above? Bro. J. is very anxious to know what is to be the final decision, that he may govern himself accordingly. Much will depend on your answer. I presume there will be no difficulty in procuring such a committee of accounts, as we spoke of when you were here, provided they do not incur any pecuniary liabilities.

Yours, ever,
Wm. Lloyd Garrison.

☞ Love to the household.

ALS: Garrison Papers, Boston Public Library. This letter was printed, in part, in *Life*, II, 237–238.

133

TO SAMUEL J. MAY

Boston, Oct. 30, 1838.

My dear bro. May:

I am truly sorry to disappoint any of the friends who may assemble in convention at Hingham to-morrow,[1] by not being present with you; especially since it has been announced from the pulpit, that I would deliver a lecture to-morrow evening. But, within the last three or four days, my inveterate enemy, the scrofula, has made its appearance upon the fore-finger of my right hand, causing great inflammation and continual pain, and swelling both the finger and the hand to huge dimensions. I am necessitated to keep a large poultice on the hand, and to bathe the swelling frequently — as yet, to no purpose. Twice, last year, I suffered in a similar manner, and therefore know the probable duration of this attack, which will be protracted for some time. As it affects my right hand, it is, of course, very painful for me to write. It would be to little purpose, that I should come and deliver some brief extemporaneous remarks; for you know that I am fastidious, on this point; and as to writing an address, now, I have neither time, nor will my hand allow me to do so. I have made a desperate attempt, and written a few pages — but was necessitated to stop.

Another consideration. This number of the Liberator[2] is a very important one, with regard to the approaching election. The replies of the various candidates to the questions propounded to them, will be coming in up to the time the paper goes to press, and will need comments. I must try to write something adapted to the crisis, painful as it is for me to hold a pen. To be absent from the office, even an hour, will hardly be allowable, under these circumstances.

My regret, in causing any disappointment at Hingham, is mitigated by the fact, that there will be present several able speakers to prevent any failure of a meeting — viz. yourself, Quincy, Phelps, Ryder,[3] &c.

I beg you will apologize to the meeting for my absence, and promise the friends in Hingham that, Deo volente, I will shortly give them an address, according to their wishes.

I know how my respected friend, Jairus Lincoln,[4] will feel, in consequence of this failure — but if I am really disqualified from performing well my part at H., in consequence of the state of my hand, (which affects my whole system,) he will excuse me. My best regards to him.

I want to see you, my dear friend, as a lover yearns to catch a glance at the mistress of his heart. The "non-resistance" theory, you perceive, is stirring up opposition from friends and foes. Is it therefore unsound? No; for men did not originate it, neither can they overthrow it. My confidence in it is strong and joyful. What is the present state of your mind respecting it?

Sister Sarah left us, yesterday, for Brooklyn, via Providence, in rather a feeble state of health. We expect Mrs. Benson to be with us very soon.

Charlotte Coffin [5] spent the day with us on Friday last. She is an excellent girl, deserving of an excellent husband.

I trust your meeting will be "ultra" and "fanatical," in the modern understanding of those terms — then it will be ardent, zealous and rationally benevolent.

Give my cordial remembrances (and also Helen's) to Mrs. May. We shall be glad to see you both at our house.

Yours, with a brother's love,

Wm. Lloyd Garrison.

ALS: Garrison Papers, Boston Public Library.

1. The semi-annual meeting of the Plymouth County Anti-Slavery Society, scheduled for Wednesday, October 31, at 10 a.m., at the Baptist meeting-house. The notice of the meeting in *The Liberator* (October 26, 1838) announced that "Messrs. Phelps and Garrison are expected to be present."

2. November 2, 1838.

3. Thomas P. Ryder was secretary of the Plymouth County Anti-Slavery Society, an agent of the Massachusetts Anti-Slavery Society in 1839–1840, and previously an agent of the Temperance Society. *The Liberator*, August 16, 1839, printed a letter from Ryder, dated Providence, Rhode Island, August 6, 1839, to Garrison, in which he wrote of his antislavery and temperance efforts. See also, in the same issue of *The Liberator*, a letter from Thomas P. Richmond, dated Bristol, Rhode Island, July 16, 1839, concerning Ryder. A Thomas P. Ryder (born in 1806), a graduate of Harvard College in 1828 and later a constable of Boston, died in the Insane Asylum of Boston, November 21, 1852. (Fremont Rider, comp., *Rider [Ryder] Families in the United States*, Middletown, Conn., 1959, vol. III, n. p.)

4. There were at least two persons by the name of Jairus Lincoln in Hingham, Massachusetts, in 1838: Jairus Lincoln (b. Boston, 1794; d. Northboro, Massachusetts, 1882), an elementary school teacher and, later, a farmer, the author of *Anti-Slavery Melodies*, published in Hingham by Elijah B. Gill in 1843; also, Jairus B. Lincoln (b. Weymouth, 1792; d. Hingham, 1870), a shipmaster. In 1863 and 1864 he was president of the Boston Marine Society. The former was probably the person referred to by Garrison. (Waldo Lincoln, comp., *History of the Lincoln Family*, Worcester, 1923, p. 259; Xerox of letter from Julian C. Loring to Mrs. Randolph, dated Hingham, Massachusetts, August 30, 1970; letter from Nancy Sahli to Louis Ruchames, dated Philadelphia, Pennsylvania, Sept. 2, 1970.)

5. Samuel J. May's sister-in-law, his wife's sister.

134

TO MARY BENSON

Boston, Dec. 23, 1838.

Dear sister Mary:

"Charity endureth all things, believeth all things." [1] Charity means love. If you have any love for me, then I am emboldened to believe that you have patiently *endured* my long silence, *believing* that it has not been owing to any want of brotherly affection, but rather to a multiplicity of cares and duties. How much I respect and esteem you, I shall not now say — because such an expression is needless.

Ever since your arrival in Providence, we have been confidently hoping to welcome you to our snug little tenement in Nassau-Court. But, it seems, you have made up your mind not to visit us at present. Well, I am sincerely sorry for this. I hope you are not taking advantage of my "non-resistance" principles; for you know I cannot coerce you. True, in resolving to remain in Providence, you are far from being blameworthy; because it is certain that you can spend your time much more pleasantly and profitably there than in Boston. Yet I would fain intercede for at least "a flying visit" — promising that you shall return whenever time goes heavily, or the attractions of home are stronger than the novelties of a crowded city. Had you not better revoke your decision? The annual meeting of our State Anti-Slavery Society will be held on the 23d of January; and will be well worth your attendance, on the score of interest. I anticipate an animated, almost a stormy scene. Facts are daily coming to my ears, which show that the spirit of sectarianism is busy at its old game of division — working in darkness, and secretly endeavoring to transfer our sacred cause to other hands. The leaders in this work of mischief are clerical abolitionists. The plot is extensively laid, and the wires are pulled skilfully. It will be managed much more ingeniously than was the "Clerical Appeal" affair. Torrey,[2] of Salem, (formerly of Providence,) is one of the most active of the plotters. I understand the plan is, to rally at our annual meeting, elect a different board of managers, start a new anti-slavery paper, to be the organ of the Society — &c. &c. The "woman question" is also to be met and settled so as to suit the priest-hood, or the probability is, there will be a division. Here, then, are materials for an excited anniversary. I do not mean that my annual report shall be a quiet document. Now, will you not come and be a spectator? And bring, if practicable, our true-hearted friend Phebe [3] with you. We shall be happy to welcome her under our roof. What will be the result of this matter is now problematical. I think, however, that the counsels of the froward will be carried headlong. Perhaps, after all, the plotters will be afraid to divulge their purposes, and will conclude that discretion is the better part of valor. I hope so; for every such outbreak but encourages the common enemy, and breeds mutual distrust and jealousy.

The Anti-Slavery Fair, in this city, was held three days, and closed on Friday evening. The proceeds amounted to $1100 — a sum much larger than has been taken on any previous occasion. Three years ago, it could not have been held without a riot. It presented an animated scene. The hall was tastefully decorated, and the tables were covered with useful and beautiful articles, adapted to every variety of taste. Every thing was conducted with propriety and order. After the Fair closed, there remained on hand a valuable stock of articles, which will be sold as opportunity offers. So much for the skill, industry, liberality and enterprise of the female abolitionists of Boston and vicinity. The ladies of Salem are to try their luck next, on Christmas day; and then our Lynn friends, who intend giving a share of their receipts to the support of the Liberator.

Bro. H. C. Wright was with us last week, but has returned to Newburyport to rest a short time in the bosom of his family. He has prepared a tract on human governments, which, when published, will doubtless stir up the feelings of community. It shows, in a simple and lucid manner, that national organizations, as now constructed, are essentially anti-christian, and utterly at war with the gospel of Christ. The more I look into the subject, the deeper is my conviction that the principles of the Non-Resistance Society are immutably true; that whoever feels unable or unwilling to forgive all manner of injuries, and the worst of enemies, has no right to rank himself among the followers of Christ; that the attempt of men to govern themselves by external rules and physical penalties is and ever must be futile; and that from the assumption, that man has a right to exercise dominion over his brother, has proceeded every form of injustice and oppression with which the earth has been afflicted. Modern christianity is, to a great extent, an imposture. There is much said about the cross of Christ — but who is willing to endure that cross? We hear much about the necessity of having faith in God — but who believes the record that he has given? A great ado is made about regeneration — but who receives the Messiah as one able to cleanse from all sin — now and forever?

I agree with Phebe, respecting Elleanor Eldridge.[4] Her case is certainly a hard one; and yet she is comparatively in affluent circumstances. I do not marvel that she desires to get justice, but I fear her heart is set upon the perishable things of earth. What I said in the Liberator about her, was cheerfully written — yet it was extorted by her importunity. She has had bad advisers, who have led her to think that her case is one of *national* importance, and that abolitionists universally would bestir themselves mightily in her behalf! — She brought with her to Boston, 200 copies of her Memoirs, expecting to sell them forthwith. Weeks have elapsed — and notwithstanding my recommendation of her work, not ten copies have been sold. I have on hand in the house, 160 copies. When she went away, she said she intended to return shortly, and bring another trunk full with her. It is about time to expect her. I wish, therefore, that you or Phebe would tell her not to come — at least, not to send any more copies. I will do the best I can with what is on hand.

You will be glad to know that the health of dear mother is much better than it was in Providence. She considers herself "perfectly well." Helen has had a troublesome cough, but is now better. Cecilia has taken a severe cold, but is able to keep about. George Thompson has had the influenza, which has puffed up his face like a London Alderman's. As for little Willie, he is sprightly, intelligent, charming — a pearl, a paragon, a non-pareil — &c. &c. &c. He is just eleven months old — can say ma and pa — walks very readily about the room, without any help — and is still remarkable for his benignity. I love him dearly, but incomparably less than I do one of the simplest principles of the government of God. If I did not, I should not be worthy of my Master.

We all felt much indebted to you for your letter, and also to Phebe for her friendly note. I hope to be able to write to her shortly. Give our united regards to her and her mother, who, I hope, enjoys her health better than formerly. Our kind remembrances must also be given to Mrs. Flagg and her husband.[5] We shall be glad to see them at our house, at any time. It is needless to add, that we send special remembrances to sister Charlotte and husband. If our bro. George is in P., say to him that I deem it of real importance that he should be at our annual meeting, if possible. He must send on as many stanch friends as he can, on that occasion. Are there any persons in Providence, who are willing to subscribe to our contemplated non-resistance publication?[6] It will be open to free discussion. Let us hear from you again soon — and remember that a trip from Providence to Boston is almost as easy as a ride from Providence to Pawtucket.

Your loving brother,

Wm. Lloyd Garrison.

☞ If Elleanor should want her books returned, or any number of them, I will forward them according to her directions. It is not probable that one half of them will be sold, because her case is a *local* one, and not actually one of suffering.[7]

ALS: Garrison Papers, Boston Public Library. A portion of this letter was printed in *Life*, II, 253.

1. A variation of I Corinthians 13:4, 7.
2. The Reverend Charles T. Torrey (b. Scituate, Massachusetts, November 21, 1813; d. Baltimore, Maryland, May 9, 1846) was corresponding secretary of the anti-Garrisonian Andover Anti-Slavery Society at its formation in 1835; he approved of the clerical appeals, and was one of several clergymen who protested against a resolution adopted at the New England Anti-Slavery Convention on May 24, 1838, inviting women to become members and to participate in the business of the organization. Torrey was also corresponding secretary of the Essex County Anti-Slavery Society. In 1839, he sought to persuade the society to repudiate Garrison but failed. In 1840 he seceded, with other opponents of Garrison, from the American Anti-Slavery Society and helped to form the American and Foreign Anti-Slavery Society. He was also sympathetic to political abolition. In his last years, he regretted his earlier opposition to Garrison. During the winter of 1841–1842 he was in Washington as correspondent for a number of Boston and New York newspapers, was arrested, released, and spent the next two years helping runaway slaves, of whom he helped about four hundred to freedom. He was arrested in Baltimore in June 1844 and sentenced to six years in the penitentiary for aiding in the escape of fugitive slaves. For further information about Torrey, see Joseph C. Lovejoy, *Memoir of Rev. Charles T. Torrey Who Died in the Penitentiary of Maryland, Where he Was Confined for Showing Mercy to the Poor* (Boston, 1847), and William W. Patton, *Freedom's Martyr, A Discourse on the Death of the Rev. Charles T. Torrey . . .* (Hartford, 1846). See also the interesting evaluation of Torrey by Louis Filler, *The Crusade Against Slavery, 1830–1860* (Harper Torchbooks, New York, Evanston, and London, 1963), pp. 163–164.
3. Phebe Jackson.
4. On November 30, 1838, *The Liberator* published the following notice:
"*Memoirs of Elleanor Eldridge.* This is a little book just published in Providence, the express purpose of which is 'to give a helping hand to suffering and persecuted merit.' Elleanor belongs to that race which a republican and christian people (alas! what a mockery of terms!) have for two hundred years classed among the brute creation, and treated with the utmost barbarity. Happily, she was never a slave, though she has been deeply injured. . . . By dint of unremitted toil, she was at last enabled to purchase a small estate in Providence, and had nearly succeeded in liquidating the cost, when advantage was taken of her temporary absence from the State, and the property was sold, without any public notice being given, at an enormous sacrifice, by one who held a mortgage upon it. Thus, most unrighteously, and in an hour, she was rendered houseless and homeless, and all the fruits of a life of industry and prudence wrested from her by fraud and violence. All the particulars of the case, and of her present situation, are detailed in this attractive narrative, which was written by a lady of great literary merit, and a warm-hearted friend of the colored race. Copies of the work may be obtained at 25, Cornhill, and we trust will find a ready sale. Accompanying it is a likeness of Elleanor, and also high recommendations of her character from some of the most respectable families in Providence."
5. John Foster Brewster Flagg (1802–1872) practiced dental surgery in Providence during 1825–1840 and perhaps also a little later. He was the author of *Ether and Chloroform; Their Employment in Surgery, Dentistry, Mid-wifery, Therapeutics, etc.* (Philadelphia, Lindsay & Blakeston, 1851), and was the first professor of anatomy and physiology in the old Philadelphia College of Dental Surgery chartered in 1852 and reorganized as the Pennsylvania College of Dental

Surgery in 1856. (Letter to Louis Ruchames, November 7, 1969, from John B. Blake, Chief, History of Medicine Division of the National Library of Medicine; Bernard Wolf Weinberger, *An Introduction to the History of Dentistry in America*, St. Louis, 1948, II 138, 196.)

6. The *Non-Resistant*. On December 21, 1838, *The Liberator* carried an announcement that "The Executive Committee of the Non-Resistance Society have resolved to publish, without delay, a specimen number of a new semi-monthly periodical, to be called 'THE NON-RESISTANT.' Terms one dollar per annum. . . . All moneys forwarded either to C. K. Whipple, Treasurer, or to the editor of the Liberator, shall be duly acknowledged. . . ."

7. The postscript was written along the edge of the last page.

IV POLITICS AND WOMEN – DIVISIONS WITHIN THE RANKS: 1839

THE CONFLICT which had simmered within the anti-slavery movement in 1838 broke out with renewed force in 1839 over the issues of political action and the participation of women in the movement. The leaders of the anti-Garrisonian efforts were Alanson St. Clair, Amos Phelps, Charles T. Torrey of Salem, the Reverend Nathaniel Colver of Boston, and Henry B. Stanton. Meeting with failure at the annual meeting of the Massachusetts Anti-Slavery Society in January, in their effort to secure the establishment of a newspaper to replace *The Liberator* and in another effort to censure Garrisonians for their refusal to vote and for their willingness to permit the participation of women, Garrison's enemies decided to issue the *Massachusetts Abolitionist*, which first appeared on February 7, 1839, and to form a competing Massachusetts antislavery organization. The new society was formed after the annual New England Anti-Slavery Convention at the end of May, and called itself the Massachusetts Abolition Society. During this period, the already strained relations between the Massachusetts Anti-Slavery Society and the executive committee in New York of the American Anti-Slavery Society deteriorated further when the New York committee advised the Massachusetts board that due to the latter's failure to raise its previous year's pledge of $10,000 to the national organization, independent agents would be sent into Massachusetts to raise the amount due. Fortunately, after much public wrangling, the amount was raised before May 1.

But if this source of conflict was eliminated, others soon took its place. These were reflections of the intensifying view of the anti-Garrisonian abolitionists of New York and elsewhere that the antislavery movement would have to place increasing reliance upon antislavery votes and the formation of an antislavery political party in combatting slavery. This emphasis could be seen in James Birney's letter in the *Emancipator* on May 2, 1839, in which he argued that those whose conscience did not permit them to vote ought to leave the American Anti-Slavery Society. The conflict over political action and the role of women continued at the annual meeting of the American Anti-Slavery Society in New York from May 7 to May 10. Again, the Garrisonians emerged victorious after bitter wrangling.

During the remainder of the year, several antislavery leaders continued to urge the formation of an antislavery political party and to nominate candidates for President and Vice-President during the 1840 elections. On this issue, even the anti-Garrisonians were divided, with Myron Holley of Rochester and James Birney urging its formation, and Lewis Tappan opposing.[1]

Dissension between the leaders of the Massachusetts Anti-Slavery Society and the executive board of the national organization in New York continued over the failure of the Massachusetts organization to meet its financial quota for 1839. In a public exchange of letters, the national board asked for permission to send its own fund raisers into the state. The Massachusetts board denied the request, attributing the situation to the attacks of the national board upon the Massachusetts abolitionists. In the midst of this crisis, there arrived the news of the passing of Benjamin Lundy, the veteran antislavery leader, on August 22, 1839.

135

TO SAMUEL J. MAY

Boston, January 4, 1838. [1839]

Beloved Friend:

According to the chronology of man's invention, another new year has come round. Doubtless, many have been the good wishes that have greeted your ears within the last three days. Allow me to add mine to the number. They extend beyond the boundaries of the present year, and include all time — eternity. I desire that you may be happy always. I believe few possess a more equable, loving and cheerful spirit than yourself. It is because you delight in doing good, from the purest motives. You are not ashamed to be a disciple of Jesus, the crucified. The cross which he bore has for you no terrors. In him you behold the righteousness of the law fulfilled, and great is your gratitude that he has left you an example, that you should walk in his steps. You believe that if you lose your life for his sake, you

---

1. For the most penetrating evaluation of the issues involved in this controversy, see Aileen S. Kraditor, *Means and Ends in American Abolitionism; Garrison and His Critics on Strategy and Tactics, 1834–1850* (New York, 1967), pp. 118ff.

shall certainly find it again. Hence, you have ceased to fear those who can kill the body. It must follow, that you are a happy man. "Great peace have they who love thy law, and nothing shall offend them." [1] I hold to a state of permanent bliss on earth. If we may rejoice in God to-day, we may always. It is said of the Captain of our salvation, that he was "a man of sorrows, and acquainted with grief." [2] But, surely, he was not unhappy, in the popular acceptation of the term. He was without sin, and therefore without misery. Yet he could weep — his bosom was troubled — he was shelterless; yea, he was "despised and rejected of men." [3] So we may weep, and be filled with anguish of spirit, in view of the sin and wretchedness of the world; our names may be cast out as evil; and yet, at the same time, we may be filled with that "peace of God, which passeth all understanding." [4] For myself, I know not what it is to be disconsolate. All my desires, interests, expectations, are swallowed up in the sufficiency and love of God. "Whom have I in heaven but him? there is none on earth that I desire beside him." [5]

I thank you for the two letters recently forwarded to me. It seems you have been preaching on the subject of Peace at Hingham. Mr. Lincoln [6] speaks of them in glowing terms, though he does not feel prepared in spirit to adopt the principles. I am anxious to know the precise state of your mind, with regard to our Non-Resistance Society. Edmund Quincy and Robert F. Walcutt [7] are now both members of our Executive Committee, and have arrived at clear satisfaction. My confidence in the soundness of the sentiments set forth in the Declaration, is equal to my trust in God — and that is perfect. I hesitate not to affirm, with all modesty, that those sentiments are invulnerable, let the opposition come from what quarter it may. Already, they are exciting much discussion, and attracting general attention. Last evening, the question of non-resistance was discussed at the Odeon, before the Boston Lyceum — in the presence of three thousand persons. There were three speakers in favor of the war side, though every one of them distinctly admitted that war is repugnant to the principles of Christianity; but they said that, in the present state of the world, those principles could not be carried out, either by individuals or nations. They were applicable only to a future age! Amasa Walker advocated the pacific policy, taking care to say that he was no believer in the doctrines of the Non-Resistance Society. His hobby was a Congress of Nations. The vote was almost unanimous in favor of biting, scratching, mutilating and killing our enemies, whether foreigners or natives. And the audience claims to be enlightened and christianized! It manifested a tiger-spirit.

You inquire after the manuscripts of Dr. Worcester. [8] They have never been put into my possession. You will have to write to the editor of the Register [9] on the subject.

Our annual meeting is at hand.[10] It threatens to be a stormy one. You must not fail to be present, if practicable. There is a conspiracy going on in our midst, to an extent deplorable and alarming. It is the old leaven of sectarianism working afresh, and determined hostility to the Liberator. Under pretence of regard for the cause, the design is to start another weekly anti-slavery publication, to be the official organ of the State Society, and to be managed upon "orthodox" principles — in the hope of subverting the Liberator, and thus driving me from the field. The game, thus far, has been so adroitly played, that not a few well-meaning abolitionists have been drawn into it. Phelps and Torrey are foremost in the matter, backed up by Stanton, St. Clair, and others. They expect, by drilling, to be able at the annual meeting to so change the present Board of Managers as to be able to do as they please. There is no mistake in all this — and it is a sad revelation. Our Board fully understand the movement; and, in order to counteract it, as far as possible, have this day resolved to publish a monthly sheet, (rather larger than the Human Rights,)[11] to be called "The Abolitionist," and to be edited by a committee, consisting of Wendell Phillips, Edmund Quincy, and myself, for gratuitous distribution on the part of auxiliary societies. More than this our cause does not require. An effort will be made, by the plotters, at the annual meeting, to wholly change this publication — and perhaps with success. The "woman question" will also be another bone of contention. Whichever way it may be decided, we may expect to see a withdrawal from the Society; but if it be decided right, I care not how many of the sectarians leave. The less we have of them, the better. I am inclined to think that bros. Scott [12] and Colver [13] will both go in favor of a new paper. If this hostility to the Liberator were carried on openly, I should care little about it; but it is fomented secretly, and in a mean and treacherous manner. I could tell you some instructive facts and occurrences, had I more room.

I feel very much relieved in mind, that our beloved and true-hearted friends Francis Jackson, Edmund Quincy, and William Bassett, have consented to take charge of the pecuniary concerns of the Liberator, so far as to hold themselves accountable for all the moneys received and expended in publishing it.[14] Mr. Knapp is now merely employed as a printer, and has no connection whatever with the accounts. Our book-keeper (Mr. Blake) is one of the best in the wide world. This arrangement will be highly satisfactory to the friends of the Liberator. In view of it, perhaps a letter from you, at this time, for the paper, would prove serviceable, if published before the annual meeting. Do you [15] as you think best about it. In the next paper, I mean to throw out signals, to call in to the annual meeting all the unflinching and trusty friends of our cause in this State and elsewhere. I shall call no names, but plainly allude to what is brewing.

Our house has been for some time cheered with the presence of Mrs. Benson;[16] and yesterday, Mary came from Providence, and will remain with us till after the meeting. ☞ You must stay with us when you come to the city — for we "will not take no for an answer" — remember that. ☜ I trust bro. George will be able to be with us, but it is somewhat uncertain. We are all in good health, except Helen, who is afflicted with a cold and ague, though some better. She cordially joins with me in proffering to Mrs. May, yourself, and Charlotte,[17] the congratulations of the new year, trusting you will all consider our house your home whenever you visit the city. Mother and Mary desire to be affectionately remembered.

Having lost my penknife, I have been compelled to write with a steel pen. You will be puzzled to read this scrawl, which you had better burn as soon as you decipher it.

Yours, unalterably,

Wm. Lloyd Garrison.

[☞ Since this letter was written, yours of the 4th is received, with the parcel of "mouse ear," for which I thank you and the kind old colored woman. Within two days, my head has troubled me, something after the manner of last winter. My Report [18] is not yet begun, but it shall be ready, rely upon it. It will be perfectly convenient for us to entertain you.] [19]

ALS: Garrison Papers, Boston Public Library. The letter was actually written in 1839. Garrison misdated the year. It was reprinted, in part, in *Life*, II, 262–263.

1. Psalms 119:165.
2. Isaiah 53:3.
3. *Ibid.*
4. Philippians 4:7.
5. Psalms 73:25, with "him" substituted for "thee."
6. Jairus Lincoln.
7. The Reverend Robert F. Walcutt.
8. The Reverend Dr. Noah Worcester (b. Hollis, New Hampshire, November 25, 1758; d. Brighton, Massachusetts, October 31, 1837), prominent Congregational clergyman and author. He occupied pulpits in Massachusetts and New Hampshire until 1813, when he settled in Brighton. Editor of the *Christian Disciple* from 1813 to 1818, and of *The Friend of Peace* from 1819 to 1829, he was also a founder of the Massachusetts Peace Society in 1815 and its secretary until 1828. He published works on theology, wrote much on social issues, and was a close friend of William Ellery Channing. (*ACAB.*)
9. The *Christian Register* had been founded in 1821 in Boston by David Reed, as a Unitarian publication. Dr. Noah Worcester was one of its contributors (*Memorial History of Boston*, III, 633.)
10. The annual meeting of the Massachusetts Anti-Slavery Society was to convene on January 23, 1839.

11. A small folio paper issued monthly by the American Anti-Slavery Society (*Life*, I, 483).

12. The Reverend Orange Scott (1800–1847), a Methodist minister in Massachusetts and Rhode Island, who joined the abolitionist ranks in 1833 and thereupon embarked upon an effort to convert the Methodist conferences to abolition. At the beginning of 1835, he contributed a series of antislavery articles to *Zion's Herald*, in which he expressed such Garrisonian principles as immediate emancipation and opposition to colonization (Oliver Johnson, *William Lloyd Garrison and his Times*, Boston, 1880, p. 237). He served as an agent of the American Anti-Slavery Society for almost two years and in 1842 he withdrew from the Methodist church to form the Wesleyan Methodist church. (*Weld-Grimké Letters*, I, 292n.) In 1848, in New York, there appeared his biography, *The Life of the Rev. Orange Scott*, by Lucius C. Matlack. See also Dwight L. Dumond, ed., *Letters of James Gillespie Birney, 1831–1857* (Gloucester, Mass., 1966), I, 450n.

13. The Reverend Nathaniel Colver.

14. A statement "To the Friends of the Liberator," signed by Jackson, Quincy, and Bassett, appeared in *The Liberator*, January 4, 1839.

15. So in manuscript.

16. Mrs. Sarah T. Benson.

17. Charlotte Coffin, Samuel J. May's sister-in-law.

18. The report for the annual meeting of the Massachusetts Anti-Slavery Society.

19. This postscript appears at the top of the first page.

136

TO GEORGE W. BENSON

Boston, Jan. 5, 1839.

My dear George:

If this year be not the happiest of your life, it shall not be my fault, if an abundance of good wishes can avail any thing. Think not, however, that these wishes extend only through the current year: in my mind your everlasting felicity is included. The same good things I desire for *you*, I also desire for *yours* — for Catherine and your dear children; yea, and for my beloved and estimable sisters Anna and Sarah. We may all be happy, if we choose; and one way to be so is to try, as we shall have opportunity, to make all the world happy, "beginning at Jerusalem" — i.e. in our immediate vicinity.

The household at Brooklyn is now fairly divided between us. The presence of mother has cheered us for some weeks; and on Wednesday, our joy was augmented by the arrival of sister Mary from Providence. She will remain with us till after the annual meeting. I had almost despaired of her coming; but a letter which I sent to her, telling her she must not take advantage of my non-resistance principles, (for I could not compel her *vi et armis*,) [1] had the effect to subdue and attract her. So that, reckoning Cecilia and little Fred,

417

(or *Ted*, as George calls him,) we have a considerable slice of the village of Brooklyn added to No. 2, Nassau Court.

It is sometime since I wrote to the sisters, and I regret my silence. How it has happened, I could tell, if that would mend the matter — but it will not. My time, as you may easily imagine, is very much occupied, and there will be little chance for a respite, probably, while I remain in the city; though, as soon as friend Johnson gets fully installed in office,[2] I hope to find a little more leisure for private correspondence.

I have many things to say to you all, on the score of friendship and brotherly affection; but these must give place to business matters affecting the integrity of the anti-slavery cause in this State.

Let me say, then, without further preliminary, that you must be present at our annual meeting on the 23d instant, if practicable, and induce as many sound, *ultra* abolitionists to attend as you can. When you were here, I believe you had some intimations that the clerical snake was coiling in the grass for a spring, and that an attempt would probably be made to subvert the Liberator, by the establishment of another anti-slavery periodical. Since that time, many facts have come to light, confirmatory of our suspicions. The conspiracy seems to be very extensive, and to have embraced a large number of high profess-ing abolitionists. The three most active in it are Phelps, Torrey and St. Clair. Stanton is ready to go with them. So will, unquestionably, Orange Scott, because of his strong dislike of the non-resistance discussion; and so, to some extent, I imagine, will Colver. John W. Browne,[3] of Lynn, was ensnared for a time, but I think will go straight. The plot is, by drilling before-hand, to rally such a number at the annual meeting as to change the present Board of Managers of the State Society — then to get a vote for the establishment of a new weekly paper, to be under the control of the new Board, and to be the organ of the Society. How mean, how ungrateful, how con-temptible, is conduct like this! I should not greatly care for it, if it had openly manifested itself — but every thing about it has been managed as secretly as possible. To counteract this revolutionary movement, as far as practicable, I made a proposition at our Board meeting to raise a committee, to report upon the expediency of pub-lishing a monthly periodical, as the organ of the Society, for the use of auxiliaries, &c. Phelps was not present — but he was nominated by one of his friends,[4] and Edmund Quincy and myself. It happened that he did not return in season from Haverhill to consult with us, and we accordingly made our report to the Board on Friday — to wit, that such a monthly ought to be printed, officially, to be called "The Abolitionist," and to be edited by a committee of three, to be elected by ballot. This report was strenuously opposed by Mr. P's friend (Ayres,)[5] on the ground that a weekly paper was called for, and would doubtless be established — that it would be better to defer the whole matter to the annual meeting — that the probability was, there would be a change in the Board, &c. Thus we had "the cat let out of the bag." The report was, however, accepted, and Wendell Phillips, Edmund Quincy and myself were elected editors. We shall have the specimen number issued forthwith, in season for the annual meeting. What will be the issue of the whole matter, it is difficult to foresee. I intend to sound a note of warning in the next Liberator,[6] in some-what guarded, yet significant language, so that there may be a general rallying of the true-hearted. Mrs. Chapman [7] is active in correspond-ence. Phillips, Quincy, Sewall, Loring, Jackson,[8] &c. will be true. I intend writing to D. L. Child,[9] but hardly expect he will be able to come. Besides getting up a new paper, the design is to settle the "woman question" against us. Thus we have all the materials for a warm and earnest collision. You remember Dr. Hawes's [10] letter last summer. That showed the plot in embryo — it is now nearly con-summated. It will come up in a plausible shape, under color of a deep regard for the cause, and with no *avowed* hostility to the Liberator. A deep impression will be made, because so many of our agents will be against us — Phelps, Torrey, St. Clair, Scott, Stanton, &c. &c. But I think, if the thing be fairly understood, that we shall be able to frustrate their hopes and expectations. In view of this state of things, I am sure you will come, if you can. Bro. May will be on hand, and will of course go right. I am in great haste, and can so [11] no more — only that we are all well, and send most affectionate remembrances to all the family.

Ever yours,
Wm. Lloyd Garrison.

ALS: Garrison Papers, Boston Public Library. This letter was reprinted in part in *Life*, II, 262–263n.

1. "By force and arms."
2. With the appointment of the committee of three to superintend the finances of *The Liberator*, Oliver Johnson assumed the post of General Agent of *The Liberator*, "to whom all remittances are to be made, and all letters addressed relating to the pecuniary concerns of the paper." (Masthead, *The Liberator*, January 4, 1839.)
3. John White Browne (b. Salem, Massachusetts, March 29, 1810; d. May 1, 1860). A lawyer, a classmate and most intimate friend at Harvard of Charles Sumner, he graduated from Harvard in 1830, and then attended Harvard Law School. He began his law practice at Lynn, was elected to the state legislature as representative of Lynn in 1837, but declined to run for the senate in 1838, though nominated. He later moved to Boston, where he spent the remainder of his life in the practice of law. In 1842, he married Martha Lincoln of Hingham. Throughout his life, he was a devoted friend of the antislavery cause, of woman's

rights, the poor, the temperance movement, and prison reform. (*In Memoriam, J. W. B.*, Boston, 1860, 90 pp.)

4. The name of the friend, as given in *Life*, II, 263n, was Joseph H. Eayrs.

5. Undoubtedly the same "friend" alluded to earlier.

6. The "note of warning" appeared in *The Liberator*, January 11, 1839, as an editorial entitled "Watchman, What of the Night?"

7. Maria Weston Chapman.

8. The last three mentioned were Samuel Edmund Sewall, Ellis Gray Loring, and Francis Jackson.

9. David Lee Child.

10. The Reverend Joel Hawes.

11. So in manuscript.

137

TO MARY S. PARKER

Boston, Jan. 8, 1839.

Esteemed Friend:

The Female Anti-Slavery Society having kindly presented me with a donation of $100, to sustain me in my efforts to "undo the heavy burden, and let the oppressed go free,"[1] I desire, through you, to proffer to the Society my very grateful acknowledgments. This money I could not accept as a personal favor; and I am sure it was not given with any such intention. It is the product of industry, economy and self-denying exertion. It shall be expended in strict conformity to the desire of the donors *i.e.* to carry on the holy warfare between Liberty and Slavery, Mercy and Cruelty, Justice and Violence, in our unhappy, guilty, oppressive country.

If I have been at all instrumental in awakening the nation to a lively sense of its guilt and danger, the credit does not in the least belong to me. If I had not spoken the truth, in the love of it, with boldness and sincerity, my labors would have been in vain. But, for that truth, no one is indebted to me, because it is of God; and had not my heavenly Father quickened me by its power, I should have been indifferent or hard-hearted even to this day; therefore, be all the praise and glory rendered to Him, "in whom we live, and move, and have our being."[2] There shall no flesh glory in his presence; and in this I feel happy. "Let everything that hath breath praise the name of the Lord" —[3] let man be forgotten.

I know we are accustomed to speak of the toils and sacrifices of individuals, in terms of panegyric; but this we may do, only by way of contrast. Our world is so stocked with selfishness, that when any one manifests a disinterested and benevolent spirit, he is apt to be hailed as "a bright, particular star" [4] — as a phenomenon in the moral world. But, in reality, it is not possible for us to make any sacrifice in the name of Christ; because as the record is infinitely glorious, the sacrifice, instead of being a loss, is in fact a gain. To reign with Christ is the consequence of suffering with him. By absolving, we exalt ourselves. The declaration of the Son of God is — "Every [one that hath foresaken houses, or brethren, or sisters, or father, or mother, or] wife or children or lands, for my [name's] sake, shall receive a hundred fold, and shall inherit everlasting life." [5]

If my soul is cheered to see what has been accomplished in our blessed enterprise, it is equally affected to see what remains to be done. Sure I am, that, unless we have that faith which overcomes the world — unless we are enabled to possess our souls in patience — unless the principles we profess to cherish are written upon our hearts — unless the flame of our zeal is kept alive by that love of God and man which many waters cannot extinguish — we shall grow weary of well-doing, become discouraged, and finally settle down into a state of apathy, from which we may be roused only by the thunders of retributive wrath. But, though mountainous obstacles remain to be overcome, let us put on the whole armor of God [6] — not a part of it, but the whole — that we may be able to stand in this evil day; so shall we be conquerors through Him who hath loved us, and given himself for us.

I remain,
Yours in the cause of bleeding humanity,
Wm. Lloyd Garrison.

Mary S. Parker.

Typed copy: Smith College Library.

1. Isaiah 58:6.
2. Acts 17:28.
3. Psalms 150:6.
4. Shakespeare, *All's Well That Ends Well*, I, i.
5. Matthew 19:29.
6. Ephesians 6:11.

138

TO GEORGE W. BENSON

Boston, Jan. 14, 1839.

My dear George:

Your letter to friend Johnson [1] was duly received to-day. The action of the anti-slavery society of Windham county, at Thompson, with regard to the Liberator,[2] is timely. The proceedings shall appear in the paper on Friday.[3] It was pleasant to me to see the names of my esteemed friends Coe and Scarborough among the movers.[4] I am sorry to say, that there is no doubt of our having a severe and painful conflict at the annual meeting. Facts are constantly coming to my knowledge, respecting the movements of Torrey,[5] & Co. — all going to show, that the plot is extensive, and that many are involved in it who have hitherto stood well in our ranks. On Saturday evening,[6] John E. Fuller called to see me for the first time on the subject, and we neither of us kept back any thing. He is an altered man, and "all high" for a new paper. [I suppose he is to be the agent for it, to drive subscriptions, &c.] I hardly expected such a defection, but he has lifted his heel against us — though, of course, he does not avow openly hostility, only he goes about saying that the Liberator is an injurious publication — that I have lost all interest in the anti-slavery cause, &c. &c. He is trying to influence our colored friends to think well of the new project; but he finds they are true as steel, and therefore angrily tells them that he believes that if Garrison should go to hell, they would go with him. I have not seen Phelps since my article, "Watchman, what of the night?" appeared. As soon as he read it in the anti-slavery office, Knapp says anger reddened his face, his lips quivered, and he pronounced me to be a wicked man, utterly unfit to be engaged in any moral enterprise, &c.[7] The fact is, I have sounded an alarm, and suddenly sprung a mine, and the plotters are greatly confounded, and of course very indignant. My belief is, that they will manage the affair with so much plausibility, and will have so many able and influential speakers on their side, as to be able to carry their point. If they should fail in doing so, they are determined to start a paper on their own hook — perhaps some of them will secede. If they should triumph, there would be no union in our Society, and of course no strength. You can hardly imagine how artfully it is all managed by the advocates of the new paper. But one thing let me say — we are to have a hard conflict — the crisis is truly momentous — ☞ *you must be here without fail* ☜ — no matter about your engagements in Connecticut — not one of them can be so important as to authorise your absence from Boston, I think. You can leave Brooklyn by the stage on Tuesday afternoon for Providence, and be here by the cars on Wednesday morning. Now, do not fail us, in this emergency. If friend Coe, or Scarborough, one or both, or any others, could also come, we shall be glad to see them in the city. More I would write, if the mail did not close in a few minutes. But let this suffice.

Mother, Mary, Helen, and all of us, are well and happy. We congratulate you and Catharine upon the birth of so fine a babe.[8] May he be worthy of his parentage.

My best regards to Mr. Coe and family, and all other friends in B.[9]

We send loving remembrances to all at home.

Yours, truly,

Wm. Lloyd Garrison.

☞ Destroy this and my last letter.

ALS: Garrison Papers, Boston Public Library. The greater part of this letter was printed in *Life*, II, 268–269.

1. Oliver Johnson.

2. A meeting of the Windham County Anti-Slavery Society, held in Thompson, Connecticut, on Tuesday, January 8, 1839, unanimously adopted a resolution which, after alluding to Garrison's opponents and praising *The Liberator* and Garrison for their contributions to the antislavery cause, resolved "That at this important crisis of our cause, we earnestly recommend the Liberator, as worthy of the patronage, of all the abolitionists of this county, and elsewhere; and we most sincerely bid the fearless and uncompromising editor, William Lloyd Garrison, God speed." (*The Liberator*, January 18, 1839.)

3. January 18, 1839.

4. The resolution was offered by the Reverend William Coe. The announcement of the resolution, in the form of a letter to "Brother Garrison," carried the signature of Philip Scarborough, recording secretary of the Windham County Anti-Slavery Society.

5. Charles Turner Torrey of Salem.

6. January 12, 1839.

7. Garrison had not mentioned any names in his editorial. But as his biographers have suggested, "those whom the coat fitted were, as we have seen in Phelps's case, quick to put it on." Phelps was working with the opposition in seeking to establish a rival antislavery newspaper. (*Life*, II, 270.)

8. The reference is to the birth of George Benson on January 7.

9. Brooklyn, Connecticut.

139

TO HARRIET FOSTER

Boston, Jan. 14, 1839.

Esteemed Friend:

Your kind letter of the 5th instant, enclosing a donation of $100, from the Salem Female Anti-Slavery Society, was safely delivered. I shall find it difficult to express my feelings, in view of this generous token of regard for my humble, though successful endeavors to arouse my country to a lively apprehension of its guilt and danger, in trading, like Babylon accursed, in slaves and souls of men.[1] If I had any property of my own, or if the subscriptions to the Liberator were sufficient to allow me an editorial stipend, I could not properly or willingly accept of this gift. Nor could I do so, if I thought the donors viewed it in the light of a personal favor, aside from the promotion of that sacred cause which lies so near all our hearts. I consent to receive it only as an anti-slavery steward, upon whom are resting the highest and most solemn obligations to be faithful to the cause of Humanity, through evil as well as good report, in pecuniary matters as well as in the inculcation of fundamental principles, let what may happen to me or mine — faithful even unto death. For it is not in the power of any individual, or of any association, to make it appear, that my labors deserve any special remuneration. Poor I am, and poor I ever expect to be on earth, from principle; for my spirit yearns too strongly over a world involved in misery and ruin by its alienation from God, to be tied down to the gainful pursuits of a grovelling age. I trust that my career, thus far, witnesses that I am not to be seduced from the path of duty by favors, nor intimidated by frowns. My testimonies must be delivered in plain, unequivocal language, let who will be offended; so shall reformation advance, and my own soul obtain perfect satisfaction. The spirit of your letter is so excellent and catholic, as greatly to cheer my own. You allude to the time when I almost stood alone, in the conflict with the demon of slavery. That was the great trial-hour of my regard for principle, of my faith in God, of my sincerity in espousing an odious and persecuted cause. No one can realise how great was the pressure that then rested upon me. O, to find all ears deaf, all eyes closed, all hearts obdurate — to be abandoned as a madman by near and dear friends — to be the object of universal reproach and hatred — to be ridiculed, despised, threatened, abused — to be contending, single-handed, against the wise and mighty, the rulers in Church and State, the pretended lights of the age — yet not to flinch, nor waver, nor compromise, nor surrender at discretion — surely, to be placed in such a situation, and to be resolute and confident under all circumstances, furnishes at least some evidence of sincerity of purpose, and filial reliance upon that good Being, who allows himself to be called by the endearing appellation of "Father." Many are the accusations brought against me; but no one has ever ventured to arraign me as at any time lacking in fidelity to the cause of my perishing countrymen.[2] I have the witness in my own bosom, that my course has been consistent and upright; and my enemies acknowledge that it is so. These things I write with humility: for whereof have *I* to glory? It is only through Christ strengthening me, that I have been able to stand in the evil day. In him, therefore, will I glory, who is the captain of my salvation.

You speak of the host now associated with me for the overthrow of slavery. Truly, they shake the earth as they march onward to the conflict, and the sound of their voices peals in the ears of affrighted tyranny like a burst of thunder. O, may they remain united in spirit, be lifted above all party and sectarian feelings, and give no opportunity to the enemy to divide and scatter them!

I am much pleased with the following sentence in your letter: — "However our opinions may differ on other subjects of equal importance, yet we trust in the cause of abolition our interest is mutual, our hopes and desires, our end and aim, one." This is noble. If all in our ranks possessed so catholic a spirit, there could be no jealousies, no rivalries, no divisions, no plottings for supremacy, among us. We should be invincible in our strength. I trust that I have ever manifested this spirit, though it has not always been exhibited toward me. I have taken, with equal cordiality, all by the hand, who were willing to extend the right hand of fellowship to my colored brother, of whatever party or sect. The Lord is my witness, that I neither cherish nor feel any thing of an exclusive spirit in this common enterprise of mercy. When I see a man compassionating the condition of one who has fallen among thieves, pouring wine and oil into his wounds, and lifting him up from his fallen state, I ask not, I care not, whether he is a Trinitarian or Unitarian, Baptist or Methodist, Whig or Democrat. Of one thing I am assured; he is acting the part of a good Samaritan, and the blessing of him that was ready to perish shall come upon his head. For the Priest and the Levite, who, in their selfishness, pride or pharisaical exclusiveness, coldly pass by on the other side, a holy scorn takes possession of my breast.[3] They are abhorred by Jehovah of hosts.

May we be faithful, not only in this single work of mercy, but in all things. While we are striving to emancipate the slave from his galling fetters, let us see to it that our own souls are enfranchised by divine love — that iniquity may no longer hold dominion over us, but perfect redemption be found for us.

Yours in every holy enterprise,
Wm. Lloyd Garrison.

ALS: Essex Institute, Salem, Massachusetts; printed in *The Liberator*, April 26, 1839.

Harriet Foster, the former Harriet Brooks of Salem, married Isaac Plummer Foster (1792–1881), who had moved to Salem in 1810. In 1816, her husband joined her father, Thomas Brooks, in his business, and soon after succeeded him in it. Harriet Foster, who had four daughters and two sons, died on May 2, 1880. (Frederick Clifton Pierce, *Foster Genealogy, Being the Record of the Posterity of Reginald Foster*, Chicago, 1899, p. 255.)

The letter to which this is a reply was also printed in *The Liberator* for April 26, 1839, immediately preceding Garrison's letter. In it, Harriet Foster, as corresponding secretary of the Salem Female Anti-Slavery Society, announced that the society, at a meeting held on December 29, 1838, had voted "that the sum of $100 be presented to you." The letter enclosed the amount and explained that it was being sent as an expression of gratitude to Garrison "for all that you have done and suffered in behalf of the oppressed and degraded millions. . . . We have regarded you as a pioneer in the glorious cause of emancipation in this country. . . . But we rejoice that you do not now stand alone. . . ."

1. Revelation 18:13.
2. *The Liberator* at this point has the following note: "This was true at the time when it was written, but it is true no longer. Mr. Garrison is now virtually charged with recreancy to the cause of the slave, because, from conscientious scruples, he abstains from voting at the polls. J."
3. The story of the good Samaritan is told in Luke 10:30–37.

---

1 4 0

TO JOHN QUINCY ADAMS

[February 8, 1839.]

SIR — There are two parties in this country, who are equally puzzled to reconcile your abhorrence of slavery, with your determination not to vote for its abolition in the District of Columbia — the slaveholders of the South, and the abolitionists of the North. In your theory of human rights, the former understand that you agree in principle with those, who, by the help of God, are resolved upon subverting a foul and bloody system. In your unwillingness to carry that theory into practice, the latter perceive that you are acting in concert with all that is despotic and inhuman in the land. You are claimed and rejected by both, at the same moment. If you would abandon your theory, the slaveholders would cease to be alarmed; and by giving it a practical application, you would insure for yourself the entire confidence of the abolitionists. Resolving to do neither, you serve but to awaken suspicion on the one hand, and to give annoyance on the other.

It seems that you are in bodily peril. For discharging, as a representative of the people, those duties which you are sworn to perform, you are warned that your days are numbered, and that you will not survive the present session. Be not alarmed. All danger of assassination is past. In avowing your unchangeable opposition to the prayer of those who are supplicating Congress to let the oppressed go free under its jurisdiction, you have avoided the pains, and will not therefore receive the honors of martyrdom. Sir, it is by your imprudence, that you have endangered your existence. Some time has elapsed — sufficient, at least, to admit of a radical change in your views — since you avowed your fixed determination to oppose the abolition of slavery in the District of Columbia. In this interval, you have written and uttered the most scorching sentiments against the slave system and all its abettors. You have used an abolition dialect, and allowed of no compromise with slavery. It was supposed by 'our southern brethren,' that you were in earnest, and meant all that your language implied. By this imprudence, you stirred up murderous feelings in their hearts; and hence their threats of assassination. Your case, however, is not without a precedent. There is more than one instance on record, in which a *lapsus linguae* has subjected a man not only to danger, but to death.

Let me assure you, that, so long as you are known to entertain your present views, with regard to the abolition of slavery in the District, not a hair of your head will be harmed, not a drop of your blood will be shed, by any southern desperado. As fire is extinguished by the application of water, so is the wrath of the slaveholder appeased by the assurance that the immediate emancipation of his slaves is not a religious duty. True, by the faithful presentation of the numerous anti-slavery petitions entrusted to your care, you cannot cease to give offence to southern representatives — not, indeed, as an object of their dislike personally, but as a witness of the amazing growth of anti-slavery sentiment in the country; but they will no longer glare upon you like the demons of Hades, nor threaten your existence, assassins as they are in spirit. No, sir, you have no cause to apprehend bodily harm. If, when about to present a fresh number of abolition petitions, you are careful to preface the act with the statement, that you 'go with the South' in opposition to the prayer of the petitioners, rely upon it, you will be treated with all due civility. It may not suit the temper of the House to accede to your proposition, to refer the memorials to a committee, select or otherwise; but no such explosion will follow as has been witnessed on other occasions. It has been your misfortune to be misunderstood by the 'chivalry of the South,' and hence the peril of your situation.

There are three classes of Americans, who are exempted by the South from the inflictions of Lynch law, and the doom of martyrdom. The first are those who are against meddling with the slave system: the second, those who advocate a gradual emancipation, to be consummated 'half way between now and never:' the third, those who insist upon transporting our free colored citizens to the coast of Africa. All these may participate in the benefits arising from 'our glorious Union,' and find protection under the wings of the American eagle. For a fourth class, there is no law, no constitution, no country. They are against banishing citizens on account of their complexion; against the gradual abandonment of atrocious iniquity; against letting slavery and its abettors alone. They believe in the duty of immediate repentance — of shivering every fetter, that holds a fellow-being in bondage, at a blow; in recognizing and treating man as man, irrespective of clime or complexion; in the oneness and equality of the human race. For this cause, they are placed under a ban of ostracism, and treated as outlaws.

To which of these parties do you belong? Not to the last, as you have expressly declared in your recent speech. Not to the first, it is certain; for you do not feel indifferent to the existence of slavery, and you evince a longing desire to have the merits of the whole question open to discussion on the floor of Congress. As to the scheme of African expatriation, I am not aware that you have given to it any countenance; a fact which justly entitles you to the gratitude and admiration of the colored race universally. In their name, I thank you for having kept yourself aloof from that stupendous folly and most unnatural crusade. Unless I greatly err in my conjectures, you are willing to be identified with the party of gradualists. You truly remark, at the close of your speech, that all such persons are at once set down by abolitionists as enemies of the cause. It is an intelligible, self-evident proposition, that he who is for the continuance of slavery, on whatever pretext, or for any duration of time, is the enemy of liberty. He may persuade himself that he is doing God service: it is not so much a question of motive, as it is of fact. I care not by what process of reasoning the conclusion is drawn, that it is right for one man to retain his fellow-man in bondage. It degrades humanity; and the consequence is the same, whether it be the result of blindness of vision, or malignity of spirit.

That you can suffer yourself, in the year 1839, to be deluded into the belief, that the gradual emancipation of our slaves is compatible with the claims of humanity and the dictates of reason, is matter of grief and surprise. That southern men have been justified in inferring from the premises you have laid down, as to the inherent wickedness of slavery, that you were in favor of immediate abolition, is quite apparent. Here is a paragraph extracted from your eloquent introduction to the memoir of Elijah P. Lovejoy: [1]

'If the African slavery be piracy, human reason can not resist, nor can human sophistry refute the conclusion, that the essence of the crime consists not in the *trade*, but in the *slavery*. Trade has nothing in itself criminal by the law of nature, or that can be made so by any law or compact of nations. It is one of the natural rights flowing from the condition of man; from reciprocal wants and reciprocal good will. Trade, therefore, can be made criminal only by the nature of the article in which it is carried on. It is the slavery, and not the purchase and sale, or the transportation of the slave, which constitutes the iniquity of the African slave trade. The moral principle, then, which dictated the interdict of the African slave trade, *pro-nounced at once the sentence of condemnation upon slavery.'*

This argument cannot be invalidated: it is clear and conclusive. If it be right to hold men as property, it is also right to sell them as property. If the system of slavery ought not to be abolished immediately, there ought to be no prohibition of the slave trade. Slave-traders are no more worthy of death than slaveholders. When, therefore, Congress pronounced the foreign slave-trade to be piracy, it stamped the brand of piracy (not technically, but in essence) upon the slave-system; and in dooming all those, who should be detected in carrying on the former, to an ignominious death, it declared that every slaveholder ought to be capitally punished as a pirate. I maintain that if the law of Congress be founded in reason and equity, then, instead of allowing slaveholders to occupy seats in either branch of the national legislature, we ought to treat them as the greatest felons of our race. Of the motives of those who engage in the foreign slave-trade, the national statute takes no cognizance. It is immaterial for what purpose, or on what pretext, men prosecute that trade: if they are caught in the act, their death-warrant is sealed. So, it matters not what are the motives or the intentions of slaveholders: the slaves being found in their hands, they are equally deserving of the same fate. In either case, as you justly remark, 'the essence of the crime consists not in the trade, but in the slavery.'

No wonder, sir, after the utterance of such sentiments, that the slaveholding banditti drew the inference that you were an abolitionist, and that henceforth it was your determination to labor for the immediate abolition of slavery at the Seat of Government. No wonder they have threatened to destroy your life, unless you will satisfy them that you do not mean what you say. Especially had they good cause to regard you as among the most 'fanatical' abolitionists, when they read the following sentiments, contained in a letter written by you to some of your constituents,[2] pending the late election in your own district:

'Should the people of the 12th Congressional District of Massachusetts again see fit to station me as their sentinel on the watch-tower of the nation, *they will not expect from me consent, acquiescence, or compromise, with this system, or with* ANY OF ITS PARTS. Unyielding hostility against it is interwoven with every pulsation of my heart. Resistance against it, feeble and inefficient as the last accents of a failing voice may be, shall still be heard, while the power of utterance shall remain, and shall never cease, till the pitcher shall be broken at the fountain, the dust return to the earth as it was, and the spirit unto God who gave it.'

This is the promise, the pledge, the dialect of an abolitionist.

When I first read this expression of your views, I was constrained to believe that you would sustain the prayer of those who supplicate Congress to emancipate the slaves in the District of Columbia. Your language was too plain to authorize any other construction. I have never understood that you endorse the doctrine of George McDuffie and John C. Calhoun, that Congress is not constitutionally empowered to abolish slavery in the District or Territory over which it has exclusive jurisdiction. In conceding the power to Congress, you acknowledge the right of that body to emancipate the slaves in the District. If I were one of your constituents, I should feel justified in saying that you have deceived me in fact, though not in intention. 'The people of the 12th Congressional District' were assured by you, that in case they saw fit to re-elect you as their representative, they might not expect from you 'consent, acquiescence, or compromise with this system [slavery,] ³ or *with any of its parts.*' The idea conveyed in this pledge was not merely that you would persevere in defending the perilled right of petition, but that you would vote, if opportunity were presented, for the overthrow of slavery and the slave-trade, in accordance with the wishes of your constituents. Great as is their veneration for you, can you suppose, for one moment, that they would have given you their suffrages, with a distinct understanding that you would join with Waddie Thompson,⁴ on the floor of Congress, to reject their prayers? No. It is for them to decide, whether you have not betrayed them. Your language now is, 'If the question were to be put this day, I would vote against it' — i.e. the abolition of slavery. 'I *now* say what my opinion is, (and I say it here, openly,) that the abolitionists and the anti-slavery societies may take, in regard to me, what course they please.' If, sir, you had been as explicit in your declarations at the time your election was pending, as you 'now' are, a majority of your constituents would have cast their votes for some other candidate. You have mitigated the rage of the South, and perhaps saved your life, by these declarations; but, many will think, at the costly sacrifice of honor and humanity.

I shall have something more to say in another letter.

Yours, respectfully,

WM. LLOYD GARRISON.

Printed in *The Liberator*, February 8, 1839.

On February 1, 1839, *The Liberator* carried the following notice:

"John Quincy Adams. This gentleman, in presenting some anti-slavery petitions to Congress on the 21st ultimo, took occasion (after stating that he was continually receiving letters threatening him with assassination) 'distinctly to say to the House, to the country, and to the world, that if the question of the abolition of slavery in the District of Columbia were to be put this day, HE WOULD VOTE AGAINST IT.' This declaration nips in the bud the hopes of many abolitionists, respecting the future course of Mr. Adams on the floor of Congress.

The loss of the right of petition is merely a consequence growing out of the existence of slavery in the District of Columbia. Mr. Adams has been zealous in protesting against an effect, and yet declares that he is resolved not to strike at the cause! This is indeed to labor in vain, and to spend one's strength for naught. What political foresight and consistency. We are glad to perceive that Mr. Adams does not deny that Congress has the constitutional power to abolish slavery in the District. It is upon the altar of *expediency* that he is disposed to immolate the inalienable rights of the victims of slavery groaning out a miserable existence within the 'ten mile square.' We lament that it is so. . . ."

1. Joseph C. and Owen Lovejoy, *Memoir of the Rev. Elijah P. Lovejoy . . .*, Introduction by John Quincy Adams (New York, 1838).
2. The letter was addressed to "Messrs. Isaac L. Hedge, Seth Sprague, Jr. and Elihu Hobart," and dated Quincy, October 27, 1838. It was printed in *The Liberator*, November 9, 1838.
3. The brackets are Garrison's.
4. Waddy Thompson, Jr. (1798–1868), a representative from South Carolina who served in Congress from 1835 to 1841 (*BDAC*.)

141

TO MARY BENSON

Boston, Feb. 10, 1839.

Dear Mary:

"Out of sight, out of mind," is a time-worn adage; but, ancient and popular as it is, true affection scouts it as false and calumnious. It may be, that, to the gross and vulgar, the bodily presence of an individual is essential to preserve his remembrance; but, to loving souls, there is a oneness and an omniprescence,[1] which no distance can separate, no barrier obstruct. So great is the triumph of spirit over matter! Nay, Love does not need, absolutely, any visual organ, in order to its creation or preservation. "No man hath seen God at any time"[2] — yet what multitudes love and adore him! The apostle Peter, in addressing the early disciples respecting Christ, says, "Whom, *having not seen*, YE LOVE; in whom, though now ye see him not, yet believing, ye rejoice with joy unspeakable, and full of glory."[3]

I am not arguing that it is of no consequence, whether you are here or in Providence. Your company, as an affectionate sister and an intelligent associate, is always desirable. I trust it will yet be so arranged, that you, and Sarah, and Anne, as well as mother, will dwell with us under the same roof; or, at least, that a very short distance only will separate us. Our sojourn on earth must necessarily be so brief, that, to me, (shall I not say, to us all?) it is very desirable we should be so situated as to be able to see each other daily. But let every thing be cheerfully submitted to the ordering of a wise and beneficent Providence.

Your recent visit to Boston was not made under the most favorable circumstances. The inclemency of the season forbade your going out freely; and I was so absorbed in my editorial details, and in preparing for the annual meeting, that I could give you very little personal attention. You must come again, when the skies are fairer, and the earth is robed in green, and all things wear a sunny aspect.

March 3, 1839.

It is three weeks ago since I wrote the first page of this letter! Here is evidence of despatch and punctuality! I think I see a smile spreading over your countenance, at my procrastination. There are others who would scold not a little, were they in your place; but they do not possess your kind and sisterly spirit. My only regret is, that Helen should have given you, by virtue of her oneness with myself, a semi-official, premature notice, that this epistle was forthcoming without delay. For almost a month, therefore, your expectation must have been daily disappointed. The blame does not all belong to me, nor to her, but we must share it between us.

It may be, that you are no longer in Providence; but I shall take it for granted, that you are still enjoying the hospitality of one who serves greatly to exalt her sex, by her many virtues and her active philanthropy; and who, instead of being corrupted by affluence, or led astray by fashion, is consecrating her time, her talents, and her means, to the service of her divine Lord and Master. Such fidelity to principle, such perseverance in well-doing, such moral courage, such clearness of vision, as characterise her life, are as rare in our degenerate world as they are worthy of all praise. I need not write her name.[4] What with apathy on the one hand, and opposition on the other, how much she has to try her spirit, I can form some estimate; but, believing that she esteems the reproach of Christ greater riches than the treasures of Egypt, and that she will endure to the end as seeing Him who is invisible, I can rejoice while I sympathize with her.

Doubtless, you wish to be informed as to the complexion of things in Boston. I can only say that, so far as the anti-slavery cause is concerned, we are (O sorrowful fact!) a divided house. That sweet fellowship which formerly prevailed in our ranks is gone, and I fear irrecoverably. Phelps has been confined to the house till within a week, since the annual meeting; but, though ill, he has been very busy with his pen against the Liberator, and in support of the new paper.[5] How he feels toward me, the articles from his pen in the Liberator painfully manifest. As for Stanton, he appears to be completely alienated. We merely interchange civilities as we meet. Jealousy, envy, and ambition, I fear, have taken possession of his breast. He told friend Knapp, the other day, that if I had declared at the annual meeting that there was no God, by merely lifting my finger I could have carried multitudes with me! What a state of heart does this evince! How false, how foolish, how cruel is such an assertion! St. Clair and Wise [6] have resigned their agencies, and are laboring with great zeal in behalf of the "Abolitionist." [7] I suppose they will be appointed agents of the American A.S. Society. You will see by the last Liberator,[8] that a collision has taken place between the New-York Executive Committee and our Board. How it will terminate, I know not. This is a sad spectacle, to present to the enemies of our holy cause; but be the responsibility upon the heads of those who are attempting to lord it over the consciences of non-resisting abolitionists. Our friends abroad, who, not being on the ground, are ignorant of what is said and done here in private, naturally feel distressed to see brethren fall out by the way; and, truly, I am filled with as much grief as any of them. They seem to think that I am opposed to the new paper, partly on selfish grounds (some of them, I mean) — as if my whole life does not prove that I have trodden under foot, with holy scorn, all considerations of self-interest! They also suppose that the originators of the new paper movement are very friendly to the Liberator, and would do nothing, designedly, to injure its circulation. How great is their error! I cannot be mistaken. I know what is the spirit that is at work, and that, under the plausible guise of friendship for the abolition cause, the design is, if possible, to subvert the Liberator, and drive me from the ranks. The Lord will make all things manifest in due time.

☞ On account of its personal allusions, you will see the propriety of destroying this half of the letter as soon as it is read. Phebe may read it [9]

Lucinda Otis called to see Helen [10] yesterday — the first time since you left; said she had been very busy respecting the new free church, and had concluded to attend Colver's meeting.[11] (By the way, he is coarse in his language, and bitter in his feelings, against non-resistance, and says he is ready to shoulder a musket any day: he hates the pacific character of the Son of God most cordially, and sneers like an infidel at the doctrine of holiness.) I did not see Lucinda, and of course had no opportunity to converse with her.

Mrs. Chapman is writing a letter to Henry Clay, in reply to his speech,[12] for publication. It will be keen and powerful, I doubt not.

Oliver Johnson is expected home from Vermont on Tuesday. If I can arrange matters with him, I shall go to Providence soon, and also to other places, for the purpose of lecturing, &c. Hope to see you before you go to Brooklyn.

Mother, Helen, and all the household, are in good health. George is a very good boy now, and improves daily — says he wants to see and kiss Aunt Mary, and also to write to her and little Anne. Dear Willie is a noble little fellow — the paragon of babes. Helen has weaned him with[in] a week, with less trouble than we anticipated. He is very hearty, and full of life and spirit. We all send the most affectionate remembrances to sister Charlotte and family, to the Chaces, to Phebe and her mother, to Dr. Flagg and wife, &c.

Your loving brother,

Wm. Lloyd Garrison.

ALS: Garrison Papers, Boston Public Library. A portion of this letter was printed in *Life*, II, 280–282.

1. Spelled thus in manuscript.
2. John 1:18.
3. I Peter 1:8.
4. Since the letter was sent to Mary, c/o George W. Jackson, Garrison is probably referring to Phebe Jackson.
5. At this point, Garrison's *Life* has the following footnote (II, 280–281n):
"The first number of the *Massachusetts Abolitionist* appeared on February 7, 1839 — a small sheet, neatly printed, and exhibiting, said Mr. Garrison (*Lib.* 9:27), both tact and talent in its selected and original articles. It made no statement of the reasons for founding it, but professed to be 'devoted exclusively to the discussion of slavery.' Its editorial conduct devolved upon a committee of twenty-seven, one-third of whom were clergymen (Lib. 9:31), till Elizur Wright was free in May to assume it. Its mottoes — 'Supremacy of the laws,' 'Liberty, the right of all — law its defence' — were an evident thrust at 'no-government' doctrines, but had an unwonted sound to the champion of the 'higher law' (*Lib.* 9:31). The subscription price was $1.00; that of the *Liberator*, $2.50."
6. Alanson St. Clair and the Reverend Daniel Wise (b. Portsmouth, England, January 10, 1813; d. December 19, 1898) of Quincy. Both had been agents of the Massachusetts Anti-Slavery Society, posts which they resigned in order to help issue the new paper. On March 1, 1839, *The Liberator* printed a letter from Wise, explaining his abandonment of *The Liberator* and his support of the *Massachusetts Abolitionist*. In the same issue, there appeared a letter from Orin P. Bacon, which was highly critical of Wise's actions. Wise came to the United States in 1833 and immediately prepared himself for the Methodist Episcopal ministry. He held various pastorates from 1837 to 1852, and from 1838 to 1848 was the publisher and editor of the *Sunday School Messenger*, the first Methodist Sunday school paper in the country. From 1852 to 1856 he was editor of *Zion's Herald* in Boston. From 1856 to 1872, he edited the Sunday school publications and tracts of the denomination. Thereafter, he was involved in a variety of literary projects. He wrote many books for young people. (*NCAB.*)
7. At this point, the following footnote appears in *Life* (II, 281n):
"It was high time for St. Clair to change sides. He had been endeavoring to win over the colored people of Fall River by false representations as to the declining circulation of the *Liberator*, and as to Mr. Garrison's own desire for a new paper — based, of course, on the latter's proposal of a monthly organ to head off the *Abolitionist* (*Lib.* 9:22, and *ante*, p. 262). Wise's coat-turning was ludicrously sudden, after having 'resolved' through the Norfolk County A. S. Society, that the *Liberator* had *not* departed from its old principles (*Lib.* 9:34). He was now recommending the *Abolitionist* because, as he said, in his dainty way, he preferred having the hairs served up in one plate, the butter in another. These worthies were assisted by the Rev. J. T. Woodbury, who charged Mr. Garrison, among other dreadful things, with being a 'Thomsonian' — 'a very good reason,' thought the latter, 'why a new anti-slavery paper should be started in this commonwealth' (*Lib.* 9:27)."

8. March 1, 1839. This refers to the decision of the executive committee of the American Anti-Slavery Society in New York, conveyed to the Board of the Massachusetts Anti-Slavery Society on February 13, that it was terminating its existing contract with the latter as to the collection of funds in that state, and was appointing independent agents who would conduct independent drives for funds.

9. This suggestion was written along the edge of the third page.

10. Helen Garrison. Lucinda Lawrence Otis (b. Boston, February 11, 1808; d. Utica, New York, May 8, 1886) married the Reverend Thorndike Cleaves Jameson, of Providence, Rhode Island, April 20, 1841. She had five children. (William A. Otis, *A Genealogical and Historical Memoir of the Otis Family in America*, Chicago, 1924, p. 288.)

11. The Reverend Nathaniel Colver.

12. *Life* has the following footnote (II, 282n):

"This speech, delivered in the U. S. Senate on February 7, 1839, apropos of the petitions for abolition in the District, was Clay's bid for the Presidency, and as such was the most notable political event of the year. It destroyed the last shred of his anti-slavery reputation at the North, except among the Friends, whom he was cunning enough to flatter, and it also cost him his nomination by the Whig party in December (*Lib.* 10:31). It was a medley of the stale charges against the abolitionists — of unconstitutional aims and measures, of endangering an immense invested capital (1200 million dollars, as he estimated), of having retarded emancipation by half a century, etc., etc. He taxed them, further, with now having abandoned moral suasion for the ballot box, with the bayonet as their next resource, and held up the old bogey of disunion and civil war. Against such a consummation he invoked the interposition of the clergy. . . . Clay's speech was printed in full in the *Liberator* (9:26). One sentence of it was destined to be reproduced many times against the author. To the moralist who objected that man could not hold property in man, Clay asserted — 'That *is* property which the law declares *to be* property.' This aphorism might fitly have found a place among the legal mottoes of the *Massachusetts Abolitionist*."

142

TO FRIENDS OF NON-RESISTANCE

Boston, Mar. 1, 1839

Dear Friend:

The Executive Committee of the N. E. Non Resistance Society at a meeting recently held, voted, that letters be addressed to all persons known to have adopted the principles of Non Resistance, or who are favourable to their free discussion, stating the claims & the wants of the Society, & requesting such pecuniary aid at their hands as the cause requires. It is in obedience to this vote that this letter is addressed to you.

It is unnecessary for us to enlarge upon the objects of the Society. They are briefly set forth in the Declaration of Sentiments which we have put forth to the world & in the Constitution of the Society.[1] We have neither time nor space to expatiate upon the infinite importance of the principles we hold, & which we would fain apply to the business

of the world as well as to the regulation of our individual hearts &
lives — principles, the adoption or rejection of which, will we are
assured determine the happiness or the misery of the human race
throughout all time, & whose influences will reach beyond the bounds
of time & stretch far into the endless ages of eternity. The law to which
we have submitted ourselves, through obedience to which we have
found rest to our souls, whose light burden & easy yoke we have
combined together that we may, in all love, persuade our brethren
to take upon themselves, is that paramount law of our being, to bring
to light & exemplify which, the Son of God came into the world and,
after a life of privation and persecution was at last nailed "for our
advantage to the bitter cross;" [2] — even the perfect and peaceable law
of Love. We are confirmed in the belief, that this is the great law of
our Nature, by beholding in the world around us the mournful signs
of the ruin which men have brought upon themselves by refusing to
obey it. We see it in the vaunted, yet vain, schemes of Government,
which they have devised for their own protection — combinations,
which crush the poor & ignorant offender, while they elevate wealthy
& instructed criminals to the rank of the makers or administrators of
their laws. We see it in the corrupt churches which make our land a
spiritual desolation. We see it in an ambitious and self-seeking Clergy,
who claiming a title from Heaven to lord it over the consciences of
their brethren, pervert souls from the right ways, teaching for doctrines the commandments of men; — teaching that the impartial Father
of all the dwellers upon the earth, sanctions the enslaving & imbruting
of His own children; that He permits the traffic in the poison which
consumes the bodies and the souls of men; that He is not displeased
at the indulgence of ambition, covetousness & revenge, provided they
be displayed in certain modes of man's own appointing; that He allows,
nay commands, man to slay his brother, if urged to the deed by the
resistance of sudden evil, if the doom of death be pronounced by a
tribunal of man's erection, or if he be called upon by the authorities
of the land to do battle with the enemies, whom he is commanded in
all cases to forgive & love. We see it in the licentiousness & vices of
private life & in the public profligacy and corruption that disgrace this
age. We discern it in the anarchy and violence which disturb our
domestic peace and in the hoarse murmurs, presaging the approach of
war, which are heard muttering along our frontier.

For all these evils which have fallen upon men through their having
forsaken the law of love, we see but one remedy — & that is immediate repentance and an instant return to their allegiance. It is to urge
upon all men this only way of safety, that we have associated together.
It is that we may be enabled to do this work vigourously & efficiently

that this application is made to you by us. Standing, a small company of men & women, banded together to war with spiritual weapons against the evil that is in the world, encompassed on every side by the bitter opposition of the powerful in church & state, cruelly misrepresented & that too by men from whom we might have expected, of whom we do still expect, better things, derided by the unthinking, feared & hated by the sagacious, to whom can we look for support & assistance, besides Him who is our strength, but to those who have assumed the same cross with ourselves, and to those who regard our warfare, though from a distance, with eyes of sympathy & interest? To all such we confidently appeal. We want increased means for propagating the truths we hold dear. Our efforts, hitherto, have been cramped by the narrowness of our resources. Still we have printed & circulated many tracts, have established the Non Resistant,[3] & have constantly employed an indefatigable & devoted agent in the field. With added means we can exert a vastly greater moral force. Able & devoted men are ready to enter upon the work, if their subsistence can be secured to them. We have materials for a mighty array of tracts. We are ready to take the field & with great effect if the sinews of this holy warfare be furnished to us. Upon those who have embarked in this great enterprise & upon those who wish it well do we rely with confidence for our supplies. Upon YOU, dear friend, we especially depend for pecuniary & other help. We know that the mere statement of our necessities is all that is needed to open your purse and heart. They who have professed before the world their devotion to this holy cause, or their sympathy with it, need no laboured appeals to excite them to a spasmodic generosity, or to overcome the selfishness which they have renounced before God. But we pray you not to delay your contribution. If this faint appeal have awakened in your breast a resolution to cast in, of your abundance or of your penury, into the treasury of the Lord, let not the holy impulse depart without accomplishing the purpose of its mission. "Hold the fleet angel fast until he bless thee."[4] Do not withold your gift because it must needs be a little one. Remember the widow's mite. Remember, too, that not many noble, not many wise, not many wealthy have been called to this odious reform. Give according to your means, yea beyond them, being assured that it will be recompensed unto you a hundred fold. Above all do what you do quickly. We cordially invite you to remit *forthwith* such an amount as you feel called upon to give, directed to either of the subscribers, or to Charles K. Whipple, treas.r [5] Should it not be convenient to transmit the money immediately, we would ask you for a pledge to be redeemed before the annual meeting in Sept.r We would further entreat you to urge upon all your neighbors who think with you on this momentous subject, the duty of sending in their funds. We pray you neglect not this request.

We have not space to urge upon you the claims of the Non Resistant. We know it is not necessary. Should you remit more than the subscription price ($1) we shall place your name upon the subscription list, if it be not already there. We hope & are confident that you will exert yourself to extend the circulation of our organ among your friends & neighbors — as well those that are willing to hear as those that have received the faith. We hope you will regard yourself as a voluntary agent to procure subscribers to it — not forgetting the indispensable condition of payment in advance.

We make no apology for this long letter. We know its object & our motives will commend themselves to your heart.

Hoping to hear speedily from you, We remain, Dear Friend, affectionately yours, in the bonds of peace & love,

> Wm. Lloyd Garrison.
> Maria W. Chapman.
> Edmund Quincy.

Lithographed form letter, Emerson Papers, Houghton Library, Harvard. Addressed to Ralph Waldo Emerson. Other copies at the Boston Public Library. The letter is not in Garrison's hand, but does bear his signature.

1. The text of the Declaration of Sentiments is printed in *Life*, II, 230–234. Both the Declaration of Sentiments and the constitution were printed in *The Liberator*, September 28, 1838.

2. Shakespeare, *Henry IV*, Part I, I, i.

3. The *Non-Resistant* "was a small folio of four columns to the page, these being the same in width as the *Liberator's* columns, to permit interchangeability of matter. It bore for its motto, 'Resist Not Evil. — *Jesus Christ.*' The editorial committee consisted of Mr. Garrison, Mrs. Chapman, and Mr. Quincy; the former's services being nominal, and the two latter assuming the chief burden of writing, in which they were assisted by Charles K. Whipple, the Treasurer of the New England Non-Resistance Society, and by H. C. Wright. Mr. Wright was the sole missionary kept in the field. . . ." (*Life*, II, 326). It may also be noted that the *Non-Resistant* was issued on the first and third Saturday of each month (*ibid.*). It "expired on June 29, 1842, for want of means" (*ibid.*, III, 79).

4. Henry Wadsworth Longfellow, *Kavanagh*.

5. Charles King Whipple (b. Newburyport, Massachusetts, November 17, 1808; d. 1900), treasurer of the New England Non-Resistance Society, also assisted in writing for the society's organ, the *Non-Resistant*. He joined the staff of *The Liberator* when the *Non-Resistant* ceased publication. (*Life*, II, 326; III, 155; IV, 421 *et passim.*) He was also the author of several pamphlets on nonresistance. In 1839, in Boston, the New England Non-Resistance Society published his *Evils of the Revolutionary War*. The Hopedale Community Press published a second edition in 1846. In 1841, he published in Boston a short nonresistance exposition of the Pauline text *The Powers that be are ordained of God*. In 1860, he wrote *The Non-Resistance Principle: With Particular Application to the Help of Slaves by Abolitionists*; and *Non-Resistance Applied to the Internal Defense of a Community*. (Peter Brock, *Pacifism in the United States, from the Colonial Era to the First World War*, Princeton, N.J., 1968, p. 585.)

143

TO JAMES MOTT

Boston, March 4, 1839.

Esteemed Friend:

"Out of sight, out of mind," is a time-worn adage; but, ancient and popular though it be, true affection scouts it as false and calumnious. It may be that, to the gross and vulgar, the bodily presence of an individual is necessary to preserve his remembrance; but, to loving souls, there is a oneness and an omniprescence,[1] which no barrier can obstruct, no distance separate. So great is the triumph of spirit over matter! Nay, Love does not need, absolutely, any visual organ, in order to its creation or preservation. "No man hath seen God at any time"[2] — yet what multitudes love and adore him! The apostle Peter, in addressing the early disciples respecting Christ, says, "Whom, *having not seen*, YE LOVE; in whom, though now ye see him not, yet believing, ye rejoice with joy unspeakable, and full of glory."[3]

You will not suppose, from the above, that I have no special desire to see you and yours, face to face. Would it were so that I could enjoy your society continually! Your claims upon my gratitude, admiration and love are too large for me ever to liquidate. From the first moment we became acquainted to the present time, you have encouraged and sustained me in my humble efforts to save this nation from ruin. Your kindness enters into the soul of my existence.

I have nothing very cheering to communicate respecting the state of affairs in Massachusetts. The Legislature of this State — now in session — I fear will do nothing to advance, but something to retard the abolition enterprise. The committee on slavery in the District of Columbia have made a report,[4] which is radically defective, and utterly contemptible; and they have the folly and impertinence to suppose, that it will be satisfactory to the abolitionists! On this point they shall be undeceived without delay, I can assure them. Then, another report[5] has been made on the petitions, praying for a repeal of all laws which proscribe, degrade and punish human beings on account of their color. It is satirical, profligate and insulting, in the highest degree — worthy to have emanated from a gang of slave-drivers, or a herd of lewd men: yet I have no doubt it will be adopted by the Legislature, without serious opposition. "We have all gone out of the way, and all become vile."[6] In this great extremity of our merciful enterprise, how soul-afflicting it is to think that jealousies, envyings, divisions, abound in our ranks, and that those who for years have stood shoulder to shoulder in the "imminent deadly breach,"[7] forgetful of their political and religious variances, now refuse to "mingle like kindred drops into one,"[8] that the stains of blood upon our country's escutcheon may be washed away! The Lord is my witness that, in seeking to undo the heavy burdens and let the oppressed go free, I have never been unwilling to associate with any man, on any pretence whatever. It has been my aim, from the first, to endeavor to secure as many friends as possible, to assist in the deliverance of my poor, fettered, guiltless countrymen from bondage — though some may say, that I have taken a strange method to do this, in using so freely the language of denunciation and rebuke. Whether I have been successful or not, let the fifteen hundred anti-slavery societies now in existence, and all the mighty machinery now in operation, determine.

Our abolition friends abroad will lament, and perhaps marvel at the division which now prevails in Massachusetts. They are not in a situation to judge correctly as to the real merits of the case. Truly, I am filled with as much grief as any of them. They seem to think, (some of them,) that I am opposed to the new paper,[9] partly on selfish grounds — as if my whole life does not prove that I have [10] always trodden under foot, with holy scorn, all considerations of self-interest! They also suppose that the originators of the new paper movement are friendly to the Liberator, and would do nothing, designedly, to injure its circulation. How great is their error! If they were here, they would think differently. The Lord will make all things manifest in due time. I cannot be, I am not mistaken. *I know* what is the spirit which is at work, and that there exists a deadly hostility to the Liberator in the breasts of those who are zealous in support of the "Abolitionist." Their determination is to destroy it, root and branch. That they will succeed, I have little doubt. The limited patronage now given to the Liberator will be divided; and the paper is now sustained only by the [the] donations of its friends. All the clergy being against it, (i. e. nearly all,) their opposition is tremendous. They will do what they can to substitute the new paper in its stead. I am inclined to believe, that the present year is to terminate the existence of the Liberator. Well, if its time has come, let it die: it has, I trust, not lived in vain. It is declared to be worthy of death, because it advocates a perfect righteousness, and maintains that the followers of Christ are bound to imitate his example in the treatment of enemies! "The head and front of its offending hath this extent — no more."[11]

How dreadful is the thought of a war between America and England, for the possession of an insignificant strip of territory![12] All religious and philanthropic efforts would be at once struck with paralysis, and the spirit of the pit would pervade the whole land. See with what eagerness and unanimity the people of Maine are preparing for a fierce and bloody conflict! They have no fear of God before their eyes — and as for the Prince of Peace, they know him not, and will not have him to rule over them. Yet they make high pretensions to christianity — hire many clergymen to preach to them — have a vast multitude of churches and meeting-houses — and are very exact in their temple worship, and in observing rites, and ceremonies, and ordinances, and sacred days! If the gospel had been preached in Maine as it was in primitive times, the war-spirit would have received, long ere this, its death-blow. But this nation is deemed [doomed?] to destruction, and the fire of God's wrath will consume both Church and State utterly.

With grateful feelings, I remain, yours with much esteem,

Wm. Lloyd Garrison.

P. S. Your letter, enclosing $5, and also the bundle containing the pamphlets on the wrongs of the red man, were duly received. The pamphlets were immediately distributed among the members of both houses of the Legislature, and I hope not without some good effect. The expense of freight and distribution was $1.50 — leaving $3.50 in my possession. What shall be done with it? I shall take the liberty to appropriate one dollar of it to pay for one year's subscription to the Non-Resistant, which will be forwarded to you regularly. I hope this will be agreeable to your feelings. Give my best regards to your dear wife, and tell her I long to know her views respecting our non-resistance principles. Helen unites with me in tendering friendly remembrances to you all.

ALS: Merrill Collection of Garrison Papers, Wichita State University Library, Wichita, Kansas.

1. So spelled in manuscript.
2. John 1:18.
3. I Peter 1:8. It may be noted that this entire paragraph is identical with the first paragraph in letter 141, to Mary Benson, February 10, 1839.
4. Garrison, in *The Liberator*, March 8, 1839, alluded to the report of the Joint Special Committee of the legislature on the subject of slavery in the District of Columbia and indicated his dissatisfaction with it. The report was reprinted in *The Liberator* on March 15, 1839. It had been issued on February 23, 1839.
5. Report of the Committee on the Judiciary, entitled "Report Respecting Distinctions of Color," House of Representatives, February 25, 1839, reprinted in *The Liberator*, March 15, 1839. The report was in response to petitions from women in Lynn, Brookfield, Dorchester, and Plymouth requesting "the immediate repeal of all laws of the State which make any distinction among its inhabitants on account of color." The immediate concern of the ladies was the Massachusetts law, on the statute books since 1705, prohibiting marriage between Negroes and whites. Garrison and other Massachusetts abolitionists had been waging a campaign against the law since the establishment of *The Liberator* in 1831. For a history of the entire issue see Louis Ruchames, "Race, Marriage, and Abolition in Massachusetts," *Journal of Negro History*, 40:250–273 (July 1955).

6. The first part has some similarity to Romans 3:12.

7. Shakespeare, *Othello*, I, iii.

8. William Cowper (1731–1800), *The Task*, Book II, "The Timepiece," line 17:

> "Mountains interpos'd
> Make enemies of nations, who had else,
> Like kindred drops, been mingled into one."

9. The *Massachusetts Abolitionist*.

10. The words, "that I have," are written twice.

11. Shakespeare, *Othello*, I, iii.

12. The dispute concerned the boundary of the United States and Canada and involved some twelve thousand square miles of land between Maine and New Brunswick. The line had been left vague in the peace treaty ending the American Revolution and early efforts to define it through mediation had failed. In the late 1830's, as a result of population expansion in Maine and New Brunswick, conflicts developed. In 1838 and 1839, fighting broke out between the New Brunswick lumberjacks intent on cutting timber in the disputed area, the valley of the Aroostook River, and Maine residents who sought to expel them. At one point, fifty Americans were captured and jailed by the New Brunswick men. Maine and New Brunswick mustered their respective militias; Congress authorized President Martin Van Buren to raise fifty thousand volunteers and appropriated ten million dollars for assistance to Maine. When it seemed that the "Aroostook War" of 1838–1839 might become a real conflict, General Winfield Scott was sent to the area and, in March 1839 arranged a truce. Each side was given the territory it actually occupied without prejudice to its basic claim. Maine was thus left in control of the Aroostook Valley. (Alexander De Conde, *A History of American Foreign Policy*, New York, 1963, pp. 155–156.)

144

TO GEORGE W. BENSON

Boston, March 19, 1839.

Dear bro. George:

I am somewhat apprehensive that this hasty scrawl will not meet your eye as promptly as I could wish; for the time is close at hand for holding our State quarterly meeting,[1] which is to decide whether our sacred enterprise shall continue under the management of its old and tried friends, or be given up to the control of politicians and sectarists. I hope you are at home — so that you may know promptly, that it is the earnest wish of myself, and others around me, that you would be present with us in this last and most important crisis. You think of coming to Boston in April. Now, just alter your arrangements so as to be with us next Tuesday.[2] Don't fail, for ordinary reasons, I pray you. As goes Massachusetts, so go the free States. By one united, vigorous effort, at this time, I am persuaded we shall succeed in utterly discomfitting all insidious plotters — but the least holding back, on our part, will prove fatal. I want to see you particularly in regard to the expediency of publishing the "Cradle of Liberty," which you saw noticed as forthcoming, in the last Liberator.[3] We shall issue a specimen number, in season for the quarterly meeting next week, and then determine at once as to the course it may be proper to pursue. I have some misgivings on the subject. It may look like a mere personal contest for patronage, though not so intended by myself. Again — I am fearful that, for us to afford a weekly paper of the size of the Abolitionist, for 50 cts. a year, containing the cream of the anti-slavery matter in the Liberator, will injure the subscription of our paper. Our friends, however, seem generally to approve of the project. If I could know your mind, I should be more decided in my own. It is thought that the issuing of this little sheet will most effectually hedge up the way of the Abolitionist, and thus defeat whatever scheme the getters up of that paper may have in view.

We may have a tolerably quiet, and again a very stormy meeting on Tuesday next. I believe the Board of Managers [4] will be sustained in the course they have pursued, by a majority of the delegates. If they should not, they will resign, as a matter of course; and the State Society will pass into other hands.

Phelps has written a long reply to the Address of the Board, respecting the doings of the N. Y. Executive Committee, which he is about issuing in a hand-bill. I did not feel obligated to give it a place in the columns of the Liberator, and declined doing so.[5]

Stanton has left the State — whether to return again, I know not; but probably he will be here at the quarterly meeting. The transformation in his feelings towards the Liberator and myself is complete. Since the annual meeting, though a large portion of the time in this city, he has had nothing to say to me. His conduct throughout has been very reprehensible, and greatly has he injured himself in the eyes of the best friends of our cause. His political hobby has well nigh ruined him and put an end to all harmonious action in Massachusetts. My soul is filled with grief on his account. — Dearly have I loved him in time past, and great have been my expectations in regard to his future career. But I fear he has made up his mind to be "a man of one idea" — for he seems to be determined to look only in one direction, and with a short-sighted vision.

There is some doubt whether Mr. Phelps will be installed at the Marlboro' Chapel,[6] on account of his hostility to the doctrine of personal and perfect righteousness. Pres. Mahan's preaching has sunk deeply into the hearts of many members of the Free Church; and you are aware, perhaps, that he advocates "perfectionism" as alone constituting christianity. He has just published a book on this subject, which I like as far as I have read it, and which will, in due time, cause some sensation among holy sinners and evangelical rebels.[7]

About 1500 subscribers are all, I understand, that have been obtained, as yet, for the Abolitionist, notwithstanding the deep hostility that is cherished toward the Liberator, and notwithstanding all the efforts of St. Clair, Phelps, Stanton, Wise, Torrey, backed up by the orthodox clergy. Not less than 5000 subscribers will be necessary to defray its expenses. These, perhaps, may be obtained, in time.

I have just received another letter from Boyle, equal if not superior to his first, and about twice as long.[8] It will make a sensation, when it is published. I shall publish it entire in the Non-Resistant, and nearly all of it in the Liberator.[9] It is the intention of friend Knapp to print it, also, in pamphlet form. Boyle ought to be here in New-England, editing a paper that shall cause every sect in Christendom (or, rather, in Babylon) to tremble. Can we not provide a way for his coming? [10] I have also received a very beautiful letter from his wife,[11] written in the same spirit.

The election in the Fourth District takes place on the 1st Monday of April. The Whigs have again nominated Nathan Brooks; [12] so that it is more than probable — almost certain — that Parmenter [13] will succeed, to the great injury of our cause. Bro. Stanton was premature in stirring up the political waters in that District.[14]

Give my brotherly regards to my friend Coe,[15] who has complimented me by giving a part of my odious name to his youngest born. I was very glad to receive his manly letter on non-resistance. It is my earnest desire that he may clearly apprehend and cordially embrace the divinely originated principles of our society. I am quite sure that he will be with us. I also desire to be remembered to his wife. Also to Mr. and Mrs. Stetson,[16] Mr. and Mrs. Scarborough,[17] and all other friends.

We received, a few days since, a joint letter from you and dear sister Anna. You have a fine babe, it seems, in George Benson — *almost* equal to my little Willie, who, being the paragon of babies, will of course not admit of an equal — notwithstanding that "all are born equal." Cover his soft cheeks with kisses for me, and also the cheeks of dear little Anne and Henry Egbert. We are glad to learn that Catherine is nearly herself again, as to health. As for us at No. 2, Nassau Court, we remain in a quiet, happy state of mind, loving many, and hating nobody in the wide world. Mother has enjoyed much better health, generally, than perhaps could have been expected. She will not return home for the present — is quite contented — but has not made up her mind how long to stay. We want her to remain with us as long as it is agreeable to her; but I presume she will wish to be with you all, during the hot summer months.

Assure my beloved sisters, Sarah and Anne, that they are as dear to me as ever; and though my letters to them are as scarce as Sybilline leaves, yet my love for them is a permanent part of my existence. Hoping to see you, without fail, on Tuesday next, when I can tell you many interesting things, I remain, as ever,

Your admiring brother,

Wm. Lloyd Garrison.

☞ Cecilia will remain with us till the 1st of May.

ALS: Garrison Papers, Boston Public Library. The major portion of this letter was printed in *Life*, II, 284–287.

1. Scheduled for March 26, 1839. The call for the meeting, in *The Liberator* of March 15, carried the names of Francis Jackson, president, and W. Phillips, recording secretary pro tem. The announced business of the meeting was to be the conflict between the Massachusetts Anti-Slavery Society and the executive committee of the American Anti-Slavery Society at New York over the control of fund-raising in the state.

2. March 26, 1839.

3. At this point, *Life* presents the following footnote (II:284n):

"The issue of this sheet was announced to be weekly at 75 cents per annum, or in large quantities at 50 cents, the contents being principally selections from the anti-slavery department of the *Liberator*, under Mr. Garrison's editorial supervision. The first number bore date of Saturday, March 23, 1839. A cut of Faneuil Hall made a pictorial heading. The motto was from John Adams: 'Great is Truth — Great is Liberty — Great is Humanity; and They must and will Prevail.' The salutatory spoke of this journal as an experiment for the benefit of those who were too poor to take the *Liberator*, or who craved a paper exclusively devoted to the subject of slavery; not as intended to be a substitute for the *Liberator*, or to interfere with it in the slightest degree. Its main object was to 'assist in preserving the integrity of the abolition enterprise in this commonwealth.' The second number bore date of April 6, after which the *Cradle of Liberty* appeared weekly, closing its first volume on March 21, 1840, and being finally discontinued with Vol. 2, No. 17, July 18, 1840; the *Monthly Offering* taking the place of it, with a difference. The size of its printed page was about 11 by 15½ inches."

4. The Board of Managers of the Massachusetts Anti-Slavery Society.

5. In *The Liberator*, March 15, 1839, in an editorial essay entitled "Free Discussion," Garrison acknowledged receipt of Phelps's communication, "which would occupy six or seven columns of our paper, reviewing the recent address of the Board of Managers of the Massachusetts A. S. Society, on the subject of the difficulties between said Board and the Executive Committee of the Parent Society. The communication . . . is in fact an extended argument against the course of the Board, and in favor of that of the Committee at New York. We decline to publish it for the following reasons:

"1. The parties to the controversy are the *Board of Managers of the State Society* and the *Executive Committee at New York*, both of which are abundantly capable of managing their own cause. We have published the Address of the Board, and shall cheerfully publish the reply of the Executive Committee whenever it may be sent to us; but we are under no obligation to open our columns to any individual or body of individuals, except the parties themselves, who are entitled to equal and exact justice at our hands. The only circumstance which can give bro. Phelps any special claim to a hearing is the fact, that he is a member of the Board; but as he has already relieved himself of all personal responsibility in the case, by stating that he does not approve the course which the Board has seen fit to take, we see not why we should be required to admit him to our columns as a champion of one of the parties.

"2. The extreme length of bro. Phelps's article, the crowded state of our columns, and an anxious desire to curtail, so far as justice to both parties will allow, a controversy of so unpleasant a character, constitute another reason in favor of our decision. It seems not a little extraordinary to us, that while the Address of the Board has been carefully excluded from the new paper, one of its prominent managers should expect us to publish an article from his pen more than twice as long as that Address; and that, too, before the Executive Committee at New York, the party concerned, has seen fit to make any reply! Our readers would have just cause to complain, if, at the present stage of the controversy, we should open our columns, indiscriminately, to what *individuals* on either side might wish to say; and to open them to brother Phelps, to the exclusion of others, would be neither courteous nor just.

"3. The approaching quarterly meeting of the State Society will furnish not only bro. Phelps, but all others who desire it, ample opportunity for the expression of their views, and thus render it unnecessary for us to fill our columns with an extended discussion, to the exclusion of much important matter."

6. *Life* has the following note (II, 285): "As pastor of the Free Church, namely. He was ultimately installed (*Lib.* 9:123), with the assistance of the Rev. Hubbard Winslow, who, though one of the most odious pro-slavery apologists among the northern clergy (*ante*, 1:478; 2:63), was yet a 'no-government' doctrinaire — for, from his (Thanksgiving) pulpit, he condemned Lovejoy's self-defence against the mob (*Lib.* 7:201)."

7. " 'Scripture Doctrine of Christian Perfection; with other kindred subjects, illustrated and confirmed in a series of Discourses, designed to throw light on the way of holiness. By Rev. Asa Mahan, President of the Oberlin College Institute' (*Lib.* 9:48). In December, 1839, an anonymous contributor to the *Liberator* is permitted to print a dialogue intended to overcome in detail the 'prejudice and misrepresentation' of which the editor was the object. We read: 'But some say he is a Perfectionist, and believes that, let him do what he will, it is no sin. — That is false. His views on the subject of holiness are in unison with those of Mr. Mahan, whom you have heard and liked' (*Lib.* 9:207)." (*Life*, II, 286n.)

Asa Mahan (1800–1889) was a minister who served in Pittsford, New York, until 1831, when he accepted a pulpit in Cincinnati. He became a trustee of Lane Seminary and supported the students in their conflict with the administration. He was president of Oberlin College from 1835 to 1850, when he accepted the presidency of Cleveland University. He resigned in 1855, served as minister for five years, and again as college president, from 1860 to 1871. He moved to England in 1871 and lived there until his death. (*Weld-Grimké Letters*, I, 79n.)

8. "The Rev. James Boyle . . . addressed a letter to Mr. Garrison touching the Clerical Appeal, Sectarianism, and True Holiness, from Rome, Ohio, which was printed in the *Liberator* for March 23, 1838 (8:45). It was a very intense and able production — 'one of the most powerful epistles ever written by man,' it seemed to the recipient (*Lib.* 8:47), who published it again in pamphlet form, with a preface and his poem 'Christian Rest' — and well calculated to inflame the hostility of the clergy to Mr. Garrison. . . ." (*Life*, II, 286n.)

9. "In the *Liberator*, 9:52, in the *Non-Resistant* of April 6, 1839; in both, under the caption, 'On Non-Resistance, — The "Powers that be," Civil, Judicial and Ecclesiastical, — Holiness.' It was dated Cincinnati, Ohio, Feb. 24, 1839." (*Ibid.*)

10. "This was in singular anticipation of a letter from Gamaliel Bailey, jr., written to Mr. Garrison on April 15, 1839, concerning Boyle, who was just leaving the employ of the *Philanthropist*. Bailey paid a very high tribute to his coadjutor, and asked if any situation could be found for him at the East, suggesting his fitness to become the salaried editor of the *Non-Resistant* (MS.). In July, 1839, Boyle was appointed lecturing and financial agent of the Ohio A. S.

Society; at which time Oliver Johnson said of him in the *Liberator* (9:122), that probably there was no man living whose religious views were more in harmony with Mr. Garrison's." (*Life*, II, 287n.)

11. "Laura P. Boyle. Her letter was printed in *Lib.* 9:56. In it, she states that she at first hesitated to join the Non-Resistance Society, being emancipated from sects, parties, and organizations generally." (*Ibid.*)

12. Nathan Brooks (b. Lincoln, Massachusetts, 1785; d. 1863) of Concord, a lawyer and insurance man, was admitted to the Middlesex bar in 1813. In 1826, he became secretary-treasurer of the Middlesex Mutual Fire Insurance Company, to which he devoted most of his time. He was, later, also involved in banking. He was at various times a member of the state legislature, as representative and senator, and was nominated several times as the Whig candidate for Congress in the Fourth District. He was interested in the reforms of the day, but was primarily involved in temperance. (D. Hamilton Hurd, *History of Middlesex County, Mass.*, Philadelphia, Pa., 1890, II, 606–607.)

13. William Parmenter (b. March 30, 1789; d. February 25, 1866) a prominent businessman and political figure in Boston, was a pioneer in the glass industry in East Cambridge; manager and agent of the New England Crown Glass Company from 1824 to 1836; president of the Middlesex Bank; a member of the state House of Representatives in 1829, of the state Senate in 1836, and a Democratic representative in Congress from 1837 to 1845. Parmenter was elected by a vote of 4,972 to 4,432 for Brooks. The vote for neither candidate, the "scattering vote" which represented the votes of antislavery people, was 512, a decline from the 731 "scattering votes" of the previous election. (*The Liberator*, April 5, 1839; *BDAC*.)

14. Henry Stanton, at the annual meeting of the New Hampshire Anti-Slavery Society in December 1838, had publicly stated that a meeting-house in which he had been scheduled to speak in Townsend, Massachusetts, had been closed to him by a friend of Nathan Brooks. Stanton recalled that Brooks's friend had stated that an antislavery lecture at that time by Stanton would be detrimental to Brooks's chances for election. (*The Liberator*, December 21, 1838.)

15. The Reverend William Coe.

16. James A. Stetson was the brother of George W. Benson's wife, Catherine.

17. Philip and Deidama Scarborough.

145

TO THE ABOLITIONISTS OF MASSACHUSETTS

Boston, March 30, 1839.

BRETHREN: — At the regular quarterly meeting of the State Anti-Slavery Society, held in this city on the 26th instant, the course which your Board of Managers felt in duty bound to pursue, in protesting against the abrupt termination of the relation heretofore subsisting between the Parent and State Societies, by the Executive Committee at New-York, was sanctioned by an overwhelming majority on the part of the delegates in attendance.[1] We are grateful for this new expression of your confidence in us. Without that confidence, we surely could not and ought not to hold our present responsible situation. Possessing it, we may calculate upon your united and hearty co-operation in every measure which is calculated to advance the interests of the anti-slavery cause, and to confer honor upon the Commonwealth.

However hasty, indiscreet, or peremptory, the Executive Committee of the Parent Society may have been, in their treatment of the Massachusetts Society, their conduct does not fairly exonerate you from redeeming the pledge of $10,000, made in your behalf, in June last, by your Board. It may, and undoubtedly will have the effect, by exciting feelings of distrust and alienation, to discourage effort, and prevent those liberal contributions which otherwise might have been made. In that case, the blame will measurably rest with the Executive Committee. But there are certainly good reasons, above all personal considerations, or the strict observance of a formal relationship between the two societies, why Massachusetts should be faithful to her promise. She is justly regarded, in this great struggle for liberty and the maintenance of human rights, (as she was in the days of the Revolution,) the pioneer State — the first and foremost to lead the way in battling with the hosts of tyranny. No other State in the Union may be expected to excel her in liberality, in zeal, or in devotedness to the cause. If *she* falter, who else will go forward? In the eyes of the enemies of emancipation, her contributions to the general anti-slavery fund will be the true test of her interest in this great and glorious enterprise. From May 1, 1837, to May 1, 1838, she put into the treasury of the Parent Society upwards of $10,000. From May 1, 1838, up to the present time, (within five weeks of the completion of another year,) she has contributed not more than half of that sum! Surely, instead of a diminution, there should have been an enlargement on her part, on the score of liberality. Surely, the Board of Managers were not rash in supposing that she would do as much to sustain the Parent Society in 1838, as she did in 1837!

Under these circumstances, the Board feel solicitous, — for the reputation of the State, the advancement of the anti-slavery cause, and the relief of the Parent Society, now deeply involved in debt, in consequence of relying upon the prompt redemption of pledges not yet cancelled by its auxiliaries, — that an *immediate*, VIGOROUS and UNITED effort be made by the various anti-slavery societies in this Commonwealth, and by individual abolitionists, to raise the sum now due, and to become due on the first of May, to the Parent Society. It is true, the time is short, and therefore the greater the necessity for prompt and efficient action, in perfect good-will, and with all possible harmony. Only five weeks intervene before the expiration of the year. Brief as is the period, it is long enough, *provided there is a will to execute the generous deed.* It is only for every abolitionist, every society, to say, resolutely and heartily, *it must*, IT CAN, IT SHALL BE DONE; and the money will be obtained without difficulty. The character of the State Society will thus be honorably redeemed, the Board will have no occasion to regret the pledge they made, and a new impetus will be given to the car of emancipation. Let no town, no society, no individual, wait to be visited by a financial agent. In such an emergency, every man ought to be his own lecturer, every society its own collector, and every town its own agent. The women of Massachusetts will do their part. The self-sacrificing spirit manifested by one of their number, who is in humble circumstances, at a late quarterly meeting, (in pledging $50 towards redeeming the State pledge, if others would come forward and co-operate with her,) was a sure token that they are ready to meet their share of the general responsibility. "What ought to be done, can be done," is a familiar maxim. The money due from this State to the Parent Society ought to be paid immediately, and IT CAN BE PAID. Let every abolitionist, whose eye is fastened upon this appeal, resolve that if it be not paid, no part of the blame shall rest upon his shoulders. Let every society replenish and empty its treasury forthwith. Let not the homely, but instructive proverb be forgotten: — "Many hands make light work." Let us, one and all, "make one last, *best* effort NOW."

The medium through which the money shall be forwarded to New York, it is, of course, optional with contributors and societies to designate. The Board, however, would with deference suggest the propriety of making the treasurer of the State Society (H. G. CHAPMAN,) [2] that medium, in accordance with the original design and form of the agreement between the Parent and State Societies. Should any money be paid over to any agent of the Parent Society, it is recommended that the society or individual, contributing it, obtain from him a promise that it shall be given into the hands of the State Treasurer, who will forward it to New York without delay. This, however, is of minor importance. "Let every man be fully persuaded in his own mind." [3] The main point is, to *redeem the pledge*. LET IT BE DONE.

In behalf of the Board of Managers of the Massachusetts Anti-Slavery Society,

FRANCIS JACKSON, *Pres.*

WM. LLOYD GARRISON, *Cor. Sec'y.*

Printed in the *Eighth Annual Report of the Board of Managers of the Mass. Anti-Slavery Society* (Boston, 1840). It was first printed in *The Liberator*, April 5, 1839, with the following legend:
"Appeal of the Board
To auxiliary anti-slavery societies, and abolitionists
generally throughout the State."

1. The vote was 143 to 23. For a complete list of the voters and their votes, see *The Liberator*, March 29, 1839. The resolution, as adopted, read: "Resolved, That the course pursued by the Board of Managers of the Massachusetts Anti-Slavery Society, in relation to the difficulty now existing between that Board and the Executive Committee of the Parent Society, meets our hearty approval."

2. Henry Grafton Chapman.

3. Romans 14:5.

146

TO HARRIET FOSTER

Boston, April 8, 1839.

Respected Friend:

At the very earliest opportunity, I shall be happy to comply with the invitation of the Board of Managers of the Salem Female Anti-Slavery Society, as conveyed to me in your interesting letter of the 5th instant. As I am now situated, — having a number of pledges to various anti-slavery societies unredeemed, — I cannot tell precisely the time I shall be able to visit Salem, but it will doubtless be in all this month. You shall be duly apprised of my coming. It is, perhaps, somewhat remarkable, — considering the proximity of the place to Boston, — that I have never given a single lecture in Salem since I began to plead for "the suffering and the dumb." Your city is not deficient in intellect, in pecuniary ability, or in hospitality to strangers; but I fear it is greatly so in *heart*. You have among you, some choice abolition spirits, of both sexes, who are "faithful among the faithless found," [1] and very much do I admire their zeal, firmness, and self-sacrificing disposition. Unfortunately, all are not abolitionists who are called such, or who make flaming pretensions on the subject of slavery. The Lord, however, is sifting us from time to time, and trying every man's work as by fire. No one can lament the divisions that exist in our ranks more than I do; but they were to have been expected, if not in their present shape, at least in some form and from some cause in the progress of our sacred enterprise.

With much respect, I remain,
Yours, ever to do good,
Wm. Lloyd Garrison.

ALS: Essex Institute, Salem, Mass.

1. John Milton, *Paradise Lost*, Book V, line 896, somewhat altered.

147

TO ARTHUR AND LEWIS TAPPAN

Boston, April 8, 1839.

Respected Friends:

It gives me real pleasure to hear that Mr. Roswell Goss, of this city, intends opening a Graham Boarding House in New-York,[1] and that you regard the enterprise with favor. Of Mr. Goss, from a long acquaintance with him, I feel authorised to speak in strong terms of commendation. He is one who reverences the voice of conscience, rejoices to walk in the light, never waits till an unpopular cause is cheered by the multitude before he supports it, walks in a state of humility, and seems to be animated by the single desire to glorify God and do good to man. In the cause of philanthropy, he has been self-sacrificing, and has given very considerable aid to the anti-slavery cause almost from its commencement. He is truly a modest man, and makes no display of himself, but is possessed of excellent business talents. He formerly kept a first-rate restorateur's[2] eating-house in this city, which was very productive, but sold out because he felt as if he ought not to cater in such a manner for the appetites of the community, and took charge of the Graham house, formerly kept by Mr. Cambell.[3] I know not what temporary assistance he will need to start his praiseworthy enterprise in New-York, but, if any, it may be extended to him with more than ordinary safety. I hope he will succeed in opening his house by the 1st of May, as it will be likely to be crowded during the anniversary week,[4] and notoriety will thus be given to it by the delegates, &c.

With undiminished affection and respect, I remain,

Your friend and fellow-laborer,

Wm. Lloyd Garrison.

Messrs. Arthur & Lewis Tappan.

ALS: Tappan Collection, Library of Congress.

1. Roswell Goss established a Graham boarding-house in New York City at 63 Barclay Street. Garrison, writing to his wife from New York on May 15, 1840 (letter 184), noted that "Goss's Graham House has been assailed by a mob, several windows broken, the door burst open, etc., etc.; though not many were engaged in this work of mischief."

2. So in manuscript.

3. David Cambell was also the editor of the *Graham Journal of Health and Longevity*, at 9 Washington Street, Boston. On September 6, 1839, *The Liberator* carried the following item:

"For the third time, in three successive years, that conscientious and worthy man, David Cambell, the publisher of the Graham Journal, has been torn from his family and business, and is now incarcerated in the Leverett street jail, for the crime of refusing to do military duty. (See his letter in another column.) His conscience would be respected if he wore the garb of a Friend; but, as he happens to be a Congregationalist, he has no right to be conscientiously opposed to bearing arms, and must therefore go to prison! Monstrous injustice! Will the enlightened citizens of this Commonwealth tolerate upon the Statute-Book a law which is so absurd and unequal in its operations? We cannot believe it." (See also Peter Brock, *Pacifism in the United States, from the Colonial Era to the First World War*, Princeton, N.J., 1968, pp. 574–575; *The Non-Resistant*, September 21, 1839.)

4. Of the American Anti-Slavery Society.

148

TO HELEN E. GARRISON

Worcester, April 22, 1839.
Monday morning.

Dear Helen — Before leaving for Groton [1] this morning, I must send you a hasty note, to say that every thing has gone off well in this place. Friend Collins [2] came up with me on Saturday, though he was extremely loath to leave on account of his wife, whom he expected in the city that day; but his anxiety to raise all the money possible, to redeem the State pledge, outweighed all other considerations. He will return this afternoon in the cars. We are stopping at Edward Earle's,[3] a very lovely man of about my age, and a member of the Society of Friends. Just before our arrival on Saturday, he had been severely cowhided in the street by a desperate cousin of his, on account of a love affair with his sister. The attack was cowardly and outrageous. Friend Earle, however, was enabled to carry out his non-resistance principles, and made no attempt to defend himself. The blows were chiefly aimed at his head and back — one struck him across the cheek, leaving the mark of the cowhide. Happily, he escaped without much injury. This affair took place in the presence of a large number of citizens, who at first made no attempt to separate the parties, being confounded at the sight. But they soon interfered, and the brutal assailant was sent to prison, to await his trial, not being able to obtain any bail. He is Earle's own cousin! Friend E. has no desire to have him punished — but the law will probably have its course.

The abolitionism of Worcester is confined to a few individuals, the women being, as usual, the most active. Formerly, the state of things here was very bad — it being dangerous to think of lecturing on slavery. Every thing is now quiet — too quiet, perhaps. I lectured, last evening, in the Methodist meeting-house, which is a small one — the friends deeming it useless to make application for any other. It was a pleasant evening, and a large throng attended — multitudes not being able to gain admittance. Not less than a thousand persons, however, contrived to wedge themselves into the house; and they listened to my address, from first to last, with marked attention. I cannot but hope that good was done. At the close, we obtained the handsome sum of about $57; and friend Collins hopes to get a hundred more to-day. Friend Earle gives $20, and his wife $5. I had in the pulpit with me friend Grosvenor,[4] who made the prayer, and Jotham Horton,[5] the Methodist minister. They both spoke to the people, sanctioning all that I had said. Grosvenor expressed the hope, that when friend Garrison next visited Worcester, he would be enabled to obtain a house that would hold at least half his audience. His remarks were very cutting.

I attended the Methodist meeting yesterday forenoon, with Collins. In the afternoon, I staid at home till tea-time, when I went to John Milton Earle's.[6]

I leave at half past 7 o'clock this morning, going direct to Groton in the stage. Dr. Farnsworth[7] will take me over to Townsend[8] this evening. I find that my appointment for Acton[9] is on Thursday, instead of Wednesday evening, so that I cannot be in Boston much before Friday noon, when I shall have to leave immediately for Salem. You had better go with me, and spend the night at friend Dean's.[10] Be in readiness when I come.

To be with you, and the dear ones, at home, is far more desirable, as a matter of choice, than to be absent even for an hour; but when duty calls, we should be willing to make a cheerful sacrifice of our own feelings and preferences upon its altar. Love to mother — and many kisses for George and Willie. They must be good boys till I return.

Ever lovingly yours,

W. L. G.

ALS· Garrison Papers, Boston Public Library.

1. Groton, Massachusetts.

2. John Anderson Collins (b. Vermont, October, 1810; d. 1879) was a student at the Andover Theological Seminary who played a leading part in revealing the "clerical plot" against Garrison. He left the seminary and became a general agent of the Massachusetts Anti-Slavery Society. He helped raise the $10,000 pledged to the American Anti-Slavery Society (*Life*, II, 292), and was sent to England in 1840 to explain the Garrisonian viewpoint and to raise money for the cause. From July 1840 to November 1841, he edited the *Monthly Garland*, a small antislavery magazine written mostly by himself. In the early 1840's, while still an agent of the Massachusetts Anti-Slavery Society, he became a follower of Fourier and was reprimanded by the abolitionists for holding Fourierist meetings following antislavery meetings. He resigned as agent to devote himself to founding a Fourierist commune at Skaneateles, New York. The commune failed and was liquidated in 1846. He was in California in 1849, where he was still living

in 1879, having more or less abandoned his efforts at social improvement. (*DAB.*)

3. Edward Earle (1811–1877), a Quaker, was born in Leicester, Massachusetts, and moved to Worcester at the age of twenty-one. There he engaged in business, first in flour, then in steel and iron, and finally in machine-carding. He married Ann Barker Buffum in 1835 and retired from business in 1869. He was a Worcester selectman (1843), a representative in the state legislature (1851), a Worcester alderman (1853), a member of the Worcester School Board (1861–1871), and mayor of Worcester (1871). He was interested in the antislavery movement from its beginning and was a friend of the Negro. (D. Hamilton Hurd, *History of Worcester County, Mass.*, Philadelphia, 1889, II, 1692–1694.)

4. The Reverend Cyrus P. Grosvenor.

5. Jotham Horton was minister of the First Methodist Meeting House in Worcester from 1838 to 1839 (Charles Emery Stevens, *Worcester Churches, 1719–1889*, Worcester, 1890, p. 98). He next ministered to the Worthen Street Methodist Episcopal Church in Lowell, from 1839 to 1840. In 1839, he was elected a vice-president of the New Organization in Massachusetts. (D. Hamilton Hurd, *History of Middlesex County*, Philadelphia, 1890, II, 143.)

6. John Milton Earle (1794–1874), a journalist and legislator, was born in Leicester, Massachusetts. He moved to Worcester in 1816. With Anthony Chase, he formed the firm of Earle and Chase, which conducted a retail business. Earle left the business in 1823, and bought the Worcester *Spy*, which had been printed in Worcester since 1775. He was its chief manager and editor until 1858. He was an early antislavery man, a Whig and Free-soiler. In 1844–1846 and 1850–1852, he was a member of the Massachusetts house, and of the senate in 1858. He also had extensive scientific interests, including pomology, conchology, and botany. He married Sarah Hussey in 1821 and had seven daughters and two sons. (Hurd, *History of Worcester County*, II, 1685–1686.)

7. Dr. Amos Farnsworth.

8. Townsend, Massachusetts.

9. Acton, Massachusetts.

10. Probably William Dean of Salem, whose wife, Lydia, was also active in the antislavery movement (see *Columbian Centinel* [Boston], April 10, 1824, for their marriage announcement).

149

TO HELEN E. GARRISON

Providence, May 5, 1839.

My dear Helen:

As a loving husband, if not as an agent of the State A. S. Society, I am in duty bound to report progress, since I kissed you and the little ones, and said to all at home, "good bye."

My trip to Taunton, on Thursday afternoon, was a quick one. Thirty-five miles in one hour and thirty-five minutes, (including stoppages,) was rapid travelling. My arrival gave much relief to the Taunton friends, who were somewhat apprehensive about it. I lectured in the evening to a pretty good audience, in Mr. Emery's meeting-house.[1] He was present, and made a prayer, though no "Garrisonite." Saw a few anti-slavery friends privately, but none of your acquaintance. Friday forenoon, I left in the stage for Fall River. Arrived at S. B.

Chace's house,[2] at 1 o'clock. He was absent, on a visit to Grafton. — Sarah Buffum[3] had gone to attend the Convention in Philadelphia. Mrs. Chace and a younger sister were at home, and gave me an agreeable entertainment. Called on several friends, and had several call on me. Addressed a good audience, in the evening, in Mr. Fowler's meeting-house. Fowler himself hates me as bad as he does a rattlesnake — chiefly because I am "a Quaker." Four or five clergymen were present, two of them in the pulpit. Yesterday morning, I left in the steam boat for this, your native place. Found that the meeting for my lecture had been appointed for the evening, in the Masonic Hall — anticipated a very thin audience, but was agreeably disappointed. The Hall was crowded — Dr. Slack[4] and his wife were among those present. Was introduced to them, and to some others. My address was listened to with profound attention. I hope it was not spoken in vain. Time will determine.

Phebe[5] gave me a welcome reception, as usual. Her mother is in comfortable health. Henry Jackson's wife[6] is staying awhile here. I have had no *controversy* with her, on any subject. She is just one of those who were "spoilt in the making" — a strange compound, most certainly. If I were fool enough to marry such a woman, I am sure I should be wise enough to run away from her — as often as circumstances might warrant. This, sub rosa. Phebe thinks she shall not be able to visit Boston this summer. Sylvia Ammidon and Miss Miller took tea with us last evening, and were present at my lecture. Sylvia is on a short visit here, and is pretty well. She and Phebe are to be present at a colored wedding this evening. I called to see Charlotte[7] yesterday afternoon — found the family all well. George Henry[8] has a very bad humor in his face, which covers both cheeks, and makes him look badly — but it does not affect his general health. While I was there, James Anthony's wife[9] came in with her babe, a girl, 6 months old, and weighing 24 pounds — a real bouncer. This forenoon, I went to the Quaker meeting — heard John Meeder[10] preach, of whom, I am told, sister Mary thought very highly as a preacher. But, if his harangue, to-day, was a fair specimen of his preaching, I should much rather he would be silent, than speak. This afternoon I am to go to Coventry, to address the Kent County Young Men's A. S. Society. Some of our modern pharisees, who have not yet learnt that a man is better than a sheep, will consider this a profanation of the Sabbath! When I return from Coventry, I will finish the remainder of this scrawl.

Monday afternoon — 3 o'clock.

I rode to Coventry in company with a young Quaker friend, Daniel Gould.[11] Stopped at his father's, and had a delightful time. There are not less than ten children in the family, (and you know I like to see a house full,) all intelligent, and thorough-going abolitionists. The two eldest daughters are interesting girls — one of them is very pretty indeed. Benjamin Green [12] and wife, and Dorcas,[13] came in while we were resting a little from our ride. The Dr. had a cold and cough, so as to prevent his accompanying them. We all started off for the meeting, carrying a small congregation with us. On arriving at the meeting-house, found it completely filled. The audience listened to my discourse with unbroken attention. After the meeting, there was quite an amicable strife among the friends, as to who should secure me at their homes for the night. I told them that I was a non-resistant, and whoever used the most compulsion would get me, of course. — It was finally agreed, that Dr. Peleg Clarke [14] should return with me to friend Gould's, where we would take tea, and then I should go home with the Dr., and stay with him all night — a distance of three miles. Benjamin Greene and his wife, and Dorcas, also stayed to tea, so that we had a very pleasant time of it. This morning Dr. Clarke brought me to town in his carriage. On the way, we called at Rowland Greene's — saw him and all the family. A most hearty reception I had from them all. The old lady was the "same old sixpence," worth at least a good many guineas. Freelove [15] was at home — also, a married sister from Albany, with a whole troop of children. Benjamin's little boy is "as fat as butter," and "as good as pie" — a bright, intelligent, dear child. Many inquiries were made after you and the children, and mother, and much love desired to you.

I dined to-day at Charlotte's. Her little Joseph [15a] pleases me prodigiously, because he resembles my sweet little Willie so closely. We had a fine time together. Charlotte looks as young and fair as she did the first time I ever saw her. Henry [16] is immersed in business.

I have just returned from a visit to Eliza J. Davis,[17] who has been staying at her mother's, for some time. She has had a severe attack of the quinsy,[18] and looks quite altered from what she did when I last saw her. Her babe resembles her strongly, and is interesting. I did not see Mrs. Chace,[19] as she was with Harriet, who is threatened with a fever. Eliza longs to see you, and to have you visit Providence — so, indeed, do a multitude of friends. Mary Chace [20] will go with friend Davis and myself to New-York this afternoon, as a delegate from the Female A. S. Society. We shall go by the way of Stonington.

I see by the papers, that an attempt was made, a few days since, to blow up the Anti-Slavery Depository in Hartford, by some villains. Considerable damage was done, but, fortunately, no one injured. I am told that bro. George was in the building at the time, writing a letter, which he coolly finished after the explosion.

Birney is out in the last Emancipator, with a long article,[21] blowing up the non-resistance abolitionists. It is unfair, unmanly, and proscriptive, and shows that there is to be a desperate struggle this week at New-York.[22] I anticipate a breaking up of our whole organization. But my mind is calm and peaceful. The Lord of hosts is my rock and refuge.

What more need I now say, than that I desire you to kiss the dear boys for me, give my love to dear mother, and accept for yourself the renewed assurances of my affection and love?

Yours, in holy bonds,

Wm. Lloyd Garrison.

☞ No intelligence from Brooklyn, except that Mrs. Robinson is dead.[23]

ALS: Garrison Papers, Boston Public Library.

1. The meeting-house was the Spring Street Church (Congregational) in Taunton, Massachusetts. Samuel Hopkins Emery (b. Boxford, Massachusetts, 1815; d. 1901), Congregational minister, graduated from Amherst in 1834 and subsequently from Andover Theological Seminary. He was installed at the Spring Street Church in Taunton in 1837. He married Julia Reed in 1838. Three years later he moved to Bedford, Massachusetts, where he remained for five years, and then returned to his original congregation in Taunton, where he stayed until 1855. In that year, he accepted a call to the First Congregational Church of Quincy, Illinois. He remained there until 1869. Thereafter, he occupied various ministerial posts until 1875, when he returned to Taunton to take charge of the Associated Charities of Taunton. He also wrote *History of Taunton, Mass.*, published in 1893. (Samuel Hopkins Emery, *History of Taunton, Mass.*, Syracuse, N.Y., 1893, "Biographical Appendix," pp. 56–57.)

2. Samuel B. Chace (b. March 11, 1800; d. December 17, 1870), of Fall River, Massachusetts, married Elizabeth Buffum, one of the five daughters of Arnold Buffum, the distinguished Quaker and abolitionist of Rhode Island and Massachusetts. In 1839 they moved to the Blackstone Valley of Rhode Island, where Samuel and his brother, Harvey Chace, "founded the great cotton manufacturing business that made them leading factors in this industry." (*Two Quaker Sisters, From the Original Diaries of Elizabeth Buffum Chace and Lucy Buffum Lovell*, New York, 1937, p. xxiv.)

3. Sarah Buffum was a daughter of Arnold Buffum and sister of Elizabeth. She married Nathaniel B. Borden, a friend of the slave, a manufacturer, and mayor of Fall River, Massachusetts, in 1843. She was his third wife. Though she did not marry until her mature womanhood, she almost married earlier, explaining, "it will be partly to keep every old shack who comes along from proposing to me." She was a prominent member of the Ladies Anti-Slavery Society of Fall River (devoted mainly to reading and discussing literature about slavery). Her house was a station on the Underground Railroad, and she was an early friend of Frederick Douglass. She died on September 10, 1854, and her obituary was printed in *The Liberator*, September 15, 1854. (L. B. C. Wyman and Arthur Wyman, *Elizabeth Buffum Chace, 1806–1899, her Life and its Environment*, Boston, 1914, I, 18, 51, 129; II, 139, 265; Frederick M. Peck and Henry H. Earl, *Fall River and its Industries*, Fall River, 1877, pp. 236–237.)

4. Dr. David Burr Slack (b. Rehoboth, May 11, 1798) was educated at Brown University and practiced medicine at North Maine Street, Providence. He married Susan W. Jackson of Providence and had ten children. He was the author of

An Essay on Human Color (Providence, 1845) and co-author with Dr. George Capron of *New England Popular Medicine* . . . (Boston, 1847). (The Reverend William Samuel Slack, *The Slack Family*, Alexandria, La., 1930, pp. 171, 179.)

5. Phebe Jackson.

6. Probably the former Maria T. Gano, the daughter of a minister, who married Henry Jackson in 1822. Henry Jackson (1798–1863) was a Baptist minister, in Charlestown, Massachusetts, from 1822 to 1836, in Hartford for about a year, and in New Bedford, Massachusetts, at the First Baptist Church, beginning in 1839. He was pastor of the Central Church in Newport, Rhode Island, from 1847 to 1863. He was the brother of Phebe Jackson. (*Biographical Cyclopedia of Representative Men of Rhode Island*, Providence, 1881, p. 279.)

7. Mrs. Henry Anthony, Helen Garrison's sister.

8 George Henry was the son of Charlotte and Henry Anthony, born on June 13, 1835. (Charles L. Anthony, *Genealogy of the Anthony Family from 1495 to 1904*, Sterling, Ill., 1904, p. 239.)

9. James Coggeshall Anthony (b. 1809) married Mary B. Smith, November 20, 1836. The baby was born November 3, 1838, and was named Julia C. Anthony. James was the brother of Henry Anthony, Charlotte's husband, and of John Gould Anthony, a naturalist, whose daughter, Annie Keene Anthony, married Garrison's son, George Thompson, in 1873. (Anthony, *Genealogy of the Anthony Family*, pp. 236, 239, 240, 243.)

10. John Meader (not Meeder) (b. Rochester, New Hampshire, 1797; d. 1860), a minister and missionary in the Society of Friends, the son of Joseph and Elizabeth Meader. He was acknowledged as minister in 1824. In 1837, he came to Providence, Rhode Island, where he preached at the Monthly Meeting. He remained until 1841, when he went on a missionary tour among the Indians west of the Mississippi. In 1850, he visited England, Ireland, and other parts of the Continent, on a mission of unity among the Friends. He returned to Providence in 1851, and preached there until 1857. (*Biographical Cyclopedia of Representative Men of Rhode Island*, p. 280.)

11. Unidentified.

12. Benjamin Greene (b. August 11, 1797, in Cranston, Rhode Island; d. April 22, 1853, in Cranston), son of Rowland Greene, helped his father conduct the Friends' School in Plainfield, Connecticut, and was its principal from 1817 to 1824. He married Hannah Sisson, the daughter of Joseph and Priscilla Sisson, on October 5, 1836. (Louise Brownell Clarke, *The Greenes of Rhode Island*, New York, 1903, p. 547.) See letter 6, to Henry Benson, January 26, 1836.

13. Dorcas was Benjamin Greene's sister.

14. Dr. Peleg Clarke, a homeopathic physician who was later president of the Rhode Island Homeopathic Society (established in 1849). Born in Richmond, Rhode Island, in 1784, he lived in Coventry, Rhode Island, most of his life. He was the son of Weeden and Thankful Clarke and married Marietta Fiske in 1819. (George A. Morrison, Jr. *The 'Clarke' Families of Rhode Island*, New York, 1902, p. 125.)

15. Freelove was the sister of Dorcas and Benjamin Greene, and the daughter of Rowland Greene. She was born in 1794. (Clarke, *The Greenes of Rhode Island*, p. 547.)

15a. Joseph Bowen Anthony, born July 16, 1837.

16. Henry Anthony.

17. Mrs. Thomas Davis, the former Eliza Chace.

18. A severe infection of the throat, accompanied by swelling and fever.

19. Mrs. William Chace.

20. Mary Chace (b. 1813), formerly Mary E. Allen, of Newport, Rhode Island, married the Honorable Oliver Chace, Samuel B. Chace's brother, on November 25, 1835. An outspoken temperance advocate and opponent of slavery, he was a banker and manufacturer, a member of the state legislature, and an

outstanding and public-spirited citizen of Fall River. (Frederick M. Peck and Henry H. Earl, *Fall River and its Industries*, Fall River, 1877, p. 248.)

21. May 2, 1839. It was entitled "View of the Constitution of the American A. S. Society as Connected with the 'No-Government' Question."

22. At the annual meeting of the American Anti-Slavery Society, which met from Tuesday, May 7, to Friday, May 10.

23. This sentence was placed along the left edge of the page.

The Brooklyn Vital Records make no mention of the death of a Mrs. Robinson in 1839.

150

TO THE EXECUTIVE COMMITTEE OF THE AMERICAN ANTI-SLAVERY SOCIETY

BOSTON, May 13, 1839.

To the Executive Committee of the American Anti-Slavery Society.

BRETHREN, — At a full meeting of the Board of Managers of the Mass. A. S. Society, held this afternoon, it was unanimously

Resolved, That this Society will use its best endeavors to pay into the Treasury of the American Anti-slavery Society a sum not less than five thousand dollars, during the ensuing year; — with the understanding that all moneys paid into the said Treasury by inhabitants of this State during the year, shall be credited towards the redemption of this pledge.

It will be observed, that the sum contemplated to be raised is fixed at "not *less* than $5,000." Should nothing occur to disturb the arrangement, the Board are not without hope that a still larger amount may be raised in this State, during the time specified, for the use of the Ex. Com. of the Parent Society. One reason why the Board do not feel prepared to name more than $5,000 as the stipulated sum, is, that they have resolved to purchase the Anti-Slavery Depository of Mr. Knapp, at a large expense, and therefore desire to *promise* no more than they can calculate promptly to redeem. It is taken for granted, that no agent of the Parent Society will be commissioned to labor in this State, by the Executive Committee, without the concurrence of the Board of the State Society.

Yours in labors for the oppressed.

WM. LLOYD GARRISON.
Cor. Sec. of the Mass. A. S. Society.

Printed in *The Liberator*, May 31, 1839; also printed in the *Eighth Annual Report of the Board of Managers of the Massachusetts Anti-Slavery Society* (Boston, 1840).

151

TO HENRY C. WRIGHT

Boston, May 20, 1839.

My dear Brother:

For two or three days, Helen and myself have been perplexed to determine, whether to visit Newburyport or Providence this week, with our two boys. You know I have long promised you a visit — particularly after our approaching Convention; but, week after next, is the annual meeting of the New-Hampshire State Anti-Slavery Society, at Concord, and I am under obligations of long standing to be present. The week after that meeting, I am pledged to lecture in Abington. So, if I do not get to my native place this week, it is very uncertain when I shall be able to do so. But, as our babes are both afflicted with the whooping-cough, we have concluded to go to Providence on Wednesday morning, where we shall remain until Monday next. Should you come to Boston in the mean time, make our house your home, as Mrs. Benson and the girl will remain, and they will give you as plain fare as a Grahamite could desire. I hope to visit Newburyport some time this summer.

At a meeting of the Executive Committee of the N. R.[1] Society on Saturday, it was decided that we have a non-resistance social meeting on Tuesday and Wednesday mornings, next week, from 7 to 9 o'clock, and a public meeting on Thursday evening.

I have just received a letter from our beloved friend Wm. Bassett, of Lynn, in which he informs me that his dear little boy William died yesterday, of a lung fever, and is to be buried this afternoon. He wished to know if you were in Boston, and would like to have you and some of the Boston friends be present at the interment. I was so situated, that I could not conveniently go down, but wrote him a brief letter of condolence. I can sympathize with him as a friend and a father.

Mrs. Chapman[2] is preparing, for publication, in season for the Convention, "Right and Wrong in Massachusetts," shewing up the present state of things in the anti-slavery ranks. It will make a stir, I am thinking — but will do good, and will cut like a two-edged sword.

Lewis Tappan has written a very bad letter, in reply to a letter of our committee, inviting him to attend the N. E. Convention. He is in a sad state of mind.

Your letter,[3] respecting Birney, is received. I mean to reply to him next week.[4]

I have lost the name of your wife, to be appended to the Declaration of Sentiments. Ask her to write it again, and write yours over again, and let us have them by Thursday or Friday, WITHOUT FAIL.

My best regards to her and the family. Believe me,

Ever yours indissolubly,

Wm. Lloyd Garrison.

ALS: Garrison Papers, Boston Public Library.
1. Non-Resistance Society.
2. Maria Weston Chapman
3. Dated Boston, May 15, 1839, it was printed in *The Liberator*, May 31, 1839.
4. The original essay by Birney and Garrison's reply were printed in *The Liberator*, June 28, 1839.

152

TO NATHANIEL P. ROGERS

Boston, May 21, 1839.

My very dear Brother:

Though it will be very inconvenient for me to attend the annual meeting of your State Society,[1] yet I cannot find it in my heart again to disappoint you and some of my other New-Hampshire brethren. Therefore, I mean to be with you, Deo volente, on that interesting occasion. "I am no orator as Brutus is, but a plain, blunt man"[2] — not quite so wicked, or so hideous, I verily believe, as some take me to be; and if there be any thing good in me, be it much or little, it must be put down to the credit of another, in whose presence no flesh shall glory. Of speech-making, you must expect very little from me; though, as you desire it, I will give you one, perhaps two addresses before I leave Concord. It is very doubtful, whether I shall be able to bring a colored brother with me. Perhaps my amiable and talented friend C. L. Remond,[3] who is now lecturing in Maine, may be induced to accompany me. I regret that you will be deprived of the presence of Wendell Phillips, as he is to leave for England immediately after the close of our N. E. A. S. Convention.

My dear Rogers, do not fail to be with us next week, I pray you. The choicest spirits here desire to take you by the hand, and to commune with you, face to face, on matters appertaining to the prosperity of our sacred enterprise. Stay not at home, except from dire necessity. My bosom is swelling with emotions, and I want to disburden it in your presence. You have an eagle vision and a discerning spirit, and have apprehended something of the truth in regard to the mournful divisions which now exist in the anti-slavery ranks in Massachusetts; but, living at a distance, and not knowing what has been daily transpiring among us, you and other dear friends abroad have not had an opportunity to decide understandingly in regard to this painful controversy. The letters of bro. Phelps, St. Clair, Wise, Scott,[4] &c. in the Liberator, show indeed what spirit they are of, at the present time; still, you have but a faint idea, probably, of the state of their minds towards the Liberator, myself, and the Mass. A. S. Society. I forbear going into any particulars here, because I hope to see you in Boston shortly. As for bro. Stanton — him whom I have loved as a part of my own soul — he is now utterly estranged from me in spirit, and is an altered man. Never did I expect to see him joining hands with the worst enemies of the anti-slavery cause, in order to blacken the character and cripple the circulation of the Liberator; but so it is. "Thus saith the Lord, Cursed is he who trusteth in man, and maketh flesh his arm."[5]

Of what stuff can their abolitionism be made, who can be thrown into hysterics by the FREE discussion of the great and solemn question of Peace? What shall be said, what thought, of those abolitionists, who, because a brother avows it as his religious conviction, that it is the duty of men literally to obey the precepts, and to imitate the example of Jesus, in relation to the treatment of enemies, are determined to drive that brother from the anti-slavery platform, as one recreant to the cause of humanity?! What evidence do they give of faith in God, or confidence in the unconquerable principles of anti-slavery, who shriek out in tones of holy horror, that the cause of emancipation will be ruined, if all discussion of the question of Peace be not instantly suppressed? How do they prove their firm assurance of their own principles being sound, who refuse or are afraid to have those principles examined? Truly, dear brother, the behaviour of some of our abolition associates, in view of the non-resistance enterprise, is as ridiculous, proscriptive and cowardly, as that of the vilest opponents of the anti-slavery cause. And it deserves special notice, that non-resistants are more furiously assailed by professed abolitionists, than by any other class of men! "How has the gold become dim, and the most fine gold changed!"[6]

Rely upon it, my brother, this sudden reverence for the governments and kingdoms of this world — this flaming zeal for politics, now manifested by certain clerical gentlemen and others among us — is hollow and deceptive. It is that old sectarian devil transformed into an angel of light, with whom we have had to contend, in some shape or other, from the beginning. It does not originate in any superior regard for the cause of the dying slave, or any special love to God or man. It comforts me to know, that time will prove what is sincere and what hypocritical, and that all things are to be made manifest in the light.

I am accused of having dragged into the abolition cause, extraneous subjects, greatly to its injury; and of attempting to make non-resistance a part of abolitionism, &c. &c. The accusation is false, proceed from what quarter it may. I have not done, or attempted to do, any such thing, at any time, or in any place. They who falsely accuse me are the real transgressors. They have committed the robbery, and then, in order to escape detection, raised the cry of "Stop thief!" They make use of abolitionism, and in their abolition character, to crush the cause of peace, and to slander my character as a man and a christian, by accusing me (as the ancient Pharisees did the Saviour) of not keeping the sabbath-day, of being opposed to the modern priesthood, who teach for hire, and divine for money, &c. &c. But when or where, as an abolitionist, have I ever reproached any abolition brother, because he belonged to this or that party or sect? Who have I refused to take by the hand, that the slave may be delivered from his fetters, because he did not agree with me in my theological or political speculations? The Lord is my witness, and my conscience sustains me in the assertion, that I have proscribed no man, shunned no man, favored no man above another, on anti-slavery ground.

Mrs. Chapman has a work in press, "Right and Wrong in Massachusetts for 1838–9," which will place this whole controversy in a clear light. It will probably be got out in season for the Convention next week.

Phelps, St. Clair, Torrey, Wise, &c., I learn, intend to organize a new and hostile society next week, which will put down the women, — the Childes, the Chapmans, the Grimkes, and the Kellys,[7] — from any active participation in anti-slavery meetings, and make it an article of faith, that it is the religious duty (!) of every man to go to the polls. All that is pro-slavery in this Commonwealth is with them.

You have managed bro. Scott to the admiration of all tried, unswerving abolitionists.[8] For your many kind words in my defence when cruelly assailed, I thank you with a full heart. My best regards to your wife, Mr. Kent,[9] &c. Yours, lovingly,

Wm. Lloyd Garrison.

ALS: Haverford College Library, Pennsylvania.

Nathaniel Peabody Rogers (1794–1846) was a New Hampshire lawyer, abolitionist, poet, and editor. In 1838, he became editor of the *Herald of Freedom*, an antislavery newspaper that had been established by the New Hampshire Anti-Slavery Society in 1835. His later views on nonresistance and no-government, which led him to oppose all organization, brought him, ultimately, into conflict with the New Hampshire Anti-Slavery Society and a severing of his connection with the newspaper as well as with Garrison. A volume of his writings was published in Concord, in 1847, by John R. French, and was entitled *A Collection from the Newspaper Writings of Nathaniel Peabody Rogers.* (Ruchames, *The Abolitionists*, pp. 156–157.)

1. The New Hampshire Anti-Slavery Society.

2. Shakespeare, *Julius Caesar*, III, ii.

3. Charles Lenox Remond (1810–1873), a Negro abolitionist of Massachusetts, has been referred to by the Negro historian Carter G. Woodson as "the ablest representative of the Negro race" prior to the appearance of Frederick Douglass. An agent of the American Anti-Slavery Society for many years, he was a Garrisonian throughout the history of the antislavery movement. After attending the London World's Anti-Slavery Conference in 1840, he remained abroad for two years, lecturing with great effectiveness in Great Britain and Ireland. Returning to Massachusetts, he played a noteworthy part in the campaign against Jim Crow railroads in Massachusetts in 1842 and 1843 and resumed his efforts in the antislavery movement. (Ruchames, *The Abolitionists*, p. 179.)

4. *The Liberator*, May 3, 1839, printed a letter from Phelps, dated Boston, April 29, 1839, in which he submitted his resignation from the Board of Managers of the Massachusetts Anti-Slavery Society and his office as Recording Secretary of the society. The letter included an attack upon the policies of the society.

St. Clair's letters were published in *The Liberator* January 25 and February 8, 1839.

Daniel Wise's letter appeared in *The Liberator*, April 26, 1839.

Orange Scott's letter was printed in *The Liberator*, April 19, 1839.

5. Jeremiah 17:5.

6. Lamentations 4:1.

7. Lydia M. Child, Maria W. Chapman, Angelina and Sarah Grimké, and Abby Kelley.

8. On April 26, 1839, *The Liberator* printed an essay entitled "Orange Scott," with the explanation that "the following is the reply of the editor of the *Herald of Freedom* to the communication of Orange Scott, published in this department last week." Nathaniel P. Rogers was then, of course, the editor of the *Herald of Freedom.* An earlier attack by Scott upon Garrison had appeared in *The Liberator* of April 5, 1839, under the heading of "J. G. Birney — Politics — No Human Government."

9. George Kent (b. May 4, 1796; fl. 1856), of New Hampshire, a graduate of Dartmouth College (1814), was admitted to the practice of law in 1817 and represented Concord in the state legislature. He was an editor and proprietor of the *New Hampshire Statesman and Concord Register*, a trustee of Dartmouth College until 1840, and a founder of the New Hampshire Anti-Slavery Society at Concord in 1834. He was host to George Thompson in 1835 when the latter was mobbed in Concord. They fled and hid in the woods together. Kent wrote poems on various occasions and was a founder of the New Hampshire Historical Society in 1823. He was later consul of the United States to Spain. (Nathaniel Bouton, *The History of Concord*, Concord, 1856, pp. 637, 731.)

153

TO THE EDITOR OF THE EMANCIPATOR

[May 31, 1839.]

DEAR SIR, — In the Emancipator of the 2d inst., appeared an elaborate essay from the pen of JAMES G. BIRNEY, giving *his* 'View of the

Constitution of the American Anti-Slavery Society, as connected with the NO-GOVERNMENT question.' [1] I read that essay with grief and amazement, and intended to make an immediate reply to it; but various engagements have prevented the completion of my design up to the present hour. This rejoinder, however, will not come at an unsuitable period.

MR. BIRNEY'S POSITIONS.

I will first briefly recapitulate the leading positions assumed by Mr. Birney, in his extraordinary exposition of the Anti-Slavery Constitution. He declares —

1. That, by the terms of the Constitution — its letter and spirit — every person who subscribes to it, and joins the Society, is under a religious obligation to go to the polls, and use the elective franchise for the abolition of slavery.

2. That, consequently, those members of the Society, who, from conscientious scruples, refrain from voting at all, on any question, 'have ceased to consent to one of the principles of the Constitution, and are virtually no longer entitled to membership.'

3. That it is the duty of all such to withdraw from the Society, on the ground of 'justice,' 'integrity,' and 'self-respect.'

4. That it must be 'productive of endless dissentions' for them to remain in the Society.

5. That they have attempted 'to compel' the great body of abolitionists 'into a crusade for abolishing government,' and have tied to the 'magnificent cause' of the slave 'a project that is hopeless, because cast out by the common sense of the nations of the world.'

6. That they are, virtually, apostates from the anti-slavery enterprise — pretenders, whose professions and practices are utterly at variance — intruders into a Society, from which, indeed, there is no power to expel them, but which they no longer sustain — heretics, who have departed from the faith once delivered to abolitionists.

7. That, in his opinion, their doctrines 'strike at the root of the social structure, and tend to throw society into entire confusion, and to renew, under the sanction of religion, scenes of anarchy and license, that have generally heretofore been the offspring of the rankest infidelity and irreligion.'

8. That, while others are 'for sustaining and purifying governments, and bringing them to a perfect conformity with the principles of the Divine government, they are for destroying *all* government.'

9. That their theory 'is but a new growth of one of the *fungi*, which sprung up in the early period of the Reformation — which soon led to the most horrible excesses — which ran its career through such scenes

of lust and blood, that Humanity could not but rejoice at its extinction.'

As an abolitionist — a member of the National Anti-Slavery Convention in 1833 — a signer of the Declaration of Sentiments — a framer, member, and manager of the Parent Society — I positively affirm, and shall undertake to prove, that the first six of the above specifications are utterly groundless.

As an advocate of 'peace on earth, and good will among men' — a supporter of government — a disciple of Christ — I as emphatically declare, that the remaining allegations are truthless, slanderous, cruel — caricatures of the pacific precepts of the gospel — phantasms of a disordered imagination — satires upon the obligations of Christianity — libels upon the character and conduct of the Prince of Peace — unsupported by any show of reasoning, any appeal to the scriptures, any presentation of evidence.

The motives which led to the publication of an essay so warily timed, so pregnant with sophistry, so crowded with misrepresentation, I leave to be judged of by the Omniscient. I am willing to believe that they were as honest and sincere, as were those which actuated Saul of Tarsus, when he became exceeding mad against the saints, and persecuted them even unto strange cities — all the while verily believing that he was doing God service. The paper was evidently drawn up with more than ordinary care, with critical exactness and cool deliberation, with legal ingenuity and skill. It admits of no apology, therefore, on the score of haste, but is to be regarded as a fair transcript of the mind of Mr. Birney, respecting the Constitution of the Anti-Slavery Society, and the principles of those who are restrained, by their religious convictions, from going to the polls.

PROTEST.

Before examining Mr. Birney's remarkable 'View,' allow me to protest, in my abolition character, against its introduction into the columns of the Emancipator, especially without a single editorial comment, as a prostitution of the official organ of the Parent Society to party purposes — as a violation of the spirit of our anti-slavery compact — as a 'thrusting in' of a topic on forbidden ground, the discussion of which is deprecated, by the writer himself, as being extremely hurtful to the abolition cause. It is as much out of place in the Emancipator, as would be an essay in favor of infant sprinkling, or the claims of the 'holy mother church.' It is a bold attack upon the pacific views entertained by a portion of the abolitionists, respecting allegiance to the will of man, the right to punish enemies, and the divine authority of government — an attack made by one dressed in the armor of an abolitionist, on the abolition platform, against abolitionists as such. If this attack be allowable, so must be a defence: hence, it opens the whole question of non-resistance, (so much dreaded by many,) for discussion and settlement in the organ of the American Anti-Slavery Society!

I enter my protest against the publication of this 'View,' at a time and under circumstances when it was calculated to mislead many honest minds, and to produce a bad impression upon the late meeting of the Parent Society, which could not be effaced by a seasonable rejoinder. I confess, it does appear to me, that nothing could be more unfair or improper than to take advantage of the last number of the Emancipator issued previous to the annual meeting, to publish such an article. Its *apparent* design was, so to mislead the judgment and obscure the vision of the delegates, as to secure the adoption of resolutions, condemnatory of non-resisting abolitionists, and in support of Mr. Birney's construction of the Constitution.

I also enter my protest against Mr. Birney's use of an epithet to denote the principles of the non-resistants, which we discard as libellous, and which has been applied to us by our enemies. It is certainly very unfair to resort to the vocabulary of our revilers, for a name by which to describe us. He calls us a 'no-government' party. He might as honestly style us a banditti. Mr. Birney is called, by the pro-slavery party, 'a fanatic,' 'a madman,' and 'an incendiary.' Would it be ingenuous to apply these epithets to him, as truly descriptive of his character? Why, then, is he so unjust as to fasten upon us a name which was coined in the mint of slander, and is circulated by the hand of falsehood? Does he venture to make, in support of his charge, a single quotation from any of our publications, official or unofficial? No — not a paragraph, not a sentence, not a word. We deny the accusation. We religiously hold to government — a strong, a righteous, a perfect government — a government which is indestructible, which is of heaven, not of men, which tolerates no evil, which is administered by an infallible Judge, an impartial Lawgiver, the King of kings, and Lord of lords. How monstrous, then, the representation, that we are 'for destroying *all* government'!! But more, on this point, in its proper connexion.

THE POLITICAL ARGUMENT.

I proceed to show, that the premises laid down by Mr. Birney, in respect to the political duties enjoined by the Anti-Slavery Constitution, are unsound; and, therefore, that his conclusions are all false.

The clause in the Constitution, upon which Mr. Birney relies to sustain his position, is that which declares, that 'the Society will endeavor, in a constitutional way, to *influence* Congress to put an end to the domestic slave trade,' &c. Commenting upon this language, he says — 'It is not unworthy of remark, that whilst our fellow-citizens, generally, were to be *addressed*, Congress were to be *influenced*.' This philological distinction he seems to think so important, as to settle the question respecting the duty of every member of the Society to use the elective franchise!

Is it possible that Mr. Birney ventures to erect his political super-structure upon so slender a foundation? Why, a mere *grain* of logic will be ponderous enough to dash it to the earth! 'Congress were to be *influenced*' — very good! My reply, then, to his labored argument, occupying more than two columns, shall be compressed into a short syllogism:

To 'endeavor to influence Congress' is required by the Anti-Slavery Constitution.

But Congress can be influenced, independent of political action at the polls.

Therefore, such action is not required by the Constitution.

The first proposition needs no proof, being admitted.

The second is thus shown to be true:

Congress can be influenced by petitions, remonstrances, facts and arguments.

But these are wholly distinct from political action at the polls.

Therefore, Congress can be influenced, independent of such action.

The third follows from the other two. And hence, to arraign any man in the anti-slavery ranks, for refraining from going to the polls on account of religious scruples, or to assume that those who belong to the Anti-Slavery Society are bound to use the elective franchise, is to enforce a test of membership not required by the Constitution.

Again:

Abolitionists, by belonging to the Anti-Slavery Society, are pledged only to what is required in the Constitution.

The use of the elective franchise is not so required.

Therefore, they are not pledged, individually or collectively, to use the elective franchise.

Again:

Congress can be influenced, though it cannot be created, without a resort to the ballot-box.

But abolitionists are bound by their Constitution to influence, not to create or assist in creating Congress.

Therefore, they are not bound to resort to the ballot-box.

Again:

It is only to *creation*, but not to the exercise of an *influence*, that power is necessary.

But the Anti-Slavery Society is pledged 'to endeavor to *influence*,' not to *create*.

Therefore, the possession and exercise of the *creative power* are not requisite to membership in that Society.

Reasoning from Mr. Birney's own premises, I ask of every candid person, whether each of these syllogisms is not strictly legitimate and conclusive? 'Congress were to be influenced,' he says. Granted! But, I repeat — to *influence* AN EXISTING BODY, is one thing: to be a participant in *creating* SUCH A BODY, is another and a very different thing. Power is essential to creation; but the feeblest soul in the universe may 'influence' the most powerful body. 'God hath chosen the foolish things of the world, to confound the wise; and God hath chosen the weak things of the world to confound the things which are mighty; and base things of the world, and things which are despised, hath God chosen — yea, and things which are not, to bring to nought things that are; that no flesh should glory in his presence.' [2] The importunity of the poor widow could induce even the unjust judge, who neither feared God nor regarded man, to grant her petition. I may endeavor to influence His Holiness, the Pope, no longer to grant sinful indulgences; but I am under no obligations to endorse the rightfulness of his authority, or to assist in electing him to office. I may supplicate a military chieftain not to devastate a certain village; but this would not be sanctioning his murderous vocation. Mr. Birney concedes that 'the [nicknamed] no-government abolitionists do not object to petitioning Congress.' Then they exactly and fully comply with the terms of the Anti-Slavery Constitution! For what are the thousands of petitions annually presented to that body, but to 'influence' it to cease upholding slavery in the District of Columbia? Is it not surprising, therefore, — nay, is it not presumptuous in my brother, — that he should urge upon those who are thus faithful in discharging their anti-slavery obligations, to 'retire from the Society,' as persons disqualified from being members of it?

MORAL ACTION.

Mr. Birney also concedes, that 'ALL the action required by the Constitution is MORAL.' But moral action is a duty enjoined upon all men by the great Lawgiver, to be employed at all times, and under all circumstances; and there is no difference of opinion among abolitionists, as to the propriety and necessity of using it for the overthrow of slavery. Political action, or the use of the elective franchise, is a privilege granted, in this country, by a majority of the people — purchased with money, or obtained by a term of residence, or by naturalization — sometimes conceded to the many, sometimes monopolized by the few

— and treated, on all hands, throughout the civilized world, as something entirely distinct from obedience to God; so that, in determining
a man's character, it is never asked, 'Does he believe in the duty of
political action?' any more than an enquiry is made as to his comparative height or bulk. It is *not* dependant upon the will of man, whether
I may love the Lord my God with all my heart, and my neighbor as
myself; but it *is*, whether I may be an elector. If, then, as Mr. Birney
truly affirms, '*all* the action required by the Constitution is *moral*,' it
is a complete refutation of his political doctrines; — he has signally
answered his own reasoning. 'What God hath joined together, let not
man put asunder;' [3] but what *man* attempts to impose upon the conscience and the understanding, let it ever be resisted in a spirit worthy
of a freeman of the Lord.

THE ANTI-SLAVERY CONSTITUTION.

In this controversy, I adhere strictly to the Constitution of the
Parent Society, because it is a question affecting the right of membership, of loyalty to the cause of the slave, of rectitude of conduct, that
is under consideration; because it matters not what is contained in
other anti-slavery documents, or what may have been published on
individual responsibility; and because Mr. Birney declares that, by
the requirements of the Constitution, I am no longer — nor are such
brethren as Samuel J. May, Isaac Winslow, Orson S. Murray, Effingham L. Capron, George W. Benson, (all signers of the Anti-Slavery
Declaration with myself,) Henry C. Wright, Amos Dresser, Edmund
Quincy, &c. &c. — entitled to a place upon the abolition platform! I
throw Mr. Birney's argument into the following shape:

The Constitution requires of those who subscribe to it, the exercise
of the elective franchise:

Those who are disqualified by law, or through conscientious scruples,
from voting at the polls, are not entitled to be members:

But women, minors, aliens, Covenanters, Non-Resistants, many of
the Society of Friends, some of the signers of the Anti-Slavery Declaration of Sentiments, and also of the framers of the American A. S. Constitution, and other persons, are thus disqualified:

Therefore, all such persons, if now members of the Parent Society,
are required by 'justice to those with whom they are associated, and
to the slave,' and also by their 'integrity' and 'self-respect,' to withdraw
from the Society; and thus 'relieve the abolition cause from an incubus, that has so mightily oppressed it'!!

In other words, the American Anti-Slavery Society ought and was
designed to be, a thoroughly POLITICAL ORGANIZATION!

I think I do no injustice to the sentiments of Mr. Birney. If he does

470

not mean all this, he has written to no purpose. Ever since I began my labors in the anti-slavery cause, I have rejoiced in believing, that all persons who hold and inculcate the doctrine, that slaveholding is under all circumstances a crime against God and man, and ought to be immediately abandoned, — of whatever party or denomination, tribe or nation, complexion or sex, — might be members of the Anti-Slavery Society; but, it seems, I have been cherishing a delusion, if Mr. B's 'View' be correct. Who, now, has been guilty of 'straining and distorting the principles of the organization, so as to make them applicable to cases, to which all concerned know they were never intended to apply,' if it be not himself? It is marvellous, truly, after passing wholesale condemnation upon myself, and some of the choicest abolition spirits in the land, and 'logically' (?) proving that for us any longer to remain in the Society would be *contra bonos mores*, — evincive of a lack of integrity, self-respect, and a sense of justice to those with whom we are now improperly associated, — he should acknowledge that

'The American Society have no *Board of Inspection* appointed to scrutinize the qualification of persons proposing themselves for membership. They publish their constitution — submit it to all — leaving it to the integrity of every one to decide for himself, whether he possesses the qualifications it requires, or not.'

So I have always thought; and therefore I marvel the more, that my friend should resolve himself into such a 'Board of Inspection,' and venture to occupy ground which the Parent Society has never felt authorized to assume!

NON-RESISTANTS WILL NOT LEAVE THE SOCIETY!

But what is to be done? Pass ten thousand resolutions in anti-slavery meetings, that political action is a religious duty, and still they would all avail nothing — so long as Mordecai the Jew is seen sitting at the king's gate. 'These sectaries,' the 'no-government' abolitionists, 'insist that their views are altogether harmonious with what is required for membership by the constitution,' — and 'it is presumed that every one *honestly* considers himself qualified for membership at the time of uniting,' and just so long as he consents to remain in the society. Hence, not one of them is disposed to withdraw from the present anti-slavery organization; for they appreciate it too highly to make a disturbance, and secede, merely because their brethren entertain different views of the gospel of peace from their own. They believe that 'both the no-government and the government men can act under the constitution, according to the dictates of their consciences respectively.' 'But is this really so?' Mr. Birney asks, with an air of incredulity. I answer — *it is really so*: so it has been for years, and so it may be till the jubilee come, if we truly 'remember them that are in bonds as bound with them,'[4] and do not attempt to make our individual views of religion or politics — of the Church or the State — the standard by which to measure the whole body. We are all perfectly agreed as to the sin of slaveholding, the duty of immediate emancipation, and the obligation which every abolitionist virtually takes to *carry out his principles* wherever he can act conscientiously, whether in the church or out of it, at the ballot-box or elsewhere. Why, then, in the name of humanity and of brotherly love, should we fall out by the way, and insist upon a separation, because we are not all united in opinion on political or theological points? Before I can be guilty of such unnatural conduct, I am sure that my right hand will forget its cunning, and my tongue cleave to the roof of my mouth.[5] In the sacred cause of emancipation, I have known no man after the flesh, and been no respecter of persons, of creeds, or sects, or parties. I have given the right hand of fellowship to all who believe in the duty of immediately letting my fettered countrymen go free, and have refused to associate with none on account of a disagreement of views on other subjects. But how coldly, how invidiously, how like an abhorred Samaritan, have I been treated by many in the anti-slavery ranks, on account of my religious opinions!

ON TRIAL AS ABOLITIONISTS.

Commenting on the fact, that 'the no-government (!) abolitionists do not object to petitioning Congress,' Mr. Birney remarks, in a strain of sarcasm — 'So far, so good. If this seems an absurdity to others, it may not to them. They may have some method of accommodating their principles to such a proceeding, of which others are ignorant. . . It is nothing more than what often happens to good men who embrace absurd dogmas, to which their practical humanity and common sense cannot be brought entirely to submit.' I dismiss this fling by saying, that, allowing it to be merited — what then? True, it may serve to convict non-resisting abolitionists of glaring inconsistency, as *non-resistants*; but it as conclusively shows that, *as abolitionists*, they faithfully abide by the A. S. Constitution, in thus endeavoring to 'influence Congress.' And it must be kept in mind, that they are now on trial AS ABOLITIONISTS, not AS NON-RESISTANTS.

POLITICAL INCONSISTENCY.

Consistency is said to be a jewel. Mr. Birney gives us a rare specimen of it, on the part of the 'pro-government abolitionists.' He tells us in one breath, that, from the moment they endorsed the A. S. Constitution, they were as sacredly bound to use their elective franchise for the benefit of the slave, as to inculcate the duty of immediate emancipation. In the next breath, he makes the astonishing confession — 'For SEVERAL YEARS after the organization of the American Society, our numbers were *too few* to attempt political action [i.e. too few to perform an imperative duty!] It was, therefore, *generally* DEPRECATED AS INEXPEDIENT.' How many abolitionists are necessary to make political action a duty, we are not told. It is, certainly, a novel criterion, by which to determine the guilt or innocence of a body of men, pledged to do a certain act, the performance of which, for a series of years, they deprecate as inexpedient! I thought it was the creed of a genuine abolitionist to do right *now*, let who will delay. But, according to Mr. Birney, these 'pro-government abolitionists' have for a long time 'stepped out of the cause, into the work of producing an abstract religion, a sort of quintessence of humanity, which *they bottle up as they go along*, to be used WHEN there is *enough of it to flood the land*.' * If, then, the 'no-government abolitionists' have acted inconsistently *in petitioning Congress*, what shall be said of the conduct of our 'pro-government' brethren, in neglecting for years to vote at the polls against slavery?

THE TRUE ABOLITION PLATFORM.

The ballot-box is the final abolition argument, says Mr. Birney. 'THE BALLOT-BOX IS NOT AN ABOLITION ARGUMENT' † says Elizur Wright, Jr. The witnesses are both 'pro-government' men, and yet they do not agree in this matter.

Again:

'Abolitionists have but one work: it is *not to put any body into office, or out of it*, but TO SET RIGHT THOSE WHO MAKE OFFICERS. It is not an action *upon Church or State*, but UPON THE MATERIALS OF BOTH. Success will certainly develope itself, both through those who make human laws, and those who interpret the divine. But it would seem the natural order, that it should show itself first through the latter. The interpreters of divine law are, in fact, the chief sinners. They have given license, *ad libitum*, to man-stealing; and it cannot be expected that the statutes of a State should be better than its religion.' ‡

Again:

'The great end at which we aim is, to subvert the relation of master

---

* Fourth Annual Report of the Parent Society.

† Quarterly A. S. Magazine for January, 1837.

‡ Idem.

and slave — *not by machinery*, POLITICAL OR ECCLESIASTICAL, but by establishing in the hearts of men a deep and wide-spreading conviction of *the brotherhood of the human race*; that God hath indeed made of one blood all nations of men for to dwell on all the face of the earth; that all men who mean to obey the divine appointment, and honestly get their bread by their labor, have a common interest in sustaining the principle, that the laborer is worthy of his hire.' §

This is a correct representation of the ground-work of abolitionism. The Anti-Slavery Society is not an organization to determine the question, whether Church or State, as now constituted, is, *per se*, right or wrong — but, simply, to 'influence' both, by 'the foolishness of preaching' the doctrine, that slaveholding is man-stealing. Its *principles* are immutable, and purely religious; its *measures*, 'such only as the opposition of moral purity to moral corruption — the destruction of error by the potency of truth — the overthrow of prejudice by the power of love — and the abolition of slavery by the spirit of repentance.' ‖

THE CHURCH AS WELL AS THE STATE TO BE PURIFIED.

It is as truly a part of its mission to purify the Church, as it is to reform the State; but not to arraign either as based upon a wrong foundation, nor to sanction either as inherently good or absolutely indispensable. As to the utility of sectarian organizations, or what constitutes the church of Christ, its members are not agreed; neither do they see eye to eye as to the proper elements of civil government. Who is so blind as not to perceive, that if such 'questions of doubtful disputation' had been brought forward in the National Anti-Slavery Convention, in 1833, for discussion and settlement, no Declaration of Sentiments could have been put forth to the world, no Anti-Slavery Society organized, on that occasion? Individual abolitionists may or may not adopt a creed, or take an oath of allegiance, and yet be faithful members of the Parent Society; but, surely, it does not come within the scope of THE SOCIETY, *or its organ*, to defend the Church, or to uphold the State, in a partisan character. This, I think, is too clear to need an additional argument. I write for the satisfaction of honest minds, not to silence hairsplitting cavillers. When, therefore, it is officially declared, that 'there are, at the present time, the highest obligations resting upon the people of the free States, to remove slavery by moral and political action, as prescribed in the Constitution of the

§ Fourth Ann. Report of the Parent Society.
‖ Declaration of the Anti-Slavery Sentiments.

United States,' ¶ and that 'the Society will endeavor, in a constitutional way, to *influence* Congress,' ** language is not used arbitrarily or dogmatically, so as to interfere with the rights of conscience, but *in a popular sense* — implying, merely, that as slavery has found a refuge in the hall of legislation as well as the temple of religion, and is sustained by the laws of the land as well as by the practices of the church, it is the grand object of the Anti-Slavery Society so to affect public sentiment, and touch the issues of religious and political action, and alter the views and feelings of the people in regard to the crime of slaveholding, that all classes of society, churchmen and politicians, law-makers and law-executioners, those who can use the elective franchise, and those who cannot, may be induced to rally together, *en masse*, for the entire abolition of slavery, whatever else that is unsound in opinion, or corrupt in practice, they may be disposed to cherish or tolerate. Seen in this clear light, how victorious are the principles, how rational the measures, how harmonious the elements of the anti-slavery association! But, contemplated in Mr. Birney's 'View,' it is a house divided against itself, the occupants of which are engaged in personal conflicts with each other, instead of defending themselves and their cause from the fierce attacks of a besieging enemy! Which course do policy, reason, justice, union, self-preservation, dictate as the true one to be pursued? Which construction of the constitution is more consonant with true charity, sound argument, and individual liberty of conscience?

AN ABSURDITY.

In reply to the statement, that many good men, some of the earliest abolitionists in the field, have been united with the American Society from its organization, and yet remain members, who are, in principle, opposed to using the elective franchise on any occasion, he says —

'The conclusion from these premises, to which the new constructionists (!) come, is, that the constitution is *consistent* with this state of things. But, if it prove any thing logically, it is, that if sectaries be not expelled from an institution, and are content themselves to remain in it, that, therefore, the rules of the institution consist with their heresy: which is absurd.'

The real, the palpable, the monstrous absurdity of the thing is, in assuming (as Mr. Birney does) that such men as SAMUEL J. MAY and ISAAC WINSLOW would deliberately sign a Declaration, and assist in framing a Constitution, by which they solemnly pledged

¶ Idem.
** Constitution of the Parent Society.

themselves to do an act which they did not mean to perform, and could not in conscience — thus proving themselves to be hypocrites, or dullards, too ignorant to understand the meaning of language! And it is particularly ridiculous, — a specimen of folly closely allied to cool effrontery, — to address them reproachfully as 'Sectaries;' to censure them for not having separated themselves from the American Society; to remind them, that, if they are not expelled, it is because their presence is tolerated by sufferance: to insinuate that they are dishonest, devoid of 'common sense,' lost to 'self-respect,' and neglectful of 'duty,' to remain in the Society; to represent them as 'an incubus' upon the anti-slavery enterprise; to accuse them of aiming to 'destroy *all* government' — and holding doctrines which 'tend to throw society into entire confusion, and to renew, under the sanction of religion, scenes of anarchy and license'!!!

AN IMPORTANT DISTINCTION.

I am quoted, by Mr. Birney, as 'having set the example of voting for a professed abolitionist, and encouraging others to do the same.' As to this citation — *cui bono*? [6] I humbly conceive, that it concerns no man, or body of men, to know how many or how few times I have voted since the adoption of the A. S. Constitution; or whether I have, or have not, changed my views of politics within a few years. What *I* may have said and done, and what the *Constitution* enjoins, are wholly distinct questions. I deny to no individual abolitionist the right to inculcate the doctrine, that it is the religious duty of every man to go to the polls; but when he assumes that the Constitution of the Parent Society maintains that doctrine, and aims to get it endorsed by the Society, as such, in the hope that he shall thus be able to create a schism in the abolition ranks, I pronounce him a disorganizing spirit, however pathetically he may talk about breaking the chains of 'the poor slaves,' or of his fears that they will be left to perish, unless he can succeed in making others swallow his political dogmas. It is quite remarkable, that some of those who have been foremost in protesting against being reckoned my followers — who have been loudest in their boasts, that they follow no man — who have been unwilling that I should be regarded as the mouth-piece of the Anti-Slavery Society, in any sense — who have repelled the slightest intimation from the enemies of abolition, that the Society is responsible for the sayings and doings of the Liberator — I say, it is quite remarkable, that, all at once, in the eyes of those persons, I have become an official organ, an unerring oracle, the Magnus Apollo of the whole land, whose speech and example are to be followed implicitly — because they have ascertained that, since the year 1833, I have actually voted *once* at the polls!

They shall not make me vain. I perceive the design of this incense-offering — to cast me off from the anti-slavery cause, (paradoxical as the statement may seem,) in order to secure 'the co-operation of the ☞ GREAT MASS OF THE INTELLIGENT MIND [i.e. the aristocracy, the rabbies and scribes] of the nation.' I am not willing to be made a tool for their convenience — to be crowned this hour, that I may be deposed the next! for it is not true, that the Liberator has ever been the official journal of any society or body of men, or that any other person, besides its editor, is responsible either for the religious or political sentiments contained in its columns.

A FALSE ACCUSATION.

'What can be more unjust,' Mr. Birney asks, 'to those who originally associated for the reasonable and single purpose of abolishing slavery, than the attempt to compel them into a crusade for abolishing government? What more unjust to the suffering slave, than to tie on to his magnificent cause a project that is hopeless, because cast out by the common sense (!) of the nations of the world?' To these interrogations I answer — that, whoever charges me, or any of my brethren of the Non-Resistance Society, with having at any time introduced our peculiar views of government into the meetings of abolitionists, or attempted to make use of the Anti-Slavery Society to give them currency, bears false witness. The charge is utterly untrue. Our accusers are the real transgressors. They have not scrupled, as abolitionists, in the official organs of the anti-slavery cause, in the capacity of abolition lecturers, in the meetings of abolition societies, to make war upon the pacific views of a portion of their brethren — views which these brethren carefully avoided promulgating as connected with the objects of the A. S. Society. Among those who have thus unfairly made use of their abolition standing and influence, in an official manner, to carry on their belligerous crusade against the friends of non-resistance, James G. Birney, Henry B. Stanton, Elizur Wright, jr., Amos A. Phelps, and Orange Scott, may be included. I never expected to receive such treatment from these brethren: — their conduct fills me with surprise and grief. To accuse me, and those who agree with me in respect to political action, with designing and striving to 'tie on' to the abolition cause THAT OF NON-RESISTANCE, so that the latter may obtain an adventitious support, is plainly to declare us devoid of all honesty, and to represent us as false and treacherous men. If we have indeed fallen so low in the estimation of our 'pro-government' associates, then not only should they desire no longer to be with us in the anti-slavery organization, but they should shun our company on ordinary occasions. If what they allege against us be true, then we are as unprincipled as the slaveholders are oppressive. But we deny the allegation, and demand the proof. We are very certain that we are 'more sinned against than sinning.' [7] As men, as citizens, as Christians, we confess that we have advocated the heaven-originated cause of Non-Resistance, and shall continue to do so, until we are convicted of error; *but not as abolitionists.* 'The head and front of our offending hath this extent — no more.' [8]

THE NON-RESISTANCE THEORY EMBODIED IN THE ANTI-SLAVERY CONSTITUTION AND DECLARATION OF SENTIMENTS.

Mr. Birney sums up his accusations against us as follows:

'They carry out, to the full extent, the non-resistance theory. To the first ruffian who would demand our purse, or oust us from our houses, they are to be unconditionally surrendered, unless *moral suasion* be found sufficient to induce him to decline from his purpose. Our wives, our daughters, our sisters, our mothers, we are to see set upon by the most brutal, without any effort, on our part, except argument, to defend them; and even they, themselves, are forbidden to use, in defence of their purity, such powers as God has endowed them with for its protection, if resistance should be attended with injury or destruction to the assailant.'

I shall not attempt to vindicate the principles of Non-Resistance, in this already too protracted reply. What I wish to remark is, that all that Mr. Birney alleges against us, in the paragraph just quoted, he and the great body of abolitionists have repeatedly enjoined upon the slave population of this country — i.e. *in no case to resist evil.* The solemn and affecting language of the Anti-Slavery Declaration of Sentiments, (which, according to Mr. Birney, 'although possessing no *obligatory* force, is the highest evidence that can be had, apart from the Constitution, of what was intended by the *body* of abolitionists in that instrument,') is to this effect:

'*Their* [our revolutionary fathers'] principles led them to wage war against their opponents, and to spill human blood like water, in order to be free. *Ours* FORBID THE DOING OF EVIL THAT GOOD MAY COME, and lead *us* to reject, and to entreat the *oppressed* to reject, the use of *all carnal weapons* for deliverance from bondage — relying *solely* upon those which are *spiritual*, and mighty through God to the pulling down of strong holds.'

Here is strong and emphatic condemnation of the conduct of those who achieved the independence of this country, in forcibly resisting their oppressors; here is a solemn declaration, that, such are the 'PRINCIPLES' of the signers of that instrument, they cannot defend themselves by a resort to physical force, in any case; and here the slaves are entreated to see their 'wives, daughters, sisters, mothers,' set upon by the most brutal, without any effort, on their part, to defend them, except by 'moral suasion' — and to unconditionally surrender themselves to the first slaveholding ruffian, who may be disposed to plunder them — because they may not do evil, that good may come — i.e. may not seek to deliver themselves, from the most horrible fate, by the use of 'such powers as God has endowed them with for their protection, if resistance should be attended with injury or destruction to the assailants'!! The cases are precisely analogous. Now, is it not one article in the creed of abolitionists, that the rights of a black man are equal to those of a white one — and that what may be justified in one, may be done by the other, under similar circumstances? Here, then, are the doctrines of non-resistance in a nut-shell!

Again: The last clause of the second article of the Constitution of the American Anti-Slavery Society is in these words:

'But this Society will *never*, IN ANY WAY, countenance the oppressed in vindicating their rights by a resort to physical force.'

This is tantamount to what is laid down as *a moral duty* in the DECLARATION. It is non-resistance to the most brutal tyrants that ever preyed upon the human race. Yet some of the very men, who have subscribed to that Constitution, are the most violent in their detestation of the non-resistance doctrines, and say that they 'hate them with a perfect hatred'!! Yes, those who have solemnly promised, before heaven and earth, that they will 'NEVER, *in any way*, countenance the oppressed in vindicating their rights by a resort to physical force,' now scout the doctrine of passive submission as most absurd and wicked, and are full of the spirit of war! '*Never* countenance' — it is not, therefore, because it would be *inexpedient* to do so, to-day, next week, or peradventure next year — but because it would be *always* contrary to the will of God, to the spirit of the Gospel, and the example of Christ! 'Whatsoever ye would that men should do to you, do ye even so to them' [9] — *negroes though they be.* 'Never, IN ANY WAY, countenance the oppressed' — mark that! How can Messrs. Birney, Phelps, Scott, &c. more directly encourage the slaves to rise against their masters, than by avowing, as they do, that self-defence against brutal assailants, by the use of carnal weapons — clubs, swords and pistols — is not only right, but a sacred duty? Non-resistants are the only persons in the land, and especially in the anti-slavery organization, who do not, 'in any way,' either in theory or practice, by precept or example, 'countenance the oppressed in vindicating their rights by a resort to physical force!' Yet, because they follow the letter and spirit of the anti-slavery constitution, in this particular, they are compared to the bloody-minded Anabaptists, and represented as being disqualified to act as members of the Parent Society!

INCONSISTENCY OF ABOLITIONISTS.

If it be said, in reply, that those who endorsed the pacific views of the Declaration of Sentiments and A. S. Constitution, did not mean to be understood as sanctioning the principles of non-resistance, as applied to all classes and descriptions of men, I answer —

1. Whatever they may have meant, it is certain that a fair interpretation of their language commits them in favor of the doctrine of universal non-resistance, as a religious duty, binding upon every individual suffering unjustly, whether white or black.

2. If they do not mean what their language obviously implies, why do they not alter the phraseology of the Constitution?

3. It is certain that to reject the use of all carnal weapons, even in cases of extreme peril and suffering, and to rely solely upon those which are spiritual, for succor and deliverance, is to declare ourselves non resistants in principle.

4. Up to the hour that Lovejoy fell, abolitionists made high pretensions to the character of 'ultra peace men' — they did not resist evil — they took up no weapons in self-defence but those of prayer, and the sword of the spirit, though cruelly treated by their enemies; and how united, invincible, victorious, they were at every onset! How, in their weakness, the omnipotence of God was made manifest, to the utter discomfiture of the enemies of emancipation! Since that time, so radical has been the change effected in the views and feelings of abolitionists, on this subject, that the following resolution, (drawn up by John G. Whittier) was rejected at the annual meeting of the Parent Society in 1838, by a vote of 19 in the affirmative, and 44 in the negative!!

'Resolved, That we earnestly desire, that the agents and members of this Society, while engaged in advocating the pure and *pacific* principles of emancipation, may continue patient under their manifold provocations, forgiving their enemies, not relying upon physical strength for their defence against the violence of others; but, by their patient endurance of evil, evince the spirit of their Master, whose mission was one of 'peace on earth, and good will to men.'

It was a body of 'ultra peace men,' who could vote down that harmless resolution! Alas! 'how has the gold become dim, and the most fine gold changed!' [10]

Let me not be misunderstood. I do not mean to affirm, that either the signers of the Declaration, or the members of the Parent Society, really intended, at any time, to take the ground now occupied by those who are technically called 'non-resistants,' or 'no-government men.' That they laid down and sanctioned all the principles of non-resistance, cannot be denied; but I do not believe that, as a body, they understood how far they had, in fact, committed themselves. They were agreed that the starved, lacerated, down-trodden slaves had no right to fight for liberty; but they did not exactly mean that they themselves were not to use carnal weapons, when *their* 'wives, daughters, sisters, mothers,' and their own sacred persons, should be put in jeopardy by 'the most brutal'! They did not perceive that, in stripping those who are the most terribly abused and outraged, of all right to lift a finger in self defence, they also deprived themselves, and all others, of such right! They did not understand that the rule was to work both ways! All this I readily admit. What I mean to say is, that, by a strict and fair construction of the instruments above alluded to, *non-resistance is more explicitly enjoined upon abolitionists, than the duty of using the elective franchise.* I cannot, therefore, think highly of the fair-mindedness of Mr. Birney, in that, while he attempts to prove that abolitionists are bound to go to the polls, by torturing the words, 'will endeavor to influence Congress,' &c. into such an obligation, he says not one word about the pacific principles embodied in the Constitution and Declaration, while attacking non-resisting abolitionists.

ABOLITION AT THE BALLOT BOX.

Once more, I beg not to be misapprehended. I have always expected, I still expect, to see abolition at the ballot-box, renovating the political action of the country — dispelling the sorcery influences of party — breaking asunder the fetters of political servitude — stirring up the torpid consciences of voters — substituting anti-slavery for pro-slavery representatives in every legislative assembly — modifying and rescinding all laws which sanction slavery. But this political reformation is to be effected solely by a change in the moral vision of the people; — not by attempting to prove, that it is the duty of every abolitionist to be a voter, but that it is the duty of every voter to be an abolitionist. By converting electors to the doctrine, that slavery ought to be immediately abolished, a rectified political action is the natural consequence; for where this doctrine is received into the soul, the soul-carrier may be trusted any where, that he will not betray the cause of bleeding humanity. As to the height and depth, the length and breadth of CHRISTIANITY, it is not the province of abolition to decide; but only to settle one point — to wit, that slaveholding is a crime under all circumstances, leaving those who believe in the doctrine to carry out their principles, with all fidelity, in whatever sphere they may be called upon to act, but not authoritatively determining whether they are bound to be members of the church, or voters at the polls. It has never been a difficult matter to induce men to go to the ballot-box; but the grand difficulty ever has been, and still is, to persuade them to carry a good conscience thither, and act as free moral agents, not as the tools of party.

EFFECTS OF NON-RESISTANCE UPON POLITICAL ACTION.

I go still further. I not only expect to see abolition at the polls, but I feel as sure as that day will follow night, that the political action of this country will be purified and renovated, in exact proportion to the prevalence of the great conservative doctrines of non-resistance! This may seem, to many, absurd, paradoxical, impossible; but it is strictly natural, rational, philosophical. As in the presence of Christianity, idolatry is made hideous even in the eyes of the idolators, and conscience is stimulated to put away the grosser forms of iniquity; so, revealed in the light of Non-Resistance, the kingdoms and governments of this world are seen in their real deformity, and those who sustain them are beginning to be ashamed of the work of their own hands, and to feel how awful are the responsibilities resting upon them, in assuming the power of life and death over each other. Non-Resistance measures every law of man by the law of God; and, already, the result of its examination is appalling. Suddenly there is a mighty stir in community! Priests have become politicians, and are holding up political action almost as 'the one thing needful.' [11] Formerly, they shrunk from this work as from the touch of foul contamination. In their opinion, religion had the slightest possible connection with politics; and the christian who seldom ventured into the turbulent arena was deemed the wisest man. Between the Church and State there was declared to be an impassable gulf. The dead were told to bury their dead, but the living instructed to follow CHRIST, as King of kings and Lord of lords, upon whose shoulders rested the only righteous government in the universe. Now the pulpit and the religious press are teeming with homilies upon the religious duty of going to the polls — upon the divine institution of human government — upon the criminality of those professedly good men, who neglect to use the elective franchise, or allow themselves to be made the tools of party — upon the solemn obligations resting upon the people, (in the language of Mr. Birney,) 'to sustain and purify governments, and bring them to a perfect conformity with the principles of the divine government'! Men who refuse to meddle with politics are marked as dangerous citizens! Truly, we may exclaim, in view of this extraordinary change of sentiment, '*Mirabile dictu!*' And to what is it to be attributed, but to the preaching of the sublime doctrines of Non-Resistance? For it is certain that, as these doctrines have spread, our 'pro-government' brethren have obtained new views of duty at the polls, and are indebted for their awakened consciences and rectified vision to the despised and calumniated non-resistants. They are not prepared to adopt the theory of this humble class; they cannot wholly forsake houses and lands, relations and friends, and lose their lives, for Christ's sake; they are not willing, in all cases, to forgive evil-doers, and do not believe in overcoming evil with good, but rely upon physical force for protection and redress; yet they are forced to perceive how hideously defective is the government which they cherish, and to confess that it bears little or no resemblance to the gospel of Christ. Hence, in order to justify their conduct, and to refute the charges of non-resistants, they have set themselves to work in good earnest, (a small portion only,) to repeal wicked and oppressive laws, to soften the severity of the penal code, to elect better men to office, to obliterate the lines of party, and to make conscience and the fear of God attendants at the polls. In all this I rejoice. I hail such an altered state of political feeling as the harbinger of a mighty reformation.

That non-resistance will essentially aid, instead of injuring the anti-slavery cause, politically and morally, is proved to a demonstration.

In the first place, no person can be a non-resistant, without being a whole-hearted abolitionist — (the greater includes the less, always) — though a man may be an abolitionist, and yet not a non-resistant.

Secondly, the principles of non-resistance have taken root more deeply, and spread more widely, in Massachusetts, than in any other State. All who embrace them are abolitionists. What State can compare with her for devotion to the cause of the slave, — for abolition integrity, activity, intrepidity, — in liberal contributions and self-sacrificing efforts to redeem the captives in our midst — in vigorous political action at the polls? To what State are the eyes of the South turned with so much anxiety and alarm, as to Massachusetts? Is she not regarded, every where, as the leader of the States in this great struggle?

Thirdly, the principles of non-resistance have been discussed in the columns of the Liberator, with more or less freedom, for the last three or four years. What has *made* the abolitionism of Massachusetts, (I do not say this boastingly, but as a historical fact, pertinent to the present argument,) but the Liberator? I appeal to Henry B. Stanton, and to every other agent who has lectured in or out of Massachusetts, whether, as a general rule, those who take the Liberator are not the very salt of the anti-slavery enterprise — the most uncompromising, clear-sighted, active, generous, among abolitionists — the most faithful to their principles, the most to be relied on at the polls? If this be not so, then these agents have testified falsely. Again and again have they declared, that, in going into a new field of labor, or even into an old one, almost their first inquiry has been, — 'Who takes the Liberator?' — because they felt sure of finding a genuine abolitionist, whether the subscriber proved to be a man or *woman.*

I repeat it, as the stirring conviction of my heart, and the logical deduction of my understanding, that Non-Resistance is destined to pour new life-blood into the veins of Abolition — to give it extraordinary vigor — to clothe it with new beauty — to inspire it with holier feelings — to preserve it from corruption — though not necessarily connected with it.

IMPORTANT FACT.

It is remarkable, that while Mr. Birney is disposed to dwell upon the *political* features of the anti-slavery cause as strikingly obvious and attractive, he should overlook the following resolution, which was adopted at the annual meeting of the American Anti-Slavery Society, no longer ago than last year!

'Resolved, That George Bourne, Charles W. Denison, Wm. Lloyd Garrison, Beriah Green, Samuel J. May, *Amos A. Phelps, Orange Scott, John G. Whittier,* and Hiram Wilson,[12] be a committee to declare a Declaration, which shall announce the judgement of the American Anti-Slavery Society, concerning the *common error* that our enterprise is of a POLITICAL, and not *religious* character.'

This resolution is a clear refutation of the elaborate reasoning contained in Mr. Birney's political essay. The reader will observe — 1. that it deprecates the notion, that the anti-slavery enterprise is of a political character, as false and pernicious; 2. that it eschews, not *party* merely, but *political action*; 3. that it makes a broad distinction between *political* and *religious* character; 4. that it implies, that, 'in the judgment of the American Anti-Slavery Society,' there is no relationship between politics and religion, any more than between light and darkness!

FAMILY GOVERNMENT.

Alluding to the non-resistants, Mr. Birney says:

'Denying to civil governments the right to use force, they easily deduce, that family governments have no such rights. Thus, they would withhold from parents any power of personal chastisement or restraint for the correction of their children.'

Without stopping to examine the truthfulness of this grave charge, I venture to make the inquiry, whether it is the appropriate business of Mr. Birney, as one of the Secretaries of the Parent Society, and in its official organ, to determine for abolitionists, whether they may or may not use the birch or the cowhide in the management of their children? If so, I do not see why he may not as properly sit in judgment upon our dietetic habits and our theological speculations — and thus act as a 'Board of Inspection appointed to scrutinize the qualifications of persons proposing themselves for membership,' touching all questions relating to law, physic, or divinity, as well as to the abolition of slavery.

DENIAL OF A CRUEL CHARGE.

I have thus attempted — with what success the readers of the Emancipator must judge — to reply to the political arguments of Mr. Birney, and to show precisely the attitude in which those stand, who are for making political action at the polls the test of membership in the anti-slavery organization. To the assertion of Mr. B., that 'the no-government theory is but a new growth of one of the *fungi* which sprung up in the early period of the Reformation, and soon led to the most horrible excesses,' I shall now merely oppose a naked denial of its truth. The *onus probandi* [13] rests upon the accuser, not upon the accused. It is for him to maintain his assertion, if he can — and, failing to do so, to acknowledge that he has done gross injustice to those, whose moral deportment he cannot impeach, and who (as he confesses) 'wholly deny and repudiate' what he supposes to be the legitimate consequences of their scheme. The principles and measures of the Non-Resistants are as opposite to those which formerly characterised the Anabaptists in Germany, as is holiness to sin, light to darkness, and mercy to cruelty! Thus saith the Lord — 'Cursed are all they who trust in man, or who make flesh their arm.' [14] 'Blessed are the peace-makers; for they shall be called the children of God.' [15]

Yours fraternally,

WM. LLOYD GARRISON.

Boston, May 31, 1839.

Printed in *The Liberator*, June 28, 1839.

The numbered notes are the editor's; all others are Garrison's.

Immediately following this letter in *The Liberator* there appears the text of the remarks of the editor of the *Emancipator*, Joshua Leavitt, which had served as an introduction to Garrison's letter when printed in the *Emancipator*. Garrison then replies to the introductory remarks. Since they are not actually a part of Garrison's letter, they are omitted here.

1. *The Liberator* of June 28, 1839, reprinted Birney's essay as well as Garrison's reply.
2. I Corinthians 1:27–29.
3. Mark 10:9.
4. Hebrews 13:3.
5. Psalms 137:5–6 (slightly paraphrased).
6. What does it accomplish?

7. Shakespeare, *King Lear*, II, i.
8. Shakespeare, *Othello*, I, iii.
9. Matthew 7:12.
10. Lamentations, 4:1.
11. A variation of Luke 10:42.
12. Hiram Wilson was one of the Lane student rebels who served as an anti-slavery agent, one of the "seventy," in Ohio in 1836. He later worked in Canada assisting fugitive slaves, and founded the British-American Manual Labor Institute. First conceived in 1838, by Wilson and Josiah Henson, for the training and education of fugitive slaves, the institute was not established until 1842. Wilson served as its principal for seven years. Its student body increased from fourteen to sixty during the first ten years of its existence. Although originally planned primarily for fugitive slaves, it later accepted interested whites, and Indians. It made an important contribution to the spiritual and physical well-being of the escaped slaves in Canada. However, because of divided counsels among the school's leaders, it declined after 1855. (Carter G. Woodson, *The Education of the Negro Prior to 1861*, New York and London, 1915, pp. 252–296.) Wilson also served as receiving agent for the Underground Railroad at St. Catherine's, Canada West, and arranged with the authorities to admit supplies for the refugees, free from custom duties. (Wilbur H. Siebert, *The Underground Railroad from Slavery to Freedom*, New York, 1898, pp. 194, 199, 202, 206.)
13. The burden of proof.
14. Jeremiah 17:5, slightly adapted.
15. Matthew 5:9.

154

TO WENDELL PHILLIPS

BOSTON, June 4, 1839.

TO WENDELL PHILLIPS:

Esteemed Coadjutor — The Board of Managers of the Massachusetts Anti-Slavery Society, in view of your contemplated visit to Europe in quest of health for your beloved companion,[1] cannot allow you to depart without giving you a letter, expressive of the estimation in which you are held by them, individually and collectively. We desire you to lay it before the friends of negro emancipation across the Atlantic, in such manner as you may think proper, that they may cordially extend to you the right hand of fellowship, as the representative of the abolitionists of Massachusetts and of New England.

We feel that, in a worldly sense, few in the extended ranks of American abolitionists have made larger sacrifices upon the altar of Humanity than yourself. Descended from a highly respectable lineage — the son of a father who has 'done the State some service,' and whose memory is endeared to the people of this Commonwealth [2] — connected with an elevated class in society — possessed of rare abilities which qualified you to reach and to fill high and responsible offices in the gift of the nation — in the spring-time of manhood, when the love of popular applause, rather than of doing good, generally inflames the youthful mind, you turned your back upon the blandishments of a seductive world, repudiated all hope of political preferment and legal eminence, made yourself of no reputation for the benefit of the perishing bondman, and became the associate of those, who, for seeking the abolition of slavery by moral and religious instrumentalities, are up to this hour subject to popular odium, to violent treatment, to personal insult. You buckled on the abolition armor when there were 'blows to take, as well as blows to give' — in one of the darkest periods of our righteous enterprise; — and from that hour to the present, we have ever found you in the front rank of the conflict, ready to leap into the 'imminent deadly breach,'[3] reckless of all consequences growing out of a faithful adherence to principle, and giving YOURSELF as a free-will offering to the sacred cause of human liberty.

As a member of your Board, we tender you our thanks for the important aid which you have rendered the cause, in helping to sustain the heavy responsibilities resting upon us, and in giving us the benefit of your enlightened counsel in all our deliberations. In the most difficult and trying periods, your vision has been clear, your faith unfaltering, your course unswerving from the strict line of duty. We shall regard your absence as a real loss to the Board, to the Society we represent, and to the great anti-slavery organization in the land — a loss which cannot be made up: and we are reconciled to your departure, only as it seems required by a sacred regard to the health of the partner of your bosom, and promises to be of signal benefit to the cause of emancipation on both sides of the Atlantic.

As the General Agent of the Massachusetts Anti-Slavery Society, for the last five months, your labors have been arduous, indefatigable, and in a high degree successful. For those labors, you have refused to accept even a slight compensation.

As an abolitionist, we are happy to be represented ourselves, across the great waters, by one so strong in principle, so far-sighted, so generous in spirit, so eloquent in thought and speech, as yourself. The warm approval of your contemplated visit, which has just been given, unanimously, by the New England Anti-Slavery Convention,[4] also testifies that the abolitionists of New England regard you as preeminently qualified to represent their principles, sentiments and wishes, in your intercourse with their trans-Atlantic coadjutors, who are sparing no efforts to effect the speedy abolition of slavery and the slave-trade throughout the world. Though your tour is mainly for a private end, and you do not go out as the OFFICIAL AGENT of any association — and therefore we cannot expect, we cannot ask you to consecrate even a moiety of your time to the furtherance of the anti-slavery enterprise, — yet we know that you will be both willing and happy to seize every convenient opportunity that may be presented, to open your mouth for the suffering and the dumb, and 'in the cause of all such as are appointed to destruction' [5] — whatever may be the complexion of their skin, or the tribe or country to which they belong. That you will be listened to with respect, and treated, not as a foreign intermeddler, but as a man and a brother, we cannot entertain a doubt. May you be guided in all that you may be called upon to say or do, by that wisdom which is profitable to direct; and be sustained by an omnipotent arm.

We need not suggest to you in what manner to present the claims of American abolitionists to the sympathy and co-operation of all humane men across the Atlantic. Your own sagacious mind will be your best director as to matter and manner, time, place and circumstances. In regard to the progress of the anti-slavery cause in the United States, it may gratify and encourage our abolition brethren abroad to learn the following, among a multitude of similar facts: —

In the year 1829, an isolated drop appeared on the surface of the land; in the year 1839, that drop is swallowed up and lost in a great ocean of humanity, which is swelling and dashing against the walls of the American Bastile with a might that is irresistible. Ten years ago, a solitary individual stood up as the advocate of immediate and unconditional emancipation, with scarcely one to cheer him to the conflict with American slavery. Now that individual sees around him, in amicable league, hundreds of thousands of persons, of both sexes, members of every sect and party, from the most elevated to the humblest rank in life, the rich and the poor, the learned and the ignorant. In 1829, not an anti-slavery society, of a genuine stamp, was in existence. In 1839, there are nearly two thousand societies, swarming and multiplying in all parts of the free States. In 1829, there was but one anti-slavery periodical in the land. Now there are not less than fourteen. In 1829, scarcely a newspaper, of any religious sect or political party, was willing to disturb the 'delicate' question of slavery. In 1839, there are multitudes of journals that either openly advocate the doctrine of immediate emancipation, or permit its free discussion in their columns. In 1829, scarcely one tract or pamphlet, in opposition to American slavery, could be readily found. In 1839, it is impossible to calculate the whole number that is scattered over the land, thicker than rain-drops and as nourishing to the soil of freedom. Including the issues of the regular anti-slavery periodicals, the estimate may be safely reckoned by millions. In 1829, not an anti-slavery agent was in the field; now there are scores, whose labors are as untiring as their appeals prove irresistible. In 1829, a lecture on slavery was an anomaly.

In 1839, the lectures and sermons delivered on the subject are too numerous to be estimated. Ten years ago, scarcely an ecclesiastical or political body dared to assail, even indirectly, the slave system. Now, synods, conferences, general associations, and legislative assemblies, are lifting up their voices against its continuance. Then, hardly a church, of any denomination, made slaveholding a bar to communion and christian fellowship; now, multitudes refuse to hear a slaveholder preach, or to recognize him as a brother. In 1829, scarcely one, if any petition, was sent to Congress, praying for the abolition of slavery in the District of Columbia, &c. &c. Now, in one day, a single member of the House of Representatives, (John Quincy Adams,) has presented one hundred and seventy-six in detail. It was ascertained, at the last session but one, that not less than seven hundred thousand persons had memorialized Congress on this and kindred subjects. In 1829, that scourge of the colored race, and most inhuman association, the American Colonization Society, was flourishing like a green bay-tree, having secured the approbation of both Church and State, and laughing to scorn all opposition. In 1839, there are few so poor as to do it reverence, in the free States, — though the traffickers 'in slaves and the souls of men' [6] regard it as the sheet anchor of their piratical ship. Its popularity has given place to abhorrence — its honor is changed to infamy — and it lies prostrate, helpless, bankrupt — a broken and blasted monument of God's displeasure. In 1829, where ten slaves escaped from their prison-house, now a hundred find their way to the north, and are safely landed in Canada, to receive liberty and protection under the flag of Victoria. May their numbers increase, from day to day, and from hour to hour, and God send them a good deliverance, is the prayer of every true-hearted abolitionist. In 1829, the free colored population of the United States were bowed to the earth in despair. Before the combined influences of those twin monsters, Slavery and Colonization, they withered like a green herb in a time of drought. Their spirits were broken, their energies paralyzed, their expectations of future good cut off. In 1839, they are quickened into life (through the power of abolitionism) as by a mighty resurrection. Now they begin to be filled with the spirit of enterprise, and are eager for moral and intellectual improvement. In various places, they have well-furnished libraries, debating societies, scientific clubs, temperance and moral reform societies, &c. &c. They have also two periodicals, very ably conducted, by men of their own complexion. Two of their members are members of the Executive Committee of the American Anti-Slavery Society, and are thus practically entrusted with the management of the anti-slavery enterprise. But we must forbear. The contrast between the state of things in 1829 and at the present time, (which we have barely glanced at,) presents almost miraculous transformations to the vision of every candid person. No revolution in public sentiment, during the same time, has ever been more extraordinary, more hopeful, or more important. Truly, before heaven and earth we attest, that it is solely the Lord's doing, and it is very marvellous in all eyes. Shall he not, then, have all the glory?

Tell our British brethren, that the apathy which once brooded over the land, like the spell of death, is broken forever. Tell them there is no part of our immense national domain, which is not agitated with the great question of human rights. For into what circle or society, what political or religious body, what legislative or ecclesiastical assembly, has the discussion not been carried? What a mass of intellect has been quickened, what generous sympathy for the oppressed excited, what intense abhorrence of slavery every where called into activity! Yea, what sacrifices have been made, what labors and sufferings joyfully encountered, by multitudes, that the yokes and fetters of twenty-five hundred thousand American bondmen might be broken, at once and forever! We do not believe, that what brought the people of England to repentance, in America serves to harden the national heart; — that the same principles, which, on moral and religious grounds, effected the abolition of slavery in one country, are calculated to perpetuate that horrid system, by their promulgation in another.

Among the distinguished band of British philanthropists, whom it will be your privilege to take by the hand, will doubtless be our beloved and eloquent coadjutor, GEORGE THOMPSON. Joyful, most joyful, will be the meeting between you. Convey to him the renewed assurances of our gratitude for his invaluable services in this country, our admiration of his philanthropic labors in Great Britain, and our deep interest in his present and future welfare. There are thousands and thousands in this country, who are fondly anticipating the time when he will again visit the United States. In his new field of benevolent enterprise, we heartily bid him God speed, as well as all those who are associated with him.

We bid you an affectionate farewell. We trust that your amiable partner, (whose generous donations to our cause have greatly helped to advance it,) will be fully restored to health, and that you will be both safely returned to us, through the mercy and goodness of God.

FRANCIS JACKSON, President.

WM. LLOYD GARRISON, Cor. Sec'y.

Printed in *The Liberator*, June 14, 1839.

1. Wendell Phillips had married Ann Terry Greene (1813–1886) in October 1837, the daughter of Benjamin Greene, who was a brother of Sarah Greene Chap-

man, the mother of Henry Grafton Chapman, Maria Weston Chapman's husband. It was Wendell Phillips's wife who converted her husband to the antislavery cause. She was an invalid at the time of her marriage, and she remained so for the rest of her life. (George Lowell Austin, *The Life and Times of Wendell Phillips*, Boston, 1888, pp. 86–87; *Life*, II, 49n; IV, 404.)

2. His father, John Phillips (1770–1823) had served in both houses of the Massachusetts legislature, and was a judge of the Court of Common Pleas, a member of the 1820 convention for the revision of the state constitution, and the first mayor of Boston (Austin, *Wendell Phillips*, pp. 21–25). The quotation is from *Othello*, v, iii.

3. Shakespeare, *Othello*, I, iii.

4. The sixth New England Anti-Slavery convention, which had met in Boston, at the Chardon-Street Chapel, on May 28–30, 1839, had, on May 30, unanimously adopted several resolutions concerning Phillips' trip. In one it commended Phillips to the abolitionists of England "as one of the most devoted, uncompromising, and eloquent advocates of the slave, and as a true representative of the feelings and sentiments of the great body of New-England Abolitionists; and that we regard his contemplated visit to England as calculated to strengthen the bonds of union between us, and to give a new impulse to the cause of humanity on both sides of the Atlantic." (*The Liberator*, June 7, 1839.)

5. Proverbs 31:8.

6. Revelation 18:13.

155

TO GEORGE W. BENSON

Boston, June 15, 1839.

Dear bro. George:

In the ear of my imagination, it is whispered to me that every member of the dear household in Brooklyn is saying, "Bro. Garrison is growing less and less attentive to us, in his epistolary interchanges." I admit the fact, with some confusion of face; but it is not and can never be true, that one particle of my affection for you all is lost, or that you are not always held in loving remembrance. It is wholly useless for me to plead, in extenuation, the multiplicity of my engagements; for though I have really been burdened uncommonly of late, yet had I more executive power, more industry, more application, more method, I could find time to write to some of you much oftener than I do. Well, if I am incorrigible in this matter, do not, I pray, any of you imitate my bad example; but see to it that I am shamed out of my dilatory, procrastinating habits by the frequency with which you write to me or dear Helen.

Bro. Collins has just handed me your letter to him. We are afflicted to learn that you have been seriously injured by an accident on your way from Hampton to Brooklyn, but rejoiced at the same time that you and friend Coe fared no worse. It was truly a narrow escape for you both, and for yourself in particular. Pray, be careful of yourself, and do not attempt to labor until you are thoroughly recovered. Give both my sympathy and congratulation to friend Coe, my regards to his wife, and some hearty kisses for me to his dear boys. — Blessings on them all!

For a month past, Helen and myself have been talking about taking the children into the country, to recruit their health, (which has been much affected by the whooping-cough,) — and we had about concluded to go to Providence — spend a few days there — from thence to Brooklyn, and tarry a week — and then home again via Worcester. But the children are now greatly recovered in health — Phebe Jackson intends visiting us next week — I have much to do in the city, and therefore cannot leave; so we must forego the pleasure of visiting Brooklyn this season. I intend carrying Helen and the children to Newburyport, immediately after the 4th of July.

You may easily imagine, that we greatly miss dear mother, and scarcely know how to be resigned to her absence. I feel very grateful to her, for consenting to remain so long with us, and taking such incessant and parental care of the children. Since she left us, we have had Lavinia remain with us; and we shall endeavor to keep her awhile longer. When will sister Sarah gladden us by her presence, or either of the other precious ones? I hope one of them, at least, will conclude to make us a visit immediately.

I see by your letter, that you decline coming into this State to reside, at present. I hope, however, that you will be able to make such arrangements by the fall, as to insure your labors as one of our State agents without fail. I am sorry you cannot come now — for "now's the day, and now's the hour," [1] when a great battle is to be fought, not for this Commonwealth only, but for the nation. As goes Massachusetts, so goes the land.

We are greatly disappointed in not being able to secure the invaluable aid of our friend C. C. Burleigh. He has a strong desire to be with us, but he feels as if he could not leave his broad field of labor in Pennsylvania. He will remain a few days in Plainfield, (for which place he left here yesterday,) and I hope you will see him, and talk over the subject. Charles, I think, is now fully enlightened as to the real spirit which actuates the disorganizers in this State, and his visit has been very serviceable to us as well as to himself.

We have just achieved a great triumph in old Essex. The annual meeting of the Essex Co. Society was held at Topsfield on Wednesday last.[2] I was not able to be present, having to lecture in Abington on that day — (they gave me a crowded house.) [3] For some weeks prior to the county meeting, Torrey, Phelps, St. Clair and Wise, were busy in endeavoring to secure a full attendance on the part of spurious abolitionists; and they were sanguine that they should succeed in their design — viz. to exclude the women, brand the non-resistants as recreant to the cause, and make the society auxiliary to the new organization instead of the State Society. They met with a real Waterloo defeat. The vote, admitting women to participate in the proceedings, was adopted by an overwhelming majority. That part of Torrey's report, which related to political action, was stricken out by a vote of 106 to 32.[4] — Our non-resistant brother, Wm. Bassett of Lynn, was elected President of the Society, and J. P. Boyce, of ditto, Cor. Sec. in the place of C. T. Torrey! It was a grand meeting — and, as friend Burleigh was present, he will give you further particulars respecting it. I attended it the second day, and was cordially received. Resolutions were adopted, approving of the Mass. Board, the Liberator, Cradle of Liberty, &c. Torrey and ten others withdrew, and organized a rival county society! What a farce! — But my sheet is full. I hope to hear from you soon. Great love to all.

Yours, indissolubly,

Wm. Lloyd Garrison.

ALS: Garrison Papers, Boston Public Library.

1. Robert Burns, "Scots, Wha Hae."

2. *The Liberator*, June 21, 28, July 5, 1839, carried a report of the meeting of the Essex County Anti-Slavery Society, which was held on Wednesday and Thursday, June 12 and 13, in the Congregational Church in Topsfield. One hundred sixty-three delegates from twenty towns in the county attended. Garrison did attend the Thursday session.

3. *The Liberator*, June 7, 1839, carried the following notice: "The Fourth Annual Meeting of the Abington Anti-Slavery Society will be holden in the Rev. Mr. Alden's meeting-house on Wednesday, the 12th of June next, at 2 o'clock P. M. An Address will be delivered by Wm. Lloyd Garrison." Garrison's account of the meeting appeared in *The Liberator*, June 21, 1839.

4. One section of the report apparently condemned abolitionists who refused to vote. This section was stricken out. The meeting passed two resolutions bearing upon this question. They were the following:

"Resolved, That the vast majority of the members of this Society hold to the duty of using the ballot-box for the slave; and it is believed that all its members assent to the doctrine, that every abolitionist who regards it morally right to use the ballot-box at all, and yet refuses or neglects so to use it as to promote the cause of emancipation, fails to perform his duty.

"Resolved, That in voting to strike out a portion of the annual report relating to political action, this society does not mean to be understood as opposing the use of the elective franchise as a means of promoting the anti-slavery cause, but only as declining to set up a political test of membership, or to declare it the duty of any man to vote who cannot do so without a violation of conscience." (*The Liberator*, June 21, 1839.)

156

TO SAMUEL J. MAY

Boston, June 22, 1839.

Dear bro. May:

Thanks for your kind letter of the 15th inst. I shall endeavor to hold myself in readiness to be with you on the 4th of July,[1] though I have not, as yet, written a single word of my address, and am just as ignorant as you are of what will be its topics.

Helen and the children will probably accompany me; but you may not expect us until the morning of the 4th — and we shall probably return to Boston the same evening. We shall decide about this more definitely, as the time draws near. Your proferred hospitality is gratefully appreciated.

I showed your letter to Mrs. Child and Mrs. Chapman, and hope they will forward some resolutions to you, according to your desire. Possibly I may send a few, but do not rely upon me. They all ought to be *apropos* to the day and the occasion.

Have you any hope or expectation, that Mr. Adams [2] will be present? I presume he would decline, if an invitation should be extended to him. How would it answer to examine, in my address, some of his objections to abolitionism?

I shall not be prepared to discourse to your people, respecting the essentials of Christianity, for the present.

Our little non-resistance circle, in this city, have been much enlivened, the present week, by the presence of Samuel Bradford, of Greenfield, Lagrange Co., Indiana.[3] He has been deputed, by some brethren in the far West, to visit this city, expressly for the purpose of seeing the friends of non-resistance, and laying before us some very interesting facts in relation to a pacific organization which has been formed in his own town and vicinity. He is a self-taught, uneducated man, but has an excellent simplicity of character, and a naturally vigorous and philosophical cast of mind. He has been an avowed and practical non-resistant for the last ten years; and his principles have been unto [him], for preservation, better than the musket or bowie-knife, or the sword of magistracy. Others have been associated with him for some time past; and though they reside in a frontier State, where they are continually exposed to outrage and danger, the Lord has protected them from all harm. They have formed themselves into a church, on the principles of non-resistance, and subscribed their names to a Declaration of Sentiments. They hold to baptism by immersion, and the breaking of bread every first day of the week: in this particular, they are a sect — and, so far, in my opinion, are in legal bondage. Bro. Bradford is very catholic in his spirit, and yet very sanguine that all non-resistants will be organized in a body, precisely after the model of the western experiment! He is certainly mistaken. There never has been, there never can be, a union of all professed christians, so long as temple-worship, the observance of forms and ceremonies, the administration and reception of ordinances, the sanctification of a particular day, &c. &c. are made essential to christian character and fellowship. About all these, theologians and polemics may wrangle, until they are all voiceless with *bronchitis* in vain: they but gender to bondage, to variance, to wrath, to perpetual strife — while the moral precepts of the gospel admit of no controversy, but commend themselves to every man's conscience, and overleap or swallow up all sects and parties, as such. O, there is nothing like the liberty which is enjoyed by those who are the sons of God! They are indeed the Lord's freemen. No man, no body of men, may say to them, "Go to this mountain in Samaria," or "Go to Jerusalem," to worship; or "Observe this rite," or "Partake of that ordinance." Christian worship is nothing but Christian obedience; and obedience is not a thing of form, or locality, or time, or circumstance. The whole gospel is summed up in a word of four letters — LOVE — that love which worketh no ill to his neighbor, and is the fulfilling of the law. Christianity is a dispensation of glorious realities: — why, then, should we cling to husks — shadows — burnt-offerings and sacrifices?

I find I am getting into a discussion, when I only intended to write a mere paragraph in answer to yours.

Notwithstanding the clamor that is raised about the non-resistance principles and doctrines, I am more and more satisfied that they constitute the very kingdom of heaven which the Prince of Peace came to establish; and also the real atonement which Jesus died to make, that the world might be reconciled unto God. They are, in fact, the end of the law for righteousness, to every one that *believeth*.

In the Emancipator of the present week, I have made a reply [4] to Mr. Birney's article, respecting the Constitution of the American A. S. Society and the "no-government" question, which, if you find time, please give a careful perusal. It occupies five columns. Bro. Leavitt's introductory remarks show a disturbed state of mind.

Susan Coffin spent the evening and night at our house the day before yesterday. Mr. Coffin's health is improving; but there is, probably, no hope of his recovery, unless he could go through several courses of the Thompsonian medicine.

I send, with my own, Helen's kind remembrances to Mrs. May, and yourself. Whether madman or heretic, I am

Your admiring friend,

Wm. Lloyd Garrison.

ALS: Garrison Papers, Boston Public Library.

1. Garrison was scheduled to deliver the address at the annual meeting of the Plymouth County Anti-Slavery Society on July 4 at Samuel J. May's meeting house in South Scituate. The text of the address was printed in *The Liberator*, July 19, 1839.

2. John Quincy Adams.

3. Samuel Bradford (b. Hillsboro county, New Hampshire, December 20, 1800; d. Greenfield, La Grange county, Indiana, December 3, 1845), a Free-Will Baptist minister and lineal descendant of George Bradford of the *Mayflower*, went to La Grange county in 1831, after having lived in Ohio for five years, and in Pennsylvania, Monroe county, New York, and elsewhere previously. He withdrew from the Free-Will Baptist church in about 1837, when he became an anti-slavery man and a nonresistant and formed a pacifist church known as the "Congregation of Saints." He was also a member of the La Grange Phalanx at the time of his death. (*Counties of Lagrange and Noble*, Chicago, 1882, pp. 268–269; Peter Brock, *Pacifism in the United States, from the Colonel Era to the First World War*, Princeton, N.J., 1968, pp. 573–574. I am indebted to Miss Caroline Dunne, Librarian, William Henry Smith Memorial Library, Indiana Historical Society, Indianapolis, Indiana, for the material from the first source.)

4. The reference is to Garrison's letter (153) of May 31, 1839.

157

TO AMOS A. PHELPS

Tuesday Morning, July 9. [1839]

Bro. Phelps:

Enclosed is your note, which I return to you, because I am not willing to make you appear ridiculous, by publishing it in the Liberator. If you wish to know what was said of your course at Templeton, by Messrs. Collins [1] and Johnson,[2] just apply to them, and I doubt not they will frankly tell you. But do not show yourself to be unduly sensitive and weakly credulous, by giving heed to any such statements as have been made to you by one who was not at the meeting, and who undertakes to report what was said in private conversation, as stated to him by "a young man."

Yours, as in auld lang syne,

Wm. Lloyd Garrison.

ALS: Phelps Papers, Boston Public Library.

Garrison refers to a letter from Phelps, dated Boston, July 8, 1839. Phelps wrote of having received a letter from a stranger, who had in turn been told by someone who had attended a meeting of the Worcester North Division Anti-Slavery Society at Templeton, Massachusetts, that at the conclusion of the meeting "some half dozen Garrisonians got around him and warned him to beware of A. A. Phelps, D. Wise, O. Scott, A. St. Clair, E. Wright, Jr., & others, declaring them to be *Traitors, Colonizationists,* & *bad men!*" Phelps closed his letter with a bitter warning to the public to beware of himself and the others who were so accused, and asked Garrison to publish the letter in *The Liberator*. The manuscript of Phelps's letter is in the Boston Public Library.

1. John A. Collins.
2. Oliver Johnson.

158

TO THE ABOLITIONISTS OF MASSACHUSETTS

[July 17, 1839.]

FELLOW-CITIZENS: — Entrusted by you with the general supervision of the anti-slavery enterprise in this Commonwealth, it behooves us, by the solemn obligations we have assumed, to watch over that enterprise as those who must give account, not only to yourselves as our constituents, but to God as our Judge. Impressed with this consideration, we offer no apology for addressing you at a time when an attempt is making, by some who have hitherto stood prominent in the abolition ranks, to destroy our old and excellent organization, and substitute another less catholic and efficient in its place — to sunder the cords of brotherly love, and weaken the bonds of mutual confidence — to array into hostile parties those who have stood shoulder to shoulder up to the present hour, fire-proof against corruption, and storm-proof against all the assaults of the enemies of emancipation. We solicit your candid attention at this time, and look to you for a final and an enlightened decision upon the merits of the controversy now existing among the professed friends of the slave in Massachusetts.

A STRANGE SPECTACLE.

The strange and unnatural spectacle is now presented to the public, of two State societies in this Commonwealth,[1] each claiming to be genuine — each charging the other with having left the old anti-slavery platform — and both assuming to speak in the name of the abolitionism of the State. It is obvious that, arrayed in this attitude of hostility, one or the other must be in the wrong — one is genuine, the other is spurious — one is loyal, the other schismatical. If they were united in spirit, they would not be divided in action. The fact, that they separately exist, proves that there is a radical difference of views between them. The allegations which they bring against each other show that they can neither coalesce, nor labor together harmoniously as separate bodies. The success of the one depends upon the extinction of the other.

THE NEW SOCIETY SCHISMATICAL — CONDUCT OF THE EXECUTIVE COMMITTEE OF THE AMERICAN SOCIETY.

Of the causes which have led to this unhappy state of things, we shall speak hereafter. According to the spirit of our anti-slavery league, and the arrangements which have been mutually agreed upon between the parent, state, and local societies, the formation of a new State Society in any State where one is already in existence, is a virtual declaration of war upon the whole anti-slavery organization. It is a precedent, which, if widely imitated, would turn the weapons of abolitionists against each other instead of the common enemy, and lead to certain discomfiture and ruin. In saying this, we do not mean to affirm, that there can no circumstances arise, which shall not only justify but absolutely require a new organization. We concede, that if any existing state anti-slavery society shall at any time depart from the original ground of union, — change its principles, or corrupt its doctrines, — it will be the duty of the faithful minority to array another society against it; and the new organization should be countenanced and applauded by every other uncorrupted association in the land. But the case should be clearly made out, to the satisfaction of the great body of American abolitionists, in order to warrant such a procedure; and when that has been done, no quarters should be given to the recreant society. Both societies cannot be properly countenanced at the same time, by the Executive Committee of the Parent Society. Under such circumstances, they are bound to exercise a sound judgment — to approve but one state society in each state. For if they may countenance as auxiliaries, two state societies in one commonwealth, they may also twenty; and thus the order and harmony of the national organization be entirely destroyed. Even if both societies should adopt precisely the same constitution, still we conceive that it would be the duty of the Executive Committee to frown upon the new society as a disturber of the anti-slavery peace. But, in this instance, they have done no such thing. — On the contrary, that Committee, through their acknowledged organ, has countenanced the disorganizing movement in this State, and actively co-operated with those who are engaged in it, in order to ensure its success; while they still continue to acknowledge the legitimacy of the old society. Their conduct, in this particular, has been blameworthy. The Emancipator hails the organization of the 'Massachusetts Abolition Society' — and, with strange infatuation, some other anti-slavery periodicals speak of it in commendatory terms. They forget that this is not a local matter, but a precedent which threatens the existence even of the American Anti-Slavery Society itself. Indeed, so essential was it deemed, after the formation of that society, that there should be perfect uniformity of action and order of arrangement among the various auxiliary associations, that our present state society relinquished its title of 'New-England,' and substituted that of 'Massachusetts." But it would never have consented to make this change, and take this subordinate position, had it foreseen such a state of things as now exists in this Commonwealth. We are constrained to believe, that, had it not been for the unwise and unjustifiable interference of prominent members of the Executive Committee, at New York, with the anti-slavery affairs in this State, the 'Massachusetts Abolition Society' would not have been formed.

PREDICTION FULFILLED — THE NEW SOCIETY PRIVATELY FORMED.

A short time prior to the annual meeting of the State Anti-Slavery Society, in January last, the pioneer journal in the abolition cause declared that a scheme was in embryo, hostile to ourselves as a Board, and to the State Society as an organization — and that it was also the design of those who were implicated in the scheme to supersede that journal by the establishment of a rival print.[2] This declaration excited much surprise, and was read with incredulity by many, at that time; but subsequent developements have sustained it, to the letter — though its truth was stoutly denied by those who have since left our ranks, and who are now found in active hostility to us. The proposition for a new anti-slavery paper, as the organ of the State Society, virtually to crush the Liberator, was rejected at the annual meeting, by an almost unanimous vote. Nevertheless, the rival paper was issued almost immediately afterwards. The attempt to organize another state society was not made till just before the meeting of the N. England A. S. Convention in May last: and the manner in which that society was brought into existence is worthy of special notice, proving as it does its illegitimacy. Most certainly, if the seceders had wished to obtain a fair and full expression of the sentiments of the abolitionists in Massachusetts, relative to the necessity or utility of a new organization — if they had felt satisfied that their proceedings would be sustained by a large majority of the tried friends of emancipation in this Commonwealth — if they had not been conscious that they constituted but an insignificant minority — they would have notified, in the most public manner, all persons interested in the cause of human freedom, of the time and place of their meeting, and invited a full attendance. But they knew that they were acting in opposition to the

views and feelings of abolitionists generally; and therefore they held
a select, private meeting at the Marlboro' *Hotel* on the 27th of May,
1839, and then and there organized the Massachusetts Abolition Society, by the adoption of a constitution, the appointment of various
committees, &c. A subsequent meeting was held at the Marlboro'
Chapel, Hall No. 1, on the 29th of May, to complete the arrangements
— at which such persons only as were friendly to the new society
were invited to be present, by a notice read in the N. E. A. S. Convention.

REASON FOR DELAY.

We have forborne taking any official notice of this extraordinary
procedure until now, in consequence of the delay of the Executive
Committee of the Abolition Society in laying the justification of their
conduct before the public. After the lapse of six weeks, they have at
length issued an Address to the People of Massachusetts, in which
they set forth 'the reasons which have led them to separate from those
with whom they once rejoiced to co-operate,' but to whom they can
no longer extend the right hand of fellowship. Before proceeding to
examine these 'reasons,' we shall briefly state

THE CHARACTER AND OBJECT OF THE ANTI-SLAVERY ORGANIZATION.

1. Its object is, the abolition of American slavery. In *support* of this
awfully atrocious system, persons of both sexes, of almost every sect
and party, and utterly discordant in their views and feelings upon
other subjects — ministers and laymen, doctors of divinity and doctors
of law, the pious and profane, those who have votes to give, and those
who have none, law-makers and law-breakers, church-members and
church-contemners — were united in feeling, purpose and sentiment,
as though they were of one mind and one heart, in regard to all other
matters. For the *overthrow* of slavery, it was evident that a union
of its enemies, not less general and formidable, was just as essential
and practicable. In the nature of our common humanity, it could not
be true, that if the foes of human freedom could co-operate together
upon common ground, its friends could not all stand upon one platform. The doctrine which had created slavery, and was perpetuating
it, was, that it was right, under certain circumstances, to hold human
beings in bondage as property, subjected to the irresponsible control
of another; that slaveholding was not a *malum in se*; [3] that the descendants of Africa belonged to an inferior order of the human race,
and therefore ought not to stand upon the same footing of equality
with the white species; that, if slavery ought to cease at any period,

it should disappear by an almost imperceptible process; and that, as fast as slaves became emancipated on our soil, they should be transported to Africa as the price and condition of their freedom. Whatever might be their views on other subjects, or in whatever sphere they might be called to act, those who subscribed to this doctrine gave their support to the slave system which curses and disgraces our country.

2. The doctrine which alone could destroy this system by moral and peaceable means, and unite the wise and good of every name in opposition to it, must of course be antagonistical to that above stated. Hence, it has ever been the great object of the anti-slavery organization to inculcate upon the consciences of the slaveholders, the duty of letting their oppressed vassals go free — leaving them without excuse for continuing to hold property in their fellow-men. It sits in judgment upon nothing but the guilt of the nation, in reducing one-sixth portion of the people to brutal servitude. It arraigns no man for his religious creed or governmental opinions. It takes no cognizance of any dispute respecting the holiness of one day in seven, or the divine authority of the priesthood, or the validity of any religious rites and ordinances. It is not a theological controversy, nor a political crusade. In its official, organized form, it appeals to all sects and parties for support, while it expresses no opinion as to their distinctive character, or their lawful existence. It takes men in masses just as it finds them: — talks of cleansing every church in the land from the abominations of slavery, just as earnestly as if it approved of every such organization, though it has no authority to determine which is orthodox or which heterodox: — discourses largely upon the duty and necessity of reforming the government, so that there may be an abrogation of all laws upholding slavery — just as freely as though there was a perfect agreement among its members as to the rightful supremacy of government. In this aspect, it is not inconsistent, but tolerant: It recognizes only the fact, that slavery is protected both by Church and State, and therefore must, in the order of events, be overthrown by influencing Church and State to cease from their oppression. In order that the Church may be purified, it does not require abolitionists to be united with any such organization; for such a requisition it has no right to exact. In order that the State may be reformed, it addresses itself only to those who feel that they are bound to participate in State affairs; for it may not coerce or violate the conscience of any man, who, from religious scruples, refuses to connect himself with the Church, or to mingle in the political affairs of the State. It simply condemns men out of their own mouths — measures them by their own acknowledged standard of action — sentences them according to

their own confessions of guilt. 'For though it be free from all men, yet it is made servant unto all, that it may gain the more. And unto the Jew, it becomes as a Jew; to them that are under the law, as under the law, that it may gain them that are under the law; to them that are without law, as without law, (being *not without law to God*, but UNDER THE LAW TO CHRIST,) that it might gain them that are without law.' [4] In short, it enforces its claim upon all orders and conditions of men, irrespective of their views of religion or politics. It predicates the duty of ecclesiastical or political action, not upon the inherent excellence of ecclesiastical or civil organizations, but upon the fact of their existence as props of the slave system, and upon the views and professions of those who are allied to them by choice.

The anti-slavery enterprise, from its commencement, has claimed to be pre-eminently a moral enterprise. It has addressed itself to the conscience, the heart, and the understanding of every man; and has depended for success upon the power of truth alone. It does not aim to reconcile the conflicting views of men on any other question beside that of the inherent criminality of slaveholding, and the right and duty of every human being to bear testimony against it, and to labor for its suppression. It claims of every abolitionist, that he shall remember those who are in bonds as bound with them; that he shall act consistently and conscientiously, according to his anti-slavery professions; and that he shall not sacrifice the cause of bleeding humanity to any sectarian or party object whatever. Occupying, therefore, this extensive field, it has ever welcomed to its ranks every human being who is willing to recognize the poor despised negro as 'a man and a brother.'

IMPORTANT DISTINCTION.

As individuals, abolitionists may utter sentiments, which, in their associated capacity, they may not express. He who becomes an abolitionist, is under no obligation to change his views respecting the duty of going to the polls, or of belonging to a sect; they are those of an individual, and not binding at all upon any other member of the anti-slavery society. But if the society itself presume to endorse those views as sound and obligatory upon all its members, then it violates the spirit of its own constitution; or, if not, then it is not true that it welcomes to its aid all men, of whatever creed or party, and hence does not stand upon 'the broad ground of a common humanity.' This distinction between the liberty of an individual, and of an association composed of many elements, is important, and essential as much to the harmony of the whole body as it is to personal free agency.

Having thus exhibited the ground-work of abolitionism, we now proceed to examine the reasons which are offered for the formation of the State Abolition Society.

THE NEW SOCIETY PARTIAL AND PROSCRIPTIVE.

And, first, we would premise, that it it is shown to be a partial and proscriptive association, because no invitation was given to the great body of Massachusetts abolitionists to be present at its organization. Had such an invitation been given, the proposition to form such a society would have been rejected by an overwhelming majority. It was concocted in private conclave. Hence, in assuming to represent the abolitionism of the Commonwealth, it is guilty of imposture.

It has not received the approbation of any anti-slavery society in the State — at least, we are ignorant of the fact, if it be otherwise. On the contrary, it has been strongly condemned, with scarcely a dissenting voice, by many societies.

It did not originate with THE PEOPLE, the ABOLITION LAITY, but with a few clerical gentlemen. And it is a fact worthy of special notice, that all (or nearly all) who are publicly engaged in its advocacy are clergymen. Messrs. Phelps, Torrey, St. Clair, Wise, Cummings, Scott, Allen,[5] &c. are all clergymen. We do not make this remark invidiously, but the coincidence is admonitory. Neither the management of the anti-slavery cause, nor that cause itself, belongs to any professional body. If the new society is not schismatical — if it commends itself to the good sense and sober judgment of abolitionists — if it stands upon the old platform — if it is not a sectarian and professional affair in its spirit — how does it happen that all its prominent advocates are of the clerical order?

THE NEW SOCIETY EXCLUSIVE IN ITS MANAGEMENT.

Another of its features (not less remarkable than instructive) is, the manner in which its affairs are to be managed. By the seventh article of its Constitution, each auxiliary society is to be entitled to a representation at its meetings, of one for every twenty-five members, though it may send a delegate if it has less than that number. By the eighth article, it is stipulated that 'the business of the society shall be transacted in meetings constituted, first, of the OFFICERS and AGENTS of the society; and second, of such GENTLEMEN as may be sent as delegates [in the proportion of 1 to 25!] from auxiliary societies.' Remarking upon this very objectionable feature, the Executive Committee use this significant language: — 'We have availed ourselves of the opportunity to guard against a DEFECT in the former organization, in regard to the composition of its business meetings. The transaction of its business will be confined to meetings composed of its officers and agents, and such a delegation as will secure an adequate and equitable representation from every auxiliary.' And the Committee gravely add — 'The provision on this subject is the same in principle as that regulating the ratio of representation in the House of Representatives of the Commonwealth'!! What analogy exists between a legislative assembly and a voluntary benevolent enterprise, we are unable to perceive. This seems to us a bold attempt to place the control of the anti-slavery cause out of the hands of the people into those of a select body. Whoever dreamed, until now, that it was a capital 'defect' in the old organization, to allow as many delegates from auxiliary societies to participate in the proceedings of the American or State Anti-Slavery Society as might choose to attend? Who ever supposed, until now, that the government of the State Society should be modelled by that of the State Legislature? What vigilant, true-hearted abolitionist believes, that a few select persons can be more safely entrusted with the management of our great and responsible cause than the people themselves? Hitherto, the utmost pains have been taken by the Parent and State Societies to ensure a crowded delegation from local associations; and the more that have rallied at their call, the more interesting and important have been their anniversaries, and the better it has been for the safety and integrity of the cause. So long as farmers, mechanics and workingmen are allowed a full and unobstructed participation in all its proceedings, the anti-slavery cause is safe. Limit this right to the few, instead of extending it to the many, and courage will give place to timidity, principle to expediency, integrity to corruption, and liberty to conservatism. Nothing has been more galling to the chief priests, scribes and pharisees, who are resolute in their hostility to the anti-slavery principles and measures, than the 'ultra' republican aspect of our cause; for, as yet, not many wise, noble or mighty have been enlisted in its support. If there were no other objection to the new society, this exclusive system of management is, in our opinion, enough to condemn it.

ALLEGED REASONS FOR DIVISION.

The causes of division in this State are stated in the Address of the Executive Committee to be three: 1. 'The Woman Question.' 2. 'Political Action.' 3. 'No Human Government Views.' The Committee 'have witnessed, with grief unspeakable, the perversion, in this State, of our associations to purposes and objects not contemplated in our bond of union, foreign to our original objects, not necessary to their attainment, and, in view of the reflecting, fatal to our prospects of ultimate success.' To allow women to sit and act in anti-slavery meetings as

equal, human beings is, in their opinion, 'a violation of good faith —
such as might justly impair the public confidence in our integrity, and
multiply hindrances to the eventual success of our efforts' — and is 'a
mill-stone to sink to the depths of a bottomless ocean the hopes of enslaved millions'! Hence, for this reason, 'the only alternative for the
dissentients is constant contention, silent submission, or final separation.' Either they must be excluded, or the women silenced, because
(to quote their own words) 'the object of our exertions is important
and onerous enough to demand *all* our efforts — our *undivided* efforts'!
The very reason why the aid of the women is deemed to be indispen-
ible by abolitionists!

'THE WOMAN QUESTION' — THE OLD SOCIETY ON CONSTITUTIONAL GROUND.

It thus appears that 'the head and front of the offending' [6] of the
Massachusetts A. S. Society is, that women as well as men are permitted in its meetings to vote, speak and act, as duty may seem to
dictate. This alone is urged as a sufficient reason why there should
be a separation, and an impassable gulf placed between the two
organizations. It is a matter of *conscience* with our seceding brethren.
Many (if not all) of them 'consider the contemplated change in the
sphere of female action, a moral wrong — a thing forbidden alike by
the word of God, the dictates of right reason, the voice of wisdom,
and the modesty of unperverted nature.' It is not for 'the noblest hearts
that beat responsive to the call of mercy for the down-trodden' to lift
up their voices in the presence of *men*, in an *anti-slavery* meeting, in
supplicating tones for the deliverance of twelve hundred thousand of
their sex from pollution and slavery! How the seceding party can
suppose that their plea of 'conscience' will be respected, while they
act as though they had none, in this respect, is matter of surprise. They
cannot belong to the State Society, it seems, because it admits women
to equal membership; but they can make their own organization
auxiliary to the American Society, which is guilty of the very same misdemeanor! * We are constrained to say, in their own language, that
'we cannot but regard this as evidence of conscious wrongdoing:
we are pained to be compelled to expose conduct so dishonorable.'
Why should they treat as unpardonable in one society, what they
wink at in another? Why make war upon an auxiliary society for
doing that which is sanctioned by the parent society? Why single

* The American Society has even gone beyond the Massachusetts
Society, by appointing women on committees. The State Society has
never done this.

out the Massachusetts Anti-Slavery Society as worthy to suffer death, while other societies, equally guilty, (!) are not even arraigned for their conduct? If there be nothing personal, nothing sectarian, nothing ulterior, on the part of the seceders, why this strange inconsistency of conduct? In the Eastern (Penn.) Society, women have been enrolled as members, acted on committees, &c. But who has heard of any outbreak, in consequence, among the abolitionists of that State? Is there no 'conscience' on this subject in that quarter? If not, *why* not? In the same manner, women have actively participated in the proceedings of the Rhode Island Society; and they have also been received as delegates in the Connecticut Society. The Massachusetts A. S. Society stands precisely in the same attitude as the American Society, the New England Convention, the Rhode Island, Connecticut, Pennsylvania and Ohio Societies; and, therefore if it ought not any longer to be upheld by abolitionists, all the rest deserve to be treated in the same manner. We call upon the friends of emancipation to note, that *this violent attack upon the State Society is also an attack upon the American Society.* It is true, the new organization is made auxiliary to the latter; but only in the vain hope that the American Society 'will retrace its steps' at the next annual meeting. Should it adhere to its recent decision, then an attempt will doubtless be made to organize a rival national society, to be managed by a small conservative body, after the pattern of the Massachusetts Abolition Society. We trust that this warning will not be disregarded or forgotten. We cannot believe that this disorganizing movement will receive any countenance from genuine abolitionists, to any considerable extent, either in this State or elsewhere.

The Executive Committee ask in their Address — 'What has this question to do with the deliverance of the bond-slaves of our country — whether, as a matter of right, females should exercise all the social, political and religious rights, discharge all the corresponding duties, and be subject to all the connected liabilities attached to them, equally with the other sex?' *No anti-slavery society has attempted to settle this question.* What rights women ought to enjoy in the church or in social life, or whether they ought to be allowed to use the elective franchise or be eligible to political office, are questions which abolitionists have never attempted to discuss: they are foreign to the object they have in view, namely, the utter extinction of slavery. On this point we are happy in being able to quote the language of the Executive Committee of the Parent Society, as expressing our deliberate conviction. Alluding to the admission of women at the late annual meeting of that society, in their recent address to the abolitionists of the United States, they justly say — 'The vote of the society, being grounded on the phraseology of its constitution, *cannot be justly regarded as committing the society in favor of any controverted principle, respecting the equal rights of women to participate in the management of public affairs.*' It should also be remembered, that the language of the resolutions which have been adopted by the Massachusetts Society, inviting individuals to participate in its proceedings, *has been in exact conformity with the terms of its constitution* — including all '*persons*' in favor of immediate emancipation, &c. The only offence, therefore, of which the Society is guilty, is that of refusing to declare that women, who have complied with all the requirements of the Constitution, are not 'persons' within the meaning of that instrument! In other words, it will not *exclude* from a free participation in its proceedings, on account of their *sex*, 'persons' who agree with it in principle and cheerfully contribute to its funds! It will not say to its own annual and life-members, when they present themselves at its meetings, 'Stand aside — your sex renders it improper that you should act with us in our efforts to redeem the slave from his bondage!' In *principle*, therefore, the society stands just where it has stood from the beginning on the firm basis of its Constitution. At its annual meeting as long ago as 1836, it adopted the following resolution by an *unanimous* vote: 'Resolved, That we consider the anti-slavery cause the cause of philanthropy, with regard to which *all human beings*, white men and colored men, citizens and foreigners, MEN and WOMEN, HAVE THE SAME DUTIES AND THE SAME RIGHTS.' For acting in accordance with the principle thus emphatically laid down, *more than three years ago,* the society is now arraigned as unworthy of confidence!

The anti-slavery society is a voluntary association, of temporary character, amenable to no ecclesiastical tribunal or political body. In deciding for itself the conditions of membership, it takes no cognizance of what is either allowed or prohibited by any other association. In allowing all *persons* who are hostile to slavery to enrol their names as members, and to open their mouths in the cause of the suffering and the dumb, it confines itself to 'its appropriate sphere,' and is doing its legitimate work. It does not necessarily endorse what is advanced by any speaker, and it throws the whole responsibility upon every *person* who takes any part in its proceedings.

It is argued that an unfair construction is put upon the word *persons*. But it has been decided by the American and other societies, that this construction is the proper one. Either the phraseology of the Constitution must be altered, or women must be admitted to equal privileges.

It is further argued, that no women participated in the formation of the Parent Society, nor have taken any part in its meetings until recently. The fact that, for a time, they neglected or declined to co-operate in this manner, does not prove that it is either unconstitutional or improper for them to do so now. As soon as the question was raised, whether they had a right to act as members and delegates, it was settled in the affirmative. Yet, in all that they have uttered in our meetings, they have not occupied the space of a single hour! No desire has ever been manifested, on their part, to crowd themselves forward; and in the few words that have dropped from their lips, they have spoken with great propriety, and been listened to with respect. Is it for this that the Massachusetts and American Societies are to be broken up, if they will not 'retrace their steps'?

> 'Think of the frantic mother,
>   Lamenting for her child,
> Till falling lashes smother
>   Her cries of anguish wild!
> Shall we behold, unheeding,
>   Life's holiest feelings crushed?
> *When woman's heart is bleeding,*
>   *Shall woman's voice be hushed?*' [7]

Hushed, too, in a meeting, the exclusive object of which is to break the yokes and fetters of slavery! Will it prove 'a mill-stone to sink to the depths of a bottomless ocean the hopes of enslaved millions'?

We are confident that this subject will be seen in its true light by all candid, reflecting abolitionists; and that enough has been advanced to show that no valid excuse has been offered by the Executive Committee of the new society, for their withdrawal from the anti-slavery ranks.

POLITICAL ACTION.

The next charge brought by this Committee against the State Anti-Slavery Society is, that it 'repudiates or looks coldly upon political action,' for the abolition of slavery, and has virtually sanctioned what are styled the 'no human government views.' This charge is utterly groundless. We give it our emphatic denial, whether it be insinuated covertly, or alleged openly. This Society and its Board feel as deeply interested in the application of its principles to political action, at the present time, and hold the same opinions respecting the use of the elective franchise, as they have done from the beginning. The only proof that is adduced by the Committee to make good their charge is this: — At the last annual meeting of the State Society, the following resolution was offered by A. St. Clair, at the close of a warm discussion of political action:

'Resolved, That it is the imperious duty of every abolitionist, who can conscientiously exercise the elective franchise, to go promptly to the polls and deposit his vote in favor of some man, who, if elected, will use his utmost constitutional power for the immediate overthrow of slavery.'

On motion of W. L. Garrison, the following was adopted in its stead:

'Resolved, That those abolitionists, who feel themselves called upon, by a sense of duty, to go to the polls, and yet purposely absent themselves from the polls whenever an opportunity is presented to vote for a friend of the slave — or who, when there, follow their party predilections to the abandonment of their abolition principles — *are recreant to their high professions,* AND UNWORTHY OF THE NAME THEY ASSUME.'

For adopting this admonitory resolution, (rebuking political hypocrisy and inconsistency in professed abolitionists,) in preference to the one offered by Mr. St. Clair, the State Society is charged with having abandoned political action, 'suffered the staff of accomplishment to pass from its hands,' and endorsed the sentiments of the Non-Resistance Society!!! Such a charge is indeed too ridiculous to need any refutation. The resolution speaks, not of abandoning the elective franchise, but of the guilt and condemnation which must rest upon those abolitionists who shall neglect or refuse to carry out their principles at the ballot-box, in their blind subserviency to party politics. It is one of the cardinal doctrines of the new organization, that it is the religious duty of every man to be a voter, his conscientious scruples to the contrary notwithstanding. What, then, would have been gained by the adoption of Mr. St. Clair's hypothetical resolution? Referring to these two resolutions, and the action of the society upon them, the Executive Committee of the new society make the following extraordinary commentary:

'A resolution is presented, affirming the old anti-slavery doctrine, that the use of the elective franchise for the slave is duty. Non-governmentism opposes it, and offers a substitute. The society yields, refuses to affirm its doctrine of duty, and adopts the non-government one of consistency. What, under such circumstances, is refusal to affirm, but denial of the doctrine? What, but a repudiation of human politics in the case, and a shaping of abolition in conformity with that model? What, but the adoption of a non-political, non-government abolition'? (!!)

Nothing can be more absurd, sophistical or slanderous, than assertions like these. It is declared that Mr. St. Clair's resolution 'affirms the old anti-slavery doctrine,' &c. But the language of that resolution is merely hypothetical, — refers only to those 'who can *conscientiously* exercise the elective franchise' — and is indisputably less strong and expressive than the one adopted by the society. We can hardly believe that the public will be frightened by the word 'non-governmentism,' seeing that it is defined to mean ☞ only the stern condemnation of such abolition voters as 'follow their party predilections to the abandonment of their abolition principles'! If this be 'non-political, non-government abolition,' and 'a repudiation of human politics,' 'a distinct and deliberate sacrifice of principle,' then all other anti-slavery societies in the land are equally guilty in this matter!

At the late annual meeting of the Ohio State A. S. Society, the following resolution was introduced by James G. Birney:

'Resolved, That the elective franchise is a power conferred in the providence of God on the citizens of the United States for good — which they ought to use, and invariably, for the election to legislative and other stations of trust, of those only who, being of good moral character, are known to be favorable to human rights, and the abrogation of all distinctions in right founded on color.'

The only objection, says the Philanthropist, which was made to this resolution, was, that its passage would conflict needlessly with the peculiar notions of the Covenanters, who were members of the Society, and who, believing that the government of the United States was wrong, refrain, on conscientious grounds, from voting. The resolution was accordingly modified, so as to read, after the first clause, ending with the word 'good' — '*which those who can conscientiously vote, ought to use inviolably for the election,*' &c. The Ohio A. S. Society, therefore, (according to the doctrine of the seceders here) has given up 'the staff of accomplishment,' and gone over to 'non-governmentism'!!

The following resolutions were unanimously adopted at the late New-England A. S. Convention, held in Boston:

'Resolved, That the Constitution of the American A. S. Society is silent as to the duty of abolitionists, as such, to use the elective franchise.

Resolved, That it is not essential to membership in that Society, that a man must believe either in the propriety or impropriety of voting at the polls.

Resolved, therefore, That those who, in the anti-slavery ranks, are pointing the finger of reproach at some of their brethren who do not feel bound either as abolitionists or as Christians to be political voters in any case, violate the fraternal spirit of our sacred league, and act as schismatics.'

Therefore, the New-England A. S. Convention is a 'non-government body'!

In the Emancipator of August 5th, 1837, then under the control of the Corresponding Secretary of the new organization, and editor of the Massachusetts Abolitionist, (Elizur Wright, Jr.) is the following editorial declaration:

'With the abstract question of *the rightfulness of human govern-ments,* AS AN EDITOR OF THE ANTI-SLAVERY SOCIETY, WE HAVE NOTH-ING TO DO; ☞ *nor will our publications cudgel any man for his sentiments on this question.'*

This is the position assumed by the Massachusetts A. S. Society — one of neutrality. Yet the same individual, who made the above decla-ration in his official character as the mouth-piece of the American Society, is now placed at the head of an anti-slavery journal,[8] in this State, for the express purpose of cudgelling all those in the abolition ranks who do not agree with him on 'the abstract question of the rightfulness of human governments'! And a new organization has been formed, to hold up to obloquy such abolitionists as feel com-pelled, by a sense of religious duty, not to go to the polls on any occasion! Let all candid and impartial minds determine, who are guilty of dragging into the abolition cause foreign questions, and thus throwing our ranks into confusion — whether they are not those who are charging the State Society with acting thus treacherously.

In our last annual report, we denied 'that it is competent for any anti-slavery society, by its votes or through its organ, to arraign either the political or religious views of its members. It may with no more propriety decide, that one man is *morally* bound to cast a vote at the polls, than that another man is morally bound to unite himself to the church. On this subject, there are many conflicting but honest opinions entertained by abolitionists.' For thus vindicating the rights of con-science, and conceding to every abolitionist the right to enjoy his own opinions respecting Church and State, the Executive Committee of the new organization falsely and foolishly declare that 'this is saying, in almost so many words, that every anti-slavery society is, of course, a no-human-government society'!! Such puerility certainly betokens a clouded intellect, a jaundiced vision, or an uncharitable state of mind. We are deeply conscientious in this matter, and therefore feel no disposition to trample upon the consciences of others.

The views which are entertained by us on this subject, are excellently expressed by the Editor of the Emancipator,[9] in the following para-graphs: Speaking for himself, he says —

'The writer of this is free to declare, that after diligent and repeated examination, he is unable to find any such principle laid down in the con-stitution, as that 'it is the religious duty of every person to whom the State grants the privilege, to vote at the polls,' or any thing equivalent to it.'

'It is a well known fact, that there have been, from the beginning, many members of the Society, who have conscientiously abstained from voting at the polls, some for one reason and some for another. The Covenanters, or Reformed Presbyterians, as a sect, wholly abstain from taking a part in elections or holding office, under our National Constitution, because it contains no recognition of the government of God. Many members of the Society of Friends keep aloof from the polls, because the Constitution countenances slavery. Others have different reasons. Many conscientious individuals have kept away through disgust of the ordinary methods of electioneering. Yet these persons voluntarily consented to the 'principles of the Constitution,' and became members of the Society, and no man could constitutionally challenge their right to membership. If there was any difficulty, it lay in their minds, and if they saw it not, it was the same as if it did not exist. Contemporaneous and uniform usage has therefore settled the question, that those who conscientiously abstain from voting may be constitutionally members. . . . BECAUSE THE DUTY OF VOTING IS A POINT WHICH THE CONSTITUTION HAS LEFT UNDECIDED.'

'It should be always borne in mind, that there are other modes of 'political' action, besides voting, as there are other modes of 'moral action' besides church discipline. Petitioning Congress or the State Legislature, is political action. Abstaining from voting, for the purpose of thereby influencing the measures of government, is political action. Questioning candidates is also political action. So, refusing to unite with a church, because that church is supposed to countenance slavery, is moral action. A thousand questions may arise in the detail, concerning which it is competent for the Society to decide, so far as its organized action is concerned, but on which it has no power to bind the conscience or coerce the will of members acting in their individual capacity, and no right to preclude from membership those who refuse to go with the majority. In regard to all these matters, a just discrimination, a kind and confiding spirit, and a paramount devotion to the ONE OBJECT which unites us, will doubtless prevent all severe collisions. But any appearance of a desire for domination, an intolerant spirit, or a design to thrust in other objects, and make them ride on the anti-slavery car, will infallibly create resistance, jealousy and discord.'

Let this catholic, fraternal spirit be ever cherished by all the sincere friends of emancipation, and it will go well with us and our enterprise to the final consummation of our wishes.

The Executive Committee of the new organization, in an appendix to their Address, have grouped together various political resolutions that have been adopted by anti-slavery societies, from time to time — the views of individual abolitionists, respecting political action, &c. &c. — in order to prove that it was among the original, fundamental doctrines of abolitionism, that the exercise of the elective franchise is obligatory upon every member of the Anti-Slavery Society, entitled to this privilege. They attempt to show, that this doctrine has recently been rejected by the State Society, and, consequently, that 'the old pioneer society has fallen, having thrown away its principles, and with them the staff of its power.'

This long array of quotations is entirely useless, because it is certain that, from the organization of the American A. S. Society down to the present schism, it was never imagined that none could be sound members of the society, except those who believed in the rightfulness of existing human governments, and held to the use of the elective franchise. Among the signers of the Declaration of Sentiments at Philadelphia, and those who adopted the Constitution of the Parent Society, were several individuals who had religious scruples about going to the polls. Of course, they never supposed that, in endorsing the one, or subscribing their names to the other, they were bound to give up those scruples as heresies too monstrous to be tolerated in the breast of any individual connected with an anti-slavery organization. 'In the mouth of two or three witnesses, every word shall be established.' [10] At the late meeting of the New-England A. S. Convention, no less than six of the signers of the Declaration just alluded to were present, viz. Effingham L. Capron, Isaac Winslow, Nathan Winslow,[11] Samuel J. May, George W. Benson, and Wm. Lloyd Garrison. These all rose successively, and explictly stated that, in affixing their names to that instrument, and in assisting in the formation of the national society, they never supposed, (nor did they believe any of their associates cherished the idea,) that those who could not conscientiously act as electors were not qualified to be members of the anti-slavery organization. Such a doctrine was never heard of until within a few months in Massachusetts; and it is too proscriptive to receive the sanction of any considerable number of abolitionists in any part of the country. The utmost harmony had invariably prevailed in all our meetings, in the passage of political resolutions, until a disposition was manifested, by those who have gone out from among us, to arraign those abolitionists, who hold non-resistance opinions, as recreant to their anti-slavery obligations. The real ground of division, therefore, is, not that the Massachusetts Society has sanctioned, directly or indirectly, the peculiar doctrines of non resistants, but that it has refused to condemn them, or to make itself a party, in any way, to the controversy which is now going on between the friends and opponents of the non-resistance enterprise. In short, to use the language of the Corresponding Secretary of the new Society in 1837, it believes, and has acted on the belief, that '*with the abstract question of the rightfulness of human government,*' it has and should have 'NOTHING TO DO!' It has refused to '*cudgel any man for his sentiments on this question,*' because it has neither the right nor the power, under its Constitution, to do so.

Again: The mass of political evidence which has been industriously accumulated by the Executive Committee of the new organization, to sustain them in their schismatical conduct, is nothing to the purpose — because a large portion of it is quoted as the sentiments of individual abolitionists, for which neither the Massachusetts nor any other anti-slavery society is responsible; because another considerable portion of

it is of a *negative* character — merely declaring that abolitionists ought
not to prostitute their suffrages by voting for pro-slavery candidates,
&c. &c. in which all are agreed; and because the remainder of it, in
which political action is enjoined upon abolitionists as a duty, is expressed in language *used in a general and popular sense, and which
was never understood nor intended to be invidious or proscriptive in
its application.* It is certainly true, that the Anti-Slavery Society has
always contemplated the use of POLITICAL as well as MORAL action
for the abolition of slavery, *because the moral and political action of
the nation is enlisted in support of that dreadful system.* Hence, in
addressing its appeals to the people, it measured them by their own
views of duty, whether orthodox or heterodox, whigs or democrats;
without sitting in judgment upon either their religious or political
opinions. In making men abolitionists, it did not contemplate any
alteration in their views on other subjects; and as the great mass of
the people held to the use of the elective franchise, it enjoined upon
them the duty of carrying their abolition principles to the ballot-box,
instead of allowing themselves to be made the tools of party and the
instruments of oppression.

But, it is said, resolutions on the subject of political action are
now rejected in anti-slavery meetings, though expressed in language
which was formerly deemed unobjectionable. To what is this change
to be attributed? It is an impeachment of the integrity of abolitionists
to say that they have abandoned any of their principles; it is an outrage upon truth to represent them as passive instruments in the hands
of any man or body of men; it is flagrant injustice to accuse them of
being 'no human government men,' on this account. ☞ The only reason
why such resolutions are now rejected is, that whereas they were
once passed without any invidious meaning, they are now presented
for the express purpose of giving them a proscriptive application —
of impeaching the abolition fidelity of some of the earliest and best
friends of our cause, and making a division in the anti-slavery ranks.
☜ Such intolerance will ever be frowned upon by genuine abolitionism.

It is claimed by the new organization, that various anti-slavery
periodicals, in other parts of the country, have welcomed its birth.
True — *but not in its true character — as a rival of the Massachusetts
A. S. Society.* In their ignorance of the real facts in the case, these
journals have taken it for granted, that the two societies might co-
operate together harmoniously. Had they examined the subject attentively, — and, especially, had they remembered that the abolitionists
of this Commonwealth are more competent to decide correctly than
themselves upon the merits of this controversy, and that *their* verdict

is almost unanimously against the new society, — they would have spoken in a different tone.

The charges which are brought by the Executive Committee of the *Abolition* Society against the State Anti-Slavery Society, are of a vital character. They accuse it of being 'perverted to purposes and objects not contemplated in our bond of union' — of attaching to the cause 'a mill-stone to sink to the depths of a bottomless ocean the hopes of enslaved millions' — of 'dishonorable conduct and conscious wrong-doing' — of having abandoned, with reference to political action, 'the original doctrines and measures of our associations' — of making 'a distinct and deliberate sacrifice of principles to the sectarian dogmas' of a few individuals — of being 'fully identified with the sectarian views of its individual members' — of adopting 'non-political, non-government abolition' — of having 'fallen,' and 'thrown away its principles, and with them the staff of its power'!!

To these accusations, in the name of the Massachusetts Society, we plead not guilty. If they are true, then this Society ought to be abandoned by every friend of God and man. If they are slanderous, then the new organization deserves to receive the severest condemnation. In either case, it is insulting to both parties to say that they may act fraternally together! How can two walk together, except they are agreed? In our judgment, the abolitionists of Massachusetts should give no countenance to the new organization, by their regard for the honor, purity and success of their great enterprise. As to the innumerable misrepresentations which are put in circulation by the agents and friends of that organization, against the State A. S. Society, — though they may deceive and mislead many, for a time, — they will ultimately recoil upon the heads of those who give them currency. We claim to stand or fall upon our official acts and publications, and are ever ready to challenge investigation.

In conclusion — we rejoice to believe that the disaffection in our ranks has extended itself to a very small number, and that the main body of abolitionists in this State are sound to the core. We place the utmost reliance upon their intelligence, discernment and integrity. They are too strongly influenced by PRINCIPLE to be easily led astray. Let them watch and pray, lest they enter into temptation. United they stand — divided they fall. Let them mark those men who counsel division. Our sole reliance must be upon God, not upon men. We believe that the anti-slavery cause is founded upon a rock, — THE ETERNAL ROCK, — and cannot be overthrown. We blush at the want of faith in its divine origin and holy invincibleness exhibited by those professed abolitionists, who cry out against the free discussion, by individuals, of any question, — whether it relate to peace or war, a human or divine government, religion or politics, Church or State, — as endangering the life of our enterprise! — Abolition thrives in exact proportion to the growth of free discussion on all moral and political subjects. The examination and discussion of no other question can possibly injure it. Its single object is to extirpate slavery from the American soil, and whatever is not oppressive in spirit has nothing to apprehend in its progress. It must and will prevail.

FRANCIS JACKSON, *President.*

WM. LLOYD GARRISON, *Secretary.*

Boston, July 17, 1839.

Printed in The Liberator, July 19, 1839.

This public letter was in response to an address by the executive committee of the newly formed Massachusetts Abolition Society (*Life*, II, 306).

1. The Massachusetts Anti-Slavery Society and the Massachusetts Abolition Society. The latter was officially organized on May 27 and 29 in Boston, by secessionists from the annual meeting of the New England Anti-Slavery Convention, which convened on May 28. Elizur Wright, Amos Phelps, and Charles T. Torrey were among its leaders (*Life*, II, 306–307). The secession was the culmination of differences over the role of women in the antislavery movement and over the questions of political action, nonresistance, and matters of religious doctrine such as the Sabbath.

2. The reference is to Garrison's editorial, "Watchman, What of the Night?," in *The Liberator*, January 11, 1839, in which he warned that "there is a deep scheme laid by individuals, at present somewhat conspicuous as zealous and active abolitionists, to put the control of the anti-slavery movements in this Commonwealth into other hands."

3. An evil in itself.

4. A variation of I Corinthians 9:19–21.

5. Those named are the Reverend Daniel Wise, the Reverend Asa Cummings, the Reverend Orange Scott, and the Reverend George Allen of Shrewsbury.

The Reverend Asa Cummings (1790–1856), Congregationalist, born in Andover, Massachusetts, was the son of Deacon Asa Cummings. He graduated from Harvard in 1817 and from Andover Theological Seminary in 1820. He held a pastorate in Yarmouth, Maine, from 1821 to 1825, and continued as honorary pastor there until 1829, when he retired as a result of ill health. He was editor of the *Christian Mirror* for twenty-nine years, beginning in 1826. It was a Congregational newspaper, of which he became proprietor in 1846. Apparently, he was a very "prudent" antislavery man. (George Mooar, comp., *The Cummings Memorial, A Genealogical History of the Descendants of Isaac Cummings*, New York, 1903, pp. 297–300.)

6. *Othello*, I, iii.

7. Elizabeth M. Chandler, "Think of Our Country's Glory," second and fourth stanzas, in Benjamin Lundy, ed., *The Poetical Works of Elizabeth Margaret Chandler* (Philadelphia, 1836), p. 64.

8. The *Massachusetts Abolitionist.*

9. Joshua Leavitt.

10. Deuteronomy 19:15; Matthew 18:16.

11. Nathan Winslow (b. Falmouth, Maine, March 27, 1785; d. Portland, Maine, September 9, 1861), a Quaker and hardware merchant, the brother of Isaac Winslow, was one of Garrison's earliest supporters, a subscriber to *The Liberator* from the date of its first issue until his death, one of its most reliable

financial supporters, and, with his brother, a founder of the American Anti-Slavery Society. He later became the father-in-law of Samuel E. Sewall. (*Life*, I, 289; II, 479; David Parsons Holton and Mrs. Frances K. Holton, *Winslow Memorial*, New York, 1888, II, 885–886.)

159

TO SAMUEL OSGOOD

[August 2, 1839.]

DEAR SIR:

I thank you for your letter of the 7th instant.[1] You do me great injustice to suppose that it is 'altogether probable' that I shall think and speak 'contemptuously' of your suggestions. Whatever is written in a kind spirit, (and you seem to be animated by such a spirit,) I hope ever to reciprocate in a charitable frame of mind. It does not necessarily follow, that he who uses severe and denunciatory language in rebuking hypocrites and time-servers, will use the same language in all cases, and under all circumstances. I cannot forget, that it is no less a christian duty to 'be courteous,' and to 'speak evil of no man,'[2] than it is to be faithful in admonishing the guilty, and to preach the truth, 'whether men will hear, or whether they will forbear.'[3]

If you have attentively read the documents that have been issued by the Managers of the Massachusetts Anti-Slavery Society, in vindication of the Society and of themselves from the charges which have been brought against them by the leading friends of the new organization, it will not be necessary for me to make an extended reply to your letter, because in those documents, you will find an elaborate refutation of many points alluded to by you; and it will hardly be profitable for me again to travel over the same ground. If you have carefully marked the rise and progress of the division in the anti-slavery ranks in this Commonwealth, and weighed the reasons which are urged in favor of a new State organization, you can no longer, with any show of consistency or propriety, hope or expect, that the two societies 'will labor apart' harmoniously, and 'emulate one another in every good work.' If you have candidly read both sides of the controversy, you ought not any longer to marvel at the alienation which exists between the friends of the old and the new organization.

You 'was not in favor of the new organization from the beginning.' You 'did believe that a little mutual condescension would remove the difficulties.' You express the belief, that if I, and the friends of the old society, 'will manifest a kinder spirit towards our opponents, all dissensions may be healed, and there may yet be but one society in

Massachusetts.' You are 'not a member of the new society, or of the old Massachusetts Society,' but think you could 'work for the cause under the banners of either.' You 'cannot perceive what we expect to gain by carrying on a warfare with the new society.' You express regret that I opposed a resolution brought forward in the last New-England Anti-Slavery Convention, by brother May, to attempt a 'compromise.'⁴ And it seems to you that I have feared (!!) that the dissensions which exist 'would be amicably settled by mutual concession, and that by such a healing measure,' I would 'lose some portion of the great influence'(!!) I have in the old society — &c. &c.

At all this I am disposed to smile and wonder. Allow me to say, that, though you make a show of candor and magnanimity, your letter is deficient in fairness and discrimination. Nothing can be more disingenuous than your attempt to account for the new organization on the score of my unkindness of spirit, or severity of language, or 'the unsparing abuse which has been poured out upon the clergy, through the columns of the Liberator.' Unless you mean to impeach the honesty and veracity of those who have seceded from the old society, you have certainly made a false issue; and, hence, your letter is destitute of any intrinsic value. You know, or ought to know, that the reasons which you have given for the schism in our ranks are not those which are alleged by the Massachusetts Abolitionist, or by the leading friends of the new movement. How can you, as a fair and candid man, thus change the entire ground of the controversy? As to 'the manner in which the clergy have been treated in the Liberator,' I have the public testimony of Orange Scott, that it has not been too severe; that all that I have said against them, as a body, is true, and warranted by the facts in the case; that I have been too lenient rather than too uncharitable. And let me assure you that if you expect the course of the Abolitionist, on this subject, will be different from that which has been pursued by the Liberator, you are greatly mistaken — unless a radical change shall take place in the views and feelings of its editor, respecting those who are 'blind leaders of the blind,' the greatest stumbling-blocks in the way of every moral reformation. Just turn to an editorial article in the last number of that paper, respecting a letter from President Lord,⁵ as a sample of what is to come. Elizur Wright, Jr. is not the man to complain of my treatment of a hireling priesthood — of those who (to quote his own expressive language) 'are emphatically a disgrace to the pastoral office' — who 'raise a bitter cry about irreverence towards their pastoral rights and dignity' — and who are 'lost in the pulpit for want of size.' A great deal of clamor is raised by certain self-convicted chief priests, who have never opened their lips on the subject of slavery but for apology, about my 'attacks upon the clergy;' but I can truly affirm with my friend Wright, 'I wage no war with the ministry, but with the clerical drones with which it is so shamefully burdened.' I hold to the office of the ministry, though my views as to the manner in which that office should be filled and occupied may differ very widely from yours. I clearly perceive the artifice that is resorted to by the corrupt men who have crept into that office. They hold up their office as a shield to protect them from the assaults of truth and justice; and when thus assailed, cry out that attempts are making to disparage or destroy the ministerial office. Cunning men! They shall be caught in their own craftiness. Now, the *office* is one thing — but the character of those who are in it is quite a different consideration. *That office I have never assailed*; but I plead guilty to the charge of having rebuked many of those who are fast bringing it into contempt, in the eyes of the ungodly, by their time-serving policy. Yet, even of this class, the Liberator has not published severer things than have appeared in the Emancipator, the Friend of Man, the Herald of Freedom, and other anti-slavery periodicals; or than have been uttered by such men as Orange Scott, A. A. Phelps, Nathaniel Colver, James T. Woodbury, Charles Fitch, Joshua Leavitt, and Alanson St. Clair — all clergymen. The truth is, during my editorial labors in this cause, I have written comparatively but very little — certainly, not a tenth part so much as I ought to have done, or at least should have been justified in doing — in condemnation of the exceedingly criminal course which, up to this hour, has been pursued by the great body of American clergymen, on the subject of slavery. I challenge any one to quote any thing which has fallen from my lips or pen, in relation to these men, which is not true to the letter, and which I cannot prove to be merited by the testimony of 'a thousand witnesses' — all occupants of the pastoral office. I do not remember to have seen a single fair quotation made from my strictures upon the clergy, by those who accuse me of treating them unjustly. Why is all this? Even you, Dr. Osgood, join in the hue-and-cry, and *mildly* and *charitably* talk about 'the *unsparing abuse* which has been poured out upon the clergy through the columns of the Liberator.' Now, I deny that I have indulged in any such 'abuse,' at any time; and, remember, I shall hold you responsible to make good your charge. If you wish to examine the files of the Liberator, they are at your service. You say — 'I utterly deny that *all* whom you have so often and so severely censured have deserved it.' Your denial is too general to avail any thing. Will you please to specify? Show me the men whom I have unduly censured — quote me fairly — and then let the public decide whether 'these men are true philanthropists, who have no sympathy with the slaveholders, who would do any thing to benefit the slave.' Excuse me if I hold you to this point — if I insist upon your *naming the men*, and *producing the evidence.* — You further charge me with having 'involved the entire mass of *non conformists* among the clergy in an indiscriminate condemnation; when there are a variety of grades in their ranks, from the deliberate apologist for the system of slavery, down to the man who is almost persuaded to join the abolitionists.' If you mean, by this language, that I have been no respecter of persons, but have rebuked all those who have refused to open their mouths 'in the cause of all such as are appointed to destruction,' and joined in assailing anti-slavery principles and measures, then the charge is true. If you mean by it, that I have assailed any minister who has gloried in the unpopular name of 'abolitionist,' and who has not failed to maintain that slave-holding is a crime under all possible circumstances, and therefore ought to be immediately abandoned, then I deny the accusation, and call for the proof. *The class against whom I have written has been as clearly defined, and as unquestionable in character, as southern slave-holders themselves.* My arrows have never been discharged at random. I have not been 'indiscriminate' in my 'condemnation.' Such men as A. A. Phelps, Orange Scott, Joshua Leavitt, Joshua V. Himes, Samuel J. May, &c. &c., have never winced under any of my strictures upon the pro-slavery character of the clergy; for the very good reason that the coat did not fit them, and they knew, *and all the people knew*, that it was not made for their backs. You ask — 'Because a clergyman, from motives of *prudence*, (!) refuses to join the ranks of the abolitionists, and perhaps *throws his influence into the* [*scale of the*] *opposite party*, is he to be held up to his people and the community as a man who has forfeited all claims to their confidence, and as deserving of reprehension?' I answer, YES — and all true-hearted, clear-sighted abolitionists will unitedly respond in the affirmative. They are con-strained to believe that the man who will not only stand aloof from their ranks, but will join with their opponents, and throw the weight of his influence into the scale of slavery, and strike hands with thieves, and consent with adulterers, is unworthy to be regarded as 'a watch-man upon the walls of Zion,' [6] or a minister of Him who came 'to bind up the broken-hearted — to proclaim liberty to the captives, and the opening of prisons to them that are bound.' [7]

Again you say — 'You have not appeared to think that the same laws govern the minds of clergymen, that you would acknowledge in reference to other intellectual men.' In this you are mistaken. It is because I have believed them to be governed by the same laws as other men, and to be influenced by similar motives, that I have thus freely animadverted, from time to time, upon their conduct. They can be as easily corrupted, as easily inflated with pride, as easily led to take the part of time-servers and parasites, and as cheaply bought with money, as other men. *As a body*, they are 'dumb dogs that cannot bark,' [8] and 'hirelings who care not for the sheep.' [9] Among them are some of the most self-sacrificing and devoted men of the age, who fear not the face of man, who glory in tribulation, and trample under foot all earthly considerations, so that they may win Christ, and fight the good fight of faith — but they are, alas! — 'like angels' visits' [10] — few and far between.

Again you remark — 'Some fully believe that you have, from the beginning, been aiming a blow, in a covert manner, at the permanency of the ministerial office,' &c. But you do not credit the charge. Then why allude to it? Is it worth your while to rake up and publish scandalous accusations which you do not believe, and which are certainly false? 'Some fully believe' — or pretend to believe — that abolitionists mean to deluge the land in blood — but what of all this? You have been *told* that I once said, in reference to an individual — 'The only way to make that man feel is to knock him down' — and you gravely remark upon this apocryphal story, 'I have not so learned Christ.' You have *heard it said*, that I have expressed a wish that the clergy 'would draw off from the subject of emancipation.'! Dr. Osgood, is it worthy of you to retail such flying rumors? Are you indeed so straitened for evidence to condemn me, that you must resort to what may be said of me by the tongue of scandal to sustain your accusations? Is this doing as you would be done by?

I am just leaving the city to attend the national anti-slavery convention at Albany,[11] and have therefore written this letter in great haste. Some other parts of your communication shall receive my attention on my return. In the mean time, I desire you to remember, that the reasons offered by you and the leaders of the new organization for that schismatical movement *are totally dissimilar.* You attribute it to my unsparing abuse of the clergy, &c. They assert that it is because women are admitted to equal membership in our society, that the Massachusetts Anti-Slavery Society is no longer what it once was, that it has thrown away 'the staff of accomplishment,' &c. &c. To what purpose, then, have you written?

       Yours, for truth and consistency,

S. Osgood.   WM. LLOYD GARRISON.

Printed in *The Liberator*, August 2, 1839.

    Dr. Samuel Osgood (b. February 3, 1784; d. December 8, 1862) was pastor of the First Church of Christ in Springfield, Massachusetts, from 1809 to 1854. His theological beliefs were orthodox. An active Mason, he was an officer and leader in the organization. From 1856 to 1862 he was a member of the Springfield school committee. At the first meeting of the Hampden County Anti-Slavery Society, held at his church in January, 1838, he was elected a vice-president,

although he was not a Garrisonian. He had earlier joined the American Colonization Society. (Mason A. Green, *Springfield 1836–1886, History of Town and City,*
Springfield, 1884, pp. 375–376, 442–443, 490, 606–607; Charles Wells Chapin,
Sketches of the Old Inhabitants and Mansions of Springfield, Springfield, 1893,
pp. 291–294.)

1. The letter from Samuel Osgood, dated Springfield, July 7, 1839, was printed
in *The Liberator,* August 2, 1839, together with Garrison's reply.

2. Titus 3:2.

3. Ezekiel 2:5, 7.

4. This refers to one of two resolutions introduced by Samuel J. May on
Thursday, May 30, 1839. The resolutions were:

"Resolved, that no reasonable and earnest effort should be omitted to heal
the division which has taken place among abolitionists and threatens to become
permanent and to extend itself.

"Resolved, therefore, that a Committee of seven be appointed to confer with
the members of the new organization, and to ascertain without delay, if practicable,
on what grounds or conditions, they will return to their former connexion, and
that in case the Convention has adjourned before the proposed conference is
concluded, the committee report to the Board of Managers of the Massachusetts
Anti-Slavery Society."

According to the report of the meeting in *The Liberator* (June 7, 1839),
Garrison spoke in favor of the first resolution and against the second. The first
resolution was carried, while the second "was indefinitely postponed."

5. The Reverend Nathan Lord (1792–1870), Congregational minister, became
president of Dartmouth College in 1828. He continued as president until 1863
when he was obliged to resign as a result of his proslavery views, expressed in a
book published in 1863, entitled *A True Picture of Abolition.* (*DAB.*) In 1839, he
considered himself an abolitionist. His views were printed in *The Liberator* on July
26, 1839.

6. "I have set watchmen upon thy walls, O Jerusalem . . ." (Isaiah 62:6.)

7. Isaiah 61:1.

8. Isaiah 56:10.

9. John 10:13.

10. The Reverend John Norris (1657–1711), English clergyman, theologian,
and author, "The Parting," *Collections of Miscellanies* (1678).

11. The National Convention of Abolitionists, called for July 31, 1839, by the
New York executive committee of the American Anti-Slavery Society. The
proposed meeting was approved by the American Anti-Slavery Society Convention in May. The invitation to the convention was extended to "such *freemen*
of the United States as adopt the principles embodied in the Constitution of the
American Anti-Slavery Society," the obvious intention being to exclude women.
The purpose of the convention was to be "the thorough discussion of those great
principles which lie at the foundation of the abolition enterprise, throughout the
civilized world; and of the measures which are suited to its accomplishment in
the United States, and especially those which relate to the proper exercise of the
right of suffrage by citizens of the free States. All questions and matters foreign
to this object will be cautiously avoided in the deliberations of the occasion."
(*Life,* II, 307–308.)

160

TO OLIVER JOHNSON

Brooklyn, (Ct.) Aug. 5, 1839.

BRO. JOHNSON:

Having just returned from the great National Convention in Albany,[1] I sit down to give you a brief account of it; — a brief account, I say, because I am very much fatigued with my journey, and for a better reason, because the entire proceedings have been reported by a skilful stenographer, and will be published without delay. I presume you have received, ere this, a printed slip from the office of the Emancipator, containing all the resolutions that were adopted, and other business items. The official intelligence thus promptly conveyed to you, you will, of course, lay before the readers of the Liberator this week.[2]

The number of delegates in attendance exceeded my expectations — about FIVE HUNDRED having placed their names upon the roll. Had the Convention been called two or three months later, I am confident, that not less than one thousand or fifteen hundred persons would have been convened together. Why the hottest and busiest season of the year was selected as the time for holding this meeting, I do not know. Unpropitious as it was, however, many more persons would have been present, I have reason to believe, had it not been for the exclusive spirit evinced in the call, and the attempt to make the Convention, in advance, on the part of some of our editorial brethren, an affair altogether political. On this account, but very little interest was taken in the Convention by the great body of abolitionists in Massachusetts; and hence, you will find, on reference to the list of delegates, that our State had a very small representation, aside from the mustering of a score of individuals in favor of the new organization, under the guidance of Messrs. Scott, St. Clair, Torrey, and Wise. As for myself, you know that, almost up to the last moment, I was undecided in my mind, whether to attend the Convention, or remain at home; solely on the ground that the Committee of Arrangements[3] had not given an invitation to the *abolitionists* of the United States, but to 'such *freemen*' only as subscribe to the principles of the American Anti-Slavery Society. I knew, indeed, that the Committee were not authorized to issue such a call; but as they had taken the liberty to use a restricted phraseology, I took it for granted that the Convention would assume a peculiar and novel aspect. Doubtless, many warm-hearted friends of the cause, in various parts of the country, were induced to remain at home, for these and other considerations.

As soon as the Convention was organized by the choice of officers, I rose and called upon the Committee of Arrangements to explain for what reasons, or on whose authority, they had confined their invitation to the 'freemen' of the United States — as I was confident they could show no warrant for the course they had taken. I made this inquiry as a matter of duty, without having previously consulted any of the delegates on this subject. The President of the Convention (Alvan Stewart) ruled it to be out of order! — a most extraordinary decision, truly. A brief discussion followed. It was contended, by Orange Scott and others, that no action could be taken in the premises, because the Committee were not amenable to the Convention, but only to the American A. S. Society, by whom they had been appointed; because, whether they had done right or wrong, it was too late to sit in judgment upon their conduct; and because the call was specific, and under it the delegates had assembled together — &c. To this reasoning it was replied, that though the Committee were directly amenable to the Parent Society, and would doubtless be censured at its next annual meeting, yet that it was competent for the Convention to decide, in view of the facts in the case, whether they had not exceeded the limits of their authority; that it was usual, in all anti-slavery convocations, to determine by vote, irrespective of the terms of any public advertisement, who should be invited to participate in the proceedings; and that, unless the Committee would explain whom they meant to include or exclude in their call, some persons present might be in doubt whether they had a right to be considered members — &c. It was announced by one of the Committee, that they had no explanations to make. I then moved, that inasmuch as the Committee had refused to explain, and as their call was somewhat indefinite, the word 'freemen' be interpreted to mean all persons, &c. This motion was lost by a large majority. Subsequently, I entered a Protest, signed by myself alone, which was read to the Convention, and ordered to be printed with the proceedings of the Convention. This was afterwards endorsed by more than sixty of the delegates. Had special pains been taken to procure signatures, I am persuaded that more than double that number could have been obtained. I send you the protest, with a list of those who approved it. You will see, at a glance, that its signers belong to various States, and generally rank among the best friends of the anti-slavery enterprise. I had no intention of getting any one to sustain me; but, as soon as my Protest was read, delegates rose in various parts of the house, and asked leave to have their names appended to it.

On the naked question of abolition, there was great unanimity of sentiment. The genuineness of the principles of the delegates was tested upon a resolution, giving a pledge not to vote for any man who would not avow himself to be in favor of immediate emancipation, whether a candidate for the office of President or Vice President of the United States, Governor or Lieutenant Governor of a State, or member of any legislative assembly. There were, I believe, but eleven names recorded in the negative. The vote was taken by ayes and noes. Of course, this resolution shows that neither Henry Clay nor Martin Van Buren may hope to receive the suffrage of a single genuine abolitionist in the United States. For the National Whig Convention, (which is soon to convene at Harrisburg,) to nominate Henry Clay as a candidate for the Presidency, would be a suicidal act.[4] *His election is wholly out of the question* — a hundred times more hopeless than the re-election of Martin Van Buren. There is not, in all this country, an individual more objectionable in the eyes of American abolitionists, than Henry Clay — not excepting John C. Calhoun or George McDuffie. There is not a more deadly foe to human freedom — not a more profligate politician — not a greater foe to the colored race — not a sterner advocate of perpetual slavery — than Henry Clay. He makes a very suitable President of the American Colonization Society; but he is totally unfit to be the President of the United States. As for Martin Van Buren, the abolitionist who would give him his support, would also sell his country for gold, and his birthright for a mess of pottage.

A few individuals in the Convention argued in favor of organizing a distinct political party; but, I am happy to say, the suggestion met with no response whatever from the great body of members present. It was ably opposed by our estimable coadjutor, Ellis Gray Loring, in a speech replete with good sense, nice discrimination, wise forecast, and timely admonition. Though restricted by the rules as to time, his brief remarks made a very salutary impression upon the minds of the audience. So long as the abolitionists refuse to step into the political arena, as a distinct party, so long their cause will prosper, their integrity be revered, and their influence over all other contending parties be irresistible.

The Convention was in session three days. In the forenoon of the last day, the Business Committee reported a resolution, submitting a proposition for the nomination of candidates for the offices of President and Vice President of the United States, to the judgment of American abolitionists. This was laid upon the table by a large majority. In the afternoon, however, within an hour of the time fixed for the dissolution of the Convention, it was called up, and, after two or three warm speeches in its favor, hurried through before any reply could be made. I offered the following amendment, which was immediately seconded, but not put to the meeting by the President.

'Resolved, as the deliberate sense of this Convention, that any attempt, on the part of the abolitionists of the United States, to nominate candidates for the offices of President and Vice President of this republic, or to organize a distinct political party, would be liable to put in imminent peril the integrity and success of the anti-slavery enterprise.'

If this resolution had been adopted by the Convention, (as I have little doubt it would have been, if it had been offered at an earlier period in full meeting,) I should have regarded it as amply repaying for the time, trouble and expense incurred by this great national meeting. It only remains for the several anti-slavery societies to take it up (or one substantially like it) for discussion, give it their approval, and thus crush in embryo this attempt to organize a new political party; for it is not possible for abolitionists to put in nomination candidates for office, without forming a distinct party. What society will be the first to set the ball in motion?

Though the Committee of Arrangements had promised, in their call, that all 'extraneous subjects' would be kept out of the Convention, the meeting had scarcely been organized before the 'no government question' was dragged in by two or three of the disorganizers from Massachusetts, (Rev. Messrs. Scott, Cummings,[5] &c.) and a large portion of the time of the meeting occupied in ridiculous harangues against non-resistants, and in favor of the 'imperious duty' of every abolitionist to go to the polls. A strenuous attempt was made to get a resolution adopted, of a proscriptive and binding character; but it was rejected by an overwhelming majority. To the attacks made upon non-resisting abolitionists, I made no reply, as a matter of principle, for, as I have never intruded my views of peace and government upon any anti-slavery meeting, so I will not stand up in their defence at any such meeting, however unjustly they may be assailed. The spirit of the Convention was liberal and just, and not at all in accordance with that which actuates the Executive Committee of the Parent Society, or the new organization in Massachusetts. I trust the rebuke thus given by the Convention will have a salutary effect.

Great disappointment was felt at the absence of Gerrit Smith; but he was suddenly taken ill on his way to Albany, and had to return home.

There was a great deal of intellectual and moral power in the Convention, though the speeches generally were not of a high order. The temper exhibited in the discussions was excellent, with a very few exceptions. On the whole, the result of our deliberations was much better than I had anticipated.

The first of August was celebrated in the evening by an address from the Rev. John Scoble, of London, Secretary of the British Society for the abolition of slavery and the slave-trade throughout the world.[6] Mr. Scoble has just returned from the West India islands, where he has been making a tour of investigation, for some time past, as to the actual working of the Emancipation Act,[7] in company with our beloved brother Charles Stuart. The spacious house was crowded to overflowing, and never was an audience more interested by the words of a speaker. The facts communicated by Mr. Scoble were of great importance and of overwhelming interest, and were listened to up to a late hour with unbroken attention by the immense throng of spectators. As Mr. Scoble will come to Boston shortly, I shall make a more particular notice of his visit hereafter. He was my bosom friend in London, and to him I am greatly indebted for the success that attended my English mission. Let abolitionists every where give him the right hand of fellowship.

In great haste, yours truly,
WM. LLOYD GARRISON.

Printed in *The Liberator*, August 9, 1839.

1. The National Convention of Abolitionists met in Albany, on Wednesday, Thursday, and Friday, July 31, August 1, and August 2. W. L. Chaplin, chairman of the committee of arrangements, called the meeting to order. Alvan Stewart of Utica was appointed president of the convention. The convention had been called by the executive committee of the American Anti-Slavery Society, which was becoming more and more hostile to Garrison and his Massachusetts followers. As indicated in an earlier note (letter 159, to Samuel Osgood, August 2, 1839, note 11), the official call had invited "such *freemen* of the United States as adopt the principles embodied in the Constitution of the American Anti-Slavery Society," thereby apparently excluding women from participation. The ultimate purpose of the convention apparently was to stimulate the creation of an anti-slavery political party.

2. A short description of the convention, including the resolutions adopted, appeared in *The Liberator*, August 9, 1839. The same issue printed a "Protest" submitted by Garrison to the convention, which condemned both its procedure and the substance of its deliberations.

3. The committee of arrangements included William Goodell, Henry Stanton, and Joshua Leavitt.

4. William H. Harrison was the candidate of the Whig party in 1840 and was, of course, elected President.

5. The Reverend Asa Cummings.

6. On November 16, 1840, Sarah Pugh, a Philadelphia antislavery Quaker, sent a poem by Abby Kimber, another Philadelphia antislavery Quaker, to Elizabeth Pease (Anti-Slavery Letters, Boston Public Library). The poem read as follows:

"John Scoble, John Scoble
The Slave's wrongs thou canst show well
And from Thames to the Tweed tell the tale
Yet the less thou canst say
Of Wm. Lloyd by the way

The more perchance truth will prevail
John Scoble!
The more perchance truth will prevail."

John Scoble and Joseph Sturge, another British antislavery leader (see letter 180, to Lucretia Mott, April 28, 1840), had investigated the apprenticeship system among Negroes in the West Indies in 1837. In 1844 Scoble and George W. Alexander, the treasurer of the British and Foreign Anti-Slavery Society, made an extended visit to France. In 1852 Scoble took over the direction of the British-American Institute, a manual-labor training institute for Negroes, at Dawn, near Dresden, Canada West, and remained there for fifteen years. Despite Scoble's efforts, the institute finally failed, primarily because of divided leadership. Scoble, while in Canada, was also active in reform politics. He returned to England in 1867. (William H. and Jane H. Pease, *Black Utopia*, Madison, Wisconsin, 1963, pp. 74–81; Dwight L. Dumond, *Letters of James G. Birney, 1831–1857*, New York and London, 1938, II, 583.)

Although originally Garrison's friend, in 1840 Scoble joined Garrison's opponents on the participation of women in the antislavery movement and on the woman question in general. He helped edit the *British and Foreign Anti-Slavery Reporter* while secretary of the British and Foreign Anti-Slavery Society. For more information about his views see Scoble's Introduction to Lewis Tappan's pamphlet, *Reply to Charges Brought Against the American and Foreign Anti-Slavery Society* (London, 1852, 24 pp.); Richard D. Webb, *The National Anti-Slavery Societies in England and the United States*, (Dublin, 1852), pp. 9–11; Edmund Quincy, *An Examination of the Charges of Mr. John Scoble and Mr. Lewis Tappan Against the American Anti-Slavery Society* (Dublin, 1852, 28 pp.).

7. This refers to the act passed in England in August 1833, freeing 800,000 slaves in the British West Indies.

161

TO GEORGE THOMPSON

Boston, Aug. 23d 1839.

Sir:

The Board of Managers of the Massachusetts Anti-Slavery Society, at a meeting held at their Rooms, in Boston, on the 17th instant, voted: That a letter be addressed by the President and Secretary, on behalf of this Board, to the Executive Committee of the British India Society informing them of the joy they feel at the inception of this new enterprize for the elevation of a long neglected & much injured portion of the human family, & of the sympathy & interest with which they regard their philanthropic efforts. In compliance with this vote we have the honor to address you at the present time, & to request you to lay this communication before the Committee.

In expressing the sentiments entertained towards your enterprize by the representatives of the earliest American advocates of the principle of the Sinfulness of all Slaveholding, & of the consequent duty and safety of Immediate Emancipation, we are confident that we utter those of all true American Abolitionists. We have not failed to learn from the contemplation of the great truths we have received & from the persecutions & trials we have endured for their sake, that all the great interests of humanity are so intertwined with each other, that one cannot be neglected without danger to the others, & that no one can be promoted without imparting a healthful impulse to all the rest. We have been taught, by our own experience, that the rights of the Slave are identical with those of the Freeman, & have been made to feel that it is only by achieving his liberties that we can secure our own. We have had occasion to observe the tendency of all truly benevolent enterprizes among ourselves to prepare the minds of men for the reception of the odious truths of the Anti-Slavery creed; while we have, at the same time, beheld the renewed life & vigour which the Abolition spirit has breathed into Organizations devoted to other departments of christian benevolence. And we are persuaded that no strenuous effort can be made in any part of the world for the subversion of tyranny & the restoration of their rights to any portion of the family of man, that will not hasten the deliverance of our downtrodden countrymen. "Our Country is the world, our countrymen are All Mankind." [1] We believe that all the inhabitants of the earth are members of the body, which must needs, by the Divine Law of their existence, sympathize with each other in health & in disease, in life & in death. We believe that all good causes will flourish & succeed more prosperously & certainly together than apart; & that every attempt for the removal of inveterate evils from the lot of any portion of mankind, made in the true spirit of Christianity, must help to alleviate the miseries & redress the wrongs of trampled humanity in every other part of the world.

It was in the firm belief of these truths that we watched with the intensest interest the noble efforts of British Abolitionists for the emancipation of their enslaved fellowmen in the Colonies; that we hailed with thanksgiving their triumph; and accepted the peaceful & blessed deliverance of the West India bondman as a happy omen of the liberation of the imbruted American. We therefore rejoice to see the devoted men who have achieved this great victory for humanity, undismayed by the toils they have endured, not contented with the triumph they have won, directing their arms towards a distant & untried field, and renewing, without an interval of repose, their holy warfare for the rights of Man. With all our hearts we bid you God Speed on your onward march. It is no wild crusade to which you have devoted yourselves. The Cross you have assumed is no badge of a fruitless fanaticism, but the blessed emblem of a practical devotion of your hands & hearts to the succour of those that have none to help them. In this enterprize you have the Author of all Good for your guide & leader. Under His guidance your ultimate triumph is certain. May His wisdom direct you & His blessing crown your efforts with success!

We could not feel this joy at your generous undertaking, or watch your movements with the unqualified satisfaction with which we expect your progress, did we think that the miseries of the wretched East Indian, which you have banded together to alleviate, would blind your eyes or harden your hearts to the far more miserable estate of the American Slave. But we know that your hearts will still bleed, that your eyes will still overflow, at the remembrance of his sufferings & his wrongs. We know that you will not fail to do all that your hands can find to do to sever his chains & heal his broken heart. We are assured that you will leave nothing undone to wipe away the disgrace which his helpless condition reflects upon the whole of Christendom, as well as upon his most guilty country. We are convinced that you will still help to swell that irresistible tide of the Public Sentiment of the civilized World which is to sweep forever from the face of the earth this cruel relic of a barbarous & pagan age. We still rely upon your efforts to make the unrepentant slaveholder a byeword & a hissing to all mankind. We trust greatly to you to make the self-glorifying robber of God's poor release his prey for very shame. We trust to you chiefly to signify to the petty despots of this (so called) free country, & to their apologists, that they must make their election between Justice at home and Infamy abroad; that they must either restore to their victims their ravished rights — the rights of labourers to their hire, of parents to their children, of husbands to their wives, of women to their virtue — or be put under the ban of the civilized world & shunned as the Pariahs of Christendom!

In the strength of this confidence & of these hopes we would once again bid you God speed in your noble enterprize for the rescue of millions of immortal men from political servitude, from physical wretchedness, from mental darkness — from the miseries & vices of which Ignorance & Tyranny are ever the fruitful parents. With the blessing of God upon your efforts, of which you are sure, if you pursue your Godlike ends by means of which He approves[,] your success is certain! May it also be speedy! Being persuaded that you will believe that it is the fulness of our hearts that speaks in this expression of our sympathy with you at the outset of your new career, we feel certain that you will not consider it as either ill-timed or superfluous. With all our hearts we shall rejoice to hear of the prosperity of your cause.

May the smile of God & the blessing of them that are ready to perish be your encouragement & your reward.

We remain, respectfully & affectionately

Your brethren in the cause of

universal humanity,

Francis Jackson, President.

Wm. Lloyd Garrison, Cor. Secretary.

George Thompson.

Sec'ry of the British

India Society.

MS.: University Library, Cambridge, England. The letter is not in the handwriting of Garrison, but is signed by him.

1. Garrison's slogan on the masthead of *The Liberator*.

162

TO EDMUND QUINCY AND HENRY C. WRIGHT

Saturday evening.

[September 14, 1839]

My dear friends, Quincy and Wright.

My worthy friend, Nathan Merriam,[1] of Worcester County, has just made another visit to this city,[2] chiefly to see some of the friends of moral and religious reform on various scriptural topics. I am sorry that I happen to be so situated as to time, that I cannot devote an hour to him; but, that his visit might not be in vain, I have taken upon me the liberty to send him to Quincy, to spend the Sabbath with you. He is somewhat apprehensive that we non-resistants are not inculcating our principles exactly in the right manner, as respects our language towards governments, &c., and has some thoughts to offer upon that subject. He is a man of strong, original mind, one who has searched the scriptures with a great deal of attention, and perhaps with no inconsiderable success. I think you will all be benefitted by a free interchange of sentiments — for, as iron sharpeneth iron, so does the face of a man his friend. Let us seek the truth with all diligence, and ever rejoice in it, that the Author of it may be glorified, and our highest good secured.

Yours, lovingly,

Wm. Lloyd Garrison.

N. B. Perhaps friend Merriam may wish to tarry until Monday morning. If so, could you make it convenient to accommodate him?

ALS: Garrison Papers, Boston Public Library. The date, September 14, 1839, is written twice on the back of this letter, in handwritings that differ from Garrison's.

1. Nathan Merriam (b. Princeton, Worcester county, Massachusetts, March 21, 1791; d. March 28, 1845) is listed in the Princeton list of selectmen for 1834–1835 and of assessors for 1835. He was apparently active in the anti-slavery and other reform movements of the day. (Letter to Louis Ruchames from Mrs. Harold Merriam, Brookfield, Mass., July 17, 1969.)

2. Boston.

163

TO GEORGE W. BENSON

Boston, Sept. 30, 1839.

My dear George:

Our Non-Resistance Convention is over,[1] and the peace and blessing of heaven have attended our deliberations. Such a mass of free mind as was brought together I have never seen before in any one assembly. "Not many mighty," "not many rich," "not many honorable," were found among us — of course; but there was much talent, and a great deal of *soul*. Not a single *set* speech was made by any one, but every one spoke in a familiar manner, just as though we constituted but a mere social party. In the course of the discussion, considerable light was thrown upon some obscure points, and many difficulties were removed from inquiring minds. The resolutions that were adopted were of the most radical and "ultra" stamp, and will create, I think, no little agitation in community.[2] Bro. Wright held two public discussions with Colver,[3] and acquitted himself very well; though he does not shine as a debater. Colver fairly unmasked himself, and showed that he was possessed of a devilish spirit. Gurley [4] never more shamefully calumniated abolitionists, than C. did the non-resistants. He accused them of being non-descripts, infidels, jacobins, atheists, outlaws, &c.; of seeking to destroy the church; of stabbing the hands that protected them; of abusing their benefactors; of reproaching the memories of the revolutionary patriots. I was shocked to hear such things from his lips: for they were exactly calculated to stir up a mob. He is really mad against us. The Lord have mercy upon him. Phelps lent him what assistance he could. You will see an account of the discussion in the Non-Resistant.[5]

We missed your presence greatly. I presume your regret, in not being able to attend, was equal to our own. We feel anxious to hear how Catherine is, and whether, in case she is better, you intend to come this way soon. Supposing that William M. Chace will see you in Providence, and give you all the particulars respecting the Convention, I need not say any thing more about it.

To-day and to-morrow we shall be busily engaged in moving to Cambridgeport, about two miles from the city. I have taken a house on lease for two years, at $250 per annum. It is not a *roomy* house, but very neat in its appearance. It is on the corner of Broadway and Elm-streets. The omnibus goes in and comes out every half hour, and will leave any one at our door. Bro. Johnson [6] and wife are to board with us. At present, I am greatly embarrassed for the want of money. I have so many articles of household furniture to buy — carpets, chairs, kitchen furniture, stores, grates, &c — as to make a pretty considerable sum. There is due me on my editorial salary nearly $150, and also some from the Mass. A. S. Society; but we are all out of funds, and I must wait awhile until money can be collected. I have had to pay for bro. James,[7] in order to get him released from the Navy Yard, over $40, as security; and this helps to cripple me. I do not wish to run in debt to A. B. & C. for my household articles; and therefore need the cash to pay for them. This forenoon, I have borrowed $100 from Philbrick,[8] and $100 from Francis Jackson, to enable me to make my purchases; promising to return it, if practicable, in all this week. They will expect me to fulfil my word. My object in writing to you is to know whether you can borrow that amount for me, so as to give me more time to "turn myself." Friend Chace [9] thought you would be able to accommodate me, without much difficulty. If it were possible for you to get me $300, instead of $200, on interest, until the end of this year, it would aid me still more. I shall be enabled easily to repay it by that time. If you cannot conveniently obtain more than the $200, I must make that answer. Perhaps you will be so situated, that you cannot get either amount for me; if so, I must look to some other source; but I am very anxious to pay Philbrick and Jackson promptly, because I have promised to do so, and because they are at this moment really pinched for means themselves. Let me hear from you as soon as convenient. I send this to you at Providence, hoping it will reach you more promptly than at Brooklyn.

Bro. James is slowly improving in health, but his case is a bad one. He has already taken three courses of the Thompsonian medicine, and will continue to take them until he is cured. I shall write to the Secretary of the Navy, at Washington, to see if I can get him discharged.

We are all in pretty good health. Little Willie limps as he walks, but we cannot discover the cause of it. Geo. Thompson is a difficult child to manage, as he has a tremendous will of his own, and he is very passionate.

Yours, with true affection,

Wm. Lloyd Garrison.

N. B. I will send you my note for whatever money you can get for me, as soon as it is received. Friend Chace paid Helen her $30, which came for timely.

ALS: Garrison Papers, Boston Public Library. The greater part of this letter is printed in *Life*, II, 328–329.

1. The first annual meeting of the New England Non-Resistance Society was held on September 25–27 in Boston in the Chardon-Street Chapel. Delegates were present not only from New England but from states in other sections as well. Pennsylvania and Ohio sent Lucretia Mott and Amos Dresser, respectively. Effingham Capron was chairman; Garrison read the annual report, which he had written; and the business committee consisted of Samuel J. May, Edmund Quincy, Henry C. Wright, Garrison, Lucretia Mott, Maria W. Chapman, Lydia M. Child, Thankful Southwick, the wife of Joseph Southwick, and Adin Ballou, a Universalist clergyman at Mendon, Massachusetts, who later helped found the Hopedale Community (*Life*, II, 327–328). A detailed account of the meeting appeared in *The Liberator*, October 11, 1839.

2. The resolutions passed at the convention were printed in *The Liberator*, *ibid*.

3. Henry C. Wright and Nathaniel Colver.

4. R. R. Gurley.

5. "Non-Resistant, I: [77]" (*Life*, II, 329).

6. Oliver Johnson.

7. James Holley Garrison (1801–1842), William Lloyd Garrison's older brother, who at an early age began to devote himself to wine, women, and song, went to sea as a merchant and naval seaman. His health wrecked by years of excessive drinking, James was confined to the Navy Yard when his ship docked in Boston in the fall of 1839. Garrison, concerned that his brother be given the best possible care, asked for permission to take him home until the restoration of his health. Apparently, the commodore in charge asked for security, which Garrison paid. When three months passed without any real improvement in James's health, Garrison asked that his brother be discharged from the Navy. After some difficulties, James was discharged and moved in with his brother and Helen. He remained with them until May 1840, when Garrison was scheduled to sail for Europe and Helen was pregnant and therefore unable to care for her brother-in-law. He then went to stay with the Bensons in Brooklyn, Connecticut. (*Life*, I and II *passim*.) For further material on James H. Garrison, see Walter M. Merrill, *Behold Me Once More: The Confessions of James Holley Garrison, Brother of William Lloyd Garrison* (Boston, 1954).

8. Samuel Philbrick.

9. William M. Chace of Providence.

THE LIBERATOR

IS PUBLISHED WEEKLY
AT NO. 25, CORNHILL, BY
ISAAC KNAPP.

Wm. Lloyd Garrison, Editor.

THE LIBERATOR

VOL. VIII.   OUR COUNTRY IS THE WORLD, OUR COUNTRYMEN ARE ALL MANKIND.   NO. 29.

BOSTON, MASSACHUSETTS.   FRIDAY, JULY 20, 1838.

REFUGE OF OPPRESSION.

HISTORICAL.

WHO ARE THE RIOTERS?

Boston, Nov. 1, 1839.

Dear Sir:

It is with great pleasure I introduce to you
the bearer of this, Dr. Madden, a gentleman of high
literary attainments, probably well known to you as
the author of an excellent work on West-India Slavery, &c. He comes from Havana, and is connected
with the Court of Mixed Commission on the slave
trade. He is here to show up the character of Consul
Trist, and especially to do all that can be done to
prevent the African prisoners of the Amistad being
sent back to Cuba. Let him, then, be received by
the friends of bleeding humanity as an angel of mercy.
He has in his possession a large amount of valua-

and are very much pleased with him. He will
go to England shortly. I need not add any more
to insure him a good reception in New-York.

Yours, truly,

Wm. Lloyd Garrison.

Letter 164, opening and conclusion

164

TO LEWIS TAPPAN, *ET AL.*

Boston, Nov. 1, 1839.

Dear Sir:

It is with great pleasure I introduce to you the bearer of this, Dr. Madden, a gentleman of high literary attainments, probably well known to you as the author of an excellent work on West-India Slavery, &c.[1] He comes from Havana, and is connected with the Court of Mixed Commission on the slave trade. He is here to show up the character of Consul Trist,[2] and especially to do all that can be done to prevent the African prisoners of the Amistad[3] being sent back to Cuba. Let him, then, be received by the friends of bleeding humanity as an angel of mercy. He has in his possession a large amount of valuable information, which comes at a very important crisis. I trust you will have a meeting of the Executive Committee, on his account. I regret that I have not been able to show him more attention, on account of absence from the city. Several of our abolition friends have had an interview with him, and are very much pleased with him. He will go to England shortly. I need not add any more to insure him a good reception in New-York.

Yours, truly,

Wm. Lloyd Garrison.

ALS: American Missionary Archives, Fisk University, Nashville, Tennessee.
    The letter was addressed as follows:

    "For   Lewis Tappan,
                    Arthur Tappan,
                    Joshua Leavitt, or
                    James G. Birney,

To introduce ⎫
Dr. Madden   ⎭   New York City."

1. R. R. Madden, *Letter to W. E. Channing, D. D., On the Subject of the Abuse of the Flag of the United States in the Island of Cuba, and the Advantage Taken of Its Protection in Promoting the Slave Trade* (Boston, William D. Ticknor, 1839, 32 pp.).
    Dr. Richard R. Madden (b. Dublin, August 22, 1798; d. 1886), an Irishman, was a traveler, philanthropist, and author. A former stipendiary magistrate in Jamaica, he was appointed in 1835 as protector of liberated Africans and arbitrator in the Mixed Commission Court. The Mixed Commission Courts had been set up after Spain had agreed in 1817 to close her slave trade between Africa and the West Indies and to give it up altogether after 1820. One court existed in British territory at Sierra Leone, the other in Spanish territory at Havana. The members of each court consisted of two arbitrators and two commissary judges, with each category represented by one appointee from each of the powers. Madden was a strong antislavery man, and later published other

works, including *Poems by a slave in the Island of Cuba, recently liberated, translated from the Spanish, with the history of the early life of the Negro poet, written by himself; to which are prefixed two pieces descriptive of Cuban Slavery* . . . (London, 1840); and *The Island of Cuba; its resources, progress, and prospects, considered in relation especially to the influence of its prosperity on the interests of the British West India Colonies* (London, 1849 and 1853). (William Law Mathieson, *Great Britain and the Slave Trade, 1839–1865,* 1929, reprinted, 1967, by Octagon Books, New York, pp. 19, 64–65, 116–117, 118.) From 1850 to 1880, Madden was secretary to the Loan Fund Board, at Dublin Castle, Ireland, to help the Irish peasantry. (*DNB.*)

2. Nicholas Philip Trist (b. Charlottesville, Virginia, June 2, 1800; d. Alexandria, Virginia, February 11, 1874) studied at West Point and in the law office of Thomas Jefferson, whose granddaughter he married. His first political appointment was a clerkship in the State Department. He was consul in Havana, Cuba, from 1833 to 1841. He was accused of failure to support the rights of American citizens, of subservience to Spanish officials, and of collaboration in the slave trade. In 1840, Congress and the State Department investigated the charges and found them to be lacking substance. He was recalled in 1841. He conducted the negotiations ending the Mexican War, and despite his recall, which he ignored, he negotiated the Treaty of Guadalupe Hidalgo. (*DAB.*)

3. The Amistad case involved a cargo of forty-nine African slaves who had been kidnaped and brought to Havana, whence they were being shipped to Puerto Principe in Cuba, aboard the vessel *Amistad*, a Spanish schooner. Led by Joseph Cinque or Cinquez, the slaves revolted, killed the captain and the cook, and seized the vessel. They ordered the crew to take them to Africa, but instead they were brought into American waters, taken into custody by the United States revenue cutter *Washington*, and taken to New London, Connecticut, on August 29, 1839. Three abolitionists especially, the Reverend Simeon S. Jocelyn, Joshua Leavitt, and Lewis Tappan, were prominent in their defense. After a struggle which awakened wide interest, the United States Supreme Court pronounced them free and ordered them returned to their native country. (*Life,* II, 326.)

165

TO AN UNIDENTIFIED FRIEND

Cambridgeport, Dec. 2, 1839.

My dear Friend:

Your Thanksgiving present of a fine fat turkey was very *apropos* to the occasion; for which I beg you to accept my very hearty thanks, as well as for a long catalogue of other favors, "too numerous to mention." I had it served up for my table, with all due "pomp and circumstance." It was cooked with absolute perfection, carved quite scientifically, and eaten with a keen relish. "The house I live in" was strengthened and renovated from the cellar to the attic; in other words, the whole frame-work of my "earthly tabernacle," to wit, my mortal body, received new support to shield it from the ravages of time. Hence, every fibre, muscle and ligament, every vein and artery, every bone and joint in my system, is indebted to you in the first instance, and to the turkey in the second. The same holds good in regard to some eight or ten others, who participated in that *fowl*, yet exceedingly *fair* banquet. So you see what a wholesale benefactor you have been!

I could have wished that you had been present with us, under such pleasant circumstances; but I presume you spent the day quite happily at home. It could not easily have been otherwise with one so cheerful in disposition, so equal in temperament, and so philosophical in mind, as yourself. No day can be a miserable one to him whose continual desire is, that the will of God be done, and not his own.

In looking over my audience at Weymouth, last evening, before I began my lecture, I observed a head bent down so as to hide the face, which, for all the world, satisfied me that it could be no other than your own! And so it turned out to be. You fairly took me by surprise. Happy as I am to see you, I was not a little disturbed by your presence! I could not but heartily sympathize with you. To be bored with the same address, "word for word, letter for letter, comma for comma," which you had heard some three or four times before, was a little too bad! Well, if you will persist in listening to "a man of one idea," and of course of one address, I cannot help it. I must say that you stood fire to the end like a good soldier; thus showing that your powers of endurance run *pari passu* with your desires to do good. I am happy to add, that, at the close of my lecture, the A. S. Society passed some complimentary resolutions respecting the same; so that I trust it was not spoken altogether in vain. Even the parson expressed his satisfaction with it.

I returned home last evening, and suppose you did also, but could not get an opportunity to speak to you. The next time you come to hear me lecture, look out for "Monsieur Tonson come again!" [1] But I hope you will hear something new.

It is a turbulent, blustering day; but, whether the wind blow high or low, whether the temperature be at zero or at blood heat, it cannot affect the personal esteem and gratitude that is due to you from

Your much obliged friend,

Wm. Lloyd Garrison.

ALS: Boston Athenaeum.

1. Monsieur Tonson is an imaginary character in the play *Monsieur Tonson* (1821) by W. T. Moncrieff, an English playwright. The phrase Garrison quotes is used as a refrain in the play. (For a synopsis of the play, see William S. Walsh, *Heroes and Heroines of Fiction*, Philadephia and London, 1914, p. 360.)

166

TO THE EXECUTIVE COMMITTEE OF THE AMERICAN ANTI-SLAVERY SOCIETY

Boston, Dec. 6, 1839.

At a special meeting of the Board of Managers of the Massachusetts Anti-Slavery Society, held on the 2d instant, a letter was read by the Corresponding Secretary, from James G. Birney and Henry B. Stanton, in behalf of the Executive Committee of the Parent Society, stating the pecuniary embarrassments of the Parent Society, and requesting either "prompt and liberal aid from the Treasury of the Massachusetts Anti-Slavery Society," or permission to send agents into this State, "to raise funds from such sources as are accessible."

The Board having duly deliberated upon the subject, hasten to convey to the Executive Committee a frank and friendly expression of their views and feelings.

While we cannot but regret, that any thing has occurred to cripple the operations or weaken the energies of the Parent Society, we are not surprised to learn that the receipts into the treasury of that Society have been greatly lessened within the last six months. The causes of this diminution are, doubtless, various. Two only are specified in the letter of Messrs. Birney and Stanton.

"First, the unprecedented pecuniary embarrassments of the country."

Unquestionably, the extraordinary pressure in the money market has tended, to some extent, to retard the progress of the anti-slavery cause, in common with other benevolent and religious enterprises. When the business of a nation becomes deranged, and private credit is impaired and public confidence shaken, it is to be expected that the efforts of Philanthropy will be more or less impeded, until the earthquake shock shall have passed away. But, confiding as we still do in the liberality and self-sacrificing spirit of a large portion of American abolitionists, — tried as they have been in former periods of national pecuniary distress, and not found wanting, — we cannot believe that the state of the money market has had very much to do with the present embarrassments of the Parent Society. Three years ago, when there was a far greater panic in the land than now exists, and almost universal bankruptcy seemed to be the order of the day — when specie payments were generally suspended throughout the country, and men's hearts were failing them for fear — a larger amount was contributed to the treasury of the Parent Society than had been realized in any one preceding year, in the palmy reign of uninterrupted prosperity. The more abolitionists became restricted in their resources, the greater was their fellowship in suffering with the despoiled and imbruted slave population. In the "abundance of their poverty," the "riches of their liberality abounded." [1] At the present time, many of them are giving substantial proofs that they are not afraid to "trust in the Lord, and do good," [2] though the earth should be removed out of its place.

"2d. The restricting resolution passed by the Parent Society at its last annual meeting, and the action of the State Societies under it, by which the Committee have been virtually prohibited from making efforts for the collection of funds within the several States; while, at the same time, the State Societies, as such, have contributed nothing to the funds of the national society."

This last is regarded as the chief cause of their embarrassment by the Executive Committee. They therefore call for a repeal or modification of said restriction, so that they may send financial agents into this Commonwealth to collect funds in aid of the Parent Society; preferring, however, "to receive prompt and liberal aid from the treasury of the State Society."

If the arrangement made at the last annual meeting of the Parent Society, in relation to the State auxiliaries, has so greatly reduced the income of the Society, it has operated in a manner not anticipated at that time. The plan of independent State action was proposed and adopted, in order to give greater efficiency to the whole anti-slavery movement. Its design was, to prevent collision in the collection of funds, to lessen and divide the responsibilities of the Executive Committee, and to increase mutual confidence and harmony among abolitionists. As it gave the laboring oar to each State auxiliary, it doubtless contemplated some reduction of the income of the Parent Society, but, certainly, not to an extent that would involve the latter Society in bankruptcy, or make its existence little better than nominal. In short, while it aimed to infuse more vitality among auxiliary societies, it also supposed that the parent association would continue in vigorous operation.

To prove that this plan was not selfish or exclusive in its inception, it will suffice to state, that when it was first adopted in 1838 by the Massachusetts and New York State Societies, each society agreed to pay into the treasury of the National Society ten thousand dollars during the current year — making an aggregate of twenty thousand dollars contributed by two auxiliaries only. This pledge was redeemed. If, therefore, since the annual meeting in May last, not a single State

Society, as such, has contributed a dollar directly in aid of the Parent Society, it is matter of grave inquiry, and calls for a faithful investigation into the causes of this delinquency. It behooves each State Society to answer for itself: all that we deem it incumbent upon us to do is, to exonerate the Massachusetts Anti-Slavery Society from all blame in this matter, and to show that it is justified in declining to aid the Parent Society from its own treasury at this crisis, or to open a door for the admission of the financial agents of that society into this Commonwealth.

It does not seem to have occurred to the Executive Committee at New York, that, in addition to the two causes which they suppose have lessened the receipts into the national treasury, there is a third, still more important; and that is, a growing distrust in their clear-sightedness, sound judgment, rigid impartiality, and anti-sectarian spirit. For all that they have done (and they have done much) to advance the sacred cause of emancipation, since they assumed the arduous responsibilities of their station, the abolitionists of the United States have felt, and will ever feel, truly grateful: — still, the manner in which they have acted on various trying emergencies, to the great injury of our cause, has gradually tended to weaken that full and perfect confidence, which abolitionists once reposed in their ability to manage so great an enterprise. We are constrained to believe, that *they* are mainly accountable for the present empty state of the treasury of the Parent Society, rather than any derangement in the finances of the country, or any inefficiency on the part of State auxiliaries. Painful as it is to us to make this impeachment, we feel obliged to do so, in justice to the State Society which we represent, and to the common cause in which we are engaged. It is far better to receive the faithful rebukes of a friend, than the deceitful kisses of an enemy; and in friendship we speak on this occasion.

Standing as watchmen upon the walls of Liberty and Humanity, and surveying the whole field of anti-slavery operations, it is expected that the Executive Committee will be the first to discover when peril threatens our glorious enterprise, and in what guise it makes its appearance; and the first to sound the tocsin of alarm. If, in any part of the country, an attempt be made to lower the abolition standard, or to create division in our ranks, or to conciliate the implacable spirit of sectarianism, or to take the management of our cause out of the hands of the people, and transfer it to those of a titled body of men, they should be foremost in exposing the treason, and registering their testimony against it. Such attempts have been made, from time to time; but, in such instances, the Executive Committee have been found either sleeping at their post, or incapable of discerning any danger, or disinclined to speak out in trumpet-tones, until the battle has been fought and won by local societies. In those instances, moreover, their official organ, the Emancipator, has been found remiss, when it should have sounded the key-note for every other anti-slavery periodical in the land.

We proceed to specify two of these instances, and to sustain our allegations.

In the history of the anti-slavery reform, the "Clerical Appeal" conspiracy marks an important crisis. In the summer of 1837, a bold attempt was made by five clergymen in Boston and its vicinity, (professed abolitionists,) to cast odium upon the whole anti-slavery movement, by bringing against its most active supporters, (without, however, calling them by name, and therefore stabbing in the dark,) almost every accusation which had ever been falsely urged by the enemies of the colored race — such as using "hasty, unsparing, and almost ferocious denunciation," making "wicked and false insinuations," scattering "fire-brands, arrows and death," "scourging, and lashing men up to the work," heaping "abuse upon ministers of the gospel, and other excellent Christians, who do not feel prepared to enter fully into the efforts of anti-slavery societies," "beating off those, whose hearts bleed for the oppressed, from active exertion in behalf of the slaves, by their unjustifiable measures." &c. Those clergymen who refused to read anti-slavery notices from their pulpits were justified in their time-serving conduct; and such as haughtily stood aloof from the anti-slavery cause, were complimented as "men who have a quick sense of propriety"!! Had all this been said and done by open foes, it would have excited no surprise, and have been scarcely worthy of notice; but, coming from five anti-slavery clergymen, one of whom had been an agent of the Parent Society, and another of whom was a member of our own Board, it caused no little amazement and agitation. It was a blow aimed at the integrity of the anti-slavery enterprise in general, and at the existence of the Massachusetts Anti-Slavery Society in particular. It came in such a shape as to threaten much evil; and loud were the exultations of the pro-slavery party over it. Great anxiety and distress of mind extensively prevailed among the watchful friends of emancipation in the several States, and especially throughout New-England. By strenuous and energetic action, the conspiracy was crushed in the bud. Multitudes of anti-slavery societies, as far west as Ohio, denounced it in emphatic terms; and, by dealing their blows thick and fast, they save our precious cause from ruin. In such a perilous emergency, what was the course pursued by the Executive Committee at New York? They took no action whatever upon the subject, but left the Massachusetts Anti-Slavery Society to conquer or perish alone; being, seemingly, indifferent as to the manner in which the struggle might terminate. Their silence was construed, by the clerical appellants and their supporters, as well as by the enemies of abolition, into an approval of this disorganizing, sectarian movement. Letters of expostulation were sent to leading members of the Committee, complaining of their ominous silence, and entreating them to be either cold or hot — to either approve or condemn the sentiments of the Clerical Appeal. Answers were returned, that they were determined to take no part in the controversy; that they regarded it as purely local; and that, if they should take any action upon it, they would (most extraordinary impartiality!) censure both parties! Struggling for its very existence, at that eventful period, as was the Society whom we represent, it may be rationally supposed, that such conduct on the part of the Executive Committee was deemed by Massachusetts abolitionists as "the unkindest cut of all," [3] and produced considerable alienation of feeling, and much distrust respecting the action of the future. As the clerical appellants were all of one denomination, and as at least three-fourths of the Executive Committee were members of the same sect, it was both feared and believed, by multitudes, that the solution of this unnatural conduct was found in sectarian sympathy. Additional irritation was produced among the tried friends of abolition in this State, by the employment, at that time, of the Rev. James T. Woodbury, of Acton, as an agent of the Parent Society, by the Executive Committee; an active participant in this disorganizing movement, who, by his agency, had every facility afforded him to sow the seeds of division in our ranks, and thus to annihilate the Massachusetts Society. Afflicted and surprised at such treatment, this Board sent an official protest to the Executive Committee against the agency of said Woodbury; and "asking as an act of justice to the Massachusetts Society, that his appointment may be recalled as soon as practicable, and not renewed until he signify his readiness to co-operate with us, heartily, and in good faith." No reply was made to this Protest.

Not only did the Committee refuse to take any official notice of the schism existing in this Commonwealth, but the Emancipator also was dumb! Though it was deemed worthy the attention of anti-slavery societies in near and remote parts of the country; though it was a subject of animadversion in every other anti-slavery periodical; and though the eyes of the friends and foes of our cause, universally, were fastened with more or less intensity upon that memorable struggle; yet the official organ of the Parent Society had no opinion, and could find no voice, on that occasion; it was silent as the grave; and "silence gives consent," said the schismatics — and they privately claimed it to be on their side. It was not until the conspiracy was effectually quelled, and its opinion was of no special service, that the Emancipator could speak in condemnatory terms of this affair.

It cannot be denied, that, from that period, the confidence of a large portion of the abolitionists in this Commonwealth and other parts of the country, in the vigilance, courage and sagacity of the Executive Committee and their organ, has gradually lessened; while their interest in the several State organizations has proportionably increased. So that whatever has been lost to the Parent Society, has been more than made up to its auxiliaries. Hence no occasion of triumph is furnished to the enemies of our righteous cause, on the ground of the emptiness of our national treasury. Abolition is not "dying away," but obtaining new vigor and extending its conquests continually. Never was more money contributed in its support, never were more active or more successful efforts made to propagate it, than at the present time.

Notwithstanding this extraordinary conduct of the Executive Committee in 1837, the Massachusetts A. S. Society felt disposed to regard it with forbearance and charity, in the hope that no such cause of complaint would again be afforded by the Committee, and that perfect harmony might be restored throughout the anti-slavery ranks. Accordingly, immediately after the annual meeting of the National Society in 1838, the State Society pledged itself to pay into the treasury of the parent, the sum of ten thousand dollars during that year. Owing to various causes, (which, as they have been publicly specified on another occasion, it is needless to recapitulate in this connexion,) the quarterly installments were not met so promptly as had been anticipated at the time of making the pledge. This unavoidable delay led to the most arbitrary and offensive proceedings on the part of the Executive Committee. Though made acquainted with all the facts in the case — though aware of the utter inability of the State Society instantly to liquidate the sum that was due — though assured that the Society would exert itself to the utmost to redeem its entire pledge within the time specified, and that, if the co-operation of one or two of the financial agents of the Parent Society could be secured, there was no occasion to doubt that this could be done — the Executive Committee peremptorily demanded the instant payment of the money due, declaring that, in case the demand was not complied with, they should regard the contract as null and void, and at once send their agents into Massachusetts to obtain funds, without any regard to the remonstrances of the State Society or its Board of Managers. *They did so* — and the consequence was, a most painful collision between the parties. The conduct of the Executive Committee was beheld with surprise and grief by the friends of emancipation out of the Commonwealth, and served greatly to increase the distrust of the abolitionists of this State towards the Committee. Still, the State Society, though thus unjustly treated, and its contract hastily nullified, determined soon after its quarterly meeting in March, (through its Board,) that the pledge should be redeemed within the period agreed, if unprecedented labor could accomplish it. At that meeting, a delegation appeared from New York, in behalf of the Executive Committee. They witnessed in the meeting, the greatest anxiety of mind to see the pledge promptly paid. It was only necessary for them to agree to co-operate in its collection, and joy and tranquillity would have pervaded the Commonwealth: not a doubt could remain that the money would be immediately raised: otherwise, it seemed almost certain, that a considerable amount would remain uncollected. The olive-branch which was held out to them they positively rejected, and proclaimed their entire want of confidence in any new promises of the State Society. That the pledge was promptly and seasonably redeemed under such adverse circumstances, is matter of surprise, and must ever redound to the magnanimity and forbearance of Massachusetts abolitionists.

Prior to this event, one of the Corresponding Secretaries of the Parent Society, (Mr. Stanton,) had been laboring in this State, seemingly in good faith towards the Massachusetts Anti-Slavery Society. Just before the annual meeting in January, however, it was discovered that the same malignant spirit of sectarianism which concocted the Clerical Appeal, for the purpose of dividing the abolition ranks, was busy in a new guise in fomenting jealousies and divisions among us. In order to carry its point, and hoping thus to cut off or expel certain obnoxious individuals, whose religious scruples would not allow them to wield the elective franchise, it attempted to enforce the dogma, as an anti-slavery test, that every abolitionist is religiously bound to vote at the polls. This dogma Mr. Stanton was the first publicly to broach; and, countenanced by such a leader, the faction in this State at once raised the cry of extermination against the Massachusetts Society, because it would not endorse a doctrine which was obviously at war with the spirit of the anti-slavery organization, and would lead to the destruction of the old broad platform of our common humanity. A new paper, called the Abolitionist, was started in Boston, in opposition to the Liberator, and edited (it is understood) for a time, by Mr. Stanton, who spared no pains to make discord and disunion in the Commonwealth, among those who had hitherto stood shoulder to shoulder in the conflict with the demon of slavery. The mischief that he did was incalculable. At the quarterly meeting in March, Mr. Lewis Tappan, a member of the New-York Executive Committee publicly counselled the division in our ranks, which has since taken place. Since that time, Mr. Elizur Wright, Jr. another member of that Committee, has become the editor of the Abolitionist, and is waging unceasing warfare against the Massachusetts Anti-Slavery Society, charging it with having given up "the staff of accomplishment," and abandoned principles and measures which are fundamental to the overthrow of slavery.

In view of developments like these, it should have excited no surprise, if the abolitionists of Massachusetts had refused to retain confidence any longer in the impartial and catholic spirit of the Executive Committee. It was too apparent that that Committee had no real fellowship with the Massachusetts Society, and was willing to see a new and proscriptive organization established upon its ruins. But even this unnatural treatment, up to the time of the annual meeting of the Parent Society in May last, was received in a magnanimous spirit by the State Society: and a yearning desire was felt by it to forgive and forget all that had passed, if, peradventure, for the future, there might be harmony of action. At that meeting, the committee on finance reported the sum of $32,500 as the amount which the abolitionists of the country should raise the current year for the use of the Executive Committee, and appropriated $5000 as the sum to be collected by Massachusetts. Alvan Stuart and others argued in favor of the sum of $15,000, as being amply sufficient; but no one spoke in favor of a larger amount than the sum reported by the financial Committee. Their report was laid upon the table, and nothing definite was agreed upon by the delegates.

To show their readiness to sustain the operations of the Parent Society to the amount apportioned to this State in New-York, if all just cause of complaint against the Executive Committee could be removed, the Board of Managers of the Massachusetts Society, at a special meeting on the 13th of May, on motion of Ellis Gray Loring,

"Voted, That this Board will use its best endeavors to pay into the treasury of the American Anti-Slavery Society, a sum *not less* than $5,000, during the ensuing year; with the understanding, that all monies paid into said treasury by inhabitants of this State, during the year, shall be credited toward the redemption of this pledge."

This vote was immediately transmitted to New York, accompanied by a letter explaining why a larger sum was not named, (in consequence of the pecuniary liabilities of the Society, &c.) and adding — "It is taken for granted, that no agents of the Parent Society will be commissioned to labor in this State by the Executive Committee without the concurrence of this Board."

Before a reply to this proposition was received, a letter was sent to this Board, by H. B. Stanton, in behalf of the Ex. Committee, stating that they had two agents then laboring in this State, (Messrs. St. Clair and Wise,) and wishing to know whether the State Society would consent to their continuing their labors in Massachusetts. On this point, the Executive Committee could not have entertained a doubt as to our views and feelings; for the two agents alluded to were notoriously hostile to the State Society, and actively engaged in seeking its overthrow, and had been induced to resign their agencies in the same on account of their opposition to it. Such a letter, under such circumstances, was a mockery in fact, if not in intention. On being read to the Board, the following resolution was adopted, and forthwith transmitted to New York.

"Whereas, the Board have already made arrangements to employ agents throughout the Commonwealth; and as, in the present state of the cause, it is desirable, for the sake of harmony and the utmost efficiency of action, that these arrangements should not be interrupted by the presence and efforts of any agents of the Parent Society, *who are unwilling to co-operate with the State Society*; therefore,

Resolved, That the Corresponding Secretary be directed to inform the Executive Committee, that it is the wish of this Board, that the agents of the Parent Society, now employed in this State, (Messrs. St. Clair and Wise,) be withdrawn from the Commonwealth."

These agents were not withdrawn until after the organization of the Massachusetts Abolition Society in June, when it was probably known that they would be employed by that Society to sow the seeds of division in our midst. Comment is here needless.

The prompt and liberal offer of the State Anti-Slavery Society was rejected by the Executive Committee, by the adoption and transmission to this Board of the following resolution:

"Resolved, That this Committee will gratefully receive any sums that may be given to our treasury by a State Society, or any other auxiliaries, as well as by individuals; and that all moneys be acknowledged by States as heretofore; but that *we do not think it expedient to make any arrangement*, by which donations made directly to our treasury shall be credited to another Society, except at the will of the donors."

At this time, the plot which had been for some months in embryo to crush the Massachusetts Anti-Slavery Society, was fully developed in the formation of the Massachusetts Abolition Society, in a private meeting. The plea for this new organization was, that the old society had widely departed from the true anti-slavery standard, and become recreant to its principles and professions; and, hence, was a mighty obstacle in the way of the cause of bleeding humanity! It was the duty of the Executive Committee of the Parent Society to take official notice of these charges; if true, to bear their testimony against such a dereliction from the path of rectitude — if slanderous, to rebuke those who were giving them currency under an abolition garb. Two State auxiliaries in one Commonwealth, openly arrayed against each other, they could not properly recognize; one or the other deserved to be frowned upon as schismatical. But they chose to give countenance to the division, first, by their silence in view of its existence; and, secondly, by allowing the Emancipator to sustain the disorganizing course of the new society. In vain have the great body of abolitionists in this State officially condemned that society as schismatical; in vain has the New England Anti-Slavery Convention lifted up its voice against it; in vain have numerous county and town societies pronounced it to be bad in its spirit, and treacherous in its origin; the Emancipator has not deigned to take any notice of these expressions of sentiment, but has left its readers to infer that the old society finds "none so poor as to do it reverence!" [4] Much that would serve to aid the Massachusetts Abolition Society, or to disparage the old pioneer society, the Emancipator has seemed willing to publish in its columns.

It is under such circumstances, that the Executive Committee make their appeal to this Board to save the Parent Society from bankruptcy! Having aided in getting up a Society in this Commonwealth, the grand object of which is to destroy the old organization, they now appeal to us as those, "who alone have direct access to the abolitionists of this State," to afford them pecuniary aid! That aid, if we had the disposition, it is not in our power to give. Our treasury is exhausted in efforts to preserve the integrity of our cause, and the State Society from extinction. All this the Executive Committee might have foreseen. How they could expect to fan the flames of division in this State, and yet to reap a pecuniary harvest, is to us inexplicable. If we should allow their financial agents to come into Massachusetts at this crisis, we fear, from past experience, it would be to the injury of the society and the cause we represent, and would throw our own arrangements into confusion. We cannot consent to this, much as we regret the embarrassment in which they now find themselves. So long as two hostile societies exist in this or any other State, the Committee must not expect much aid from either. Already this division has cost the anti-slavery cause not less than $10,000, which otherwise might have been at the disposal of the Parent Society.

If the Massachusetts Anti-Slavery Society were at present in funds, this Board would still deem it a matter of grave inquiry, how far it would be expedient or proper to assist the Parent Society, so long as there is just ground to apprehend, that the very assistance that might be thus given would be used by the Executive Committee to the injury of the State Society. We feel constrained to say, that we regard the course pursued by that Committee, in several particulars, as not in accordance with the spirit or genius of universal emancipation. Whether it be an error of judgment simply, or originate in sectarian feelings or false views of duty, the injury to the cause of human freedom is the same. We regret the necessity which calls for this declaration of our sentiments, and earnestly hope that we shall find no occasion for reproof or complaint in the future course of the Executive Committee toward the Society which we have the honor to represent. In that case, we will guarantee to them the hearty, united and liberal co operation and friendship of the abolitionists of Massachusetts.

Submitting this statement in vindication of the Massachusetts Anti-Slavery Society from all blame in regard to the present pecuniary embarrassments of the Parent Society, we conclude by the adoption of the following preamble and resolves:

Whereas, it has been officially communicated to this Board, that the American Anti-Slavery Society is at present deeply involved in pecuniary embarrassments;

And whereas, "prompt and liberal aid" has been solicited of the Massachusetts Anti-Slavery Society; or, in case that cannot be given, leave has been asked by the Executive Committee at New York to send their financial agents into this State to collect moneys;

And whereas, the State Society is now struggling, at great expense, to preserve the integrity of the anti-slavery cause from the assaults of a hostile association, which has virtually received the sanction of said Executive Committee:

And whereas, the official organ of the Parent Society has done much to cripple the resources of this Society, by its approval of the new organization; therefore,

Resolved, That this Society must decline granting the desired aid to the Parent Society.

Resolved, That justice to the Society which we represent, and to the cause we espouse, forbids our compliance with their request, that the financial agents of the Parent Society may come into this State, at the present time.

By order of the Board,

FRANCIS JACKSON, *President.*

WM. LLOYD GARRISON, *Cor. Sec.*

Printed as Appendix to the *Eighth Annual Report of the Board of Managers of the Massachusetts Anti-Slavery Society,* presented on January 22, 1840; reprinted in *The Liberator,* February 14, 1840.

The Liberator, in reprinting the letter, accompanied it with the following introductory paragraphs:

"The following letter from the Board of Managers of the Massachusetts Anti-Slavery Society to the Executive Committee of the Parent Society, is of sufficient importance to commend it to the attention of abolitionists throughout the country, and shows in a lucid manner what are the relations at present subsisting between the two societies. It forms a part of the Eighth Report of the State Society, and was cordially approved at the late annual meeting. The Board feel that though the task of making such a development of facts is painful, yet fidelity to the Society and the cause of the slave demands its performance. For several months past, the Executive Committee at New-York have from time to time set forth the pecuniary embarrassments of the Parent Society, and urged the necessity of immediate aid being given to save it from bankruptcy. It appears that, since the last May meeting, not a single State Society has contributed any of its funds directly to the treasury of the Parent. Under these circumstances, there was no other alternative left to the managers of the Mass. A. S. Society, than either to allow unmerited reproach to be cast on themselves and the Society, on the ground of indifference or remissness, or to explain the causes which had conspired to prevent their bearing an equal share of the pecuniary burdens of the Parent Society. . . .

"At the late special meeting of the Parent Society, it was resolved that the sum of $10,000 be apportioned amongst the several State societies, in order to relieve the Executive Committee from their present liabilities, &c. Of this sum, $1250 were assigned to be raised by the Mass. A. S. Society. The Board decline complying with this arrangement, for the reasons set forth in the letter which is here annexed."

1. II Corinthians 8.2, somewhat altered.
2. Psalms 37:3.
3. Shakespeare, *Julius Caesar*, III, ii.
4. *Julius Caesar*, III, ii.

167

TO JAMES K. PAULDING

Boston, Dec. 14, 1839.

Hon. J. K. Paulding,
Secretary of the Navy.

Sir — I have a brother, James H. Garrison, who is now attached as a seaman to the U. S. ship Columbus, at the Navy Yard, in Charlestown. He has been in the naval service of his country for the long period of sixteen years. It is rather more than four months since his last enlistment. During nearly all this time, he has been on the sick list, wholly incapacitated to perform any labor. His disease is a difficult one to eradicate from the system, if it be not immedicable; and must, for an indefinite period, render him of little or no value to the navy. It is a fistulous abscess, of a cancerous nature, situated at the base of the back bone, and badly affecting the spine, and shattering the constitution. Through the kindness of Com. Downes [1] and Capt. Storer,[2] I have been permitted to take him to my house for a few weeks past, in order to procure for him such medical treatment, and pay him such attention, as his case demands, and a brother's affection could prompt. He is now in a somewhat better condition than when he was removed, but it is wholly uncertain how much he may yet be called to suffer under surgical operation, or how soon he will be able (if ever) to discharge the duties of a seaman in the U. S. service. Of course, under these circumstances, to have him remain under pay, cannot be a very desirable object to the Government, the burdens of which should be lessened wherever and whenever it is practicable. My object, therefore, in writing this letter, is respectfully and earnestly to solicit of you the immediate discharge of my brother from the navy, upon the usual conditions. I cannot doubt your kindness in this matter, and shall gratefully appreciate its exercise.

It may have additional weight with you to add, that, during the sixteen years in which he has done, not only "the State," but the country, "some service," [3] it has not been my privilege to enjoy his society more than a fortnight, until his recent sickness! He is an only brother, in whose welfare I feel a deep interest; and none the less, because of the buffetings and perils through which he has been called to pass from boyhood. You will, I am sure, make the case your own, and act accordingly.

Trusting that you will immediately communicate a favorable letter to Com. Downes or Capt. Storer, (whom I have notified that I should ask for my brother's discharge, and whose kindness I shall not easily forget,)

> I remain,
>
> Yours, respectfully,
>
> Wm. Lloyd Garrison.

P.S. My brother will append to this letter a few lines, expressive of his wishes respecting his discharge.

ALS: National Archives and Records Service, Naval Records Collection.

James Kirke Paulding (1779–1860) was already a distinguished author when he was appointed secretary of the Navy under President Martin Van Buren. It must have been especially difficult for Garrison to appeal to Paulding, who was ardently segregationist and proslavery and had in 1836 published a strong defense of slavery in his book *Slavery in the United States* (New York, 1836).

Paulding replied on January 11, 1840: "Your letter for the discharge of your brother from on board the Rec'g ship *Columbus*, at Boston, has been received and referred to Commodore Downes, with directions to examine into his case, and, if found to correspond with your statement, he is authorized to discharge him, provided he is not in debt to the U. States." (*Life*, II, 330n.)

1. Commodore John Downes (b. Canton, Massachusetts, 1784; d. Charlestown, Massachusetts, 1854) was appointed a midshipman in 1802 and promoted to lieutenant in 1807. He participated actively in the War of 1812 on the *Essex* and the *Essex Junior*. He was made a master commandant in 1813. After 1830 he was given command of the frigate *Potomac* and the Pacific Station and participated in the first American naval action in the Orient in 1832. From 1835 to 1842 and 1849 to 1852 he was commandant of the Boston Navy Yard. From 1843 to 1845, he was port captain at Boston. (*DAB.*)

2. Captain George Washington Storer (b. Portsmouth, New Hampshire, 1789;

d. 1864) was a godson of George Washington; he entered the Navy as a mid-shipman in 1809 and served on the *Independence* in the Mediterranean station in 1815–1816, and on the *Constitution* in 1823–1824. He was made commandant in 1828 and captain in February, 1837. He commanded the receiving ship *Columbus* in 1839 and the *Potomac* at the Brazil station in 1840–1842. From 1845 to 1846 he commanded the Navy Yard at Portsmouth, New Hampshire, and thereafter served in a variety of commands until his retirement in 1862, when he was promoted to the rank of rear admiral on the retirement list. (Malcolm Storer, *Annals of the Storer Family*, Boston, 1927, p. 56; *Navy Register of the United States*, Washington, 1840.)

3. "I have done the state some service, and they know it"; Shakespeare, *Othello*, V, ii.

168

TO THE HON. CALEB CUSHING

Boston, Dec. 16, 1839.

Sir:

Though we may not agree, precisely, as to the principles and measures of American abolitionists, yet of one thing I am quite certain — viz. your readiness to confer a favor upon any of your fellow-citizens who may solicit such at your hands. Hence my freedom in making the present application.

Enclosed is a letter from me to the Secretary of the Navy, requesting the discharge of my brother, James H. Garrison, from the naval service. He has been about sixteen years in that service, but is now an invalid. His last enlistment was on board of the U. S. ship Columbus, at the Navy Yard in Charlestown, rather more than four months since. During nearly all this time, he has been on the sick list, wholly incapacitated to perform any labor. His disease is a difficult one to cure, if it be not immedicable — it being a fistulous abscess, situated at the base of the back bone, and badly affecting the spine, etc. Through the kindness of Com. Downes, I have been allowed to take him to my house for a few weeks past, in order to procure for him such medical treatment, and pay him such attention, as his case demands, and a brother's affection could prompt. As he is (and is likely to be, for an indefinite period) a mere bill of expense to the government, it cannot be an object to the same to retain him in the service. It is, however, a somewhat difficult matter, usually, to get seamen discharged; and therefore it is that I trouble you with the accompanying letter, requesting you to deliver it personally into the hands of the Secretary of the Navy. Perhaps all this is needless — perhaps my letter to him would alone be sufficient; but I wish to make "assurance doubly sure," [1] on account of the affection I feel for my brother, and my great anxiety for his welfare. For the last sixteen years, I have not enjoyed his society a single fortnight, until his present illness. He is anxious to get his discharge, and has signified his wishes to the Secretary in my letter.

I am sure you will pardon me for giving you this trouble. Your kindness will be duly appreciated by

Yours, respectfully,

Wm. Lloyd Garrison.

Hon. Caleb Cushing.

ALS: Chicago Historical Society.

At this time, Cushing was a Whig representative in Congress (1835–1843). As Walter Merrill notes (*Against Wind and Tide, A Biography of Wm. Lloyd Garrison*, Cambridge, Mass., 1963, p. 162), it must have been hard for Garrison to write to Cushing, because they had quarreled some years before. But Garrison did not permit this to stand in the way of his brother's needs. Garrison's *Life* notes that Cushing wrote to Garrison on March 11, 1840: "Receiving yours of the 6th, I have called again on the Secretary of the Navy, and he said he would reconsider the whole matter; and I think he is now satisfied that your brother's absence with you was a mere technical violation of law, and involved no injury to the service, but the contrary, and that he will give such additional orders as to close the case in the manner desired. But if otherwise, please to let me know, and I will press him further on the subject" (II, 330n). In an earlier letter to Garrison, dated Washington, January 28, 1840, Cushing had written: "Soon after I received your letter, I called on Mr. Paulding, & delivered your letter addressed to him, & solicited in my own name the release of your brother. He assured me it should be done, if (as he did not doubt) the facts should prove to be as represented. I inquired of him again today; & he said that he had sent orders to the Navy Yard for the discharge of your brother, if, on examination there, the facts were found conformable to the representations made. If any further difficulty interferes, please to let me know that I may interfere for its removal." (MS: Boston Public Library; see Letters 170 and 173 to Cushing, dated February 10 and March 6, 1840.

Cushing's biographer writes, justifiably, that the response to Garrison's request for help "is highly creditable to Cushing's generosity of spirit and forgiving nature, in view of Garrison's earlier strong attacks upon him and the fact that Cushing was not the representative from Garrison's district." (Claude M. Fuess, *The Life of Caleb Cushing*, New York, 1923, I, 272–273.)

1. Shakespeare, *Macbeth*, IV, i.

V THE GREAT SCHISM AND THE EUROPEAN PILGRIMAGE: 1840

THE CONFLICT within abolitionist ranks reached its height in 1840 over two key issues: antislavery political action in the presidental election of 1840 and control of the American Anti-Slavery Society. A convention held in Albany on April 1, 1840, by antislavery men who were favorably disposed toward creation of an antislavery political party, nominated James Birney and Thomas Earle, of Pennsylvania. A second convention, on May 13 and 14 in New York City, confirmed their nomination as the candidates of the newly formed Liberty party.

The annual meeting of the American Anti-Slavery Society, which convened on May 12, 1840, in New York City, witnessed the final split between the Garrisonian and anti-Garrisonian forces. With the predominance of the Garrisonian view regarding the participation of women in the councils of the society, the anti-Garrisonian minority seceded and, on May 15, formed the American and Foreign Anti-Slavery Society, with Arthur Tappan as president, James G. Birney and Henry B. Stanton as secretaries, and Lewis Tappan as treasurer. Since the old executive committee of the American Anti-Slavery Society had transferred the society's newspaper to the new society, a new official organ, *The National Anti-Slavery Standard*, was created and began publication on June 11, 1840.

The World's Anti-Slavery Convention, called by the British and Foreign Anti-Slavery Society for June 12 in London, was one of the highlights of the year, indeed, of Garrison's career. Because of the need for his presence at the meeting of the American Anti-Slavery Society in New York in May, he arrived in London several days after the opening of the convention. By that time, the female delegates from Massachusetts and Pennsylvania had been excluded from the convention. In protest, Garrison sat in the balcony with the ladies and other males who protested the ladies' exclusion and refused to participate in the proceedings. The remainder of his trip was spent in traveling throughout England, Scotland, and Ireland, reviving old friendships, and being fêted by luminaries of the British antislavery movement. Garrison left England on August 4 and arrived in Boston on August 17.

During the latter months of the year two events were most noteworthy. The presidential election in November witnessed the triumph of General William Henry Harrison, the Whig candidate, over Martin Van Buren, the Democratic candidate, with the Liberty party candidate, James Birney, receiving only 7,100 votes nationally. To Garrison, the ignominiously low vote for Birney seemed a total vindication of his opposition to the creation of an abolitionist political party, as an impractical and divisive force within the abolitionist movement.

The Chardon-Street Convention, called to evaluate the Christian Sabbath, the ministry, and the church, met on November 17, 1840, for three days, at the Chardon-Street Chapel in Boston. Its participants and deliberations have been notably depicted in Emerson's famous essay. Although Garrison did not sign the call to the convention, he did publish it in *The Liberator*, and managed to collect for himself a substantial portion of the denunciation that was subsequently heaped upon the convention by its critics.

Garrison's thoughts, as he celebrated his thirty-fifth birthday on December 10, 1840, were expressed in a sonnet which he wrote for the occasion.

SONNET

On completing my thirty-fifth year, Dec. 10, 1840.

If to the age of threescore years and ten,
   God of my life! thou shalt my term prolong,
   Still be it mine to reprobate all wrong,
And save from woe my suffering fellow-men.
Whether, in freedom's cause, my voice or pen
   Be used by Thee, who art my boast and song,
   To vindicate the weak against the strong,
Upon my labors rest Thy benison!
O! not for Afric's sons alone I plead,
   Or her descendants; but for all who sigh
In servile chains, whate'er their caste or creed:
   They not in vain to Heaven send up their cry;
For all mankind from bondage shall be freed,
And from the earth be chased all forms of tyranny.

169

TO GEORGE W. BENSON

Boston, Jan. 4, 1840.

Dear George:

A host of good wishes is springing from my heart for your happiness, and that of every member of our dear family circle, not only during the present year, but for all time — all eternity. I know not how months, weeks and days go with you, (though I can easily guess) — but with me they pass like lightning flashes. I know not what it is to have a moment hang heavily on my hands, from one year's end to another. O, how many things I find it in my heart to do — and yet, alas! how very few of them I accomplish! Still, I am busy, busy — all the time busy — almost too busy to find time to eat. On my very knees, I beg you all at Brooklyn graciously to pardon me for not writing to you oftener. Indeed, I hardly write, now-a-days, at all. And yet I love you all dearly — as much so, as if I sent you a whole quire of letters daily. Though out of sight, none of you are out of mind — O no! It is only those who are destitute of affection — who do not know what love is — who can forget.

The new year finds us, at home, in the enjoyment of perfect health, and happy in mind, though empty in purse. The boys are thriving finely — but Willie is a none-such! Though not yet two years old, he talks with almost as much fluency as George. O, he is a darling! so fair, so plump, so good-natured, so cheerful, so every thing that is good! George goes to school quite regularly, and bids fair to be a good scholar. He is slowly improving in his temper, and his paroxysms of disobedience are becoming fewer and less violent. But he has a tremendous will of his own, and is even more obstinate than his father — "a chip of the old block," and something more.

We are looking for mother daily. Helen will rejoice to see her, and so shall I. It is some time, however, since we heard any thing from her. Helen wrote to her a few days ago, but no reply has been received. We take it for granted that she is at Charlotte's, and trust she is well.

After a great deal of trouble, we have finally got our arrangements made with friend Knapp.[1] The committee of reference awarded him $175 [2] — being $125 less than was proposed to him in the conference of friends at Loring's office. He is in a very miserable state of mind, and very much embittered in his feelings, I am sorry to say, toward us all, and myself in particular. I have scarcely had any conversation with him, on this account. You will be glad to perceive, that Loring and Philbrick are added to the committee of finance for the Liberator — making a very respectable and solid committee. It is of great service to the paper to have such men act in such a capacity. The prospect before us is fair, and full of encouragement. I anticipated a great falling off of subscribers at the close of the volume; but I think we have never had so few leave us before. This is certainly very remarkable. We have had some discontinuances, to be sure; but many new subscribers have been added to our list. We start with entirely new materials in our printing-office, and the appearance of the paper is much improved.

How sorry I am to say, that it will be utterly out of my power to be with you at Hartford on the 8th inst.[3] But what I cannot do, I cannot. I know how great will be the disappointment of the Connecticut friends — your own — and all the household at Brooklyn. And, what is worse, Quincy [4] tells me that he will not be able to go. He made the attempt before [5] — got half-way, or part way — was forced to stay in the cars all night, and then return home, in consequence of the storm. The annual meeting of our State Society takes place on the 22d. With a thousand other things I have to do between that brief space and this, I have the Annual Report to write, reviewing the events of the past year — which must, of necessity, be a very long and elaborate document. O, I groan to think of it! Not a syllable of it is yet prepared — nor can I get one hour to devote to it; and yet it *must* be all written before the meeting. Dear George, you see how I am situated: therefore, apologize for my absence to the friends at Hartford. If I can possibly get time, I mean to write a letter to Cowles,[6] to be read at the meeting — but it is doubtful whether I shall succeed. I will do the best I can, and who can do more? Do not fail to be at the meeting yourself, and save Connecticut abolitionism from the political gulf which yawns to devour. And by all means be at our annual meeting on the 22d, if possible: we shall need your presence on many accounts. Love to dear Mary, Sarah, Anna, Catharine, &c.

Yours, lovingly,

Wm. Lloyd Garrison.

☞ I am distressed and mortified to think that I cannot send you, in this letter, the money that is due you. I have $400 owing to me on my salary, &c. but cannot get any of it at present. In the course of this month, shall doubtless get it all. My creditors annoy me by their duns — but they must wait.

ALS: Garrison Papers, Boston Public Library. A portion of this letter was printed in *Life*, II, 334–335.

As happened in the past, Garrison initially dated his first letter of the new year, "1839." It was then crossed out and replaced by "1840," whether by Garrison or by a later editor is unclear.

1. On December 20, 1839, in its prospectus for the ensuing year, *The Liberator* announced that "the pecuniary affairs of the paper are to be managed by a financial committee consisting of the following widely known and well-tried friends of emancipation — Francis Jackson, Ellis Gray Loring, Edmund Quincy, Samuel Philbrick, and William Bassett."

On January 3, 1840, *The Liberator* printed a communication, "To the Friends of the Liberator," dated Jan. 1, 1840, bearing the names of the five members of its financial committee. After noting that a committee of three of the undersigned had been in charge of the financial operations of the paper during the past year, as an experiment to learn the necessary facts concerning the paper's financial operation and to ascertain "whether the expenditures of the paper could be covered by its receipts," the paper announced a reorganization of its operation. "An arrangement has accordingly been made with Mr. Knapp, who has relinquished his interest in the paper, receiving therefor a certain consideration; and an attempt will now be fairly made to conduct the concern with the most rigid regard to economy."

On May 15, 1842, in a letter to Elizabeth Pease, Garrison explained the change in administration more fully. "A committee was appointed to confer with Mr. Knapp, in order to effect the desired arrangement in an amicable and equitable manner. This he entered into with much reluctance, of course. As a matter of experiment, it was agreed that he should waive all right and title to any part of the *Liberator* for the term of two years — he being paid such remuneration as impartial referees might feel disposed to award. It was further agreed that, during this period, the pecuniary concerns of the paper should be managed by a responsible committee, in whom its friends could feel the utmost confidence; and, consequently, the present committee kindly consented to act in this capacity. . . .

"When the question of remuneration was submitted to the referees, (who were all quite friendly to Mr. Knapp), they summoned a number of practical printers as witnesses to determine the amount that ought to be awarded to Mr. Knapp. On being asked, of what pecuniary value a newspaper could be which sunk one or two thousand dollars per annum over and above its receipts, they, of course, said, none whatever. . . . As a matter of kindness and good-will, rather than of equity, the referees decided that I should pay Mr. Knapp $150 — half of it to be paid yearly. This decision was cheerfully met on my part.

"To say that I separated from my friend Knapp with great reluctance and pain of mind — that I exerted myself to the utmost to retain him as printer of the *Liberator* — that I greatly compassionated his forlorn condition, and did everything in his behalf that friendship and sympathy could suggest — is simply to assert the truth, which all my friends in this quarter know full well. But the *existence of the Liberator depended upon this new arrangement*; and justice to those who had to sustain it required that it should be made.

"This arrangement was to expire in two years by its own limitation   that is, on the first day of January, 1842." (Quoted in *Life*, II, 331 332.)

2. *Life*, II, 332, notes that Garrison's account here differs slightly from his later account to Elizabeth Pease, "in respect to the amount of the pecuniary award," which was there stated to be $150.

3. The reference is to a meeting of the Connecticut Anti-Slavery Society at Hartford on Wednesday morning, January 8. The meeting was to be a continuation of one previously held at Hartford on December 18, 1839. Because of a severe snowstorm, the number present had been small. After some business had been transacted the meeting adjourned to meet again on January 8. (*The Liberator*, January 3, 1840.)

4. Edmund Quincy.

5. He had tried to attend the December 18 meeting.

6. Samuel Smith Cowles (b. Farmington, Connecticut, December 9, 1814; d. there, December 5, 1872) was then secretary of the Connecticut Anti-Slavery Society. As a youth he had learned the trade of printer at Windsor, Vermont. In 1837, he came to Boston as a journeyman printer. A year later, he began to edit and print the *Charter Oak*, an antislavery newspaper, in Hartford. He returned to his native village in 1843, where he held many prominent positions, including justice of the peace, notary public, judge of the Probate Court, member of the legislature, and commissioner of the Supreme Court. (Colonel Calvin D. Cowles, comp., *Genealogy of the Cowles Families in America*, New Haven, 1929, pp. 529–530.)

170

TO CALEB CUSHING

Boston, Feb. 10, 1840.

Dear Sir:

I offer you my very grateful acknowledgements for your kind interposition to obtain the discharge of my sick brother from the navy; and also for your letter of the 28th ultimo, wishing to know whether any further difficulty stood in the way, that you might interpose for its removal. I should have written to you at a much earlier period, had his case been settled; but it was not until Saturday, that I was able to procure my brother's discharge, and then accompanied by such conditions as induced me not to accept it, until I could hear from the Secretary of the Navy again. Enclosed is a letter which I have addressed to Mr. Paulding, giving a plain statement of the facts in the case. I send it to you unsealed, in order that you may possess yourself of its contents by a perusal; — after which, you may seal it, if you think proper, before handing it to Mr. P.

In regard to my brother's leave of absence, I have been waiting, ever since the first week of his removal to my house, to have him summoned back to the ship; and have marvelled not a little at the indulgence granted to him, but supposed that it was given in consequence of his being unfit to perform any active service. Com. Downes says he specified, in his note to Capt. Storer, "a few days absence." True; but Capt. Storer, in the receipt he gave me for the $36 I put into his hands as security for my brother's return, made nothing definite as to time; and hence I felt authorized to keep James as long as no special inquiry was made after him. It seems to me that either the Commodore or the Captain was in fairness bound to explain to me the rules of the ship, respecting absentees, at the time of James's removal, as I was wholly ignorant of them. They did not do so — and the consequence has been, that, owing to a wrong impression in my own mind, he has been absent a much longer period than the law allows. Still, there is no criminality justly attaching to either of us; and I conceive that it would be an act of extreme cruelty and injustice to brand and punish him as "a deserter." If Com. Downes really regarded him as such, why did he not tell me so in the first instance, when I applied for his discharge? Why did he not order a search to be made for him, and offer a reward for his seizure? I cannot but feel surprised, and somewhat indignant, at such treatment. The fact, I suppose, is really this — both Com. Downes and Capt. Storer very well knew that my brother was in all probability beyond cure, and therefore they gave themselves no concern about his absence, as long as he said nothing about receiving wages, and as long as I had paid over the bounty money to the Captain. But when, as he was about getting his discharge, his claim to the bounty and wages was urged, (in consequence of his being discharged as an invalid,) then it was convenient to make him out, technically, a deserter, and thus leave him penniless and helpless, in the midst of his sickness. What a farce it was to have a medical examination of the person of "a deserter," in order to know if he could be discharged as an invalid! I am disposed to hope that the Secretary of the Navy will act with magnanimity and generosity in the present case — that he will allow my brother wages and his bounty up to the time of his discharge — and that, if an error has been committed by me, through ignorance and misapprehension, in keeping my brother in the city so long a time, he will wink at it, in view of the illness of that brother, and especially on the ground of his eighteen years' service in the navy. What a wretched compensation it will be, at best, for all that James has endured and perilled in behalf of his country!

I send you herewith, Capt. Storer's receipt for the money I paid him as security. The Secretary may wish to see the original. Please return it to me.

James shipped at Charlestown on the 3rd of August last, for a term of three years.

I verily believe it is far easier to get a southern slave manumitted at the south, than it is to get a seaman discharged from the U. S. navy.

I am sorry to trouble you with this matter again; but as you have kindly renewed the offer of your services, I make free to ask you to see Mr. Paulding, and use your influence with him to effect a just and amicable settlement of the case.

> Yours, very thankfully,
>
> Wm. Lloyd Garrison.

Hon. C. Cushing.

ALS: Merrill Collection of Garrison Papers, Wichita State University Library, Wichita, Kansas.

171
TO CHARLES STEARNS

Boston, Feb. 10, 1840.

MY DEAR BROTHER:

In the midst of pressing engagements, I hasten to reply to your letter of the 31st ultimo.[1] Deeply do I sympathize with you in your present situation, and strong is my admiration and love for you as one desirous to have a conscience void of offence toward God and man, and breathing nothing but peace and good-will to all the human race. I know, by experience, that, though a jail is not a desirable residence as a matter of choice, nevertheless,

'Stone walls do not a prison make,
Nor iron bars a cage' — [2]

for the spiritually enfranchised soul is not to be trammelled by such devices. He whom Christ makes free, can never be bound, except bodily; and though his body be confined, he is still free indeed.

I will not stop to say what I think of the barbarism and tyranny of Connecticut, in trampling upon the rights of conscience, and consigning to prison such of her citizens as believe that they are forbidden by the gospel to do military duty. After ages will look upon this matter with astonishment. It is the opprobrium of the nineteenth century.

You inquire, what my opinion is, in regard to its being right or wrong to pay a military fine, for not doing military duty; and whether it is not a compromise of principle to pay such a fine.

I answer, first, that the friends of peace are by no means agreed on this point; some believing that they may pay the fine, without doing wrong — and others, that it would be an abandonment of principle for them to do so. It is obvious that no one man can determine for another what is wrong. 'Let every man be fully persuaded in his own mind.'[3] Let us be careful to give heed to what conscience may seem to dictate; but let us also aim to have an enlightened conscience, that we may not err in obeying it.

Without designing to go into an extended argument at this time, I would say, that in the application of the principles of peace to existing customs and governmental requisitions, there will doubtless often difficulties occur to perplex the mind, as to what really is or is not a violation of those principles. Still, if we have a sincere desire to know the truth, and seek the guidance of the Spirit of Truth, I think we shall not be long in discovering the path of rectitude.

Again. As for myself, though I was for a time of a different opinion,

I see no reason why a military fine may not be paid, as well as any other exacted by a government based on physical force. If I refuse to bear arms — if I will not procure a substitute — if I bear an open and uncompromising testimony against the military system — I do all, in my opinion, that is required by Christianity. In paying that which is exacted of me, in consequence of my refusing to train, I by no means assent to the justice of the exaction, but act in the spirit of the precept — 'He that will take thy coat, let him have thy cloak also.' [4] In parting with my goods, unresistingly, whenever they are demanded by government, I may suffer wrong, but I do no wrong to others. I shed no blood, but am known to be opposed to its being shed by my fellow-men. If the government take my money, and with it hire others to do the work of butchery, mine is not the responsibility. The government is doubly guilty: first, in exacting the money — and, secondly, in perverting it to such a horrid use.

You say — 'I consider the imprisonment as a punishment for not paying the fine, not for refusing to do military duty.' I do not see any clear distinction in this view of the case. The law presents three alternatives, every one of which is equally unjust. First, do military duty — or, second, pay so much money — or, third, go to jail. The cause of your imprisonment is, primarily, *your refusal to train*. Remember that almost all the duties and taxes levied by government are absorbed in supporting the army and navy, and upholding the arm of violence. If, in paying a military fine, you countenance the militia system; then, in paying your ordinary taxes to government, you sanction its rightful authority, and are responsible for its acts. But, I conceive, it is not so. In neither case do you *necessarily* manifest your approval. You submit to pay tribute, be it ever so unjust, or for whatever purpose it may be used by government — in accordance with the injunction of the apostle — 'not only for wrath, but for conscience sake.' [5] This is gospel non-resistance. At the same time, you bear your testimony against whatever is sinful in the government or the people, at whatever peril to your person or property.

You illustrate the subject by a reference to the theatre — and ask, whether a christian could pay a fine for refusing to attend it, without committing sin. I answer, as before, that, in paying the fine, he does not sanction either the theatre or the extortion. *He submits to be robbed.* If he should attempt to compare the acts of government with the gospel, he would find that they are nearly all of them wrong, and that the government itself is hostile to the dominion of the Son of God. Now, what shall he do? To sustain it directly, he cannot. Its offices, its honors, its powers, he will not share. Yet, if it demands his property, he will part with it, rather than *seem* to be rebellious.

Jesus, the Messiah, was a true non-resistant. He came expressly to set up a kingdom that should break in pieces and destroy all others. Yet he paid tribute, and also caused his disciples to do so, to a tyrannical, bloody, idolatrous government. In this respect, as well as in many others, I think he 'left us an example that we should follow his steps.' [6] Who will say, that, in paying this tribute, he sanctioned or made himself responsible for any of Caesar's doings? And if *he* could pay money that went not merely to support 'a theatre,' but gladiatorial shows, armed and bloody resistance to evil, and gross idolatry, may *we* not pay the exactions of the American government without doing wrong, or participating in its sanguinary proceedings? Provided, of course, that we make it manifest to all, as did the Saviour, that we belong to a kingdom which is not of this world — that we are willing to suffer the loss of all things that we may win Christ — that our treasure is not on earth, but in heaven — that we desire the forgiveness, and not the punishment of enemies.

My sheet is full, and I must stop. If I have written anything that may serve to enlighten or relieve your mind, I shall be glad. Honoring you greatly for the reverence which you are disposed to pay to duty and conscience, I remain,

Your sympathizing brother,

WM. LLOYD GARRISON.

Printed in *The Liberator*, February 14, 1840.

Charles Stearns, a young journalist as well as pacifist and Garrisonian abolitionist, and a native of Massachusetts, was imprisoned in Hartford, Connecticut, for refusing to report for militia duty. He was soon released, and returned to his antislavery and pacifist activities. In 1855 he moved to Lawrence, Kansas, where he gave up his nonresistance views, explaining that "When I live with men made in God's image, I will never shoot them; but these pro-slavery Missourians are demons from the bottomless pit, and may be shot with impunity." He took part in the defense of Lawrence in September 1856, under the leadership of John Brown, against the attack of 2,300 Missourians. He moved to Central City, Colorado, in 1861, where he stayed for more than four years. During the Civil War he and his wife, who was an uncompromising abolitionist though raised in Kentucky, decided that if the war ended in the emancipation of the slaves, they would go South to help the freedmen. But she died before they could go. He left Colorado in 1865, and returned to Massachusetts, passing through Boston and proclaiming in the newspapers his intention to go South to work for the Negro's education, right to vote, and right to own land. Arriving in Savannah in May 1866, with his three-year-old daughter and new wife, Hetta, he bought a 1,500-acre farm in Columbia County, Georgia, which he named Hope On, Hope Ever Plantation. He stayed on the plantation for six years, suffering many tribulations, and returned to Boston around 1872. In 1876, he wrote to Garrison asking him to become president of the National Southern Emigration Society, whose purpose was to sponsor a movement of antislavery northerners to the South. He was active in radical and labor reform movements in the 1880's and 1890's. In 1902, still interested in the Negro, he attended the Annual Tuskegee Conference. He wrote and published several books, the most noteworthy being *The Black Man of the South and the Rebels*, New York and Boston, 1872. (Much of the material in this biographical sketch is from *The Black Man*, etc. See also Peter Brock, *Pacifism in the United States, from the Colonial Era to the First World War*, Princeton, N.J., 1968, pp. 612, 679; Aileen S. Kraditor, *Means and Ends in American Abolitionism* . . . , New York, 1969, p. 89; a letter from James M. McPherson to Louis Ruchames, Princeton, New Jersey, dated July 31, 1969, cites Stearns to B. T. Washington, Feb. 2, 1902, Washington Papers, Library of Congress.)

1. The letter to Garrison from Charles Stearns, dated Hartford County Jail, Connecticut, Jan. 31, 1840, appeared, with Garrison's reply, in the same issue of *The Liberator*. "I wish to inquire," wrote Stearns, "what your opinion is, in regard to its being *right* or *wrong* to pay a *military* fine — for not doing military duty. I have always regarded it as being a part of the system, and that, by so doing, you countenance that system — virtually acknowledging it to be right; and consequently have supposed it to be wrong to pay a fine, and have made up my mind to suffer imprisonment, rather than do it. I have lately had an opportunity to bring my principles to the test. I was fined for refusing to do military duty, refused to pay it, and am now suffering imprisonment in consequence; from which, unlike the Massachusetts law, *there is no release*. I must either pay this fine, or remain here as long as I live. Since I have been here, some of my friends have tried to persuade me, that I am in the wrong concerning this matter; that by paying the fine, I do not countenance the military system, as I do it unwillingly; I as much countenanced it by coming to jail, as by paying the fine. They say, here are two penalties for refusing to train; you are at liberty to choose between them; and, certainly, you ought to choose the least."

Garrison's reply was prefaced by the following remarks in *The Liberator*: "By the law of Massachusetts, a military fine is liquidated by imprisonment for the space of six days; but it appears from the letter of Mr. Stearns, that, by the law of Connecticut, no provision is made for the relief of those who cannot conscientiously pay such a fine. They must either pay it, or be imprisoned for life, or at least until they can procure the pardon (!) of the Executive. If — as we suppose — the Friends are allowed in Connecticut to enjoy their rights of conscience without molestation, the case assumes a still more aggravated aspect. Imprison a man on account of his pacific principles. And in a State boasting of its republicanism and Christianity. And because he is, peradventure, connected with the Congregational or Methodist denomination, and not with the Society of Friends. There is a specimen of enlightened and righteous legislation, in the nineteenth century of the Christian era — in the 'land of the free and the asylum of the oppressed!' Tell it not in Burmah! publish it not in the streets of China! . . ."

2. Richard Lovelace (1618-1658), English poet, "To Althea: From Prison."
3. Romans 14:5.
4. Matthew 5:40, slightly adapted.
5. Romans 13:5.
6. I Peter 2:21, slightly adapted.

172

TO THE ABOLITIONISTS OF THE UNITED STATES

[February 28, 1840.]

DEAR BRETHREN:

The sacred enterprise in which we are enlisted has been called to encounter many imminent perils, and to pass through various fiery ordeals. No outward opposition, however, has been able to arrest its progress, or to intimidate or divide its friends. Calumny, persecution, outrage, have served only to quicken its growth, awaken sympathy in its favor, and multiply the number of its adherents. The reformation which has been effected in public sentiment, on the subject of slavery, within the last six years, is truly astonishing. Until within a short period, the union of abolitionists has been perfect, their love and respect for each other mutual, their spirit catholic, their mode of action uniform, their understanding of the philosophy of anti-slavery reform clear and harmonious. Waging no war against any religious sect or political party, as such, but appealing to them all, in the sacred names of RELIGION and JUSTICE, to assist in emancipating our enslaved countrymen, — and relying solely upon moral suasion for success in our great undertaking, — we have made proselytes among all sects and parties, with a rapidity almost unexampled in the history of national regeneration, and have thickly planted our associations in every free State. But we are now in the midst of a crisis, perhaps more threatening in its aspect, and more trying to the spirit, than any which has been surmounted in our struggle with the powers of darkness. We are no longer an unbroken phalanx — our foes are they of our own household — our ranks are, to some extent at least, schismatically affected — there is, we fear, less faith in God, and more reliance upon human wisdom, than formerly — a growing disposition to underrate the power of truth — an active determination, on the part of some, to manufacture and impose new tests of anti-slavery character, which shall divide us asunder — and, in certain quarters, a sectarian exclusiveness of purpose, in respect to the management of our cause.

The basis of our union as a society is, and in the nature of things only can be, an agreement in the heinousness of the sin of slave-holding, and in the duty of immediate emancipation. Upon this basis, it has been found practicable to bring together individuals of almost every conceivable variety of opinion on other subjects. Upon this basis alone, is there any hope that slavery will ever be peaceably abolished, and our country saved from the horrors of a civil and servile war. Upon it, every man is left free to cherish his own peculiar views of Church and State — to belong to whatever sect or party he may choose to select; pledging himself only to this one thing — that, for the sake of his sect or party, he will not sacrifice the cause of bleeding humanity — and that he will stand by his anti-slavery principles in good faith, and at all hazards, in whatever station he may occupy, or among those with whom he may be disposed to associate.

Already, not less than three movements have been made, calculated if not designed to abridge this common platform, and to substitute in its place one conceived and fashioned by the spirit of exclusiveness.

The first attempt was to exclude from an equal participation in the proceedings of our organization, one half of the warmest, most self-sacrificing, most successful friends of the slave, on account of their sex — to make certain sectarian views, respecting the equality of woman, the views of our whole body, instead of leaving every individual to enjoy his or her own ideas of duty and propriety in this matter, being responsible only to God.

This conduct has justly been frowned upon by the great body of abolitionists.

The next movement that was calculated to divide our ranks was a violent attack upon those abolitionists, whose religious scruples do not allow them to participate directly in the politics of the country, by using the elective franchise. It was declared that a belief in the religious duty of every man to vote at the polls (if he has the right legally,) and in the divine authority of government, is indispensable to sound membership in our society. Such a test, it is obvious, is contrary to the genius and scope of abolitionism, and would exclude from our platform some of the earliest and most efficient friends of our cause, who have been eminently instrumental in arousing this nation to a sense of its guilt and danger in perpetuating slavery. A new organization in this State, having such a test, has been formed during the last year; and is now endeavoring to destroy the Massachusetts A. S. Society for refusing to enforce this dogma upon its members!

The third and latest movement that has been made, to the serious interruption of our harmony as a body, comes in the form of a proposition to organize a distinct political party, in open hostility to the whig and democratic parties, as such. This proposition has been very fully and ably discussed in the anti-slavery periodicals during the past year; and overwhelmingly rejected by abolitionists throughout the country, as inexpedient, improper, and dangerous to the integrity and peace of our organization. The State Anti-Slavery Societies of Massachusetts, Rhode Island and Connecticut, have *unanimously* voted it down; and a multitude of other societies, in various sections of the country, have coincided in this decision. No one has given it an approval, to our knowledge. The national anti-slavery convention, which assembled at Albany in August last, with special reference to the subject of political action, declined taking any definite position in regard to a third party.

Notwithstanding these strong and gratifying expressions of sentiment, the EMANCIPATOR (the official organ of the American Anti-

Slavery Society) continues to advocate the formation of such a party! This conduct, in our opinion, is exceedingly unwise, and reprehensible. Nor can we but deeply regret the course pursued by the Executive Committee of the Parent Society; inasmuch as they necessarily, by their silence, seem to countenance all that is advanced in the Emancipator on this subject; and inasmuch as the Society which they represent stands publicly pledged to 'open no road to political preferment,' and has constantly deprecated the formation of a distinct political party by abolitionists.

In the Fourth Annual Report of the Parent Society, it is declared that 'the great end at which we aim is, to subvert the relation of master and slave — *not by machinery, political or ecclesiastical*, but by establishing in the hearts of men a deep and wide-spreading conviction of the brotherhood of the human race,' [1] &c. And it is added in the same Report, that 'the best safeguard' against the entrance of political adventurers into our ranks, 'is for abolitionists, while they firmly refuse to vote for a man who will not support abolition measures, *to avoid setting up candidates of their own.*' [2]

At the fifth annual meeting of the Society, a large committee was appointed 'to prepare a declaration, which shall announce the judgment of the American Anti-Slavery Society concerning the common error, that our enterprise is of a *political* and not *religious* character.' [3]

In the third Report of the Society,[4] the following language is held:

'This Society has *no rewards to bestow*, but those of a good conscience. We have opened, *and shall open*, NO ROAD TO POLITICAL PREFERMENT. The moment the cause shall have become popular, it will have accomplished its object; and if any have hoped to ascend by it to earthly glory, they will find themselves on the ground. The strength of our cause must be in the humble, fervent prayer of the righteous man, which availeth much, and the blessing of that God, who hath chosen the weak things of this world to confound the mighty.'

Judge Jay, in a letter addressed to the Vermont Anti-Slavery Society in 1836, says: [5]

'The exhibition of TRUTH in christian faithfulness, appears to me the great instrument by which we are to operate. Should *political* Anti-Slavery ever be substituted for *religious* Anti-Slavery, the consequences would probably be disastrous to the cause of human rights, and to the welfare of our common country. So long as abolitionists seek only the removal of slavery in the *States* through the voluntary action of the masters, there will, in my opinion, be no danger of a dissolution of the Union; but should they become a *political* party, striving for office and power, they would be joined by a corrupt and selfish herd, and losing their moral feeling and moral influence, might prove dangerous to the peace and stability of our Republic.

As abolitionists, like others, differ about men and measures, they cannot honestly unite as a body on topics unconnected with emancipation, and it is earnestly to be hoped that the cause of abolition will remain uncontaminated by state politics. It is, however, a serious question, whether an abolitionist can conscientiously vote for a candidate for Congress who is known to be in favor of perpetuating the abominations of the District of Columbia. At the same time, the expediency of nominating 'abolition candidates,' as such, is certainly doubtful.'

In the Quarterly Anti-Slavery Magazine for January, 1837, the following view is entertained of the distinguishing characteristic of the anti-slavery enterprise:

'The abolition of slavery has a legitimate claim to be regarded as A GREAT RELIGIOUS ENTERPRISE. . . *It savors not of the selfishness and ambition of* A POLITICAL PARTY SCHEME — it has no sympathy with such motives — it disdains such measures, and partakes not at all of that spirit. It seeks to accomplish *a great religious object* purely by *religious and moral means.* . . The friends of the cause of abolition ought to prosecute it AS a *religious* enterprise . . . Possibly it may have been, for the moment, forgotten that this cause is the cause of God — is really a great religious enterprise, and ought to be prosecuted as such, and *as nothing else.* . . It is a controversy against sin, and never can succeed, except by the power of truth and holiness. Then let us clothe us with this power, and hold it forth before the world as it is. . . Political economy is too weak to contend against the giant passions which sustain slavery. So is the principle of fear. . . Make this a great religious enterprise — make it such in spirit, in argument, in appeal — make it such in all our measures and operations, and we cannot fail of success.'

In an Address to the People of the United States, issued by the New England Anti-Slavery Convention in 1834, it is said: [6]

'The Anti-Slavery Society, which is now growing so rapidly in every part of our country, although its seeds were sown among the weeds and thorns of popular prejudice, is not a new sect or *party, coming forward to mingle in the strife of politics,* or the controversies of religion. It is intended to engage the friends of justice in every party; and it is actually composed of men of almost all the different religious and political denominations in our country.'

The following resolution was adopted at the New-England A. S. Convention in 1837, on motion of William Goodell: [7]

'Resolved, That while abolitionists are called upon carefully to avoid a course which might identify them with either of the political parties of the country — *and while their policy* EQUALLY *requires them to abstain from organizing a political party of their own* — they are nevertheless bound by their principles to withhold their votes from those who either oppose freedom of speech and of the press, or who decline to act in favor of human rights, so far as the Constitution will permit, in the State and National Legislatures, to which they may belong.'

In May last, the Executive Committee of the American A. S. Society issued an address to the abolitionists of the United States, in which they declared —

'Abolitionists are associated for a single object; — to change the civil, social and moral condition of the colored people. We believe this can be brought about, *without destroying existing organizations in the State or in the Church.* There is no statesman of any political creed, — no religionist of any sect, — who may not consistently give us his aid.'

But it is not our object, in this address, to prove (as we might) by a strong array of evidence, that the abolitionists of this country have, from an early period in their cause, regarded the formation of an anti-slavery political party as at war with sound policy, and incompatible with the unity of the anti-slavery organization. It is very apparent, that any attempt to force such a measure upon them must necessarily produce collision and discord, if not disorganization.

Our special object now is, to call upon the various anti-slavery societies and periodicals in the country, to give no countenance to a 'National Anti-Slavery Convention for Independent Nominations,' which has just been called by a meeting of abolitionists in Genessee county, N. Y. to be held at Albany on the first of April next. The call is presumptuous, comes with no authority, and should receive general condemnation. It is evident that there is, in the western part of New York, a small but talented body of restless, ambitious men, who are determined to get up a third party, come what may — in the hope, doubtless, of being lifted by it into office. Though the voice of the abolitionists of the country has been raised, clearly and emphatically, against such a movement, — and though it is certain that, without the sanction and co-operation of the great body of American abolitionists, a third party would be utterly powerless, and even with their approval would at present be practically inefficient, — yet they give no heed to these things, but are for precipitate and distinct political action!

We feel no small amount of surprise and regret in view of their conduct. Whether it be an error of judgment, or a desire for preferment, on their part, the injury inflicted on our righteous cause is the same. They should be promptly rebuked before all the people. We do not doubt, we readily concede, that there are disinterested, truehearted abolitionists in New-York, and in other States, who are disposed to favor this new political project; and we would not cast any imputation upon their motives, whatever may be our opinion of the clearness of their vision, and the soundness of their judgment. Still, we are constrained to believe that it is an ambitious, selfish spirit which has given birth and shape to the movement; and we speak of it accordingly.

For the honor and purity of our enterprise, we trust that the abolitionists of the several States will refuse to give any countenance to the proposed convention at Albany. Let their verdict be recorded against it as unauthorised, unnecessary, premature. Let the meeting be insignificant and local, and thus rendered harmless. Whenever the exigencies of the times shall demand another national anti-slavery convention, let the call be made through an official medium: let the Executive Committee of the Parent Society, after having clearly ascertained the views of the managers of the several State societies in relation to it, send forth an invitation. Let us not sanction a precedent, which shall encourage, nay authorize a few, irresponsible individuals at any time to appoint a national gathering of abolitionists, as it may suit their caprice or ambition, in order to promote some selfish or local purposes. The annual meeting of the American Anti-Slavery Society will be held in New York city early in May; and at that meeting (which will be the most important in its bearings upon the purity and success of our cause of any that has preceded it,) let there be an overwhelming attendance of the tried and faithful friends of immediate emancipation, to deliberate and act not only upon the political, but upon every other aspect of our holy enterprise.

By order of the Board of Managers of the Massachusetts Anti-Slavery Society.

FRANCIS JACKSON, *Pres.*

Wm. Lloyd Garrison, *Cor. Sec.*

Printed in *The Liberator*, February 28, 1840.

1. *Fourth Annual Report of the American Anti-Slavery Society, with the Speeches Delivered at the Anniversary Meeting Held in the City of New York, on the 9th May, 1837, and the Minutes of the Meetings of the Society for Business* (New York, 1837), p. 105.

2. *Ibid.*, p. 114.

3. The committee members were George Bourne, Charles W. Denison, Garrison, Beriah Green, Samuel J. May, Amos A. Phelps, Orange Scott, John G. Whittier, and Hiram Wilson (*The Liberator*, May 18, 1838).

4. The report presented to the annual meeting in May 1836.

5. William Jay's letter was dated February 11, 1836, and was printed in the second annual report of the Vermont Anti-Slavery Society, p. 17 (letter dated May 12, 1969, from Alan D. MacKinnon, Museum Staff, Vermont Historical Society).

6. For the text, see *The Liberator*, September 6, 1834.

7. *The Liberator*, June 2, 1837, "Political Action."

173

TO CALEB CUSHING

Boston, March 6, 1840.

Dear Sir:

Some three or four weeks ago, I forwarded a letter to you, by mail, respecting the case of my brother; in which was enclosed a long epistle to the Secretary of the Navy, detailing certain facts in relation to the conduct of Com. Downes and Capt. Storer, who, (though he was declared on examination by the naval physician and surgeon, to be an invalid who could be of no further use to the navy,) refused to discharge my brother, except on such conditions as I felt unwilling to comply with, until I could hear again from Mr. Paulding. Since my letter was written, Mr. Paulding has informed me, (I suppose at the request of Com. Downes,) that I must abide by the decision of Com. D.; but as he makes no allusion to the letter which I addressed to him, through your care, and as I have had no reply from you acknowledging the receipt of my communication, I am apprehensive that the packet I addressed to you has miscarried. If so, I shall regret the loss and delay exceedingly, but will send you another copy of the letters immediately. Please let me hear from you by return of mail, if convenient. I feel reluctant to give you this additional trouble; but the interest which I feel in my brother's welfare, and a desire to have justice done in his case, must be my apology. I know you will aid me to the extent of your ability.[1]

    With much respect, I remain,
     Your much obliged friend,
      Wm. Lloyd Garrison.

Hon. Caleb Cushing.

ALS: Merrill Collection of Garrison Papers, Wichita State University Library.

1. See Garrison's letters to Cushing of December 16, 1839 (168) and February 10, 1840 (170).

174

TO GERRIT SMITH

[Boston, March 27, 1840.]

ESTEEMED FRIEND — In the Liberator of August 30, 1839, I inserted a letter from you, complaining of the course which I and many others

thought proper to pursue at the last annual meeting of the American
A. S. Society, on the subject of political action. It was published without note or comment. In a recent communication to the Friend of
Man, you remind me that I have not attempted to answer your objections, as I promised to do. It is not too late, even now, to make a
reply, the delay of which has been wholly unintentional.

After expressing your gratification at the almost unanimous adoption of a resolution at the meeting in New-York, declaring, in substance, that the exercise of the elective franchise is not essential to
membership in the Anti-Slavery Society, you proceed to express your
surprise and regret, that I and many others voted against the adoption
of another resolution, which virtually maintains an entirely different
doctrine! As follows:

'Resolved, That this Society still holds, as it has from the beginning,
that the employment of the political franchise, as established by the Constitution and laws of the country, so as to promote the abolition of slavery,
is of high obligation — a DUTY, which, *as abolitionists*, we OWE to our
enslaved fellow countrymen, groaning under legal oppression.'

One of two things must be true: — the Constitution of the Parent
Society either makes the duty of employing the elective franchise
obligatory upon every one of its members entitled to vote, or it does
not. If it does, then you are right in saying that we, who opposed the
adoption of the above resolution, performed an unconstitutional act;
then non-resistants cannot properly belong to the Parent Society, because they cannot comply with the requirements of the Constitution;
then the resolution which was passed, conceding that no such test is
required, ought to be rescinded. If it does not, then we had a perfect
right to record our votes against the resolution above quoted, and no
man may rightfully reprove us for our conduct. That resolution, be it
remembered, was introduced and sustained by the very men who
profess to believe, that those who cannot in conscience vote at the polls
are disqualified from being members of the Society — by J. G. Birney,
A. A. Phelps, H. B. Stanton, A. St. Clair, C. T. Torrey, Daniel Wise;
and their design was, to proscribe all those who do not agree with
them on the subject of political action. They supported the resolution,
because, in their opinion, it expressed precisely the doctrine, the
absurd and disorganizing doctrine, that a Covenanter, a Non-Resistant,
any man who refrains from going to the polls for conscience' sake,
necessarily stands beyond the pale of the anti-slavery organization.
Had you been present, and listened to the extraordinary language of
those who sustained the resolution, I am strongly inclined to believe
that your name would have been recorded among those who opposed
its adoption. Mr. Burleigh's substitute [1] was an excellent one — strong,

explicit, satisfactory — and would have been adopted by an over-whelming majority, if the other had not been forced upon the meeting by a call of the previous question, on the part of Orange Scott.

You suppose I was led to vote against the resolution, because of my 'new views on the subject of civil government.' NOT AT ALL — I did not oppose it as *a non-resistant*, but as *an abolitionist* — and I would have as strenuously contended against its passage in 1833 as in 1839. It seems to me, dear brother, that I must have fallen in your estimation, if even the *suspicion* can enter your mind, that I am 'loading down the anti-slavery cause with [my] peculiar views' — that I desire to torture the Constitution of the Society into an accommodation to my change of sentiments — that I would sacrifice one particle of the Constitution to my conscience, &c. &c. I will not believe it. Yet, what is conveyed by your language, but this imputation? I again assert, plainly and unequivocally, that I would have as stoutly resisted the new political construction of our Constitution in 1833, as at the present time, *without any reference to the non-resistance doctrines*; because it is a test which is at once useless, proscriptive, and invidious. Believe me, I shall never think of making the Anti-Slavery Society 'conform to the various and varying consciences of its members.' No, indeed.

You remark — 'I presume you admit, that the Constitution of the American A. S. Society contemplates the duty of political action *in its broadest sense*.' If you mean by the words I have placed in italic, that I admit that the Constitution makes the use of the elective franchise a condition of membership in the Society, and the duty of every individual, you are mistaken. I admit no such thing. I never dreamed of such an interpretation. I affirm that the Constitution contemplates no such duty. If I believed otherwise, it would be my duty to withdraw from the Society, and I would not remain a member of it one day longer. If you mean by the phrase, 'in its broadest sense,' nothing more than that it is and ever has been the design of the Anti-Slavery Society to change the political action of the country, as far as practicable, from upholding to abolishing slavery, as fast as those who go to the polls shall become converted to the fundamental doctrines of the Society as to the sinfulness of slaveholding, and the duty of immediate emancipation, then we are perfectly agreed in opinion. It is simply saying, that those abolitionists, who use the elective franchise, are expected to be faithful at the polls in the cause of the slave; but it enjoins upon no man the duty of going to the polls, if his conscience will not allow him to do so. Hence, when a resolution, like the following, is offered for adoption, it passes in our meetings without a dissenting voice — none giving a more hearty response to it than bro. Birney's 'no-government' abolitionists:

'Resolved, That those abolitionists, who feel themselves called upon, by a sense of duty, to go to the polls, and yet purposely absent themselves from the polls whenever an opportunity is presented to vote for a friend of the slave — or who, when there, follow their party predilections to the abandonment of their anti-slavery principles — are recreant to their high professions, and unworthy of the name they assume.'

Such a resolution was drafted by myself, and adopted at the annual meeting of the Massachusetts A. S. Society, in January, 1839. The faction who are at work to break up our old organization, declare that this is to lower the abolition standard; and Elizur Wright, Jr. hesitates not to say, that it is a virtual sanction of my 'no-government' (!) views!! 'This one act is enough,' he exclaims. Hence a new organization, hostile to the State Society, is called into being. I shall be very slow to believe, that you have any sympathy with such a movement, whatever may be your views of the heaven-born principles of non-resistance.

You remark, respecting those who framed the Constitution, 'Most certainly, not one of them would, at that time, have declared it immoral to vote.' Most certainly — I reply — at least three of them had at that time conscientious scruples about going to the polls, and had not voted for years, nor ever intended to vote again — viz. Isaac Winslow, Samuel J. May, and George W. Benson. There were, I doubt not, (especially among the Friends,) others who entertained the same scruples. Now, is it to be supposed, for one moment, that such men would frame a Constitution, solemnly binding themselves to do an act which they had no intention of doing — no conscience to perform? This would go to impeach their intelligence or their honesty.

There is, I think, a fallacy in your reasoning, that because the Constitution admits that each slave State 'has the exclusive right to legislate in regard to its abolition in said State,' therefore, 'it is an implicit declaration of the duty to legislate for its abolition.' *It is only the recognition of a constitutional fact.*

I do not see the analogy between the cases of the atheistical abolitionist and the non-resistant. The being of a God is expressly acknowledged in our Constitution, but not a word is said about going to the polls.

You express your belief that I opposed a 'constitutional resolution,' because of the change that had taken place in my views of civil government. I must again say, that you are mistaken. I opposed the resolution on principle, *as an abolitionist.*

You add — 'I cheerfully admit that, in both cases, the charge justifies the withholding of an affirmative vote; but that it does, in any degree, justify a negative one, I cannot perceive.' But does not silence give consent? Is there such a thing as neutrality upon a moral question? 'All who are in favor of the passage of the resolution will say, Ay!' 'All who are opposed to its passage will say, No!' According to your argument, I am bound to remain silent, and allow the vote to be declared unanimous! Is that my liberty as an abolitionist?

You continue — 'The American A. S. Society should leave its members perfectly free to become Non-Resistants, Perfectionists, Agrarians, or what not.' How can it grant this license, if its Constitution enjoins upon its members the doctrine of the resolution I opposed, that abolitionists are in *duty* bound to employ the elective franchise for the overthrow of slavery — 'a duty which they *owe* to their enslaved fellow-countrymen'? You are wholly at variance with Messrs. Birney, Stanton, Phelps and Scott; for they maintain that Non-Resistants are bound, in good faith, by the terms of the Constitution, to withdraw from the Society, as men who have abandoned a great principle, a fundamental doctrine, an essential measure!

Non-resistants do not wish to 'incumber,' 'impede,' or 'modify' the action of the Society, or to alter the Constitution in consequence of 'their peculiarities.' They are perfectly satisfied with the Constitution as it is, and can heartily subscribe to it. And, as to political action, it is the legitimate, philosophical tendency of their doctrines, in their opinion, to purify and elevate that kind of action.

Yours, fraternally,
WM. LLOYD GARRISON.

Printed in *The Liberator*, March 27, 1840.

1. C. C. Burleigh's amendment read:
"That the abolitionist who regards it as his duty to use the elective franchise, and yet uses it against, or neglects to use it *for* the promotion of the cause of emancipation, is false to his own principles and clearly fails to do his duty." (*The Liberator*, May 24, 1839.)

175

TO DELEGATES OF THE MASSACHUSETTS ANTI-SLAVERY SOCIETY

Boston, April 9th, 1840.

Dear Friend,

You have been duly appointed a delegate to represent the Massachusetts Anti-Slavery Society, at the Annual Meeting of the American Anti-Slavery Society, to be held in New York, on the 12th of May next.

You are earnestly requested to be present, as business of great importance, involving the integrity of the Anti-Slavery cause, is expected to be brought before the Society.

574

In behalf of the Board of Managers of the Massachusetts Anti-Slavery Society,

Francis Jackson Pres't
Wm. Lloyd Garrison, Sec.

LS: Schomburg Collection, New York Public Library; signed but not written by Garrison.

176

TO JOSHUA T. EVERETT
PRESIDENT, WORCESTER COUNTY NORTH DIVISION
ANTI-SLAVERY SOCIETY

Boston, April 14, 1840.

MY DEAR FRIEND:

As I have been advertised to be at the Leominster meeting to-morrow,[1] and have held out the hope that I might be able to do so, I fear that my absence will create some disappointment to those beloved associates, who may give their attendance. But, knowing as I do, that I could be of very little service even were I present — that, doubtless, brothers Lincoln,[2] and Chace, yourself and other speakers, will be at the meeting — and, especially, that our large-hearted and eloquent brother James C. Jackson,[3] so recently restored to us from the very jaws of death, will also be with you, to pour forth his soul under the inspiration of divine love — my mind is greatly relieved, and I have no doubt that you will have an interesting and profitable gathering.

✿   ✿   ✿   ✿   ✿

At the present time, we are passing through a trying and fearful crisis. The love of many in our ranks has waxed cold — the faith of many, in the omnipotence of truth, has given way to unbelief — our house is, to some extent, divided against itself — and some of the most prominent individuals in our cause seem bent, not merely upon narrowing down our platform to their sectarian or political views, but even upon destroying the American Anti-Slavery organization altogether! In such an emergency, we need much of that wisdom which is of God — unfailing trust in his great and precious promises — deliverance from that fear of man which brings a snare — the sympathy of JESUS yearning in our bosoms for the suffering and the dumb — an eye that is single, that our whole body may be full of light [4] — a disposition that can cheerfully make frequent and liberal sacrifices in the cause of bleeding humanity — a spirit of earnest supplication, that the will of God, and not our own, may be done on earth as it is in heaven — perfect emancipation from sectarism and party thraldom — the one baptism of the Holy Ghost — and that faith which overcomes the world. Believing that our sacred enterprise was commenced upon right principles; that, sooner or later, in some form or other, it must triumph; that, of a truth, it has been owned and blessed of God, in a signal manner, since its commencement; that there are multitudes of good men and women in our land, who never will abandon it, come what may, new organization or disorganization, persecution or toleration, condemnation or applause; and, knowing as I do, through what trials and perils it has victoriously passed, each time coming forth from the fiery ordeal purer and more precious than ever, I cannot allow my mind to be filled with despondency, even in view of all that is transpiring around or among us. Our numbers may be diminished by apostacy — our ranks divided by faction — our operations, for a time, impeded by political ambition and sectarian animosity: but these are not, necessarily, evidences either of the unsoundness of our cause, or the uncertainty of its final success. No! Blessed be God, that with all possible confidence and exultation we may exclaim, no! The real trouble is, that the people are too many — in other words, that we have multiplied too fast for the purity and efficiency of our enterprise; and it is only those who are 'fearful and afraid,' who are disposed to bow down upon their knees to drink, that now turn from the conflict with the Midianites. So long as there remain three hundred souls, who put their trust in God, and have faith to take him at his word, the cause is safe, our triumph is certain, and the day of jubilee shall be ushered in with thanksgiving and praise, and with the grateful confession — 'Not unto us, O Lord, not unto us, but unto thy name be the glory!' [5] Trusting that there will be none but *'lap-water* abolitionists' at your meeting to-morrow, I remain,

  Yours, in opposition to all iniquity,

          WM. LLOYD GARRISON.

Printed in *The Liberator*, May 1, 1840.

 Joshua Titus Everett (b. Princeton, Massachusetts, January 6, 1806; d. Westminster, Massachusetts, February 10, 1897) was active in various reform movements of his day, an early convert to the antislavery cause, and a personal friend of Garrison, May, Phillips, and Frederick Douglass. He was president of the Worcester County North Division Anti-Slavery Society for many years. He was a member of the Massachusetts legislature in 1833–1835 and a selectman and assessor in Princeton in 1834 and 1835. (Edward Franklin Everett, *Descendants of Richard Everett*, Boston, 1902, p. 250.)

 1. *The Liberator*, April 10, 1840, carried the following announcement:

 "Worcester North. Our anti-slavery friends in Worcester North Division are reminded that the county meeting is to be holden in Leominster on Wednesday next, 15th inst. Let them be strong, prompt and multitudinous in their attendance!"

2. Probably Jairus Lincoln. See letter 133, to Samuel J. May, Oct. 30, 1838.

3. James Caleb Jackson (b. Manlius, New York, March 28, 1811; d. July 11, 1895) edited the *National Anti-Slavery Standard* in its earliest days. His father was a successful physician and surgeon. As early as his teens, he became involved in temperance and antislavery activity. He was an agent for the New York State Anti-Slavery Society in Essex county (1839), corresponding secretary of the American Anti-Slavery Society, editor of *The Standard* (1840) and of the Madison county (New York) *Abolitionist*, and editor and proprietor of the Albany *Patriot*. In 1846, in failing health, he went to Cuba, New York, to Dr. Silas O. Gleason's water cure. Enthusiastic about the cure, he formed a partnership with Dr. Gleason, and together they opened a water cure, called Glen Haven, at Skaneateles Lake, in Cayuga county, New York. Three years later, he purchased Gleason's interest. He earned a medical degree at the Medical College in Syracuse, New York. In 1858, he removed to Dansville, New York, where he opened the Jackson Sanatorium. There he also edited a health journal, *The Laws of Life*. His treatment emphasized the formation of proper health habits and abjured the use of drugs. He lived the last nine years of his life in North Adams, Massachusetts. (A. O. Bunnell, ed., F. I. Quick, comp., *Dansville, 1789–1902*, Dansville, n. d., pp. 176–180.)

For a description of the illness which brought Jackson to the verge of death, see his letter to Garrison of March 6, 1840, in *The Liberator*, March 20, 1840.

4. Adapted from Matthew 6:22 or Luke 11:34.

5. Psalms 115:1; see also Judges 7:1–7.

177

TO THE ABOLITIONISTS OF THE UNITED STATES

[April 24, 1840.]

BRETHREN: — The approaching anniversary of the American Anti-Slavery Society is calculated to fill the breast of every true-hearted abolitionist with more than ordinary solicitude. It cannot be disguised — it should not be, if it could — that serious dissensions have arisen in our ranks, to the detriment of our cause, and to the imminent peril of our whole organization. As these dissensions were commenced in Massachusetts — as a new organization has been formed in this State, claiming to occupy the ground of the Society we represent — as there seems to be a disposition, in various quarters, to excite in your minds any other than fraternal feelings towards the Massachusetts Anti-Slavery Society, and to ourselves as its Board of Managers, apparently for no good purpose — we deem it proper to make the following appeal to your good sense and sober judgment, trusting that it will not be made in vain.

We beg leave to call your attention, once more, to the basis of anti-slavery fellowship — to the length and breadth of the platform upon which we all professedly stand — to the object of our organization.

I. THE BASIS OF ANTI-SLAVERY FELLOWSHIP. What is it? Perfect agreement in opinion, that all men have an inalienable right to liberty; that to enslave a human being, or to retain him in slavery, under any circumstances, is an impious and cruel act; that it is the duty of the slaveholder immediately to relinquish his claim of property in man, and to liberate all whom he holds in bondage; that to colonize or proscribe any portion of the American population, on account of their complexion, is to insult HIM who has made of one blood all nations of men, to violate the spirit and precepts of our holy religion, and to make war upon our common humanity.

II. THE LENGTH AND BREADTH OF THE ANTI-SLAVERY PLATFORM. In the foregoing sentiments, persons of every sect and party can unite for the overthrow of slavery, in an associated capacity, and join hand-in-hand and stand shoulder to shoulder upon common ground, without compromising any of their distinctive peculiarities, or having their liberty of conscience or of speech trammelled on any subject. Accordingly, for the express purpose of uniting, in one unbroken phalanx, as many of our countrymen as believed in the doctrine of immediate emancipation, irrespective of their views on other subjects, the New-England (now the Massachusetts) Anti-Slavery Society was formed in 1832; from which have originated the American Anti-Slavery Society and its two thousand auxiliaries. Until somewhat recently, the experiment has proved successful, in an eminent degree. The utmost harmony of feeling and sentiment has prevailed in all our associations, and a more delightful spectacle of christian charity and brotherly love has never been exhibited to the world. Astonished to behold such a union, and regarding it as ominous of the downfall of their cherished system, the holders of slaves have been seized with fear and trembling. To show how perfectly agreed abolitionists have been, in relation to the nature and design of their organization, we quote the following resolutions, which were unanimously adopted at the fifth annual meeting of the Parent Society held in New-York, May 2, 1838:

'Resolved, That, in our efforts to abolish slavery, we meet each other, not as members of any religious or political party; but as abolitionists, on the broad ground of our common brotherhood and humanity — as moral and accountable beings, entitled to equal rights and privileges.

'Resolved, That it is the glory of the anti-slavery cause, that its principles are of such fundamental importance to the welfare of the whole human family, that men who differ widely from each other on political and theological subjects, can labor harmoniously together for its promotion; and that no political party, or religious denomination, which is not in itself corrupt, has any thing to fear from its progress or final triumph.' [1]

Similar resolutions have been adopted by anti-slavery societies, in all parts of the country, with perfect unanimity.

III. The object of the anti-slavery organization. What is it? The abolition of slavery, and the improvement and elevation of our colored population. By what instrumentality? By the promulgation of the doctrine of immediate emancipation, and the application of truth to the consciences and hearts of a pro-slavery people. Not by exacting a conformity of views, among the friends of emancipation, with regard to any theological or political dogma; not by arraigning any man for believing, or refusing to believe, in the divinity of the Church or State; not by assuming that any existing civil or ecclesiastical government is either good or evil in itself; not by making it obligatory upon any abolitionist to be a voter at the polls, or a member of any religious denomination; not by refusing to give the right hand of fellowship to any man, or body of men, on account of conscientious scruples entertained respecting subjects foreign to the anti-slavery enterprise. For, if any such test were required, it is certain that there could be no such thing as a union of all sects and parties for the overthrow of slavery; and it would be perfectly absurd to talk of a *common* platform of humanity. While, however, no member of our organization may attempt to convert it either to his peculiar religious or political views, nor denounce those who do not embrace those views as abolitionists, he does not, nevertheless, by consenting to become a member of our organization, surrender his right to proselytize to the extent of his ability, apart from abolitionism, as a man or a christian — either as a member of any sect or party, or as one who stands aloof from all sects or parties; provided, of course, he never makes the cause of bleeding humanity subordinate to any political or sectarian considerations, but bears a faithful and consistent testimony against the sin of slavery. A Methodist clergyman, for example, in joining an anti-slavery society, has no right to obtrude his views of Methodism upon it, with a design to give them currency; but, when not acting in the society, he has an indisputable right to attempt to make as many converts to his religious faith as possible; and no abolitionist may justly complain of his conduct. This is a common sense view of the subject. In an official address to the public, issued by the Executive Committee of the American A. S. Society, August 24, 1837, it is truly declared —

'The Constitution, after setting forth the principles of the Society, declares that whoever consents to these principles, not being a slaveholder, may, on making a pecuniary contribution, become a member. Hence, good faith obviously requires, not only that those who enter the Society should sincerely embrace its avowed principles, but also that ☞ THE SOCIETY SHOULD ABSTAIN FROM ALL INTERFERENCE WITH SUCH OTHER PRINCIPLES AS MAY BE HELD BY ITS MEMBERS. ☜ *Of course, no member is required, by his connection with the Society, to re-*

frain from expressing (on his own responsibility) his individual opinions on any subject whatsoever. We believe there is among the abolitionists, A MOST CORDIAL AND UNANIMOUS ASSENT TO THE GREAT MORAL TRUTHS PROCLAIMED IN OUR CONSTITUTION, *while on many other and important topics, they maintain very opposite and irreconcileable sentiments.*

Some of these sentiments being promulgated in anti-slavery papers, and advocated by one or more abolitionists, have been used to prejudice the anti-slavery cause. ☞ ON THE SENTIMENTS ALLUDED TO, THE EXECUTIVE COMMITTEE HAVE NO AUTHORITY TO SIT IN JUDGMENT; ☜ *but, whether true or false, they receive no sanction from the Society, and every member is at liberty to assail or defend them.*

The great diversity of sentiment entertained by abolitionists, on political and religious subjects, instead of being, as our enemies vainly imagine, an indication of our weakness, is a demonstration of our strength, and an omen of our ultimate triumph. That cause cannot belong to a sect or a party, which is espoused by men of all sects and of all parties. The rights for which we are contending, are the rights of our common nature, and their advocacy cannot safely be committed to any sect or party, nor can any sect or party be exempted from rebuke, which takes the attitude of hostility to these rights.' [2]

It would be needless to dwell upon this point, were it not that a new construction has lately been given to the language of the Constitution, by a few individuals who are somewhat prominent in our ranks, and especially by the official organ of the American A. S. Society; evidently with a design to create odium against other members of the Society, and, if possible, to induce them to withdraw from the same, in consequence of their religious scruples against participating in the politics of the country. This construction is, that every member of the Society, who is entitled to the elective franchise, is bound to use it, by the terms of the Anti-Slavery Constitution — a construction which has already produced much discord among abolitionists, which is as false as it is pernicious, which would exclude from our organization some of the earliest and best friends of the slave, and which would not merely abridge our common platform, but inevitably break it into fragments.

Slavery pollutes the Church, and corrupts the State. In order, therefore, to effect its abolition, both Church *and* State need to be purified. It is the avowed object of the Anti-Slavery Society to enlist on the side of emancipation, 'moral *and* political action.' As the American people are upholding slavery by their religious and political power, it assumes that they are under the strongest obligations to use such power for the overthrow of that hideous system: i.e. it speaks in popular language, without meaning to concede, or deny, the inherent rightfulness of human governments or church establishments, because it is not necessary for the Society to make any such concession or denial. Now, if the State cannot be purged from the stain of slavery, unless abolitionists go to the polls; neither can the Church, unless they connect themselves with it. But what would be the consequence, if it should be made an abolition test, that every member of the Anti-Slavery Society is in duty bound to connect himself with the Church, on the ground that such a connection is essential to its anti-slavery purification, and that abolitionists have pledged themselves to do all that is lawfully in their power for the abolition of slavery? Discord and division throughout our extended ranks! The same disastrous effect, to a considerable extent, has already been produced by the attempt to introduce a political test of membership into the Society.

In one thing abolitionists are perfectly agreed, namely, that duty to God and humanity requires of them fidelity to their anti-slavery principles and professions, in whatever sphere they may be called to act — in the church, or out of it — at the ballot-box, or away from it — in all places, under all circumstances, and at all times. No other agreement is practicable, among those whose religious and political sentiments so widely differ   none other is necessary to insure the onward progress of our sacred cause. Why, then, should there be any collision in our ranks, in reference to any extraneous question?

The unhappy controversy which has been carried on in this Commonwealth, during the past year, may have been regarded by you, dear brethren, as purely local or personal in its bearing. It has not been so viewed by us. So far as we have been called to participate in it, we have felt that, in resisting the efforts of those who have sought to destroy the Massachusetts Anti-Slavery Society, we have been contending for the purity and integrity of our whole organization — of our common cause. We proceed to show, that if the Society has done any thing to justify a withdrawal of confidence from it, and especially the formation of a rival association, then the Parent Society and its auxiliaries, having departed as widely from the path of anti-slavery rectitude, should also be superseded by other organizations.

The first charge which was brought against the Society, as justifying a new organization in this State, was, that WOMEN were allowed to participate in its proceedings. For refusing to put a gag into their mouths, and for giving liberty to all *persons* to speak and act, in its meetings, for the emancipation of hundreds of thousands of enslaved men and *women*, it was declared, by those who have since seceded from us, to be 'a violation of good faith,' and 'connecting with our cause A MILL-STONE, to sink to the depths of a bottomless ocean the hopes of enslaved millions'! — so that 'the only alternative for the dissentients was, constant contention, silent submission, or final separation.' *

* See the Address of the Executive Committee of the Massachusetts Abolition Society to the Public.

It is not our design, in this Address, to *argue* this or any other question, but simply to state *facts*. If, therefore, because the Massachusetts A. S. Society does not deny to its members, without distinction of sex, the right to sit on equal terms in its meetings, it ought to be denounced and abandoned; then, as its Board of Managers, we have done wrong in vindicating its course, and in condemning the conduct of those who have gone out from us; and it remains for you, brethren, at the approaching meeting of the National Society, to join with our opponents in efforts to crush the old Pioneer Society. If, on the other hand, the Society, by this decision, has acted in strict accordance with the spirit, design and scope of the anti-slavery enterprise, then it has a claim to the support and approval of every anti-slavery society and periodical in the land.

On this subject, the State Societies of Rhode-Island, Connecticut, New-York, New-Jersey, Pennsylvania, and Ohio, stand committed *in the same manner*, and also a multitude of minor societies. Nay, so does the National Society itself — at the last annual meeting of which, it was decided, that women, as well as men, were entitled to vote and act in its proceedings.

We are not aware that in any other State besides our own, any attempt has been made, or thought of, to establish a new State Society, on the ground above stated. But why should there not be a Rhode-Island, a New-York, a Pennsylvania, or an Ohio *Abolition* Society, as well as a *Massachusetts* Abolition Society? We ask, in the name of justice and brotherly kindness, why the Massachusetts Anti-Slavery Society, — which has done more to advance our sacred enterprise than any other, should be singled out for destruction, for refusing to exclude the most zealous, faithful and laborious friends of bleeding humanity from our common platform, and to suppress the convictions and emotions of such women as a Mott, a Grimke, a Chapman, a Child, and a Kelley?

The other charge against this Society is, that it has given up the 'staff of accomplishment,' and become a non-resistance society, because it refuses to declare that it is the *religious* DUTY of every abolitionist, to whom the State grants the PRIVILEGE, to use the elective franchise; and leaves every one of its members to decide for himself, what duty requires in this particular. It is well known, that, in the anti-slavery ranks, there are many persons whose religious scruples will not allow them to vote at the polls, in any case — 'some for one reason, and some for another.' The Covenanters, or Reformed Presbyterians, as a sect, wholly abstain from taking a part in elections or holding office, under our National Constitution, because it contains no recognition of the government of God. Many members of the

Society of Friends keep aloof from the polls, because the Constitution countenances slavery. Others have different reasons. Many conscientious individuals have kept away through disgust at the ordinary methods of electioneering.** They who subscribe to the doctrine of non-resistance also decline being voters at the polls. All these persons, (and none have shown themselves more efficient or indefatigable in our cause,) must be excluded from membership in the Anti-Slavery Society, by such a political test. To enforce it, therefore, would be a violation of the rights of conscience — at war with common sense and common charity — utterly nugatory as an expedient to stimulate political action — subversive of our anti-slavery platform — and disastrous to the hopes of our enslaved countrymen.

The charge against the Massachusetts A. S. Society, that it has become subservient to the principles of non-resistance, is utterly false. Whether those principles are right or wrong, *it lies not in the province of the Society to determine.* It has never, in any manner, directly or indirectly, given them its sanction. A very large majority of its members do not embrace them. Its resolutions, on the subject of political action, have ever been of the most uncompromising character. Its addresses to the anti-slavery electors of the Commonwealth, through its Board, have also been equally strong and emphatic. In short, it occupies precisely the same ground, on this subject, as other kindred associations. Its abolitionism, both morally and politically, is and ever has been of the purest and best quality, and marked by a vigor and an efficiency unsurpassed, if equalled, in any other State. We do not speak boastingly in its behalf; but when the worst calumnies are circulated against it, and it is falsely represented by some who wear an abolition garb to have fallen to the earth, we may be pardoned for asking, with some degree of complacency — 'What State is so well abolitionized as Massachusetts? What Society contributes so much money to sustain the anti-slavery movement? Where has political abolitionism achieved such victories as in this State? What other Legislature, besides that of Massachusetts, has demanded the immediate abolition of slavery in the District of Columbia? Upon what State has the Parent Society hitherto relied so confidently for aid as Massachusetts?' The answers to these questions furnish the best refutations of the cruel aspersions which have been so profusely cast upon the Society.

This, then, is the true position of the Massachusetts A. S. Society: — It leaves its members free to act in its meetings, as they shall deem proper, and refuses to pass censure upon such of them as conscientiously abstain from using the elective franchise. For which of these

** Emancipator of April 11, 1839.

acts, brethren, will you take up stones to cast at it? Because it thus acts, is it to be branded as a 'rotten-hearted, no-human-government, woman's rights institution'? * * * — or does it not deserve the approbation of every enlightened mind, and every genuine lover of freedom?

Brethren, the spirit which has sought to take the life of the Massachusetts A. S. Society, is now plotting the overthrow of the American Society, with all its auxiliaries! It has thrown its mask aside, and unblushingly declares that our sacred cause cannot be safely trusted in the hands of 'the common people' — the farmers, mechanics, and working-men — but must be placed under the control of a select body of men, in order to give it respectability and success! Such a proposition has been made in the Emancipator,[3] and is to be carried, if possible, at the annual meeting of the Parent Society, in May next. We believe you will reject it with indignation as evil in its design, and fatal in its tendency.

In whatever part of the country you reside, we call upon you to rally at that meeting as one man, by all the sacrifices which you have made, and all the perils through which you have passed — by your abhorrence of bigotry and intolerance on the one hand, and political ambition and profligacy on the other — by the hopes which have been raised in the bosoms of the friends of freedom on both sides of the Atlantic, and of those who are pining in bondage on our own shores, in view of our national anti-slavery organization — by your faith in HIM who has chosen the weak things of the world to confound the things which are mighty! Our cause is in peril among false brethren; and upon the result of the meeting in New York, great events will depend. They who are for placing it in other hands, or, in case they cannot succeed, are for annihilating the National Society in the expectation of disbanding every other, will spare no pains to muster as strong an array as possible, on that occasion. Will the true-hearted men and women, whose love for the anti-slavery cause has thus far surmounted every obstacle, and outlived all persecution, and whose purpose it is to stand by the old platform, come what may, be less prompt or numerous in their attendance? Never has there been a crisis like the present, and it must be met with unfaltering spirits and invincible courage.

The attack upon the integrity of our organization, brethren, will present itself in various forms, at our approaching anniversary; it being manifest that there are those among us, who care not in what manner they succeed in their disorganizing purposes. They have ceased to be animated by the catholic and disinterested spirit of genuine

* * * Letter of Orange Scott in Zion's Herald.

abolitionists. Having endeavored to excite division among us, and not without success, they adduce it as a reason why we ought to consent to disband our forces. Be not deceived by any of their expedients. They will endeavor —

1. To get the vote reconsidered, by which women were declared, at the last anniversary of the Society, to be entitled to all the rights and privileges of membership. They assert that it was not in accordance with your wishes; that it was carried by a packed meeting; and they confidently maintain that you will obliterate it from the records of the Society at its next meeting. Should they be disappointed, however, they have intimated that they will secede, as they have done in this State, and start an American *Abolition* Society! They can do no less, if they do not mean openly to proclaim themselves men devoid of conscience, — judging them out of their own mouths; unless, indeed, they are willing, in the spirit of perfect toleration and christian magnanimity, to retrace their steps! Or,

2. To pass resolutions, asserting the duty of abolitionists to engage in the politics of the country, conscientious scruples on the part of any to the contrary notwithstanding; with the deliberate intention to impeach the abolition integrity of such as religiously abstain from using their elective franchise, and in the hope of effecting their withdrawal from the Society. Or,

3. To limit the number of delegates to the annual meeting, after the manner of legislative bodies — they deeming it extremely unsafe to allow all *persons*, who are members of anti-slavery societies, to participate in its proceedings, according to present usage! They will offer an amendment to the Constitution, to this effect. Or,

4. To commit the Society in favor of a third political party, and thus accomplish its ruin by division. Or, at least,

5. To procure the sanction of the Society to the nomination of the Albany Convention, of anti-slavery candidates for the Presidency and Vice Presidency of the United States. Or,

6. To induce the Society to recommend to its auxiliaries not to pass any judgment upon the political action of such abolitionists as choose to get up independent nominations, but to leave anti-slavery conventions to manage the machinery of politics. As if it were foreign to the design of our organization, to exercise careful supervision over the political aspects of our cause, as well as over its moral and religious bearings! Or,

7. To disband the American Anti-Slavery Society, on the ground that it has been superseded by the State organizations, or that it is divided against itself, and therefore cannot and ought not to stand. Or,

8. To effect a secession from the Society, for the purpose of form-ing another, less broad in its platform, less tolerant in its spirit, and more under the control of the rulers in Church and State. Or,

9. To effect the formation of an 'Independent Anti-Slavery Board,' for conducting our enterprise, to be called 'The American Board of Commissioners for the Abolition of Slavery' — the same 'to be inde-pendent, possessing powers similar to those of the A. B. C. F. M.' — to be clothed with irresponsible power, and to have the right of per-petuating itself by filling its own vacancies!! Instead of State So-cieties, the Board to appoint State committees in each State, auxiliary to itself!! [1] Or,

10. To encourage the formation of sectarian societies, with a view to the speedy abandonment of existing organizations. Already, a Con-vention of Baptists has been summoned at New-York, for the purpose of forming an American Baptist Anti-Slavery Society! The Wesleyan Observer,[5] in this State, of which Orange Scott is one of the editors, advocates the formation of an American Methodist Anti-Slavery So-ciety! Then we may expect a proposition for forming an American Presbyterian, an American Unitarian, an American Whig, an American Democratic Anti-Slavery Society — &c. &c. &c. Against every sectarian or political scheme of this kind, we protest in the name of our com-mon humanity. Whatever may be plausibly urged in its defence, or whatever may be the motives of those who favor it, we are constrained to regard it with disapprobation, and to speak of it in terms of con-demnation. For it has been the boast and glory of the anti-slavery enterprise, that men of all sects and parties rally around its standard, forgetful of all sectarian and political differences; and who that has watched its astonishing growth but must acknowledge, that it has received the smiles of Heaven, and that it occupies the only ground upon which freemen and christians can either successfully or con-sistently unite for the deliverance of the oppressed millions in our land from chains and slavery?

We call upon you, brethren, to frown indignantly upon each and every attempt thus to dissolve our noble organization into its original elements, for the purpose of obstructing the growth of spiritual free-dom and human progress — of gratifying personal envy or ambition — of fostering the great and relentless enemy of humanity, SECTARISM. If you would not see our broad platform in any degree narrowed — if you would preserve it from the spirit which is seeking to dash it into fragments — if you would still rally under an anti-sectarian banner, and unite with the wise and good of every name for the salvation of your country, and the deliverance of the oppressed — then you will throng to the anniversary of the Parent Society on the 12th of May next, in despite of hard times, from all parts of the country, in such numbers as to put down all machinations for the dissolution of an organization, which is the terror of the oppressor and bigot alike, and upon the existence of which depends, under God, in all probability, the peaceful abolition of slavery in the Republic.

In behalf of the Board, we are yours, fraternally,

FRANCIS JACKSON, *President.*

WM. LLOYD GARRISON, *Cor. Sec.*

Printed in *The Liberator*, April 24, 1840.

1. *The Liberator*, May 13, 1838.
2. *The Liberator*, September 1, 1837. Two paragraphs are omitted from the original.
3. This refers to a suggestion made by the Reverend David Root. See note 4 and the paragraph to which it pertains.
4. This recommendation was made by the Reverend David Root. See *The Liberator*, April 24, 1840; also, letter 179, to Nathaniel P. Rogers, April 24, 1840.
5. The *American Wesleyan Observer* was published in 1839 by Orange Scott and Jonathan Horton. Its purpose was to abolitionize the Methodist church at the General Conference of 1840. (Dwight L. Dumond, *Letters of James Gillespie Birney, 1831–1857*, Gloucester, Mass., 1966, p. 450n.)

178

TO GEORGE BRADBURN

Boston, April 24, 1840.

My dear Bradburn:

Your note of yesterday, requesting letters of introduction to Anti-Slavery friends in England, has just come. As you intimate that you may leave to-morrow, and Francis Jackson informs me that he has a bundle for you, you see I have scarcely a moment to comply with your request. But George Thompson will be sufficient to obtain for you an introduction to a host of noble men and women across the Atlantic. How glad, how *very* glad I am, that Lucretia Mott and her husband are going to the Convention! [1] And how sorry, how *very* sorry I am, that I cannot go with them and with you! My dear Bradburn, it is not probable that I shall arrive in season to be at the opening of the Convention; [2] but, I beseech you, *fail not to have women recognized as equal beings in it.* Interchange thoughts with dear Thompson about it. I know he will go for humanity, irrespective of sex.

God speed you!

Your friend,

Wm. Lloyd Garrison.

To George Bradburn.

Transcript: Garrison Papers, Boston Public Library; published in *Life*, II, 354.

The Reverend George Bradburn (b. Attleboro, Massachusetts, March 4, 1806; d. Melrose, Massachusetts, July 26, 1880), a Unitarian minister and abolitionist, was elected in 1839 to the Massachusetts legislature as Whig representative from Nantucket. He was one of the leaders in the movement to repeal the state antimiscegenation law. He served for three years. In 1839, too, Bradburn was appointed an agent of the American Anti-Slavery Society. In 1840, he was a delegate to the World's Anti-Slavery Convention in London. ([Frances H. Bradburn], *A Memorial of George Bradburn*, by his wife, Boston, 1883, *passim.*)

1. The British and Foreign Anti-Slavery Society, founded in London in April 1839, sponsored the World's Anti-Slavery Convention of "friends of the slave," called for June 12, 1840, in London.

2. Because of his required attendance at the national antislavery convention in New York in May.

179

TO NATHANIEL P. ROGERS

Boston, April 24, 1840.

My dear Rogers:

A single moment is allowed me to thank you for your note of the 21st. I am with you in spirit continually, sympathizing with you in all your trials, yet rejoicing to believe that, though you are called to pass through a fiery ordeal, your gold will thereby be made brighter and purer. You have, at length, roused up the demon-spirit of sectarianism in New-Hampshire; and, as it shall develope itself more and more clearly to your vision, you will agree with me, I think, in branding it as the deadliest foe of God and man. Remember that Babylon is to be destroyed — and what are all these different sects, which are biting and aiming to devour each other, but part and parcel of Babylon? Well, blessed be God, a kingdom has been established by our dear Redeemer, which can never be shaken. Happy are all they who have entered into it, to go no more out forever, and to feel no uneasiness or alarm, though the mountains be cast into the midst of the sea, and though the earth be moved out of its place!

You see, dear Rogers, that the new organization spirit is seeking to pervert our whole anti-slavery organization. What a monstrous proposition is that put forth in the Emancipator, by David Root! [1] It is high treason against the life of our glorious cause. And then the reasons he adduces in its favor! It is to give *respectability* and *popularity* to abolitionism! O, my soul is sick to witness such folly and madness in such a quarter!

I know not how you can be spared from New-Hampshire, at such a crisis, to go to the World's Convention; and yet I am extremely desirous that you should accompany me to that interesting meeting. In my judgment — all things considered — if the means can be raised, you had better go. An absence of three months, during the hot summer-time, will do you much good, I verily believe, in body and soul; and, in the sequel, our cause, I am sanguine, will be the gainer for it. I am sure it will be very painful for you to leave your dear wife and children, even for so short a time; and very painful to them to have you go; but we are not to live to ourselves, but unto God. Say to Mrs. Rogers,[1a] that I shall enter into her feelings as a wife and mother, in case you make the voyage to England; for I know how my own dear Helen feels, and how my own heart is affected at the thought of separation from her and our precious children — especially as I shall be called to leave her in circumstances of delicacy, and, consequently, of some peril.

Our friend Miss Clark leaves to-day for Concord.[2] She is a most sterling and estimable woman, "of whom" new organization "is not worthy"!

I shall depend upon seeing you at my house before you go to New-York. I shall not leave here until Monday afternoon, May 11th.[3]

☞ Blow one good blast in the Herald [4] about the May meeting.

Yours, lovingly,

Wm. Lloyd Garrison.

ALS: Charles Roberts Autograph Collection, Haverford College, Pennsylvania.

1. The Reverend David Root. See letter 6, to Henry E. Benson, January 26, 1836. Root's letter in the *Emancipator* was reprinted in *The Liberator*, April 24, 1840. In it he announced that at the next annual meeting of the American Anti-Slavery Society he would "move for the calling of a General Convention of the friends of abolition for the purpose of discussing the question of forming a National Anti Slavery Board for conducting our enterprise. . . ." If such a board were formed, "The American Society should therefore become defunct." Root's proposal meant by-passing the American Society because of its pro-Garrisonian influence.

1a. The former Mary Porter Farrand (1796–1890) married Nathaniel P. Rogers in 1822. Of their eight children, one died in childhood. (Ezra S. Stearns, *History of Plymouth, New Hampshire*, Cambridge, Mass., 1906, vol. II, pp. 577–579.)

2. Mary Clark of Concord, New Hampshire. See letter 1, to Henry E. Benson, January 9, 1836.

3. The New England Garrisonians chartered the steamboat *Massachusetts*, which left for New York from Providence, Rhode Island, on May 11. Most of the Massachusetts delegation gathered at the railroad depot in Boston, whence trains took them to Providence. The national antislavery meeting in New York began on May 12 in the afternoon.

4. The *Herald of Freedom*, of which Rogers was editor.

180
TO LUCRETIA MOTT

Boston, April 28, 1840.

Esteemed Friend:

It is the sentiment of my heart, that, among all the friends and benefactors of the human race with whom it has been my privilege to become acquainted on this side of the Atlantic and in England, no one has impressed me more deeply, or filled me with greater admira tion, on the score of intellectual vigor, moral worth, and disinterested benevolence, than yourself. I make this avowal with the more freedom, inasmuch as it is no part of my character to play the flatterer; and, particularly, on account of my delinquencies as a correspondent. When I reflect upon the many kindnesses which have been manifested toward me by yourself and your estimable husband, running through a period of ten years, and then remember how few have been the expressions of gratitude on my part, and how seldom I have written to either of you, I am filled with surprise and regret. Believe me, however, that, though my epistles have been "few and far between"[1] — though I have not been voluble in the utterance of my gratitude — I have felt more than words could express, and shall ever retain a lively sense of your goodness. Well do I know that you neither ask nor desire a profusion of acknowledgments for any thing that you may have done, and therefore I have abstained from dealing in "words, words, words,"[2] even though those words would have been spoken in all sincerity.

For your favor of December last, by Isaac Winslow, (accompanied by the present of a fine silk handkerchief,) and your letter of the present month, enclosing $20 as a gift from my generous but unknown friend Sarah Pearson,[3] (to whom I shall forward a letter of thanks,) I am greatly obliged. The sight of your handwriting is ever cheering to me, and is next to seeing you personally.

For the tracts recently put forth by Friends, on the subject of slavery, which you have kindly forwarded to me, be pleased also to accept my thanks. These tracts all contain excellent sentiments; and yet nearly in all of them something is wanting. The phraseology of Friends' documents is generally peculiar, and sometimes obscure. The duty of immediate emancipation they do not set forth in explicit terms; and the plunderers of God's poor are addressed in a style far different from that used by Isaiah, Jeremiah, and Ezekiel. For example — in "An Address to a portion of our Southern Brethren," &c. which is written in admirable temper of mind, there seems to be something like an attempt to propitiate the spirit of these cruel and ungodly oppressors, in a way which I do not like. The second paragraph commences — "We are aware of the peculiar and trying situation wherein you are placed, in relation to slavery. You have been reared from the tenderest infancy as in its lap," &c. &c. I do not regard this as either a philosophical or the christian method to bring such men to repentance. It really looks like hunting up excuses for their nefarious conduct! At least, they will not be slow to regard them as palliatives for defacing the image of God, and transforming human beings into cattle and creeping things. God, in calling individuals and nations to repentance, never tells them, *in limine*, how unfortunate they have been, and how trying is their situation; but he always takes it for granted that they are without excuse, and calls upon them to break off their sins by righteousness without delay.

The Address speaks of the circumstances thrown around the southern man-thief, (*you* will pardon me for using "plain language," though I am not a member of the Society of Friends,) as "leading them to believe it lawful and *right* to hold their fellow-creatures in unconditional bondage." They believe no such thing: — they never did, they never can believe it! What! talk of those who "hold these truths to be SELF-EVIDENT — that *all men are created* EQUAL — that they are endowed BY THEIR CREATOR with certain INALIENABLE RIGHTS — that among these are life, LIBERTY, and the pursuit of happiness" — talk of such believing it "lawful and right" to trade in slaves and souls of men, to keep back the hire of the laborer by fraud, to hold their fellow-beings in chains and slavery! It is all moonshine, and can never melt ice.

My dear friend Edward Needles is somewhat disturbed by a resolution, which was lately adopted by the Essex Co. Anti-Slavery Society at Lynn, severely censuring the Friends, as a body in the United States, for their timidity and indifference in relation to the anti-slavery cause.[4] The Lord forbid that I should accuse them of what they are not guilty; but, while I am willing to make many honorable exceptions, I am nevertheless constrained to rank them among the corrupt sects of the age.

I have scarcely left any room to tell you how delighted I am to learn that you and James are soon to embark for England, in order to be at the World's Convention.[5] My heart leaped at the intelligence; for I could not be reconciled to the thought that you were to remain behind. I am pleased beyond measure, and have only to regret that I shall not be able to go over in the same packet with you both; but duty requires me to be at the anniversary of the Parent Society, which is pregnant with good or evil to our sacred cause. It will be a trying occasion, but I think the right side will prevail. A most afflicting change has come over the views and feelings of E. Wright, Jr.[,] Leavitt, Goodell, Phelps, &c.; especially in regard to myself personally, whom they seem now to hate and despise more than they once apparently loved and honored. My peace and happiness, however, are derived from God, in whom I live and shall rejoice evermore: therefore, it is, it ever will be, in my estimation, a small thing to be judged of man's judgment.

It is somewhat uncertain, whether I shall go to England, because it is impossible to foresee what may transpire at New-York; but it is my intention to go, if practicable. As you will anticipate me in your arrival, I wish you to convey to Elizabeth Pease the respect and esteem of an admiring friend, and assure her that I have the strongest desire to be personally acquainted with her. Also remember me most affectionately to George Thompson, Joseph Sturge,[6] John Scoble, Fowell Buxton, and Wendell Phillips and wife.

My best regards to James, and to all the members of your family — in which dear Helen cordially unites. Heaven bless and preserve you!

Your grateful friend,

Wm. Lloyd Garrison.

☞ I regret that the Lundys are unwilling to trust me to write the biography of my lamented friend Benjamin, but I make no complaint.[7]

ALS: Swarthmore College Library. Published, with some changes, in Anna Davis Hallowell, ed., *James and Lucretia Mott: Life and Letters* (Boston, 1884), pp. 139–142.

1. Thomas Campbell (1777–1844), Scottish poet, *Pleasures of Hope*, Part II.
2. *Hamlet*, II, ii.
3. Sarah Pearson was an active antislavery participant. Since there were many antislavery men and women who wished to buy only free produce — not made by slave labor — she opened a free-produce store in Hamorton, Pennsylvania, and kept it for fourteen years. (R. C. Smedley, M. D., *History of the Underground Railroad in Chester and Neighboring Counties of Pennsylvania*, Lancaster, Pa., 1883, p. 254.)
4. An account of the meeting, which took place on March 10 and 11 in the Christian Chapel at Lynn, Massachusetts, and the text of the resolution passed there, appeared in *The Liberator*, March 20, 1840.
5. James and Lucretia Mott were among the delegates of the Pennsylvania Anti-Slavery Society to the convention. Lucretia Mott was also chairman of a delegation sent by the Philadelphia Female Anti-Slavery Society, and one of the representatives of the American Anti-Slavery Society to the World's Convention. (Hallowell, ed., *James and Lucretia Mott: Life and Letters*, p. 144; *Life*, II, 353.)
6. Joseph Sturge (1793–1859), a member of the Society of Friends in England, was instrumental in organizing the British and Foreign Anti-Slavery Society in 1839, which called the World's Convention. He had been active in the movement for emancipation in the West Indies and after emancipation continued his efforts to abolish the indenture system, which had replaced slavery there. He was co-author, with Thomas Harvey, of *The West Indies in 1837; Being the Journal of a Visit to Antigua, Montserrat, Dominica, St. Lucia, Barbadoes, and Jamaica, Undertaken for the Purpose of Ascertaining the Actual Condition of the Negro Population of those Islands* (London, Hamilton, Adams & Co., 1838,

192 pp.). Sturge was also the author of *A Visit to the United States in 1841* (London, 1842, 192 pp.).

At the World's Convention, Sturge opposed the participation of women (*Life*, II, 352, 353, 367, 369, 474; *Weld-Grimké Letters*, p. 512n; Dwight L. Dumond, *A Bibliography of Antislavery in America*, Ann Arbor, Mich., 1961, p. 107).

7. Lundy had died in Illinois on August 22, 1839. Years earlier, Garrison had promised Lundy that he would write his biography if he should survive him. On September 20, 1839, Garrison, in an obituary editorial in *The Liberator*, entitled "The Pioneer Fallen," had written that "the biography of Benjamin Lundy should be given to the public as speedily as practicable. It will afford me great satisfaction to prepare it, provided I can be put in possession of his papers and documents. I gave him to understand, during our connexion in Baltimore, that, if it should be my lot to survive him, I would be his biographer. Unfortunately, he lost a large portion of his most valuable papers and journals at the burning of Pennsylvania Hall — a loss that is irreparable; but there are sufficient materials left to make an interesting volume."

On December 27, 1839, *The Liberator* reprinted an item from the *Emancipator* which noted: "It is proposed that Mr. Garrison, who was associated with him [Lundy] at Baltimore, before the anti-slavery societies began, should write a memoir. We do not think it could be in more suitable hands. All persons possessing letters, papers or facts calculated to aid such a memoir, are requested to communicate them to Wm. L. Garrison, at Boston."

However, the Lundy family apparently questioned Garrison's ability to present a sympathetic picture of Lundy, in view of their differences and estrangement during the latter years. The first sign of this mistrust was a notice in *The Liberator*, February 7, 1840, which requested that manuscripts, letters, and other documents relating to Lundy's life be sent to Joseph Lundy, Benjamin Lundy's father, at the Anti-Slavery Office in Philadelphia. This was confirmed in a letter from Joseph Lundy to Garrison, dated Rancocas, January 16, 1840, which, after noting Garrison's intention to do Lundy's biography, stated: "having been acquainted with the fact, that he had commenced the work himself some time before his death, at the urgent solicitations of his friends, which no doubt would have been completed if they [his manuscripts] had not been destroyed by the burning of 'Pennsylvania Hall,' or his life had been prolonged a short time longer — which circumstances prove he had not selected thee, nor any one else, at that period, to do it. Add to this, the circumstance thrown around him by thyself, has induced, or rather constrained us to prefer or make choice of another hand to narrate the history of his eventful life, of which thee could have been informed previous to the notice above alluded to, if his relations had been aware of thy intention. We exceedingly regret to be under the necessity of conveying this information to thee. . . ."

This letter, printed in *The Liberator*, March 20, 1840, was prefaced by Garrison's comment: "It seems, by the following rather singular letter from his father, that it would not be agreeable to the feelings of his relatives to have us undertake the task: we therefore relinquish it, not doubting that it will be executed in a better manner by someone else, though we are certain that no one can be found to pay a warmer tribute to the memory of BENJAMIN LUNDY, than we find it in our heart to bestow. The tone of the letter does not seem to be particularly respectful or cordial, which we regret. We do not know, precisely, what is meant by the language — 'the *circumstance* thrown around him by thyself' — but this we know, that if our venerable friend supposes that, because in a single instance we disagreed with certain views entertained by our departed brother, we should not be disposed to write an impartial biography, he is altogether ignorant of our character. It is in our nature to be more liberal in the bestowment of praise, on that very account. Whatever else we may lack, we hope that we are not destitute of magnanimity. It is proper to add, that we have never had an interview either with Benjamin Lundy's father or relatives."

1 8 1

TO RICHARD P. HUNT

Boston, May 1, 1840.

Esteemed Friend:

I am informed, in a letter from my excellent friend Thomas M'Clintock,[1] that you have kindly forwarded to the care of Charles Collins,[2] at New-York, 4 yds. of super olive mixed, made at the Waterloo Factory, *free from the taint of slavery,* intended as a present to me, prior to my embarkation from the commercial emporium for the World's Convention. It is scarcely necessary for me to say, that this token of your friendship and respect is peculiarly acceptable at the present time, for which I beg you to accept my heartfelt thanks, and which cannot fail to be regarded with interest and pleasure on the other side of the Atlantic, as well as on this. If a multiplicity of words were any proof of gratitude, it would be easy for me to fill up the remainder of this sheet with grateful expressions. Having said that your gift is highly prized by me, especially as it is the product of free labor, you will need nothing more.

How melancholy is the thought, that oppression, violence and fraud taint almost all the products of human industry throughout the earth! Truly, the whole creation groans, waiting impatiently for its redemption. Thanks be to God, the promise is that it shall be redeemed. The Son of God has not died in vain. Strong as Satan is, his empire of darkness shall be destroyed, and upon its ruins be erected the kingdom of heaven. Jesus is mightier than the great Adversary, and, having overcome the world, he shall assuredly "reign from sea to sea, and from the river to the ends of the earth."[3] How peaceful, how happy, how glorious will be his reign! Every man shall sit under his own vine and fig-tree, and there shall be none to molest or make afraid. None!

> "No war, or battle's sound,
> Was heard the world around,
> No hostile chiefs to furious combat ran:
> But peaceful was the night,
> In which the Prince of Light,
> His reign of peace upon the earth began!"[4]

So let it be, now and evermore! Why should not man be reconciled to his fellow-man, and all be swallowed up in the will of God? Has not one God created us, and are we not all made of one blood? Are we not all brothers and sisters — members of the same family — under the same obligations and duties — mutually dependent upon each other —

destined to the same immortality? Let us rejoice in hope. Let us exercise that faith which triumphs over every obstacle. If Truth is mighty, and must prevail, then, at some time or other, in some way or other, Error is destined to perish. The conflict may be long and terrible; but it can never be a matter of doubt, to the mind of the christian, on which side victory is ultimately to rest.

Whatever may be said or done at the World's Convention, the mere fact that the nations, by their representatives, are about to meet and embrace each other in love, and to devise ways and means for the deliverance of all who groan in slavery, is indescribably joyous to my soul. As a precedent for many similar conventions yet to be held, for other glorious purposes, it is full of moral sublimity, and pregnant with mighty consequences. It is an epoch in the history of human regeneration.

It is a favorite idea of mine, that the time is coming when there shall be but one speech among mankind. The diversities of language in the world are the results of man's alienation from God, and demonstrative proofs that the world is in a fallen state. Nations will never be fully reconciled to each other until they all use the same dialect, and understand each other without the aid of interpreters. Language is subject to the will of man, and can be modified or changed at his pleasure. It is not the will of God, I firmly believe, that human speech should be so full of confusion. I prophesy, therefore, that, just in proportion to the prevalence of righteousness in the earth, this Babel confusion will be done away; and I confidently anticipate the time when there will be a World's Convention to agree upon a common dialect for all people, kindreds, tongues and tribes under heaven! Perhaps you will smile at my enthusiasm, and think me Utopian in my views; and perhaps you will agree with me that the idea is rational, and at some future period may be realized.

Our mutual friend Thomas M'Clintock is one for whom I entertain a very high regard. I desire to be affectionately remembered to him and his family. Hoping to see you both at the anniversary of the Parent A. S. Society in New-York, I remain,

Your much obliged friend,

Wm. Lloyd Garrison.

ALS: Waterloo Library and Historical Society, Waterloo, New York.

Richard P. Hunt, an antislavery Quaker and prominent businessman and civic leader in Waterloo, New York, was the first secretary of the Waterloo Woolen Manufacturing Company, "for years the largest village industry." For many years, he and his wife maintained an Underground Railroad station in their home, on the outskirts of Waterloo. (Letter from John S. Genung, Curator-Historian, Waterloo Library and Historical Society, to Walter M. Merrill, March 24, 1967.)

1. Thomas McClintock was a village druggist and Quaker. "The Hunt and McClintock ladies were among those who issued the call for the first women's rights convention in 1848, and met at the Hunt home in Waterloo to draft the invitation." (Letter from John S. Genung to Walter Merrill, March 24, 1967.)
2. Unidentified.
3. Psalms 72:8.
4. John Milton, "Hymn. On the Morning of Christ's Nativity," with some variations.

182

TO GERRIT SMITH

[May 8, 1840.]

DEAR FRIEND:

So little weight did I suppose your letter addressed to me in the Liberator of 30th of August last, in relation to the Constitution of the American Anti-Slavery Society, would have with abolitionists generally, that I allowed several months to glide away, before I attempted to refute its reasoning. It is true, I expressed, at the time, my intention to make an immediate rejoinder, because I thought one was required of me, at least on the score of courtesy, and because your letter was by no means satisfactory to my understanding or my heart; but — as in several other instances — such was the pressure of other matters upon my hands, I failed to perform what I purposed to do. Nor should I refer to that letter at this late day, if you had not seemed wholly to misapprehend the cause of my silence. If I am rightly informed — and if I may judge from your frequent reference to it, in the anti-slavery newspapers — you have been disposed to regard your letter as unanswerable, and have exhibited a state of mind on the subject, closely bordering on ostentation. Far be it from me to blame you for doting upon that production; but as no one else seems to have regarded it as a remarkable, or even as an ingenious effort, would it not be well for you to think and speak of it less frequently, or, at least, with a somewhat different air? If you have alluded to my silence, in your private intercourse with others, as a proof that I was conscious that I could not overthrow your constitutional exposition, I can only say that you have done me great injustice.

Hearing that you were making a bad use of my silence, I published a brief reply to your letter in the Liberator of the 27th March. This was not satisfactory to you. In your rejoinder,[1] (see Liberator of the 24th ultimo,) you say:

'The issue between us is, substantially, whether in a meeting where the obligations of the Constitution of the American A. S. Society are recognized, it is proper to forbid the unconditional assertion of the doctrine, that to go to the polls is a duty. If it is proper, then you are right, and I am wrong.'

You maintain, in a broad and unqualified manner, that the 'Constitution regards political action as a duty' — not the duty of any particular portion, but of all the members of the society. For you add —

'The distinction you set up, viz: that the Constitution makes political action the duty of *some* persons, and not of others, I have not the optics, and I wonder that you have, to discover in that instrument.'

And in your letter to Henry C. Wright,[2] alluding to myself, you say, in an apparently ruffled state of mind that betrays you into the use of reproachful language —

'How can he [Mr. Garrison] have the *assurance* to ascribe the new "movement" on the subject of voting, to any others than himself and his fellow "non-resistants?" Verily, such *measureless draughts on human credulity*, and such *confidence in the inexhaustibleness of one's stock of reputation for ingenuousness and infallibility*, are rarely witnessed.'

I receive the taunt without offence, merely remarking that what has elicited it is, my resolute determination not to consent to the slightest abridgement of the anti-slavery platform. As to 'infallibility,' I make no pretensions to it, but ever expect to grow in knowledge, as I hope to grow in grace. Of the integrity of my spirit, and the singleness of my heart, I am more confident — though 'I am what I am, by the grace of God.'

To return to the point at issue. Are those, who become members of the American Anti-Slavery Society, under a constitutional obligation to use the elective franchise?

Yes, is your declaration. No, is my reply.

What then is the language of the Constitution?

'1. The Society shall aim to convince all our fellow-citizens, by *arguments* addressed to their understandings and consciences, that slaveholding is a heinous crime in the sight of God, and that the duty, safety, and best interests of all concerned, require its immediate abandonment, without expatriation.'

'2. It will also endeavor, in a constitutional way, to influence Congress to put an end to the domestic slave trade, and to abolish slavery in all those portions of our common country which come under its control, especially in the District of Columbia; and likewise to prevent the extension of it to any State that may be hereafter admitted to the Union.'

A third object of the Society is, the improvement and elevation of the free colored population.

It is the second section upon which you rest your political construction.

I have to remark —

1. That there is not one word in that section, respecting the use of the elective franchise, or the political duties of abolitionists. This is plain. But, you reply, the Society aims at legislative action; and "that being the highest form of political action, it is no more than a legitimate inference, that the Constitution contemplates all the lower forms, such as voting, petitioning, &c." This I deny, if you mean that 'the Constitution contemplates' political action as the 'duty' of all who are members of the Society. *How* Congress is to be influenced is not specified. Not even a hint is given that the ballot-box is to be the instrument; but, the 'legitimate inference' from the construction and language of the second article of the Constitution is, that Congress is to be influenced precisely in the same manner as are the people of the United States, namely, 'by arguments addressed to their understandings and consciences, that slaveholding is a heinous crime,' &c. &c.; in other words, by moral suasion — by religious action. At the time that Constitution was written, I hesitate not to affirm, as my deliberate conviction, that there was not an individual who subscribed to it, who expected that the Society would act at any time as a political body, or who regarded it in any other light than as a moral and philanthropic association. There were three ways in which the Society hoped to influence Congress: — 1. By 'arguments addressed to the understandings and consciences' of the members. 2. By petitions, appeals, remonstrances, &c. to that body, in relation to slavery in the District of Columbia, &c. 3. By the dissemination of light and truth among the people, and so turning their political action, (i. e. such of them as used the elective franchise) in favor of the cause of bleeding humanity, instead of allowing it to be given to the support of slavery. The one grand object of the Society, therefore, was, is, and should be, not to meddle with any religious sect or political party, as such, any farther than the presentation of arguments, showing the heinous nature of slavery, and the duty of immediate emancipation, would prove an interference. For the Society to attempt to get up a religious sect, or form a political party, for the purpose of abolishing slavery, would assuredly be wandering from its 'appropriate sphere' — and not less reprehensible would be any attempt to establish a religious or political test as a condition of membership. I do not mean to 'overlook four words' — to wit, that 'the Society is to endeavor to accomplish its object *in a constitutional way.*' What was meant by those 'four words'? That voting at the polls is a religious duty, or binding upon any body? No — that notable discovery belongs to the

school of new organization! What then? Why, nothing more than that the Society did not seek to transcend the limits of the U. S. Constitution, and was neither seditious nor unlawful in its object and tendency. It was at an early period charged upon abolitionists, that they trampled the Constitution under foot, and were acting in a treasonable manner. This was an official denial of the charge, and a public pledge and declaration, that abolitionists, as a body, desired to do nothing, except *'in a constitutional way'*: — inasmuch as, under the Constitution of their country, they found ample scope and verge enough to do all they desired. This I present as a true exposition of those 'four words,' which have been so absurdly construed; for I testify of that which I do know — and I call upon any of those who adopted the Anti-Slavery Constitution, and who have not departed from our original platform, to contradict this statement, if they can. Not less absurd and mischievous has been the construction put upon the following words in the Preamble, 'to do all that is *lawfully* in our power.' As if, because it is *lawful* for abolitionists to organize a third party, or start a sect hostile to all other sects, or abstain from the products of slave labor, or do a thousand and one other things, therefore they are 'constitutionally' *bound* thus to act! Truly, this is to mould language like dough, or stretch it like India rubber! I affirm that the phrase was intended merely as another declaration, that the Society was disposed to do only what was lawful and right in itself — and not to designate in what manner, or through what medium, its members should act for the overthrow of slavery. *They* must determine, each for himself, what it is or what it is not 'lawfully' in their power to do; and it is not for the majority, who happen to agree in opinion respecting a particular measure, to oppress the minority, by establishing any other test of sound membership, than a hearty advocacy of the doctrine of immediate emancipation.

2. Your construction is a political absurdity, because it requires an impossibility! By whom is Congress to be influenced? By 'THE *Society*,' as such. Can the Society vote at the polls? No. How, then, did it expect to influence Congress? By believing, in the language of the Preamble, 'that it is practicable, by appeals to the consciences, hearts and interests of the people, to awaken A PUBLIC SENTIMENT *throughout the nation*, that will be opposed to the continuance of slavery [not merely at the Seat of Government, but] *in any part of the republic*' — and that rectified public sentiment operating upon Congress in multifarious forms, and through a multitude of channels! How simple — rational — philosophical! As individuals, the members of the Society were left free to exert an influence upon Congress in such manner as conscience and duty would allow; but, as a Society,

they could wield no other than a strictly moral influence, which, however, would naturally operate upon the political action of the country.

3. If your interpretation of the language of the Constitution be right, then it follows that the anti-slavery platform, instead of being very broad, is exceedingly narrow — and, instead of being common, is very select: for if that instrument requires of those who sign it, not only a belief in the 'divinity' of a man-made government, but to pledge themselves, one and all, to wield the elective franchise — then, truly, non-resistants cannot belong to the Society, nor can women, nor can the Reformed Presbyterians, nor can a large portion of the Society of Friends, nor can a still larger portion of the free colored people, nor can foreigners not naturalized, nor can children and youth, nor can *Gerrit Smith himself*! — for even you, I am assured, with all your zeal for political action, have conscientious scruples that will not permit you to vote either for James G. Birney, or for any other man, to be President or Vice President of the United States, or a member of Congress, or Governor of the State of New-York! 'Thou that teachest another, teachest thou not thyself?' [3] Thou that sayest, a member of the American A. S. Society is morally or legally bound, by subscribing to its Constitution, to wield the elective franchise — dost thou wield it? I marvel at your inconsistency. Out of your own mouth you stand condemned. If you say, the question is not as to your consistency, but what does the Anti-Slavery Constitution require, I reply, true — but, until you repent politically, and comply with the terms of that Constitution, (as you construe it,) you ought to hold your peace, and cease from rebuking others.

4. The Constitution, you admit, does not 'make political action the duty of some persons, and not of others' — but of all. How, then, if this be so, can you either consistently or properly be a member of the Society? How can any man, who has conscientious scruples against going to the polls, or is deprived of the privilege, belong to it? It is idle to talk of allowing persons to be members on the score of courtesy, or as a matter of sufferance. A free spirit would spurn to be received on such terms, — conscious of its innate abhorrence of every form of tyranny, and of its burning devotion to the cause of the oppressed. Besides, if the requirements of the Constitution may be set aside to accommodate the peculiarities of some, of what value is it? How much better is it than a nose of wax? I do not see how you can honestly escape from this dilemma. You must either give up your present interpretation of that instrument, or withdraw from the Society on account of your inability to comply with its terms, or remain in the same as a delinquent member, or concede that the anti-slavery platform is, after all, of petty dimensions.

In your letter of June 3,[4] you say — 'That a man may be a sound and thorough abolitionist, and yet be conscientiously opposed to all participation in politics, is undeniable.' I should like to be informed if the Constitution requires something more of an individual, in order to be a consistent and an exemplary member of the Society, than that he is 'a sound and thorough abolitionist'? If political action be 'the staff of accomplishment,' how can you say that it is a matter of no consequence, whether an abolitionist uses it or not?

Again — you lay it down as 'a true doctrine,' that 'the American A. S. Society should leave its members perfectly free to become Non-Resistants, Perfectionists, Agrarians, or what not' — but how can it do so, if, by its Constitution, it arrays itself against persons entertaining these views? or if 'it is not,' as you declare, 'a Society to conform to the various and varying consciences of its members'?

You argue that as long as voting is 'a constitutional way' to influence Congress, so long it will be incompetent for me, or any other person, to deny its rightfulness. This is to assert, but not to prove. I have no right — no other man has a right — to do wrong, in order to do good. Congress may be influenced in a way that is not righteous — am I therefore bound to resort to that mode? or to sanction it? or to say nothing against it? Observe — the language of the Constitution is not, in *every*, but in 'a constitutional way,' to influence that body — and by all means 'that are *lawfully* in our power' — i.e. in accordance with the will of God and the gospel of his Son.

In my last letter,[5] I stated that at least three of the signers of the Declaration of Sentiments, (Isaac Winslow, George W. Benson, and Samuel J. May,) had conscientious scruples, at the time of signing that instrument, 'which had kept them from going to the polls for a series of years;' and I argued that, 'to suppose, for one moment, that such men would frame an instrument, solemnly binding themselves to do an act which they had no intention of doing, and no conscience to perform,' would be to impeach their intelligence or their honesty. The manner in which you attempt to evade a fact so formidable, so perfectly conclusive, is, I think, hardly ingenuous.

You reason thus — 'The reply speaks of their conscientious scruples on the subject of voting. This is wholly different from their declaration, that it is immoral to vote.' This looks like hair-splitting. If a person is debarred from performing an act, by conscientious scruples, is it not because he deems the act wrong in itself? 'I infer,' you say, 'not that they had made up their minds never to vote again, but only that they had not made up their minds to vote again'! Most ingenious distinction! But what does it avail? You concede that their consciences might not have allowed them to vote; and yet charge them with having

601

deliberately affixed their signatures to an instrument, which required them to violate their consciences! Surely, this is an impeachment either of their *intelligence* or their *honesty*. It is of no consequence, whether they deemed it 'immoral to vote,' or whether they could not vote on account of 'conscientious scruples:' in either case, they failed to discharge their anti-slavery obligations, according to your interpretation of the Anti-Slavery Constitution. I have lately interrogated these brethren on this subject. Messrs. Winslow and Benson inform me, that, some years before the National A. S. Convention was held in Philadelphia, 'they had made up their minds never to vote again,' on the ground of religious duty. Mr. May says, (to adopt your phraseology,) 'that he had not made up his mind to vote again,' but had retired in disgust from all participation in politics, on account of the corruption of the political parties. Politically, therefore, to all practical purposes, they stood where the Covenanters and Non-Resistants now stand.

You put it to my candor, whether the Constitution of our Society recognizes God any more distinctly than it does political action. To this I reply, in the words of our mutual friend J. C. Hathaway [6] —

'No man has a right, in an anti-slavery meeting, to introduce a resolution, simply asserting the existence of God, and the duty of abolitionists to believe in and worship him — [i.e. as an abolition test.] If introduced, an infidel has a perfect right to oppose it, and the introducer will be responsible for dragging in infidelity, because it is no part of the legitimate business of an anti-slavery meeting to establish or destroy a belief in the existence of a Supreme Being, assert or deny the duty of abolitionists in relation to him.' [*]

My dear brother, my soul is wearied and disgusted with this verbal criticism. I had supposed that you were not one of those whom the letter kills, but one made alive by the spirit. If I have relied upon any man in our ranks to vindicate the catholic and all-embracing principles of our organization, and to oppose every attempt to narrow the anti-slavery platform, it has been yourself. I am greatly disappointed at your course. There is not one of all the band of disorganizers in this State, more pertinacious or more arbitrary in his political views of the Anti-Slavery Constitution, than yourself. The ground you occupy is not tenable — the foundation upon which you have erected your constitutional exegesis is sandy. Why it is that you have thus suddenly become the political champion of new organizationism, both in relation to a third party and the duty of using the elective franchise, while at the same time you are not disposed to vote at the

[*] Letter in the Friend of Man, of April 8th, [1840].

polls, is to me inexplicable. You are as zealous in this matter as any political partizan in the land; and yet, at the same time, and almost in the same breath, you speak quite contemptuously of political instrumentalities! I quote your very words, in your letter to H. C. Wright of February 29: [7]

'Compared with *moral suasion* — with addresses to the consciences of men and the throne of God — *political action is almost a contemptible instrumentality.*'

Again, in a letter to the editor of the Emancipator, you say —

'I have not written this letter because I place great reliance on political instrumentalities — for, in point of fact, *few men place less on them.* Let me but know that the abolitionist has not been guilty of dishonoring his principles by voting against them — and I care comparatively little, whether he is in favor of voting between, or over the heads of the parties — or, indeed, *whether he votes at all.*'

Again you say —

'Albeit, I attach so little importance to voting, as *not even to vote myself.*'

Anon, you are full of enthusiasm for 'independent nominations,' and eagerly disposed to measure weapons with any man who presumes to say, that he comes under no obligation to vote at the polls, by joining the American Anti-Slavery Society! Then, again, with surprising inconsistency, you declare —

'I should be as much opposed as yourself to a Constitution which should enjoin voting'! †

Yea, and in the course of an earnest advocacy of a third party as essential to the success of our cause, you frankly confess —

'I am still unable to see how the proposed independent organization will supply this lack of fidelity.' ‡

Further — whilst you are trying to prove that non-resisting abolitionists are, by the Anti-Slavery Constitution, tied up to the duty of using their right of suffrage, you claim for yourself the right to think, say and do as you please, in relation to politics, under that instrument! With an air of independence which I commend, you say —

'To know whether I may vote — or what is included in the right to vote — whether I may not designate for my candidate whom I will — *I do not look into the structure or provisions of the Anti-Slavery Society*:

† Letter addressed to me in the Liberator of February 22, 1839.
‡ Letter to William Goodell, of Feb. 8, 1840.

for when I joined the society, I had as little idea of having disfranchised myself by the connection, as by my connection with the temperance society. I could have no patience with efforts that should be made to convince me that, by uniting with the Anti-Slavery Society, I have lost my right to vote.'

In the same independent spirit you will allow me to say, that, to know whether I may or may not use the elective franchise, I do not 'look into the structure or provisions of the Society,' — in joining which, I had 'as little idea' of binding myself to be a voter at the polls, as I had to make myself a slave; and that I protest against the efforts 'made to convince me, that, by uniting with the A. S. Society, I have lost my right' to decline being a voter. The liberty which you are determined to possess in your own case, you seem unwilling to grant to others. For one, as an abolitionist, I am and always have been the friend and advocate of perfect toleration and equality, on this subject, in the anti-slavery ranks. And I will further say that, in no instance, to my knowledge, have the friends of non-resistance ever attempted to commit the anti-slavery cause in favor of their pacific enterprise, but have uniformly, and with all possible integrity, protested against making either of these enterprises responsible for the other. No man has yet been able to show, that either Henry C. Wright, or myself, or any other non-resistant, has on any occasion attempted to discuss the subject of non-resistance in any anti-slavery meeting, or to procure the adoption of resolutions in favor of non-resistance, or to prevent the adoption of such as required abolitionists to carry their anti-slavery principles with them to the ballot-box. On the contrary, we have firmly, uniformly and scrupulously refused, even when our views as non-resistants have been most shamefully misrepresented and furiously assailed by our brethren, to stand on the defensive, and have deprecated the 'dragging in of extraneous topics.' This I assert with a good conscience, and without fear of any evidence being produced to the contrary. Yet you do not hesitate to charge bro. Wright and myself with having 'engrafted non-resistance on the anti-slavery enterprise'! And how do you prove this? Why, by showing that we do not agree with you on a point of *inference* merely, as to the meaning of a particular clause in our Constitution! You have accused H. C. Wright and J. C. Jackson of having been 'guilty of dragging' non-resistance before the Bloomfield Convention,[8] because they dissented from Myron Holley's [9] political assumptions on that occasion; but these brethren, and others who were at the Convention, have explicitly denied your accusation, and you have retracted it — though not after your usual hearty manner.

There are several other points upon which it was my design to comment: but this letter is already too long. I can only add, in conclusion, that, in saying that you had suddenly turned a political 'summerset,' I did not mean to use an offensive term, nor to impeach the purity of your motives. Nor were you in the minds of the Massachusetts Anti-Slavery Board, when in their address to the abolitionists of the United States, in opposition to the Albany Convention, they expressed the opinion, that some who were zealous in getting up that Convention were actuated by ambitious desires. Whilst multitudes are deploring the course you are pursuing, few, if any, are disposed to attribute it to any other cause than a confusion of the head.

How much I love and admire you, my acts, (however you may misinterpret them,) and not my words, shall show. Conceding, as you have done, on various occasions, that Jesus Christ was a non-resistant — that his disciples are bound to be such — that the doctrines of non-resistance are divine — and that you are often led to inquire of yourself, whether it be not owing to the small measure of your Christian faith, and to your but partial trust in God, that you do not embrace these doctrines — I feel much solicitude on your account, lest, in your present temper of mind on the subject of politics, you should quench the Spirit of God which is manifestly striving with you, and close your eyes to the heavenly light which has burst upon you, and once more ally yourself to the kingdoms of this world, which are all to be destroyed by the brightness of the coming of Christ. Let there be no delay in making up your mind. If the Lord be God, serve him; if Baal, serve him. My prayer is for your perfect salvation.

Your faithful friend,

WM. LLOYD GARRISON.

Printed in *The Liberator*, May 8, 1840.

1. Gerrit Smith's letter to Garrison in *The Liberator*, April 24, 1840, was addressed, very frigidly, to "Dear Sir" and was dated Peterboro, April 6, 1840.

2. Smith's letter to Henry C. Wright, in *The Liberator*, April 24, 1840, addresses Wright as "My Dear Brother," and is dated Peterboro, April 1, 1840. It is in reply to Wright's letter to *The Liberator*, dated Waterloo, March 12, 1840, in which he enclosed copies of an exchange of correspondence with Myron Holley, and a letter to Gerrit Smith.

3. Romans 2:21.

4. The correct date is June 7, 1839. *The Liberator*, July 19, 1839, announced: "Our friend Gerrit Smith will see in the crowded state of our columns this week the reason why his communication is delayed. It shall appear next week."

In the following issue, July 26, Garrison announced that Smith's letter had been "accidentally mislaid," but that he would "make another careful search for it."

On August 23, *The Liberator* carried the following notice: "Gerrit Smith has very kindly forwarded to us, at our request, a copy of the communication which he transmitted to us some weeks since, and which was lost in an unaccountable manner, though we have repeatedly made the most diligent search after it, in vain. It shall appear next week. We regret the delay which has taken place. It has been basely insinuated by some of the schismatics in the anti-slavery ranks, that we purposely mislaid or were unwilling to publish Mr. Smith's letter! Even Lewis Tappan said to us, a few days since in New York, — 'Did you not know that Gerrit Smith intended that his letter should be published in *The Liberator* before the Convention was held at Albany?' — Thereby intimating that we had designedly withheld its publication! What cool effrontery is this! And we may add, further, that, so anxious is Mr. Tappan to colonize us beyond the pale of anti-slavery, he urged us to leave the cause, and devote ourselves to some other pursuit, which he thought would be more congenial with our feelings!! *Et tu, Brute?* What the disorganizers expect to find in Mr. Smith's letter, to bolster them up in their factious course, we cannot imagine. That letter was not written with any such design, we can assure them. . . ."

The letter of June 7, 1839, was finally printed in *The Liberator* on August 30, 1839.

5. Garrison's letter (174) of March 27, 1840, to Gerrit Smith.

6. Joseph C. Hathaway's letter, dated Waterloo, February 24, 1840, was reprinted in *The Liberator*, March 6, 1840, from *The Friend of Man*. Joseph Comstock Hathaway (b. Farmington, New York, April 20, 1810; d. Dansville, New York, Sept. 21, 1873) was an antislavery man of Waterloo, New York. He was a Quaker and farmer. In 1832, he married Esther Aldrich. (Elizabeth Starr Versailles, *Hathaways of America*, Northampton, Mass., 1965, p. 250.)

7. Gerrit Smith's letter to Wright, dated February 29, 1840, as well as a letter dated Waterloo, February 26, 1840, from Wright to "My Brother," apparently Garrison, were printed in *The Liberator*, March 13, 1840. Smith's letter is a reply to one by Henry C. Wright to *The Liberator*, dated West Bloomfield, February 6, 1840, printed in *The Liberator*, February 21, 1840, in which Wright provided an account of a convention of the abolitionists of western New York. In the same issue of *The Liberator*, there appears, too, a letter dated Alleghany, Pennsylvania, December 25, 1839, from Wright to Gerrit Smith.

8. For an account of the convention at West Bloomfield, New York, see the letter by Henry C. Wright, dated West Bloomfield, New York, Feb. 6, 1840, in *The Liberator*, February 21, 1840. He refers to the convention of abolitionists of Western New York as having just closed after two days of meetings.

9. Myron Holley (b. Salisbury, Connecticut, April 29, 1779; d. Rochester, New York, March 4, 1841), lawyer, book-seller, politician, and editor, moved to Canandaigua, New York, in 1803, where he soon gave up the practice of law in favor of book-selling. He was county clerk in 1810–1814 and was elected a state assemblyman in 1816. He was a strong partisan of the building of the Erie Canal. As a member and treasurer of the board of commissioners from 1816 to 1824, he played an important part in bringing the project to completion. He subsequently moved to Lyons, New York, where he was active in the anti-masonic movement. In 1831, he became editor of the Lyons *Countryman*, an antimasonic journal, which ceased publication after three years. He then edited the *Free Elector* in Hartford, Connecticut, for one year, returned to Lyons, and then moved to Rochester, New York, where he edited the Rochester *Freeman* and lived for the remainder of his life. Holley was one of the earliest advocates of an abolitionist political party and a founder of the Liberty Party. (*ACAB.*)

183

TO OLIVER JOHNSON

New-York, *Tuesday noon, May* 12, 1840.

Dear Friend:

I hasten to send you a few lines, respecting our anti-slavery proceedings thus far, as the present anniversary of the National Society excites unusual interest in every quarter of the country.

I need not tell you — for you were present to behold the stirring scene with your own eyes — what a rallying there was at the Depot in Boston, yesterday noon, of the earliest, the truest, the most untiring and zealous friends of our old anti-slavery organization, in accordance with the arrangements that had been made to convey them to Providence, and from thence to this city. A few came from the land of 'down east,' and from the thick-ribbed hills of the Granite State; — but, especially from the counties of old Essex, and Middlesex, and Norfolk, and Plymouth, and Suffolk, in Massachusetts, they came promptly and numerously at the summons of Humanity, in spite of 'hard times' and the busy season of the year, to save our heaven-approved association from dissolution, and our broad platform from being destroyed. An extra train of cars had been engaged for the occasion; but, so numerous was the company, another train had to be started — our numbers continually augmenting at every stopping-place between the two cities. O, it was a heart-stirring and rare spectacle — such as has never before been witnessed in the progress of our all-conquering enterprise; and many were the spectators, who were looking on with wonder and surprise at such a gathering of fanaticism, and such a 'dying away' of abolitionism. On arriving at Providence, the company embarked on board of the steam-boat Rhode-Island, which had the American flag flying in the breeze, (the flag of Liberty has not yet been fashioned,) a considerable number of delegates from Bristol county and from the city of Providence joining us; so that, huge and capacious as were the dimensions of our chartered boat, it was very difficult to move about with facility, notwithstanding the *accommodating* disposition of all on board. On making an enumeration, it appeared that there were about 450 anti-slavery men and women in our company, of whom about 400 were from Massachusetts.[1] [Probably another hundred went by other routes.] There never has been such a mass of '*ultraism*' afloat, in one boat, since the first victim was stolen from the fire-smitten and blood-red soil of Africa. There were persons of all ages, com-

607

plexions, and conditions — from our time-honored and veteran friend SETH SPRAGUE,[2] through ripened manhood down to rosy youth. They were, indeed, the moral and religious *elite* of New England aboli- tionism, who have buckled on the anti-slavery armor to wear to the end of the conflict, or to the close of life. It was truly a great and joyful meeting, united together by a common bond, and partaking of *the one spirit of humanity.* Such greetings and shaking of hands! such interchanges of thoughts and opinions! such zeal, and disin- terestedness, and faith! Verily, it was good to be there! And hundreds more, I am now confident, would have been with us, had the arrange- ment been made one week earlier, and the knowledge of it more widely conveyed; for it was, you know, entered into at a late hour. Some of the towns are remarkably well represented; but I believe our friends at Plymouth — the old PILGRIM ROCK — have surpassed all others.

We had an uncommonly pleasant trip to this city. The north- easterly storm which had lasted for several days previous, cleared up finely just as we left Providence and a glorious sunset and a bright moonlight evening followed. All was tranquil — all happy. In the course of the evening, spirited addresses were made by Wm. M. Chace, Dr. Manford,[3] C. M. Burleigh,[4] Samuel J. May, N. P. Rogers, and J. A. Collins, which were frequently responded to in an en- thusiastic manner.

I have just come from the anniversary meeting. The meeting- house was crowded to excess with delegates alone! How many names will be enrolled I will not attempt to *guess*; but there is considerable excitement, and the new organization have rallied pretty numerously. This afternoon will probably determine the fate of the Parent Society.

The meeting was most eloquently addressed by a colored brother, from Oneida Institute, named Henry H. Garnet [5] — Patrick Henry never spoke better, on any occasion. He was followed by Luther Lee [6] and Lewis Tappan — the latter making some very interesting state- ments respecting the Amistad prisoners. No action was taken upon the Annual Report, a portion of which was read by Joshua Leavitt, but which I have not time to comment upon.

I have little doubt that the right side will prevail. How our Penn- sylvania friends stand at this crisis, you will learn by the following resolutions, which have just been adopted at the annual meeting of the Eastern Pa. Anti-Slavery Society by an overwhelming majority.

Whereas, a Convention recently held in Albany, and styled a National Convention of the friends of immediate emancipation, has nominated candi- dates for the Presidency and Vice Presidency of the United States, to be supported at the approaching election, on abolition grounds exclusively; —

And whereas, the abolitionists of the country, and the anti-slavery societies, are liable to be held, in the public estimation, responsible for this measure; —

1. Resolved, That we protest against the voice of that Convention being regarded as the voice of American abolitionism; because

1st. The abolitionism of the country was almost wholly unrepresented in the Convention, there being but one hundred and twenty-one delegates enrolled, of whom one hundred and four were from the State of New York, and more than half of these from Albany and Troy — not one from Pennsylvania, nor from either of seven other free States; and

2d. The nomination was opposed by a large proportion of the delegates present, was voted against by 33, and sustained by only 44, and was therefore carried by little more than one-third of the whole number enrolled. (Adopted 93 to 27.)

2. Resolved, That without intending to pass any censure on the persons composing that Convention, we regret the course which it pursued, as inexpedient and injurious to the cause, which, we doubt not, it was designed to promote.

3. Resolved, That while we entertain a very high respect for the gentlemen whose names have been so injudiciously brought forward as nominees of that Convention, our opinion is, that any efforts made by us to promote their election, would be not only wholly futile, but a diversion of our energies from a channel in which they might be spent with service to the cause of humanity.

4. Resolved, That we heartily deprecate all measures which have for their object or tendency the organization of abolitionists, as such, into a third political party.

5. Resolved, That it is the duty of abolitionists, by diffusing the principles of light, and liberty, and love, to convert men of all parties, to truth in doctrine, and right in practice; to make abolitionists of partisans, not partisans of abolitionists.

6. Resolved, That we do not express these sentiments from hostility to political action in itself considered, nor from preference to either of the candidates of the great political parties.

7. Resolved, That we fully concur in the sentiment, that no consistent abolitionist can vote for any candidate for office, who will not use his official power whenever he rightfully can, in promoting the repeal of all laws, and the change of all constitutional provisions, which tend to uphold slavery; and that, in our estimation, the candidates of both the great parties have evinced a subserviency to the slave power, which renders them utterly unworthy of the suffrages of the true friends of freedom. (Adopted unanimously.)

8. Resolved, That it is expedient, under present circumstances, for abolitionists, at the approaching presidential contest, to scatter their votes, or entirely absent themselves from the polls. (Resolutions 2, 3, 4, 5, 6, 8, adopted 74 to 23.

Yours truly,
WM. LLOYD GARRISON.

N.B. I shall probably sail for Liverpool, in company with bro. Rogers, on Saturday.

Printed in *The Liberator*, May 15, 1840. A portion of this letter was reprinted in *Life*, II, 346–348.

Garrison wrote this letter on the first day of the annual convention of the American Anti-Slavery Society, which was held in the Fourth Free Church of New York from May 12 to May 15, 1840. This was the convention which culminated in the fatal division of the antislavery movement into two national societies.

1. *Life*, II, 347n, notes the following: "Of the large body of delegates from Massachusetts, only 27, as Edmund Quincy pointed out (*Non-Resistant*, July 8, 1840), were known Non-Resistants; the remainder, of course, adhering to Mr. Garrison solely upon anti-slavery grounds, without assenting either to his views of peace or to the peculiar religious sentiments on account of which he was assailed, but with fixed resolve to see fair play in the anti-slavery ranks. A very large proportion of them were members of orthodox churches. Seth Sprague was among the most prominent Methodist laymen in New England."

2. Seth Sprague (b. July 4, 1760; d. July 8, 1847), of Duxbury, one of the most prominent Methodist laymen in New England, father of Peleg Sprague. He served in the Revolutionary War, though still a boy, and engaged in fishing as a livelihood from 1778 to 1790. After earning a moderate competence in trade and navigation, he retired from business activity to husbandry. His public activities included forty years as justice of the peace and of the quorum and twenty years as member of the state legislature, and he served twice as a member of the electoral college. He actively favored the War of 1812. As a prominent reformer, he participated in the temperance movement, presiding over the first temperance meeting in Duxbury, and was always an active Abolitionist sympathizer. (Justin Winsor, *History of the Town of Duxbury, Massachusetts . . .* , Boston, 1849, pp. 318–320.)

3. "Alias John Colman. His titulary name, like his anti-slavery profession, was put on [*Lib.* 10:111, 131, and MS. July 16, 1841, Oliver Johnson to W. L. G.]" (*Life*, II, 348n). On July 10, 1840, *The Liberator* carried the following item: "Caution. We deem it to be our duty to caution our friends against placing any confidence in the individual who has been known in Boston and vicinity, for some time past, as 'Doctor Manford.' There is too much reason to believe that this was not his real name. He has disappeared under circumstances which make this caution necessary." On August 14, 1840, *The Liberator* indicated that "Dr. Manford" had admitted the deception, but gave little additional information about him.

4. Cyrus Moses Burleigh (b. Plainfield, Connecticut, February 8, 1820; d. Sunnyside, Pennsylvania, March 7, 1855), brother of Charles Calistus Burleigh. He was a lecturer on temperance and slavery and edited the *Pennsylvania Freeman* in 1855. He married Margaret Jones of Philadelphia on February 3, 1855. He was the son of Rinaldo Burleigh of Plainfield and Woodstock, Connecticut, and his other brothers were William Henry, the Reverend Lucian, George Shepard, and John Oscar. (Charles Burleigh, *Genealogy of the Burley or Burleigh Family of America*, Portland, Me., 1880, p. 228.)

5. The name is misspelled Henry S. Garret in *The Liberator*. The address was printed in *The Liberator*, May 22, 1840. The Reverend Henry Highland Garnet (1815–1882) was a former slave in New Market, Kent county, Maryland, who had escaped in 1824. After living and studying in New York, he entered Oneida Institute and became a Presbyterian minister and lecturer. He was an agent of the American Anti-Slavery Society until 1843, when he delivered a militant speech at the Convention of Colored Americans at Buffalo in 1843. The speech, entitled "An Address to the Slaves of the United States," was a call to the slaves to rebel and slay their masters. His address was not endorsed by the convention. In fact, it was repudiated by Frederick Douglass and the American Anti-Slavery Society. Thereafter, he no longer served as agent of the society, but was pastor of the Liberty Street Presbyterian Church in Troy, New York, from

1843 to 1848. His congregation was white. In 1850 he went to England on a speaking tour, served as a missionary in Jamaica in 1852, and several years later, succeeded the Negro preacher and abolitionist, the Reverend Theodore S. Wright, as minister of the Shiloh Presbyterian Church in New York City. During the Civil War, he was a minister in Washington, D.C. He died while serving as United States minister to Liberia in 1882. (*DAB.*)

6. Luther Lee (1800–1889), clergyman, originally of Schoharie, New York, joined the Methodist Episcopal church in 1821 and, after several years, became an itinerant missionary and preacher. He began to preach against slavery in 1836 and became active in the antislavery movement following the death of Elijah Lovejoy in 1837. He assumed the initiative in forming antislavery societies among the Methodists and in 1840 took part in the formation of the Liberty party. In 1841, he established and edited *The New England Christian Advocate,* an antislavery journal, at Lowell, Massachusetts. He seceded from the Methodist church in 1842 and began a weekly journal, *The True Wesleyan.* When the Wesleyan Methodist connection was organized as an antislavery organization, he became a pastor of that church in Syracuse, New York. After the Civil War, he returned to the Methodist Episcopal church. He lived in Michigan from 1867 to the end of his life. (*ACAB, NCAB.*)

184

TO HELEN E. GARRISON

New York, May 15, 1840.
Friday afternoon.

My dear Helen:

Our campaign has just closed, and a severe siege we have had of it, and a glorious triumph we have achieved. It was our anti-slavery boat-load that saved our society from falling into the hands of the new organizers, or, more correctly, *disorganizers.* They had drummed up recruits from all quarters, by the most dishonorable means; and a formidable appearance they presented at the opening of the meeting on Tuesday. The first subject that came up to try the strength of the parties was the appointment of Abby Kelly on the Business Committee. The vote stood about 560 in her favor, to 450 against her. Where these 450 belonged, or who they were, we had no means of ascertaining, because the question was not taken by yeas and nays. The minority finally seceded, and formed a society with the title, "The American and Foreign Anti-Slavery Society." Arthur Tappan declined a re-election, and Lindley Coates,[1] one of the signers of the Philad. Declaration of Sentiments, was chosen in his stead. Not one of the Executive Committee was re-elected, except James S. Gibbons.[2] We have made clean work of every thing — adopted the most thoroughgoing resolutions — and taken the strongest ground — with *crashing* unanimity. The excitement in the city has been great. The spirit of mobocracy has been roused, in consequence of so many of the "Garrison Party" having come from Massachusetts; and our delegation have been driven out of the halls we had engaged, and had to go from pillar to post to find a place where to lay their heads. Goss's Graham House has been assailed by a mob, several windows broken, the door burst open, &c. &c.; though not many were engaged in this work of mischief. What particularly excited these "lewd fellows of the baser sort" [3] was, the mixing of our white and colored friends on terms of equality. One of our friends from Oberlin was severely injured. As Rogers [4] and myself have been stopping with our colored friend Van Ranssalaer,[5] we have seen nothing of the mobocrats. It has not amounted to any thing like a popular tumult.

But I need not even begin to tell you any thing of our proceedings, as bro. Johnson will give you and the rest of the dear household all the particulars.

Yesterday forenoon, in the meeting, your little package was put into my hands; and my heart was delighted to read the hasty note which you penned for me. I am rejoiced and strengthened greatly to see with how much fortitude and composure you bear our separation.[6] Nobly done, dear Helen! May the Lord be with you in spirit, and enable you to sustain your mind until we meet again, which I trust will be in the course of three or four months. I assure you that nothing but a strong sense of duty will ever lead me to separate myself from you; for there is no place so dear to me in the world as my home, and I am never so happy as when by your side. You know I am not given to making many professions; but I do not feel the less, but *the more*, on this account. O no! Be assured, that you shall hear from me frequently, when I am across the "big waters."

You shall have a long letter from me before I leave this city, which will be on Tuesday afternoon next, in the fine large ship Columbus, for Liverpool. Rev. C. P. Grosvenor,[7] Wm. Adams, C. L. Remond, and Rogers, will go with me.

Bro. George leaves this afternoon for Brooklyn, with James C. Jackson. I have serious thoughts of going with him; but, as there is some danger that I cannot get back in season, I suppose I must not go. Bro. George will come for James [8] and dear little George, (bringing sister Anne with him,) on Friday or Saturday next, unless bro. Johnson and wife shall conclude to go to Brooklyn. Oliver will explain matters to you about this. It is bro. G's opinion, that James's health will be much improved by going to Brooklyn, where he will give him some Thompsonian courses, if he thinks best to take them. George says you need have no anxiety whatever about dear little Georgy in B.[9]

Be sure and use your composition tea freely — and get some Checkerberry leaves (if they are good) to drink, and take all possible care of yourself. Cover the cheeks of my dear boys with kisses daily on my account, and tell them to be good little children until my return, when father will bring them some pretty things from England, which will please them very much. I wish I had time to write more, but you shall hear from me again in a day or two.

> Yours, with all possible affection,
> W. L. G.

N. B. Any thing for me may be sent as late as Monday afternoon train, Bro. J.[10] will see to it. I want several copies of the Declaration of Sentiments [11] forwarded in frames, and also a regular file of the Non-Resistant & Liberator from the first of January.

ALS: Garrison Papers, Boston Public Library. Much of this letter is printed in *Life*, II, 355–357. The original was first dated "May 14, Thursday morning." The "14" and "Thursday morning" were then crossed out and "May 16, Friday afternoon," was substituted. A hand other than Garrison's, probably one of his sons, has crossed out "16" and substituted "15." The reason for the change is that Friday afternoon, the day the American Anti-Slavery Society convention ended, was May 15.

1. Lindley Coates (b. March 3, 1794; d. June 3, 1856), notes *Life* (II, 355n), had not signed the Declaration of Sentiments. He lived in Sadsbury, Lancaster county, Pennsylvania, and was one of the earliest active abolitionists. He helped to form the Clarkson Anti-Slavery Association, before the formation of the American Anti-Slavery Society. He was a member of the Pennsylvania Constitutional Convention in 1837, and sought to prevent the limitation of the franchise to whites only. Chosen president of the American Anti-Slavery Society in 1840, he held the office until replaced by Garrison in 1843. He was active in the Underground Railroad, his house serving as a station. (R. C. Smedley, *History of the Underground Railroad in Chester and Neighboring Counties of Pennsylvania*, Lancaster, Pa., 1883, pp. 84–89.)

2. James S. Gibbons (b. Wilmington, Delaware, July 1, 1810; d. 1892), Quaker and a son-in-law of Isaac T. Hopper. He lived in Philadelphia until 1835, where he was a prosperous dry-goods merchant and opponent of slavery. He married Abigail Hopper in 1833 and two years later moved to New York where he continued as businessman and banker. He was author of books on banking and taxes. He was a member of the executive committee of the American Anti-Slavery Society and a devoted supporter of the *National Anti-Slavery Standard*, the new organ of the American Anti-Slavery Society established in 1840. He once mortgaged his furniture to raise funds for the *Standard*. Both he and his father-in-law were disowned in 1842 by the New York Monthly Meeting of the Society of Friends for their support of the *Standard* and the American Anti-Slavery Society. (See Anna Davis Hallowell, ed., *James and Lucretia Mott: Life and Letters*, Boston, 1884, pp. 211, 212, 217, 226.) However, he continued to attend meetings despite this action. He wrote the popular Civil War song, "We are Coming Father Abraham, three hundred thousand strong." (*DAB.*)

3. Acts 17:5.

4. Nathaniel P. Rogers.

5. Thomas Van Rensalaer. See letter 124, to Oliver Johnson, August 14, 1838; also, *Life*, II, 355–356n.

6. "Mrs. Garrison was on the eve of her third confinement" (*Life*, II, 356n).

7. "Of Worcester, Mass. Grosvenor, together with the Rev. Nathaniel Colver,

of Boston, and the Rev. Elon Galusha, of Perry, N. Y., had been deputed to attend the World's Convention by the body called the National Baptist A. S. Convention organized in New York on Apr. 28–30, 1840 (*Mass. Abolitionist*, 2:53). Colver was also a delegate of the Mass. Abolition Society, and Galusha of the American and Foreign A. S. Society (*ibid.*, 2:111, and *Lib.* 10:118)." (*Life*, II, 356n.)

8. Garrison's brother.
9. Brooklyn, Connecticut.
10. Oliver Johnson.
11. Of the American Anti-Slavery Society.

185

TO HELEN E. GARRISON

New-York — Saturday noon.
[May 16, 1840.]

My dear Love:

I came very near going back to Boston yesterday, with the multitudinous throng of friends on board of the Rhode-Island, to give you one more fond embrace, and to hug our dear Willie and Georgie after my old manner; but, as there would be some risk about my getting back in season to take the packet for Liverpool on Tuesday, and as I feared if we should meet again to be again separated in the course of forty-eight hours, our hearts would be lacerated afresh, I concluded it would be best for me to remain here. I should have gone with George, however, to Brooklyn, if I could have been certain about arriving here seasonably. The friends gave me a cordial adieu; and, though my heart was somewhat saddened at the idea of a separation, I put on a cheerful air, and urged them to go onward with unfaltering steps in the great reform of the age. Say to friend Johnson, that J. C. Jackson, bro. George, N. P. Rogers, and myself, were down at the Fulton ferry, and saw the Rhode-Island[1] go by with her glorious company. Whether any of them saw us, we could not tell.

As I have lost my credentials from the Mass. A. S. Society,[2] I wish bro. Johnson to see Francis Jackson forthwith, and ask him to write a certificate, and sign it, and have it forwarded to me in the bundle to be sent on Monday afternoon. That bundle may be directed either to the Anti-Slavery Office, or to Thomas Van Ranssalaer. Whatever is intended for me must be sent by that conveyance; as the packet will sail on Tuesday noon, unless there be stormy weather.

Last evening, bro. Rogers and myself went over to Brooklyn, to stay at friend Truesdell's,[3] until we sail. He has got a fine house, and we had a very gracious reception at the hands of Mrs. T. — of course.

Friend Adams, of Pawtucket, who is going to Liverpool with us, is also at friend T's.

I am writing this scarcely intelligible scrawl at the house of James S. Gibbons, in a room where a lively discussion is going on between Rogers, C. C. Burleigh, Abby Kelly, and others; you will therefore excuse me if I make out a meagre epistle; for my head is perfectly confused, and my body not yet recovered from its weariness. My health, however, is excellent, and every thing looks fair and promising for our voyage.

The British Queen has just arrived, in 16 days from London. I wish it were so that we could go out in her; but she will not sail till the 1st of June.

I hope, dear H., to receive a letter from you and bro. Johnson in the bundle. You shall have a better letter from me before I leave. Give my loving regards to dear mother, James,[4] Mrs. Johnson, Oliver,[5] & remember me to Caroline,[6] and kiss the boys a thousand times over for their father's sake. I must close abruptly, or I shall lose the mail.

Yours, indissolubly,

Wm. Lloyd Garrison.

ALS: Garrison Papers, Boston Public Library. The date is in the original manuscript, written by a hand other than Garrison's.

1. The boat carrying the New England delegation on its return trip to Providence.
2. To the World's Anti-Slavery Convention. Garrison attended the convention as a delegate of the Massachusetts Anti-Slavery Society.
3. Thomas Truesdell.
4. Garrison's brother.
5. Oliver Johnson.
6. Unidentified.

186

TO HELEN E. GARRISON

New-York, May 19, 1840.

Beloved Wife:

To-day, at 12 o'clock, was the time advertised for the sailing of the Columbus. The wind, however, is "dead ahead," so that the packet will not sail until to-morrow; and perhaps not till the day after, should the wind not haul round. This delay renders it more than probable that we shall not arrive in season to be at the *opening* of the World's Convention. No doubt, our new organization opponents are hoping that we shall have a long voyage; for they now understand, that, if we are present when the Convention commences, the "woman question" will inevitably be brought up, or, rather, the question, whether the delegates appointed by the American Anti-Slavery Society (among whom is Lucretia Mott) shall be entitled to seats in the Convention. Father Bourne,[1] who goes against "woman's rights," is now sitting by my side; and he predicts, with all confidence, that no woman will be allowed a seat in the Convention. Such a thing, he says, was never heard or thought of in any part of Europe. It is, perhaps, quite probable, that we shall be foiled in our purpose; — but the subject cannot be agitated without doing good — and you and the dear friends of human rights may be assured, that we shall not easily allow ourselves to be intimidated or put down.

Expecting to go this forenoon, bro. Rogers and myself have had a busy time of it in packing up our things, and getting ready to bid our native land farewell — though I hope not a long or last farewell. As usual, I had many things left undone, and felt very badly about leaving in such haste; especially as I supposed no opportunity would be afforded me to send you another letter before my departure. Our trunks were all carried down to the wharf, before we ascertained that the packet would not sail to-day. Just before we fastened them up, the bundle arrived from Boston, containing letters from you, from Johnson[,] H. G. Chapman, &c. [. . .] have miscarried, [. . .] Office, to the Anti-[Slavery] [. . .] tely, it ar- [. . .]

Your letter, dear H., comforted me exceedingly. I am sure that I love you far more than words can express; and therefore it is that I have never been prodigal of words on this subject. I am equally certain that you fully reciprocate my love, and that we are mutually endeared to each other. You speak of your feelings in consequence of our separation. I can not only imagine it all, but realize it all. It is very trying to my spirit, that I cannot catch a glimpse of your countenance, and hold sweet converse with you face to face, and play and prattle with my two darling boys. Now that I am here detained another day, how much do I regret that I did not return to Cambridgeport in the Rhode-Island with the true spirits which came from our good State to the rescue of Freedom's perilled cause! — As it was, I should have returned, had I not supposed that the pain of separation, a second time, would have been greater than before.

I find it difficult to persuade myself, that I am about to depart for the shores of old England, over the broad Atlantic. Every thing seems dream-like. A few days will dispel this visionary feeling, and wake me up to the reality of a sea-voyage. When I am absent from you, it is impossible for me not to feel as if I had not suffered a bereavement. I have not had one good night's sleep since I left

Boston; and yet my health is remarkably good. How sweet, how rapturous will be our meeting on my return, if life and health be vouchsafed to us! How rich will be the compensation for any loss that we may have sustained! Ah! even now, in imagination, I embrace you, and imprint upon your cheek the kiss of purity and love. As for dear George and Willie, I know not how to be separated from them. I almost feel as if they had been taken from me, and I were once more childless. Precious gifts of God! precious tokens of nuptial felicity! Tell my darling Willie, that I hope he will always be a dear good boy, and remember that the good God sees him by day and night, and loves all good children. Tell [. . .] not come now, un [. . .] He goes to [. . .] may not [. . .] Dear Willie wants all the little slaves to be set free, and he is willing that his father shall go a great way off to break their chains. — Kiss him morning, noon and night, for my sake. Many pretty things will I bring him when I come back. And George shall have some too, if he is a good boy. When he goes to Brooklyn, I hope he will try to learn all that he can at school, so that when I come back, he will be able to read the nice little books I shall bring him. You may kiss him as often as you do Willie, for they are equally dear to my heart.

My poor dear brother James! I am sorry to hear that his health does not seem to improve, and that he has another ulcer internally; but let us hope that the warm weather, with proper care and treatment, will yet restore him. I love him with all a brother's affection — of that, he cannot doubt. Earnest is my prayer to God, that he may be led to review his past life, and to perceive how widely he has departed from the path of rectitude, to the ruin of his immortal soul. O that he may be led to speedy and hearty repentance, that he may rejoice in God, and be made an heir of glory, through Jesus Christ our Saviour! But, without repentance, there can be no reconciliation; and unless we are reconciled to God, how can we be happy? I shall think a great deal about dear James during my absence, and shall endeavor to write to him soon. A letter from him would be regarded as a special token of his love by me. Whether he had better go to the Hospital, or to Brooklyn,[2] in view of his present situation, George can decide far better than myself.

Rogers[3] and myself have been very hospitably entertained at Mrs. Truesdell's. He is still quite unwell with his cold, and has rather a hard cough. Poor man! he sighs [as] badly as I do to think about home, and wife, and children, (he has seven [. . .] as much delighted to get a letter [. . .] addresses for the [. . .] midnight, I [. . .] to me with [. . .] ate terms. She is a first-rate woman, and in all respects worthy of such a man. The more I see of Rogers, I love him; and his friendship for me is ardent and sincere. He has never before been separated from his family; and you may naturally imagine how home-sick he must feel. Yet he is full of pleasing anticipations as it respects the Convention in London, and longs to be on the water.

Last evening, I addressed a very respectable audience of colored people in T. S. Wright's [4] meeting-house, in relation to the difficulties which had arisen in our cause, and to the charges brought against myself. I went into the matter, root and branch — Lewis Tappan and La Roy Sun[derland being present] — neither of whom ventured to deny or [. . .]

Yester[day   Mr.] Covo, &c. &c. [. . .]

N.B. I meant to have written a letter to friend Johnson for public[a-tion this w]eek, but have not got it completed. Hope to send a [. . .] to-morrow or next day.[5]

AL: Garrison Papers, Boston Public Library. Printed, in part, in *Life*, II, 357–358. The bottom portion of the first page is torn off and the end of the letter is torn in different places.

1. The Reverend George Bourne, originally of England. See letter 8, to Isaac Knapp, February 3, 1836.
2. "He went to Brooklyn, Conn." (*Life*, II, 358n.)
3. N. P. Rogers.
4. See letter 30, to Helen, May 25, 1836.
5. The postscript is written upside down at the top of the last page.

187

TO HELEN E. GARRISON

New-York — Wednesday forenoon — May 20, 1840.

Dear Love:

I have no hope of hearing any thing from you until after my arrival in England; for you, of course, suppose that I am now launched upon the boundless deep, receding farther and farther from you and home. But here I remain, detained (as yesterday) by a northeasterly storm — and how can I improve this unexpected opportunity more agreeably to my feelings, than by sending you another token of my love? I have nothing new to communicate; but the mere assurance that I continue in good health will be more gratifying to you than pages of the every day events of life. Of this city, I am thoroughly sick. Here Mammon reigns in filthy splendor, and Humanity finds none to sympathize with it. All is heartless, selfish, exclusive. I am writing in Wall-street, where the money-changers congregate, and where affluence and beggary are seen side by side, but acknowledging no relationship by creation, and at mutual enmity with each other. It is rightly named — *Wall*-street — for those who habitually occupy it in quest of riches at the expense of mankind, are *walled* in from the sympathies of human nature, and their hearts are as fleshless and hard as the paving-stones on which they tread, or the granite and marble buildings which they have erected and dedicated to their idol Gain. Love — pure, benignant, all-sympathizing, all-embracing Love — where art thou? Son of God, whose aim and end were to do good even to enemies — to reconcile man to man by reconciling man to God — to bind up the broken hearted, succor the distressed, and rescue the fallen — where is thy blessed spirit to be seen? How many, in this great city, have more than heart can wish, and are revelling in luxury and affluence! How many are deprived of the necessaries of life, and know not, when the sun goes down in the west, where to lay their head! How many are overfed — surfeited — banqueted upon daintiful things! How many hunger and thirst, and consume by a slow famine! Yesterday, as I went up this street, to drop a letter for you into the Post-Office, a little ragged boy asked of me a pittance to buy him some bread. An occurrence like this is a reproach to the whole city. Either the Creator of men is a partial, malevolent Being, or man is horribly selfish and wicked. "Let God be true, and every man a liar." [1] All misery, all want, all suffering from famine and nakedness, is contrary to the will of God. He desires that all may be fed with the abundance of fatness, and that every man should sit under his own vine and fig-tree, and have none to molest or make him afraid.[2] That time shall yet arrive — for Jesus has not died in vain. He shall save his people from their *sins* — and, being saved from these, they will be saved from all the consequences of sin; for they will then love their neighbor as themselves, and love "worketh no evil". [3]

This detention by the storm makes it almost certain that we shall be too late to be at the opening of the World's Convention. I am not impatient, however, nor do I feel any disposition to grieve. My confidence in the wisdom, forecast, benevolence of God is perfect. He is, ever has been, and ever will be, infinitely good and gracious. Nothing can be unjust which he devises, nothing malevolent which he orders. "The Lord reigns — let the earth rejoice." [4]

Being detained here, my spirit naturally yearns to see you. Could I have sailed from Boston, instead of New-York, how much more preferable would it have been, as a matter of choice, to my heart! But all things are ordered wisely — and He, who sees the end from the beginning, knows what is best. Though I shall sail from New-York, I shall aim to return to Boston direct.

Through what scenes or vicissitudes we may be called to pass during our separation, it is impossible for us to foresee; but, how grateful am I to God, that he has given me a free wife, and free children! I shall not be tortured with the apprehension, that you may be sold to some hyena-spirited slave-speculator, or that George and Willie may be kidnapped, and reduced to slavery. Nor will your bosom be torn with anguish at the thought, that I may be claimed and hurried off as the property of another. In the course of three months, or, at the longest, four months, (I shall hasten back with all loving speed,) we may hope to see each other, and mingle joyful congratulations with gushing tears of gratitude. The time, though it may seem long to us, is, in fact, very brief. My heart bounds as I think of the babe which may be presented to me on my return. Heaven grant you a safe and easy delivery! Would that I could be near you in the hour of child-birth. I *shall* be, in spirit, though not in a bodily presence. It is a great relief to my mind to think that you will lack for nothing — that you are to have a skilful *female* physician, a good nurse, and dear mother and sister Anne with you, and our estimable friend Mrs. Johnson, and such an active and excellent housewife as Caroline. Your caution is so large, that I need not urge you to take all possible care of yourself, both before, at the time, and after your sickness.

I shall send this letter to you in a bundle, by Mr. Snow,[5] of Cambridgeport, who has just called in, and informed me that he returns home this afternoon. The other letters and packages you may hand to friend Johnson, to be taken into the city without delay. Mr. Snow has kindly promised me that he will call and see you immediately on his return. I hope, therefore, you will receive this as early as to-morrow noon.

Inform friend Chace that the Liberator volumes, and anti-slavery pamphlets, &c. which I bought at auction, came to $9.76 — for bringing which to the Anti-Slavery Depository, I paid 50 cts. — making $10.26. I authorize him to get the money of H. G. Chapman, and to give a receipt for the same in my name.

You mention that dear little Willie has had an attack of the croup, but was better when you wrote. I trust he has had no relapse. Should he have a cough, I know of nothing better than the balsam of liverworth, with an injection occasionally. Farewell! I go, but leave my heart behind me, and shall try to come back for it without delay. This is probably the last letter I shall be able to send you on this side of the water. Love to all the household.

Your affectionate husband,

W. L. G.

ALS: Garrison Papers, Boston Public Library. Printed, in part, in *Life*, II, 358–359.

1. Romans 3:4.
2. Micah 4:4, slightly adapted.
3. Romans 13:10.
4. Psalms 97:1.
5. Unidentified.

188

TO HELEN E. GARRISON

New-York, May 21, 1840.
Thursday forenoon.

My dear Helen:

The storm still continues — and the notice is, that the Columbus will not sail until to-morrow at 11 o'clock — which means, that she cannot get out of the harbor with the present head-wind, even if that wind should continue a week longer. The transition in the weather, during the past week, has been very great. Up to Tuesday, the heat was overwhelmingly oppressive. To walk any considerable distance covered me with profuse perspiration. Since then, the weather has been, not as cold, perhaps, as Greenland, but almost as uncomfortable; so that a fire has been as much needed as in February. It rained very hard all last night, and to day it drizzles, drizzles, drizzles. The clouds, however, are beginning to pass away, and the wind is hauling round a little more to the north. We shall undoubtedly succeed in weighing anchor to-morrow. I am very glad that this storm came on before we sailed; for if we had been all this while beating against a head wind close on a lee shore, it would have been dismal indeed. We shall doubtless have very pleasant weather after this. I expect to be quite sea-sick, however, whether it rain or shine, blow high or low. The moment I begin to think of being rocked upon the billows, my stomach grows very sensitive, and is almost ready to heave. A thorough vomiting will do me as much good as a lobelia emetic. After the first three or four days at sea, I expect to be able to devour any thing that may be set before me in the shape of food, and to grow like a young pig in fatness.

As soon as I came over from Brooklyn [1] this morning, (for Rogers and myself are still making our head-quarters at Mrs. Truesdell's,) who should I see but Wm. M. Chace and James C. Jackson, just arrived from Boston, via Connecticut! The sight was as unexpected as it was pleasant. Many inquiries about home and friends were quickly made on my part, and as quickly answered on theirs. William informed me that dear Anne [2] was with you, and that bro. James and dear little Georgie came with him to Killingly,[3] in good spirits, and well pleased with the prospect before them. Georgie behaved very well indeed — sleeping a little on the way, but, when wide awake, watching the motion of the cars, and asking questions, after his usual manner. I was glad to hear that he expressed no desire to return home, but seemed perfectly contented. You will miss him, no doubt, very much; but his absence will be a relief to you at the present time. Unless there should be special reasons for his coming home at an earlier period, I would let him remain in Brooklyn until my return from London. How Willie will miss his father and Georgie! The dear child! Was there ever one so precious given to parents before?

It is friend Chace's opinion, that James was somewhat improved in health. Bro. George will manage him with all ease, and watch over him with the care of a brother.

I am gratified to hear that the Board of Managers in Boston are disposed to act in a very liberal and spirited manner, in reference to the National Society. Friend C. informs me that the Boston Female Society will pay over to the national treasury, in the course of a few weeks, the sum of $500. This is noble. The abolitionists of the country will yet be constrained to acknowledge, as one man, that the Massachusetts Anti-Slavery Society has been shamefully calumniated by those who have seceded from our ranks. Everything will come out right, if we only put unshaken trust in God, and care not what evil-minded persons may say or do to us.

If I could have spent a few days with the dear household in Brooklyn, before my departure for Europe, my heart would have been refreshed beyond measure. I long to see sister Mary and Sarah, and Catherine and the children. Especially do I desire to see sister Anne, whom I love with very strong affection. I hope she will like the quietude of our situation at Cambridgeport, and the scenery interspersed between our house and Cambridge college. I wish it were so that I could be at home now, to make some evening excursions with you both; but I will hope to do so on my return. If dear Anne cannot wholly supply my place in your mind, she will do more to solace you, in your lonely moments, than any other being, during my absence. Had I been permitted to bid her a parting farewell, I should have claimed a brother's privilege to imprint upon her cheek a brother's kiss. It must now be given by proxy; and I authorize you to bestow the same, promising to remunerate you by and by.

My thoughts revert occasionally to the little garden attached to our dwelling, and I long to get a peep at it with my visual organs. In imagination, I see your beans, and peas, and radishes, and what not, modestly peeping out of the ground, and beginning to thrive finely.

Mrs. Johnson [4] and Caroline will keep an eye upon their growth, no doubt. If I were at home, I could do my share in eating the products of the garden; but, as for taking care of it, I should make as poor a figure at it, as one of the medical faculty does in administering calomel to a patient who is down with the pleurisy. Let as many flowers be cultivated as convenient; for they very beautifully "set off" a place like ours.

I have had a good many letters to write since I have got over the fatigue of the annual meeting, as well as many other things to attend to. Hence, together with the continual anxiety of my mind about the packet, I have not felt in the mood of writing any thing in relation to the anti-slavery controversy, for the Liberator. Rogers has scarcely done any better for the Herald of Freedom. His cough still continues, and his spirits flag a little. I have luckily been able to buy some balsam of liverwort for him, and have administered a few doses, to good effect. Last evening, we had a long talk about his native place, and the hills and valleys, and lakes, and rivers of New-Hampshire; and it revived him exceedingly. Between us both, it is difficult to say which has the stronger yearning after home, and the wife, and children, and friends, which cluster around that sacred spot.

Friend Chace is now writing an epistle at the same table with me — probably to his beloved Mary. I can enter into the glow and ardor of his feelings, by remembering the days of our courtship — rather let me say, by the pleasure I feel in communicating with my dear wife at the present moment.

To-morrow morning, before I go on board of the packet, I hope to get a glimpse at this week's Liberator. Dear Johnson, I feel that he has an arduous task to perform in editing the paper,[5] and super-intending the concerns of the printing establishment. May his health and his spirits not fail him. I am, dearest,

Yours, most affectionately,

Wm. Lloyd Garrison.

☞ It must be taken for granted, that I send affectionate remem-brances to mother, Anne, Mr. and Mrs. J.[6] Give my regards to Mr. and Mrs. Knight,[7] Calista,[8] &c. Do not fail to have letters forwarded to me by the British Queen on the first of June. She will probably arrive out as soon as the Columbus; and it will be very cheering to receive intelligence some ten days later.

☞ Tell friend Johnson to send the Liberator, without fail, from this week, to John H. Murray,[9] 329, Greenwich-street, New-York city — (a new subscriber) — by mail, and charge one year's subscription to friend Chace, to whom I have paid the money. Be careful to send this week's paper.

My olive mixt suit of clothes I have not yet worn. It fits me very well. The pantaloons were about one inch too long, and I have had them altered accordingly. I shall feel, and perhaps look, rather oddly in a frock coat. I am so attached to black, that I shall probably wear my black suit nearly all the time in London. H. G. Chapman has sent me a bill of exchange for £30, so that I shall have funds enough to carry me through.

Adieu! adieu! dear Helen. Think of our future meeting, ere long, (the Lord willing,) and wipe all tears away.

ALS: Garrison Papers, Boston Public Library. Printed, in part, in *Life*, II, 359–360

1. Brooklyn, New York.
2. Anne Benson.
3. Windham county, Connecticut. Garrison spells it Killingley.
4. Mrs. Oliver Johnson.
5. Johnson was editing *The Liberator* in Garrison's absence.
6. Mr. and Mrs. Oliver Johnson.
7. Unidentified.
8. Unidentified.
9. Otherwise unidentified.

189

TO GEORGE W. BENSON

Thursday afternoon. [May 21. 1840]

Dear bro. George:

Shakespeare somewhere says — "The rain, it raineth every day" [1] — and, sure enough, it comes puttering down, drizzle, drizzle, drizzle — the wind (a strong northeaster) dead ahead since Tuesday at sunrise, and the sky all involved in melancholy. Hence, I am still occupying the "sky parlor" of our friend Van Ransalaer, where you and bro. Wright [2] exhibited your professional skill upon each other as pugilists of the first order, and where so many beautiful compliments were bestowed by you upon each other and bro. Rogers. It is far better to be here, however, than to be just on the edge of the coast, contending with such a gale in hopeless strife. We shall be off to-morrow, if the wind changes, which will probably be the case. How happy should I have been, if I could have been permitted to spend a few days under the family roof at Brooklyn, before my departure! Tell dear Mary and Sarah, that they are by no means forgotten, and that they possess a large share of my affections. Sister Anne, I rejoice to hear, is now with dear Helen. W. M. Chace and J. C. Jackson arrived this morning; and by them I learn that brother

James and my darling boy Georgie are both in Brooklyn.[3] It seems as if I *must* go and see you all. Say to dear James, that I love him as I do my own soul; that I hope he will be careful of his health; that he has my prayers for the divine guidance and blessing; and that I hope to see him much improved in health on my return. I think he will soon feel perfectly at home with you. I need not ask you to keep an oversight of little Georgie — for I know you need no prompting on this point. Give him many kisses for my sake; and tell him father means to bring him something pretty from London in the big ship, if he is a good boy. Give my kind regards to Catherine, and my salutations on the cheek with the lips to each one of your precious babes — write to me at London, to the care of J. H. Tredgold,[4] 27, New-Broad-street, — and believe me that no one loves you more than does

Your ultra, fanatical brother,

Wm. Lloyd Garrison.

N. B. Bro. Rogers sends his kind regards to you and bro. James. He has still a bad cold and cough, but will easily throw it off, I hope, at sea. Remember me to friend Scarborough and family, and all the Brooklyn friends as one.

ALS: Garrison Papers, Boston Public Library. The date in the original manuscript was inserted by a hand other than Garrison's.

1. *Twelfth Night*, V, i.
2. Henry C. Wright.
3. Brooklyn, Connecticut.
4. J. H. Tredgold (1798–1842) was secretary of the British and Foreign Anti-Slavery Society. Garrison spelled the name "Treadgold," incorrectly.

190

TO OLIVER JOHNSON

On Board of the packet ship Columbus,
Near Sandy Hook, May 22, 1840.

MY DEAR FRIEND:

After a detention of three days by a northeasterly storm, we are now on our way to the Atlantic for the old world, which, under God, is yet to be renovated and made wholly new. In the judgment of the most enlightened friends of our common humanity, on both sides of the Atlantic, it is my duty to attend the World's Convention in London, on the 12th of June next, — the first which has been held since the dispersion of the human race at the building of the tower of Babel. The object of the Convention is not the gratification of an impious ambition, but the promotion of the cause of philanthropy and religion; — not to get unto itself a name, by attempting to scale the walls of heaven, but to overthrow a worse than Babel fabric, which exalts itself above all that is called God; — not to increase the power of the few, but to secure the rights of the many; — not to perpetuate the dominion of man over man, but to enforce the great, self-evident, all-pervading truth, that liberty is the birth-right of mankind, and that oppression and slavery, under all circumstances and modifications, in all climes and among all people, are in opposition to the will of God, and hostile to the interests of our race. I do not allow myself to pause and inquire, how much will the Convention accomplish. I am sure it cannot prove a failure. Whether the number of delegates be few or many, whether few or many nations be represented, it will not have been summoned in vain. The acorn must first be planted, before the oak can lift its stately form to the sky, or spread out its branches for shelter and shade. Before the Temple of Liberty can be reared, its foundation must first be laid broad and deep. The husbandman buries his seed in the earth, and then waits patiently for the ripened harvest. To the unintelligent mind, which takes no cognizance of cause and effect, such a process may seem like labor lost. 'He that hath ears to hear, let him hear.' [1] Mankind are to be reconciled together. They shall cease to enslave, to destroy, to hate each other. They shall mingle together like the kindred drops of ocean, and their feelings, desires and purposes roll in unison like the waves of the sea. Their country shall no longer be hemmed in by geographical boundaries, or bounded by any number of square miles less than the whole globe. All seas, all mountains, all territories, shall be held as the common property of our race. The confusion of tongues shall cease, and one speech be spoken as it was before the universal dispersion.

> 'The noise of war shall cease from sea to sea,
> And married nations dwell in harmony.'

These blissful events must happen, it seems to me, or the Son of God has come into the world in vain. My faith is perfect in his ability to overcome the evil that is in the world, through the power and by the agency of divine love. That the first World's Convention will do something toward hastening such an epoch, I think cannot reasonably be doubted. What does the first imply but a second, a third, and a final Convention, to prepare the whole earth to celebrate one universal jubilee?

Knowing how many enfranchised spirits I leave behind me, who will be anxious to receive the earliest intelligence of the proceedings of the Convention, I shall write to you by the first conveyance. How that body will be organized, or how comprehensive will be the spirit which may pervade it, it is not for me to predict. The object of the Convention is to promote the interests of Humanity. It is, then, a common object, in which all who wear the human form have a right to participate, without regard to color, sex or clime. With a young woman placed on the throne of Great Britain,[2] will the philanthropists of that country presume to object to the female delegates from the United States, as members of the Convention, on the ground of their sex? In what assembly, however august or select, is that almost peerless woman, Lucretia Mott, not qualified to take an equal part?

I have no wish to mar the harmony, or disturb the repose of the Convention, by the introduction of any topic; but I cannot consent to have one human being excluded from the World's Platform, even for the sake of peace. If I should be outvoted on this particular point, I may enter my protest against the decision, but neither secede nor 'new organize.'

It is with difficulty I tear myself away from home, friends and country, at this trying crisis in the anti-slavery enterprise. Though my absence is a matter of very little consequence, I cannot help feeling a strong desire to remain behind. And yet my visit may not be wholly useless on the other side of the Atlantic. I anticipate a kind reception at the hands of my British friends, and feel a thrill of pleasure at the prospect of once more embracing my beloved coadjutor George Thompson. May the spirit of love and of a sound mind be with me, and success be given to my mission, as far as it is in accordance with the will of God.

I hope to hear from you, and many other dear friends, from time to time, and shall try to reciprocate all epistolary favors.

The pilot is about leaving the ship, and I must close this hastily written letter to send by him. Farewell! Be faithful and true to the end.

With great regard, I remain,
Your friend and brother,
WM. LLOYD GARRISON.

N.B. I would gratefully acknowledge the kindness of my friend Thomas Van Rensalaer, of New-York city, and of Thomas Truesdell and family, of Brooklyn, N.Y. in extending to me a most hospitable reception during my stay in the commercial emporium.

Printed in *The Liberator*, May 29, 1840. Printed, in part, in *Life*, II, 360–361. There it is suggested, without evidence, that the letter may have been written to Maria W. Chapman. Johnson, who was then editor of *The Liberator*, seems more probable.

1. Mark 4:9.
2. Victoria, Queen of England from 1837 to 1901.

191

TO AN UNIDENTIFIED CORRESPONDENT

[May 22, 1840.]

'As the Rhode Island swept down the East River, on her return voyage, she made a majestic appearance, with her multitudinous company crowding her spacious decks. How did my heart bless those devoted men and women, who, in the midst of great pecuniary embarrassments, and at considerable expense, left their business and families at the call of duty, and rushed to the rescue of a despised and buffeted cause, even at the certainty of being misunderstood, calumniated, hated, both by professed friends and open foes! Bros. Rogers, Jackson, George W. Benson, and myself, watched your boat until it dwindled to a speck, and vanished out of sight.'

Printed in *The Liberator*, May 22, 1840. *The Liberator* printed this item with the comment: "The following is an extract of a private letter written by Mr. Garrison while in New York."

192

TO HELEN E. GARRISON

In the Gulf Stream, May 28, 1840.
Lat. 39, 30, long. 69.

My dear Wife:

Six days at sea, and yet not more than one day's sail from New-York! We left that city on the 22d inst. at noon, and were towed down to Sandy Hook by a little pigmy of a steam-boat, with the formidable name of SAMSON, which gallantly grappled with our huge packet-ship, and carried her through the water as though she were scarcely an incumbrance. The dismal northeasterly storm, which had detained us so long in port, had almost wholly passed away, and the wind (though light) appeared to be in the right quarter. The pilot left us at about 3 o'clock, at which time I began to feel quite seasick, and vomited quite freely. It was with the utmost difficulty I was able to write a very brief epistle to bro. Johnson, which I gave to a colored young man to put into the New-York Post Office, and which I hope was not forgotten or mislaid, as it was intended for publication in the Liberator. Day after day, we have been baffling about from north to south, and from south to north, making scarcely any headway direct — now aiming for Charleston, S.C. and now for Halifax, N.S. till at last we find ourselves in the Gulf Stream, almost entirely becalmed. We have had, however, this consolation, (not a selfish one, I trust,) that we have overtaken and distanced several vessels, and have had none to go ahead of us. The weather, moreover, has been uniformly clear, mild, delightful, with scarcely a cloud to be seen in the horizon, the sun looking down upon us with a smile of complacency, the shoreless birds following in our wake on tireless wing, the waves heaving softly and harmoniously together, and occasionally a swarm of fish trooping gaily around us. Still, here we are, and with very little prospect that we shall be in London in accordance with our hopes and expectations at the time of our departure. It is all right, and I feel nothing of impatience or disquietude in my mind at our situation and prospects; because I know that the Almighty can never do aught amiss, and that he is disposed and has the ability to govern winds, waves and ocean in the best possible manner. All my fears, anxieties, cares, I have thrown upon him; and, let what may happen, I feel within me a spirit which says, "Not my will, but thine be done, O God" [1] — a spirit of cordial, hearty acquiescence, not of forced submission.

As for our ship, she is five years old, about 660 tons burthen, strongly made, rides upon the billows gracefully, and is considered a good "sea-boat." She has three cabins, one for the ladies, and one for gentlemen, below, and one for the latter on deck. These are handsomely fitted up with maple and rose-wood, but do not present so showy an appearance as those of some of the other packet-ships. The captain and mate claim for her the credit of being a fast sailer; but, as yet, we have not had a fair opportunity to test her speed. Capt. Cropper [2] is a Virginian, of Herculean stature, free and easy in his manners, and not at all disposed to display his authority, or to act the part of a despotic commander. The first mate is a coarse, blunt man, of good sense and considerable information, and hails, I presume, from old England.

Our passengers constitute rather a motley assemblage. In the steerage, there are between forty and fifty, mostly Irish and Scotch. In the cabins, we have about thirty, — American, German, Scotch, Irish, English, &c. Of Americans, there are not more than two or three, beside Grosvenor, Rogers, and myself. There are some half a dozen women, but none of them appear to be of cultivated minds — one of them has two small children with her. The men (with the exception of us three, and one other person,) are a prayerless, godless, drinking, card-playing, low-minded set, boisterous in their merriment, coarse in their manners, and disposed to make light of every thing serious and sacred. To attempt to reason with them is like casting pearls to swine. We have had some serious conversations with them on various topics, and not altogether in vain; but they are awfully estranged from God, and from the spirit of his dear Son. They treat us, however, quite respectfully, and feel themselves restrained in our presence, to some extent. The thought of being associated with them for three or four weeks longer, is by no means agreeable. If such were to be my companions throughout eternity, how miserable should I be, especially if there were any affinity between my spirit and theirs! I hope we shall do them some good; and, if so, I shall not regret that we have fallen into their company. O, how large a portion of mankind live like beasts, "without God and without hope in the world," [3] enemies to each other, caring for nothing but the gratification of their lusts and appetites, and dead in trespasses and sins!

A word as to our fare. We take breakfast at 8 o'clock — lunch at 12 — dinner at 4 — and supper at 8. Our table is daily made to groan with dishes of various food — roast beef, mutton, lamb, turkey, chickens, &c. &c. by way of meats — pies, custards, tarts, and puddings of all kinds — apples, oranges, figs, raisins, almonds, &c. Nearly all the passengers indulge pretty freely in drinking brandy, wine, porter, &c. They banter us occasionally for our cold water habits, and we rebuke them quite as often for their tippling.

As for our health — dear Rogers came on board in a very feeble condition, and with a bad cough; and, until yesterday, has been very poorly indeed. He has been, in fact, a sufferer, but his cough is now gone, and yesterday and to-day he has seemed much better. I have been almost all the time very qualmish, and for the first three days could relish no kind of food. I have now fairly passed the Rubicon, and can eat my three meals a day without having any unpleasant sensation in my stomach. But, O, as for sleep, as yet I have scarce[ly] known what it is. My bed is almost as hard as a plank, an[d I] toss and turn in vain to get repose. The moment I lie down, my mind turns instinctively homeward, and there it hovers until dawn of day. I have written a little poetical effusion to describe my feelings — the first verse of which I here append:

> "As to her nest some wandering bird
>   Returns to cheer her helpless brood,
> Her breast by anxious care disturbed,
>   And throbbing with solicitude;
> So, tossed upon the restless deep,
>   My spirit, doomed afar to roam,
> Flies swiftly, robbed of rest and sleep,
>   To that all-hallowed spot — sweet home."

Yes, dear Helen, in thought, fancy, spirit, I am with you at all hours, and the dear children whom God has given us.

On Monday, we spoke the packet-ship St. Patrick, 28 days from Liverpool for New-York, with an immense number of cabin and steerage passengers. She sent her boat alongside, and gave us some English newspapers. I tried to write a hasty letter to you, and did so, but lost my chance by a single minute, as the boat went off in a very few moments. Perhaps I shall be able to send this by some chance conveyance. If not, I shall forward it to you from Liverpool, with another announcing our arrival. You must not neglect writing to me, and giving me such details of family affairs and domestic events as you may judge will be interesting to me. Your letters shall be destroyed as soon as read, if that assurance will induce you to write more frequently. After your confinement, let me have a letter from some one of the household without delay. In that hour of trial, may you have all needed fortitude, and be safely delivered.

I think a great deal of my dear children, and long to hear their pleasant voices — more vocal to my spirit than the melody of birds. But I must leave you all in the hands of Him who is infinitely wise and good, trusting that we shall all meet around the family board again, before the month of September shall have entirely passed away. Distribute my affectionate remembrances among all at home, and all inquiring friends, and never for a moment doubt the fidelity and affection of

Your faithful and loving husband,

Wm. Lloyd Garrison.

ALS: Garrison Papers, Boston Public Library. A portion is printed in *The Liberator,* July 31, 1840.

1. Luke 22:42.

2. Captain Thomas B. Cropper (born c. 1810; d. San Francisco, 1855), of Accomac county, Virginia, was a captain on the Liverpool Black Ball Line. At various times, he was captain of the *Columbus,* the *New York II,* and the *Isaac Webb.* He was "one of six captains to receive gold medals from the British government for heroic services in which the lives of 64 men from British vessels were saved in November of 1840." (Robert G. Albion, *Square Riggers on Schedule,* Princeton University Press., Princeton, N.J., 1938, p. 334; letter to Louis Ruchames, dated November 10, 1969, from Mark G. Eckhoff, Director, Legislative, Judicial and Diplomatic Records Division, National Archives and Records Service, Washington, D.C.)

The *Columbus* "was built at Newburyport, Massachusetts in 1834. She was a sizable full-rigged ship of 663 tons" and operated between New York and Liverpool from 1834 to 1845. "She was a fair but not a fast sailor, her average for all westward crossings being 36 days. . . . in 1835 [she] took the biggest cargo eastward to Liverpool officially recorded for any transatlantic packet." (Letter to Louis Ruchames, dated October 27, 1969, from Pamela McNulty, Reference Librarian, G. W. Blunt White Library, Mystic Seaport, Marine Historical Association, Inc., Mystic, Conn.)

3. Ephesians 2:12: ". . . having no hope, and without God in the world."

193

TO MARIA W. CHAPMAN

In the Gulf Stream, June 3, 1840.

—— It seems to be settled that we are not to participate largely in the World's Convention. We were detained three days in New-York by a northeasterly storm, and our progress, since we took our departure, has been tedious in the extreme. For the first eight days we had a succession of head winds, so that we were not more than two days good sailing from New-York. This completes our twelfth day, and yet not more than one fourth of our passage is made. What say you to a voyage of forty-eight days? We are consoled, however, by the assurance, that when we shall have passed the Grand Banks, fair winds may be expected to the end of our journey. You must not conclude that our ship is a dull sailer; on the contrary, she can scarcely find a competitor on the ocean. We have already overtaken and passed quick a number of vessels — and have, therefore, the consolation of knowing that we are *progressing* as fast as any vessel could do under similar circumstances, except a steam packet. Still, it is highly probable that the Convention will have nearly closed by the time that we arrive in London. If so, I shall retrace my steps homeward without much delay; for 'my heart is in my native land,'[1] and I long to be at my old post. For some cause or other, which I find is more easily felt than expressed, it has been impressed upon my mind that I could be of more service to the anti-slavery cause by remaining at home, than by going to England; and with the dull prospect now before me, be assured that this impression is deepened. It is for me to do all I can to promote the grand object of my mission, and to leave the event with God. His will I hold to be infinitely paramount to my own, in all things.

[After some remarks upon the influence of the World's Convention upon the emancipation of the colored race universally, Mr. Garrison proceeds:]

But the mere abolition of slavery is not the reconciliation of the world to God, or of man to his brother man; though there can never be any such reconciliation without it. I want to see a World's Convention that shall have for its object the recognition and approval of Jesus, the Messiah, as the only King and Ruler on earth — the establishment of his kingdom to the subversion of all others — the prostration of all national barriers, castes, and boundaries — the mingling of the whole human race, 'like kindred drops into one'[2] — the forgiveness of enemies, without any resort to brute force, even after the example of Christ — the overthrow of all military and naval power, by the substitution of spiritual for carnal weapons — the adoption of a common language, to the suppression of the Babel dialects which now divide and curse mankind. Such a Convention I hope to see and attend before this mortal shall have put on immortality. It will produce a mighty sensation throughout the earth, and be more terrible to tyranny and misrule than 'an army with banners.' [3] Seizing upon it by faith, and yearning to behold it as a reality, I am constrained to exclaim,

> 'How long, dear Savior, oh how long
>   Shall that bright hour delay?
> Fly swifter round, ye wheels of time,
>   And bring the welcome day!' [4]

O for the establishment of a pure religion on earth! the religion of peace and good will to all mankind! Let the truth be told, though the whole of Christendom be thereby convicted of infidelity. That religion which can enslave a human being, from any cause or on any pretext whatsoever — which can justify war for the attainment of any good, in self-defence, or as a means of preventing evil — which can punish its enemies by imposing fines, or inflicting imprisonment or death — which relies upon physical force for its safety and prevalence — which denies the equality and oneness of the human race, and divides them into separate castes, conditions and tribes — which graduates human sympathy and love by geographical boundaries and sectional divisions — is essentially and eternally a defective religion, hostile to the spirit of the gospel, and at enmity with the cross of Christ. Yet this is the religion of the United States, of England, of Turkey — of every nation, whether Protestant, Catholic, Mahomedan or Pagan. Christianity must and will supplant it.

June 12. We have had very favorable winds for the last ten days, and are now within four hundred miles of Cape Clear. In four days more we hope to be in Liverpool. To-day the Convention meets in London. May it lay a broad foundation upon which to build the superstructure of Humanity! If it shall exclude from a participation in its proceedings a single human being, on account of complexion or sex, it will excite the pity and amazement of after ages. I am inclined to think it will act upon the 'new organization' basis, and while it will not proscribe color, will make a distinction in sex. If so, there will not be a delegate more forward to condemn such conduct than

Your friend,

WM. LLOYD GARRISON.

Printed in *The Non-Resistant*, August 12, 1840; the part of the letter dated June 12 is reprinted in *Life*, II, 362. The material in brackets was inserted by the editor of *The Non-Resistant*.

1. Garrison was probably thinking of an anonymous poem which was later published in a collection made by George B. Cheever, *The Poets of America* (Hartford, 1850), pp. 252–253. The poem begins:

"My thoughts are in my native land,
My heart is in my native place."

2. William Cowper, *The Task*, Book II, "The Timepiece."
3. The Song of Solomon, 6:4, 10.
4. Unidentified.

194

TO JAMES GARRISON

Near the Grand Banks,⎱
June 4th — noon — 1840.⎰

Dear bro. James:

The sun shines brightly to-day, and, favored by a tolerably fair wind, our ship is gallantly going ahead at the rate of 8 or 9 knots. Our progress, however, since we left New-York, (as the date of this letter sufficiently shows,) has been very slow and tedious. — For the first eight days, we had a succession of head winds, so that we were not more than two days' ordinary sailing from the place of our departure! This day completes our thirteenth day — and yet not one third of our passage is made! This is quite remarkable at this season of the year, when westerly winds are found usually to prevail. You must not infer, that our ship (the Columbus) is a dull sailer: on the contrary, she has never been beaten since she was launched upon the deep. We have already overtaken and passed quite a number of vessels — and have, therefore, the consolation of knowing, that we are getting along as fast as any other vessel, except a steam-packet, could do under similar circumstances. Capt. Cropper says he has never had such luck before. His longest voyage from New-York to Liverpool has never exceeded twenty-two days — his last occupied but sixteen: unless we have uncommon good luck the remainder of our trip, we shall be at least one month between the two ports. Hence, it is highly probable that the World's Convention will have nearly closed its session by the time that we arrive in London. If so, my trip will have been almost in vain, and I shall retrace my steps homewards without much delay — probably by the first of August. I have come hither against my own inclinations, from the first; and now, with such a prospect before me, I sigh to think where I am, and that it is too late to beat a retreat.

Nothing has occurred, of special moment, since we left. We have seen a fair proportion of whales, porpoises, dolphins, &c. but not the sea-serpent. Mother Carey's chickens [1] have followed in our wake on tireless wing. In one day, one of our passengers (a Dr.) ensnared eleven, and stuffed them for preservation. We have had one or two smart gales, but nothing very serious. The Columbus is a tight sea-boat, of about 660 tons burthen, and throws aside the highest waves with all possible ease. In our cabin we have about thirty passengers — very few Americans — mostly English and Scotch. I can almost imagine that I am in the Cave of the Forty Thieves. A more uncongenial set I never was doomed to associate with — and grateful shall I be to see the day that will rid me of their company. Card-playing, gambling, drinking, swearing, and boisterous merriment, constitute the order of the day. It is horrible to my spirit, as well as to dear Rogers' — but in vain do we enter our protest against it. I am sorry to say, that the Captain rather encourages than frowns upon these proceedings.

I seal this letter hastily, as a vessel is approaching, by which I hope to send this letter to you. God bless you! Love to all the dear household at Brooklyn! [2]

Ever your loving brother,

Wm. Lloyd Garrison.

P.S. The vessel proves to be an English brig, called the Emma, of Newport, bound to Portsmouth, N.H. Her captain treated us very shabbily — came within hailing distance, desired to be reported, but asked us no questions, though from the manner in which he came down to us, we supposed he was in distress, and we accordingly altered our course and took in some of our sail, in order to give him all needed aid. He has hoaxed us completely: consequently, passengers very cross.

June 11 — lat. 48, 40 — long. 25, 04.

Since I penned the foregoing pages, we have been favored with favorable winds, and have come with much speed — some of the time, at from 12 to 13 knots an hour. To-day we are averaging 10 or 11, with a quiet sea and a bright sky. The prospect now is that, in four or five days more, we shall be in Liverpool. This makes our twentieth day since we left, but it has seemed to me longer than six months at home. It is quite clear that I was not born to be any thing better than a land-lubber. I doubt whether I shall ever be tempted to cross the Atlantic again, if I shall be spared to reach my native land in safety. Commend me to dry land.

I have thought much about you, dear James, since I left. I am anxious to hear how you are in body and in mind — how you like

Brooklyn, and farming, and the quietude of nature, and every thing that appertains to a coun[try] life. O, how I long to see you not only restored to sound health, but reconciled to God in your spirit! I want to sing praises with you through all eternity, in company with dear mother, and our departed sisters, and with an innumerable host of the wise and good in all ages, now redeemed from sin and the power of the devil. When I consider how mercifully, almost miraculously, God has preserved your life to the present time, I cannot abandon the hope that he will yet pluck you as a brand from the burning, and make you an heir of glory. If we have sinned, and are willing to oonfoss and forsake our sins, he is ready to forgive us. Let his goodness lead us to repentance. His name is Love, and his forbearance, long-suffering and mercy are infinite. Let us not distrust him — despair is suicidal — it is but to follow Christ, to imitate his example, to receive him in faith, and pardon will be vouchsafed to us, and heaven will be our portion. Why should we be fiends, if we may become angels?

My mind is becoming more and more concerned for the poor sailors. Their condition is a pitiable one. They are awfully oppressed, degraded and contemned, as a class. If my life be spared, I will lift up my voice mightily in their behalf. Their wrongs shall be redressed.

My heart throbs violently as I think of dear Helen — the children — friends, and home. Tell my darling first-born, Georgie, that I will bring him some nice presents from London, if he is a good boy, and also some for dear Willie. God grant that we may all be permitted to see each other again on earth, in health, peace and safety, is the prayer of

Your affectionate brother,

W. L. G.

Tuesday, June 16. Have safely arrived in Liverpool, and hope to be in London to-morrow.[3]

ALS: Garrison Papers, Boston Public Library. Printed, in part, in *Life*, II, 362.

1. **Any of** numerous sea birds. The origin of the name is unknown.
2. This paragraph was written in pencil.
3. Penciled along right edge of page.

195

TO AN UNIDENTIFIED CORRESPONDENT

At Sea — lat. 49, 54, long. 20, 45 — June 12, 1840.

The further I find myself removed from you, the nearer do I find yourself to me. You will readily understand this paradox, without any explanation. The bodily separation of true-hearted friends but cements their souls the more closely together. The date of this letter shows you that I am not, this day, where it was my hope to have been when I left New-York — namely, at the opening of the Convention in London. We have now been twenty-one days on our passage, and shall need four or five more of good sailing before we can land at Liverpool. It is not probable, therefore, that we shall be able to take our seats in the Convention much, if any, before Monday, June 22d. We have had 'Jonah's luck' as to head-winds and calms, but, for the last eight days, our speed has been of a galloping character. All things are ordered wisely by Providence, and this conviction makes me very patient and submissive. I cannot better improve a leisure hour to-day, than by addressing a few hasty lines to you, as a token of my friendship. But I warn you that this is no place in which to generate 'thoughts that breathe,' [1] or from which to enunciate 'words that burn.' [2] If my brain be not sea-sick, I am quite sure that my heart is sick of the sea. Not that I love ocean less, but that I love my mother earth more. I am content to be a land-lubber, and no sailor — at least, until there be a second deluge; and then I will go into the ark, if I may be permitted, as a matter of self-preservation. What a multiform thing is habit! Here I am, only three weeks on

'The sea, the sea, the open sea,
The ever bright, the ever free.' [3]

and yet 'sighing like a furnace' [4] to get a glimpse at *terra firma*, and to place my feet upon something more stable than a billowy foundation; — while the first mate of the ship assures me that he is never so contented as when at sea, and cannot spend more than three or four days ashore before he becomes miserable! 'Every one to his trade — every man to his liking.'

Dear Rogers and myself have had our share of sea sickness, but are now in good condition, and expect to be all the better for our voyage — physically better, I mean, and I hope not morally worse; though I assure you that we are in a poor school to improve our morals. If one can derive any benefit from an association, at once constant and inevitable, with men 'whose god is their belly,' [5] whose mouths are an open sepulchre, whose lips are full of profanity and pollution, whose time is consecrated to drinking, card-playing, gambling, and bawling, why then we are favored in an extraordinary manner. This is a faithful description of a large proportion of our cabin passengers. They are all pro-slavery, to the back-bone; one of them boasts of having been engaged in the slave trade, not long since; another, an Englishman, and for many years a resident in

Philadelphia, exults in the burning of Pennsylvania Hall; and all of them agree with our most celebrated doctors of divinity, that slavery is a 'patriarchal' institution, and that, if abolitionists will persist in their work of 'agitation,' they must not complain at any treatment they may receive. To be 'cabined' with such associates, who neither fear God nor regard man, is certainly most unfortunate, and adds immensely to the unpleasantness of our situation. We have borne a faithful testimony against them, but it is only throwing pearls before swine.

You may easily conceive that, what with sea-sickness, and what with the uproar of these excitable 'gentlemen,' — added to my growing aversion to pen, ink and paper, — I have not felt in a mood to read or write since my embarkation. The only journal I have kept has been written upon my memory, not upon paper or parchment. I remember that, day after day, we had head-winds or were becalmed; that, sometimes, the ocean 'slept like an unweaned child,' and anon 'lifted up its voice on high'; that we have spoken two vessels, and seen several others; that we have seen several whales, porpoises, dolphins, &c. &c.; that we have caught and stuffed (not eaten) several of mother Cary's chickens; that we have had one or two rough days, but generally very beautiful weather; that we have acted the boy, and sent a large kite heavenward, till it looked no bigger than a paper bird, (if you can imagine the size;) that, in the Gulf Stream, our thermometer stood at 80 and upwards, and on the Grand Banks at 40 and 45; — and all these things, and others equally important and marvellous, I might have duly and succinctly chronicled in a journal, from day to day as they transpired, but I have chosen to give you a specimen only, and the remainder must, alas! be lost to you and the world.

Extract: printed in *The Liberator*, July 31, 1840.

This item and several others, dated "Within sight of land, June 14, 1840"; "320 miles from Liverpool, June 14, 1840"; "Monday morning, June 15"; "Near Hollyhead, 70 miles from Liverpool, Monday afternoon, June 15, 1840 — 5 o'clock"; "London, June 29, 1840"; and "July 3" were printed in *The Liberator*, July 31, 1840, with the following introductory remarks: "From a number of private letters, written by Mr. Garrison since his embarkation for England, we have copied the following extracts, presuming that the space they will occupy in the Liberator could be filled with nothing more gratifying to our numerous readers. We copy according to the order of the respective dates."

1. Thomas Gray, *The Progress of Poesy*, Part III, Stanza 3, line 4.
2. *Ibid.*
3. Barry Cornwall (Bryan Waller Procter), 1787–1874, "The Sea." Cornwall's poem reads somewhat differently:

> "The Sea! the sea! the open sea!
> The blue, the fresh, the ever free!"

His *English Songs and Other Smaller Poems* was published in England in 1832.

He wrote a biography of Charles Lamb in 1864 and was a member of the circle of Lamb, Hazlitt, and Leigh Hunt. He earned his livelihood as a solicitor in London. (E.E.)

4. Shakespeare, *As You Like It*, II, vii.
5. Philippians 3:19.

196

TO EDMUND QUINCY

At Sea, June 13th, 1840

My dear Quincy:

There are more flowers, and blossoms, and trees, on your beautiful little estate in Dorchester, than I have yet seen on this great circular and apparently interminable Atlantic; though I have been travelling, with all attainable speed, for the space of twenty two days. But then, your Charles River must succumb to "this great and wide sea, wherein are things innumerable, both small and great." [1] Its dolphins, and porpoises, and whales, are insignificant monsters, in comparison with such as hover about my trackless path. We are now going at the rate of twelve knots an hour — but still it is "water, water, every where." [2] Around me is as perfect a deluge as ever Noah beheld; for I hesitate not to affirm, that his vision extended no further than does my own. He may have been, moreover, near-sighted — and so am I; but he could not have had so excellent a pair of spectacles as now bestride my nose — for there was no optician in his day equal to Pierce in Washington Street. Besides, he was not furnished with a spy-glass, which gives extension to the watery waste, and widens the dome of heaven at its base; and therefore the deluge which he saw was no great affair, after all. In some respects, the inmates of his Ark were more curious and odd than those which swarm in the one in which it is my lot to be enclosed. Nevertheless, we have beasts, both wild and tame; but the mischief is, that the former occupy the cabin, and the former [3] are confined to the long boat. We have a cow, sheep, pigs, turkeys, geese, ducks, hens, &c. &c.; and their company is infinitely to be preferred to that of the creeping things, and "slow bellies," [4] and wild cattle, which, in the shape of human bipeds, thrust themselves upon me for companionship. Now and then we see a ship in the distance, which makes a very beautiful landscape, as a fanciful son of the Emerald Isle is reputed to have written to a friend, when for the first time, he found himself out of sight of land, and discovered a sail ahead. Should the wind continue fair, we hope to tread upon dry land in the course of three days. We abound in vultures, but have no dove to send out, to bring us information respecting the abatement of the waters; but the refusal of Mother Carey's chickens any longer to keep company with us is a cheering indication of "Land O"!

You see, by the gaiety of this epistle, that moping Melancholy and myself are not on very friendly terms. Still, my disappointment is none the less real, on finding myself this day "at sea," instead of occupying a seat in the World's Convention, which began its session yesterday. If sighing or crying would remedy the matter, I would put myself at once into the melting mood, and make the ocean my debtor; but it will not, and hence my philosophy teaches me to be patient and serene. I am so small an atom in this great Universe, that it is of very little importance to what point of the compass I may float. I have consented to come on my present mission against my own convictions, and with a sincere distrust of my ability to sustain its responsibilities. There are those, no doubt, on both sides of the Atlantic, who would rejoice if brother Rogers and myself should be detained by adverse winds until the dissolution of the Convention; but there are probably more who will regret our absence from it. The former will have no just cause for exultation; and the latter may console themselves with the reflection, that — all things are wisely ordered by Providence.

My mind has been greatly exercised on the subject of non-resistance since I left New York. It magnifies itself wonderfully as I reflect upon it. It is full of grandeur, sublimity, glory. It is a mine, the riches of which are inexhaustible; an ocean of disinterested benevolence, at once shoreless and fathomless. Aside from it, there is no such thing as our being "crucified unto the world, and the world unto us." [5] It is the consummation of the Gospel of peace, for it is that perfect reconciliation which the Messiah died to make between God and Man, and among the whole human race. It makes babes and fools more sagacious and intelligent than the wisest statesmen, the deepest Philosophers, and the most acute political economists, — Its principles and doctrines receive the cordial detestation of all that is selfish, ambitious, violent and lustful on earth. A notable proof of this has been given in this ship. Our passengers (a profane, lewd, gambling, brandy-loving company, with scarcely an exception) scoff at the idea of non-resistance, as the crucifiers of the Son of God railed at him upon the Cross. They cannot find words to express their contempt and abhorrence of it! And not less heartily do they despise the *Niggars* and the Abolitionists, and all such fanatics; and it is difficult to decide, whether they regard Slavery or "the powers that be" with the greater admiration — though as far as they can do so, with impunity, they do not hesitate to trample all law, both human and divine, under their feet! Let the same test be applied among the desperately wicked throughout the Globe, and their verdict will be the same.

I have brought six bound volumes of the Non-Resistant with me but regret that I have no loose copies of the paper for distribution in war making, glory loving England.

Dear Rogers enjoins upon me to give his affectionate regards to you and yours. We have "taken sweet counsel together" [6] and mingled our sympathies and joys in common. My situation would be intolerably irksome without his company. We wish you to remember both of us kindly to all enquiring friends, of whom we can feelingly say —

"Though out of sight, still in remembrance dear." [7]

My special regards to Mrs. Quincy, and a kiss for each of your children —

Yours affectionately,

Wm. Lloyd Garrison.

London, June 30, 1840.

My dear Quincy — The original of the foregoing scrawl is in the possession of a friend, who, for a particular purpose, has given me this copy as a substitute. The Convention is over, and its proceedings will be duly put into your hands by means of the press. It refused to allow the women delegates from the U.S. a place among the other delegates, and, consequently, Rogers and myself, with C. L. Remond and Wm. Adams of Pawtucket, declined taking seats in the same. The rebuke we thus gave is making a deep and salutary impression upon the public mind. We have been most hospitably entertained.

W. L. G.

Transcript sent by Garrison with ALS of June 30 (last paragraph): Smith College Library.

1. Psalms 104:25.
2. Samuel Taylor Coleridge, *The Rime of the Ancient Mariner*, Part II.
3. So in manuscript.
4. Titus 1:12.
5. A variation of Galatians 6:14.
6. Psalms 55:14.
7. George Linley (1798–1865), "Song. Attr. to Linley. *Notes and Queries*, Ser. 5, Vol. X, p. 417" (*Oxford Dictionary of Quotations*, second edition, p. 314), The original reads, "Tho' lost to sight, to mem'ry dear/ Thou ever wilt remain."

197

TO HELEN E. GARRISON

Within sight of land, June 14, 1840.

My dear Wife:

I take up my pen hastily, to commune with you to the extent of a letter-sheet. Since I penned a few lines to you in the Gulf Stream, nothing of special importance has occurred to break the monotony of a sea voyage. Our passengers (of whom I complained) have not improved either in their manners or morals, and most cordially hate me for the burning rebukes which I have faithfully administered to them. Unspeakably happy as I should be to enjoy your society at the present time, I have felt thankful that you did not accompany me; for no virtuous woman could tolerate, for one moment, the language and conduct of such immoral creatures. Not a good thought, not a sensible remark, has fallen from any of their lips since we started; but swearing, drinking and smoking have been the order of the day. Fortunately, we have been highly favored as to wind and weather, for the last ten days, and have almost made amends for our first twelve days of ill-luck. It would have made your heart glad to see how swiftly we ploughed the great deep; for, though the distance between us is widening momently, yet it only serves the sooner to bring us together. And, O! how my soul yearns to be again by your side! All last night, I lay in my birth,[1] unable to obtain the least repose, and thinking of you, your situation, the children, home, and friends. This I have done repeatedly, till my heart has been borne down by the rush of tumultuous emotions, and the weight of affectionate longings. In airy visions I embrace you, but feel only the more wretched as I awake to a sense of my loneliness. "What has become of your philosophy?" you may rationally inquire. I have enough of it left to be resigned to my lot, but not enough to cure me of home-sickness. Dear Helen, I can truly affirm, that I have never absented myself one hour from you as a matter of choice, but only as duty and friendship imperatively demanded the sacrifice. The strength of my love you will probably never fully know; for I am not accustomed to the use of fond terms, and feel a thousand fold more than I can express. Sometimes you have hinted that I was too ready to go away from home; and such a charge would have made me often very unhappy, if I could have persuaded myself that you meant it as a reproach. I have always excused it on the ground of your affection for me, which I know to be pure and intense; and happy am I that my presence at all times is a delight to your heart. It seems to me as if a large part of the year had passed away since our separation; but it will not be five weeks until to-morrow! How like lightning flashes would those five weeks have passed, at home! But now, every hour "drags its slow length along,"[2] and weeks are months. But a truce to complaint.

The weather has been very fine, as a general thing, and the sea far from being boisterous, except in two or three instances, when we have had moderate gales of wind: — I say *moderate* gales; for though they may have seemed somewhat impassioned to us who have never been caught on the ocean by a real hurricane, yet, in the eyes of old seamen, they amounted to just nothing at all. Yesterday was, perhaps, the most *unsteady* day we have encountered. Our noble ship had a stern encounter with many a ruffian billow, whose staggering blows made her shake from stem to stern. It was a stormy night last night, but this morning the sun has risen in full-orbed effulgence, the wind sets in the right quarter, the sea is briskly tumultuous, and our ship goes bounding like an Arabian steed toward the land, the dim outlines of which now faintly appear in the distance, to the joy of all on board. It is Cape Clear, the very extremity of the Irish coast. We have now a fair prospect of being in Liverpool on Tuesday, which will make our passage twenty-five days.

To-day is the Catholic, Protestant, Jewish Sabbath, but not the Christian. It makes the fourth I have spent on the bosom of the Atlantic. Happily, the God I worship is no longer to be reverently approached at particular times and seasons, or by any outward forms or ceremonies; — but, in Christ Jesus, he has broken every outward yoke: therefore, I allow no man to judge me in meat or drink, or in respect to a holy day, or the new moon, or the sabbath; for having, as I humbly hope, obtained the substance, I do not need the shadow. Happily, too, neither at Jerusalem, nor on the mountain of Samaria, nor in any meeting-house, (whether "orthodox" or "heterodox,") are we required to be found, at any time or for any reason, to render acceptable worship to the Most High.

Painful and almost impracticable as it is to write under the peculiar circumstances which surround me, this letter will make the seventh *[3] (closely written) which I shall have completed since I recovered from my sea-sickness — namely, two for you, — one for Francis Jacks[on] — one for Edmund Quincy, — one for Mrs. Chapman, — one for Wm. M. Chace, — and one for bro. James at Brooklyn, of the state of whose health I am extremely anxious to hear. Will you

---

* Add three more to the number.[4]

not give me some credit for resolution and perseverance? I shall write letters to bro. Johnson on my arrival at Liverpool, and send the whole package by the packet-ship which is to leave for New-York on Friday next, the 19th instant. It is doubtful whether they will arrive as soon by this conveyance, as they would if they were forwarded by the British Queen, which sails from London on the 1st of July; but there will not be much difference, probably, between the two. You may expect to receive letters from me by the latter, when I hope to be able to give you a sketch of the proceedings of the Convention. I understand that the Great Western will sail from Bristol for New-York on the 1st of August; in which Rogers and myself propose to embark for home, but may see cause to alter our minds hereafter.

By this time I conclude that you have passed through the perils of child-bed.[5] Would that some carrier-pigeon could bring me swift intelligence of the result! I cannot but hope that all has gone well with you and the new-born babe. The idea of having a third child, to be called my own, is almost as pleasing and novel to me as it was at the prospect of the birth of dear little Georgie. Should I hear good tidings from you, perhaps my Muse may manufacture some verses in honor of the new comer; though I ought first, in order, to celebrate the advent of my little paragon, Willie Wallie. Well, he shall not be forgotten. I shall love all my children, (and mine are thine, dearest,) equally well. Take heed to yourself that you do not take cold; and, in case of sickness, use your Thompsonian medicines in preference to any others. Dear sister Anne will know how to administer them. Within three hundred miles from Liverpool, and three thousand from New-York, I send on the wings of the wind a thousand kisses for you and the children, my dearest regards to mother and Anne, my kindest remembrances to Mr. and Mrs. Johnson, my compliments to Mr. and Mrs. Knight, Catharine, &c. &c.

> Your loving husband,
> Wm. Lloyd Garrison.

ALS: Massachusetts Historical Society. Printed, in part, in *Life*, II, 362–364.

1. Garrison's spelling.
2. Alexander Pope (1688–1744), English poet, "An Essay on Criticism."
3. Garrison initially wrote "eighth," then crossed it out and wrote "seventh" above it.
4. Written by Garrison in pencil.
5. The Garrisons' third child, named Wendell Phillips, was born on June 4, 1840.

198

TO AN UNIDENTIFIED CORRESPONDENT

320 miles from Liverpool, June 14, 1840.

'Land O!' is the animating cry on deck; and, sure enough, there is Cape Clear right ahead of us, at some distance, and in a rather misty condition; so that it is by no means as *clear* as our sight is disposed to demand. In a very short time, however, the entire elevation will be made manifest to the dullest vision. As you may readily imagine, all our passengers are much exhilarated by the prospect; especially as our voyage has been one week longer than we anticipated at the time of our embarkation. But, as I believe you have never been out of sight of your mother earth, you cannot fully understand how cheering is the shout of 'Land O!' All eyes are strained to trace the dim outlines of the coast, as though it had been suddenly cast up from the bottom of the deep by a mighty earthquake — a new creation emerging from another universal deluge! Every house, every tree, every object, will be scanned with intense interest. The ocean is not a fit place for a residence; and few there are who exchange it reluctantly for *terra firma*, if they have been tossed upon its billows for any considerable time. I do not include seamen in this category, because

> 'Their march is o'er the mountain wave,
> Their home is on the deep.' — [1]

though very many of them would gladly follow some other employment, if they knew what to do. We have now a fair prospect of being in Liverpool on Tuesday; though vessels are sometimes a week, and even a fortnight, in going up the channel. The distance is more frequently run in forty-eight hours. Of course, every thing depends upon the wind; and who or what, whether on the land or the sea, that has a fair wind, cannot make progress?

✿   ✿   ✿   ✿   ✿

The place at which the packet-ship Albion was wrecked a few years ago, and nearly every soul on board was lost, may now be faintly discerned in the distance. It is invariably inquired for by all travellers on this route, and will probably be regarded with melancholy interest during the present century. Strange that such an event should excite more commiseration than the slaughter of a hecatomb of human beings upon the field of battle! Surely, it is cause for far greater lamentation to see men voluntarily engaged in the awful work of self-destruction, than to behold them whelmed in the deep 'by the visitation of God.'

We are now directly opposite to Cork, but at too great a distance from it to see it even in miniature. A fishing-boat, having on board three or four wretched looking Irishmen and as many squalid boys, is bearing down upon us for the purpose of selling us some fresh fish. Not being able to keep up with the speed of our ship, we have thrown them a rope, and are thus towing them along until we can make an exchange (by means of the rope) of some corned beef and pork for some fine flounders and haddock. Both parties appear to be well pleased with their bargain. I have just excited the hot indignation of a medicinal doctor on board, (an otherwise intelligent but profligate Englishman,) because, on his declaring that every haddock bore the mark of the fingers of Jesus, ever since Peter made his memorable draught of fishes, I pleasantly pronounced it 'a fish story' — not supposing, for one moment, that he gave credence to so ridiculous a fable, for he is no Catholic. He instantly took fire at my 'impeachment of his veracity' — said the miracle was as duly authenticated as any other performed by the Saviour — admonished me that we were drawing near his native land, and that it behooved me to be careful how I came across his track — and with a menacing air gave me to understand, that if I were a non-resistant, he was not! All this would have been quite ludicrous, had he not been in his cups. It is proper to add, that I have excited his animosity, as well as that of others in the cabin, on various occasions, on account of my reprobating the use of brandy, whisky, wine, and every other intoxicating drink — profane language — gambling, &c.

A Philadelphia packet-ship (which sailed two or three days before the Columbus) is just ahead us, and looks 'for all the world' like a fine large dwelling house afloat, with chimneys, windows, and other appurtenances. The illusion, at this distance, is complete, and not less curious than unique. We are fast gaining upon her, however, and shall soon alter her 'questionable shape.' [2] As yet, we have distanced every competitor.

I am very much struck with the unerring precision of nautical skill and science. Here we have come some three thousand miles across a trackless ocean, and have been for three weeks out sight of land — yet aiming, all the while, for Cape Clear; and, lo! the first object that meets our eyes is the Cape, the immediate approach to which was foretold by our captain half an hour before it became visible to any on board. This closely approximates to the perfection of knowledge.

The abridgment of my liberty, and the company with which I

have been compelled to associate, since the 22d ultimo, make me a more earnest advocate of immediate emancipation than ever. My day of jubilee I hope is at hand. It shall be my first object, as soon as I touch that soil which sets every captive free, to assist in liberating all who pine in slavery throughout the globe.

Extract: printed in *The Liberator*, July 31, 1840. The name of the person to whom this letter was addressed is not given.

1. A variation of Thomas Campbell (1777–1844), English poet, "Ye Mariners of England."

2. *Hamlet*, I, iv.

199

TO HELEN E. GARRISON

Monday morning, June 15, 1840.

Dear Helen:

Providence is smiling upon us most benignly. Since I finished my scrawl to you of yesterday, every thing appertaining to sky, air and water has been of the most delightful character. We are now within 125 miles of Liverpool, with a tranquil sea, and going at the rate of 8 or 10 knots an hour; so that there is scarcely a doubt that we shall be walking in the streets of Liverpool in the course of twenty-four hours. But there is a homely adage, "Do not halloo until you get out of the woods" — and another to this effect, "There is many a slip between the cup and the lip" — so I will not allow myself to be too sanguine on this point. Should we not be disappointed, however, we shall remain to-morrow night in Liverpool, and on Wednesday morning take the cars for London, which will soon carry us to "the capital city of mankind." Last night it was very beautiful — the moon shone brightly, illuminating the joyous sea with its beams, pouring a radiant tide of light upon our gallant bark, and revealing to us in the distance the outlines of the Irish coast — and the stars looked down upon us with their angelic eyes, as if to steal away our hearts — and the waves chanted melodious music — and "all went merry as a marriage bell." [1] Feelingly I exclaimed with the poet —

"Most glorious night! thou wast not made for slumber!" [2]

and so I continued to pace the deck until a late hour, musing upon many things, and now and then giving a yearning look toward the blue West, where lies the dearest home of all the homes on earth — i. e. the dearest to *me*. At midnight, I threw myself into my birth, and found (what I could not the night previous) repose and sleep. The morning has broken upon us splendidly. I begin to feel as if I were not wholly lost to mankind, and could be of some little service to somebody in this suffering world. God grant that my mission to England may not be in vain! My weakness is perfect, but his strength is infinite; my judgment fallible — his wisdom unerring; my ignorance excessive — his knowledge vast and exhaustless. Aid me, O God, at this crisis! Make my tongue as the pen of a ready writer; fill my mind with great and good thoughts; give me a double portion of thy grace; and exert over me a loving mastery in all things!

I have been reading to dear Rogers the following exquisite poetical tribute, taken from "The Mirror of Literature, Amusement, and In-struction" [3] — and as it is expressive of the feelings of my heart in view of an incident which I trust has safely transpired, for the third time, at home, I cannot deny myself the pleasure of copying it, my love, for your perusal — not doubting that you will be as much pleased with it as I have been.

TO A NEW VISITANT. by J. H. Wiffen.[4]
"Welcome, dear child, with all a father's blessing,
  To thy new sphere of motion, light, and life!
After the long suspense, the fear distressing,
  Love's strong, subduing strife.

Sealed with the smile of Him who made the Morning,
  Though to the matron charge of Eve consigned,
Com'st thou, my radiant babe, the mystic dawning
  Of one more deathless mind.

'Tis a strange world, they say, and full of trouble,
  Wherein thy destined course is to be run:
Where joy is deemed a shadow, peace a bubble,
  And true bliss known to none.

Yet to high destinies it leads, — to natures
  Glorious, and pure, and beautiful, and mild, —
Shapes all impassive to decay, with features
  Lovelier than thine, fair child!

To winged Beatitudes, for ever tending,
  Rank above rank, to the bright source of bliss,
And, in ecstatic vision tranced, still blending
  Their grateful love with His.

Then, if thou'rt launched in this benign direction,
  We will not sorrow that thy porch is past: —
Come! many a picture waits thy young inspection,
  Each lovelier than the last.

What shall it be? On Earth, in Air, in Ocean,
    A thousand things are sparkling, to excite
Thy hope, thy fear, joy, wonder, or devotion,
    Heiress of rich delight.

Wilt thou, when Reason has her star implanted
    On thy fair brow, with Galileo soar?
Rove with Linneus through the woods, or haunted
    Be by more charmed lore?

Shall sky-taught Painting, with her ardent feeling,
    Her rainbow pencil to thy hand commit?
Or shall the quivered spells be thine, revealing
    The polished shafts of Wit?

Or, to thy fascinated eye, her mirror
    Shall the witch Poesy delight to turn,
And strike thee warm to every brilliant error
    Glanced from her magic urn?

Heed her not, darling! she will smile benignly,
    So she may win thine inexperienced ear;
But the fond tales she warbles so divinely,
    Will cost thee many a tear.

She has a Castle, where, in death-like slumbers,
    Full of wild dreams, she casts her slaves; some break,
After long hurt, their golden chains; but numbers
    Never with sense awake.

She it was, dear, who in Greek story acted
    Such tragic masques; who, in the grape's disguise,
Choked sweet Anacreon, Sappho's soul distracted,
    And seared old Homer's eyes:

Tasso she tortured; Savage unbefriended;
    O'er Falconer's bones the matted sea-weed spread;
Chatterton poisoned; Otway starved; and blended
    White with the early dead!

She too, with many a smile, thy sire has flattered,
    Promising flowers, and fame, and guerdons rare;
Till youth was past, and then, he found, she scattered
    Her vows and wreaths in air.

Shun, then, the Syren! spurn her laurelled chalice,
    Though the bright nectar dance above the brim;
Lest she should seize thee in her mood of malice,
    And tear thee limb from limb!

But, to selecter influences, my beauty,
  Pay thy young vows, — to Truth, that ne'er beguiles,
Virtue, fixed Faith, and unpretending Duty,
  Whose frowns beat Fancy's smiles!

Look on me, love, that in these radiant glasses
  Thy future tastes and fortunes I may trace; —
O'er them alternate shade and sunshine passes,
  Enhancing every grace.

Peace is there yet, and purity, and pleasure;
  With a fond yearning o'er the leaves I look;
But the lid falls — farewell the enchanting treasure!
  Closed is the starry book!"

Yours, ever, W. L. G.[5]

ALS: Garrison Papers, Boston Public Library. Also printed, in part, in *The Liberator*, July 31, 1840.

1. George Gordon Byron, Lord Byron (1788–1824), *Childe Harold's Pilgrimage*, Canto III, stanza xxi.
2. *Ibid.*, Canto III, stanza xciii.
3. A monthly magazine published in London from 1822 to June 1847.
4. Jeremiah Holmes Wiffen (1792–1836), English author, poet, translator of Tasso, and librarian at Woburn Abbey (*DNB*).
5. Written in pencil.

200

TO HELEN E. GARRISON

Near Hollyhead, 70 miles from
Liverpool, Monday afternoon, June 15, 1840 — 5 *o'clock.*

My beloved Helen:

I again seize my pen to fill up another sheet for your perusal, which will be the last you may expect from me until after my arrival in London — if, peradventure, we shall be permitted to reach Liverpool in safety. I say *if* — for, within an hour, our situation has been changed from one of apparent security to one of very great peril. For the last week, we have been favored so remarkably as to wind and weather, that I was led to say to Capt. Cropper to-day noon, that, if they had been placed under his control, he could not have fashioned them more to his mind. Since morning, up to the time at which I am now writing, our speed has been swift, to an extraordinary degree; and at this moment, aided by a strong current, it is very great. But a violent gale has suddenly set in, accompanied by a dense fog, and our path is momently becoming more and more perilous. We are close in the neighborhood of Hollyhead, a high rocky elevation, to pass which, safely, will require no little seamanship, as we are situated; and it is evident that our captain (than whom no one can easily be found better qualified to meet such an emergency) regards it as a serious matter. The noisy uproar of our dinner-table has given place to a silent concern for the issue, and every countenance wears a grave aspect. Our danger lies not so much in the gale, as in the fog; for, with clear weather, every rock and shoal could be discerned, and avoided without much difficulty. It is peculiarly trying to be shrouded in a thick mist at the very moment when light and vision are most needed.

6 o'clock P.M. Both the wind and fog are increasing, but we have passed Hollyhead in safety. We have escaped one danger, however, only to encounter others equally formidable; for the navigation up the channel is continually growing more intricate and difficult, all the way to Liverpool. Happily, we are expecting soon to obtain a pilot — and who is to be compared to "the pilot who weathers the storm"?[1] Perhaps the fog will prevent our being seen. One thing is certain: without a pilot, there will not be much quietude of mind among our passengers to-night. We have shortened sail, and retarded the speed of our ship, and are proceeding onward with all possible wariness.

7 o'clock. The gale continues, but now and then the fog clears up, so that we are enabled to ascertain our position. The Welsh mountains are on our right, and, with their robes of mist, look grim and spectre-like. All eyes are strained to discern a pilot-boat, and, to our great relief, one is seen bearing down upon us. A ship is just ahead of us, also waiting for a pilot. The boat is now along side of her, and has supplied her with one. Will she see our signal? — and, if so, can she also accommodate us in the same manner? Here she comes — and now she takes a wide circuit, passes us, and evidently is not prepared to give us any aid. A new and sad sensation is beginning to be felt. Our ship is now "laying to." I can now understand why it is that seamen dread to be embayed in a storm, and infinitely prefer to be on the ocean, in such an emergency, where they can find plenty of sea-room.

8 o'clock. Another pilot-boat comes dancing over the waves to the wild music of the gale, and is evidently intending to reach us. Now she makes a circuit around us, having a light skiff or wherry floating at her stern, with the pilot and two or three oarsmen in it, ready to be cast off, that he may be put on board; now it is alongside — and now the man of all men, at this crisis, leaps on to the deck — and now we all breathe freely once more. It is astonishing to see how in-

stantaneous has been the relief afforded by his presence. Once more we are under weigh, slowly and cautiously. All at once, too, we are in the midst of a great hubbub! The pilot has brought a copy of the Liverpool Chronicle of June 13, in which are detailed, at great length, the particulars of an attempt to assassinate Queen Victoria and her husband Prince Albert, by a youth only 17 years of age, named Edward Oxford. As these particulars will be spread before you in the Boston papers quite as soon as the contents of this sheet will meet your eye, I will not attempt to make even a synopsis of them here. Suffice it to say, the mad attempt at murder proved abortive. As a large proportion of our passengers are Englishmen, the news created no little sensation in their breasts; but when, on reading the account aloud at their request, I came to the statement, that "the prisoner's father was a mulatto, and his grandfather was a black," they yelled like so many fiends broke loose from the bottomless pit — (remember! they have been to America, and have got the *virus* of slavery and prejudice infused into their veins!) — swore that Oxford "ought to be strung up, without judge or jury, and cut in pieces," in true Lynch law style — the whole "nigger race" made to suffer for so foul an act, ay, and all those who are disposed to act as their advocates! I have seldom seen so horrid an exhibition of fiendish exultation and murderous malignity. It was useless, of course, to attempt to argue the matter, especially as some of them were none the better for strong drink. Why it is any worse for a colored man or boy to perpetrate a crime than for a white one, I have never been able to understand. I ventured to remind one of the most violent, who was in favor of killing Oxford *instanter*, without any trial, that the law presumed every person to be innocent until he is proved to be guilty, and that it was possible, nay probable, that the lad was deranged; but he scouted it all, and declared that it was *not possible* that he could be insane. O no! Because he had some colored blood in his veins! For a colored person, who does wrong, to be insane at the time, is an impossibility! More was made of this affair, because bros. Grosvenor, Rogers and myself were known to be abolitionists, on our way to attend the World's Convention. Poor creatures! they know not what they do. Their hearts are full of the spirit of murder, while they are professing to be horror-struck in view of an attempt to commit murder! Well, let them rave, and let all the enemies of the colored race shriek in concert. "He that sitteth in the heavens shall laugh; the Lord shall have them in derision;"[2] — and, peradventure, they may yet find, that "it is a fearful thing to fall into the hands of the living God"[3] — the God of the oppressed — the God of justice! One of them said that he should not have cared if it had been an attempt to assassinate Daniel O'Connell! They all cordially detest O'Connell, because he is an "agitator" and an "abolitionist."

10 o'clock. The gale has abated, but, in consequence of the hazy state of the atmosphere, our ship will lay to during the night. We expect to be in the dock by 10 o'clock to-morrow morning.

Past midnight. The aspect of the sky is dark and wild, and the wind begins to rise in its strength; but, fatigued with writing, and by the events of the day, I seek my birth, in order to snatch a few hours of rest.

Tuesday morning, 11 o'clock. Safely arrived at Liverpool! *Laus Deo!* I feel very grateful for all the mercies that have been vouch-safed to us on our passage. We are all now grouped together in the Custom House waiting to have our trunks examined. I have just heard that all our anti-slavery friends, who preceded us, have arrived, and are now in London. We shall be there tomorrow afternoon, *Deo volente.* O for an opportunity to obtain rest — rest — rest!

It is pleasant once more to tread upon the solid earth. For the second time in my life, I am "a *foreigner*" — and yet there is not a man upon the surface of the globe, whom I am not willing to recognize as "a man and a brother." [4] Let all geographical distinctions between nations cease, so far as they serve to divide the human family into castes, and let love abound universally.[5] Wishing to be affectionately remembered to all inquiring friends, I remain, my love,

Yours devotedly,

Wm. Lloyd Garrison.

ALS: Garrison Papers, Boston Public Library. Also printed, in part, in *The Liberator,* July 31, 1840.

In the original manuscript, "My beloved Helen" is crossed out, probably for publication in *The Liberator,* where the salutation is omitted.

1. George Canning (1770–1827), English statesman and poet, "Song for the Inauguration of the Pitt Club, 25 May 1802."

2. Psalms 2:4.

3. Hebrews 10:31.

4. "Am I not a man and a brother?" was the legend on the medallion designed by Josiah Wedgwood, and adopted as the seal of the London Anti-Slavery Society.

5. The remainder of this letter is crossed out, probably for publication. It is omitted in *The Liberator.*

2 0 1

TO HELEN E. GARRISON

London, June 29, 1840.

My dear Helen:

I have now been in London eleven days, and, for the first time since my arrival, take up my pen to send you a hasty epistle by the British Queen — having been too busy to despatch any letters home until now. Accompanying this, you will receive several others, which were written during my voyage to Liverpool, and which would have been forwarded to you from that port, had I not supposed that they would reach you sooner by the B. Q. than by the packet-ship. If bro. Johnson shall feel disposed to make any extracts from them, for the Liberator, or from any of the letters I have sent to other friends, he can do so. It will not be possible for me to write much for the paper directly.

The first thing which you and the household, and all our anti-slavery friends, will wish to hear about, is the Convention. On the score of respectability, talent and numbers, it deserves much consideration; but it was sadly deficient in freedom of thought, speech and action, having been under the exclusive management of the London Committee, whose dominion was recognized as absolute. At the opening of the Convention, Wendell Phillips moved that the female delegates from the U. S. be admitted to seats therein; which motion he sustained in a spirited manner, and was followed by Bradburn and Prof. Adam,[1] and one or two others, on the same side. It was rejected, however, by a very large majority, on the ground of custom and usage. George Thompson deprecated its introduction, and urged Wendell to withdraw it! All this was some days before our arrival. As soon as we learnt the result, — and, especially, that the London Committee assumed to take the management of affairs into their own hands, we (i.e. Rogers, Remond, Wm. Adams of Pawtucket, and myself,) refused to take a seat in the Convention, or to enrol our names on the list of delegates. This created much uneasiness on the part of that body, and no pains were spared to seduce us from our position; but we remained inflexible to the end — looking on, as silent spectators, from the galleries, from day to day.

I am quite certain, from all that has transpired, that, had we arrived a few days before the opening of the Convention, we could have carried our point triumphantly. As it is, we have not visited this country in vain. The "woman question" has been fairly started, and will be canvassed from the Land's End to John o'Groat's house.[2]

Already, many excellent and noble minds are highly displeased at the decision of the Convention, and denounce it strongly. The new organizers have done what they could to injure us, and have succeeded in creating some prejudice against us, especially on the part of the clergy; but the effect will be temporary. We have all been treated with the utmost respect and hospitality, and invitations to go here and there are pouring in upon us from all quarters. An excellent Protest [3] against the exclusion of women was drawn up by Prof. Adam, and signed by himself, Phillips, Bradburn, Mott, Col. Miller,[4] &c., and presented to the Convention, which, on motion of Colver, seconded by Scoble, was laid on the table, and refused a place among the printed proceedings! We, who refused to connect ourselves with the Convention, shall have a separate Protest of our own, which we shall publish in some one of the London newspapers. Rely upon it, we have acted most wisely in this matter; but I cannot now go into particulars. For the proceedings of the Convention, I refer you to the papers accompanying this. It was in session only ten days, but disposed of a considerable amount of business. On Wednesday, a public meeting was held in Exeter Hall, and went off with great eclat. The assembly was immense, and the various speakers were received in the most enthusiastic manner. When O'Connell made his appearance, the applause was absolutely deafening. He made a speech of great power, and denounced American slaveholders in blistering language — at the same time paying the highest compliments to American abolitionists. No invitation was given to Thompson, Phillips, or myself, to speak; but Birney [5] was assigned a part, and so was Stanton.[6] Remond stepped forward of his own accord, and was repeatedly cheered by the audience. He took them by surprise, and acquitted himself very creditably. Prejudice against color is unknown here.

Rogers and I have boarded at the same house with Stanton and his wife, Colver, Grosvenor, James & Lucretia Mott, Isaac Winslow and daughter, Abby Southwick, (who are all well,) and several other delegates.[7] Mrs. Stanton [8] is a fearless woman, and goes for woman's rights with all her soul. Stanton voted right in Convention on the question. We have been to see Westminster Abbey, the Museum, the Tunnel, the Tower, St. Paul's, &c. &c. The talk now is, that we shall leave for Scotland in the course of a week, under the care and guidance of George Thompson. I feel considerable curiosity to see Glasgow and Edinburgh, and the Scottish highlands; yet can I truly say, "there's no place like home." Some of the Irish delegates insist upon it that I shall take a trip to Ireland. Perhaps we may conclude to visit Dublin. I have shaken hands with O'Connell repeatedly.[9]

A thousand thanks for your affectionate letter, received by the

British Queen. Every line it contained was full of interest, and served greatly to relieve my mind from a heavy load of anxiety. May all things go prosperously with you, dearest! And may the protection of Heaven be graciously vouchsafed to the dear children, and to us all! My heart is swelling with tender emotions. O, how I yearn to clasp you in my arms!

I have been introduced to Lady Byron, the Countess of Brunswick, Mrs. Opie, Mary and William Howitt, Elizabeth Fry, Anna Braithwaite,[10] and other noted women. A splendid soiree has been given to the foreign delegates, at which I spoke.[11] Several elegant entertainments have also been made for us.[12] I let out all my heresies, in my intercourse with those who invite us together, and have made no little stir in consequence.[13] Slavery out of the question, our country is a century in advance of England on the score of reform, and of general intelligence and morality. We, in New-England, scarcely dream of the privileges we enjoy, and the enviable condition in which we are placed, as contrasted with the state of things here.

Dear Thompson has not been strengthened to do battle for us, as I had confidently hoped he would be. He is placed in a difficult position,[14] and seems disposed to take the ground of non-committal, publicly, respecting the controversy which is going on in the United States. Yet I trust he will soon see his way clear to speak out in our behalf.

Perhaps I may conclude to return home in the Great Western, which is to sail from Bristol on the 25th July. If not, I shall aim to take the steamer Acadia, for Boston via Halifax, 4th August.

I am waiting, with all a husband's and a parent's anxiety, to hear from you. May the intelligence prove pleasurable to my soul! Dearest, I am

Your loving husband,
Wm. Lloyd Garrison.

☞ My darling, precious, unrivalled boys! Are they well? Do they inquire after father, or have they forgotten him already? How their memory is entwined around my heart-strings! A myriad of kisses for them and their mother.

☞ It is needless for me to say, that you must give my affectionate remembrances to all at home, and to all inquiring friends. My health was never better. I shall endeavor to take all possible care of myself. Rogers sends his love to all.

ALS: Garrison Papers, Boston Public Library. Also printed, in part, in *The Liberator*, July 31, 1840, and in *Life*, II, 381–385.

1. William Adam, professor of Oriental languages at Harvard College. Born in Scotland, Adam spent fifteen or twenty years in India, in the service of the

East India Company. He later migrated to the United States, where he lived for several years, teaching at Harvard College. A staunch friend of Garrison, N. P. Rogers, George Thompson, and Wendell Phillips, he was a delegate of the Massachusetts Anti-Slavery Society to the World's Convention and favored the participation of women in the convention. After the convention, he served as an officer of the British India Society and wrote *The Law and Custom of Slavery in British India in a Series of Letters to Thomas Fowell Buxton* (Boston, 1840, 279 pp.). (*The Liberator*, October 16, 1840; *Life*, II, 353, 369, 373, 382.)

2. Land's End is a cape at the extreme west point of England. John O'Groat's octagonal house was at the northernmost point of Scotland. The meaning is, from one end of England to the other. (For John O'Groat, see William S. Walsh, *Heroes and Heroines of Fiction*, Philadelphia, 1915, p. 207.)

3. The text was printed in *The Liberator*, July 31, 1840.

4. Colonel Jonathan P. Miller (1797–1847) of Vermont. "He had served in Greece with Lord Byron (Stanton's 'Hist. Woman Suffrage,' 1:439). For his conversion to abolition by Orson S. Murray, see the Cincinnati *Price Current*, June 18, 1885" (*Life*, II, 370n). Born in Randolph, Vermont, he served as a private in the United States Army, and attended the University of Vermont. He went to Greece in 1824, aided the Greeks in their fight for freedom, and returned to Vermont in 1826. After lecturing on behalf of the Greek cause in New York and New England, he returned to Greece with several cargoes of clothing and provisions. In 1827, he was back in Vermont. He settled in Montpelier, studied law, and was admitted to the bar. Elected to the Vermont legislature in 1833, he introduced resolutions calling upon the Vermont representatives in Congress to demand the abolition of slavery and the slave trade in Washington, D.C. He was a delegate from his state to the World's Anti-Slavery Convention and participated actively thereafter in the antislavery movement. (*ACAB.*)

5. James Birney.

6. Henry B. Stanton.

7. At Mark Moore's, No. 6 Queen St. Place, Southwark Bridge, Cheapside (Anna Davis Hallowell, ed., *James and Lucretia Mott: Life and Letters*, Boston, 1884, p. 149).

8. Elizabeth Cady Stanton (1815–1902) married Henry B. Stanton just before they sailed for London on May 12, 1840. She was to become an outstanding reformer and leader in the woman's rights movement. In 1848, with Lucretia Mott, she organized the first woman's rights convention. (*CVDE; ACAB.*)

9. "In this year O'Connell began his famous agitation for 'Repeal.' Mr. Garrison related that he, together with friends, one day called upon him, and as it was known that he was about to make an important speech in Parliament, they feared to find him busy. He was, on the contrary, taking a rest before going to the House of Commons, and, stretched upon a sofa, was enjoying one of Dickens's novels." (*Life*, II, 383n.)

10. Those mentioned here are identified as follows:

Lady Byron (1792–1860), born Anne Isabella Milbanke, was a poet and scholar interested in theology and mathematics; she was somewhat puritanical. She married Lord Byron in 1815 and separated from him in 1816. She led a retired life after the separation, devoting much of her time to religion and charity. According to Harriet Martineau, her later life was devoted to educating the children of the poor and in promotion of various philanthropic projects (Harriet Martineau, *Biographical Sketches*, London, 1867, pp. 316–325). Harriet Beecher Stowe later wrote *Lady Byron Vindicated* (Boston, 1870). See also *DNB*, II, 584–607.

The Countess of Brunswick is otherwise unidentified.

Mrs. Amelia Opie (1769–1853) was a novelist and poet. She married John Opie, a painter, in 1798. Her husband died in 1807. She originally wrote novels and poetry. Coming under the influence of Joseph John Gurney, brother of Elizabeth Fry and Samuel Gurney, she became a Quaker in 1825 and stopped writing novels. Instead she wrote didactic essays. In 1833, she published a book of poems called *Lays for the Dead*. She spent her time chiefly in philanthropic and reform projects. She attended the World's Anti-Slavery Convention in 1840 as the delegate from Norwich. She loved clothes and good society more than other Quakers. (*DNB*). See also George Bradburn's account of her in [Frances H. Bradburn], *Memorial of George Bradburn* by his wife (Boston, 1883), p. 111.

Mary Howitt (1799–1888), a writer, was the daughter of a prosperous Quaker of Straffordshire, England. She married William Howitt, a writer, in 1821, and began a career of literary collaboration with him. In 1827, she published *The Desolation of Eyam and Other Poems*. In 1837, she and her husband moved to Esher, where she began writing stories for children which proved very popular. From 1840 to 1843, the Howitts lived in Heidelberg, Germany, to advance the education of their children. There Mary translated the novels of Frederika Bremer and many tales of Hans Christian Andersen. In her old age, she converted to Catholicism. In 1889, her daughter, Margaret, published her biography, *Life of Mary Howitt*. (*DNB*.)

William Howitt (1792–1879) was a writer whose father had joined the Society of Friends. He was also a chemist and druggist. His writings included *A Popular History of Priestcraft in All Ages and Nations* (1833), *Visits to Remarkable Places* (1840, 1842) and a five-volume *Popular History of England* (1856–1862). He wrote more than a hundred articles on spiritualism. He and his wife settled in Rome in 1870. (*DNB*.)

Elizabeth Fry (1780–1845) was a prominent prison reformer, sister of Samuel Gurney. At twenty-nine she was recognized as a Quaker Minister, and in 1820 she married Joseph Fry, a tea merchant and banker. She had an unusual aptitude for influencing people and reforming the most hardened criminals. She was most involved in helping the female prisoners of Newgate. She established centers in London to shelter the homeless and to help them find jobs. Although her husband went bankrupt in 1828, she continued her efforts in reform and philanthropy. (*DNB*).

Anna Braithwaite (1788–1859) of Kendall was the wife of Isaac Braithwaite, whom she married in 1808. Her father, Charles Lloyd, was a banker who also had an interest in the iron trade. He was a Quaker who was active with other Quakers in the antislavery movement. Isaac Braithwaite, also a Quaker, was in the dyeing trade and had a thorough scientific education. In 1815, Anna Braithwaite was acknowledged as a Quaker minister. As such, she traveled throughout England and went on three trips to the United States, in 1823, 1825 and 1827, her husband accompanying her on the last two trips. On her first trip she visited North Carolina, where she first witnessed the horrors of slavery. She met Elias Hicks in 1824 in the United States, and had several talks with him on their differences in Quaker theology. However, she and her husband remained opposed to what they believed to be Hicksite mysticism. (Joseph Bevan Braithwaite, *Memoirs of Anna Braithwaite*, London, 1905, *passim*; Rufus M. Jones, *The Later Periods of Quakerism*, London, 1921, pp. 441, 459, 492; J. Bevan Braithwaite, *A Friend of the Nineteenth Century*, by His Children, London, 1909, pp. 17–27 and *passim*.) *Life*, II, 384, notes that "a dinner on June 20 at Isaac and Anna Braithwaite's lodgings, 'in company with Garrison, Rogers, whom I like better and better, and others,' is recorded by Mrs. Mott in her diary. . . ."

11. "At the Crown and Anchor Tavern. 'Stanton made the first speech. He was followed by M. Duclos de Boussais in a very brief speech. Next came Garrison, who talked of "woman's rights" — blaming the Convention for its disregard of them — of universal suffrage in Ireland, and the necessity of a universal language' ('Memorial of G. Bradburn,' p. 95). William Adams's report ran (*Lib.* 10:127): 'At a soirée, W. L. Garrison was so loudly called for by the people that he stepped forward, and bore a faithful testimony against the unfaithfulness of the friends of the cause who went to America, and did not do their duty on that subject while there; especially Joseph John Gurney, Drs. Cox, Hoby, &c. He spoke fearlessly of the conduct of the Committee in calling such a con-

vention, and then denying it; also of war, and of woman slavery, which had been exercised over the female delegates. Our new organizers made no reply.' " (*Life*, II, 384n.)

12. "As at William Ball's, Tottenham, on June 25, where 'William L. Garrison spoke at length, very well,' *teste* Mrs. Mott . . ." (*Life*, II, 384n).

13. "Thus, William H. Ashurst to Mr. Garrison, on June 30: 'If you have a copy of the pamphlet upon non-resistance which you read at my house, to spare, or can tell me where I can procure it in this country, may I trouble you just to drop me a line, saying in so many words it may be had in such a place? Pray make arrangements so that I shall receive from America the *Liberator* for the next twelve months, and tell me unto whom and how I shall remit my subscription. I should like to arrange also to receive from America a copy of anything that shall appear officially, or from any of our known friends, upon the woman question. Their emancipation from serfdom is next in importance to the slavery question.' (MS.)" (*Life*, II, 384n.)

14. "Miss Harriet Gairdner wrote from Edinburgh on Nov. 25, 1840, to J. A. Collins, that Thompson was not his own master while in the employ of the British India Committee, and was obliged to have regard to his family necessities" (*Life*, II, 385n).

---

2 0 2

TO HELEN E. GARRISON

London, July 3, 1840.

My dear Love:

Yesterday morning, I was joyfully electrified by the receipt of a letter from bro. Johnson,[1] giving me the intelligence of your safe delivery of a fine boy on the 4th ult. Every thing appears to have transpired in the best possible manner. The relief which has been given to my anxious mind is more than words can express. Most sincere and heart-felt is my gratitude to the Giver of every good and perfect gift. James and Lucretia Mott, Isaac Winslow and company, and many other friends, both English and American, are pouring in their congratulations. What name shall be given to our new comer? is the question. I will not attempt to decide, until my return. Elizabeth Neal[l][2] says, call him Charles Follen[3] Garrison. Lucretia Mott and bro. Rogers think the name should be Edmund Quincy Garrison. There are many dear friends, and many good names, from which to make a selection. The lock of hair, forwarded by bro. J.,[4] is pronounced by all to be very beautiful, and I gaze upon it with rapturous delight. The babe is a boy — ah! you are disappointed, and so am I; for we had both fondly hoped that it would prove to be a girl. But the gift is none the less precious, and I am thankful, very thankful for it. Bro. J. intimates that the lad has uncommonly good lungs, and thinks he may be heard almost across the Atlantic. He begins early to make a noise in the world. O that I had him in my

arms to smother him (not quite) with kisses! What sort of features
has the dear little fellow? I can hardly think that he will be a match
for Willie or George; but perhaps the last may be first. So! I am now
the father of three boys! Why, it was only the other day that I was
a babe myself! How all these things come to pass, I cannot tell: it
must be that I am growing old: and yet how imperceptibly one glides
away on the stream of time! Well, if all the rest of the world are
moving forward, why should we remain behind? The reign of time
is impartial.

I had made up my mind to return to-morrow in the steamer
Brittania,[5] which sails from Liverpool for Boston; but, at the solicitations of the British friends, and especially to gratify dear Rogers,
who wishes to see Scotland before his return, I have concluded to
stay another month, and (Deo volente) shall sail from Liverpool
for Boston in the steamer Acadia, on the 4th of August; so that I
shall hope to embrace you by the 20th of next month. After the
receipt of this, therefore, it will be useless to send me any letters or
papers, as I shall have left for home before their arrival. Along with
bro. J's letter came a Liberator of June 12th, which was a real treat.
I have also received a copy of the Anti-Slavery Reporter,[6] and of the
Emancipator of 12th ult. Bro. Rogers is exceedingly anxious to hear
from his wife, and to get hold of a copy of the Herald of Freedom.
The intelligence of the victory over "new organization" in New-
Hampshire makes him feel twenty years younger. I do not believe
he can be induced to leave his Granite Hills, and take charge of the
Anti-Slavery Standard. He shrinks from the post, on account of its
vast responsibility, but especially because of his strong attachment
for his native State. Our friends will do well to have some other person
in view, in case he cannot be induced to leave his little Herald. I
shall do what I can to locate him in New-York.

Nearly all our party are stopping at the same house. We have
more invitations than we can meet, and can find no time either to
read or write, — scarcely any to sleep. I am completely worn out.
The hospitality of our English friends is unbounded. Several splendid
entertainments have been given to us — one, by the celebrated Mrs.
Opie, and another by the rich Quaker banker, Samuel Gurney.[7] He
sent seven barouches to convey us to his residence, (one of the most
beautiful in the world,) a few miles from the city; and a great
sensation did we produce as we paraded through the streets of
London. The dinner was magnificent, and all the arrangements on
the most liberal and elegant scale. After the banquet was over, we
had several speeches — one from Buxton,[8] another from Birney,[9]
another from myself, &c. The Duchess of Sutherland,[10] (who ranks

next to the Queen, and is celebrated for her beauty,) accompanied by her daughter,[11] an interesting young lady, and Lord Morpeth,[12] honored us with their presence. The Duchess came in a splendid barouche, drawn by four fine horses, with postillions, &c. She behaved very graciously, and, on parting, shook me cordially by the hand. She has given £20 to aid the fugitive slaves in Upper Canada. Her husband is the richest man in the kingdom, and she is noted for her liberality. She has since expressed a wish to have an interview with me, but I think it doubtful whether I shall find time to call. Haydon,[13] the celebrated artist, is now engaged in making a painting of the Convention, 10 feet by 7, in which he will group the most distinguished personages who were present, nearly as they sat in that body. His portraits will be from life. He has already taken a large number, and has succeeded admirably. I shall sit to him to-morrow for my likeness — a copy of which has been spoken for by the Duchess aforesaid. [Don't you be jealous!] I have seen Lady Byron repeatedly, and the day before yesterday took dinner and tea with her at the house of Mrs. Read, an opulent Unitarian lady.[14] I would just add, that our colored friend Remond [15] invariably accompanies us, and is a great favorite in every circle. Surely, if dukes, lords, duchesses, and the like, are not ashamed to eat, sit, walk and talk with colored Americans, the *democrats* of our country need not deem it a vulgar or odious thing to do likewise. Charles made a short, but good speech in Exeter Hall the other day.[16] The Duchess of Sutherland has signified her wish to see him also at her palace. You see how abolitionism is rising in the world! Lucretia Mott is winning "golden opinions" on all sides, in spite of the ceaseless efforts of the Orthodox quakers to obstruct her course, because she is a Hicksite. She has spoken once in public, and is to speak again shortly. On Monday,[17] there is to be a meeting at Freemason's Hall, on the subject of India, at which O'Connell, Bowring,[18] Thompson, myself, and others, are expected to speak. On the evening of the same day, there is to be a temperance meeting in Exeter Hall — Rogers is to be among the speakers. Perhaps I may say something on the occasion. On Tuesday, I shall go with Rogers down to Ipswich, (70 or 80 miles,) to see Clarkson,[19] and get him to come out with a letter against the Colonization Society, if I can. He says Cresson [20] deceived him.[21] I shall return on Wednesday or Thursday, and shall probably leave London with Geo. Thompson and Rogers, on Friday, for Scotland, — going first to Tynemouth, near Newcastle, to spend a day with Harriet Martineau. I shall try to send you a letter by the Great Western, on the 25th inst. Mrs. Thompson is near her confinement. She is in Edinburgh, with her children. There is to be a great meeting in Glasgow on the 1st of August, which I shall probably attend. I shall also go to Ireland.

Bro. Johnson must not publish the gossip contained in this letter, as it would look like vanity on our part; but he can allude to the fact, that we have been hospitably entertained by eminent friends of the anti-slavery cause, &c. I long to get back, dearest, and mingle in the glorious conflict which is going on in our country. Tell bro. J.[22] to bear an open front and a serene countenance, and fear nothing; for, *in due time*, we shall reap, if we faint not. I have just seen the first number of the Anti-Slavery Standard. It is a beautifully printed sheet, and makes a fine appearance. I am afraid, however, that it will cripple the circulation of the Liberator, by being put at so low a rate. Remember me affectionately to mother, sister Ann, bro. J. and wife, &c. &c. Also give my special regards to Caroline. With an overflowing heart, I remain,

Your faithful and loving husband,

Wm. Lloyd Garrison.

Bro. Johnson may publish as much of my letters to you and other friends, which were written on our voyage here, as he thinks best.[23]

ALS: Garrison Papers, Boston Public Library. Also printed, in part, in the *Life*, II, 385–389.

1. Oliver Johnson.

2. Elizabeth Johns Neall (b. Bucks county, Pennsylvania, November 7, 1819; d. December 9, 1907), a Quaker, the daughter of Daniel and Sarah Mifflin Neall and granddaughter of Warner Mifflin, the Quaker reformer and antislavery man, was a delegate of the Philadelphia Female Anti-Slavery Society to the World's Convention. She married Sydney H. Gay, editor for a time of the *National Anti-Slavery Standard*, in 1845. (Hilda Justice, compiler, *Life and Ancestry of Warner Mifflin . . .* , Philadelphia, 1905, p. 20; Frank Willing Leach, *The Mifflin Family*, Philadelphia, 1932, sixth page [no pagination].)

3 After the eminent abolitionist scholar and clergyman who had drowned in a shipwreak off Long Island Sound on January 13, 1840.

4. Oliver Johnson.

5. Garrison's spelling is incorrect. It should be *Britannia*.

6. The organ of the secessionist American and Foreign Anti-Slavery Society.

7. For a more detailed description of the dinner at Samuel Gurney's, see Anna Davis Hallowell, ed., *James and Lucretia Mott: Life and Letters* (Boston, 1884), pp. 162–164. Samuel Gurney (1786–1856) married Elizabeth Sheppard in 1808. They inherited her father's house in Essex, Ham House, in 1812. Gurney was a partner in the discount house of Richardson & Overend from 1807 onward, and was responsible for its growth into the greatest discounting house in the world. He became known as "the banker's banker." He joined Fowell Buxton, Joseph Gurney, and Elizabeth Fry in their efforts at prison and legal reform. He was a patron of the newly established colony of Liberia. He moved to Nice, France, after his wife's death in 1855. (*DNB*.)

8. Thomas Fowell Buxton.

9. James Birney.

10. Harriet Elizabeth Georgiana Leveson-Gower (1806–1868), Duchess of Sutherland, the third daughter of George Howard, the sixth Earl of Carlisle. In 1823 she married her cousin, George Granville Leveson-Gower, who succeeded

his father as second Duke of Sutherland in 1833. They lived in Stafford House, St. James Palace, which, through the duchess' influence, became an important center of society and of philanthropic undertakings. The latter included the protest of the English ladies against American slavery in 1853. The duchess was appointed Mistress of the Robes on the accession of Queen Victoria, and remained in that post when the Whigs were in power, until her husband's death. She was later an admirer of Garibaldi. (*DNB.*) See also [Frances H. Bradburn], *Memorial of George Bradburn* by his wife (Boston, 1883), p. 108, for George Bradburn's adulatory description of her, in which, among other things, he notes, "She is said to be the most beautiful woman in the country."

11. Lady Elizabeth Georgiana (1824–1878), the eldest daughter of the Duke and Duchess of Sutherland, married George Douglass Campbell, later Duke of Argyll, on July 18, 1844. She was Mistress of the Robes to Queen Victoria from 1868 to 1870. (George Edward Cokayne, *The Complete Peerage*, London, 1010, I, 211 212; see also Hallowell, ed., *James and Lucretia Mott*, p. 163n.)

12. Brother of the Duchess of Sutherland. On learning of Garrison's intention to visit Ireland, Lord Morpeth gave him a letter of introduction to a government official at the Castle in Dublin (*Life*, II, 387n). George William Frederick Howard (1802–1864), Lord Morpeth, reformer, member of Parliament, was appointed chief secretary for Ireland in April 1835, a post that he held for six years. In May of the same year he was admitted to the Privy Council. He advocated various Irish reform bills. In 1839, he was admitted to the Cabinet. After resigning his offices, he visited the United States and Canada in 1841. He became chancellor of the duchy of Lancaster in 1850, which he resigned in 1852. He was installed rector of the University of Aberdeen in 1853. He was Lord Lieutenant of Ireland in 1858 and 1859 to 1864. He also wrote widely in prose and verse. In 1853, he wrote the preface for an English edition of *Uncle Tom's Cabin*. (*DNB.*)

13. Benjamin Robert Haydon (1786–1846), English painter, noted primarily for his historical paintings (*EE*).

14. See reference to this dinner in Hallowell, ed., *James and Lucretia Mott*, pp. 164–165. Mrs. Elizabeth Jesser Reid (Garrison misspells it "Read"; b. December 25, 1794 or 1795; d. London, March 3, 1866) was a widow who resided at 6 Grenville Street, Brunswick Square, London. According to George Bradburn (spelling her name "Reed"), she had one of her rooms adorned with busts of Dr. Channing and other clergymen (*Memorial of George Bradburn*, p. 109). The daughter of William Sturch, ironmonger and theologian, she was a Unitarian who followed W. J. Fox out of the faith and a founder of Bedford College. She was a substitute nurse and a faithful visitor of Harriet Martineau's, as well as her closest friend. She had married John Reid, M.D., in 1821. He died in 1822. "She was remarkably absent minded, lacked quickness and dexterity, often said stupid things, and was amazingly awkward. . . . Yet Miss Martineau, who said she never spilled, broke, or lost a thing, put up with all this awkwardness for the sake of what Mrs. Reid had to offer — the cleverest letters she received, her thoughts on life, her moral insight. . . ." (R. K. Webb, *Harriet Martineau, A Radical Victorian*, New York and London, 1960, p. 17; Frederick Boase, *Modern English Biography*, Truro, England, 1901, III, 98.)

15. Charles Lenox Remond.

16. See letter 201, to Helen Garrison, June 29, 1840.

17. July 6, 1840.

18. Dr. (afterwards Sir John) Bowring (1792–1872), a member of Parliament and of the World's Anti-Slavery Convention, reformer and author. A brilliant linguist, he translated numerous works from the French, Italian, Spanish, Swedish, Danish, Russian, Polish, Magyar, Arabic, and Chinese, among others, into English. He was an ardent advocate of free trade, and close friend, biographer, and publisher of the works of Jeremy Bentham. In 1847, he went to China as English consul at Canton. In 1854, he was appointed plenipotentiary to China and gov-

ernor, commander-in-chief, and vice admiral of Hong Kong and its dependencies, as well as chief superintendent of trade in China. He was also knighted by the queen. He left the East and returned to England in 1860. (*DNB.*)

19. Thomas Clarkson (1760–1846), prominent English antislavery agitator, joined as early as 1787 in the movement to suppress the slave trade. He was a vice-president of the Anti-Slavery Society formed in 1823, which ultimately brought about the emancipation of the slaves in the West Indies in 1833. "Before he entered on the crusade slaveholding was considered, except by a chosen few, as a necessary part of social economy; it was due largely to Clarkson's exertions that long before his death it had come to be regarded as a crime." He wrote numerous works on slavery and the slave trade. (*DNB.*)

20. Elliott Cresson (1796–1854), Quaker businessman and philanthropist of Philadelphia. He was a colonizationist, an organizer of the Young Men's Colonization Society of Pennsylvania, and a life member of the American Colonization Society. He traveled widely, both in the United States and England, as an agent of the American Colonization Society, for the purpose of raising funds for and arousing interest in the society. (*DAB.*)

21. "Mr. Garrison's engagements prevented his making the intended visit, but in September he had the supreme gratification of publishing in the *Liberator* (10:154) Clarkson's renunciation of the Colonization Society. He apologized for any shortcomings in his reception of Mr. Garrison in 1833, and showed both how Cresson had hoodwinked him, and how he had regained a clear vision as to the 'diabolical scheme.' This important manifesto was forwarded by Elizabeth Pease on Sept. 3. It was begun in July (MS. [July] 18, 1840, E. Pease to W. L. G.) 'It is,' said Mr. Garrison, 'one of the results of our mission to England, and is alone a rich compensation for all the expense and trouble incurred by that mission.' (*Lib.* 10:155)." (*Life,* II, 388n.)

22. Oliver Johnson.

23. Written at the top of the first page, upside down.

203

TO OLIVER JOHNSON

LONDON, July 3, 1840.

MY DEAR JOHNSON:

I had fully made up my mind to leave for home in the Government steamer Britannia, which sails from Liverpool for Boston to-morrow; and therefore have neglected preparing any letters for publication in the Liberator, respecting the Anti-Slavery Convention in this city, which was dissolved some days since. But the importunities of the anti-slavery friends, in various quarters, for me to remain, are of such a nature, that, at the eleventh hour, I have come to the conclusion to remain in England until the 4th of August, — making, in the mean time, a tour to Scotland and Ireland. The mail is to be closed in less than an hour, and I can only say, that all the delegates from the United States are in good health, and, on the score of hospitality, have had no occasion to complain of their British friends. I have forwarded the London papers, containing pretty full reports of nearly all the proceedings of the Convention, which will furnish you with matter enough to occupy the columns of the Liberator until my return. In publishing the discussions and speeches, I wish you to give precedence to what fell from the lips of the great and eloquent O'Connell — especially his scorching, blistering, burning speech, delivered in Exeter Hall. On our arrival, we found that the Convention had adopted a rule, excluding all female delegates from a seat in it, and thus refusing to let the voice of the American Anti-Slavery Society be heard in behalf of bleeding humanity, except by proxy! Could we do less — by our regard for consistency and justice, and as representatives of a Society which makes no distinction among its members on account of complexion, condition or sex — than to refuse (I mean such of us as were *allowed* to become members) to connect ourselves with such a body? No — no. Accordingly, N. P. Rogers, Charles L. Remond, William Adams and myself, came severally, spontaneously and unanimously to the determination, not to place our names upon the list of delegates. Hence, we were mere spectators during the sittings of the Convention. All possible entreaties were made to induce us to alter our decision, but in vain. We felt that, by bearing such a testimony, on such an occasion, and under such circumstances, we should do incomparably more for the slaves of our country, and for the whole human race, than by consenting to recognize the principle, that the delegates sent to a 'World's Convention' by any anti-slavery society might properly be excluded from the same, and that the anti-slavery platform is to be measured by the corrupt usages of the world. We could not consent to see any of those, who were associated with us to represent the American Society, thrust out of a meeting convened for the purpose of breaking the yokes and fetters of slavery, and ourselves permitted to enjoy rights and privileges at their expense. We felt that, in excluding any one of our delegation, the Convention excluded all and hence the decision to which we came. How it will be viewed by those who sent us thither, I can scarcely entertain a doubt. I believe they will sustain us by their approving voices.

Wishing to be affectionately remembered to all the beloved friends at home, I remain, in much haste,

Yours for perfect freedom,

WM. LLOYD GARRISON.

Printed in *The Liberator*, July 24, 1840.

2 0 4

TO OLIVER JOHNSON

LONDON, July 3, 1840.

DEAR JOHNSON — I send you the accompanying Protest against the exclusion of a portion of the American delegates from the General Anti-Slavery Convention in this city, and also against some of the proceedings of that body, for insertion in the Liberator.[1] It was drawn up by Prof. Adam, of Harvard University, who has signalized himself for his fidelity to the cause of human rights, and his un-compromising regard for the principles of genuine reform. Those only who were members of the Convention have signed this Protest. The delegates who were excluded from the same will prepare one of their own, which will be forwarded to you by the earliest conveyance.

The Protest was read, at the close of the Convention, by Wendell Phillips, and produced a strong sensation. It was treated in the most disrespectful manner; and, on motion of *Rev. Nathaniel Colver, of Boston,* seconded by Rev. John Scoble, was *laid on the table,* in imitation of the example of the slaveholders and their tools in the American Congress, respecting the petitions of abolitionists. The request to have it printed with the proceedings of the Convention was denied, in the spirit of cowardice and injustice. Such conduct must inevitably produce a reaction. O'Connell, Bowring, Ashurst,[2] and other eminent men, have expressed their disgust and indignation at the exclusion of the American women, and the result will, I am sure, be most advantageous to the cause of our common humanity.

Yours, faithfully,

WM. LLOYD GARRISON.

Printed in *The Liberator,* July 31, 1840.

1. Printed in *The Liberator,* July 31, 1840.
2. William Henry Ashurst (February 11, 1792–October 13, 1855), a London solicitor and philanthropist. See letter from Ashurst to Garrison, dated Muswell Hill, June 18, 1840 (*Life,* II, 376–377). In that letter, Ashurst suggests that a "Protest" against the refusal of the convention to seat women be drawn up and submitted to it. As Garrison's letter to Johnson indicates, the suggestion was followed. A radical, influenced by the writings of Tom Paine and Benjamin Franklin, and a friend of Robert Owen, the socialist, Ashurst was one of the first to announce on the walls of his house that he would pay no taxes until the Reform Bill of 1832 was passed. He was active in numerous other reform activities. He advocated the political and social equality of women. A friend of Mazzini, he helped found the Friends of Italy in 1851 and the People's International League in 1852. (*DNB.*)

Nathaniel Colver, Samuel Gurney, and Thomas
Clarkson, portrait studies by Benjamin Robert
Haydon, 1840

The World's Anti-Slavery Convention, 1840, painted by Benjamin Robert Haydon

2 0 5

TO ELIZABETH PEASE

London, July 13, 1840.

Esteemed Friend:

On the eve of embarking for Scotland, I cannot refrain even at this late hour (midnight) from saying on paper — what, perhaps, it is quite needless for me to say at all — that your manifold kindnesses, since my arrival in this city, have imposed upon me obligations which I shall never be able to cancel; that our acquaintance has been to me of the most pleasant and instructive nature; and that in you I have found one whom I shall ever esteem it an honor and a privilege to place among the highest on my list of friends. The deep interest which you have so long manifested in the anti-slavery cause led me, while on the other side of the Atlantic, to hope that it might be my privilege to see you on my arrival in this country; but I did not imagine that it would happily fall to my lot to enjoy so much of your society. On my return home, it will afford me peculiar satisfaction to state to Mrs. Chapman, Mrs. Child, and other anti-slavery women, how genuine a woman, in the best sense of the term, I found Elizabeth Pease to be, and how much she is entitled to the gratitude and esteem of all who are laboring to undo the heavy burdens, and to let the oppressed go free. You know me too well, I trust, to suppose that I am dealing in mere compliment; and you must not be offended with me for thus undisguisedly stating my real estimation of your character. My good opinion may not be of any value; but I cannot withhold the expression of it. May every christian grace ripen in you to perfection; may you be enabled to perceive and follow duty, at whatever sacrifice, in all things, under all circumstances; may that peace, which the world can neither give nor take away, ever be yours; and may the blessings of those who are ready to perish rest upon your head. I hope to see you in Liverpool, before I bid a final adieu to England; but should any circumstances prevent, I will still cherish the hope of greeting you and other dear friends here, at no distant day, on the soil of New-England, at my own beloved home. I shall carry the remembrance of all that you have done across the Atlantic, even to the verge of life. It will give me great pleasure to hear from you, at any time, in relation to the various benevolent and moral enterprises of the age, in which we both feel a lively interest. Your epistolary favors shall be fully reciprocated. Much more I find it in my heart to say, but time will not permit. Wishing you all possible felicity in this life, and an eternity of happiness, I shall ever remain,

Your faithful and much obliged friend,

Wm. Lloyd Garrison.

Elizabeth Pease.

ALS: Villard Papers, Houghton Library, Harvard.

---

2 0 6

TO HELEN E. GARRISON

Edinburgh, July 23, 1840.

My Beloved Wife:

I am now in the capital city of world-famous Scotland, having arrived from London the day before yesterday, in company with Geo. Thompson, N. P. Rogers, and C. L. Remond. How was my heart gladdened to receive your long and affectionate letter of the 28th ultimo! And yet there were portions of it which gave me pain and uneasiness. The sudden death of Mrs. Collins [1] was assuredly in an afflicting form, and excites my strongest sympathies. Poor little Willie, it seems, has been ill, and is yearning to behold the face of his absent father. Tell him that father expects to see him in a very short time; that he hopes and prays that the good God, who lives in heaven, will bring him safely back to Cambridgeport, in the big ship, across the great ocean; that Willie must love and kiss his little baby-brother, and be himself a good boy, for father means to bring him a nice present; and that he must be obedient to his dear mother, his grandmama, and his aunt Ann. I am delighted to hear such good news from Brooklyn. Dear Georgie has in him, if a father's partiality does not becloud my judgment, all the elements of a noble man; and if he be judiciously managed by us, by reason rather than by physical coercion, kindly but resolutely, I doubt not that he will, in an eminent manner, fulfil the desires of our hearts. I think you had better let him remain in Brooklyn until my return home. "And when will that be?" is the question, above all others, you desire to have answered. I hope to see and embrace you and the dear children in the course of a month. It is now my intention to leave Liverpool on the 4th of August, in the new government steamer Acadia, which will sail for Boston via Halifax. Bro. Rogers will accompany me. We have neither of us, however, yet secured a passage, but have written on to Liverpool about it. Should she, unfortunately, be already supplied with a full complement, we shall then take the next packet-ship — unless we can succeed in obtaining berths in the new steamer President, which is to sail about the same time. We shall not return in the President, if we can help it — as she asks about sixty dollars more than the Acadia. Much do I regret — and in this regret there are thousands in England, Scotland and Ireland who deeply participate — that I have not more time to spend in this country, with a just regard to the best interests of the anti-slavery cause in the United States, and to the claims which a loving wife and growing family have upon me, especially at this great crisis. Though the spirit of new organization has poisoned many in England, and found other unclean spirits congenial with its own, yet the kind, and, in several instances, the enthusiastic manner in which I have been received by the people, has made a very deep impression upon my memory, which time can never efface. It has been my privilege to become acquainted with some of the noblest spirits of the age, both men and women; and much do they sympathize with us in the arduous struggle we are making in America against slavery, and its formidable ally sectarianism. Among the meetings it has been my happiness to attend, was a temperance meeting in Exeter Hall,[2] (the largest and most enthusiastic I ever saw,) at which that sturdy champion of Irish liberty, and most wonderful among the statesmen and orators of the age, Daniel O'Connell, made a powerful speech in favor of the doctrine of total abstinence. He was received with a storm of applause that almost shook the building to its foundations. The spectacle was sublime and heart-stirring beyond all power of description on my part. George Thompson, N. P. Rogers, and myself, addressed the immense concourse, and were flatteringly received, as were also Rev. Messrs. Grosvenor and Galusha.[3] I shall send a report of some of the speeches to bro. Johnson, which appears in the Temperance Journal.[4] As I had no opportunity to revise the sketch made by the reporter, you must take it as you find it. It has also been my privilege to attend a similar meeting in Edinburgh. On arriving in this city, on Tuesday afternoon,[5] and carelessly walking through the streets, I observed placards conspicuously posted in various directions, stating that Geo. Thompson, C. L. Remond, and W. L. Garrison, were in the city, and would be present at the temperance meeting that evening, and address the auditory! Though I had not been consulted by any one on the subject, and was wholly taken by surprise, yet I felt that I could not, as a professed friend of bleeding humanity, as a thorough "teetotaller" of fourteen years' standing, as an American citizen, refuse to lift up my voice in favor of the first great moral enterprise which I ever publicly espoused, especially as I was told that, as yet, in Scotland, it had made comparatively small progress, and was generally treated by "gentlemen of property and standing," and the priesthood, very much as the anti-slavery cause is by those classes in the United States. Our friends Thompson, Rogers, and Remond, accompanied me to the meeting, and made excellent speeches. A glorious sight it was to behold! There were about two thousand persons present — and never was there assembled, on any occasion, a more interesting or enthusiastic multitude. On our entering the hall, they received us with cheers and deafening applause, which were renewed as we severally proceeded to make our addresses. You may form some faint idea of the spirit which animated the crowded assembly when I tell you that the meeting commenced at 7 o'clock in the evening, and did not disperse until 2 o'clock in the morning! There was no appearance of fatigue or drowsiness to the end, except on the part of sundry little children and infants, who quietly slept in their mothers' arms.

To-morrow morning, a public breakfast is to be given to Rogers, Remond and myself, at which it is expected there will be a choice collection of some of the most respectable and eminent friends of humanity in Edinburgh. The honor is a very great one, and will be duly appreciated by us all.[6] We have been urged to have a public meeting, but time will not allow of it. To-morrow afternoon we shall make an excursion to the highlands,[7] and then proceed to Glasgow — at which place we expect to attend a great anti-slavery meeting on Monday evening next, which will be called expressly for our accommodation. We shall then proceed immediately to Dublin, and from thence to Liverpool.

Though I like England much, on many accounts, I can truly say that I like Scotland better.

I have not written much for the Liberator, because it has been out of my power to do so — my engagements have been so numerous; and because I think it best to reserve what I have to say about this visit, and the London Convention, until my return. We are in the full enjoyment of health, and in excellent spirits; and though we have felt that in thus widely separating ourselves from our families and friends, we have made no small sacrifice, yet we are satisfied that the cause of humanity on both sides of the Atlantic, and throughout the world, will be greatly aided by our present mission. Our joy and consolation are great in beholding the signs of the times, and our faith and hope remain steadfast as the pillars of the universe. I trust we are animated with the single desire, that all sin may be banished from the world, and that the will of God may be done on earth as it is done in heaven. I feel, I have long felt, that my feet are planted upon the eternal Rock, and though a hurricane is raging around me, and the billows of persecution are swelling against me, my rest is perfect. God is my rock and refuge; and in Christ Jesus I have found eternal life. How happy I am to be accounted worthy to assist in filling up the measure of the sufferings of Jesus!

The Liberator for June 12th and 19th has this moment been put into [my] hand, as well as the last number of the Non-Resistant, and also a cheering letter from my beloved friend Johnson. The great moral conflict on our shores continues to increase in intens[ity,] but, thanks be to God! I am glad to perceive no faltering on the part of the tried friends and champions of humanity. But, O! what heart-sickening, what astounding, what almost incredible developments of character are making on the part of those who have seceded from the old anti-slavery platform! Well, whatever is hidden must and should be made manifest in the light. If it must be so, let God be true, and every man a liar. I pant to be in the conflict, and at my old post, which I will be — Deo volente, — in the course of four or five weeks.

George Thompson is with us, in heart and spirit, and clearly perceives which party has truth, justice and freedom on its side in America. Mrs. T.[8] has just presented him with another babe, — a girl, — and is doing well.

I am greatly rejoiced to hear that the health of dear brother James is improving, and that he finds Brooklyn a pleasant residence. May God bless him, and Jesus save him! The intelligence respecting the safe accouchement of Mrs. Chapman is also very pleasing. Dearest, I have written this letter in the utmost haste, but if there be any part of it which will furnish friend J.[9] with an editorial article, let him have it. A million remembrances to all the friends!

Yours, devotedly,

Wm. Lloyd Garrison.

ALS: Garrison Papers, Boston Public Library. Also printed in *Life*, II, 395–398.

1. Mrs. John A. Collins. A search of *The Liberator* does not reveal any allusion to her death, its date or causes.

2. July 6, 1840. See letter 202, to Helen Garrison, July 3, 1840.

3. The Reverend Elon Galusha of Perry, New York, was a delegate of the National Baptist Anti-Slavery Convention, organized in New York on April 28–30, 1840, to the World's Convention. He was also a delegate of the American and Foreign Anti-Slavery Society (*Life*, II, 356n).

4. The *Temperance Journal* was published in Boston by the Massachusetts Temperance Union from 1833 to 1847. From 1837 to 1840 its name was the *Temperance Journal and Total Abstinence Gazette*. (*Union List of Serials*.)

5. July 21, 1840.

6. "It took place at the Royal Hotel, with Adam Black as second chairman (*Lib.* 10:142). The editor of the Edinburgh *Witness*, who had expected Mr. Garrison's manner to be bold and even boisterous, reported, on this occasion, that 'His appearance as a speaker is exceedingly becoming — his manner is calm, gentlemanlike, and impressive — and his utterance polished and agreeable.' (*Lib.* 10:134)." (*Life*, II, 397n.)

7. "The route was by way of Sterling and Callander, through the Trosachs,

across Loch Katrine, 'and over a rough defile to Loch Lomond'; thence to Glasgow (*Lib.* 11:147)" (*Life*, II, 397n).

8. Thompson.

9. Oliver Johnson.

---

2 0 7

TO MARCUS GUNN

Glasgow, July 27, 1840.

Dear Sir:

In the midst of the most pressing engagements, I have found time to read your Essay on the Domestic Policy of the United States, and have been greatly pleased with it. It evinces much discrimination, and is a just exhibition of the superiority of the American form of government over every other now existing in the world. Its publication in this country, at the present time, I am inclined to think, would be serviceable to the sacred cause of human rights. A monarchy is accompanied by many evil and bitter things, and is destined to pass away, in the fulness of time, in whatever country it may at present be found. I am for no other change, however, than such as may be effected by peaceable and moral means; for "they that take the sword, shall perish with the sword." [1] God grant a speedy deliverance to all mankind from all their burdens, and bring them under his own government, which is the best in all the universe!

As slavery in America is justly the reproach of that country, and tends to bring our republicanism into disrepute in Europe, I would suggest to you the propriety of adding to your Essay a burning rebuke on that subject; stating the important fact, that that horrible system is not the fruit of our republican form of government, but is contrary to it, and will yet be destroyed by the genius of republicanism.

Yours, for universal liberty,

Wm. Lloyd Garrison.

ALS: Garrison Papers, Boston Public Library. Printed in *Life*, II, 398–399.

Addressed to Temperance Coffee House,

5, Nicholson Street

Edinburgh

Mr. Gunn is unidentified.

1. Matthew 26:52.

2 0 8

TO JOSEPH PEASE

Liverpool, August 3, 1840.

Esteemed Friend:

At your request, I sit down to give you my opinion as to the prospect of the speedy and peaceable overthrow of slavery in the United States. Let me say, then —

1. That Christianity sanctions the use of nothing but moral and religious means and measures for the suppression of any sin, or the overthrow of any system of iniquity — in other words, it forbids the doing of evil that good may come, however vast the good to be achieved, or small the evil to be resorted to for its accomplishment. To bring the products of free labor into competition with those of slave labor, and thus secure the abolition of slavery and the slave trade throughout the world, is a peaceable, legitimate and Christian measure, which commends itself to the approval of all good men.

2. That [though Truth is mighty, and must ultimately prevail,] [1] there is not any instance recorded, either in sacred or profane history, in which the oppressors and enslavers of mankind, except in individual cases, have been induced, by mere moral suasion, to surrender their despotic power, and let the oppressed go free; but, in nearly every instance, from the time that Pharaoh and his hosts were drowned in the Red Sea, down to the present day, they have persisted in their evil course until sudden destruction came upon them, or they were compelled to surrender their ill-gotten power in some other manner.

3. That the emancipation of the eight hundred thousand bondmen in the British West India Colonies forms no exception to this lamentable truth — as it was effected by the colossal power of the mother country, and in opposition to the feelings and wishes of the West India planters. That power, it is true, was stirred up by the moral and religious action of the people of England; but, had the liberation of the West India slaves depended upon the triumph of moral suasion *in the colonies* over the depravity of the planters, there is not the slightest probability that it would have taken place. Indeed, it is certain that the planters would never have allowed any anti-slavery agitation among them. The mere suspicion, a few years since, that the Wesleyan and Baptist missionaries sympathized with the slave population, and were hostile to slavery, raised such a tempest of fury against them, that their chapels were ruthlessly destroyed, and they were either cast into prison, or compelled to flee for their lives. The

slaveholding power, wherever it holds absolute sway, will never tolerate any movement for its overthrow. There is, therefore, no liberty of speech or of the press in the slave States of America, and, consequently, no chance for the exercise of moral influence against slavery in that section of the country.

4. That, of all oppressors and tyrants who have cursed and afflicted mankind, none have ever equalled the enslavers of the colored race, — *especially American republican slaveholders,*— in ferociousness of spirit, moral turpitude of character, and desperate depravity of heart. I regard their conversion, as a body, to the side of bleeding humanity, by appeals to their understandings, consciences, and hearts, about as hopeless as any attempt to transform wolves and hyenas into lambs and doves, by the same process. Their understandings have become brutish, their consciences seared as with a hot iron, and their hearts harder than adamant.

5. That nothing will induce them to manumit their slaves but an utter inability to compete with the labor of freemen, in raising those productions which now give life and sustenance to the slave system; in connection with a rectified public sentiment, that shall every where regard them as the deadliest enemies of the human race.

6. That it is by the cultivation of cotton alone, and the purchase of that article by British manufacturers, that American slavery puts at defiance the opinions of the civilized world, baffles the efforts of the abolitionists of England and America for its speedy overthrow, and raises an impenetrable wall of defence against the attacks of its enemies.

7. That if England would supply herself with free cotton from some other part of the world, to the exclusion of all slave grown cotton, it is quite certain that, within seven years, American slavery would be peaceably abolished, from absolute necessity, as well as from the moral change which will by that time have been wrought in the free States of America, in opposition to that hideous system of plunder and outrage.

8. That it now seems to be placed beyond all doubt, that cotton can be grown by free labor at a much less expense, and in far greater abundance, in British India, than it is now done by slave labor in the United States: hence, that England, as a matter of self-interest, as well as on the score of humanity, should without delay redress the wrongs of India, give protection and encouragement to its oppressed and suffering population, and thus obtain a cheap, permanent and abundant supply of free cottton from her own vast and fertile possessions in the East.

I am sure that your British India movement will fill the hearts of

American slaveholders with dismay. May speedy and complete success attend it! — I see no reason why it should not receive the zealous and hearty support of the friends of humanity in Great Britain, especially of all genuine abolitionists on both sides of the Atlantic. For all that you are doing to promote it, (and no man can be doing more,) and for all your previous efforts in the cause of West India emancipation, I honor and praise you. Be not weary in well-doing, and you cannot fail of success. The case is one of great urgency. Let no time be lost, therefore, in laying all the facts respecting India before the people. Those facts can never be listened to with indifference by them, but will cause their hearts to burn like fire. They will rally *en masse* under the broad banner of universal emancipation, and their motto will be — "Justice for India! Freedom for the American slave! Prosperity to England! Good will to all mankind!"

I remain, dear sir, with the highest respect,

Your faithful friend and coadjutor,

Wm. Lloyd Garrison.

Joseph Pease.

ALS: Garrison Papers, Boston Public Library. Printed, in part, in *Life*, II, 391–394.

Joseph Pease (b. Darlington, England, January 28, 1772; d. there, March 16, 1846) was a wealthy Quaker, woolen manufacturer, railroad promoter, philanthropist, and abolitionist. He was the first Quaker member of the House of Commons and a founder, with George Thompson, of the British India Society. He was the father of Elizabeth Pease. (*Life*, II, 183, 372, 469).

1. This clause was crossed out by Garrison in the original.

209

TO GEORGE W. BENSON

Boston, August 18, 1840.

Dear bro. George:

I am most happy to give you the assurance, over my own "sign manual," that my journeyings abroad have come to an end, and that I am once more safely restored to the bosom of my family, and to a choice circle of near and dear friends. A fortnight ago, this day, I was in Liverpool! Our trip across the Atlantic, in the new steam-ship Acadia, occupied only about 12 days — which is altogether unprecedented in the annals of navigation. Ask dear bro. James what he thinks of it. By the way, my heart is gladdened to hear how contented he has been in Brooklyn, and that his health is much better. How happy I am to get back again, it is impossible for me to find words to say. My heart is almost as full of delight as the Atlantic is of water. Give me the land of my nativity above all other lands! And yet England, Scotland, and Ireland, are all beautiful — very beautiful. I have been received, in each of those kingdoms, in the most flattering manner, and could not have desired a warmer reception. But, the Lord willing, I mean to see you and all the dear ones, face to face, on Friday afternoon. Helen and the babe will accompany me; and probably friend Johnson. We shall remain with you until Monday. All are well at home. I long to see dear little Georgie, as well as your own dear children. My brotherly regards to Mary, Sarah, and Catharine, and affectionate remembrances to friends Coe,[1] Scarborough,[2] &c.

Yours, ever,

Wm. Lloyd Garrison.

N.B. We shall leave in the one o'clock train, P.M. on Friday. Can you meet us at the Killingley Depot?[3]

[Catharine says you must come if you possibly can. Mary is quite sick says if you can get the constitution water or powder you may, it is excellent for her complaint.[4]]

ALS: Garrison Papers, Boston Public Library.

1. The Reverend William Coe.
2. Phillip Scarborough.
3. Written along the left edge of the page.
4. This note is not in Garrison's handwriting; it is probably in Helen's.

210

TO ANTI-SLAVERY FRIENDS AND COADJUTORS

[August 19, 1840.]

To my Anti-Slavery Friends and Coadjutors.

I stand once more upon my native soil, ready to mingle with you in the great and glorious conflict which is going on in this country between the friends and the enemies of God — the lovers and the haters of man. Devoutly recognizing the kindness of that Providence, which has permitted me to visit and commune with the free and brave spirits of England, Scotland and Ireland — which has followed me wherever I have travelled, and made my path pleasant and agreeable in the highest degree, — and which has returned me in safety and health to the bosom of my family, — I seize the earliest opportunity to say to you, that, instead of faltering in your course, you have every possible inducement to rejoice in spirit, and to redouble your exertions to bring to a speedy termination that terrible system of slavery, which is the shame and curse of our country. That system cannot endure much longer: there are causes in operation, which, in the course of a very few years, will assuredly emancipate every American slave. Once more, then, to the onset!

Only three months have transpired since I left the United States; yet, during that brief period, I have travelled nearly eight thousand miles, — have visited the principal cities and towns in Great Britain, — have attended and participated in various public meetings, — have had many important interviews with some of the noblest spirits of the age, — and have labored incessantly, and I trust not in vain, to promote the great work of Reform, in all its various branches. My reception has been cordial and flattering in the extreme, in connection with those who were associated with me in the mission to England. Especially are we all under the deepest obligations to our anti-slavery friends in Scotland and Ireland. They spared no pains to make our visit satisfactory and delightful, and to show us how deeply they sympathized with us in all our trials and toils on this side of the Atlantic. To some of them, I shall have occasion to allude in a more particular manner hereafter.

Of the London Convention, I shall speak without reserve in future numbers of the Liberator. It was any thing but a free anti-slavery meeting. It was a mere automaton in the hands of a self-constituted body in London, who, having invited the abolitionists of America to meet the abolitionists of all the world in convention, most unjustly decreed that a portion of their delegates should not be recognized on that occasion. In excluding any one of the delegates of the American Anti-Slavery Society from a seat in the convention, the credentials of all of them were virtually dishonored; for they all stood on the same ground, and all acted by the same authority. The American abolitionists, therefore, have a right to complain, that they have been deceived, and treated with indignity. They will be careful not to be deceived a second time. There will never be another such convention held in London, or any where else. If there be any one act of my life, of which I am particularly proud, it is in refusing to join such a body, on terms which were manifestly reproachful to my constituents, and unjust to the cause of liberty. If I have been at any time serviceable to the cause of our common humanity, I have never done better than in bearing my testimony against the exclusive organization of the *pseudo* 'World's Convention.' My worthy associates, Messrs. Rogers, Adams,[1] and Remond, nobly refused to allow their names to be placed upon the roll of the convention, although strongly importuned to join it.

Since I left this country, it has been my privilege to travel in company with my excellent coadjutor Nathaniel P. Rogers, from whose luminous pen much may be expected in regard to our anti-slavery mission. He has won for himself the esteem and admiration of the best friends of our cause on the other side of the Atlantic, and done much to promote the great object so dear to the hearts of all faithful abolitionists in the United States.

As soon as I shall have recovered from the fatigues of the voyage, I shall resume the editorial duties of the Liberator, and endeavor to meet them with more zeal and devotion.

WM. LLOYD GARRISON,

Boston, August 10th, 1840.

Printed in *The Liberator*, August 21, 1840.

1. William Adams of Pawtucket, Rhode Island.

211

TO JAMES G. BARBADOES, THOMAS COLE, J. T. HILTON

Boston, August 19, 1840.

Beloved Friends:

I have received your affectionate and heart-melting letter,[1] congratulating me on my return in safety to the land of my nativity, and inviting me, in behalf of the colored citizens of Boston, to attend a public meeting to-morrow evening, for the purpose of receiving 'their hearty welcome, and the assurance of their continued attachment and unshaken confidence.' For this fresh token of your love, I can find no words to express the gratitude of my heart. Most joyfully do I accept of the invitation which you have extended to me. There are none among the whole human race so dear to me as my colored friends in this city; because they were the first to give me the right hand of fellowship, and to bid me God speed in my warfare against that monster of monsters, American slavery. Your proffered reception I shall ever regard as the greatest honor that can be conferred upon me by mortals; and in itself will be a rich compensation for all that I may have suffered in prosecuting the anti-slavery enterprise. All, that I claim for myself is, that I have borne a faithful, consistent and uncompromising testimony against slavery and all its abettors, in the midst of danger, and at no little personal hazard. Less I could not have done, and discharged a duty which I owe to God and suffering humanity. For this, no special praise is due to me. In your approval of my course, I find a panegyric which is truly to be prized.

For reasons which will be laid before you in due season, I did not connect myself with the London Convention; but I was none the less zealous in pleading your cause throughout Great Britain. My mission, I trust, has been of real service — the fruits of which, time alone can fully develope.

It is exceedingly gratifying to me to know, that my beloved and invaluable companion, Nathaniel P. Rogers, is also to be included in the public welcome which you propose to give to me. He is worthy of any mark of approbation that you can bestow upon him, and will gratefully appreciate this token of your regard for his labors in the anti-slavery field.

Begging each member of the Committee to accept the assurances of my personal esteem and regard, and pledging myself afresh to the cause of universal freedom, I remain,

Your grateful friend and faithful advocate,

WM. LLOYD GARRISON.

James G. Barbadoes, ⎫
Thomas Cole,   ⎬ *Committee.*
J. T. Hilton.   ⎭

Printed in *The Liberator*, September 11, 1840.

James G. Barbadoes (d. June 22, 1841, at St. Ann's Bay, Jamaica, West Indies, aged forty-five) was a prominent Negro abolitionist of Boston, a member of the Massachusetts delegation of six to the founding convention of the American Anti-Slavery Society in 1833. He was a devoted Garrisonian. He earned his livelihood as a barber. In August 1839 he moved his barbershop from Elm Street to No. 62 Court and Tremont Streets. For a copy of an advertisement publicizing his shop, see *The Liberator*, August 30, 1839. He went to Jamaica as one of a group of Negroes who planned to settle there, but the group was apparently duped by West India proprietors, and Barbadoes and two of his children died there. (*The Liberator*, August 6, 1841.)

Thomas Cole died in Boston on June 9, 1847, at the age of forty-two. He had been active in the Negro community of Boston, and in the antislavery and temperance movements. (*The Liberator*, June 25, 1847.)

For information on Hilton, see letter 32, to Helen, June 1, 1836.

1. Printed in *The Liberator*, September 11, 1840, together with Garrison's reply.

212

TO HENRY C. WRIGHT

Brooklyn, August [23,] 1840.

My dear bro. Wright:

I receive your "welcome home" with heart-felt satisfaction. It is impossible for me to find words to convey to you the joy which I feel on finding myself once more on the soil of New-England; for, though my reception abroad has been all that my soul could desire, and far more enthusiastic than I had any reason to expect, yet I can truly say, "America, with all thy faults, I love thee still" [1] — better, far better, as a place of residence, than any other land on the surface of the globe. Putting our heaven-defying slave system, and our infernal prejudice against the colored man, out of the question, in all things else appertaining to the intelligence, equality and happiness of the people, Great Britain falls far in the rear of the United States, and her population have many and grievous burdens to bear, which are unknown to the white inhabitants of this highly favored country. But, alas! slavery and prejudice cannot be put aside, but must be taken into the general account. We have, it is true, no monarchy, no royalty, no nobility — but we have something infinitely more frightful than them all. Americans may boast that "no castled lord" can be found in all their wide-spread territory; but many a "cabined slave" clanks his chains, and shows his scars, even by the side of their tall liberty-pole!

How much I desire to see you! I will not attempt to give you even a synopsis of the events which transpired during my brief sojourn in England, Scotland and Ireland — not, at least, until we shall be permitted to see each other, face to face. Let me just assure you, that I regard my mission as one of the most important movements of my life; that every thing looks well for our side of the question across the great waters; that the rejection of the American female delegation by the London Convention, and the refusal of Rogers, Remond, Adams, and myself, to become members of the same, have done more to bring up for the consideration of Europe the rights of woman, than could have been accomplished in any other manner; that, wherever we travelled, notwithstanding our contumacious (!) behaviour toward the Convention, we were hailed as the benefactors of our race; that we "sifted into" the minds of those with whom we came in contact, all sorts of "heresies" and "extraneous topics," in relation to Temperance, Non-Resistance, Moral Reform, Human Rights, Holiness, &c. &c.; that we have secured the personal acquaintance and friendship of some of the noblest spirits of the age, who will co-operate with us in all our efforts to subvert the empire of Satan; and that, in due season, the fruits of our mission will be made manifest to all eyes. On the subject of non-resistance, I had very much to say in England, Scotland, and the Emerald Isle; especially in view of the monuments and statues erected in honor of naval and military warriors, and of the numerous castles, and forts, and arsenals, and armed troops, which were every where to be seen. I carried out with me six bound volumes of the Non-Resistant, six copies of the engraved Declaration of Sentiments, and a bundle of non-resistance tracts, all which I distributed in the most judicious manner, and to great acceptance. Some converts were made before our departure, and many minds are laboring with the great question. As the temperance cause is somewhat unpopular in England, and the great mass of abolitionists there are in the daily habit of using wine, porter, and other intoxicating liquors, I said much privately and publicly in favor of total abstinence, and rebuked them faithfully for their criminal indulgence.[2] In short, I did what I could for the redemption of the human race.

Dear Rogers was my companion on all occasions, and assisted me in my labors very materially. He was exceedingly well-received, and has won for himself a good reputation. It is somewhat doubtful whether he will go to New-York; but I think he will not be able to resist our importunities. Indeed, *he must go* — and greatly will our new organization antagonists tremble on seeing him actually in the editorial chair of the "Standard" — and so will all, who are endeavoring to stop the march of reform through this country and the world.

As to George Thompson, I can say, that he is with us, through evil report and through good report, — for better, for worse, — on the woman question, — on the side of non-resistance, old organization, &c. His speech at the London Convention was unfortunate and incoherent, which he now ridicules, and of which he is ashamed, but which was extorted under peculiar circumstances, and without reflection. "Richard's himself again,"[3] and nobly will he do battle for us.

You tell me that since I left, no effort has been spared by Leavitt, Phelps, Goodell, &c. to make my name odious. Very well — it gives me no uneasiness whatever. I compassionate and pity their present state of mind, and dread nothing but the frown of my Saviour, to whose cause I am devoted for life, and for whose sake I am willing to suffer the loss of all things.

I desire you to give my affectionate regards to our true-hearted brother Dr. Hudson,[4] and to accept for yourself the assurances of my unfeigned love and lasting regard. In haste,

Your faithful coadjutor,

Wm. Lloyd Garrison.

ALS: Garrison Papers, Boston Public Library. Printed, in part, in *Life*, II, 409–410. The date was inserted in the manuscript by another hand.

1. William Cowper, *The Task*, Book II, "The Time-Piece," line 206, "England, with all thy faults, I love thee still — "
2. "Thus, his declining the wine proffered at William Ashurst's led the latter to ask Mr. Garrison's reasons for such a departure from usage. The discussion which ensued ended, upon further reflection, in Mr. Ashurst's becoming a total

abstainer on principle. A similar testimony at Wincobank Hall sufficed to banish the decanter ever after from Mrs. Rawson's table. Many like instances might be adduced. Indeed, Mr. Garrison's temperance testimonies began on his former visit to England in 1833, and were still uttered on his final visit in 1877." (*Life,* II, 410n.)

　　3. Colley Cibber (1671–1757), English playwright, *Richard III, Altered,* V, iii.
　　4. Erasmus D. Hudson.

---

2 1 3

TO ELIZABETH PEASE

Boston, August 31, 1840.

Esteemed Friend:

The Acadia leaves to-morrow, on her return to Liverpool. It would be unpardonable in me not to send an epistle to one, for whom I entertain the most profound respect and the strongest friendship; and to whom I am indebted, on the score of generosity, personal kindness, and anti-slavery sympathy and co-operation, far more than any return of thanks, however eloquently expressed, can ever repay.

It is impossible for me to tell you what were my feelings, on discovering that the little steamer, which brought us alongside of the Acadia in the Mersey, had returned to the dock without my knowledge — carrying you and the other dear friends, who had come so far to see us embark, entirely out of sight — perhaps never to behold each other again on earth. Dear Rogers felt as deeply as myself at this circumstance. We were so troubled in seeing to our luggage, and in ascertaining where we were to be located during the voyage, that we did not discover, till it was too late, that you had left us. I felt very unhappy about it, I assure you; and if tears of regret could have availed any thing, we should not have wept in vain. It was our intention to have given you all the last waive of our hats and handkerchiefs, and to have watched you closely till distance should hide you from our sight. What must you have thought of us! Our conduct must have seemed inexplicable. We felt very badly about our warm-hearted friend Richard D. Webb,[1] in particular, in consequence of his having come all the way from Dublin to bid us farewell. But I will not dwell on this painful subject. Rest assured that the choice circle of friends, with whom it was our privilege to become acquainted in England, Scotland and Ireland, will never be forgotten by us, nor their names be erased from the tablets of our hearts. Heaven bless them!

You remember what sort of a place you found the "forward cabin" to be. When you left us, Rogers and myself had about come to the conclusion, that we should have to remove ourselves from the uncomfortable quarters we had selected, and take births in the "after cabin." However, though we were told that we could not associate with the other passengers, nor sit at the same table with them, if we persisted in retaining our place forward, we nevertheless resolved, *as a matter of anti-slavery self-denial and economy*, not to change our position. Rev. Mr. Galusha, and a gentleman belonging to Halifax, joined us; but we all found just occasion to complain of the treatment we received. You would have smiled, and perhaps felt somewhat indignant, to have seen the table that was made for us. It was merely a pine board, just narrow enough to hold a plate, behind which it was difficult to get access, and under which it was equally ludicrous and painful to see so tall a man as our friend Galusha attempt to crawl. The food that was served up to us was generally not fit to be eaten, and very little withal as to quantity. We were scantily supplied with fresh water; so that we could not get enough to wash our faces decently. As to towels, they were few and far between. As a dernier resort, we took a sheet, and wiped upon that, nearly all the way over the Atlantic. We complained to the head-steward of our treatment, and he promised to make it better — saying that we were entitled, substantially, to the same fare as those obtained in the after cabin — but he did not fulfil his promise. Happily, our voyage was a short one (though it seemed to us almost interminable, so anxious were we to see home, and to be delivered from such a pitiable situation) — only twelve days and a half — the shortest ever made by any other vessel. The mammoth steamer President, which sailed three days before us, did not arrive in New-York until after the arrival of the Acadia in Boston!

There were few incidents that occurred on our passage, that would be of any interest to you. A sea-voyage is usually very monotonous; and, situated as dear Rogers and myself were, ours was uncommonly so. We saw *quantum suff.* of "mother Carey's chickens," spouting whales, tumbling porpoises, and winged flying-fishes. Now and then we saw (and it is always a pleasant sight at sea) a sail in the distance, but did not speak any, except in a single instance. We were surrounded by a dense fog for several days, which impeded our progress, and made it dangerous to run at full speed: it hindered us at least one day on the passage. The weather was generally very fine: only for about forty-eight hours did the wind blow a gale against us. The Acadia is a fine sea-boat, and worthy of much commendation. There was [a] circumstance that took place on board, of a melancholy nature. The third officer of the ship, who was quite unwell when he came on board, died on the passage, and was thrown overboard the day before we arrived at Halifax. The captain read [a] church service over him, in the presence of the crew and passengers, before committing him to the deep. It was a novel and solemn scene — the presentation of death in a new and peculiar form.

When within one hour's sail of Halifax, we were detained by a fog for nearly twelve hours! On going up the harbor, all the inhabitants turned out to receive us, and with their cheers to make the welkin ring. Halifax is beautifully situated, and reminded me very forcibly of the place of my nativity — Newburyport. Although we took the "Bostonians" by surprise, they nevertheless rushed to the wharves by thousands, and gave the Acadia a grand reception. It was one of the most thrilling scenes I ever witnessed; and as it was the termination of my voyage, I could not help weeping like a child for joy. Never did home before look so lovely.

On landing at Boston,[2] we were warmly received by a deputation of our white and colored anti-slavery friends, from whom I received the pleasing intelligence, that my dear wife and children were all well. These I soon embraced in my arms, gratefully returning thanks to God for all his kindness manifested to us during our separation. I need not attempt to describe the scene.

Our refusal to join the London Convention is warmly applauded by the tried and true-hearted abolitionists of this country. The London Committee will hear from them shortly.

I suppose this will find you at your own delightful residence in Darlington. Though it is not worth answering, I will cherish the hope of hearing from you, in reply, without delay. I have mentioned your kindness to the excluded delegates to Mrs. Chapman and other friends, and they all appreciate it highly. Wishing to be affectionately remembered to your father and brother, and all inquiring friends, I remain,

Your grateful friend,

Wm. Lloyd Garrison.

ALS: Garrison Papers, Boston Public Library. Printed in *Life*, II, 404–406.

1. Richard Davis Webb (b. Dublin, February 19, 1805; d. there, July 14, 1872), a printer by occupation, was a Quaker who left the society when he learned that they did not welcome "disturbers." He had been converted to the antislavery cause by George Thompson in 1837, and first met Garrison in 1840. He remained Garrison's life-long and devoted friend. In London in 1861 there appeared his biography of John Brown, entitled *The Life and Letters of Captain John Brown*. In a letter to Wendell Phillips Garrison, dated Roxbury, July 27, 1872, Garrison wrote that "though not a graduated scholar, he was, nevertheless, very broadly educated by his own industry and aptitude for the acquirement of general knowledge; and his reading was of the most varied and extensive character." (Garrison Papers, Boston Public Library.) Webb was also "an indefatigable (and illegible) correspondent of Mrs. Chapman and her sisters — indeed he said he had a 'perfect passion for Westons.'" (R. K. Webb, *Harriet Martineau, A Radical Victorian*, New York and London, 1960, pp. 17–18, *Life*, II, III, IV, *passim*.)

2. August 17, 1840.

2 1 4

TO ELIZABETH PEASE

Boston, Sept. 1, 1840.

Dear Friend:

I find that, during my absence in England, the spirit of "new organization" spared no pains, and let slip no opportunity, to make me odious with the public, and, especially, to alienate the affections of the colored people from me. They well know that, so long as I retain the confidence of my colored friends, all their machinations against me will prove abortive. Thus far, it has only been the viper gnawing against the file. You will see, by the last number of the Liberator,[1] an account of a great meeting which was held in the Marlboro' Chapel, in this city, by the colored inhabitants, in conjunction with their white friends, in order to give a public welcome to dear Rogers and myself on our return from abroad.[2] It was a most interesting, affecting and sublime spectacle. We were received with great enthusiasm, and deemed it as great an honor as could be conferred upon us by mortals. I wish you could have looked in at the meeting just at the moment when my estimable and much respected colored friend, John T. Hilton, gave me the right hand of fellowship in the presence of the great assembly, and in the name of the colored citizens of Boston. If you could have seen the fervor of his grasp, and the visible emotions of his soul, you would have concurred with me in opinion, that such a reception would more than compensate for a whole life of toil and sacrifice in behalf of "the suffering and the dumb." On the preceding evening, a meeting was got up by the new organizers for Messrs. Colver and Galusha, but it did not amount to any thing: they were largely indebted to the friends of the old society, for their audience. Colver was vulgar and abusive, as usual — perhaps rather more so.

A similar public welcome has since been given to me by the colored inhabitants of Salem, and most delightful it was to my spirit.[3] At the close of my address in their meeting-house, an elegant entertainment was served up in the Masonic Hall, in which some eighty persons, male and female, participated — and at the conclusion of which, highly complimentary speeches were made by a number of white and colored friends. It was, indeed, a joyous occasion. After all the manifestations of gratitude and kindness which have been made towards myself by the colored population of the United States, for so many years past, — to say nothing of the obligations which rest upon me as a moral being, — for me to abandon their cause, come what may to my person or reputation, would be base in the extreme. It is my exalted privilege to be one of their advocates, and I want no other.

Mrs. Chapman was delighted to hear about our movements in England, and particularly all we had to say about yourself. She is as buoyant and active in spirit as ever, and, if possible, even more arduous in her labors. Noble woman!

There is to be a State Anti-Slavery Convention in New-Hampshire next week,[4] and another in Massachusetts during this month,[5] at both of which Rogers and myself are expected to be present, to give an account of that which never existed — to wit, the World's Convention. We shall show it up in its true light, London Committee and all!

And now for a specimen of American *orthodox* Quakerism, as it relates to prejudice against a colored complexion. Perhaps our mutual friend William Bassett has sent it to you already: if so, you will excuse the repetition. In one of the numbers of "The Friend," [6] published in Philadelphia, an extract was inserted from a letter written in London by John T. Norton,[7] (one of the delegates to the Convention,) giving an account of the manner in which respectable colored persons were treated on your side of the Atlantic, and of the absence of that prejudice which is so disgraceful to America. Such was the excitement, it seems, created by that little paragraph among the *quiet* readers of the Friend, that the editor had to come out with the following apology! Hear him!

"Within a few days past, we have received more than one intimation, from *respectable* sources, that we *have been guilty of an indiscretion,* by inserting, the week before last, the article headed, "Colored People in London." In answer we may say, that it was copied from one of our exchange papers, *with no other view* than as showing the kind of feeling with which colored people were regarded there; and, being unaccompanied by note or comment, it was only by *a strained inference* that we could be supposed *to hold it up as an example for imitation among ourselves.* WE SHOULD BE VERY SORRY TO BE SO UNDERSTOOD. We are not, nor ever have been connected with the anti-slavery societies; and, although among those associated with them are many estimable individuals, and not a few of them in the list of our particular friends, yet we have uniformly believed, that *one of the greatest mistakes committed by the anti-slavery people,* is the mixing up with the abolition question, *the warfare against what* THEY ARE PLEASED TO CALL *prejudices in regard to the colored race.*"

Spirits of Fox, Woolman and Benezet! [8] Here we have the full manifestation of that hateful spirit, which hunts the colored man with blood-hound ferocity on these shores, and makes his life full of wretchedness and misery. Such Quakerism as this is of Satan's own manufacture. I shall wait with some curiosity to see how it will be treated by the Society of Friends in England. I hope you will lay it before them, that we may have a response in due season.

William Bassett has been cut off from the Society in this country! [9] He will, doubtless, give you all the particulars about it. He is a martyr to the cause of humanity, and has been expelled only because the Society is too corrupt to retain such purity. — His spirit, however, is just as peaceful, his countenance just as benignant, his purpose just as steadfast, as they were before this shameful treatment. The proscription of such a man is one of the most conclusive proofs of the awful condition into which the Society of Friends has fallen in this negro-hating country.

The dear babe that was born during my absence is even more beautiful than was either of his brothers at his age. He was very unwell just before my return, so that it was supposed he could not recover; but he was mercifully spared. I have not yet given him a name! Shall we call a "World's Convention" to decide upon it? If so, remember women are not to be included in the call! And yet I am determined to have their decision in the case.

Much do I wish to see you and the other dear friends in England; but as this wish cannot be gratified at present, do not fail to let me hear from you soon. Remember me affectionately to your father, mother, brother, &c.

Yours, truly,

Wm. Lloyd Garrison.

ALS: Garrison Papers, Boston Public Library. Printed in *Life*, II, 411–413.

1. August 28, 1840.
2. The meeting was held on August 20, 1840.
3. The meeting was reported in *The Liberator*, September 18, 1840.
4. The convention was held in Concord, New Hampshire, on September 9 and 10 and was reported in *The Liberator*, September 18, 1840.
5. Actually, the Massachusetts Anti-Slavery Convention was held on October 6 and 7 in Worcester, and was followed by another state convention in Springfield on October 8 and 9.
6. *The Friend*, subtitled "A Religious and Literary Journal," was the oldest periodical of the Society of Friends. It was founded in 1827, during the Hicksite controversy, and was under the control of the Philadelphia Yearly Meeting. From 1827 to 1851, its editor was Robert Smith, III. Its orientation was generally conservative. (Frank Luther Mott, *A History of American Magazines, 1741–1850*, New York and London, 1930, pp. 562–565.)
7. John Treadwell Norton (b. April 28, 1795; d. Farmington, Connecticut, June, 1869) had been a prominent merchant in Albany, New York, and a partner in the firm of Corning and Norton, from 1825 to 1829. He was also president of the New York Central railroad during that period. He moved to Farmington, and built the largest house in town (thirty-four rooms) in 1832. His business activities in Connecticut included sponsorship of the Farmington canal and dam, the Farmington River Water-Power Company, and the raising of Jersey cattle.

He was vice-president of the American Anti-Slavery Society in 1839 and 1840. (Dwight L. Dumond, ed., *Letters of James Gillespie Birney, 1831–1857*, Gloucester, Mass., 1966, I, 558n. This source refers to Norton as "Rev.," although there is no evidence that he was a minister.) In 1842, he sought to reunite the abolitionist factions. (See circular to Garrison, Joshua Leavitt, John G. Whittier, Lewis Tappan, Gerrit Smith, and Theodore D. Weld, dated December 12, 1842, in Weston Papers, Boston Public Library; *Farmington, Connecticut, The Village of Beautiful Homes*, Farmington, 1906, p. 79; J. H. Trumbull, *The Memorial History of Hartford County*, Boston, 1886, I, 213; II, 200.)

8. George Fox (1625–1691) was the English founder of the Society of Friends and an early critic of slavery (*EE*).

John Woolman (1720–1772), was a prominent American Quaker and early opponent of slavery. He was the author of *Some Considerations on the Keeping of Negroes: Recommended to the Professors of Christianity of Every Denomination* (Part I, 1754; Part II, 1762), perhaps the most widely read antislavery work of its day. He traveled thousands of miles in preaching against slavery and was one of the most effective antislavery agitators. (*DAB*.)

Anthony Benezet (1713–1784) has been called the foremost antislavery propagandist of the late eighteenth century. Born in France, he came to the United States at the age of eighteen, two years after he had joined the Society of Friends. A merchant in his early years, he devoted the last forty years of his life to teaching and writing. Deeply influenced by Woolman, he spoke and wrote prolifically against slavery and for Negro equality. His works include *Observations on the Inslaving, Importing and Purchasing of Negroes* (1759; second edition, 1760); *A Short Account of that Part of Africa Inhabited by the Negroes* (1762; second and third editions, 1763); *A Caution and Warning to Great Britain and her Colonies, in a Short Representation of the Calamitous State of the Enslaved Negroes in the British Dominions* (1766); and *Historical Account of Guinea; Its Situation, Produce and the General Disposition of Its Inhabitants* (1771). Louis Ruchames, *Racial Thought in America*, vol. I, *From the Puritans to Abraham Lincoln*, New York, 1969, p. 124.

9. For background information on William Bassett, see letter 107, to George W. Benson, January 15, 1838; see also Bassett, *Proceedings of the Society of Friends in the Case of William Bassett* (Worcester, Mass., 1840), in which he defines his own position; for an English defense of Bassett, see *Society of Friends in the United States: Their Views of the Anti-Slavery Question, and Treatment of the People of Colour* (Darlington, England, 1840).

215

TO JOSEPH PEASE

Boston, Sept. 1, 1840.

Esteemed Friend:

I salute you from the shores of the "new world." My return voyage occupied only twelve days and a half — the shortest ever made across the Atlantic. Happily, I found all my family and friends in the enjoyment of good health; and I need not say that our rejoicing on beholding each other was great and mutual. We could fervently respond to the grateful language of David — "O, give thanks unto the Lord; for he is good; for his mercy endureth forever." [1] And, surely, his mercy attended our footsteps across the mighty deep; and in our sojourneyings among you, it was signally manifested to us by day and by night. How can we better show our gratitude to God, than by consecrating ourselves anew to the cause of bleeding humanity?

I hope that, ere this, you have had your contemplated meeting in Manchester, in reference to the British India question; [2] that the great advocate of the human race, the fearless and eloquent O'Connell, and that no less eminent and faithful friend of all mankind, George Thompson, were present on the occasion, to lift up their inspiring voices in behalf of the poor natives of India; that a mighty impetus was given to your movement, which nothing shall be able to resist; and that it is the determination of the Committee of the British India Society to take bold and decisive measures, both in relation to the people and government of Great Britain, that justice may not be delayed, and that the grand remedy for slavery and the slave trade may be speedily applied. Why should there be any hesitancy in the matter? Is not India groaning under the weight of British oppression? Are not millions of her inhabitants systematically plundered not only of their most sacred rights, but even of the food which is necessary to sustain life? In the midst of fertility and abundance, are they not visited by the most frightful famines, in a manner unexampled in the history of a downtrodden people? And are not the people and government of England responsible for it all? And is it not clear that, by relieving India, and giving full scope to the cultivation of cotton by the remunerated labor of her population, the prosperity of England will be greatly advanced, her character redeemed in the eyes of mankind, and India saved from starvation and ruin? Is it not equally clear, that, if Great Britain will but supply herself with free grown to the exclusion from her market of our slave-grown cotton, a blow will be struck at the American slave system, from which it can never recover? It seems very strange, nay, quite incomprehensible to me, that the abolitionists of England do not espouse the British India movement *en masse*. Already, there is much consternation on this side of the Atlantic, among the planters and their northern adherents, in relation to that movement. My eye at this moment rests upon a copy of the New-York Herald,[3] (a violent pro-slavery journal,) in which a tocsin of alarm is sounded in the ears of the slaveholding States. The editor cries out lustily against "the villanous designs of the abolitionists to destroy the interests of the southern planter," and adds — "Much as we detest the conduct and principles of the insurgent and scandalous abolitionists, we feel bound to give them, [i.e. the facts in relation to your India movement,] in order to put our southern friends on their guard against the infamous designs of these crazy scoundrels." This is a high panegyric upon your proceedings, and should mightily encourage you to go forward in your great work of human redemption.

I have consulted Henry Chapman & Co. with regard to the Bill of Exchange (£30) on the Barings,[4] which I left in your possession. They authorize me to say, that if you have received the money for it, you will oblige them by paying the same to the Barings, to be credited to their account; or, if it be still in your possession, they wish you to return it to the Barings, that it may be put to their account with that house. Please let me hear from you or Elizabeth, as to the disposal of the Bill

We are now in the midst of a hot political excitement in this country, in relation to the Presidency. The whole nation is politically insane, and reason will not be restored, (if then,) until the question be settled, whether Martin Van Buren or William Henry Harrison be the successful candidate. Both of them are mortally hostile to the anti-slavery cause, and deserve to be covered with infamy, rather than with laurels. O, the inconsistency of my countrymen!

My mind constantly returns to England, and I often think of the pleasant interviews we enjoyed together. It is possible, perhaps probable, that we may never meet again on earth; but I will cherish the hope that it may be otherwise.

Wishing to be cordially remembered to your wife, Elizabeth, and son, I remain, gratefully,

Your friend and coadjutor,

Wm. Lloyd Garrison.

P.S. Please to inform Elizabeth, that the Protest,[5] about which so much stir was made, has been forwarded to John Scoble by the steamer Acadia. Fortunately, the manuscript was carefully preserved after the publication of the Protest in the Liberator. So, that matter is rectified. Inform her, also, that Rev. Messrs. Hubbard Winslow and Nehemiah Adams,[6] of Boston, (two of the most deadly foes of the anti-slavery cause,) are now on a tour to England. Let them be put to open shame.

ALS: Garrison Papers, Boston Public Library. A portion of this letter is printed in *Life*, II, 393n.

1. I Chronicles 16:34.

2. Garrison is referring to a meeting held on Wednesday evening, August 26, 1840, in the Corn Exchange, Manchester, England, for the formation of a Northern Central British India Society, "for bettering the condition of our fellow subjects, the natives of British India." Among the speakers were Daniel O'Connell and George Thompson. (*The Liberator*, October 9, 16, 1840.)

3. The New York *Herald* was founded on May 6, 1835, by James Gordon Bennett (1795–1872) as the *Morning Herald*, a penny daily. Although the *Herald's* editorial policy was presumably independent, it was strongly anti-

abolitionist. *Life* (III, 281), referring to a meeting of the American Anti-Slavery Society in May 1850, remarks: "the air was full of coming violence, of which a truly Satanic Scotchman, James Gordon Bennett, editor of the New York *Herald,* was the prime invoker." For additional material on Bennett's view of the abolitionists, see Bertram Wyatt-Brown, *Lewis Tappan and the Evangelical War Against Slavery* (Cleveland, 1969), pp. 157, 197, 208, 236. See also Frederic Hudson, *Journalism in the United States, from 1690 to 1872* (1873; republished as J. & J. Harper Editions, New York and Evanston, 1969), pp. 428–490.

4. Baring Brothers was a prominent English banking firm, founded in 1770.

5. This is the Protest, dated "London, June 23, 1840," to which Garrison alluded in his letter (204) of July 3, 1840, to Oliver Johnson, and which was printed in *The Liberator,* July 31, 1840.

6. Nehemiah Adams (1806–1878), Congregational clergyman, was born in Salem, Massachusetts. A graduate of Harvard College and Andover Theological Seminary, he was pastor of the First Congregational Church in Cambridge from his graduation to 1834 and of the Essex Street Church (Congregational) of Boston from 1834 to his death. After a visit to the South in 1854 he wrote *A South-Side View of Slavery* (Boston, 1854), which emphasized the virtues of slavery and attacked the abolitionists. In 1863, he wrote *The Sable Cloud,* which was a reply to his critics. (*ACAB.*)

216

TO NATHANIEL P. ROGERS

Boston, Sept. 4, 1840.

My dear Rogers:

With my whole body and soul, I can fully enter into all your feelings of lassitude and prostration, experienced since your return from England. I am now somewhat recovered, however, and trust you are better than when you wrote. You want me to be at your Concord meeting next week,[1] to help make out a story about our mission. It will be extremely inconvenient for me to attend — for bro. Johnson is now at Nantucket, and is not expected back for some ten days. Yet, as I love you very much, "which nobody can deny" — as I wish to see some of the brave and faithful spirits in New-Hampshire, who behaved so gallantly and triumphed so gloriously during our absence abroad — and as it is taken for granted that you will be present at our State meeting in Worcester next month — I am resolved to be with you, if Providence permit, as a looker-on, if not as an active participant in your proceedings. Nevertheless, you must not expect me till Wednesday noon.[2] I hope to be able to remain with you till Friday morning, when I must return to this city without fail. Delighted as I should be, under other circumstances, to visit Hanover, especially in company with yourself, it will not be in my power. I am frightened to think of the responsibilities of my position, and how much work I have got to do. The annual meeting of the Non-Resistance Society is at hand, and

691

my poor brains have got to be severely tasked to make out an annual report in readiness for the occasion.³ Time no longer flies with leaden wings and cumbrous weight, as he did when we were straying three thousand miles from home; but his flight is now like the eagle's, and as brilliant but evanescent as the lightning's flash. O, the comforts, the endearments, the joys of home! Are there any other two such spots in all this wide world as are to be found in Concord and Cambridge-port? What say you? Thanks to the impartial Giver of all good gifts, there are many others, besides ourselves, whose love for wife, children, friends and home is as ardent and pure as our own; who, separated from these, sigh and droop as we did on the other side of the great, tumultuous, terrible Atlantic; and whose relish for domestic bliss is perfect.

I went to Brooklyn after my dear little George Thompson, the morning that you left to catch a glimpse, and to receive the embraces and congratulations of the members of your sweet family. Helen and the babe went with me, and it proved a most pleasant jaunt. The weather was delightful, and our ride without any fatigue or incon-venience. We went by rail-road from Boston to Worcester, and from Worcester to Killingley, which is within three or four miles of Brook-lyn. Within seven years, it was a long and tedious day's ride from Boston to Brooklyn. We had to start as early as three o'clock in the morning. Now the distance is performed in five hours, in a truly luxurious manner. So much for making a straight path, levelling the hills and exalting the valleys, and using steam-power! So it will be with our moral rail-roads. The spirit of man will ride easily by and by, methinks! We must dig, and drill, and blast awhile longer, before a dead level can be made on which to try the speed of the great loco-motive engine of Truth. "It's coming yet, for a' that." ⁴

Little Georgey met us at the Killingley depot. He was so over-joyed to see us, that he could not recover his equilibrium for some time. He was particularly glad to see his little baby-brother, whom he had never seen before, and in whose existence he had stoutly re-fused to believe — ⁵ [En *passant* — I have named the [. . . house-] hold at Brooklyn were well, but I [. . .] George at home. He had gone to Pro[vidence . . .] nian courses to Mrs. Davis, wife of [. . .] of Wm. M. Chace. She is in a decline, [. . .] her recovery. I found bro. James in [. . .] when I left. He looked quite farmer-like, [. . .] useful. He inquired particularly after you, for whom he has [. . . re-] spect and esteem. I hope he may be prevailed upon to remain in Brooklyn during the winter, but he is rather anxious to be in Boston again.

Bro. Johnson ⁶ accompanied me to B.⁷ We went to Canterbury, to see the house in which Miss Crandall kept her school. Andrew T. Judson's [8] house is on the opposite side of the street. We saw that unhappy and guilty man sitting at his front-door. Without he repents, "it were good for that m[an] that he had never been born." [9]

One thing I must enjoin upon you seriously. You must not expect me to make any formal address to any audience in Concord. I cannot do it. My head is too much confused to think of a regular speech. I have forgotten all that I ever knew — which was not much. — I will join in your discussions as well as I am able.

Think as you will about it, your speech at the Marlboro' Chapel [10] (all personal allusions in it to myself out of the question,) was a very neat and acceptable one. It was well received by the audience who heard it, and the report of it has been read with pleasure by others.

I will return your thanks to Mr. and Mrs. Southwick as soon as I see them. Your stay with them was their rich compensation.

It makes me feel both sorrowful and indignant to hear that there are abolitionists in New-Hampshire and Massachusetts, who avow [11] [. . .]ey are certainly infatuated; or some-[. . .] moral sense, and inflict a se[. . .] sist in their purpose.

[. . .]lem gave me a public welcome and [. . .] last week. I wish, and they wished, that [. . .] on the occasion.

Give my strong regards to bro. Chandler, [12] George Kent, and other esteemed friends in Concord. Dear Helen unites with me in sending much love to your excellent wife, whom, with yourself, we shall be at all times most happy to see at our house.

Our mutual friend Mary Clark will be the bearer of this to you. It was very pleasant to meet her in the city. You will be equally glad to see her in Concord.

Your loving friend,

Wm. Lloyd Garrison.

ALS: Charles Roberts Autograph Collection, Haverford College, Pennsylvania. The third and fourth pages of the original manuscript are torn.

1. The New Hampshire Anti-Slavery Convention of September 9 and 10.
2. September 9.
3. The Non-Resistance Convention, the second annual meeting of the Non-Resistance Society, was held at Chardon-Street Chapel on September 23 and 24.
4. Robert Burns, "A Man's A Man for A' That" (1795).
5. The next page is torn.
6. Oliver Johnson.
7. Brooklyn, Connecticut.
8. See letter 18, to George W. Benson, April 10, 1836, n. 8.
9. Matthew 26:24.
10. This was at the meeting of August 20, to welcome back Garrison and N. P. Rogers from England, reported in *The Liberator*, August 28, 1840.
11. The page is torn here.
12. John B. Chandler of Concord, New Hampshire (b. February 13, 1805;

d. August 3, 1864). An ardent abolitionist, he was called "a local doctrinaire" by the Reverend Henry McFarland, the minister of the First Congregational Church in Concord. He caused an uproar in Concord and elsewhere by refusing to be married by a clergyman. Instead, he married Maria Church, another abolitionist, by mutual declaration, in the presence of witnesses, at the breakfast table. He was present at the meeting in Concord on September 9 and 10 and proposed a resolution opposing N. P. Rogers' removal to New York as editor of the *Standard*. He was a clockmaker and a deacon of the North Church from 1836 to 1837, when he transferred his commitment to the South Church (Congregational), which was then organized. He was deacon there until 1842, when he was dismissed because of his abolitionism. He is reported to have become "deranged" by spiritualism, and died in the New Hampshire Asylum. (*Sixty Years in Concord and Elsewhere, Personal Recollection of Henry McFarland*, Concord, 1899, pp. 21–22; George Chandler, *The Descendants of William and Amos Chandler*, Boston, 1872, pp. 646, 1007.)

217

TO AMOS FARNSWORTH

Boston, Sept. 6, 1840

My dear friend:

Your letter of the 1st inst, inviting me, in behalf of the Groton Antislavery Society, to visit your place for the purpose of giving one or more lectures on slavery is another proof among numerous others that have been given, that my course on the other side of the Atlantic meets with the cordial approval of my antislavery friends and associates in this country. I am gratified & strengthened by it. How soon I shall be able to comply with the invitation it is now quite difficult for me to say. Our Non-Resistance Anniversary is rapidly approaching, and I have yet a long Report to draw up for the Society: then follow the State Convention to be held in Worcester & Springfield early in October. On Wednesday morning I must go to Concord, N.H. to be present at the State Convention, and to assist in determining the question, whether Rogers shall go to New York to edit the Standard. Our friends in the Granite State naturally feel reluctant to give him up, and he himself shrinks from occupying so conspicuous and important a post; but I am decidedly of opinion that he ought to go, and that, if he should decline going, it would be very injurious to the subscription list of the Standard — which, I doubt not, has been considerably augmented by the expectation, that, on his return from abroad, he would occupy the national editorial chair. Besides, the seceders from us, I think, fear his caustic racy pen more than that of any other man we could send to New York. It is, however, very doubtful whether he can be persuaded to go; for his local attachments are very strong, and there are some difficulties in the way.

If I had time, I should like to fill this and a much larger sheet with giving you some particulars of my trip to the old world; but I have many letters to write, and a great many engagements on hand, besides a vast amount of documents, pamphlets, newspapers &c. to wade through, which have accumulated during our absence. I will reserve therefore what I have to say about matters & things in England, Scotland and the Emerald Isle, until we are permitted to see each other face to face.

So beautiful, so like a Paradise is all England, that since my return, our lands every where look wild and uncultivated; and scenes which were once full of attraction now seem to be quite homely, as well as homelike in their aspect. Perhaps even Groton may suffer by the comparison; and yet, for fineness of locality, beauty & grandeur of scenery and extension of prospect, I am not sure that there are many places abroad to surpass it. At least I am anxious to take another peep at it as soon as practicable, and especially to take you by the hand, and enjoy once more your faithful friendship and generous hospitality.

Henry G. Chapman is now somewhat ill, having had another attack of bleeding internally. How he is today I have not heard. I know not that he is considered dangerous. The worst of it is, he is in the hands of a regular physician! There's a thrust for you! Peradventure, all may go well.

I wish to return to the Anti Slavery Society my thanks for their kind invitation, and to be remembered to Messrs Hawley, Boutelle, Hall [1] and other friends, in affectionate terms —

Your much obliged friend,
Wm. Lloyd Garrison.

Transcript: Garrison Papers, Boston Public Library.

1. The Reverend Silas Hawley (b. Amherst, Massachusetts, August 15, 1815; d. November 3, 1888) of Groton, Massachusetts, was editor of the *Christian Reformer*, a paper devoted to the subject of Christian union. His family moved to central New York when he was a child, and remained there until 1839. He was opposed to slavery even during his student days, before the establishment of *The Liberator*, though his father was a colonizationist. He was present at the organization of the New York Anti-Slavery Society in Utica, New York, in October 1835. He was pastor, for some time, of the Congregational Church of Cazenovia, near Peterboro, New Hampshire, and resigned because of broken health. Thereafter he traveled widely and spoke on church unity and national reform. In the fall of 1839, he came to Groton as guest of Amos Farnsworth, to serve as lecturer and antislavery agent for the Massachusetts Anti-Slavery Society. After 1840, his main interest became Primitive Church unity. He founded the Christian Church in Groton and became its first minister in 1840, and left in 1841. In 1873, he retired to Beaver Dam, Wisconsin, where he continued his evangelical labors. (Silas Hawley, *Reminiscences of Groton during the Years 1839, 1840 and 1841*, Groton, 1886, a pamphlet; Elias S. Hawley, *The Hawley Record*, Buffalo, N.Y., 1890, p. 568.)

Elder Luther Boutelle (b. Groton, May 4, 1806) had a shoe shop and home on Hollis Street in Groton, frequented by antislavery workers. He was an advocate of temperance, antislavery, and other social and religious reforms. At first a

Congregationalist, he later became an Adventist, under the influence of William Miller, who predicted that "the Lord would come (in 1844)." He later went to Grafton, Vermont, and then to other parts of New England and the middle states, where he preached as an Adventist. At the time of his ninetieth birthday he was living in Chelsea, Massachusetts. (Isaac C. Wellcome, *History of the Second Advent Message and Mission, Doctrine and People*, Yarmouth, Me., 1874, pp. 219–220; Samuel Abbott Green, ed., *Groton Historical Series*, Groton, 1899, IV, 233–235; Clara Endicott Sears, *Days of Delusion: A Strange Bit of History*, Boston and New York, 1924, p. 188 *et passim*.)

Benjamin Hall of Groton, Massachusetts, was also a follower of William Miller in 1840. Clara Endicott Sears, in *Days of Delusion*, pp. 188–189, refers to Hall as "a fire-eater in fanaticism, who was ostensibly a follower of William Miller, but who in reality disseminated some theories of his own which were wholly at variance with the latter's doctrine, the result being that the confusion of ideas in regard to what was portending was well-nigh distracting to those awaiting the end. Groton had acquired some reputation as a centre of rebellion to orthodox creeds, and a few years before, in 1840, had held a convention of followers of Prophet Miller and Come-Outers. It had attracted the notice of the public and a number of persons went there largely from curiosity to learn upon what grounds they based their theories, and among others were Theodore Parker, A. Bronson Alcott, George Ripley, of Brook Farm fame, and Christopher P. Cranch, of Newton, who walked there from Concord."

218

TO SAMUEL J. MAY

Boston, Sept. 6, 1840.

My dear bro. May:

Your kind "Welcome home again!" comes joyously to my ears, among the thousand congratulations that have been given to me on my safe return from the old world. During my absence, I saw much that was magnificent, wonderful, curious, strange, pleasant, afflicting; but my mind is too much confused, by the multitudinous array of objects and incidents, to allow me to state any thing accurately. All that the Tower, Westminster Abbey, St. Paul's, the British Museum, and many other famous places contain, I have seen, and gazed upon, till my eyes were weary of sight-seeing. England, in beauty, order, and cultivation of soil, is indisputably the Eden of the world; but, alas! the old serpent is in it, and as full of falsehood and mischief as ever. Oppression, degradation, vice, starvation are there, side by side with monarchy, royalty, aristocracy, monopoly. England is on a volcano, which, if it explode, will cover her with desolation. Should Victoria suddenly expire, in all probability there would be a revolution that would scatter to the four winds her present form of government, and establish a republican one in its place. But the people need more light as well as more bread, and they are determined to have both, or perish in the attempt. I could not enjoy the beautiful landscapes of England, because of the suffering and want staring me in the face, on the one hand, and the opulence and splendor dazzling my vision, on the other. O, to think that God — our kind, merciful, loving Creator — has filled this earth with abundance for all, and yet that nine-tenths of mankind are living in squalid poverty and abject servitude in order to sustain in idleness and profligacy the one-tenth!

I was much pleased with Scotland — better pleased than with England. Her scenery, indeed, is not so beautiful, but it is far more grand and sublime; and she has enough of beauty to atone for what is wild and rude in her formation. I like her people better than I do the people of England: they are more like New-Englanders in their appearance and manners. I was exceedingly pleased with the Irish friends I saw in Dublin, and received from them a welcome most cordial and ardent. But I must wait till I see you, and then you shall hear all about the "gipseying" of bro. Rogers and myself. I must contrive to come down and see you on some Saturday, and remain with you till Monday, lecturing on Sabbath evening, if agreeable. This I will try to do in the course of two or three weeks. On Wednesday, I must go to Concord, N.H. to attend a State Convention, and help determine the question, whether bro. Rogers shall go to New-York to edit the Standard. I want him to go — and so do the anti-slavery friends generally; but he shrinks from the post, and his New-Hampshire friends very naturally desire him to remain in Concord. Many persons have subscribed for the Standard, solely on the supposition that he would be the editor of it; and it would go hard with the paper, I fear, if he should disappoint them. Besides, it would be very difficult for us to find an acceptable substitute. James C. Jackson, who has edited the Standard up to this time with so much ability, could not be prevailed upon to be the permanent editor; and we ought not to confine so able a lecturer to an editorial chair.

I am happy to find that, in refusing to connect myself with the London Convention, I have acted in accordance with the views and feelings of the friends of old organization, both white and colored. The Convention embodied a great amount of talent, respectability and philanthropy, but it was entirely under the control of the London Committee, whose usurpation ought to have been resisted in the spirit of the Lord's freemen. They will be caught, however, in their own sectarian craftiness, and made to lament what they have done.

The greatest honor I ever received in my life was conferred upon me by the colored citizens of Boston in the meeting called by them at the Marlboro' Chapel — the proceedings of which you have doubtless seen in the Liberator. Their reception of me was affectionate and cordial beyond my powers of description, and most deeply affecting to my heart. The colored people in Salem also gave me an elegant entertainment, and a very welcome reception. How faithful and true ought I to be to them! how ardent should be my zeal, how incessant my labors, in their behalf!

I have been to Brooklyn since my return, with Helen and the babe, in order to bring little Georgie home. It was indescribably pleasant to see that dear spot again, around which cluster some of my fondest recollections. All the members of the household were well, but bro. George was absent during our stay. I lectured, on Sabbath evening, in Elder Coe's meeting-house, to a small audience, in reference to the London Convention.

Sister Anne and mother are still with us. The former had a severe fall upon the face from our door-steps a day or two since, knocked out a tooth, and bruised herself considerably. She is now better.

Henry G. Chapman is quite unwell, at present. He has had another attack of bleeding internally, and, what is worse, is in the hands of a regular physician. I do not know that any serious danger is apprehended, but I think I know what kind of treatment he needs. All the other Boston friends, I believe, are well, and in good spirits. My own health has been much improved by my visit abroad.

Are not Howitt's and O'Connell's letters,[1] in reference to the exclusion of our female delegates, excellent and important?

I take it for granted that you will be present at the Non-Resistance anniversary. It will be a good one, I trust, and blessed of the Lord.

Helen, mother and Anne desire to be cordially remembered to Mrs. May and yourself. I long to see you both.

Every lovingly yours,

Wm. Lloyd Garrison.

ALS: Garrison Papers, Boston Public Library.

1. Daniel O'Connell's letter, dated "16 Pall Mall, 20th June, 1840," appeared in *The Liberator*, September 4, 1840, together with a letter from Lucretia Mott to O'Connell, dated "London, 6th mo. 17, 1840." Mrs. Mott's letter had asked for O'Connell's opinion concerning the refusal of the London Anti-Slavery Convention to seat the female American delegates. O'Connell's reply stated that he had originally opposed their admission, but that on receiving Mrs. Mott's letter he had given the matter further thought and had arrived at the opposite opinion. "My mature consideration of the entire subject convinces me of the right of the female delegates to take their seats in the Convention, and of the injustice of excluding them. I do not care to add, that I deem it also impolitic; because that exclusion being unjust, it ought not to have taken place, even if it could also be impolitic."

The letter from William Howitt, a Quaker, philanthropist, and man of letters, dated "London, June 27th 1840," to Lucretia Mott, appeared in *The Liberator*, August 28, 1840. He condemned the refusal to admit the ladies to the convention, in which he had not taken part, and attributed their rejection to Quaker sectarianism. "I heard of the circumstance of your exclusion at a distance, and immediately said — 'Excluded on the ground that they are women?' No, that is not the real cause — there is something behind. Who and what are these female delegates? Are they orthodox in religion? The answer was, 'No, they are considered to be of the Hicksite party of Friends.' My reply was, 'That is enough — *there* lies the real cause, and there needs no other. . . . But what a miserable spectacle is this! The 'World's Convention' converting itself into the fag-end of the yearly meeting of the Society of Friends!'"

219

TO MRS. HENRY WALKER

Boston, Sept 8, 1840.

Dear Madam:

After I parted from you at the Rotherham Fair, (an interview which I shall ever remember with pleasure,) I visited York, Newcastle, Tynemouth, Melrose, Edinburgh, Glasgow, Paisley, Dublin, and many other intermediate places; and the reception I every where met with, not only as a stranger from another country, but as the friend and advocate of the colored race, was such as to fill my heart with gratitude, and to lay me under the heaviest obligations — obligations which I fear I shall never have an opportunity to discharge. On arriving in Liverpool to embark for the United States, I found that your box of contributions for the anti-slavery cause in this country had safely arrived; but I was compelled to leave in such haste, that I could not get time to send you even a brief note, acknowledging its receipt. In your letter accompanying the box, you intimated that it might be as well to send it to the New-York instead of the Bangor Fair, but kindly allowed me to make such disposal of it as I might think proper. As I know of no Fair to be held in New-York, and as the beautiful articles you have sent would not probably sell so well in so small and remote a place as Bangor, and as we are soon to have a grand Fair at Worcester and in Boston, I have taken the liberty to consign them to the care of our celebrated Mrs. Chapman,[1] who will see that they are disposed of to the best advantage, and will doubtless send you a letter of thanks. May the proceeds be instrumental in breaking the yokes and fetters of the millions who are grinding in the American prison-house of bondage, and the Lord Almighty reward you for your kindness!

I left Liverpool on the 4th of August, in the steamer Acadia, and arrived home after a passage of only twelve days and a half — the shortest ever yet made across the Atlantic. Short as it was, it seemed very long to me — so anxious was I once more to be in the bosom of my family, and at my old post, conflicting with the enemies of human freedom. How swift is the flight of the mind! How it annihilates time and space, and overleaps mountains and seas as though they were aids rather than hindrances! What a laggard is the lightning, compared with thought! How easy it is, in imagination, to pass from Boston to Rotherham! More than three thousand miles in less than a moment! Such perfect mastery has spirit over matter — so much more agile is the soul than the body!

I found my beloved family in the enjoyment of good health, though the dear babe that was born during my absence had had a very narrow escape from death by sickness. My friends were overjoyed to see me. But nothing could exceed the enthusiasm of the colored population of Boston. They immediately called a public meeting in the Marlboro' Chapel, (the largest in the city,) to give me a public welcome; and a most thrilling and affecting occasion it was to my spirit. Persecuted, but excellent people! To suffer with them is my highest ambition, and to know that they hail me as their faithful friend and advocate is the greatest honor I can desire.

The refusal of the London Convention to receive the American female delegates has greatly impaired its beauty and power in the eyes of the genuine abolitionists of this country. It was an act that would commend itself to the slaveholder, but not to the slave. Let every soul that wishes to bear its testimony against the fiendish system of slavery be gratified to the utmost. In Christ Jesus, all are one.

I am now in the land of prejudice and slavery. O, if these could only be eradicated from it, there would be no land to compare with it under heaven. Putting these out of the question, (alas! they cannot be!) our people, in general intelligence, equality, comfort and enterprise, are far, very far in advance of any other people on the face of the globe. We therefore sin against the clearest light, and in the most awful manner. But a spirit of repentance and reformation is beginning to prevail extensively in the land, on this subject. We shall not much longer tolerate slavery in our borders. It is contrary to our Declaration of Independence, our Constitution, and our theory of government; and being also diametrically opposed to the spirit of the gospel, it must die soon, and die ignominiously.

I shall ever remember my visit to Sheffield and Rotherham with unmingled delight and the purest satisfaction. The pleasant scenes of Winco Bank [2] are constantly before my eyes, and I long to be once more under the roof of Mrs. Rawson [3] — a lady whose kindness I can never too highly appreciate, and for whom I entertain the very highest respect. Should you happen to see her, you will greatly oblige me by giving my friendly and grateful remembrances to her, her mother, sister, &c. I wish also that my respects may be given to the

Countess of Effingham [4] and James Montgomery,[5] and also to Mr. Walker.

It will give me much pleasure to hear from you or any of the friends in your vicinity, at any time. Any information I can give in return shall be cheerfully comunicated.

Yours, with great regard,

Wm. Lloyd Garrison.

Mrs. Walker.

ALS; Lilly Library, Indiana University. The letter is addressed to Clifton House, near Rotherham, England.

Mrs. Henry Walker is otherwise unidentified.

1. Maria Weston Chapman.

2. At about the middle of July 1840, Garrison, Rogers, Remond, and Thompson visited Sheffield, where they enjoyed the hospitality of the Rawsons of Wincobank Hall (*Life*, II, 395).

3. Mrs. Mary A. Rawson (d. Sheffield, England, August 11, 1887, aged eighty-five). Otherwise unidentified. (*Life*, IV, 408.)

4. The Countess of Effingham (d. 1864), whose maiden name was Lady Charlotte Primrose, was the eldest daughter of Neil, third Earl of Rosebery. In 1800 she married Kenneth Alexander Howard (1767–1845), the first Earl of Effingham of the second creation, a general and a Whig. She remarried in 1858. (*DNB*.)

5. James Montgomery (1771–1854), "'beloved bard of Negro freedom'" (*Life*, II, 395), was one of Garrison's favorite poets (*Life*, IV, 314). His father was a Moravian minister in Irvine, Ayrshire, Scotland. The Sheffield *Register*, to which he had contributed, became his property in 1795. He was an opponent of Negro slavery in the West Indies and of the slave trade. In 1807, he was asked to write a poem about the abolition of the African slave trade by the British Parliament during that year. The result was the publication in 1809 of "The West Indies," a poem in four parts. He also wrote "Songs of the Abolition of Negro Slavery in the British Colonies, August 1, 1834." In 1858, *The Poetical Works of James Montgomery* was published in Boston in five volumes (*DNB*; Eva B. Dykes, *The Negro in English Romantic Thought*, Washington, D.C., 1942, *passim.*)

220

TO GEORGE W. BENSON

Boston, Sept. 17, 1840

My dear George:

I am in a hurry, and must write a very short letter. The long and short of it shall be, that you must be at our non-resistance meeting next week.[1] Let nothing, I pray you, that is *surmountable*, keep you away. Remember how important is the meeting, and how necessary it is that every one of us should be found in his place on that occasion. Remember, too, that I have not seen you since I crossed the Big Lake, — visited the great English Babel, London, — ascended the highlands of Scotland, — sailed across Loch Katrine and Loch Lomond,

— saw Rob Roy's cave where he used to hide from his pursuers,[2] — went into Holyrood Palace, where the unfortunate Queen Mary used to reside, and where her favorite Secretary David Rizzio was murdered almost before her own eyes — &c. &c. O, but I *must* see you — so, come along, and bring as many non-resistants along with you as possible.

I have written a few lines to bro. James. If he can make up his mind to stay in Brooklyn during the winter, I shall be glad. His health is, probably, not sufficiently restored to make it safe for him, at present, to try a voyage at sea. He could not be in Boston, or Cambridgeport, without being in the way of strong temptation, which it would be difficult, if not impossible, for him to resist. This is now not to be regarded in him as a fault, but as a misfortune. I am quite sure that James wishes to lead a virtuous and sober life; but, if he would succeed in his purpose, he must remain awhile longer in the country. I have told him that you would counsel him as a brother, and that your interest in his welfare is equal to my own. I have told him, further, that, whatever clothing or other necessaries he might need, you and I would freely supply him with them. He told me that he wanted to be where he could be earning something, and not to feel dependant.[3] I assured him that there was no dependance about it, and that we should not regard him as laboring under special obligation to either of us. Pray try to satisfy him on this point.

But I must stop. Let me see you next Wednesday. Love to Catharine, Sisters Mary and Sarah, and kind remembrances to the Scarboroughs.

Yours, ever,

Wm. Lloyd Garrison.

ALS: Garrison Papers, Boston Public Library.

1. The second annual convention of the New England Non-Resistance Society, called for September 23, 1840, in Boston.

2. Rob Roy (1671–1734), Scottish freebooter and outlaw whose true name was Robert MacGregor. He was popularized by Sir Walter Scott's novel, *Rob Roy*. (*CVDE.*)

3. So spelled in manuscript.

221

TO JAMES GARRISON

Boston, Sept. 17, 1840.

My dear James:

It is with me all the time, hurry, hurry, hurry; else I should have written to you before. Not that I have much to say, but it is pleasant to say "how d'ye do?" to a brother, if nothing more; especially if the health of that brother be somewhat impaired by disease. I did not express to you when I was in Brooklyn, (for I could not find words to do it,) how cheering it was to my spirit to find you in such good condition of body and mind, after my rambles on the other side of the Atlantic. I hope your health has continued to improve since I saw you, and that you have become more attached to the place than ever. It seems to me, as one loving you as I do my own soul, and desirous of giving you good advice, that the best thing you can do will be to remain with bro. George through the winter. This will give you time to recover your strength as fully as possible by the time that spring opens, when you can (if you think best) go to sea again; though I could wish that you would not have the disposition ever again to try the "billowy main." Be that as it may, you are probably not well enough to go on a voyage at present. As for living in or near Boston, I would not advise you to try the experiment. You know, dear James, your liability to fall into temptation; and though you may think that you can guard yourself, and that there is no danger, yet experience must have taught you that, under the pressure of temptation, surrounded by shipmates, you are not able successfully to resist — gladly as you would do so, if the thing were possible.

Your safety, health, improvement, and true happiness, will all be promoted by remaining in Brooklyn. Bro. George and the family will delight to do every thing in their power to make your abode an agreeable one. We shall be able to correspond with each other frequently, which will be next to conversing with each other, face to face. Whatever you want of clothing, books, papers, &c. you shall have, on making it known to me or bro. George. You shall not lack for any thing to make you comfortable. My rich recompense will be in seeing you rising in the scale of improvement, and towering up consciously as one "made but a little lower than the angels." [1] Brooklyn is a beautiful home; and in the company of the dear household there, and of the Scarboroughs, and others, time may be made to pass pleasantly and rapidly.

You must be careful not to work too hard. You are naturally very ambitious, and will therefore be in continual danger of going beyond your strength. Take every thing "fair and easy" — moderately — and "make yourself at home." This is as much the wish of bro. George as it [is] my own. He loves you like a brother. Give due heed to whatever he may advise you, for his judgment is very sound, his forecast remarkable, and his kindness disinterested and pure. It will be of real service to you occasionally to take a Thompsonian course, and he will be as good a doctor as you can obtain elsewhere. May Heaven bless and guide you, and make the remainder of your life as honorable and happy as either of us could desire.

There is nothing new with us at Cambridgeport. Friend Johnson has been spending some time at Nantucket. His wife is now in Vermont. Mr. Knight has broken up housekeeping, and sold all his furniture. He is very much involved in debt, even to utter bankruptcy. The house in which we live has been attached. The part occupied formerly by Mr. Knight is still vacant, and there is little or no probability that it will be let this winter. We are all in good health. Sister Anna has recovered from the effect of the fall which she had from the door-step a short time since. We have named our little babe Wendell Phillips. He is growing finely, and is certainly one of the best babes in all creation. His good nature is continual: he sleeps quietly all night long, is afraid of nobody, and is decidedly pretty. George and Willie are rousing lads, full of life and spirit, and still somewhat hard to manage. George goes to school pretty regularly, but is not disposed to be very scholastic. He says he does not like Cambridgeport, but wishes to go into the country, to Brooklyn, to live. He often speaks of you all, Mr. Scarborough, Herbert, Lucy,[2] &c.

The Whig Bunker Hill parade was a very great one, but I did not happen to see it, as I was on a visit at the time to Concord, N.H. It was a foolish affair, got up, of course, for political effect. It seems now, almost beyond a doubt, that Gen. Harrison is to be the next President.

I saw Rogers at Concord. He kindly inquired after you. It is somewhat doubtful whether he goes to New-York to take charge of the Standard. I did what I could at the Concord meeting to get him to remove. His decision will soon be made up.

Tell bro. George that we all expect he will be at the Non-Resistance meeting in this city next week. He must not disappoint us. I shall expect to receive a letter from you by him.

Bro. Collins, Johnson, Chace, and all at home, desire to be cordially remembered to you. Give our love to all the dear friends in Brooklyn.

Your affectionate brother,
Wm. Lloyd Garrison.

ALS: Garrison Papers, Boston Public Library.

1. Psalms 8:5.
2. The references are to Philip Scarborough; Herbert, the son of Philip and Deidamia Scarborough, and the brother of Lucy, born on April 6, 1820 (typescript of Vital Records of Brooklyn, Connecticut, in New England Historic Genealogical Society, p. 58); and Lucy Scarborough.

2 2 2

TO PHEBE JACKSON

Boston, Sept. 19, 1840.

My dear friend:

I am anticipating a great deal of pleasure in the confident expectation of seeing you and many other beloved friends and acquaintances, at the non-resistance meetings to be held in this city on Wednesday and Thursday next. Dear Helen joins with me in offering you the hospitality of our house, such as it is, in Cambridgeport; and in expressing the hope that nothing will hinder you from coming to see us. Our meetings in Boston will doubtless be highly interesting; and as their object is peace on earth and good will to all mankind, after the pattern of the Son of God, our adorable Redeemer, who laid down his life for his enemies, it is very desirable that all who are interested in it, in this region, will be present on the occasion. True, they who would seem in any way to countenance, ay, even to tolerate our proceedings, especially by their presence, must run the hazard of suffering reproach, and being reckoned among the off-scouring of all things; but this, I am sure from what I know of your spirit, will rather stimulate you to come than to keep away. In your experience, you have been able to verify the declaration of the Savior — "*Blessed are ye when men shall revile you, and persecute you, and shall say all manner of evil against you falsely, for my sake.*" [1] For myself, I can truly say, that I rejoice, and am exceeding glad, to be ridiculed and denounced for my views of the gospel of peace. In the correctness of those views, I am more and more confirmed. They fill my soul with tranquillity and joy, and ally it to the spirit of the Messiah. Surely, if all mankind would embrace these views, there would no more blood be shed, the use of all carnal weapons would cease, every man would sit under his own vine and fig-tree, and there would be none to molest or make afraid. How insane, therefore, are they who say that non-resistance will lead to anarchy and bloodshed!

Since I saw you last, you know I have been a sojourner in the old world, whereof I have much to tell you when we meet. I have seen all manner of things, strange, beautiful, curious and sublime. England, Scotland and Ireland are crowded with all heroic, classical, historical incidents; so that almost every inch of ground upon which the traveller treads is associated with some important or remarkable event. In fact, I was fairly tired of sight-seeing; and yet "the eye is not satisfied with seeing, nor the ear with hearing." [2] Our country in nothing resembles England. We have (and I rejoice that we have) no ruined priories and abbeys, no towers, no castles, no royal palaces, and but few monuments. Our buildings declare nothing of antiquity. We are of yesterday, as a people, and can point to nothing which was the work of the Romans, Saxons, Normans, or Danes. Nature, or, rather, Nature's God, has done much for our country; for its mountains, rivers, cataracts, wildernesses, and vast domains, are far superior to any that the United Kingdom can show. England, however, is far more beautiful — so beautiful, indeed, that, since my return home, every thing looks very much deteriorated, and I can scarcely find a captivating spot. But there is one exception to be made. Thanks to the goodness of God, I am restored in safety to my home; and I challenge all Europe, the whole world, to produce a more delightful place. "There is no place like it," at least to me. Surrounded by my dear wife and children, and feeling reconciled to God and no enmity toward any human being, I am very happy. My enemies are numerous, active, bitter; but they only distress their own souls — not mine. It gives me no uneasiness to read what they allege against me as an "infidel," a "disturber of the peace," and "a pestilent fellow." They know, quite as well as I do, that the truth is not in them, and that they bear false witness.

Some time during this fall, I hope to visit Providence, and perhaps give a public lecture. I wish to see, face to face, the true-hearted men and women (few though they may be) in your city, and to assure them of my high appreciation of their labors in the cause of our common humanity.

I wish to be specially remembered to your mother, with whom I sympathize on account of her being an invalid; but I doubt not that she finds, even in a sick chamber, that the grace of God is sufficient for her. May the light of his reconciled countenance ever shine upon her! Remember me, also, in terms of friendship, to Dr. Flagg and wife, whose kindness, as manifested to me on various occasions, I shall ever gratefully appreciate.

We are all well at home. Anna and mother are still with us. Mother will probably return home in a few days, with bro. George. I have named the dear babe that was born during my absence, Wendell Phillips. He is, of course, a none-such. I am commissioned to give our united love to you, your mother, &c. &c.

Yours, with great esteem,

Wm. Lloyd Garrison.

ALS: New York Public Library.

1. Matthew 5:11.
2. Ecclesiastes 1:8.

2 2 3

TO ELIZABETH PEASE

Boston, Sept. 30, 1840.

My dear friend:

I admit that I deserve a good scolding, for having lost the opportunity (by about 15 minutes only!) of sending letters to you and other dear friends in England by the Acadia, on her return passage. It is not, however, in your nature to scold, and therefore I shall escape. I had written sundry letters to send by the Acadia, but, owing to a misunderstanding (which was general among our citizens) as to the hour of her departure, failed to get them into the mail-bag. My regret, as you can easily imagine, was very great. A Liberator was forwarded to you, informing you of our safe arrival home, and of the reception given to us by our white and colored friends; and this consoled me not a little.

As many thanks as there are waves in the Atlantic for the epistle received from you by the Britannia. You see what liberty I have taken with it, and some others brought me by our mutual friend George Bradburn, in the last number of the Liberator.[1]

Thomas Clarkson's letter,[2] repudiating the Colonization Society, is of great value, and will make a salutary impression upon the public mind. I am overjoyed to think that the dear old man has publicly abandoned that wicked combination, and left it to perish in infamy. It would have been most afflicting to all the genuine friends of bleeding humanity, if he had gone down to the grave even ostensibly as a supporter of that Society. I am surprised, nevertheless, that, in stating his objections to it, he does not say one word about its impious doctrines and pro-slavery principles. He really seems to be wholly ignorant of them!

Little did I think, my dear friend, that you would so soon see among you another of our anti-slavery band in Massachusetts; but I am as happy to introduce to you, (as I doubt not you will be to see him,) my esteemed friend and coadjutor, John A. Collins, the General Agent of the Massachusetts Anti-Slavery Society, and a member of our Board of Managers. He is a free spirit, a lover of universal reform, most zealous and efficient as an advocate of emancipation, one who has made large sacrifices for our cause, is thoroughly conversant with all the schisms that have taken place in our ranks, and is generally successful in whatever he undertakes. The object of his mission he will lay before you and the other choice spirits in England, so that I need not go into any details in this letter. Suffice it to say, that, in consequence of the political excitement now raging like a whirlwind in this country — the embarassed state of the times — and, especially, the blow which our third party abolitionists and the new organizationists have given to the anti-slavery enterprise — we are really in a more critical situation than we have ever been before; and, unless we can get some aid from abroad, I am apprehensive that the American Anti-Slavery Society, with the National Standard, Rogers and all, must sink. We have, you may rest assured, strained every nerve to sustain ourselves; and it is with the greatest reluctance that we send our bro. Collins on his mission. It is a dernier resort, "for better, for worse." We are well aware how many are the calls made upon our British friends, to promote objects of charity, mercy and religion; but we know, too, that they have realized the truth of the Saviour's declaration, that "it is more blessed to give than to receive." In attempting to put away the evil that is in the world, we must forget all national distinctions and geographical boundaries, and remember that we are indeed members of one family, to whom there is nothing foreign, nothing remote. I have told my friend Collins of the difficulties that will lie in his path, especially in consequence of the introduction of the new organization spirit among you in England. He goes out, therefore, with very moderate expectations; for even a little assistance will amount to a great deal at this juncture. We trust, for our sakes, that his mission will be short, for we cannot spare him long abroad. I rely very much upon your judgment, and also that of Geo. Thompson, in this emergency. Do counsel my friend Collins, for he will need to be wise as a serpent, and harmless as a dove. He goes out in behalf of the American Society, the Executive Committee of which, I presume, will send an address by him to the anti-slavery friends in England. Our Board, also, will furnish him with some credentials.

Next week, we are to have a State Anti-Slavery Convention in Worcester, at which Rogers and myself must be present to give an account of our doings in England. I wish *you* could be present. There is hardly another person in all the world that I desire to see so much as yourself. I hope we shall have a whole shipload of British abolitionists, *of the right stamp*, imported to these shores, ere long. We must have a World's Convention in Boston.

My dear Helen feels very grateful to you for your numerous kindnesses to me, and would be glad of an opportunity to return like for like. My family are all well, and my own health continues good.

You must let me hear from you as often as convenient. I will *try* to be punctual in giving letter for letter. My time here is very much absorbed in the anti-slavery and non-resistance enterprises; and I cannot write so frequently as I should otherwise be glad to do. I have not, as yet, said much about the state of things in England in the *Liberator;* but intend to as soon as our State meetings shall have been concluded.

As soon as a correct report of your grand meeting in Manchester, in behalf of British India, shall reach me, I will commence the publication of the proceedings.[3] I still look to that movement with the deepest interest, and shall aid it to the utmost of my poor ability.

Mary S. Parker has been quite ill for some time, and is evidently in a consumption.

I wish I was in Darlington to-day, provided I could return home to-morrow — or, rather, provided the Atlantic did not roll between. All I can do is, to desire to be affectionately remembered to your father, mother, brother, and all inquiring friends. In haste,

Yours, in every good work,

Wm. Lloyd Garrison.

ALS: Garrison Papers, Boston Public Library; printed, in part, in *Life,* II, 416–418.

1. *The Liberator,* September 25, 1840, printed letters from Elizabeth Pease (Liverpool, September 3, 1840), George Thompson (Liverpool, September 4, 1840), Charles L. Remond (Manchester, England, August 31, 1840), Richard D. Webb (Dublin, July 2, 1840), and others. In an explanatory comment, Garrison remarked that "By the arrival of the steamer Britannia at this port, we have received several letters and newspapers from our anti-slavery friends in England, containing much interesting intelligence; and although the former (excepting the venerable Clarkson's letter) were written for our private perusal, in great haste, yet we have taken the liberty to publish such portions of them as we believe will be gratifying to our readers."

2. The letter, addressed to Garrison, was printed in *The Liberator* on September 25, 1840.

3. See *The Liberator,* October 9 and 16, 1840.

224

TO JOSEPH PEASE

Boston, Sept. 30, 1840.

Esteemed Friend:

The bearer of this is John A. Collins, the General Agent of the Massachusetts Anti-Slavery Society, and now deputed by the Executive Committee of the National Society to visit England for a special purpose, which he will communicate to you. I recommend him as a good soldier in the anti-slavery struggle, full of zeal, energy and devotion, and ready to espouse every good enterprise, however unpopular it may be. We are, at present, beset by foes within and without, and we need succor from abroad to enable us to stand our ground. If our national society must be given up, it shall not be until we have laid our case before those who feel a deep interest in its success.

When I read the account of your grand meeting in Manchester, in reference to British India, I felt a thrill of satisfaction, and longed to see you, face to face, to give you my congratulations upon so auspicious a commencement of your magnificent enterprise. O for the arrival of that time when the blood-stained cotton of America will no more be able to find a purchaser in all England, and when the free cotton of India, pure and white as the snow of heaven, shall be manufactured by British industry, to the overthrow of slavery and the slave-trade throughout the world! The Lord speed it!

Wishing you all possible happiness in your declining years, and great success in your undertaking, I remain,

　　　　　　　　　　Your friend and coadjutor,

　　　　　　　　　　　　Wm. Lloyd Garrison.

Joseph Pease, Sen'r.

N.B. I am requested to say, by Henry Chapman & Co. that you may give the Letter of Credit for £30 on Baring, Brothers & Co. which I left in your care, (or an equivalent in money,) to John A. Collins, who will give you a receipt for the same.

ALS: Garrison Papers, Boston Public Library.

225

TO MARIA W. CHAPMAN

Boston, Oct. 5, 1840.

My dear Mrs. Chapman:

You will see by the last Liberator, that the meeting of the Middlesex County A. S. Society is to be holden at Groton on Wednesday of next week;[1] the same day that you propose to have a meeting of your Society in this city.[2] Now, no man can be in two distant places at one and the same time; and as I am pledged to Dr. Farnsworth to be present at the Groton meeting, (and you know he will be very much disappointed, as well as some others, if I should break my pledge,) I do not see how I can be one of the speakers at your meeting on the evening of the 14th inst. I would not have you alter the time of your meeting, on my account; yet, if my presence at it be desirable, and the arrangement can be made without any inconvenience, I would propose the evening of the 16th inst. (Friday,) as the time for the Boston meeting. Submitting the matter to your good judgment, I remain,

Your faithful friend,

Wm. Lloyd Garrison.

Mrs. M. W. Chapman.

ALS: Chicago Historical Society.

1. The meeting of the Middlesex County Anti-Slavery Society, at Groton, Massachusetts, had been called for Wednesday, October 14, at 10 a.m. The notice of the meeting announced that "The question of political action in reference to the ensuing election will be considered." (*The Liberator*, October 2, 1840.)

2. The annual meeting of the Boston Female Anti-Slavery Society had been called for Wednesday, October 14, at 10 a.m., and was to be held in Marlboro' Chapel. The date was not changed. (*The Liberator,* October 9, 1840.) See letter 227, to Maria W. Chapman, October 13, 1840.

226

TO HIS EDITORIAL CHAIR

WORCESTER, Oct. 6, 1840.⎫
Tuesday Night. ⎭

To MY EDITORIAL CHAIR:

Up to this hour, you and I have had very little to do with each other since my return in pursuit of the World's Convention on the other side of the wild-heaving and awful Atlantic. That Convention, you know, was *non est inventus.*[1] As soon as I can get through with the numerous engagements which have been imposed upon me, in consequence of my mission, I hope to occupy you to good purpose.

I write now from Worcester. 'The heart of the Commonwealth' is not yet perfectly sound in relation to our great anti-slavery enterprise, though it is in a more healthy condition than it was formerly. As to the effect of slavery upon the nation, it may be scripturally affirmed that the whole head is sick, and the whole heart faint — and from the crown of our head to the sole of our foot, we are full of wounds, and bruises, and putrefying sores.[2] But there is some hope of recovery.

I left Boston this morning in company with a choice number of old organized abolitionists, to be present at the State Anti-Slavery Convention in this place. We have not had a more pleasant day since the present year was ushered into existence. As pleasing evidence of the change which is gradually taking place in public sentiment on the subject of prejudice, I will state that no distinction between white and colored travellers is now made on the Worcester rail-road.

711

All who behave decently are treated accordingly. There were several colored delegates to the Convention in the cars, but I could not perceive that the feelings of any individual were ruffled on that account. Custom will soon make it, I trust, a matter of course in all our steam-boats, stage-coaches, rail-road cars, and other conveyances. The prejudice which persecutes and degrades a brother on account of the color of his skin is manifestly unreasonable, vulgar, unnatural, impious. It must be abandoned universally in this country, or our republicanism and Christianity will continue to be a jest and by-word.[3]

No meeting-house could be obtained for the use of the Convention but the Methodist, which is a small one, but very neat. The notice of the meeting had not been given from any of the pulpits in this town, or in any newspaper except the Christian Reflector;[4] so that the inhabitants generally were not apprised of our intention. In consequence of the present political excitement in this State, and the fact that another Convention is to be holden at Springfield on the 8th and 9th inst., I did not anticipate a large meeting. The number of delegates in attendance, however, is about 200, which will doubtless be increased to-morrow. They are fine specimens of genuine, unshackled abolitionism. The Convention assembled at 10 o'clock, A.M., and was called to order by Oliver Johnson, one of the Committee of Arrangements. John M. Fisk,[5] of North Brookfield, was chosen President, and Wm. C. Coffin [6] Secretary, pro tem. A committee of nomination of officers was appointed, as follows: — Oliver Johnson, Wm. Bassett, Wm. B. Earle,[7] N. P. Rogers, and Richard Clapp,[8] who reported the names of the following individuals: — President, Dr. Amos Farnsworth, of Groton; Vice Presidents, John M. Fisk,[9] of West Brookfield; E. L. Capron, Uxbridge; N. Johnson,[10] New Bedford; W. Buffum,[11] Worcester; Richard Clapp, Dorchester. Secretaries, Wm. C. Coffin, New Bedford; J. S. Wall,[12] Worcester. The following persons were appointed a Business Committee: — Wm. Lloyd Garrison, N. P. Rogers, Abby Kelley, W. B. Earle, Francis Jackson, Wm. Bassett, Hiram A. Morse,[13] Mary P. Kenney.[14] Several important resolutions were discussed and adopted with perfect unanimity. But I have not time to go into particulars. Nearly four hundred dollars were collected this evening, in pledges and money, in the course of a few minutes. About one hundred dollars was also taken at the Anti-Slavery Fair. It is truly good to be here.

In great haste, I remain,

Your faithful occupant,

WM. LLOYD GARRISON.

Printed in *The Liberator*, October 9, 1840.

1. "He is not to be found"; the return of a sheriff on a writ when the person to be served is not found in his jurisdiction.

2. Isaiah 1:5–6; slightly paraphrased.

3. Since they first came into public use in the mid-1830's, the railroads of Massachusetts had segregated Negro and white passengers. The final elimination of such segregation took place in 1843, as the result of a prolonged campaign by the abolitionists. For a history of segregation on the railroads of Massachusetts, see Louis Ruchames, "Jim Crow Railroads in Massachusetts," *American Quarterly*, 8:61–75 (Spring 1956).

4. The *Christian Reflector* was published in Worcester, Massachusetts, from July 1838 to May 1848. It was managed by a board of fifteen Baptists, seven clergymen and eight laymen, and edited by the Reverend Cyrus P. Grosvenor. It was a strong antislavery newspaper. (William Lincoln, *History of Worcester, Massachusetts*, Worcester, 1862, p. 427.)

5. Unidentified.

6. William C. Coffin (born c. 1816) is listed in the New Bedford *Directory* for 1838, page 53, as bookkeeper in the Mechanics Bank, and as boarding at 40 South Second Street. He later became treasurer of the New Bedford Institute for Savings. After the division in the antislavery movement between old and new organization, he remained a staunch Garrisonian and, on various occasions, also helped to provide shelter for fugitive slaves. (See letters to Maria W. Chapman, in 1840 and 1842, Weston Papers, Boston Public Library.) He married Sarah C. Barney, the daughter of Paul and Mary Barney of New Bedford, in 1845. (Leonard Bolles Ellis, *History of New Bedford and Vicinity*, Syracuse, N.Y., 1892, p. 517; *Vital Records of New Bedford*, Boston, 1932, II, 125.)

7. William B. Earle (b. December 20, 1802; fl. 1886) of Leicester, Massachusetts, was the son of Pliny Earle, the largest manufacturer in the country of card-clothing for the spinning of cotton. He conducted his father's business from 1819 to 1832, when, at the death of his father, he assumed complete responsibility. He was also an inventor in his own right. He was blind during the last thirty years of his life. A Quaker, he was present at the first annual meeting of the New England Non-Resistance Society in 1839. (The Reverend A. H. Coolidge, *A Brief History of Leicester, Massachusetts*, Leicester, 1890, pp. 31–32; Pliny Earle, comp., *The Earle Family: Ralph Earle and his Descendants*, Worcester, 1888, pp. 110–111.)

8. Richard Clapp (b. Dorchester, July 24, 1780; d. December 26, 1861), a tanner by trade, lived on Pond Street, near Five Corners, Dorchester. He held various political offices in the town: chairman of the Board of Selectmen, Overseer of the Poor and of Highways, and member of the School Committee. He was also president of the Dorchester Anti-Slavery Society. (Ebenezer Clapp, comp., *The Clapp Memorial: Record of the Clapp Family in America*, Boston, 1876, p. 274.)

9. Colonel John Mellon Fisk of West Brookfield was born in New Braintree, Massachusetts, July 14, 1798, and died at West Brookfield on December 31, 1854. He apparently owned a store in West Brookfield and was active in town affairs as well as in the antislavery movement. For many years he was president of the Worcester County South Anti-Slavery Society. His father, the Reverend John Fisk (1770–1855) was a minister at New Braintree beginning in 1796, helped in the founding of Amherst College, and received the degree of D.D. from Amherst College in 1844. (Letter to Louis Ruchames from Mrs. Harold Merriam, Brookfield, Mass., dated July 17, 1969; obituary printed in *The Liberator*, January 17, 1855.)

10. A Nathan Johnson, Negro, is listed in the New Bedford *Directory* for 1838, page 77, as a confectionary, at 23 Seventh Street, residing at 21 Seventh Street. He was one of a committee of three chosen at a meeting of the Negro citizens of New Bedford in November 1837 to interrogate all candidates for legislative office concerning their views on slavery and the slave trade. In 1836

he signed a call for a temperance convention of the people of color in New England, to be held in Providence on May 17, 1836. (*The Liberator*, November 17, 1837; May 14, 1836.)

11. Unidentified.

12. *The Liberator*, June 28, 1839, carried a letter from Joseph S. Wall, dated Worcester, June 15, 1839, which enclosed $3.00 in payment of a year's subscription to *The Liberator*, as well as for several copies of an earlier issue. The letter indicates that Wall was then a member of the Society of Friends and that he was dissatisfied with that organization's failure to oppose slavery. He attended the second annual meeting of the New England Non-Resistance Society in 1840 (*The Non-Resistant*, October 14, 1840). *The Liberator* of May 8, 1840, announced the establishment of a weekly newspaper by Joseph S. Wall, entitled *Health Journal and Advocate of Physiological Reform*.

13. Hiram Morse, of Holliston Massachusetts, died on May 10, 1858, aged fifty-seven. He had been active in the temperance and antislavery movements for more than twenty years (obituary by G. W. S., dated Milford, May 17, 1858, in *The Liberator*, May 28, 1858). He was also a supporter of the nonresistance movement in 1840 (*The Non-Resistant*, October 14, 1840).

14. Unidentified.

227

TO MARIA W. CHAPMAN

BOSTON, Oct. 13, 1840.

MRS. MARIA W. CHAPMAN

ESTEEMED FRIEND — As I am pledged to be present at the quarterly meeting of the Middlesex County Anti-Slavery Society, which is to be holden at Groton to-morrow, it will not be in my power to address the members of the Boston Female A. S. Society, in accordance with your invitation. Under these circumstances, the best and only thing I can do is to say, on paper, that, if it were possible for me to be in two places at the same time, it would give me the greatest satisfaction to participate in the proceedings of your meeting.

I congratulate the Boston Female Anti-Slavery Society on the fact, that, notwithstanding its demise has been 'officially' proclaimed to the country,[1] it is still in existence, animated with more than pristine zeal and courage, — devising ways and means for the furtherance of our great anti-slavery enterprise, — undisheartened by the secession of treacherous friends and the assaults of open foes, — and resolved to keep the field until liberty be proclaimed throughout all the land unto all the inhabitants thereof. I congratulate the Society that it is once more a united body, having one faith, one spirit, one purpose; that the evil spirit of sectarianism has been cast out of it, and sent to its own place; that though among its members are found persons of almost every religious persuasion in the land, there is, nevertheless, benevolent sympathy and true Christian charity among them all, leading them to forget all theological disputes and sectarian distinctions in the cause of suffering humanity; and that it has lost nothing, but gained much, by the withdrawal of those whose love of sect is stronger than their abhorrence of slavery.

The Boston Female Anti-Slavery Society does not need any panegyric from me, or from others, to establish its claims to the admiration and applause of the friends of emancipation universally. Its deeds shine like the stars, and are seen as clearly on the other side of the Atlantic as on this. For a time, indeed, its light was obscured by mists and vapors, but now breaks forth from a cloudless sky. In the troublous times of mobocracy, the Society stood erect, as self-possessed in spirit and dauntless in mien as though no danger were apprehended or known. At the present crisis, more searching than any that has preceded it, it is found having its lamps trimmed and burning, steadfast in its integrity, and sleepless in its vigils.

These are the times that try the souls of WOMEN, as well as men. The Moloch of slavery has, from the first, sought to frighten them from an equal participation in the anti-slavery cause, by howling about the indelicacy of their publicly pleading for their imbruted sex. Pro-slavery at the North admonishes them to beware how they travel out of their 'appropriate sphere,' and piously quotes scripture to prove that they ought to be dumb on the anti-slavery platform, especially in the presence of men! Time-serving priests and profligate politicians are out in full cry against such of them as dare to act on the doctrine, that, in Christ Jesus, there is neither bond nor free; neither male nor female, but all are one — and if one, then not two — then not superior and inferior — then not high and low. Associated with these in the same unrighteous crusade are seen many professed abolitionists, whose clamor is more noisy, whose behavior is more outrageous, and whose spirit is more frantic, than those in whose company they are found. So hostile are they to the freedom of the soul — so determined to make their own theological interpretation of scripture the test of anti-slavery fellowship — so unwilling to co-operate in the same society, on equal terms, with all who believe in the sinfulness of slaveholding — so opposed to allowing every soul to act freely, in view of its own accountability — that, failing to carry their despotic purposes into effect, they have seceded from our hitherto unbroken ranks, organized new and hostile societies, held up to public scorn and reprobation their old anti-slavery associates, and waged a war of extermination against every anti-slavery society that recognizes no distinction in sex. The leaders in this work of mischief are the very individuals who were loudest in their approval of the course pursued by Angelina E. and Sarah M. Grimke, at the

715

time those eminent women were lecturing to promiscuous assemblies in New-England. What do they plead now, in justification of their present schismatical conduct? *Conscience!* Where was their conscience at that period? And when have they been required to vote in an anti-slavery meeting against the convictions of their conscience? Let it be kept constantly in mind, too, that they have not left us merely that they may prosecute the anti-slavery reform in their own way, leaving their former coadjutors, in the spirit of christian toleration, to follow the dictates of their own consciences, and pursue their own measures. Had they done this, their conduct would have been far more excusable than it now is. But they have not been willing to concede to others what they are determined to enjoy themselves, namely, LIBERTY OF CONSCIENCE. Hence, they have spared no pains to make the old anti-slavery organization detestable, and to hold it up as a dangerous body, unworthy of the support or countenance of good men! They have tried to supplant it by every means in their power, and up to the present hour their hostility is virulent in the extreme.

The effect of this abusive conduct and sectarian movement has been to purify our ranks, inspire woman with a just sense of her own equality, and advance the cause of universal reform.

There is, however, a mighty work yet to be done, and they who are not prepared to make liberal sacrifices, and encounter much reproach, and 'lap water with their tongues,'[2] and have grown weary in well-doing, had better retire from the conflict. While the spirit which now animates the Boston Female Anti-Slavery Society shall continue to dwell in it, I cannot believe that any thing will arise to induce it to forsake the cause, or compromise its principles, or sully its character. Having done so much, I doubt not it will stand, and endure even unto the end. May the God of the oppressed bless and prosper it abundantly!

With assurances of my high regard for your intellectual and moral worth, and your extraordinary labors in this righteous enterprise, I remain, dear madam,

Your grateful friend and faithful coadjutor,

WILLIAM LLOYD GARRISON.

Printed in the *Liberator*, October 16, 1840.

1. The "Seventh Annual Report of the Boston Female Anti-Slavery Society," printed in *The Liberator*, October 30, 1840, carried the text of a letter from M. V. Ball to Elizabeth Pease, dated "Boston, May 6, 1840," which announced "that the Boston Female Anti-Slavery Society has been DISSOLVED, and another formed in its place. Our *no-government* friends being resolved to carry their *peculiar views* along with them in the anti-slavery car, became so annoying in their movements, that it was found impracticable to continue united with them; and the consequence has been in our Female Society *dissolution*, and I fear it will be in many others. . . . With this I send you the *Massachusetts*

Abolitionist, containing the minutes of the last meeting of the Society, and another noticing the formation of the Massachusetts Female Society."

This letter reflected a partisan, anti-Garrisonian view of certain events at the quarterly meeting of the Boston Female Anti-Slavery Society on April 8, 1840.

Divisions similar to those that had formed within the American Anti-Slavery Society and the Massachusetts Anti-Slavery Society had also appeared within the Boston Female Anti-Slavery Society. There were differences not only over policy but also over who the true officers of the society were. At the quarterly meeting on April 8, 1840, with the legitimacy of the society's officers being disputed, a resolution to dissolve was passed by a vote of 142 to 10. The report of the meeting, dated April 13, 1840, was filed by "Mary S. Parker, *President,* and L. L. Otis, *Sec'y,*" and printed in *The Liberator,* April 17, 1840. A counter-statement, published beside the other report, in the same issue of *The Liberator,* and bearing the names of "Lydia Maria Child, *Pres. pro tem.,* and Caroline Weston, *Sec. pro tem.,*" of the Boston Female Anti-Slavery Society, disputed the former statement. It stated that "a part of the board of officers of the Boston Female Anti-Slavery Society for the year 1839, have, in the fourth month of 1840, for which *they were not elected,* pronounced the Society dissolved, and advertised the same extensively. This renders it necessary that the Society should instantly issue its Journal of the recent transactions, with this brief statement and DENIAL, for the information of its absent and distant members." It went on to state that those who had originally claimed to be the society's officers for 1840 had actually been defeated by a vote of 82 against them. However, "instead of recording the fact that they were defeated, they suppressed 17 votes, and recorded that they were elected. . . . To prevent action upon the minutes, with which they had involved the question of their re-election . . . they introduced, *while those minutes were before the meeting,* a resolution to dissolve the Society. This resolution came upon the Society with the most astounding unexpectedness. The members opposed to a dissolution all refused even to vote on the proposition. The acting President, in the midst of long and loud and reiterated remonstrances, pronounced the Society dissolved by a vote of 143 to 10.

"This announcement of the self-constituted President and Secretary, WE, THE BOSTON FEMALE ANTI-SLAVERY SOCIETY, (in public meeting assembled, agreeably to notice given on the spot, and advertised in the Liberator, Transcript and Mercantile Journal,) DECLARE INVALID." A postscript announced that the statement had been "unanimously" adopted "by the 120 members present."

2. The reference is to Judges 7:5ff.

228

TO JOHN A. COLLINS

Boston, Oct. 16, 1840.

My dear Collins:

By this time, I suppose you are very near the shores of old England — perhaps fairly landed. That all possible success may attend your mission is the ardent desire of my heart; because it is connected with the peaceable triumph of our great anti-slavery enterprise. Nothing special has transpired since you left. Your absence, as yet, has not excited any particular inquiry. When asked where you are gone, we say to England; deeming it both useless and needless to feign or affect mystery about it. Neither the Emancipator nor the Abolitionist has noticed your departure; but I suppose both of them will do so, in due season. In his last number, Leavitt virtually threatens to prosecute the Standard, if it be not careful how it speaks of him! The Emancipator, by the way, is pretty near "death's doors." Our tried friend, J. S. Gibbons, in a letter just received from him, says an 'old friend met him a day or two since in New-York, who said — "There's to be a meeting this afternoon, aint there?" "Don't know. Where, and about what?" "Why, at No. 9, Spruce-street, to consult whether the Emancipator shall go on, or stop." Leavitt has started a penny daily, to advocate the third party project. He calls it "The Ballot-Box." It will doubtless place him, and all who are concerned in it, in a sad "box," ere long. We shall know, in the course of a few weeks, how many abolitionists are disposed to countenance that unwise movement. I think the number will be found to be small indeed; at least, I hope so, for the integrity of our cause. The third party is only another name for new organization. They twain are one.

You will, of course, wish to hear how our State Conventions at Worcester and Springfield went off. I refer you to the Liberator of to-day for an account of the proceedings.[1] The meeting at Worcester [2] was very interesting, but the number of delegates in attendance not large. Some three or four hundred dollars were collected in pledges and cash, and about two hundred were raised by the Fair. The meeting at Springfield [3] came very near being a total failure. The time and the place chosen for it were highly unfavorable. There were not enough present in the forenoon to warrant an organization. In the afternoon, some thirty persons were present, and in the evening less than a hundred. The next day, there was very little increase, though in the evening there were, perhaps, two hundred persons in the audience. The principal speakers were Rogers, Abby Kelley, Johnson, Chace, "Rev. Dr." Osgood,[4] and myself. Dr. Osgood received all the female delegates to his house, and was very solicitous to have Rogers and myself take shelter under his roof, but we declined — preferring to stop with Dr. Church.[5] He said, in our meeting, that he did not wish to be called Dr.; that he was sick of the title; that he had never sought it, &c. &c. He also said that he had a very high opinion of his brother Garrison, and liked the Liberator very much, though he was in hourly expectation of being put into the Refuge of Oppression. He behaved, on the whole, very well, and did not say one word in favor of the new, or against the old organization. It happened that there was a tremendous Whig gathering on the very day of our Convention; and, consequently, the whole town was in commotion. There were long processions, public harangues, illuminations, transparencies, &c. What a work is to be done for our cause in the western part of this State! But where are the laborers? [6]

I have just returned from the Middlesex County Convention at Groton.[7] In the forenoon, about a dozen persons were present; in the afternoon, twice that number; and in the evening, one hundred: not half a dozen of whom were from all the other towns in the county! The fact is, bro. Collins, and we cannot and ought not to hide it, a large proportion of the abolitionists in this State, and elsewhere, are determined to go with their party at the approaching election; and they will not attend our meetings until after election, even if at all. This is not less humiliating than true. Besides this, new organization has benumbed the sensibilities and paralyzed the energies of very many who were once actively engaged in our cause. It is the worst foe that liberty has to conte[nd with] — the most dangerous form of pro-slavery.

This morning I go to Methuen, to attend the Essex County Convention.[8] I expect we shall have to address bare walls; but, no matter. After all, believing that God is with us, we may confidently affirm that we are multitudinous as to number, and victorious as to principle. Abby Kelley will attend the meeting. She spoke eloquently and impressively at Springfield. She also addressed a public meeting of the Boston Female Anti-Slavery Society, in the Melodeon, last Wednesday evening.[9] I was at Groton; but I hear that she acquitted herself well. Mrs. Southwick [10] was in the chair.

Rogers has consented to write regularly for the editorial department of the Standard. Bro. Johnson is now in New-York, and will probably remain until your return, superintending the paper. — But the Executive Committee are suffering for the want of funds, and the Standard must soon, I fear, be ingloriously furled, in the presence of our enemies, unless some aid can be promptly obtained from abroad. There are some, at least, in England, who will try to help us.

I was very unfortunate on my return from the Worcester Convention, having lost my wallet, containing upwards of fifty dollars in money, and an order to the amount of thirty dollars, besides sundry valuable papers. There is now no probability that I shall ever recover it. It is a severe loss for me in my poverty, though not a very large sum. I feel like an animal that has been denuded of its fur. But, "the Lord is my shepard," [11] and he will not fail to watch over me and mine.

We are all in good health at home. My three boys are in fine condition; but I cannot tell which of them I love best, or which is the handsomest. The babe Wendell Phillips promises to be a formidable rival of his brothers. Helen desires to be very cordially remembered to you.

I did intend to write, by the Caledonia, to my beloved friends George Thompson, Elizabeth Pease, Richard D. Webb, John Dunlop,[12] C. L. Remond, &c.; but I can only beseech you to give them the assurances of my brotherly love for them all. They shall hear from me, Deo volente, by the next steamer. Let us hear from *you* as often as possible. The Lord bless and prosper you!

Yours, truly,

Wm. Lloyd Garrison.

ALS· Garrison Papers, Boston Public Library. Printed in *Life*, II, 418–420.

1. October 16, 1840.
2. October 6, 7, 1840.
3. October 8, 9, 1840.
4. These are N. P. Rogers, Oliver Johnson, William M. Chace, and Dr. Samuel Osgood.
5. Dr. Jefferson Church (b. Middlefield, Massachusetts, October 21, 1802; d. April 11, 1885) of Springfield, who served as president of the convention. He studied medicine at the Berkshire Medical Institute in Pittsfield, Massachusetts, and entered medical practice in Peru, Massachusetts, in 1825. He moved to Springfield the following year, where he practiced medicine for nearly fifty years. Together with Dr. Edwin Seeger, he edited and published *Tully's Materia Medica*. He was an early antislavery man. (Charles Wells Chapin, *Sketches of the Old Inhabitants and Mansions of Springfield*, Springfield, 1893, p. 141; see Garrison's letter of introduction for Church, written to Henry I. Bowditch, July 13, 1854.)
6. "Rogers took a more rosy view of the Convention at Springfield. Writing to Francis Jackson, October 24, 1840, he says (MS): 'We had a grand time at Springfield — a really grand time. I behaved tolerably well there myself. Garrison and Chace and Johnson and Abby [Kelley] did wondrously. It made Springfield stare. By the way, Abby is taking the field like a lion. What a speech in the *Liberator* (10:171), and how superbly reported' — doubtless by Mrs. Chapman." (*Life*, II:419.)
7. The meeting was held on Wednesday, October 14.
8. Called for Friday, October 16, in Methuen, Massachusetts.
9. October 14, 1840.
10. Thankful Southwick, president of the Boston Female Anti-Slavery Society.
11. So in manuscript.
12. John Dunlop kept a bachelor hall at Randolph Cliff, England. A strong antislavery man, he had traveled in the United States, where he had acquired a portrait of Daniel Webster. By 1840, because of Webster's proslavery position, he had turned the portrait around to face the wall. ([Frances Bradburn], *Memorial of George Bradburn*, by his wife, Boston, 1883, p. 118.)

2 2 9

TO GEORGE W. BENSON

Boston, Nov. 1, 1840.

My dear George:

When I was on the other side of the Atlantic, father Time hobbled along upon his crutches in the slowest and most painful manner; but now his speed outstrips that of every locomotive in the land. I cannot keep up with him, nor within sight of him; and this must be my excuse for not having answered your letter sooner. In regard to bro. James's case, I am cheered to hear that he has improved in health, so far even as to gain flesh. You say that he is anxious to visit Boston. Of course, I do not wish to have him remain in Brooklyn, contrary to his desires; nor do I wish you to be put to any expense or trouble on his account. Yet I do earnestly desire that he will remember, that it is not in his power (in spite of all his good resolves) to visit this city, without falling in the way of temptation, and being overcome by it. He can find safety only in absenting himself from the company of seamen, at least as much as possible. I know this may seem hard, and almost insupportable, to dear James; but is it not much worse, much more hard, for him to be a degraded and miserable man? Still, if he inclines to come to Boston, let him do so, and I will do the best for him that lies in my power. I do not want him to feel that he is a prisoner; for nothing permanently will be gained, except it be carried by moral suasion. Bro. May informs me that he had several interesting conversations with James, and thought he had improved very considerably. If he could make up his mind to remain in Brooklyn during the winter, it would be the best thing he can do.

I am truly rejoiced (and so is Helen) to hear that mother is willing to come to Cambridgeport again, and be with us during the winter. To Helen, her company and assistance are invaluable. I am at a loss to know how we can do without her. I am aware that there is nothing particularly attractive at our house to win her from Brooklyn; and this makes it more kind in her to be willing to take up her abode with us. The meeting of the Rhode-Island State Society will take place (I believe) on the 23d and 24th inst.[1] If convenient, I wish mother would be in Providence at that time, so as to return with me. Let me beseech you not to fail to be at that meeting. Something must be done to prevent the last state of Rhode-Island being worse than the first. Remember your former connexion with the State Society, and do not at so perilous a crisis leave it to perish ignominiously. If we resolve upon it, we can have a good meeting.

The call for the Sabbath, ministerial and church Convention is beginning to make a mighty stir among the priesthood, and even to fill with dismay some of our professed anti-slavery friends. Cowards! not to know that truth is mightier than error, and that it is darkness, and not light, that is afraid of investigation. Several of our subscribers have already discontinued their papers on account of the publication of the Call in the Liberator,[2] and more, I suppose, will soon follow their example. The New-Hampshire Panoply, Vermont Chronicle, New York Observer, Zion's Herald, Boston Transcript, Greenfield Gazette, Lynn Puritan, American Sentinel,[3] &c. &c. are out in full blast about it. They attribute it all to me, of course; some of them insisting that my name is appended to the call. You will see, in the next Liberator, what they have said. This will be the occasion of a fresh attack upon my devoted head, and also upon the Liberator, to crush it. — But, truly, none of these things disturb me. I can "smile at Satan's rage, and face a frowning world," for my trust is in the Lord, and Christ is my Redeemer. Dear George, come on to the Convention, and do not say, "I cannot." Bring bro. Wright with you, and friend Coe,[4] and as many of the Brooklyn friends as possible. These are solemn, glorious, stirring times to live in! Let us do with our might what our hands find to do. So, come along!

The barrels of apples that you sent was [5] truly acecptable. Give my thanks (and Helen's also) to friend Scarborough [6] for his very timely and acceptable present of quinces. They were very nice; and if he will come to Cambridgeport, he shall have "a taste of their quality" as they are preserved. Bro. May speaks of his visit to Brooklyn with a great deal of pleasure. He will be at the Sabbath Convention. I hope the health of sister Sarah is improved. Poor Eliza Davis, it seems, is near the termination of her earthly career. "What shadows we are!" [7] Love to all the household. In great haste,

Your loving brother,   Wm. Lloyd Garrison.

ALS: Garrison Papers, Boston Public Library. Printed, in part, in *Life*, II, 423–424.

1. The meeting was called for November 24 and 25, 1840, in Providence.
2. The call appeared in *The Liberator*, October 16, 1840, and occupied the greater part of a column. In a paragraph signed by Edmund Quincy, chairman, and Maria W. Chapman, secretary, immediately preceding the call, it was explained that "a numerous meeting of the friends of Universal Reform was held on Thursday, the 24th of Sept. 1840, in the Chardon Street Chapel, Boston, for the purpose of considering the expediency of calling a Convention to examine the validity of the views which generally prevail in this country as to the divine appointment of the first day of the week as the Christian Sabbath, and to inquire into the origin, nature and authority of the institutions of the Ministry and the

Church, as now existing. Edmund Quincy was appointed Chairman; and Maria W. Chapman Secretary. It was unanimously agreed upon, that such a Convention should be held during the present autumn. Edmund Quincy, Maria W. Chapman, A. Bronson Alcott, Thankful Southwick, and John A. Collins were appointed a Committee to issue a Call, specifying the time, place, and purposes of the meeting." The call, dated September 25, 1840, carried twenty-four signatures, and included, in addition to those already named, Henry C. Wright, Abby Kelley, William H. Channing, William Bassett, Theodore Parker, and Oliver Johnson. It set Tuesday, November 18, 1840, as the date, and the Chardon-Street Chapel in Boston as the place of the meeting.

3. Of the papers mentioned here, The Boston *Transcript* was established in 1830, by Dutton and Wentworth, who were the state printers. Its first editor was Lynde M Walter, a Harvard graduate, who continued in that office until 1840, and who died in 1842. The newspaper was politically and economically conservative. (Frederic Hudson, *Journalism in the United States, from 1690 to 1872*, J. & J. Harper Editions, New York and Evanston, 1969, p. 386; Frank Luther Mott, *American Journalism*, revised edition, New York, 1950, p. 217.)

The Greenfield *Gazette* was first issued in Greenfield, Massachusetts, in 1792, as *The Impartial Intelligencer*, by William Coleman and Thomas Dickman. Six months later its name was changed to the Greenfield *Gazette*. In the ensuing years, its name and ownership were again frequently changed. In 1840, it was being published by Ansel Phelps and Charles J. J. Ingersoll as the *Gazette and Mercury*. It was politically conservative. (Francis Thompson, *History of Greenfield*, Greenfield, 1904, I, 289, 548–553.)

The Lynn *Puritan* was founded in 1840 as a combined religious and secular newspaper. Its religious department was edited by the Reverend Parsons Cooke, minister of the First Church of Lynn, who was distinguished for his love of controversy, and who continued as editor until 1862. The secular department was edited by James R. Newhall, a journalist and historian. The paper was soon moved to Boston and merged with the Boston *Recorder*. (Alonzo Lewis and James R. Newhall, *History of Lynn*, Boston, 1865, pp. 407–408, 475–477.)

The *American Sentinel* was published in Middletown, Connecticut, from 1823 to 1898. It was founded by William D. Starr and William H. Niles. Its proprietorship and management remained in the Starr family, with some interruptions, for many years. In 1833, it merged with the *Witness* and was thereafter called the *Sentinel and Witness*. (Norris G. Osborn, *History of Connecticut*, New York, 1925, pp. 178–179.)

4. The Reverend William Coe.

5. So in manuscript.

6. Philip Scarborough.

7. Edmund Burke (1729–1797), "Speech at Bristol on Declining the Poll, 1780."

230

TO JOHN A. COLLINS

Boston, Dec. 1, 1840.

My dear Collins:

Two months have now elapsed since you left us, and yet no one has received a word of intelligence directly from you; — and were it not that, in a letter to me, Elizabeth Pease had announced your safe arrival, and your visit to Darlington,[1] we should all be in a state of disquietude on your account. The Acadia, Britannia, Caledonia, British Queen, and Great Western, have all arrived since you landed in England. You may have written by some one of these conveyances: if so, your letters have never come to hand. We shall expect to hear from you, without fail, by the next packet. I wrote a letter to you by the Caledonia, on her previous trip, and sent it by the surgeon; but, instead of dropping it into the Post-Office at Liverpool, he had the boldness to break open the seal, and read its contents, and keep it in his possession! He has since been dismissed, and Dr. M'Tear,[2] a young friend of mine, of Glasgow, has taken his place, by whom the letter has been returned to me, I shall put it in the mail-bag to-day for you, although it contains nothing of special importance.

Elizabeth speaks of your visit to Darlington with a great deal of pleasure. I knew it would be refreshing to her spirits to see another specimen of old organization abolitionism. Is she not a truly superior woman? She is apprehensive that you will not meet with much success in collecting funds; and should her fears be realized, you will, of course, hasten home as soon as practicable — for we need your presence here exceedingly at the present juncture. She will not be able to give much herself, on account of her heavy expenditures in aid of the East India movement, as well as in various other ways. Her heart is large and liberal.

Nothing of special importance has transpired since you left. On the score of health, I believe in the circle of our anti-slavery acquaintance all are well, except the wife of Thomas Davis of Providence, (Wm. M. Chace's sister,) whose demise is almost daily expected.

What has created the greatest stir among us is our recent Sabbath Convention, in Chardon-street Chapel. About fifty clergymen were present at various times, though scarcely one of them deigned to enrol his name as a member of the body. The champions in favor of the commonly received views of the Sabbath were nearly all new organized abolitionists — viz. A. A. Phelps, (who spoke nearly four hours at one time, with a good deal of tact and spirit) — Nathl. Colver, who exhibited his vulgarity and personal malice at full length — C. T. Torrey, who said very little to the purpose — Dr. Osgood, of Springfield, who reasoned fairly and in good temper. Luther Lee was also on hand, charged to the muzzle with "logic," but, unfortunately, he could not get an opportunity to fire it off. Bro. Hawley[3] was likewise anxious to give the anti-Sabbatarians a blast, but failed to get the floor. J. V. Himes and P. R. Russell spoke at some length, in a declamatory manner, in favor of the Sabbath. The latter has discontinued his Liberator, and several others have done so, since the Call of the Sabbath Convention was published in its columns; among them our friend John Smith of Andover,[4] (he has stopped two or three copies,) who has virtually turned his back upon the anti-slavery cause, gone back to his pro-slavery minister Jackson,[5] acknowledged his faults, and connected himself again with the church — and all to show his regard for religion, and his abhorrence of heretics! Phelps made the best argument in favor of the Sabbath at the Convention, but the foundation of it was a supposition, and the key-stone an inference. I was sorry that I could get no opportunity to reply to him. On being pushed as to the meaning of the declaration, "There remaineth, therefore, a rest for the people of God," [6] he said it meant the first day of the week!! Taylor, the "sailor preacher," [7] behaved in a most outrageous manner, and exhibited a dreadfully malignant spirit. There was a great deal of rambling discussion, to very little purpose. — Mrs. Folsom [8] interrupted the proceedings continually, and spoke in a very disorderly manner. Mellen [9] had a word to say at the eleventh hour. But you will see the proceedings hereafter. The clergy are out now, every Sabbath, preaching it up as a divine institution; [10] but He who is Lord of the Sabbath, and who is himself the true rest, will confound them.

Gen. Harrison is elected President by an overwhelming majority. At the late election, the great body of abolitionists violated their solemn pledges, and voted for party. George Bradburn at the East, and John Rankin [11] at the West, did a great deal of harm by supporting Harrison. On Nantucket, there was but 1 scattering vote! Poor Birney, it is estimated, has received some five or six thousand votes out of two millions and a half! [12] The farce is equally ludicrous and melancholy. Yet the Emancipator, Friend of Man, and Abolitionist, seem determined to keep it up.

New organization is drooping to its death. Aside from the third party movement in this State, it has no vitality. In our meetings, we denounce it as the worst form of pro-slavery.

Rogers [13] has his hands full in New-Hampshire, but he is a moral Richard cœur de lion, and gives his blows thick and fast. He writes both for the Standard and the Herald of Freedom. Bro. Johnson [14] has been in New-York for some weeks past, and will probably remain there during the winter, superintending the Standard.

James C. Jackson [15] is actively engaged in lecturing in western New-York. How they are getting along at New-York, I do not know. In this State, we are doing almost nothing. We have not a single agent in the field — and yet this is the very season of the year when we ought to be up and doing. I lecture as often as I can conveniently,[16] but it is very difficult for me to be absent from Boston. Bro. Bishop [17] is still at 25, Cornhill, but he seems to have a sort of Paul Pry disposition, and has given me an article for publication in the Liberator, calling upon the Board to answer a variety of questions which he propounds to them, &c. &c. Some of them he very well knows cannot be answered until your return from England. What his motive is, I cannot imagine. I do not think I shall publish his communication.

I attended the State meeting of the R. I. A. S. Society at Providence,[18] a few days since. It was pretty well attended, and passed some strong resolutions. Abby Kelley was present, and spoke.

Of course, you and dear Thompson have become acquainted with each other, long ere this. Give my choicest remembrances to him and his lady, to E. Pease,[19] C. L. Remond, Wm Smeal,[20] &c. &c.

> Yours, faithfully,
>
> Wm. Lloyd Garrison.

ALS: Garrison Papers, Boston Public Library; printed, in part, in *Life*, II, 427–429.

    1. Where Elizabeth Pease resided.

    2. Probably John McTear, who also conveyed a letter to Garrison from William Smeal of Glasgow, which was printed in *The Liberator* on March 12, 1841; he is otherwise unidentified.

    3. The Reverend Silas Hawley.

    4. John Smith (b. Brechin, Scotland, May 19, 1796; d. Andover, Massachusetts, February 25, 1886) was a master millwright in Scotland who had learned the latest techniques of making textile machinery in Glasgow. He came to the United States near the end of 1816, and worked in Waltham, Massachusetts, in the mill of the Boston Manufacturing Company for two and a half years. In the spring of 1822, he was involved in a partnership for the making of machinery in Plymouth, Massachusetts. He and his partners moved to Andover, two years later, where they built and operated a machine shop. After seven years he bought the entire business, which had become very lucrative. He entered the flax-spinning business in 1835, gradually withdrawing from his earlier venture. He was an early reformer and antislavery man. (D. Hamilton Hurd, *History of Essex County, Massachusetts*, Philadelphia, 1888, II, 1646–1649.)

    5. The Reverend Samuel Cram Jackson (b. Dorset, Vermont, March 13, 1802; d. July 26, 1878), of Andover, Massachusetts. His father, Dr. William Jackson, was a classical scholar. He was a graduate of the Andover Theological Seminary in 1826, and served as first minister of the West Church at Andover from 1827 to 1850. During the ensuing twenty-two years, he functioned as assistant state librarian. His special interest was education. (*Ibid.*, pp. 1603–1605.)

    6. Hebrews 4:9.

    7. "Rev. Edward T. Taylor, commonly called Father Taylor, an eccentric Methodist clergyman, pastor of the Bethel Church in North Square, Boston, and one of the famous pulpit orators of that city. See Harriet Martineau's chapter on 'Originals,' in the second volume of her 'Retrospect of Western Travel.'" (*Life*, II, 427–428n.)

The Reverend Edward Taylor (b. Richmond, Virginia, December 25, 1793; d. Boston, April 5, 1871) went to sea at seven, spent ten years on shipboard, then came ashore and was converted to Methodism. He was captured by the British while serving on the *Black Hawk* during the War of 1812. After the war he came to Boston and worked as a peddler for a junk dealer. He was admitted in 1819 to the New England Conference of the Methodist Episcopal church, and spent ten years ministering in towns along the coast. In 1829, the Methodists formed the Port Society of Boston "to further the moral and religious welfare of sailors." The next year they established the Seamen's Bethel, and chose Taylor as their preacher. Remaining there for many years, Taylor became a legend, receiving tributes from many outstanding thinkers and writers of the day. He was famous for his dramatic and salty oratory and was the model for Father Mapple in Melville's *Moby Dick*. (*DAB*; Gilbert Haven and Thomas Russell, *Father Taylor, The Sailor Preacher*, Boston, 1873.)

8. Mrs. Abigail Folsom (b. England, c. 1792; d. Rochester, New York, August 8, 1867), "a worthy but insane woman, 'that flea of conventions,' as Emerson called her. The patient and humane toleration of her, year after year, on their platform, by the abolitionists, in ostensible regard for free speech, not only sadly interfered with their proceedings, but brought endless ridicule and misrepresentation upon them. Non-resistance also had here its practical disadvantages." (*Life*, II, 426–427n.) She came to the United States in 1837, interested herself in the condition of the colored people, and became an antislavery advocate. She delivered several addresses at meetings of the American Anti-Slavery Society between 1842 and 1845. She was frequently carried out of antislavery meetings because of her excessive desire to speak. She often climaxed her remarks with the exclamation: "It's the capitalists!" On one occasion she was carried out of a hall on her chair by Wendell Phillips, Oliver Johnson, and one other, whereupon she loudly commented that she was more fortunate than her Lord, for he had only one ass to ride, but she had three to carry her. After her marriage, she lived a retired life and rarely appeared at public meetings. She was the author of "Letter from a Member of the Boston Bar to an Avaricious Landlord," Boston, 1851. (*NCAB*.)

9. Dr. George W. F. Mellen. A chemist at 49 Chatham Street, Boston, he lived at 117 Washington Street; "another deranged spirit, who became even more troublesome than Mrs. Folsom, because easily made the tool of those who enjoyed the fun of egging him on and disturbing anti-slavery meetings." (*Life*, II, 428.) Mellen was also an author who, in the summer of 1841, published a book on the unconstitutionality of slavery. *Life* (III, 33n) comments: "Noteworthy is the appearance of a book (midsummer madness, one might think it, considering the time of year, the deranged author, and the vain doctrine) by G. W. F. Mellen (*ante*, 2:428), entitled, 'An Argument on the Unconstitutionality of Slavery.' Mr. Garrison, on a hasty reading, judged it to deserve attention (*Lib.* 11:123); but when, at the Millbury quarterly meeting of the Mass. A. S. Society, in August, Mellen, in conjunction with S. S. Foster, attempted to embody this argument in a resolution, they were defeated (*Lib.* 11:139). It will be seen hereafter how the doctrine was forced upon the Third Party."

10. *The Liberator*, December 4, 1840, carried the following editorial item: "Since the Sabbath Convention was held in Boston, and from the time that the Call for it was issued, the clergy, far and near, have been denouncing it, and preaching with even more than ordinary zeal and fervor in favor of the holiness of the first day of the week. This was what we expected, and to this we do not object. We only hope that laymen will be led to search the scriptures afresh, for *themselves*, on this important question; and we would recommend the holding of local conventions for the purpose of eliciting a full and free discussion of the subject."

11. The Reverend John Rankin (b. near Dandridge, Jefferson county, Tennessee, February 4, 1793; d. 1886), a Presbyterian minister and early abolitionist who began speaking against slavery as early as 1818. For forty-four years, beginning in 1821, he served as minister in Ripley, Ohio. The author of many antislavery pamphlets, he was best known for his book, *Letters on American Slavery, addressed to Mr. Thomas Rankin, Merchant at Middlebrook, Augusta County, Virginia*, published at Ripley, Ohio, in 1826, 118 pp. The book was reprinted, serially, in the second volume of *The Liberator*, in 1832, and republished as a book by Garrison & Knapp in 1833, and in other years thereafter.

(*ACAB.*) Later, he was a lecturer for the American Anti-Slavery Society. (Dwight L. Dumond, *Anti-Slavery: The Crusade for Freedom in America,* Ann Arbor, Mich., 1961, p. 91; *Life,* I, 305.)

12. Birney received 7,059 votes. For an account of the election and Birney's role in it, see Betty Fladeland, *James Gillespie Birney: Slaveholder to Abolitionist* (Ithaca, N.Y., 1955), pp. 187–189.

13. N. P. Rogers.

14. Oliver Johnson.

15. "He had, till relieved by Oliver Johnson, been doing yeoman service in editing the *Standard*" (*Life,* II, 428n).

16. He spoke in Milford, New Hampshire, on Tuesday, November 12 and in Middleboro, Massachusetts, at the semiannual meeting of the Old Colony Plymouth County Anti-Slavery Society, on Thursday, December 10, 1840. (*The Liberator,* November 20, 27, 1840.)

17. Joel Prentiss Bishop (1814–1901), "an intermittent student at Oneida Institute from 1829 to 1833, became in 1835 an antislavery agent for the New York State Anti-Slavery Society and was later assistant editor of its organ, *Friend of Man,* and financial secretary of the society. In 1842 he studied law at Boston, practised, and wrote numerous legal treatises, two of which became classics of the law: *A Commentary on Marriage, Divorce and Separation* (1891), and *New Criminal Procedure* (1896)." (*Weld-Grimké Letters,* I, 71n.) During the Civil War he wrote a book entitled *Secession and Slavery.*

18. *The Liberator,* November 27, 1840, described the meeting, which took place on Wednesday and Thursday, November 25 and 26, 1840.

19. Elizabeth Pease.

20. William Smeal (b. Leith, Scotland, June 13, 1793; d. Glasgow, August 15, 1877), an active British abolitionist and Quaker, with whom Garrison spent some time during his 1840 trip to England and who remained a lifelong friend. Beginning in 1843, he and Robert Smeal edited *The British Friend* of Glasgow, a monthly, which took a strong stand for the emancipation of American slaves. In August 1840, William Smeal and four other Friends of Glasgow, in a letter to the Glasgow *Argus,* dissociated themselves from the Hicksite views of Lucretia Mott, who had spoken in Glasgow several days earlier as a minister of the Society of Friends. (See Anna D. Hallowell, ed., *James and Lucretia Mott: Life and Letters,* Boston, 1884, pp. 175–179; Rufus M. Jones, *The Later Periods of Quakerism,* London, 1921, II, 943; *Life,* II, 298, 402; IV, 283, 411.)

231

TO ELIZABETH PEASE

Boston, Dec. 1, 1840.

My dear friend:

The Brittannia sails this day for Liverpool. So strong is my desire to see once more, face to face, you and the other choice friends with whom it was my privilege to become acquainted in England, that, despite my great aversion to a sea-voyage, I feel as if I could cheerfully encounter the terrors of the Atlantic, even at this inclement season of the year, to appease the yearnings of my spirit. Whether we shall ever meet again on earth is at least problematical. Nothing is so perishable as life — nothing so uncertain as the future. I long for the time when "there shall be no more sea" [1] — nothing to obstruct the communion of kindred souls. Till that time come, by this mortal putting on immortality, we must avail ourselves of such facilities of intercourse as may be granted to us.

Your long epistle by the Caledonia was altogether too short! I send you more thanks in return than there are words contained in it. Much do I regret that I am necessitated to send you so brief an epistle in reply. It was a great relief to us all to hear of the safe arrival of our friend J. A. Collins; but, had you not announced the fact in your letter, we should have been ignorant of it up to the present hour — for, by some strange negligence, we have not received a line from him since his departure. I see that you are not sanguine as to the success of his mission, on various accounts; nor have I been at any time; and nothing but the extreme exigency of the case, and the appalling prospect that was before us, would have reconciled me to his going to England for the purpose of procuring pecuniary aid. I did not suppose, dear friend, that you would be able to give him much assistance; for I am too well aware of the liberal expenditures you are continually called to make in the cause of philanthropy, — especially in support of the glorious East India movement, the success of which is so intimately connected with the overthrow of slavery and the slave trade throughout the world. It is not necessary that you should contribute a farthing in our aid, at this crisis, to convince any of us that we have not a more generous or faithful friend on earth than yourself. You have expended a very large amount of money, directly and indirectly, in the anti-slavery enterprise, since you espoused it. This I know you will not claim as a merit; but Heaven will reward you — nay, I doubt not that you have already been richly recompensed in your own soul. I hope, however, that J. A. Collins' mission will not be wholly in vain; for, unless some pecuniary aid be obtained from our English friends, we must, I fear, stop the publication of the National Standard, and dissolve our National Society — and that, too, very shortly.

I feel anxious to know how far the spirit of "new organization" has poisoned the minds of our anti-slavery friends on the other side of the Atlantic. The true-hearted abolitionists here regard it as the worst, and indeed the only active foe now in the field, to retard the cause of emancipation. It is the more dangerous, because it assumes the form, but denies the power of abolitionism. It has filled our once unbroken ranks with confusion, caused the love of many to wax cold, excited personal animosity, and, as far as it has prevailed, has made the last state of community, on the subject of slavery, even worse than the first. By consulting the Liberator, you will see how it is spoken of by the old anti-slavery societies.

Mr. Birney returned in the Great Western, a few days since. I see that he and Stanton have taken a pretty extensive tour through England, Scotland and Ireland; [2] and I am glad that they have been so well-received, as American abolitionists. The result of the election for President makes the nomination of Mr. Birney [3] to that office perfectly ridiculous. Out of more than two millions of votes that have been cast, he has not received more than five or six thousand! A large number of abolitionists refrained from going to the polls; and a still larger number, I blush to say, voted either for Harrison or Van Buren, and thus violated their most sacred pledges. George Bradburn was among the number. How far it will affect his anti-slavery character hereafter remains to be seen. I fear he is politically ambitious. You will see his letter to me in the Liberator. [4] It is very sophisticated, and in it George Thompson is quoted in a manner that I think is incorrect.

Dear Rogers is leading the little anti-slavery band in New Hampshire gallantly forth to battle. He is beset on all sides by false friends and implacable foes; but his faith and courage rise with the emergency, and never has he been so active or efficient as at the present time. Should you not receive many letters from him, his excuse must be that he has to edit both the Herald of Freedom and the Standard, and also to act as an anti-slavery lecturer. He entertains a very exalted opinion of Elizabeth Pease. Since his return, he has made some very severe strictures upon the abolitionism of England, as such; and especially upon the conduct of the London Committee. The refusal of that Committee, and also of the Convention, to acknowledge the American female delegates, has received very general condemnation among the abolitionists in this country.

Mrs. Chapman is well, and in fine spirits, as usual. You will see the Annual Report of the Boston Female A. S. Society, from her pen, in the Liberator: [5] in it is contained a reply to the accusation of M. V. Ball against the Society, contained in a private letter to you. [6] Miss Ball has not ventured to make any rejoinder. She thus stands publicly convicted of slander and falsehood.

The fair of the "Massachusetts *Emancipation* Society," (Miss Ball's,) takes place this day. It will be a small affair. That of the Boston Female A. S. Society will be held toward the last of this month, and I expect will eclipse every other that has preceded it.

It delights me to hear that there is a growing interest in your East India movement in England. Though there is not a great deal said about it publicly by the slaveholding and pro-slavery party in this country, yet I know that they are very much concerned about it. The Lord prosper it right speedily!

We have recently had a very interesting Convention in this city, to discuss the question, whether the first day of the week is to be regarded as a Sabbath — a "holy day." There were some fifty clergymen present. It is making no small stir in community, and bringing fresh vials of wrath upon my devoted head as a heretic, an infidel, &c. [See the Liberator.]

Your admiring friend,

Wm. Lloyd Garrison.

☞ Give my affectionate regard to dear Thompson, Remond, Collins, your father, mother, &c. Let me hear from you as often as convenient, even though I may not send you letter for letter.

ALS: Garrison Papers, Boston Public Library.

1. Revelation 21:1: ". . . and there was no more sea."
2. Birney returned to New York on November 24, 1840. For an account of Birney's trip to Europe in the company of Henry and Elizabeth Cady Stanton, who had just been married, with Birney and Henry Stanton also serving as delegates to the World's Anti-Slavery Convention, see Betty Fladeland, *James Gillespie Birney: Slaveholder to Abolitionist* (Ithaca, N.Y., 1955), pp. 190–206.
3. Birney was the nominee for President of the Liberty party.
4. November 20, 1840. The letter is dated Nantucket, November 9, 1840. An earlier letter by Bradburn, dated Nantucket, October 22, 1840, appeared in *The Liberator* on October 30, 1840. It was in the former letter that Bradburn alleged that George Thompson, with whom he had spoken while abroad, agreed with his point of view on political action by abolitionists.
5. October 30, 1840.
6. The letter from Martha V. Ball to Elizabeth Pease, dated Boston, May 6, 1840, appeared in the Seventh Annual Report of the Boston Female Anti-Slavery Society together with Elizabeth Pease's letter of reply. See letter 227, to Maria Weston Chapman, October 13, 1840.

Index of Recipients

(References are to letter numbers)

Abolitionists, 22, 145, 158, 172, 175, 177, 210
Adams, John Quincy, 140
Anti-Slavery Conventions, 7, 23, 176

Barbadoes, James G., 211
Benson, Anna, 69
Benson, George, 58
Benson, George W., 2, 16, 18, 38, 49, 56, 65, 66, 70, 78, 85, 91, 94, 95, 98, 104, 107, 110, 111, 119, 132, 136, 138, 144, 155, 163, 169, 189, 209, 220, 229
Benson, Henry E., 1, 3, 6, 33, 35, 41, 44, 46, 48, 50, 52, 55, 59, 61, 62
Benson, Mary, 68, 128, 134, 141
Benson, Sarah, 64, 130
Benson, Sarah Thurber, 63, 79, 108, 109, 118
Birney, James G., 17
Boyce, James P., 97
Bradburn, George, 178
Buckingham, Joseph Tinker (editor of the Boston *Courier*), 73, 74, 76, 77

Capron, Effingham L., 54
Chace, William, 34
Chapman, Maria W., 193, 225, 227
Child, David L., 47
Clarke, John S. (President of Providence Anti-Slavery Convention), 7
Cole, Thomas, 211
Collins, John A., 228, 230
Courier (Boston), 73, 74, 76, 77
Cushing, Caleb, 67, 80, 168, 170, 173

Davis, Edward M., 106

Editorial Chair (Garrison's), 226
Emancipator, 153
Everett, Joshua T., 176
Executive Committee of the American Anti-Slavery Society, 150, 166

Farmer, John, 84
Farnsworth, Amos, 217
Fifield, Hannah, 103
Foster, Harriet, 139, 146

Garrison, Helen E., 14, 15, 20, 21, 24, 25, 26, 28, 30, 31, 32, 39, 60, 72, 82, 86, 113, 114, 117, 127, 129, 148, 149, 184, 185, 186, 187, 188, 192, 197, 199, 200, 201, 202, 206

Garrison, James H., 194, 221
Goodell, William, 11
Gunn, Marcus, 207

Hilton, John T., 211
Hudson, Erasmus D., 125
Hunt, Richard P., 181

Jackson, Francis, 120, 122
Jackson, Phoebe, 101, 222
Johnson, Oliver, 9, 89, 124, 160, 183, 190, 203, 204

Kimball, Joseph H., 90
Knapp, Isaac, 8, 27, 37, 40, 42, 43, 51, 53, 87, 116

Leavitt, Joshua (editor of *Emancipator*), 153

May, Samuel J., 4, 5, 36, 57, 75, 105, 112, 123, 126, 131, 133, 135, 156, 218
Mott, James, 143
Mott, Lucretia, 180
Murray, Orson S., 88

New England Spectator, 45, 99
Non-Resistants, 142

Osgood, Samuel, 159

Parker, Mary S., 137
Paulding, James K., 167
Pearce, Dutee J., 12
Pease, Elizabeth, 102, 205, 213, 214, 223, 231
Pease, Joseph, 208, 215, 224
Phelps, Amos A., 71, 83, 157
Phillips, Wendell, 154
Porter, William S. (editor of N. E. *Spectator*), 45, 99

Quincy, Edmund, 121, 162, 196

Rogers, Nathaniel P., 152, 179, 216

Scott, William H., 23
Smith, Gerrit, 174, 182
Stearns, Charles, 171

Taber, Isaac C., 96
Tappan, Arthur, 147
Tappan, Lewis, 10, 13, 93, 147, 164

Thompson, George, 29, 115, 161

Unidentified, 165, 191, 195, 198

Walker, Mrs. Henry, 219
Woodbury, James T., 92
Wright, Elizur, Jr., 100
Wright, Henry C., 19, 81, 151, 162, 212

Erratum

On page 85 the source of Letter 22, To Friends of the Anti-Slavery Movement, April 18, 1836, should be given as follows: Weston Papers, Boston Public Library.

Index of Names

The following abbreviations are used: AA-SS, American Anti-Slavery Society; MA-SS, Massachusetts Anti-Slavery Society; NEN-RS, New England Non-Resistance Society; WLG, William Lloyd Garrison.

Abington, Mass., 460, 492, 493
Abington Anti-Slavery Society, 493
Abolitionist, The, xxviii, 415, 418–19
Abolitionist (Madison county, N.Y.), 577
Abolitionist. See *Massachusetts Abolitionist*
Academy Anti-Slavery Society (Leicester, Mass.), 68, 69
Acadia (steamship): WLG plans to return home on, 656, 660, 668, 669; WLG's voyage on, 675, 682–84, 688, 699; mentioned, 682, 690, 707, 724
Acton, Mass., 293, 453
Adam, William: identified, 656–57; at World's Convention, 654, 655, 666
Adams, Charles P., 353
Adams, John, 282; quoted and identified, 38, 41
Adams, John Quincy: identified, 181; letter to, 426–30; eulogy on Madison, 180; WLG praises, 204–05; speaks at Newburyport, 271, 275; letter from, read at AA-SS convention, 352; and abolitionism, 268, 426–31, 494; introduction to volume on Lovejoy, 348, 428–29, 431, threatened, 426–27; and slavery in Washington, D.C., 426–31, 489; mentioned, 146
Adams, Nehemiah: identified, 691; and Pastoral Letter, 323; in England, 690
Adams, Robert, 353
Adams, William: identified, 353; opposes Clerical Appeal, 303; in New York, 351, 615; sailing for England with WLG, 612, 615; at World's Convention, 641, 654, 665, 677, 680
Adams, William Tindall, 353
Adventists, 183, 696

Advocate and Family Guardian, 99
Africa, 285, 319, 607
African Repository, 48
Agency Committee of the Anti-Slavery Society, 231
Alabama, 105
Albany, N.Y.: National Convention of Abolitionists at (1839), 521, 522, 523–27, 565; National Anti-Slavery Convention for Independent Nominations at (1840), 553, 568–69, 605, 606, 608–09
Albany *Patriot,* 577
Albert, Prince, 652
Albion (packet-ship), 645
Alcott, Abigail, 367; identified, 367–68
Alcott, Amos Bronson, 119; identified, 62; weeps at WLG's sonnets, 60; poverty of, 367; married life of, 367–68; and nonresistance, 401; and Prophet Miller, 696; and Chardon-Street Convention, 723
Alcott, Lousia May, 62
Alcott, William Andrus, 118; identified, 119
Alden, Rev. Mr., 493
Alexander, George W., 528
Alexander, S. R., 309; identified, 310
"Algernon Sidney" (pseudonym of Walter Colton): identified, 222; letters to editor of *Courier* in reply to, 217–221, 223–31, 246–51; S. J. May reveals identity of, 233, 234
Allen, Rev. George, 42, 503; identified, 43
Allen, J. M., 209
Allender, Dr. Walter T., 259
Alta Californian, 222

Alton, Ill.: death of Lovejoy at, xxviii, 329, 331, 332

American, The, 43

American Academy of Arts and Sciences, xxix

American and Foreign Anti-Slavery Soceity: various founders of, xxix, 100, 111, 355, 410; Galusha delegate of to World's Convention, 100, 671; formation of, 553, 611; *Anti-Slavery Reporter* organ of, 662

American Anti-Slavery Almanac, 274; identified, 276

American Anti-Slavery Society: letters to Executive Committee of, 459, 538–48; letter for MA-SS delegates to, 574–75; letter to Abolitionists of the United States in anticipation of Convention, 577–87; annual meetings: (1835), 113; (1836), 68, 91, 93, 98–99; (1837), 211, 233 and 234, 253, 254, 257, 260–61, 265; (1838), 333, 344, 346, 347, 355, 357, 566; (1839), 413, 451, 452; (1840), 553, 569, 584–92 *passim,* 595, 602–08, 610, 611–12; (1850), 691; convention to train Seventy Agents of, 184–85, 187–88, 201, 202; Convention at Albany, 521, 522, 523–27, 524, 565; publications of, xxvi, 26, 154, 158, 348, 357; flourishing condition of, 2; founding convention, 33, 187, 189, 466, 474, 602; G. Smith joins, 46, 47; helps *Liberator,* 50–51; and Rhode Island legislative committee, 125, 130; sending agent to West Indies, 146, 151, 153, 159, 160–61; nonviolent principles of, 228–29, 239–40, 478–81, 610; Constitution, 239–40, 350, 351, 353, 464–85, 495, 510, 512, 513, 522, 596, 597; Declaration of Sentiments, 240, 466, 470, 474, 475, 478–81, 513, 611, 613; Ann G. Chapman's bequest to, 252, 253, 256; and Clerical Appeal, 290, 298–300, 303, 304, 308, 541–42; and jurisdiction over slavery, 308, 350, 573; conflicts with MA-SS, 412, 413, 433 and 435, 443, 445–46, 447–49, 538–49, 583, 622; and political action, 467–70, 472–76, 484, 485, 495, 510–13, 525–26, 565–68, 571–74, 579–80, 597; broad basis of, 473–74, 500–02, 567–68, 607; Negroes on Executive Committee of, 489; and Massachusetts Abolition Society, 498–500, 546–47; in danger of ruin, 498–99, 575, 584–87, 589, 708, 719, 729; participation of women in, 505, 506–08, 522, 527, 582; secession from, to form American and Foreign Anti-Slavery Society, 553, 586, 610, 611; delegates to World's Convention, 592, 616, 677; various founders of, xxix, 36, 46, 80, 96, 100, 111, 112, 122, 128, 209, 210, 216, 217, 354, 357, 679; various agents of, xxx–xxxi, 36, 54, 112, 160, 202, 297, 310, 336, 355, 357, 386, 417, 433, 464, 486, 588, 708; mentioned, xxv, xxviii, xxix, 35, 47, 72, 100, 111, 171, 217, 251, 308, 329, 364, 410, 535, 577, 610, 688, 691, 717, 727

American Asylum for the Deaf and Dumb (Hartford), 378, 380

American Baptist Anti-Slavery Society, 586

American Board of Commissioners for Foreign Missions, 100, 343, 586

American Colonization Society: decline of, 2, 489; Joseph Tracy and, 25; Gerrit Smith and, 46, 47, 192 and 193; R. R. Gurley and, 48; Harriet Martineau and, 59; Leonard Bacon and, 76; meeting in New York, 99, 100; R. J. Breckinridge and, 167; free Negroes not fooled by, 319; Henry Clay and, 525; Thomas Clarkson repudiates, 661, 664, 707 and 709; Elliott Cresson and, 664; mentioned, 110, 278, 279, 295, 522

American Education Society, 111

American Female Guardian Society, 99

American Journal of Science, 179

American Methodist Anti-Slavery Society, 586

American Missionary Association, 73, 111

American Peace Society: WLG on defects of, 278–80; and William Ladd, 278; and George Beckwith, 393. *See also* New England Non-Resistance Society

American Philosophical Society, xxix

American Quarterly Anti-Slavery Review. See *Quarterly Anti-Slavery Magazine*

American Sentinel, 722; identified, 723

American Sunday School Union, xxix

American Tract Society, xxix

American Union for the Relief and Improvement of the Colored Race: identified, 25; William Ladd abandons, 94; and Clerical Appeal, 312, 313; and Sidney Willard, 392

Index of Names

American Wesleyan Observer, 586; identified, 587
Ames, Fisher, 87–88; identified, 89
Amherst College, 161
Amistad (ship), 535, 536, 608
Ammidon, Miss, 78
Ammidon, Melania, 3, 194; identified, 4
Ammidon, Sylvia, 194, 455; identified, 4
Andover, Mass., 238, 245
Andover Anti-Slavery Society, 410
Andover Theological Seminary: "Appeal of Abolitionists of the Theological Seminary," 300, 302, 303, 304–05, 323; J. A. Collins leaves, 453
Andrew, Gov. John A., xxx
Andrews, Ethan Allen, 75
Ann, 366–67
Ann, Anna. *See* Benson, Ann Elizabeth
Anthony, Annie Keene, 458
Anthony, Frederick Eugene, xxiii
Anthony, George Henry, 455; identified, 458
Anthony, Henry: identified, 7–8; in New York as usual, 91–92; mentioned, xxiii, 176, 256, 394, 396, 409, 458
Anthony, Mrs. Henry (Charlotte Benson): identified, xxiii; WLG visits, 90, 102, 455, 456; caring for Henry Benson, 102, 150; mentioned, 7–8, 70, 122, 137, 146, 151, 191, 202, 256, 394, 403, 409, 434, 555
Anthony, James Coggeshall, 455; identified, 458
Anthony, Mrs. James Coggeshall (Mary B. Smith), 455; identified, 458
Anthony, John Gould, 458
Anthony, Joseph Bowen, 456; identified, 458
Anthony, Julia C., 455; identified, 458
Anthony, Mary Gould, xxiii
Anthony, Sarah, 92; identified, xxiii
Anthony, Susan B., 26
Antigua, 40
Anti-Slavery Bugle (Salem, O.), xxvi
Anti-Slavery Reporter, 660; identified, 662
"Appeal of Clerical Abolitionists . . ." *See* Clerical Appeal
Appleton, Gen. James, 108; identified, 112
Aristides, 192
Arkansas: admission of to Union, 75, 76, 82, 84, 287–89; petitions against admission, 84–85; WLG's lost article on, 91
Arnold (*Liberator* subscriber), 162–63

Arnold, Benedict, 72, 217, 280
Aroostook War, 440–41, 442
Ashurst, William H.: identified, 666; mentioned, 659, 681–82
Atlas. See Boston *Daily Atlas*
Attleborough, Mass., 204
Atwell, Samuel Young, 132; identified, 134
Augusta (Ga.) *Chronicle*, 229
Austin, Tex., 73
Austin, James T.: identified, 331; *Remarks on Dr. Channing's Slavery*, 245, speech on Lovejoy, 331
Ayres (or Eayres), Joseph H., 419, 420

Babcock, Archibald D.: identified, 291; mentioned, 84, 117, 118, 290, 390
Babcock, Mrs. Archibald D., 390
Babylon, 284
Bacon, Leonard, 192; identified, 76; reviews by, 75; "out on" Henry C. Wright, 259
Bacon, Orin P., 434
Bailey, Gamaliel: edits *Philanthropist* and *National Era*, 69; praises James Boyle, 446–47
Bakewell, Robert, 178, 179
Ball, Lucy M., 10, 23, 26
Ball, Rev. Mason, 13
Ball, Martha V., 716–17, 730, 731
Ball, William, 659
Ballot Box, The, 718
Ballou, Rev. Adin, 334, 534
Baltimore, Maryland, xxix, 80
Bancroft, George, 111
Baptists, xxii; and abolitionism, 113, 140, 586
Barbadoes, James G.: identified, 679; letter to, 678–79
Barclay, Robert: identified, 168; and Sabbath, 166, 173, 368
Baring Brothers, 690, 710; identified, 691
Barnes, Mr. (stage-driver), 76
Barnes, Gilbert H., 54
Barnstable District, Mass., 204
Barry, C. C., 13
Barry, Samuel, 128
Bassett, William: identified, 336; disowned by Society of Friends, 336, 687, 688; and *Liberator*'s finances, 415, 417, 557; son dies, 460; president of Essex County Anti-Slavery Society, 493; mentioned, 311, 335, 393, 686, 712, 723
Bassett, William (son of above), 460
Bean, Benning M., 289

737

Beckwith, Rev. George C., 390; identified, 393

Beecher, Rev. Edward: identified, 355; *Narrative of Riots at Alton* quoted, 329; letter read at AA-SS convention, 352

Beecher, Rev. Henry Ward, 66, 355

Beecher, Rev. Lyman, 64, 355; identified, 66; speech on Sabbath, 2, 144, 145, 148, 156, 160, 166, 208

Bell, James (bank robber, *alias* Laidley), 93

Belsham, Thomas: identified, 168; and Sabbath, 168, 173, 368

Beman, Rev. Nathaniel Sydney Smith, 248; identified, 251

Benezet, Anthony, 686; identified, 688

Benjamin Franklin (steamboat), 90, 97, 215

Bennett, James Gordon, 690–91

Bennington, Vt., xxv

Benson, Ann Elizabeth (also Anne or Anna): identified, xxiii; letter to, 206–08; letters received from, 114, 116, 118, 180, 181, 304, 444; health of, 156, 698, 704; diffidence of, 175, 392, 397; WLG's appreciation of, 188, 330, 444–45; still mourning Henry Benson, 211; staying with Helen in WLG's absence, 620, 621, 622, 624, 644; visiting Garrisons, 698, 706; mentioned, 77, 90, 182, 186, 188, 198, 256, 274, 395, 417, 623, 662, 668

Benson, Anna Elizabeth (daughter of George W. Benson): identified, xxiv; health of, 3, 7, 92, 121, 127, 129, 136, 145, 151; weighed, 174; homesick, 396; mentioned, 5, 64, 90, 330, 398, 434, 444

Benson, Charlotte. *See* Anthony, Mrs. Henry

Benson, Eliza Davis, xxiv

Benson, Frances, xxii

Benson, George (often referred to as "Father"): identified, xxii; letter to, 179–81; death of, 3, 190, 192, 196, 208, 254; and T. P. Ives, 103–04; dotes on grandson, 121, 122; anxiety for Henry Benson, 155, 175; visits Plainfield with WLG, 160, 163; and WLG's board money, 181; WLG's appreciation of, 188; and naming of George W. Benson's child, 311–12; mentioned, 4, 15, 17, 58, 60, 142, 143

Benson, Mrs. George (Sarah Thurber, often referred to as "Mother"): iden-

tified, xxii; letters to, 193–95, 254–56, 336–38, 338–40, 362–64; health of, 70, 210, 233, 254, 409, 422, 433; WLG's appreciation of, 188, 329–30, 492; WLG comforts on death of husband, 193; expected to visit Garrisons, 395, 398, 403, 406, 555, 721; visiting Garrisons, 416, 417, 460, 620, 698, 706; mentioned, 303, 367, 431, 453, 457, 615, 623, 644, 668

Benson, George (son of George W. Benson), 444; identified, xxiv

Benson, George W.: identified, xxiii–xxiv; letters to, 6 7, 00–03, 70–72, 134–35, 157–58, 176–77, 200–02, 203–04, 210–12, 251–53, 266–68, 290–91, 302–03, 304–07, 311–13, 329–31, 335, 341–42, 344–45, 365–67, 403–04, 417–19, 421–23, 442–45, 491–93, 532–34, 555–56, 624–25, 675–76, 701–02, 721–22; letter quoted, 1; and bank robber, 92; health of, 122, 339, 491; plans for Newport hearing, 129–30; attends Henry Benson in sickness, 150, 191; letters received from, 181, 200, 266, 304, 340, 444; enthusiasm for Thomsonian medicine, 274, 339; and MA-SS, 207, 307, 338, 409, 416, 418, 422, 492; birth and naming of sons, 311–12, 337, 423; in New Haven, 349; success in business, 353; and WLG's salary, 366; going on excursion, 388–89; house-hunting with WLG, 391, 394; and NEN-RS, 391, 395, 701, 704; and explosion in Hartford, 456; scruples about voting, 513, 573, 601–02; and James Garrison, 612, 622, 703; pugilistic skills, 624; WLG's eagerness to see, 701–02; urged by WLG to attend Sabbath Convention, 722; mentioned, 43, 47, 83, 89, 121, 136, 145, 156, 167, 175, 179, 180, 191, 202, 254, 255, 271, 345, 392, 396, 398, 399, 470, 614, 628, 692, 698, 706

Benson, Mrs. George W. (Catharine Knapp Stetson): identified, xxiv; health of, 136, 533, 444; birth of children, 312, 423; WLG's love for, 330; mentioned, 64, 65, 71, 90, 128, 129, 145, 175, 176, 202, 417, 556, 622, 625, 644, 676, 702

Benson, Helen Eliza. *See* Garrison, Mrs. William Lloyd

Benson, Henry Egbert: identified, xxiv; letters to, 3–4, 8–10, 21–24, 119–22, 125–28, 142–43, 145–46, 149–51,

155–57, 158–60, 165–67, 174–75, 181–83, 186–89, 190–92; and MA-SS, 2, 13, 79, 116, 118, 121–22, 199; urged to attend Providence convention, 24; health of, 60, 63, 68, 70, 71, 79, 82, 90, 102, 107, 117, 125–26; 142–43, 144, 145, 155, 159, 162, 165, 179–80, 181, 188, 196, 200, 201, 203, 204; George Thompson's letter to, 104, 109, 120; WLG's anxiety for, 115, 149–50, 185, 201, 204; visits Philadelphia to settle A. Buffum's accounts, 120–21, 122, 126–27, 162; letters received from, 123, 155, 158–59, 174; letter quoted, 157; wants to hear from Knapp, 101–02, may go on trip for health, 162, 174; medical experiments of, 176, 177, 191, 196; staying with Southwicks, 179–80; impending death of, 196–97; death of, 199, 205–06, 208, 211, 254; Ann G. Chapman's solicitude for, 252, 255; WLG settles accounts of, 207; George W. Benson's son named after, 311–12; mentioned, 1, 59, 65, 95, 102, 124, 136

Benson, Henry Egbert (son of George W. Benson), 444; identified, xxiv; birth and naming of, 311–12; weight of, 337; health of, 396, 403

Benson, Mary: identified, xxii–xxiii; letters to, 205–06, 394–96, 407–10, 431–34; visits Uxbridge with WLG, 146; WLG's appreciation of, 188, 330, 624; sick, 274; invited to wedding of A. E. Grimké, 349; visiting Garrisons, 416, 417, 432; mentioned, 7, 110, 155, 173, 174, 175, 303, 349, 351, 352, 397, 431, 434, 455, 556, 622, 676, 702

Benson, Mary (daughter of George W. Benson), xxiv

Benson, Sarah (daughter of George W. Benson), xxiv

Benson, Sarah Thurber: identified, xxiii; letters to, 196–98, 399–400; WLG's appreciation of, 188, 330, 444–45, 624; WLG hopes for visit of, 201, 252, 255, 395, 398, 399, 400, 403, 406, 492; health of, 210, 722; mentioned, 77, 271, 389, 401, 402, 417, 431, 556, 622, 676, 702

Benson, Thomas Davis (son of George W. Benson), xxiv

Benson, William Collins, 272

Benson, William P. R., 272

Bensonville, Mass. (later Florence), xxiii

Bentham, Jeremy, 663

Bible: withheld from slaves, 285; quoted, *passim*

Bird, Mrs., 392

Birney, James G.: identified, 35; letters to, 66–69, 535; WLG's letter to *Emancipator* in reply to essay of, 464–85; and Kentucky antislavery societies, 33; tribulations of, 34, 35, 45, 61, 173, 230, 232; Channing's letter to, 61, 222; and *Philanthropist*, 61, 69, 232; quoted, 242; visits J. Q. Adams, 268; and AA-SS, 349, 352, 357; and political action, 412, 413, 464–85, 510, 571; "View of the Constitution of the American Anti-Slavery Society as Connected with the 'No Government' Question," 457, 459, 460, 461, 464–85, 495; and MA-SS, 538; secretary of American and Foreign Anti-Slavery Society, 553; Liberty party's presidential nominee, 553, 554, 725, 728, 730 and 731; in Great Britain, 655, 660, 730, 731; mentioned, 248, 264, 293, 464, 572, 600

Bishop, Joel Prentiss, 725–26; identified, 728

Bishop, Lyman, 329

Black, Adam, 671

Blagden, Rev. George Washington: identified, 110; convention at meeting-house of, 108; accused of being slaveholder, 275, 299, 301–02

Blain, Rev. John, 139; identified, 141

Blake, Mr. (bookkeeper for *Liberator*), 404, 415

Blake, George, 64; identified, 66

Blake, James M., 131; identified, 133

Blake, William, 68

Bloodgood, Justice, 257, 260

Bloomfield Convention, 604, 606

Bolus, Dr., 101

Bond, George, 331

Booth, Mr. (teacher at American Asylum for the Deaf and Dumb), 377–78

Borden, Nathaniel B., 457

Boston, Mass.: mobs in, xxv, xxx, 186, 189, 247, 268, 365; antislavery fairs in, xxv, 194, 195, 408, 699; reception of George Thompson in, xxx; WLG leaves for Brooklyn, 1, 199; abolitionism in, 13–14, 19, 180, 199, 432–33; Henry Benson in, 63, 162, 179–80; WLG urged to return to, 73–74, 75, 78, 109; WLG's impression of, 83;

WLG plans to return to, 143, 156, 177, 381, 389; disturbances at, 151, 152, 154, 162, 164; slave cases in, 170, 171, 195; Garrisons return to, 290, 291, 333, 389–90, 400; Grimkés in, 345, 346, 347; Garrisons to rent Phelps's house in, 399, 400, 403; colored citizens welcome WLG home, 678, 684, 685, 697–98, 700; James Garrison and temptations of, 702, 703, 721; mentioned, xxv, 59, 213, 233, 333, 494, 554, 668, 699, 705, 710, 711, 725 *et passim*

Boston, Anti-Slavery Intelligence Office (36 Brattle Street), 118

Boston, Anti-Slavery Office (25 Cornhill), 59, 254, 725

Boston, Belknap-Street Church (African Baptist Church), 318, 319, 321

Boston, Chardon-Street Chapel: meeting of NEN-RS in, 534; Chardon-Street Convention held in, 554, 722. *See also* Chardon-Street Convention

Boston, Congress Hall, 209

Boston, Faneuil Hall: George Thompson at, xxx; meeting on Lovejoy's death, 331; meeting on Texas, 335, 336

Boston, Free Church: identified, 367; and A. A. Phelps, xxviii, 213, 215; and MA-SS, 209; and Clerical Appeal, 290; decrease of Negro worshippers at, 318, 319

Boston, Lyceum, 414

Boston, Marlborough Chapel: identified, 367; dedication of, 365–66; WLG to speak at, 374, 375; WLG and N. P. Rogers welcomed home at, 685, 693, 697–98; and Phelps, 443, 446; Massachusetts Abolition Society meets at, 500; mentioned, 390, 392, 711

Boston, Marlborough Hotel: MA-SS meeting at, 209; Massachusetts Abolition Society organized at, 500

Boston, Music Hall, xxx

Boston, Odeon: identified, 343; Grimkés speak at, 342, 345 and 346; nonresistance discussed at, 414

Boston, Young Men's Anti-Slavery Society of, 79, 183

Boston *Commercial Gazette*, 189

Boston *Courier*, 222; identified, 221; letters to, 217–21, 223–31, 234–44, 246–51

Boston *Daily Advocate*, 108; identified, 111

Boston *Daily Atlas*, 74, 75, 245

Boston Female Anti-Slavery Society: letter to Maria W. Chapman for, 714–16; Maria W. Chapman and, xxiv; mobbed, xxv, 189, 247, 393; annual reports of, 8, 10–11, 716, 730; contributions to antislavery cause, 23, 26, 108, 420, 622; petitions against admission of Arkansas, 85; fairs, 194, 195, 408, 699; Ann G. Chapman's bequest to, 253; WLG can't address, 710–11, 714; divisions in, 714–17; mentioned, 4, 8, 10, 83, 719

Boston *Free Press and Advocate*, 111

Boston *Illuminator*, 98; identified, 99

Boston *Post*, 111

Boston Quarterly Review, The, 347; identified, 348

Boston *Recorder*: identified, 149; anti-Garrisonism, 147, 172, 294; mentioned, 25, 381, 723

Boston Reformer, 347; identified, 348

Boston *Register*, 415; identified, 416

Boston Samaritan Asylum for Indigent Colored Children, 252, 253–54, 255, 263

Boston *Transcript*, 722; identified, 723

Boston True Thomsonian, 342–43

Botany Bay, 39; identified, 41

Bourne, George: identified, 35–36; letter to Rhode Island Convention, 34, 35; speaks, 88, 108, 117, 276; against women's rights, 616; mentioned, 109, 115, 290, 484, 569

Boussais, Duclos de, 658

Boutelle, Elder Luther, 695; identified, 695–96

Bowring, John, 661, 666; identified, 663–64

Boyce, James P., 84, 493; identified, 311; letter to, 310–11; at Peace Convention, 393

Boyce, Mrs. James P. (Julia Ann Purrinton), 310; identified, 311

Boyce, Jonathan, 311

Boyer, Jean Pierre, 146

Boyle, Rev. James: identified, 346; letter on Clerical Appeal, 345, 368; letter on nonresistance, 444, 446; and Gamaliel Bailey, 446–47; closeness of religious views to WLG's, 447

Boyle, Mrs. James (Laura P.), 444; identified, 447

Bradford, Dr. Gamaliel, 60; identified, 62

Bradburn, George, 707; identified, 588; letter to, 587; at World's Convention, 654, 655; supports Harrison in election, 725, 730; and political action, 730, 731

Bradford, Samuel, 494–95; identified, 496

Braithwaite, Isaac, 658

Braithwaite, Mrs. Isaac (Anna Lloyd), 656; identified, 658

Branch, Elder Nicholas, 162; identified, 164

Brandon *Telegraph*, 307, 308

Breckinridge, Robert J.: identified, 167; debates with George Thompson, 165–66, 167, 170, 171, 231; WLG wants copy of his will, 263; opponent of abolitionism, 263

Bright, John, xxx

Bristol county, R.I., 607

Bristol County (Mass.) Anti-Slavery Society, 308–09, 310, 313

Britannia (steamship), 724, 728; letters from England received by, 707, 709; WLG considered sailing on, 660, 664

British-American Institute (Dawn, Canada), 486, 528

British and Foreign Anti-Slavery Reporter, 528

British and Foreign Anti-Slavery Society: calls World's Convention, 553, 588; Sturge helped organize, 592; mentioned, 113, 528, 625

British Friend, The, 728

British India Movement: MA-SS encourages, 528–31; WLG's enthusiasm for, 674–75; progress of, 689–90, 730; meeting at Manchester, England, on, 689, 709, 710; Elizabeth Pease and, 724, 729

British India Society: letter to George Thompson for, 528–31; George Thompson and, xxx, 659; WLG's hopes for, 689

British Queen (packet-ship): letters forwarded by, 623, 654, 656; mentioned, 615, 644, 724

Bronson, Rev. Asa, 140; identified, 141

Brooklyn, Conn.: Bensons' farm "Friendship's Vale," xxii, xxiii, 95, 101, 109, 186, 252, 254, 341; S. J. May in, xxvii, 143; considerations on WLG's staying in, 1, 73–74, 75; WLG in, 1, 63, 116, 123, 199, 210–11, 268–69, 274, 291, 333, 368, 371, 692, 698; WLG plans to visit, 1, 71, 109–10, 252, 267, 345, 381, 389, 676; Henry Benson urged to go to, 63, 150, 156, 175; Weld to visit, 159; Garrisons postpone going to, 210–11, 492; de-

scriptions of, 271, 312, 376; meeting of Windham Co. Anti-Slavery Society at, 345; WLG wishes he could have visited, 614, 622, 624; James Garrison at, 612, 617, 625, 703, 721; George Thompson Garrison at, 612, 617, 668, 704; WLG writes from, 3–32, 36–52, 63–75, 119–28, 134–35, 142–78, 269–88, 368–89, 523–27; mentioned, 5, 271, 290, 291, 457, 704 *et passim*

Brooklyn, N.Y., 614, 621

Brooks, Nathan, 444; identified, 447

Brougham, Lord Henry Peter, 36; identified, 40

Brown, Dr. (Thomsonian), 397

Brown, David Paul, 362; identified, 364

Brown, John: Gerrit Smith and, 47; A. M. Milligan and, 112; Charles Stearns and, 562; R. D. Webb's biography of, 684

Brown, John E., 101; identified, 103

Brown, Moses, xxiv; identified, 103; WLG visits, 102; near death, 175, 176

Brown, William C., 42; identified, 43

Brown, Benson & Ives, xxii

Browne, John W., 418; identified, 419–20

Brownell, Dr. Richmond, 150; identified, 151

Brownson, Orestes A., 347; identified, 348

Brunswick, Countess of, 656

Bryant, William Cullen, 13

Buchanan, James, 111

Buckingham, Joseph Tinker: identified, 221; letters to (as editor of *Courier*), 217–21, 223–31, 234–44, 246–51

Buffalo, N.Y., Convention of Colored Americans at, 610

Buffum, Arnold, 113, 457; identified, 122, disagreement about *Liberator* accounts of, 120–22, 126–27

Buffum, James N., 311

Buffum, Sarah, 95, 96; identified, 457; at convention in Philadelphia, 455

Buffum, W., 712

Bullard, Elder, 70

Bunker, Capt. (of *Benjamin Franklin*), 97

Bunker Hill, Battle of, 278, 334, 704

Bunker Hill (steamboat), 378

Burgoyne, Gen. John, 280

Burke, Edmund, quoted and identified, 32, 33; 189; 722, 723

Burleigh, Charles Calistus: identified, 72; helps edit *Liberator*, 1, 2, 116, 118, 169, 178; visits WLG, 70, 177;

speaks, 108, 113, 117, 124, 139, 379; at Newport for hearing, 132; laboring in Pennsylvania, 492; enlightened about new organization, 492; resolution on elective franchise, 571–72, 574; mentioned, 72, 115, 159, 161, 493, 610, 615

Burleigh, Cyrus Moses, 608; identified, 610

Burleigh, George Shepard, 610

Burleigh, John Oscar, 610

Burleigh, Rev. Lucian, 610

Burleigh, Rinaldo, 72, 610

Burleigh, William H.: identified, 178–79, opposes Clerical Appeal, 303; mentioned, 177, 610

Burns, Robert (N.H. delegate to Congress), 289

Burns, Robert (poet), quoted and identified, 31, 33; 226–27, 232; 492, 493; 692, 693

Butler, Charles, 113, 118

Buxton, Thomas Fowell, 592, 662; identified, 61; height, 58, 61; speaks at Gurney's banquet, 660

Byron, Lord, 657; quoted and identified, 229, 232; 647, 650

Byron, Lady (Anne Isabella Milbanke): identified, 657; WLG sees, 656, 661

Caledonia, 720, 724, 729

Calhoun, John C., 525; identified, 154; his "Bill of Abominations," 135; proposes bill censoring mail, 138; a mere politician, 154; quoted on abolitionists, 239, 245; and slavery in District of Columbia, 430

California, 222

Calista, 623

Calvin, John: identified, 168; and Sabbath, 166, 173, 297, 314, 315, 368

Cambell, David, 451; identified, 451–52

Cambell, John R., 13

Cambridge Anti-Slavery Society, 392

Cambridgeport, Mass., 702, 704, 721; Garrisons move to, 533

Campbell, Thomas, quoted and identified, 590, 592; 645, 647

Canada: dispute between United States and, 440–41, 442; fugitive slaves in, 486, 489, 661; British-American Institute in, 486, 528

Canning, George, 651, 653

Cannon, Gov. Newton, 170

Canterbury, Conn.: Prudence Crandall's school in, xxvii, 73; WLG visits, 692–93

Cape Clear, Ireland, 643, 645

Caples, Charles V., 115; identified, 116; speaks, 113, 117

Capron, Effingham L., 470, 513; identified, 113; letter to, 171–73; and MA-SS, 13, 712; at New England Anti-Slavery Convention, 110; and NEN-RS, 390, 391, 395, 534

Capron, Mrs. Effingham L. (Lydia B. Allen), 110, 172; identified, 173

Caroline, 615, 620, 623, 662

Carter, Edwin B., 71; identified, 72

Cassey, Joseph: identified, 122; proposed arbiter between WLG and Buffum, 120, 122, 127

Catherine (or Catharine). *See* Benson, Mrs. George W.

Catholicism, 178, 281, 348

Cecelia: WLG sends for, 394, 397–98, 400; mentioned, 393, 403, 409, 417

Chace, Eliza J. (later Mrs. Thomas Davis): identified, 157; and Frank Farley, 156; helps Helen with children, 201, 208; visits Garrisons, 307; illness of, 456, 692, 722, 724; mentioned, 167, 216, 271, 308

Chace, Harvey. *See* Chase

Chace, Oliver, 458

Chace, Mrs. Oliver (Mary E. Allen), 456; identified, 458

Chace, Samuel B., 458; identified, 457; WLG visits family of, 454–55

Chace, Mrs. Samuel B. (Elizabeth Buffum), 455; identified, 457

Chace, William, 157; family, 102, 256, 272, 434

Chace, Mrs. William, 456

Chace (Chase), William M. (son of above): identified, 8; letter to, 123–25; George W. Benson's business partner, xxiii; WLG sees, 89, 349, 351, 621, 624; goes to New York, 90, 92; seeks lawyer for Newport hearing, 129; and Henry Benson, 151, 196, 201; at convention of AA-SS agents, 185; speaks, 575, 608, 718, 720; writing to Mary, 623; mentioned, 7, 35, 157, 216, 217, 268, 389, 394, 398, 533, 534, 620, 622, 643, 692, 704, 724

Chandler, Elizabeth Margaret: identified, 164; Lundy editing her writings, 163; quoted, 508, 516

Chandler, John B., 4; identified, 693–94

Channing, William Ellery: identified, 5; *Slavery*, 2, 3, 5, 9, 14–15, 16, 22,

43–45, 47, 59, 74, 75, 223–24, 241–42, 245; and abolitionists, 44–45, 61, 222, 223–24, 372; and WLG, 56, 57, 59, 61, 83; Harriet Martineau staying with, 59–60, 61; and "Algernon Sidney," 222, 223, 250; speech on Lovejoy's death, 331; mentioned, xxvii, 25, 84, 131, 392, 416

Channing, William H., 723

Chaplin, W. L., 527

Chapman, Miss (Mary Gray?), 78

Chapman, Ann Greene, 3, 194; identified, 4; death and bequests of, 252, 253, 255–56

Chapman, Henry, 349(?); identified, 11; helps *Liberator*, 9; Knapp cannot get money from, 177, 179(?); gives $100 to WLG, 202; and Company, 690, 710

Chapman, Mrs. Henry (Sarah Greene), 490

Chapman, Henry Grafton: identified, 25; and MA-SS, 13, 22, 449; and money matters, 177, 179(?), 620, 624; illness of, 695, 698; mentioned, 11, 60, 62, 298, 300(?), 349(?), 490, 616

Chapman, Mrs. Henry Grafton (Maria Weston): identified, xxiv–xxv; letters to, 632–33, 710–11, 714–16 (see also 627n); edits *Liberty Bell*, xxiv, xxviii; WLG visits, 55, 60, 78, 81; quoted on WLG and Channing, 57, 61; family, 57; hymns selected by, 118 and 119; at Convention of American Women, 356, 362, 363, 364, 366; illness, 366, 367; WLG's salary, 366; and NEN-RS, 390, 391, 393, 395, 398, 534; writing to Henry Clay, 433; and *Non-Resistant*, 438; writes Boston Female Anti-Slavery Society's annual reports, 460, 463, 730; and Elizabeth Pease, 667, 684, 686; safe accouchement of, 671; and Sabbath Convention, 722–23; mentioned, 11, 25, 56, 60, 194, 343, 347, 360, 419, 463, 491, 494, 582, 643, 684, 699, 720

Chaptal, Jean Antoine, 335

Chardon-Street Convention, xxxi, 393; identified, 554, 722–23; denunciations of, 722, 727; WLG describes, 724–25, 731

Charleston, S.C., 14; mail robberies in, 34–35, 30; railway, 230, 232

Charlestown, Mass., 549, 559

Charter Oak, The, 179, 386

Chase (or Chace), Harvey, 140, 457; identified, 141

Cherokee Indians, 217

Chickasaw (brig), 152

Child, David Lee: identified, 134; letter to, 152–54; going to Matamoras with Lundy, 78, 80; at Newport, 132, jailed for debt, 154; and *Emancipator*, 154; mentioned, 79, 347, 419

Child, Mrs. David Lee (Lydia Maria): identified, 79; on Executive Committee of AA-SS, xxv; *Appeal* of, xxviii; going to Matamoras with Lundy, 78, 80; WLG's sympathy with, 152; and antislavery fair, 194, 195; to attend American Women's Anti-Slavery Convention, 356; at NEN-RS Convention, 534; and divisions in Boston Female Anti-Slavery Society, 717; mentioned, 81, 134, 347, 463, 494, 582, 667

China, 663–64

Choate, Mr., 171

Christian Advocate and Journal (New York), 43, 354

Christian Disciple, 416

Christian Freeman (Hartford), 179

Christian Mirror (Portland, Me.), 294, 345; identified, 149; anti-Garrisonism, 147, 172; Asa Cummings editor, 516

Christian Reflector, 712; identified, 713

Christian Reformer, 695

Christian Register, 415; identified, 416

Christian Soldier, xxv

Christian Spectator, 75, 76

Christian Witness, 178, 300, 302

Christiana, 60, 62, 79

Church, Dr. Jefferson, 718; identified, 720

Church, Maria, 694

Cibber, Colley, quoted and identified, 342, 340, 681, 682

Cincinnati, O.: Birney in, 35, 69, 230, 232; railroad to South Carolina, 230, 232. See also Lane Theological Seminary

Cincinnati *Weekly Herald and Philanthropist*, 69

Cincinnati Abolition Society, 232

Cinque (or Cinquez), Joseph, 536

Clapp, Daniel, 338; identified, 340

Clapp, Richard, 712; identified, 713

Clark, Mary: identified, 4; mentioned, 3, 589, 693

Clark, Dr. William: identified, 342–43; WLG at his Thomsonian infirmary, 341–42

Clarke, John S.: letter to, as president

of Rhode Island Anti-Slavery Society, 28–32

Clarke, Dr. Peleg, 393, 456; identified, 458

Clarkson, Thomas, 192; identified, 664; WLG plans to visit, 661, 664; repudiates Colonization Society, 664, 707, 709

Clarkson Anti-Slavery Association, 613

Clay, Henry: Maria W. Chapman writing to, 433; and abolitionists, 435, 525

Clerical Appeal: identified, 275; WLG's review of, 273, 275; silence of New York Executive Committee on, 290, 298–300, 303, 304–06, 541–42; Woodbury praises, 297; clerical protests following, 299, 300, 374 (see also Andover Theological Seminary); quoted on *Liberator's* treatment of Elipha White, 300–01, and G. W. Blagden, 301–02; reactions to, 303, 305–06, 307, 312–13; Phelps and, 304, 347; Boyle's letter on, 345, 346; sectarian spirit of, 544; mentioned, 11, 200, 263, 274, 291, 292, 309, 311, 321, 407, 453

Coates, Lindley, 611; identified, 613

Coe, Rev. William: identified, 335; and nonresistance, 335, 444; moves resolution encouraging *Liberator*, 422, 423; in accident with George W. Benson, 491–92; mentioned, 396, 676, 698, 722

Coffin, Charlotte, 406, 416; identified, 406

Coffin, Joshua, 81

Coffin, Peter, 81, 495

Coffin, Mary Ann, 79, 268; identified, 81

Coffin, Susan, 79, 495; identified, 81

Coffin, William C., 712; identified, 713

Cohasset, Mass., 79

Colburne, John, 53

Cole, Thomas: identified, 679; letter to, 678–79

Coleman, William, 13

Coleridge, Samuel Taylor, 639, 641

Collins, Charles, 594

Collins, John Anderson: identified, 453–54; letters to, 717–20, 723–26; and MA-SS pledge to AA-SS, 452, 453; and A. A. Phelps, 496; death of wife, 668; mission to England, 707–08, 709–10, 717–18, 726, 729; and Chardon-Street Convention, 723; mentioned, 491, 608, 659, 704, 731

Collins, Mrs. John A., 668, 671

Colman, John. *See* Manford, Dr.

Colonization Society. *See* American Colonization Society

Colonization Herald, 222

Colored American, 217, 354

Colored Samaritan Asylum, 252, 253–54, 255, 263

Colton, Walter: identified, 222; identity as "Algernon Sidney" revealed, 233, 234. *See also* "Algernon Sidney"

Columbia (mail packet), 36

Columbus (packet ship), 623, 646; identified, 631; letters written from, 625 650 *passim*; WLG to sail on, 612; departure delayed, 615, 621; WLG tells about, 629–30, 632, 634–35

Columbus (receiving ship), 549, 550, 551

Colver, Nathaniel: identified, 336; WLG's admiration for, 342; anti-Garrisonian efforts of, 412, 415, 418; hostility to nonresistance, 433, 532; vulgarity of, 685, 724; mentioned, 335, 338, 519, 613–14, 655, 666

Come-Outers, 696

Committee for the Abolition of the Slave Trade, 356

Concert of Prayer, 180

Concord, N.H.: New Hampshire Anti-Slavery Society meetings at (1836), 109, 113, 116; (1837), 264; (1839), 460; (1840), 686, 687, 691, 693, 694, 697; Young Men's Anti-Slavery Convention at, 282, 288; mentioned, 4, 33, 704

Congregationalist Journal, 173

Congress, U.S.: debates to be published in *Liberator*, 4, 23; petitions to for abolition of slavery in the District of Columbia, 7, 9, 24, 37, 48–49, 204, 205, 253, 289, 326, 335, 489; treatment of antislavery petitions, 9, 204–05, 214, 215, 253, 286, 287, 435; and slavery in District of Columbia, 14, 20, 72, 253, 289, 430; and admission of Arkansas, 75, 76, 82, 84–85, 289; and censorship of mails, 137–38; and fugitive slaves, 170; authority over slavery in states, 308, 350, 429; and annexation of Texas, 326; ways of influencing by abolitionists, 467–70, 472, 512, 598–601; mentioned, 53, 86, 132, 230, 287, 567, 666

Connecticut: 75, 378; lacks state anti-slavery society, 29, 33; abolitionism in, 70, 383, 386, 556; legislature, 133,

164, 349, 367; conscientious objectors in, 560, 563

Connecticut Anti-Slavery Society, 346; formation of, 340, 377; participation of women in, 506, 582; WLG cannot attend meeting of, 556, 557; opposes antislavery political party, 565

Connecticut Evangelical Magazine and Religious Intelligencer, 259

Constitution, U.S.: and abolitionists, 55, 567; and slavery, 170, 286, 350, 474–75, 700; failure of, 325; reasons for not voting under, 511–12; mentioned, xxv, xxviii, 253

Constitutional Union Party, 203

Cooke, Rev. Parsons, 723

Cork, Ireland, 646

Cornell's (stage-coach stop?), 176

Cornell, Rev. William M., 275

Cornish, Samuel E., 216; identified, 217

Cornwall, Barry, quoted and identified, 637, 638

Covenanters, refusal to vote, 470, 510, 511, 571, 582

Coventry, R.I.: WLG asked to speak at, 268, 271, 274; WLG visits, 455–56

Coventry Temperance Union, 340

Cowles, Samuel Smith, 556; identified, 558

Cowper, William: quoted and identified, 32, 33; 106, 107; 182, 183; 215, 216; 330, 331; 440, 442; 632, 634; 680, 681

Cox, Dr. Abraham Liddon: identified, 96; WLG visits, 94, 261; WLG wants copy of Breckinridge's will from, 263

Cox, Rev. Francis A: identified, 113; mentioned, 109, 359, 658

Cradle of Liberty: identified, 445; plans for, 442–43; resolution approving, 493

Cranch, Christopher P., 696

Crandall, Almira (Mrs. Rand), 163; identified, 164

Crandall, Prudence (Mrs. Calvin Philleo): identified, 164; happiness of with husband, 163; mentioned, xxvii, 72, 73, 137, 178

Crandall, Dr. Reuben, 136; identified, 137

Cresson, Elliott, 107; identified, 664; and Clarkson, 661

Crocker, Rev. Nathan Bourne, 136; identified, 138

Cropper, James, 225; identified, 231

Cropper, Capt. Thomas B., 634, 650; identified, 631; described, 629

Cross, Rev. John(?), 351; identified, 354

Cross, Rev. Joseph Warren(?), 351; identified, 354

Cuba, 535, 536

Cummings, Rev. Asa: identified, 516; and *Christian Mirror*, 149; and Massachusetts Abolition Society, 503; at Albany Convention, 526

Curtis, B. R., 171

Curtis, C. P., 171

Cushing, Caleb: identified, 205; letters to, 204 05, 256, 551–52, 558–59, 570; WLG and, 552

Cushman, Samuel, 289

Cutler, Rev. Calvin, 23; identified, 27

Cutts, John Smith. *See* Smith, John Cutts

Dansville, N.Y., 577

Danville, Ky., 33

Darlington, England, 684, 723, 724, 709

Dartmouth College, 522

Davis, Edward M.: identified, 334; letter to, 333–34; going to Europe, 351, 355

Davis, Thomas: identified, 308; mentioned, 307, 349, 456

Davis, Mrs. Thomas. *See* Chace, Eliza J.

Dawn, Canada, 528

Dean, Lydia, 454

Dean, William, 453; identified, 454

Declaration of Independence, U.S.: quoted, 591; mentioned, 226, 235, 286, 384, 700

Declaration of Sentiments (of AA-SS), 210, 240, 242, 293, 305, 332, 470

Democratic party, 161, 348

Democratic Review, 348

Demosthenes, 181, 183

Denison, Rev. Charles Wheeler, 484, 569; identified, 354; edits *Emancipator*, 26; speaks in New York, 351

Dickens, Charles, 657

District of Columbia. *See* Washington, D.C.

Dixon, William, 257; identified, 259

Dole, Ebenezer: identified, 11; supports *Liberator*, 9; withdraws from Peace Convention, 393

Dorchester Anti-Slavery Society, 713

Dorr, Thomas Wilson: identified, 131; chairman of R.I. legislative committee, 125, 130, 132

Douglass, Frederick, 457, 404, 576, 610

Douglass, Robert, 359; identified, 361

Douglass, Sarah H., 361
Downes, Commodore John: identified, 550; and James Garrison, 549, 558, 559, 570
Dresser, Rev. Amos, 470; identified, 202; to be at MA-SS meeting, 201; Augusta *Chronicle* on, 229; at NEN-RS Convention, 534
Drew, Charles: identified, 84; mentioned, 83, 117, 192, 310
Dublin, Ireland, 682; WLG plans to visit, 655, 670; WLG's visit to, 697, 699
Dumond, Dwight L., quoted, 54, 185
Dumont, Rev. Henry A., 97–98; identified, 99
Dunlop, John, 720
Durfee, Gilbert Hathaway, 65, 68; identified, 66

Earle, Edward, 452, 453; identified, 454
Earle, Mrs. Edward (Ann Barker Buffum), 453, 454
Earle, John Milton, 453; identified, 454
Earle, Pliny, 713
Earle, Thomas, 553
Earle, William B., 712; identified, 713
East India Movement. *See* British India Movement
Eastern Pennsylvania Anti-Slavery Society, 506, 608–09
Easton, Rev. H., 116
Eayres. *See* Ayres
Edinburgh, Scotland: George Thompson to lecture in, 59; WLG in, 668–71; temperance meeting in, 669–70; mentioned, 655, 661, 699
Edinburgh, Royal Hotel: public breakfast for WLG at, 671
Edinburgh *Witness*, 381, 671
Edom, 284, 325
Effingham, Countess of (Charlotte Primrose Howard), 701
Eldridge, Elleanor, 408–10; identified, 410
Elliot (or Elliott), Rev. David, 263; identified, 264
Emancipation Act, 527, 528
Emancipator: identified, 26; letter to editor of, 464–85; R. G. Williams jailed for circulating, 12; editorship of, 24, 42, 46, 153, 154, 213, 214–15, 216, 354; Goodell's essays on "Human Rights" in, 45, 47; silence on Clerical Appeal, 298–300, 303, 304, 305, 306, 308; and death of Lovejoy, 332; and Birney's letter on nonresist-

ing abolitionists, 457, 459, 464–65, 466–67, 485, 495, 496; hails Massachusetts Abolition Society, 498, 547; and political action, 510, 511–12, 565–66, 725; remissness of, 541–43; proposition to form National Anti-Slavery Board published in, 584, 588, 589; Gerrit Smith's letter to editor quoted, 603; near death's doors, 718; mentioned, xxix, 23, 165, 263, 378, 381, 519, 523, 553, 660, 718
Emerson, Ralph Waldo, 57, 554; quoted, 727
Emery, Rev. Samuel Hopkins, 454; identified, 457
Emma (English brig), 634
England. *See* Great Britain; World's Anti-Slavery Convention
Essex county, Mass., 607
Essex county, N.Y., 577
Essex County (Mass.) Anti-Slavery Society; various meetings of, 109, 113, 117, 118, 309, 310, 719; organization of, 112; C. T. Torrey corresponding secretary of, 410; Garrisonian triumph in, 492–93; censures Friends, 591, 592
Essex Courant (Newburyport), xxvi
Eunice, Cousin, 101, 143
Everett, Gov. Edward, 201; identified, 202
Everett, Joshua T.: identified, 576; letter to, 575–76
Exeter Hall. *See* London, Exeter Hall

Fairbanks, Drury, 13, 78; identified, 80
Fairhaven, Mass., 310
Fall River, Mass.: WLG invited to speak in, 121, 123, 143; WLG hung in effigy in, 137, 140; WLG speaks in, 135, 140, 454–55; described, 140; A. St. Clair's activities in, 434
Fall River (Mass.) Anti-Slavery Society, 125, 137, 141
Fall River (Mass.) Female Anti-Slavery Society, 140, 456
Farley, Frank, 167, 169; identified, 157; sickness of, 156
Farley, Rev. Frederick Augustus, 143, 157; identified, 131; WLG hears sermon by, 130
Farmer, John, 4; identified, 266; letter to, 264–66
Farnsworth, Dr. Amos: identified, 168–69; letter to, 694–95; and MA-SS, 13, 712; mentioned, 167, 453, 710
Farr, Jonathan: identified, 168; critical letter, 166–67

Fessenden, Gen. Samuel, 108; identified, 110–11

Fifield, Dr. Noah, 328

Fifield, Mrs. Noah (Hannah Cranch Bond): identified, 328; letter to, 328

Filler, Louis, 12

Filmer, Sir Robert, 218, 220; identified, 222

Finney, Charles Grandison, 6

First of August (British West India Emancipation Day): observances of, 143, 151, 152, 527, 662; WLG speaks in New York on, 376, 378, 386

Fisk, John M (of West Brookfield), 712; identified, 713

Fisk, John M. (of North Brookfield), 712

Fitch, Rev. Charles: identified, 111; WLG praises, 139; plans to leave Free Church, 213, 290; and clerical appeals, 273, 275, 300–02, 305, 374; Woodbury's letter to quoted, 297–98; WLG's chastisement of, 300; rallying forces, 303, 307; discourse on dedication of Marlboro' Chapel, 366; mentioned, 26, 108, 276, 312, 313, 316, 319, 519

Flagg, Dr. John Foster Brewster: identified, 410–11; mentioned, 409, 434, 706

Flagg, Mrs. John Foster Brewster, 409, 434, 706

Florence, Mass., xxiii

Florida, 105

Follen, Charles: identified, 16–17; and MA-SS, 12, 15; speaks at MA-SS meeting, 22, 25; before Massachusetts legislative committee, 56, 58, 64, 65; Memoir of, 57; speaks at Peace Convention, 390; mentioned, 60, 78, 120, 659, 662

Follen, Mrs. Charles (Eliza Lee Cabot), 56, 78; identified, 57

Folsom, Abigail, 725; identified, 727

Forbes, Abner, 13

Foreign and Home Missions, 275, 280, 299

Foster, Abby Kelley, 308

Foster, Festus, 65; identified, 66

Foster, Isaac Plummer, 425

Foster, Mrs. Isaac Plummer (Harriet Brooks): identified, 425; letters to, 423–25, 450

Foster, John, 173

Fosters, the, 127

Fourier, François, 453

Fourth of July, 235, 333; WLG speaks on, 121, 123, 140, 272–273, 374, 375, 494, 496; WLG on inconsistencies of, 138–39

Fowler, Rev. Orin: identified, 141; WLG speaks at meeting-house of, 140, 455

Fox, George, 686, 688; identified, 168; and Sabbath, 166, 173, 368

France, 283; E. M. Davis going to, 355; Scoble and Alexander visit, 528

Franklin, Benjamin, 666

Franklin, John Hope, 217

Frederick: identified, 393–94; mentioned, 392, 394, 395, 397, 399, 417

Free Elector (Hartford, Conn.), 606

Free Press, xxvi

Freedom's Journal, 217

Free-Soil party, 43, 221, 454

Friend, The, 686; identified, 687

Friend of Man, The: identified, 24, 46; opposes Clerical Appeal, 300, 302, 303, 305; supports antislavery political party, 725; J. P. Bishop helps edit, 728; mentioned, 519, 571, 602

Friend of Peace, The, 416

Friends, Society of (Quakers): Van Buren cowers before, 71, 72; and peace movement, 94, 279; and abolitionism, 233–34, 258, 591, 592, 686–87; disowns William Bassett, 336, 687, 688; unnatural manner of preachers, 359; excommunicates members present at marriage of A. E. Grimké, 360; and military service, 389, 452, 563; and vote, 470, 512, 583, 600; and Hicksites, xxvii, 359, 661, 687, 698–99, 728; and Sabbath, 368; flattered by Clay, 435; and slavery, 590–91; disowns I. T. Hopper and J. S. Gibbons, 618; R. D. Webb leaves, 684; and color prejudice, 686; various members mentioned, xxii, xxvii, 103, 113, 118, 122, 334, 340, 348, 353, 361, 373, 392, 452, 454, 455, 516, 592, 596, 606, 613, 657, 658, 662, 664, 675, 688, 713, 714, 728; other mentions, 86, 102, 163, 327, 455

Friendship's Vale. See Brooklyn, Conn.

Fry, Elizabeth: identified, 658; mentioned, 656, 657, 662

Fugitive Slave Act: (1850), xxvii, 62; (1793), 171

Fuller, John E.: identified, 60; WLG's appreciation of, 62; and Clerical Appeal, 290; in Philadelphia, 360; an altered man, 422; mentioned, 13, 182, 213, 274, 276, 347, 351

Gaines, Edmund Pendleton, 169–70; identified, 171
Gairdner, Harriet, 659
Gale, George W., 96
Galusha, Rev. Elon, 98, 683; identified, 100; delegate to World's Convention, 614, 671; speaks at temperance meeting, 669; feebly welcomed home, 685
Gannett, Rev. Ezra Stiles: identified, 84; unhappy state of mind, 83; at Peace Convention, 390–91
Garnet, Henry H., 111; identified, 610–11; speaks at AA-SS Convention, 608
Gavitt, George W., 131; identified, 133
Garrison, Andrew, 183; identified, 184
Garrison, Edwin William, 272
Garrison, George Thompson: identified, 25; birth expected, 1, 22; birth of, 2, 60, 105, 115, 644; naming of, 52, 72, 311–12; WLG's reflections on free birth of, 62, 340, 620; character and development, 63–64, 121, 313, 356, 363–64, 372, 375, 433–34, 533–34, 555, 668, 704; WLG misses, 79, 82, 269–70, 616, 617, 676; health of, 58, 107, 115, 118, 156–57, 173, 174, 180, 182, 189, 191, 194, 197, 201, 204, 208, 211, 233, 252, 255, 261, 271, 303, 313, 330, 350, 360, 409, 460, 492; travels of, 129, 135–36, 186–87, 622; receives presents from Boston Female Anti-Slavery Society fair, 194; visits Brooklyn, 267, 617, 622, 625; misses Brooklyn, 291; reaction to new baby, 336, 337; can play in yard, 392, 395, 397, 399; mentioned, 54, 65, 70, 83, 90, 109, 127–28, 136, 143, 151, 216, 260, 362, 303, 418, 453, 458, 494, 614, 622, 636, 656, 660, 692, 698
Garrison, James: identified, 534; letters to, 634–36, 702–04; WLG arranges discharge from navy, 533, 549–50, 551–52, 558–59, 570; health of, 533, 549, 551, 612, 617, 671; WLG's hopes for, 617, 625, 635–36, 702; in Brooklyn, Conn., 675, 692, 721; mentioned, 615, 622, 643
Garrison, Wendell Phillips, 692, 698; WLG anticipates birth of, 620, 644, 648; birth of, 659–60; sickness of, 687, 700; naming of, 687, 704, 706; promise of, 704, 719–20
Garrison, William, 272

Garrison, William Lloyd
personal concerns: finances, 2, 8, 10, 49–52, 73, 75, 109, 177, 202, 252, 255, 291, 366, 371, 420, 533, 556, 690, 719; children, 2, 60, 62, 105, 115, 269–70, 333, 335, 336–38, 340, 620, 631, 644, 648, 659–60, 719 (see also individual names); persecutions and calumnies of, 2, 19, 137, 140, 167, 224, 250, 296, 305–08, 313, 314–15, 323–24, 363, 364, 369, 371–72, 374, 383–85, 391, 424, 426, 463, 592, 606, 640, 678, 700, 722 *et passim*; encomiums on, 24, 115, 207, 208, 209, 312, 313, 423, 426, 537; poetry by, 60, 62, 238, 245, 281, 327, 368, 370, 554, 630; urged to return to Boston, 73–74, 75; health of, 95, 101, 102–03, 104, 109, 115, 121, 142, 144, 156, 163, 165, 169, 172, 174, 182, 185, 188, 189, 194, 199, 274, 330, 338–39, 341–42, 344, 346, 350, 360, 368, 371, 375, 379–80, 396–97, 400, 405, 416, 617, 621, 637, 656, 670, 691, 708; *Thoughts on African Colonization*, 111, 122, 209, 231; not chosen editor of E. M. Chandler's poems, 164; matrimonial bliss, 255, 616, 642; on separation from Helen, 269–70, 352, 589, 612, 616–17, 619–20, 636, 642–43; considers subordinating abolitionism to reforms in general, 291; espousal of antislavery cause, 326, 333–34, 381–82, 383–84, 420–21, 463; and colonization, 355, 664; love of home, 453, 675–76, 679–80, 684, 688, 692, 706; not to write biography of Lundy, 592, 593; voyage to England, 628–53 *passim*; in Great Britain, 653–75 *passim*; voyage home, 675, 682–84, 688, 699; welcomed home, 676–77, 678, 685, 693, 696, 697–98, 700, 707

living arrangements: goes to Brooklyn, Conn., 1, 73–74, 75, 116–17, 121; disposes of Brighton Street house, 22–23, 26; returns to Boston, staying at Parkers', 3, 121, 176, 177, 201, 252; in Brooklyn for summer 1837, 199, 267, 268–69, 274; returns to Boston, 290, 291; in Brooklyn for summer 1838, 333, 345, 366, 367; returns to Boston, rents Phelps's house, 381, 389, 391–92, 394, 397–98, 399, 403, 407; takes house in Cambridgeport, 533, 622–23, 704

comments on: weather, 7, 101, 117–

18, 121, 174–75, 194, 204, 256, 259, 270, 271, 312, 398, 621, 629, 643, 647, 650–53; freedom of speech, 20, 30–31, 218, 286, 462, 516, 674; public speaking, 71, 108, 187, 189, 271, 275, 374–75, 387, 405, 494, 693; his luck, 76–77, 215, 637; "hard language," 86, 224, 246–51, 306, 334, 372, 519–20; self as correspondent, 104, 117, 119–20, 125, 135, 161–62, 186, 187, 196, 201, 206, 233, 251–52, 254, 329–30, 338, 340, 350, 356, 407, 418, 432, 445, 491, 555, 702–03, 708–09; mortality, 114–15, 155–56, 165, 190, 193, 196–97, 200–01, 205–06, 211–12, 252, 254–55, 283–84, 310, 340, 728–29; health, 125–26, 142, 145, 159; Thomsonian medicine, 189, 194, 339, 341–42, 344, 346, 387; separation from friends, 193, 375–78, 431, 439, 636–37; time, 201, 206, 329, 335, 555, 692, 699–700, 721; love of money, 211, 618–19; patience, 619, 640; ocean, 637, 639–40, 645

on abolitionism: nature and objects of, 14, 17–19, 29–31, 37–38, 282, 474–75, 500–04, 579–80; progress of, 19–20, 29, 86, 106, 212, 267, 296, 324–26, 355, 381–82, 424–25, 440, 488–90, 541–47, 563–64; tribulations of abolitionists, 30, 31, 45, 67–68, 86–87, 106, 129, 186, 218, 225, 230, 247–48, 282, 286–87, 331, 362–63, 365, 371, 427–28, 612; and church, 140, 166, 263, 474–75, 481–82, 501, 580–81, 586; and political action, 154, 324, 426, 464–85, 493, 504, 508–15, 516, 525, 544, 565–69, 571–74, 579–85 *passim*, 607 605, 608–09, 718, 719, 725, 730; and nonresistance, 234–44 *passim*, 248, 251, 332, 433, 457, 462–63, 464–85 *passim*, 493, 513, 582–83, 604; and Clerical Appeal, 273, 290, 298–300, 303, 304–06, 312–13, 541–42; and new organization, 312, 351, 493, 517, 576, 588, 599, 633, 655, 660, 669, 685, 708, 718, 719, 724, 725, 729; broad basis of, 383–84, 385, 425, 471, 475, 500–02, 504, 507, 564–65, 567, 577–81, 586, 602; divisions within, 432–33, 439–40, 461–62, 475, 497–516, 517–21, 564–65, 575–76, 577–87, 715–16; inevitable triumph of, 576; desperate situation of, 588, 708, 725, 729

on slavery: and church, 19, 20, 86, 139, 145, 263, 580–81: resistance to, 32, 55, 224–30, 234–44, 334, 479; and emancipation, 32, 38–40, 187, 333–34, 355, 427–28, 673; evils of, 105–06, 138–39, 285–86, 326, 334, 500–01, 673–74, 689, 700, 710, 711 *et passim*

on travel: by stage-coach, 76–77, 89, 128–29, 136, 155; by railroad, 77, 191, 206, 215, 260, 607, 692, 711–12; by steamboat, 91, 93–94, 94–95, 97–98, 184, 186–87, 215–16, 260, 349, 360, 378, 607–08; by ship, 628–53 *passim*, 682–84

on women: in antislavery cause, 108–09, 326, 407, 415, 419, 449, 463, 493, 504–08, 521, 565, 581–82, 714–16; antislavery convention of, 362–63, 366; and Peace Convention, 390, 395; and World's Convention, 587, 616, 627, 633, 641, 654, 658–59, 665, 666, 677, 680, 698, 700, 730

views on: peace and nonresistance, 32, 237, 258, 276–80, 328, 332, 365, 387–88, 406, 408, 414, 435–36, 452, 464–85 *passim*, 494–95, 526, 560–63, 571–74, 604, 640–41, 680–81, 705; free Negroes, 106, 257, 318–20, 367, 379, 422, 439, 489, 597, 661, 678, 685–87, 697–98, 700, 711–12; Sabbath, 144, 145, 147–49, 156, 160, 166–67, 172–73, 297, 298, 306, 314–20, 328, 359, 368, 374, 385, 388, 455, 643; government, 147–48, 154, 258, 297, 298, 305, 306, 332, 368, 374, 436, 501, 572, 580–88; religion, 188, 258–59, 274, 281, 285, 297, 305, 306, 316–17, 352, 359, 368–69, 374, 385, 436, 495, 632–33, 643; temperance, 280, 669–70, 680–82; organizations, 287–88, 402; eventual unity of languages, 595, 626, 633; monarchy and republicanism, 672

Garrison, Mrs. William Lloyd (Helen Eliza Benson): identified, xxii, xxiv; letters to, 54–56, 58–61, 76–79, 81–83, 89–90, 90–93, 93–94, 101–03, 107–10, 114–16, 116–18, 135–37, 184–85, 215–16, 260–61, 269–72, 349–50, 350–53, 358–60, 389–92, 396–98, 452–53, 454–57, 611–13, 614–15, 615–18, 618–20, 621–24, 628–31, 642–44, 647–50, 650–53, 654–56, 659–62, 668–71; going to Brooklyn, Conn., 1, 74, 267, 676, 692, 698; and birth of George Thompson Garrison, 1, 2, 60, 63, 115; letters received from, 58, 399, 612, 616, 655–56; wants basket-cradle, 65; health of, 74, 107, 114–15, 116, 121,

129, 165, 174, 189, 191–92, 194, 197, 198, 201, 204, 205, 208, 252, 273–74, 313, 330, 356, 379, 386–87, 400, 409, 416, 422, 433; patience with WLG's absences, 81, 612, 642; WLG's appreciation of, 81, 135, 255, 260, 616, 642–43; shopping, 145, 268; irksome confinement of, 180, 201, 291; in Providence, 184, 269, 397–98; goes to New York, 186–87; anxiety for Henry Benson, 196, 200, 202, 205; helpers for, 201, 208, 252, 255, 338, 366–67, 394, 396, 397–98, 721; WLG on separation from, 209–70, 352, 589, 612, 619–20, 636, 642–43, 656; visits S. J. May, 302–03, 307, 494; and naming of G. W. Benson's son, 312; birth of William Lloyd Garrison, Jr., 336–37; and Thomsonian medicine, 342, 387, 644; WLG warns against excessive affection, 352; wants WLG to burn her letters, 353; calls on Abigail Alcott, 367; and A. A. Phelps's house, 392, 394, 397, 403; going to Newport with family, 492; birth of Wendell Phillips Garrison, 589, 620, 644, 659; Anna Benson staying with, 620, 621, 622, 624, 644; mentioned, 70, 154, 173, 180, 181, 185, 198, 210, 274, 308, 338, 360, 373–74, 406, 432, 433, 441, 460, 492, 496, 555, 615, 693, 705, 708, 720 *et passim*

Garrison, William Lloyd, Jr.: birth of, 333, 335, 336–38, 340; naming of, 337; health of, 352, 387, 397, 399–400, 460, 492, 533, 620, 668; character of, 409, 434, 555; wants little slaves to be set free, 617; WLG's gratitude at his freedom, 620; mentioned, 356, 360, 362, 375, 379, 444, 453, 456, 494, 614, 616, 622, 636, 644, 656, 660

Garrison Junior Choir, 195

Gates, Horatio, 280

Gay, Sydney Howard, 662

Gayle, Gov. John: identified, 12; correspondence with Gov. Marcy, 9, 10, 12, 13

Geers (Geer), William D., 23; identified, 26

Genius of Temperance (New York), 46, 72

Genius of Universal Emancipation, 80, 231, 348

Genessee county, N.Y., 568

Georgia, 105, 217, 562

Gibbons, James S.: identified, 613; mentioned, 611, 615, 718

Gilbert, Gad S., 73

Gill, John: identified, 168; and Sabbath, 166, 173

Gilman, Rev. and Mrs., 61

Gilpin, John, 215, 216

Glasgow, Scotland: George Thompson in, 59, 167; WLG plans to visit, 655, 670; First of August meeting in, 662; WLG writes from, 672

Glasgow *Argus*, 728

Glasgow *Chronicle*, 105, 115

Glasgow Emanicipation Society, 167, 231

Gleason, Dr. Silas O., 577

Goodell, William: identified, 46–47; letter to, 43–46; and Garrison, 22, 24, 293, 592, 681; and *Emancipator*, 24, 26, 42, 213, 215; and Channing's *Slavery*, 44–45, 47; and Massachusetts legislative committee, 55, 56, 60, 64; at Newport hearing, 124, 129; and politics, 567; Gerrit Smith's letter to quoted, 603; mentioned, 23, 60, 63, 65, 99, 260, 265, 268, 527

Gordon, Henry C., 128

Goss, Roswell: identified, 451; WLG's letter of recommendation for, 451; Graham House assailed, 612

Gould, Daniel, 455–56

Gould, Joseph D., 260; identified, 261

Gove, Mr., 618

Goodyear, Rev. George, 13

Graham, Sylvester: identified, 272; boarding houses, 260, 451; followers of, 271, 339, 367, 460

Graham Journal of Health and Longevity, 451

Gray, Rev. Frederick Turrell, 194, 393; identified, 196

Gray, Frederick Turrell, Jr., 393

Gray, George, 270

Gray, John: identified, 25–26; expecting baby, 22; errand for, 134; sells house, 175; mentioned, 58, 60, 61, 180, 194, 196, 205, 303, 393

Gray, Mrs. John (Sarah S. Paine): identified, 272; expecting baby, 22; carpeting for, 134; mentioned, 25, 270

Gray, Thomas, quoted and identified, 310, 311; 637, 638

Great Britain: abolitionism in, xxx, 38–39, 61, 113, 231, 326, 673–75, 689, 730; George Thompson in, xxx, 225, 490; and abolition of colonial slavery,

39–40, 48, 168, 490, 528, 673; Lewis and Paul in, 49–52, 53; Thomas Spencer going to, 104, 106, 120; abolitionists from, in America, 113, 359, 361, 658; E. M. Davis going to, 355; apprenticeship system in, 356; J. A. Collins's mission to, 453, 707–08, 709–10, 717–18, 726, 729; C. L. Remond in, 464; Wendell Phillips going to, 486–90; WLG's visit to, 553–54, 653–75 *passim*, 660, 664, 669, 676, 677, 679, 680, 695, 696–97, 699, 701, 705–06, 708, 709; Bradburn going to, 587; WLG's anticipations of, 627, 632, 648; nonresistance in, 641, 680; lack of color prejudice in, 655, 661; compared to America, 656, 680, 695; temperance cause in, 661, 669–70, 680, 681–82; WLG's departure from, 668, 682–83, 699; beauty of, 676, 695, 696–97, 708; Society of Friends in, 687; Winslow and Adams touring, 690; necessity of aid from, 719; Birney and Stanton in, 730; mentioned, xxx, 21, 117, 231, 326, 440–41, 442, 527, 535, 554, 592, 613, 616, 670, 676, 682, 685, 686, 687, 690, 691, 707, 709, 728. *See also* British India Movement

Great Western, 644, 656, 661, 724

Greece, 226, 657

Greeley, Horace, xxvi

Green, Beriah: identified, 96; speaks, 185, 187, 351; and political action, 484, 569; mentioned, 94, 248, 293, 332, 349

Green, Daniel, 162–63

Green, Gen. Duff, 239; identified, 245

Green, Russell, 162

Greene, Albert Daniel, 26

Greene (Green), Benjamin, 26, 456; identified, 458

Greene, Mrs. Benjamin (Hannah Sisson), 456; identified, 458

Greene, Benjamin (father of Mrs. Wendell Phillips), 490

Greene, Dorcas: identified, 26; mentioned, 23, 456, 458

Greene, Freelove, 26, 456; identified, 458

Greene, Rowland, 23, 164; identified, 26; WLG visits, 160, 163, 456

Greeneville, Tenn., 80

Greenfield, Lagrange co., Ind., 494, 496

Greenfield (Mass.) *Gazette and Mercury*, 722; identified, 723

Greenville (S.C.) *Mountaineer*, 54

Gregg, Jarvis, 245

Grimké, Angelina E.: identified, 103; marriage to Theodore D. Weld, 53, 111, 333, 349, 350, 356, 359, 360, 361; WLG talks with, 101, 102, 359; *Appeal* of, 182, 183; speaks, 185, 199, 323, 342, 343, 345, 346, 347, 348, 715–16; and nonresistance, 258, 332; and Ladies Anti-Slavery Convention, New York, 261; asks about changing *Liberator*, 291; exhausted, 322, 323; attacked in Pastoral Letter, 323; speaks at Pennsylvania Hall, 362, 363, 364; mentioned, 268, 274, 307, 324, 327, 358, 361, 463, 582

Grimké, Sarah M.: identified, 103; speaks, 185, 199, 323, 345, 346, 347, 715–16; and nonresistance, 258, 332; and Ladies Anti-Slavery Convention, New York, 261; WLG sees, 322, 358, 359; attacked in Pastoral Letter, 323; mentioned, 268, 274, 291, 307, 327, 361, 463

Grosvenor, Rev. Cyrus Pitt: identified, 112; speaks, 108, 453, 669; crossing ocean with WLG, 612, 629; Baptist delegate to World's Convention, 613–14; editor of *Christian Reflector*, 713; mentioned, 13, 25, 652, 655

Groton, Mass., 452, 695; antislavery convention at, 710, 711, 719

Groton Anti-Slavery Society, 694, 695

Gulliver, Deacon John: identified, 313; and *New England Spectator*, 26, 215, 313; to invite Phelps to Free Church, 213; anti-Garrisonian activities, 312, 315

Gunn, Marcus, letter to, 672

Gurley, Rev. Ralph Randolph: identified, 48; Gerrit Smith's letter to, 46, 47; at NEN-RS Convention, 502

Gurney, Joseph John, 657, 662; identified, 361; sermon of, 359; WLG criticizes, 658

Gurney, Samuel, 657, 658; identified, 662; gives banquet for abolitionists, 660

Haiti, 146, 159

Hale, David, 42

Halifax, 684

Hall, Benjamin, 695; identified, 696

Hall, Rev. Robert Bernard, 208; identified, 210

Hallett, Benjamin Franklin, 108; identified, 111

Hallock, Gerard, 42

Hallowell, Morris L., 364
Hamorton, Pennsylvania, 592
Hampton, Conn., 274, 276
Hampton County Anti-Slavery Society, 521
Hancock, John, 282
Harriet, 456
Harrington, Dr. Reuben: identified, 181; treating Henry Benson, 179, 188, 191, 196, 197, 201, 203; mentioned, 182, 192, 307
Harrington, Judge Theophilus. *See* Herrington
Harrisburg, Pa., 243, 525
Harrison, William Henry: identified, 72; and abolitionists, 3, 690, 730; and presidential election of 1840, 527, 554, 704, 725
Harrisonian, The, 72
Hartford, Conn.: antislavery convention in, 340; riotous spirit in, 377; Deaf and Dumb Asylum in, 377–78; attempt to blow up Anti-Slavery Depository in, 456; mentioned, 342, 376, 380, 556, 557
Hartford, Conn., Temperance Hotel, 376–77, 380
Harvard College, xxviii, xxix, 65, 110, 161, 203, 656–57, 666
Harvey, Thomas, 592
Hathaway, Joseph Comstock, 602; identified, 606
Havana, Cuba, 535, 536
Haverhill *Gazette*, 113
Haydon, Benjamin Robert, 661; identified, 663
Hawes, Rev. Joel, 342, 419, 420; identified, 343
Hawley, Rev. Silas, 169, 695; identified, 695; at Chardon-Street Convention, 724
Hayne, Gov. Robert Young, 32; identified, 33
Hazard, Benjamin: identified, 130–31; and R.I. legislative committee on abolitionists, 130, 131, 132
Hazard, Thomas T., 131; identified, 132
Health Journal and Advocate of Physiological Reform, 714
Henry, Patrick, 226, 608
Henshaw, Daniel, 12
Henson, Josiah, 486
Herald of Freedom: identified, 27; and N. P. Rogers, 463, 623, 660, 725, 730; opposes Clerical Appeal, 300, 302, 303, 305; mentioned, 4, 24, 288, 464, 519, 589

Herald of Peace, 4, 15; identified, 5
Herrington, Judge Theophilus, 41
Hewitt, Dr., 303
Hicks, Elias, 658
Hicksites. *See* Friends, Society of
Higginson, Stephen, 61
Hildreth, Dr. Charles Trueworth: identified, 80–81; mentioned, 79, 336, 352
Hill, Gov. Isaac, 289–90
Hill, Rev. Stephen P., 108; identified, 112
Hillard, George Stillman: identified, 62; and abolitionists, 00, 05, 214, 215; speaks on Lovejoy, 331
Hilton, John Telemachus: identified, 118–19; letter to, 678–79; counsellor of MA-SS, 13; speaks, 113, 117; gives WLG right hand of fellowship, 685
Himes, Rev. Joshua Vaughan: identified, 183; to leave church, 182; Thomsonian treatment, 339, 341–42; and WLG's treatment of clergy, 520; at Chardon-Street Convention, 724
Hinckley, Albert, 160; identified, 161
Hinckley, Vincent, 160; identified, 161
Hingham, Mass., 347, 405, 406
Hitchcock, D. K., 276
Hoby, Rev. James, 359, 658; identified, 113
Holbrook, James, 72; identified, 73
Holley, Myron, 605; identified, 606; and politics, 413, 604
Holyhead, Wales, 651
Hopedale Community, 534
Hopper, Abigail, 613
Hopper, Isaac T., 613
Hope On, Hope Ever plantation, 562
Hornblower, Judge Joseph Coerton, 170; identified, 171
Horton, Rev. Jotham, 453, 587; identified, 454
Howitt, William: identified, 658; WLG meets, 656; on rejection of women from World's Convention, 698–99
Howitt, Mrs. William (Mary Botham), 656; identified, 658
Howland, Gen. Asa, 13
Hubbard, William J., 51; identified, 53
Hudson, Erasmus D., 681; identified, 386; letter to, 381–85
Human Rights, 303, 415; identified, 417
Hunt, Richard P.; identified, 596; letter to, 594–95
Hyde (theology student), 166, 172–73

Ide, Rev. Jacob, 13
Illinois Anti-Slavery Society, 355

Independent, xxvi, xxviii

India. *See* British India Movement

Indians, American, 105–06, 217, 441

Ingenac (Inginac), Joseph Balthazar, 146; identified, 146–47

Ingersoll, Charles J. J., 723

Investigator and General Intelligencer, 46

Ipswich, England, 661

Ireland: WLG plans to visit, 655, 662, 664; Lord Morpeth and, 663; WLG's visit to, 676, 677, 680 81, 697, 705; Birney and Stanton in, 730; mentioned, 464, 554, 658, 669, 676, 680, 682, 695

Ives, Thomas P., 102; identified, 103–04

Jackson, Andrew: and censorship of mail, 137–38; letter on Gaines, 169–70, 170–71; and Duff Green, 245

Jackson, Charles, 152

Jackson, Francis: identified, xxv; letters to, 368–70, 373–75; and MA-SS, 13, 419, 614, 712; vindicates WLG's character, 370, 373, 374; and finances of *Liberator*, 415, 417, 557; co-signs letters with WLG, 449, 490, 516, 531, 575; WLG borrows from, 533; mentioned, 4, 182, 268, 372, 445, 587, 643, 720

Jackson, George W., 152, 434

Jackson, Rev. Henry, 152, 455; identified, 458

Jackson, Mrs. Henry (Maria T. Gano), 455; identified, 458

Jackson, James C.: identified, 577; speaks, 575, 725; and nonresistance, 604; and *Standard*, 697, 728; mentioned, 612, 614, 621, 624

Jackson, Phoebe (Phoby) identified, 151–52; letters to, 322, 705–06; WLG's appreciation of, 256, 432, 434; to visit Garrisons, 492, 705; mentioned, 26, 151, 397, 398, 407, 408, 409, 433, 434, 455, 458

Jackson, Richard, 151–52, 398

Jackson, Mrs. Richard (Nabby Wheaton, "Phebe's mother"): identified, 398; sickness of, 397, 400, 706; mentioned, 409, 434, 455

Jamaica, 202, 611, 679

James, Rev. John Angell, 225; identified, 231

Jay, John, 99, 251

Jay, Judge William, 248; identified, 99–100; at AA-SS Convention, 98, 349, 351, 353; letter quoted, 566–67, 569

Jefferson, Thomas, 536; quoted and identified, 226, 231, 232; 287, 325, 327

Jeffrey, Louisa, 56, 60; identified, 57

Jeffreys, George, 224; identified, 231

Jenkins, William, 101, 102; identified, 103

Jenkins, Mrs. William (Anna), 175

Jerusalem, 284

Jews, 178, 179, 247, 281, 316, 320

Jocelyn, Rev. Simeon S., 536

Joel, Cousin, 136; identified, 138

John Edward. *See* May, John Edward

John O'Groat's House, 654, 657

Johnson, Israel H., 364

Johnson, Nathan, 712; identified, 713–14

Johnson, Oliver: identified, xxv xxvi; letters to, 36–40, 281, 376–80, 523–27, 607–09, 625–27, 664–65, 666; quoted, xxviii, 447; and *Liberator*, 267, 275, 301–02, 366, 371, 375, 404, 418, 419, 623, 654, 662, 665, 671; at AA-SS Convention, 351, 353; WLG receives letters from, 374, 616, 659, 671; and NEN-RS, 398, 401; and A. A. Phelps, 496; to board with Garrisons, 533; WLG sending letters to, 618, 620, 628, 644, 669; at MA-SS Convention, 712, 718, 720; and *Standard*, 719, 725, 728; and Chardon-Street Convention, 723; mentioned, 22, 281, 390, 396, 421, 433, 613, 614, 615, 623, 644, 662, 691, 693, 704, 727

Johnson, Mrs. Oliver (Mary Ann): identified, xxvi; house-hunting for Garrisons, 391, 394; to board with Garrisons, 533; to be at Helen's delivery, 620; mentioned, 351, 390, 615, 623, 704

Journal of the Times, xxv

Judson, Curtis, 377; identified, 380

Judson, Andrew T., 72, 693; identified, 73

Kansas, 562

Kaufman, Abram, Jr., 238; identified, 245

Kelley, Abby: identified, 364; speaks, 363, 718, 719, 720, 726; at Peace Convention, 390, 393; at AA-SS Convention, 611; and Chardon-Street Convention, 723; mentioned, 463, 582, 615, 712

Kenney, Mary P., 712

Kendall, Amos, 137

Index of Names

Kenrick, John, xxii

Kent County Ladies Anti-Slavery Society, 271

Kent County Young Men's Anti-Slavery Society, 455

Kent, George, 463, 693; identified, 464

Kentucky, 29, 33, 35, 54

Kilton, George, 270

Kilton, Rev. George W., 182, 270; identified, 183

Kilton, Mrs. George W., 270

Kimball, John S.: identified, 25; mentioned, 13, 22, 78, 182

Kimball, Joseph Horace, 161; identified, 288; letter to, 281–88

Kimber, Abby, 527

Kingsbury, Benjamin, Jr., 42; identified, 43

Knapp, Isaac: identified, xxvi; letters to, 33–35, 97–99, 131–33, 138–41, 144, 161–63, 169–70, 273–75, 357; and *Liberator*, 1–2, 4, 9, 23–24, 26–27, 50–51, 67, 91, 144, 166, 169, 184, 415, 555–56, 557; and Henry Benson, 63, 95, 161–62, 188, 203; revisits Newburyport, 115, 274; and Arnold Buffum's accounts, 120, 121, 122, 126; writing habits of, 143, 160, 161–62, 176, 271; and WLG's finances, 176, 177, 181, 208, 291, 366; prints Boyle's letters, 345, 444; MA-SS to purchase Anti-Slavery Depository of, 459; final arrangements with, 555–56, 557; mentioned, 13, 59, 78, 83, 107, 117, 118, 182, 192, 261, 368, 398, 422, 432

Knapp, Mrs. Isaac, xxvi, 274, 398

Knight, Mr. and Mrs., 623, 644, 704

Kraditor, Aileen S., 413

Ladd, William: identified, 95; speaks on peace, 94, 97, 98; and American Peace Society, 278, 279–80; at Peace Convention, 389, 391, 400

Ladies Anti-Slavery Convention (N.Y.), 261

Lafayette, Marquis de, 334

Laidley. See Bell, James

Lambert, Daniel, 58; identified, 61

Land's End, 654, 657

Lane Theological Seminary, 53, 160, 202, 355, 486

League of Brotherhood, 202

Lathrop (Lothrop), Rev. John, 373; identified, 375

Lavinia, 492

Lawrence, Kans., xxviii, 562

Laws of Life, The, 577

Leavitt, Rev. Joshua: identified, 216; letter to, 535; and N.Y. *Evangelist,* 6; and *Emancipator,* 26, 215, 308, 718; speech, 349; remarks on WLG's reply to Birney, 485, 495; quoted on voting, 511–12, 516; and clergy, 519, 520; and *Amistad* case, 536; change in feelings toward WLG, 592, 681; starts *The Ballot Box,* 718; and *Standard,* 718; mentioned, 216, 527, 608

Lee, Gen. Charles, 280

Lee, Rev. Luther: identified, 611; at AA-SS Convention, 608; at Chardon-Street Convention, 724

Lee, Richard, 222

Lee, Rev. Samuel, 351; identified, 354

Leggett, William, 259

Leicester, Mass., 68, 69

Leominster, Mass., 575, 576–77

LeRow, George: identified, 79; mentioned, 78, 82, 83

Leveson-Gower, Lady Elizabeth Georgiana, 661; identified, 663

Lewis, Alonzo, 12

Lewis, Israel, 49; identified, 52–53

Lexington (steamboat), 349

Lexington, Ky., 33

Lexington, Mass., xxvii

Liberator, The: identified, 1; letter to editorial chair of, 711–12; letters printed in, 17–21, 28–32, 33–35, 36–40, 85–88, 97–99, 131–33, 138–41, 144, 217–21, 223–31, 234–44, 246–51, 264–66, 276–80, 281, 281–88, 292–97, 314–20, 357, 376–80, 381–85, 423–25, 426–30, 447–49, 459, 464–85, 486–90, 497–516, 517–21, 523–27, 538–48, 560–62, 563–69, 570–74, 575–76, 577–87, 596–605, 607–09, 625–27, 628, 631, 636–38, 645–47, 650, 653, 656, 664–65, 666, 676–78, 678–79, 711–12, 714–16; and Henry Benson, xxiv, 2, 9, 23–24, 199, 206; finances of, xxv, 8, 9, 10–11, 22, 25, 50–51, 141, 192, 193, 267, 291, 371, 372, 373, 404, 408, 415, 417, 419, 423–24, 434, 533, 556 and 557; Oliver Johnson helps edit, xxv–xxvi, 275, 523, 527, 613, 623, 628, 654, 665; Isaac Knapp and, xxvi, 1–2, 9, 23, 26–27, 91, 166, 167 68, 169, 208, 273, 557; Tappans and, xxix, 306; arrangements for during WLG's absence, 1–2, 109, 116, 144, 269, 623 and 624; C. C. Burleigh helps edit,

754

1, 2, 116, 118, 169, 178; S. J. May helps with, 2; subscribers to, 3, 22, 23, 45, 66–67, 162, 516–17, 623, 659; E. M. P. Wells dislikes, 9, 22; resolutions praising, 24, 207, 208, 312, 313, 422, 423, 493; Gerrit Smith and, 52, 192, 193, 570–71, 596; WLG urged to return to Boston for sake of, 73–74, 75; disagreement with A. Buffum about, 120–22, 126–27; WLG unable to write for, 144, 184, 623, 670; and sectarianism, 166, 178; to be expanded, 199, 208, 210, problems with clergy, 199–200, 440, 518–21; connection with MA-SS, 208, 210, 290–91; peaceable attitude of, 238–39, 483–84; and A. A. Phelps, 263, 275, 443, 445–46, 496 and 497; and Clerical Appeal, 273, 275, 299, 300, 303, 304, 312, 313; WLG considers changing nature of, 291, 313; and J. T. Woodbury, 297; E. Wright disapproves conduct of, 305; WLG cannot leave, 308, 405; hostility to, and efforts to subvert, 314, 384, 412, 415, 418, 419, 422, 432, 433, 434, 440, 444, 462, 499, 516; bright prospects of, 335, 556; and *Massachusetts Abolitionist*, 433, 440, 499, 544; and *Non-Resistant*, 438; and *Cradle of Liberty*, 443, 445; as creator of Massachusetts abolitionism, 483–84; and Chardon-Street Convention, 554, 722, 724–25; WLG takes file to England, 613; and *Standard*, 622; Dr. Osgood likes, 718; mentioned, xxiii–xxviii *passim*, 113, 122, 186, 190, 209, 245, 257, 259, 263, 306, 309, 335, 368, 386, 395, 444, 446, 485, 660, 671, 677, 685, 707, 709 *et passim*

Liberia, 380, 611, 662
Liberty Bell, xxiv, xxviii
Liberty League, 47
Liberty party: and presidential election of 1840, xxix, 553, 554, 731; mentioned, 35, 47, 112, 308, 606
Liggins, Mr., 39
Lincoln, Abraham, xxx
Lincoln, Jairus: identified, 406; mentioned, 405, 575, 577
Lincoln, Jairus B., 405(?); identified, 406
Lincoln, Levi, 256; identified, 257
Linley, George, 641
Litchfield County Anti-Slavery Society, 381, 383, 386
Liverpool, England: WLG on way to,

635, 637, 643, 645, 647, 650; WLG arrives at, 636, 653; WLG leaves from, 668, 699; WLG writes from, 673–75; mentioned, 58, 59, 612, 615, 644, 667, 670, 675, 682
Liverpool *Chronicle*, 652
London: peace conference in, 161; WLG writes from, 654–68 *passim*; London Committee of World's Convention, 654, 677; World's Convention meeting in, 553–54, 633; lack of color prejudice in, 686; mentioned, 636, 637, 653, 661, 677. *See also* World's Anti-Slavery Convention
London, Crown and Anchor Tavern, 658
London, Exeter Hall: antislavery meetings at, 39, 655; O'Connell's speech at, 655, 665; temperance meeting at, 661, 669
London, Freemason's Hall, 661
London Anti-Slavery Society, xxx, 356
London Convention. *See* World's Anti-Slavery Convention
London *Patriot*, 167, 171
Longfellow, Henry Wadsworth, 437, 438
Longley, Thomas, 65; identified, 66
Lord, Rev. Nathan, 518; identified, 522
Loring, Ellis Gray: identified, 57; as abolition lawyer, 55, 56, 83, 129, 170, 171, 214; delivers panegyric on WLG, 207, 209; opposes antislavery political party, 525; on financial committee of *Liberator*, 556, 557; mentioned, 13, 60, 61, 78, 182, 349, 353, 419, 545, 555
Loring, Mrs. Ellis Gray (Louisa Gilman): identified, 79; mentioned, 78, 194, 347
Lothrop. *See* Lathrop
Lovejoy, Elijah: identified, 329, death of, xxviii, 328, 331–32, 480; portrait sent to G. W. Benson, 335; and Edward Beecher, 355; *Memoir* of, 347, 348, 428, 431
Lovejoy, Mrs. Elijah, 329
Lovejoy, Joseph C.: *Memoir of the Rev. Elijah P. Lovejoy*, 348, 428, 431
Lovejoy, Owen: letter on death of Elijah Lovejoy, 332; *Memoir* of Lovejoy, 348, 428, 431
Lovelace, Richard, 560, 563
Lowell, James Russell, xxviii–xxix, 79
Lowell, Robert, xxv
Lowell, Mass., 23, 27, 347
Lowell (Mass.) Young Men's Anti-Slavery Society, 23, 27, 347

Lucy, Cousin, 360
Lundy, Benjamin, xxii, 348; identified, 80; plans for colony at Matamoras, 78, 80; edits E. M. Chandler's poems, 163, 164, 516; death of, 413; WLG not trusted to write biography of, 592, 593
Lundy, Joseph, 592, 593
Lunt, George, 2, 57, 58, 79
Luther, Martin: identified, 168; and Sabbath, 166, 173
Lyman, Theodore, Jr., 12
Lynch, Charles, 10
Lynn, Mass.: people of, 233–34, 310, 311; antislavery meetings in, 233–34, 256, 591, 592; antislavery fair, 408
Lynn (Mass.) Female Anti-Slavery Society, 364
Lynn *Puritan*, 722; identified, 723
Lynn *Record*: identified, 12; mentioned, 9, 23, 27
Lyon, George, 162
Lyons (N.Y.) *Countryman*, 606
Lyttle, Robert T., 232

McClintock, Thomas, 594, 595; identified, 596
McDowall, Rev. John Robert, 98; identified, 99; death of, 192, 193
McDuffie, Gov. George: identified, 10; message to S.C. legislature, 10, 14; quoted and identified, 20, 21; 31, 33; 139, 141; 243, 245–46; and slavery in District of Columbia, 430; mentioned, 8, 74, 228, 525
McFarland, Rev. Henry, 694
M'Goun, Dr., 182
M'Intyre, Dr. ("the botanical doctor"): treats WLG's catarrh, 90, 92, 95, 103, 121; unwell, 203–04
M'Tear, Dr. John, 724; identified, 726
Madden, Richard R., 535; identified, 535–36
Madison, James, death of, 180, 181
Madison County (N.Y.) *Abolitionist*, 577
Mahan, Asa, 443; identified, 446
Main (Maine), Job, 150; identified, 151
Maine, 33, 112, 133, 461; and Aroostook war, 442
Maine Anti-Slavery Society, 33, 111
Manchester, England: antislavery meeting at, 38–39; British India meeting at, 689, 690, 709, 710
Manford, Dr. (*alias* of John Colman), 608; identified, 610
Mann, Horace, xxvii

Mapple, Father, 727
Marcy, Gov. William Learned: identified, 12; message of, 9, 14, 20; correspondence with Gov. Gayle, 9, 10, 12, 13; and abolitionists, 15–16; speech, 23
Martin, Rev. Mr. (of New York), 273
Martineau, Harriet: identified, 16; and meeting of WLG and Channing, 57, 61; WLG meets, 59–60, 84; and Elizabeth Reid, 663; mentioned, 15, 56, 79, 101, 657, 661, 726
Mary. *See* Benson, Mary
Mary Stuart, Queen, 702
Mason, Gov. Stevens Thomson, 230; identified, 232
Massachusetts: letters to abolitionists of, 447–49, 497–516; legislative committee on abolitionists, 2, 55–56, 57, 60, 62, 64, 65–66, 79, 81; constitution, 55, 154, 170, 228, 277; legislature and abolitionists, 64–65, 133, 199, 207, 209, 233, 252, 253, 342 and 343, 439; slavery abolished in, 195; and antislavery petitions to Congress, 214, 215, 253, 256; abolitionism in, 324, 462, 483–84, 492, 523, 577, 581, 583, 693, 725; legislature and slavery in District of Columbia, 439, 441, 583; legislature's "Report Respecting Distinctions of Color," 439, 441; nonresistance in, 483; new organization in, 499–500, 725; Address to the People of, by Massachusetts Abolition Society, 500; abolitionists from, rallying at AA-SS Convention (1840), 607, 610, 612; mentioned, 65, 203, 205, 441, 444, 464, 513, 526, 553, 563, 725
Massachusetts (steamboat), 91, 589
Massachusetts Abolition Society: formation of, 412, 499–500, 516, 546–47; MA-SS's response to organization of, 497–516; Address to the People of Massachusetts by, 500, 509, 516; faults of, 503–04; efforts to compromise with, 517–18; mentioned, 27, 506, 514–15, 581, 582
Massachusetts Abolitionist: identified, 434; establishment of, 412, 544; plans for, 415, 418, 422, 444, 499; and *Liberator*, 440 and 442, 443, 499; and politics, 725; mentioned, 111, 432, 433, 434, 510, 511 and 516, 518, 545, 716–17, 718
Massachusetts Anti-Slavery Society: letters written on behalf of, 447–49,

486–90, 497–516, 528–31, 538–49, 563–69; letter to be read at meeting of, 17–21; letter to delegates of, 574–75; annual meetings (1836), 4, 5–6, 8–9, 11, 13–15, 17–21, 21–22, 24; (1837), 204, 207–08, 209; (1838), 333, 335, 336; (1839), 407–08, 412, 415–18 *passim*, 422, 499; (1840), 556; state convention, 686, 687, 691, 694, 708, 711–12, 718–19, 720; quarterly meetings, 233, 234, 256, 303, 304, 307, 442–48 *passim*, 727; Henry Benson and, 2, 13, 79, 116, 118, 121–22, 199, 208; successor to New England Anti-Slavery Society, 6, 33, 499, 578; difficulties in finding meeting-places, 8–9, 11, 199, 204, 712; Board of Managers of, 10, 12–13, 22, 162 and 164, 182, 415, 418, 419, 447, 448, 493, 568–69, 605, 726; annual reports by WLG, 14, 16, 261, 262, 333, 347, 416, 417, 556; and Massachusetts legislative committee, 55, 57, 64–65; wants WLG to return to Boston, 73–74, 75; and WLG's finances, 73, 109, 177, 366, 533; participation of women in, 195, 407, 505, 506–08, 581–82, 584; and *Liberator*, 208, 210, 290, 291; delegates to World's Convention, 209, 614, 657; A. A. Phelps becomes agent of, 213, 215, 262; oppugns insurrection, 240–41, 242; financial embroilments with AA-SS, 412, 413, 433, 435, 443, 445–46, 447–49, 452, 453, 459, 538–40, 543–46, 622, and J A Collins, 452, 453, 707, 709; divisions and antagonisms within, 415–19, 462, 499, 504–15, 521, 546, 577, 581–83; and political action, 511, 513, 565, 573, 582–84; and Massachusetts Abolition Society, 515, 517, 518; and Clerical Appeal, 541–42; mentioned, xxiv, xxv, xxviii, 10, 12, 29, 33, 80, 84, 113, 161, 168, 183, 210, 263, 310, 323, 348, 364, 434, 605, 695, 717

Massachusetts Colonization Society, 25

Massachusetts Female Society, 716–17

Massachusetts Historical Society, xxix

Massachusetts Peace Society, 416

Matamoras, Mexico, 78, 80

May, John Edward, 3, 15; identified, 5

May, Joseph: identified, 25; mentioned, 22, 25, 60, 83, 174

May, Samuel Joseph: identified, xxvi–xxvii; letters to, 13–15, 17–21, 128–30, 177–78, 232–33, 331–32, 346–47,

375–76, 386–89, 401–02, 405–06, 413–16, 494–96, 696–98; helps with *Liberator*, 2, 4; and W. E. Channing, 5, 16, 59; birth of child, 22, 25; before Massachusetts legislative committee on abolitionists, 55, 56; and Henry Benson, 63, 208; speaks, 79, 108, 139, 143, 151, 152, 162, 208, 390, 608; visiting Brooklyn, 117, 121, 123, 143, 253, 307, 313; plans of, 143, 160, 163, 169, 176–77; and Farr's letter to WLG, 167; WLG's appreciation of, 180, 375–76, 386, 413–14; and identity of "Algernon Sidney," 222, 233, 234; and Ann G. Chapman, 252 and 255; on death of Lovejoy, 331–32; pacific resolution at AA-SS Convention, 350; and WLG's salary, 366; and Sabbath, 388, 722; and NEN-RS, 389, 391, 393, 395, 401, 403, 406, 414, 534; and anti-slavery Declaration of Sentiments, 475, 513; and politics, 484, 509; and new organization, 518, 522; scruples about voting, 573, 601–02; and James Garrison, 721; mentioned, xxii, xxiv, 4, 13, 15, 17, 54–55, 60, 62, 82, 83, 94, 98, 117, 118, 124, 132, 137, 150, 153, 157–58, 169, 174, 175, 183, 197, 248, 261, 269, 272, 294, 322, 323, 332, 346–47, 349, 367, 386, 396, 402, 403, 414, 416, 419, 470, 404, 406, 520, 576

May, Mrs. Samuel Joseph (Lucretia Flagge Coffin): identified, 62; has baby, 22, 25; lively as ever, 60; and children, 82–83; mentioned, 13, 55, 83, 110, 117, 169, 253, 375, 406, 496

Mazzini, Giuseppe, 666

Meader, John, 455; identified, 458

Med, case of, 195

Mellen, Dr. G. W. F., 725; identified, 727

Melrose, Scotland, 699

Merriam, Nathan, 531; identified, 532

Merritt, Rev. Timothy, 352, 357; identified, 354

Methodist Church, 586, 587

Methuen, Mass., 719

Mexico, 170, 265, 536

Middlebury, Vt.: antislavery conventions at, 33, 36, 41; State Convention on Peace at, 276, 278

Middlesex County (Mass.) Anti-Slavery Society, 347, 354, 607, 710, 711, 714, 719

Midnight Cry, The (N.Y.), 100
Mifflin, Warner, 662
Millbury, Mass., 727
Miller, Miss, 455
Miller, Col. Jonathan P., 655; identified, 657
Miller, William, 696
Milligan, Alexander McLeoud, 112
Milligan, Rev. James, 108; identified, 112
Milton, John, quoted and identified, 28, 32; 450; 594, 596
Mirror of Literature, Amusement and Instruction, 648, 650
Missouri, 82, 84, 91, 562
Mixed Commission Courts, 535
Moncrieff, W. T., 537
Monmouth Courthouse, battle of, 278, 280
Montgomery, James, 701
Monthly Garland, 453
Monthly Offering, 445
Montpelier, Vt., xxv
Moore, Mark, 657
Moore, Dr. Robert, 127; identified, 128
Moore, Mrs. Robert (Esther), 127, 364; identified, 128; speaks, 363
Morpeth, Lord (George William Frederick Howard), 661; identified, 663
Morris, Robert, 86; identified, 88
Morse, Hiram A., 712; identified, 714
Morse, Jedidiah, 381
Morse, Richard Carey, 381
Morse, Samuel F. B., 381
Morse, Sidney Edwards, 149, 378; identified, 381
Moseley, Ebenezer, 57
Mott, James: identified, xxvii–xxviii; letter to, 439–41; and A. Buffum's accounts, 120, 122, 127; visits WLG in Philadelphia, 358; at World's Convention, 655; mentioned, 126, 334, 351, 355, 587, 590, 591, 592, 659
Mott, Mrs. James (Lucretia Coffin): identified, xxvii–xxviii; letter to, 590–92; on Executive Committee of AA-SS, xxv; speaks at Pennsylvania Hall, 363, 364; and NEN-RS, 534; and World's Convention, 616, 627, 698; speaks in England, 661; mentioned, 327, 334, 355, 358, 582, 587, 655, 657, 659
Mott, Maria, 334
Mott, Thomas, 334
Mount Pleasant, O., 80
Murray, John H., 623

Murray, Rev. Orson S., 308, 470; identified, 104; letter to, 276–80; speaks on antislavery, 102, 108
"My Mother's Gold Ring," 94, 95

Nantucket, Mass., 691, 704, 725
Nashville, Tenn., 202
National Anti-Slavery Convention for Independent Nominations, 553, 568–69, 605, 606, 608–09
National Anti-Slavery Standard: Oliver Johnson edits, xxvi, 725; Edmund Quincy edits, xxviii; establishment of, 553, 662; J. C. Jackson edits, 577; and N. P. Rogers, 660, 681, 694, 697, 704, 725, 730; may have to be furled, 708, 719, 729; Leavitt threatens to prosecute, 718; mentioned, xxiv, 169, 386, 613
National Baptist Anti-Slavery Convention, 100, 671
National Convention of Abolitionists (Albany, N.Y.), 521; call, 522; WLG's account of, 523–27; political stand, 565
National Enquirer and Constitutional Advocate of Universal Liberty, 80
National Era (Washington, D.C.), xxix, 69
National Intelligencer (Washington, D.C.), 96
National Philanthropist (Boston), 46
National Southern Emigration Society, 562
National Whig Convention, 525
Neall, Elizabeth Johns, 659; identified, 662
Needles, Edward, 358, 591; identified, 361
Needles, Mrs. Edward (Mary Hathaway), 358; identified, 361
Nell, Henry, 53
Neville, Morgan, 232
New Bedford, Mass., 308–09, 310, 713
New Bedford Port Society, 309–10
New Bedford Young Men's Anti-Slavery Society, 309
New Brunswick, Canada, 442
New England: progress of antislavery cause in, 29 and 33, 258, 324; reaction to Clerical Appeal in, 298, 305, 541; compared to England, 656, 697; Grimkés lecturing in, 716; mentioned, 290, 444, 667, 679–80, 714
New England Anti-Slavery Convention: (1834), 567; (1836), 68, 69, 71, 78, 80, 102, 103, 104, 107–09, 114–15,

119, 120, 139, 194; (1837), 262–63, 265, 267, 269, 567; (1838), 366, 367, 410, 412; (1839), 460, 463, 487, 491, 499, 506, 510, 513, 516, 518, 522; mentioned, 21, 112, 252

New England Anti-Slavery Society: becomes MA-SS, 6, 24, 33, 499; organization, 187, 189, 209, 578; constitution, 239; mentioned, xxii, xxv–xxx *passim*, 57, 62, 80, 100, 122, 161, 210

New England Arena, 72

New England Non-Resistance Society: letter on behalf of, 135–38; and Henry C. Wright, xxvi; formation (see also Peace Convention), 333, 391, 395; Declaration of Sentiments, 401, 403–04, 414, 435–38; WLG on principles of, 408; meetings of, 460, 532, 534, 691, 693, 694, 701, 702, 705; and abolitionists, 477, 509; mentioned, 113, 335, 447, 713, 714

New England Spectator, 23; identified, 26; letters to editor of, 147–49, 314–20; and clerical appeals, 111, 215, 275, 300, 345; anti-Garrisonism of, 172, 313; Woodbury's letter in, 297–98

New England Thomsonian Convention, 343

New Englander, 76

New Hampshire, 27; abolitionism in, 133, 134, 282, 286–89 *passim*, 588, 660, 693; and N. P. Rogers, 623, 694, 697, 725, 730

New Hampshire Anti-Slavery Society, 29, 464; letter to John Farmer for, 264–66; and *Herald of Freedom*, 27, 463; founding, 33; meetings, 109, 113, 116, 264, 447, 680, 687; WLG plans to attend meetings of, 460, 461, 464, 691, 693, 694, 697

New Hampshire Depository, 173

New Hampshire Observer, 172; identified, 173

New Hampshire Panoplist, 173

New Hampshire Panoply, 722

New Hampshire Statesman and Concord Register, 464

New Hampshire Young Men's Anti-Slavery Convention, letter to J. H. Kimball for, 281–88

New Haven, Conn., 168, 367, 377

New Haven *Religious Intelligencer*, 259

New Jersey, 171

New Jersey Anti-Slavery Society, 582

New organization: progress of, 312, 313, 351, 353, 493, 517, 588, 660, 685,

708, 718, 719, 724, 725; and AA-SS constitution, 599; effect of in England, 655, 669, 729; mentioned, 633. *See* Massachusetts Abolition Society; Massachusetts Anti-Slavery Society

New Richmond, O., 69

New Rowley, Mass., 309

New York *Advocate of Moral Reform*, 98; identified, 99

New York Anti-Slavery Society: founding convention, 28, 32, 47, 695; *Friend of Man* organ of, 24, 46; and *Emancipator*, 26; financial arrangements with AA-SS, 539; participation of women in, 582; mentioned, xxix, 29, 99, 308, 354, 357, 577

New York City: AA-SS conventions in, 3, 211, 233, 253, 254, 260–61, 344, 346, 347, 349, 584, 592, 595, 611–12; abolitionists in, 50–51, 133, 290, 298–300, 303, 725; bank robbery in, 92, 93; WLG writes from, 93–95, 97–99, 184–85, 215–16, 260–61, 349–57, 607–25 *passim*; WLG mobbed in, 186, 189; Helen's trip to, 186–87; lack of protection for free Negroes in, 257; WLG delivers First of August speech in, 376, 378, 386; WLG sick of, 618–19; N. P. Rogers's reluctance to go to, 660, 681, 694, 697, 704; mentioned, xxiii, 92, 93, 216, 257, 259, 451, 725, 728

New York City, Broadway Tabernacle, 376, 378, 379, 381

New York City, Female Benevolent Society, 99

New York City Anti-Slavery Society, 111

New York *Commercial Advertiser*, 245

New York *Courier and Enquirer*, 95; identified, 96–97

New York *Evangelist*, 4, 357; identified, 6

New York *Evening Post*, xxvi, 10; identified, 13

New York Executive Committee. *See* American Anti-Slavery Society

New York *Herald*, 689; identified, 690–91

New York *Independent*, 76

New York *Journal of Commerce*: identified, 41–42; mentioned, 40, 167, 204, 378, 379

New York *Observer*: identified, 381; mentioned, 25, 259, 294, 345, 379, 722

New York *Spectator*, 277

New York state, Gov. Marcy and abolitionists in, 12, 15–16, 20
New York *Sun*, 155
New York *Tribune*, xxvi, xxviii
New York *World*, 97
Newburyport, Mass., xxvi, 684; Essex County Anti-Slavery Society meets in, 113, 115, 117; WLG wants to hear about, 274; J. Q. Adams speaks in, 274, 275
Newburyport *Free Press*, 221
Newcastle, England, 699
Newcastle-upon-Tyne, England, 238, 245
Newhall, James R., 723
Newport, R.I., 97; hearing of abolitionists at, 123–24, 125, 126, 131–33
Nichol, John, 327
Nichol, Mrs. John. *See* Pease, Elizabeth
Niles, William H., 723
No, 283–84
Non-Resistant, The: identified, 438; establishment of, 409, 411; Edmund Quincy edits, xxviii; and James Boyle, 444 and 446, 447; WLG takes file to England, 613, 641, 681; mentioned, xxi, 335, 361, 441, 446, 532, 534, 634, 671
Non-Resistant Society. *See* New England Non-Resistance Society
Norfolk, Conn., 381, 383, 386
Norfolk county, Mass., 607
Norris, Rev. John, 521; identified, 522
Norris, Rev. Samuel, 208; identified, 209
North American (Philadelphia), 222
North American Review, 203
North Carolina, 71, 72
Northampton, Mass., xxix, 23, 27, 79
Northampton Association of Education and Industry, xxiii
Northern Central British India Society, 690
Northern Chronicler (Newburyport), xxvi
Northfield, N.H., 36
Norton, John Treadwell, 686; identified, 687–88
Norwich, England, 658
Norwich (Conn.) *Aurora*, 72; identified, 73

Oakes, William: identified, 167; mentioned, 13, 113, 166
Oberlin, 612
Oberlin College, 161
O'Connell, Daniel, 75; identified, 41; speaks on antislavery, 39, 655, 665;

and passengers on *Columbus*, 653; WLG meets, 655, 657; speaks at British India meeting, 661, 689, 690; and exclusion of women from World's Convention, 666, 698; speaks on temperance, 669
Ohio, 35, 45, 69, 80, 486, 534
Ohio Anti-Slavery Society: formed, 29, 33; *Philanthropist* organ of, 69; and James Boyle, 346, 446; participation of women in, 506, 582; and political action, 510
Old Hampshire Anti-Slavery Society, 27, 79
Old Silsbee Street Debating Club, 311
Oliver (from Baltimore), 390
Olivet Institute, 202
Oneida Institute, 94, 96, 608, 728
Opie, Mrs. John (Amelia Alderson): identified, 657–58; WLG meets, 656; entertains abolitionists, 660
Osceola, 105; identified, 107
Osgood, Rev. Samuel: identified, 521–22; letter to, 517–21; speaks at MA-SS Convention, 718; at Chardon-Street Convention, 724
Otis, Harrison Gray, 91; identified, 93
Otis, Lucinda, 433, 717; identified, 435
Owen, Robert Dale, 348, 666
Oxford, Edward, 652

Packard, Dr. Theophilus, 13
Paine, Thomas, 384, 666
Paisley, Scotland, 699
Paley, William: identified, 168; and Sabbath, 166, 173
Parker, the Misses, 15, 55, 78, 83, 110, 117, 180, 192, 213
Parker, Abigail, 17
Parker, Asa, 189
Parker, Eliza: identified, 16; mentioned, 192, 198, 290
Parker, Lucy: identified, 17; mentioned, 198, 213, 274, 322, 353, 366, 391, 394
Parker, Mary S.: identified, 17; letter to, 420–21; health of, 189, 192, 198, 709; to attend women's antislavery convention in Philadelphia, 347, 356; and Boston Female Anti-Slavery Society, 717; mentioned, 201, 202, 260, 261, 290, 389–90, 392
Parker, Theodore, 269, 696, 723
Parish (Parrish), John: identified, 4–5; death of, 3
Parmenter, William, 444; identified, 447
Parrish, Joseph, Jr., 364

Pastoral Letter of the General Association of Massachusetts . . . , 199–200, 323

Patton, John Mercer, 335; identified, 336

Patriot and Democrat; *Patriot and Eagle*, 73

Paul, Rev. Nathaniel, 49–52; identified, 53

Paul, Susan, 194; identified, 195

Paul, Rev. Thomas: identified, 321; at Belknap Street Church, 318, 319; mentioned, 195, 320

Paul, Thomas (son of above), 195

Paulding, James Kirke: identified, 550; letter to, 549–50; and discharge of James Garrison from navy, 533, 551, 552, 558–59, 570

Pawtucket, R.I., 96

Peace Convention: Declaration of Sentiments of, 333, 391, 395; plans for, 387, 389; WLG on, 390, 395, 398, 400; mentioned, xxxi, 389. *See also* New England Non-Resistance Society

Pearce, Dutee J.: identified, 49; letter to, 48–49

Pearl, Philip, 345

Pearson, Sarah, 590; identified, 592

Pease, Elizabeth: identified, 326–27; letters to, 323–26, 667–68, 682–84, 685–87, 707–09, 720, 728–31; later letter to quoted, 557; sends money to WLG, 323, 324, 327; WLG's appreciation of, 667–68, 682, 729; and J. A. Collins, 707, 708, 723, 724; M. V. Ball's letter to, 716–17, 730–31; mentioned, 527, 592, 664, 675, 690, 726, 730

Pease, Joseph, 327; identified, 675; letters to, 673–75, 688–90, 709–10

Peck, Miss, 271

Peck, Harriet, 272

Peck, Joanna, 272

Peck, Lydia, 272

Peck, Mary Ann, 272

Peck, Perez, 338; identified, 340

Peckham, Rev. Samuel H.: identified, 112; speaks in Newburyport, 108, 113

Penn, William, 192, 217; identified, 173; and Sabbath, 173, 368

Pennsylvania: legislature on free speech, 133; sends delegate to NEN-RS Convention, 534; abolitionists in oppose Albany Convention, 608–09; mentioned, 243, 553, 613

Pennsylvania, Young Men's Colonization Society of, 664

Pennsylvania Anti-Slavery Society, 88, 592; *Christian Witness* organ of, 176; constitution quoted, 243

Pennsylvania Freeman, xxvi, 72, 80

Pennsylvania Hall. *See* Philadelphia, Pennsylvania Hall

Pennsylvania School for the Deaf and Dumb, 380

Pennsylvania Society for Promoting the Abolition of Slavery, xxii

Perkins, Rev. Jonas, 275

Perry, Rev. Gardner B., 13

Peterborough, N.Y., 32

Phelps, Rev. Amos Augustus: identified, xxviii; letters to, 211–14, 262–63, 496; and *Emancipator*, 42, 52, 153, 213, 214–15; at Newport for hearing, 129, 132; speaks, 185, 405, 406, 724, 725; becomes agent of MA-SS, 215, 262, 268; and Clerical Appeal, 274, 275, 290, 306, 347; E. Wright's letter to, 307–08; WLG rents home of, 333, 391–92, 394, 397–98, 399, 400, 403; anti-Garrisonian efforts of, 412, 415, 418, 419, 422 and 423, 432, 462, 463, 464, 492, 592, 681; and *Abolitionist*, 418, 419; reply to Address of MA-SS Board, 443, 445–46; and *Massachusetts Abolitionist*, 444; and nonresistance, 477, 479, 532; and political action, 484, 569, 571; WLG returns note of, 496–97; and Massachusetts Abolition Society, 503, 516; mentioned, 6, 71, 82, 103, 135, 168–69, 216, 245, 261, 275, 290, 293, 294, 307, 309, 399, 443, 519, 520

Phelps, Mrs. Amos Augustus (Charlotte), 394; identified, 396

Phelps, Ansel, 723

Philadelphia: founding convention of AA-SS in, xxvii, 187, 189, 332; WLG's early lecture in, 85–86, 88; Henry Benson visits, 126, 162; anti-Garrisonian sentiment in, 164; WLG writes from, 358–60; riots at during Women's Anti-Slavery Convention, 362–63, 364, 365, 371; mentioned, xxii, xxvii, 71, 120–21, 122, 128, 344–45, 347, 349, 360, 379

Philadelphia, Franklin Institute, 85–86, 88

Philadelphia, Pennsylvania Hall: identified, 361; WLG describes, 358–59; meetings at, 333, 362–64; burning of, 363, 365, 371, 593, 638

Philadelphia *Album*, 88

Philadelphia Female Anti-Slavery Society, xxvii, 128, 592
Philadelphia *Inquirer*, 86, 88
Philadelphia Junior Anti-Slavery Society, 364
Philadelphia *World*, 354
Philadelphia Young Men's Anti-Slavery Society: letter to William Scott for, 85–88; meeting to be held, 82, 83
Philanthropist, 66, 68; identified, 69; efforts to suppress, 35, 61, 232; WLG praises, 67; and political action, 510
Philbrick, Samuel, 347; identified, 348; WLG borrows money from, 533; on financial committee of *Liberator*, 556, 557
Philip, King, 105; identified, 107
Philleo, Rev. Calvin, 163; identified, 164
Philleo, Mrs. Calvin. *See* Crandall, Prudence
Phillips's (stagecoach stop?), 176
Phillips, John, 486; identified, 491
Phillips, Jonathan, 336
Phillips, Joseph, 120; identified, 107
Phillips, Miriam, 110
Phillips, Wendell: identified, 257; letter to, 486–90; maiden antislavery speech of, 234; speaks on Lovejoy, 331; at Peace Convention, 391; to edit *Abolitionist*, 419; General Agent of MA-SS, 487; commended to abolitionists of England, 491; converted to antislavery by wife, 491; at World's Convention, 654, 655, 666; mentioned, 110, 256, 327, 349, 353, 399, 445, 461, 576, 592, 657, 727
Phillips, Mrs. Wendell (Ann Terry Greene): identified, 490–91; mentioned, 327, 486, 592
Pierce, Dutee J. *See* Pearce
Pierce, Franklin, 111, 289
Pinckney, Henry Laurens: identified, 49; mentioned, 48, 135, 154, 289
Plaindealer, 257; identified, 259
Plainfield, Conn., 160, 163
Plum Island, Mass., 274, 275
Plumer, William Swan, 263; identified, 264
Plymouth county, Mass., 322, 323, 607
Plymouth County Anti-Slavery Society, 405, 406, 494, 496
Poles, 226
Pomeroy, Rev. Swan L., 98; identified, 100
Pomfret, Conn., 162
Pomfret Landing, Conn., 136, 137
Pope, Alexander, quoted and identified, 341, 343; 643, 644

Pope, Eliza, 260; identified, 262
Porter, William S., 26; identified, 149; letters to, as editor of *Spectator*, 147–49, 314–20
Portland *Mirror*. See *Christian Mirror*
Potter, Rev. Ray: identified, 96; conduct of, 208, 214, 215; mentioned, 94, 129, 145, 184
Powers, Rev. Mr., 390
Prentice, John, 94; identified, 96
Presbyterian Church, 263–64, 301
President (steamboat), 91
President (mammoth steamship), 669, 683
Price, Rev. Thomas, 170, 225; identified, 171
Priestley, Joseph, 368; identified, 370
Procter, Bryan Waller ("Barry Cornwall"), 637, 638–39
Protest of Clerical Abolitionists, 300
Providence, Rhode Island: letter to president of antislavery convention at, 28–32; WLG speaks in, xxiv, 455; antislavery meetings in, 15, 24, 182, 183, 721–22, 726, 728; WLG to visit, 70, 71, 78, 82, 140–41, 156, 271, 272–73, 322, 706; bank robbery in, 92, 93; Henry Benson in, 150, 176, 177, 203; Helen in, 184, 269, 397–98; WLG writes from, 33–35, 89–93, 101–03, 128–30, 135–37, 138–41, 454–57; mentioned, 8, 55, 63, 93, 159, 322, 347, 409, 607. *See also* Rhode Island Anti-Slavery Society
Providence, African Church, xxiv
Providence Anti-Slavery Society, xxiv
Providence Female Anti-Slavery Society, 71, 141, 157
Providence Society for the Abolition of the Slave Trade, xxii
Puerto Principe, Cuba, 536
Pugh, Sarah, 527
Purvis, Robert, 364
Putnam, O., 33

Quakers. *See* Friends, Society of
Quarterly Anti-Slavery Magazine, 158, 322; identified, 158; quoted, 473, 567
Quincy, Edmund: identified, xxviii–xxix; letters to, 371–73, 531, 639–41; and *Liberator*, xxv, 415, 417, 557; speaks, 352, 357, 405; and Peace Convention, 389, 391, 393; and NEN-RS, 401, 403, 414, 534; to edit *Abolitionist*, 415, 418, 419; and *Non-Resistant*, 438; and Sabbath Convention, 722–23; mentioned, 399, 419, 470, 528, 556, 610, 643, 659

Quincy, Mrs. Edmund (Lucilla P. Parker), xxviii, 373, 641
Quincy, Josiah, xxviii
Quincy, Mass., 531

Ram's Horn, 380
Rand, Mr., 163
Rand, Mrs. See Crandall, Almira
Rankin, John: identified, 727–28; mentioned, 253, 357, 725
Rantoul, Robert, Jr.: identified, 62; mentioned, 25, 60, 65
Raritan Bay Union, 354
Rawson, Mary A., 682, 700; identified, 701
Raymond, Rev. J. T., 378; identified, 380
Read, N. C., 232
Rebecca, 252, 255
Reed, John, 204; identified, 205
Reed, William, 68, identified, 69
Reese, David M., 43
Reid (Read, Reed), Mrs. Elizabeth, 661; identified, 663
Remarks on Dr. Channing's Slavery, 241–42, 245
Remond, Charles Lenox: identified, 464; lecturing in Maine, 461; and World's Convention, 641, 654, 665, 677, 680; speaks at Exeter Hall, London, 655, 661; in Edinburgh, 668, 669–70; mentioned, 612, 709, 720, 726, 731
Revolution, American: and peace principles, 98, 278; as justification of resistance, 225–26, 235, 240, 244, 334, 478; trials of, 282–83; mentioned, 38, 253, 331, 610
Rhode Island, planned hearing of abolitionists before legislature of, 123–24, 125, 130, 131–33, 134
Rhode Island (steamboat), 607, 614, 616, 628
Rhode Island Anti-Slavery Society: founding convention, 6–7, 10, 13, 15, 22, 24, 27, 33–35, 65; letter to founding convention, 28–32; arrangements for hearing of abolitionists, 123, 125, 130–31, 132; meetings, 152, 182, 183, 313–14, 721–22, 726, 728; participation of women in, 506, 582; votes against antislavery political party, 565; mentioned, xxiv, 134, 141
Rhode Island Homeopathic Society, 458
Richmond, Va., 113
Richmond Enquirer, 72
Richmond Whig, 229

Right and Wrong in Boston, xxiv, 38–39, 460, 463
Rights of All, 217
Ripley, George, 696
Rizzio, David, 702
Rob Roy, 702
Robbins, Dr. Edward Hutchinson, 209
Robeson, Andrew, 371, 372; identified, 373
Robespierre, Maximilien, 217; identified, 221
Robinson, Mrs., 457, 459
Robinson, Daniel Chapman, 134, 174; identified, 135
Robinson, Martin, 55; identified, 56
Robinson, Vine: identified, 157; mentioned, 135, 156, 312, 313
Rochester (N.Y.), Freeman, 606
Rogers, Nathaniel Peabody: identified, 463–64; letters to, 461–63, 588–89, 691–93; edits Herald of Freedom, 27, 288, 623, 660, 725, 730; in New Hampshire, 588, 725, 730; misses home, 617–18, 623; sails on Columbus with WLG, 629, 630, 637; and World's Convention, 640, 641, 654, 665, 677, 680, 686; WLG's appreciation of, 641, 678, 681; and Standard, 660, 681, 694, 697, 704, 719, 725, 730; speaks on temperance in Great Britain, 661, 669, 670; welcomed home, 679, 685, 693, 718; returns on Acadia with WLG, 682 84; at MA-SS conventions, 708, 712, 718, 720; mentioned, 266, 392, 608, 609, 612, 614, 615, 616, 621, 624, 625, 628, 641, 648, 652, 655, 657, 659, 660, 661, 668, 697, 708
Rogers, Mrs. Nathaniel Peabody (Mary Porter Farrand), 463, 589; identified, 589; Rogers misses, 617 18, 623; mentioned, 463, 589
Root, Rev. David, 358; identified, 27; Thanksgiving sermon, 23, 27; proposal to create independent antislavery board, 586, 587, 588, 589
Rotherham, England, 699, 700
Royal Tar, 183
Russell, George, 13
Russell, Rev. Philemon R., 309, 724; identified, 310
Russwurm, John B., 217
Ryder, Thomas P., 405; identified, 406

Sabbath Convention. See Chardon-Street Convention
Sabine, Rev. Mr., 262
St. Clair, Rev. Alanson: identified, 210;

praises WLG, 208; poverty of, 309; lectures at Hingham, 347; and non-resistance, 391, 401; anti-Garrisonian activities of, 412, 415, 418, 419, 433 and 434, 462, 463, 492; and MA-SS, 433, 434, 546; and Massachusetts Abolition Society, 503; and political action, 463, 508–09, 571; mentioned, 308, 349, 360, 390, 444, 497, 519, 523

St. Louis, Mo., 106

St. Patrick (packet ship), 631

Salem, Mass.: ladies of to hold fair, 408, 423–24, 425–26, 450; abolitionism in, 450; WLG going to, 453; colored citizens welcome WLG home, 685, 698

Salem and Vicinity Anti-Slavery Society, 107

Samaritan Asylum. *See* Boston Samaritan Asylum

Samson (steamboat), 628

Sanford, Rev. David, 275

Sarah. *See* Benson, Sarah

Saratoga, battle of, 278, 280

Sargent, Henrietta, 81, 194; identified, 83

Sargent, Lucius Manlius, 94, 97; identified, 95

Savannah, Georgia, 14

Scarborough family, 625, 702, 703

Scarborough, Herbert, 704

Scarborough, Lucy: identified, 269; mentioned, 268, 367, 704

Scarborough, Philip: identified, 269; mentioned, 422, 423, 444, 676, 704, 722

Scarborough, Mrs. Philip (Deidama), 269, 444

Scituate, Mass.: S. J. May in, 79, 163; Sarah Benson visits, 398, 400, 402, 403

Scoble, Rev. John, 592, 690; identified, 527–28; speaks on West Indies, 527; at World's Convention, 655, 666

Scotland: George Thompson in, 59; WLG plans to visit, 655, 660, 661, 664, 667; WLG's visit to, 668–71, 672, 677, 680, 697, 701–02, 705; Birney and Stanton in, 730; mentioned, 554, 676, 682, 695

Scott, Rev. Orange, 13, 497; identified, 417; anti-Garrisonian activities of, 415, 418, 419, 462, 463, 464; and nonresistance, 477, 479; and political action, 484, 569; and Massachusetts Abolition Society, 503; and WLG's

attitude toward clergy, 518, 519, 520; at Albany Convention, 523, 524, 526; letter quoted, 584; editor of *American Wesleyan Observer*, 586, 587

Scott, Walter, 97, 99

Scott, William H., 122; letter to, 85–88

Scott, Gen. Winfield, 442

Searl, Sarah A., 275

Sears, Willard, 209

Selden, John: identified, 168; and Sabbath, 166, 173

Seminole Indians, 107

Seneca Falls, N.Y., xxviii

Sentinel and Witness, 723

Seventy Agents. *See* American Anti-Slavery Society

Sewall, Samuel E.: identified, 56–57; and Massachusetts legislative committee, 55; as abolition lawyer, 129, 170, 171; mentioned, 13, 78, 182, 195, 214, 419, 517

Sewall, Mrs. Samuel E., 195, 196

Shakespeare, William: quoted and identified — *Merchant of Venice*, 37, 41; *Hamlet*, 74, 75; 124, 125; 304, 307; 590, 592; 646, 647; *As You Like It*, 89, 90; 359, 361; 637, 639; *Julius Caesar*, 124, 125; 461, 464; 542, 549; 547, 549; *Much Ado about Nothing*, 161, 164; *King Lear*, 282, 288; 478, 486; *Macbeth*, 372, 373; 551, 552; *Othello*, 440, 442; 478, 486; 486, 487, 491; 505, 516; *Twelfth Night*, 624, 625

Sharp (Sharpe), Granville, 4; identified, 5

Sharpe, Robert D., 3; identified, 4

Shaw, Lemuel, 152, 194; identified, 195

Shaw, Mrs. Lemuel (Hope Savage), 194; identified, 195

Sheffield, England, 700

Shipley, Simon G., 13

Shipley, Thomas, 120, 127; identified, 122

Sidney, Algernon: identified, 222; *Discourses on Government* quoted, 218, 219–21, 227–28; as abolitionist, 219, 224, 251; mentioned, 217–18, 221, 228. *See also* "Algernon Sidney"

Signs of the Times, 183

Silliman, Benjamin, 178; identified, 179

Simmons, Rev. Charles, 204; identified, 205

Simmons, James Fowler, 132; identified, 134

Sims, Thomas, 62

Sisson, Hannah. *See* Greene, Mrs. Benjamin

Sisson, Joseph, 392, 458

Sisson, Mrs. Joseph (Priscilla Taylor), 392, 458

Sisson, Susanna (or Susan), 390; identified, 392–93

Slack, Dr. David Burr, 455; identified, 457–58

Slack, Mrs. David Burr (Susan W. Jackson), 455, 457

Slade, William, 37, 82; identified, 40–41

Slavery. See Channing, W. E.

Smeal, Robert, 728

Smeal, William, 726; identified, 728

Smith, Miss, 215

Smith, Gerrit: identified, 47; letters to, 596–605, 570–74; WLG's strictures on, 45–46, 52, 54; contributes to support of *Liberator*, 52, 192, 193; contributes to Oneida Institute, 94; at AA-SS meetings, 98, 99, 349, 352, 353, 357; letters to WLG from, 570–71, 596–97, 605–06; correspondence with H. C. Wright, 597, 605, 606; mentioned, 32, 129, 132, 248, 293, 307, 308, 380

Smith, Dr. James McCune: identified, 354–55; speaks at AA-SS Convention, 352, 357

Smith, John, 725; identified, 726

Smith, John Cutts, 82; identified, 83

Smith, Dr. Thomas, 264

Snow, Mr., 620

Snowden, Rev. Samuel, 319–20; identified, 321

Sommerville, William, Jr., 120

Songs of the Free, and Hymns of Christian Freedom, 118, 119

South: and abolitionists, 2, 14, 16, 20, 30, 31, 61, 74, 75, 125, 137–38, 229, 239, 241, 250, 286, 287, 293, 324–25; North compared to, 13–14, 24, 257; and antislavery petitions to Congress, 48; and admission of Texas, 75, 286; and resistance to oppression, 228–31, 242; and J. Q. Adams, 426–27; and British India movement, 689–90; mentioned, 133, 134, 159, 326, 562

South Americans, 226

South Carolina, 10, 21, 33, 49, 54, 103, 243

South Scituate, Mass., xxvii, 160, 161, 494, 496

Southard, Rev. Nathaniel: identified, 100; edits *Youth's Cabinet,* 267, 269; edits *Anti-Slavery Almanac,* 276; mentioned, 98, 139, 261, 262, 263, 274, 275

Southwick, Abby, 655

Southwick, Joseph: identified, 80; Henry Benson staying with, 179–80; and petitions, 182; mentioned, 12, 78, 347, 392, 393, 396

Southwick, Mrs. Joseph (Thankful Hussey): identified, 393; caring for Henry Benson, 179–80; and NEN-RS, 391, 395, 534; and Boston Female Anti-Slavery Society, 719 and 720; and Chardon-Street Convention, 723; mentioned, 347, 392, 398, 693

Spalding, Dr. John: identified, 144; mentioned, 142, 165, 175

Spaulding, Edward, 71; identified, 73

Spear, Charles, 68; identified, 69

Spectator. See New England Spectator

Spencer, Thomas: identified, 107; going to England, 104, 106, 120

Sprague, Seth, 608; identified, 610

Spring, Marcus, 354

Spring, Mrs. Marcus (Rebecca Buffum), 351; identified, 354

Springfield, Mass., MA-SS convention in, 687, 694, 712, 718–19, 720

Standard. See National Anti-Slavery Standard

Stanton, Henry Brewster: identified, 54; WLG praises, 52, 233, 268; lectures, 102, 108, 109, 112, 113, 117, 185, 201, 208, 215, 234, 444, 447; expected to be at Newport, 124, 128, 129, 132; cautious about Clerical Appeal, 290; in New York for AA-SS meetings, 260, 349, 352, 357; anti-Garrisonian activities, 412, 415, 418, 419, 432–33, 443, 444, 462, 544; and nonresistance, 177; and Albany Convention, 527; letter to MA-SS Board, 538, 546; and political action, 544, 571; secretary of American and Foreign Anti-Slavery Society, 553; in Great Britain, 655, 658, 730 and 731; marriage, 657; mentioned, 115, 135, 143, 202, 214, 252, 255, 261, 263, 483

Stanton, Mrs. Henry Brewster (Elizabeth Cady): identified, 657; mentioned, 308, 655, 731

Starke (Stark), John, 38; identified, 41

Starr, William D., 723

State Eagle (Conn.), 73

Stearns, Charles: identified, 562–63; letter to, 560–62

Stedman, Jesse: identified, 370; Francis Jackson vindicates WLG to, 368, 373, 374

Stedman, John W., 73

Stetson, James A.: identified, 128; mentioned, 127, 210, 444

Steward, Austin, 53

Stewart, Alvan, 307, 349; identified, 308; speaks, 351, 352, 360; at AA-SS Convention, 350, 351, 352, 357, 545; at Albany Convention, 524, 527

Storer, Capt. George Washington: identified, 550; and James Garrison, 549, 550, 558, 559, 570

Storrs, Rev. George, 34, 288; identified, 36

Stow, Rev. Baron, 393

Stowe, Harriet Beecher, 355

Stuart, Charles: identified, 16; *Life of Granville Sharp*, 5; WLG praises, 14; speaks, 108, 109, 113, 117, 185, 187; touring West Indies, 527; mentioned, 21, 102, 115

Sturge, Joseph, 528, 592; identified, 592-93

Suffolk county, Mass., 607

Sumner, Charles, 62

Sunday School Messenger, 434

Sunderland, Rev. La Roy: identified, 217; mentioned, 216, 245, 618

Supreme Court, U.S., 170, 536

Sutherland, Duchess of (Harriet Elizabeth Georgiana Leveson-Gower), 660-61; identified, 662-63

Swaim's Panacea, 189, 194, 339

Syracuse, N.Y., xxvii

Taber, Isaac C.: identified, 309-10; letter to, 308-09

Tappan, Arthur: identified, xxix; letters to, 298-300, 451, 535; founder of N.Y. *Evangelist*, 6; founder of N.Y. *Journal of Commerce*, 41-42; and Nathaniel Paul, 49-52; and C. C. Burleigh, 72; and J. R. McDowall, 99; president of American and Foreign Anti-Slavery Society, 553; declines re-election as president of AA-SS, 611; mentioned, 19, 216, 248, 293, 378

Tappan, Julia Ann, 349; identified, 350

Tappan, Lewis: identified, xxix; letters to, 42-43, 49-52, 298-300, 451, 535; founder of N.Y. *Evangelist*, 6; persuades Helen Garrison to visit New York, 186; religious differences with WLG, 188; feelings toward WLG,

290, 306, 308, 460, 606; opposes formation of antislavery political party, 413; and American and Foreign Anti-Slavery Society, 528, 553; and *Amistad* case, 536, 608; counsels division in antislavery ranks, 544-45; mentioned, 35, 43, 216, 293, 349, 351, 352, 357, 618

Tarbox, Mr., 175

Taunton, Mass., 454

Taylor, Mr. (of Virginia), 117

Taylor, Daniel A., 155, 165; identified, 157

Taylor, Rev. Edward T.: identified, 726-27; compared to Snowden, 321; at Chardon-Street Convention, 725

Taylor, Zachary, 12

Temperance Journal, 669; identified, 671

Templeton, Mass., 496-97

Texas, 102, 268; WLG on prospect of annexation of, 75, 265-66, 286, 326; invasion of, 170, 285-86; meetings on, 230, 276, 335, 336; mighty agitation against admission of, 267; WLG speaks on, 282, 308

Thacher, Rev. Moses, 12

Thome, James Anthony, 159, 288; identified, 160-61

Thompson, George: identified, xxix-xxx; letters to, 104-07, 355-56, 528-31; and Henry Benson, xxiv, 120; resolution in remembrance of, 14, 16; volume published on, 24, 27; mobbed, 45, 189, 464; letters received from, 58-59, 61, 109, 120, 233, 709; children, 59, 117; quoted on abolitionists' reputation, 87; announces birth of G. T. Garrison in Scotland, 115; debates with Breckinridge, 165-66, 167, 170, 171, 231; "Algernon Sidney" on, 224, 225; nonviolent principles of, 228, 236-38, 241, 244, 245; accused of advocating violence, 245; and British India Movement, 531, 659, 661, 675, 689, 690; at World's Convention, 654, 681; to guide WLG in Scotland, 655, 668; and controversies of American abolitionists, 656, 659, 671, 681; speaks at temperance meeting, 669-70; and political action, 730 and 731; mentioned, 19, 21, 26, 52, 76, 79, 113, 151, 169, 173, 219, 360, 490, 587, 592, 655, 657, 684, 708, 720, 726, 731

Thompson, Mrs. George (Anne Erskine): identified, 27; arrives in Liv-

erpool, 59; son born, 117; daughter born, 671; mentioned, 24, 115, 356, 661, 726
Thompson, Waddy (Waddie), Jr., 430; identified, 431
Thompson, William Lloyd Garrison, 117, 120
Thompson, Conn., 76, 77, 421–22, 423
Thomson, James, quoted and identified, 7; 125, 128; 165, 167
Thomson, Samuel, 183
Thomsonian Scout, The, 343
Thoughts on African Colonization, 111, 122, 209, 231
Thurston, Rev. David, 108; identified, 111–12
Tillotson, Rev. George J., 71, 156; identified, 73
Tillson, Joseph: identified, 118; mentioned, 116, 121–22
Tolman, John B., 12
Tonson, Monsieur, 537
Topsfield, Mass., 492–93
Torrey, Rev. Charles T., 68; identified, 410; anti-Garrisonian activities of, 407, 412, 415, 418, 419, 422, 444, 463, 492, 493; and Massachusetts Abolition Society, 503, 516; and Albany Convention, 523; and political action, 571; at Chardon-Street Convention, 724
Torringford Anti-Slavery Society, 386
Toussaint L'Ouverture, 146
Towne, Rev. Joseph Hardy: identified, 263; prudence of, 262–63; and Clerical Appeal, 273, 275, 297, 305; and other clerical protests, 300, 302, 374; and anti-Garrisonian plans, 303, 312
Townsend, Mass., 447, 453
Tract and Bible and Education Societies, 275, 299
Tracy, E. Carter, 149
Tracy, Rev. Joseph: identified, 24–25; mentioned, 22, 149, 192
Trask, Rev. George, 97, 389; identified, 99
Treat, Selah, 377; identified, 380
Tredgold, J. H., 625
Trench, William, 73
Trist, Nicholas Philip, 535; identified, 536
Troy, N.Y., 123–24, 125, 129, 610–11
Truesdell, Thomas: identified, 353; WLG stays with, 350, 378, 614–15, 627
Truesdell, Mrs. Thomas, 351, 614–15, 617

Turner, Nat, 229
Turpin, (Rev. Mr.?), 52; identified, 54
Tynemouth, England, 661
Tyre, 284

Underground Railroad, xxvii, 457, 486, 595, 613
Union Herald, 303
Union Humane Society, 80
Unionist, 72, 178
United States: letters to the abolitionists of, 563–69, 577–87; abolitionists and Union, 15, 29–30, 49, 61, 72, 75, 85, 289; financial depressions in, 50, 211, 212, 259, 538–39; WLG on condition of, 282–86, 325, 700; compared to Great Britain, 680, 706; political excitement in, 690, 708; superior form of government of, 672. *See also* Arkansas; Texas
United States Telegraph, 245
Utica, N.Y., 32, 46, 47
Uxbridge, Mass., 146, 171–72

Van Buren, Martin: and abolitionists, 3, 525, 690, 730; and slavery in District of Columbia, 71, 72, 233, 234; defeat of, 554; mentioned, 154, 259, 442, 550
Van Rensalaer, Thomas: identified, 380–81; speaks on First of August, 378; WLG stays with, 612, 614, 624, 627
Van Rensalaer, Mrs. Thomas, 379, 614
Vermont: abolitionism in, 36–37, 41, 133, 307, 657; WLG denounced in, 369, 370, 372; peace convention in, 276, 278; mentioned, 22, 29, 33, 38, 607, 704
Vermont Anti-Slavery Society: letter to Oliver Johnson for, 36–40; formation of, 29 and 33; mentioned, 104, 566, 569
Vermont Chronicle: identified, 149; mentioned, 25, 147, 172, 259, 294, 345, 722
Vermont Telegraph, 104, 277, 305, 307
Vermont Watchman, xxv
Victoria, Queen: identified, 627; mentioned, 627, 652, 661, 696
Virginia, 229
Voice of the West, 183

Walcutt (Wallcutt), Rev. Robert F., 401, 414; identified, 402
Walker, Amasa, 260; identified, 161; not the man to go to West Indies, 159; at Peace Convention, 389, 390

Index of Names

Walker, Henry, 701
Walker, Mrs. Henry, letter to, 699–701
Wall, Joseph S., 712; identified, 714
Walley, Samuel Hurd, Jr., 64; identified, 66
Walter, Lynde M., 723
Wampanoag Indians, 107
War of 1812, xxv, 235, 283, 610
Ward, Joshua Holyoke, 65; identified, 66
Wardlaw, Dr. Ralph, 225; identified, 231
Ware, Rev. Samuel, 68; identified, 69
Warren, Gen. Joseph, 220, identified, 232
Washington, George, 4, 6, 217, 280, 282, 294, 334, 384, 551
Washington, D.C.: petitions against slavery in, 7, 37, 48–49, 71, 182, 183, 204–05, 289, 335, 357, 431, 469, 489, 598; politics and slavery in, 14, 20, 37, 71, 72, 133, 234, 287, 289, 426–30, 567; Massachusetts legislature and slavery in, 214, 215, 253, 439, 441, 583
Washington (cutter), 536
Waterloo, N.Y., 595
Watts, Rev. Isaac, 155–56; identified, 157
Wayland, Francis, 45, 277; identified, 47; *Elements of Moral Science*, 46, 48
Webb, James Watson, 97
Webb, Richard Davis: identified, 684; mentioned, 528, 682, 709, 720
Webster, Daniel, 33, 41, 71, 720
Wedgwood, Josiah, 356, 653
Weekly Advocate, 217
Weekly Herald and Philanthropist, 69
Weeks, Joseph, 289
Weld, Lewis, 377; identified, 380
Weld, Theodore, D.: identified, 53–54; WLG anxious to see, 52, 159; mobbed at Troy, N.Y., 123–24, 129, 132; urged to attend Newport hearing, 123–24, 125, 128, 129, 130; lecturing for AA-SS, 160; leading convention of "Seventy," 184, 185, 187; urged to attend Massachusetts legislative committee hearing, 214, 215; missing, 216; ill health of, 257, 261; and Angelina Grimké, 333, 349, 350, 356, 359, 360, 361; sectarianism of, 359; mentioned, 35, 44, 103, 111, 163, 201, 202, 364, 377, 380
Weld, Mrs. Theodore D. *See* Grimké, Angelina E.

Wells, E. M. P.: identified, 11–12; dislikes *Liberator*, 9, 22; and MA-SS, 10, 12, 15, 16, 22; at AA-SS Convention, 352, 357
Wesley, John, 36; identified, 40
Wesleyan Observer, 586; identified, 587
West Bloomfield, N.Y., 604, 606
West Indies (West India): emancipation in, 39–40, 378, 379, 528, 529, 592, 664, 673; Henry Benson may visit, 146, 151, 162; AA-SS sending agent to, 153, 159, 160–61; apprenticeship system in, 529, 592; Madden's book on slavery in, 535; mentioned, xxx, 231, 376, 527, 679
West Newbury, Mass., xxx
West Point, 277
Western New York, convention of abolitionists of, 606
Western Reserve College, 96, 111
Westminster Review, 57
Weston family: identified, 57; mentioned, 55, 56, 60, 78
Weston, Ann(e), 57
Weston, Ann (Anne or Anna): identified, 57; mentioned, 194, 391, 395
Weston, Caroline: identified, 57; mentioned, 194, 347, 717
Weston, Deborah, 57
Weston, Hervey Eliphaz, 57
Weston, Lucia, 57
Weston, Warren, 57
Weymouth, Mass., 328, 537
Weymouth Anti-Slavery Society, 537
Whiffen, Jeremiah Holmes, 648–50
Whipple, Charles K., 411, 437; identified, 438
Whitby, Daniel: identified, 168; and Sabbath, 166, 173
Whitcomb, Dr. James B., 63, 70; identified, 65
White, Rev. Elipha: identified, 300–01; accused of being slaveholder, 275, 299
White, Lydia, 127; identified, 128
Whittier, John Greenleaf: quoted and identified, 134, 135; 243–44, 246; 265, 266; and *Pennsylvania Freeman*, 80; peace resolution at AA-SS Convention, 349, 350, 480; and political action, 484, 569; mentioned, 13, 62, 113, 214, 233, 268, 290, 294, 350, 358, 360
Wilberforce, William, 166, 167; identified, 168
Wilberforce, Canada, 53

Wilbour, Charles, 141; identified, 141–42

Wilde, Judge, 171

Willard, Sidney, 390; identified, 392

William, Cousin, 270; identified, 272

Williams, Mrs. (daughter of), 110, 113

Williams, Joseph: identified, 5; mentioned, 3, 113, 232

Williams, Julia, 261, 360

Williams, Ransom G.: identified, 12; mentioned, 9, 15, 216

Williams, Rev. Thomas, 94, 98; identified, 96

Willimantic Anti-Slavery Society, 71

Willis, Nathaniel, 140

Wilson, Hiram, 484, 569; identified, 486

Wilson (Willson), Rev. Luther, 4, 22; identified, 6

Windham County, Conn., and vote on suffrage, 367

Windham County Anti-Slavery Society: WLG to address, 274, 276, 282; praises *Liberator*, 421–22, 423; mentioned, xxii, 4, 72, 161, 345, 346

Windham County Advertiser, 26, 73

Windham County Gazette, 72

Winslow, Miss, 194

Winslow, Harriet, 195

Winslow, Hubbard: identified, 75–76; mentioned, 75, 446, 690

Winslow, Isaac: identified, 209; and voting, 475, 513, 573, 601–02; mentioned, 13, 208, 470, 516, 590, 655, 659

Winslow, Jeremiah, 209

Winslow, Louisa Maria, 196

Winslow, Lucy Ellen, 195

Winslow, Nathan: identified, 516–17; mentioned, 195, 209, 513

Wise, Rev. Daniel, 497; identified, 434; efforts for *Massachusetts Abolitionist*, 433, 444; anti-Garrisonian activities of, 434, 462, 463, 464, 492, 503; appointed AA-SS agent, 444, 546; and Albany Convention, 523; and voting, 571

Witherspoon, Rev. John, 263; identified, 264

Women, Anti-Slavery Convention of: Mary Benson attends, xxii; Susan Paul vice-president of, 195; Mary Parker thinks of attending, 347; planned, 356; WLG attends and describes, 333, 362–63, 364; M. W. Chapman's fever after, 360

Woodbury, Rev. James Trask, 434, 519; identified, 297–98; letter to, 292–97;

letter to WLG, 297–98, 300, 305; rallying forces, 303, 307; E. Wright and L. Tappan on WLG's letter to, 305–06; agent of AA-SS, 542

Woodbury, Levi, 297

"Woolman." *See* Greene, Rowland

Woolman, John, 686; identified, 688

Wooster, Dorastus, 41

Worcester, Dr. Noah, 414; identified, 416

Worcester, Mass.: abolitionism in, 43, 452–53; MA-SS meetings in, 304, 307, 687, 691, 694, 708, 711–12, 718, 719; young men's antislavery convention at, 398, 399, 403; antislavery fair, 699, 712, 718; mentioned, xxx, 313, 315

Worcester County North Division Anti-Slavery Society; letter to president of, 575–76; mentioned, 496–97, 576–77

Worcester County South Division Anti-Slavery Society, 43, 713

Worcester Spy, 454

Workmen's party, 348

World's Anti-Slavery Convention (also called London Convention): identified, 553–54; refusal to seat female delegates, 553, 587, 616, 627, 633, 641, 654, 659, 665, 666, 677, 680, 698–99, 700, 730; WLG's delight that Motts will attend, 587, 591, 592; N. P. Rogers urged to attend, 588–89; WLG's anticipations of, 595, 615–16, 619, 625–27, 632–40 *passim*; WLG on, 654–55, 665, 677, 686, 711; WLG's refusal to connect himself with, 679, 684, 697; protests against, 666, 690 and 691; mentioned, xxvii, 100, 209, 353, 593, 594, 614 and 615, 618, 644, 657, 663, 665, 670, 684, 687, 698, 708, 731

Wright, Elizur, Jr.: identified, 111; letter to, 321–22; WLG writes to, 153; editor of *Quarterly Anti-Slavery Magazine*, 158, 322; Breckinridge's charges against, 165–66, 167; criticizes WLG's course, 303, 305–06, 307–08; and *Massachusetts Abolitionist*, 434, 545; and political action, 473, 477, 510, 573; and Massachusetts Abolition Society, 516, 573; change of feelings toward WLG, 592; mentioned, 108, 157, 185, 216, 293, 497, 518, 519

Wright, Fanny, 348

Wright, Rev. Henry Clarke: identified, xxx–xxxi; letters to, 73–75, 257–59,

460–61, 531, 679–81; and MA-SS, 10, 12, 13, 15, 22 and 25; resolution on northern responsibility for slavery, 21, 24; asks WLG to return to Boston, 73–74; speaks, 94, 108, 113, 117; regrets connection of *Liberator* with MA-SS, 290–91; in Philadelphia with WLG, 358–60; and Peace Convention, 389, 390, 393; and NEN-RS, 401, 438, 532, 534; prepares tract on human governments, 408; Gerrit Smith's correspondence with, 597, 603, 604, 605, 606; and Chardon-Street Convention, 722, 723; mentioned, 78, 98, 115, 216, 332, 351, 364, 470, 624
Wright, Mrs. Henry Clarke, 461

Wright, Pauline, 308
Wright, Rev. Theodore S.: identified, 111; mentioned, 99, 108, 113, 115, 117, 378, 611, 618

Yates, Rev. James D., 9; identified, 11
York, England, 699
Young, Edward, quoted and identified, 142, 144; 325, 327
Young, John Clarke, 52; identified, 54
Young Mother, The, 118; identified, 119
Youth's Cabinet, 267, 274; identified, 269

Zion's Herald (Boston): identified, 43; mentioned, 42, 217, 354, 417, 434, 584, 722